Malaysia, Singapore & Brunei

Langkawi,
Kedah
& Perlis
(p191)

Penang
(p158)

Perak
(p125)

Kuala Lumpur
(p54) ✪

Selangor & Negeri
Sembilan (p106)

Melaka
(p215)

Peninsular Malaysia's
Northeast
(p282)

Pahang &
Tioman Island
(p252)

Johor (p237)

Singapore
(p488) ✪

Darussalam
(p468)

abah
(p314)

Sarawak
(p392)

D1545168

Simon Richmond,
Brett Atkinson, Lindsay Brown, Austin Bush, Ria de Jong,
Damian Harper, Anita Isalska, Anna Kaminski

Contents

PLAN YOUR TRIP

Welcome to Malaysia,
Singapore & Brunei 6

Malaysia, Singapore &
Brunei's Top Experiences. . .10

Need to Know 20

First Time 22

What's New 24

Month by Month 26

Itineraries 28

Outdoor Adventures. . . . 34

Eat & Drink
Like a Local 42

Regions at a Glance. . . . 49

ON THE ROAD

KUALA LUMPUR 54
Sights 55
Activities 67
Courses 69
Festivals & Events 70
Sleeping 70
Eating 77
Drinking & Nightlife 94
Entertainment 98
Shopping 99

SELANGOR & NEGERI
SEMBILAN 106
Selangor 108
Batu Caves 108

Forest Research
Institute Malaysia 109
Genting Highlands 109
Bukit Fraser 110
Putrajaya 113
Petaling Jaya &
Shah Alam 115
Klang &
Pelabuhan Klang 116
Kuala Selangor 118
Negeri Sembilan 119
Seremban 119
Kuala Pilah 121
Sri Menanti 122
Port Dickson 123

OMAR ALI SAIFUDDIEN
MOSQUE, BRUNEI P470

NASI LEMAK P47

Contents

PERAK 125
Ipoh. 127
Gopeng & Around. 134
Cameron Highlands. 136
Pulau Pangkor 143
Kuala Kangsar. 148
Taiping 151
Kuala Sepetang 155
Belum-Temenggor
Rainforest 156

PENANG. 158
George Town 160
Greater Penang. 183
Air Itam & Penang Hill. . . 183

Batu Ferringhi. 184
Teluk Bahang & Around. . . 186
Balik Pulau &
Kampung Pulau Betong. . . 188
Southeast Penang
Island 190

LANGKAWI, KEDAH
& PERLIS 191
Kedah 192
Pulau Langkawi 193
Alor Setar 209
Around Alor Setar 212
Kuala Kedah 212
Perlis 213
Kangar 213
Around Kangar 214

MELAKA. 215
Melaka City 217
Ayer Keroh. 235
Alor Gajah 236

JOHOR 237
Johor Bahru 238
Muar 244
Mersing 246
Seribuat Archipelago. . . .248
Endau-Rompin
National Park 250

PAHANG &
TIOMAN ISLAND . . . 252
Pulau Tioman 253
The Coast. 262
Tanjung Gemok. 262
Pekan 262
Kuantan 263
Cherating. 268
The Interior 270
Temerloh & Around 270

Jerantut 272
Taman Negara. 273
Kuala Lipis. 279
Raub 280

PENINSULAR
MALAYSIA'S
NORTHEAST 282
Kelantan. 283
Kota Bharu 283
Around Kota Bharu 291
Terengganu 293
Pulau Perhentian 293
Pulau Redang 301
Pulau Kapas 304
Kuala Terengganu. 305
North of Kuala
Terengganu 312
South of Kuala
Terengganu 312

SABAH 314
Kota Kinabalu 316
Tunku Abdul Rahman
National Park 329
Pulau Manukan. 330
Pulau Mamutik 330
Pulau Sapi 330
Pulau Gaya 331
Pulau Sulug. 331
Northwestern Sabah . . 331
Mt Kinabalu &
Kinabalu National Park . . . 332
Around Mt Kinabalu. 339
Northwest Coast 341
Island Getaways 344
Eastern Sabah. 345
Sandakan. 346
Sepilok 351
Sandakan Archipelago. . . 356
Deramakot
Forest Reserve 357

HINDU TEMPLE AT BATU
CAVES P108

Sungai Kinabatangan ...358
Lahad Datu 363
Danum Valley
Conservation Area......365
Tabin Wildlife Reserve ...367
Semporna 367
Semporna Archipelago ...369
Tawau.................376
Tawau Hills Park........379
Maliau Basin
Conservation Area......380
Southwestern Sabah... 381
Beaufort Division 385
Pulau Tiga
National Park 387
Pulau Labuan 388

SARAWAK 392
Kuching 393
Western Sarawak 413
Bako National Park 414
Santubong Peninsula ... 417
Semenggoh Wildlife
Centre 420
Annah Rais Longhouse ...420
Kubah National Park 421
Bau & Around 423
Lundu................424
Gunung Gading
National Park 425
Tanjung Datu
National Park 427
Talang-Satang
National Park 428
Batang Ai Region 429
Central Sarawak......430
Sibu 430
Batang Rejang 434
Bintulu 438
Similajau National Park...441
Niah National Park......443
Lambir Hills
National Park 445

Miri 446
Northeastern Sarawak...453
Gunung Mulu
National Park 453
Kelabit Highlands.......459
Limbang Division 465

BRUNEI
DARUSSALAM 468
Bandar Seri Begawan...470
Tutong &
Belait Districts 482
Tutong 482
Jalan Labi 482
Seria.................483
Temburong District ...483

Bangar 484
Batang Duri...........485
Ulu Temburong
National Park 485

SINGAPORE 488
Sights................489
Activities 517
Courses 520
Tours.................520
Festivals & Events 520
Sleeping..............531
Eating................536
Drinking & Nightlife.....546
Entertainment.........552
Shopping 553

Contents

LITTLE INDIA,
SINGAPORE P501

GIBBON IN FOREST,
SABAH P314

PITCHER PLANT, BAKO
NATIONAL PARK P414

UNDERSTAND

History 564

People, Culture &
Politics 576

Religion 582

Arts, Architecture &
Media 586

Environment 592

SURVIVAL GUIDE

Directory A–Z 598

Transport 606

Health. 611

Language 616

COVID-19

We have re-checked every business in this book before publication to ensure that it is still open after the COVID-19 outbreak. However, the economic and social impacts of COVID-19 will continue to be felt long after the outbreak has been contained, and many businesses, services and events referenced in this guide may experience ongoing restrictions. Some businesses may be temporarily closed, have changed their opening hours and services, or require bookings; some unfortunately could have closed permanently. We suggest you check with venues before visiting for the latest information.

SPECIAL FEATURES

Outdoor Adventures . . . 34

Eat & Drink
Like a Local. 42

Regional Specialities. . . .81

The Mega-Diversity
Region 521

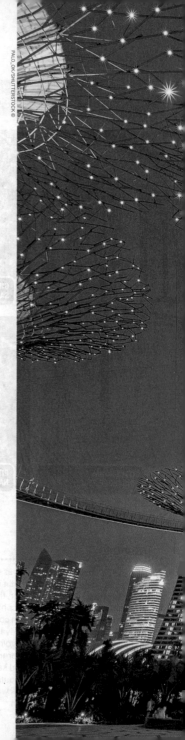

Right:
Supertrees
by night,
Gardens by the
Bay (p489),
Singapore,
designed by
Wilkinson Eyre
and Grant
Associates

WELCOME TO
Malaysia, Singapore & Brunei

For Southeast Asia in a microcosm, you can't beat this trio of fascinating countries. I've always enjoyed the diversity of cultures, the delicious cuisine, combining Malay, Chinese and Indian dishes, as well as the dynamic arts and architecture of the principal cities of Kuala Lumpur and Singapore. One day you can be exploring the heritage cityscape of George Town, the next riding longboats into the deepest recesses of Sarawak or scuba diving off gorgeous tropical islands – it's all one huge adventure in the company of welcoming people.

By Simon Richmond, Writer
For more about our writers, see p640.

Peninsular Malaysia & Singapore

VIETNAM **PHILIPPINES**
THAILAND
**MALAYSIAN
BORNEO**
**PENINSULAR
MALAYSIA** **BRUNEI** Sabah
Sarawak
SINGAPORE Borneo
INDONESIA
Sumatra Sulawesi

*Gulf of
Thailand*

Hat Yai

Padang
Besar
Satun
PERLIS THAILAND Yala
Taman Bukit Kayu
Negara Hitamo
Perlis Kangar
Pulau
Langkawi
Alor Setar
KEDAH Sungai Petani Kerob
Gerik
Penang
National
Park
PENANG Butterworth
George Town
Pulau
Penang

Kota Bharu
Hub of traditional
Malay culture (p283)

Narathiwat
Tak Bai
Pengkalan Kubor
Sungai Kolok **Kota
Bharu**
Rantau
Panjang
Kuala Krai
Merang

Perhentian Islands
(Pulau Perhentian)
Pulau Lang Tengah
Pulau
Redang
**SOUTH
CHINA
SEA**

Kuala Terengganu
Pulau Kapas
Marang

*ANDAMAN
SEA*

PERAK
Taipingo Kuala
Kangsar
Ipoh
Gopeng Tanah Rata
Pulau
Pangkor Laut Lumut
Bidor

Royal Belum
State Park
*Tasik
Temenggor*

KELANTAN
Gua
Musang
Gunung Taman
Tahan Negara
(2187m) National
Park
Kenong Rimba
State Park
Kuala Lipis

*Tasik
Kenyir* **TERENGGANU**

Dungun

Taman Negara
Malaysia's premier
national park (p273)

Cherating

PAHANG
Jerantut

Kuantan

Cameron Highlands
Tea plantations and
pleasant walks (p136)

Slim
River
Kuala Kubu Bharu
SELANGOR
Kuala Selangor
Shah Alam **KUALA LUMPUR**
Pelabuhan Klang Putrajaya
(Port Klang)
Morib KLM
Port Dickson

Bukit Fraser
(Fraser's Hill)
Temerloh

Pulau Tioman
Beautiful island ideal
for chilling (p253)

Pulau
Tioman
Seribuat
Archipelago

Kuala Lumpur
Chinatown's historic, cultural
and culinary delights (p54)

Melaka
Vibrant World Heritage–
listed city (p215)

**NEGERI
SEMBILAN**
Seramban
Gemas
Endau-Rompin
National Park
MELAKA
Melaka
Muar

JOHOR
Mersing
Pulau
Ting

Pula
Ting

*Selat Melaka
(Strait of Melaka)*
Batu
Pahat
Kluang
Kota Tinggi

**SUMATRA
INDONESIA**

Dumai

Pontian Kecil
SINGAPORE

**Johor
Bahru**
SINGAPOR

ELEVATION
1500m
1000m
500m
200m
0m

Singapore
Amazing urban green spaces,
National Gallery (p488)

Strait of Singapor

Pakanbaru

N 0 ─── 100 km
0 ─── 50 miles

Malaysian Borneo & Brunei

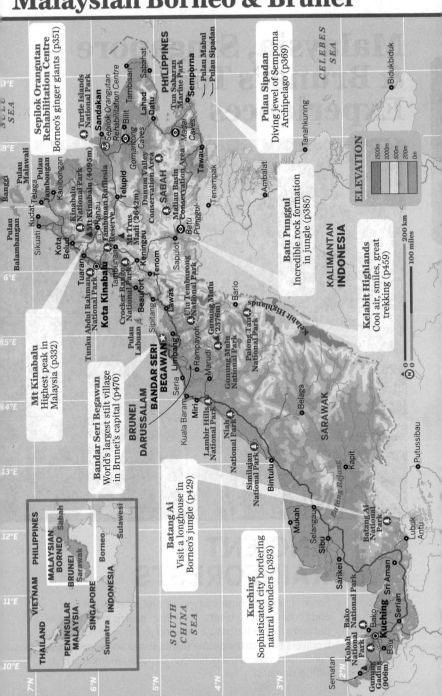

Sepilok Orangutan Rehabilitation Centre (p351)
Borneo's ginger giants

Pulau Sipadan
Diving jewel of Semporna Archipelago (p369)

Mt Kinabalu
Highest peak in Malaysia (p332)

Bandar Seri Begawan
World's largest stilt village in Brunei's capital (p470)

Batu Punggul
Incredible rock formation in jungle (p385)

Kelabit Highlands
Cool air, smiles, great trekking (p459)

Batang Ai
Visit a longhouse in Borneo's jungle (p429)

Kuching
Sophisticated city bordering natural wonders (p393)

ELEVATION

1500m
1000m
500m
200m
0m

200 km
100 miles

Locations

Bidukbiduk
Tanahkuning
Ambalat
Tenampak
KALIMANTAN INDONESIA
Putussibau
Lubuk Antu
Sri Aman
Serian
Sematan

SOUTH CHINA SEA
CELEBES SEA
SULU SEA

THAILAND
VIETNAM
PHILIPPINES
PENINSULAR MALAYSIA
MALAYSIAN BORNEO Sabah
BRUNEI
Sarawak
Borneo
SINGAPORE
INDONESIA
Sumatra
Sulawesi

Malaysia, Singapore & Brunei's Top Experiences

1 ANCIENT RAINFORESTS

Large chunks of primary jungle are protected by national parks and conservation projects. The foliage seems impenetrable, but join a ranger-led nature walk and you'll see mind-boggling biodiversity, from the pitcher plants, lianas and orchids of the humid lowlands, to the conifers and rhododendrons of high-altitude forests.

Taman Negara, Pahang

Inside Malaysia's premier national park, giant trees with buttressed roots dwarf luminescent fungi and orchids. This dense rainforest is home to everything from flying squirrels, lizards and monkeys to elephants and tigers. p273

Left: Canopy walk; Right: Macaques, Taman Negara

Ulu Temburong National Park

Only a tiny fraction of this 500-sq-km area of pristine rainforest (pictured, above) is accessible to the public but it is still a highlight of a visit to Brunei. Observe butterflies or go swimming in the cool waters of Sungai Temburong. p485

Gunung Mulu National Park

World Heritage–listed Gunung Mulu National Park offers some of the planet's most incredible (and accessible) caves, brilliant old-growth tropical rainforest and the jagged Pinnacles formation on Mt Api. p453

Above: Wind Cave, Gunung Mulu National Park

2 WILDLIFE ENCOUNTERS

The most common sightings in the region's parks and natures reserves will be of insects or colourful birdlife, but you could get lucky and spot a foraging tapir, a silvered leaf monkey, or an orangutan swinging through the jungle canopy. The oceans are just as bountiful: snorkel or dive among shoals of tropical fish, paint-box-dipped corals, turtles, sharks and dolphins.

Sepilok Orangutan Rehabilitation Centre

Orangutan combine raw power and gentle restraint, stupid amounts of cuteness and deep reserves of what we can only call wisdom and, sometimes, sadness. All these complicated observations occur at once at Sabah's Sepilok Orangutan Rehabilitation Centre. p351
Below right: Mother and baby orangutans

TUM3000/GETTY IMAGES ©

Pulau Sipadan

Sometimes it seems as if the world's most colourful marine life considers the seawall of Sipadan to be prime real estate – from the commonplace to utterly alien fish, molluscs and reptiles. p369
Above: Porcelain crabs

Singapore Zoo

Singapore's zoo is one of the world's most inviting, enlightening animal sanctuaries. Open-air enclosures allow freedom for the animals to roam and unobstructed visitor views. p511
Right: White tiger, Singapore Zoo

3 ISLAND ESCAPES

DIDIER MARTI/GETTY IMAGES ©

Between them, Malaysia, Singapore and Brunei have 975 islands, most of them uninhabited. Whether it's the simple pleasure of stepping from a beach hut straight into balmy turquoise waters or embracing the luxury of a five-star resort, the chances are high that you'll find your own island paradise.

Pulau Tioman

Pulau Tioman is blessed with dozens of serenely beautiful beaches, myriad jungle trails, waterfalls and even serious surf off the island's east coast.
p253

ABC Village (p257), Pulau Tioman

Pulau Langkawi

The Jewel of Kedah, Langkawi has white-sand beaches, isolated luxury resorts, diving opportunities and pristine jungles. Off-the-beaten-track–type exploration will also reveal that this large island still retains its endearing *kampung* (village) soul.
p193

Pulau Ubin

Singapore's very own rustic island getaway offers a glimpse of the *kampung* life that was a big part of Singapore as recently as the 1960s. Cycle past tin-roof shacks, ramshackle shrines and lazing monitor lizards; end the day by digging into a simple seafood meal by the sea.
p509

4

CULINARY PLEASURES

There's no shortage of superb restaurants in these countries, but take it from us, the best food is served in the humblest surroundings. Countless vendors serve delicious dishes from mobile carts, stalls and shophouses, many using generations-old recipes and techniques.

George Town

George Town's dining scene is breathtakingly diverse. On a single street you can find quality Malay, Chinese, South Indian and Western cuisines. p160

Top: Morning market, George Town

Ipoh

Ipoh's old town is packed with grab-and-go eats. The must-try dish is tauge ayam, tender poached chicken served with fat bean sprouts and rice cooked in chicken broth (pictured, above left). p127

Singapore

Chicken rice, satay, sweet and sour rojak, spicy barbecue sambal stingray: Singapore's hawker food is the stuff of legend – you'll even find two Michelin-starred stalls! p488

Above right: Singapore food stalls

5 CULTURAL RICHES

NATALIIA SOKOLOVSKA/SHUTTERSTOCK ©

SAMCI3P/SHUTTERSTOCK ©

For accessing the region's arts and crafts and understanding more about its complex history, a visit to Malaysia, Singapore and Brunei's excellent museums and galleries is essential.

Islamic Arts Museum Malaysia

The dazzling collection of objects housed in this fine Kuala Lumpur museum proves that religious devotion can be married with exquisite craftsmanship. p61

Top left: Jewel-encrusted gold pipe, Islamic Arts Museum

National Gallery Singapore

Art-lovers could spend hours wandering the world-class collection of 19th-century and modern Southeast Asian art housed across two of the city's most iconic heritage buildings. p495

Asian Civilisations Museum

Travel back through time at Singapore's engrossing ode to Asia's cross-cultural connections. You'll find the region's most comprehensive collection of pan-Asian treasures within this museum's walls p495

Bottom left: Buddhist statue, Asian Civilisations Museum

6 AMAZING ARCHITECTURE

The region's range of architecture spans the gamut from traditional Malay wooden houses to colonial era edifices and eye-popping glass and steel skyscrapers. Not to be missed are the World Heritage listed urban zones of George Town and Melaka.

Sarawak Longhouses

Essentially a whole village under a single roof, these dwellings can be longer than two football pitches and contain dozens of family units. To find longhouses least affected by modern life take a boat up the remote Batang Ai. p417
Top left: Longhouse at Sarawak Cultural Village

Kampong Ayer

The largest water village in the world, Kampong Ayer (pictured, left) is a fascinating juxtaposition of nostalgia and development. p470

Petronas Towers

It's impossible to resist the magnetic allure of these 452m-high twin towers (pictured, top right), designed by architect César Pelli, an embodiment of Malaysia's development. p55

7 SCENIC VISTAS

Whether it's the glittering lights and gleaming towers of urban metropolises such as KL and Singapore, or the natural landscapes of Borneo and peninsula Malaysia, this region offers the sweetest of scenic eye candy.

Mt Kinabalu

If the weather is on your side, attaining the summit of the region's highest mountain will also serve up amazing views stretching to the Philippines. Or it will be cloudy. Whatever: the climb is still exhilarating. p332

Below, right: Summit of Mt Kinabalu

FUJITAMIN/SHUTTERSTOCK ©

Gardens by the Bay

Spanning a whopping 101 hectares, Gardens by the Bay, designed by Wilkinson Eyre and Grant Associates, is Singapore's hottest horticultural asset. Don't miss the Supertrees (pictured, above). p489

Cameron Highlands

Misty mountains, Tudor-themed architecture, 4WDs, scones, strawberries and scenic tea plantations all converge in this distinctly un-Southeast Asian destination (pictured, below right). p136

8 RELIGIOUS SITES

PRASIT RODPHAN/SHUTTERSTOCK ©

From incense-wreathed Chinese temples to magnificent mosques, this region is peppered with atmospheric and visually stunning religious sites – in cities, on hillsides and even in caves.

Batu Caves

A giant limestone outcrop a few kilometres north of Kuala Lumpur is the location of this polychromatic Hindu shrine (pictured, above). A 43m gilded statue of Lord Murugan guards the 272 steps to the main Temple Cave. p108

Kek Lok Si Temple

On the island of Penang, Malaysia's largest Buddhist temple is a multi-level complex of pagodas and pavilions, watched over by a 36.5m bronze statue of the goddess of mercy. p184

Masjid Jamek Sultan Abdul Samad

This 1907 onion-domed mosque is a stunner – and looking even more splendid having recently been given a thorough restoration as part of Kuala Lumpur's River of Life city beautification project. p60

Need to Know

For more information, see Survival Guide (p597).

Currency
Malaysian ringgit (RM),
Singapore dollar (S$),
Brunei dollar (B$)

Language
Bahasa Malaysia, English, Chinese dialects,
Tamil

Visas
Generally not required
for stays of up to 60
days (Malaysia), 90
days (Singapore) and 30
to 90 days (Brunei).

Money
ATMs widely available.
Credit cards accepted
by most businesses.

Mobile Phones
Local SIM cards can be
used in most phones.
Other phones must be
set to roaming.

Time
GMT/UTC plus eight
hours

When to Go

Penang ●
GO Mar–Nov

Kota Bharu
GO Mar–Nov

Kuala Lumpur
GO Mar–Nov

Singapore
GO Mar–Nov

Kuching
GO Mar–Nov

Tropical climate, rain year-round
Tropical climate, wet & dry seasons

High Season
(Dec–Feb)

➡ School holidays
followed by Chinese
New Year inflate
prices and mean
advance booking of
transport and hotel
rooms is important.

➡ It's monsoon
season for the east
coast of Peninsular
Malaysia and western
Sarawak.

Shoulder
(Jul–Nov)

➡ From July to
August, vie with
visitors escaping
the heat of the Gulf
States as the region
enjoys what it calls
Arab Season.

➡ It's monsoon
season down the
west coast of
Peninsular Malaysia
until September.

Low Season
(Mar–Jun)

➡ Avoid the worst
of the rains and
humidity.

➡ The chance to
enjoy places without
the crush of fellow
tourists.

Useful Websites

Brunei Tourism (www.brunei tourism.travel) Information on travel in the sultanate.

Lonely Planet (www.lonely-planet.com) Destination information, hotel reviews, traveller forum and more.

Malaysia Asia (http://blog.malaysia-asia.my) Award-winning travel blog packed with local insider info.

Tourism Malaysia (www.tourism.gov.my) Official national tourist information site.

Visit Singapore (www.visit singapore.com/en) Official tourism board site.

Important Numbers

Country code	Malaysia ☎60; Singapore ☎65; Brunei ☎673
International access code	Malaysia & Brunei ☎00; Singapore ☎001
Police	Malaysia & Singapore ☎999; Brunei ☎993
Ambulance & fire	Malaysia ☎994; Singapore ☎995; Brunei ambulance ☎991, fire ☎995
Directory assistance	Malaysia ☎103; Singapore ☎100; Brunei ☎113

Exchange Rates

Australia	A$1	RM2.95
Canada	C$1	RM3.18
Euro	€1	RM4.80
Indonesia	100Rp	RM0.028
Japan	¥100	RM3.70
New Zealand	NZ$1	RM2.70
Thailand	100B	RM12.28
UK	£1	RM5.45
USA	$1	RM4.15

For current exchange rates, see www.xe.com.

Daily Costs

Budget: less than RM100/ S$200/B$80

➡ Dorm bed: RM15–50/ S$25–45/B$10–50

➡ Hawker centres and food-court meals: RM5–7/S$5-6/ B$1–4

➡ Public transport per trip: RM1–2.50/S$1.40–2.50/ B$1–2

Midrange: RM100–400/ S$200–400/ B$80–160

➡ Double room at midrange hotel: RM100–400/S$150–300/B$60–80

➡ Two-course meal at midrange restaurant: RM40–60/S$80/B$5–15

➡ Cocktails at decent bar: RM30–40/S$20–30

Top end: more than RM400/ S$400/B$160

➡ Luxury double room: RM450–1000/S$350–800/ B$140–170

➡ Meal at top restaurant: RM200/S$300/B$10–20

➡ Three-day diving course: RM800–1000

Opening Hours

Banks 10am–3pm Monday to Friday, 9.30am–11.30am Saturday

Bars and clubs 5pm–5am

Cafes 8am–10pm

Restaurants noon–2.30pm and 6pm–10.30pm

Shops 9.30am–7pm, malls 10am–10pm

Arriving in Malaysia, Singapore & Brunei

Kuala Lumpur International Airport Trains (RM35) run every 15 minutes from 5am to 1am; 30 minutes to KL Sentral. Buses (RM10) leave every hour from 5am to 1am; one hour to KL Sentral. Taxis cost from RM75 to RM100; one hour to KL.

Changi International Airport Frequent MRT train and public and shuttle buses into Singapore from 5.30am to 11.18pm, S$1.70–9. Taxis cost S$20 to S$40, 50% more between midnight and 6am.

Brunei International Airport Buses (B$1) run frequently to Bandar Seri Begawan until 5.30pm. Taxis cost B$25. Both take around 15 minutes.

Getting Around

Bus There's hardly anywhere you can't get by bus on Peninsular Malaysia and Singapore, but they are more limited on Brunei.

Train & MRT Malaysian trains have a far less extensive network than buses; still useful for access to a few remote locations. ETS trains are fast but not so frequent. The MRT is the best way to get around Singapore.

Car Good idea to hire one to explore Malaysia and Brunei's hinterlands; avoid using in cities though.

Flights Planes go to major cities, islands and more remote destinations.

Ferries For island-hopping and connections between Malaysia and Singapore.

For much more on **getting around**, see p607.

PLAN YOUR TRIP NEED TO KNOW

First Time

For more information, see Survival Guide (p597).

Checklist

➡ Make sure your passport is valid for at least six months past your arrival date.

➡ Get any vaccinations you might need and pack medications in their original, clearly labelled containers.

➡ Arrange for appropriate travel insurance.

➡ Check your airline's baggage restrictions.

➡ Inform your debit-/credit-card company you're heading away.

What to Pack

➡ Umbrella

➡ Small day-pack or cross-body bag

➡ Sunglasses

➡ Sunscreen

➡ Flip-flops (thongs)

➡ Mosquito repellent

➡ A bandana to keep sweat at bay

➡ Tissues and hand sanitiser

➡ Deodorant

➡ Electrical adaptor (not necessary for UK appliances)

Top Tips for Your Trip

➡ Leave rigorous outdoor activities for early morning or late afternoon to avoid the sweltering midday heat.

➡ Party early: there's no shortage of bars offering good-value happy-hour deals, mostly between 5pm and 8pm or 9pm.

➡ Carry a packet of tissues: handy for mopping hands at hawker centres and for use in toilets which may not have toilet paper.

What to Wear

The region's lowlands are pretty much always hot and sticky, so pack lightweight clothes made from natural fabrics such as cotton and linen that dry quickly. Flip-flops (thongs) may be too flimsy to withstand a few days of exploring a city; opt for sturdier leather sandals or lightweight canvas sneakers.

For the cooler highlands, warmer clothing will be needed. A fleece, sweater and woolly socks can also come in handy for the frigid air-conditioning in trains, long-distance buses and cinemas.

Erring on the side of modesty (covering your shoulders and down to the knees) will be seen as respectful by Malaysians and will attract less attention. Put on smarter clothes and shoes if you're heading out on the town.

Sleeping

Accommodation options in these three countries range from simple, shared backpacker dorms to some of Asia's most luxurious resorts. Book well ahead for holiday periods such as Chinese New Year and around big events such as the F1 night race in Singapore.

➡ **Hostels** Mainly found in the biggest cities and resort areas, including several flashpacker options.

➡ **Guesthouses & homestays** Seldom fancy but also a great way to meet locals. Also consider staying in tribal longhouses in Borneo.

➡ **Hotels** Ranging from rock-bottom basic to hyper luxurious.

Eating

Nestled between South and East Asia, it's no surprise that the dishes of Malaysia, Singapore and Brunei have incorporated elements of these heavyweight cuisines – plus the best bits of Southeast Asia. In this region, it's possible to start the day in India, lunch in China and dine in Malaysia. And that doesn't even touch on snacks and dishes that are somewhere in between, nor some of the most fragrant, delicious fruit imaginable. Is there a better place to eat in the world? We don't think so.

Money

ATMs widely available. Credit cards accepted by most businesses.

Bargaining

At *pasar malam* (night markets) and other street markets a certain amount of bargaining is fine for souvenir-type goods, but avoid being too aggressive as that's not part of the region's shopping culture. Smile, be polite and don't get stuck on small differences of price.

Tipping

Tipping is not generally expected, but leaving a small contribution for exceptional service is appreciated.

➡ **Hotels** Tipping is most common for services in top-end hotels.

➡ **Restaurants** Many restaurants in the major cities add a service charge of around 10% onto the bill.

INMAGINEASIA / GETTY IMAGES ©

Malaysian family enjoying a meal

Etiquette

➡ **Visiting mosques** Cover your head, arms and legs.

➡ **Eating** Use your right hand only if eating with your fingers.

➡ **Modesty** Don't embrace or kiss in public.

➡ **Greetings** A *salam* involves both parties briefly clasping each other's hand then bringing the same hand to touch their heart. Malay women don't shake hands with men – smile and nod or bow slightly instead.

Language

English is widely understood, but linguists will be pleased to tackle a multitude of other languages spoken here. The national language of Malaysia and Brunei is Bahasa Malaysia (Malay). All Malaysians speak Malay, and many are fluent in at least two other languages common in the region including Tamil, Hokkien, Cantonese and Mandarin. There are also Chinese dialects, various other Indian and Orang Asli languages and even, in Melaka, a form of 16th-century Portuguese known as Kristang. See Language (p616) for more information.

What's New

The global COVID-19 pandemic has had an unprecedented economic and social impact on Malaysia, Singapore and Brunei, closing borders between the neighbouring countries for the first time in history.

COVID-19

When the UK released its 'Green List' of countries it considered safe to travel to in May 2021, both Singapore and Brunei made the cut – a reflection of the relative success the pair have had in controlling the spread of the coronavirus. Singapore has taken various approaches in its careful resumption of travel, including setting up Connect@Changi, a short-stay facility for business travellers to meet without having to serve quarantine. For updates on travel rules and local situations check the following:

Brunei www.moh.gov.bn/SitePages/COVID-19.aspx

Malaysia www.pmo.gov.my/special-contents/2019-novel-coronavirus-2019-ncov

Singapore www.moh.gov.sg/covid-19

Merdeka 118

Edging towards completion is the gleaming skyscraper Merdeka 118 atop Petaling Hill in Kuala Lumpur. So named because it has 118 storeys, the 644m tall building will be Malaysia's tallest structure, and the second tallest in the world. A Park Hyatt hotel will occupy the tower's upper floors along with an observation deck. The complex, which is on schedule for completion in 2024, will also include a theatre, separate residential towers, shopping mall and landscaped grounds.

Dewakan 2.0

In December 2019, acclaimed restaurant Dewakan (p115) opened the doors to its new home on the 48th floor of a central KL tower. Chef Darren Teoh's unique culinary skills, which transform rare and forgotten

---

LOCAL KNOWLEDGE

WHAT'S HAPPENING IN MALAYSIA, SINGAPORE & BRUNEI

Simon Richmond, Lonely Planet writer

In late February 2020, Malaysia's coalition government, led by Dr Mahathir Mohamad, collapsed. A week later, many Malaysians were shocked that UMNO, the party of disgraced former PM Najib Razak, had stepped back into government with the help of defecting politician Muhyiddin Yassin, who became the new prime minister. In January 2021, parliament was suspended under a state of emergency announced to deal with the spike in coronavirus cases. Critics claim this was also a ploy by Muhyiddin to keep his unstable government in power.

The People's Action Party (PAP) has governed Singapore since the country's birth in 1965. The general election of 2020 didn't change that, but the PAP did suffer a reduced majority. The Workers' Party gained 10 seats and its leader Pritam Singh is now Official Leader of the Opposition – the first time any opposition leader in Singapore has been considered relevant enough to hold the post.

Malaysian ingredients into fine dining dishes, now come with the added glitter of city skyline views.

Batu Caves

Since being given a rainbow coloured paint job, the 272 steps leading up to the Temple Cave at Selangor's celebrated Batu Caves have been trending on Instagram. The local heritage authorities may not be very pleased at this unorthodox revamp of a national heritage site but the caves are more popular than ever with visitors.

Sky Mirror

Another recent Insta-image smash has been a sandbar that appears for just four days, twice a month at the mouth of the Kuala Selangor river. Those in the know have been flocking to Kuala Selangor, 70km northwest of KL, to join a boat tour (www.skymirrortour.com) to what has been dubbed the Sky Mirror. With the weather on your side its possible to snap stunning photos of the reflections in the film of water covering the surface of the sandbar.

Desaru Coast

Looking for a new tropical beach getaway? Just over an hour's drive from Johor Bahru, the **Desaru Coast** (https://desaru coast.com) offers pristine sand as well as a fun waterpark, golf course, fruit farms, natural mangroves and several swanky new resort hotels including the luxurious **Anantara** (www.anantara.com/en/desaru-coast) and **One&Only Desaru Coast** (www.oneandonlyresorts.com/desaru-coast).

Sarawak Museum Complex

Scheduled to open in mid-2021, the modern and innovative Sarawak Museum Complex (p400) incorporates several floors of interactive and hands-on exhibitions showcasing the various communities, cultures and history of the state. Surrounded by parkland and including a cafe, the spectacular building is inspired by traditional Islamic architecture. Some of the most interesting ethnographic exhibitions dis-

For inspiration and up-to-date news, visit www.lonelyplanet.com/malaysia/articles

LISTEN, WATCH AND FOLLOW

BFM (www.bfm.my) Malaysia's only independent radio station focussing on business and current affairs has many great podcasts.

Zafigo (https://zafigo.com) Travel tips and ideas for and by local Asian women.

LadyIronChef (www.ladyironchef.com) Reports from a man who loves nothing more than eating his way around Singapore and beyond.

The Scoop (www.thescoop.co) News, commentary, culture and life in Brunei.

FAST FACTS

Food trend Locally sourced ingredients

Number of islands in Malaysia Over 20,000

Region's highest peak Mt Kinabalu (4095m)

Population Malaysia 32 million, Singapore 5.6 million, Brunei 422,680

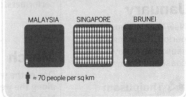

MALAYSIA   SINGAPORE   BRUNEI

≈ 70 people per sq km

played at the old Sarawak Museum will be re-installed here.

Raffles Returns

After shutting its doors for over two years, storied hotel Raffles Singapore (p532) reopened in October 2019. The property has been meticulously revamped with all the finest modern comforts but without losing one iota of charm. Among the hotel's new restaurants are **BBR by Alain Ducasse** in the old Bar & Billiard Room, and **La Dame de Pic** showcasing the culinary stylings of Michelin-starred chef Anne-Sophie Pic.

Month by Month

TOP EVENTS

Thaipusam, January or February

Chinese New Year, January or February

Chingay, February

Hungry Ghost Festival, August

Rainforest World Music Festival, July

January

New Year is a busy travel period. It's monsoon season on Malaysia's east coast and Sarawak.

✯ Thaipusam

Enormous crowds converge at the Batu Caves north of KL, Nattukottai Chettiar Temple in Penang and in Singapore for this dramatic Hindu festival involving body piercing. Falls between mid-January and mid-February. (p584)

February

Chinese New Year is a big deal throughout the region and a busy travel period. Book transport and hotels well ahead.

✯ Chinese New Year

Dragon dances and parades mark the start of the new year. Families hold open houses. Celebrated on 1 February 2022, 22 January 2023 and 10 February 2024.

✯ Chingay

Held over two nights during the first weekend of Chinese New Year, Chingay delivers Singapore's biggest street parade, featuring lion dancers, floats and performers. (p531)

March

One of the wettest months along the west coast of Malaysia, so bring an umbrella and watch out for flash flooding.

✯ Birthday of the Goddess of Mercy

Offerings are made to the popular Chinese goddess Kuan Yin at temples across Malaysia. The goddess is also honoured three times more during the year, in April/May, July/August and October/November.

May

While the east coast is relatively dry, on the west coast the monsoons are starting.

✯ Wesak Day

Buddha's birth, enlightenment and death are celebrated with processions in KL, Singapore and other major cities, plus various events including the release of caged birds to symbolise setting free captive souls. Celebrated on 16 May 2022, 4 May 2023 and 22 May 2024.

June

School holidays and one of the hottest months, so get ready to sweat it out.

✯ Gawai Dayak

Held on 1 and 2 June but beginning on the evening of 31 May, this Sarawak-wide Dayak festival celebrates the end of the rice-harvest season.

✯ Dragon Boat Festival

Commemorates the Malay legend of the fishermen who paddled out to sea to prevent the drowning of a Chinese saint, beating drums to scare away any fish that might attack him. Celebrated from June to August, with boat races in Penang.

🎆 Hari Raya Aidilfitri

The end of Ramadan is followed by a month of breaking the fast parties, many public occasions where you can enjoy a free array of Malay culinary delicacies.

🔒 Great Singapore Sale

The Great Singapore Sale sees retailers around the island cut prices (and wheel out the stuff they couldn't sell earlier in the year). There are bargains to be had if you can stomach the crowds. Go early! (p531)

July

Busy travel month for Malaysian Borneo, so book ahead for activities, tours and accommodation.

☆ Rainforest World Music Festival

A three-day musical extravaganza held in the Sarawak Cultural Village near Kuching as well as Kuching itself, which hosts a Fringe Festival. (p404)

🍴 Singapore Food Festival

A two-week celebration of all things edible and Singaporean. Events taking place across the city include tastings, special dinners and food-themed tours. (p531)

🎆 Sultan of Brunei's Birthday

Colourful official ceremonies are held on 15 July to mark the sultan's birthday and include an elaborate military ceremony presided over by the supremo himself.

🎆 George Town Festival

This outstanding arts, performance and culture festival in Penang includes international artists, innovative street performances and also has a fringe component in Butterworth on the mainland. (p171)

August

With a big influx of Arab and European tourists to the region during this time, it pays to book ahead for specific accommodation.

🎆 Hungry Ghost Festival

Chinese communities perform operas, host open-air concerts and lay out food for their ancestors. Celebrated towards the end of the month and in early September.

🎆 Malaysia's National Day

Join the crowds at midnight on 31 August to celebrate the anniversary of Malaysia's independence in 1957. There are parades and festivities the next morning across the country.

🎆 Singapore National Day

Held on 9 August, Singapore National Day is a hugely popular spectacle of military parades, civilian processions, air-force fly-bys and fireworks. Tickets are snapped up well in advance; however, you can watch all the aerial acts from Marina Bay Sands. (p531)

September

Haze from forest and field clearance fires in Indonesia create urban smog across the region.

☆ Formula One Grand Prix

The F1 night race screams around Marina Bay. Off-track events include international music acts. Book accommodation months in advance and be prepared to pay through the nose. (p533)

November

In the run-up to Deepavali, the region's Indian communities are packed with stalls selling textiles and celebratory sweets.

🎆 Deepavali

Tiny oil lamps are lit outside Hindu homes to attract the auspicious gods Rama and Lakshmi. Indian businesses start the new financial year, with Little Indias across the region ablaze with lights.

December

A sense of festivity (and monsoon rains in Singapore and east-coast Malaysia) permeates the air as the year winds down. Christmas is a big deal mainly in Singapore, with impressive light displays on Orchard Rd.

🎆 ZoukOut

ZoukOut is Singapore's biggest outdoor dance party, held over two nights on Siloso Beach, Sentosa. Expect A-list international DJs. (p547)

Itineraries

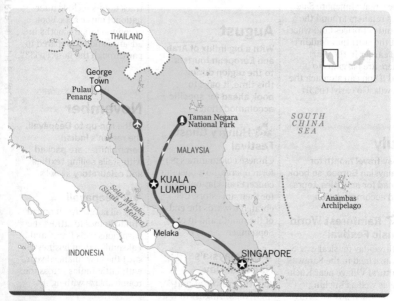

THAILAND

George Town
Pulau Penang

Taman Negara
National Park

MALAYSIA

KUALA LUMPUR

Selat Melaka
(Strait of Melaka)

Melaka

SOUTH
CHINA
SEA

Anambas
Archipelago

INDONESIA

SINGAPORE

Essential Malaysia & Singapore

This itinerary cherry picks the best of the two countries with a focus on urban adventures but also with the chance to experience the region's amazing biodiversity.

Spend your first three days in Malaysia's capital **Kuala Lumpur** (KL) where you can explore cultural diversity in Chinatown, marvel at the soaring steel-clad Petronas Towers and discover the treasures of the Islamic Arts Museum.

Next head inland to **Taman Negara**. Even on a two-day visit to this magnificent national park you can clamber across the canopy walkway and do some short jungle hikes. Return to KL and hop on a flight to Penang where three days will give you a good taste of the heritage districts of **George Town** and other island highlights such as Kek Lok Si Temple.

Historic **Melaka**, another Unesco World Heritage Site, deserves a couple of nights but visit midweek to avoid the crowds. Then head across the causeway to **Singapore** where you can spend your final four days enjoying everything from maxing out your credit card at glitzy shopping malls and sampling delicious hawker food to visiting the eye-boggling space age architecture of Marina Bay and the excellent zoo and night safari.

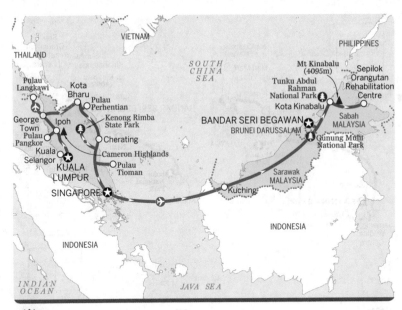

The Grand Tour

6 WEEKS

Starting on the Peninsula and finishing in the wilds of Borneo, this itinerary includes classic sights, some off-the-beaten-track gems and time to relax and take it all in.

Schedule a week in **Kuala Lumpur** and surrounds for sightseeing and acclimatisation. Day trips could include Batu Caves and Putrajaya, a showcase of modern Malaysian architecture. The sleepy old royal capital of **Kuala Selangor**, near to which you can observe the dazzling natural display of fireflies, is also only a couple of hours' drive from KL.

After a pit stop in **Ipoh**, which has some great colonial-era architecture and places to eat, your second week is spent in the cooler climate of the **Cameron Highlands** where you can take walks past verdant tea plantations. Return to the coast and hop across to **Pulau Pangkor**.

The urban delights of **George Town**, on Penang are up next; the city's Unesco World Heritage district is packed with colourful, fascinating sights. This large island is also Malaysia's number one food destination. A quick flight away are the resorts, gorgeous beaches and jungle hinterlands of **Pulau Langkawi**.

Into week four and it's time to cross the mountainous spine of the peninsula to **Kota Bharu**, a great place to encounter traditional Malay culture. Island- and beach-hop down the east coast, pausing at **Pulau Perhentian**, **Cherating** and **Pulau Tioman**. **Kenong Rimba State Park** offers jungle adventures without the crowds.

Singapore can easily swallow up a week of shopping, museum viewing and world-class eating. From here you can fly to **Kuching** in Sarawak, a good base for a longhouse excursion or for arranging a trek in **Gunung Mulu National Park**. Rack up the visa stamps by taking the overland and river route from Sarawak to Sabah via Brunei stopping in the capital **Bandar Seri Begawan**.

Having made it to **Kota Kinabalu**, relax for a few days dipping into the art scene of Sabah's capital or heading to the nearby islands of the **Tunku Abdul Rahman National Park**. Your final challenge, should you choose to accept it, is to climb **Mt Kinabalu**. Alternatively, it's difficult to resist the chance to eyeball close up the supercute ginger apes at **Sepilok Orangutan Rehabilitation Centre**.

Sabah–Sarawak Sampler
2 WEEKS

This abridged itinerary for the time-challenged offers a sample of the best of Malaysian Borneo, including top national parks, snaking rivers and time spent lounging on longhouse verandahs.

Start in **Kota Kinabalu** (KK), which encapsulates Southeast Asian city life on a manageable scale and where you'll be obliged to spend a day or two sorting permits to tackle Sabah's star attraction, **Mt Kinabalu**. Consider a day-trip cruise (including buffet dinner) down one of the tea-brown rivers in the **Beaufort Division**, or learn a little about the local culture at the **Mari Mari Cultural Village**.

Leapfrog by plane from KK to Miri and then on to **Gunung Mulu National Park**, home to the world's largest caves, and several challenging jungle treks, including the marathon Headhunters Trail. Pass through Miri once more for a flight down to **Kuching**. Sarawak's capital is a real charmer and will easily keep you occupied for several days. Break up your time in town with a visit to **Semenggoh Wildlife Centre**, **Bako National Park** and, if you have time, to a longhouse such as **Annah Rais Longhouse**.

Ultimate Borneo
4 WEEKS

On this grand tour of Borneo tackle the island's top five treks and enjoy some world-class diving and snorkelling plus encounters with endangered wildlife.

From **Kuching** explore the local longhouses and **Bako National Park**. Fly to **Miri**, which is the base for trips to the impressive **Niah National Park** and **Bario** in the vine-draped Kelabit Highlands.

Travel overland to **Bandar Seri Begawan**, Brunei's capital. Also schedule in the sultanate's **Ulu Temburong National Park**, a pristine sliver of primary rainforest.

Chill out in **Kota Kinabalu** before setting off for **Mt Kinabalu**. Catch some ape love at the **Sepilok Orangutan Rehabilitation Centre**, followed by a layover in historic **Sandakan**. The mighty **Sungai Kinabatangan** offers wildlife enthusiasts plenty of photo fodder. If you've got the time (and the dime), head deep into Sabah's green interior for a trek through the **Danum Valley Conservation Area**. The magnificent dive sites of the **Semporna Archipelago** accessed from **Semporna** provide an ideal climax.

3 WEEKS Jewels of the North

Idyllic islands, Malay culture, rainforests and hill stations all feature on this tour around the north of Peninsular Malaysia.

Explore **Kuala Lumpur** for a few days before heading to the east-coast resort of **Cherating**. Move on to **Kuala Terengganu**, with its pretty Chinatown and the Kompleks Muzium Negeri Terengganu.

Next come the classic **Perhentian islands**, accessed from Kuala Besut. Pulau Perhentian Besar tends to be less crowded and just as gorgeous as its more popular twin, Pulau Perhentian Kecil. Back on the mainland, linger a day or two in **Kota Bharu**, for its museums, cultural events and night market, then head to the remote **Royal Belum State Park** in northern Perak.

Access more Malay culture in Kedah's capital **Alor Setar** before taking the ferry from Kuala Perlis to **Pulau Langkawi** for sunbathing, island-hopping and jungle exploration. Fly to **George Town**, the essential stop on Penang, then cool down in the hill station of **Bukit Fraser** (Fraser's Hill) before returning to KL.

3 WEEKS Southern Comforts

The southern end of Peninsular Malaysia is no slouch in offering up a diverse range of travel experiences, plus there's easy access to and from Singapore, the logical start and finish to this trip.

Leave yourself several days to soak up the island state of **Singapore's** manifold attractions. If you're strapped for cash then **Johor Bahru** just across the causeway is a cheaper base. It's a decent hangout, not least for street food and nearby Legoland.

The lethargic riverside town of **Muar** has a colonial-era district that's worth a look, and can be used as a base for assaults on Gunung Ledang, Johor's highest mountain, located within the **Gunung Ledang National Park**. Recover in Unesco World Heritage Site–listed **Melaka** where you can spend several days enjoying the enduring Portuguese and Dutch influence.

Explore the last remaining stands of lowland forest on the peninsula in **Endau-Rompin National Park**. Stunning **Pulau Tioman** is the epitome of an island paradise. Alternatively, indulge in some island-hopping and diving around the 64 gems of the **Seribuat Archipelago**.

Malaysia & Brunei: Off the Beaten Track

MYANMAR

VIETNAM

TAMAN NEGERI PERLIS

Home to a vast system of caves and Malaysia's only semideciduous forest, rich in wildlife, this small and remote state park runs 36km along the Thai border. (p214)

DABONG

Lined with flowers and trees, this attractive village, reached by the Jungle Railway, is an excellent exploration base for Kelantan's interior, including the amazing waterfalls in the Gunung Stong State Park. (p293)

PULAU LANG TENGAH

This idyllic, tiny island off the northeast coast of Peninsular Malaysia is a good diving base and, with just three resorts, is quieter and less-developed than neighbouring islands such as the Perhentians. (p302)

KENONG RIMBA STATE PARK

A far less visited alternative to Malaysia's premier national park, this sprawling area of lowland forest rises to the limestone foothills bordering Taman Negara itself. (p280)

SUNGAI BANTANG RECREATIONAL FOREST

Accessed from the town of Bekok in Johor, this forest offers trekking routes, campsites, waterfalls and gently cascading rivers in which you can swim. (p246)

PULAU BESAR

Said to resemble a pregnant woman lying on her back in the sea, this small, placid island, 10km off the southeast coast of Melaka, was once a retreat for Muslim mystics. (p236)

THAILAND

Gulf of Thailand

TAMAN NEGERI PERLIS

Kangar

Alor Setar

Kota Bharu

PULAU LANG TENGAH

Kuala Terengganu

George Town

DABONG

Taiping

KENONG RIMBA STATE PARK

Ipoh

Strait of Melaka

MALAYSIA

Kuantan

Medan

KUALA LUMPUR

Putrajaya

Seramban

SUNGAI BANTANG RECREATIONAL FOREST

Melaka

Johor Bahru

PULAU BESAR

SINGAPORE

Sibolga

SUMATRA INDONESIA

INDIAN OCEAN

0 ⎯⎯⎯⎯⎯⎯ 500 km
0 ⎯⎯⎯⎯⎯⎯ 250 miles

SOUTH CHINA SEA

IMBAK CANYON CONSERVATION AREA

You need to be on a tour to access this 25km-long canyon lying deep in the heart of Sabah, lined with pristine rainforest and hemmed in by immense sandstone cliffs. (p357)

PHILIPPINES *Sulu Sea*

PULAU SELIRONG RECREATIONAL PARK

At the northern tip of Brunei's Temburong District, this 25-sq-km mangrove-forested island is an untamed habitat for proboscis monkeys and flying lemurs. (p485)

Kota Kinabalu

○Sandakan

PULAU SELIRONG RECREATIONAL PARK

BANDAR SERI BEGAWAN

IMBAK CANYON CONSERVATION AREA

SABAH MALAYSIA

BRUNEI DARUSSALAM

BATU PUNGGUL

○Semporna

Celebes Sea

KUCHING WETLANDS NATIONAL PARK

○Kuching

SARAWAK MALAYSIA

BATU PUNGGUL

Not far from the Kalimantan border, deep in Murut country, this 200m jungle-topped limestone outcrop riddled with caves is a bucket-list challenge for rock climbers. (p385)

KUCHING WETLANDS NATIONAL PARK

This seaside park's majestic mangroves are a habitat for monkeys, fireflies, estuarine crocodiles and countless varieties of fish and prawns. Snub-nosed Irrawaddy dolphins can be spotted in the offshore waters. (p419)

KALIMANTAN INDONESIA

Java Sea

Plan Your Trip

Outdoor Adventures

The region's national and state parks offer everything from easy nature trails to challenging hikes into the heart of virgin rainforests. There are also mountains to climb, caves to explore and tropical seas teeming with marine life to dive, as well as other aquatic-based activities such as surfing and white-water rafting.

Best Outdoors

Best Jungle Treks

Taman Negara (p273), Maliau Basin (p380), Kelabit Highlands (p464), Endau-Rompin National Park (p250)

Best Mountain Climbing

Mt Kinabalu (p332), Gunung Ledang (p245), Gunung Mulu (p453), Gunung Tahan (p275), Mt Trusmadi (p383)

Best Diving & Snorkelling

Semporna Archipelago (p369), Pulau Perhentian (p293), Pulau Redang (p301), Pulau Tioman (p253), Seribuat Archipelago (p248)

Best Caving

Gunung Mulu National Park (p453), Niah National Park (p443), Gomantong Caves (p358), Wind Cave (p423)

Hiking & Trekking

Fancy seeing what life might have been like 100 million years ago? Trekking into the deepest parts of the region's jungles will give you a clue as they were largely unaffected by the far-reaching climatic changes brought on elsewhere by the Ice Age. Significant chunks of these rainforests have been made into national parks, in which all commercial activities apart from tourism are banned.

The British established the region's first national park in Malaya in 1938. That was the basis for what is now Taman Negara (p273), the crowning glory of Malaysia's network of national parks, which crosses the borders of Terengganu, Kelantan and Pahang. In addition to this and the 27 other national and state parks across the country (23 of them located in Malaysian Borneo), there are various government-protected reserves and sanctuaries for forests, birds, mammals and marine life.

Even in the heart of KL, it's possible to stretch your legs hiking in the KL Forest Eco Park (p60) or Taman Tugu (p61). Alternatively, head a little north of the city to find a network of serene forest trails at the Forest Research Institute of Malaysia (p109).

Only 1 sq km of Brunei's 500-sq-km Ulu Temburong National Park (p485) is accessible to the public but what a treat it presents, being one of the most pristine slices of rainforest in the region. Even Singapore offers up several hiking possibilities: the country's National Parks Board manages 10% of the island's total land area, which comprises over 300 parks and four nature reserves, including Bukit Timah Nature Reserve (p512).

When to Go

The region has wet months and less wet months. Global warming has also affected the monsoons so that year to year precipitation varies widely. In short, no matter where you go and when, you're likely to get wet – and if not from rain then certainly from sweating!

What is seasonal, however, is the number of other travellers you'll be competing with for experienced guides and lodgings. Northern hemisphere residents often come to the region during the summer holidays in their home countries, so if you plan to trek in July or August book a tour far in advance. Also watch out for regional travel high points such as Chinese New Year holidays and the so-called Golden Week of holidays that Japanese people usually take late in April or early May.

Permits, Guides & Bookings

Many of the region's national parks and natural beauty spots charge a nominal entrance fee (around RM10). At a few, if you wish to trek or engage in other activities such as fishing or mountain climbing, then there may be additional permits to purchase and guides to hire. In particular, Mt Kinabalu has stringent visitor regulations, as does Gunung Mulu National Park.

Accommodation is generally not a problem when visiting most national parks. Various types are available, from hostel to luxury resorts. Transport and accommodation operations are increasingly being handled by private tour companies, who require you to book in advance and pay a deposit.

Many national parks have well-marked day trails and can be walked unaccompanied. But for almost all overnights, only a fool would set out without a local guide.

CYCLING

The region's excellent roads make it one of the best places in Southeast Asia for bike touring. Perhaps the most popular route is the one up the east coast of Peninsular Malaysia, with its relatively quiet roads. However, if you're fit and energetic, you may prefer the hillier regions of the peninsula's interior or Malaysian Borneo – ideal for mountain biking. Attracting some of the world's top cyclists is **Le Tour De Langkawi** (☏03-7734 2999; www.ltdl.my; ☉Mar), a week-long multistage race, which despite its name is staged at locations across Peninsular Malaysia.

Remember, trail maps of any sort are completely unavailable and signage along remote trail networks is nonexistent. A good guide will be able to gauge your abilities and push you a little, rather than taking the easiest way as a matter of course. Try a shorter guided hike before setting off on an overnight adventure to get a sense of how you fare in tropical trekking conditions.

Especially in Sabah, Brunei and Sarawak, the national parks are very strict about allowing only licensed guides. We've heard stories of groups being turned back when they arrived with an uncertified leader. Before you fork over any cash, compare notes with other travellers and ask to see the guide's national-park certification.

Guides for day walks can sometimes be hired at national park HQ, but for overnights you'll need to contact either a freelance guide or a tour agency. Budget anything from RM50 to RM200 per day for a guide depending on the duration and difficulty of the trek you are planning.

Mountain & Rock Climbing

Towering above the forests of Borneo are some brilliant mountains. Even non-climbers know about 4095m Mt Kinabalu, the highest peak between the Himalayas

RESPONSIBLE HIKING

Jungle hiking can be one of the highlights of a trip to the region. However, to the un-initiated, it can be something of a shock – like marching all day in a sauna with a pile of bricks strapped to your back. To make the experience as painless as possible, it's necessary to make some preparations:

➡ On overnight trips, bring two sets of clothing, one for walking and one to wear at the end of the day (always keep your night kit separate and dry in a plastic bag). Within minutes of starting, your hiking kit will be drenched and will stay that way throughout your trip.

➡ If you'll be passing through dense vegetation, wear long trousers and a long-sleeved shirt. Otherwise, shorts and a T-shirt will suffice. Whatever you wear, make sure it's loose-fitting.

➡ Bring fast-drying synthetic clothes. Once cotton gets wet, it won't dry until you take it to the laundry back in town.

➡ It can be cool in the evening, so bring a fleece top to keep warm.

➡ Unless you like a lot of support, consider hiking in running shoes with good traction. You could also go local and buy a pair of 'kampung Adidas' – a Malaysian jungle version of a hiking shoe, shaped like an Adidas soccer cleat but made out of rubber (like a souped-up Croc). They're cheap (under RM10 a pair) and popular with porters and guides.

➡ Buy a pair of light-coloured leech socks – they're not easy to come by in the region so buy them online before coming.

➡ Drink plenty of water. If you're going long distances, you'll have to bring either a water filter or a water-purification agent like iodine (most people opt for the latter to keep pack weight down).

➡ Get in shape long before coming to the region and start slowly, with day hikes before longer treks.

➡ Always go with a guide unless you're on a well-marked, commonly travelled trail.

➡ Wear loose underwear to help prevent chafing. Bring talcum powder to cope with the chafing caused by wet undergarments.

➡ If you wear glasses, treat them with an antifog solution (ask at the shop where you buy your glasses).

➡ Consider putting something waterproof over the back padding to keep the sweat out of your pack, or consider a waterproof stuff sack.

➡ Keep your camera in a waterproof container, with a pouch of silica gel or other desiccant.

➡ Pack sunscreen, insect repellent, a water bottle and a torch (preferably a head-lamp to keep your hands free).

The following points are also worth bearing in mind if you're planning a mountaineering or caving adventure:

➡ Hire a local guide – it's the best way to make sure you're in touch with local customs and concerns as you move through tribal lands.

➡ Follow the golden rule of rubbish: if you carried it in, carry it out. Never bury your rubbish – it may be out of sight, but it won't be out of reach of animals.

➡ Where there isn't a toilet, bury your waste in a small hole 15cm deep and at least 100m from any watercourse. Use toilet paper sparingly and cover everything with soil and a rock.

➡ Always stick to the marked trails, however indistinct they may be. Carving your own path through the jungle can disrupt local people, not to mention plants and wildlife.

Hikers crossing a suspension bridge in Gunung Mulu National Park (p453)

and the island of New Guinea. This craggy monster simply begs to be climbed, and there is something magical about starting the ascent in humid tropical jungle and emerging into a bare, rocky alpine zone so cold that snow has been known to fall. But beyond the transition from hot to cold, it's the weird world of the summit plateau that makes Mt Kinabalu among the world's most interesting peaks. It's got a dash of Yosemite and a pinch of Torres del Paine, but at the end of the day, it's pure Borneo.

Sabah's second-highest peak, Mt Trus Madi (2642m), is a far more difficult peak to ascend than Mt Kinabalu – and a more difficult trip to arrange.

Gunung Mulu (2376m) isn't quite as high but it's almost as famous, thanks in part to being a Unesco World Heritage Site. If you're a real glutton for punishment, you'll probably find the five-day return trek to the summit of this peak to your liking. Those who make the journey experience a variety of pristine natural environments, starting with lowland dipterocarp forest and ending with rhododendron and montane forest.

Pulau Berhala in the Sandakan Archipelago is also a prime destination for rock climbers, although there are no local operators leading tours here.

On the peninsula, Gunung Ledang (p245; 1276m) is a good introduction to tropical mountaineering. There are also several good climbs in Taman Negara, including Gunung Tahan (2187m), an expedition that can take between seven to nine days. At Juara on Pulau Tioman there's also a rock-climbing operation.

Costs

Guide fees could be anything between RM150 and RM250 per day. There will also be national park entry fees (RM1 to RM15) and climbing permits (RM200 in the case of Mt Kinabalu) to consider.

Pre-Trip Preparations

Climbing one of Malaysia's mountains is like a jungle trek except more so – more physically exhausting, more psychologically challenging and especially more vertical. Be prepared for ascents that turn your legs to rubber and much colder weather.

As with longer treks, book well ahead. Many of the agencies that handle trekking also offer mountain ascents. Some of the more experienced guides in Sarawak's Kelabit Highlands can take you to two rarely climbed peaks, Batu Lawi and Gunung Murud.

Keen mountain climbers may want to search out a copy of *Mountains of Malaysia – A Practical Guide and Manual* (1988) by John Briggs. Online resources include Climb Malaysia (www.climb.my).

Caving

Slice one of Malaysia's limestone hills in half and chances are you'll find that inside it looks like Swiss cheese. Malaysians have been living, harvesting birds' nests, planning insurgencies and burying their dead in these *gua* (caves) for tens of thousands of years. These days, the country's subterranean spaces – including some of the largest caverns anywhere on earth – are quiet, except for the flow of underground streams, the drip of stalactites and the whoosh of the wings of swiftlets and bats.

Sarawak's Gunung Mulu National Park is a place of spelunking superlatives. It's got the world's second-largest cave passage (the Deer Cave, 2km in length and 174m in height), the world's largest cave chamber (the Sarawak Chamber, 700m long, 400m wide and 70m high) and Asia's longest cave (the Clearwater Cave, 107km in length). Several of the park's caves are – like their counterparts in Niah National Park – accessible to nonspelunkers: you can walk through them on well-maintained walkways.

Other caves open to the public include the Dark Cave at the Batu Caves; various caverns in and around Gunung Stong State Park; those in Taman Negara; and the Gomantong Caves in Sabah.

Pre-Trip Preparations

A pitch-black passageway deep in the bowels of the earth is not the ideal place to discover that you can't deal with narrow, confined spaces. Before heading underground, seriously consider your susceptibility to claustrophobia and fear of heights (some caves require scaling underground cliffs). If you have any concerns about a specific route, talk with your guide beforehand.

MALAYSIA'S TOP 10 NATIONAL & STATE PARKS

PARK	FEATURES	ACTIVITIES	BEST TIME TO VISIT
Bako	beaches, proboscis monkeys	coastline walks, trekking	May-Sep
Batang Ai	primary forest crawling with wild orangutan	trekking	year-round
Endau-Rompin	lowland forest, unique plants, waterfalls and rivers	trekking, wildlife spotting	Apr-Sep
Gunung Mulu	caves, the Pinnacles, Headhunters Trail	caving, trekking, mountain climbing	May-Sep
Kinabalu	Mt Kinabalu	mountain climbing	May-Sep
Niah	caves	caving, trekking	May-Sep
Penang	meromictic lake, monkeys	trekking	Apr-Jul
Perlis	Gua Wang Burma cave, stump-tailed macaques, Malaysia's only semi-deciduous forest	caving, trekking	Jun-Aug
Taman Negara	canopy walkway, hides, jungle trails, rivers	trekking, wildlife spotting, river trips	Apr-Sep
Tun Sakaran	sand-fringed islands, technicolour reefs	snorkelling, diving	year-round

TOP WILDLIFE SPOTS

Taman Negara (p273) Malaysia's oldest and most prestigious national park is home to everything from fireflies to elephants.

Royal Belum State Park (p156) Home to 10 varieties of hornbill and the majority of Malaysia's big mammals.

Sungai Kinabatangan (p358) Spot wild orangutans and pygmy elephants along the banks of Sabah's longest river.

Bako National Park (p414) The park's coves and trails are one of the best places to spot proboscis monkeys.

Deramakot Forest Reserve (p357) Sabah home to leopard cats, civets and deer.

Singapore Zoo (p511) One of the world's best, along with the Night Safari and the River Safari experience.

Ulu Temburong National Park (p485) Breathtaking views from canopy walkway in Brunei's Temburong region.

Be prepared to crawl through muck, including bat guano, and bring clothes you won't mind getting filthy (some guides and agencies supply these).

Aquatic Adventures

Diving & Snorkelling

Reasonable prices, an excellent variety of dive sites and easy access make Malaysia a great diving choice for both first-timers and old hands. Island-based boat dives are the most common, but a few areas, like Sabah's Pulau Sipadan, have some cracking sites right off the beach. You may also come across live-aboard boats to get you to more remote spots.

The standards of diving facilities in Malaysia are generally quite high and equipment rental is widely available. Most places offer the universally recognised Professional Association of Diving Instructors (PADI) certification.

When to Go

The northeast monsoon brings strong winds and rain to the east coast of Peninsular Malaysia from early November to late February, during which time most dive centres simply shut down. Visibility improves after the monsoon, peaking in August and September. On the west coast, conditions are reversed and the best diving is from September to March. In Malaysian Borneo the monsoons are less pronounced and rain falls more evenly throughout the year, making diving a year-round activity.

Costs

Most dive centres charge around RM200 to RM300 for two dives, including equipment rental. A three-dive day trip at Sipadan costs between RM750 and RM850 (some operators include park fees, other don't – be sure to ask). PADI open-water courses range from RM1000 to RM1200. Many resorts and dive operators also offer all-inclusive dive packages, which vary widely in price.

Pre- & Post-Trip

While it is possible simply to show up and dive at some of the larger dive centres like Pulau Tioman, it's a good idea to make arrangements in advance, if only to avoid waiting a day or two before starting. Diving at Sipadan is capped at 120 divers per day; book in advance.

Note that it is unsafe to dive directly after flying due to poorly pressurised cabins and dehydration. It's also a serious health risk to fly within 24 hours of your last dive.

Kayaking & White-Water Rafting

Malaysia's mountains plus rainforests equals fast-flowing rivers, which result in ideal opportunities for river-rafting and kayaking enthusiasts.

On the peninsula, has become the white-water hot spot, with rafting and

PLAN YOUR TRIP OUTDOOR ADVENTURES

LANO LAN/SHUTTERSTOCK ©

Top: Diver at Layang
Layang (p345), Sabah

Bottom: White-water
rafting on the Kiulu
River (p321), Sabah

RESPONSIBLE DIVING

Consider the following tips when diving or snorkelling, and help to preserve the ecology and beauty of the reefs:

➡ Do not use anchors on the reef, and take care not to ground boats on coral.

➡ Avoid touching living marine organisms with your body or dragging equipment across the reef.

➡ Be conscious of your fins. Clouds of sand or even the surge from heavy fin strokes can damage delicate organisms.

➡ Major damage can be done by divers descending too fast and colliding with the reef, so practise buoyancy control across your trip.

➡ Resist the temptation to collect (or buy) coral or shells from reefs of dive sites. Some sites are even protected from looting by law.

➡ Ensure that you take home all your rubbish and any litter you may find.

➡ Don't feed the fish; this can disturb their habits or be detrimental to their health.

kayaking organised along the Sungai Selangor; PieRose Swiftwater (p112) is a reputable company.

White-water rafting has become quite the craze in Sabah, with Kota Kinabalu-based operators taking travellers south of the city to the Beaufort Division for some Grade III to IV rapids on the Sungai Padas (Padas River). Calmer water at Sungai Kiulu near Mt Kinabalu is a tamer option for beginners.

Kayaking is offered by several operators in Kuching.

Boating

Yachting clubs offer chances for those interested in a sailing trip around the region or learning how to sail, including **Royal Selangor Yacht Club** (☑03-3168 6964; www.rsyc.com.my; Jln Shahbandar), Pelabuhan Klang; and Avillion Admiral Cove (p124), Port Dickson.

Boating adventures can also be had on the region's lakes, rivers and mangrove-lined estuaries. Taking a sundown boat ride through the mangroves of Kuching Wetlands National Park to spot crocodiles and fireflies can be a magical experience. Firefly-spotting boat trips out of Kuala Selangor are also popular.

On larger rivers, transport is by 'flying coffin' – long, narrow passenger boats with about 70 seats, not including the people sitting on the roof. Thanks to their powerful engines, these craft can power upriver against very strong currents.

Surfing

Malaysia is no Indonesia when it comes to surfing, but Cherating and Juara on Pulau Tioman in Malaysia receive a steady stream of surfers during the monsoon season when the swells are up, as does the Tip of Borneo (Tanjung Simpang Mengayau) in Sabah.

You can also rent paddleboards in Tioman and Cherating, kitesurfing gear in Cherating and take courses in all of those sports in both locations.

Plan Your Trip
Eat & Drink Like a Local

Eating like a local in Malaysia, Singapore and Brunei is a snap. The food is absolutely delicious, hygiene standards are among the highest in Southeast Asia, and most vendors speak English. And an almost perverse obsession with food among the locals means that visitors are often smothered in culinary companionship.

The Year in Food

As might be expected of a people consumed with food and its pleasures, Singaporeans, Malaysians and Bruneians mark every special occasion with celebratory edibles.

Chinese New Year (January/February)

In the weeks leading to Chinese New Year, every table is graced with *yee sang* (*yue sang* or *yu sheng*; 'fresh fish'), a mound of grated raw vegetables, pickles, pomelo segments and crispy, fried-dough pieces topped with sliced raw fish.

Ramadan

During Ramadan, celebrated in the ninth month of the Islamic calendar (typically between May and August), special food markets swing into action in the late afternoons, offering a wide variety of Malay treats.

Deepavali (October/November)

During the Indian Festival of Lights, make your way to a Little India, where you'll find special sweets such as *jalebi* (deep-fried fritters soaked in sugar syrup) and savoury snacks like *muruku* (crispy fried coils of curry leaf–studded dough).

Food Experiences
Meals of a Lifetime

Rebung (p92), **Kuala Lumpur** Seemingly endless buffet of traditional Malaysian dishes.

Nipah Deli (p147), **Pulau Pangkor** Watch the sun set over seafood steamboat, or fish and tamarind curry, at this attentive beachfront restaurant.

Singh Chapati (p141), **Cameron Highlands** Feast on potato masala, palak paneer and freshly made chapati at the Cameron Highlands' best Indian restaurant.

Seng Huat Bak Kut Teh (p117), **Klang** Rich pork-rib stew is slow-cooked to perfection at this unassuming place under Klang Bridge.

Kedai Kopi Ambassador (p289) **Kota Bharu** Select Thai, Malay or Chinese from separate stalls and chefs within this busy sidewalk restaurant under the red archway entrance to KB's Chinatown.

Lepau (p407), **Kuching** Organic and sustainable ingredients combine with the traditional cuisine of Sarawak's indigenous Iban and Bidayuh people.

Kocik Kitchen (p230), **Melaka** Prawns and pineapple bathed in a coconut sauce is a must, rounded off with flavourful *cendol* (shaved-ice dessert with green noodles, syrups, fruit and coconut milk) at this authentic Peranakan place, tucked away in Melaka's Chinatown.

Teksen (p176), **George Town** Shophouse-bound legend that does nearly faultless Chinese and Chinese/Malay fare.

Jumbo Seafood (p538), **Singapore** Breezy riverside restaurant serving up Singapore's best chilli crab. Prepare to get messy.

Cheap Treats

Jalan Alor (p79), **Kuala Lumpur** KL's premier eats street has something for everyone.

Pasar Besar (p120), **Seremban** Hunt out Seremban's most flavoursome beef noodles at the main food market; our favourite is stall 748.

Yap Kee (p117), **Klang** Banana-leaf spreads never tasted better than at Klang's cult favourite, an Indian restaurant within a Chinese shophouse.

Ansari Famous Cendol (p153), **Taiping** The *cendol* is sweet, creamy and perfectly balanced at this third-generation vendor.

Funny Mountain Soya Bean (p132), **Ipoh** Crowds gather for silky-textured *tau fu fah,* sweet bean-curd pudding, freshly made at this legendary stall since 1952.

Muhibah Bakery & Cafe (p289), **Kota Bharu** A bright and clean bakery with row upon row of sweet treats, including pandan cake and iced doughnuts and very good coffee.

Restoran Golden Dragon (p310), **Kuala Terengganu** Bustling Chinese restaurant with fresh seafood, cold beer and plastic furniture spreading out onto the sidewalk.

Choon Hui (p406), **Kuching** Get an early start to beat the mid-morning crowds enjoying what is reputedly Kuching's best Sarawak laksa.

Restoran Reaz Corner (p241), **Johor Bahru** Take a corner seat to watch the world go by round the clock in this small open-air curry house in the heart of town.

Lorong Baru (New Lane) Hawker Stalls (p177), **George Town** Basically everything that's tasty and cheap about Penang all in one narrow lane.

Kuah Night Market (p206), **Langkawi** Graze your way from chicken satay stall to fruit seller to mee goreng (fried noodles) at this roving night market held at a different location each day of the week.

A-Square Night Market (p325), **Kota Kinabalu** Over three dozen food stalls to choose from, including superlative laksa and indigenous dishes.

COOKING COURSES

A standard one-day course usually features a shopping trip to a local market to choose ingredients, followed by the preparation of curry pastes, soups, curries, salads and desserts.

➡ LaZat Malaysian Home Cooking Class, Kuala Lumpur (p69)

➡ Nazlina Spice Station, George Town (p169)

➡ Penang Homecooking School, George Town (p169)

➡ Bumbu Cooking School, Kuching (p403)

➡ Top Peak Travel, Kota Kinabalu (p320)

➡ Food Playground, Singapore (p520)

Top Spot Food Court (p407), **Kuching** Super-fresh seafood abounds at this hugely popular Kuching institution on top of a car park.

Hong Kong Soya Sauce Chicken Rice & Noodle (p539), **Singapore** You'll have to queue for the world's cheapest Michelin-starred meal at this humble hawker stall, but it's so worth it.

Dare to Try

Bak kut teh Order this comforting Chinese-Malaysian stewed pork dish 'with everything' and be converted to porcine bits and bobs.

Kerabu beromak On Langkawi, coconut milk, chillies and lime juice dress this 'salad' of rubbery but appealingly briny sea-cucumber slices.

Perut ikan This Penang Nonya coconut-milk curry made with fish innards, pineapple and fresh herbs is spicy, sweet, sour and – yes – a little fishy.

Siat When stir-fried, plump sago grubs from Sarawak turn golden and crispy and boast a savoury fattiness recalling pork crackling.

Sup torpedo Malaysia's bull's penis soup is said to enhance sexual drive.

Local Specialities

Malaysia, Brunei and Singapore have similar populations, share a tropical climate and were all at one time home to important trading ports along the spice route. As a result, their cuisines are characterised by comparable flavours and are built on a shared foundation of basic ingredients. Yet there are some regional differences.

Malaysia

Asam laksa Thick rice noodles in a tart, fish- and herb-packed broth; one of Penang's most famous dishes.

Ayam tauge Tender boiled chicken served with crunchy bean sprouts is a favourite in Ipoh.

Cendol Fine, short strings of green-bean flour dough in coconut milk sweetened with Melaka's famous palm sugar, and topped with shaved ice; the city's signature dessert.

Char kway teow Closely associated with Penang is this dish of silky rice noodles stir-fried with plump prawns, briny cockles, chewy Chinese sausage, crispy sprouts, egg and a hint of chilli.

Chicken rice balls Hokkien-style chicken and rice combined in the form of small globes; one of Melaka's most beloved dishes.

Curry debal A fiery curry with origins in Melaka's Kristang (Portuguese-Eurasian) community.

Hinava Raw fish marinated with lime juice and herbs; a dish associated with Sabah.

Maggi goreng Fried instant noodles; a late-night snack ubiquitous in KL.

DINING DOS & DON'TS

If eating with your hands, do:

➡ wash your hands first; in Malay restaurants use water from the 'teapot' on the table while holding your fingers over the tray;

➡ use only your right hand, and scoop food up with your fingers;

➡ serve yourself from the communal plate with utensils, never your fingers.

Don't:

➡ offer alcohol or pork to Muslims (and don't mention pork to Muslims);

➡ stick your chopsticks upright in a bowl of rice; it symbolises death to Chinese people.

Nasi kerabu Rice tinted light blue from a flower, tossed with herbs and seasonings, and served with various toppings; a dish beloved in Kelantan.

Sarawak laksa Thin rice noodles served in a curry broth topped with shrimp, chicken and a shredded omelette.

Tuak Rice wine brewed by Sarawak's indigenous inhabitants.

Singapore

Chilli crab Eat the stir-fried crab with your fingers, then mop up the spicy, eggy chilli and tomato sauce with French bread or deep-fried *man tou* (Chinese-style buns).

Fish-head curry Allegedly invented by an Indian cook and relying on a cut of fish beloved by the Chinese, this example of Singaporean fusion is much better than it sounds.

Katong laksa Singapore's signature laksa has thick noodles cut into short segments (making chopsticks unnecessary), a rich coconut milk–based broth and a unique garnish of fish cakes.

Kaya toast Grilled bread served with *kaya* (coconut jam), often accompanied by soft boiled eggs and strong coffee, is Singapore's emblematic breakfast.

Brunei

Ambuyat Use a long bamboo fork to dip this sticky, stringy, sago flour–derived 'porridge' into various dips.

Daging masak lada hitam A popular beef dish that combines elements of a stir-fry, curry and stew.

Udang sambal serai bersantan Prawns served in a rich coconut milk–based curry.

How to Eat & Drink
What to Eat

Rice Long-grained rice is boiled in water or stock to make porridge (congee or *bubur*); fried with chillies and shallots for nasi goreng (fried rice); and packed into banana-leaf-lined bamboo tubes, cooked, then sliced and doused with coconut-and-vegetable gravy for the Malay dish *lontong*. Rice flour, mixed with water and allowed to ferment, becomes the batter for Indian *idli* (steamed rice-and-lentil cakes) and

Top: Set of *ambuyat*

Bottom: *Nasi kerabu*

COLEONG / GETTY IMAGES ©

Durians

apam (crispy-chewy pancakes cooked in special concave pans). Glutinous (sticky) rice – both white and black – is a common ingredient in local sweets.

Noodles Many varieties of noodle are also made from rice flour, both the wide, flat *kway teow* and *mee hoon* (or *bee hoon;* rice vermicelli). Round yellow noodles form the basis of the Muslim Indian dish *mee mamak*. The Chinese favourite *won ton mee,* found anywhere in the region, comprises wheat-and-egg vermicelli, a clear meat broth and silky-skinned dumplings.

Meat and fish A person's religion often dictates a dish's protein. *Babi* (pork) is *haram* (forbidden) to Muslims but is the king of meats for Chinese. *Ayam* (chicken) is tremendously popular in Malaysia and Singapore, but more of a special-occasion meat in Brunei (as is beef or buffalo). Tough local *daging* (beef) is best cooked long and slowly, for dishes like coconut-milk-based rendang. Indian Muslims do amazing things with *kambing* (mutton). Lengthy coastlines and abundant rivers and estuaries mean that seafood forms much of the diet for many of the region's residents.

Vegetables Vegetable lovers will have a field day. Every rice-based Malay meal includes *ulam,* a

selection of fresh and blanched vegetables – wing beans, cucumbers, okra, eggplant and the fresh legume *petai* (or stink bean, so-named for its strong garlicky taste) – and fresh herbs to eat on their own or dip into sambal. Indians cook cauliflower and leafy vegetables like cabbage, spinach and roselle (sturdy leaves with an appealing sourness) with coconut milk and turmeric. Other greens – *daun ubi* (sweet potato leaves), *kangkong* (water spinach), Chinese broccoli and yellow-flowered mustard – are stir-fried with *sambal belacan* or garlic.

Sweets The locals are passionate about *kuih* (sweets); vendors of cakes and pastries lie in wait on street corners, footpaths and in markets. Many *kuih* incorporate coconut, grated or in the form of milk, and palm sugar, often combining sweet and savoury flavours to fantastic effect.

What to Drink

Caffeinated drinks Half the fun of taking breakfast in one of Singapore's or Malaysia's Little Indias is watching the tea wallah toss-pour an order of *teh tarik* ('pulled' tea) from one cup to the other. Locals love their leaves; tea is also brewed with ginger for *teh halia,* drunk hot or iced, with or without milk (*teh ais* or *teh-o ais*), and soured with lime juice *(teh limau).* Kopi (coffee) is also extremely popular, and the inky, thick brew owes its distinctive colour and flavour to the fact that its beans are roasted with sugar.

Juices, etc Caffeine-free alternatives include freshly squeezed or blended vegetable and fruit juices, sticky-sweet fresh sugar-cane juice (nice with a squeeze of calamansi), and *kelapa muda,* or young coconut water, drunk straight from the fruit with a straw. Other, more unusual drinks are *ee bee chui* (barley boiled with water, pandan leaf and rock sugar), *air mata kucing* (made with dried longan) and *cincau* (herbal grass jelly).

Beer This is the most ubiquitous drink in the region, generally available at Chinese-run restaurants and stalls. Choose from local brands, such as Tiger, to foreign brands brewed under licence, such as the deliciously malty Guinness, as well as an increasing number of imports and locally brewed craft beers.

Wine Typically only available at fancy restaurants and, due to hefty import taxes and duties, at a premium.

Cocktails In the larger cities, you'll find an increasing number of mixologists doing their thing, although prices aren't cheap.

FRUIT FOR THOUGHT

Fruit such as *nenas* (pineapple), watermelon, papaya and green guava are available year-round. April and May are mango months, and come December to January and June to July, follow your nose to sample notoriously odoriferous love-it-or-hate-it durian. Should the king of fruits prove too repellent, other lesser-known tropical fruits you may come across at markets and street stalls include:

Belimbing The yellow flesh of the starfruit is sweet and tangy and believed by many to lower blood pressure.

Buah nona The custard apple; a knobbly green skin conceals hard, black seeds and sweet, gloopy flesh with a granular texture.

Buah salak Known as the snakeskin fruit because of its scaly skin; the exterior looks like a mutant strawberry and the soft flesh tastes like unripe bananas.

Cempedak The Malaysian breadfruit; a huge green fruit with skin like the Thing from the *Fantastic Four;* the seeds and flesh are often curried or fried.

Ciku The dull brown skin of the sapodilla hides supersweet flesh that tastes a bit like a date.

Duku Strip away the yellowish peel of this fruit (also known as *dokong* and *langsat*) to find segmented, perfumed pearlescent flesh with a lychee-like flavour.

Durian Due to its intense odour and weapon-like appearance, the durian is possibly Southeast Asia's most infamous fruit, the flesh of which can suggest everything from custard to onions.

Durian belanda Soursop has a fragrant but tart granular flesh and hard, black seeds; it's only ripe when soft and goes off within days, so eat it quickly.

Jambu merah Rose apple; elongated pink or red fruit with a smooth, shiny skin and pale, watery flesh. It's a good thirst quencher on a hot day.

Longan A tiny, hard ball like a mini lychee with sweet, perfumed flesh; peel it, eat the flesh and spit out the hard seeds.

Manggis A hard, purple shell conceals the mangosteen's delightfully fragrant white segments, some containing a tough seed that you can spit out.

Nangka Considered the world's largest fruit, jackfruit takes the form of a giant green pod with dozens of waxy yellow sections, the taste of which reminds us of Juicy Fruit chewing gum.

Limau bali Like a grapefruit on steroids, pomelo has a thick pithy green skin hiding sweet, tangy segments; cut into the skin, peel off the pith then break open the segments and munch on the flesh inside.

Rambutan People have different theories about what rambutans look like, not all repeatable in polite company; the hairy shell contains sweet, translucent flesh, which you scrape off the seed with your teeth.

Local booze Across Malaysia, you'll still find a handful of places serving sugar-palm-based alcohol, and in Sarawak, the sticky rice-based booze known as *tuak*.

When to Eat

To those of us used to 'three square meals', it might seem as if the locals are always eating. In fact, five or six meals or snacks is more the order of the day than strict adherence to the breakfast-lunch-dinner trilogy.

Breakfast is often something that can be grabbed on the run: *nasi lemak* (rice boiled in coconut milk served with *ikan bilis* – small, dried sardines or anchovies – peanuts and a curry dish) wrapped to go *(bungkus)* in a banana leaf or brown waxed paper, a quick bowl of noodles, toast and eggs, or griddled Indian bread.

Come late morning a snack might be in order, perhaps a *karipap* (deep-fried pastry filled with spiced meat or fish and potatoes). Lunch gener-

FASTING & FEASTING

In general, there's no need to be deterred from visiting Malaysia during Ramadan, the Muslim holy month of sunrise-to-sunset fasting. Indian and Chinese eateries remain open during the day to cater to the country's sizeable non-Muslim population and, come late afternoon, Ramadan bazaars pop up all over the country. These prepared-food markets offer a rare chance to sample Malay specialities from all over the country, some of which are specific to the festive season or are rarely found outside private homes. One of the country's biggest Ramadan markets is held in KL's Malay enclave of Kampung Baru. Cruise the stalls and pick up provisions for an evening meal – but don't snack in public until the cry of the muezzin tells believers it's time to *buka puasa* (break the fast).

During Ramadan in Brunei, hotel room service is just about the only place that will serve food during the daytime.

ally starts from 12.30pm, something to keep in mind if you plan to eat at a popular establishment.

The British left behind a strong attachment to afternoon tea, consumed here in the form of tea or coffee and a sweet or savoury snack like *tong sui* (sweet soups), various Indian fritters, battered and fried slices of cassava, sweet potato, banana and – of course – local-style *kuih*.

Dinner spans from sundown until late. Among Malays, there's often a generous time window, with diners lingering over cups of sweet tea, while the Chinese generally tend to approach dinner earlier and more efficiently.

Late at night, *pasar malam* (night markets) spring up, which in predominantly Malay areas might offer items such as grilled or fried chicken and lots of sweets, or in more diverse areas, Chinese dishes such as fried noodles.

Where to Eat

Hawker stalls Many locals would argue that the best (and best-value) food is found at hawker stalls, and who are we to argue? Most of these dishes can't be found in restaurants and when they are, they're rarely as tasty, so hawker-stall dining is a must if you really want to appreciate the region's cuisines in all their glory. To partake, simply head to a stand-alone streetside kitchen-on-wheels, a

coffee shop or a food court; place your order with one or a number of different vendors; find a seat (shared tables are common); and pay for each dish as it's delivered. After you're seated you'll be approached by someone taking orders for drinks, which are also paid for separately.

Kopitiam Generally refers to old-style, single-owner Chinese coffee shops. These simple, fan-cooled establishments serve noodle and rice dishes, strong coffee and other drinks, and all-day breakfast fare like soft-boiled eggs and toast to eat with *kaya*.

Restoran (restaurant) Eateries ranging from casual, decades-old Chinese establishments to upscale places boasting international fare, slick decor and a full bar. Between the two extremes lie Chinese seafood restaurants where the main course can be chosen live from a tank, as well as the numerous cafes found in Malaysia's many shopping malls.

Pasar (markets) Consider grazing at one or more *pasar*. Morning markets usually have Chinese-owned stalls selling coffee and Indian-operated *teh tarik* stalls offering freshly griddled roti. Triangular *bungkus* (packages) piled in the middle of tables contain *nasi lemak;* help yourself and pay for what you eat.

Pasar malam (night markets) Also good hunting grounds, where you'll find everything from laksa to fresh-fried doughnuts.

Regions at a Glance

Kuala Lumpur

Food
Shopping
Art Galleries

Fantastic Food

Allow your stomach to lead the way around Kuala Lumpur. Tuck in with locals at the fantastic hawker stalls along Jln Alor, at Imbi Market or in Chinatown. Sample Indian food in Brickfields, Malay delights in Kampung Baru, and a brilliant array of international options in KLCC and Bangsar.

Super Shopping

KL sports a multiplicity of malls, classic Southeast Asian fresh-produce day markets and several atmospheric night markets, the most famous of which is along Chinatown's Jln Petaling. The art deco Central Market is strong on arts and crafts.

Contemporary Art

Access Malaysia's vibrant contemporary art scene at the National Visual Arts Gallery, the ILHAM gallery or exhibitions at smaller commercial spaces such as Wei-Ling Gallery.

p54

Selangor & Negeri Sembilan

Wildlife
Food
Architecture

Wildlife Encounters

Encounter monkeys up close at FRIM and Batu Caves. Go bird-watching at Bukit Fraser (Fraser's Hill), Cape Rachado Forest Reserve near Port Dickson, and the coastal mangroves near Kuala Selangor.

Eating Adventures

Head to Klang's Little India for authentic tastes from the subcontinent and the flavourful pork soup *bak kut teh*. Seremban has taste sensations ranging from beef-ball noodles to *cendol*.

Architectural Wonders

Putrajaya is stacked with monumental contemporary architecture around an artificial lake. The Istana Lama is a beautiful black hardwood palace in Sri Menanti.

p106

Perak

Architecture
Food
Nature

Colonial-Era Architecture

Ipoh and the surrounding Kinta Valley are virtual time warps into colonial-era Malaysia. Taiping also has its share of visit-worthy historic buildings, while Kuala Kangsar sparkles with mosques and royal palaces.

Regional Chinese Cuisine

Ipoh, Perak's largest city, is one of Malaysia's top culinary destinations, home to excellent regional Chinese food as well as some great Malay food and artisan coffee shops.

Jungles & Mangroves

Perak is home to the deep jungles of Royal Belum State Park and the slightly muddier forests of Matang Mangrove Forest Reserve. Gopeng, outside of Ipoh, also has a burgeoning nature scene.

p125

Penang

Architecture
Food
Museums

World Heritage

There's a good reason why George Town is a Unesco World Heritage Site: the city is home to countless protection-worthy antique shophouses, mansions, Chinese Clanhouses, markets and temples.

Culinary Capital

George Town is the culinary capital of Malaysia and our favourite place to feed in Southeast Asia. Quality hawker centres, street vendors, and a contemporary eating and drinking scene.

Museums & Galleries

The streets of George Town are already something of an open-air museum, but the city's excellent museums and contemporary art galleries ensure you'll be both educated and entertained for days.

p158

Langkawi, Kedah & Perlis

Beaches
Nature
Eating

Splendid Beaches

Pulau Langkawi's beaches are world famous for a reason: the sand is white and fine, the water is clear, and there's been less development here than in other Southeast Asian destinations.

Mountainous Jungle

View Langkawi's mountainous landscape from Panorama Langkawi cable car, or see it close up at one of the numerous waterfalls. Alternatively, head for the limestone hills of Taman Negeri Perlis along the Thai border.

Food

Pulau Langkawi is home to an admirable spread of foreign restaurants, from Thai to Turkish. Also sample amazing fish-head curry in Alor Setar.

p191

Melaka

Heritage
Food
Shopping

Architectural Delights

Learn about the history, culture and architecture of Melaka at abundant museums. Better yet, experience it wandering past Chinese shophouses, Dutch colonial-era architecture, Chinese and Hindu temples, mosques and churches.

Sit-Down Meals

Take a dim sum breakfast, eat curry off a banana leaf for lunch, and dine on Peranakan specialities for dinner. Melaka isn't swarming with hawker stalls but also offers a great choice of international and regional cuisines.

Shopping Options

Shop Chinatown's trinkets and beaded Peranakan shoes, or go modern in massive air-con malls for electronics and name brands. Don't miss Jonker Walk Night Market.

p215

Johor

Nature
Diving
Nightlife

Malaysia's Wilds

Endau-Rompin National Park isn't nearly as well known as Taman Negara in Pahang, but that's what makes it so magical. Hike through dense rainforests and along clear rivers to several impressive waterfalls.

Off-the-Radar Islands

The Seribuat Archipelago is where all the in-the-know expats living in Singapore and southern Malaysia go. Here you'll find low-key beaches, spectacular diving and family-friendly lodgings.

Duty-Free Booze

The Zon is Johor Bahru's duty-free port and several drinking holes and nightclubs clog the area. Hop from one to the next without spending all your ringgit.

p237

Pahang & Tioman Island

Beaches
Jungles
Food

Beach Life

Coastal Pahang offers the supremely chilled-out surf town of Cherating. Pulau Tioman has no less than eight great beach areas to choose from.

Jungle Adventures

The vast jungle preserve of Taman Negara offers plenty of hiking and wildlife-spotting opportunities. Pulau Tioman's trails will make you glad you packed hiking boots.

Culinary Travel

Kuantan is a food lover's city, from the cheap and delicious food stalls next to the bus station to the hard-to-find but oh-so-worth-it seafood paradise of Ana Ikan Bakar Petai restaurant. Culinary travellers will want to make a pilgrimage to taste Raub's famous fish-head curry.

p252

Peninsular Northeast

Beaches & Islands
Adventure Activities
Culture

Aquatic Adventures

Home to some of Southeast Asia's loveliest and most accessible islands, east-coast Malaysia is a magnet for those looking to dive, snorkel and swim.

Mountains & Waterfalls

Travellers are few in Kelantan's wild interior. Make the pretty jungle town of Dabong your base for mountain treks, river tracing and caving, and visiting breathtakingly steep waterfalls.

Cultural Insights

The geographical blending zone between Muslim Malaysia and Buddhist Thailand, Kelantan is amazingly rich in opportunities for cultural exploration. Further south, Terengganu offers visitors the chance to explore Malay culture.

p282

Sabah

Wildlife
Hiking & Trekking
Diving

Rare Species

Sabah is home to some of the world's rarest animal species such as the iconic orangutan, while the surrounding seas are home to an abundance of colourful marine life.

Jungle Trekking

Sabah's mountainous hinterland is a trekker's delight, taking adventurers past raging rivers that flow out of and through some of the most primordial forests in the world.

Marine Marvels

To say Sabah is known for its diving scene is like saying France is known for its cuisine. The diving in spots like Layang Layang and, of course, the famous Sipadan is – no hyperbole – some of the best in the world.

p314

Sarawak

Hiking & Trekking
Caves
Wildlife

Hiking

Hiking from Bario to Ba Kelalan or to the summit of Gunung Mulu will exhilarate experienced hikers, but even a relaxed stroll through one of the national parks around Kuching will envelop you in equatorial rainforest.

Cave Exploration

The Wind Cave, Fairy Cave and Niah National Park boast huge caverns with stalactites and bats, but for sheer size and spectacle you can't beat Gunung Mulu National Park, famed for the Deer Cave and the 700m-long Sarawak Chamber.

Jungle Life

Wild proboscis monkeys munch leaves at Bako National Park, orangutans swing through Semenggoh Nature Reserve and estuarine crocodiles lurk in the muddy waters of Kuching Wetlands National Park.

p392

Brunei Darussalam

Food
Architecture
Nature

Dining Abundance

Booze might be banned but there is no limit on gastronomic indulgence, a pleasure taken seriously in these parts. The sultanate is food mad and the opening of a restaurant is typically a major social event.

Architectural Diversity

Between the sultan's glittering palace, the opulent Empire Hotel, gaudy mosques and the largest water village in the world, this nation compensates for its small size with some huge construction projects.

Primary Rainforest

The sultanate has done an admirable job of preserving its tracts of primary jungle. An excellent, tightly controlled national park gives green breathing space to Borneo's many beasties.

p468

Singapore

Food
Shopping
Museums

Culinary Creativity

Food in Singapore is both a passion and a unifier across ethnic divides, with Chinese, Indian, Indonesian and Peranakan specialities. Find legendary hawker centres and food courts, plus experimental, fine-dining hot spots.

Boutiques & Malls

All bases are covered, from lavish malls and in-the-know boutiques, to heirloom handicraft studios and galleries peddling contemporary local art.

Cultural Storehouses

World-class museums offer evocative insights into the region's history and culture. While giants like the National Museum of Singapore are a must, make time for lesser-known NUS Museum and the Changi Museum & Chapel.

p488

On the Road

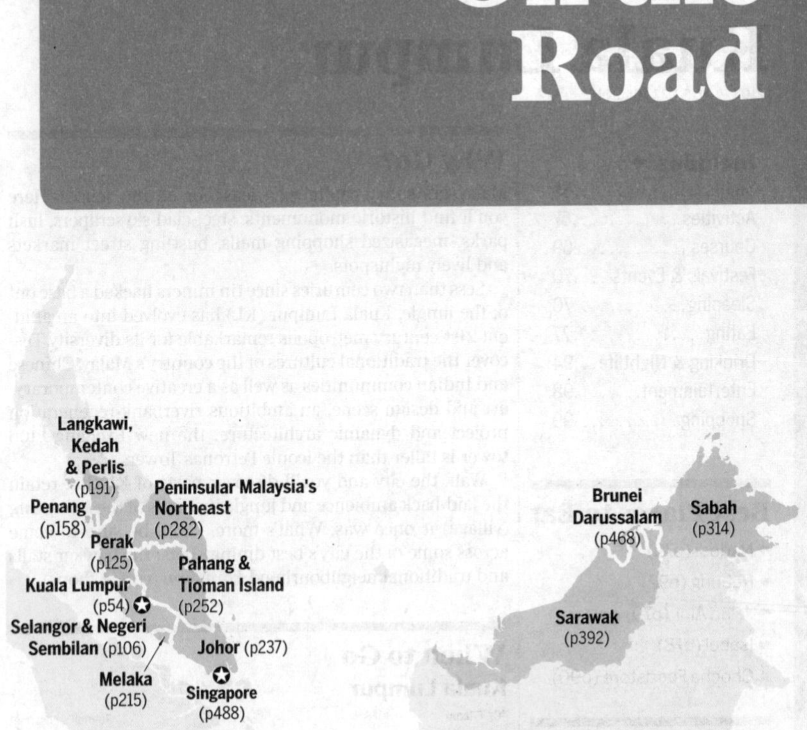

Langkawi, Kedah & Perlis (p191)

Penang (p158)

Perak (p125)

Peninsular Malaysia's Northeast (p282)

Kuala Lumpur (p54) ✪

Selangor & Negeri Sembilan (p106)

Pahang & Tioman Island (p252)

Johor (p237)

Melaka (p215)

Singapore (p488) ✪

Brunei Darussalam (p468)

Sabah (p314)

Sarawak (p392)

Kuala Lumpur

🔊 03 / POP 1.77 MILLION

Includes ➡

Sights 55
Activities 67
Courses 69
Festivals & Events 70
Sleeping 70
Eating 77
Drinking & Nightlife . . .94
Entertainment 98
Shopping 99

Best Places to Eat

➡ Nadodi (p79)
➡ Rebung (p92)
➡ Jalan Alor (p79)
➡ Isabel (p78)
➡ Chocha Foodstore (p90)

Best Places to Stay

➡ Villa Samadhi (p71)
➡ Mingle Hostel (p71)
➡ Hotel Stripes (p75)
➡ Majestic Hotel (p75)
➡ BackHome (p71)

Why Go?

Malaysia's sultry capital is a feast for all the senses. Here you'll find historic monuments, steel-clad skyscrapers, lush parks, megasized shopping malls, bustling street markets and lively nightspots.

Less than two centuries since tin miners hacked a base out of the jungle, Kuala Lumpur (KL) has evolved into an affluent 21st-century metropolis remarkable for its diversity. Discover the traditional cultures of the country's Malay, Chinese and Indian communities as well as a creative contemporary-art and design scene, an ambitious riverbank-regeneration project and dynamic architecture: the new Exchange 106 tower is taller than the iconic Petronas Towers.

Walk the city and you'll discover parts of KL that retain the laid-back ambience and jungle lushness of the *kampung* (village) it once was. What's more, you'll be sure to come across some of the city's best dining spots: the hawker stalls and traditional neighbourhood *kopitiam* (coffee shops).

When to Go
Kuala Lumpur

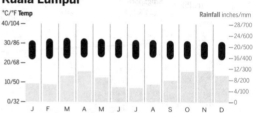

Jan & Feb Enjoy the Chinese New Year and the dramatic Hindu festival Thaipusam.

Apr & May Catch the Standard Chartered KL Marathon and Wesak Day celebrations.

Aug & Sep Celebrate Independence and Malaysia Day, then the arts fest DiverseCity.

History

In 1857, 87 Chinese prospectors in search of tin landed at the apex of the Klang and Gombak rivers and imaginatively named the place Kuala Lumpur, meaning 'muddy confluence'. Within a month, all but 17 of the prospectors had died of malaria and other tropical diseases, but the tin they discovered in Ampang attracted more miners and KL quickly became a brawling, noisy, violent boomtown.

The local sultan appointed a proxy (known as Kapitan China) to bring the unruly Chinese fortune-seekers and their secret societies into line. The successful candidate Yap Ah Loy (Kapitan China from 1868 to 1885) took on the task with such ruthless relish that he's now credited as the founder of KL.

Yap had barely established control, however, when fighting broke out between local sultans for the throne of Perak. KL was swept up in the conflict and burnt to the ground in 1881. This allowed the British government representative Frank Swettenham to push through a radical new town plan that transferred the central government from Klang to KL. By 1886 a railway line linked KL to Klang; by 1887 several thousand brick buildings had been built; and in 1896 the city became the capital of the newly formed Federated Malay States.

After a brutal occupation by Japanese forces during WWII, the British temporarily returned, only to be ousted when Malaysia declared its independence here in 1957.

KL's darkest hour came on 13 May 1969, when race riots mainly between the Malays and Chinese communities claimed hundreds, perhaps thousands, of lives. A year later local government elections were suspended – ever since, KL's mayor has been appointed by the Federal Territories Minister. In 1974 the sultan of Selangor ceded the city's land to the state so it could officially become the Federal Territory of Kuala Lumpur.

Celebrations broke out across KL following the May 2018 general election, when the reformist alliance led by 93-year-old Dr Mahathir Mohamad unseated the Barisan Nasional (BN) coalition from six decades of rule. There's pressure now for locals to vote for a city mayor.

Meanwhile, KL keeps evolving with major infrastructure projects including the Tun Razak Exchange (the centrepiece of which is Exchange 106, a 106-storey 492m tower that is the country's tallest building), expansion of the mass rapid transit (MRT) system and urban beautification and conservation programs.

◉ Sights

KL's city centre is compact – some of the sights are so close together that it's often quicker to walk than take public transport (which can easily become snarled in traffic and KL's tortuous one-way system).

◉ Bukit Bintang & KLCC

★ Petronas Towers
TOWER

(Map p58; ☑ 03-5039 1915; www.petronastwintowers.com.my; Jln Ampang, KLCC; adult/child RM80/33; ⊙ 9am-9pm Tue-Sun, closed 1-2.30pm Fri, last admission 8.30pm; 🖟; 🚇 KLCC) Resembling twin silver rockets plucked from an episode of *Flash Gordon*, the Petronas Towers are the perfect allegory for the meteoric rise of the city from tin-miners' hovel to 21st-century metropolis. Half of the daily allocation of tickets for 45-minute tours – which take in the Skybridge on the 41st floor and the observation deck on the 86th – are sold in advance online. Otherwise, turn up early to be sure of scoring a ticket to go up.

First stop on the tour is the Skybridge where you can look down 170m as you walk across the glass-walled connection corridor between the two towers. Next you take the lift up to the 86th-floor observation deck to see the city from 370m.

★ KLCC Park
PARK

(Map p58; www.suriaklcc.com.my/attractions/klcc-park; off Jln Ampang, KLCC; 🚇 KLCC) At the heart of the mammoth KLCC development, this excellent park offers a 1.3km soft-surface jogging track, a great children's playground and paddling pool. Crowds gather here in the early evening to watch the glowing towers punching up into the night sky and the Lake Symphony fountains play at 8pm, 9pm and 10pm in front of the Suria KLCC.

★ ILHAM
GALLERY

(Map p58; ☑ 03-2181 3003; www.ilhamgallery.com; 3rd & 5th fl, Ilham Tower, 8 Jln Binjai, KLCC; ⊙ 11am-7pm Tue-Sat, to 5pm Sun; 🚇 Ampang Park) **FREE** This thought-provoking contemporary-art gallery is an excellent excuse to step inside the glossy, 60-storey ILHAM Tower. The artwork selected for ILHAM's rotating exhibitions spans various media and is curated to provoke debate: expect anything from black-and-white documentary photography to neon-coloured paintings of *kampung* houses.

Kuala Lumpur Highlights

1 **Petronas Towers** (p55) Admiring the glittering exterior, then heading up to the observation deck.

2 **Islamic Arts Museum** (p61) Being dazzled by the exquisite craftsmanship of this religious collection.

3 **Petaling Street Market** (p100) Exploring this busy day and night market and the surrounding sights of Chinatown.

4 **Lake Gardens – Tun Abdul Razak Heritage Park** (p65) Relaxing in this lush swath of greenery which includes a wonderful bird park.

5 **Merdeka Square** (p61) Standing at KL's colonial heart surrounded by a handsome ensemble of heritage buildings.

6 **Jalan Alor** (p79) Diving into the outdoor dining adventure of KL's most famous strip of hawker stalls.

7 **Thean Hou Temple** (p64) Taking in the hilltop view from this fabulous Buddhist temple.

8 **Masjid Jamek Sultan Abdul Samad** (p60) Enjoying this historic riverside mosque and garden.

9 **Kampung Baru** (p65) Discovering the few remaining traditional wooden homes of this old Malay village in the city's heart.

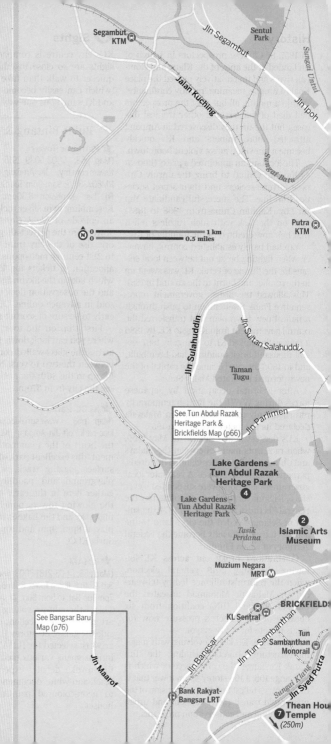

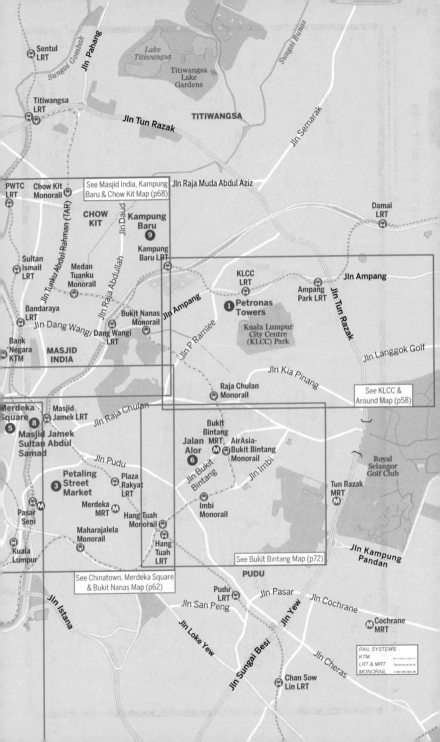

Sentul
LRT

Lake
Titiwangsa

Titiwangsa
Lake
Gardens

Sungai Bunus

Jln Pahang

Sungai Gombak

Titiwangsa
LRT

Jln Tun Razak

TITIWANGSA

Jln Semarak

PWTC
LRT

Chow Kit
Monorail

See Masjid India, Kampung
Baru & Chow Kit Map (p68)

Jln Raja Muda Abdul Aziz

Damai
LRT

**CHOW
KIT**

Jln Daud

**Kampung
Baru**
9

Sultan
Ismail
LRT

Kampung
Baru LRT

KLCC
LRT

Jln Ampang

Medan
Tuanku
Monorail

Jln Tunku Abdul Rahman (TAR)

1 **Petronas
Towers**

Ampang
Park LRT

Jln Tun Razak

Bandaraya
LRT

Jln Dang Wangi

Jln Raja Abdullah

Bukit Nanas
Monorail

Jln Ampang

Kuala Lumpur
City Centre
(KLCC) Park

Jln Langgok Golf

Bank
Negara
KTM

Dang Wangi
LRT

Jln P Ramlee

**MASJID
INDIA**

Jln Kia Pinang

See KLCC &
Around Map (p58)

Raja Chulan
Monorail

Merdeka
Square
5 **8**

Masjid
Jamek LRT

Jln Raja Chulan

**Masjid Jamek
Sultan Abdul
Samad**

Bukit
Bintang
MRT

**Jalan
Alor**
6

AirAsia-
Bukit Bintang
Monorail

Jln Pudu

Jln Bukit Bintang

Jln Imbi

**Petaling
Street
Market**
3

Plaza
Rakyat
LRT

Tun Razak
MRT

Royal
Selangor
Golf Club

Pasar
Seni

Merdeka
MRT

Hang Tuah
Monorail

Imbi
Monorail

Maharajalela
Monorail

Jln Kampung
Pandan

Kuala
Lumpur

Hang
Tuah
LRT

See Bukit Bintang Map (p72)

PUDU

See Chinatown, Merdeka Square
& Bukit Nanas Map (p62)

Pudu
LRT

Jln Pasar

Jln Cochrane

Jln Istana

Jln San Peng

Jln Yew

Cochrane
MRT

Jln Loke Yew

Jln Sungai Besi

Jln Cheras

RAIL SYSTEMS
KTM
LRT & MRT
MONORAIL

Chan Sow
Lin LRT

KLCC & Around

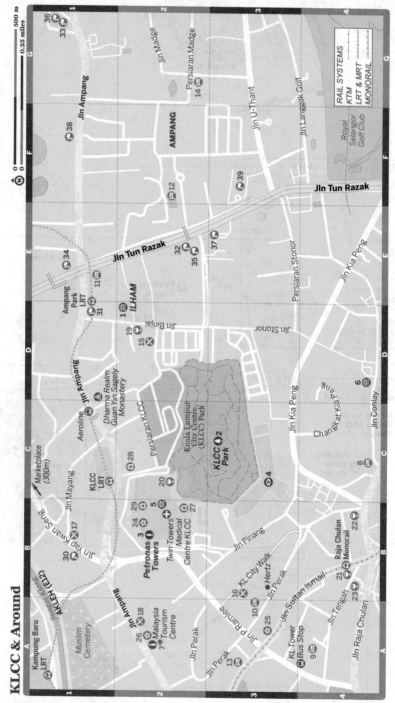

500 m
0.25 miles

RAIL SYSTEMS
KTM
LRT & MRT
MONORAIL

KLCC & Around

◎ Top Sights
1 ILHAM	D2
2 KLCC Park	C3
3 Petronas Towers	B2

◎ Sights
4 Aquaria KLCC	C3
5 Galeri Petronas	B2
Petrosains	(see 5)
6 Rumah Penghulu Abu Seman	D4

❹ Activities, Courses & Tours
7 MikesBikes	A2

◎ Sleeping
8 Banyan Tree Kuala Lumpur	C4
9 E&O Residences Kuala Lumpur	A4
Element Kuala Lumpur	(see 1)
10 Fraser Place Kuala Lumpur	A3
11 G Tower Hotel	E1
12 MiCasa All Suite Hotel	F2
13 The Bed KLCC	A3
14 Villa Samadhi	G2

◎ Eating
15 Acme Bar & Coffee	D2
16 Beta KL	B3
Fuego	(see 19)
Malaysia Boleh!	(see 28)
17 Nadodi	B1
18 Nasi Kandar Pelita	A2

Yun House	(see 28)

◎ Drinking & Nightlife
19 Claret	D2
20 Delirium Café Kuala Lumpur	C2
DivineBliss	(see 11)
21 Heli Lounge Bar	B4
22 Nakd Bar	B4
23 Suzie Wong	B4

◎ Entertainment
24 Dewan Filharmonik Petronas	B2
25 KL Live	A3
26 WOW KL!	A2

◎ Shopping
27 Farah Khan	B2
28 Shoppes at Four Seasons Place	C2
29 Suria KLCC	B2

❶ Information
30 Australian High Commission	B1
31 British High Commission	D1
32 Canadian High Commission	E2
33 Dutch Embassy	G1
34 French Embassy	E1
35 German Embassy	E2
36 Irish Embassy	G1
37 Singapore High Commission	E3
38 Thai Embassy	F1
39 US Embassy	F3

Aquaria KLCC AQUARIUM
(Map p58; ☎03-2333 1888; www.aquariaklcc.com; Concourse, KL Convention Centre, Jln Pinang, KLCC; adult/child RM65/56; ☉10am-8pm, last admission 7pm; 🖚; 🚇 KLCC) The highlight of this impressive aquarium is its 90m underwater tunnel: view sand tiger sharks, giant gropers and more up close. Daily feedings of various fish and otters are complemented by special sessions feeding arapaimas and sharks on Monday, Wednesday and Saturday (see website for schedule). Wheelchair accessible.

Galeri Petronas GALLERY
(Map p58; ☎03-2051 7770; www.galeripetronas. com.my; 3rd fl, Suria KLCC, Jln Ampang, KLCC; ☉10am-8pm Tue-Sun; 🚇 KLCC) **FREE** Swap consumerism for culture at this excellent art gallery showcasing Petronas' art collection, including photography and paintings. It's a bright, modern space with interesting, professionally curated shows that change every few months.

Petrosains MUSEUM
(Map p58; ☎03-2331 8181; www.petrosains.com. my; 4th fl, Suria KLCC, Jln Ampang, KLCC; adult/ child RM28/16.50; ☉9.30am-4pm Tue-Fri, to 5pm Sat & Sun; 🖚; 🚇 KLCC) Fill an educational few hours at this interactive science discovery centre with all sorts of buttons to press and levers to pull. Many of the activities and displays focus on the wonderful things that fuel has brought to Malaysia – no prizes for guessing who sponsors the museum.

Rumah Penghulu Abu Seman HISTORIC BUILDING
(Map p58; ☎03-2144 9273; www.badanwarisan malaysia.org; 2 Jln Stonor, Bukit Bintang; suggested donation RM10; ☉tours 11am & 3pm Mon-Sat; 🚇Raja Chulan) This glorious wooden stilt house, which was once the family home of a village headman in Kedah, was built in stages between 1910 and the 1930s and later moved to KL. Interesting tours of the property provide an explanation of the house's architecture and history and of Malay customs and traditional village life. You can wander around outside tour times (and since it's built with ventilation in mind, you can easily look in).

Dharma Realm Guan Yin
Sagely Monastery   BUDDHIST TEMPLE
(Map p58; ☑ 03-2164 8055; www.drba.org; 161 Jln Ampang, KLCC; ☺ 7am-4pm; 🚇 Ampang Park) **FREE** The calm spaces, potted plants, mandala ceilings and giant gilded statues create an appropriately contemplative mood for quiet meditation at this colourful modern temple. The complex is dedicated to Kuan Yin, the Buddhist goddess of compassion, represented by the central statue in the main building.

⊙ Chinatown, Merdeka Square & Bukit Nanas

★ **Menara Kuala Lumpur**   TOWER
(KL Tower; Map p62; ☑ 03-2020 5444; www.menara kl.com.my; 2 Jln Punchak, Bukit Nanas; observation deck adult/child RM44/29, open deck adult/child RM99/52; ☺ observation deck 9am-10pm, last tickets 9.30pm; 🚇 KL Tower) Although the Petronas Towers are taller, the 421m Menara KL, rising from the crest of Bukit Nanas, offers the best city views. The bulb at the top contains a revolving restaurant, an interior **observation deck** at 276m and, most thrilling of all, an **open deck** at 300m, access to which is weather dependent. Risk vertigo to take your photo in the **sky box**, which puts nothing but glass between you and the ground below (no young children allowed).

A free **shuttle bus** (☺ 8am-10.30pm) runs from the gate on Jln Punchak, or you can walk up through the KL Forest Eco Park and its canopy walkway.

★ **KL Forest Eco Park**   NATURE RESERVE
(Taman Eko Rimba KL; Map p62; ☑ 03-2026 4741; www.menarakl.com.my; Bukit Nanas; ☺ 8am-6pm; 🚇 KL Tower) **FREE** KL's urban roar is replaced by buzzing insects and cackling birdlife at this forest of tropical hardwoods, covering 9.37 hectares in the heart of the city. One of the oldest protected jungles in Malaysia (gazetted in 1906), the park is commonly known as Bukit Nanas (Pineapple Hill). Don't miss traversing the lofty canopy walkway.

The canopy walkway is easily reached from the Menara KL car park; signposts display walking routes. For longer forays, pick up a basic map to the trails from the **Forest Information Centre** (Map p62; ☑ 03-2026 4741; www.forestry.gov.my; Bukit Nanas; ☺ 9am-5pm; 🚇 KL Tower) on Jln Raja Chulan (trails lead directly from here).

★ **Masjid Jamek Sultan**
Abdul Samad   MOSQUE
(Friday Mosque; Map p62; 64 Jln Tun Perak, Chinatown; ☺ 10am-12.30pm & 2.30-4pm Sat-Thu; 🚇 Masjid Jamek) **FREE** This graceful, onion-domed mosque, designed by British architect AB Hubback, borrows Mogul and Moorish styles with its brick-and-plaster banded minarets and three shapely domes. Located at the confluence of the Gombak and Klang rivers, Masjid Jamek was the first brick mosque in Malaysia when completed in 1907. It remained the city's centre of Islamic worship until the opening of the National Mosque in 1965.

KUALA LUMPUR IN...

Two Days

Breakfast at **Imbi Market** then get your bearings of the city from atop **Menara Kuala Lumpur**, enjoying the view from the open-air deck if weather (and your head for heights) permits. Hike back down Bukit Nanas along the **canopy walkway**, keeping an eye peeled for monkeys.

Spend the afternoon exploring **Chinatown**, going souvenir shopping at the **Central Market** and admiring the heritage architecture around **Merdeka Square**. End the day at **Jalan Petaling** for food and the night market.

On day two, explore the Lake Gardens, dropping by the **KL Bird Park** and the **Islamic Arts Museum** or **National Museum**. Hit the Kuala Lumpur City Centre (KLCC) at dusk to see the **Petronas Towers** beautifully illuminated. Browse the superb mall **Pavilion KL**, trawl the night food stalls of Jalan Alor and grab a nightcap at **Suzie Wong**.

Three Days

There are great views of the city skyline from **Lake Titiwangsa**, where you can also visit the **National Visual Arts Gallery**. Amble through the Malay area of **Kampung Baru**, then take a taxi to the splendid **Thean Hou Temple**. Enjoy a sundowner at **Heli Lounge Bar** followed by a memorable meal at **Nadodi**. Hit **No Black Tie** for late-night jazz and cocktails.

⭐ **Sin Sze Si Ya Temple**   BUDDHIST TEMPLE
(Map p62; ☑ 03-2072 9593; Jln Tun HS Lee, Chinatown; ⊙ 7am-5pm; 🚇 Pasar Seni) **FREE** Kuala
Lumpur's oldest Chinese temple (1864) was
built on the instructions of Kapitan Yap Ah
Loy and is dedicated to Sin Sze Ya and Si Sze
Ya, two Chinese deities believed instrumental
in Yap's ascension to Kapitan status. Several
beautiful objects decorate the temple, including two hanging carved panels, but the best
feature is the almost frontier-like atmosphere.

Merdeka Square   SQUARE
(Dataran Merdeka; Map p62; 🚇 Masjid Jamek)
The huge open square, where Malaysian independence was declared in 1957, is speared
by a 95m flagpole, one of the world's tallest.
In the British era, the square was used as a
cricket pitch and called the Padang (field).

The square is surrounded by heritage buildings including the magnificent **Sultan Abdul
Samad Building** (Map p62; Jln Raja; 🚇 Masjid
Jamek) and **St Mary's Anglican Cathedral** (Map p62; ☑ 03-2692 8672; www.stmarys
cathedral.org.my; Jln Raja; ⊙ 8am-5pm; 🚇 Masjid
Jamek), both designed by AC Norman.

Sri Mahamariamman Temple   HINDU TEMPLE
(Map p62; ☑ 03-2078 5323; 163 Jln Tun HS Lee, Chinatown; ⊙ 6am-8.30pm; 🚇 Pasar Seni) **FREE** Rising
almost 23m above this lively Hindu temple
is its *gopuram*, a tower decorated with colourful Hindu gods. Founded in 1873, making
it one of the oldest such temples in Malaysia, it is decorated in South Indian style and
named after Mariamman, the South Indian
mother goddess (also known as Parvati). Her
shrine is at the back of the complex. On the
left sits a shrine to the elephant-headed deity
Ganesh, and on the right one to Lord Murugan.

◉ **Lake Gardens, Brickfields &
Bangsar**

⭐ **Islamic Arts Museum**   MUSEUM
(Muzium Kesenian Islam Malaysia; Map p66; ☑ 03-
2092 7070; www.iamm.org.my; Jln Lembah Perdana,
Lake Gardens; adult/child RM14/7; ⊙ 10am-6pm;
🚇 Kuala Lumpur) Inhabiting a building every bit
as impressive as its collection, this museum
showcases Islamic decorative arts from around
the globe. Scale models of the world's best
Islamic buildings, fabulous textiles, carpets,
jewellery and calligraphy-inscribed pottery all
vie for attention; the 19th-century recreation
Damascus Room is a gold-leaf-decorated
delight. Don't forget to gaze up at the building's intricate domes and tile work.

RIVER OF LIFE
....
The River of Life project – an ambitious
federal undertaking to transform the
Klang river from a polluted sinkhole into
a clean and liveable waterfront – had its
first phase completed in 2017. Improve-
ments centre on Chinatown and Merdeka
Sq, where pavements have been widened,
streets beautified with public art by local
artists and directional signage improved.

The original steps down to the
river behind Masjid Jamek have been
uncovered and the area around the
mosque and along the riverbank has
been regenerated, with new pedestrian
walkways, plazas and a bridge linking
up to Merdeka Sq. At night this section,
dubbed the **Blue Pool**, is illuminated
with azure lights and wreathed in fog
effects as fountains dance at the river
confluence between 8pm and 11pm.

⭐ **KL Bird Park**   WILDLIFE RESERVE
(Map p66; ☑ 03-2272 1010; www.klbirdpark.com;
Jln Cenderawasih, Lake Gardens; adult/child
RM67/45; ⊙ 9am-6pm; 🚌; 🚇 Muzium Negara)
More than 3000 birds flutter and soar
through this 21-hectare aviary. Some 200
species of (mostly) Asian birds can be spotted here, from strutting flamingos to para-
keets. The park is divided into four sections:
in the first two, birds fly freely beneath an
enormous canopy. Section three features the
native hornbills (so-called because of their
enormous beaks), while section four offers
the less-edifying spectacle of caged species.

⭐ **National Museum**   MUSEUM
(Muzium Negara; Map p66; ☑ 03-2267 1111; www.
muziumnegara.gov.my; Jln Damansara, Lake Gardens;
adult/child RM5/2; ⊙ 9am-6pm; 🚇 Muzium Negara)
This excellent modern museum offers a good
primer on Malaysia's history, from prehistoric
to present-day. The country's geological features and prehistory are tackled in one gallery
(which features a replica of the 11,000-year-
old Perak Man, Malaysia's most celebrated
archaeological discovery). The gallery of
modern history is even more interesting, with
recreations of temple walls, royal beds and
ceremonial garb from across the centuries.

Taman Tugu   PARK
(www.tamantuguproject.com.my; Pers Sultan Salahuddin; ⊙ 7am-7pm; 🚇 Muzium Negara) **FREE** The
first stage of this major new 27-hectare park

KUALA LUMPUR

Chinatown, Merdeka Square & Bukit Nanas

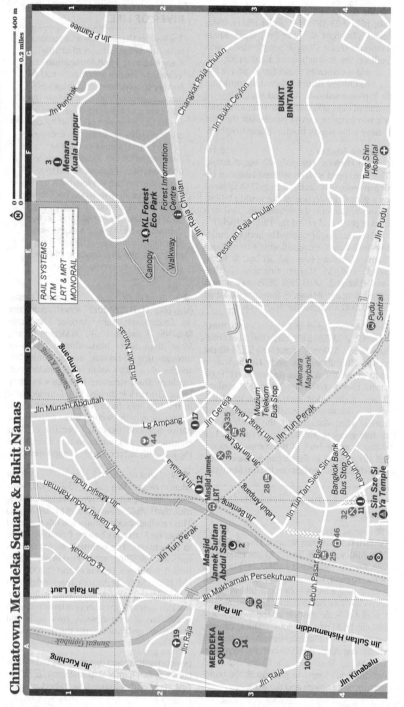

400 m
0.2 miles

RAIL SYSTEMS
KTM
LRT & MRT
MONORAIL

Jln P Ramlee

Jln Punchak

Menara
Kuala Lumpur
3

Changkat Raja Chulan

Jln Bukit Ceylon

BUKIT
BINTANG

KL Forest
Eco Park
1

Forest Information
Centre

Canopy
Walkway

Jln Raja Chulan

Pesiaran Raja Chulan

Jln Pudu

Tung Shin
Hospital

Jln Bukit Nanas

5

Menara
Maybank

Pudu
Sentral

Jln Munshi Abdullah

Sungai Klang

Jln Ampang

Lg Ampang

44

17

Jln Gereja

35
26

Jln Hang Lekiu

Muzium
Telekom
Bus Stop

Jln Tun Perak

Jln Melaka

Jln Tun HS Lee

39

12

Masjid Jamek
LRT

Jln Benteng

Lebuh Ampang

28

Jln Tun Tan Siew Sin

Bangkok Bank
Bus Stop

Lebuh Pudu

4 **Sin Sze Si**
Ya Temple

32
11

Lg Tuanku Abdul Rahman

Jln Masjid India

Lg Gombak

Jln Tun Perak

Masjid
Jamek Sultan
Abdul Samad
2

Jln Makhamah Persekutuan

25

46

6

Lebuh Pasar Besar

Jln Sultan Hishamuddin

Jln Raja Laut

Sungai Gombak

19

Jln Kuching

Jln Raja

20

MERDEKA
SQUARE
14

Jln Raja

Jln Raja

10

Jln Kinabalu

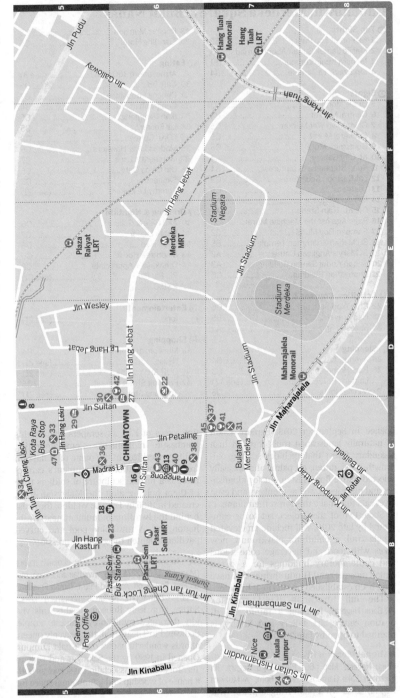

Chinatown, Merdeka Square & Bukit Nanas

◎ Top Sights

1	KL Forest Eco Park	E2
2	Masjid Jamek Sultan Abdul Samad	B3
3	Menara Kuala Lumpur	F1
4	Sin Sze Si Ya Temple	B4

◎ Sights

5	Brave Mural	D3
6	Central Market	B4
7	Chinatown Wet Market	C5
8	Cockerel Mural	C5
9	Goldsmith Mural	C6
10	KL City Gallery	A4
11	Kuen Stephanie Sculptures	B4
12	Lat Cartoon Sculptures	C2
13	Lostgens'	C6
14	Merdeka Square	A3
15	Old KL Train Station	A7
16	Rage Against the Machine Mural	C6
17	Sampan Boy Mural	C2
18	Sri Mahamariamman Temple	B5
19	St Mary's Anglican Cathedral	A2
20	Sultan Abdul Samad Building	A3
21	Zhongshan Building	C8

◉ Activities, Courses & Tours

22	Chin Woo Stadium	D6
23	Han Travel	B5
24	Majestic Spa	A7

◉ Sleeping

25	Avenue J	B4
26	BackHome	C3
	Lantern Hotel	(see 47)
27	Mingle Hostel	D6
28	Reggae Mansion	C3
29	Tian Jing Hotel	C5

◎ Eating

	Atmosphere 360	(see 3)
30	Cafe 55	D5
31	Chocha Foodstore	C7
32	Geographer	B4
33	Ikan Panggang	C5
34	Lai Foong	C5
35	LOKL Coffee	C3
36	Madras Lane Hawkers	C5
37	Merchant's Lane	C7
38	Old China Café	C6
39	Sangeetha	C3
	Tommy Le Baker	(see 21)

◎ Drinking & Nightlife

40	Aku Cafe & Gallery	C6
41	Botak Liquor	C7
42	Deceased	D6
43	Moontree House	C6
44	Omakase + Appreciate	C2
	Piu Piu Piu	(see 21)
45	PS150	C7

◎ Entertainment

	fono	(see 21)

◎ Shopping

46	Museum of Ethnic Arts	B4
	Naiise	(see 21)
	OUR ArtProjects	(see 21)
47	Petaling Street Market	C5
	Tandang Store	(see 21)

opened in September 2018. Explore 1.5km of naturally landscaped trails through lush secondary forest that includes soaring old-growth trees, rattan, oil palms and specially selected native flora. Listen out for kingfishers and magpies as well as monkeys and even civet cats that make this forest their home.

Stage two of the project, set to be completed by late 2019, will include an elevated jungle trail, a children's playground, new lakes with food and beverage concessions and contemporary buildings for a *surau* (small mosque) and Hindu shrines that have long been established on this lush hillside.

The full Khazanah ILMU complex (⊠ Bank Negara), housing a rainforest education centre, art gallery and library, is planned to open by late 2020.

National Monument · MONUMENT

(Tugu Negara; Map p66; Plaza Tugu Negara, Jln Parlimen, Lake Gardens; ☺ 7am-6pm; Ⓜ Muzium Negara) FREE On a palm-fringed plaza, with fine views of KL's skyscrapers, stands this bombastic monument. Commemorating military sacrifices in the name of Malaysian freedom, the National Monument's centrepiece is a bronze sculpture of soldiers (one of them holding aloft the Malaysian flag), created in 1966 by Felix de Weldon, the artist behind the Iwo Jima monument near Washington, DC. A royal-blue pool and curved pavilion heighten the grand impression.

★ Thean Hou Temple · BUDDHIST TEMPLE

(Map p66; ☎ 03-2274 7088; www.hainannet.com.my; 65 Pers Endah, off Jln Syed Putra, Taman Persiaran Desa; ☺ 8am-10pm; ☑ Tun Sambanthan) FREE Sitting atop leafy Robson Heights, this vividly decorated multistorey Chinese temple, dedicated to Thean Hou, the heavenly queen, affords wonderful views over Kuala Lumpur. Opened in 1989 by the Selangor and Federal Territory Hainan Association, it serves as both a house of worship and a functional space for events such as weddings. In recent years it's also become a tourist attraction in its own right, especially during Chinese festival times and the birthdays of the various temple gods.

Old KL Train Station HISTORIC BUILDING
(Map p62; Jln Sultan Hishamuddin; ⓡ Kuala Lumpur) One of KL's most distinctive colonial buildings, this grand 1910 train station (replaced as a transit hub by KL Sentral in 2001) was designed by British architect AB Hubback in the Mogul (or Indo-Saracenic) style. The building's white plaster facade is crumbling, but you can still admire its rows of keyhole and horseshoe arches, providing ventilation on each level, and the large *chatri* (elevated pavilions) and onion domes adorning the roof.

Sekeping Tenggiri GALLERY
(Map p76; ☏ 017-519 6552; www.sekeping.com/tenggiri; 48 Jln Tenggiri, Bangsar; ⊙ by appointment; ⓡ Abdullah Hukum) FREE For art lovers it's worth making an appointment to view architect Ng Seksan's superb collection of Malaysian contemporary art, so large that he's turned over a whole house to store and display it. View pieces by top talents including Phuan Thai Meng, Samsudin Wahab and Justin Lim.

Perdana Botanical Garden PARK
(Map p66; ☏ 03-2617 6404; www.klbotanicalgarden.gov.my; Lake Gardens; ⊙ 7am-8pm; 🚻; Ⓜ Muzium Negara) FREE Strolling around KL's oldest public park, established in the 1880s, you'll admire native and introduced flora, including 800 species of orchid, mahogany trees more than 300 years old and countless hibiscus blooms (the country's national flower). Ferns, edible and aquatic plants each have their own gardens, all prettily arranged with gazebos and a boardwalk around a lake with fountains.

KL Butterfly Park WILDLIFE RESERVE
(Taman Rama Rama; Map p66; ☏ 03-2693 4799; www.klbutterflypark.com; Jln Cenderasari, Lake Gardens; adult/child RM24/13; ⊙ 9am-6pm; ⓡ Kuala Lumpur) This is a great place to get up close with a hundred or so of the 1100-plus butterfly species found in Malaysia, including the enormous and well-named birdwings, the elegant swallowtails, and the colourful tigers and Jezebels. There's also a bug gallery where you can shudder at the size of Malaysia's giant centipedes and spiders.

Masjid Negara MOSQUE
(National Mosque; Map p66; www.masjidnegara.gov.my; Jln Lembah Perdana, Lake Gardens; ⊙ 9am-noon, 3-4pm & 5.30-6.30pm, closed Fri morning; ⓡ Kuala Lumpur) FREE The elegant design of this gigantic 1960s mosque was inspired by Mecca's Masjid al-Haram. Able to accommodate 15,000 worshippers, it has an umbrella-like blue-tile roof with 18 points symbolising the 13 states of Malaysia and the five pillars of Islam. Rising above the mosque, a 74m-high minaret issues the call to prayer, which can be heard across Chinatown. Non-Muslims are welcome to visit outside prayer times; robes are available for those who are not dressed appropriately.

Royal Museum MUSEUM
(Muzium Diraja; Map p66; ☏ 03-2272 1896; www.jmm.gov.my; Jln Istana, Robson Heights; adult/child RM10/5; ⊙ 9am-5pm; 🚌 Tun Sambanthan, then taxi) You can tour the first two floors of this grand mansion, originally built as a family home in 1928 by Chinese tin tycoon Chan Wing. From 1957 it served as the official KL residence of Malaysia's head of state, until the opening of the new National Palace in the city's north in 2011. The museum's exterior, with its eclectic European style, looks much the same as it did in Chan Wing's day.

◉ Masjid India, Kampung Baru & Northern KL

★ National Visual Arts Gallery GALLERY
(NVAG, Balai Seni Lukis Negara; ☏ 03-4026 7000; www.artgallery.gov.my; 2 Jln Temerloh, Titiwangsa; ⊙ 10am-6pm; 🚌 Titiwangsa, ⓡ Titiwangsa) FREE

ⓘ WALKING TO THE LAKE GARDENS

Lake Gardens – Tun Abdul Razak Heritage Park (Map p66; ⊙ 7am-8pm; Ⓜ Muzium Negara) can seem like an island of greenery cut off from the city by railway lines and highways. However, it's possible to walk to here from Chinatown or the National Museum.

From Chinatown take the pedestrian bridge across from the Central Market to Kompleks Dayabumi and then head south around the back of the post office to the underpass leading to the Masjid Negara. Another set of overhead pedestrian bridges leads to the Old KL Train Station from Pasar Seni LRT station, from where you can also walk up to the gardens.

Both a pedestrian bridge and a tunnel under the highway link the gardens with the National Museum.

Tun Abdul Razak Heritage Park & Brickfields

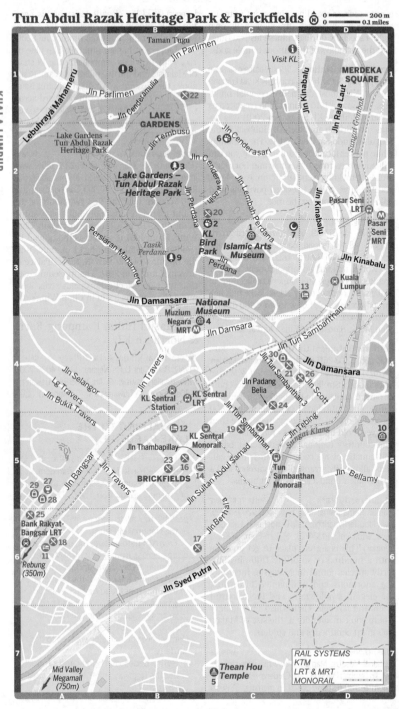

Tun Abdul Razak Heritage Park & Brickfields

◎ **Top Sights**
1 Islamic Arts Museum C3
2 KL Bird Park.. C3
3 Lake Gardens – Tun Abdul Razak
   Heritage Park.................................. B2
4 National Museum............................... B4
5 Thean Hou Temple........................... C7

◎ **Sights**
6 KL Butterfly Park................................ C2
7 Masjid Negara.................................... C3
8 National Monument.............................B1
9 Perdana Botanical Garden................. B3
10 Royal Museum.................................... D5

🛏 **Sleeping**
11 Alila Bangsar..................................... A6
12 Aloft Kuala Lumpur Sentral................ B5
13 Majestic Hotel.................................... D3
14 PODs.. B5

✕ **Eating**
15 ABC Stall.. C5

16 Ammars B5
17 Annalakshmi Vegetarian
   Restaurant B6
18 Botanica + Co A6
19 Brickfields Pisang
   Goreng.. C5
20 Hornbill Restaurant............................ C2
21 Lawanya Food Corner C4
22 Rebung B1
23 Restoran Sin Kee............................... B5
24 Restoran Yarl.....................................C4
25 Southern Rock Seafood...................... A6
26 Vishal... D4

🍷 **Drinking & Nightlife**
27 Coley A5

🛍 **Shopping**
28 Kedai Bikin A5
29 Nala's Kampung House....................... A5
30 Wei-Ling Gallery................................. C4

For their inventiveness and sheer scale, the artworks on display at the NVAG are worth a trip out of central KL. In rotating exhibitions by regional artists, themes of Malaysian politics and local identity positively leap from canvases. Upper galleries are accessed by a spiral-shaped ramp that recalls the Guggenheim Museum.

Titiwangsa Lake Gardens PARK
(Taman Tasik Titiwangsa; Jln Tembeling, Titiwangsa; ⓖ Titiwangsa,ⓖ Titiwangsa) For a postcard-perfect view of the city skyline, head to Lake Titiwangsa and the relaxing tree-filled park that surrounds it. It's a pleasant spot for jogging and boating on the water; however, at the time of research, much of the park was cordoned off as part of upgrading works connected to the city's River of Life beautification program.

Kampung Baru Gateway GATE
(Map p68; Jln Raja Abdullah & Jln Raja Muda Musa, Kampung Baru; ⓖ Kampung Baru) A modern concrete and blue glass gateway marks the entry to this neighbourhood of traditional Malay wooden houses. Gazetted by the British in 1899, Kampung Baru's low-slung charms are best revealed by simply wandering its streets. Along the way, enjoy tasty home-cooked Malay food at unpretentious roadside cafes and stalls.

Loke Mansion HISTORIC BUILDING
(Map p68; ☎03-2691 0803; 273a Jln Medan Tuanku, Chow Kit; ⊙by appointment; ⓖMedan Tuanku) Rescued from the brink of dereliction by the law firm Cheang & Ariff, this was once the home of self-made tin tycoon Loke Yew. The Japanese high command set up base here in 1942. Access to the interior of the beautifully restored mansion is by appointment only, but you're welcome to pause in the driveway and admire the whitewashed exterior.

Bank Negara Malaysia Museum & Art Gallery MUSEUM
(☎03-9179 2784; www.museum.bnm.gov.my; Sasana Kijang, 2 Jln Dato Onn; ⊙10am-6pm; ⓖ Bank Negara, then taxi) FREE This well-designed complex of small museums focuses on banking, finance and money and is not dull in the least. Highlights include a collection of ancient coins and money (and a slick interactive screen to examine their history), a gallery of the bank's private art collection, a surreal 3m-long tunnel lined with RM1 million (in the Children's Gallery), and a history of the Islamic banking system (which must comply with sharia law, including prohibitions against usury). Get a taxi from Bank Negara.

🏃 Activities

★**Spa Village** SPA
(Map p72; ☎03-2782 9090; www.spavillage.com; Ritz-Carlton, 168 Jln Imbi, Bukit Bintang; treatments RM420-930; ⊙10am-10pm; ⓜBukit Bintang) A beautifully landscaped pool with waterfalls and greenery creates a tranquil setting for this first-rate spa. Signature treatments include the traditional Royal Malay couples spa experience (including a massage, scrub,

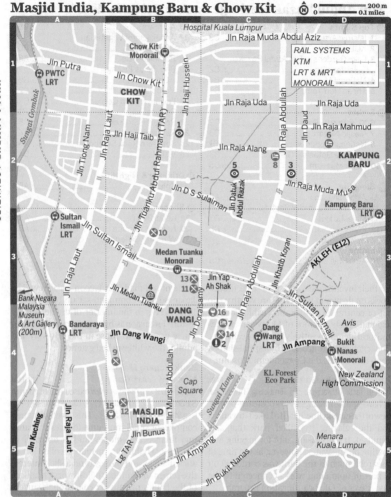

scented body steaming and shared herbal bath in a private garden area) and a Chinese Peranakan treatment involving a rattan tapping massage, and pearl and rice facial.

Bike With Elena
CYCLING

(☎013-850 0500; www.bikewithelena.com; tours from RM250) Knowledgeable Elena (aka Mei Yun) and her guides offer several cycling tours on classic Malayan bikes, the most popular option being the four-hour pedal that starts in Merdeka Sq and continues through Chinatown towards Kampung Baru. Along the way you'll stop for snacks and drinks, all included in the cost.

Chin Woo Stadium
SWIMMING

(Map p62; ☎03-2072 4602; www.chinwoo.org. my; Jln Hang Jebat, Chinatown; swim adult/child RM5/2.50; ⊙2-8pm Mon-Fri, 9am-8pm Sat & Sun; ☐Pasar Seni) This historic sports stadium sits atop a hill overlooking Chinatown. The highlight here is its 50m outdoor pool. Note that all swimsuits must be tight-fitting (ie no baggy shorts even with an inner mesh lining) and you need a cap as well.

MikesBikes
CYCLING

(Map p58; ☎017-673 7322; www.mikebikes.my; Malaysia Tourism Centre (MaTiC), 109 Jln Ampang, KLCC; 2/4hr tour from RM125/210; ☐Bukit Nanas) Using

Masjid India, Kampung Baru & Chow Kit

⊙ **Sights**
1 Bazaar Baru Chow Kit.........................B2
2 Courage to Dream mural.....................C4
3 Kampung Baru Gateway......................C2
4 Loke Mansion..................................B3
5 Master Mat's House...........................C2

⊖ **Sleeping**
6 Bagasta Boutique Guesthouse............D2
7 Hotel Stripes...................................C4
8 Tamu Hotel & Suites..........................C2

⊗ **Eating**
9 Capital Café.....................................B4
10 Kin Kin...B3

11 Limapulo...B3
12 Masjid India Pasar Malam...................B5
13 Peter Hoe Cafe.................................B3
14 Yut Kee...C4

⊖ **Drinking & Nightlife**
15 Coliseum Cafe..................................B5
16 Gavel..C4

⊗ **Entertainment**
Timbre @ The Row....................(see 13)

⊖ **Shopping**
Peter Hoe at the Row.................(see 13)

modern versions of the Dutch grandmother-style bicycle from the Netherlands, these guided bike tours take you around central city areas including Kampung Baru and Chow Kit. MikesBikes also runs sunset tours starting at 5pm for a slightly less sweaty pedal.

Hammam Spa SPA
(Map p76; ☎03-2282 2180; www.hammamspas.com; 3rd fl, Bangsar Village II,15 Jln Telawi 2, Bangsar; treatments RM116-398; ⊙10am-10.30pm; ⧉822) The Moroccan steam bath comes to KL at this small and beautiful mosaic-tiled spa. Couples and singles packages are available with sumptuous titles such as the Royal Couple (RM730) and the Sultan's Daughter's Wedding (RM456), or you can go for a simple steam and scrub (*gommage;* RM168).

Majestic Spa SPA
(Map p62; ☎03-2785 8070; www.majestickl.com; Majestic Hotel, 5 Jln Sultan Hishamuddin, Lake Gardens; treatments RM410-995; ⊙10am-10pm; ⧉Kuala Lumpur) Charles Rennie Mackintosh's Willow Tea Rooms in Glasgow are the inspiration for the Majestic's delightful spa, where treatments are preceded by a refreshing tea or Pimm's cocktail. After your pampering, there's a pool for a dip and sunbathe.

Simply Enak FOOD & DRINK
(☎017-287 8929; www.simplyenak.com; tours RM260) Daily tours to places such as Chow Kit and Petaling St to experience authentic Malaysian food with resident experts.

⚓ **Courses**

★**LaZat Malaysian Home Cooking Class** COOKING
(☎019-238 1198; www.malaysia-klcookingclass.com; Malay House at Penchala Hills, Lot 3196, Jln Seri Penchala, Kampong Sungai Penchala; RM290; ⊙8.30am-2pm Mon-Sat) A market tour is followed by a hands-on cooking class in a traditional Malay home in the leafy northwestern suburb of Sungai Penchala. A different menu is taught on each day of the week, with vegetarian fare on Monday and dishes with a Malay, Malaysian Chinese or Peranakan slant on other days.

myBatik ART
(☎012-257 9775; www.mybatik.org.my; 34 Jln Mengkuang, Ampang Hilir; batik course RM55-720; ⊙8am-5pm; ⧉300, 303) Founded by friendly artist Emilia Tan, this is the best place in KL to learn the skill of batik – using wax to paint with coloured dyes on fabric. On offer are demonstration sessions and DIY batik classes for adults and children (weekends are popular with families). There's also a shop selling unique products made from their own batik fabrics.

Sarang Cookery COOKING
(Map p72; ☎012-210 0218; www.sarangcookery.com.my; 8 Jln Galloway, Bukit Bintang; 4hr classes RM250; ⊙9am-1pm & 2-6pm Mon-Fri, cafe 11am-9.30pm; ⧉Hang Tuah) Learn to cook four different Peranakan (Nonya), Malay or Indian dishes at these fun, hands-on cooking classes run by B&B owners Christina and Michael at one of their properties. Ingredients from the herb garden such as lemongrass, turmeric and basil are incorporated into the dishes, which are consumed at the end of the class in a sit-down meal.

Also here is a cafe serving a good range of classic Malaysian dishes and drinks.

✳ Festivals & Events

Cooler Lumpur Festival ART
(www.coolerlumpur.com; ☻Sep) Multidisciplinary arts festival with a different annual theme and events staged at Publika (p101).

DiverseCity CULTURAL
(www.diversecity.my; ☻Sep) KL's international arts festival runs throughout September and offers a packed program of contemporary and traditional dance, music shows, literature readings, comedy and visual-arts events.

KL International Jazz & Arts Festival MUSIC
(www.klinternationaljazz.com; ☻Sep) A cracking line-up of artists perform at this festival, held at several venues including the campus of the University of Malaya.

Urbanscapes ART
(www.facebook.com/urbanscapes; ☻Nov) Held in various venues across the city over three weekends, this long-running festival brings together art, music, film and design with a series of performances and events.

🛏 Sleeping

KLites' love of brands is reflected in the city's many international hotel chains. You can often grab great online deals for top-end accommodation, and there are also some excellent new boutique-style midrange options. Budget sleeps are plentiful, too, but the best places fill up quickly, so book ahead – especially over public holidays.

Practically all midrange and top-end places offer promotions that substantially slash rack rates; booking online will almost always bring the price down. Room discounts will not apply during public holidays.

🛏 Bukit Bintang & KLCC

Paper Plane Hostel HOSTEL $
(Map p72; ☑03-2110 1676; www.paperplanehostel.com; 15 Jln Sin Chew Kee, Bukit Bintang; dm/d with shared bathroom RM65/100; ❄🛜❄; 🚇Hang Tuah, 🚉Hang Tuah) Hand-painted murals, exposed brick walls and high-ceilinged rooms impart a sophisticated air to this hostel in a 90-year-old shophouse. Mixed and women-only dorm rooms are attired in tasteful monochrome, while loft-room dorms have dizzying, custom-made three-tier bunks. Service is companionable and the entire place is fairy-godmother clean.

★The Bed KLCC DESIGN HOTEL $
(Map p58; ☑03-2715 2413; www.thebedklcc.com; Vortex KLCC, 12 Jln Sultan Ismail, KLCC; dm/s/d incl breakfast from RM59/140/180; ❄🛜❄; 🚇Bukit Nanas) On the lower floors of the circular Vortex tower, this innovative hotel offers two styles of capsule rooms – 10-bed dorms where you crawl into the capsule from the front and ones which are really the same as regular dorm cubicles. It's all very stylishly done with an excellent lounge, library and kitchen area.

Classic Inn GUESTHOUSE $
(Map p72; ☑03-2148 8648; www.classicinn.com.my; 36 & 52 Lg 1/77A; d/tw incl breakfast from RM70/99; ❄@🛜; 🚇Imbi) Check-in is at the newer, more upmarket branch of Classic Inn at No 36, where there are spotless rooms all with private bathrooms and a pleasant verandah cafe. The original yellow-painted shophouse at No 52 continues to be a retro-charming choice with plain but perfectly agreeable private rooms, a small grassy garden and welcoming staff.

KL FOR CHILDREN

There are dozens of attractions around KL set up specifically to keep little ones entertained. A good starting point is the Lake Gardens, particularly the KL Bird Park (p61) and the playground and boating pond in the Perdana Botanical Garden (p65). The waterfall splash pool in the KLCC Park (p55) is also great for waterbabies, as is the adjacent adventure playground and the Aquaria KLCC (p59).

Kids will also enjoy KL's malls. Berjaya Times Square has an indoor **theme park** (Map p72; ☑03-2117 3118; www.berjayatimessquarethemeparkkl.com; Berjaya Times Square, 1 Jln Imbi, Bukit Bintang; adult/child RM57/47; ☻noon-10pm; 🚇Imbi). There are more theme parks dotted around KL, including the wet and wild park at Sunway Lagoon (p115).

Brave kids and teens will be thrilled by the chance to make like a monkey in the treetops by traversing the canopy walkways and trails at KL Forest Eco Park (p60) and Taman Tugu (p61).

Paloma Inn HOTEL **$**
(Map p72; ✆03-2110 6677; www.hotelpalomainn.
com.my; 12-14 Jln Sin Chew Kee, Bukit Bintang; dm/s/d
RM40/85/110; ❇@🛜; 🚇Hang Tuah, 🚍 Hang Tuah)
Set on a backstreet of prewar shophouses, Paloma is well run and quiet, with simple, mostly
wooden-floored rooms, featuring occasional
flashes of magenta, pleasingly modern bathrooms and a shady garden out front. Rates are
slightly higher Friday and Saturday.

★**Kuala Lumpur Journal** BOUTIQUE HOTEL **$$**
(Map p72; ✆03-2110 2211; www.kljournalhotel.
com; 30 Jln Beremi, Bukit Bintang; d incl breakfast
from RM280; ❇🛜❄; Ⓜ Bukit Bintang) This
hip hotel, with an urban vibe and appeal-
ing retro design, is located steps away from
Bukit Bintang's shopping and nightlife.
Rooms feature blown-up prints of KL street
life by local photographer Che Mat and floor-
to-ceiling windows to take in the city views.
The rooftop saltwater pool and bar is a plus.

★**Mov Hotel** BOUTIQUE HOTEL **$$**
(Map p72; ✆03-2781 9888; www.movhotel.com;
43 Jln Berangan, Bukit Bintang; r from RM230;
❇@🛜❄; Ⓜ Bukit Bintang) A contemporary
sculpture of a white tiger prowling the lobby
and a slide into its restaurant are just a couple of the fun, creative touches at this stylish
property just steps from nightlife hub Changkat Bukit Bintang. The top-tier loft rooms
offer double-height ceilings and penthouse
furnishings.

Element Kuala Lumpur HOTEL **$$**
(Map p58; ✆03-2771 3388; www.elementkuala
lumpur.com; Ilham Tower, 8 Jln Binjai, KLCC; r from
RM340; ❇@🛜❄; 🚇 Ampang Park) 🅿 Book
in advance for some very good deals at this
stylish hotel that occupies the top floors
of the Foster + Partners–designed Ilham
Tower. Rooms are stylishly decorated, spa-
cious and offer good views. A nice touch is
that they include filtered water dispensers
instead of plastic bottles. The swimming
pool uses saline rather than chlorine.

★**Villa Samadhi** HOTEL **$$$**
(Map p58; ✆03-2143 2300; www.villasamadhi.
com.my; 8 Persiaran Madge, Ampang; d from RM577;
❇🛜❄; 🚇 Ampang Park) It's hard to believe
you're in the heart of KL when staying at this
gorgeous boutique property that epitomises
Southeast Asian chic. The black polished
concrete, bamboo and reclaimed-timber
rooms combine with luxurious light fixtures,
idyllic central pool, lush foliage, poolside
bar (serving complimentary cocktails) and

SLEEPING PRICE RANGES

The following price ranges refer to a
double room with bathroom.

$ less than RM100
$$ RM100–400
$$$ more than RM400

intimate modern Malay restaurant Mandi
Mandi to conjure an antidote to urban stress.

Banyan Tree Kuala Lumpur LUXURY HOTEL **$$$**
(Map p58; ✆03-2113 1888; www.banyantree.
com; 2 Jln Conlay, Bukit Bintang; r/ste from
RM830/1200; ❇🛜❄; 🚇Raja Chulan) There are
only 55 rooms at this luxury hotel occupy-
ing the loftiest floors of a 59-storey build-
ing – which guarantees sweeping views all
around. You'll pay a premium for the rooms
facing either the KL or Petronas Towers, but
whatever the aspect, the interiors are spa-
cious, plush and hushed.

G Tower Hotel HOTEL **$$$**
(Map p58; ✆03-2168 1919; www.gtowerhotel.com;
199 Jln Tun Razak, KLCC; r from RM400; ❇@🛜❄;
🚇 Ampang Park) There's an exclusive atmosphere at this slickly designed property atop an
office complex, where the facilities include a
gym, infinity pools and a top-floor lounge, restaurant and bar. Arty black-and-white prints
set a sophisticated tone in the bedrooms.

🛏 Chinatown

★**BackHome** HOSTEL **$**
(Map p62; ✆03-2022 0788; www.backhome.
com.my; 30 Jln Tun HS Lee, Chinatown; all incl
breakfast dm/d/tr with shared bathroom from
RM50/138/168; ❇@🛜; 🚇 Masjid Jamek) This
chic pit stop for flashpackers offers polished-
concrete finishes, Zen decoration, rain
showers (all rooms share bathrooms) and
a blissful central courtyard sprouting spin-
dly trees. There are mixed, women-only and
couples' dorms (sleeping four). Also on site
is pleasant LOKL Coffee (p91).

★**Mingle Hostel** HOSTEL **$**
(Map p62; ✆03-2022 2078; www.minglehostels.
com; 53 Jln Sultan, Chinatown; dm/s/d with shared
bathroom from RM42/78/98, d RM135; ❇@🛜;
🚇 Pasar Seni) Occupying a 1920s building once
owned by a Chinese tycoon, this clued-up hostel has a naturalistic feel with venerable stone
walls and lounge zones open to the air. Dorms
and rooms feel ample, each bed with its own

Bukit Bintang

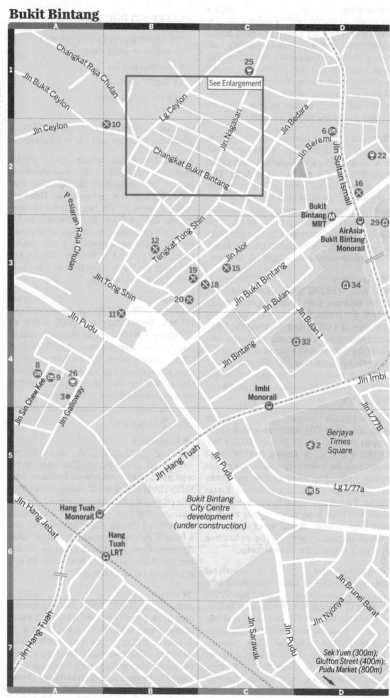

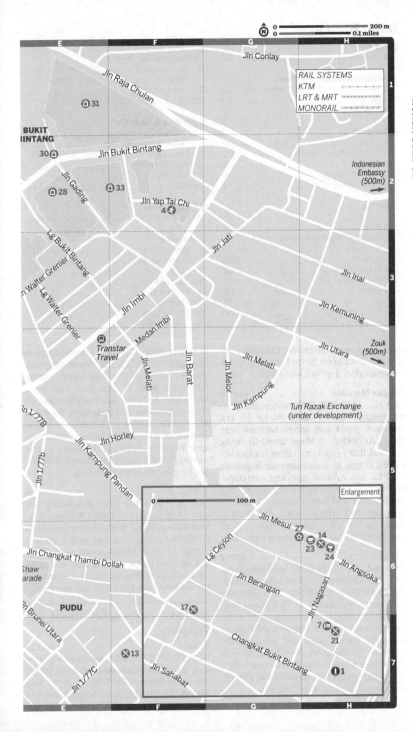

Bukit Bintang

◉ Sights
1 Mural Alley...H7

◉ Activities, Courses & Tours
2 Berjaya Times Square Theme Park.... D5
3 Sarang Cookery....................................A4
4 Spa Village..F2

◉ Sleeping
5 Classic Inn D5
6 Kuala Lumpur Journal.........................D2
7 Mov Hotel H7
8 Paloma Inn..A4
9 Paper Plane Hostel..............................A4

◉ Eating
Ben's..(see 31)
10 Bijan...B2
11 Blue Boy Vegetarian Food Centre.......B4
Brasserie Fritz.............................(see 16)
Enak KL..(see 33)
12 French Feast...B3
13 Imbi Market at ICC Pudu......................F7
14 Isabel...H6
15 Jalan Alor...C3
Lot 10 Hutong.............................. (see 29)
16 Mr Chew's Chino Latino Bar................D2

17 Pinchos Tapas Bar...............................F6
18 Restoran Beh Brothers.......................C3
19 Restoran TKS.......................................B3
Sisters Noodle............................ (see 18)
20 Wong Ah Wah.......................................B3
21 Wurst...H7

◉ Drinking & Nightlife
22 Blueboy Discotheque..........................D2
23 Feeka Coffee Roasters.......................H6
24 Pisco Bar...H6
25 Taps Beer Bar......................................C1
TWG Tea .... (see 31)
26 VCR..A4

◉ Entertainment
27 No Black Tie..G6

◉ Shopping
British India................................ (see 31)
28 Fahrenheit88.......................................E2
29 Lot 10..D3
30 Pavilion Elite.......................................E2
31 Pavilion KL...E1
32 Plaza Low Yat......................................D4
33 Starhill Gallery....................................F2
34 Sungei Wang Plaza.............................D3

air-con and electrical sockets. Occasional antiques and old brass lamps hark back to the building's glory days as a social hall.

Reggae Mansion HOSTEL $
(Map p62; ☎03-2072 6877; www.reggaehostels malaysia.com/mansion; 49-59 Jln Tun HS Lee, Chinatown; dm/d with shared bathroom from RM30/120; ✻@🖥; 🚇 Masjid Jamek) Grooving to a beat that's superior to most backpacker places, Reggae Mansion instantly impresses with its faux-colonial style and contemporary touches, including a lively rooftop bar, mini-cinema and flash cafe-bar. Container-style beds feel private though one dorm is very large (24 beds). Ask for a quieter room away from the bar if you're not a night owl.

Lantern Hotel HOTEL $
(Map p62; ☎03-2020 1648; www.lanternhotel. com; 38 Jln Petaling, Chinatown; d/tw incl breakfast from RM90/105; ✻🖥; 🚇 Pasar Seni) You can't get more central to Chinatown than this slickly designed, contemporary hotel. Simple, whitewashed rooms have lime or tangerine feature walls and private bathrooms – the cheapest ones have no windows. Take a breather on the terrace with a cityscape mural, creeper plants and a bird's-eye view of Petaling Street Market.

Tian Jing Hotel BOUTIQUE HOTEL $$
(Map p62; ☎03-2022 1131; www.tianjinghotel. com; 66-68 Jln Sultan, Chinatown; s/d incl breakfast RM180/250; ✻🖥; 🚇 Pasar Seni) Dark-wood four-poster beds are handsomely offset by crisp white sheets at this boutique hotel that successfully channels Chinatown's atmosphere minus the kitsch. Some of the rooms sport balconies, but it's a busy area, so you're unlikely to be hanging out there unless you like people- and traffic-watching.

Avenue J HOTEL $$
(Map p62; ☎03-2022 3338; www.avenuejhotels. com; 13 Jln Lebuh Pasar Besar, Chinatown; d incl breakfast from RM140; ✻🖥; 🚇 Pasar Seni) Right beside the Klang river and with a picture-postcard view of Masjid Jamek as you walk out the door, this is a handy, new and pleasant midrange option. Rooms are compact and the cheapest ones don't have any windows.

🛏 Lake Gardens, Brickfields & Bangsar

PODs HOSTEL $
(Map p66; ☎03-2276 0858; www.podsbackpacker. com; G-6, 30 Jln Thambipillay, Brickfields; dm/s/d with shared bathroom RM35/65/75; ✻🖥; 🚇KL Sentral) This friendly, basic backpackers offers some of the cheapest beds in town. Note par-

titions between the rooms are flimsy and mattresses are on the floor. There's a pleasant cafe on the ground floor for breakfast and a rooftop deck. Rates are slightly higher on the weekend.

Sekeping Tenggiri   GUESTHOUSE $$
(Map p76; ☑017-519 6552; www.sekeping.com; 48 Jln Tenggiri, Bangsar; d RM220-330; ✳🔊💺; 🔲 Abdullah Hukum) Providing access to architect Ng Seksan's superlative private collection of contemporary Malaysian art – displayed in the rooms of the adjoining house – this is a lovely place to stay. The rough-luxe mix of concrete, wood and wire decor (with cleverly recycled materials making up lamp fixtures) is softened by abundant garden greenery and a cooling plunge pool.

Aloft Kuala Lumpur Sentral   HOTEL $$
(Map p66; ☑03-2723 1188; www.starwoodhotels.com/alofthotels; 5 Jln Stesen Sentral, Brickfields; d from RM250; ✳@🔊💺; 🔲 KL Sentral) Designed for the Google generation of young creatives, Aloft is industrial chic meets plastic fantastic. Staff are super friendly and you have to smile at the witty cartoon art in each of the spacious, well-designed rooms. Place a big tick against its infinity rooftop pool and bar with one of the best views in KL.

★ **Alila Bangsar**   DESIGN HOTEL $$$
(Map p66; ☑012-228 1373; www.alilahotels.com/bangsar; 58 Jln Ang Seng, Brickfields; r from RM440; Ⓟ✳🔊💺; 🔲 Bank Rakyat-Bangsar) Having established its brand in Bali, Alila (which means 'supreme' in Bahasa Indonesia) has opened one of KL's most appealing new hotels. The pared-back design, integrating concrete, wood and plenty of plants, suits the tropics and there are great views from the spacious rooms, which run between the 35th and 40th floors.

★ **Majestic Hotel**   HISTORIC HOTEL $$$
(Map p66; ☑03-2785 8000; www.majestickl.com; 5 Jln Sultan Hishamuddin, Lake Gardens; d/ste incl breakfast from RM358/483; ✳@🔊💺✳; 🔲 Kuala Lumpur) Originally opened in 1932 and the pre-WWII KL equivalent of Raffles in Singapore, the impeccably restored Majestic is one of the city's top luxury hotels. Whether you stay in the original building or the new attached tower block (where the majority of rooms are) you are guaranteed comfort and style. Other appealing features include an orchid-filled conservatory and two swimming pools.

🛏 Masjid India & Kampung Baru

★ **Hotel Stripes**   HOTEL $$
(Map p68; ☑03-2038 0000; www.stripeskl.com; 25 Jln Kamunting, Dang Wangi; r from RM340; ✳🔊💺; 🔲 Dang Wangi) Blown-up black-and-white photos of what this area looked like 50 years ago feature in the stylish rooms of this new small luxury hotel. Light filters in through the lattice of brickwork that forms

---

SERVICED APARTMENTS

Some of KL's best accommodation deals, particularly for longer stays, are offered by serviced apartments. Studios and suites tend to be far larger and better equipped than you'd get for a similar price at top-end hotels. There are usually pools and gyms within the complexes, too. There are quite a few of these complexes scattered across the city. For short stays, breakfast is usually included. Our top picks:

E&O Residences Kuala Lumpur (Map p58; ☑03-2023 2188; www.eoresidences.com; 1 Jln Tengah, Bukit Bintang; 1-bed apt from RM450; ✳@🔊💺; 🔲 Raja Chulan) Chances are, once you spend a night in these elegantly designed apartments, with their clean-line furnishings and striking contemporary art, you will not want to leave. There's a good gym and large outdoor pool in the landscaped courtyard garden.

MiCasa All Suite Hotel (Map p58; ☑03-2179 8000; www.micasahotel.com; 368b Jln Tun Razak, Ampang; apt from RM250; ✳@🔊💺; 🔲 Ampang Park) A choice of one-, two- or three-bedroom suites – all reasonably priced, with wood floors and well-equipped kitchens. Relax beside the large, palm-tree-fringed pool, or enjoy the small spa. Facilities include a gym and coin-operated laundry.

Fraser Place Kuala Lumpur (Map p58; ☑03-2118 6288; http://kualalumpur.frasershospitality.com; Lot 163, 10 Jln Perak, KLCC; apt from RM350; ✳@🔊💺; 🔲 Bukit Nanas) Good workspaces and walk-in closets feature in these colourfully designed apartments. The facilities, including an outdoor infinity pool, gym, sauna and games room, are top-notch.

Bangsar Baru

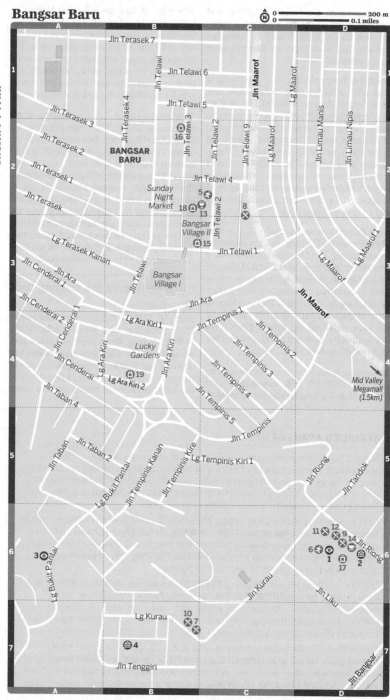

Bangsar Baru

◎ Sights
1 APW D6
2 Galeri Prima D6
3 Kebun-Kebun Bangsar A6
4 Sekeping Tenggiri B7

✚ Activities, Courses & Tours
5 Hammam Spa C2
6 Uppercase D6

⊟ Sleeping
Sekeping Tenggiri .... (see 4)

⊗ Eating
7 Baba Low's 486 .... B7
8 Bangsar Sunday Market C2
9 Breakfast Thieves D6
10 Ganga Cafe B7
11 Kaiju D6
12 Proof D6

⊕ Drinking & Nightlife
13 Mantra Bar KL C2
14 Pulp by Papa Palheta D6

⊟ Shopping
15 Bangsar Village I & II B3
16 I Love Snackfood B2
17 Khoon Hooi D6
18 Nala Muse B2
19 Pucuk Rebung B4

the facade and there's a fab rooftop terrace pool with views towards KL tower.

Bagasta Boutique Guesthouse GUESTHOUSE **$$**
(Map p68; ☑03-2698 9988; www.facebook.com/bagastaboutiquehotel; 56 Jln Raja Alang, Kampung Baru; d from RM120; ❋❄; ⬚ Kampung Baru) Even though it's not in one of the old wooden mansions of Kampung Baru, this small hotel in a modern block is at the heart of the area. Its simple rooms incorporate local crafts and a sprinkling of Malay design (wood from old *kampung* houses was used to make headboards), giving it more character than other midrange options.

Tamu Hotel & Suites HOTEL **$$**
(Map p68; ☑03-2603 1777; www.tamuhotel.com; 120 Jln Raja Abdullah, Kampung Baru; r incl breakfast from RM240; ❀❋❄❅; ⬚ Kampung Baru) The comfortable, butterscotch and blue decorated hotel rooms occupy the 15th to 26th floors of this new 40-storey tower – a forerunner of how much of currently low-rise Kampung Baru will likely end up. There's a great wrap-

around pool with views towards the city's skyline and over the Malay village (while it lasts).

✖ Eating

KL is a nonstop feast. You can dine at elegant white-tablecloth restaurants or mingle with locals at street stalls, taking your pick from a global array of cuisines. Ingredients are fresh, cooking is high quality and hygiene standards are excellent. Most vendors speak English, and the final bill is seldom heavy on the pocket.

✖ Bukit Bintang & KLCC

Blue Boy Vegetarian Food Centre CHINESE **$**
(Map p72; ☑011-6695 0498; Jln Tong Shin, Bukit Bintang; mains RM5-10; ⊙8am-6pm; ✗; ◻Imbi) Run by Chung Ching Thye and his son since the mid 1970s, this remarkable hawker-style cafe at the base of a backstreet apartment block serves only vegetarian dishes. If you bypass a couple of stalls that use egg, it's also vegan. Try the *char kway teow* (broad noodles, clams and eggs fried in chilli and black bean sauce).

Nasi Kandar Pelita MALAYSIAN **$**
(Map p58; ☑03-2162 5532; www.pelita.com.my; 113 Jln Ampang, KLCC; mains RM8-15; ⊙24hr; ◻ KLCC) There's round-the-clock eating at the spiffy Jln Ampang branch of this chain of excellent *mamak* (Indian Muslim) food courts. It's cheap, clean and offers plenty of choice: browse *roti canai* (flat, flaky bread served 4pm to 11am), chicken cooked in the tandoor (cylindrical oven) and biryani (spiced rice dishes) before you decide.

Malaysia Boleh! MALAYSIAN **$**
(Map p58; www.shoppeskl.com; Level B1, Shoppes at the Four Seasons, Jln Ampang, KLCC; mains RM9-12; ⊙10am-10pm; ◻ KLCC) Meaning 'Malaysia can!', this popular slogan is used to good effect at this eye-catchingly designed food court that gathers together the best loved dishes from around the country. Sample Penang fried oyster omelette, *bak kut teh* (pork-rib soup with hints of garlic and Chinese five-spice) from Klang, Kuantan's take on *nasi lemak* (rice boiled in coconut milk, served with *ikan bilis* – small deep-fried anchovies – peanuts and a curry dish) and much more.

Lot 10 Hutong HAWKER **$**
(Map p72; www.lot10hutong.com; basement, Lot 10, 50 Jln Sultan Ismail, Bukit Bintang; dishes RM9-18; ⊙10am-10pm; Ⓜ Bukit Bintang) Lot 10 was the first mall to encourage top hawkers to open branches in its basement food court. The

KUALA LUMPUR EATING

well-designed space houses names such as Soong Kee, which has served beef noodles since 1945. Look also for Kong Tai's oyster omelettes, Hon Kee's Cantonese porridge, Kim Lian Kee's Hokkien mee (yellow noodles fried with sliced meat, boiled squid, prawns and strips of fried egg) and Penang Famous Fried Koay Teow.

★ Isabel
SOUTHEAST ASIAN **$$**

(Map p72; ☑ 03-2110 6366; www.isabel.com.my; 21 Jln Mesui, Bukit Bintang; mains R28-125; ⊙ noon-3pm & 6-10pm, bar closes midnight; ☑ Raja Chulan) Isabel is pure charm and a great addition to KL's dining scene. Both in terms of its menu and contemporary tropical decor, the restaurant provides a sophisticated twist on local classics, with dishes from across the region including a delicious Laotian chicken *larb* (salad), a mango kerabu salad and luscious oxtail stew as well as various curries.

Beta KL
MALAYSIAN **$$**

(Map p58; ☑ 03-2181 2990; www.facebook.com/betakualalumpur; 163 Fraser Place, 10 Jln Perak, KLCC; set lunch RM25-40, mains RM27-80; ⊙ noon-3pm & 5-9.45pm Tue-Sun; ☑ Bukit Nanas) Hats off to Beta KL for trying to do something different with traditional Malaysian cuisine, but not being too precious about it. There is a 10-course set menu (RM198), but it's fine to order à la carte with dishes such as ox tongue, inverted curry puff and twice-cooked duck leg being made to share.

Yun House
CANTONESE **$$**

(Map p58; ☑ 03-2382 8888; www.fourseasons.com/kualalumpur; Four Seasons Hotel Kuala Lumpur, 145 Jln Ampang, KLCC; dim sum RM21-48; ⊙ noon-2.30pm & 6-10.30pm Mon-Fri, 10am-3pm & 6-10.30pm Sat & Sun; ☑ KLCC) Superb dim sum (the barbecue chicken buns melt in the mouth like clouds) and other expertly made Cantonese dishes, plus a beautiful dining room overlooking KLCC park, make this the perfect spot for a leisurely treat of a lunch.

ⓘ GOOD FOOD BLOGS

Eat Drink KL (www.eatdrinkkl.blogspot.com)

FriedChillies (www.friedchillies.com)

The Yum List (www.theyumlist.net)

CC Food Travel (www.ccfoodtravel.com)

KYspeaks.com (www.kyspeaks.com)

Burpple (www.burpple.com/kl)

Bijan
MALAYSIAN **$$**

(Map p72; ☑ 03-2031 3575; www.bijanrestaurant.com; 3 Jln Ceylon, Bukit Bintang; mains RM33-88; ⊙ 4.30-10.45pm; ☑ Raja Chulan) One of KL's best Malaysian restaurants, Bijan offers skilfully cooked traditional dishes in a sophisticated dining room that spills out into a tropical garden. Must-try dishes include a rendang curry made with duck, *masak lemak ikan* (fish curry with turmeric) and *opor rusuk* (beef ribs in a coconut and palm sugar sauce).

Enak KL
MALAYSIAN **$$**

(Map p72; ☑ 03-2782 3807; www.feastvillage.com/enak-kl; Feast fl, Starhill Gallery, 181 Jln Bukit Bintang, Bukit Bintang; mains RM33-61; ⊙ noon-11pm; Ⓜ Bukit Bintang) One of the better options in Starhill's (Map p72; ☑ 03-2782 3800; www.starhillgallery.com; ⊙ 10am-10pm) Feast floor, Enak is worth searching out for its finely presented Malay cuisine with a sophisticated twist.

Mr Chew's Chino Latino Bar
FUSION **$$**

(Map p72; ☑ 03-4065 0168; www.mr-chew.com; The Penthouse, WOLO Bukit Bintang, Jln Bukit Bintang, Bukit Bintang; mains RM25-120; ⊙ 11.30am-2.30pm & 6-10.30pm, bar 5pm-12.30am; Ⓜ Bukit Bintang) Drop dead gorgeous, Mr Chew's owns its multilevel penthouse space combining slick restaurant and various cosy lounges for cocktails. If the Chinese and Latin American mash-up of a menu seems like a bit of a mouthful, that's because it is. Some dishes work better than others – we liked the nori tacos and catfish *char siu* buns best.

Fuego
LATIN AMERICAN **$$**

(Map p58; ☑ 03-2162 0886; www.troikaskydining.com; Level 23a, Tower B, The Troika, Persiaran KLCC, KLCC; mains R25-140; ⊙ 6pm-midnight; ☑ Ampang Park) There's a Latin American twist to Fuego, which is famed for its ceviche, tacos, tapas and DIY guacamole – served in granite bowls for mashing the avocado with various other ingredients. With its huge open-air deck facing square on to the Petronas Towers, it's also a show-stopper of a place to sip a beer or cocktail.

Ben's
INTERNATIONAL **$$**

(Map p72; ☑ 03-2141 5290; www.thebiggroup.co/bens; Level 6, Pavilion KL, 168 Jln Bukit Bintang, Bukit Bintang; mains RM25-78; ⊙ 11am-11pm; ☎; Ⓜ Bukit Bintang) The flagship brand of the BIG group of dining outlets delivers on both style and substance. There's a tempting range of Eastern and Western comfort foods, appealing living-room design and

DON'T MISS

JALAN ALOR

The collection of roadside restaurants and stalls lining **Jalan Alor** (Map p72; ⊗ most vendors 5pm-4am; Ⓜ Bukit Bintang) is the great common denominator of KL's food scene, hauling in everyone from sequinned society babes to penny-strapped backpackers. From around 5pm till late every evening, the street transforms into a continuous open-air dining space with hundreds of plastic tables and chairs and rival caterers shouting out to passers-by to drum up business (avoid the pushiest ones!). Most places serve alcohol and you can sample pretty much every Malay Chinese dish imaginable, from grilled fish and satay to *kai-lan* (Chinese greens) in oyster sauce and fried noodles with frogs' legs. Thai food is also popular. Recommended options:

Restoran TKS (Map p72; 32 Jln Alor; small mains RM15-35; ⊗ 6pm-4am;) for mouth-tingling Sichuan dishes.

Restoran Beh Brothers (Map p72; 21a Jln Alor; dishes RM5-10; ⊗ 24hr), one of the few places open from 7am for breakfast, where **Sisters Noodle** (Map p72; noodles RM7; ⊗ 7am-4pm) serves delicious 'drunken' chicken mee (noodles) with rice wine, and there's also a good Hong Kong–style dim sum stall.

Wong Ah Wah (WAW; Map p72; ☑ 03-2144 2463; 1-9 Jln Alor; chicken wings per piece RM3.30; ⊗ 5pm-4am) is unbeatable for addictive spicy chicken wings, as well as grilled seafood, tofu and satay.

nice touches such as a box of cards with recipes and talk topics on each table.

Brasserie Fritz　　　　　　BRASSERIE **$$**
(Map p72; ☑ 03-4065 0876; www.brasseriefritz. com; ground fl, WOLO Bukit Bintang, Jln Bukit Bintang, Bukit Bintang; mains R15-40; ⊗ 8am-midnight; Ⓜ Bukit Bintang) This elegantly decorated space occupies a prime Bukit Bintang corner, making it a handy pit stop for anything from breakfast to supper and a nightcap. There's a good bakery here, too.

Pinchos Tapas Bar　　　　　TAPAS **$$**
(Map p72; ☑ 03-2145 8482; www.pinchos.com.my; 18 Changkat Bukit Bintang, Bukit Bintang; tapas RM18-66; ⊗ food 5-11pm, bar to 3am, Tue-Sun; ⊟ Raja Chulan) This is the real deal for tapas, run by a Spaniard and packed with KL's approving Spanish-speaking community. A great place for a solo meal and drink or fun with a group while you munch your way through the wide-ranging menu.

Wurst　　　　　　INTERNATIONAL **$$**
(Map p72; ☑ 03-2781 9801; B1 fl, Mov Hotel, 43 Jln Berangan, Bukit Bintang; mains R16-49; ⊗ 6.30am-10pm; Ⓜ Bukit Bintang) A key, fun feature of this restaurant dedicated to sausages is that you can enter it using a twisting slide (don't worry – there's also a lift here, too). The halal bangers are house-made from lamb, veal, beef and chicken and are very tasty – order them in platters that include sides of coleslaw, salad and toasted bread buns.

★ **Nadodi**　　　　　SOUTH INDIAN **$$$**
(Map p58; ☑ 03-2181 4334; www.nadodikl.com; Lot 183, 1st fl, Jln Mayang, KLCC; 7-/9-/12-course menus from RM396/473/495; ⊗ 6-11pm Mon-Sat; ☑; ⊟ KLCC) The recipes and ingredients of Tamil Nadu, Kerala and Sri Lanka are the foundation for the sensational tasting menus served at Nadodi (which means nomad). We highly recommend the vegetarian option – 12 courses may sound like a lot, but the sizes of each beautifully presented plate are just right, allowing the chef's artistry to shine.

Acme Bar & Coffee　　　INTERNATIONAL **$$$**
(Map p58; ☑ 03-2162 2288; www.acmebarcoffee. com; unit G1, The Troika, 19 Persiaran KLCC, KLCC; mains RM44-99; ⊗ 11am-midnight Mon-Thu, to 1am Fri, 9.30am-1am Sat, to midnight Sun; ⊟ Ampang Park) Blink and you might be in a chic bistro in New York, Paris or Melbourne. The menu changes seasonally so there's always something new to try, from tasty nibbles such as salted, egg yolk–battered chicken strips to bigger dishes like chargrilled cod steak with ABC *kicap* (a type of soy sauce), chickpea ratatouille and papaya-pineapple salsa.

French Feast　　　　　　FRENCH **$$$**
(Map p72; ☑ 03-2110 6283; www.frenchfeast.com. my; 20 Tengkat Tong Shin, Bukit Bintang; mains RM55-115; ⊗ 6.30-10.30pm Tue-Fri, 9am-3pm & 6.30-10.30pm Sat & Sun; Ⓜ Bukit Bintang) Occupying a tastefully restored old home, French Feast offers classic French bistro–style dishes including cassoulet, house-smoked sausages

KUALA LUMPUR EATING

PUDU DINING

Once a Chinese village on the edge of KL, Pudu is now firmly part of the city and is worth visiting for several great eating experiences.

Perfect for breakfast or brunch is **Imbi Market at ICC Pudu** (Map p72; Jln 1/77C; dishes RM5-10; ⏰6am-2pm Tue-Sun; 🚇 Pudu), a modern food court and market serving mouthwatering food. Top eats include rice-flour noodles at **Ah Fook Chee Cheong Fun**; rice with rich, spicy sambal and myriad accompaniments at **Ann Nasi Lemak**; oyster peanut porridge from **Ong Bee Khing**; and **Sisters Crispy Popiah** serving exquisite wraps.

The popular hawker stall alley **Glutton Street** (Pudu Wai Sek Kai; Jln Sayur; noodles RM5-10; ⏰most stalls 5pm-midnight; 🚇 Pudu) comes to life at night. Evening grazing could include addictive fried chicken, *chai tow kway* (radish cake stir-fried with soy sauce, bean sprouts and egg), prawn fritters and barbecued dried squid, all for bargain prices.

Occupying the same handsome art deco building for the past six decades, **Sek Yuen** (📞03-9222 0903; 315 Jln Pudu; mains RM15-35; ⏰noon-2.30pm & 5.30-9pm Tue-Sun; 🚇 Pudu) is a Pudu institution. Some of the aged chefs toiling in the wood-fired kitchen have served three generations the same old-school Cantonese dishes. The *kau yoke* (pork belly), village chicken and crispy-skin roast duck are all classics.

with puy lentils and imported cheeses and wines. There's also an indulgent weekend brunch menu accompanied by freshly baked pastries and breads.

🍴 Chinatown

⭐ Madras Lane Hawkers HAWKER $
(Map p62; Madras Lane, Chinatown; noodles RM5-6; ⏰8am-4pm Tue-Sun; 🚇 Pasar Seni) This hidden-away alley of hawker stalls is best visited for breakfast or lunch. Among its standout operators is one offering 10 types of *yong tau fu* (vegetables stuffed with tofu and a fish and pork paste). The *bak kut teh* and curry laksa stalls are also good.

Ikan Panggang HAWKER $
(Map p62; 📞019-315 9448; Jln Hang Lekir, Chinatown; mains RM6-15; ⏰5-11pm Tue-Sun; 🚇 Pasar Seni) Tuck into spicy fish and seafood dishes and luscious chicken wings from this stall labelled only Ikan Panggang (which means grilled fish) outside Hong Leong Bank. Order ahead: it generally takes 20 minutes for your foil-wrapped pouch of seafood to cook, allowing time to explore the market.

Lai Foong HAWKER $
(Map p62; 138 Jln Tun Tan Cheng Lock, Chinatown; noodles RM8; ⏰7am-4.30pm; 🚇 Pasar Seni) The stall that lends its name to this old-school hawker cafe has been dishing up beef ball noodles since 1956; ask for its special 'steak and balls' soup made with beef penis and testicles.

Sangeetha INDIAN $
(Map p62; 📞03-2032 3333; 65 Lebuh Ampang, Chinatown; mains RM13.50-18; ⏰8am-11pm; 📞;

🚇 Masjid Jamek) This well-run vegetarian restaurant serves lots of North Indian delights such as *idli* (savoury, soft, fermented-rice-and-lentil cakes) for breakfast and *masala dosa* (rice-and-lentil crepes stuffed with spiced potatoes) throughout the day. Its Punjabi *chaat* (snacks), including vegetable samosas and *pani puri* (stuffed dough balls), are perfect for afternoon munchies.

⭐ Chocha Foodstore ASIAN $$
(Map p62; 📞03-2022 1100; www.facebook.com/chocha.foodstore; 156 Jln Petaling, Chinatown; mains RM22-60; ⏰11am-11pm Tue-Sun; 🚇Maharajalela) Behind the raw concrete and timber facade of the old Mah Lian Hotel is this restaurant and teashop with a plant-filled courtyard and the original hotel tiles. Chocha's 'tea sommelier' serves an extensive selection of speciality brews between 11am and 7pm, but it's the delicious modern Asian cooking using fresh farm-to-table ingredients that's the standout.

Geographer INTERNATIONAL $$
(Map p62; 📞03-2022 2193; www.geographer.com.my; 93 Jln Tun HS Lee, Chinatown; mains RM25-30; ⏰11am-11pm Sun-Thu, until midnight Fri & Sat; 📶; 🚇 Pasar Seni) Melaka's long-running Geographer Cafe brings its winning formula of local and international cuisine and drinks to the heart of KL. Take your pick between Malaysian favourites such as fried rice or laksa noodles, or go for the salads, sandwiches or burgers – it's all good. Cocktails and beers are affordable and the old Malaya ambience appealing.

(Continued on page 91)

Regional Specialities

Malaysia, Singapore and Brunei collectively form a hungry traveller's dream destination – a multiethnic region boasting a wide-ranging cuisine shaped over centuries by the Muslim, European, Indonesian, Indian and Chinese traders, colonisers and labourers who have landed on its shores.

Above *Asam laksa*

Local Flavours

If the region has any single culinary constant at all, it's undoubtedly noodles. But even these differ from country to country and coast to coast. *Asam laksa,* the Penang take on laksa, combines toothsome round rice noodles doused with a tart, fishy, herbal broth, while across the South China Sea in Sarawak, laksa is breakfast food, and residents wake up to a spicy, coconut-rich curry soup packed with rice vermicelli, omelette strips, chicken and prawns.

Rice also features prominently across the region. *Nasi lemak,* an unofficial 'national dish' of Malaysia, is rice steamed with coconut milk and cream, and topped with *ikan bilis* (small, dried sardines or anchovies), peanuts, sliced cucumber, sweet-hot sambal and half a

hard-boiled egg (curry optional); *thali* – rice served on a banana leaf 'plate' with a choice of curries – is daily Indian fare.

For the best of multi-culinary Malaysia, Penang is generally regarded as the region's gastronomic ground zero. KL residents have been known to make the four-hour drive to Penang for a single meal, and hungry Singaporeans pack out hotels on weekends. In addition to regional Chinese food, *mamak* (halal Indian) specialities, southern Indian treats and Malay dishes, the peninsula is a hot spot for Peranakan or Nonya cooking, born of intermarriage between Chinese immigrants and local Malays. Culinary fusion is also a theme in Melaka, the former Portuguese outpost where you'll find Kristang (a

1. Dishes on display at a market stall in Kota Kinabalu (p316) 2. Chinatown (p499), Singapore 3. *Kuih*

blend of Portuguese and local cooking styles) dishes such as *debal*, a fiery Eurasian stew.

If it's all a bit too overwhelming, head to the peninsular east coast – the heartland of traditional Malay cooking. The states of Kelantan and Terengganu have been considerably isolated from the rest of the country, and have received few Chinese and Indian immigrants. Consequently, regional specialities have remained staunchly Malay. Graze the region long enough and you may develop a few cavities; local cooks excel at making all manner of *kuih*, Malay-style sweets, and even savoury dishes have a noticeably sweet edge.

And if you're looking to diverge from the local cuisine altogether, then look no farther than Singapore; the island nation's high-end dining scene is second to none in Southeast Asia. Whether you're hankering for handmade papardelle (pasta), steak frites, sparklingly fresh sashimi or a molecular gastronomic morsel quick-frozen in liquid nitrogen and bedecked with foam, you'll find it in a posh restaurant there.

PIXELBLEED/SHUTTERSTOCK ©

1. *Char kway teow* **2.** Street-food stall in George Town (p160), Penang **3.** *Hor fun* **4.** *Otak otak*

SVETLANA SF/SHUTTERSTOCK ©

Penang

Penang is known for its Peranakan or Nonya cuisine, a fusion of Chinese and Malay (and sometimes also Thai) ingredients and cooking techniques. Examples include *kerabu beehoon*, rice vermicelli tossed with sambal and lime juice and garnished with fresh herbs, and *otak otak*, curried fish 'custard' steamed in a banana leaf.

It is also the home of *nasi kandar*, rice eaten with a variety of curries, a *mamak* speciality named after the *kandar* (shoulder pole) from which ambulant vendors once suspended their pots of rice and curry.

Penang's hawker food is a must. Wide, flat *kway teow* noodles are stir-fried with prawns, cockles, egg and bean sprouts for the hawker speciality *char kway teow*. Other don't-miss dishes include the laksa twins: *asam* (round rice noodles in a hot and sour fish gravy topped with slivered pineapple, cucumber, mint leaves and slightly astringent torch ginger flower) and *lemak* (with a coconut milk-based broth).

Kedah, Perlis & Perak

Thai culinary influence extends to foods in Malaysia's west-coast states of Perlis and Kedah, where fish sauce is as common a seasoning as *belacan*. Here, look for laksa *utara*, a lighter but still spicy and intensely fish-flavoured version of Penang's *asam laksa*.

Farther south is Ipoh, the mostly Chinese capital of Perak state and a town with a reputation for excellent eating. Pasta lovers rave over Ipoh's rice noodles, said to derive their exceptional silky smoothness from the town's water. Judge for yourself with the local version of Hainanese chicken – served with a side of barely blanched bean sprouts and noodles instead of rice – and *hor fun*, rice noodle soup with shredded chicken breast.

1. *Satay celup* 2. *Mee rebus* 3. *Ayam percik* 4. *Nasi kerabu*

JPLDESIGNS/GETTY IMAGES ©

Melaka

Melaka's specialities include *ayam pong teh* (chicken cooked with soybean paste, dark soy sauce and sugar), *ikan cili garam* (fish curry), *satay celup* (skewered meat, seafood, and vegetables cooked at the table in a tub of peanut-based sauce) and Hainanese chicken served with rice moulded into balls.

Often overlooked here is Kristang cuisine, the edible result of intermarriage between Portuguese colonisers and locals that's an intriguing blend of Chinese/Peranakan, Indian, Malay and, of course, European ingredients.

Johor & Pahang

Johor state boasts two tasty Malay noodle specialities: *mee bandung*, yellow noodles topped with a zippy, tomatoey shrimp gravy; and *mee rebus,* the same type of noodles doused with a sweet-savoury sauce thickened with sweet potatoes. The state also has its own variation on the laksa theme, consisting of spaghetti in a thin spicy fish gravy topped with chopped fresh herbs.

Pahang's rivers are known for *ikan patin*, known in English as silver catfish, a freshwater fish that's a local delicacy.

Kelantan & Terengganu

Kelantan state's capital, Kota Bharu, boasts Malaysia's most beautiful wet market, as well as plenty of places to try specialities like *ayam percik* (chilli paste–marinated chicken, grilled and doused with coconut sauce) and visually arresting *nasi kerabu* (rice tinted blue with natural colouring obtained from dried pea flowers).

In Terengganu state, a vendor dishing up mounds of red rice signals *nasi dagang*. The slightly nut-flavoured grain is cooked with coconut milk and eaten with fried chicken and sambal.

1. *Pan mee* with chicken broth 2. *Roti canai* 3. *Kari kepala ikan*
4. Fried carrot cake

SYIBLI/SHUTTERSTOCK ©

Kuala Lumpur, Selangor & Negeri Sembilan

Almost all of Malaysia's specialities can be found in KL, but two dishes in particular are more easily found here than elsewhere: *pan mee* (literally 'board noodles'), thick and chewy wheat noodles tossed with dark soy and garnished with chopped pork, *ikan bilis* and shredded cloud ear mushrooms; and *sang har mee* ('fresh sea noodles'), huge freshwater prawns in gravy flavoured with rice wine and prawn fat served over crispy noodles.

Farther south, in Negeri Sembilan state, descendents of Minangkabau, who immigrated from the Indonesian island of Sumatra hundreds of years ago, dish up a mean *nasi padang* – rice accompanied by a parade of fiery curries, *gulai* (fish and vegetables cooked in mild coconut milk gravy), soups and sambal.

Singapore

Singapore's culinary landscape is a near replica of Malaysia's, but in miniature. Still, Singaporeans do lay special claim to a few dishes, including crab stir-fried with black pepper, and fried carrot cake, which despite its name, is actually a savoury dish of squares of radish-flour cake stir-fried with bean sprouts, chilli sauce and salted radish. *Kari kepala ikan* (fish-head curry) was allegedly invented by a Singaporean-Indian cook playing to the Chinese love of fish cheeks. Hainanese chicken-rice, a plate of rice flavoured with garlic and broth, tender poached chicken, sliced cucumber and dipping sauces, assumes similarly iconic status here.

Singaporeans love their *roti prata* (the equivalent of Malaysia's *roti canai*) for breakfast, and have their own version of laksa – called Katong laksa for the neighbourhood that birthed it – noodles in a prawn and coconut-milk-based, highly spiced soup.

Fish on display at a market stall in Kota Kinabalu (p3)

Malaysian Borneo (Sarawak & Sabah)

Sarawak's highlanders specialise in dishes cooked in bamboo, like the chicken dish *ayam pansuh* (a special occasion dish of chicken wrapped in tapioca leaves and cooked with water inside a length of bamboo).

If you're in Kota Kinabalu, consider splurging on a meal of bounty from the South China Sea, chosen by your own self from a fish tank and cooked to order at one of the city's many seafood restaurants. Another seafood speciality worthy of mention is *hinava* (sometimes called *umai,* and also found in Sarawak), raw fish seasoned simply with lime juice, herbs and chillies.

Brunei

If Brunei had a national dish, it would be *ambuyat*, a glutinous mass made from the pith of the sago tree, ground to a powder and mixed with water. Served by twisting around chopsticks or long-twined forks, *ambuyat* is usually dipped into *cacah*, a *sambal belacan*- and tamarind-based sweet-and-tart sauce, and accompanied by boiled or smoked seafood and salads. *Ambuyat* itself doesn't have a taste – it's the sauce that gives it its zing. Shrimp-and-chilli mixes are the most popular, although you can technically dip the dish in anything you'd like.

If you are invited to a Bruneian home, you'll probably be served *bahulu* with your tea. This simple dessert is made from eggs, flour and sugar. *Kuripit sagu*, a biscuit-like version of *bahulu*, is jazzed up with mild coconut flavours.

(Continued from page 80)

LOKL Coffee
INTERNATIONAL **$$**

(Map p62; 📞03-2072 1188; http://loklcoffee.com; 30 Jln Tun HS Lee, Chinatown; mains RM16-30; ⏰8am-5pm Mon, Wed-Sun, until 3pm Tue; 🛜; 🚇 Masjid Jamek) Coffees served Western- or Malay-style (with a sticky splosh of condensed milk) are equally good at this welcoming cafe. On the menu are filling brunch dishes such as cornmeal waffles and omelettes, as well as comfort foods such as dessert toasties.

Merchant's Lane
FUSION **$$**

(Map p62; 📞03-2022 1736; www.facebook.com/merchantslane/home; Level 1, 150 Jln Petaling, Chinatown; mains RM20-32; ⏰11.30am-10pm Mon, Tue, Thu & Fri, 9.30am-10pm Sat & Sun; 🛜; 🚇 Pasar Seni) Stairs lead up from a narrow doorway to this high-ceilinged charmer of a cafe. Staff nurture an easygoing vibe and customers are united by enthusiasm for Instagramming the greenery-draped venue and its fusion cuisine. East-meets-West dishes like 'Italian chow mein' and chicken with green-stained pandan rice are hit and miss, but the venue is a delight.

Old China Café
MALAYSIAN **$$**

(Map p62; 📞03-2072 5915; www.oldchina.com.my; 11 Jln Balai Polis, Chinatown; mains RM15-41; ⏰11.30am-9.45pm; 🚇 Pasar Seni) Step through swinging, saloon-style doors into the old guild house of a laundry association, now a charming Peranakan restaurant. Calligraphy and old photographs cover the walls, and grandfather clocks and dainty marble-topped tables add to the quaint ambience. Beef rendang, succulent Nonya fried chicken and *babi masak asam* (tamarind pork stew) feature on the menu of Peranakan comfort food.

Cafe 55
CAFE **$$**

(Map p62; 📞019-222 0262; www.facebook.com/55JalanSultan; 55 Jln Sultan, Chinatown; mains RM18-28; ⏰7.30am-6pm; 🛜; 🚇 Pasar Seni) All-day breakfast options here include local flavours such as pandan or *kaya* spread on the toast. Or you could go for a *yee sang soba,* where you get to toss the noodles with colourful, healthy salad ingredients. It's all served up in a shabby chic, renovated shophouse that is spot on for 21st-century Chinatown style.

Atmosphere 360
MALAYSIAN, INTERNATIONAL **$$$**

(Map p62; 📞03-2020 2121; www.atmosphere360.com.my; Menara Kuala Lumpur, 2 Jln Punchak, Bukit Nanas; buffet lunch/afternoon tea/dinner RM92/61/208; ⏰11.30am-1pm, 3.30-5.30pm & 6.30-11pm; 🚇KL Tower) There are 360-degree views from this tower-top revolving restaurant.

WEEKEND NIGHT MARKETS

The weekly **Bangsar Sunday Market** (Pasar Malam; Map p76; car park east of Jln Telawi 2, Bangsar; hawker food RM4-6; ⏰1-9pm Sun; 🚌822), though mostly for fresh produce, is also a fine hawker food grazing zone. Stalls sell satay and a variety of noodles including *asam laksa* (laksa with a prawn paste and tamarind-flavoured gravy), *chee cheong fun* (rice noodles) and *char kway teow*.

Stalls pack out the length of Lg Tuanku Abdul Rahman, the alley between Jln TAR and Masjid India, for the **Masjid India Pasar Malam** (Map p68; Lg Tuanku Abdul Rahman, Masjid India; street food RM5-10; ⏰3pm-midnight Sat; 🚇 Masjid Jamek). Amid the headscarf and T-shirt sellers are plenty of stalls serving excellent Malay, Indian and Chinese snacks and colourful soya- and fruit-based drinks.

The lunch and dinner buffets offer an ample choice of Malay dishes, though they can be hit and miss. Book ahead (you can do this online) for meals, especially sunset dining, but you can usually just drop in for high tea.

Note there's a smart-casual dress code in the evening and it costs extra to sit by the window (per table RM25 at lunch and RM50 at dinner).

🍴 Lake Gardens, Brickfields & Bangsar

★ Restoran Yarl
SRI LANKAN **$**

(Map p66; 📞016-272 4009; 50 Jln Padang Belia, Brickfields; meals RM10-15; ⏰7am-10pm Tue-Sun; 🚇KL Sentral) Discover the spicy and delicious cuisine of northern Sri Lanka at Yarl. Help yourself from clay pots of spicy mutton, chicken and fish *peratal* (dry curry), squid curry, aubergine *sothi* (mild curry with coconut milk) and vegetable dishes. Don't miss the house speciality, crab curry – try a ladle of the sauce if you don't fancy grappling with claws.

Tugu Cafe
MALAYSIAN **$**

(📞016-263 3379; 515 Persiaran Sultan Salahuddin, Lake Gardens; mains RM4-7; ⏰8am-6pm Mon-Fri, until 3pm Sat; Ⓜ Muzium Negara) Occupying a handful of stalls outside the Civil Servants Club House (PPTD), this rustic food court is rightly famed for its superb fish-head curry, deep-fried free-range chicken and banana fritters.

Steps lead up here from beside the National Monument (p64).

Ganga Cafe
INDIAN $

(Map p76; ☑03-2284 2119; www.theganga.com.my; 19 Lg Kurau, Bangsar; mains RM8.50-10.50, Sun brunch buffet RM21; ⊗8am-10pm Mon-Sat, 10am-3pm Sun; ⚑; ⋒ Bank Rakyat-Bangsar) This bright little cafe on Lg Kurau is a great spot for wholesome vegetarian Ayurvedic chapatis, wholewheat naans, *parathas* (bread made with ghee and cooked on a hotplate), *dosas* (crispy pancakes), curries, lassis and special masala tea. On Sundays it's a self-service brunch buffet.

Baba Low's 486
PERANAKAN $

(Map p76; ☑03-2284 8486; www.facebook.com/babalowslorongkurau; 11 Lg Kurau, Bangsar; mains RM7.50-8.50; ⊗7am-10pm; ⋒ Bank Rakyat-Bangsar) The 486 in the name refers to the street number of the original restaurant in Melaka of this mini-chain specialising in freshly made, authentic staples of Peranakan cuisine, *ayam pong teh* (miso soy chicken), spicy fish paste patties *otak otak* and – of course – laksa.

Annalakshmi Vegetarian Restaurant
INDIAN $

(Map p66; ☑03-2274 0799; www.annalakshmi.com.my; Temple of Fine Arts, 116 Jln Berhala, Brickfields; dinner mains RM10-18; ⊗11.30am-3pm & 6.30-10pm Tue-Sun; ⚑; ⋒ KL Sentral) This well-regarded vegetarian restaurant has set prices at night and a daily lunch buffet for RM18 (RM21 Friday to Sunday); or you can eat at the humbler **Annalakshmi Riverside** next to

the car park behind the main building, where it's 'eat as you wish, give as you feel'.

Vishal
INDIAN $

(Map p66; ☑03-2274 1995; 22 Jln Scott, Brickfields; meals from RM7; ⊗7.30am-10.45pm; ⚑; ⋒ Tun Sambanthan) Sit at one of the tables and allow the army of servers to dollop out the great-tasting food on to a banana leaf for you. If you're hungry, supplement the standard meal with a good range of side dishes or a huge mound of chicken biryani. Good for tiffin snacks and a refreshing lassi, too.

★ Rebung
MALAYSIAN $$

(Map p66; ☑03-2276 3535; www.restoranrebung datochefismail.com; 5th fl, 1 Jln Tanglin, Lake Gardens; buffet lunch/dinner RM40/50; ⊗8.30am-10.30pm; ✱⛁; ⋒ Masjid Jamek, then taxi) Occupying the top level of a multistorey car park overlooking the Botanical Garden, flamboyant celebrity chef Ismail's restaurant is one of KL's best. The seemingly endless buffet spread is splendid, with all kinds of dishes that you'd typically only be served in a Malay home. Go hungry and book ahead at weekends when it's super busy.

Restoran Sin Kee
CANTONESE $$

(Map p66; ☑03-2274 1842; 194 Jln Tun Sambanthan, Brickfields; mains RM15-20; ⊗11am-2.30pm & 6-9.30pm Tue-Sun; ⋒ KL Sentral) This restaurant with a retro vibe is a vestige of 1970s KL, promising a trip to yesteryear with its signature *mun fan* (braised rice). The dish is served on a plate covered with an upturned bowl, which upon removing, reveals a heap

---

BRICKFIELDS STREET EATS

Brickfields has several street vendors serving tasty snacks well worth sampling while you explore the area.

Lawanya Food Corner (Map p66; ☑016-220 2117; 1077/8 Lg Scott; meals RM8; ⊗6am-4pm; ⋒ KL Sentral) Don't be put off by the low-key appearance of this simple joint with a few ramshackle tables lined up against a lime green wall under a sheet of corrugated iron. The same family has been preparing delicious curries here for more than 30 years, with a spread of meat and vegetarian dishes served from clay pots.

ABC Stall (Map p66; Jln Tun Sambanthan 4; cendol RM2.20; ⊗10am-5.30pm; ⋒ Tun Sambanthan) Cool down with fresh coconut water (RM4.50), *ais cendol* (shaved ice) and other desserts.

Ammars (Map p66; Asia Parking, Jln Tun Sambanthan; vadai RM1; ⊗8am-8pm; ⋒ KL Sentral) In a parking lot across the road from KL Sentral, the family who run this stall fry up tasty Indian snacks, such as lentil *vadai* (fritters) flavoured with fennel seeds, in giant woks.

Brickfields Pisang Goreng (Map p66; ☑012-617 2511; cnr Jln Thambipillay & Jln Tun Sambanthan 4; banana fritters RM1.40; ⊗11am-5pm; ⋒ Tun Sambanthan) Offers banana fritters so tasty that they can get away with charging a bit more for them than other vendors. The stall also sells curry puffs (RM1.60).

DON'T MISS

APW – A PRINTING WORKS REBORN

Art, good food and drink, landscape design and community events, including free yoga, pop-up markets and live music, all feature at **APW** (Map p76; ☏03-2282 3233; www.apw. my; 29 Jln Riong, Bangsar; ☐ Bank Rakyat-Bangsar). Standing for Art Printing Works, this is one of Malaysia's top printing companies for books and magazines, based in Bangsar since 1965. However, as the printing business has evolved in the early 21st century, the owners have creatively converted parts of their plant into something less industrial and more like a lifestyle park.

Check out the regularly changing exhibitions at **Galeri Prima** (Map p76; ☏03-2724 8300; www.facebook.com/galeri.prima; 31 Jln Riong, Bangsar; ☺10am-6pm Mon-Fri), which promotes local art heavyweights and emerging names like Zarina Abdullah and Anassuwandi Ahmad. **Uppercase** (Map p76; ☏03-2724 7111; www.uppercase.asia; 29 Jln Riong, Bangsar; ☺co-working space 9am-6pm Mon-Fri, yoga 9am-10pm Sat), a co-working space during the week, often hosts free yoga classes on Saturdays as well as other events and classes.

Permanent fixtures include the atelier of fashion designer **Khoon Hooi** (Map p76; ☏03-2788 3667; www.khoonhooi.com; ☺10am-7pm) and a gathering of fine cafes, bars and restaurants, including Breakfast Thieves for creative brekkie and lunch dishes, **Kaiju** (Map p76; ☏03-2788 3796; www.facebook.com/kaijucompany; mains RM30; ☺noon-2.30pm & 6-10.30pm Tue-Sun) for a fun mash-up of Thai and Japanese, **Proof** (Map p76; ☏03-2788 3613; www.facebook.com/proofpizzaAPW; pizza RM24-61; ☺12.15-3pm & 6-10.30pm; ☏) for artisan pizza and wine, and third-wave coffee hub **Pulp by Papa Palheta** (Map p76; ☏03-2201 3650; www.papapalheta.com.my; ☺7.30am-10pm Mon-Thu, to 11pm Fri, 9am-11pm Sat, to 10pm Sun; ☏).

of rice smothered in gravy, meat, vegetables, Chinese sausages and shrimp.

Botanica + Co   INTERNATIONAL $$
(Map p66; ☏011-2600 8188; www.botanica.com. my; ground fl, Alila Bangsar, 58 Jln Ang Seng, Brickfields; mains RM24-70; ☺8am-9.30pm; ☐ Bank Rakyat-Bangsar) True to its name, Botanica + Co presents a lush, plant-filled environment that's a pleasure to linger in. A crowd-pleasing menu packs in bumper sandwiches, gourmet pizzas and fresh salads as well as great interpretations of local fare – chef Sam's special laksa is a winner.

Southern Rock Seafood   SEAFOOD $$
(Map p66; ☏03-2856 2016; www.southernrock seafood.com; 32-34 Jln Kemuja, Bangsar Utama; mains RM32-65; ☺10am-10pm; ☏; ☐ Bank Rakyat-Bangsar) The fishmonger to some of KL's top restaurants has its own operation and it's a corker. The fish and seafood – in particular the wide range of oysters – is top quality, simply prepared to allow the flavours to sing. The blue-and-white decor suggests nights spent on the sparkling Med rather than the muddy Sungai Klang.

Breakfast Thieves   BREAKFAST $$
(Map p76; ☏03-2788 3548; www.breakfastthieves. com; APW, 29 Jln Riong, Bangsar; mains RM25-32; ☺9am-5pm Tue-Sun; ☏; ☐ Bank Raykat-Bangsar)

The only crime these thieves are guilty of is stacking their all-day brunch menu with so many delicious options (such as the Mr Terry Benedict, which pairs 24-hour braised ox cheek with porcini on an egg muffin) that one visit here is simply not enough.

Hornbill Restaurant   INTERNATIONAL $$
(Map p66; ☏03-2693 8086; www.klbirdpark.com; KL Bird Park, 920 Jln Cenderawasih, Lake Gardens; mains RM17-30; ☺9am-7.30pm; ☏; ☒Muzium Negara) Providing a ringside view of the feathered inhabitants of KL Bird Park, the Hornbill offers good food without fleecing the tourists too much. Go local with its *nasi lemak* and fried noodles, or please the kids with fish and chips or the homemade chicken or beef burgers.

Masjid India, Kampung Baru & Northern KL

Kin Kin   CHINESE $
(Map p68; 40 Jln Dewan Sultan Sulaiman, Chow Kit; noodles RM7.50; ☺8am-6.30pm Tue-Sun; ☒Medan Tuanku) This bare-bones shop is famous throughout the city for its chilli *pan mee* (board noodles). These 'dry' noodles, topped with a soft-boiled egg, minced pork, *ikan bilis*, fried onion and a special spicy chilli sauce, are a taste sensation. If

LOCAL KNOWLEDGE

BANGSAR'S COMMUNITY GARDENS

A century ago Bangsar's hills were covered by a rubber plantation. Long since a residential area, the area is going back to its roots with a couple of green-fingered projects.

Having given away over 21,000 trees and plants since it was set up in 2013, the environmental NGO **Free Tree Society** (www.freetreesociety.org; Jln Limau Purut; ⊙9.30-11.30am Tue & Sat; 🚌822) showcases its work at a compact and lushly designed garden that is open twice a week for visits. Info boards around the beds of tropical plantings cover subjects such as landscaping and pond life. It also boasts perhaps the prettiest toilet in the city. There's an image of an endangered animal hidden on each of the info boards as a way of making it fun for kids to learn about the natural environment.

For several years a community group led by local architect Ng Seksan had been campaigning to create a garden on a 3-hectare linear strip of land reserved for the national electricity company's pylons as they march through Bangsar. In 2017 the hillside garden **Kebun-Kebun Bangsar** (Map p76; www.facebook.com/kebunkebunbangsar; Lg Bukit Pantai; ⊙7am-7pm; 🚇 Kerinchi) started to bloom in spectacular fashion. Join volunteers to help tend terraces packed with indigenous plants, flowers, fruits and vegetables – there's even a section of rice paddy. Beehives, creative gazebos and landscaping elements add to the charm.

Guided tours of both gardens can be arranged via Airbnb.

you don't eat pork, staff do a version topped with mushrooms.

Capital Café
MALAYSIAN $

(Map p68; 213 Jln TAR, Masjid India; dishes RM5-7; ⊙7.30am-7.30pm Mon-Fri, 10.30am-7.30pm Sat; 🚇 Bandaraya) In a formula little changed since it opened in 1956, Capital Café has no frills, only fabulously old-fashioned Malay food. Chinese, Malay and Indian chefs work together to rush plates of mee goreng, *rojak* (salad doused in a peanut-sauce dressing) and satay (evenings only) to hungry diners; on busy days, you may have to share a table.

Yut Kee
CHINESE $

(Map p68; ☎03-2698 8108; 1 Jln Kamunting, Dang Wangi; meals RM7.50-16; ⊙7.30am-4.30pm Tue-Sun; 🚇 Dang Wangi) This beloved *kopitiam* (in business since 1928), run by a father-and-son team and their crew of friendly, efficient staff, serves classic Hainanese and colonial-era food: try the chicken chop, *roti babi* (French toast stuffed with pork), toast with homemade *kaya*, or Hokkien mee.

★Eat X Dignity
INTERNATIONAL $$

(☎03-4050 3387; http://eatxdignity.business. site; 25-G, Jln 11/48a, Sentul Raya Blvd, Sentul; mains RM11-18; ⊙10.30am-9pm; 🚇 Sentul Timur) Barack Obama visited this worthy project run by Dignity, a Malaysian foundation providing education for the poor and refugees. Students gain work experience at this attractive cafe, which serves excellent renditions of local favourites, including *nasi lemak* and laksa, alongside salads, burgers and pasta.

★Limapulo
MALAYSIAN $$

(Map p68; ☎03-2698 3268; 50 Jln Doraisamy, Masjid India; mains RM17-45, set lunches RM9.90; ⊙noon-3pm & 6-10pm Mon-Sat; 🚇 Medan Tuanku) Its tag line is 'baba can cook', the baba being genial Uncle John who is often to be found greeting guests at this atmospheric and justly popular restaurant. The Nonya-style cooking is very homely, with dishes such as *ayam pong teh* and shrimp and petai beans cooked in sambal. The set lunches are good value.

Peter Hoe Cafe
CAFE $$

(Map p68; ☎018-223 5199; 1st fl, The Row, 56 Jln Doraimsamy, Dang Wangi; mains RM20-49; ⊙11.30am-6pm; 📷; 🚇 Medan Tuanku) Peter Hoe brings the same colourful and creative attention to this casual cafe as he does to his adjacent interior design shop. Fresh salads and quiches are a standout.

🍷 Drinking & Nightlife

🍸 Bukit Bintang & KLCC

★Suzie Wong
COCKTAIL BAR

(Map p58; ☎017-226 6480; Wisma Lim Foo Yoong, 86 Jln Raja Chulan, entrance on Jln Tengah, Bukit Bintang; ⊙9pm-3am Mon-Sat; 🚇 Raja Chulan) Push aside the heavy curtain at the end of a club-by bar to discover the wild goings-on at this old-Hong Kong–style speakeasy cocktail bar. Expect a glamorous drag cabaret, live music and handheld fireworks to accompany the popping of champagne corks and swilling of drinks in carved-out coconuts.

If you're lucky enough to find a seat, be aware that there will be a hefty minimum table charge on Friday and Saturday nights. The noodle stall just outside the main entrance is another fun touch for a pre- or post-party supper.

★ **Heli Lounge Bar** COCKTAIL BAR
(Map p58; ☑03-2110 5034; www.facebook.com/Heliloungebar; Level 34, Menara KH, Jln Sultan Ismail, Bukit Bintang; ☺5pm-midnight Mon-Wed, to 2am Thu, to 3am Fri & Sat, to 11am Sun; ☎; ☐Raja Chulan) There are plenty of rooftop bars in KL, but none sport the exhilarating 360-degree views of this prime place for sundowners. Steady your hands carrying your daiquiri or lychee martini upstairs from the gleaming bar to the helipad, where bird's-eye views prompt selfies galore.

Go early to catch the sunset and for the 6pm to 9pm happy-hour prices (the helipad opens at 6pm). After 9pm a dress code applies and your group will need to stump up for a bottle in order to enter. Women get free drinks on Thursday 'ladies' night'.

★ **Feeka Coffee Roasters** CAFE
(Map p72; ☑03-2110 4599; www.facebook.com/feeka.coffeeroasters; 19 Jln Mesui, Bukit Bintang; ☺8am-11pm; ☎; ☐Raja Chulan) Set in a minimally remodelled shophouse on hip Jln Mesui, Feeka delivers both on its premium coffee (choose from microlot beans or espresso-based drinks) and its food, with breakfast items served from 8am to 3pm, and a menu including omelettes and pulled-pork sandwiches served from noon to 11pm, as well as delicious cakes.

VCR CAFE
(Map p72; ☑03-2110 2330; www.vcr.my; 2 Jln Galloway, Bukit Bintang; ☺8.30am-11pm; ☎; ☐HangTuah) Set in an airy prewar shophouse, VCR serves first-rate coffee, all-day breakfasts (RM19 to RM35) and desserts to a diverse crowd of backpackers and laptop-wielding locals.

Delirium Café Kuala Lumpur CRAFT BEER
(Map p58; ☑03-2162 7888; www.facebook.com/deliriumcafekl; Suria KLCC, KLCC; ☺10am-midnight; ☐ KLCC) In a country where craft beers have yet to gain a foothold, the opening of a bar showcasing the products of Belgium brewery Delirium is a major event. You can get very merry indeed working your way through the 100-plus beers on the menu here – so much so that you may think the huge pink elephant in the bar is for real.

RGB At The Bean Hive CAFE
(☑03-2181 1329; www.rathergoodbeans.com; 35 Jln Damai, Ampang; ☺8am-5.30pm Mon-Fri, 9am-6pm Sat & Sun; ☎; ☐ Ampang Park) This is what you get when a boutique coffee roaster teams up with health-conscious cooks in a quiet green oasis. RBG serves excellent hand-drip coffees and espresso-based drinks as well as vegan and vegetarian breakfasts, sandwiches and pastas, all in a spacious bungalow with an inner courtyard and big grassy yard.

Claret WINE BAR
(Map p58; ☑03-2162 0886; www.troikaskydining.com/claret; Level 23a, Tower B, The Troika, Persiaran KLCC, KLCC; ☺4pm-1am; ☎; ☐ Ampang Park) This sophisticated wine and cocktail bar is the first space you'll encounter out of the lift

KUALA LUMPUR DRINKING & NIGHTLIFE

REDEVELOPING KAMPUNG BARU

The Malay enclave of Kampung Baru originates from colonial British times. Worried about the declining number of Malay residents in the capital, the British set aside 224 hectares of land in the late 1890s – on what was then the outskirts of Kuala Lumpur – as protected Malay agricultural land. Settlers were encouraged to plant crops in this new village: Kampung Baru.

Up until a few years ago, in what seems like a miracle amid a city that has conspicuously reached for the skies, Kampung Baru remained very much like a Malay village – albeit minus the vegetable patches and rice paddies. Alongside well-maintained traditional homes such as **Master Mat's House** (Map p68; off Jln Datuk Abdul Razak; ☐ Kampung Baru) were less well-maintained wooden structures. It's still largely like this with around 1350 plots of land owned by some 5300 people.

However, the village has shrunk to around 90 hectares and only about 30% of the land owners still live here, with immigrant Indonesians and Thai Muslims making up the bulk of the residents. A masterplan has been draw up for the area's phased redevelopment. Major new projects, including the 40-storey Tamu Hotel & Suites (p77) and construction of the MRT2 line, are among the first wave of such developments that will change Kampung Baru forever.

to the collection of bars and restaurants that make up Troika Sky Dining. It's a pleasant, intimate spot with comfy low chairs.

Taps Beer Bar
CRAFT BEER

(Map p72; ☑03-2110 1560; www.tapsbeerbar. my; One Residency, 1 Jln Nagasari, Bukit Bintang; ☺5pm-1am Mon-Sat, noon-1am Sun; ☎; ☐Raja Chulan) Taps specialises in ale from around the world, with some 80 different microbrews on rotation, 14 of them on tap. There's also a menu of Malay and American-style comfort food (mains RM24 to RM30). There's live music Thursday to Saturday at 9pm and regular beer festivals and events.

Pisco Bar
BAR

(Map p72; ☑03-2142 2900; www.piscobarkl.com; 29 Jln Mesui, Bukit Bintang; ☺5pm-1am Tue, Thu & Sun, to 2am Wed, to 3am Fri & Sat; ☐Raja Chulan) Take your pisco sour in the cosy, exposed-brick interior or the plant-filled courtyard of this slick tapas joint. The chef is half Peruvian, so naturally the ceviche here is good. DJs regularly spin the decks at the upstairs dance space on Friday and Saturday nights.

Zouk
CLUB

(☑03-2110 3888; www.zoukclub.com.my; TREC, 436 Jln Tun Razak, Ampang; admission RM20-55; ☺10pm-3am Sun-Tue, to 4am Wed, to 5am Thu-Sat; Ⓜ Tun Razak Exchange) Zouk remains one of KL's premier dance clubs. Among its seven party spaces are the Main Room, which reverberates to electro, techno and trance; and Ace, a hip-hop and R 'n' B club. Wear your flashiest threads (no T-shirts or sandals for men).

Admission charges depend on what sections of the club you want access to and what day and time of the night you visit. Bring your passport, as tourists get free entry before 1am.

TWG Tea
TEAHOUSE

(Map p72; www.twgtea.com; Level 2, Pavilion KL, 168 Jln Bukit Bintang, Bukit Bintang; ☺10am-10pm; Ⓜ Bukit Bintang) Offering a mind-boggling range of more than 400 teas and infusions, this KL offshoot of the original Singaporean TWG is a luxurious place to refresh during your rounds of the mall. The teas are beautifully packaged for gifts. As well as afternoon tea (2pm to 6pm), it also serves brunch from 10am to 3pm and meals from noon to 10pm.

☕ Chinatown

★ Botak Liquor
COCKTAIL BAR

(Map p62; ☑03-2022 1100; www.facebook. com/BOTAKLiquor; 156 Jln Petaling, Chinatown;

☺5.30pm-1am Tue-Sun; ☐ Pasar Seni) Hanging baskets and lush potted plants framing the bar set the leafy, botanical tone for the superior cocktails made by mixologist Jon Quek at Botak. Ingredients such as pandan, jasmine, tarragon and kaffir lime feature in the drinks, which include liquors infused with pumpkin seeds, pineapple and jackfruit.

★ PS150
COCKTAIL BAR

(Map p62; ☑03-7622 8777; www.ps150.my; 150 Jln Petaling, Chinatown; ☺6pm-2am Tue-Sat, 3-10pm Sun; ☐ Pasar Seni) The southern end of Jln Petaling's evolution into a hip 'hood is helped along by this cocktail bar concealed behind a fake toyshop in a building that was once a brothel. Inside, the dim red lights and vintage-style booths bring to mind the films of Wong Kar-Wai. Sit around the convivial bar at the back and watch expert mixologists ply their trade.

Omakase + Appreciate
COCKTAIL BAR

(Map p62; www.facebook.com/OmakaseAppreciate; basement, Bangunan Ming Annexe, 9 Jln Ampang, Chinatown; ☺5pm-1am Tue-Fri, 9pm-1am Sat; ☎; ☐ Masjid Jamek) This cosy, retro cocktail bar is one of KL's top-secret drinking spots. The expert mixologists here each have their own menu of speciality cocktails or, if nothing appeals, ask them to create a drink tailored to your tastes. Part of the fun is finding the entrance: look for the sign saying 'no admittance'.

Deceased
COCKTAIL BAR

(Map p62; ☑03-2715 7492; www.facebook.com/ thedeceasedkl; 55 Jln Sultan, Chinatown; ☺6.30pm-3am; ☐ Pasar Seni) Bloody severed hands (made of rubber), a skull mask smoking a cheroot, or a wooden shoe (for beating purposes!) are part of the gimmicky, Instagram friendly accoutrements for the cocktails at this death- and horror-themed cocktail bar.

It's on the rooftop of Mingle Hostel (p71); residents get 20% off the bill. You'll find the entrance next to Cafe 55 (p91).

Aku Cafe & Gallery
CAFE

(Map p62; ☑03-2857 6887; www.oldchina.com.my/ aku.html; 1st fl, 8 Jln Panggong, Chinatown; ☺11am-8pm Tue-Sun; ☎; ☐ Pasar Seni) This intimate, art-filled cafe serves good hand-drip brews, ice-blended drinks, and juices from pressed apple to banana smoothie. Light meals and pasta dishes are outshone by the inventive dessert menu. There are some unusual craft souvenirs for sale, too.

Keep climbing the stairs to find the contemporary-arts space Lostgens' (Map p62;

KL'S STREET ART

Following in the wake of Penang's street-art revolution, KL is also turning to street artists to brighten up its urban landscape with murals. Lithuanian artist Ernest Zacharevic's **Sampan Boy** (Map p62; Wisma Allianz, 33 Jln Gereja, Bukit Nanas; ⊟ Masjid Jamek) depicts a boy in a traditional wooden boat, while his **Rage Against the Machine** (Map p62; 12-14 Jln Sultan, Chinatown; ⊟ Pasar Seni) props up half of an actual yellow school bus against a car park wall, accompanied by paintings of smoke billowing out from the vehicle and attacking students surrounding it.

Other murals to look out for are the huge painting of a **boy in a tiger hat** (Map p62; Jln Raja Chulan; ⊟ Muzium Telekom) opposite the Muzium Telekom; artist Kenji Chai's giant **cockerel** (Map p62; Jln Tun Tan Cheng Lock, Chinatown; ⊟ Plaza Rakyat) on the side of the Nando's building on Jln Tun Tan Cheng Lock as well as his 25-storey-tall **Courage to Dream** (Map p68; Menara M101 Dang Wangi, 3 Jln Kamunting, Dang Wangi; ⊟ Dang Wangi) painting that has made the record books as Malaysia's tallest mural; and Russian artist Julia Volchkova's evocative **goldsmith** (Map p62; Jln Panggong, Chinatown; ⊟ Pasar Seni) on the end of a terrace of shophouses in Chinatown.

As part of the River of Life project, a number of sculptures have been commissioned, including red-painted metal sculptures by **Kuen Stephanie** (Map p62; Bangkok Bank Sq, Lebuh Pudu, Chinatown; ⊟ Masjid Jamek) depicting scenes from Malaysian life in the style of paper cuttings. These can be seen on Bangkok Bank Sq and Lebuh Pudu. Fun, life-size sculptures based on cartoonist **Lat's** (Map p62; Jln Melaka, Chinatown; ⊟ Masjid Jamek) humorous characters are dotted along the trail from Jln Melaka to the KL Forest Eco Park on Jln Raja Chulan.

Also look out for **Mural Alley** (Map p72; off Changkat Bukit Bintang, Bukit Bintang; Ⓜ Bukit Bintang), painted to resemble a stream cascading through the jungle – it looks particularly effective at night when the neon clouds above glow brightly.

www.facebook.com/lostgens; 3rd fl, 8c Jln Panggong, Chinatown; ⊗1-7pm Tue-Sun; ⊟ Pasar Seni) FREE.

Bangsar

⭐**Coley** COCKTAIL BAR
(Map p66; ☑019-270 9179; www.facebook.com/LongLiveColey; 6-G Jln Abdullah, Bangsar Utama; ⊗5pm-1am Mon-Sat; ⊟ Bank Rakyat-Bangsar) Revive your parched taste buds with inventive libations, such as whisky and guava bubble tea, or coconut gin, at this sleek and sultry bar that's one of Asia's best. It's named after Ada Coleman, a female bartender in 1920s London and creator of the Hanky Panky cocktail – a fixture on the menu here.

⭐**Mantra Bar KL** ROOFTOP BAR
(Map p76; ☑017-344 8299; www.mantrabarkl.com; Bangsar Village II, 15 Jln Telawi 2, Bangsar; ⊗4.30pm-1.30am Sun & Tue-Thu, to 3am Fri & Sat; ⊟822) This sophisticated bar on the rooftop of Bangsar Village II has an indoor lounge and outdoor deck with spectacular views over the leafy, low-rise suburbs to the city skyline beyond. A dress code applies on Friday and Saturday nights, when DJs play to a fashionable crowd.

Masjid India & Outside Central KL

Gavel CRAFT BEER
(Map p68; ☑03-2856 0509; www.facebook.com/YapAhShak; 20 Jln Yap Ah Shak, Dang Wangi; ⊗8am-9pm; ⊟Medan Tuanku) With bars in KL serving craft beers still thin on the ground, Gavel stands out for its bottled collection. The tasting notes on the menu are very helpful if you're not familiar with the ales sourced from Japan, the US, Australia and the UK.

Coliseum Cafe BAR
(Map p68; ☑03-2692 6270; www.coliseum1921.com; 100 Jln TAR, Masjid India; ⊗10am-10pm; ⊟ Masjid Jamek) The kind of bar in which colonial planters and clerks would have knocked back stouts and G&Ts, this retro watering hole (in business since 1921) oozes nostalgia. The bar is worth visiting even if you don't eat a meal at the adjoining grill room, where little seems to have changed since Somerset Maugham tucked into its famous sizzling steaks.

LGBTIQ+ KL

KL has a small but friendly LGBTIQ+ scene that is fairly fluid. Rainbow Rojak (www.face book.com/RainbowRojak) organises occasional LGBTIQ+-friendly dance parties. Also check www.utopia-asia.com for the latest places to go.

DivineBliss (G Tower Rooftop; Map p58; 03-2168 1881; www.facebook.com/groups/divinebliss; The View, G Tower, 199 Jln Tun Razak, KLCC; RM45; 10pm-3am Sat; Ampang Park) On Saturday nights the spacious rooftop bar at the G Tower hotel hosts this popular LGBTIQ+ event. A young, lively crowd pack the dance floor until the early hours. Bring photo ID for entry.

Blueboy Discotheque (Map p72; 03-2142 1067; www.facebook.com/pg/blueboy discotheque; 50 Jln Sultan Ismail, Bukit Bintang; admission incl 1 drink RM38; 9pm-3am, to midnight Sun; Bukit Bintang) An incredible survivor of the KL gay scene since the 1980s, Blue Boy has undergone a makeover to emerge as a surprisingly stylish but still trashily fun venue in which to watch glam drag shows and dance till the early hours.

Nakd Bar (Map p58; 03-2710 0348; www.facebook.com/nakdbar; Lot 64, ground fl, Wisma Conway, Jln Raja Chulan, Bukit Bintang; 5pm-1am Mon-Thu, to 3am Fri, 10pm-3am Sat; Raja Chulan) Get an eye-full of topless male bar tenders on Friday and Saturday nights.

Moontree House (Map p62; 03-2031 0537; www.moontree-house.blogspot.com; 1st fl, 6 Jln Panggong, Chinatown; 10am-8pm Wed-Mon; ; Pasar Seni) Relaxed cafe where you can tap into KL's discreet lesbian scene.

☆ Entertainment

KL has plenty of entertainment options, but you have to keep your ear to the ground to discover the best of what's going on. Conservative tastes and censorship mean that quite a lot of what is on offer can be bland and inoffensive, but occasionally controversial and boundary-pushing performances and events are staged.

If you'd like to see and hear traditional Malaysian dances and music, there's a free show at the Malaysia Tourism Centre (p102) at 3pm Monday to Saturday. If you miss that, there's also an evening dance show at 8.30pm daily (combined with a buffet dinner) in nearby WOW KL! (Map p58; 03-2161 0122; www.wowkl.my; 139 Jln Ampang, KLCC; buffet & show RM130; show 8.30-9.30pm, buffet 7-10pm; Bukit Nanas).

★ **No Black Tie**   LIVE MUSIC
(Map p72; 03-2142 3737; www.noblacktie.com.my; 17 Jln Mesui, Bukit Bintang; live music RM40-50; 5pm-1am Mon-Sat; Raja Chulan) Blink and you'd miss this small live-music venue, bar and bistro, hidden as it is behind a grove of bamboo. NBT, as it's known to its faithful patrons, is owned by Malaysian concert pianist Evelyn Hii, who has a knack for finding the talented singer-songwriters, jazz bands and classical-music ensembles who play here from around 9pm.

★ **Kuala Lumpur**
Performing Arts Centre   PERFORMING ARTS
(KLPAC; 03-4047 9000; www.klpac.org; Sentul Park, Jln Strachan, Sentul; Sentul) Part of the Sentul West regeneration project, this modernist performing-arts complex puts on a wide range of progressive theatrical events including dramas, musicals and dance. Also on offer are performing-arts courses and screenings of art-house movies.

Dewan Filharmonik Petronas   CONCERT VENUE
(Map p58; 03-2051 7007; www.dfp.com.my; box office, Tower 2, Petronas Towers, KLCC; box office 10.30am-6.30pm Tue-Sat; KLCC) Don't miss the chance to attend a show at this gorgeous concert hall. The polished Malaysian Philharmonic Orchestra plays here (usually Friday and Saturday evenings and Sunday matinees, but also other times), as do other local and international ensembles. There is a smart-casual dress code.

Istana Budaya   PERFORMING ARTS
(National Theatre; 03-4026 5555; www.istana budaya.gov.my; Jln Tun Razak, Titiwangsa; tickets RM100-300; Titiwangsa, Titiwangsa) Large-scale drama and dance shows are staged here, as well as music performances by the National Symphony Orchestra and National Choir. The building's soaring roof is based on a traditional Malay floral decoration of betel leaves, while the columned interior invokes a

provincial colonialism. There's a dress code of no shorts and no short-sleeved shirts.

KL Live
LIVE MUSIC

(Map p58; ☑03-2162 2570; www.lifecentre.com. my; 1st fl, Life Centre, 20 Jln Sultan Ismail, Bukit Bintang; ☺ Raja Chulan) A boon to KL's live-music scene, this spacious venue packs in rock and pop fans with a decent line-up of overseas and local big-name artists and DJs.

Timbre @ The Row
LIVE MUSIC

(Map p68; ☑03-2602 2623; www.timbre.com.my; 60-64 Jln Doraisamy, Dang Wangi; ☺5pm-midnight Tue-Thu, to 1am Fri & Sat, to 11pm Sun; ☺ Medan Tuanku) This sleek live music bar and restaurant is the KL outpost of a successful Singaporean operation of the same name. Musicians, mainly playing jazz and light pop and rock, take to the stage here from Wednesday to Sunday.

🔒 Shopping

Kuala Lumpur is a prizefighter on the Asian shopping parade, a serious rival to retail heavyweights Singapore, Bangkok and Hong Kong. On offer are appealing handicrafts, major international brands (both legit and fake versions), masses of malls and decent sale prices. The city's traditional markets are hugely enjoyable and atmospheric experiences, regardless of whether you have a purchase in mind.

🔒 Bukit Bintang & KLCC

★ Pavilion KL
MALL

(Map p72; ☑03-2118 8833; www.pavilion-kl.com; 168 Jln Bukit Bintang, Bukit Bintang; ☺10am-10pm; ☜; Ⓜ Bukit Bintang) Pavilion sets the gold standard in KL's shopping scene. Amid the many familiar international brands, there are some good local options, including for fashion **British India** (Map p72; ☑03-2141 0395; http://britishindia.com.my; Level 2) and the more affordable Padini Concept Store. For a quick trip to Japan, head to the Tokyo Street of stalls on the 6th floor.

There's also an excellent food court in the basement. Note that when you enter the mall from Jln Bukit Bintang, you are already on level 3. The mall is connected to its new extension **Pavilion Elite** (Map p72; 166 Jln Bukit Bintang).

Lot 10
MALL

(Map p72; ☑03-2782 3566; www.lot10.com.my; 50 Jln Bukit Bintang, Bukit Bintang; ☺10am-10pm; Ⓜ Bukit Bintang) Fronted by branches of fashion

retailers H&M and Zara, this mall's star turn is **Isetan The Japan Store**, a department which curates the best of Japanese products.

Suria KLCC
MALL

(Map p58; ☑03-2382 2828; www.suriaklcc.com. my; Jln Ampang, KLCC; ☺10am-10pm; Ⓜ KLCC) Even if shopping bores you to tears, you're sure to find something of interest at this fine shopping complex at the foot of the Petronas Towers. It's mainly international brands.

You'll find some local retailers here too, including Royal Selangor for pewter, Vincci for shoes and accessories and **Farah Khan** (Map p58; www.farahkhan.com; ground level) for designer women's fashion.

Sungei Wang Plaza
MALL

(Map p72; ☑03-2148 6109; www.sungeiwang.com; Jln Sultan Ismail, Bukit Bintang; ☺10am-10pm; Ⓜ Bukit Bintang) A little confusing to navigate but jam-packed with youth-oriented fashion and accessories, this is one of KL's more interesting malls with a focus on street fashion and bargains rather than glitzy international brands.

Fahrenheit88
MALL

(Map p72; ☑03-2148 5488; www.fahrenheit88.com; 179 Jln Bukit Bintang, Bukit Bintang; ☺10am-10pm; Ⓜ Bukit Bintang) This youth-oriented mall houses a large branch of Japanese clothes store **Uniqlo**. Shoe lovers should check out **Shoes Gallery** by Parkson and South Korean footwear emporium **Shoopen**.

Plaza Low Yat
ELECTRONICS

(Map p72; ☑03-2148 3615; www.plazalowyat.com; 7 Jln Bintang, Bukit Bintang; ☺10am-10pm; Ⓜ Imbi) Malaysia's largest IT mall offers eight floors of electronic goods and services. Head to the top-floor shops for repairs.

There have been reports of credit-card details being recorded after transactions, so if possible use cash here, or be vigilant about the stall you're dealing with.

🔒 Chinatown

★ Museum of Ethnic Arts
ANTIQUES

(Map p62; ☑03-2148 2283; www.facebook.com/pg/ahg12345; 2nd fl, the Annexe, 10 Jln Hang Kasturi, Chinatown; ☺11am-7pm; Ⓜ Pasar Seni) Although billed as a museum, the bulk of items are for sale in this extraordinary private collection of tribal arts from Borneo. You'll also find Nonya ceramics, Tibetan *thangka* paintings, Chinese paintings and porcelain, embroidered wall hangings, hand-carved boxes and doors, and all manner of delights from Malaysia and the region.

Central Market
MARKET

(Map p62; ☑ 03-2032 2399; www.centralmarket. com.my; Jln Hang Kasturi, Chinatown; ⊕ 10am-10pm; 🚇 Pasar Seni) This 1930s art deco building (a former wet market) was rescued from demolition in the 1980s and transformed into a touristy arts-and-crafts centre. Nonetheless, there are some excellent finds – paper art, hand-cut soaps, jewellery and T-shirts – among its 350 shops. The adjacent **Kasturi Walk** – the arch is a series of *wau bulan* (moon kites) – is bordered by handsome restored shophouses.

Petaling Street Market
MARKET

(Map p62; Jln Petaling, Chinatown; ⊕ 10am-10.30pm; 🚇 Pasar Seni) Malaysia's relaxed attitude towards counterfeit goods is well illustrated at this popular night market bracketed by fake Chinese gateways. Traders start to fill Jln Petaling from midmorning until it is jam-packed with market stalls selling everything from fake designer handbags to jackfruit. Visit in the afternoon if you want to take pictures or see the market without the crowds.

🏠 Brickfields & Bangsar

★Nala's Kampung
House
FASHION & ACCESSORIES

(Map p66; www.naladesigns.com; 18 Jln Abdullah, Bangsar; ⊕ 10am-7pm; 🚇 Bank Rakyat-Bangsar) Lisette Scheers is the creative force behind the Nala brand of homewares, stationery, accessories and other arty items. All her products embody a contemporary but distinctly local design aesthetic and are beautifully displayed at this concept shop in a lovely old *kampung*-style house.

Bookmark the last Sunday of the month for its **Bazaar Malam** (5pm to 10pm) when tasty food and drink stalls are set up in the surrounding garden and there's live music and DJs.

For more of Lisette's designs also drop by **Nala Muse** (Map p76; ☑ 03-2633 5059; www. naladesigns.com; Bangsar Village II, 15 Jln Telawi 2, Bangsar; ⊕ 10am-10pm; 🚌 822) or the outlet in Robinsons at **Shoppes at Four Seasons Place** (Map p58; ☑ 03-2026 5085; www. shoppeskl.com; 145 Jln Ampang, KLCC; ⊕ 10am-10pm; 🚇 KLCC).

★Pucuk Rebung
ART

(Map p76; ☑ 03-2094 9969; www.pucukrebung.com; 18 Lg Ara Kiri 2, Bangsar; ⊕ 10am-6pm Mon-Fri, to 7pm Sat & Sun; 🚌 822) Specialising in antiques and fine arts, this is one of the best places in KL to find quality pieces of local craft as well as pricier Malay ethnological items. It's worth dropping by for a browse and a chat with the affable owner, ex-banker Henry Bong.

Bangsar Village I & II
MALL

(Map p76; ☑ 03-2282 1808; www.bangsarvillage. com; 15 Jln Telawi 2, Bangsar; ⊕ 10am-10pm; 🚌 822) These twin malls, the main focus of Bangsar, are linked by a covered bridge. Together they offer plenty of upmarket fashions, including local designers as well as pretty much all your other shopping needs from groceries to hardware.

I Love Snackfood
VINTAGE

(Map p76; ☑ 03-2201 7513; www.ilovesnackfood. com; 17a Jln Telawi 3, Bangsar; ⊕ 11am-8pm;

TRADITIONAL WET & DRY FOOD MARKETS

Western-style supermarkets are far more common in KL than the semioutdoor wet (produce) and dry food markets found across Asia. However, a few such traditional markets still exist and are worth searching out.

Pudu Market (Pasar Besar Pudu; Jln Pasar Baharu, Pudu; ⊕ 4am-2.30pm; 🚇 Pudu) Arrive early to experience KL's largest wet market at its most frantic. Here you can get every imaginable type of fruit, vegetable, fish and meat – from the foot of a chicken slaughtered and butchered on the spot to a stingray fillet or a pig's penis.

Bazaar Baru Chow Kit (Chow Kit Market; Map p68; 469-473 Jln TAR, Chow Kit; ⊕ 8am-6pm; 🚇 Chow Kit) This daily wet-and-sundry market serves the Chinese and Malay working class of Chow Kit. It's a warren of tight paths and hangers loaded with fruit, veggies, and all manner of cheap clothing and electronic items. You can also sample hawker and *kopitiam* food and drinks here in hole-in-the-wall outlets that haven't changed in decades.

Chinatown Wet Market (Map p62; Jln Sang Guna, Chinatown; ⊕ 7am-1pm; 🚇 Pasir Seni) Come here for freshly plucked chickens. The market is squished in darkened alleys between Jln Petaling and Jln Tun HS Lee and it's where locals shop for their groceries.

DON'T MISS

ZHONGSHAN BUILDING

A repurposed block of interconnected 1950s shophouses that once housed the Selangor Zhongshan Association is now **home** (Map p62; ☑016-660 2585; www.facebook.com/thezhongshanbuilding; 80-84 Jln Rotan, Kampung Attap; ◪Maharajalela) to a hip collection of creative businesses, including a cool art gallery and gift boutique, a couple of cafes, a bespoke tailor, bookstore, design archive and even a LGBTIQ+ support organisation.

Start your explorations at the anchor tenant **OUR ArtProjects** (Map p62; ☑03-2276 2624; www.ourartprojects.com; ◷11am-7pm Tue-Sat), a gallery specialising in contemporary works by regional artists. Monthly changing exhibitions may include painting, sculpture, photography and mixed media. Next door is the groovy design concept store **Naiise** (Map p62; ☑016-428 6250; www.naiise.com.my; ◷noon-7pm Tue-Fri, 11am-6pm Sat & Sun), which opens up onto the internal courtyard in which you'll find ace bakery and cafe **Tommy Le Baker** (Map p62; ☑03-4043 2546; www.tommylebaker.wordpress.com; sandwiches RM17-26; ◷10.30am-8pm Tue-Fri, 9.30am-6pm Sat & Sun). Head upstairs for the recorded music shop **Tandang Store** (Map p62; ☑016-333 0475; www.tandangstore.com; ◷1-9pm) and the cool cafe **Piu Piu Piu** (Map p62; ☑010-406 3695; https://piupiupiu.business.site; ◷11am-7pm Tue-Sun). Up on the top floor is **fono** (Map p62; www.instagram.com/fono.kl), which hosts live music performances, DJs and film screenings.

◪822) There's always something attractive to discover at this concept store specialising in kitsch interior decor, vintage collectables (think typewriters, trunks and globes), books and stationery.

Kedai Bikin HOMEWARES
(Map p66; ☑03-2201 5503; www.kedaibikin.com; 8 Jln Abdullah, Bangsar Utama; ◷10am-7pm Mon-Fri, 11am-6pm Sat; ◪Bank Rakyat-Bangsar) Managed by home-grown architects and designers, this furniture and home accessories shop turns retro furniture into contemporary showpieces. For example, the famous cord chairs – once staples of Malaysian homes – are given an updated look by adding timber armrests or a rattan weave support. Collaborations with craftspeople from across Malaysia give their products a unique, local touch.

Wei-Ling Gallery ART
(Map p66; ☑03-2260 1106; www.weiling-gallery.com; 8 Jln Scott, Brickfields; ◷10am-6pm Mon-Fri, to 5pm Sat; ◪KL Sentral) The top two floors of this old shophouse have been imaginatively turned into a contemporary gallery to showcase local artists. Note the artwork covering the metal security gate in front of the shophouse next door.

🏠 Masjid India & Outside Central KL

Peter Hoe at the Row HOMEWARES
(Map p68; ☑018-223 5199; 1st fl, The Row, 56 Jln Doraisamy, Dang Wangi; ◷10am-7pm; ◪Medan Tuanku) Peter Hoe's explosively colourful and creative emporium is a KL institution. It stocks all manner of original fabric products, such as tablecloths, cushions and robes (many handprinted in India for the shop), as well as woven baskets, lanterns, silverware, candles and knick-knacks galore.

★Publika MALL
(www.facebook.com/PublikaGallery; 1 Jln Dutamas 1, Solaris Dutamas; ◷10am-10pm) Art, shopping, dining and social life are all in harmony at this innovative mall, 10 minutes' drive north of Bangsar. There's a good handicrafts market on the last Sunday of the month.

Mid Valley Megamall MALL
(☑03-2938 3333; www.midvalley.com.my; Lingkaran Syed Putra, Mid Valley; ◷10am-10pm; ◪Mid Valley) Mega is the only way to describe this enormous mall, where you could easily lose yourself for days in the hundreds of shops, two department stores (**Metrojaya** and **Aeon**), multiplex cinema, huge food court and even a colourful Hindu temple.

Royal Selangor Visitor Centre ARTS & CRAFTS
(☑03-4145 6122; https://my.royalselangor.com; 4 Jln Usahawan 6, Setapak Jaya; ◷9am-5pm; ☎; ◪Wangsa Maju) FREE Located 8km northeast of the city centre, the world's largest pewter manufacturer offers some very appealing souvenirs made from this malleable alloy of tin and copper. Also for sale are the company's silver pieces under the Comyns brand and its Selberam jewellery. Selangor's products are sold at its retail outlets in KL's malls including Suria KLCC and Pavilion KLCC.

ℹ Information

IMMIGRATION OFFICES

Immigration Office (☑ 03-6205 7400; www.imi.gov.my; 69 Jln Sri Hartamas 1, off Jln Duta; ⊙ 7.30am-1pm & 2-5.30pm Mon-Thu, 7.30am-12.15pm & 2.45-5.30pm Fri; Ⓜ Semantan, then taxi) Handles visa extensions.

INTERNET ACCESS

Internet cafes are rare these days, but if you're travelling with a wi-fi-enabled device, you can get online at hundreds of cafes, restaurants, bars and many hotels for free.

MEDIA

Look out for magazines **Vision KL** (www.visionkl.com) and **Unreserved** (www.unreservedmedia.com). For current events, check out the online **Time Out KL** (www.timeout.com/kuala-lumpur).

MEDICAL SERVICES

Pharmacies are all over town; the most common is Watsons, in most malls.

Hospital Kuala Lumpur (☑ 03-2615 5555; www.hkl.gov.my; Jln Pahang; ⓠ Titiwangsa, ⓐ Titiwangsa) City's main hospital, north of the centre.

Tung Shin Hospital (Map p62; ☑ 03-2037 2288; www.tungshin.com.my; 102 Jln Pudu, Bukit Bintang; ⓐ Plaza Rakyat) A general hospital with a Chinese traditional medicine clinic.

Twin Towers Medical Centre KLCC (Map p58; ☑ 03-2382 3500; www.ttmcklcc.com.my; Level 4, Suria KLCC, Jln Ampang, KLCC; ⊙ 8.30am-6pm Mon-Sat; ⓐ KLCC) Handily located in the mall attached to the Petronas Towers, with a second clinic near KL Sentral.

MONEY

Most banks and shopping malls provide international ATMs (typically on the ground floor or basement level). Money changers frequently offer better rates than banks for changing cash and (at times) travellers cheques; they're usually open later and at weekends and are found in shopping malls.

POST

General Post Office (Map p62; ☑ 03-2267 2267; www.pos.com.my; Jln Tun Tan Cheng Lock, Chinatown; ⊙ 8.30am-5.30pm Mon-Fri, to 1pm Sat; ⓐ Pasar Seni)

TOURIST INFORMATION

Malaysia Tourism Centre (MaTiC; Map p58; ☑ 03-9235 4900; www.matic.gov.my/en; 109 Jln Ampang, KLCC; ⊙ 8am-10pm; ⓐ Bukit Nanas) Provides information on KL and tourism across Malaysia, and has a free cultural dance show at 3pm Monday to Saturday.

Visit KL (Kuala Lumpur Tourism Bureau; Map p66; ☑ 03-2698 0332; www.visitkl.gov.my; 11 Jln Tangsi; ⊙ 8.30am-5.30pm Mon-Fri; ☎; ⓐ Masjid Jamek) Come here for brochures and maps.

ℹ Getting There & Away

AIR

Kuala Lumpur International Airport (KLIA; ☑ 03-8777 7000; www.klia.com.my; ⓐ KLIA) KL's main airport has two terminals and is about 55km south of the city.

SkyPark Subang Terminal (Sultan Abdul Aziz Shah Airport; ☑ 03-7845 1717; www.subangskypark.com; M17, Subang) Firefly, Berjaya Air and some Malindo Air flights land here, around 23km west of KL's city centre.

BUS

KL has several bus stations, but most buses now leave from Terminal Bersepadu Selatan, 14.5km south of the city centre. Other long-distance bus services are operated by **Aeroline** (Map p58; ☑ 03-6258 8800; www.aeroline.com.my; Corus Hotel, Jln Ampang, KLCC; ⓐ KLCC), **Nice** (Map p62; ☑ 03-2260 1185; www.nice-coaches.com.my; Mezzanine floor, Jln Sultan Hishamuddin; ⓐ Kuala Lumpur) and **Transtar Travel** (Map p72; ☑ 03-2141 1771; www.transtar.travel; 135 Jln Imbi, Bukit Bintang; ⓐ Imbi).

Terminal Bersepadu Selatan (TBS)

Connected to the Bandar Tasik Selatan train-station hub, about 15 minutes south of KL Sentral, is **Terminal Bersepadu Selatan** (TBS; ☑ 03-9051 2000; www.tbsbts.com.my; Jln Terminal Selatan, Bandar Tasik Selatan; ☎; ⓐ Bandar Tasik Selatan, ⓐ Bandar Tasik Selatan), KL's main long-distance bus station. Operators here serve destinations to the south and northeast of KL. This vast, modern transport hub has a centralised ticketing service (CTS) selling tickets for nearly all bus companies – including services offered by major operator **Transnasional** (www.transnasional.com.my) – at counters on level 3 or online (up to three hours before departure).

Pekeliling Bus Station

Buses arrive at **Pekeliling** (off Jln Pekeliling Lama; ⓠ Titiwangsa, ⓐ Titiwangsa) from central peninsula locations, including Kuala Lipis, Raub and Jerantut. It's next to Titiwangsa LRT and monorail stations, just off Jln Tun Razak. Several companies run services to Kuantan.

Pudu Sentral Bus Station

Steps from Chinatown and also close to Bukit Bintang, this **bus station** (Puduraya; Map p62; Jln Pudu, Chinatown; ⓐ Plaza Rakyat) serves only a few destinations, including the Genting Highlands, Seremban and Kuala Selangor.

CAR

KL is the best place to hire a car for touring the peninsula, though driving out of KL is complicated by a confusing one-way system and contradictory road signs that can throw off your sense of direction – use a navigation device. All the major rental companies have offices at KLIA. City offices – generally open from 9am to 5.30pm weekdays and 9am to 1pm Saturday – include **Avis** (Map p68; 03-2162 2144, outside office hours 1800-882 847; www.avis.com.my; Rennaissance KL Hotel, 128 Jln Ampang; ☺8am-6pm; ☐ Bukit Nanas) and **Hertz** (Map p58; 03-2181 0658; www.simedarbycarrental.com; Soho Suite KLCC, Jln Perak, KLCC; ☺8am-6.30pm Mon-Sat, to 1.30pm Sun; ☐ Raja Chulan).

TRAIN

All long-distance trains depart from **KL Sentral** (1300-889 933; www.klsentral.com.my), hub of the KTM (p104) national railway system. The information office in the main hall can advise on schedules and check seat availability.

There are daily connections with Ipoh, Butterworth (for Penang) and Padang Besar (on the border with Thailand). Heading south to Johor Bahru you will need to change trains at Gemas. Fares are cheap.

KL is also on the route of the opulent **Eastern & Oriental Express** (www.belmond.com/eastern-and-oriental-express) on its journey between Singapore and Bangkok. Check the website for details of infrequent departures.

KL Sentral runs a coupon system for taxis – look for the counters near the exits from the KLIA Ekspres/Transit lines and main KTM/KTM Komuter lines.

ⓘ Getting Around

KL Sentral is the hub of a rail-based urban network consisting of the KTM Komuter, KLIA Ekspres, KLIA Transit, LRT and Monorail systems. Unfortunately, the systems – all built separately – remain largely unintegrated. Different tickets generally apply for each service, and at stations where there's an interchange between the services, they're rarely conveniently connected. That said, you can happily get around much of central KL on a combination of rail and monorail services, thus avoiding the traffic jams that plague the inner-city roads.

TO/FROM THE AIRPORTS
KLIA

The fastest way to the city (30 minutes) is the comfortable **KLIA Ekspres** (www.kliaekspres.com; adult/child one-way RM55/25; ☺5am-1am), with departures every 15 to 20 minutes. From KL Sentral you can transfer to your final destination by monorail, light rail (LRT), KTM Komuter train or taxi.

The **KL Transit** train also connects KLIA with KL Sentral (35 minutes), stopping at three other stations en route (Salak Tinggi, Putrajaya and Cyberjaya, and Bandar Tasik Selatan).

If flying from KL on Malaysia Airlines, Malindo Air or Cathay Pacific, you don't have to haul your luggage to the airport. You can check in your

---

KLIA TRANSIT HOTELS

If all you need to do is freshen up before or after your flight, KL has a number of decent transit-accommodation options.

Capsule by Container Hotel (03-7610 2020; www.capsulecontainer.com; L1-5, Gateway, KLIA2, Sepang; s for 6/9/12hr from RM90/100/110, d for 6/9/12hr RM190/210/230, not incl breakfast; ☒@☎; ☐KLIA) Grab forty winks at this contemporary crash pad, where the capsule rooms are housed in adapted transport containers. Bathrooms are shared and there are women-only zones. During the day a bed for up to six hours costs only RM55. Located next to KLIA2.

Sama-Sama Express KLIA (03-8787 4848; www.samasamaexpress.com; mezzanine level, Satellite A Bldg, KLIA, gate C5; d not incl breakfast for 6/12hr RM270/540; ☒☎; ☐KLIA) Located inside the terminal (air side), this hotel offers rooms with private bathrooms and TVs. There's a lounge package (RM74) if you just want a few hours' access to hot drinks, snacks, shower facilities and comfy couches. For a more luxurious overnight stay, head to **Sama Sama Hotel** (03-8787 3333; www.samasamahotels.com; Jln CTA 4B, Sepang; d/f not incl breakfast from RM510/630; ☐☒@☎☒; ☐KLIA).

Tune Hotel KLIA2 (03-8787 1720; www.tunehotels.com; lot PT 13, Jln KLIA 2/2; d not incl breakfast from RM230; ☒☎; ☐KLIA2) A decent option if you have an early flight, the Tune Hotel is connected to the airport terminal via a covered walkway. There is a cafe-bar and a convenience store on the ground floor. Day-use rooms include a meal and drink (7am to 7pm, from RM119).

baggage at KL Sentral before boarding a train to KLIA for your flight.

The **Airport Coach** (☑ 016-228 9070; www.airportcoach.com.my; 1-way/return to KL Sentral RM12/18; ⏰ 5.30am-12.30am, every 30min) takes an hour to reach KL Sentral; for RM18 it will take you to any central KL hotel from KLIA and pick you up for the return journey for RM25. The bus stand is clearly signposted inside the terminal. Other bus companies connecting KLIA to KL Sentral are **Skybus** (☑ 016-217 8496; www.skybus.com.my; one-way/return RM11/20) and **Aerobus** (☑ 03-3344 8828, 24hr 010-292 3888; www.aerobus.my; one-way adult/child RM9/5).

Taxis from KLIA operate both on a fixed-fare coupon system and the meter. Buy your taxi coupon before you exit the arrivals hall; standard taxis cost RM75 (for up to three people), premier taxis for four people cost RM103 and family-sized minivans seating up to eight cost RM200. The journey will take around one hour. Given the extra charges on the metered taxis for tolls and pick-up at the airport (RM2), plus the unknown traffic factor, the fixed-fare coupon is the way to go.

Going to the airport by taxi, make sure that the agreed fare includes tolls; expect to pay RM65 from Chinatown or Jln Bukit Bintang.

SkyPark Subang Terminal

KTM Komuter trains (www.ktmb.com.my; from RM1.40; ⏰ 6.45am-11.45pm) Run from KL Sentral to SkyPark Terminal stopping at Subang Jaya along the way. The one-way fare is adult/child R15/7.50 and the journey takes 30 minutes. From KL Sentral, services leave roughly every hour between 5.30am and 9.30pm, from SkyPark Terminal between 7.50am and 11.20pm.

SkyPark Shuttle (☑ 019-276 8315; one-way RM10) Connects Subang Airport with KL Sentral. Services take one hour and run on the hour between 9am and 9pm. There's also a service to KLIA and KLIA2.

Taxis charge around RM40 to RM50 into the city, depending on traffic, which can be heavy during rush hour.

BICYCLE

KL has recently been promoting cycling as a means of getting around, creating some blue-painted bike paths in the city centre – although on many you'll still have to jostle with cars, motorbikes and scooters and pedestrians!

As a visitor you'll likely be better off joining a cycle tour such as those run by Bike With Elena (p68) and MikesBikes (p68).

The rental service **oBike** (www.o.bike/my) is available in Kuala Lumpur. Download its app and you can rent out its bicycles for a refundable deposit of RM109 and a usage charge of RM1 per 15 minutes. There are no official docking stations – instead you use the app to unlock the locks on the silver and yellow bikes themselves. oBikes

can usually be found next to **KL City Gallery** (Map p62; ☑ 03-2691 1382; www.klcitygallery.com; 27 Jln Raja, Merdeka Sq; RM5; ⏰ 9am-6.30pm; 🚇 Masjid Jamek) and at the junction of Jln Tun Sanbanthan and Jln Sultan Abdul Samad in Little India, Brickfields, as well as many other scattered locations. Be warned that many bikes are in poor condition.

Cycling Kuala Lumpur (cyclingkl.blogspot.com) Online map of bike routes and plenty of detail on how to stay safe on KL's roads.

Bike Kitchen (www.facebook.com/bikekitchenkl) Nonprofit community group that helps people learn about fixing bicycles and cycling in general.

BUS

Most buses are provided by **Rapid KL** (☑ 03-7885 2585; www.rapidkl.com.my; RM1-5; ⏰ 6am-11.30pm). The main local bus station is at **Pasar Seni** (Map p62; Jln Sultan Mohamed, Chinatown; 🚇 Pasar Seni) in Chinatown. Rapid KL buses have their destinations clearly displayed. They are divided into four classes:

Bas Bandar ('city bus') Services run around the centre (RM1).

Bas Utama Buses from the centre to the suburbs (RM1 to RM3).

Bas Tempatan ('local bus') Services around the suburbs (RM1).

Bas Ekspres Express buses to distant suburbs (RM3.80).

Apart from Pasar Seni, useful stops in and around Chinatown include Bangkok Bank on Lebuh Pudu, Medan Pasar on Lebuh Ampang, Kota Raya on Jln Tun Tan Cheng, and Muzium Telekom on Jln Raja Chulan.

The free **GO-KL City Bus** (☑ 1800-887 723; www.gokl.com.my; ⏰ 6am-11pm Mon-Thu, to 1am Fri & Sat, 7am-11pm Sun) has four circular routes, with stops at KLCC, KL Tower, KL Sentral, the National Museum and Merdeka Sq. Buses run every five minutes during peak hours and every 10 to 15 minutes at other times.

KL MONORAIL

The air-conditioned **monorail** (www.myrapid.com.my; RM0.90-4.10; ⏰ 6am-midnight) zips from KL Sentral to Titiwangsa, linking many of the city's sightseeing areas. There can be waits of up to 15 minutes between services and it gets packed during morning and early evening rush hours.

KTM KOMUTER TRAINS

There are three main KTM Komuter lines: Tanjung Malim to Pelabuhan Klang, Batu Caves to Gemas and KL Sentral to Terminal Skypark (for Subang Airport). Trains run every 15 to 20 minutes during peak hours but there can be intervals of up to 45 minutes between trains at off-peak times.

TRAVEL CARDS

If you're flying into KL and only staying for a day or two, then the best-value card is the **KL TravelPass** (www.kliaekspres.com). Included in the cost of a single (RM70) or return (RM115) transfer on the KLIA Ekspres train with the international airport is two days of rides on the city's LRT, MRT and monorail lines.

If you're staying for an extended period in KL, consider the prepaid **MyRapid card** (www.myrapid.com.my), valid on Rapid KL buses, the monorail and the Ampang and Kelana Jaya LRT lines. It costs RM20 (including RM5 in credit) and can be bought at monorail and LRT stations. Just tap at the ticket gates or when you get on the bus and the correct fare will be deducted. Each time you reload this card with credit, RM0.50 will be deducted as a reload fee.

The **Touch 'n Go card** (www.touchngo.com.my) can be used on all public transport in the Klang Valley, at highway toll booths across Malaysia and at selected parking sites. The cards, which cost RM10 and can be reloaded with values from RM10 to RM500, can be purchased at most petrol stations, KL Sentral, and the central LRT stations KLCC, Masjid Jamek and Dang Wangi.

LIGHT RAIL TRANSIT (LRT)

As well as buses, Rapid KL runs the **Light Rail Transit** (LRT; ☎ 03-7885 2585; www.myrapid.com.my; from RM0.80; ⊙ every 6-10min 6am-11.45pm Mon-Sat, to 11.30pm Sun) system. There are three lines: the Ampang line from Ampang to Sentul Timur; the Sri Petaling line from Sentul Timur to Putra Heights; and the Kelana Jaya line from Gombak to Putra Heights. The network is integrated with the MRT and monorail lines but because all were constructed by different companies at different times, you may have to follow a series of walkways, stairs and elevators, or walk several blocks down the street to make connections.

Buy single-journey tokens or MyRapid cards from the cashier or electronic ticket machines. An electronic control system checks tickets/tokens as you enter and exit via turnstiles (you tap the token on the way in and insert it in the gate on the way out).

MASS RAPID TRANSIT

Construction is ongoing for KL's **MRT** (Mass Rapid Transit; ☎ 1800-82-6868; www.mymrt.com.my; from RM0.80) system. This rail-based public-transport network aims to ease the road-traffic congestion that plagues the Greater Kuala Lumpur/Klang Valley region.

The Sungai Buloh–Kajang line is operational, while construction is ongoing for the Sungai Buloh–Serdang–Putrajaya (SSP Line) – phase one of this line to Kampung Batu is scheduled to open by July 2021, with phase two to Putrajaya to be completed a year later.

TAXI

KL has plenty of air-conditioned taxis, which queue up at designated taxi stops across the city. You can also flag down moving taxis, but drivers will stop only if there is a convenient place to pull over (these are harder to come by when it's raining and during peak hours). Fares start at RM3 for the first three minutes, with an additional 25 sen for each 36 seconds. From midnight to 6am there's a surcharge of 50% on the metered fare, and extra passengers (more than two) add 20 sen each to the starting fare. Blue taxis are newer and more comfortable and start at RM6 for the first three minutes and RM1 for each additional 36 seconds. Night surcharges of 50% also apply.

Unfortunately, some drivers refuse to use the meter, even though this is a legal requirement. Taxi drivers lingering outside luxury hotels or tourist hot spots such as KL Bird Park are especially guilty of this behaviour. Note that KL Sentral and some large malls such as Pavilion and Suria KLCC have a coupon system for taxis where you pay in advance at a slightly higher fee than the meter.

One of the easiest ways to get a taxi is to download the app Grab to your smartphone or tablet. This way you will also know in advance what your fare will be.

Selangor & Negeri Sembilan

Includes ➡

Selangor............108
Batu Caves 108
Forest Research
Institute Malaysia....109
Genting Highlands...109
Bukit Fraser.........110
Putrajaya 113
Petaling Jaya &
Shah Alam..........115
Klang &
Pelabuhan Klang 116
Kuala Selangor......118
Negeri Sembilan.....119
Seremban 119
Port Dickson 123

Best Places to Eat

➡ Dewakan (p115)
➡ Yap Kee (p117)
➡ Pasar Besar (p120)
➡ Haji Shariff's Cendol (p120)

Best Places to Stay

➡ Avillion Port Dickson (p124)
➡ Thistle Port Dickson Resort (p124)
➡ Ye Olde Smokehouse Fraser's Hill (p111)
➡ Pullman Putrajaya Lakeside (p114)

Why Go?

Teeming jungles, fishing villages and seaside resorts are scattered across the states of Selangor and Negeri Sembilan, in easy reach of high-octane Kuala Lumpur.

Selangor's top attractions are barely outside the city limits, such as the staggering Batu Caves and orderly administrative capital Putrajaya. Kuala Selangor wins hearts with its fireflies and unhurried village culture unfolds on islands around Klang. Lost-in-time Bukit Fraser (Fraser's Hill) is almost hidden by the encroaching jungle.

Fiendish traffic follows you across much of Selangor but all is calm southeast, in Negeri Sembilan. Venture here for less-touristed temples, Minangkabau culture and Port Dickson beach life.

Big-hitter attractions are easily toured from KL using public transport, but hiring a car enables you to soak up the countryside: stilt villages, ancient stones and cruising along the coast.

When to Go
Kuala Selangor

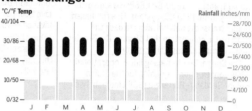

Jan & Feb During the festival of Thaipusam, the Batu Caves are mobbed by pilgrims.

Mar Watch the raptors' annual northern migration at the Cape Rachado Forest Reserve.

May & Jun Escape the lowland heat at Bukit Fraser's International Bird Race.

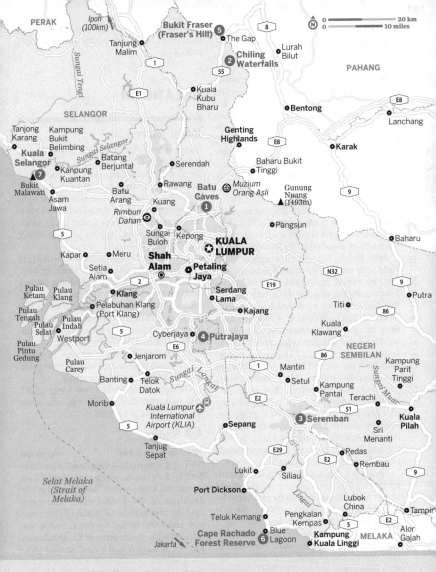

Selangor & Negeri Sembilan Highlights

1 Batu Caves (p108)
Exploring Hindu shrines at Malaysia's most famous cave temples.

2 Chiling Waterfalls (p112)
Hiking (and wading) to reach 20m-tall cascades.

3 Seremban (p119)
Taking a whistle-stop tour of Minangkabau culture

and pausing to slurp beef noodles.

4 Putrajaya (p113)
Touring the monumental architecture and serene gardens of Malaysia's modern administrative capital.

5 Bukit Fraser (p110) Bird-watching and hiking at a lush colonial-era hill station.

6 Cape Rachado Forest Reserve (p123) Hearing a forest chorus on hikes to hidden beaches or the crowning lighthouse.

7 Kuala Selangor (p118)
Gazing up at a synchronised natural light show where fireflies glow in the trees.

History

In the 15th century, all of what is now Selangor and Negeri Sembilan was controlled by Melaka.

Negeri Sembilan's Minangkabau people, settlers from Sumatra, enjoyed protection from the Melaka Sultanate and then the Johor Sultanate. However, they felt increasingly insecure with the rising power of the Bugis (a seafaring group of warrior-like settlers from Sulawesi) in Selangor, so they turned to their former homeland for protection. Raja Melewar, a Minangkabau prince from Sumatra, was appointed the first *yang di-pertuan besar* (head of state) of Negeri Sembilan in 1773. Out of this initial union emerged a loose confederation of nine *luak* (fiefdoms). The royal capital of Negeri Sembilan was established at Sri Menanti.

After Melaka fell to the Portuguese in the early 16th century, control of Selangor was hotly contested, partly because of its rich tin reserves. By the middle of the 18th century, the Buginese had established a sultanate, based at Kuala Selangor. A century later the success of the tin trade and the growing wealth of the Chinese communities in the fledgling city of Kuala Lumpur led to conflicts both among and between the Selangor chiefs and the miners. The outcome was a prolonged civil war, which slashed tin production and destroyed KL. In 1874, with the civil war over, the British took control. The sultan was forced to accede to the installation of a British Resident at Klang, and for the next 25 years the state prospered, largely on the back of another boom in tin prices.

Negeri Sembilan was also rich in tin, so for much of the 19th century it too suffered unrest and political instability motivated by greed. After Raja Melewar's death, the title of *yang di-pertuan besar* was taken by a succession of Sumatran chiefs, until a series of protracted tin-related wars from 1824 to 1832 led to the severance of political ties with Sumatra.

British Resident Frank Swettenham cajoled the sultans of Selangor, Negeri Sembilan, Perak and Pahang into an alliance that eventually became the Federated Malay States in 1896. The federation was centrally administered from a phoenix-like KL, which had become a well-ordered and prosperous city by the turn of the 20th century. In 1974 Selangor's sultan ceded KL as a federal territory, and Shah Alam took over the role of capital of Selangor. In the late 1990s, Putrajaya was also cleaved off from Selangor and built up as Malaysia's federal administrative capital.

SELANGOR

Batu Caves

Guarded by a monumental statue of Hindu deity Lord Murugan, the **Batu Caves** (⊕ Batu Caves) are a Malaysian national treasure and an unmissable day trip from Kuala Lumpur. These limestone caves harbour Hindu temples where dioramas of mythic scenes glow beneath stalactites, bats flutter in the shadows, and monkeys prey on tourists hiking the 272 stairs to Temple Cave.

American naturalist William Hornaday is credited with discovering the caves in 1878, though they were known to Chinese settlers (who collected guano) and to local indigenous peoples. The caves are always a colourful experience, but never more so than in late January or early February when hundreds of thousands of pilgrims converge for the three-day Thaipusam festival, in which devotees in a semi-trance walk in procession from KL's Chinatown to the caves.

The cave complex is 13km north of KL and each cave has a different admission price (Temple Cave is free).

◎ Sights

★ **Ramayana Cave**   HINDU SHRINE
(RM5; ⊗ 8.30am-6pm; ⊕ Batu Caves) No cave at Batu is more spectacularly embellished than Ramayana Cave, which boasts psychedelic dioramas of the Indian epic 'Ramayana'. Pass the green, 15m-tall statue of Hanuman and cross the bridge to enter. Inside you can't miss the giant statue of Kumbhakarna, brother of Ravana and a deep sleeper (note the attempts to wake him with arrows and cymbals). Climb the stairs to a shrine featuring a naturally occurring lingam, a stalagmite that is a symbol of Shiva.

Temple Cave   HINDU SHRINE
(⊗ 8am-8.30pm; ⊕ Batu Caves) FREE Centrepiece of the Batu Caves complex and one of Malaysia's most photographed sights, Temple Cave sits atop 272 steps populated by scampering monkeys. Guarded by a 42.7m statue of Lord Murugan, erected in 2006 and said to be the world's largest, the dome-shaped cavern

is the focal point of the yearly Thaipusam festival (p584). Temple Cave has been a Hindu shrine since K Thambusamy Pillai, founder of KL's Sri Mahamariamman Temple, placed a statue of Lord Murugan here in 1890.

Dark Cave CAVE
(☑012-3715001; www.darkcavemalaysia.com; adult/child RM33/24; ☺10am-5pm Mon-Fri, 10.30am-5.30pm Sat & Sun; ☒Batu Caves) Selangor's natural limestone labyrinths are home to trapdoor spiders, bats, flatworms and other creatures, and 45-minute guided tours of Dark Cave offer a glimpse of the ecosystems at play. On the stairs up to Temple Cave, branch left to join a tour along 850m of limestone passageways within this conservation site. In seven different chambers you'll see dramatic stalactites and flowstones, pits used for guano extraction, and possibly 10 species of bat among hundreds of other life forms.

❶ Getting There & Away

KTM Komuter trains terminate at Batu Caves station (RM2.60 from KL Sentral, 30 minutes, every 15 to 30 minutes).

A taxi from KL costs around RM30 to RM40.

Forest Research Institute Malaysia

Birdsong and wall-to-wall greenery replace droning traffic at the 545-hectare **Forest Research Institute Malaysia** (FRIM; ☑03-6279 7592; www.frim.gov.my; per car/adult/bicycle RM5/5/1; ☺8.30am-7.30pm; ☒Kepong Sentral) in Kepong, 17km northwest of KL. A serene, green day trip from the city, FRIM is also the heart of tropical forestry research in Malaysia. Mining and farming tore away Kepong's natural greenery in 1925, prompting the first forest research officer, FW Foxworthy, to establish a forest nursery. The institute was founded in 1929 and over decades the forest, and the accompanying scientific research, have flourished.

Today FRIM is an exemplary ecotourism destination, with walking and cycling paths winding through rare dipterocarp trees, picnic spots by shallow waterfalls, and traditional village houses preserved for posterity.

Knowledgeable guides lead group **walking tours** (☑03-6279 7592; frim_enquiry@frim. gov.my; hour-long tour per group RM120) of the main trails – Salleh, Keruing and Engkabang – for groups. Trekkers undaunted by insects should book a night walk (per group

RM250) for insights into the forest's nocturnal wildlife. Book at least a week ahead by phone or email.

Hire a **bike** (☑03-6275 0129; Clubhouse; ☺8am-5pm Sat & Sun) to pedal around the sealed roads within the FRIM grounds. There's a set fee for the first hour (adult RM7 to RM15, child from RM5), followed by a charge of RM3 for each subsequent hour.

❶ Getting There & Away

Take a KTM Komuter train to Kepong Sentral (RM2.40) and then a taxi (RM7 to RM10); arrange for the taxi to pick you up again later.

A round trip by taxi from central KL, including a couple of hours of waiting time, will cost upward of RM90.

Genting Highlands
☑03

The razzle-dazzle of **Resorts World** (☑03-2718 1888; www.rwgenting.com; ☺casino 24hr) dominates the Genting Highlands, 50km north of Kuala Lumpur. These mist-cloaked heights, topping out at 1800m, have the crisp temperatures of other hill stations, but they've been bulldozed, landscaped and built up into a vast entertainment complex:

an open-all-hours casino, malls, amusement parks, bars and 10,000 hotel rooms.

Aside from a few walking trails and a valley cable-car ride, the great outdoors appears to have been almost entirely eradicated from the Genting experience. Genting is popular with Malaysian weekenders, and they generally aren't here for nature so much as cool air and buzzing indoor entertainment.

Between the golf course and Resorts World, on a forested cliff, stands a temple that's both awe-inspiring and blood-curdling. **Chin Swee Caves Temple** (www.chinswee.org) was completed in 1994, the brainchild of Resorts World founder Tan Sri Lim Goh. A nine-storey pagoda and monumental lotus-seated Buddha impress, but it's the **Journey to Enlightenment** pathway – 10 gory dioramas of punishments in hell – that will be seared into your brain. Don't bring the kids.

With amusement parks and malls the prime focus for visitors, it's surprisingly easy to weekend here without even glimpsing the rippling valleys. Fortunately, the **Awana Skyway** (☑03-6251 8398; www.rwgenting.com/attractions/awana-skyway; SkyAvenue Station; one-way RM7; ☉7am-midnight) cable car whisks visitors out from the malls and high above the dense forest at a speed of 6m per second. The journey between upper SkyAvenue Station and the lower **Awana Station** takes 10 minutes.

❶ Getting There & Away

Genting Express Bus operates 10 daily services between 7.30am and 7pm from Kuala Lumpur's Pudu Sentral bus station (adult/child RM12.20/10.90, 1½ hours). The same service is offered almost hourly between 8am and 8pm from KL Sentral (RM11.90/10.80). The price includes the return cable-car trip from Awana Station to the top of the hill.

A taxi from KL costs at least RM100.

Bukit Fraser

☑09 / POP 1000

A leaf-cloaked stone clock tower heralds your arrival at the exceedingly British hill station of Bukit Fraser (Fraser's Hill), 100km north of Kuala Lumpur. Here amid Tudor-style buildings and creaky inns, colonial ambience has been conserved in amber: it's a tiny, somnolent kingdom of golfers and bird-watchers, where accommodation is authentically dusty and you're as likely to dine on beef and English ale as nasi goreng.

Spread across seven densely forested hills in the Titiwangsa Range at an altitude ranging from 1220m to 1524m, this cool, quiet and relatively undeveloped station is a desirable spot for keen bird-watchers and ramblers seeking respite from the lowland heat.

◉ Sights & Activities

Fraser's Hill is all about the great outdoors. As well as bird-watching and hiking you can play **golf** (☑09-362 2129; Jln Genting; green fees RM30-40; ☉clubhouse 8.30am-1pm & 2-4.30pm Sun-Thu, 8.30am-noon & 2.45-4.30pm Fri), go **horse riding** (☑09-362 2195; Jln Valley; short rides adult/child RM8/6, archery per person RM10; ☉8.30am-6.30pm Sun-Thu, 8.30am-noon & 2.45-6pm Fri) and hire a pedal boat (RM8 per 15 minutes) to explore Allan's Waters, a former reservoir.

Bird Interpretive Centre   MUSEUM
(☑09-362 2007; ☉10am-5pm Sat & Sun) FREE
For an overview of the birding scene, visit the Bird Interpretive Centre on the 2nd floor of the golf-course clubhouse, across the village square. Hours are spotty; ask at the Puncak Inn (p112) if it isn't open.

Mr Durai   BIRD-WATCHING
(☑013-983 1633; durefh@hotmail.com; Shahzan Inn Fraser's Hill, Jln Lady Guillemard; per group half-/full day RM200/600) For one of Malaysia's top birding guides, contact the eagle-eyed Mr Durai, who has been taking people bird-watching for almost 30 years.

Hiking

Hemmant Trail   HIKING
This fern-fringed, relatively flat and wide path runs above the golf course for 1km. The trailhead is a few minutes' walk up from the village square.

Pine Tree Trail   HIKING
(Jln High Pines) Start early if you want to tackle Bukit Fraser's best-known hike, the steep 5.5km Pine Tree Trail (seven to 10 hours return). The challenge is rewarded by thick jungle and fresh, fern-framed views of the hills. A guide isn't essential, but you must register at the village **police station** (☑09-362 2222; Jln Gap) first.

Note that it's a long walk to the trailhead (nearly 2km west of the main roundabout) for those without a vehicle.

Jeriau Waterfall   WATERFALL
About 4km northwest of the town centre, along Jln Air Terjun, is Jeriau Waterfall,

Bukit Fraser (Fraser's Hill)

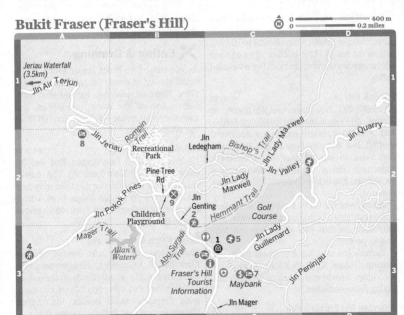

0 ——— 400 m
0 ——— 0.2 miles

Bukit Fraser (Fraser's Hill)

⊚ Sights
1 Bird Interpretive Centre C3

⊕ Activities, Courses & Tours
2 Hemmant Trail...B2
Mr Durai..(see 7)
3 The Paddock D2
4 Pine Tree Trail...A3
5 Royal Fraser's Hill Golf Club C3

⊜ Sleeping
6 Puncak Inn B3
7 Shahzan Inn Fraser's Hill C3
8 Ye Olde Smokehouse Fraser's Hill A2

⊗ Eating
9 Hill View...B2

⊕ Drinking & Nightlife
Scott's Pub & Restaurant ....(see 6)

where you can swim. It's a 20-minute climb from the road to reach the falls.

🎊 Festivals & Events

International Bird Race SPORTS
(☺ May/Jun) Bukit Fraser hosts an International Bird Race in which teams of bird-watchers compete to observe and record the highest number of species in a set time period.

Ask for details locally, or enquire through Tourism Pahang (www.pahangtourism.org.my).

🛏 Sleeping

There's a good range of accommodation, from bare-bones hotel rooms to colonial-era suites, but keep expectations of modern

amenities low. Prices increase steeply at weekends and on public holidays.

Note that air-conditioning doesn't come as standard as it isn't needed at this cool hill station.

★ Ye Olde Smokehouse
Fraser's Hill HOTEL **$$**
(☑ 09-362 2226; www.thesmokehouse.my; Jln Jeriau; d incl breakfast RM308-495; P ☎) Exposed beams, log fires, four-poster beds and chintz – the Smokehouse goes for broke on its English-charm offensive. Rooms are individually tailored, from the doll's-house-like 'Charlotte' to grand 'Scott', with a brick chimney and elegant furnishings. Full English breakfast is included.

Even if you don't stay here, consider dropping by for a pint at the bar, or a well-made pie or roast at lunch (mains RM28 to RM70). Afternoon tea (RM28) is from 3pm to 6pm on the garden terrace, overlooking a wooded valley.

Puncak Inn   HOTEL $$
(☑ 09-362 2007; http://puncakinn.pkbf.gov.my; Jln Genting; d incl breakfast from RM110, apt RM150-400; [P][@][🛜]) Standard rooms are small and scuffed, but friendly Puncak Inn offers the best value in Bukit Fraser. The location is supremely central, the information centre is on site and English is spoken. Wi-fi in reception only.

Apart from the hotel, it also offers studios, two- and three-bedroom apartments and four cottages that can sleep between four and 15 people.

Puncak Inn also has a pleasant patio restaurant (mains RM5 to RM6) overlooking the village square with a mix of Western and Malay dishes on offer.

Shahzan Inn Fraser's Hill   HOTEL $$
(☑ 09-362 2300; http://shahzaninn.com; Jln Lady Guillemard; d RM312-369, ste RM408-853, incl breakfast; [P][🛜]) Overlooking the golf course (p110), Shahzan Inn has 92 well-sized rooms, simply attired in white and beige. Like everywhere in Bukit Fraser, it isn't gleaming and modern, but it's the most contemporary accommodation in town.

🍴 Eating & Drinking

As you come into Bukit Fraser, you'll find a small cluster of shops for self-catering supplies. There are also two hawker-stall complexes: one off the main roundabout, and the other a 10-minute walk up the hill from the village square.

Hill View   CHINESE $$
(☑ 09-362 2231; 3 Food Garden, Pine Tree Rd; mains RM9-20; ⊙10am-9pm; ☑) The family that has run this stall for a couple of generations serves up simple dishes from salted-fish rice to braised bean curd and various veggie specials.

Scott's Pub & Restaurant   PUB
(www.thesmokehouse.my; Jln Genting; ⊙noon-10pm Thu-Tue) A pleasingly accurate rendition of a British country pub stands on the corner of Bukit Fraser's main roundabout, complete with fireplace, wood beams, Manchester United scarves and Fuller's London Pride.

ℹ Information

Fraser's Hill Tourist Information (☑ 09-517 1623; http://puncakinn.pkbf.gov.my; Puncak Inn, Jln Genting) Located in the Puncak Inn lobby (and staffed whenever there's someone

---

KUALA KUBU BHARU & CHILING WATERFALLS

White-water rafting and wading to waterfalls draw scores of weekenders to Kuala Kubu Bharu, 70km north of Kuala Lumpur. The river-splashed trail to Chiling Waterfalls is the prime attraction, but this sleepy town (known locally as KKB) has become a modest hub for white-water rafting and kayaking on the Sungai Selangor. Well-established **PieRose Swiftwater** (☑ 013-361 3991; www.raftmalaysia.com; 11 Jln Damai 7; rafting per person from RM180; ⊙8am-6pm), run by a husband-and-wife team, can arrange guided trips on the white water.

Thirteen kilometres east of KKB on Federal Rte 55, just a short distance past the Selangor Dam, look right for the entrance to the Santuari Ikan Sungai Chiling (Chiling River Fish Reserve). On weekends you can't miss the spot, as dozens of cars will be parked outside.

Within the reserve you'll find a rough camping ground and a highly popular trail up to the 20m-tall **Chiling Waterfalls** (⊙8am-6pm Fri-Sun) FREE on the Sungai Chiling (Chiling River). Be prepared to get very wet on the exhilarating 1½-hour hike, which starts from the small pedestrian bridge across the lot from the camping ground. Register at the ranger's cabin (RM1) by the bridge before you cross.

The route up is clearly marked, but we recommend going with a group or guide, since you have to cross the river five times and there is a risk of flash flooding. For a full-day tour in the company of an upbeat, spiritually inclined guide, contact **Happy Yen** (☑ 017-369 7831; www.happyyen.com; tours per person RM550).

The falls have a large natural swimming area at the bottom, which to many is the whole purpose of the hike up. But the river area around the camping ground is also pleasant and loaded with fish. Note that the falls and camping ground are only open on weekends, and there is nowhere to buy food or water.

at reception), this information centre can supply maps, brochures and bird-watching advice.

Maybank (Jln Lady Guillemard; ⊘ 9.15am-4.30pm Mon-Thu, to 4pm Fri) Accepts credit cards and has an ATM.

🛈 Getting There & Away

Only private cars can get to Bukit Fraser, 100km north from Kuala Lumpur, but note the road is narrow, winding, fringed by jungle on both sides and prone to sudden monkey crossings. Hardened cyclists pedal their way here from Kuala Kubu Bharu (40km).

There's no petrol station in Bukit Fraser itself; the nearest ones are found at Raub and Kuala Kubu Bharu.

If coming by public transport from KL, take a KTM Komuter train (RM8.70) to Kuala Kubu Bharu and then a taxi (RM80 to RM100). There are few taxis at KKB, so rather than showing up and hoping for the best, have your hotel arrange one for you. From KL a taxi will cost around RM200 to RM250.

Putrajaya

📞 03 / POP 90,000

An eye-catching array of monumental architecture amid manicured greenery is on display in Putrajaya, 25km south of KL and 20km north of Kuala Lumpur International Airport (KLIA). Covering 49 sq km of former rubber and oil-palm plantations, the federal government's administrative hub (almost exclusively Muslim in population) was but a twinkle in the eye of its principal visionary – former prime minister Dr Mahathir – as late as the early 1990s. It's still a long way off its envisioned population of more than 300,000 and can feel eerily quiet at weekends.

From marbled minarets to the trim gardens, it's immediately clear that Putrajaya is a planned city – a marvel of engineering that is rather missing a soul. At its heart is a 6-sq-km artificial lake fringed by landscaped parks and an eclectic mix of buildings and bridges, best viewed when illuminated at night.

⊙ Sights

★**Putra Mosque**   MOSQUE
(Dataran Putra, Presint 1; ⊘ 9am-12.30pm, 2-4pm & 5.30-6pm Sat-Thu, 3-4pm & 5.30-6pm Fri) An apparition in rosy-pink granite, Masjid Putra has a captivating delicacy of design. Capped by an ornate pink-and-white dome and starring a 116m minaret, the mosque is a marriage between graceful Middle Eastern and traditional Malay styles. It was the first of Putrajaya's buildings to be completed (1999) and can hold 15,000 worshippers.

Non-Muslim visitors are welcome outside of prayer times. Even modestly dressed visitors, particularly women, may be required to wear one of the mosque's fetching maroon robes.

Taman Botani   GARDENS
(Botanical Gardens; 📞 03-888 7770; Presint 1; ⊘ garden 7am-7pm, visitor centre 9am-5pm) **FREE** Laid out in 1977, this 93-hectare site is Malaysia's largest botanical garden. More than 700 types of plant flourish in the tropical gardens; there's also a visitor centre, a lakeside restaurant and a beautifully tiled **Moroccan Pavilion** (adult/child RM3/1). A tourist tram (RM4) trundles between the flower beds and trestles, and you can hire bicycles (RM4 per hour). You'll need to take a taxi to get here.

Taman Wetland   PARK
(📞 03-888 7774; Presint 13; ⊘ 9am-5.30pm Mon-Fri, to 6.30pm Sat & Sun) A short taxi ride from Dataran Putra is this serene, contemplative space with peaceful nature trails, aquatic animals and 100 species of waterbird (climb the 18m **lookout tower** for the best views).

Canoes, kayaks and bikes can be rented at the **boathouse** (from 9am to 7pm), which is about 1km from the **Nature Interpretative Centre** (open 9am to 5pm Tuesday to Sunday) by road or walkway.

China-Malaysia Friendship Garden GARDENS
(Anjung Floria; Presint 4) **FREE** It's worth dropping by this peaceful Chinese-style garden, located next to the **Seri Saujana Bridge**. The design of the garden incorporates elements of Lingnan architecture, a style originating in Guangdong and nearby provinces of China, and includes bonsai trees, a pretty pagoda, rockery and pond. Plants are labelled in English.

Tuanku Mizan Zainal Abidin Mosque MOSQUE
(Iron Mosque; 25 Jln Tuanku Abdul Rahman, Presint 3) One of the most striking sights in Putrajaya is metal-domed Tuanku Mizan Zainal Abidin Mosque glinting in the sun. It's Putrajaya's second-most important mosque after Putra Mosque, though it's double the size.

Istana Kehakiman   ARCHITECTURE
(Palace of Justice; Persiaran Perdana) One of the most impressive photo ops in Putrajaya is the five-storey Palace of Justice. Its central domes and tall archways represent a union of styles, from neoclassical and Mogul to

SELANGOR & NEGERI SEMBILAN PUTRAJAYA

Indo-Saracenic (an echo of the Sultan Abdul Samad Building in Merdeka Sq in Kuala Lumpur, which it was designed to replace).

Kompleks Perdadanan Putrajaya
ARCHITECTURE

(Putrajaya Corporation Complex; Persiaran Perdana) The front of this corporate building has an unusual arch gateway composed of a lattice of steel blades. Through the arch sight lines you can see the Tuanku Mizan Zainal Abidin Mosque (p113) across what is known as the Kiblat Walk, a plaza atop a skyway to the mosque.

Putrajaya Convention Centre
NOTABLE BUILDING

(📞 03-8887 6000; Presint 5) Resembling a flattened alien spaceship, the brutalist-style Putrajaya Convention Centre squats at the southern end of Persiaran Perdana. You'll need private transport, but it's worth cruising past, not only for the UFO-like building but also for the expansive views over Putrajaya and Cyberjaya.

🏃 Activities

Skyrides Balloon
BALLOONING

(📞 03-8893 0185; www.skyridesputrajaya.com; Sky Rides Festival Park, Jln P2M, Presint 2; 15min rides per person RM73; ☉ 10am-10pm Sun-Thu, to midnight Fri & Sat) There are great views of Putrajaya and the lake from this tethered helium balloon, which floats to 150m from near the **Millennium Monument** (Monumen Alaf Baru; Lr Ehsan, Presint 2).

👉 Tours

Putrajaya Sightseeing
TOURS

(📞 03-8890 4788; Putrajaya Sentral, Presint 7; adult/child RM50/25; ☉ 11am & 3pm Sat-Thu, 3pm Fri) Departing from the bus station (ground level at the train station), these bus tours are a convenient way to zip through Putrajaya's most significant landmarks. Touring half a dozen sights over two or three hours, most stops are brief, but there's a solid half-hour to explore the impressive Putra Mosque (p113). Purchase tickets on the spot.

It's worth calling ahead to confirm departure times, or asking at a tourist office in Kuala Lumpur.

Cruise Tasik Putrajaya
BOATING

(📞 03-8888 5539; www.cruisetasikputrajaya. com; Jeti Putra, Presint 1; sightseeing cruise adult/child from RM25/18, dinner cruise adult/child from RM130/88; ☉ 11am-6.30pm Mon-Fri, 10am-7pm Sat & Sun) Choose from half-hour sightsee-ing cruises (10am weekends, 11am and noon weekdays) or book ahead for a dinner cruise, where you can pick from a Malay buffet while gliding across Putrajaya Lake. Most atmospheric are the regular cruises aboard a *lepa-lepa* (adult/child RM40/26) – these wooden vessels were traditionally used as houseboats.

✨ Festivals & Events

MyBalloonFiesta
AIR SHOW

(Putrajaya International Hot Air Balloon Fiesta; www. myballoonfiesta.com; Sky Rides Festivals Park; ☉ Mar) Hot-air balloons float over Putrajaya Lake in morning and evening sessions at the annual balloon festival, a colourful fixture of Putrajaya's events calendar for a decade. The highlight of the event is **night glow**, when pilots light up their (grounded) balloons by igniting their burners in a synchronised display accompanied by music and fireworks.

Royal Floria
FAIR

(http://floriaputrajaya.com.my; China-Malaysia Friendship Garden, Presint 4; admission RM4-24; ☉ late Aug/early Sep) Flower gardens, from fairy tale to psychedelic, create a riotously colourful spectacle at Royal Floria, the largest garden festival in Malaysia.

🛏 Sleeping & Eating

Pullman Putrajaya Lakeside
RESORT $$

(📞 03-8890 0000; www.pullmanputrajaya.com; 2 Jln P5/5, Presint 5; d RM240-400, apt from RM470; ❄ @ 🛜 ⩵) Close to the Convention Centre and beside Putrajaya Lake, this elegantly presented resort incorporates traditional Malaysian elements (rugs, ornate murals and tilework) into its design. The best rooms have balconies with lake views.

Pulse Grande Putrajaya
HOTEL $$

(📞 03-8887 8888; www.pulsegrande.com.my; Taman Putra Perdana, Presint 1; d from RM320; ❄ @ 🛜 ⩵) This elegant hotel has spacious, contemporary rooms with occasional nods to Malay style and great hillside views across to Putrajaya Lake. Good-value weekend packages are available, and there are frequent online promotions.

Alamanda
FOOD HALL $$

(📞 03-8888 8882; www.alamanda.com.my; Jln Alamanda, Presint 1; mains from RM15; ☉ 10am-10pm) A fairly standard shopping mall, albeit with grand entrances flanked by bamboo, Alamanda has an above-average food hall. Take your pick of *roti canai* (flaky, flat bread), *nasi campur* (buffet of curried meats, fish and vegetables, served with rice) and fresh sugar-cane juice. Popular with families.

ℹ️ Information

i-Centre (Dataran Putra, Presint 1; ⊙ 9am-1pm & 2-5pm, closed 12.45-2.45pm Fri) A very helpful booth. Electric vehicles (two-seater electric cars) can be hired here (RM100 per hour) for zipping around the city, and at weekends bicycles are also available to rent (RM6 per hour).

ℹ️ Getting There & Around

KLIA transit trains from KL Sentral (RM14, 20 minutes) and KLIA (RM9.40, 18 minutes) stop at Putrajaya Sentral (Putrajaya & Cyberjaya).

The 502 bus runs from the train station to close to Dataran Putra (3km) between 6am and 10pm. A taxi is RM15.

Putrajaya's attractions are dispersed across a large area. If you aren't driving, you'll need to make use of taxis or hop aboard the sightseeing bus.

Petaling Jaya & Shah Alam

🗹 03

Heading southwest of Kuala Lumpur along the Klang Hwy, the Kota Darul Ehsan ceremonial arch marks the transition between the city and Selangor. Just over the boundary, the mall-heavy suburb of Petaling Jaya (known locally as PJ) blends into Shah Alam, the state capital, with its famous Blue Mosque.

Spreading across a large, pedestrian-unfriendly area and threaded by roaring highways, sights in Shah Alam and Petaling Jaya can only be toured by private vehicle. Make heavy use of local taxis and avoid rush hour at all costs.

👁️ Sights & Activities

Masjid Sultan Salahuddin
Abdul Aziz Shah   MOSQUE
(Blue Mosque; 🗹 03-5159 9988; www.mssaas.gov. my; Shah Alam; ⊙ 9am-4pm Mon-Thu, to 6pm Sat & Sun, Fri Muslims only; 🚆 Shah Alam) Southeast Asia's second-biggest mosque is a dazzling sight: four 142m-high minarets stand sentry around its latticed blue dome, the largest in the world for a religious building. The prayer hall can hold as many as 24,000 worshippers. Allow time to walk around the ornate building. Modestly dressed visitors are allowed inside, though menstruating women, warns a sign, are not.

It's worth the inconvenient journey to get there. Get a taxi from Shah Alam and ask the driver to wait for you.

Sunway Lagoon   AMUSEMENT PARK
(🗹 03-5639 0182; http://sunwaylagoon.com; 3 Jln PJS, 11/11 Bandar Sunway, Petaling Jaya; adult/child RM169.80/141.50; ⊙ 10am-6pm; 🚼; 🚆 Setia Jaya) An impressive multizone theme park, flanked by high-rises and adjoining Sunway Pyramid (p116), occupies the site of a former tin mine and quarry. Its 90-plus attractions include the world's largest artificial surf beach (thrashing out 2.5m waves), rides that plummet from 11 storeys, a 360-degree rotating ship and fairground games for smaller kids. Ideal for cooling off on hot days.

If splashing around in water doesn't cool you down sufficiently, there is also an **ice rink** (🗹 03-7492 6800; www.sunwaypyramidice. com; Mon-Fri RM18.80, Sat & Sun RM23.50, incl skate hire; ⊙ 10am-8pm Mon-Fri, 9am-9pm Sat, 9am-6pm Sun) right in the centre of Sunway Pyramid.

🍴 Eating

⭐ Dewakan   MALAYSIAN $$$
(🗹 03-5565 0767; www.dewakan.my; lower ground fl, KDU University College, Jln Kontraktor U1/14, Shah Alam; menus RM285-350; ⊙ 6.30-10pm Mon-Sat; 🚆 Batu Tiga) Darren Teoh heads a team of exciting young chefs at this innovative restaurant based at the KDU University College in Shah Alam. Chefs get playful with local flavours and whimsical presentation, such as their black banana porridge, prawns in starfruit juice, and goat tartare. It's absolutely worth the journey from Kuala Lumpur for this evening-long fine-dining experience. Reservations essential.

☆ Entertainment

⭐ Merdekarya   LIVE MUSIC
(🗹 016-207 1553, 016-202 0529; www.merdekarya. com; 1st fl, 352 Jln 5/57, Petaling Garden, Petaling Jaya; ⊙ 7pm-1am Tue-Thu, to 2am Fri & Sat; 🚆 Petaling) Tap into the local music scene at this grungy, arty venue, which hosts concerts and open-mic nights (and shakes up a decent cocktail). Happy hour is reliably 6pm to 9pm, but see the website for upcoming events. Performers are paid through tips, so fill the jar generously.

🔒 Shopping

1 Utama   MALL
(🗹 03-7710 8118; www.1utama.com.my; 1 Lr Bandar Utama, Petaling Jaya; ⊙ 10am-10pm Sun-Thu, to 10.30pm Fri & Sat; 🚆 LRT Kelana Jaya) The main reason to visit this mall is its 2790-sq-metre

Secret Garden, one of the largest roof gardens in the world, with more than 500 varieties of plants (weekends and public holidays only). There's also a mini-rainforest in the mall's atrium and the climbing centre **Camp5** (☑ 03-7726 0410; www.camp5.com; 5th fl; day pass adult/child RM36/16, 1hr taster session incl equipment RM55; ☺ 2-11pm Mon-Fri, 10am-8pm Sat & Sun; Ⓜ Bandar Utama).

Jaya One   MALL
(☑ 03-7957 4933; http://jayaone.com.my; 72A Jln Universiti, Petaling Jaya; ☺ 10am-10pm; Ⓜ Asia Jaya) Home to the performing-arts centre **PJ Live Arts** (www.pjlivearts.my), which hosts regular music, comedy and family-friendly shows, Jaya One is chock-full of shops and places to eat. It's also the venue for **Markets** (www.facebook.com/marketsmy), a huge bazaar of vendors selling new and old items, as well as handicrafts, held almost every month; check its Facebook page.

Sunway Pyramid   MALL
(☑ 03-7494 3100; www.sunwaypyramid.com; 3 Jln PJS, 11/11 Bandar Sunway, Petaling Jaya; ☺ 10am-10pm; Ⓡ Setia Jaya) Distinguished by its monumental Ancient Egypt–style decor, including a crowning pyramid, this vast mall buzzes with high-end brands, restaurants and a good food court. A central ice rink (p115) allows skaters to pirouette in full view of shoppers. Other entertainments include a bowling alley, multiplex cinema and the adjoining water park, Sunway Lagoon (p115).

❶ Getting There & Away

The Kelana Jaya LRT line connects Putra Heights with central Kuala Lumpur, passing numerous stations in Petaling Jaya on the way.

KTM Komuter trains run from KL Sentral to Shah Alam (RM4, 30 minutes, every 20 to 30 minutes) via Petaling station (RM2.10).

Klang & Pelabuhan Klang
☑ 03 / POP 276,730

Unless they're making use of ferries to Sumatra, most travellers will cruise through Selangor blissfully unaware of the existence of Klang. The town is split between frenetic Klang town and its port, Pelabuhan Klang (7km east). This is a colourful place where traffic jams are made worthwhile by colonial-era architecture, and day trips beckon to islands such as culture-rich Carey and low-slung Ketam. Meanwhile, a discerning population of local food lovers are queuing for

perfectly balanced *bak kut teh* (stewed pork ribs) and feeding an ever-growing coffee scene.

Klang, 35km west of Kuala Lumpur, is easily accessed via the KTM Komuter train.

◉ Sights

Klang is small enough to explore on foot. Jln Tengku Kelana is the heart of the town's colourful **Little India**.

Tourism Selangor also offers a free, 2½-hour guided **walk** (☑ 03-5513 2000; www.tourismselangor.my; ☺ 9-11.45am Sat & Sun) **FREE** covering nine of the town's heritage sights.

★**Galeri Diraja Sultan Abdul Aziz**   MUSEUM
(☑ 03-3373 6500; www.galeridiraja.com; Jln Stesen, Klang; ☺ 10am-5pm Tue-Sun; Ⓟ) **FREE** Housed within a well-restored colonial-era building are treasures of the Selangor Sultanate, which dates back to 1766. The building, designed by prolific architect AB Hubback and built in 1909, is reason enough to visit. Inside, collections of royal seals, silver cigar cases and celebrity-autographed golf clubs offer insights into the royal lifestyle. Bonus: there's some bizarre taxidermy.

Towards the end of the gallery there's some intriguing regional miscellany; look out for the skull of a 6.5m crocodile captured from the Klang River in 1961.

It's five minutes' walk south from the train station.

Masjid Diraja Sultan Suleiman   MOSQUE
(off Jln Kota Raja, Klang; Ⓟ) There's something a little sci-fi about the soaring concrete domes and rocket-ship minaret of this former state mosque. Opened in 1934 it's a striking blend of art deco, neoclassical and Middle Eastern influences. Four sultans are buried here.

Dress modestly and, provided there's someone to usher you in, you can step inside the octagonal prayer hall to admire the stained-glass dome.

Klang Fire Station   MUSEUM
(Balai Bomba Klang Selatan; ☑ 03-3371 4444; Jln Gedung Raja Abdullah, Klang; ☺ 8am-6pm) **FREE** This vividly red-and-white-striped fire station has occupied the same Victorian-style building since the 1890s and now also houses a small museum dedicated to the history of Klang's fire service.

If you're lucky the fire station chief himself might be on hand to show you the exhibits, which include a wind-up siren from 1945, historic fire extinguishers, uniforms, hoses and nozzles.

ISLAND DAY TRIPS FROM KLANG

If you're looking for an off-the-beaten-track day trip from Klang (or indeed, from Kuala Lumpur), try Pulau Ketam, reached by ferry, or Pulau Carey, reached by road.

Pulau Ketam (Crab Island; www.pulauketam.com) This charming fishing village built on stilts over the mudflats gets its name from the abundance of crabs found here. There's little to do other than wander around the village's wooden buildings, snap pictures and enjoy a Chinese seafood lunch at one of several restaurants, but most find this good enough. Ferries (return adult/child RM15/9) depart from Klang's local ferry terminal, across the street from Pelabuhan Klang Station.

Pulau Carey This island, 40km southwest of KL (reachable by road), is home to the **Mah Meri Cultural Village** (☑03-2282 3035, 010-252 2800; http://mmcv.org.my; Kampung Orang Asli Sungai Bumbun; RM20; ☺9am-6pm Sat & Sun, book ahead Mon-Fri). It's well worth a visit to learn about the distinct culture and traditions of the Mah Meri, a subgroup of the Senoi people who live along the coast of Selangor. The Mah Meri are renowned for masterful woodcarving and expressive masks worn during dance rituals to represent ancestral spirits. Call or email before making the journey, as the cultural village mostly caters to visiting groups. If you don't have your own wheels, hire a taxi to Pulau Carey from Klang (a round trip with a couple of hours on the island costs RM160).

🛏 Sleeping & Eating

Talents Motor Park Inn   MOTEL $
(☑03-3167 0052; http://talentsmotorparkhotel.com; Lot 29700, Persiaran Raja, Muda Musa, Kampung Raja Uda; d/tr/q not incl breakfast RM95/130/168; ▣❄❈) Talents succeeds surprisingly well in its attempt to export Australia-style motor inns to Malaysia. The result involves simple, clean rooms with fridges, kettles and wet-room bathrooms, each facing its own parking space and with friendly staff presiding over it all. Ideal if you have wheels; otherwise, it's a lonely location between the port and Klang town.

★ Yap Kee   MALAYSIAN $
(20 Jln Besar, Klang; mains from RM11.50; ☺10.30am-4.30pm) This spartan banana-leaf restaurant in an old shophouse, two blocks to the right as you leave the train station, usually has only a couple of choices available. But it's legendary in Klang: fish, crunchy fried chicken and expertly cooked vegetable curries laid onto banana leaves. No fanfare, just good food – a formula unchanged for more than 70 years.

Seng Huat Bak Kut Teh   MALAYSIAN $$
(☑012-309 8303; www.senghuatbakkutteh.com; 9 Jln Besar, Klang; mains RM11-20; ☺7.30am-12.30pm & 5.30-8.30pm; ☑) Klang is famous for *bak kut teh*, pork stew made by simmering ribs in a fragrant broth of star anise, ginseng, orange peel and other spices. Welcoming Seng Huat, beneath Klang Bridge, has been busy finessing the recipe since 1979 and we think it's the best in town – get here early before the meat sells out.

It's two blocks to the right as you exit the train station.

🍷 Drinking & Nightlife

★ Seraph Awaken   COFFEE
(☑012-290 6860; www.facebook.com/seraph awaken; 28 Jln Stesen 1, Klang; ☺noon-7pm Mon, Thu & Fri, 10am-6pm Sat & Sun) Coffee making is approached with scientific precision by Cheau See and Chun Hoong, who serve hand-brewed drip coffee from a counter laden with beakers and rubber tubes. The couple started out with a roadside coffee stall before moving into a beautiful, plant-filled *kopitiam* (coffee shop) dating from 1928. Watch the website for live music and cultural events at the cafe.

Coffee Ink   CAFE
(☑03-3319 3591; www.facebook.com/coffeeinklg; 19 Jln Remia 3, 1st fl, Bandar Botanik; ☺11am-11.30pm Tue-Sun; ☈) Seven kilometres south of Klang town there's a chic set of art-cafes and coffee haunts, and one of the best is Coffee Ink. Abstract art, wooden birdcages and cloud-like lamps add whimsy to this high-ceilinged coffee lounge. Sandwiches, fries and rice dishes are offered, but the brews are best.

ℹ Getting There & Away

KTM Komuter trains run from KL Sentral to Klang (RM5.20, one hour, every 20 to 30 minutes).

Klang's bus station is on the other side of the river from the main sights. To get here from the train station, head right and then cross the bridge. On the other side, the main bus station can be seen straight ahead (regular buses to Kuala Lumpur, RM9, take around one hour but you're at the mercy of the traffic).

For buses to Kuala Selangor turn left after crossing the bridge and wait under the overpass about a block past the 7-Eleven. Buses run every hour or so (RM6).

Taxis to Pulau Carey (RM160 return, including waiting time) can be hired directly outside the train station.

Five stops down the KTM line from Klang is Pelabuhan Klang station (RM2.30/6.40 from Klang/KL), which is across the road from local and international ferries. To the left as you face the water is a **jetty** (Pelabuhan Klang) with boats to Pulau Ketam (return adult/child RM15/9).

To the right are ferries serving two locations in Sumatra, Indonesia: Tanjung Balai (one way/return RM110/190, four hours, one daily except Sunday) and Dumai (one way/return RM110/170, 3½ hours, 10am Tuesday, Thursday and Saturday). To check ferry times, call the **International Ferry Terminal** (☑ 03-3167 7186; Pelabuhan Klang). Unless you speak the language, this isn't an easy (or especially enjoyable) crossing.

Kuala Selangor

☑ 03 / POP 205,000

Best known for nightly light shows of fireflies along the Sungai Selangor, Kuala Selangor has a friendly *kampung* (village) atmosphere and a smattering of worthwhile sights. A former military fort crowns the town, and is worth a ramble for its museum and lighthouse. At the foot of the hill is a nature park in the mangroves, while the city centre is a cheery assemblage of *kedai kopi* (coffee shops) and shops.

If you have your own vehicle, the town is an easy jaunt from Kuala Lumpur (70km southeast), with plenty of pretty countryside to explore nearby.

◉ Sights & Activities

Taman Alam Kuala Selangor   NATURE RESERVE
(☑ 03-3289 2294; www.mns.my/kuala-selangor-nature-park-ksnp; Jln Klinik; adult/child RM4/1; ⊙ 9am-6pm) On the estuary of Sungai Selangor, at the foot of Bukit Malawati, this 240-hectare park features three ecosystems to explore: secondary forest, an artificial lake and a mangrove forest with views out to sea. Cover them all on a 3km trail that includes a raised walkway above the mangroves and several lookout towers. This is a wonderful place to spot wildlife, including birds (September begins the migratory season), wild pigs, mudskippers and silvered leaf monkeys.

If you want to stay overnight, accommodation at the park entrance includes no-frills A-frame huts (RM30) or two-bed (one single, one queen) wooden chalets with fan and attached bathroom (RM60). There's no food available, but the restaurants in town are less than 10 minutes' walk away.

Bukit Malawati   HISTORIC SITE
FREE It's a short walk through landscaped parklands to the top of Bukit Malawati, with views across the mangrove-dotted coastline. Once an administrative and military fort, all that remains today are sections of wall, cannons and a **well**, formerly filled with various poisons and used to torture traitors. At the summit is a picturesque British **lighthouse** (dating from 1907) and a small **museum** (History Museum; ☑ 03- 3289 7167; ⊙ 9.30am-5.30pm Sun-Thu, 9.30am-noon & 2.45-5.30pm Fri) **FREE** of local history.

The fort here was briefly conquered by the Dutch when they invaded Selangor in 1784; Sultan Ibrahim took it back a year later. The town later became embroiled in the Selangor Civil War (1867–73), which saw the fort partly destroyed.

The road up Bukit Malawati starts from the edge of town and does a clockwise loop of the hill; you can walk up and around in less than an hour. Further down the hill is the **Royal Mausoleum**, the burial ground for the first three sultans of Selangor.

Tame silvered leaf monkeys hang out here, but resist feeding them.

Kampung Kuantan   WILDLIFE WATCHING
(per boat RM53; ⊙ 7-10pm) The main place for viewing fireflies around Kuala Selangor is Kampung Kuantan, 8km east of the city. Malay-style wooden boats (leaving on demand) take up to four people for a 45-minute river trip to the 'show trees' and their dazzling displays, rather reminiscent of a light-spangled Christmas tree. Bring insect repellent. It's most easily reached with your own vehicle.

Trips aren't recommended on full-moon or rainy nights as the fireflies are not at their luminous best.

⏤ Sleeping

VI   BOUTIQUE HOTEL **$$**
(☑ 03-3281 2219; www.facebook.com/viboutique hotel; 1 Jln Sri Penambang; d/ste not incl breakfast RM110/237; 🅿 ❄ 🀫 🐾) Plump modern beds set against a pared-down industrial aesthetic...always a satisfying combination. The 48-room VI is one of Kuala Selangor's more

contemporary accommodation options. It adjoins an excellent cafe and it's 2km north of the centre. Wi-fi's at reception only.

It books up quickly at weekends due to tour groups; reserve ahead.

De Palma Hotel Kuala Selangor   HOTEL **$$**
(☑ 03-3289 7070; www.depalmahotel.com; Jln Tanjung Keramat; d/ste incl breakfast from RM160/240; P ✽ @ 🛜 ☒) Surrounded by palm trees, 1.5km north of the entrance to Bukit Malawati, is this modest, Muslim-owned miniresort. Wooden cabins, brightened by colourful feature walls, are in a reasonably good state of repair and there's a decent outdoor pool. Wi-fi at reception only.

Firefly Park Resort   HOTEL **$$**
(☑ 03-3260 1208; www.facebook.com/FireflyPark Resort; Jln Haji Omar, Kampung Bukit Belimbing; chalets for 4 not incl breakfast from RM159; P ✽ ☒) In a village setting ideal for firefly watchers, this midrange resort has plainly decorated, comfortable four-person chalets perched on stilts over the river and pleasant landscaped grounds. Boat trips to watch the fireflies cost RM25/9 for adults/children. It's 8km northeast of central Kuala Selangor.

🍴 Eating & Drinking

For seafood in a casual setting, head to **Pasir Penambang**, a fishing village on the northern side of the river, where a number of chaotic seafood restaurants are clustered. If you don't have your own transport, ask your hotel to arrange a taxi (RM10 to RM15).

Auntie Foo   MALAYSIAN, CAFE **$**
(Jln Raja Abdullah; breakfasts from RM3, mains from RM5; ⊙ 8.30am-6.30pm; 🛜) A block southeast of stalwart **Auntie Kopitiam** (☑ 03-3289 7289; C3, Jln Sultan Ibrahim; meals RM5-12; ⊙ 6.30am-6pm) is younger, fresher Auntie Foo, which attracts a mixed crowd of locals and tourists...mainly for the coconut shakes. There's a good choice of Malay mains and desserts: *nasi lemak* (rice boiled in coconut milk, served with fried *ikan bilis* peanuts and a curry dish) with spicy beef rendang, followed by shaved-ice and green-noodle dessert *cendol,* is a classic.

★ Café Lumière   CAFE
(☑ 018-291 2799; www.facebook.com/cafelumiereks; 50 Jln Stesen; ⊙ noon-5pm Wed-Mon) With guitars, clocks and rock icons set against its whitewashed brick walls, Café Lumière has a loose Parisian theme and an upbeat atmosphere. Daily food specials rotate between spaghetti bolognese, bangers and mash, sticky lemon chicken and various Europetinged recipes, while the coffee is consistently excellent. Pricey by Kuala Selangor standards but wholly worthwhile.

ℹ Getting There & Away

Catch bus 740 to/from Klang (RM5, one hour, half-hourly) or bus 100 to/from Kuala Lumpur's Medan Pasar bus hub, just up from Central Market (RM9, two hours, half-hourly).

A taxi one way from Kuala Lumpur will cost around RM80, but it may be difficult to persuade a KL taxi driver to take you only one way; consider renting a taxi for a day or half-day, if you aren't driving. Alternatively, join a firefly tour from KL with a company such as Viator (www. viator.com).

NEGERI SEMBILAN

Seremban
☑ 06 / POP 620,100

Seremban, 70km southeast of Kuala Lumpur, wears its charms lightly. Its ramshackle district of Chinese shophouses, regal colonial buildings dotted alongside attractive Lake Gardens, and famous beef noodles are enjoyable diversions if you're looking for a detour between KL and Melaka, or heading towards Port Dickson's beach resorts.

Like KL, Seremban's roots lie in the discovery of tin in the late 19th century, which saw prospectors flock to the village originally known as Sungai Ujong. Today Negeri Sembilan's state capital, its atmosphere is more low-key than it was during the old tin-mining boom times.

◉ Sights

★ Muzium Negeri Sembilan   MUSEUM
(Kompleks Taman Seni Budaya; ☑ 06-763 1149; Jln Sungai Ujong; ⊙ 9am-5pm Sat-Thu, 9am-12.15pm & 2.45-5pm Fri) FREE State history, from traditional weapons to blow-by-blow accounts of European invasions, is well presented at this museum 2.5km southwest of central Seremban. The main building has a Minangkabau-style peaked roof; even more interesting are the two wooden stilt houses outside, the **Istana Ampang Tinggi** (1860s) and the **Rumah Negeri Sembilan**, both transported and reconstructed here from elsewhere in the state. They're superb

examples of Minangkabau architecture – clamber up the ladders for a closer look at their wooden ornamentation.

Note the beautifully carved foliage panels on the outer walls of the Istana Ampang Tinggi. The Rumah Negeri Sembilan has the curved roof (like buffalo horns) common to Minangkabau buildings and was constructed without using any metal nails.

If you don't have your own vehicle, a taxi from town will cost less than RM10, or you can drop in on the way to Sri Menanti.

📛 Sleeping

Port Dickson and KL are less than an hour away by road, each with a broader and better set of accommodation options, so it's worth considering Seremban as a day trip.

Royale Chulan Seremban   HOTEL $$

(☑ 06-7666666; www.royalechulan-seremban.com; Jln Dato AS Dawood; d RM320-477, ste RM646, incl breakfast; P❋🛜😺) Large rooms with big writing desks walk the line between business and chic at this beige-toned behemoth next to the Lake Gardens. This is Seremban's classiest place to stay, and while some rooms feel worn, the facilities are grand: a landscaped outdoor pool and Jacuzzi, traditional spa and a big international breakfast spread.

🍴 Eating & Drinking

Pasar Besar   HAWKER, MARKET $

(Main Market; off Jln Pasar; noodles RM5.50; ⊘7am-noon) Seremban's main food market (1975) is a local institution, with dozens of stalls flowing out from its central wet market. Take your pick of vendors dishing up Seremban's signature beef noodles – **stall 748** makes a rich, delicious version of the dish. Go early for the biggest choice.

★Haji Shariff's Cendol   DESSERTS $

(44 Jln Yam Tuan; cendol from RM1.50; ⊘10.30am-6pm Sat-Thu) Since the 1930s the Shariff family has been serving up refreshingly sweet bowls of *cendol* (an icy dessert made with pandan noodles, coconut milk and jaggery syrup). Order from the counter inside this green 1919 shophouse: *cendol biasa* gets you the dessert plain (a clean, fresh taste), but it's even better with chewy red bean (*kacang*) or glutinous rice (*pulut*).

It also serves a local version of *mee rojak* (noodles with a spicy tomato rather than soy sauce; RM4.50).

Kee Mei Siew Pao   MALAYSIAN $

(cnr Jln Dr Krishnan & Jln Dato Bandar Tunggal; pork bun RM1.80; ⊘8am-6pm, closed every 2nd & 4th Tue of month) This basic shop is a great place to pick up some of Seremban's famous *pao* (golden pastry pork buns).

Also worth a nibble are the black sesame and *kaya* (coconut-cream jam) puffs.

La Roasteria   CAFE

(☑010-546 8200; www.facebook.com/laroasteria coffee; 16 Jln Kong Sang; ⊘8am-6pm Tue-Sun; 🛜) Western-style coffees come with a correspondingly high price tag at La Roasteria, but we still can't resist its iced coffee and banana-croissant pudding. Travel miscellany such as suitcases makes the charcoal-walled interior even cosier.

THE LAKE GARDENS & COLONIAL DISTRICT

The **Lake Gardens** (Taman Tasik Seremban; Jln Taman Bunga) are the centrepiece of the old colonial-era district; start here for a short walking tour into Seremban's past. Pinched between two busy roads, the gardens aren't exactly serene, but their walking paths and lawns are refreshing to stroll. Dip southeast for a quick look at 1923-founded **King George V School** (Jln Za'aba), Seremban's premier colonial-era academic institution and still a functioning school.

Walking northeast along Jln Dato Hamzah, which follows the far side of the park, you'll see **Masjid Negeri Sembilan** (State Mosque; Jln Dato Hamzah), the state mosque, with its nine external pillars representing the nine original fiefdoms of Seremban. Continuing north note the **Kompleks Kraf Negeri Sembilan** (☑06-767 1388; cnr Jln Bukit & Jln Sehala) in a handsome 1912 mansion that was once home to British Resident Captain Murray. From the same era is the even grander neoclassical **State Library** (off Jln Dato Hamzah), once the offices of the colonial administration. It was built in 1912 and designed by AB Hubback, the architect responsible for many heritage buildings in KL and beyond. Across the road is the **Istana Besar**, home of the Sultan of Negeri Sembilan.

Seremban

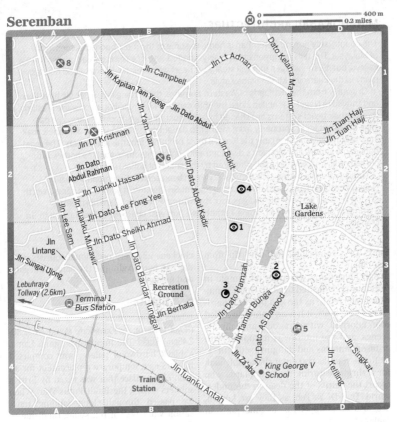

Seremban

◉ Sights
1 Kompleks Kraf Negeri Sembilan C3
2 Lake Gardens C3
3 Masjid Negeri Sembilan C3
4 State Library C2

🛏 Sleeping
5 Royale Chulan Seremban D4

🍴 Eating
6 Haji Shariff's Cendol B2
7 Kee Mei Siew Pao A2
8 Pasar Besar A1

🍸 Drinking & Nightlife
9 La Roasteria A2

🛈 Getting There & Away

KTM Komuter trains shuttle between KL Sentral and Seremban (RM8.70, 1¼ hours, half-hourly).

There are also buses to/from Kuala Lumpur and many large centres such as Melaka (RM7.50 to RM8.80, 1½ hours, hourly) leaving from the **Terminal 1 bus station** (off Jln Tuanku Munawir).

Long-distance taxis operate from outside both the train station and the bus station and have fixed prices to various destinations. A one-way fare to a beach resort at Port Dickson is around RM60 to RM70.

Central Seremban is walkable. Taxis line up near Terminal 1 and around Pasar Besar. Journeys within town should cost less than RM10.

Kuala Pilah

🗹 06 / POP 66,000

Rows of Chinese shophouses set a colourful scene in Kuala Pilah, 40km east of Seremban, but the centrepiece of this valley town is the ornate temple **Sansheng Gong** (Sansheng Temple; Jln Dato Undang Johol; ⊙ 7am-

MINANGKABAU ARCHITECTURE

The countryside around Seremban is home to some of the most bucolic scenes in all of Malaysia. The hills are green and densely wooded, and rice fields spread across the valleys, but it's the villages that will steal your heart with their traditional wood houses, many in the charming Minangkabau style.

Originally from the highlands of Western Sumatra, the Minangkabau people have lived and thrived in Negeri Sembilan since the 15th century. Minangkabau people are Muslims, though their belief systems are shaped by adat, customs that predate Islam. The passage of Minangkabau property from mother to daughter has endured for centuries, making the Minangkabau arguably the world's most prominent matrilineal society. The most noticeable feature is the region's distinct traditional architecture, such as homes with curved roofs and pointed gables inspired by the shape of buffalo horns.

Good examples of this architectural style can been seen in Seremban's Muzium Negeri Sembilan (p119) and the old royal town of Sri Menanti. If you have a car it's worth driving through some of the villages, too: **Kampung Pantai** is 10km northeast of Seremban on Federal Rte 86, while **Terachi** is 27km east on Rte 51 at the turn-off to Sri Menanti.

6pm). It's a compelling half-day trip from Seremban.

Sansheng Gong was the first temple in the country dedicated to Guan Gong, sometimes referred to as the god of war. Guarded by stone lions, it has an impressive tiled roof adorned with dragons and mythic scenes, and the interior is festooned with crimson lanterns and dangling sculptures.

To the right as you enter the temple look for a shrine featuring the two guards who escort the spirits of the dead to the underworld. Dua Di Ya Peh, as they are known, are also worshipped as fortune gods in Malaysia.

Across the road from the temple is a *pailou* (archway) dedicated to Martin Lister, the first British Resident (1889–97) of Negeri Sembilan.

❶ Getting There & Away

There are regular buses to/from Seremban (RM4, one hour, half-hourly). Buses from Kuala Pilah also link to Kuala Lumpur (RM10, two hours, half-hourly).

Sri Menanti

🕗 06

The palatial architecture dotted around Sri (or Seri) Menanti belies its languid pace. Nestled in a highland valley, this sleepy hamlet was first settled over 500 years ago by Minangkabau immigrants from Sumatra. Sri Menanti became Negeri Sembilan's royal capital in the 18th century. Today the silence is only interrupted by birdsong, scampering chickens and very occasional tourists, who day trip here to glimpse the palace, museum and mosque.

◉ Sights

Istana Lama MUSEUM, PALACE
(Royal Museum; 🕗10am-6pm, closed Fri 12.30-2.45pm) FREE The impressive Istana Lama, a black hardwood palace, was completed in 1908 as a temporary replacement for an even older palace that was razed by British soldiers during the Bukit Putus War. When we passed through, long-standing renovation work was in full swing (and due to finish in 2020), but visitors could tour the grounds and the outside of the palace.

Note the ornate, gilt eaves and the roof, assembled using a traditional method known as *lipatan gunting* (folding scissor) technique.

Arranged over four floors, with long galleries, and a distinctive gabled tower in the centre, the palace was fashioned without the use of metal nails. It's elevated on 99 pillars, many of them carved with foliated designs, with each post said to represent one of the legendary 99 *luak* (clan) warriors of Negeri Sembilan. Climb to the top floor for views over the gardens.

Inside are displayed the king and queen's bedchambers, the children's playroom, a large dining room and huge dining table, as well as kris weaponry and royal regalia.

It's located straight across the main roundabout as you drive west along Sri Menanti's main road.

Istana Besar
PALACE

Just beyond Sri Menanti's tiny Lake Gardens is Istana Besar, the impressive modern white palace of the Yamtuan Besar (the head of state) of Negeri Sembilan. It was built in the 1930s and is not open to the public.

Makam Diraja
CEMETERY

(Royal Cemetery) Next to the brass-domed mosque, visible almost immediately as you turn right onto Sri Menanti's main road from N29, is the royal cemetery, which has a distinctive Victorian/Moorish pavilion. Shaded by large green domes immediately inside the gates is the prominent grave of Tuanku Abdul Rahman, the first *yang di-pertuan agong* (or 'king') of independent Malaysia.

ⓘ Getting There & Away

You'll need private transport to reach Sri Menanti, which lies an easy 30km drive east and south from Seremban (6km off the Seremban–Kuala Pilah road, Federal Rte 51). A round-trip taxi from Seremban costs around RM100.

Port Dickson

☑ 06

The closest beach area to Kuala Lumpur, Port Dickson (PD) is popular with locals, Singaporeans and resident foreign expats. Compared to the enticing shores elsewhere in Malaysia, Port Dickson's beaches don't compete, but if you're seeking a family-friendly, amenity-packed resort experience, it's an easy escape from KL – provided you have your own transport.

Note that when people talk about Port Dickson they're usually referring to the coastline and not Port Dickson town, a small and unexciting settlement slightly inland.

◉ Sights & Activities

There's close to 24km of coastline, much of it undeveloped, with several popular public beach areas outside the resorts. If you visit the public beaches be aware that local Malay rules of propriety prevail: dress modestly (cover up with T-shirt and shorts over skimpy swimsuits) and if you're a couple, keep the PDA to a minimum.

★ Cape Rachado Forest Reserve
NATURE RESERVE

(Tanjung Tuan Forest Reserve; Jln Pantai; RM1; ⏰ 7am-6pm) A world away from the resorts is 80-hectare Cape Rachado Forest Reserve. A paved road (pedestrians only) leads through towering jungle to brilliant-white Tanjung Tuan lighthouse, Malaysia's oldest.

In 1606 the seas around the cape blazed with a naval battle between the Portuguese and Dutch armadas; the Portuguese outgunned the Dutch but were later forced to capitulate. Since 1921 the area's been a nature reserve, visited annually by 300,000 migratory birds and used as an egg-laying site by turtles.

The reserve is 2km down a turn-off from the main road through Port Dickson. You can park at the Ilham Resort and then hike through the forest. Stick to the marked trails unless you're a trained survivalist.

The lighthouse, a 20-minute uphill hike from the park entrance, isn't open to the public, but you can walk around it for great sea views. On a clear day you can see Sumatra, 38km away across Selat Melaka (Strait of Melaka).

SELANGOR & NEGERI SEMBILAN PORT DICKSON

ANCIENT MEGALITHS

There are hundreds of megaliths scattered across Peninsular Malaysia, most concentrated in Melaka and Negeri Sembilan. Their origin and purpose remains obscure, as does their age, though they are often found in Muslim cemeteries. The megaliths here could be a few hundred years old, from the time of the Minangkabau arrival, or they could be thousands of years old. Locals call them Batu Hidup (Living Stones), which may be a reference to the fact they seem to grow over the years, the result of land erosion around them. Surprisingly, megaliths aren't believed to be sacred.

When we last visited, some stones that had been previously left in the open air were being taken away for study and display in museums, but you can see a good example at the **Pengkalan Kempas Megalith Site** (Kampung Batu China), a 15th-century Muslim cemetery 20km east of Port Dickson.

Avillion Admiral Cove
BOATING

(☑06-647 0888; www.avillionadmiralcove.com; 5½ mile, Jln Pantai) This large resort and marina has various water-sport options for nonguests; ask at reception. You can rent kayaks (per hour RM47) and banana boats (per person RM24 to RM33), hire a jet ski (RM118 for 15 minutes) or take a 30-minute boat cruise (per boat RM470, individual prices depend on group size).

✻✫ Festivals & Events

Raptor Watch Festival
WILDLIFE

(https://mnsraptorwatch.wordpress.com; per person RM1; ☉Mar) At the height of the bird migratory period, usually in early March, the Raptor Watch Festival offers one or two days of bird-watching walks through Cape Rachado Forest Reserve. Register when you arrive and BYOB (bring your own binoculars).

🛏 Sleeping

Rates are usually 15% lower on weekdays, and 10% higher on peak public holidays.

Avillion Admiral Cove
RESORT $$

(☑06-647 0888; www.avillionadmiralcove.com; 5½ mile, Jln Pantai; d incl breakfast RM202-350; P❄@☎❄) Rooms at Avillion Admiral Cove are modestly decorated, their beds screened off from the living area. The 'panorama' rooms gaze at glinting views of the marina, but the less expensive 'superior' rooms are just as ample. The water sports available on site are reason enough to stay, but the fixed-priced buffet dinners (and enormous breakfast banquets) seal the deal.

PNB Ilham Resort
RESORT $$

(☑06-662 6800; www.ilhamresort.com; Batu 10, Tanjung Biru; d/apt incl breakfast from RM238/330; P❄☎❄) This large resort has a quiet stretch of white-sand beach to itself, and classic, wood-floored rooms encircling a large central pool. Ilham has a low-slung, casual feel compared to some of the other resorts (and some rooms feel fusty), but the location is ideal for rambles into Cape Rachado Forest Reserve.

★ Avillion Port Dickson
RESORT $$$

(☑06-647 6688; www.avillionportdickson.com; Jln Pantai; d RM325-515, chalet RM420-1530, incl breakfast; P❄☎❄) Beautifully designed and lushly planted with lily ponds, birds of paradise, bromeliads and palms, this highly awarded five-star has over-the-water chalets evoking a traditional Malay fishing village, only with luxurious amenities. Even the cheaper rooms are classier than just about anywhere else in Port Dickson, with hardwood floors, elegant wood furnishings, flagstone bathrooms and loads of natural light.

Thistle Port Dickson Resort
RESORT $$$

(☑06-648 2828; www.thistle.com.my/portdickson; Jln Pantai; d/f incl breakfast from RM400/736; P❄@☎❄) This exclusive resort, set in 36 hectares of landscaped grounds, features a private 3km beach, golf course, magnificent pool, beautiful views, a fitness centre and more.

🍴 Eating

All resorts have restaurants (and some bars) on the premises, and most are open to nonguests.

If you have a vehicle, it's worth seeking out the local food stalls that pop up along the main road. Seafood is the speciality, but you can also get Thai curries, Malay staples and snacks such as satay, *cendol* and coconut shakes.

PD Famous Cendol
DESSERTS $

(Kampung Teluk Kemang; cendol RM2-5; ☉11am-7pm) *Cendol* takes a variety of colourful forms at this roadside dessert shop: durian flavour, topped with rice or red beans, or perhaps with a scoop of ice cream. We also recommend the coconut shakes.

There are stalls selling savoury food too, such as *cucur udang* (prawn fritters) and curry noodles.

Crow's Nest
MALAYSIAN $$

(☑06-647 6688; http://avillionportdickson.com; Avillion Port Dickson, Jln Pantai; mains RM35-55; ☉11am-11pm; P☎) For a mix of Malay and Western food (think burgers, nasi goreng and soups), this swish modern restaurant at Avillion Port Dickson is a reliable bet. Grab a terrace table for excellent views of the coast.

ℹ Getting There & Around

Port Dickson is best reached and explored by private transport, but it's possible to get here using public transport. First take the KTM Komuter train from Kuala Lumpur to Seremban (RM8.70) and then a taxi (RM60, or around RM45 through a ride-share app such as Grab) from the Terminal 1 bus station.

There's little to no public transport around the beach areas. Ask your resort to order you a taxi should you need one, and be prepared to wait a while for it.

Perak

♩05 / POP 2.48 MILLION

Includes ➜

Ipoh. 127
Gopeng & Around. . . .134
Cameron Highlands . . .136
Pulau Pangkor 143
Kuala Kangsar. 148
Taiping 151
Kuala Sepetang 155
Belum-Temenggor
Rainforest 156

Best Places to Eat

➡ Restaurant Lou Wong (p132)

➡ Nipah Deli (p147)

➡ Singh Chapati (p141)

➡ Lim Ko Pi (p131)

➡ Ansari Famous Cendol (p153)

Best Places to Stay

➡ Pangkor Laut Resort (p147)

➡ The Happy 8 (p129)

➡ Banjaran Hotsprings Retreat (p129)

➡ The Shop (p150)

➡ Adeline's Villa (p136)

➡ Belum Eco Resort (p157)

Why Go?

This rugged swath of Peninsular Malaysia is as rewarding for trekkers as for gastronomes. Perak (literally 'silver', a nod to its tin-mining boom times) receives only a modest stream of international travellers, but to Malaysians, its attractions are totemic: white coffee, colonial-era relics, limestone bluffs.

Nostalgia is rife in Ipoh and Taiping, Perak's largest and most appealing towns. But Perak is most interesting beyond its population centres: surrounding Ipoh are temples posing dramatically on cliffs; west of Taiping is a mangrove reserve. Things get wetter and wilder at river-rafting centre Gopeng, and north in Royal Belum State Park, where pristine rainforest is interspersed with lagoons.

Perak is also a good starting point to explore the Cameron Highlands (technically in Pahang) and its breezy hill stations, where days are spent hiking and slathering cream onto scones.

When to Go
Ipoh

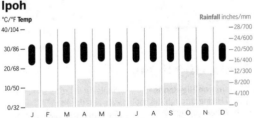

Dec–Feb Sizzle on Pangkor's beaches or ring in Chinese New Year in Ipoh or Taiping.

Jun–Aug Bird-watch in Belum or hike the Cameron Highlands before heavier rains set in.

Oct & Nov During Perak's wetter months, take a city break in Ipoh or Taiping.

Perak Highlights

1 **Cameron Highlands** (p136) Hiking through the cool highlands, enjoying tea and scones.

2 **Temple Caves** (p128) Marvelling at the spiritual retreats in Perak's serrated limestone cliffs.

3 **Ipoh** (p127) Strolling a mural-laden old town,

indulging in Ipoh's signature eats and drinks.

4 **Pulau Pangkor** (p143) Spotting hornbills from a beach hammock at a popular island getaway.

5 **Gopeng** (p134) Exploring caves and getting thrillingly river-splashed at this adventurous outpost.

6 **Royal Belum State Park** (p156) Muddying your hiking boots on a guided walk through a dam-flooded jungle reserve.

7 **Taiping** (p151) Meandering past elegantly wasted colonial buildings in between bites of street food.

History

Perak can lay claim to some of the most ancient roots in Peninsular Malaysia, thanks to archaeological findings in the Lenggong Valley that date back to the Palaeolithic era.

Today's sultanate of Perak dates back to the early 16th century, when the eldest son of the last sultan of Melaka, Sultan Muzaffar Shah, began a new dynasty on the banks of Sungai Perak (Perak River). The state's rich tin deposits quickly made it a target of both covetous neighbours and foreign forces.

Dutch efforts in the 17th century to monopolise the tin trade were unsuccessful, but remains of their forts can still be seen on Pulau Pangkor (Pangkor Island) and at the mouth of Sungai Perak. In the 18th century, the Bugis from the south and the Siamese from the north made concerted attempts to dominate Perak, but British intervention in the 1820s trumped them both.

The British had remained reluctant to meddle in the peninsula's affairs, but growing investment in the Strait settlements, along with the discovery of tin ore in Perak in 1848, encouraged their interest. The mines also attracted a great influx of Chinese immigrants, who soon formed rival clan groups allied with local Malay chiefs, all of whom battled to control the mines.

The Perak sultanate was in disarray, and fighting among successors to the throne gave the British their opportunity to step in, making the first real colonial incursion on the peninsula in 1874. The governor, Sir Andrew Clarke, convened a meeting at Pulau Pangkor at which Sultan Abdullah was installed on the throne instead of Sultan Ismail, the other major contender. The resultant Pangkor Treaty required the sultan to accept a British Resident, and to consult him on all issues other than those relating to religion or Malay custom. One year later, Sultan Abdullah was forced, under threat of deposition, to accept administration by British officials on his behalf.

Various Perak chiefs united against this state of affairs, and the Resident, James WW Birch, was assassinated at Pasir Salak in November 1875. Colonial troops were called in to fight the resulting, brief Perak War. Sultan Abdullah was exiled and a new British-sanctioned sultan was installed. The next British Resident, Sir Hugh Low, had administrative experience in Borneo, was fluent in Malay and was a noted botanist –

he even had a pitcher plant named after him (*Nepenthes lowii*). He assumed control of taxes from the tin mines and practised greater intervention in state affairs. In 1877 he introduced the first rubber trees to Malaysia and experimented with planting tea and coffee as well. The sultans, meanwhile, maintained their status, but were increasingly effete figureheads, bought out with stipends.

The first railway in the state, from Taiping to Port Weld (now known as Kuala Sepetang), was built in 1885 to transport the wealth of tin; the result was rapid development in Taiping and Ipoh. In 1896 Perak, along with Selangor, Pahang and Negeri Sembilan, became part of the Federated Malay States. The system of British Residents (and later Advisers) persisted even after the Japanese invasion and WWII, ending only when Perak became part of the Federation of Malaya in 1948. Perak joined the new independent Malaysia in 1957.

When the tin industry declined in the 1980s, once-thriving towns began to empty and Kuala Lumpur drew increasing numbers of jobseekers out of Perak. Tourism is slowly helping Perak to bounce back, with steadily increasing visitor numbers throughout the late 2010s.

Ipoh

⏱ 05 / POP 710,000

Perak's finest colonial architecture stands side by side with rickety *kedai kopi* (coffee shops) in chameleonic Ipoh. The capital of Perak is flanked by towering white cliffs, some with magnificent cave temples pocketed in the limestone. Sliced into old and new towns by the Kinta River, Ipoh charms with its street and street food – rather like a languid version of George Town.

Ipoh is more than a gateway to the Cameron Highlands or a way station en route to Penang. Shaped by the 1920s tin-mining boom, Ipoh's wealth and population ebbed away after the mines' closure. But an old-town renaissance has revived its time-worn buildings into boutiques, hotels and gorgeously kitsch cafes.

Food is reason enough to visit. Malaysian and Singaporean gastronomes arrive in droves for Ipoh's *tauge ayam* (chicken bean sprouts) and to argue over who serves the best *kopi putih* – white coffee, the town's signature drink.

◉ Sights

Most of Ipoh's grand colonial architecture is found in the old town, west of the Sungai Kinta. Start at the 1917 vintage **train station** (Jln Panglima Bukit Gantang Wahab), a harmonious Moorish and Victorian architectural masterpiece, framed by wide arches and capped with a broad white dome. It was designed by AB Hubback who is also responsible for the nearby gleaming white **town hall** (Dewan Bandaran; Jln Panglima Bukit Gantang Wahab; ☺8am-5pm) dating back to 1916 and the **courthouse** (Jln Panglima Bukit Gantang Wahab) completed in 1928.

On your way into the old town you won't fail to miss the **Birch Memorial Clock Tower** (Jln Dato' Sagor) FREE, erected in 1909 in memory of James WW Birch, Perak's first British Resident. Birch was murdered in 1875 at Pasir Salak by local Malay chiefs. A frieze featuring Moses, Buddha, William Shakespeare and Charles Darwin was intended to illustrate the growth of civilisation. Look for the ghostly outline of a figure representing Mohammed, long ago painted over.

Don't miss atmospheric **Concubine Lane** (Jln Panglima), **Jalan Market** and **Jalan Bandar Timah** – look out for murals with tender portraits of Ipoh life by Lithuanian artist Ernest Zacharevic.

Muzium Darul Ridzuan   MUSEUM
(☎05-241 0048; http://muzium.perak.gov. my; 2020 Jln Panglima Bukit Gantang Wahab; ☺9.30am-5pm Sat-Thu, 9.30am-12.15pm & 2.45-5pm Fri; ℗) FREE North of the *padang* (field), this museum is housed in a 1926 villa built for a wealthy Chinese tin miner. The museum features displays on the history of tin mining (downstairs) and forestry (upstairs) in Perak. Most intriguing are the WWII-era bunkers behind the building. The museum is affected by periodic closures and renovations; check ahead before making a special trip.

DON'T MISS

IPOH'S TEMPLE CAVES

Ipoh's surrounds are a honeycomb of caves, many of which have powerful spiritual associations. Several clifftop meditation spots grew into large complexes. The following three temples make a convenient day trip by car. Ipoh Secrets offers informative guided excursions, or you can hire a local driver such as **Mr Raja** (☎012-524 2357).

Perak Tong (Gua Perak; Jln Kuala Kangsar; ☺8am-4pm; ℗) FREE Developed in 1926 by Chinese Buddhists Chong Sen Yee and his wife, this temple (7km north of Ipoh) is popular for its mesmerising murals and panoramic views. The first staircase leads to a majestic seated Buddha (12m tall) in the main chamber. Some of the surrounding murals were painted as recently as the 1990s. Follow the staircase up and outside; after 450 steep steps you'll reach expansive views across Ipoh and its hilly beyond. Buses bound for Kuala Kangsar can stop near Perak Tong on request.

Kek Look Tong (Gunung Rapat; ☺8am-7pm; ℗) FREE With a craggy cave mouth beneath a towering cliff, Kek Look Tong (1920) has the most impressive approach of all Ipoh's temples. Three Sages dominate the central cavern, while towards the back a cheerful Chinese Buddha of Future Happiness sits in the company of three bodhisattvas. Beyond the main chamber, the cave passage opens onto a lagoon and picturesque gardens, bookended by forested cliffs. It's 8km southeast of central Ipoh. The landscaped gardens deserve attention for their miniature statues, depicting scenes from the life of the Buddha, and reflexology footpath (take off your shoes for the textured walkway). A taxi costs around RM35 each way.

Sam Poh Tong (Gunung Rapat; ☺8am-3.30pm; ℗) FREE First discovered by a monk in 1890, this temple, 5km south of Ipoh, is still used by nuns and monks pursuing solitary meditation. To the right of the entrance is an ornamental garden with ceramic lions, miniature shrines and Buddha statues encircling a rock-studded pond. Continue through the main chamber to a breathtaking scarlet-tiered pavilion with sheer limestone behind. Opposite is a turtle pond: these armoured reptiles are said to rebalance karma when they're released (or fed slices of tomato). The temple can be reached by Gopeng-bound buses from Ipoh.

PAT, R

6864

RESORT STAYS

The opulent **Banjaran Hotsprings Retreat** (☏05-210 7777; www.thebanjaran.com; 1 Persiaran Lagun Sunway 3, Sunway City; villas incl breakfast RM1250-1650; ☏❄@🛜🏊), 8km northeast of Ipoh, offers spacious villas – some overlooking water, others garden-facing – designed to organic effect with wood, stone and rattan. The feather beds are hard to get out of, the private plunge pools even more so.

With a focus on golf, fishing and bird-watching, **Clearwater Sanctuary** (☏05-366 7433; www.cwsgolf.com.my; Batu Gajah; chalet not incl breakfast RM250-475; ☏❄🛜🏊) is a carefully sculpted fresh-air idyll, 15km south of Ipoh. Its wooden chalets, in a contemporary style, overlook an artificial lake. Guests busy themselves on the 18-hole golf course, or spotting purple heron preening in the reeds. Activities include badminton, angling and swanning around in a Jacuzzi.

🏃 Activities & Tours

Use the *Ipoh Heritage Trail* maps 1 and 2, sporadically available at Ipoh's tourist information centre (p133), for a self-guided walking tour of colonial Ipoh, or check out the billboards around Kong Heng Sq.

Taman Rekreasi
Gunung Lang
BOATING, OUTDOORS

(off Jln Kuala Kangsar; boat rides adult/child RM3/1.50; ⊙boats 8.30am-6pm Sun-Thu, 8.30am-noon & 3-6pm Fri) This cliffside recreation park, 4km north of Ipoh, is a relaxing place to enjoy a boat ride, spot turtles gliding across the lake, or feel mist from the waterfall (sorry, it's artificial). We suggest skipping the miniature zoo.

Ipoh Secrets
DRIVING, WALKING

(☏012-521 2773; https://ipohsecrets.com) From cultural walks in Ipoh (from RM150 per person) to private tours of the cave temples (RM720 per car), Ipoh Secrets offers info-packed excursions to Perak's top sights. This efficient operator can also take visitors off the beaten track (pottery making, the historic Lenggong Valley) or create tailor-made itineraries. Tours in English or Mandarin.

Ray the Tour
HISTORY, CULTURAL

(☏Singapore 00 65 8428 3884; www.raythetour.com; tour for 2/3 people from RM536) Based out of Singapore, this family business has guides who've spent years living in Ipoh, and their local knowledge shines. Typical itineraries include nostalgia-steeped tours around the old town, cave temples and **Kellie's Castle** (Jln Batu Gajah-Gopeng; adult/child RM10/8; ⊙9am-6pm; 🅿), including plenty of well-chosen stops for food and hotel pick-up (minimum group of two). Reserve at least a few days ahead; ideally a fortnight or more.

🛏 Sleeping

East of the Sungai Kinta, in the new town, there's plentiful accommodation for all budgets, catering to business travellers and weekenders. Some of the most appealing midrangers are in Ipoh's outskirts.

Vloft Backpackers Hostel
HOSTEL $

(☏012-502 0187; https://vloft-backpackers-hostel.business.site; 115A Jln Sultan Iskandar; dm not incl breakfast RM24-28; ❄🛜) Perched between Ipoh's old and new towns, Vloft offers simple, spick-and-span accommodation in a high-ceilinged, century-old shophouse (a 12-bed and four-bed dorm). Each bed has its own locker and there's a shared pantry and little terrace overlooking the din of the main road.

★The Happy 8
BOUTIQUE HOTEL $$

(☏05-243 8388; www.thehappy8.com.my; 46 Jln Pasar; d not incl breakfast RM170; ❄🛜) Hidden behind a leafy, statue-festooned entryway, Happy 8's hand-crafted feel and intimate on-site cafe are a winning combination. Upcycled wood, hand-painted murals and stone-effect bathrooms give rooms a quirky, retro feel; the best have balconies peeking through the leaves.

Even if you aren't staying overnight, take a break in the charming **cafe**, decked out in bamboo and wood, and see if you can get a seat on the mesh platform (there's water beneath your feet).

★Sekeping Kong Heng
BOUTIQUE HOTEL $$

(☏012-227 2745; www.sekeping.com/kongheng; 74 Jln Bandar Timah; s RM55, standard d RM95-130, r & ste RM220-800, not incl breakfast; ❄🛜🏊) At the heart of Ipoh's old-town renaissance, this startling hotel and hostel harnesses history and modern design

Ipoh

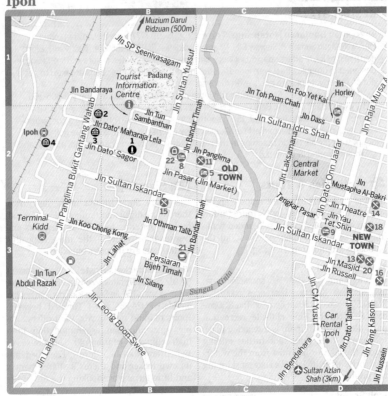

to impressive effect. The experience depends on what you book: cheaper rooms are rough-hewn and occasionally dank; others are larger with an attractive, industrial style. Outdoor lounge areas have wire-frame seats and old-fashioned shutters, providing an ideal vantage point over the old town.

Be aware that some apartments are open-air with mesh walls; not ideal for light sleepers.

There's a small, open-air pool.

M Roof   DESIGN HOTEL $$
(☑ 05-547 1777; https://mroof.mboutiquehotels. com; Jln Dato Lau Pak Kuan; d RM162-204, ste/ apt from RM366/450, not incl breakfast; P ✳ ☎) Some of Ipoh's most chic accommodation is out of town, such as M Roof, a glamorously monochrome hotel in a high-rise 5km northeast of the old town. Rooms are gorgeously modern with high-quality mattresses, duck-feather pillows, urban

artwork and sleek, honeycomb-tiled bathrooms.

MU Hotel   HOTEL $$
(☑ 05-240 6888; https://muhotel.com; 18 Jln Chung On Siew; d incl breakfast from RM169; P ✳ @ ☎) This reinvented Ibis Styles hotel has a tasteful pomelo-inspired colour scheme and 113 snazzy rooms. The amenities befit a business hotel (good wi-fi, a small gym, four complimentary shuttle buses to the old town), but it's as popular with weekenders as business travellers. A pleasant haven from the busy new town.

Hotel French   HOTEL $$
(☑ 05-241 3030; www.frenchhotel.com.my; 60-62 Jln Dato' Onn Jaafar; d not incl breakfast RM148-178; P ✳ ☎) Fetching and minimalist in style, this no-frills hotel rather lacks the promised French flair, though rooms are brightly lit and contemporary, all with safes and fridges (though a few lack windows).

Ipoh

◎ Sights

1 Birch Memorial Clock Tower B2
2 Courthouse A2
3 Town Hall..A2
4 Train Station..A2

🛏 Sleeping

5 The Happy 8 .... C2
6 Hotel French...D2
7 MU Hotel...E4
8 Sekeping Kong Heng B2
9 Vloft Backpackers Hostel...................D3
10 WEIL Hotel...F3

✖ Eating

11 Concubine Lane Tau Fu Fa................ C2
12 Cowan Street E2
13 Famous Mee Hakka D3
14 Funny Mountain Soya Bean..............D3
15 Lim Ko Pi..B3
16 M Salim D3
17 Ming Court..E2
18 Restaurant Lou Wong...........................D3
19 Vnam Kitchen.. E1
20 Xin Quan Fang D3

◎ Drinking & Nightlife

21 Sin Yoon Loong B3

◎ Shopping

22 Kong Heng Square Artisan
    Market..B2

PERAK IPOH

★ **WEIL Hotel** BUSINESS HOTEL **$$$**
(☑ 05-208 2228; www.weilhotel.com; 292 Jln Sultan Idris Shah; d RM335-468, ste from RM526, incl breakfast; P❋🤶🏊) Central Ipoh's poshest business hotel smoulders with down-lit dining areas, lavish breakfasts and a small rooftop pool and cocktail bar. Rooms are fitted with exceedingly comfortable beds and polished, glass-fronted bathrooms, with chic touches such as monochrome prints of Ipoh landmarks. 'WEIL', if you're wondering, is the founder's name backwards.

Indulgence Living BOUTIQUE HOTEL **$$$**
(☑ 05-255 7051; www.indulgencerestaurant.com; 14 Jln Raja Dihilir; d incl breakfast RM420-790; P❋🤶) Resembling an English country mansion improbably plonked next to a main road, Indulgence has a set of individually decorated rooms, from rococo to antique Chinese in style (we liked the chic, Italianate 'Giulianna' room). Rooms are showing signs

of age, but unique decor and gourmet extras, including upmarket European-style breakfasts, make it one of Ipoh's more interesting places to stay.

✖ Eating

Lim Ko Pi MALAYSIAN, CHINESE **$**
(☑ 05-253 2898; http://ipohlimkopi.com; 10 Jln Sultan Iskandar; mains RM12-17; ⊙ 8am-5pm Tue-Sun) From colourful tiles to secluded inner dining nooks, this relaxing cafe in a 1920s building has a strong whiff of Ipoh's glory days. Considering the setting, breakfasts are good value (from RM5 for eggs, toast and white coffee). Lunches include generous portions of prawn fried rice, curry noodles and smoky-but-sweet stewed pork. Service is unrushed compared to elsewhere in town.

Concubine Lane Tau Fu Fa CHINESE **$**
(8 Jln Panglima; per bowl RM2.50; ⊙ 10.30am-4.30pm; ☑) Historic Jln Panglima, aka 'Concubine Lane', is elbow to elbow with

visitors on weekends, but it's worth squeezing through for a brimming bowlful of *tau fu fah* (bean-curd pudding) at this hole-in-the-wall canteen. Freshly prepared each morning, each bowl is topped with sugar or ginger and black sesame.

Hours vary because when the pudding's gone, it's gone.

M Salim
MALAYSIAN, INDIAN $

(cnr Jln Yang Kalsom & Jln Che Tak; mains from RM6; ⏱ 6.30am-9.30pm Sat-Thu, 6.30am-1pm & 2-9.30pm Fri) This busy, no-frills halal place will feed you a mountain of nosh for a few ringgit. Pile your plate by pointing at whatever's freshly cooked that day (village-style chicken, spicy okra, eggs), or order fragrant biryani and its signature mutton curry.

Xin Quan Fang
HAINAN, MALAYSIAN $

(174 Jln Sultan Iskandar; mains from RM5.50; ⏱ 7am-1pm) You'd better come early (seriously, 7am) for the chance to sample Hainanese curry noodles and pork and bean sprouts. These two dishes are pretty much all Xin Quan Fang churns out, but they are excellent, as testified by the lines that stretch around the block for this family-run favourite.

★ Restaurant Lou Wong
MALAYSIAN $$

(📞 05-254 4190; 49 Jln Yau Tet Shin; mains from RM14; ⏱ 11am-9.30pm Sat-Thu) Ipoh's signature dish, *tauge ayam*, has been perfected at perennially popular Lou Wong. The restaurant is unadorned, with plastic seats spilling into the street, but the sole dish on offer is immensely satisfying: smooth poached chicken on soy-drenched cucumber, and crunchy bean sprouts sprinkled with pepper. Side dishes are either rice or noodles, and a bowl of chicken stock.

Lou Wong's popularity has spawned a number of imitators with suspiciously similar names nearby.

Vnam Kitchen
VIETNAMESE $$

(📞 05-254 2633; 32 Jln Seenivasagam; mains RM11-17; ⏱ noon-10pm) Reliable Vietnamese fare, from lemongrass pork and crystal spring rolls to enormous soups, is served up

---

IPOH'S BEST EATS

They say it's the water: Ipoh has a glowing reputation as a food city, and locals believe that deposits from the rich karst formations around town seep into the groundwater, giving the city's food a special quality. The city has a number of signature dishes.

Tauge ayam This is probably the dish most closely associated with Ipoh: tender poached chicken served with Ipoh's fat bean sprouts and rice (the latter cooked in chicken broth) or a bowl of rice noodles. Restaurant Lou Wong is the heart of a clutch of *tauge ayam* places, but many locals swear by **Cowan Street** (📞 012-520 3322; cnr Jln Raja Ekram & Jln Sultan Abdul Jalil; half-chicken RM26; ⏱ 6-9.30pm Thu-Sun).

Kopi putih Known in English as Ipoh white coffee, this method of roasting beans with palm-oil margarine was allegedly invented at **Sin Yoon Loong** (📞 05-241 4601; 15a Jln Bandar Timah; ⏱ 6am-5.30pm Mon-Sat, to 1pm Sun), but every local has a different favourite venue. If you have a car, try the rich brews at Jié Cafe (p133).

Hakka mee Flat wheat noodles topped with salty ground pork and served with a side bowl of broth with fish and pork balls and tofu; best at **Famous Mee Hakka** (Paris Restaurant; 163 Jln Sultan Iskandar; mains from RM3.30; ⏱ 7am-noon).

Curry mee Join the queue early (we promise it's worth it) for pork and bean sprouts and Hainanese curry noodles at **Famous Mee Hakka** (Paris Restaurant; 163 Jln Sultan Iskandar; mains from RM3.30; ⏱ 7am-noon). The family running the show has been making the dish for decades, and didn't get its loyal following by rushing.

Tau fu fah Soft, warm and scooped straight from a wooden barrel, this sweet bean-curd pudding is found at some excellent places in Ipoh. **Funny Mountain Soya Bean** (49 Jln Theatre; pudding RM3, soy milk RM2.50; ⏱ from 10.30am; 📷) is almost legendary.

Dim sum Tourist favourite **Ming Court** (📞 05-255 7134; 36 Jln Leong Sin Nam; dim sum RM2.40-5.30; ⏱ 6am-noon Fri-Wed) has reliably tasty pork *bao* (steamed buns) and other dim sum whisked around the sit-down dining room by staff. Point, eat and then point again. Arrive early.

at this efficient and friendly restaurant with a soothing lotus backdrop.

Drinking & Nightlife

Ipoh's old town quietens down after dark, except at beer joints such as the **Sinhalese Bar** on the corner of Jln Bijeh Timah and Jln Market. But there are decent boozers in the new town, particularly northwest of Ipoh Parade. Try the Irish- and English-style pubs on Jln Raja Ekram and Jln Lau Ek Ching. (Don't miss frosty thirst-quencher, 'snow beer'.)

For something glamorous, WEIL Hotel (p131) has a memorable rooftop cocktail bar.

Jié Cafe　　　　　　　　　　　　CAFE
(☑ 012-527 6771; 61 Persiaran Tokong, Taman Hoover; ☺ 9.30am-5pm Thu-Sun) In a neighbourhood that fills to bursting with lunchtime crowds, antique-styled Chinese cafe Jié stands out for its rich, sweet version of traditional white coffee. It's 1.5km south of Ipoh's new town.

Shopping

★ **Kong Heng Square**
Artisan Market　　　　　ARTS & CRAFTS
(Jln Panglima; ☺ 11am-5pm Wed-Mon) During the colonial era, these walls formed the city's large single shop block. Today a cluster of craft stalls has sprung up around this light-flooded atrium in Ipoh's old town.

Don't miss pausing to slurp an ice ball at **Bits & Bobs** (RM5) or browsing the cutesy pachyderm-themed purses and trinkets at **Why Not Elephants**.

Ipoh Parade　　　　　　　　　MALL
(☑ 05-241 0885; http://ipoh.parade.com.my; 105 Jln Sultan Abdul Jalil; ☺ 10am-10pm) Shiny, brand-filled shopping mall in Ipoh's new town, featuring fashion, electronics and a food court.

❶ Information

Ipoh Hospital (☑ 05-208 5000; http://hrpb.moh.gov.my; Jln Raja Ashman Shah) Located about 1.5km northeast of Ipoh's new town. Has an emergency room.

Kinta Medical Centre (☑ 05-242 5333; www.kintamedicalcentre.com; cnr Jln Chung Thye Phin & Jln Chamberlain Hulu) Medical centre in the new town with a 24-hour emergency room.

Tourist Information Centre (☑ 05-208 3155; http://ipohtourism.mbi.gov.my; 1 Jln Bandaraya; ☺ 10am-5pm Mon-Fri)

❶ Getting There & Away

AIR
Ipoh's airport, **Sultan Azlan Shah Airport** (☑ 05-318 8202; https://ipoh.airport-authority.com), is about 4km southeast of the city centre; a taxi here from central Ipoh costs about RM20. At the time of writing Scoot

PERAK IPOH

BUSES FROM IPOH

DESTINATION	PRICE (RM)	DURATION (HR)	FREQUENCY
Alor Setar	24-29	3½-4	at least 10
Butterworth (Penang)	15-25	2-3½	half-hourly, 8am-10pm
Cameron Highlands	20-25	2-4	at least 7, 9.30am-6.30pm
Gerik (for Royal Belum State Park)	17-20	2-2½	at least 5
Hat Yai (Thailand)	55	6-7	2 (one day, one night service)
Johor Bahru	53-70	7½	at least 10, morning & evening only
KLIA	30-40	3½	at least 5
Kota Bharu	34-39	7	at least 6, morning & evening only
Kuala Kangsar	5	1-1½	half-hourly to hourly
Kuala Lumpur (TBS)	20-35	2½-3	at least hourly, 4.15am-10.20pm
Lumut (for Pulau Pangkor)	9-11	3	10, 8am-8pm
Melaka	33-43	4-5	at least 8, 8.30am-12.30am
Singapore	65-100	8	half-hourly, 9-10.30am & 8.30pm-midnight
Taiping	10	1-1½	10 daily

(www.flyscoot.com) offered direct flights to Singapore (from RM340).

BUS

Most travellers will arrive at Ipoh's intercity bus station, **Terminal Amanjaya** (📞05-526 7818, 05-526 7718; www.peraktransit.com.my; Persiaran Meru Raya 5), approximately 8km north of Ipoh. Bus 116 (RM2.40, half-hourly) goes between Amanjaya and the train station until 8pm, while taxis cost roughly RM25 to RM30 (less with a ride-share service such as Grab).

At the time of writing, some buses within Perak (and to the Cameron Highlands) were still running to/from city-centre **Terminal Kidd** (Jln Tun Abdul Razak) and Perak Road-ways services to Lumut still departed across the road at the Shell Station. Check the departure station ahead of time, but Amanjaya is your likeliest bet, with the biggest choice and frequency.

It's worth checking timetables or booking ahead using an online ticket service such as www.easybook.com.

TRAIN

Trains run to Kuala Lumpur (RM24 to RM37, 2½ to 3¼ hours, 10 daily) and Butterworth (RM33 to RM42, two hours, five daily). Check www.ktmtrain.com for the latest info on fares and schedules.

❶ Getting Around

Ipoh's old and new towns are easy to explore on foot, and **taxis** (📞05-253 4188) or ride-share services such as Grab can be used to zip between the two.

For attractions out of town, you'll need public or hired transport. **Car Rental Ipoh** (Kereta Sewa Maju Jaya; 📞012-520 3588, 019-556 2158; www.carrentalipoh.com; Jln CM Yusuf; ⊘8am-8pm) has good rates for small cars (from RM100 per day); call between 8am and 8pm, or book by email. There are a few fuelling stations in town, including **Shell** (Jln Tun Abdul Razak).

Gopeng & Around

The best of Perak's rugged beauty is accessed from Gopeng, a former tin-mining outpost 17km southeast of Ipoh. The area surrounding this easygoing town is flush with forest, pocketed with caves (notably the impressive Gua Tempurung), and the thrashing Kinta River has carved out a regional river-rafting and waterfall-trekking scene.

Gopeng is easiest to explore by car, though all-inclusive resorts and some guest-houses can package up meals, accommodation, activities and transfers.

◉ Sights

Gua Tempurung   CAVE
(📞014-220 4142; aptguatempurung@gmail.com; self-guided adult/child RM20/10, tour adult/child from RM40/20; ⊘9am-5pm Sat-Thu, 9am-12.30pm & 2.30-5pm Fri) If you only do one thing in Gopeng, explore the 'Coconut Cave', named for its domelike interior. The easy option is the 'Golden Flowstone' walk, a self-guided 40-minute stroll along boardwalks that wind between hulking stalactites. Or you can get thrillingly wet and muddy on scrambles of various lengths through the cave tunnels (book ahead – not for the claustrophobic). It's 9km south and east from Gopeng town; follow Rte 1 and the signs.

If you don't have your own transport, many resorts in Gopeng arrange tours. Last entry 4.15pm.

Kinta Nature Park   WILDLIFE RESERVE
(Taman Alam Kinta; www.facebook.com/KintaNP; ⊘8am-6pm) Tin-mining ponds surrounded by tangles of forest have turned into a home for herons, egrets and 150 different bird species. Long ignored by all but the most dedicated bird-watching enthusiasts, the area was gazetted as a state park in 2017. Bring your binoculars to spot stork-billed kingfishers, baya weavers, otters and butterfly lizards. It's 6km south of Batu Gajah.

It is possible to visit independently by bike, but we recommend using a guide with a 4WD, as roads are rough. Gopeng resorts and Ipoh-based guides offer excursions.

Gaharu Tea Valley   FARM
(📞05-351 1999; www.gaharu.com.my; off Jln Kampung Sungai Itek; tours adult/child RM10/5; ⊘9am-6pm) A Cameron Highlands experience in miniature, this valley grows *gaharu* (agarwood) for premium-priced, caffeine-free teas. It's touristy, emphasising the healing powers of *gaharu* and its role in Middle Eastern and Chinese cultures, with contrived attractions such as 'Lovers' Tree'. But with viewing platforms and a cafe serving goji and *gaharu* tea, and tea-stained eggs, it's a pleasant detour.

Find it 3km southeast of Gopeng town, well signposted off the main road.

❊ Activities

Thrashing around in rivers and waterfalls is the main draw in Gopeng. Activity

KINTA VALLEY HERITAGE LOOP

Perak is thought to derive its name (Malay for silver) from shimmering tin ore, with much of the area surrounding Ipoh built on the tin trade. The Kinta Valley boom towns that sprang up during the 1870s may have lost their sheen (metallic and otherwise), but they form an interesting day trip from Ipoh by road.

Leaving Ipoh, head southwest on Hwy 5 for 15km to reach sparsely populated **Kampung Papan**. This small town has some attractive period houses, though most are depressingly dilapidated. **Istana Raja Billah** (1896), a mansion at the village's north-westerly edge, is now a private home.

Seven kilometres further southeast you'll reach **Batu Gajah**, an important settlement since the early 19th century. The town's name, meaning stone elephant, comes from two pachyderm-shaped rocks submerged in the Kinta River. If arriving in the morning, you can grab fresh roti and coffee at a local Indian restaurant such as **Ganapathi** (155 Jln Besar, Batu Gajah; mains RM3-10; ⊙6am-8pm).

Batu Gajah is awash with colonial buildings, including a neoclassical **Court House** (1892), the custard-yellow **St Joseph's Church** (1882), the **Old Railway Station** and **Kinta Gaol**, built to hold more than 450 prisoners. Other photo ops include the modern, gold-domed **mosque** and the well-kept **God's Little Acre Cemetery**. For an in-depth tour, consult the *Batu Gajah Heritage Driving Trail* map, available at Ipoh's tourist office.

Leaving town, drive 9km south to the **TT5 Tin Dredge** (☑014-904 3255; www. facebook.com/tanjungtualangno5; 9th Km Jln Batu Gajah-Tanjung Tualang, Tanjung Tualang; adult/child RM10/5, tour RM20/10; ⊙9am-6pm). A rusty relic of Perak's tin-mining glory days, this 75m-long, 4500-tonne dredging apparatus is a surprisingly interesting site.

Belly rumbling? Tanjung Tualang is home to a clutch of seafood restaurants such as **Luen Fong Restaurant** (☑05-360 9267; cnr Jln Pasar & Jln Besar; mains RM20-48; ⊙noon-2pm & 5-7pm). Settle in for steamed fish or the local speciality, freshwater prawns.

Returning to Batu Gajah, turn east along Hwy A8, where after about 7km you'll reach Kellie's Castle (p129). Steeped in tragic legend, this Gothic- and Moorish-style castle was commissioned by wealthy Scottish planter William Kellie Smith and abandoned after his sudden death.

About 500m west of the castle is a **Hindu temple**, built for the artisans by Smith after the Spanish flu killed dozens of their workforce. The workers placed a figure of Smith, dressed in a white suit and pith helmet, on the temple roof.

Continue east for about 7km until you reach Hwy 1, where you can return north to Ipoh after 13km.

Ipoh-based operators such as Ipoh Secrets (p129) and Mr Raja (p128) can arrange bespoke tours.

guides and resorts go hand in hand – you can book accommodation and excursions together, or book day excursions and stay elsewhere.

Guided activities include white-water rafting and river boarding (RM150), wet abseiling (RM100), caving (RM70) and rafflesia trekking (RM60), with guided walks to the blooming site of this pungent, parasitic flower – sightings aren't guaranteed. Rafting and some caving excursions are only for groups of eight or more; in general, prices are cheaper the larger your group. If you're solo or in a small group, book a couple of weeks ahead as it may be possible to join a larger group.

🛏 Sleeping & Eating

Accommodation and outdoor activities are intertwined in Gopeng – most likely you'll book them as a package through one of the resorts. Aside from Gopeng Guest House, reserving well ahead is crucial. Many resorts are more accustomed to group bookings than lone travellers so check-in hours can be spotty...particularly when staff embark on all-day rafting excursions.

If you don't have wheels, arrange a pick-up. Oh, and don't expect good wi-fi.

Gopeng Guest House　　GUESTHOUSE **$**
(☑017-486 6845; https://gopengguesthouse. wordpress.com; Jln Sungai Itek; s/d/f incl breakfast RM50/90/120; 🛜) Furnished *kampung*

(village) style, with fabrics, wooden shutters and tinted glass, this Gopeng town guesthouse has a magically nostalgic atmosphere. If you prioritise privacy and modern trappings, the fan-cooled, communal experience isn't for you. For everyone else, adventurous host Jaja seals the deal with her local tips, bike rental (RM30) and outdoor activities on offer. Near Gopeng bus station.

There's also a **cafe** serving *asam pedas* (spicy fish soup), *tauge ayam* and other regional specialities.

Nomad Adventure Earth Camp GUESTHOUSE **$**
(📱016-201 1219, 03-7958 5152; www.nomad adventure.com; Kampung Chulek; dm/tw/q halfboard RM59/158/356; 🅿 🛜) 🍴 The originator of river rafting in Gopeng, Nomad draws an adrenaline-charged clientele for its accommodation and activity packages (mostly groups). Located 2.5km north of Gua Tempurung, Nomad has basic dorms, treehouses and chalets for a back-to-nature experience. Everything's crafted from repurposed wood, with upcycling touches like pipe shoe racks, and it grows its own bananas and sweet potato for communal meals.

Fans give relief from the heat and bathrooms are shared, except in the four-person Matahari Villas. Mosquito nets on request. Book accommodation and activities (rafting, waterfall abseiling, kayaking, zip lining and climbing) at least 24 hours in advance.

It may be possible for solo and small-group travellers to join larger groups for excursions, but it's essential to enquire ahead.

⭐ **Adeline's Villa** RESORT **$$**
(📱05-359 2833; www.adelinevilla.com; Jln Kampung Pintu Padang; per person shared/tw bungalow incl meals from RM220/270; 🅿 ❄) A laid-back pace is instantly established at Adeline's, 6km east of Gopeng. The resort stretches across flourishing gardens, with its 21 chalets fitted in a contemporary *kampung* style: wooden beams, thatched roofs and the occasional zany wall mural. Some sleep up to 12 people.

Adeline's specialises in accommodation and activity packages (rafting, caving, trekking...). Book at least one month ahead.

Mee Kari Ami NOODLES **$**
(noodles RM6; ⊙8.30am-7pm Thu-Tue) Specialising in *mee kari* (spicy noodles), this out-of-the-way food stall is in a verdant

setting, 3.5km southeast of Gopeng town. It's friendly, and the food's moreish and in generous portions. Ask directions before you set out; it's off the road towards Gaharu Tea Valley (p134).

ℹ️ Getting There & Away

Private transport makes life much easier in and around Gopeng. Buses run between Gopeng's bus station and Ipoh (RM3 to RM4, 30 minutes, half-hourly 6.30am to 10pm) and Lumut (RM10, 1½ hours, hourly). Sri Maju buses from Kuala Lumpur's Pudu Sentral towards Ipoh Amanjaya stop in Gopeng (RM19.30).

Cameron Highlands

Emerald tea plantations unfurl across Malaysia's largest hill-station area. Temperatures in these 1300m to 1829m heights rarely top 30°C, inspiring convoys of weekenders to enjoy tea and strawberries in the restorative climate. Though technically in Pahang, the highlands are accessed from Perak.

The Cameron Highlands encompass a string of townships, including (north to south) Kampung Raja, Tringkap, Brinchang, Tanah Rata and Ringlet. Named after explorer Sir William Cameron, who mapped the area in 1885, the highlands were developed during the British colonial period. Gardens, bungalows and a golf course sprang up during the 1930s, cementing the highlands' reputation as a refuge for heat-addled Brits to mop their brows.

Tourism is big business, so views are occasionally blighted by building sites for yet another megaresort; Brinchang in particular felt like a construction site when we last visited. But between trekking and genteel tea culture, there is serenity amid the touristic hubbub.

◉ Sights

Many attractions around the Cameron Highlands are glorified souvenir shops, peddling lavender or honey without much of a visitor experience. Tea plantations are as worthwhile for the views as the brews.

⭐ **Sam Poh Temple** BUDDHIST TEMPLE
(Map p138; off Jln Pecah Batu, Brinchang; ⊙7am-6pm) This scarlet-and-yellow temple complex, just below Brinchang, about 1km off the main road, is peopled with huge burnished statues and magnificent tilework. Inside the first hall are statues of the defend-

PERAK CAMERON HIGHLANDS

ers of Buddhist law; continue to the inner temple building (remove your shoes), where hundreds of ceramic tiles feature intricately hand-painted Buddha images.

The temple, built in 1972, is dedicated to medieval admiral and eunuch Zheng Ho and is allegedly the fourth-largest Buddhist temple in Malaysia.

A taxi from Tanah Rata costs RM15.

Lata Iskandar WATERFALL
(Tapah) A picturesque, thoroughly refreshing stop if you're driving route 59 up to the Cameron Highlands, this cascade tumbling over granite boulders is popular with paddling families. Banana, durian and snack stalls abound nearby. It's 20km south of Ringlet.

Ee Feng Gu Honey Bee Farm FARM, SHOWROOM
(Map p138; ☑05-496 1951; www.eefenggu.com; Kea Farm; ⊗8am-7pm; ☑) FREE One of the better honey-themed attractions in the highlands, this working apiary has landscaped flower gardens where you can watch bees buzzing around hibiscus flowers and there's a little museum explaining how the sweet stuff is produced. Only the indoor kids' maze carries an entry fee (adult/child RM3/2). It's 4km north of central Brinchang.

There's a huge attached souvenir shop in which to pick up flavoured honey by the stick (RM1), jars of honey (from RM10) and all manner of bee-shaped gifts.

PERAK CAMERON HIGHLANDS

HIKING TRAILS

Besides getting in touch with your inner Englishness via tea and strawberries, the Cameron Highlands' main attraction is its web of hiking trails. It's crucial to ask locally before embarking on any trail – a couple of routes have become prowling grounds for robbers, and there have even been a few reports of sexual assaults. But the overwhelming majority of hikers in the Cameron Highlands enjoy the rippling hills and blessedly cool temperatures without incident.

Talk to the well-informed staff at Father's Guest House (p139) for the latest, or better yet, join a guided hike with **Eco Cameron** (Map p140; ☑ 05-491 5388; www.ecocameron. com; 72-A Persiaran Camellia 4, Tanah Rata; tours per person RM50-180; ⊗ 8am-9.30pm) or **Jason Marcus Chin** (☑ 010-380 8558; jason.marcus.chin@gmail.com; half-/full-day tour from RM50/70).

The usual safety rules apply. Trails aren't well signposted and some are treacherous and steep. Always carry water, some food, and rain gear, and don't set out in the mid-afternoon (darkness descends quickly). Let your guesthouse know your planned route and predicted return time.

The following are the most popular trails. **Trail 1** was closed when we last visited and **Trails 9 & 9A** are to be avoided because of robberies and assaults targeting tourists, and packs of dogs.

Trails 2 & 3 Tricky Trail 2 (1½ hours) and linked Trail 3 to Gunung Beremban (2½ hours) suit experienced walkers. The terrain's overgrown but hikers with a good level of fitness will enjoy the exhilarating scramble.

Trail 4 Warning: we heard a report of assault on this popular trail, so ask locals before setting out. Just past Century Pines Resort in Tanah Rata, the trail leads to Parit Falls (30 minutes), though you might find this small waterfall murky and the site strewn with garbage. Another route to the waterfall is from the main road leading south from the southern end of the golf course.

Trails 5 & 7 Moderate Trail 5 and very challenging Trail 7 climb the flank of Gunung Beremban (1840m). Don't attempt the old route for Trail 6, from Gunung Jasar to Bharat Plantation, without a guide – it's left off present maps for good reason.

Trail 8 This trail splits off Trail 9 just before Robinson Falls and is a steep three-hour approach to Gunung Beremban. Only experienced hikers should attempt this strenuous trail.

Trail 10 For lofty views this enjoyable 3km, three-hour route winds upward from Carnation Park (1km northwest of Tanah Rata's main road) to Gunung Jasar before descending back to Tanah Rata along the road.

Cameron Highlands

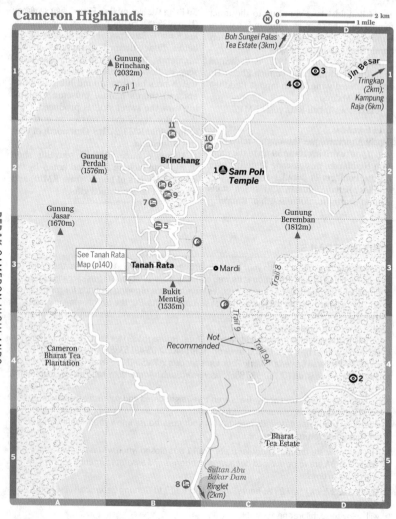

Cameron Highlands

◉ Top Sights
1 Sam Poh Temple.....................................C2

◉ Sights
2 Boh Tea Garden......................................D4
3 Ee Feng Gu Honey Bee Farm.................D1
4 Raaju's Hill Strawberry Farm................C1

🛏 Sleeping
5 Bala's Holiday Chalet B3
6 Casa de la Rosa.....................................B2
7 Hotel De'La Ferns B2
8 The Lakehouse......................................B5
9 Smokehouse B2
10 Snooze C2
11 Strawberry Park Resort.......................B2

Boh Tea Garden   PLANTATION
(Map p138; ☎ 05-493 1234; www.bohtea.com;
Jln Boh, Ringlet; ⏰ 9am-4.30pm Tue-Sun) FREE
Velvety green views are glorious from this
out-of-the-way tea plantation, though it's
a white-knuckle drive to get here (allow
40 minutes from Tanah Rata; it's six snaking
kilometres off the main road). Sip tea on an

idyllic outdoor terrace, buy boxes of tea or ramble with your camera ready.

Raaju's Hill Strawberry Farm   FARM

(Map p138; ☑019-575 3867; Brinchang; ⊘ 8.30am-6.30pm) Locals believe that the way the evening mist hits this valley-tucked berry farm is the reason its fruit tastes so sweet. If berry picking (RM30 for two people for 500g of strawberries) sounds like hard work, you're sure to find something – thick strawberry milkshakes (RM8) or the strawberry 'steamboat', where fruit is drowned in chocolate sauce (RM20) – to tempt you in the cafe.

☞ Tours

With considerable distance between sights and barely-there public transport, guided tours are popular. Many tours focus on tea plantations and strawberry picking – guides don't add much to these activities so consider a taxi instead.

If you're interested in hiking or highland flora and fauna, we highly recommend hiring a guide or joining a group walk. Recommended guides include Eco Cameron (p137) and Jason Marcus Chin (p137).

🛌 Sleeping

Tanah Rata is the heart of the highlands, with the main bus station, a glut of restaurants and a correspondingly large range of places to stay across budgets. Brinchang, 4km north, also has several hotels. Study a map before booking, as hotels outside Tanah Rata (eg in Ringlet or Tringkap) may only suit travellers with their own vehicle.

The highlands are busy during school holidays in April, August and December; book well in advance. Prices rise by around 25% at weekends and during holidays.

Air-con is not essential in the breezy Cameron Highlands, and few hotels have it. Note also that connectivity in the Cameron Highlands can be patchy, so take hotel wi-fi claims with a grain of salt.

★Father's Guest House   GUESTHOUSE $

(Map p140; ☑016-566 1111; www.fathersguesthouse.net; 4 Jln Mentigi, Tanah Rata; dm RM30, d from RM96, d/tr/q without bathroom from RM75/96/128, not incl breakfast; P@🛜) Old-school hostel friendliness meets modern amenities at Father's. Pleasant private rooms and clean 10-person dorms elicit sighs of relief from travellers checking in. The staff are an indispensable source of knowledge about hiking

trails. Other perks include free tea and coffee, plus an on-site cafe serving real bacon.

★Westwood Highland   HOSTEL $

(☑05-498 1611; http://westwoodhighland.com; 4B Jln Batu 51, Kampung Raja; dm/s/d/tr not incl breakfast RM65/100/210/230; P🛜) Tucked away 10km north of Brinchang, Westwood treads a pleasing line between contemporary hostel and farmstay experience. There are four-bed dorms and private rooms (shared bathroom) and everything's shiny, clean and free from damp (which is never guaranteed in these humid highlands). It's best to have your own transport, but you can request a pick-up if arriving by bus.

Cameronian Inn   GUESTHOUSE $

(Map p140; ☑05-491 1327; www.thecameronianinn.com; 16 Jln Mentigi, Tanah Rata; dm/d RM25/80, f RM160-200, not incl breakfast; P🛜) Surprisingly calm for its location, 300m south of Tanah Rata's busy main road, the family-run Cameronian Inn offers outstanding value for its basic dorms and private double and family rooms. Breakfast is available at the cafe (RM2.50 to RM4.90) but scones with homemade jam (RM8.50) are the menu's highlight.

★Bala's Holiday Chalet   GUESTHOUSE $$

(Map p138; ☑05-491 1660; bala.reservations@gmail.com; off Jln Besar; r RM140-250, ste RM280-380, not incl breakfast; P@🛜) In a sea of faux-colonial mansions, Bala's is the real deal. Formerly a boarding school, Bala's has 35 rustic rooms (plus split-level suites for families) speckled across tangled English country gardens, where giant ferns and lemon trees burst forth. It's a period building so rooms feel a little aged, but the view amply compensates – particularly when accompanied by afternoon tea.

With notice, Bala's can arrange great-value trekking excursions and tours to the Orang Asli village (from RM25).

Bala's is up a steep road 1.5km north of Tanah Rata, so it's best to have your own wheels.

Casa de la Rosa   HOTEL $$

(Map p138; ☑05-491 1333; www.hotelcasadelarosa.com.my; Jln Circular; d RM204-306, tr from RM369, q from RM433, incl breakfast; P🛜) Regal, well-maintained Casa de la Rosa is cut from familiar Cameron Highlands cloth: black-and-white Tudor facade, hardwood furnishings and a dash of European style. The 30-room property is clean, efficiently

Tanah Rata

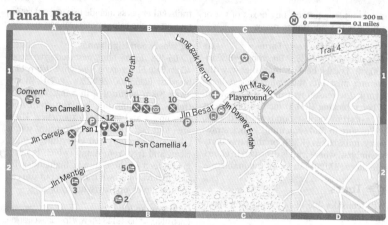

Tanah Rata

Activities, Courses & Tours
1 Eco Cameron.......................................B2

Sleeping
2 Arundina...B2
3 Cameronian Inn...................................A2
4 Century Pines Resort..........................C1
5 Father's Guest House.........................B2
6 Heritage Hotel.....................................A1

Eating
7 Barracks Cafe......................................A2

8 KouGen...B1
   May Flower....................................(see 1)
9 Restaurant Bunga Suria......................B2
10 Restoran Sri Brinchang......................B1
11 Singh Chapati.....................................B1

Drinking & Nightlife
12 Travellers Bar.....................................B2

Information
13 New Highlands Laundry......................B2

run and many rooms have lovely valley views. It might not have history, but it does everything jolly well.

Arundina GUESTHOUSE $$
(Map p140; ☑ 05-491 1129; www.arundina.com; 17 Jln Mentigi, Tanah Rata; d RM180-307, tr RM233-392, incl breakfast; 🅿🛜) This welcoming guesthouse on the outskirts of Tanah Rata has 12 pleasant, high-ceilinged rooms, many of which overlook a flower garden. The mauve colour scheme is a nod to *Arundina graminifolia,* the bamboo orchid for which the guesthouse is named. Effervescent staff and communal balconies complete the guesthouse's friendly atmosphere. Coffee and tea on tap.

Hotel De'La Ferns HOTEL $$
(Map p138; ☑ 05-491 4888; www.hoteldelaferns.com.my; 39 Jln Besar, Tanah Rata; s/d/tr/q from RM230/250/300/320, ste RM449-620, incl breakfast; 🅿@🛜) In quintessential Cameron Highlands style, this mock-Tudor hotel harbours kingly rooms inspired by an English

manor: white walls, wooden fittings and suites with wow factor, featuring throne-like beds and big TVs. The olde-English charm might be manufactured, but it's a pleasing package, partly thanks to the helpful staff.

Located about 1.5km north of Tanah Rata, en route to Brinchang.

Snooze GUESTHOUSE $$
(Map p138; ☑ 016-666 2102; www.facebook.com/SnoozeCH; 4 Jln Besar, Brinchang; d/tr/q not incl breakfast from RM110/150/180; 🛜) The cupcake colour scheme might be a little kitsch for some, but this clean guesthouse is one of Brinchang's better-value places to stay. There are bright sitting areas in which to chill or play, plus a fridge and laundry facilities.

Century Pines Resort HOTEL $$
(Map p140; ☑ 05-491 5115; www.centurypines resort.com.my; 42 Jln Masjid, Tanah Rata; d RM230-300, ste RM450-900, incl breakfast; 🅿🛜) Stepping into Century Pines' lobby gives the

impression of an upmarket hotel from the '80s (statement pillars, marble floors) but thankfully rooms have been modernised since then. They're in a tasteful style with wet-room bathrooms.

Heritage Hotel HOTEL $$

(Map p140; ☑05-491 3888; www.heritage.com.my; Jln Gereja, Tanah Rata; d RM180-340, ste RM300-1000, incl breakfast; P 🛜) At this faux-Tudor hotel, 'heritage' means vintage carpets, furnishings in need of TLC and doors that require a rattle to access your room. The most comfortable and modern rooms are in the 'new' (decade-old) wing. Amenities for families are the prime reason to book: arcade games, washing machines, pool tables, gardens and a bar – ideal for those rainy highland days.

Smokehouse BOUTIQUE HOTEL $$$

(Map p138; ☑05-491 1215; www.smokehousehotel.com; Ringlet; d/ste incl breakfast from RM400/680; P 🛜) This charismatic 1939 property looks as though it was lifted straight out of the English countryside with its exposed beams, four-poster beds and even a red phone box. Six of the rooms date to the 1930s, though the rest follow a similar style: expect heavy wooden furnishings and the occasional fireplace, plus modern conveniences such as mosquito screens.

There's also a fine restaurant serving cream teas and classic British fare, with a few vegetarian dishes. Smokehouse is located about 2km north of Tanah Rata, by the golf course on the road to Brinchang.

Strawberry Park Resort RESORT $$$

(Map p138; ☑05-491 1166; www.strawberrypark resorts.com; Brinchang; d RM600, ste RM800-1100, not incl breakfast; P @ 🛜 ☲) Primo pampering and exceptionally classy rooms lift Strawberry Park above its resort competition. All room types are elegant, from the ample doubles to family chalets with balconies, while tennis courts, pool and Balinese spa allow plenty of opportunity for R&R. It's a winding 2km north from the main road and only viable if you have a car. Significant discounts online.

The Lakehouse BOUTIQUE HOTEL $$$

(Map p138; ☑05-495 6152; www.lakehouse-cameron.com; Ringlet; d RM700-880, ste RM810-1350, incl breakfast; P ✳ 🛜) This 1960s-built country manor is a sophisticated choice. Furnished with writing desks, four-poster beds and wood-beamed ceilings, the 19

sumptuous rooms hark back to a genteel era, while the bathrooms are sparkling and modern. There's a 2km loop trail into the forest right by the door, plus a classy on-site restaurant specialising in British cuisine.

It's 10km south of Tanah Rata.

🍴 Eating & Drinking

Tanah Rata has the majority of the area's restaurants. Cuisines include Chinese, Indian, Malay and a colonial hangover of English breakfasts and scones – but the quality is similarly variable. Brinchang has a smaller spread, including restaurants serving Chinese and steamboat (a DIY hotpot where meat and veggies are submerged in broth). Elsewhere tea, honey and strawberry-themed attractions ensure a constant supply of snacking opportunities.

★ Singh Chapati INDIAN $

(Map p140; ☑017-578 6454; www.facebook.com/singhchapati; cnr Lg Perdah & Jln Besar, Tanah Rata; mains RM11-21; ⏰2-9pm; 🖊) On a lofty perch behind Tanah Rata's main drag, Singh's is the sweetest Indian joint in town. Dig in to fragrant biryanis, excellent veggie mains like butter paneer and smoky aubergine, and its famous chapati (flatbreads), and wash it down with mango lassi or masala tea.

This no-frills restaurant benefits from a slightly secluded setting; try to bag a terrace table looking towards hills and mock-Tudor mansions.

Restaurant Bunga Suria INDIAN $

(Map p140; 66a Persiaran Camellia 3, Tanah Rata; mains from RM5.50; ⏰7am-10pm; 🖊) Thoroughly local but friendly to tourists, the least manic of Tanah Rata's Indian canteens has great-value banana-leaf meal specials and satisfying breakfasts including *idli* (savoury, soft fermented-rice-and-lentil cakes) popped from the steamer to be dipped in coconut chutney. We prefer its masala tea (less sugar, more cardamom) to the other places in town.

Restoran Sri Brinchang INDIAN $

(Map p140; 25 Jln Besar, Tanah Rata; breakfast from RM3.20, mains from RM7.50; ⏰7.30am-10pm; 🖊) The most popular of the Indian restaurants on Tanah Rata's main road, this busy place heaps vegetable curries, pappadams and rice onto banana leaves for its filling lunches and prides itself on spring chicken served straight from the tandoor. Breakfasts include outsize *masala dosa*

PERAK CAMERON HIGHLANDS

(rice-and-lentil crepe stuffed with spiced potatoes).

★ Barracks Cafe INTERNATIONAL $$
(Map p140; ☎ 011-1464 8883; https://barrackscafe. business.site; 1 Jln Gereja, Tanah Rata; mains RM17-40; ⊗2-10pm Tue-Fri, noon-10pm Sat & Sun) Former military barracks rarely look this idyllic, with marble tables set among flower gardens. The hipster-pleasing menu offers Indian and British dishes, and great mocktails in mason jars. Indian fare such as lamb masala and butter chicken aren't the most authentic, but everything's tasty and well presented. The burgers and soups served in bread bowls are the best choices.

KouGen JAPANESE, KOREAN $$
(Map p140; ☎ 012-377 0387; 35 Jln Besar, Tan-ah Rata; mains RM21-29; ⊗noon-9pm Thu-Tue) Claypot roast pork, fried rice in kimchi, teriyaki burgers and sushi – KouGen pre-pares an impressive spread of Japanese and Korean fusion dishes from its open kitchen. Go the whole hog with sides such as *yaki-tori* (grilled chicken skewers) and freshly steamed soy beans. Perk: it's not at all hectic, despite the main-road location.

May Flower CHINESE $$
(Map p140; ☎ 05-491 4793; 81a Persiaran Camel-lia 4, Tanah Rata; steamboat per person RM25; ⊗noon-10pm; ☑) Steamboat is the quintes-sential Cameron Highland experience, and May Flower is one of the most reliable places to huddle around a steamy vat of broth. Take your pick of clear, spicy or half-half stocks and nibbles to dunk therein: choices are as varied as chicken, fish balls, jellyfish, mixed vegetables and tofu.

Travellers Bar PUB, BAR
(Map p140; ☎ 017-525 9001; www.facebook.com/ TravellersBistroPub; 66a Persiaran Camellia 3, Tanah Rata; ⊗noon-midnight) Somewhere be-tween a cosy pub and a wannabe cocktail bar is Travellers Bar. Propped up near Tanah Rata's main street, it's a beacon to hikers in need of cold beers and comfort food, and expats, backpackers and locals all mingle here. In a region with limited nightlife, it's a respectable all-rounder: pub meals, draught beers, sports screenings and decent cocktails.

ℹ Information

Medical Clinic (Klinik Kesihatan; Map p140; ☎ 05-491 1257; cnr Jln Besar & Jln Langgak Mercu, Tanah Rata)

New Highlands Laundry (Map p140; Persiaran Camellia 3, Tanah Rata; ⊗10.30am-7pm)

Police Station (Map p140; ☎ 05-491 5443; Jln Besar, Tanah Rata)

Post Office (Map p140; Jln Besar, Tanah Rata; ⊗9am-5pm Mon-Fri, to 1pm Sat)

ℹ Getting There & Away

BUS

Tanah Rata's long-distance **bus station** (Termi-nal Freesia; Map p140; Jln Besar) is at the east-ern end of the main road. Buy tickets at least a day in advance for popular destinations. Daily bus and boat transfer packages also reach Taman Negara and the Perhentian Islands.

WORTH A TRIP

BREWS & VIEWS AT BOH TEA ESTATE

There's no pastime more quintessentially Cameron Highlands than sipping a local brew, pinky finger outstretched, while gazing at valleys blanketed in tea plants. **Boh Sungei Palas Tea Estate** (☎ 05-496 2096; www.bohtea.com; Brinchang; ⊗8.30am-4.30pm Tue-Sun) FREE, set in a verdant patchwork of tea plantations, has the best cuppas and pano-ramic views.

The narrow approach road leads past worker housing and a **Hindu temple** (tea pickers are predominantly Indian) to the modern visitor centre, where you can witness tea production firsthand, and a **cafe** (☎ 05-496 2096; www.bohtea.com; Brinchang; ⊗9am-4.30pm Tue-Sun) where you can sip a cuppa while surveying the plantations below. Free 15-minute tours showing the tea-making process are conducted half-hourly.

The estate is located in the hills north of Brinchang, off the road to Gunung Brinchang. Public buses running between Tanah Rata and Kampung Raja pass the turn-off to Gunung Brinchang. From there it's 4km along the winding road, after which it's another 15 minutes' walk downhill to the visitor centre.

A taxi from Tanah Rata costs RM30 each way.

DESTINA-TION	PRICE (RM)	DURA-TION	FREQUENCY (PER DAY)
Brinchang	2	20min	every 2hr, 6.30am-6.30pm
Ipoh	20	2½-3hr	7
Kuala Lumpur	35-40	4¾hr	at least 10, 8.30am-5.30pm
Melaka	70	6hr	1 (or change in KL)
Penang	32-40	5hr	at least 3
Singapore	125-140	10hr	at least 3

TAXI

Long-distance **taxi** (Map p140; ☑05-491 2355; Jln Besar, Tanah Rata) fares are posted on a board at Terminal Freesia. During our visit, rates were RM180 to Ipoh, RM400 to Penang (George Town) and RM400 to RM550 to Taman Negara.

❶ Getting Around

While we never recommend hitchhiking, some travellers do so to get between Tanah Rata, Brinchang and the tea plantations beyond.

BUS

Buses run between Tanah Rata and Brinchang between 6.30am and 6.30pm every two hours or so (from RM2). Mention your main-road destination when boarding and the driver will likely drop you close.

TAXI

Taxis from Tanah Rata operate at fixed rates and all prices are posted on a board at Terminal Freesia. At the time of writing, rates from Tanah Rata were Brinchang (RM10), Boh Sungei Palas (RM30), Raaju's (RM20), Tringkap (RM25) and Mossy Forest (RM120). For touring around, a taxi costs RM25 per hour.

Pulau Pangkor

POP 25,000

From a swaying hammock on Coral Beach, Pulau Pangkor's turbulent past feels a world away. 'Beautiful Island' is a former pirate hideout and bit player in the battle to control the Selat Melaka (Strait of Melaka). In the 17th century the Dutch built a fort here in their bid to monopolise the Perak tin trade, and were swiftly driven out. In 1874 a contender for the Perak throne sought British backing and the Pangkor Treaty was signed, ushering in the colonial period.

These days the only ruckus is from monkeys, hornbills – big-beaked birds that are abundant on Pangkor – and Malaysian

VALE ECO CENTER

Immerse yourself in biodiverse Teluk Rubiah forest with a little help from this informative eco centre. An offshoot of green NGO EcoMY (www.ecomy.org), the **Vale Eco Center** (☑012-284 2881; www.vale.com; Jln Telok Muroh, Lumut; ☺8.30am-6pm) educates visitors about the 100 plant and 128 bird species in the forest and promotes minimum-impact tourism (plastics are banned in the park). For guided walks, email a month ahead; otherwise embark on three marked forest trails (allow 2½ hours). An excellent stop before boarding a ferry to jungly, hornbill-packed Pangkor Island.

For optimum bird-watching opportunities and mild temperatures, tour the forest between 8.30am and noon.

weekend warriors. Few foreign visitors wash ashore, probably because the beaches aren't Malaysia's best.

Beyond resort centres such as Teluk Nipah and Pasir Bogar, there's a subdued, villagey feel. Stroll Sungai Pinang Kecil (SPK) or colourful Teluk Gedong to experience a slower pace...if you can bear to leave that hammock.

❍ Sights

The island's east coast is its workaday side, home to two fishing villages, **Sungai Pinang Kecil** (SPK) and **Sungai Pinang Besar** (SPB). The road that runs along the east coast turns west at **Pangkor Town**, home to most of the island's amenities, then crosses the island to **Pasir Bogak**, which has a good (though crowded) beach. From there the road veers north to the village of **Teluk Nipah**, another busy beach, and a good destination for water sports and snorkelling. Continuing north, **Coral Beach** is the best (public) beach on Pangkor.

Foo Lin Kong   TEMPLE
(Map p144; Sungai Pinang Besar; ☺7am-7pm) The most attractive temple on Pulau Pangkor is colourful Foo Lin Kong, a landscaped site with flower gardens, dragon-roofed pavilions and a miniature Great Wall of China threading the site. Climb the stairs to overlook the temple's glittering tiled roofs and the hills beyond. It's 500m west of the main road between Pangkor Town and Sungai Pinang Kecil.

Pulau Pangkor

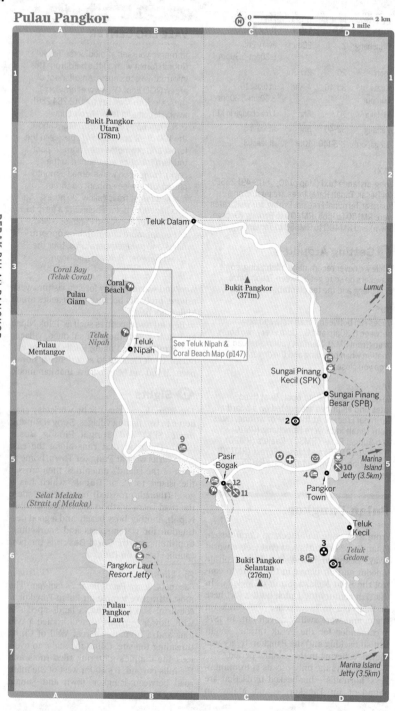

0   2 km
0   1 mile

Bukit Pangkor
Utara
(178m)

Teluk Dalam

Coral Bay
(Teluk Coral)

Coral
Beach

Pulau
Giam

Bukit Pangkor
(371m)

Lumut

Teluk
Nipah

Teluk
Nipah

See Teluk Nipah &
Coral Beach Map (p147)

Pulau
Mentangor

Sungai Pinang
Kecil (SPK)

Sungai Pinang
Besar (SPB)

2

5

9

Pasir
Bogak

7
12
11

Selat Melaka
(Strait of Melaka)

4

10

Marina
Island
Jetty (3.5km)

Pangkor
Town

6

Pangkor Laut
Resort Jetty

Teluk
Kecil

3

8
1

Teluk
Gedong

Bukit Pangkor
Selantan
(276m)

Pulau
Pangkor
Laut

Marina Island
Jetty (3.5km)

Pulau Pangkor

⊙ Sights
1 Batu Bersurat......................................D6
2 Foo Lin Kong.......................................C5
3 Kota Belanda......................................D6

⊜ Sleeping
4 BestStay Hotel....................................D5
5 Pangkor Guesthouse SPK...................D4
6 Pangkor Laut Resort...........................B6

7 Pangkor Sandy Beach Resort..............C5
8 Tiger Rock Resort................................D6
9 Vikri Beach Resort..............................B5

⊗ Eating
10 Pangkor Kopitiam...............................D5
11 Restoran Fong Leong.........................C5
12 Restoran Pasir Bogak.........................C5

There's a theme-park atmosphere thanks to the cartoonish statues and souvenir stands. Donations are encouraged; place them in the tin sentrymen at the entrance.

A taxi from Pangkor Town costs RM6.

Kota Belanda RUINS
(Dutch Fort; Map p144; Teluk Gedong) FREE The remains of a Dutch fort with a turbulent history are attractively preserved 2km south of Pangkor Town. Built in 1670 to store supplies of Perak's precious tin, it was sacked by Malays in 1690. The Dutch managed to rebuild the fort in 1743, only to abandon it five years later after repeated attacks from local warrior chiefs.

The old fort was totally swallowed by jungle until 1973, when it was reconstructed as far as the remaining bricks would allow. Nowadays it's a well-managed site framed by palm trees and trim lawns.

A taxi from Pangkor Town costs RM16.

Batu Bersurat HISTORIC SITE
(Sacred Rock; Map p144; Teluk Gedong) Close to the waterfront at Teluk Gedong is this mammoth stone carved with the symbol of the Dutch East India Company (Vereenigde Oost-Indische Compagnie; VOC) and other graffiti, including a faint depiction of a tiger stealing a child.

Lin Je Kong Temple TEMPLE
(Map p147; Coral Beach) FREE A small, psychedelic, open-air temple, adorned with statues of giant mushrooms, Chinese dragons and – for some reason – cartoon mice, perches above the northern edge of Coral Beach. Popular with photo-snapping families, Lin Je Kong visits are as much about the sea views as the shrine.

✦ Activities

Snorkel gear, boats and jet skis can be hired at hotels or on the beach at Pasir Bogak and Teluk Nipah; a 15-minute **banana boat ride** costs RM15 to RM25, and a small boat to take you **snorkelling** at pocket-sized nearby islands costs from RM25 per person.

🛌 Sleeping

Teluk Nipah has a big buffet of budget to midrange beach resorts. To the south, Pasir Bogak has several bigger, midrange resorts. Lodgings in Pangkor Town and Sungai Pinang Kecil (SPK) offer a more local feel, though they're distant from good beaches.

Rates vary between peak (weekends and holidays) and off-peak prices. Finding a bed during major holidays, such as Chinese New Year, can be near impossible without advance reservations.

🛏 Teluk Nipah

Nazri Nipah Camp CHALET $
(Map p147; ☑ 05-685 2014; Lot 4445; d hut with fan only RM60, tr/f RM80/160, not incl breakfast; ❋ 🛜) Accommodation ranges from simple A-frames to bungalows with private bathrooms at this backpacker favourite, strung with maps, flags and other travel regalia. The garden-set lodgings are very basic – avoid if you have a terror of insects – but Nazri Nipah has many fans for its relaxing ambience and beer garden. Staff are so laidback you might not find them.

Ombak Inn B&B $$
(Map p147; ☑ 05-685 5223; www.ombakinnchalet.com; Lot 4440; d RM100-180, f RM180-250, incl breakfast; ❋ 🛜) Chilled-out Ombak Inn is stretched across a bougainvillea-draped garden, with walkways shaded by leaves larger than your head. Lodgings are priced by size and quality – we recommend the modern 'premium' rooms (from RM120 to RM180): they're tile floored, pastel coloured and have extras such as kettles.

Budget Beach Resort RESORT $$
(Map p147; ☑ 05-685 3529; d/tr/q not incl breakfast RM130/160/190; ❋ 🛜) The self-deprecating name doesn't do justice to Budget Beach's

simple but neat wooden chalets. Standard doubles have little garden-facing terraces while triple and family rooms are plain but well sized.

Hospitable staff and a pleasant outdoor area lift this choice above Pulau Pangkor's formulaic resorts.

MNY Resort HOTEL $$
(Map p147; ☑05-685 5588; www.facebook.com/mnyhotel; d standard RM140-230, superior RM170-265, not incl breakfast; ✹🛜❄) Rooms at MNY are clean, candy-coloured and mercifully lacking the mildewy feel that prevails in too many Teluk Nipah hotels. The better rooms have hardwood furnishings, all have TVs and a combination of fan and air-con. The highlight is the small rooftop pool with jungly views.

Anjungan RESORT $$
(Map p147; ☑05-685 1500; www.anjunganresort pangkor.com; d/tr/q incl breakfast from RM174/221/278; ✹🛜❄) On the northern stretch of Teluk Nipah's main drag, Anjungan is quieter than neighbouring resorts, with a chic, family-friendly ambience. The chalet-style rooms have tiled floors and quaint trimmings such as Dutch ceramic lamps and wicker chairs; 'deluxe' rooms all have balconies. Outdoors there's a novelty pool shaped like a ship, plus a Jacuzzi and kids' wading pool.

LOCAL KNOWLEDGE

GREEN PANGKOR

There's a battle under way to save Pangkor Island. No visitor will fail to notice the overflowing trash cans, rubbish left on beaches and the abundance of one-use plastics. But NGO **EcoMY** (http://ecomy.org) has been developing eco-tourism through a mentoring program, empowering local business owners to minimise their environmental impact. A guided jungle trek, culture tour or wildlife-spotting walk with **Pangkor Nature Guides** (☑013-444 4655; www. facebook.com/pangkornatureguides) 🖉 is an excellent way to discover the island's thickly forested interior and learn more about the ecological challenges faced by this booming holiday destination.

🛏 Pasir Bogak

Vikri Beach Resort GUESTHOUSE, CHALET $$
(Map p144; ☑05-685 4258; http://vikribeach.com; Lot 6; d/tr RM150/180, f from RM230, not incl breakfast; ✹🛜) Family-run Vikri has a dozen wooden and brick bungalows dotted around straggling gardens, with the beach just across the main road. 'Standard villas' have clashing colour schemes, but the pricier chalets (RM250) have an agreeable contemporary design. Rooms show signs of wear, but it's a peaceful, homely environment. Breakfast is an extra RM15.

Pangkor Sandy Beach Resort RESORT $$
(Map p144; ☑05-685 3027; www.pangkorsandy beach.com; 30 Jln Pasir Bogak; d/tr from RM183/242, chalet from RM320, incl breakfast; ✹🛜❄) Popular with groups, Sandy Beach has neat, if unexciting, contemporary rooms; the best of them face the cloud-shaped outdoor pool.

🛏 East Coast Villages

Pangkor Guesthouse SPK GUESTHOUSE $
(Map p144; ☑011-3551 4728; www.spkpangkor guesthouse.blogspot.com; Sungai Pinang Kecil; d with private/shared bathroom RM80/70, dm RM35, not incl breakfast; ✹🛜) To steep yourself in local life, flee the beach resorts and bed down in less-touristed fishing village Sungai Pinang Kecil. There's a pleasant terrace with hammocks and welcoming English-speaking host Joyce Guok can advise on local food and ecofriendly activities in the area.

BestStay Hotel HOTEL $
(Map p144; ☑05-685 3111; www.beststay.com.my; Lot 55, Jln Pasir Bogak, Pangkor Town; d/tr/f not incl breakfast from RM80/120/170; ✹🛜) A reliable if uncharming option for travellers needing accommodation close to Pangkor Town jetty, BestStay has thoroughly beige rooms with fast wi-fi (a rarity on Pangkor).

★Tiger Rock Resort BOUTIQUE HOTEL $$$
(Map p144; ☑019-574 7183; www.tigerrock.info; Teluk Gedong; d per person incl full board RM690-820; ✹@🛜❄) 🖉 Hidden deep in the jungle 1km south of Pangkor Town, Tiger Rock offers romantic rooms decorated with vintage flair. Local artwork and upcycled materials pile on the charm, and there's a library and bamboo-fringed outdoor pool. It doesn't accept walk-ins (literally – the road shouldn't be tackled on foot; it's rough and there are dogs). Reserve at least a fortnight ahead.

Pangkor Laut

★ Pangkor Laut Resort
RESORT $$$

(Map p144; ☑ 05-699 1100; www.pangkorlautresort. com; r RM860-2310, ste RM2990-5500, incl breakfast; ✸@�✲) An impeccably managed private island resort lies west of Pulau Pangkor, reachable only by prebooked guests on a 20-minute boat transfer from Marina Bay. The resort feels deliciously secluded: thatched-roof garden villas have luxe interiors, and sea villas perch on stilts above emerald water. Around the island are high-quality restaurants, a beachfront barbecue and sand that shimmers. Book ahead.

✗ Eating

✗ Teluk Nipah

Daddy's Café
INTERNATIONAL $

(Map p147; ☑ 05-685 1744; mains RM12-18; ⏰11am-11pm; 🛜) Reliable and adored by backpackers, Daddy's feels like a haven at the northernmost edge of Coral Beach. Food service runs throughout the day and it's hot, fresh and well presented: towers of satay skewers, seafood fried rice and (of course) ice-blended fruit drinks. Settle into a plastic chair on the sand or hide from the heat inside. Serves beer, too.

★ Nipah Deli
MALAYSIAN, CHINESE $$

(Map p147; ☑ 05-685 1416; www.facebook.com/ NipahDeli; mains RM14-25; ⏰11am-11pm; 🍴) The best dining experience in the Teluk Nipah area, this beachfront restaurant combines generous portions of mostly Malaysian home cooking with views out to sea. It's consistently very good: prawn noodles, DIY steamboat (where seafood and/or veggies are simmered in a tureen at your table) and a respectable number of vegetarian dishes.

✗ Pasir Bogak

Restoran Fong Leong
CHINESE $

(Map p144; mains RM6-20; ⏰5-10pm) Fong Leong is a place where locals gather to knock back Tiger beer over steamed fish and fried squid. Expect brusque service but tasty food.

Turn left off Pasir Bogak's main road to the beach, 100m beyond Coral Bay Resort.

Teluk Nipah & Coral Beach

N 0 —————— 200 m
   0 —————— 0.1 miles

Teluk Nipah & Coral Beach

◎ Sights
1 Lin Je Kong Temple A1

🛏 Sleeping
2 Anjungan A2
3 Budget Beach Resort B3
4 MNY Resort B3
5 Nazri Nipah Camp B2
6 Ombak Inn A3

✗ Eating
7 Daddy's Café A1
8 Nipah Deli A1

Restoran Pasir Bogak
CHINESE $$

(Map p144; mains RM8-44; ⏰6-10pm Tue-Sun) Tourists come here for a seafood splurge and beers galore (we suspect they carry every local brand). The dry chilli chicken, served with a rich, spicy paste and curry leaves, is a Chinese-Indian-Malay fusion that works a treat. The steamed seafood is expertly cooked, but do your maths on the price-by-weight menu. Go early; it's crowded by 7pm.

It's off Pasir Bogak's main road, opposite Coral Bay Resort.

✕ Pangkor Town

Pangkor Kopitiam   MALAYSIAN **$**
(Map p144; ☑018-955 9742; jetty; laksa from RM5,
mains RM7.50-17; ☺10.30am-10.30pm Wed-Mon;
❄🛜) Meals at ferry terminals aren't usually memorable, but this jetty cafe whips
up decent Thai and Western-style fast food
(chicken chop, squid fried rice, laksa, fish
and chips) along with more elaborate menus
such as whole steamed fish with pak choi.
Pleasant views of boats crowding the shore.

🛈 Information

Medical Clinic (Klinik Kesihatan Pangkor; Map
p144; ☑05-685 4048; 189 Jln Pasir Bogak,
Pangkor Town) Around 500m west of Pangkor
Town's jetty.

Police Station (Map p144; ☑05-685 1222; Jln
Pasir Bogak, Taman Desa Pangkor) Pangkor's
police station is 1km west of Pangkor Town's
jetty.

Post Office (Map p144; ☑05-685 1281; Jln
Pasir Bogak, Pangkor Town; ☺8.30am-5.30pm
Mon-Fri)

🛈 Getting There & Away

Lumut and Marina Island are the mainland gateways for Pulau Pangkor. If you miss the last bus
out of Lumut, **Brezza Hotel** (Lot 4118, Jln Sultan
Yusuf Izzuddin, Lumut), a short walk west of the
jetty, is a convenient place to crash.

BOAT

Ferries (return ticket RM14) reach Pulau Pangkor
from **Lumut Jetty** (Terminal Jeti Lumut; Lumut;
40 minutes, every half-hour or 45 minutes
between 6.30am and 8.30pm) and **Marina
Island Jetty** (☑05-680 5888; Jln Utama Marina
Island, Lumut; 15 minutes, hourly between
6.45am and 7.30pm, with services running
later in July and August). Advance booking isn't
necessary. Both jetties are near to ample open
and closed parking lots (RM10 to RM20 per day)
and have cafes and other facilities. Lumut has a
bus station.

From Lumut most ferries stop at **SPK Jetty**
(Map p144; Sungai Pinang Kecil) before continuing to the main jetty in **Pangkor Town** (Map
p144; ☑05-683 5800; Pangkor Town); don't
hop off too soon unless you're staying in SPK.

Pangkor Laut Resort (Map p144; Pangkor
Laut) is served by a separate ferry service from
Marina Island; a resort booking is required.

BUS

Lumut's scruffy bus station is a brief walk from
the jetty to Pulau Pangkor and is well connected
to major towns.

DESTINATION	PRICE (RM)	DURA-TION	FREQUENCY (PER DAY)
Butterworth	19-24	3½ hrs	10
Ipoh	9-10	2 hrs	at least 8
Johor Bahru	62-70	8½ hrs	2 (morning & evening)
Kota Bharu	48	8½ hrs	2 (morning & evening)
Kuala Lumpur	27	4-4½ hrs	at least hourly (7.30am-11pm)
Melaka	42-44	6½ hrs	5
Singapore	70-130	9 hrs	at least 2

🛈 Getting Around

In the absence of public transport, you will be
obliged to use Pangkor's candy-pink minibus
taxis, which operate between 6.30am and 9pm.
Set-fare services for up to four people from
the jetty in Pangkor Town include Pasir Bogak
(RM10), Teluk Nipah (RM16) and destinations in
the north of the island (RM20). Travel between
Teluk Nipah and Pasir Bogak will cost you
RM15. Cab drivers treat fares as non-negotiable
(we've tried).

The island can be explored by confident
motorcyclists (or hardened bike riders). Bendy
roads and distracted drivers mean it's not good
for beginners. There are numerous places at
Pangkor Town, Pasir Bogak and Teluk Nipah that
rent motorcycles at around RM50 per day and
bicycles for RM15. **Ah Toh Rental** (☑012-602
0409; per day motorbike/car from RM50/100)
loans motorbikes and, when there's availability,
cars; pick-up in Pangkor Town.

Kuala Kangsar
☑05 / POP 40,000

The epicentre for some of Malaysia's defin-
ing moments, Kuala Kangsar (KK) is the
royal seat of Perak. Orbiting its teeming
town centre are some of the state's most lavish constructions, including converted palaces and an impressive gilt-domed mosque.

In a lesser state of finery are buildings
dating to KK's colonial past. The town was
the first foothold of the British, who moved
to control the peninsula by installing Residents at the royal courts here in the 1870s.
KK was also the birthplace of Malaysia's
rubber industry and site of the first durbar
(conference of Malay sultans) in 1897. The
growth of Ipoh and Taiping over the past
century has left KK lagging behind, but it's a
worthy day trip.

⊙ Sights

Kuala Kangsar's top sights sprawl over an area southeast of the centre, best explored by car. This is not a town suited to pedestrians, due to roaring traffic and missing sidewalks.

If you arrive by public transport, consider asking a taxi driver to take you to the top trio – Istana Kenangan, Masjid Ubudiah and Sultan Azlan Shah Gallery – as a half-day excursion. Ray the Tour (p129) can arrange guided trips of KK from Ipoh that include pottery making.

★ **Sultan Azlan Shah Gallery** MUSEUM
(Istana Kota; ☑ 05-777 5362; http://gsas.perak.gov.my; Jln Istana; adult/child RM4/2; ⊙ 10am-5pm Sat-Thu, 10am-noon & 2.45-5pm Fri; P) This former royal palace, also known as Istana Kota and Istana Hulu, is a showy mash-up of Renaissance, neoclassical and Moorish styles. Completed in 1903 its marbled hallways now host exhibitions honouring the life of the 34th sultan of Perak, Sultan Azlan Shah (1928–2014): see his rotating cabinet of gem-crusted watches, sunglasses, items from his school days and a separate building sheltering his Rolls-Royces and other luxury vehicles.

Other royal family treasures include HRH's swords and kris (elaborately carved daggers with jewel-studded scabbards) and the fanciest baby cradle you've ever seen. State gifts are also displayed, including Malaysia's largest recorded fungus. The royal reaction to this mighty mushroom is not described.

When we passed through, renovation works were due to begin; check ahead before making a special trip.

Masjid Ubudiah MOSQUE
(Ubudiah Mosque; Jln Istana; ⊙ 9am-noon, 3-4pm & 5.30-6pm Sat-Thu; P) With bands of Italian marble and enormous gold domes, Masjid Ubudiah is a contender for the title of Malaysia's prettiest mosque. Commissioned by Perak's 28th sultan, Idris Shah, after his recovery from illness, Masjid Ubudiah – meaning 'mosque of self-surrender to Allah' – was masterminded by AB Hubback, the architect behind numerous colonial buildings in Perak. The mosque was completed in 1917, though the sultan didn't live to see it finished. Dress modestly.

Istana Kenangan MUSEUM
(Jln Istana; ⊙ 9.30am-5pm Sat-Thu, 9.30am-12.15pm & 2.45-5pm Fri; P) FREE Also known as the Palace of Memories, Istana Kenangan is made of wood (without a single metal nail) and bamboo woven into diamond-shaped patterns across its exterior walls. Built in 1926 it served as temporary royal quarters until the nearby Istana Iskandariah was completed. It was also used as a stopgap mausoleum for members of the royal family awaiting burial.

Clock Tower TOWER
Kuala Kangsar's gold-domed clock tower was installed in the late 1930s, in honour of the coronation of King George VI. A handy landmark, it stands in the middle of KK's traffic-clogged central roundabout.

OFF THE BEATEN TRACK

PREHISTORIC LENGGONG

One of the world's oldest complete human skeletons was discovered in the Lenggong Valley, 40km north of Kuala Kangsar. Unearthed in Gua Runtuh ('fallen cave'), scientists have verified the skeleton's age as 11,000 years. Together with other Palaeolithic and neolithic findings, Perak Man brought Lenggong to the attention of scientists worldwide. Outside the African continent, Lenggong's archaeological sites fill in the puzzle pieces for one of the longest timelines of early humans in a single place.

The region is now listed as a World Heritage Site, though Lenggong hasn't attracted much attention from tourists. Ipoh Secrets (p129) can arrange trekking tours around the waterfalls, caves and excavation sites of this ancient corner of Perak. **Lenggong Archaeological Gallery** (☑ 05-767 9700; Kampung Baru Kota Tampan, Lenggong; ⊙ 9am-6pm) FREE shines a light on the region's ancient past, but when we passed through, the museum was undergoing lengthy renovation. When it's up and running, it will be a worthy stop for anyone travelling between Ipoh and Royal Belum State Park.

Kuala Kangsar

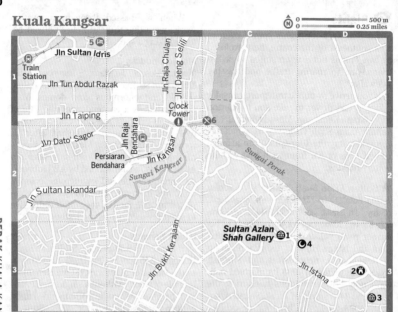

Kuala Kangsar

⊙ Top Sights
1 Sultan Azlan Shah Gallery.................C3

⊙ Sights
2 Istana Iskandariah............................D3
3 Istana Kenangan.............................D3
4 Masjid Ubudiah................................D3

🛏 Sleeping
5 The Shop A1

✕ Eating
6 Medan Cendol Dan Laksa.................C1

Istana Iskandariah   PALACE
(Jln Istana) The official residence of the sultan of Perak is arguably the most attractive royal palace in Malaysia, so it's a shame those of nonroyal blood can't get closer than a quick peek from the road. Completed in 1933, the two-floor palace is an intriguing mix of Arab and art-deco architectural styles.

🛏 Sleeping & Eating

KK's sights are easily covered in a day. If you do decide to linger, the hectic city-centre area has several budget hotels, as well as more atmospheric choices outside the centre.

The signature dish is Kuala Kangsar–style laksa, where wheat (instead of rice) noodles are submerged in a coconut and tamarind broth. KK is also well known for excellent *cendol* (shaved ice with green noodles, syrups, coconut milk and toppings such as rice and red beans).

Find both at dedicated food hall **Medan Cendol Dan Laksa** (Jln Sungai Perak; cendol from RM2, mains from RM4; ⊙11am-6pm) by the river – there are numerous noodle, coffee and dessert places and hawker stalls around here.

★ The Shop   HOTEL **$$**
(☏017-743 8401; www.facebook.com/theshop hotel; 1 Persiaran Seri Delima, Taman Seri Delima; d RM95-158, f from RM194, not incl breakfast; P❄🛜) Adjoining a fabulous coffee shop 1km east of the train station, The Shop is unquestionably Kuala Kangsar's best place to stay. The design is rough-hewn (industrial themes, chocolate-brown drapes and cushions), but it's exceedingly comfortable, from plush beds to ultramodern bathrooms. Note that the cheaper rooms don't have windows.

ℹ️ Getting There & Away

The **bus station** (Jln Raja Bendahara) is located near the city centre. Timetables and prices are vulnerable to change.

DESTINATION	PRICE (RM)	DURA-TION (HR)	FREQUENCY (PER DAY)
Butterworth	11	1½-2	2
Ipoh	5-10	1-1½	9
KLIA	45	4	5
Kota Bharu	35-39	6½	5-6
Kuala Lumpur	24-27	3¼-3¾	9
Lumut (for Pulau Pangkor)	16	2	2
Melaka	45	5½	1 (11.45am)
Putrajaya	28	4	3
Singapore	65-125	8½-9	2-3 (1 overnight)
Taiping	5-13	1	half-hourly

Kuala Kangsar's **train station** (off Jln Sultan Idris) is 1.5km northwest of the centre. Nine daily services reach Taiping (RM13 to RM14, 20 minutes), Ipoh (RM16 to RM19, 30 minutes) and Kuala Lumpur (RM44 to RM57, three to 3½ hours), and five go to Butterworth (RM25 to RM32, 1¼ hours). Check www.ktmb.com.my for the latest fares and schedules.

A paid-parking system operates in Kuala Kangsar (RM2 for five hour-long tickets). Buy vouchers from shops around Jln Temenggong (you may have to ask in a few) and scratch off the time and date.

Taiping

📱 05 / POP 245,200

Perak's second-largest town is defined by water and greenery. Locals laud it as the 'City of Peace' for trailblazing Malaysia's first museum, first railway and first newspapers in English, Malay and Tamil. But it's Taiping's 'Rain City' title that has stuck. Taiping has the biggest volume of rainfall in Peninsular Malaysia: all the better for its verdant lake gardens (and the pastime of 'rain betting', where locals take a punt on what time downpours will start and stop).

Taiping has the same ingredients as Penang and Ipoh – great food, elegantly weathered colonial architecture, street art – but on a smaller scale. It's a worthwhile detour in its own right, and a stepping stone to hill station Bukit Larut and the mangrove reserve in Kuala Sepetang. Kid-friendly attractions such as the zoo have also made it a favourite getaway for Malaysians with big families and even bigger umbrellas.

⊙ Sights & Activities

⭐ **Taman Tasik Taiping**   GARDENS

(Lake Gardens; Jln Taman Tasik; 🅿️) **FREE** Taiping's centrepiece is a 64-hectare expanse of lagoons and grassland east of town. Created in 1880 on the site of an abandoned tin mine, the gardens owe their lush greenery to Taiping's annual rainfall – thought to be the highest in Peninsular Malaysia. These artificial lakes are a pleasant place in which to picnic beneath a century-old tree, watching for the monitor lizards that glide through the algae-rich water. Alternatively, hire a paddleboat (RM10) and bob around.

⭐ **Muzium Perak**   MUSEUM

(📱05-807 2057; www.jmm.gov.my; Jln Taming Sari; adult/child RM5/2; ⊙9am-6pm; 🅿️🚻) With many of Perak's museums in dire need of more funding, Taiping's well-maintained Muzium Perak stands out. Parts of the pristine, whitewashed building date to the 1900s and inside are diverting displays about natural history (complete with a century-old elephant skeleton), state history and Malaysian customs. The silver engraving, embroidery and Orang Asli masks are highlights. Perfect for one of Taiping's many rainy days.

All Saints Church   CHURCH

(Jln Taming Sari; ⊙hours vary; 🅿️) Consecrated in 1887, this timber church is one of the oldest Anglican churches in Malaysia and is still used as a place of worship. The Gothic-inspired ensemble was designed by Australian architect George A Lefroy. Step inside to see original stained-glass windows, a pipe organ (a rarity in Malaysia), carved pews and brass plaques commemorating benefactors and parishioners past.

Zoo Taiping & Night Safari   ZOO

(📱05-808 6577; www.zootaiping.gov.my; Jln Taman Tasik; zoo adult/child RM16/8, night safari adult/child RM20/10; ⊙8.30am-6pm daily, night safari 8-11pm Sun-Fri, 8pm-midnight Sat; 🅿️🚻) Animals are always happiest in the wild, but Taiping's zoo is a well-maintained space managed by conservation-minded staff. Elephants have shade and space to bathe in dust and water, while other creatures such as lions, Malayan sun bears and orangutans have sizeable enclosures. A miniature train

Taiping

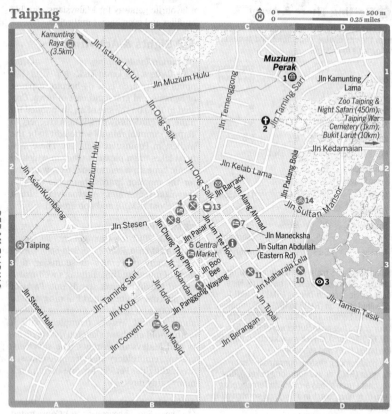

N 0 ____ 500 m
0 ____ 0.25 miles

Taiping

◉ Top Sights
1 Muzium Perak C1

◉ Sights
2 All Saints Church.............................. C2
3 Taman Tasik Taiping.......................... D3

🛏 Sleeping
4 Cherry Inn... B2
5 Legend Inn... B4
6 Louis Hotel.. B3
7 Sojourn Beds & Cafe........................ C3

✕ Eating
8 Ansari Famous Cendol....................... B3
9 Larut Matang Food Court.................. C3
10 Pusat Makanan Taman Tasik............ D3
11 Pusat Penjaja Taiping....................... C3
12 Triple Shot.. B2

🍷 Drinking & Nightlife
13 DoubleTap... C2

ℹ Transport
14 CycleDios.. D2

chugs around the site, if walking in the heat
is too much.

The **night safari** offers a chance to see
nocturnal animals beginning to stir.

Zoo Taiping is located about 2km east of
central Taiping; a taxi here will cost around
RM10. Parking costs RM3.

Burmese Pools SWIMMING
(off Jln Bukit Larut) FREE Thought to have been
discovered by Burmese soldiers in the 1920s,
these natural pools, fed by the Batu Tegoh
River, are a popular bathing spot for families. They are 3km east of central Taiping,
off the road that leads to Bukit Larut (a taxi
from the centre should cost RM10).

🛏 Sleeping

★**Sojourn Beds & Cafe** HOSTEL $
(☑05-805 4048, 012-464 3443; www.sojournbc.com; 54 Jln Kota; dm/s/d incl breakfast with shared bathroom RM34/39/84; ❄🛜) In a high-ceilinged 1930s shophouse, cheerful Sojourn has four-bed dorms with pod-style bunks – that means more privacy and less rocking from the top bunk. There's bike rental (per half-/full day RM6/10), lockers and primo local knowledge on tap. When we passed through, a new location (still in central Taiping) was on the horizon.

Cherry Inn GUESTHOUSE $
(☑05-805 2223; 17 Jln Stesen; d/q not incl breakfast from RM60/120; ❄🛜) Showcasing Chinese antiques and kitschy ornaments at every turn (including a ceramic Mao shushing noisy guests), Cherry Inn is a characterful place, plum in the centre of Taiping. Rooms are pastel-washed and well priced, with wet-room bathrooms (cheaper rooms have shared bathrooms). There's also a two-room apartment available for RM250.

★**Sentosa Villa** HOTEL $$
(☑05-805 1000; www.sentosa-villa.com; Jln 8, Taman Sentosa; r RM138-338, villa RM208-628; P❄🛜) Unquestionably Taiping's most attractive place to stay, this complex of villas is alive with durian trees, palm groves and teeming ponds. Chalets have an organic feel, with bare brick and polished wood floors, while split-level family accommodation has fun wooden ladders between rooms. Gathered in the main building are more standard hotel rooms: less sumptuous but tile-floored and well equipped.

Sentosa Villa is 3km east of the town centre. It's located off the road to Bukit Larut – follow the signs. It's best to have a car, or you can taxi to and from the centre (less than RM10).

Louis Hotel HOTEL $$
(☑05-808 2333; www.louishotel.com.my; 129-131 Jln Pasar; d/tr not incl breakfast from RM98/138; ❄🛜) Trim, surgically clean rooms are attended by friendly staff at this excellent all-rounder, opposite Taiping's wet market.

The hotel supplies parking vouchers for use on the surrounding streets. Beware: a deluge of market shoppers can create bottlenecks – ask the owner for help if your vehicle gets blocked in!

Legend Inn HOTEL $$
(☑05-806 0000; www.legendinn.com; 2 Jln Long Jafaar; d RM129-189, ste RM229-389, incl breakfast; P❄🛜) Located across a busy road from the bus station, Legend Inn has modern rooms at reasonable rates. The general feel is understated, with monochrome decor, efficient staff and it's kept nicely clean. Light sleepers should note the mosque across the road.

🍴 Eating & Drinking

★**Ansari Famous Cendol** DESSERTS $
(cnr Jln Chung Thye Phin & Jln Barrack; cendol RM1.60-3.70; ⏰10am-5pm, or earlier) Creamy and sweet with generous amounts of green noodles and *gula melaka* (dark coconut-sugar syrup), shaved-ice desserts have been dished up at Ansari since 1940. This third-generation seller gets our vote as the best *cendol* in Taiping.

Pusat Makanan Taman Tasik HAWKER $
(Jln Maharaja Lela; mains from RM3; ⏰24hr) This lakeside hawker court and coffee shop has a good selection of stalls serving dishes from *curry mee* (yellow noodles submerged in spicy broth) to *ikan bakar* (chargrilled fish) and oyster omelette.

Pusat Penjaja Taiping HAWKER $
(Jln Tupai; mains from RM3; ⏰9am-11pm) *Nasi ayam* (chicken rice), laksa and fruit-festooned ice-blended drinks are served up at this bustling, great-quality food court.

Larut Matang Food Court FOOD HALL $
(cnr Jln Panggong Wayang & Jln Chung Thye Phin; mains from RM3; ⏰11am-7pm) Busiest and best at lunch, this gritty court is half Chinese and half Malay. Look out for local favourite **Omar's Popiah** stall, where you can chomp on large rolls of crisp veggies wrapped in a wheat pancake.

Triple Shot EUROPEAN, CAFE $$
(☑05-8012957; www.facebook.com/tripleshotbedn coffee; 46 Jln Barrack; sandwiches from RM8, mains RM12-22; ⏰10am-11pm; ❄🛜) An eclectic menu, from Malaysian *kopitiam* (coffee shop) classics via fish and chips to bacon bruschetta and the occasional 'paleo' option, keeps things interesting at this trendy cafe. Many of the loyal punters are here purely for coffee: unusually for Malaysia, all servings are double shots and unsweetened.

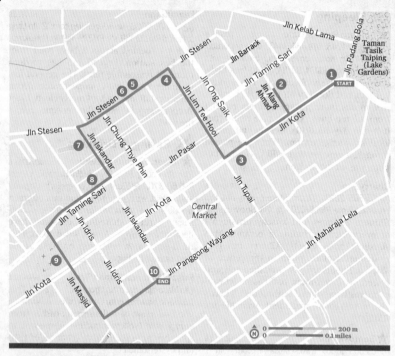

Town Walk
Colonial Taiping

START PERPUSTAKAAN TAIPING
END HOTEL PEACE
LENGTH 2KM; ONE TO TWO HOURS

Taiping's former role as a prosperous and important colonial-era outpost is still palpable in the city's well-preserved architecture. This walking tour offers the chance to admire Taiping's most notable colonial-era buildings, from religious monuments to state institutions (most can only be seen from outside).

Start at ❶ **Perpustakaan Taiping** (1882), the red-roofed public library. Nearby, the white neoclassical ❷ **District Office** is on Jln Alang Ahmad. Continue southwest along Jln Kota until you reach ❸ **Jam Besar Lama** (1890), the Old Clock Tower. It once functioned as Taiping's fire station (and later, its tourist information centre, though it was closed for a lengthy renovation when we passed through).

Turn right at Jln Lim Tee Hooi. On your left upon reaching Jln Stesen is the wood-shuttered ❹ **Town Rest House** (1894), formerly the governor's residence, in a shabby state of repair. Across Jln Stesen is

the well-preserved colonial ❺ **King Edward VII School** (1905), the classrooms of which were used as torture chambers by the Japanese during WWII. Taiping's original ❻ **train station** is a few steps west; Taiping was the starting point for Malaysia's first railway line, now defunct. Opened in 1885 it ran 13.5km to Port Weld (Kuala Sepetang).

Walking further west on Jln Stesen, you can see ❼ **St George's School** (1915). Head south on Jln Iskandar, then turn right onto Jln Taming Sari; here you'll find Taiping's tiny ❽ **Little India**. Follow the street west until Jln Masjid; opposite you'll see the ❾ **Old Kota Mosque** (1897), the oldest in Taiping, notable for its hexagonal design.

Moving south along Jln Masjid, turn left on Jln Panggong Wayang, where you'll see the ❿ **Hotel Peace**. Its Peranakan design features stained glass, stucco tiles and gold-painted lion heads roaring from stone columns. The scruffy hotel is better avoided, but the coffee shop downstairs is a serviceable spot for *kway teow* (fried noodles with fish balls) and a soda.

DoubleTap

CAFE

☎05-801 2502; www.facebook.com/doubletap taiping; cnr Jln Barrack & Jln Lim Tee Hooi; ◎8am-11pm Wed-Mon; 🛜) Catering to hip, laptop-wielding locals, Double Tap has a warehouse aesthetic (bare brick, beamed ceiling) and serves Western-style coffee (at Western prices...a flat white for RM8). It's a chic place to linger over homemade yoghurt or a tiramisu-flavoured latte.

Information

Post Office (☎05-807 7555; Jln Barrack; ◎8.30am-5.30pm Mon-Fri, to 1pm Sat) Located a block north of Taiping's major artery, Jln Taming Sari.

Taiping Hospital (☎05-820 4000; http://htaiping.moh.gov.my; Jln Taming Sari) Ask a local to call ahead, if you can.

Tourist Information Centre (355 Jln Kota; ◎10am-5pm Mon-Sat, 2-6pm Sun) Located in the former clock tower, this office was undergoing a seemingly endless period of renovation when we stopped by.

Getting There & Away

Taiping's long-distance bus station, **Kamunting Raya** (Stesen Bas Ekspres Kamunting Raya; ☎05-891 5279; Taman Medan Kamunting), is 7km north of the town centre – hop on bus 8 (RM1.20, 6am to 8.30pm) to get there to/from the local bus station, or take a taxi (RM10) to the town centre. Most southbound services pass **Medan Simpang** (cnr Rtes 74 & 1), 5km southwest of town (less than RM10 by taxi).

Prices and timetables are vulnerable to change but destinations include the following:

DESTINATION	PRICE (RM)	DURATION	FREQUENCY (PER DAY)
Butterworth (Penang)	10-15	2 hr	6
Ipoh	10	1½ hr	half-hourly (7.30am-5pm)
Kota Bharu	35	7-8 hr	1 (10am)
Kuala Lumpur	25-30	4 hr	at least hourly
Singapore	70-120	9 hr	at least 6 (morning & night)

Many regional buses leave from the **local bus station** (Terminal Taiping; Jln Masjid) across the street from Masjid Daerah Taiping. Destinations include Kuala Kangsar (RM3.90, one hour), with departures at least hourly from 6am to 7.30pm, and Lumut (for Pulau Pangkor; RM10, three hours), with three daily departures. Taxis also hang around here.

Taiping's train station is 1km west of the town centre, on the Kuala Lumpur–Butterworth line.

There are several daily trains to Kuala Lumpur (RM47 to RM62, three to six hours) and Butterworth (RM21 to RM26, one to 1½ hours), stopping at Kuala Kangsar (RM14, 20 minutes) and Ipoh (RM20 to RM24, one hour) en route.

Getting Around

Download the **CycleDios** (☎012-976 6726; http://cycledios.com; Jln Kota; per 30min RM1) app and register to use the automated city bike-rental service. There are pick-up locations across Taiping, including the zoo, lake gardens and the city centre.

Taxis can be hailed along main drag Jln Kota, especially near the market square (Halaman Pasar).

PERAK KUALA SEPETANG

Kuala Sepetang

☎05 / POP 5000

Gateway to the teeming **Matang Mangrove Forest Reserve** (RM5; ◎8am-5pm), Kuala Sepetang is a sleepy fishing port 14km west of Taiping. The mangrove forest, a natural breakwater that supports a diverse ecosystem, is an enchanting place to explore by foot or on a boat ride – to organise this, contact **KS Eco Tours** (☎012-514 5023; www.kualasepetang.com) 🌿. The reserve is best known for its fireflies, which glow like fairy lights after sundown, but it's also spellbinding by day.

Travelling from Taiping, the entrance to the reserve is about 500m before Kuala Sepetang village. If you want to stay overnight, there are basic A-frame huts, which sleep between four and eight people, perched on stilts near the river's edge. Enquire at the entrance kiosk.

The lost-in-time village – still shown on some maps under its old name of Port Weld – has a **Charcoal Factory** (☎012-573 9563; www.facebook.com/pg/KualaSepetangCharcoalFactory) FREE, a small mosque and a few riverside fish restaurants.

Getting There & Away

Blue Omnibus 77 runs every 40 minutes from 6am to 7pm between Taiping's local bus station (opposite Masjid Daerah Taiping) and Kuala Sepetang (30 minutes, RM2). Buses can drop you at the forest reserve, 500m shy of the village, on request.

WORTH A TRIP

BUKIT LARUT

Wreathed in mist and rising 1035m above sea level, Bukit Larut is Malaysia's oldest (and smallest) hill resort. It's a pleasant half-day trip from Taiping, 10km southwest.

The British established the hill station in 1884 as a retreat from the lowland heat. Its tea plantations never came to fruition, but some of the era's original bungalows still speckle the hillside. Sedan chairs have long since been replaced by Land Rovers as the mode of uphill transport, but Bukit Larut still offers a tranquil glimpse of Perak's colonial past.

Reaching the top is half the fun; from there, there's fragrant, cool air, walking trails and romantically foggy views. The hill is also a favourite with hikers, though a good level of fitness is required to complete the steep, 10km climb (it can take 2½ hours one way). The setting is serene, but the walk requires jumping out of the path of 4WDs ferrying passengers up and down the serpentine road.

From the upper station, it's a further 40 minutes' hike along a tarmac road to the **telecom tower**, a lofty lookout where you can just about peer through the jungly treeline to a misty panorama beyond. Shortly after the 12.8km marker, the trail forks, its left-hand branch plying a heavily overgrown path to **Gunung Hijau** (1448m) lookout. Due to thick vegetation (competent hikers only), you can usually only follow the path for about 15 minutes, but even on this short walk there's a good chance of seeing monkeys and numerous birds.

There are a few self-catering chalets for rent on Bukit Larut (per night RM60 to RM150). Make bookings through the **Bukit Larut Office** (☑ 05-807 7241; Jln Bukit Larut; ⊗ 8am-4pm) and bring your own food.

Private cars are not allowed on the road up to Bukit Larut – it's only open to government Land Rovers, which run a regular service (round trip RM10) from the **station** (Jln Bukit Larut) at the foot of the hill. A taxi here from Taiping should cost RM10.

Belum-Temenggor Rainforest

A mantle of primeval jungle covers Perak's northernmost tip. Bordering Thailand to its north and the Malaysian state of Kelantan to the east, Belum-Temenggor Rainforest has thrived for 130 million years. The area was partly flooded after Temenggor Dam was completed in 1972. Tree trunks still reach out from the watery depths – a ghostly sight to greet travellers, who arrive by boat.

Dam-created Lake Temenggor spiders its way through the rainforest and into 1175-sq-km Royal Belum State Park. Permits and guides are essential in the protected area, where tapirs, sun bears, tigers and elephants make their home. Mammal sightings are rare, even with a guide at dawn or dusk when animals are most active. But it's a thrill a minute for bird-watchers, with all 10 of Malaysia's hornbill species cawing from the ancient trees. Spot orchids, splash beneath waterfalls and forget about the lack of phone signal – humankind can wait.

A typical tour itinerary in Belum includes a nature hike, an excursion to look for rafflesia in remote areas of the park and a tour of the Orang Asli village (only one village in the area receives visitors). Tour operators such as Belum Eco Resort (p157) have meaningful links with the Orang Asli here, but many travellers will feel uncomfortable witnessing tourists snapping cameras at villagers. Interrogate your tour provider about what's offered and what its links are with the Orang Asli village. Equally, be wary of tours that guarantee rafflesia sightings. These heavyweight parasitic blooms are hard to find and only bloom for a few days.

Locals say butterfly-spotting is at its best in April, May and November. The best months to see hornbills are August and September, while migratory birds arrive in October and November. Otters and eagles can be seen year-round, along with an eye-popping variety of fungi, flowers and insect life.

◉ Sights

Royal Belum State Park　STATE PARK
(Belum-Temenggor Forest Reserve; www.royalbelum. my) This 1175-sq-km park within Belum-Temenggor Rainforest was gazetted in 2007 to protect a rich menagerie of tigers, tapirs,

panthers and the Sumatran rhino – though the latter is now believed to be extinct in Malaysia. The spears of submerged trees poking above the waterline of the largely dam-flooded lake are an eerie sight.

A permit and guide are needed to explore; hotels can help with both. Book a fortnight ahead to secure tours and a permit (RM20); you'll need a scan of your passport.

If applying directly, contact Perak State Park Corporation.

As in all natural wildernesses, wildlife sightings are a matter of luck (spotting elephant dung is a lucky day indeed!). Bird-watchers will have the most joy: among the 316 avian species spotted in the park are all 10 species of Malaysian hornbills, and it's common to see colourful birds such as blue-rumped parrots, red-crowned barbets and green broadbills. Flocks of birds assemble between July and October.

🛏 Sleeping

Belum Eco Resort and Belum Rainforest Resort aren't located in the state park, but each is well positioned for excursions in and around the protected zone.

⭐ Belum Eco Resort   RESORT $$
(📞012-524 9184; www.belumecoresort.com.my; all-inclusive 2-/3-night package per person from RM815/1090) 🏊 Thrillingly remote Belum Eco Resort perches on a private island, thick with jungle and teeming with wildlife. Twelve A-frame chalets (electricity evenings only) line its shore and there are plain houseboat rooms offered, too. Accommodation is basic but it doesn't get closer to nature than this: friendly pet dogs, deafeningly loud cicadas, and breakfasts on a terrace overlooking the lake.

Host Steve Khong is a wealth of local knowledge and guided tours of the area emphasise minimal impact on the environment, striving to educate visitors about native wildlife.

Book at least a week or two ahead. The rate includes a boat transfer between Pulau Banding jetty and the island, daytime activities in the park, evening entertainment and all meals. Phone reception is threadbare (a pot plant marks the only spot with good signal).

Belum Rainforest Resort   RESORT $$$
(📞05-791 6800; www.belumrainforestresort.com; Pulau Banding; d incl breakfast RM450-690; 🅿✳🛜♨) Less than 2km shy of Pulau Banding jetty is Belum's most upmarket resort. Rooms make an effort at elegance, with polished floors and textured wood panelling, but many are worn so it feels expensive for what you get. Still, the on-site restaurant is decent, staff are friendly and ponds filled with croaking frogs bring nature to your door.

The resort isn't inside Royal Belum State Park, but staff can arrange guided tours (short walk/full-day excursion RM142/358), as well as fishing trips (RM566 to RM849).

ℹ Information

Perak State Park Corporation (Kompleks Pejabat Kerajaan Negeri; 📞05-791 4543; www.royalbelum.my; Government Complex Bldg (1st fl), Jln Sultan Abd Aziz, Gerik; ⏰8am-5pm Mon-Fri) Perak's state park corporation can assist with securing a permit (RM20) to visit Royal Belum State Park.

ℹ Getting There & Away

The main gateway town to Belum-Temenggor Rainforest is Gerik, 130km north of Ipoh. To reach the state park, travel by boat from **Pulau Banding Jetty** (Jeti Pulau Banting; off Lr Timur-Barat, Pulau Banding), 40km northeast of Gerik. Private transport is the easiest way to reach the jetty.

There are two ways to arrive by public transport: take a bus to Gerik (sometimes spelt Grik and pronounced 'Greek'), where taxis at the town's bus station can take you the remaining 40km to Pulau Banding (RM60).

Alternatively, from Butterworth, Ipoh, Kuala Kangsar or Taiping, board a Kota Bharu–bound bus and ask the driver to drop you off at Pulau Banding Jetty, or near Belum Rainforest Resort, located near Hwy 76. It's not a regular stop so you'll be expected to pay the full fare to Kota Bharu. Leaving Belum, buses from Kota Bharu are unpredictable, so you'll probably have to take a taxi to Gerik and continue by bus from there.

Departures to/from Gerik's bus station include the following:

DESTINATION	PRICE (RM)	DURATION (HR)	FREQUENCY (PER DAY)
Ipoh	17	2½-4	4
Kota Bharu	30	4	1
Kuala Lumpur	33.40	4-6	3-7

Penang

Includes ➡

George Town 160
Greater Penang 183
Air Itam &
Penang Hill 183
Batu Ferringhi. 184
Teluk Bahang
& Around 186
Balik Pulau & Kampung
Pulau Betong 188
Southeast Penang
Island 190

Best Places to Eat

➡ Lorong Baru (New Lane) Hawker Stalls (p177)

➡ Teksen (p176)

➡ Nasi Padang Minang (p177)

➡ Gurney Drive Hawker Stalls (p177)

➡ Wai Kei Cafe (p175)

➡ Nan Guang (p189)

Best Places to Stay

➡ You Le Yuen (p172)

➡ 23 Love Lane (p172)

➡ Campbell House (p172)

➡ Karuna Hill (p189)

➡ Sweet Cili (p172)

➡ Lone Pine Hotel (p185)

Why Go?

If there's a more thrilling cocktail of Eastern cultures than in Penang, we've yet to find it. The state is divided both geographically and administratively into two sections: Pulau Pinang (Penang Island), a 293-sq-km island in Selat Melaka (Strait of Melaka), and Seberang Perai, a narrow 760-sq-km strip on the peninsular mainland.

Focus on the island and its cosmopolitan capital George Town. This vibrant city delivers old-world Asia in spades, from trishaws pedalling past watermarked Chinese shophouses to blue joss smoke perfuming the air. The freshest aspects of modern culture are present, too, in the exceptional art scene and free-spirited carnivals, all fed by an infectious local enthusiasm for Penang's long history and kaleidoscope of cultures.

If you can tear yourself away, the rest of the island is rich in palm-fringed beaches and fishing villages, mountainous jungle and farms growing nutmeg and durian.

When to Go
George Town

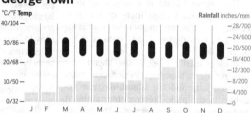

°C/°F **Temp**   Rainfall inches/mm

Jan–Feb Book ahead if visiting George Town during busy Chinese New Year.

Jul The George Town Festival keeps the city busy for a month.

Nov–Dec The most comfortable climate for visiting the island.

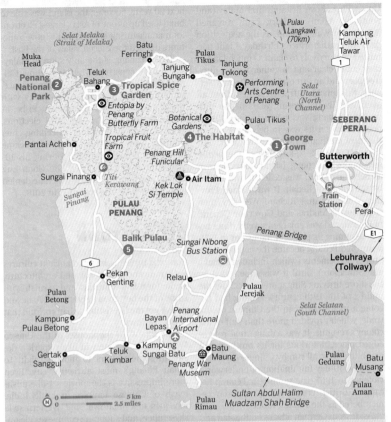

Penang Highlights

1 George Town (p160)
Exploring the architecture of the World Heritage zone, staying in a boutique heritage hotel and digging into some of Southeast Asia's most delicious food.

2 Penang National Park (p187) Hiking through virgin rainforest to beaches where monkeys scamper.

3 Tropical Spice Garden (p187) Becoming familiar with the contents of your spice rack at this aromatic garden and linked cookery class.

4 The Habitat (p184) Enjoying cool breezes and fantastic views of the island from this nature reserve located at the top of Penang Hill.

5 Balik Pulau (p188) Slowing to a relaxed pace at the durian and nutmeg farms, sleepy villages and beautiful beaches of Penang's heartland.

History

Little is known of Penang's early history. Chinese seafarers were aware of the island, which they called Betelnut Island, as far back as the 15th century, but it was little more than a way station en route to trading ports. It wasn't until the early 18th century that colonists arrived from Sumatra and established settlements at Batu Uban and the area now covered by southern George Town. The island came under the control of the sultan of Kedah, but in 1771 he signed the first agreement with the British East India Company, handing them trading rights in exchange for military assistance against Siam (present-day Thailand).

Fifteen years later Captain Francis Light, on behalf of the East India Company, took formal possession of Penang, hoisting the

Union Flag above Britain's first Malay (and Southeast Asian) territory. Light renamed it Prince of Wales Island, as the acquisition date fell on the prince's birthday. Light permitted new arrivals to claim as much land as they could clear and, together with a duty-free port and an atmosphere of liberal tolerance, this quickly attracted settlers from all over Asia. By the closing years of the 18th century, Penang was home to over 10,000 people, and on its way to becoming one of the most multicultural places on earth.

In 1800, a 189-sq-km slice of the peninsula opposite Penang Island, today known as Seberang Perai, was ceded to the British by the sultan of Kedah. It was named Province Wellesley after Richard Wellesley, then Governor of Madras and Governor General of Bengal, and was enlarged several times before assuming its present dimensions in 1874.

In 1826 Penang became the capital of the Straits Settlements (which included Melaka and Singapore), until it was superseded by the more thriving Singapore in 1832. By the middle of the 19th century, Penang had become a major player in the Chinese opium trade, which provided more than half of the colony's revenue. It was a dangerous, rough-edged place, notorious for its brothels and gambling dens, all run by Chinese secret societies. A 10-day fulmination of underworld violence in 1867 (the same year Penang became a British crown colony) is today remembered as the Penang Riots.

Aside from German attacks on Russian and French ships in its harbour, there was little action in Penang during WWI. WWII was a different story: before Japan's invasion began with overwhelming aerial bombardment, Penang's Europeans were evacuated, leaving behind a largely defenceless population. Japan took over the island on 19 December 1941, only 12 days after the attack on Pearl Harbor in the US, renaming it Tojo-to. The following 3½ years were the darkest of Penang's history, particularly for its ethnic Chinese population.

Things could never be the same after the war. Any aura of invincibility or moral authority had deserted the British, and the end of imperial rule was imminent. The Straits Settlements were dissolved in 1946; Penang became a state of the Federation of Malaya in 1948, gained independence from Britain in 1957, and became one of Malaysia's 13 states in 1963.

With its free-port status withdrawn in 1969, Penang went through several years of decline and high unemployment. Over the next 20 years, however, the island was able to build itself up as one of Asia's largest electronics manufacturing centres, and is now sometimes dubbed the 'Silicon Valley of the East'.

Today, Penang is the only state in Malaysia to have consistently elected ethnic Chinese chief ministers since independence, something that has caused relations with the Malay-led federal government to be, at times, fraught. In the May 2018 elections, Chow Kon Yeow took over as Penang chief minister from Lim Guan Eng, who became Malaysia's finance minister. During his 10-year stint as chief minister, Lim Guan Eng battled corruption charges, which he denied and of which he was acquitted in 2018.

GEORGE TOWN

🎧 04

Combine three distinct and ancient cultures with indigenous and colonial architecture, shake for a few centuries, and garnish with some of the best food in Southeast Asia, and you've got the irresistible urban cocktail that is George Town.

The timeworn shophouses of the Unesco World Heritage zone will likely spark a desire in some visitors to move straight to Pulau Pinang's most attractive city. Even more impressive is the movie-set-like mishmash of Chinese temples in Little India, mosques in Chinatown, and Western-style skyscrapers and shopping complexes gleaming high above British Raj–era architecture.

The eclectic jumble makes this a city that rewards explorers. Get lost in the maze of chaotic streets and narrow lanes, passing shrines decorated with strings of paper lanterns and fragrant shops selling Indian spices; or enjoy George Town's burgeoning street-art scene, its modern cafes and fun bars.

◉ Sights

◉ Inside the Unesco Protected Zone

★ **Blue Mansion** HISTORIC BUILDING
(Cheong Fatt Tze Mansion; Map p162; 🕿 04-262 0006; www.cheongfatttzemansion.com; 14 Lr Leith; adult/child RM16/8; ⊙ tours 11am, 2pm & 3.30pm) The most photographed building in George Town is this magnificent 38-room, 220-window mansion, built in the 1880s and rescued from ruin in the 1990s. Its distinctive blue-hued

GEORGE TOWN'S CLANHOUSES

Between the mid-1800s and the mid-1900s, Penang welcomed a huge influx of Chinese immigrants, primarily from China's Fujian province. To help introduce uncles, aunties, cousins, 10th cousins, old neighbourhood buddies and so on to their new home, the Chinese formed clan associations and built Clanhouses, known locally as *kongsi,* to create a sense of community, provide lodging and help find employment for newcomers. In addition to functioning as 'embassies' of sorts, Clanhouses also served as a deeper social, even spiritual, link between an extended clan, its ancestors and its social obligations.

As time went on, many clan associations became extremely prosperous and their buildings became more ornate. Clans – called 'secret societies' by the British – began to compete with each other over the decadence and number of their temples. Due to this rivalry, today Penang has one of the densest concentrations of clan architecture found outside China.

Khoo Kongsi (Map p162; ✆04-261 4609; www.khookongsi.com.my; 18 Cannon Sq; adult/child RM10/1; ⊙9am-5pm) This spectacular Clanhouse is one of the most impressive in George Town. Gorgeous ceramic sculptures of immortals, carp, dragons, and carp becoming dragons dance across the roof ridges. The interior is dominated by incredible murals depicting birthdays, weddings and, most impressively, the 36 celestial guardians. As impressive as it is today, Khoo Kongsi was once even more ostentatious; the structure caught fire on the night it was completed in 1901, an event put down to divine jealousy. The present building dates from 1906. On the last Saturday evening of each month, the structure is illuminated and entrance is free from 6.30pm to 9pm.

Cheah Kongsi (Map p162; ✆04-261 3837; www.cheahkongsi.com.my; 8 Lr Armenian; adult/under 5 RM10/free; ⊙9am-5pm Sun-Fri, to 1pm Sat) Looking splendid after a major restoration that ended in 2015, Cheah Kongsi is home to the oldest Straits Chinese clan association in Penang. The ornate front of the Clanhouse can be seen clearly across a grassy lawn from Lr Pantai, but the official entrance, where you need to buy a ticket, is on Lr Armenian. Besides serving as a temple and assembly hall, this building has also been the registered headquarters of several clans.

Lim Kongsi (Map p162; Lr Ah Quee) Set up in 1860, this Clanhouse is also known as Kew Leong Tong, which means Hall of Nine Dragons. The association is open to anyone with the surname Lim, no matter their origin, and is the only Clanhouse in Penang with a female patron deity. At the entrance to the shrine, look for the well of Mar Chor Poh, the patron saint of sailors, who also happens to be a Lim.

Han Jiang Ancestral Temple (Map p162; 127 Lr Chulia; ⊙9am-5pm) This beautifully decorated and maintained Clanhouse, belonging to the Penang Teochew Association, dates back to 1870. It features informative displays on the immigration and culture of the clan.

exterior (once common in George Town) is the result of an indigo-based limewash.

Hour-long guided tours (included in the admission fee) explain the building's feng shui and unique features, and relate stories about Cheong Fatt Tze, the rags-to-riches Hakka merchant-trader who commissioned the mansion for his seventh (and favourite) wife.

★Pinang Peranakan
Mansion   HISTORIC BUILDING
(Map p162; ✆04-264 2929; www.pinangperanakan mansion.com.my; 29 Lr Gereja; adult/child RM20/free; ⊙9.30am-5pm) This ostentatious, mint-green structure is among the most stunning restored residences in George Town. Every door, wall and archway is carved and often

painted in gold leaf, and the grand rooms are furnished with majestic wood furniture featuring intricate mother-of-pearl inlay. There are displays of charming antiques, and fascinating black-and-white photos of the family in regal Chinese dress grace the walls. Self-guided visits are possible, or enquire about the timing of occasional guided tours (included in the ticket price).

The house belonged to Chung Keng Quee, a 19th-century merchant, clan leader and community pillar, as well as one of the wealthiest Peranakan of that era.

After visiting the main house, be sure to also check out **Chung Keng Kwi Temple,** the adjacent **ancestral hall** and the attached **Straits Chinese Jewellery Museum,** with its

Central George Town

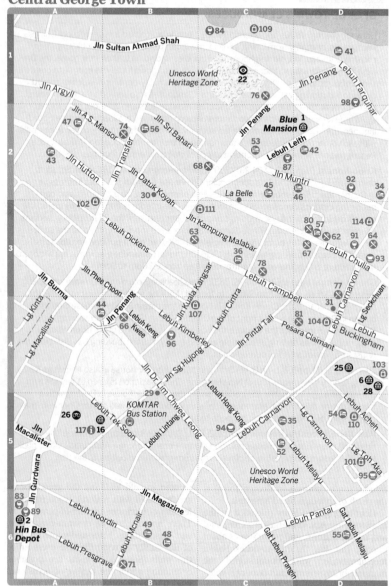

PENANG GEORGE TOWN

dazzling collection of vintage bling and glittery ornamentation; admission to all is included.

Chew Jetty
AREA

(Map p162; Pengkalan Weld) The largest and most intact of the clan jetties, Chew Jetty consists of 75 elevated houses, several Chinese temples, a community hall and lots of tourist facilities, all linked by elevated wooden walkways. It's a fun place to wander around admiring docked fishing boats while the scent of frying fish wafts across the walkways. There are numerous places to browse souvenirs and nibble snack food.

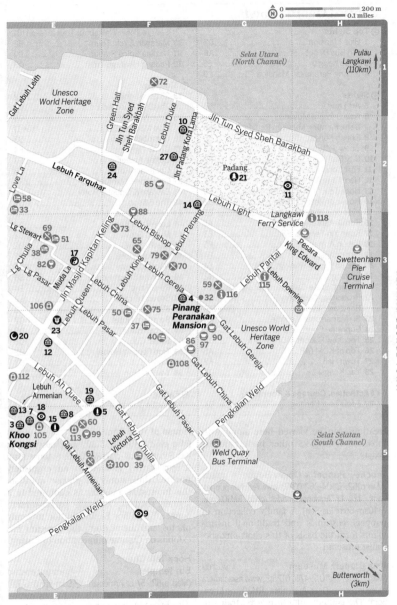

N
0   200 m
0   0.1 miles

Selat Utara
(North Channel)

Pulau
Langkawi
(110km)

Unesco
World Heritage
Zone

Jln Tun Syed Sheh Barakbah

Padang

Langkawi
Ferry Service

Pesara
King Edward

Swettenham
Pier
Cruise
Terminal

**Pinang
Peranakan
Mansion**

Unesco World
Heritage
Zone

**Khoo
Kongsi**

Weld Quay
Bus Terminal

Selat Selatan
(South Channel)

Butterworth
(3km)

PENANG GEORGE TOWN

Arrive towards sunset to take 'golden-hour' photos from the end of the jetty (you'll be in good company). For a more authentic experience, explore the less touristy jetties to the southwest: Lee Jetty, New Jetty and Yeoh Jetty.

Batik Painting Museum Penang   GALLERY
(Map p162; 04-262 4800; www.batikpg.com; 19 Lr Armenian; adult/student RM10/5; 10am-6pm) Penang artist Chuah Thean Teng is credited with applying the age-old local craft of batik (a dye-resist process) to making works of art. Several of his beautiful

Central George Town

◉ Top Sights
1 Blue Mansion D2
2 Hin Bus Depot A6
3 Khoo Kongsi E5
4 Pinang Peranakan Mansion F3

◉ Sights
5 Art Lane E5
6 Asia Camera Museum D4
7 Batik Painting Museum Penang E5
8 Cheah Kongsi E5
9 Chew Jetty F6
10 City Hall F2
11 Fort Cornwallis G2
12 Han Jiang Ancestral Temple E4
13 Hock Teik Cheng Sin Temple E5
14 House of Yeap Chor Ee G2
15 Kids on a Bicycle Mural E5
16 Komik Asia A5
17 Kuan Yin Teng E3
18 Lebuh Armenian E5
19 Lim Kongsi E4
20 Masjid Kapitan Keling E4
21 Padang G2
    Penang State Gallery .... (see 26)
22 Protestant Cemetery C1
    Rainbow Skywalk .... (see 26)
23 Sri Mariamman Temple E4
24 Supreme Court F2
25 Teochew Puppet & Opera House D4
26 Top at KOMTAR A5
27 Town Hall F2
28 Yap Kongsi D4

◉ Activities, Courses & Tours
29 Food Tour Penang B4

George Town Walkabout Tour ... (see 116)
30 Matahari Cycle Tours B2
31 Nazlina Spice Station D4
32 Penang Heritage Trust G3

◉ Sleeping
33 23 Love Lane E2
34 The 80's Guesthouse D2
35 Betel Nut Lodge C5
    Blue Mansion .... (see 1)
36 Campbell House C3
37 China Tiger F4
38 Coffee Atelier E3
39 Container Hotel F5
40 East Indies Mansion F4
41 Eastern & Oriental Hotel D1
42 The Edison D2
43 Jawi Peranakan Mansion A2
44 Loke Thye Kee A4
45 Muntri Grove C2
46 Muntri Mews D2
47 Museum Hotel A2
48 Noordin Mews B6
49 Noordin Street House B6
50 Ren i Tang F4
51 Seven Terraces E3
52 Sinkeh C5
53 Southern Hotel C2
54 Spices Hotel D5
55 Sweet Cili D6
56 Tido Penang Hostel B2
57 Tien D3
58 You Le Yuen E2

◉ Eating
59 Auntie Gaik Lean's G3

creations can be viewed here along with those of around 25 other batik painting artists.

Teochew Puppet & Opera House MUSEUM
(Map p162; 04-262 0377; www.teochewpuppet.com; 122 Lr Armenian; adult/child RM10/free; ⊙10am-6pm Tue-Sun) A family collection of puppets, costumes and traditional instruments form the basis of this charming specialist museum.

Asia Camera Museum MUSEUM
(Map p162; 012-474 0123; www.asiacameramuseum.com; 71 Lr Armenian; RM20; ⊙10am-6pm) The contents of a former portrait studio have been relocated to this shophouse on Lr Armenian. A guided tour escorts you to a camera obscura, more than 1000 old cameras (some of which you can play with), some old portraits, a darkroom and a very retro photo studio.

House of Yeap Chor Ee MUSEUM
(Map p162; 04-261 0190; www.houseyce.com; 4 Lr Penang; adult/child RM20/10; ⊙tours 10am & 3pm Mon-Fri) Housed in an exquisitely restored three-storey shophouse mansion, this interesting museum is dedicated to a former resident, itinerant barber-turned-banker, Yeap Chor Ee. In addition to family photos and mementoes, the museum has exhibits on Chinese immigration to Penang.

Hock Teik Cheng Sin Temple HISTORIC BUILDING
(Map p162; 57 Lr Armenian; ⊙9am-5pm) FREE This 1850 temple is dedicated to its patron deity, the Taoist God of Prosperity. Resplendent in red, gold and polished black columns, it has quite a few aliases, such as Poh Hock Seah, Hokkien Kongsi and Tong Kheng Seah. Why so many names? Well, besides serving as a temple and assembly hall, this building has also been the registered headquarters of several clans.

60 BTB E5
   China House ....(see 60)
61 Da Shu Xia Seafood House E5
62 Goh Thew Chik D3
63 Hameediyah B3
64 Holy Guacamole D3
65 Jaloux F3
66 Joo Hooi Cafe B4
67 Junk D3
68 Kafe Kheng Pin C2
69 Kebaya E3
70 Leaf Healthy House F3
71 Lebuh Presgrave Hawker Stalls B6
72 Medan Renong Padang Kota Lama F1
73 Merican Nasi Kandar F3
   Mews Cafe ....(see 46)
74 Nasi Padang Minang B2
75 Sri Ananda Bahwan F4
76 Sup Hameed C1
77 Teksen D3
78 Tho Yuen Restaurant C3
79 Veloo Villas F3
80 Wai Kei Cafe D3
81 Yin's Sourdough Bakery D4

⊜ Drinking & Nightlife
82 Antarabangsa Enterprise E3
83 Backdoor Bodega A6
84 Beach Blanket Babylon C1
85 Constant Gardener F2
86 Fuku Eatery & Desserts F4
87 Georgetown Wines C2
88 Golden Shower by ChinChin F2
89 Good Friends Club A6
90 Jing-Si Books & Cafe G4
   Kopi C ....(see 60)

91 Micke's Place D3
92 Mish Mash D2
93 Mugshot Cafe D3
94 Narrow Marrow C5
95 Ome by Spacebar D5
96 Out Of Nowhere B4
97 Ten Yee Tea Trading G4
98 Three-Sixty Revolving Restaurant
   & Sky Bar D1
99 Vine & Single E5

⊛ Entertainment
100 Canteen F5

⊟ Shopping
101 Barbara Moore Gallery D5
102 Batek-Lah A3
103 Bon Ton D4
104 Campbell Street Market D4
105 Fuan Wong E5
106 Gerak Budaya E3
107 Kuala Kangsar Market B4
108 Mano Plus F4
109 Moon Shop C1
110 Rozanas Batik D5
111 Sam's Batik House C3
112 Shop Howard E4
113 Sixth Sense E5
114 Unique Penang D3

ⓘ Information
115 Ministry of Tourism G3
116 Penang Global Tourism G3
117 Penang State Forestry
   Department A5
118 Tourism Malaysia H3

PENANG GEORGE TOWN

Penang Museum   MUSEUM

(Map p168; ☑04-226 1462; www.penang
museum.gov.my; 57 Jln Macalister; RM1; ⊙9am-
5pm Sat-Thu) Penang's state-run museum
includes exhibits on the history, customs
and traditions of the island's various
ethnic groups, with photos, videos, doc-
uments, costumes, furniture and other
well-labelled, engaging displays. The history gallery includes a collection of early-
19th-century watercolours by Captain
Robert Smith, an engineer with the East
India Company, and prints showing landscapes of old Penang.

On our visit, the museum's usual location
on Lr Farquhar was undergoing renovation
and exhibitions were temporarily rehoused
here at the **Penang State Museum Board**
(Map p168; ☑04-226 1461; www.penangmuseum.
gov.my; 57 Jln Macalister; ⊙9am-5pm) FREE.
When finished in 2020, it's expected to return to Lr Farquhar.

Fort Cornwallis   HISTORIC SITE

(Map p162; ☑04-263 9855; www.theesplanade
park.com.my; Jln Tun Syed Sheh Barakbah; adult/
child RM20/10; ⊙9am-10pm) Captain Light
first built a wooden fort here in 1786, thus
establishing the free port where trade
would, he hoped, be lured from Britain's
Dutch rivals. Between 1808 and 1810, convict labour built the current stone fort, with
the star-profile shape of the walls allowing
for overlapping fields of fire against enemies. For all its size, Fort Cornwallis today
isn't particularly impressive; only the outer
walls stand, enclosing a rather spare park.

Masjid Kapitan Keling   MOSQUE

(Map p162; 14 Lr Buckingham; ⊙7am-7pm) FREE
Penang's first Indian Muslim settlers (East
India Company troops) built Masjid Kapitan
Keling in 1801. The mosque's domes are yel-
low, in a typically Indian-influenced Islamic
style, and it has a single minaret. It looks

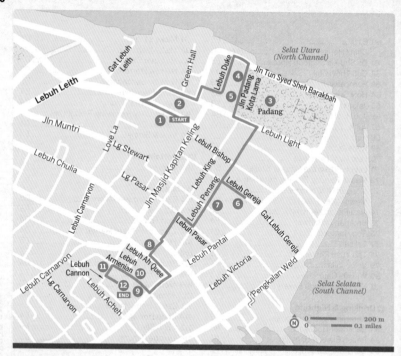

City Walk
Five Cultures on Two Feet

START PENANG MUSEUM
END KHOO KONGSI
LENGTH 2.25KM; THREE TO FOUR HOURS

This walk will give you a glimpse of George Town's cultural mix: English, Indian, Malay, Peranakan and Chinese.

Starting at the original location of the ① **Penang Museum** (Lr Farquhar), head west and then north towards the waterfront, passing the ② **Supreme Court**. Note the statue of James Richardson Logan, advocate for nonwhites during the colonial era. Walk north along Lr Duke to the waterfront, then head south along Jln Padang Kota Lama past the vast ③ **Padang** (field) and the grandiose architecture of the ④ **City Hall** and ⑤ **Town Hall**. Proceed east along Lr Light, then south on Lr Penang. A short detour east along Lr Gereja finds the impressive ⑥ **Pinang Peranakan Mansion** (p161), the former digs of one of George Town's great Peranakan (literally, half-caste, also Baba-Nonya or Straits Chinese) merchant barons.

Returning to Lr Penang, head south into Little India and take a deep breath of all that spice;

if it's around lunchtime, refuel with an authentic southern Indian–style banana-leaf thali meal at ⑦ **Sri Ananda Bahwan** (p175). At Lr Pasar, head west past shops selling milky South Asian sweets, then south at Lr King to the intersection of ⑧ **Lebuh King and Lebuh Ah Quee**, a literal example of Penang's cultural crossroads. To your south is a Chinese assembly hall and rows of fading Chinese shophouses; to your north is a small Indian mosque; and across the street is a large Malaysian restaurant.

Head east along Lr Ah Quee, then south along Lr Pantai; you're now at ⑨ **Lebuh Armenian**. Among George Town's most gentrified streets today, it was formerly a centre for Chinese secret societies and was one of the main fighting stages of the 1867 riots. Stroll west past restored shophouses until you reach ⑩ **Cheah Kongsi** (p161), home to the oldest Straits Chinese clan association in Penang.

Continue to the corner of Jln Masjid Kapitan Keling and the bright green 1924 Hokkien Clanhouse ⑪ **Yap Kongsi** (◷9am-5pm). Finally, head south on Lr Cannon and duck into the magnificently ornate ⑫ **Khoo Kongsi** (p161), the most impressive *kongsi* (clan meeting house) in the city.

UNESCO & GEORGE TOWN

In 2008, the historic centre of George Town was designated a Unesco World Heritage Site for having 'a unique architectural and cultural townscape without parallel anywhere in East and Southeast Asia'. A 'core' area comprising 1700 buildings and a 'buffer', which together span inland from the waterfront as far west as Jln Transfer and Jln Dr Lim Chwee Leong, were drawn up, and the structures within these areas have been thoroughly catalogued and are protected by strict zoning laws.

The general consensus is that the Unesco listing has been a good thing for George Town, having helped the city safeguard its age-old feel while also reaping the benefits of a facelift. The designation seems to have sparked an interest in local culture among residents, and some claim that it has also had the effect of drawing younger locals back to the city, which suffered from a debilitating 'brain drain' during the 1980s and 1990s.

However, there's no arguing that the listing has been a double-edged sword. Many once-abandoned buildings have been snatched up by developers hoping to cash in, and property values have skyrocketed. Today, some shophouses can easily sell for more than US$1 million, and 'heritage' hotels and cutesy cafes can be found on just about every street in George Town. Not all of them have been renovated according to strict heritage rules. Uncontrolled rents haven't helped either, with some landlords hiking rates to over RM10,000 a month. The consequence is that the traditional shops and trades that gave the area much of its unique flavour are being forced to close down or move out to less pricey areas of the city.

sublime at sunset. Mosque officials can grant permission to enter.

Kuan Yin Teng TAOIST TEMPLE
(Temple of the Goddess of Mercy; Map p162; cnr Jln Masjid Kapitan Keling & Lg Stewart) **FREE** This temple dedicated to Kuan Yin – the goddess of mercy, good fortune, peace and fertility – is a captivating place to observe Taoist ritual. Rebuilt in the early 19th century by the first Hokkien and Cantonese settlers in Penang, the temple stands on the site of an earlier shrine. This popular temple seems to be forever swathed in smoke from the outside furnaces, where worshippers burn paper money, and from the incense sticks being waved around inside.

Outside the Unesco Protected Zone

★ Hin Bus Depot GALLERY
(Map p162; www.hinbusdepot.com; 31A Jln Gurdwara; ☉noon-8pm Mon-Fri, from 11am Sat & Sun) **FREE** The elegant remains of this former bus station have become a vibrant hub for George Town's burgeoning contemporary art scene. Half a dozen artists studios and a gallery host exhibitions (ranging from sculpture to photography), an arts-and-crafts market every Sunday (11am to 5pm), and art-house movies and documentaries on Tuesdays. The open-air areas are bedecked with street art.

Within the grounds you'll also find several cafes, and there are several artsy bars nearby.

Komik Asia MUSEUM
(Map p162; ☑04-371 5512; www.paccm.com.my; Level 2, ICT Mall KOMTAR; RM20; ☉11am-7pm Mon-Fri, to 9pm Sat & Sun) If you don't know your Lat from your Tezuka Osamu, then this is the place to become more closely acquainted with the dynamic work of comic-book artists from across the region. Kids and not a few adults will love this remarkable collection from nine Asian countries, including Malaysia, China, Japan and South Korea. There's a good gift shop, too.

To find the museum, enter the mall from Lr Lintang and take the escalator to the 2nd floor.

Protestant Cemetery CEMETERY
(Map p162; Jln Sultan Ahmad Shah; ☉24hr) **FREE** Under a canopy of magnolia trees you'll find the graves of Captain Francis Light, the founder of the British colony of Penang, and many others, including governors, merchants, sailors, and Chinese Christians who fled the Boxer Rebellion in China (a movement opposing Western imperialism and evangelism), only to die of fever in Penang. Also here is the tomb of Thomas Leonowens, the young officer who married Anna – the schoolmistress to the King of Siam, made famous by *The King and I*.

Wat Chayamangkalaram BUDDHIST TEMPLE
(Temple of the Reclining Buddha; Map p168; 17 Lg Burma; ☉8am-5pm) **FREE** The Temple of the Reclining Buddha is a typical Thai temple; differences from Malay Chinese Buddhist temples include the design of roofs,

George Town

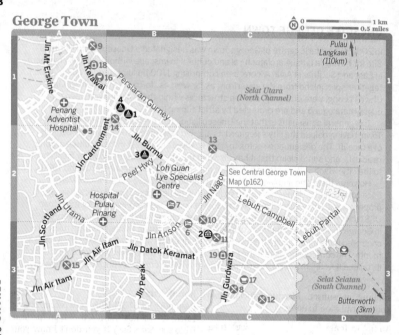

N 0 ———————— 1 km
   0 ———————— 0.5 miles

George Town

⊙ Sights
1 Dhammikarama Burmese
 Buddhist Temple...............................B1
 Penang Museum ....(see 2)
2 Penang State Museum Board............C3
3 Wat Buppharam.................................B2
4 Wat Chayamangkalaram.....................B1

✪ Activities, Courses & Tours
5 Penang Homecooking School.............A2

🛏 Sleeping
6 GLOW...B3
7 Macalister Mansion............................B2

✖ Eating
8 Cecil Street Market............................C3

9 Gurney Drive Hawker Stalls................A1
10 Kafe Heng Huat.................................C2
11 Lorong Baru (New Lane)
 Hawker Stalls...................................C3
12 Macallum Street Night Market............C3
13 Ocean Green.....................................C2
14 Pulau Tikus Hawker Centre.................B1
15 Suffolk House....................................A3

🍷 Drinking & Nightlife
16 Gravity...A1
17 Macallum Connoisseurs.....................C3

🛍 Shopping
18 Gurney Plaza....................................A1
19 Hin Pop-Up Market...........................C3

which have sharp eaves, and *chedi* (stupa; solid bell-shaped pillars) in the compound. Inside, it houses a 33m-long reclining Buddha draped in a gold-leafed saffron robe.

The temple is about 2.5km northwest of central George Town; a taxi here is about RM15.

Dhammikarama Burmese
Buddhist Temple   BUDDHIST TEMPLE
(Map p168; 24 Lg Burma; ⊙7am-6pm) **FREE**
Penang's first Buddhist temple, built in

1805, is a rare instance of a Burmese Buddhist temple outside Burma (Myanmar). There's a series of panel paintings on the life of the Buddha lining the walkways and the characters are dressed in Burmese costume, while inside typically round-eyed, serene-faced Burmese Buddha statues stare out at worshippers.

The temple, which has been significantly added to over the years, is located about 2.5km northwest of central George Town; a taxi here will cost RM15.

Wat Buppharam
BUDDHIST TEMPLE

(Map p168; 8 Jln Perak; ⊗8am-6pm) FREE This Thai temple, dating from 1942, is home to the 'Lifting Buddha', a renowned, 100-year-old, gold-leaf-encrusted Buddha statue about the size of a well-fed house cat. If you can lift the statue while concentrating on your wish, then your wish may come true. To confirm this, attempt to lift the statue a second time; if it has now suddenly become too heavy to lift then your wish *will* come true!

The temple is about 2.5km northwest of central George Town; a taxi here will cost RM15.

Top at KOMTAR
VIEWPOINT

(Map p162; ☑04-262 3800; www.thetop.com.my; Jln Penang) There are all kinds of attractions – most targeted at families – in this major revamp of part of George Town's iconic KOMTAR tower. The biggest draw is undoubtedly **Rainbow Skywalk** (☑04-262 3800; www.thetop.com.my/rainbow-skywalk; 68th fl; adult/child RM64/45; ⊗11am-10pm Sun-Tue, to 11pm Fri & Sat; ⓐ), the 68th-floor rooftop observation deck. Visitors might also be interested in the **Penang State Gallery** (☑04-262 3800; adult/child RM30/20; ⊗11am-8pm; ⓐ), providing a breezy overview of the state's history. Check the website for the full list of attractions.

Sri Mariamman Temple
HINDU TEMPLE

(Map p162; Lr Queen; ⊗8am-noon & 4.30-9pm) FREE Built in 1883, Sri Mariamman is George Town's oldest Hindu house of worship. For local South Indians, the temple fulfils the purpose of a Chinese Clanhouse; it's a reminder of the motherland and the community bonds forged within the diaspora. It is a typically South Indian temple, dominated by the *gopuram* (entrance tower).

The major festival of Thaipusam (p171), which includes a procession where some participants hang pots of milk off their bodies on wire hooks and undergo other bodily piercings, begins here. In October a wooden chariot takes the temple's deity for a spin around the neighbourhood during Vijayadasami festivities. Also known as the Dussehra, this festival marks the victory of the mother goddess Durga over the demon Mahishasura.

The temple's back entrance is on Jln Masjid Kapitan Keling.

⚏ Courses

Nazlina Spice Station
COOKING

(Map p162; ☑012-453 8167; www.pickles-and-spices.com; 2 Lr Campbell; morning/afternoon classes RM250/200) The bubbly and enthusiastic Nazlina will teach you how to make those dishes you've fallen in love with while in Penang. A course begins with a visit to the Campbell Street Market (p174) and a local breakfast, followed by instruction on four dishes including dessert. Afternoon lessons are vegan/vegetarian, with no market tour.

Penang Homecooking School
COOKING

(Map p168; ☑016-437 4380; www.penanghome cookingschool.com; 85 Taman Berjaya; classes RM280-330; ⊗9am-2pm Mon-Sat) Pearly and Chandra have opened their home to teach visitors how to make Indian, Peranakan and street dishes. Courses are flexible in terms of scope and time (see the website), and the fee varies depending on how many dishes you want to make. A half-day course includes transportation and a visit to a market. Advance booking required.

⛬ Tours

There's a huge variety of self-guided George Town tours, from food walks to those focusing on traditional trades or architecture – pick up a pamphlet of the routes at Penang Global Tourism (p181). Alternatively, there's a variety of guided tours, from the largely architecture-centric George Town Heritage Walks (p170) to the cuisine-focused Food Tour Penang (p170).

If walking isn't your thing, consider the **Hop-On Hop-Off bus route** (☑011-1230 5358; www.myhoponhopoff.com/pg; adult/child 24hr from RM115/50; ⊗8am-8pm), which winds its way around the perimeter of the Unesco-protected zone. It's a good way to get a quick overview of George Town, and you can get on and off at 17 stops.

★ Matahari Cycle Tours
CYCLING

(Map p162; ☑019-448 0440; www.cyclematahari.com; 29 Jln Datuk Koyah; tours from RM390) Balik Pulau's charm isn't apparent from its main roads. To really experience the area, from its hillside durian farms to its fishing villages, the best way is on the seat of a bicycle – ideally led by the utterly enthusiastic and professional Princilia and SJ. Their tours span a whole day, and include food and drink as well as transport.

Book via their office in George Town or online. Email for tour requests.

Penang Heritage Trust
WALKING

(PHT; Map p162; ☑04-264 2631; www.pht.org.my; 26 Lr Gereja; site visits from RM20; ⊗office

PENANG GEORGE TOWN

9am-5pm Mon-Fri) This conservation-minded entity leads well-regarded walking tours of George Town. There are two different walks, a religious-themed meander and an exploration of George Town's Little India; both are led by experienced guides. Walks require at least two people, usually last around three hours, and must be booked three working days in advance (via email).

George Town Heritage Walks WALKING
(☑ 016-440 6823; www.facebook.com/georgetown heritagewalks; tours from RM180; ⊙ 9am-5pm Mon-Sat) Discover George Town – and beyond – with Joann Khaw, a Penang native and heritage expert who leads architecture and food tours as well as tours of inland Penang, among others. Excursions require at least two people, plus advance notice and input from those booking: Joann likes to tailor her tours to meet the interests of whomever she's guiding that day.

Simply Enak FOOD & DRINK
(☑ 017-287 8929; www.simplyenak.com; RM250-270) This outfit (*enak* means 'delicious') offers two food-based walking tours of George Town.

George Town Walkabout Tour WALKING
(Map p162; ☑ 04-263 1166; www.mypenang.gov. my; Penang Global Tourism, 10 Whiteways Arcade, Lr Pantai; ⊙ 10.30am Tue, Thu & Sat) These 1½-hour walking tours, led by certified guides and history researchers, are a good way of getting a quick handle on the essentials of the heritage zone. They also cover some of the key street-art locations. Arrive at 10am to register as one of up to 20 participants.

Food Tour Penang FOOD & DRINK
(Map p162; ☑ 012-212 3473; www.foodtour penang.com; tour per person US$62) Excellent brunch (9.30am to 1.30pm) and dinner (5pm to 9pm) tours, starting from Prangin Mall, take in around half a dozen George Town street food markets and shophouse restaurants revered by locals. All food and drink is included; come with an empty stomach.

★☆ Festivals & Events

A good resource for Penang festivals is the state's official tourism website, **Penang Global Tourism** (www.mypenang.gov.my). The booklet, *Penang Tourism Calendar of Events,* available at Penang Global Tourism (p181), is a comprehensive guide to the island's

> **DON'T MISS**
>
> ### GEORGE TOWN'S STREET ART
>
> George Town's street-art craze shows no sign of abating. It's a trend that goes back to 2010, when Penang's state government commissioned the studio **Sculpture At Work** (http://sculptureatwork.com) to do a series of cartoon steel art pieces across town. Affixed to George Town street walls, these 3D artworks detail local customs and heritage with humour, while also providing a quirky counterpoint to the natural urban beauty of the historic core.
>
> It was in 2012, however, when George Town's street-art scene really took off. For that year's George Town Festival (p171), Lithuanian artist **Ernest Zacharevic** (www.ernestzacharevic.com) was commissioned to do a series of public paintings in the city centre, some of which he chose to combine with objects such as bicycles, motorcycles and architectural features. The art has been a smash hit, with his **Kids on a Bicycle** (Map p162; Lr Armenian) piece having become a major tourist attraction, complete with long lines and souvenir stalls.
>
> Zacharevic's success led to the '101 Lost Kittens' series of murals commissioned for the 2013 George Town Festival, with the intent of bringing attention to the issue of stray animals, as well as many examples of privately funded public art. Other major street artists' works to look out for include Russian artist Julia Volchkova's striking pieces (you'll see one on an alley off Lg Stewart) and UK artist **Thomas Powell** (www.thomaspowell artist.com), whose works are at the Hin Bus Depot (p167) art centre.
>
> **Art Lane** (Map p162; www.facebook.com/ArtLanePenang; 127 Lr Pantai; ⊙ 9am-7pm) is a gallery crafted from two vacant pre-WWII shophouses. Artworks run the gamut from murals of dogs, cats, flowers and Chinese opera singers to installations and a sculpture of a pink tank. Check the website for details of events held here, including yoga, craft markets and workshops.
>
> *Marking George Town,* a free map showing the location of pieces by Zacharevic and some of the other artists mentioned above, is available at Penang Global Tourism (p181).

REGULAR STREET EVENTS

Last Friday, Saturday & Sunday of the Month (www.facebook.com/LFSSPenang; ⊙last weekend of month) This series of activities and events takes place on the last weekend of each month, and revolves around themes of heritage, entertainment, culture and nature. Previous events have included Chinese opera, live classical music, cemetery tours and guided walks around Penang's Botanical Gardens. Check the Facebook page to see what's on when you're in town.

Occupy Beach Street (Legally) (www.facebook.com/occupybeachstreet; Lr Pantai; ⊙7am-1pm Sun) Every Sunday, the northern end of Lr Pantai (also known as Beach St) and linked side streets are closed to vehicular traffic and replaced by a carnival-like atmosphere of artists, performers and vendors.

annual festivals. For more niche events, seek out the **Penang Free Sheet**, available online (www.penangfreesheet.my) or in newsletter form at many guesthouses and cafes.

Chinese New Year NEW YEAR
(⊙Jan or Feb) Celebrated with particular gusto in George Town. The Khoo Kongsi (p161) is done up for the event, and dance troupes and Chinese-opera groups perform all over the city.

Thaipusam RELIGIOUS
(⊙Jan or Feb) This masochistic festival is celebrated as fervently in Penang as it is in Singapore and KL, but without quite the same crowds. The Sri Mariamman (p169), Nattukotai Chettiar and Waterfall Hilltop temples are the main centres of activity.

George Town World Heritage Day CULTURAL
(www.facebook.com/GeorgeTownCelebrations; ⊙7 Jul) A public holiday commemorating the inscription of George Town as a World Heritage city. A chance to catch many cultural and street performances around town.

George Town Festival PERFORMING ARTS
(www.georgetownfestival.com; ⊙Aug) Not to be missed, this month-long arts and performance festival brings top international talent to the city and premieres exciting new local works.

Hungry Ghost Festival CULTURAL
(Phor Thor; ⊙Aug or Sep) The gates of hell are said to be opened every year on the 15th day of the seventh month of the Chinese lunar calendar. To appease the hungry ghosts, Penangites set out food offerings and endeavour to entertain them with puppet shows and street-side Chinese-opera performances. This is a magical time to be in the city.

Lantern Festival CULTURAL
(⊙Sep/Oct) An island-wide festival celebrated by eating moon cakes, the Chinese

sweets once used to carry secret messages for underground rebellions in ancient China.

George Town Literary Festival LITERATURE
(www.georgetownlitfest.com; ⊙Nov) Malaysia's largest literary festival is held at venues in George Town over three or four days in late November and attracts both local and international writers.

🛏 Sleeping

George Town's accommodation options range from the grungiest hostels to the swankiest hotels. In particular, there are some charming boutique places converted from former shophouses in the heritage zone, although not everything advertised as a 'heritage hotel' truly fits that description.

In general, hotel prices increase on weekends and holidays. Most places fill up quickly, so book ahead – especially if a holiday, such as Chinese New Year, is approaching.

🛏 Inside the Unesco Protected Zone

The 80's Guesthouse HOSTEL $
(Map p162; ☑04-263 8806; www.the80sguesthouse.com; 46 Love Lane; dm/d incl breakfast from RM35/95; ❋@🛜) With 1950s film posters and old radios, the nostalgic theme extends much further back than the '80s, but it would be rude to quibble when the dorms and private rooms are spotless and common areas pleasantly attired with greenery and bookshelves. Single-sex four-bed and mixed six-bed dorms all share bathrooms, as do the minimalist private rooms. Lockers and towels included.

Container Hotel HOSTEL $
(Map p162; ☑04-251 9515; www.containerhotel.my/penang; 4 Gat Lr Chulia; dm/d from RM45/154; @🛜) This hotel's concept (crafted from old

PENANG GEORGE TOWN

shipping containers) is a little fudged in that there are no real containers used! Nonetheless, its dorms, which include female-only options, are spotless and offer a smidgen more design style than other backpackers. Private rooms are minimalist, compact and chic.

★ **You Le Yuen** GUESTHOUSE **$$**
(Map p162; ☑04-261 1817, 013-492 2125; www.youle yuen.com; 7 Love Lane; ste incl breakfast from RM350; ❄☎) There are just four rooms at this boutique B&B, each making the most of the lovely antique shophouse with exposed brick walls, retro furnishings and central courtyard (now used as a cafe). The duplex suites make full use of the building's height. As well as the cafe and bar, there's also a fashion boutique to browse.

★ **Campbell House** HOTEL **$$**
(Map p162; ☑04-261 8290; www.campbellhouse penang.com; 106 Lr Campbell; r incl breakfast from RM370; ❄@☎) Dating back to 1903, this once-standard hotel is seeing a new life as a sumptuous boutique property. Thoughtful details, such as fragrant, locally sourced toiletries, beautiful Peranakan tiles in the bathrooms, Nespresso machines and high-quality mattresses, make the difference here – in addition to the excellent service and overwhelmingly positive feedback from guests.

★ **Sweet Cili** BOUTIQUE HOTEL **$$**
(Map p162; ☑04-261 9986; www.sweetcili.com; 6 Gat Lr Melayu; s/d from RM130/196; ❄☎) Equal parts handsome and functional, Sweet Cili is a midrange hotel whose cool, spacious rooms, decked out with retro-themed design and furniture, all include access to an inviting communal kitchen.

Ren i Tang HOTEL **$$**
(Map p162; ☑04-250 8383; www.renitang.com; 82A Lr Penang; r incl breakfast RM220-480; ❄☎) This former Chinese medicine warehouse has been carefully restored into a boutique hotel where antique charm resounds from every creaking floorboard. Each of its 17 differently sized rooms carries reminders of the building's former life; we like the corner 'Tub Room', equipped with a wooden soaking tub, and the 'Loft Rooms', former storage attics with sloping ceilings.

Spices Hotel BOUTIQUE HOTEL **$$**
(Map p162; ☑04-261 9986; www.spiceshotel.com; 5 Lg Lumut; r/ste incl breakfast RM244/505) A 150-year-old bodhi tree sprouts from the wall in the courtyard of this appealing boutique hotel that has won an award for its archi-

tect owners. The nine rooms feature Malay, Islamic and Indian design influences. The neighbouring mosque will mean that you won't need an alarm clock for an early start.

Betel Nut Lodge BOUTIQUE HOTEL **$$**
(Map p162; ☑04-264 4100; www.betelnutlodge. com; 100 Lr Melayu; s/d RM150/210; ❄☎) Betel Nut offers tidy, homey rooms in a refurbished shophouse on a relatively untouristy street. Expect cool tiles, warm lights, soft beds and helpful, if slightly overbearing, service.

Sinkeh HOTEL **$$**
(Map p162; ☑04-261 3966; www.sinkeh.com; 105 Lr Melayu; s/d incl breakfast RM190/280; ❄☎) Yes, Sinkeh is located in an old shophouse, but modern concrete, glass and steel set the tone inside. Despite this, service is warm and the rooms are comfortable, if not particularly spacious.

Southern Hotel BOUTIQUE HOTEL **$$**
(Map p162; ☑04-262 0770; www.facebook.com/ 108southernboutique; 108 Jln Muntri; RM176-240; ❄☎) In this handsome, whitewashed heritage building, the smallest rooms are so compact as to be almost podlike – probably best for solo travellers – but are attractive and comfortable. Free coffee and water, and a convenient location, might help you get past the tight quarters.

East Indies Mansion HOTEL **$$**
(Map p162; ☑04-261 8025; www.eastindieshotel. com; 25 Lr China; r incl breakfast from RM223; ❄☎) This large heritage shophouse has been converted into a secluded-feeling small hotel. The seven rooms vary considerably, with some spanning two floors, but are united in a design theme that brings together retro touches and colourful, chunky furniture, not to mention the central open-air courtyard and other inviting communal areas. Great for families.

★ **23 Love Lane** BOUTIQUE HOTEL **$$$**
(Map p162; ☑04-262 1323; www.23lovelane.com; 23 Love Lane; r/ste incl breakfast RM544/1145; ❄@☎) Occupying a former mansion, its kitchen and stables, 23 Love Lane tastefully combines antique furniture and fixtures with modern design touches and arty accents. There are lots of open spaces and high ceilings to catch the breezes, inviting communal areas, a peaceful aura, and service that complements the casual, homey vibe.

★ **Blue Mansion** HERITAGE HOTEL **$$$**
(Map p162; ☑04-262 0006; www.cheongfatttze mansion.com/rooms; 14 Lr Leith; r/ste incl breakfast from RM568/998; ❄@☎❄) Occupying one

of George Town's most emblematic buildings, the Blue Mansion wrote the book on how to craft the ideal heritage hotel. The 18 spacious, high-ceilinged guest rooms open onto airy courtyards and have octagonal terracotta tile floors. They're all decorated with antique and retro furniture and ooze authentic colonial-era atmosphere.

★**Muntri Grove** BOUTIQUE HOTEL **$$$**
(Map p162; ☑04-261 8888; www.georgetown heritage.com/muntri-grove-hotel; 127-131 Jln Muntri; r incl breakfast RM400; ❋☑🛜❋) Tucked off a quiet street is this row of 19th-century servants' houses that have been transformed into one of central George Town's loveliest boutique hotels. The 16 large and attractive rooms include huge four-poster beds and vintage furniture. The small pool and leafy surrounds are an added bonus, and rooms on the ground floor are pet-friendly.

Seven Terraces BOUTIQUE HOTEL **$$$**
(Map p162; ☑04-261 8888; www.georgetown heritage.com/seven-terraces-hotel; 14A Lg Stewart; ste/apt incl breakfast RM700/1000; ❋@🛜❋) Crafted from a row of seven joined shophouses, surrounding a beautiful central courtyard, Seven Terraces is one of the most luxurious places to stay in central George Town. The 16 two-storey suites (including two even larger multiroom 'apartments') are vast and regal-feeling, and have been decorated with a mix of original antiques, reproductions and contemporary pieces.

The Edison BOUTIQUE HOTEL **$$$**
(Map p162; ☑04-262 2990; www.theedisonhotels. com; 15 Lr Leith; r/ste incl breakfast from RM550/850; P❋@🛜❋) Looking fabulous after a major overhaul, this spacious colonial building offers 35 tastefully decorated rooms, a light-infused courtyard, high ceilings, latticed windows and a grand entrance. There are also cabanas to lounge in next to the pool.

Tien BOUTIQUE HOTEL **$$$**
(Map p162; ☑04-263 8116; www.tienhotel.com; 348 Lr Chulia; r incl breakfast from RM578; ❋@🛜❋) This distinctive, prewar shophouse has been painted a bright shade of teal and reborn as a modern, attractive boutique hotel. The eight rooms aren't huge, but are comfortably arranged, with vast beds and functional furniture. A rooftop lounge, plunge pool and convenient location are other perks.

Coffee Atelier HERITAGE HOTEL **$$$**
(Map p162; ☑04-261 2261; www.coffeeatelier.com; 47-55 Lg Stewart; r/ste incl breakfast from RM371/428; ❋🛜) Unlike the slick heritage hotels you'll find elsewhere, the renovation of this row of 1920s shophouses has left them feeling wonderfully rustic, and the peeling paint and quirky yet appropriate furnishings provide heaps of character. Each house is divided into two units, with a second smaller bedroom on the 1st floor and huge courtyard-style bathrooms in the ground-floor rooms.

Eastern & Oriental Hotel HISTORIC HOTEL **$$$**
(E&O; Map p162; ☑04-222 2000; www.eohotels. com; 10 Lr Farquhar; ste incl breakfast from RM850; ❋@🛜❋) Dating to 1885, the E&O is one of those rare hotels where historic opulence has gracefully moved into the present day. The suites in the original Heritage Wing seamlessly blend modern comfort with colonial-era style, using hardwood antiques and vintage-themed furnishings; those with a sea view are worth the extra outlay. Rooms in the more modern Victory Annexe are no less appealing.

SELF-CATERING APARTMENTS

If, after having explored George Town, you have fantasies of living in a restored Chinese shophouse, then there's no shortage of options. Here are a couple of self-catering places that we like:

Loke Thye Kee (Map p162; ☑04-263 1929; www.lokethyekee.com; 326 Jln Penang; ste RM380; ❋🛜) The five studio-apartment-style suites in this row of old shophouses offer plenty of space, kitchenettes, big showers and a great contemporary feel. However, bring your earplugs as there's traffic noise from the busy road outside.

A string of new, ground-level suites was close to being finished when we were in town.

China Tiger (Map p162; ☑012-501 5360, 04-264 3580; www.chinatiger.info; 29 Lr China; apt RM500; ❋@🛜) Fancy feeling at home even when you're away? Then consider a stay at one of China Tiger's two open-concept, self-catering, apartment-like rooms. They accommodate up to five people and include heaps of space, natural light and functional kitchenettes.

GEORGE TOWN'S MARKETS

George Town has some wonderful old-school markets, such as **Campbell Street Market** (Pasar Lebuh Campbell; Map p162; 4 Lr Campbell; ⊙7am-noon), **Kuala Kangsar Market** (Map p162; Jln Kuala Kangsar; ⊙6am-2pm) and **Cecil Street Market** (Pasar Lebuh Cecil; Map p168; 40-48 Lr Cecil; mains from RM5; ⊙9am-7pm). You'll see butchers and fishmongers here in all their visceral glory alongside vendors of fresh fruit, vegetables and all kinds of daily goods, as well as a smattering of crafts. Cecil Street Market is a particularly good spot for grazing on hawker food, too, as is the **Macallum Street Night Market** (Map p168; Lingtan Macallum 1; mains from RM5; ⊙6-10.30pm Mon & Thu).

Modern George Town markets cater more for tourists and serve to showcase the up-and-coming talents of Penang's creative scene. The best of them is Hin Bus Depot's **Hin Pop-Up Market** (Map p168; www.hinbusdepot.com; Hin Bus Depot, 31A Jln Gurdwara; ⊙11am-5pm Sun), held every Sunday, but you might also find something interesting at the Occupy Beach Street (Legally) event (p171).

Outside the Unesco Protected Zone

Tido Penang Hostel
HOSTEL $
(Map p162; 04-251 9266; www.tidopenanghostel.com; 106 Jln Argyll; dm/r incl breakfast from RM40/90; ❄@🛜) Malay for 'sleep', Tido is one of George Town's best-designed hostels. Just the right side of industrial chic, the polished concrete walls and floors are brightened up with colourful art. There's a lift, so no carting your backpack up five floors to the ace common room with great views. Friendly staff plus bicycle and scooter rental round out the package.

★ Noordin Mews
HOTEL $$
(Map p162; 04-263 7125; www.noordinmews.com; 53 Lr Noordin; r/ste incl breakfast RM355/560; ❄@🛜🏊) These two restored shophouses boast an attractive 1920s and '30s feel, down to the antique adverts and retro furniture. Very friendly service, a pool and a secluded-feeling location away from the main tourist drag are additional draws.

Museum Hotel
HOTEL $$
(Map p162; 04-226 6668; www.museumhotel.com.my; 72 Jln AS Mansor; r/ste incl breakfast from RM300/650; ❄@🛜) Attractive and comfortable with great service, the Museum Hotel is a gem in this price range. Located in a stately block of restored shophouses, the 24 rooms range from tight but comfy singles to larger rooms, all tastefully decorated with antique- and vintage-themed design touches, and looked after by capable staff.

GLOW
HOTEL $$
(Map p168; 04-226 0084; www.glowhotels.com/penang; 101 Jln Macalister; r incl breakfast from RM230; P❄@🛜🏊) A chain with charm.

And lots of space. And a location near tonnes of street food. And it's great value! There's certainly a lot to like about this young-feeling hotel, located about 700m northwest of the intersection with Jln Penang – not least the laundry-and-transfer services, the gym, bar and restaurant, and the well-equipped pool.

Jawi Peranakan Mansion
BOUTIQUE HOTEL $$$
(Map p162; 04-261 8888; www.georgetownheritage.com; 153 Jln Hutton; r/ste incl breakfast from RM400/600; ❄🛜🏊) The latest in the GTHH collection of boutique hotels in restored heritage buildings delivers Middle Eastern chic with its tiles, carved wooden doorways and wrought-iron details. It's a little bit of a walk from the main heritage zone, but nothing too strenuous, and there's a good pool here to cool down in, too.

Noordin Street House
BOUTIQUE HOTEL $$$
(Map p162; 04-262 7173; www.noordin-streethouse.com; 71 & 73 Lr Noordin; r incl breakfast RM420-820; ❄@🛜🏊) A charming, homey boutique hotel has been coaxed out of this rambling shophouse. There are eight eclectic rooms, which share inviting public spaces, including a plunge pool and restaurant.

Macalister Mansion
BOUTIQUE HOTEL $$$
(Map p168; 04-228 3888; www.macalistermansion.com; 228 Jln Macalister; r from RM930; P❄@🛜🏊) One of George Town's more distinctive boutique hotels, Macalister Mansion offers eight elegantly designed rooms in a lovely old house that's been given a slick contemporary makeover. Its restaurant, the Dining Room (open 7pm to 11pm Tuesday to Sunday), serves excellent food and there's a very nice pool and bar area too.

The mansion is around 2km outside the heritage zone; a taxi here should cost about RM15.

Eating

Inside the Unesco Protected Zone

★ Wai Kei Cafe   CHINESE $
(Map p162; Lr Chulia; mains from RM7; ⊙11am-2pm daily, 6-9pm Mon-Fri) This gem sits in the middle of the greatest concentration of travellers in George Town, yet is somehow almost exclusively patronised (in enthusiastic numbers) by locals. Come early for *char siew* (barbecued pork) and *siew yoke* (pork belly), probably among the best versions of these dishes we've encountered in Asia.

Kafe Kheng Pin   HAWKER $
(Map p162; 20 Jln Penang; mains from RM4; ⊙7am-2pm Tue-Sun) The must-eats at this old-school-feeling hawker joint include a legendary *lor bak* (deep-fried meat rolls dipped in sauce), rice porridges and an exquisite Hainanese chicken-rice (steamed chicken with broth and rice).

Hameediyah   MALAYSIAN $
(Map p162; ☑04-261 1095; 164 Lr Campbell; mains RM8-20; ⊙10am-10pm Sat-Thu) Hameediyah dates back to 1907 and is allegedly the oldest place serving *nasi kandar* (South Asian Muslim–influenced curries served over rice) in Penang, though a renovation belies its many years. Brave the long lines and rather dreary dining room for rich, meaty curries or *murtabak* – a *roti prata* (flaky, flat bread) stuffed with minced mutton, chicken or vegetables, egg and spices.

Merican Nasi Kandar   MALAYSIAN $
(Map p162; Melo Cafe, 101 Jln Masjid Kapitan Keling; meals from RM6; ⊙9am-4pm; ☑) Step into this classic-feeling cafe for excellent *nasi kandar*. You can't go wrong with the tomato rice, topped with just about any of the rich curries, and as a bonus, Merican has more vegetable dishes than most places of its genre.

Joo Hooi Cafe   HAWKER $
(Map p162; 475 Jln Penang; mains RM3-5.50, desserts from RM2.50; ⊙11am-5pm) The hawker-centre equivalent of one-stop shopping, this hectic place assembles all of Penang's best dishes: laksa, *rojak* (a 'salad' of crispy fruits and vegetables in a thick, slightly sweet dressing), *char kway teow* and an incredibly popular *cendol*.

Tho Yuen Restaurant   CHINESE $
(Map p162; ☑04-261 4672; 92 Lr Campbell; dim sum RM1.60-8, mains from RM4.50; ⊙6am-3pm Wed-Mon) Tho Yuen is packed with newspaper-reading loners and chattering locals all morning long. It's best to arrive early for its widest array of breakfast dim sum. Mid-morning, plump pork *bao* (steamed buns) and shrimp dumplings give way to chicken rice and *hor fun* (vermicelli with beef and bean sprouts). Servers speak minimal English but do their best to explain the contents of dim sum carts.

Sri Ananda Bahwan   INDIAN $
(Map p162; ☑04-264 4204; www.srianandabahwan.com.my; 53-55 Lr Penang; mains from RM4; ⊙7am-11.30pm; ☑) This busy and buzzy chain restaurant whips up filling *masala dosa* (rice-and-lentil crepe stuffed with spiced potatoes), lip-smacking tandoori chicken and countless vegetarian Indian dishes. There's also a counter of glistening sweets, such as *laddu* (tiny cannonballs of syrup, coconut and gram flour), for takeaway nibbles.

Its vegetarian-only outlet is a few doors along the street at No 25.

Veloo Villas   INDIAN $
(Map p162; ☑04-262 4369; 22 Lr Penang; set meals RM5-13.50; ⊙7am-10pm; ☑) Service is amiable and unfussy at this cheap, cheerful banana-leaf restaurant. Come between 11am to 4pm for hearty rice-based set meals, or outside these hours for *dosa* (paper-thin rice-and-lentil crepes) and other made-to-order meals.

Goh Thew Chik   CHINESE $
(Map p162; 338A Lr Chulia; mains RM5-6; ⊙11am-5pm Wed-Mon) This simple cafe draws the crowds with its excellent Hainanese chicken-rice, so you may have to wait for a table.

Sup Hameed   MALAYSIAN $
(Map p162; ☑04-261 8007; 48 Jln Penang; mains from RM4.50; ⊙24hr) On the surface, this is very much your typical shop serving *nasi kandar*. We don't particularly recommend eating here during the day, but from around 4pm, Hameed sets out tables on the street and serves his incredibly rich and meaty soups (try *sup kambing* – mutton soup), which come with slices of white bread.

Yin's Sourdough Bakery   BAKERY $
(Map p162; ☑011-2419 5118; www.yinssourdough.com; 11 Pesara Claimant; loaves from RM3.50; ⊙7am-6pm Mon-Sat; ☑) Tired of rice? Weary of noodles? Head here for freshly baked, additive-free bread, alongside cranberry buns, cinnamon rolls and focaccia. Buy baked goods to go, or stick around for a sandwich, breakfast or pizza.

PENANG GEORGE TOWN

DON'T MISS

CHINA HOUSE

You can't really say you've been to George Town unless you've stepped inside **China House** (Map p162; 04-263 7299; www.chinahouse.com.my; 153 & 155 Lr Pantai; mains RM25-35; 9am-midnight). This block-wide amalgamation of shophouses is home to a variety of dining, drinking and shopping options. It all starts splendidly with the buzzy bakery cafe, **Kopi C** (Map p162;), serving scrumptious baked goods, serious coffee and great light meals, and it just gets better from there.

Return in the evening to experience the elegant yet relaxed restaurant **BTB** (Map p162; 04-262 7299; mains RM55-70; 9am-midnight Sun-Thu, to 1am Fri & Sat;), the cocktail and wine bar **Vine & Single** (5pm-midnight) and the live-music venue **Canteen** (183B Lr Victoria; 9am-2am Mon-Sat, to midnight Sun). And don't forget about the boutique shop and art gallery upstairs!

Leaf Healthy House
VEGETARIAN $

(Map p162; 012-448 8491; www.facebook.com/TheLeafHealthyHouse; 5 Lr Penang; mains RM8-15; 11.30am-3pm & 5.30-10pm Mon-Sat;) Fresh salads, juices, healthy rice and noodle dishes are all served at this appealing veggie cafe.

★ Teksen
CHINESE $$

(Map p162; 012-981 5117; 18 Lr Carnarvon; mains RM15-20; noon-2.30pm & 6-8.30pm Wed-Mon) There's a reason this place is always packed: it's one of the tastiest, most consistent restaurants in town (and in a place like George Town, that's saying a lot). You almost can't go wrong here, but don't miss the favourites – the 'double-roasted pork with chilli padi' is obligatory and delicious – and be sure to ask about the daily specials.

Jaloux
ITALIAN $$

(Map p162; 016-452 9882; www.facebook.com/jaloux24; 24 Lr King; mains RM28-33; noon-3pm & 6-9pm Thu-Mon) Chefs Hong and Yen have charmed Penangites at two previous venues, with their quirky style and delicious Italian food and desserts. Jaloux is their latest venture and features both minimalist decor and a pared-back menu, almost exclusively homemade pasta with maybe a soup or panna cotta for support. It's all delicious and worth the wait.

Auntie Gaik Lean's
PERANAKAN $$

(Map p162; 017-434 4398; 1 Lr Bishop; mains RM25-35; noon-2.30pm & 6-9.30pm Tue-Sun) A homey, old-school dining room serving likewise Peranakan dishes. If you're intimidated by the menu, opt for the daily set lunch, which is posted out front.

Holy Guacamole
MEXICAN $$

(Map p162; 04-261 6057; www.facebook.com/holyguac.penang; 65 Love Lane; mains RM18-20; noon-2.30am;) In a city with such amazing local food it feels wrong to recommend a Mexican restaurant, but the folks at Holy Guacamole are doing an admirable job. Admittedly, the offerings are more Austin, Texas than Mexico City. Still, there are lots of meat-free options, and Holy Guacamole doubles as a bar, with live music every night.

Junk
BURGERS $$

(Map p162; 016-438 3205; www.facebook.com/junk401; 401 Lr Chulia; mains RM20-30; noon-1am Mon-Thu, to 2am Fri-Sun) Some claim the burgers at this casual spot are the best in town. With a short drinks list and a fun, eclectic vibe, Junk also serves as a bar.

Mews Cafe
MALAYSIAN $$

(Map p162; 04-263 5125; www.georgetownheritage.com/mews-cafe; Muntri Mews, 77 Jln Muntri; mains RM25-30; 8am-11pm) Traditional local dishes such as laksa and nasi goreng (fried rice) with chicken satay are made with high-quality ingredients and served in generous portions at this stylish cafe fronting **Muntri Mews** (Map p162; 04-261 8888; r incl breakfast from RM400;). Sitting in the leafy patio, you can watch the passing parade with a drink and dessert, a lovely way to spend some time.

Da Shu Xia Seafood House
SEAFOOD $$

(Tree Shade Seafood Restaurant; Map p162; 012-474 5566; 177C Lr Victoria; mains RM20-40; 11am-3.30pm & 5-10pm Thu-Tue) This open-air shack has lost the shade of the tree it was originally named after, but it remains a place where locals go for cheap and tasty seafood. Pick your aquatic protein from the trays out front, and the staff will fry, steam, soup or grill it up for you.

Kebaya
PERANAKAN $$$

(Map p162; 04-264 2333; www.kebaya.com.my; Seven Terraces, 14A Lg Stewart; set dinner RM128; 6-10pm) This is your chance to sample Peranakan-influenced cuisine in a setting that the Baba-Nonya elite of yesteryear would have approved of. The stately dining room, part of the Seven Terraces hotel (p173), is decorated with a gorgeous collection of antiques, set to a soundtrack of live piano. Set four-course dinners are served at two sittings (starting at 6pm and 8pm).

✖ Outside the Unesco Protected Zone

★ **Nasi Padang Minang** INDONESIAN $
(Map p162; 92 Jln Transfer; mains from RM4; ⊙11am-5pm) Serve-yourself, buffet-style restaurants generally opt for quantity over quality, but the Padang-style Indonesian curries, stir-fries, soups, salads and grilled dishes here are uniformly vibrant and delicious. Come at lunch for the best, freshest selection.

Kafe Heng Huat HAWKER $
(Map p168; cnr Jln Macalister & Lg Selamat; mains RM10; ⊙11am-6pm Wed-Mon) Outside Kafe Heng Huat you'll find Soon Chuan Choo who, in her trademark red chef's hat, has been turning out some of Penang's best *char kway teow* for nearly 50 years. Adjacent stalls sell *won ton mee* (wheat- and egg-noodle soup) and other Chinese Penang staples.

Lg Selamat intersects with Jln Macalister about 500m northwest of the intersection with Jln Penang.

Nyonya Breeze Desire PERANAKAN $$
(☎04-899 9058; 3A-1-7 Straits Quay, Tanjung Tokong; mains RM10-45; ⊙11am-10pm; 🚌101, 102, 103) Although in a rather charmless setting in a mall, the food here is good, and ranges

DON'T MISS

HAWKER STALL HEAVEN

Not eating at a hawker stall in George Town is like skipping the Louvre in Paris – unthinkable! There are tonnes of hawker centres and stalls in and around town, from shophouse-bound *kopitiam* (coffee shops) to open-air markets made up of mobile stalls.

Keep in mind that hawker-stall vendors run flexible schedules, so don't be surprised if one isn't there during your visit. A good strategy is to avoid Mondays and Thursdays, when many vendors tend to stay at home.

Our favourite hawker stalls include the following:

Gurney Drive Hawker Stalls (Map p168; Persiaran Gurney; mains from RM4; ⊙5pm-midnight) One of Penang's most famous hawker complexes sits amid modern high-rise buildings bordered by the sea. Tourists and locals rush in for an almost overwhelming selection of Muslim and Chinese-Malay dishes. Gurney Drive is about 3km west of George Town. A taxi here will set you back RM20.

Lorong Baru (New Lane) Hawker Stalls (Map p168; cnr Jln Macalister & Lg Baru; mains from RM3; ⊙5-10.30pm Thu-Tue) Ask locals where their favourite hawker stalls are, and they'll generally mention this night-time street extravaganza, located about 1km west of the city centre. Prepare to battle for a spot if you're visiting at the weekend.

Pulau Tikus Hawker Centre (Map p168; cnr Solok Moulmein & Jln Burma; mains from RM4; ⊙6am-2pm) Before those bland guesthouse breakfasts get you down, consider a visit to this busy morning market area. The market is about 2.5km north of Jln Penang; a taxi from the centre of George Town is around RM20.

Sea Pearl Cafe (☎04-899 0375; 338 Jln Tokong Thai Pak Koong, Tanjung Tokong; mains from RM8; ⊙11am-10pm Thu-Tue) The excellent seafood and unique location of this basic hawker centre – seemingly hidden in a Chinese temple complex looking out over the North Channel – make the Sea Pearl one of our favourite places to eat outside the city centre. It's 7km northwest of George Town; a taxi here costs RM25.

Lebuh Presgrave Hawker Stalls (Map p162; cnr Lr Presgrave & Lr Mcnair; mains from RM5; ⊙5pm-midnight Fri-Wed) A famous vendor of Hokkien mee (yellow noodles fried with sliced meat, boiled squid, prawns and strips of fried egg) draws most folks to this open-air hawker convocation.

Medan Renong Padang Kota Lama (Map p162; Jln Tun Syed Sheh Barakbah; mains from RM3; ⊙5.30pm-midnight Thu-Tue) One side of this seaside food centre is called 'Islam' and serves halal Malay food, and the other is called 'Cina' and serves Chinese and Malay specialities, including the absolutely delicious *rojak* (a fruit-and-vegetable salad) at 101 Rojak.

from several *kerabu* (salads) to staples such as *inche kabin* (deep-fried chicken).

Straits Quay is located about 7km northwest of George Town; a taxi here costs about RM25. Search for 'Nyonya Breeze Desire at Straits Quay' on Facebook.

Ocean Green
SEAFOOD $$

(Map p168; ☑04-227 4530; 48F Jln Sultan Ahmad Shah; mains RM35-50; ⏱noon-11pm) There's a menu at this waterfront seafood smorgasbord, but talk to your server about what's fresh. The dining hall is invariably packed – if it's too busy or hot, ask about the air-con rooms in the adjacent Paramount Hotel. It's a good idea to reserve. We loved the crab *bee hoon* (vermicelli noodles) and prawns with chilli dipping sauce.

Suffolk House
INTERNATIONAL $$

(Map p168; ☑04-228 3930; www.suffolkhouse. com.my; 250 Jln Air Itam; mains RM55-65; ⏱noon-10.30pm) Dishes such as beef pot pie and prawn-crusted sea bass are on the main menu, but the best reason for heading to this beautifully restored 200-year-old Georgian-style mansion is to indulge in its traditional afternoon tea (RM45 per person), featuring freshly baked scones, dainty cakes and neatly cut sandwiches.

 Drinking & Nightlife

A lively budget-oriented nightlife area is the conglomeration of backpacker pubs near the intersection of Lr Chulia and Love Lane. Artsier bars that draw locals can be found near the Hin Bus Depot (p167).

★Mugshot Cafe
CAFE

(Map p162; www.facebook.com/themugshotcafe penang; 302 Lr Chulia; ⏱8am-midnight; 🛜) Asian breakfast not your thing? Stop into this eclectic cafe to be transported West for a meal. The options include huge mugs of coffee, wood-fired bagels, homemade yoghurt with fruit and granola in glass jars, and baked goods from the neighbouring bakery.

Antarabangsa Enterprise
BAR

(Map p162; ☑04-263 2279; 21 Lg Stewart; ⏱3pm-2am Mon-Thu, 2pm-3am Fri & Sat, 7.30-11.30pm Sun) 'Bar' is an overstatement for this booze distributor that happens to have a stack of plastic tables and chairs that customers can use. Pick your brew – allegedly Penang's cheapest – from the fridge, and stake your claim next to the grizzled regulars or backpackers keen to see what all the fuss is about. It's fun and social, and you'll probably become a regular.

Narrow Marrow
CAFE

(Map p162; ☑016-553 6647; www.facebook.com/ narrowmarrow; 252A Lr Carnarvon; ⏱10am-1am Thu-Tue) Decorated with work by local artists and dangling Chinese lamps, this space serves exceptional coffee by day and hosts live music and social events by night. Try the toddy, served plain, in a cocktail or – our favourite – with beer.

Beach Blanket Babylon
BAR

(Map p162; www.32mansion.com.my; 32 Jln Sultan Ahmad Shah; ⏱noon-midnight) The open-air setting and relaxed vibe contrast with the rather grand building this bar is linked to. Pair your drink and alfresco views over the North Channel with tasty local dishes.

Ome by Spacebar
CAFE

(Map p162; 1 Lg Toh Aka; ⏱8am-6pm Fri-Wed) This cavernous cafe carved out of an old shophouse has exposed brick and *Kinfolk*-inspired minimalism that complement its sophisticated coffee drinks, which range from pour-overs to nitro, and baked goods such as olive oil zucchini cake.

Macallum Connoisseurs
CAFE

(Map p168; ☑04-261 3597; www.facebook.com/ Macallum; 1 Gat Lr Macallum; ⏱9am-midnight; 🛜) Since they roast their own beans and train baristas at this giant warehouse space, you can rely on the place for a decent cup of coffee. On the menu are decent Western-style snacks and light meals including toasted bagels, and the compound is home to a gelato outlet.

Gravity
ROOFTOP BAR

(Map p168; ☑04-219 0000; www.ghotelkelawai. com.my; G Hotel Kelawei, 2 Persiaran Maktab; ⏱5pm-1am) Yes, it's a hotel pool bar, but the breezy rooftop location and spectacular views, both out to sea and across to Penang Hill, make Gravity one of the island's top sundowner destinations. Time your visit for happy hour (5pm to 7pm), or enjoy free-flowing house wines (RM75 per hour).

It's about 3.5km northwest of central George Town in Pulau Tikus; a taxi here should cost RM20.

Micke's Place
BAR

(Map p162; ☑012-493 8279; www.facebook.com/ mickesplacelovelane; 94 Love Lane; ⏱noon-3am Sat-Thu, 2pm-3am Fri) Graffiti-covered walls, shisha pipes and free-flowing booze: this classic formula has allowed Micke's Place to remain one of the most popular backpacker bars in George Town. Sure, Micke's lacks panache, but its crowd of travellers makes for easy mingling, so it's a good place to start your night.

GEORGE TOWN'S SPEAKEASIES

Tired of drinking at establishments with pesky signs or conventional entrances? Then George Town is your place. Alcohol consumption is above board in the town, but over the last few years, the city has seen the emergence of several 'speakeasies': semi-concealed bars, many serving cocktails revolving around local ingredients. The drinks can be hit-and-miss, but the experience is great fun.

Backdoor Bodega (Map p162; www.facebook.com/backdoorbodega; 37B Jln Gurdwara; ⊙10pm-1am Thu-Sat) With a hidden location behind an unmarked door – ask at the nearby **Good Friends Club** (Map p162; ☑016-452 9250; www.facebook.com/goodfriendsclubpenang; 39 Jln Gurdwara; ⊙7pm-1am Wed-Mon) – and a unique marketing angle (it claims to be an 'overpriced pin shop'), Backdoor Bodega might be the most elusive of George Town's speakeasies. There really are pins for sale, and a purchase comes with a free cocktail, many using locally inspired ingredients such as Thai tea and homemade coconut rum.

Golden Shower by ChinChin (Map p162; ☑012-428 2509; www.facebook.com/golden showerbychinchin; 86 Lr Bishop; ⊙5.30pm-2am Tue-Sun) Enter a glass room housing what looks like it could have been Louis XVI's bathroom only to emerge in a pastel pink lozenge that resembles a Mary Kay showroom circa 1957. For all the quirk and decadence, however, the service and drinks don't justify the sky-high tariffs.

Out Of Nowhere (Map p162; www.facebook.com/outofnowhereeee; 73 Jln Kuala Kangsar; ⊙7am-noon Mon, 7pm-1am Mon-Wed, to 2am Fri & Sat, to midnight Sun) To find this speak-easy, locate Hold Up Coffee Shop, then proceed through the giant orange refrigerator (yes, really). You'll emerge into a semi-open-air space serving drinks that are probably more visually impressive and over the top (sample ingredients: toasted bread infusion, jackfruit foam, sesame-seed tincture) than they are delicious.

Mish Mash COCKTAIL BAR
(Map p162; ☑017-536 5128; www.mishmashpg. com; 24 Jln Muntri; ⊙5pm-midnight Tue-Sun) Mixology magic takes place between the whisky- and wine-bottle-lined walls of Mish Mash. Japanese flavours come to the fore in cocktails such as the 'Pandan Paloma', with tequila and pandanus sugar. We also appreciated its well-blended mocktails such as pear and rosemary smash.

Constant Gardener CAFE
(Map p162; ☑04-251 9070; www.constantgardener. coffee; 9 Lr Light; ⊙9am-midnight Tue-Sun) A serious venue for serious coffee drinkers, this attractive place brews its lattes with coveted beans from Malaysia and beyond, and serves some pristine-looking pastries and cakes.

Ten Yee Tea Trading TEAHOUSE
(Map p162; ☑04-262 5693; 33 Lr Pantai; ⊙10am-6.30pm Mon-Sat) All major styles of Chinese tea are on sale here, but the fun part is deciding which to buy. For RM20 you choose a tea (which you can share with up to five people), then Lim, the enthusiastic owner, shows you how to prepare it the proper way.

Jing-Si Books & Cafe CAFE
(Map p162; ☑04-261 6561; 31 Lr Pantai; ⊙10am-7pm Mon-Sat, 8am-6pm Sun) An oasis of spiritual calm, this outlet for a Taiwanese Buddhist group's teachings is a wonderful place to revive in hushed surroundings over a pot of interesting tea or coffee – all of which go for RM5.

Three-Sixty Revolving Restaurant & Sky Bar ROOFTOP BAR
(Map p162; ☑04-261 3540; www.360rooftop.com. my; Bayview Hotel, 25A Lr Farquhar; ⊙4pm-1am Sun-Thu, to 2am Fri & Sat; 🐾) As the name indicates, there's a revolving restaurant (doing its thing from 6.30pm to 10pm), but we prefer the adjacent open-air Sky Bar, which boasts some of the best views of George Town.

Georgetown Wines WINE BAR
(Map p162; www.facebook.com/georgetownwines; 19 Lr Leith; ⊙6pm-1am Wed-Mon) Built into a former stable, this wine bar and restaurant is one of the city's more attractive places to have a drink. Take a walk through the cellar to choose a bottle or order house wines by the glass.

☆ Entertainment

Performing Arts Centre of Penang PERFORMING ARTS
(☑04-899 1722; www.penangpac.org; 3H-3A-1, Quay One, Straits Quay, Jln Seri Tanjung Pinang; 🚌101, 102, 103) Check the website to see what shows are on at this modern performing-arts

centre, in the shopping plaza **Straits Quay** (☑ 04-891 8000; www.straitsquay.com; ☺ 9am-1am Mon-Sat, to midnight Sun; ☐ 101, 102, 103) between George Town and Batu Ferringhi. There's an experimental theatre seating 150 people and a main stage seating 350.

It's located about 7km northwest of George Town; a taxi here will cost about RM25.

🔒 Shopping

★ Batek-Lah   FASHION & ACCESSORIES
(Map p162; ☑ 04-228 2910; www.batek-lah.com; 158 Jln Transfer; ☺ 11am-7pm Mon-Sat) Malaysian-produced batik printed cloth is made into a variety of men's and women's fashions and gift items here. Some of the more expensive designs are hand-drawn rather than block-printed, making them unique.

Staff can also arrange for clothes tailored to your request using your choice of batik cloth.

★ Unique Penang   ARTS & CRAFTS
(Map p162; 62 Love Lane; ☺ 5-10pm) Be charmed by the colourful artworks, prints and post-cards of friendly young owners Clovis and Joey, as well as the many images created by the art students they train here.

As the couple points out, paintings are hard to squeeze into a backpack, so nearly all of the gallery's art is available in postcard size, which they will even arrange to post for you at a time of your choosing.

★ Bon Ton   ARTS & CRAFTS
(Map p162; ☑ 04-262 7299; 86 Lr Armenian; ☺ 10am-7pm) Head here for fabrics – both new and antique – as well as boxes, stationery, coffee-table books, art pieces, bags and other classy Asian bric-a-brac.

There's also a branch above China House (p176), and for bigger pieces of furniture and more of Bon Ton's stock, check out **179 The House** (179 Lr Pantai).

Mano Plus   HOMEWARES
(Map p162; ☑ 04-262 8383; www.manoplus.com; 1st fl, 37A & 37B Lr Pantai; ☺ 9am-6pm Mon-Thu, to 9pm Fri-Sun) The subtle, minimalist, design-focused homewares here, some of which are made locally, include earthy ceramics, handsome stationery, wooden toys and fancy scissors. The shop is also home to a good cafe, **Fuku Eatery & Desserts** (Map p162; ☑ 016-302 2102; 🛱).

Sixth Sense   CLOTHING
(Map p162; ☑ 04-261 5813; www.sixthsensestores.com; 157 Lr Pantai; ☺ 10am-7pm Mon-Sat, noon-5pm Sun) Earthy, simple, linen-heavy clothing for

both men and women is the emphasis at this local-label store. Supplementing this is a selection of handsome, minimalist homeware.

Moon Shop   GIFTS & SOUVENIRS
(Map p162; ☑ 016-467 4011; www.facebook.com/moonshopgallery; 38/1 Lr Farquhar; ☺ 11am-8pm Mon-Sat) Tan Wei Min creates lush and beautiful terrariums in everything from small glass jars to giant globes. Buying one is like taking home a piece of the tropics. Even if you're not in the market for a plant, the shop is well worth visiting for a hand-brewed artisan coffee or matcha (powdered green tea) drink.

Barbara Moore Gallery   ART
(Map p162; ☑ 016-467 3207; www.barbaramooreart.com; 13 Lg Toh Aka; ☺ by appointment) Canadian colour-pencil artist Barbara Moore has a small gallery in her home on one of the heritage zone's more charming residential streets – worth visiting for its ambience and street art alone. Also here is the historic artefact jewellery of Ben Rogen.

Gerak Budaya   BOOKS
(Map p162; ☑ 04-261 0282; www.gerakbudayapenang.com; 78 Jln Masjid Kapitan Keling; ☺ 11am-8pm Mon-Sat) If you're looking for books about Malaysia and the region, or books written by local authors, this is the place to come – the selection here is unsurpassed. This is the fiction and poetry branch – there's a nonfiction branch at 226 Lr Pantai.

Shop Howard   ARTS & CRAFTS
(Map p162; ☑ 04-261 1917; www.studiohoward.com; 154 Jln Masjid Kapitan Keling; ☺ 10am-6pm) Pick up one of Howard Tan's distinctive photographic prints at this compact gift boutique that also sells unique postcards, art, handicrafts and books on local topics, all made by local artists.

Rozanas Batik   ARTS & CRAFTS
(Map p162; ☑ 014-247 5347; 81B Lr Acheh; ☺ 11.30am-6pm Mon-Sat) This shophouse workshop features the owner's beautiful handmade batik items. If you want to learn more about this craft, take a walk-in class (from noon to 6pm Monday to Saturday) in the adjacent studio (RM35 to RM75).

Gurney Plaza   MALL
(Map p168; ☑ 04-222 8222; www.gurneyplaza.com.my/en; Persiaran Gurney; ☺ 10am-10pm) In addition to more than 300 shops, including the department store Parkson, Penang's biggest and boldest mall includes tonnes of food and beverage outlets, a multiplex cinema, an

amusement theme park, a fitness centre and a beauty spa.

A taxi here from central George Town costs RM15 to RM20.

Fuan Wong ARTS & CRAFTS
(Map p162; ☎04-251 9463; www.fuanwong.com; 13 Lr Armenian; ⏰10am-6pm Mon-Sat) This gallery showcases the exquisite fused-glass creations of Penang artist Wong Keng Fuan. Colourful bowls and quirky sculptures are for sale.

At the rear of the store is a second branch of Shop Howard, selling the photographic prints, artworks and crafts of Howard Tan.

Sam's Batik House CLOTHING
(Map p162; ☎04-262 1095; www.samsbatikhouse.com; 183-185 Jln Penang; ⏰10.30am-8pm Mon-Sat) Nicknamed 'Ali Baba's Cave', this deep trove of silky and cottony goodness is one of the best places in George Town to buy sarongs, batik shirts and Indian fashions.

Information

INTERNET ACCESS

Nearly all lodging options offer wi-fi, and some have a computer terminal for guest use. Wi-fi is also widely available at restaurants, cafes and in shopping malls, but internet cafes are a dying breed.

MEDICAL SERVICES

The following are all a few kilometres west of central George Town, around 15 minutes away by taxi, which will cost about RM15 to RM20.

Hospital Pulau Pinang (Map p168; ☎04-222 5333; http://jknpenang.moh.gov.my; Jln Residensi; ⏰24hr) The island's largest public hospital, with general healthcare and emergency services.

Loh Guan Lye Specialist Centre (Map p168; ☎appointments 04-238 8888, emergency 04-226 6911; www.lohguanlye.com; 19 Jln Logan; ⏰24hr) For more specific health issues, head to this private hospital.

Penang Adventist Hospital (Map p168; ☎04-222 7200; www.pah.com.my; 465 Jln Burma; ⏰24hr) Not-for-profit hospital and health centre.

MONEY

Branches of major banks are on Lr Pantai and Lr Downing, near the main post office. Most have 24-hour ATMs. At the northwestern end of Lr Chulia are a few money changers, open longer hours than banks and with more competitive rates.

POST

Post Office (Map p162; ☎04-261 9222; Lr Downing; ⏰8.30am-5pm Mon-Fri, to 1pm Sat) The island's main post terminal.

TOURIST INFORMATION

Ministry of Tourism (Map p162; ☎04-262 0202; www.malaysia.travel; 11 Lr Pantai; ⏰8am-5pm Mon-Fri) Government office providing general tourism information on the country as a whole. Nearby, the agency's **Penang branch** (Map p162; ☎04-262 2093; www.tourism.gov.my; Jln Tun Syed Sheh Barakbah; ⏰8am-12.15pm & 2.45-5pm Mon-Fri) provides state-specific information. There's also an **airport branch** (☎04-642 6981; Penang International Airport; ⏰7am-10pm).

Penang Global Tourism (Map p162; ☎04-264 3456; www.mypenang.gov.my; 8B Whiteways Arcade, Lr Pantai; ⏰8.30am-5.30pm Mon-Fri) The visitor centre of the state tourism agency is the best all-around place to go for maps, brochures and local information.

Getting There & Away

AIR

Penang International Airport (☎04-252 0252; www.penangairport.com; 🚌401) is 18km south of George Town.

BOAT

Langkawi Ferry Service (LFS; Map p162; ☎04-264 2088; www.langkawi-ferry.com; PPC Bldg, Pesara King Edward; one-way adult/child RM60/45; ⏰7am-5.30pm Mon-Sat, to 3pm Sun) Boats leave for Langkawi, the resort island in Kedah, at 8.30am and 2pm and return from Langkawi at 10.30am and 3pm. The journey takes between 1¾ and 2½ hours each way. Book a few days in advance to ensure you get a seat.

Swettenham Pier Cruise Terminal (Map p162; ☎04-210 2211; www.penangport.com.my; Pengkalan Weld) International cruise ships dock here.

BUS

Most interstate and international buses to George Town arrive and depart from **Sungai Nibong Bus Station** (☎04-659 2099; www.rapidpg.com.my; Jln Sultan Azlan Shah, Kampung Dua Bukit; 🚌401, 303), just to the south of Penang Bridge. A taxi from Sungai Nibong to George Town costs around RM50.

Before heading out to Sungai Nibong, check whether you can board your long-distance bus at **KOMTAR Bus Station** (Map p162; ☎04-255 8000; www.rapidpg.com.my; Jln Ria). Note that transport to Thailand (except to Hat Yai) is via minivan. Transport can also be arranged to Ko Samui and Ko Phi Phi via a transfer in Surat Thani and Hat Yai respectively.

Buses around Penang Island are run by the government-owned **Rapid Penang** (☎5.30am-midnight hotline 04-255 8000; www.rapidpg.com.my). Fares range from

RM1.40 to RM4. Most routes originate at **Weld Quay Bus Terminal** (Map p162; ☏ 04-255 8000; www.rapidpg.com.my; 19-24 Pengkalan Weld) and most also stop at KOMTAR.

DESTINATION	PRICE (RM)	DURA-TION	FREQUENCY
Hat Yai (Thailand)	35-40	5 hrs	frequent
Ipoh	28	2½ hrs	frequent
Johor Bahru	60-70	9 hrs	frequent
Kota Bharu	39-41	7 hrs	up to 7 daily
Kuala Lumpur	38	5 hrs	frequent
Kuala Terengganu	51	8 hrs	daily
Melaka	50	7 hrs	frequent
Singapore	80	10 hrs	up to 12 daily
Tanah Rata (for Cameron Highlands)	40	5 hrs	up to 6 daily

TRAIN

Penang's train station is located in Butterworth, next to the ferry terminal and bus and taxi station.

GEORGE TOWN'S STREET NAMES

Finding your way around George Town can be slightly complicated since many roads have both a Malay and an English name. While many street signs list both, it can still be confusing. We use primarily the Malay name. Here are the two names of some of the main roads:

Malay	English
Lr Gereja	Church St
Jln Masjid Kapitan Keling	Pitt St
Jln Tun Syed Sheh Barakbah	The Esplanade
Lr Pantai	Beach St
Lr Pasar	Market St

To make matters more bewildering, Jln Penang may also be referred to as Jln Pinang or as Penang Rd – but there's also a Penang St, which may also be called Lr Pinang! Similarly, Chulia St is Lr Chulia but there's also a Lg Chulia, and this confuses even the taxi drivers.

ⓘ Getting Around

TO/FROM THE AIRPORT

Bus 401 runs to and from the airport (RM4) every half-hour between 6am and 11pm daily, and stops at KOMTAR Bus Station (p181) and Weld Quay Bus Terminal, taking at least an hour.

The fixed taxi fare to central George Town is RM44.70; expect the journey to take around 30 minutes depending on traffic.

BICYCLE

There are several places near the intersection of Gat Lr Armenian and Lr Victoria offering one-day rental of city bikes for around RM10. You can also find bicycles for rent at many places along Lr Chulia.

Alternatively, the new network with **LinkBike** (www.linkbike.my) connects nearly 30 docking stations across the island. Download the app and use the bikes from as little as RM2 per day. However, note that dedicated bike lanes are scarce in George Town.

BUS

Useful government-operated buses around George Town include the free CAT and Pulau Tikus Loop buses; they run on one-way circuits around the heritage zone and Pulau Tikus areas, respectively. See the website of Rapid Penang (p181) for details.

Most routes originate at Weld Quay Bus Terminal and most also stop at KOMTAR Bus Station and along Lr Chulia.

Privately run services on the Hop-On Hop-Off Bus (p169) can also be handy for getting around central George Town and further afield.

Bus stops to various destinations can be found along Lr Chulia.

DESTINATION	ROUTE NO	PICK-UP
Batu Ferringhi	101	Pengkalan Weld, Lr Chulia, KOMTAR
Penang Hill	204	Pengkalan Weld, Lr Chulia, KOMTAR
Penang International Airport, Teluk Kumbar	401	Pengkalan Weld, Lr Chulia
Persiaran Gurney	101, 103	Pengkalan Weld, KOMTAR
Sungai Nibong Bus Station	401, 303	Pengkalan Weld, Lr Chulia, KOMTAR
Teluk Bahang	101	Pengkalan Weld

CAR & MOTORCYCLE

La Belle (Map p162; ☏ 04-264 2717, 016-416 0617; www.facebook.com/VespaPenang; 440B Lr Chulia; motorcycle/car per 24hr from

---

ⓘ GETTING TO & FROM BUTTERWORTH

Butterworth is the main town of Seberang Perai, the mainland part of Penang state. It's usually regarded as a way station rather than a destination in its own right. It's a jumping-off point to vibrant Pulau Pinang (Penang Island), and has rail links to KL and towards the Thai border.

The cheapest way to get to George Town is via the ferry. The **Pangkalan Sultan Abdul Halim Ferry Terminal** (off E17; foot passenger adult/child RM1.20/0.60, bicycle/motorbike/car RM1.40/2/7.70; ☺5.20am-12.40am) is linked by walkway to Butterworth's bus and train stations. Ferries take passengers and cars every 10 minutes from 5.20am to 9.30pm, every 20 minutes until 11.15pm, and hourly after that until 12.40am. The journey takes 10 minutes and fares are charged only for the journey from Butterworth to Penang; returning to the mainland is free.

From **Penang Central Bus Station** (☐04-313 9888; 6 Jln Pantai) there are services to many of Peninsular Malaysia's main cities and towns, as well as to Thailand and Singapore. For schedules and bookings, check www.easybook.com/bus-terminals/butterworth-bus-terminal.

Taxis to/from Butterworth (approximately RM50) cross the 13km Penang Bridge. There's a RM7 toll payable (usually by passengers) at the toll plaza on the mainland, but no charge to return.

At least five daily trains connect **Butterworth Train Station** (☐04-323 7962; www.ktmb.com.my; off E17) with Kuala Lumpur (RM79, 3½ to four hours).

To reach Thailand, take one of 14 daily Komuter services to the border at Padang Besar (RM11, 1¾ hours). There you can connect to the International Express to Hat Yai, or take a Shuttle Train across the border.

Check www.ktmb.com.my and www.train36.com for the latest info on fares and schedules.

RM30/60; ☺9am-10pm) in George Town hires out cars. There are also several companies based at Penang International Airport, including the following:

Avis (☐04-643 9633; www.avis.com; ☺7.30am-9.30pm)

Hertz (☐04-643 0208; www.hertz.com; ☺7.30am-10pm Mon-Sat, 8am-2pm Sun)

Kasina (☐04-644 7893; www.kasina.com.my; ☺7.30am-10pm Mon-Sat, 8.30am-5pm Sun)

New Bob Rent-A-Car (☐04-642 1111; www.bobcar.com.my; ☺8am-11pm Mon-Fri, to 10pm Sat & Sun)

TAXI

Penang's taxis all have meters, which nearly all drivers refuse to use, so negotiate the fare before you set off. Typical fares to places just outside the city centre start at around RM15. Taxis can be found on Jln Penang, at the Weld Quay Bus Terminal (p182) and near KOMTAR Bus Station. Ride-sharing apps including Grab are commonly used in George Town.

TRISHAW

Bicycle rickshaws are a fun if touristy way to negotiate George Town's backstreets, and cost between RM20 and RM40 per hour depending on your negotiating skills. As with taxis, it's important to agree on the fare before departure.

GREATER PENANG

Air Itam & Penang Hill

Penang's most spectacular Buddhist temple and lush ancient rainforests are an easy day trip from George Town. It's generally about 5°C cooler at the top of Penang Hill (821m); it's one of the reasons why pukka British colonials from Francis Light onwards favoured this location as a retreat. There are still some 50 bungalows scattered around the top of the hill, though few of them are lived in full time, if at all, and a handful are in ruins.

The funicular from Air Itam makes getting up the hill easy. From there, you'll have to look hard for pockets of nature between the souvenir-selling scrum and hawker stalls, but they exist in the form of treetop walks and nature trails.

⊙ Sights & Activities

Gentle hikes along the paved roads at the top of Penang Hill are the best reason for heading up here. The Habitat (p184) offers refreshing outdoor activities including a 15m-high canopy walkway. To walk the 5km from the top of the hill to the Botanical Gardens (p184) takes around 1½ hours.

Kek Lok Si Temple
BUDDHIST TEMPLE

(Temple of Supreme Bliss; ☑04-828 3317; www.kekloksitemple.com; Jln Balik Pulau, Air Itam; ☺8am-6.30pm; 🚌204) Staggered on hillside terraces overlooking Air Itam, around 8km from the centre of George Town, Malaysia's largest Buddhist temple is a visual delight. Built between 1890 and 1905, Kek Lok Si is the cornerstone of the Malay-Chinese community, which provided the funding for its two-decade-long construction (and ongoing additions). Its key features are the seven-tier **Ban Po Thar** (Ten Thousand Buddhas Pagoda; RM2; ☺8am-6pm) pagoda and an awesome 36.5m-high bronze statue of Kuan Yin, goddess of mercy.

To reach the temple's main entrance, you'll have to run the gauntlet of souvenir stalls on the uphill path. You'll also pass a pond packed with turtles and the complex's **vegetarian restaurant** (☑04-828 8142; mains RM10; ☺10am-6.30pm; 🍴). There are a lot of stairs involved, but the final stretch up to the statue of Kuan Yin is covered by a funicular.

The Habitat
NATURE RESERVE

(☑04-826 7677; www.thehabitat.my; Penang Hill; adult/child RM50/30, after 5.30pm RM70/40; ☺9am-7pm) Bordering one of Penang's two virgin rainforest reserves, the spine of this fantastic addition to the Penang Hill experience is a finely crafted 1.6km nature trail. Along it you can access suspended walkways (thrillingly high up in the canopy), viewing platforms and pocket gardens featuring different species of tropical plants. You can explore on your own, but it's better to take one of the guided tours; ask ahead about night walks and tours suited to children.

Botanical Gardens
GARDENS

(☑04-227 0428; http://botanicalgardens.penang.gov.my; Waterfall Rd; ☺5am-8pm; 🚌10) **FREE** Once a granite quarry, Penang's Botanical Gardens were founded in 1884 by Charles Curtis, a tireless British plant lover who collected the original specimens and became the first curator. Today, the 30-hectare grounds include a fern rockery, an orchidarium and a lily pond. Follow the 1.5km Curtis Trail, which dips into the jungle, or hike up to Penang Hill.

Also known as the Waterfall Gardens, after the stream that cascades through from Penang Hill, the grounds are populated by many long-tailed macaques. Don't be tempted to feed them: monkeys do bite, and there's a RM500 fine if you're caught.

Monkeycup@Penang Hill
GARDENS

(☑012-428 9585; www.facebook.com/monkeycup.pghill; Tiger Hill Rd, Penang Hill; adult/child RM12/6; ☺9am-6pm) Weird and wonderful nepenthes (Monkey Cup) species from around the world are planted in this mossy garden. The guides will explain how these carnivorous plants feed on insects. It's a nice location on Penang Hill to go for a walk, or a ride on one of the electric buggies; there's also a cafe.

✖ Eating

Cliff Cafe
HAWKER $

(Astaka Bukit Bendera; Penang Hill; mains from RM4; ☺7am-8pm) This multilevel food-and-beverage centre atop Penang Hill serves all the local favourites, including *nasi goreng ayam* (fried chicken rice) and *char kway teow*.

David Brown's
INTERNATIONAL $$$

(☑04-828 8337; www.penanghillco.com.my; Penang Hill; mains RM55-66; ☺sky terrace 9am-11pm, restaurant 11am-10pm) Located at the top of Penang Hill, this restaurant has an open-air terrace that's probably the island's most atmospheric destination for colonial-style high tea (3pm to 6pm); the full deal for two people is RM108. It also has a good selection of Western dishes, including chunky sandwiches with fries and beef Wellington.

ℹ Getting There & Around

Bus 204 runs from both Weld Quay (p182) and KOMTAR (p181) stations in George Town to Air Itam, for Kek Lok Si Temple (RM2.70) and on to Penang Hill (RM1.40 from Kek Lok Si).

The **Penang Hill Funicular** (www.penanghill.gov.my; one-way adult/child under 6 RM15/5, fast lane adult/child under 6 RM45/5; ☺6.30am-11pm; 🚌204) is the least sweaty way to reach the top of the hill (there are various walking trails up, including popular ones from the Botanical Gardens). The **Kek Lok Si Temple Funicular** (one-way/return RM8/16; ☺8.30am-5.30pm) whisks you to the highest level of Kek Lok Si.

A taxi to either location from George Town will cost about RM25.

From the top of Penang Hill, beside the food court, hop on one of the **electric carts** (Jln Balik Pulau, Penang Hill; RM30) carrying up to five people for a 20-minute round trip to the Monkeycup@Penang Hill gardens.

Batu Ferringhi

Penang's main beach destination has a handful of classy resorts and is well geared up for family fun. While it's much touted and much visited, it doesn't entirely live up to the hype and can't compare to Malaysia's best: the water isn't as clear as you might expect, swimming often means battling jellyfish, and the beach itself can be dirty, especially on weekends when hordes of day trippers visit.

🏃 Activities

There are plenty of water-sports rental outfits along the beach; options include **jet skis** (RM80 for 15 minutes), **banana boating** (RM25 per person) and **parasailing** (RM150 per ride).

After those activities you might need a relaxing **massage**. All sorts of foot masseuses will offer you their services; expect to pay around RM40 for a 30-minute deep-tissue massage.

Chi, the Spa at Shangri-La   SPA
(☑04-888 8888; www.shangri-la.com; Shangri-La Rasa Sayang Resort, Jln Batu Ferringhi; treatments from RM188; ⊙10am-10pm; 🖵101) By a wide margin the most luxurious spa on Penang, Chi is its own little wonderland of pampering, with massages and other treatments taking place in one of 11 private villas in a lush beachside setting.

Wave Runner Watersport   WATER SPORTS
(☑012-437 5735; off Jln Batu Ferringhi; ⊙10am-7pm; 🖵101) One of several casual beachside operations offering rental of jet skis, banana boats and paragliders. It also runs trips out to Monkey Beach in Penang National Park in a boat seating up to eight people (RM350 for the boat).

🎊 Festivals & Events

Penang Island Jazz Festival   MUSIC
(www.penangjazz.com; ⊙Nov/Dec) Features local and international artists at changing venues in Batu Ferringhi.

🛏 Sleeping

There are lots of somewhat overpriced, chain-style resorts catering to families and quite a few extremely overpriced, budget homestays, but very little in between. The vast majority of accommodation is along Jln Batu Ferringhi, the town's main strip, which runs parallel to the beach.

Roomies   HOSTEL $
(☑04-881 1378; www.roomiespenang.com; 4th fl, 76C-4 Jln Batu Ferringhi; dm/r/ste incl breakfast RM50/170/200; 🌀@🛜; 🖵101) If you don't

mind sleeping communally, Roomies is by far the most appealing budget option in Batu Ferringhi. The dorm has 10 beds, and is spacious, bright and clean. There are also two private bedrooms and all rooms share a clean set of bathrooms. The rooftop area with a hydroponic lettuce garden is a plus!

Baba Guest House   GUESTHOUSE $
(☑017-554 9681, 04-881 1686; babaguesthouse 2000@yahoo.com; 52 Batu Ferringhi; r RM70-100; 🌀🛜; 🖵101) This turquoise-painted domestic compound belonging to a friendly Chinese family houses large and spotless – although bare – rooms. Half the rooms share bathrooms, while the more expensive air-con rooms come with en suite bathrooms.

Roomies Suites   HOTEL $$
(☑04-881 1378; www.roomiespenang.com; 2nd fl, 1-9B Eden Parade, Lg Sungai Emas; ste incl breakfast RM200; 🅿🌀@🛜; 🖵101) Despite being on the 2nd floor of a seemingly abandoned shopping complex, Roomies Suites is easily Batu Ferringhi's best midrange option. The 13 rooms here are stylish and spacious, and are looked after by a friendly host.

It offers the same high standards as its sister property, Roomies, which has a dorm.

Holiday Inn Resort   RESORT $$
(☑04-881 1601; www.holidayinnresorts.com/penang; 72 Jln Batu Ferringhi; r/ste incl breakfast from RM280/420; 🌀@🛜🏊; 🖵101) A big, busy resort with accommodation blocks on either side of the main road. It's a great place for families, with expansive pools and themed 'kidsuites', which come with TV and video games. There's also tennis courts and a gym for the adults. There was a renovation in progress when we stopped by.

⭐Shangri-La Rasa Sayang Resort   RESORT $$$
(☑04-888 8888; www.shangri-la.com; Jln Batu Ferringhi; r/ste incl breakfast from RM675/2310; 🅿🌀@🛜🏊; 🖵101) Spread across 12 hectares, its beachside grounds shaded by historic rain trees, the Rasa Sayang is Batu Ferringhi's top resort. It's split into two wings, Garden and Rasa, with the latter offering the more exclusive atmosphere. Rooms are large and pleasantly decorated; all have balconies and many have sea views.

⭐Lone Pine Hotel   RESORT $$$
(☑04-886 8686; www.lonepinehotel.com; 97 Jln Batu Ferringhi; r/ste incl breakfast from RM435/970; 🌀@🛜🏊; 🖵101) Dating back to the 1940s,

this is one of Batu Ferringhi's oldest – and best – resorts. The 90 rooms are spacious and bright; a few offer personal plunge pools or private gardens. The grounds have a stately, national-park-like feel, with hammocks suspended between the pines (actually casuarina trees) and a huge pool as a centrepiece.

Hard Rock Hotel   RESORT $$$
(☑04-881 1711; http://penang.hardrockhotels.net; Jln Batu Ferringhi; r/ste incl breakfast from RM504/750; ❋@☎☒; ☐101) If you can stomach the corny, hyper-corporate vibe, this resort can be a fun place to stay. There's a particular emphasis on family friendliness, with child-friendly pools, kid-friendly suites and teen-themed play areas (complete with pool table and video games).

A branch of the **Hard Rock Cafe** (☺11.30am-2am) is attached to the resort.

Golden Sands Resort   RESORT $$$
(☑04-886 1191; www.shangri-la.com; Jln Batu Ferringhi; r incl breakfast from RM410; ❋@☎☒; ☐101) You can almost imagine Julie the cruise director leading you through the orderly array of green lawn chairs, sprawling cement walkways and mushroom-like thatched huts at this family-oriented resort. Rooms move into the modern age and are spacious with marble bathrooms.

Parkroyal   RESORT $$$
(☑04-881 1133; www.parkroyalhotels.com; Jln Batu Ferringhi; r/ste incl breakfast from RM505/1105; ❋@☎☒; ☐101) This 1980s-era resort has seen a recent and extensive renovation, and is looking better than ever. The 309 rooms remain relatively standard and comfortable, and the grounds are more a reason to stay, with two pools, lots of lawn to bask on and a great strip of beach out front.

🍴 Eating & Drinking

You can get a beer at most non-halal places, but outside of the hotels, toes-in-the-sand type beach bars are few – **Bora Bora** (☑04-885 1313; www.facebook.com/boraborabysunset; 415 Jln Batu Ferringhi; ☺noon-1am Sun-Thu, to 3am Fri & Sat; ☐101), located roughly in the centre of the strip, is the exception.

Long Beach   MALAYSIAN $
(Jln Batu Ferringhi; mains from RM4; ☺6-11pm; ☐101) This buzzy hawker centre has the usual selection of Chinese noodle dishes, Indian breads and meat curries, and Malaysian seafood dishes.

Bungalow   INTERNATIONAL $$
(☑04-886 8566; www.lonepinehotel.com; Lone Pine Hotel, 97 Jln Batu Ferringhi; mains from RM28; ☺breakfast 6.30-10.30am, lunch & dinner 11am-11pm; ☎; ☐101) Back in the 1940s, the bungalow that this beachside restaurant partly occupies was the hub of the Lone Pine Hotel (p185), one of Batu Ferringhi's most historic properties. That period is evoked in dishes such as chicken chop – remnants of the era when Hainanese chefs, former colonial-era domestic servants, dominated restaurant kitchens. Other Malaysian and international dishes are available.

Lebanon   MIDDLE EASTERN $$
(☑04-881 3228; Jln Batu Ferringhi; mains RM35-50; ☺noon-midnight; ☐101) Middle Eastern visitors have brought their cuisine to Batu Ferringhi, and this is the pick of the lot. We fancy the meze platter, which brings together everything from hummus to stuffed grape leaves.

Ferringhi Garden   INTERNATIONAL $$
(☑04-881 1193; Jln Batu Ferringhi; mains RM35-50; ☺cafe 8am-5pm, restaurant 5-11pm; ☎; ☐101) Everyone falls in love with the Ferringhi Garden's outdoor setting, with its terracotta tiles and hardwood surrounded by bamboo – not to mention the seafood-heavy menu. During daytime hours, the neighbouring cafe serves good breakfast and real coffee – a relative rarity in Batu Ferringhi.

ℹ Getting There & Around

Bus 101 runs from the Weld Quay and KOMTAR stations in George Town, and takes around 30 minutes to reach Batu Ferringhi (RM2.70). A taxi here from George Town will cost at least RM40.

Most of Batu Ferringhi is accessible on foot. If you want to go further afield, consider renting a motorcycle (around RM50 a day); you'll find rental agencies along Jln Batu Ferringhi.

Teluk Bahang & Around

Most visitors come here to visit Penang National Park, which offers both accessible hiking and relaxing beach-hopping by boat. If nearby Batu Ferringhi is Penang's version of Cancún or Bali, Teluk Bahang is the quiet (sometimes deathly so) beach a few kilometres past the party.

○ Sights

★ Penang National Park
NATIONAL PARK
(Taman Negara Pulau Pinang; ☑04-881 3500; ⊗8am-5pm; P; 🖥101) FREE The old saying about good things coming in small packages suits dainty Penang National Park. At 23 sq km it's Malaysia's smallest national park, but you can fill a day with activities as diverse as jungle walks, fishing and sunbathing on quiet, golden-sand beaches. Private guides and boat operators amass near the entrance and parking lot. A one-way trip from the entrance should cost RM50 to Teluk Duyung (Monkey Beach), RM90 to Pantai Kerachut and RM130 to Teluk Kampi.

Sign in at the park entrance, which is a short walk from Teluk Bahang's main bus stop. It's an easy 1km walk to the head of the canopy walkway (now indefinitely closed), from where you have the choice of two routes: bearing west towards Muka Head (5km, up to two hours) or south to Pantai Kerachut (3km, up to 90 minutes).

The easiest walk is the 15-minute stroll west to Sungai Tukun, where there are some pools to swim in. Following this trail along the coast about 10 minutes more brings you to the private University of Malaysia Marine Research Station, where there is a supply jetty, as well as Tanjung Aling, a nice beach to stop at for a rest. From here it's another 45 minutes or so down the beach to Teluk Duyung, also called Monkey Beach (after the numerous primates who scamper about here). It's another 30 minutes to Muka Head, the isolated rocky promontory at the extreme northwestern corner of the island, where on the peak of the head is an off-limits lighthouse dating from 1883. The views of the surrounding islands from up here are worth the sweaty uphill jaunt.

A longer and more difficult trail heads south from the suspension bridge towards Pantai Kerachut, a beautiful white-sand beach that is a popular spot for picnics and a green-turtle nesting ground. Count on about 1½ hours to walk to the beach on the clear and well-used trail. On your way is the unusual meromictic lake, a rare natural feature composed of two separate layers of unmixed freshwater on top and seawater below, supporting a unique mini-ecosystem. From Pantai Kerachut, you can walk about 40 minutes onward to further-flung and isolated Teluk Kampi, which is the longest beach in the park; look for trenches along the coast – they're remnants of the Japanese occupation in WWII.

★ Tropical Spice Garden
GARDENS
(☑04-881 1797; www.tropicalspicegarden.com; 595 Mukim 2, Jln Teluk Bahang; adult/child RM29/17, incl tour RM45/20; ⊗9am-6pm; ♿; 🖥101) 🖋 This beautifully landscaped oasis of tropical flora, over 500 species in all, unfurls across 200 fragrant hectares. Armed with an audio guide (included with admission), you can wander independently among lily ponds and terraced gardens, learning about local spices, and medicinal and poisonous plants. Alternatively, join one of three daily guided tours (9am, 11am and 1.30pm) or book a kid-friendly educational tour.

Take bus 101 from George Town (RM2.70) and inform the driver that you want to get off here. Last admission 5.15pm.

The garden offers well-regarded cooking courses (www.tsgcookingschool.com; classes RM160-240; ⊗lessons 9am & 1.30pm Tue-Sun) and its restaurant Tree Monkey (☑04-881 3493; www.treemonkey.com.my; mains RM31-38; ⊗9.30am-10.30pm; 🐾), though pricey, is worth a visit for its relaxing terrace area and refreshing herb-infused lemonades. There's also a good shop, and just across the road from the gardens is a beautiful white-sand beach.

Art & Garden by Fuan Wong
GARDENS
(☑012-485 5074; www.facebook.com/ArtandGarden byFuanWong; Jln Teluk Bahang; adult/child RM30/15; ⊗9.30am-6.30pm; 🖥501) Rising up a hillside on a part of the family's durian orchard is this amazing conceptual garden where glass artist Fuan Wong marries his collection of weird and wonderful plants with his sculptures and installations. Creative works by other artists are dotted throughout the garden, which also offers breathtaking views of Penang Hill.

Escape
AMUSEMENT PARK
(☑04-881 1106; www.escape.my; 828 Jln Teluk Bahang; adult/child RM128/85; ⊗10am-6pm Tue-Sun; ♿; 🖥501) It's fun for all the family here, but be warned: adults report being more challenged than kids by the adventurous games and attractions at this play park, some of which involve climbing and jumping.

Teluk Bahang Forest Reserve
FOREST
(☑ranger's office 04-885 2388; ⊗9am-5pm; 🖥501) FREE This 873-hectare forest reserve contains a chunk of Penang's virgin rainforests. Guides are rarely available, so pick up a hiking leaflet at the ranger's office at the park entrance or at the Penang State Forestry Department (Pengarah Perhutanan Pejabat Perhutanan Negeri; Map p162; ☑04-650 5250; http://jhn.penang.gov. my; 20th fl, KOMTAR, Lr Tek Soon; ⊗9am-5pm

Mon-Fri) in George Town; the leaflets have trail maps and some information on plant identification. Also ask at either of these offices about **camping** in the reserve. There's a small **forestry museum** near the ranger's office.

There are five mapped trails in the park, although some were temporarily closed when we were in the area. The best-known is the 15.5km **Penang Hill Forest Challenge**, the longest trail in Penang, which leads all the way to the top of 821m Penang Hill. This walk is less strenuous in the downhill direction; from the Teluk Bahang end, expect the trek to take at least eight hours.

One of the better walks is the easy 800m **Monkey-Cup Forest Trail**, where you can search for carnivorous nepenthes (monkey cups), more commonly known as pitcher plants.

Intermediate trails are the 1.2km **Simpoh Gajah Trail**, which passes through virgin jungle; the 2.9km **Charcoal Kiln Trail**, which has some gnarly uphill sections through lovely forest to an old 1950s charcoal kiln; and the much more difficult 4.2km **Ridge Top Trail**, which branches off the Charcoal Kiln Trail to reach a ridge 400m above sea level. This last trail has some fantastic views over Teluk Bahang, as well as pitcher plants to look out for along the way – if you don't have too much blinding sweat stinging your eyes.

Entopia by Penang Butterfly Farm GARDENS (☑04-888 8111; www.entopia.com; 830 Jln Teluk Bahang; adult/child RM60/40; ☺9am-6pm; 📮501) Entopia is about so much more than tropical butterflies – although there's some 13,000 of these beauties from around 120 species fluttering freely around the well-designed attraction's outdoor gardens. You'll also be able to see and learn about all kinds of insects and invertebrates while wandering around this large maze-like environment.

Tropical Fruit Farm FARM (☑04-8665168,012-4971931;www.tropicalfruitfarm.com.my; Jln Teluk Bahang; tour adult/child from RM40/30; ☺9am-5pm; 📮501) About 8km south of Teluk Bahang is this 10-hectare hillside farm, which cultivates more than 250 types of tropical and subtropical fruit trees, native and hybrid. Its one-hour tours include a fruit buffet and a glass of fresh juice.

🍽 Sleeping & Eating

Teluk Bahang has mainly budget and midrange accommodation with nothing particularly outstanding. For top-end resorts,

the closest option is to stay in nearby Batu Ferringhi.

The main shopping area along the road heading east to Batu Ferringhi has a few coffee shops, where you'll find affordable Chinese dishes and seafood, as well as a couple of places selling *nasi kandar,* such as **Restoran Khaleel** (☑04-885 1469; 187 Jln Teluk Bahang; mains from RM4; ☺24hr; 📮101).

Jasmine Homestay HOMESTAY $$ (☑017-457 8681; www.facebook.com/jasminehomestayandtours; 46 Jln Hassan Abas; r from RM100; ❄; 📮101) This tidy, suburban-feeling house in the middle of Teluk Bahang's residential area hires out rooms. Boat service can also be arranged.

Hotel Sportfishing HOTEL $$ (☑04-885 2728; www.hotelsportfishing.my; Jln Nelayan; r RM130-140; ❄🛜; 📮101) The two floors of plain but clean rooms are at the edge of the beach at Teluk Bahang and look over the fishing pier. The hotel is located near the entrance to Penang National Park.

🛈 Information

Penang Nature Tourist Guide Association (PNTGA; ☑04-881 4788; ☺8am-6pm) Contact this organisation to arrange a guide for Penang National Park (p187). Guided walks for up to five people start from RM150.

🛈 Getting There & Away

Bus 101 runs from George Town every half-hour as far as the roundabout in Teluk Bahang (RM3.40). A taxi here from George Town will cost at least RM50. Bus 501 runs between Teluk Bahang and Balik Pulau (RM3.40).

Balik Pulau & Kampung Pulau Betong

Meaning 'on the other side of the island', Balik Pulau is Penang Island's main inland outpost. It's a busy market town with a strip of charming old shophouses surrounded by rice fields, and durian, clove and nutmeg orchards. The most prominent sight in town is the handsome **Holy Name of Jesus Catholic Church** (☑04-866 8545; www.hnjpenang1854.com; 11000 Jln Balik Pulau, Balik Pulau; 📮502, 401E, 501) **FREE**, which dates from 1894.

South of the town is the sleepy fishing village Kampung Pulau Betong, home to wooden houses built on stilts, flowerbeds and colourful boats bobbing in the harbour.

PULAU AMAN & BUKIT TAMBUN

For a relaxing time off the beaten track, tiny Pulau Aman (Peace Island) is perfect. Just 4.5km off the southern coast of Seberang Perai, the island is home to a fishing village of around 300 inhabitants.

It won't take you more than a couple of hours to explore the whole island. There's a small pebbly beach to the north of the village, while the southern seashore path takes you to a dead end via shady groves with rubber trees. You may also be able to persuade one of the fishermen to ferry you across to neighbouring **Pulau Gedung**, an even smaller and uninhabited island with some caves to explore.

There are no hotels on the island but it is possible to arrange a stay with **Homestay Pulau Aman** (☑013-512 4026, 013-459 0330; www.homestaypulauaman.weebly.com; 145 Pulau Aman; full board from RM70), which will be in a simple village house.

There's a simple cafe next to the jetty and one a few steps away in the heart of the *kampung* (village). All the food served is basic Malaysian dishes.

A **ferry** (return RM7; ⊙9am-7pm) departs from the pier at Batu Musang every two hours from 9am to 7pm; boats leave from Pulau Aman an hour earlier. On weekends, there are departures as frequently as every 15 minutes.

Worth a look before or after a trip to the nearby island of Pulau Aman is the attractive village of **Bukit Tambun**. The shophouses along the main street are painted with rainbow colours and murals, including images of Bruce Lee, Mr Bean, Woody from *Toy Story* and portraits of local shopkeepers. Look also for the grand but now ruined Chinese mansion near several places serving *mee udang* (prawn noodle soup).

PENANG BALIK PULAU & KAMPUNG PULAU BETONG

Nearby is Pantai Pasir Panjang, one of the island's best beaches.

Just north of Balik Pulau is Sungai Pinang, a hilly, lush area associated with agriculture, especially Penang's famous durian. An excellent guide to the area's cultural and agricultural destinations is the map *Discover Balik Pulau,* available at Penang Global Tourism (p181).

🛌 Sleeping & Eating

The greater Balik Pulau area is known for its durian, and a couple of the larger orchards in Sungai Pinang, about 8km north of Balik Pulau, have opened up their stunning grounds to accommodation.

Balik Pulau functions as a good lunch stop for anyone making a round trip of the island. Locals have been known to cross the island for the town's laksa and the area is famous for durian and other fruits.

Bao Sheng Durian Farm　　FARMSTAY **$$**
(☑012-411 0600; www.durian.com.my; 150 Mukim 2, Sungai Pinang; per person incl breakfast RM90-175; ❄🗢🏊) This popular durian farm has expanded its scope to include accommodation. The cheapest of the 16 rooms share a bathroom, while the most expensive resemble free-standing villas. During durian season (from approximately May to July), rates triple, and stays include

two durian tastings and a guided tour of the farm.

★Karuna Hill　　RESORT **$$$**
(☑016-441 4488; www.facebook.com/karunahill; 849 Bukit Kechil, Sungai Pinang; villa incl breakfast RM700-1000; ❄🗢) For a truly unique stay, consider a night or two at this working durian farm. Accommodation takes the form of spacious, modern villas perched on a hillside, overlooking jungle, a rushing stream, immense boulders, some of the world's most expensive fruit, and views that span to the sea.

Malihom　　VILLA **$$$**
(☑04-261 0190, 012-428 5191; www.malihom.com; Kiri N/t 168 Bukit Penara Mukim 6; villa incl breakfast RM540-950; ❄@🗢🏊) Accommodation at the top of this 518m-high peak takes the form of eight splendidly restored century-old rice barns, united in a private retreat. Walk around to take in the 360-degree view over hills of jungle, the estate's durian orchard, the sea and several villages. Given the isolated location, you'll likely want to upgrade to full board.

★Nan Guang　　MALAYSIAN **$**
(67 Jln Balik Pulau, Balik Pulau; mains from RM5; ⊙10am-5pm Wed-Sun; 🚌502, 401E, 501) Locals come here for *laksa asam* – thick rice noodles in a tart, herbaceous fish-based broth,

with mint leaves, pineapple slivers, onions and fresh chillies – or *laksa siam,* in which the tartness is tempered with a dollop of coconut milk. Refreshing nutmeg juice is also available.

Cafe Ko Cha Bi Balik Pulau   MALAYSIAN $
(☑012-474 5178; www.facebook.com/CafeKoChaBi; 110 Jln Balik Pulau, Balik Pulau; mains RM4.50-8; ☺10am-6pm Fri-Wed; ☒502, 401E, 501) Run by friendly folk, this pleasantly decorated cafe serves a very tasty range of local dishes including a delicious laksa, Hakka rice and noodles and desserts such as *ais kacang* (dessert of ice shavings topped with coloured syrups, brown sugar syrup and coconut milk, filled with red beans, *attap* seeds and jelly).

ℹ Getting There & Away

You can reach Balik Pulau on buses 502 and 401E from George Town and Bayan Lepas respectively (RM4), and on bus 501 from Teluk Bahang (RM3.40).

Bus 403 runs from Balik Pulau to Kampung Pulau Betong (RM1.40), stopping 2km short of Pantai Pasir Panjang.

Southeast Penang Island

There are a few attractions scattered around this southeast part of Penang Island that are worth a look. However, most visitors arrive – either flying into the international airport or being deposited at Sungai Nibong Bus Station – and don't hang around, which, for visitors with limited time, is a wise choice.

A natural destination while making a round-island tour is the fishing port at **Batu Maung.** However, the best reason for heading south is to eat freshly cooked seafood beside the lovely beach at **Teluk Kumbar.**

◉ Sights

Sam Poh Footprint Temple   TEMPLE
(Jln Maung; ☺24hr; ☒302, 307) FREE This small seaside temple overlooking fishing boats and the second Penang bridge has a shrine dedicated to the legendary Admiral Zheng He. Also known as Sam Poh, his portrait is painted on a giant boulder outside. The temple sanctifies a huge 'footprint'

in the rock that's reputed to belong to the famous 15th-century Chinese navigator.

Penang War Museum   MUSEUM
(☑04-626 5142, 016-421 3606; www.facebook.com/PenangWarMuseum; Bukit Batu Maung; adult/child RM37.10/18; ☺9am-6pm; ☒302, 307) Perched on top of the steep Bukit Batu Maung hill, this former British fort, built in the 1930s, was used as a prison and torture camp by the Japanese during WWII. Today, the crumbling buildings have been restored as a memorial to those dark days. Barracks, ammunition stores, cookhouses, gun emplacements and other structures can be explored in this eerie, atmospheric place, and there are information boards in English all over the site.

✖ Eating

Khunthai   THAI $$
(☑04-625 1155; www.khunthai.com; 1052 MK9 Pasir Belanda, Teluk Kumbar; mains RM23-32; ☺11am-midnight; ☒401, 401E) A blissful beachside setting, intimate atmosphere and daytime dining gives Khunthai the edge over the neighbouring seafood restaurants at Teluk Kumbar. The steamed fish is excellent and you can choose from all the usual Thai dishes.

Hai Boey Seafood   SEAFOOD $$
(☑013-488 1114, 04-649 3746; www.facebook.com/haiboeyseafoodpenang; 29 MK9 Pasir Belanda, Teluk Kumbar; mains RM30-40; ☺11.30am-2.30pm & 6-10.30pm; ☒401, 401E) Right on the beach at Teluk Kumbar, this is one of Penang's most famous destinations for seafood. Choose what you'd like to eat from the tanks at the entrance. It's best to reserve a table on weekends or holidays when it can be very busy.

ℹ Getting There & Away

You'll find both Penang International Airport (p181) and the Sungai Nibong Bus Station (p181), Penang's main interstate and international bus station, in the southeast of Penang Island. The area is also well connected with George Town by Rapid Penang buses (p181), including the 302 and 307 to Batu Maung and the 401 and 401E to Teluk Kumbar. Taxis to both these destinations from George Town will cost at least RM50.

Langkawi, Kedah & Perlis

Includes ➡

Kedah 192
Pulau Langkawi 193
Alor Setar 209
Around Alor Setar . . .212
Kuala Kedah 212
Perlis. 213
Kangar 213
Around Kangar 214

Best Places to Eat

➡ Selera Akmal (p206)
➡ Yasmin (p205)
➡ La Chocolatine (p205)

Best Places to Stay

➡ Temple Tree (p202)
➡ Kunang-Kunang (p202)
➡ Ambong Ambong (p203)
➡ Four Seasons Resort (p204)
➡ La Pari-Pari (p203)
➡ Soluna Guesthouse (p201)

Why Go?

The states of Kedah and Perlis represent a rural idyll that is central to the Malay identity. Limestone pillars thrust up through emerald paddy fields, which contribute to the harvest of over half of the country's domestic rice supply. Not that many foreigners see this. In fact, most travellers would draw a blank if you asked them about Kedah. That's because almost everyone knows this state by its biggest island: Langkawi. And justifiably so. Langkawi's glorious clear waters and luxurious wide beaches warrant the attention they receive.

Perlis, Malaysia's smallest state, has an even lower profile. Like Kedah it borders Thailand and most travellers simply rush through it on their way up there. Their loss; this friendly corner of the country is part of the Malay heartland and well worth a visit.

When to Go
Kuala Kedah

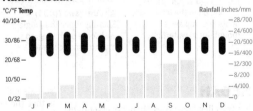

Feb & Mar Generally the region's driest months, although temperatures can be relatively high.

Apr–Oct The wettest time of year; the odd tropical storm is expected and tourist numbers are low.

Jul Typically Langkawi's coolest month.

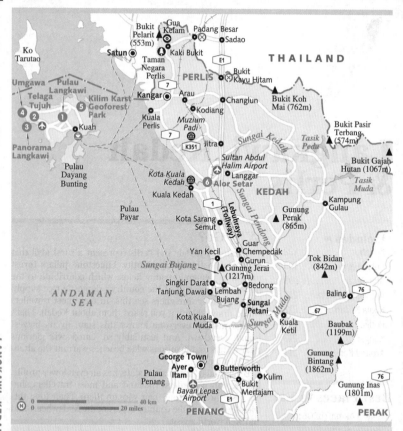

Langkawi, Kedah & Perlis Highlights

1 Pulau Langkawi (p193)
Relaxing on one of this fabled island's surfeit of perfect beaches.

2 Telaga Tujuh (p195)
Cooling off in the freshwater pools at Langkawi's mountaintop waterfalls.

3 Panorama Langkawi (p195) Riding the cable car all 708m to the top of Gunung Machinchang to enjoy the spectacular views.

4 Umgawa (p195)
Soaring above the jungle – and some of the region's most dramatic scenery –

along a pulse-pounding zip line.

5 Kilim Karst Geoforest Park (p196) Taking an eco-minded boat tour through the steamy mangroves.

6 Alor Setar (p209)
Revelling in the former glory days of royal Malaysia.

KEDAH

For travellers' purposes, there are essentially two facets to Kedah: the tropical island of Langkawi and its surrounding islets, and the rural, little-visited mainland, known as Malaysia's 'rice bowl'.

Langkawi is the stuff of tourist brochures that don't skimp on descriptions such as

'sun-kissed' and 'paradise'. The good news is that the beaches generally live up to the hype, but it's also an island destination that continues to maintain its Malay roots. If, like most, Langkawi is the only destination on your itinerary, you can rest assured that you'll still get the chance to experience both facets.

History

Settlement in Kedah goes back to the Stone Age – some of the earliest excavated archaeological sites in the country are near Gunung Jerai. Recent finds in Lembah Bujang date back to the Hindu-Buddhist period in the 4th century CE, and the current royal family can trace its line back directly to this time.

Discoveries in Lembah Bujang show that it was the cradle of Hindu-Buddhist civilisation on the peninsula – the society that would become the foundation stone for Malay culture – possibly from as early as CE 110, and it was one of the first places to come into contact with the Indian traders who would eventually bring Islam to Malaysia.

During the 7th and 8th centuries, Kedah was part of the Srivijaya Empire of Sumatra, but later fell under the influence of the Siamese until the 15th century, when the rise of Melaka brought Islam to the area. In the 17th century Kedah was attacked by the Portuguese, who had already conquered Melaka, and by the Acehnese, who saw Kedah as a threat to their own spice production.

In the hope that the British would help protect what remained of Kedah from Siam, the sultan handed over Penang to the British in the late 18th century. Nevertheless, in the early 19th century Kedah once again came under Siamese control, where it remained until early in the 20th century when Siam passed control to the British.

After WWII, during which Kedah (along with Kelantan) was the first part of Malaya to be invaded by the Japanese, Kedah became part of the Federation of Malaya in 1948, albeit reluctantly, and then part of the Federation of Malaya in 1957.

Pulau Langkawi

Dominating an archipelago of more than 100 islands and islets, Pulau Langkawi is synonymous with sandy shores, jungle-cloaked valleys and bargain shopping. Blonde beaches are the biggest draw, but this 478.5-sq-km island has been duty free since 1987, making low-cost kitchenware a close second.

Spas, seafood restaurants and beach bars are abundant, but fortunately Pulau Langkawi has not been developed beyond recognition. Beyond Pantai Cenang, the inevitable first stop for beach lovers, travellers can experience life lived in the slow lane in traditional *kampung* (villages). The island's official name is 'the jewel of Kedah' and its rugged beauty is evident in waterfalls, hot springs and forest parks – all excellent reasons to peel yourself off your beach towel.

Sights & Activities

Langkawi is big: almost 500 sq km. Kuah is the principal town but aside from a couple of good restaurants, the main reason to stop here is for the banks, ferries or duty-free shopping. The beaches are elsewhere.

If you're looking for exclusivity, the beautiful but relatively remote beaches at Teluk Datai (p196), in the island's far northwest corner, and at Tanjung Rhu (p196) on the north coast are the ones to head for. Both locations are served by luxury resorts.

Pantai Cenang

The beach here is gorgeous: white sand, teal water and green palms. There are water sports on hand and the water is good for swimming, but beware of jellyfish (p201) and speeding jet skis ripping past. There are some very fine top-end resorts at Cenang, as well as the bulk of Langkawi's budget and midrange accommodation. Come night time, an odd mix of expats, domestic tourists, backpackers and package holidaymakers take to the main road to eat, drink, window shop and generally make merry.

Underwater World AQUARIUM
(Map p198; 04-955 6100; www.underwaterworldlangkawi.my; Jln Pantai Cenang; adult/child RM46/36; 10am-6pm) With an imposing facade that makes it something of a landmark on the main Cenang strip, this aquarium features 500 species of marine and freshwater creatures as well as rockhopper penguins. Some exhibits (especially the rainforest walk) are well executed, while others seem small and in need of a clean.

Laman Padi MUSEUM
(Rice Garden; Map p198; 04-955 3225; lamanpadi@ladaeco.my; Jln Pantai Cenang; 9am-5pm) **FREE** This complex comprises rice paddies populated by water buffalo and ducks. Call in advance to arrange a tour to learn about, and even have a hand in, planting rice. There's also a museum dedicated to rice cultivation and a restaurant.

Nawa Sari Spa SPA
(Map p198; 010-512 9831; Villa Molek, Jln Teluk Baru; massage RM50-130; 10am-9pm) Here you can sigh contentedly while you're pummelled and oiled by Thai masseurs.

Pulau Langkawi

Selat Chinchin
(Strait of Chinchin)

Teluk Datai

Pulau Datai

22

19

12

11

27

23

35

14 Padang Lalang

10

38

33

13

112

4

Gunung Machinchang (708m)

Telaga Tujuh

3

18

Panorama Langkawi

20

2

21

25

17

113

Jln Teluk Yu

Gunung Raya (881m)

6

15

Pulau Burau

34

37

Kuala Muda

Padang Matsirat

30

7 Langkawi Hospital

29

Jln Padang Gaung

Langkawi International Airport

32

Kedawang

Jln Padang Matsirat

24

108

115

36

16

31

Kuah

112

Pulau Rebak Besar

28

Pulau Rebak Kecil

Pantai Cenang

39

Pulau Tepor

See Pantai Cenang & Pantai Tengah Map (p198)

116

ANDAMAN SEA

Pulau Kentut Besar

Pulau Tuba

Pulau Beras Basah

Pulau Singa Besar

Pulau Dayang Bunting

Tasik Dayang Bunting

Pantai Tengah

Compared to Pantai Cenang, this is a slightly smaller, narrower beach, with less noisy water-sports activity than on Pantai Cenang. There are a few big, all-inclusive resorts here, good restaurants and bars, and a few cheaper hotels too.

Alun-Alun Spa

SPA

(Map p198; ☎ 04-955 5570; www.alunalunspa.com; Jln Teluk Baru, Tropical Resort; massage from RM120; ⏰ 11am-11pm) With four branches across Pu-

pampering is available here with an emphasis on traditional Malay techniques – including an invigorating bamboo massage – and natural remedies, such as compresses made with herbs from the garden.

Pantai Kok & Around

The beach here is popular with locals who picnic under the trees. There are a handful of equidistant upscale resorts around here, many with their own small strips of beach.

★**Panorama Langkawi**   CABLE CAR
(Map p194; ☑04-959 4225; www.panorama langkawi.com; Oriental Village, Burau Bay; basic package of SkyCab & 3D art museum adult/child RM55/40; ⊙9.30am-7pm) The highlight of this family-friendly amusement park is SkyCab, a cable car that whisks visitors to the top of Gunung Machinchang (708m). For an extra RM5, you can walk along the 100m-high SkyBridge for knee-trembling views across the jungle canopy. Arrive early to avoid long queues at weekends and during school holidays.

SkyCab is closed for maintenance once a month; check the calendar on the website.

Other attractions, sprinkled among souvenir shops and snack stands, include an F1 simulator, 6D Cinemotion (a 3D movie simulator with splashes of water) and a 3D art museum where you can take selfies with murals of famous sights and artworks.

★**Telaga Tujuh**   WATERFALL
(Seven Wells; Map p194; Jln Telaga Tujuh) The series of freshwater rock pools at Telaga Tujuh, located at the top of a waterfall inland from Pantai Kok, makes a refreshing alternative to splashing about in the ocean. To get here, follow the road from Pantai Kok past Oriental Village (SkyCab is well signposted) until it ends at a car park. From here it's a steady 10-minute climb through the rainforest (stay to the right) to the wells at the top of the falls.

Connected by a thin trickle of refreshingly cool mountain water and surrounded by thick jungle that is home to a family of cheeky, and somewhat intimidating, monkeys (keep food out of sight), the pools also offer brilliant views of the island.

★**Umgawa**   ADVENTURE SPORTS
(Map p194; ☑013-343 8900; www.ziplinelangkawi. com; Telaga Tujuh; tours RM199-499; ⊙8.30am-4.30pm) This new outfit offers 12 zip lines spanning one of Langkawi's most rugged corners. The long course has zip lines as

lau Langkawi, Alun-Alun is accessible and gets good reviews. The spa's blended aromatherapy oils are available for purchase.

Ishan Spa   SPA
(Map p198; ☑04-955 5585; www.ishanspa.com; Jln Teluk Baru; ⊙11am-7pm) Some pretty posh

LANGKAWI, KEDAH & PERLIS PULAU LANGKAWI

Pulau Langkawi

⊙ Top Sights
1 Kilim Karst Geoforest Park E2
2 Panorama Langkawi A3
3 Telaga Tujuh A2

⊙ Sights
4 Durian Perangin D2
5 Galeria Perdana E2
6 Gunung Raya D3
7 Kota Mahsuri C3
8 Lagenda Langkawi Dalam Taman E4
9 Langkawi Wildlife Park E2
10 Pantai Pasir Hitam C2
11 Pantai Pasir Tengkorak B1
12 Temurun Waterfall B1

⊘ Activities, Courses & Tours
13 Air Hangat D2
   East Marine .... (see 39)
14 JungleWalla D2
15 Langkawi Canopy Adventures C3
16 Langkawi Coral D3
17 Rumah Holistic B3
18 Umgawa A3

⊟ Sleeping
19 Andaman Langkawi A2
20 Berjaya Langkawi A3
21 Danna B3
22 Datai Langkawi A2
23 Four Seasons Resort D1

24 Kunang-Kunang B3
25 Ritz Carlton Langkawi B3
26 St Regis Langkawi E4
27 Tanjung Rhu Resort D1
28 Vivanta by Taj – Rebak Island B4

⊗ Eating
   Gallo Nero .... (see 34)
29 Jalan Makam Mahsuri Lama
   Night Market C3
30 Kedawang Night Market B3
31 Kuah Night Market D3
32 Nasi Lemak Ultra B3
33 Padang Lalang Night Market D2
34 Padang Matsirat Night Market B3
35 Scarborough Fish & Chips D1
   Selera Akmal .... (see 34)
36 Wan Thai D3
   Wonderland Food Store .... (see 31)

⊙ Drinking & Nightlife
   Charlie's Bar & Grill .... (see 39)

⊙ Shopping
37 Atma Alam Batik Art Village B3
38 Kompleks Kraf Langkawi C2

⊙ Transport
39 Kuah Jetty D4
   Langkawi Ferry Service .... (see 39)

LANGKAWI, KEDAH & PERLIS PULAU LANGKAWI

long as 200m and as high as 80m, including a dramatic swing over Telaga Tujuh. Guides are safety oriented, wilderness educated and enthusiastic.

⊙ Teluk Datai & Around

The beaches at Teluk Datai are arguably some of the island's most beautiful and secluded, but are really only accessible if you're staying in one of the area's two luxury resorts.

Pantai Pasir Tengkorak BEACH
(Map p194; Jln Datai) This beautiful, secluded public beach, with its soft white sand, clear water, shady trees and jungle backdrop, is popular with locals on weekends; during the week it can be almost empty. The car park and entrance to the beach is on the 161 road, between Langkawi Crocodile Farm and Temurun waterfall. Note that the bathrooms here may or may not be open and there is nowhere to buy food or water.

There are several theories on the origins of the beach's name, which means 'sandy skulls'. One eerie explanation relates to the

legend of a nearby whirlpool that would swallow passing ships; the heads of the crew would later wash up on the shore.

Temurun Waterfall WATERFALL
(Map p194; Jln Datai) A brief walk from the main road up to Teluk Datai, the falls here – the island's tallest – are worth a look, though beware of food-stealing monkeys. The turn-off is on the left-hand side as you head east, 1km past Pantai Pasi Tengkorak.

⊙ Tanjung Rhu & Around

Tanjung Rhu is one of Langkawi's wider and better beaches, fronted by magnificent limestone stacks that bend the ocean into a pleasant bay. On clear days, the sunsets here give the word 'stunning' new meaning. The water is shallow, and at low tide you can walk across the sandbank to the neighbouring islands (except during the monsoon season).

★**Kilim Karst Geoforest Park** NATURE RESERVE
(Map p194; 1-4hr tour for up to 8 people per hr from RM200) The jetty near Tanjung Rhu is the

main departure point for boat trips into the extensive mangrove forests with stunning limestone formations that edge much of the northeastern coast of Langkawi. Tours usually include a stop at Gua Kelawar (a cave that's home to bats), lunch at a floating restaurant and eagle-watching.

Unfortunately, to attract eagles and please their camera-toting customers, many tour operators churn chicken fat or other foodstuff into the water behind the boats, disrupting the birds' natural feeding patterns and damaging the ecosystem. Dev's Adventure Tours (p199) and JungleWalla (p199) are outfits offering boat and kayaking trips that do not include eagle feeding.

Durian Perangin WATERFALL
(Map p194) The swimming pools here are a 10-minute walk up paved steps through the forest, with pagoda-like shaded seating areas along the way. The water is always refreshingly cool, but the falls are best seen at the end of monsoon season, from late September and early October. The waterfalls are located 2km off the 112 road, just east of Air Hangat.

Pantai Pasir Hitam BEACH
(Map p194; Jln Teluk Yu) West of Tanjung Rhu is Langkawi's much touted but ultimately disappointing 'black-sand beach'. It isn't technically a black-sand beach, but mineral oxides have added their colour scheme to the coast. There's a children's playground, a small tourist market and, as a disturbing backdrop, the Kedah cement plant, which stands out like a post-apocalyptic, smoke-belching thumb amid the green.

Galeria Perdana MUSEUM
(Map p194; 04-959 1498; www.jmm.gov.my; Jln Air Hangat, Kampung Kilim; adult/child RM10/4; 8.30am-5.30pm) Established by prime minister Dr Mahathir Mohamad, who was born in Kedah and is credited with transforming the fortunes of Langkawi by granting it duty-free status, this museum displays the sort of gifts that get passed between heads of state (Formula One race cars, Ming vases painted with the prime minister's face – that sort of thing). The vast collection is well displayed in this elegant gallery with its magnificent, hand-painted ceilings. It's located 12km north of Kuah.

Langkawi Wildlife Park ZOO
(Map p194; 04-966 5855; www.langkawiwildlife park.com; 1485 Jln Kisap, off Jln Air Hangat; adult/ child RM39/22; 8.30am-6pm) While there are plenty of animals around (with an emphasis on exotic birds), feeding is encouraged and animals are kept in relatively poor conditions. Animal welfare experts advise against human interaction. It's located about 10km north of Kuah.

Air Hangat HOT SPRINGS
(Ayer Hangat; Map p194; 04-959 1195; 16 Jln Air Hangat; entry adult/child RM5/free, private room for 2 people per hr from RM200; 9am-6pm) This spacious and rather empty-feeling 'spa village', located south of Tanjung Rhu, is known for its hot springs. There are various pools in which to soak your feet, some with pleasant views of the surrounding countryside, but to fully submerge in the hot water you'll need to book one of the private rooms.

Elsewhere on the Island

Gunung Raya MOUNTAIN
(Map p194) The tallest mountain on Pulau Langkawi (881m) can be reached by a snaking, paved road through the jungle. It's a spectacular drive to the top with views across the island and over to Thailand from a lookout point and a small teahouse (assuming there's no fog). In the evening there's a good chance of spotting great hornbills near the road.

Kota Mahsuri SHRINE
(Mahsuri's Fort; Map p194; 04-955 6055; Jln Makam Mahsuri, Kampung Mawat; adult/child RM15/5; 8am-6pm) The story of Mahsuri, a Malay princess who was unjustly accused of adultery and put a curse on Langkawi in revenge, is commemorated at this historical complex that includes Mahsuri's shrine as well as a recreation of a traditional house, a theatre, a 'diorama museum' and food outlets. The site is west of Kuah, a few kilometres off the road to the airport.

As the legend goes, Mahsuri's punishment was to be executed by stabbing. With her dying breath she cursed Langkawi with seven generations of bad luck. This took place in 1819 and not long after, the Siamese invaded the island. However, some 160 years later, Langkawi started to take off as a tourism destination when it was declared a free port in 1987.

Rumah Holistic SPA
(Map p194; 019-339 1831; www.rumahholistic. com; Lot 160, Kampung Ranggot Besar; massages from RM150; 10am-6pm) This small retreat

Pantai Cenang & Pantai Tengah

N

0 — 500 m
0 — 0.25 miles

See Inset

Jln Bohor Tempoyak

17

25

19 34 32

24

PANTAI
CENANG

13
Taxi Stand

16
26

7 46 41

43

4

37

Jln Pantai Cenang

38

44

10 22

ATM

T Shoppe

Fortune 100
Moneychanger

Taxi
Stand

Pantai
Cenang

47 12

8

2 21

28

Jln Pantai Tengah

Zon Duty Free
Shopping Centre

42

23

39

ANDAMAN
SEA

5

Inset Same scale as main map

40

11

33

27

35

30

9

36

3

15 PANTAI
TENGAH

14
Taxi
Stand

20

29 45

See Main Map

Jln Pantai Cenang

31

Jln Teluk Baru

Pantai
Tengah

18

Pulau
Tepor

Resorts World
(250m)

6

LANGKAWI, KEDAH & PERLIS

Pantai Cenang & Pantai Tengah

◎ Sights
1 Laman Padi	A1
2 Underwater World	C3

✚ Activities, Courses & Tours
3 Alun-Alun Spa	C5
4 Crystal Yacht Holidays	C2
5 Dev's Adventure Tours	C4
6 Ishan Spa	D7
7 Mega Water Sports	A2
8 Nawa Sari Spa	D3
9 Tropical Charters	C5

🛏 Sleeping
10 AB Motel	B3
Ambong Ambong	(see 6)
11 Bon Ton	B4
12 The Cabin	C3
13 Casa del Mar	A1
14 Frangipani	C5
15 Fuuka Villa	D5
16 Gecko Guesthouse	B2
17 Gemalai Village	B1
18 Holiday Villa	D6
19 Izz Room	B1
20 La Pari-Pari	D5
21 Langkawi Dormitorio	C3
22 Paretto Seaview Hotel	B3
23 Pondok Keladi	D4
24 Rainbow Lodge	B1
25 Soluna Guesthouse	B1

26 Sweet Inn Motel	B2
27 Temple Tree	B4
28 Tropical Resort	D3
29 Tubotel	A5
30 Villa Molek	C5
31 Zackry Guest House	D6

🍴 Eating
32 Bohor Tempoyak Night Market	B1
fatCUPID	(see 20)
33 Istanbul	C4
34 Kasbah	B1
35 La Chocolatine	C5
36 Melayu	C5
Nam	(see 11)
37 Orkid Ria	B2
38 Putumayo	B2
39 Red Tomato	C4
40 Restoran Rinnie	B4
Unkaizan	(see 6)
41 Yasmin	B2

🍸 Drinking & Nightlife
42 Cliff	B4
43 Kalut Bar	A2
La Sal	(see 13)
44 Nest Rooftop	B2
45 Smiling Buffalo	B5
46 Thirstday	B2
47 Yellow Café	B3

at the masseur's home, hidden in thick jungle, has just one treatment room for up to two people. While it's tricky to find (owner Eric will arrange to meet you and accompany you by car or send a local taxi driver to collect you), the rural, forest location is part of its charm.

The approach here is holistic and full-day packages can include tai chi, yoga and meditation. Bookings must be made in advance.

☞ Tours

A variety of tours can be booked at any of the numerous travel agencies at the jetty in Kuah and along Pantai Cenang, as well as at most hotels.

The most popular day trip is the island-hopping tour, offered by most tour and diving companies and costing as little as RM30 per person. Tours usually take in **Dayang Bunting** (Lake of the Pregnant Maiden), located on the island of the same name. It's a freshwater lake surrounded by craggy limestone cliffs and dense jungle, and a good spot for swimming. Other stops may include the pristine beach at **Pulau Beras Basah**, sea stacks and sea caves, and a stop for **eagle-watching**.

There are several cruise operators in Langkawi and nearly all of them offer daily dinner and sunset cruises.

JungleWalla   ADVENTURE
(Map p194; ☎ 019-590 2300; www.junglewalla.com; 1C, Lot 1392, Jln Tanjung Rhu; tours RM120-180; ⊙9am-6pm) 🌿 Since setting up this nature tour company in 1994, Irshad Mobarak has become something of a celebrity naturalist in Malaysia. On offer are bird-watching excursions, jungle walks, and mangrove- and island-hopping trips, all with an emphasis on observing wildlife. Multiday itineraries are available on request. Transportation is not included.

Dev's Adventure Tours   ADVENTURE
(Map p198; ☎ 019-494 9193; www.langkawi-nature.com; 1556 Tanjung Mali, Pantai Cenang; tours RM140-240; ⊙8am-10pm) 🌿 Cycling, mangrove excursions and jungle walks: this outfit offers a fat menu of options led by knowledgable and enthusiastic guides. Book online or by phone. Transfers are provided from most hotels.

Langkawi Canopy Adventures ADVENTURE

(Map p194; ☑ 012-466 8027; www.langkawi.travel; Lubuk Semilang; tours RM180-220) The highlight here is high-adrenaline 'air trekking' through the rainforest along a series of rope courses and zip lines. Excursions must be booked at least a day in advance and you'll need to arrange a taxi to take you to the site at Lubuk Semilang, in the middle of Langkawi.

Tropical Charters CRUISE

(Map p198; ☑ 012-316 5466; www.tropicalcharters. com.my; Jln Teluk Baru, Pantai Tengah; cruises from adult/child RM260/130) Take to the water on a day or sunset cruise, usually with lunch or dinner included. Boats depart from the pier near Resorts World, south of Pantai Tengah; transport from most hotels is included.

Tropical Charters also offers ferry transfers to Ko Lipe in Thailand (RM118).

Crystal Yacht Holidays CRUISE

(Map p198; ☑ 04-955 6545; www.crystalyacht. com; 243 Jln Berjaya, Kampung Lubok Buaya; dinner cruise from RM280) Crystal Yacht operates popular sunset dinner cruises. Boats depart from the pier at Resorts World, south of Pantai Tengah, and transport from most hotels is included.

Mega Water Sports ADVENTURE

(Map p198; ☑ 012-200 2155; www.megawater sports.com; Pantai Cenang; tours RM600-900) These guided jet-ski tours around the islands off the south coast of Langkawi get rave reviews. There are various difficulty ratings, from a family-friendly beginner level to one requiring wave-jumping experience.

Tours start and end at the northern end of Pantai Cenang.

★ Festivals & Events

Langkawi International Maritime & Aerospace Exhibition AIR SHOW

(LIMA; www.limaexhibition.com; ⊙ Mar biennially) LIMA is considered one of the world's major air shows. Hotels fill up and prices soar during this event.

🛏 Sleeping

Good accommodation on Langkawi is rarely cheap. The luxury resorts are excellent, but midrange places (even some upscale ones) can be mediocre. Budget-oriented hostels and guesthouses are generally lacklustre (and some are appalling); the few standout budget options are worth booking ahead.

During school holidays and peak tourist season (approximately November to February), advance bookings are generally necessary for all budgets. At other times, supply outstrips demand and prices are negotiable.

🛏 Kuah

St Regis Langkawi RESORT $$$

(Map p194; ☑ 04-960 6666; www.stregislangkawi. com; Jln Pantai Beringin, Kuah; ste from RM1500; ✳@🕏≋) Comprising of only suites and villas, this luxury resort shares a pleasant sandy cove with its stablemate The Westin and is within easy reach of Kuah. There's more of a Moroccan rather than Malaysian feel to the overall design, which includes a gorgeous bar, infinity pool and the dazzling Kaya Puti Asian haute cuisine restaurant.

DIVING & SNORKELLING

Strung out like several green jewels in the teal sea are the four islands that make up **Pulau Payar Marine Park**, the focus of Langkawi's dive and snorkelling expeditions. Most trips come to 2km-long Pulau Payar, although you probably won't see the interior of the island – all the action centres on a diving platform and horseshoe-bend of coast. Enquire about the water conditions before you go as it can get murky.

East Marine (Map p194; ☑ 019-409 3966; www.eastmarine.com.my; Fisherman's Wharf, Jln Pantai Dato Syed Omar, Kuah; snorkelling/diving trips from RM150/300; ⊙ 8am-6pm) Probably the most reputable diving outfit on Pulau Langkawi, East Marine conducts full-day diving and snorkelling excursions to Pulau Payar Marine Park, as well as PADI certification courses starting at RM1100.

Langkawi Coral (Map p194; ☑ 04-966 7318; www.langkawicoral.com; Plot 9-11, Tingkat 2, Komplek Cayman, Jln Penarak, Kuah; snorkelling/diving from RM350/450; ⊙ 9.30am-5.30pm) Diving and snorkelling trips to Pulau Payar Marine Park include transfers from hotels to the departure point at Kuah pier, a buffet lunch and some time for sunbathing.

Pantai Cenang & Around

★ Soluna Guesthouse   GUESTHOUSE $

(Map p198; ☑ 04-955 2764; www.solunaguesthouse.
com; Jln Bohor Tempoyak, Pantai Cenang; dm RM25,
r RM50-80; ❉ 🛜) A two-storey wooden house
serves as the centrepiece of this charming
budget enclave. Looked after by a friendly
owner (as well as what appears to be the resident cats and chickens), the rooms are simple
but bright and inviting. The cheapest rooms
are fan-cooled and share a bathroom.

Sweet Inn Motel   HOTEL $

(Map p198; ☑ 04-955 8864; www.sweetinns.
net; Jln Pantai Cenang, Pantai Cenang; r RM90;
🅿 ❉ 🛜) This is one of the cleaner budget
sleeping options in Pantai Cenang. The wi-fi
doesn't reach beyond reception and rooms
are small, plain and lacking in atmosphere,
but it does gain points for easy beach access.

Gecko Guesthouse   GUESTHOUSE $

(Map p198; ☑ 019-428 3801; rebeccafiott@hotmail.
com; Jln Pantai Cenang; dm RM25, r RM50-140;
❉ 🛜) Here you'll find a collection of bungalows, chalets and rather dingy dorms, dread-
locked folk in the common area and very
good chocolate milkshakes served at the bar.

Izz Room   GUESTHOUSE $

(Map p198; ☑ 04-955 1397; www.izzroom.blogspot.
com; Pantai Cenang; r RM50-80, villa RM150-200;
❉ 🛜) A pleasant community feel enlivens
Izz Room's basic, sparsely furnished accommodation spread around a palm-shaded
gravel courtyard. The best rooms are in the
brightly coloured block opposite reception,
while cheaper doubles have fans and shared
bathrooms.

Rainbow Lodge   HOSTEL, GUESTHOUSE $

(Map p198; ☑ 04-955 8103; http://rainbowlangkawi.
yolasite.com; Lg Surau, Pantai Cenang; dm RM18-22, r
RM40-120; ❉ @ 🛜) Set 300m back from Pantai
Cenang, this cheerfully painted place has non-
bunk dorm beds with partitions and curtains,
allowing better repose than the average hostel. Private rooms that are cheaper have fans,
while pricier ones have TV, air-con and fridge.

The friendly staff can help arrange motorbike rental and guided tours.

Paretto Seaview Hotel   HOTEL $$

(Map p198; ☑ 04-952 3457; www.facebook.com/
parettoseaviewhotel; 16 Jln Pantai Cenang, Pantai
Cenang; r RM170-275; 🅿 ❉ 🛜) Beds on packing-
crate wood with furniture to match may
not sound ideal, but Paretto makes it work.

Rooms are vast, with separate sitting rooms
and spacious bathrooms. A drinking water
dispenser and a location just across the
street from the beach are additional perks.

AB Motel   HOTEL $$

(Map p198; ☑ 04-955 1300; www.abmotel.weebly.
com; Jln Pantai Cenang, Pantai Cenang; r RM90-
180; ❉ 🛜) This hotel offers a mix of accommodation that straddles both sides of the
street. Opt for the plain, but tidy linked bungalows on the beach side. Spacious balconies
are another perk, but wi-fi is limited to the
lobby area only.

Tubotel   HOSTEL $$

(Map p198; ☑ 014-240 7022; www.tubotel.com;
Kuala Cenang; dm RM45-50, r RM128-188, all incl
breakfast; 🅿 ❉ 🛜) At the distinctive and fun
Tubotel, rooms are individual concrete pipes
whose snug interiors house surprisingly
comfy beds (bathrooms are in a separate
block); the four-bed dorms are in disused
shipping containers. A downside is the rel-
atively isolated-feeling location.

Langkawi Dormitorio   HOSTEL $$

(Map p198; ☑ 017-236 2587; www.facebook.com/
lgkdormitorio; 1556 Jln Pantai Cenang, Pantai
Cenang; dm/r from RM50/220; ❉ 🛜) Feeling
a little weary of party hostels? Dormitorio
offers a more sedate, grown-up experience
with its clean, pastel-hued dorm rooms, each
with its own bathroom. Private rooms are
bare but handsome, with en suite bathrooms.

The Cabin   HOTEL $$

(Map p198; ☑ 012-417 8499; www.thecabin.com.
my; Jln Pantai Cenang, Pantai Cenang; r RM160;

LANGKAWI, KEDAH & PERLIS PULAU LANGKAWI

LEGENDARY LANGKAWI

The name Langkawi combines the old Malay words *helang* (eagle) and *kawi* (reddish brown). Classical Malay literature claims the island is one of the resting places of Garuda, the mythological bird that became Vishnu's vehicle. The whole island is steeped in legends, and the favourite story is of Mahsuri, who was wrongly accused of infidelity by those jealous of her beauty. Before finally allowing herself to be executed, she put a curse on the island for seven generations. As proof of her innocence, white blood flowed from her veins, turning the sands of Langkawi's beaches white. Her tomb is known today as Kota Mahsuri.

A legacy of Mahsuri's curse is the 'field of burnt rice' at Padang Matsirat. There, villagers once burnt their rice fields rather than allow them to fall into the hands of the Siamese. It's said that to this day heavy rain sometimes brings traces of these grains to the surface.

Another legend concerns the naming of places around the island. Langkawi's two most powerful families became involved in a bitter argument over a marriage proposal. A fight broke out and all the kitchen utensils were used as missiles. The *kuah* (gravy) was spilt at Kuah and seeped into the ground at Kisap, which means 'to seep'. A pot landed at Belanga Perak (Broken Pot) and finally the saucepan of *air panas* (hot water) came to land where Air Hangat village is today. The fathers of these two families got their comeuppance for causing all this mayhem – they are now the island's two major mountain peaks. You can learn more at the intriguing **Lagenda Langkawi Dalam Taman** (Map p194; Jln Persiaran Putra; ⊙9am-7pm) FREE in Kuah.

⊛☏) With a vibe verging on caravan park, the Cabin features 20 duplex bungalows that are a short walk from the beach. Rooms are pleasantly cosy but, decked out with colourful furniture, have more character than most places in this price range.

Gemalai Village HOTEL $$
(Map p198; ☏04-955 3225; www.geoparkinn langkawi.com/TheGemalaiVillage; Jln Pantai Cenang, Laman Padi; r incl breakfast from RM330; P⊛☏) Gemalai is a complex of six *kampung* huts built on stilts over the paddy fields at Laman Padi. The traditionally styled rooms are comfortable and well equipped, and the bathrooms are partially open-air. An excellent Malay breakfast is served in your room.

Although the name Gemalai refers to the Bahasa Malaysia word for a gentle breeze that whispers across the paddy, light sleepers should beware that the huts' thin walls and close proximity to a road, as well as roosters and buffalo, might make their stay a little less than peaceful.

★Bon Ton BOUTIQUE HOTEL $$$
(Map p198; ☏04-955 1688; www.bontonresort. com.my; Jln Pantai Cenang; villas incl breakfast from RM484; ⊛☏☒) Bon Ton takes the form of eight Malay stilt houses perched over a grassy, coconut-palm-studded plot of land, each one decked out with dark wood and positioned to catch the breeze. With its organic accents and traditional craftwork, it's somehow regal and rustic all at once.

★Temple Tree BOUTIQUE HOTEL $$$
(Map p198; ☏04-955 3937; www.templetree.com. my; Pantai Cenang; r incl breakfast RM550-1200; ⊛☏☒) On the adjoining plot to Bon Ton, sister hotel Temple Tree raises the stakes with a collection of antique structures relocated from various points in Malaysia. An imposing Chinese mansion, a wooden villa from Penang, colonial-style shophouses and other restored structures make up the stately, park-like compound.

Linking both locations is a common thread of class, style, thoughtful service and – take this as a warning if you don't care to share your villa with Felix – cats.

★Kunang-Kunang BOUTIQUE HOTEL $$$
(Map p194; ☏04-952 3656; kunangkunang heritage@gmail.com; Jln Kampung Gelam, Mukim; villa incl breakfast RM360-600; ⊛☏☒) Like a traditional Malay village, Kunang-Kunang takes the form of a clutch of antique wooden villas. The 12 units are decked out in charming retro furniture with the occasional contemporary touch, some with heaps of room. They're not exactly near the beach, but the pool, which is set in a pond, is a unique way to cool off.

Casa del Mar BOUTIQUE HOTEL $$$
(Map p198; ☏04-955 2388; www.casadelmar-langkawi.com; Jln Pantai Cenang, Pantai Cenang; r/ste incl breakfast from RM875/1300; ⊛@☏☒) This is a sumptuous, vaguely Spanish-themed place on the quieter northern end

of Pantai Cenang. Rooms feature thoughtful design touches and techie amenities, as well as a small private garden or balcony. Various package deals are available. At peak times the 34 rooms can get booked up several months in advance.

Vivanta by Taj – Rebak Island RESORT $$$
(Map p194; 04-966 5566; www.vivantabytaj. com/rebak-island-langkawi; Rebak Besar; r/ste incl breakfast from RM630/880; ﹡＠☎❄) Lying just off Pantai Cenang, the small island of Rebak Besar plays host to this exclusive resort, which offers spacious and elegant chalets in beautifully landscaped grounds. It has all the facilities you would expect, including a gym, spa and restaurants. Access to and from the island is by speedboat and transfers from the airport are included.

The island is car-free and has its own quiet stretch of beach, making it a good option for families with children.

🚲 Pantai Tengah & Around

Zackry Guest House GUESTHOUSE $
(Map p198; 04-952 3208; zackryghouse@gmail. com; Lot 735, Jln Teluk Baru, Pantai Tengah; dm RM35, r RM70-110; ﹡＠☎) This ramshackle, family-run guesthouse has a sociable atmosphere. Rooms are basic, yet clean and cosy, and communal areas include a fridge, vending machines and places to lounge. Note that there's a two-night minimum, no phone bookings and only about half of the rooms have an attached bathroom.

★ La Pari-Pari BOUTIQUE HOTEL $$
(Map p198; 04-955 3010; www.laparipari.com; 2273 Jln Teluk Baru, Pantai Tengah; r incl breakfast RM365-395; P﹡☎❄) ✈ Tucked away in a picturesque spot just off the main Pantai Tengah strip, La Pari-Pari has a laid-back vibe. The 12 immaculate rooms, with a slightly space-age feel and huge bathrooms, are housed in chic whitewashed chalets in attractive grounds, with day beds and a pond-side beach.

It's the type of place where guests exchange life stories over cocktails at the poolside bar and restaurant fatCUPID (p206).

Pondok Keladi GUESTHOUSE $$
(Map p198; 012-536 9216; Lot 1011, Jln Pantai Tengah, Pantai Tengah; r RM120, villa RM135-180; ﹡☎) This cosy compound of six rooms and three cottages is looked after by Dee and Mark – two of the most gracious hosts on Pulau Langkawi. The free-standing cottages,

outfitted with kitchenettes and a bit more space, are the wisest options, but all rooms have access to a communal kitchen and a garden.

Fuuka Villa HOTEL $$
(Map p198; 04-955 1133; www.fuukavilla.com; Jln Teluk Baru, Pantai Tengah; r/villa RM250/480; ❄) Fuuka has spacious, modern rooms in a cosy compound. Huge bathrooms come standard and the villa has a kitchenette. Additional perks include a small pool and a peaceful, almost countryside setting at the base of a hill.

Tropical Resort HOTEL $$
(Map p198; 04-955 4075; Jln Pantai Tengah; r incl breakfast RM350-450; P﹡＠☎❄) Located inland from Pantai Tengah is this string of plain, spotless and well-run duplex bungalows. At night the soft lighting around the pool makes for a romantic setting.

★ Ambong Ambong HOTEL $$$
(Map p198; 04-955 8428; www.ambong-ambong. com; Jln Teluk Baru, Pantai Tengah; r RM880-1080, ste RM1350-1580, villa RM1800-2500, all incl breakfast; ﹡☎❄) This clutch of minimalist, contemporary structures perched on a forested hillside forms a pleasing contrast. Choose from one of six inviting studios, three large suites or two vast two-bedroom cottages; all are stylish and airy with balconies overlooking the rainforest and sea below. The steep access makes it unsuitable for people requiring wheelchair access and children under 12.

★ Villa Molek HOTEL $$$
(Map p198; 04-955 3605; www.villamolek.com; 2863 Jln Teluk Baru, Pantai Tengah; ste incl breakfast from RM553; ﹡☎❄) Those looking for a quiet, home-like stay should head here. Accommodation takes the form of 12 classy villas, each with a living room and kitchenette. The two-storey villas are set in a small, secluded garden across the road from the beach and, as children under 18 aren't welcome, draw a predominately mature clientele.

Frangipani RESORT $$$
(Map p198; 04-291 3141; www.frangipanilangkawi. com; 138 Jln Teluk Baru, Pantai Tengah; r/villa from RM580/690; ﹡＠☎❄) ✈ Friendly service, genuine efforts towards ecological conservation and its location on a quiet stretch of beach are the reasons to stay at this large resort. Rooms are spacious and comfortable, if slightly dated.

Holiday Villa RESORT **$$$**
(Map p198; ☑04-952 9999; www.holidayvillahotel
langkawi.com; Jln Teluk Baru, Pantai Tengah; r/ste
incl breakfast from RM450/820; ✷@🛜☲) This
vast resort complex retains a palpable 1980s
feel and has tennis courts, a gym, several
restaurants and an infinity pool. The airy
and brightly furnished rooms look out over
lawns and a soft white-sand beach.

Pantai Kok & Around

Ritz-Carlton Langkawi RESORT **$$$**
(Map p194; ☑04-952 4888; www.ritzcarlton.
com; Jln Pantai Kok, Teluk Nibong; r from RM1800;
✷@🛜☲) Enveloped by rainforest on a private cove, the Ritz-Carlton offers an exclusive luxury escape that's barely 10 minutes'
drive from the airport. Rooms are spacious
and super chic, and with plenty of activities
on-site (including ones for the kids), there's
little incentive to leave. Don't miss sunset
drinks at the ocean view Horizon bar.

Danna HOTEL **$$$**
(Map p194; ☑04-959 3288; www.thedanna.com;
Telaga Harbour Park, Pantai Kok; all incl breakfast
r/ste/villa from RM1200/4500/6500; ✷@🛜☲)
This imposing, sumptuous hotel embraces
its colonial-era theme with details such as
a billiard room, library and cigar room, tif-
fin lunches and speciality English afternoon
teas. Rooms are huge and come with attrac-
tive furniture and wood and marble floors.
The hotel pool is the largest in Langkawi. A
new addition has 10 free-standing pool villas.

Berjaya Langkawi RESORT **$$$**
(Map p194; ☑04-959 1888; www.berjayahotel.com;
Karong Berkunci 200, Pantai Kok; r/ste incl breakfast from RM750/1190; ✷@🛜☲) Located past
the headland at the western end of Pantai
Kok, Berjaya has 412 rooms spread over a
vast area; guests are ferried between reception and their chalets in minibuses. The
waterfront suites are the most attractive,
while the cheapest rooms can feel rather
tired. A stay includes a complimentary tour
of the adjacent jungle.

Teluk Datai

Datai Langkawi RESORT **$$$**
(Map p194; ☑04-950 0500; www.thedatai.com;
Jln Teluk Datai; r/ste/villa incl breakfast from
RM1600/3000/4560; P✷@🛜☲) Tucked in a
corner in the far northwest of Pulau Lang-
kawi and surrounded by ancient rainforest,
the Datai manages to feel both untamed and

luxurious. Along with rooms and suites in
the main hotel building, there are spacious
and modern rainforest or seafront villas to
choose from.

All have access to a small city's worth of
amenities (spas, gyms, yoga – the works),
not to mention one of the island's best
beaches. A unique luxury experience.

Andaman Langkawi RESORT **$$$**
(Map p194; ☑04-959 1088; www.luxurycollection.
com/andaman; Jln Teluk Datai, Teluk Datai; r/ste incl
breakfast from RM800/2000; P✷@🛜☲) In a
grand wooden Malay-style building seemingly dropped in the middle of the jungle is
this luxurious retreat with the usual multi-
star amenities and dining outlets. The 178
rooms are large and inviting, and the highlight here is the location, which includes a
stunning semiprivate beach.

Tanjung Rhu

⭐**Four Seasons Resort** RESORT **$$$**
(Map p194; ☑04-950 8888; www.fourseasons.com/
langkawi; Jln Tanjung Rhu, Tanjung Rhu; r/villa from
US$755/2000, all incl breakfast; P✷@🛜☲)
Sporting a youthful vibe (at least for a Four
Seasons resort) and a Moroccan theme, this
place is among Langkawi's most luxurious
resorts. Amenities are everything you'd ex-
pect at this level and the service is impecca-
ble. Bathrooms-so-big-you'll-get-lost-in-them
aside, you'll love the manicured jungle setting
and the semiprivate beach.

Tanjung Rhu Resort RESORT **$$$**
(Map p194; ☑04-959 1033; Jln Tanjung Rhu, Tan-
jung Rhu; r/ste incl breakfast from RM1550/3000;
P✷@🛜☲) This beautifully situated resort
has 54 large and comfy rooms with balconies and great views of the limestone and
green water at Tanjung Rhu. Service is a
pleasant blend of competent and friendly,
and two elegant 50m pools as well as a saltwater lagoon pool are added draws. With no
water sports, the 2.5km private beach feels
secluded and serene.

✕ Eating

Around Kuah

Wan Thai THAI **$$**
(Map p194; ☑04-966 1214; 86 Persiaran Bunga
Raya, Kuah; mains RM20-35; ⊙11am-3pm &
6.30-10pm; ✷) A reminder that Langkawi is
geographically closer to Thailand than the

Malaysian mainland comes in the form of this buzzing restaurant serving excellent traditional Thai cuisine in a large dining room where the decorators didn't scrimp on their use of ornate polished wood. Popular dishes such as chicken cooked in pandan leaf sell out early. Booking is recommended.

Wonderland Food Store CHINESE $$
(Map p194; Lot 179-181, Pusat Perniagaan Kelana Mas, Kuah; mains from RM16; ⊙6-11pm) Of the string of Chinese-style seafood restaurants in Kuah, Wonderland has been around longer than most and gets the best reviews. It's an informal, open-air place where the food (steamed fish, giant prawns, fried rice) is cheap and tasty.

Pantai Cenang & Around

Nasi Lemak Ultra MALAYSIAN $
(Map p194; ☎019-303 6129; Jln Kedawang; mains from RM5; ⊙5pm-midnight Wed-Mon) The fragrant, rich, authentic KL-style *nasi lemak* (rice boiled in coconut milk, served with fried *ikan bilis,* peanuts and a curry dish) is made by a friendly, English-speaking family who are passionate about the dish. Accompany your rice spread with rendang, fried chicken or one of the other sides made on a daily basis.

Restoran Rinnie MALAYSIAN $
(Map p198; Jln Kuala Muda; mains from RM5; ⊙9am-6pm Sat-Thu) Above-average *nasi campur* (buffet of curried meats, fish and vegetables, served with rice), including a few vegetable options, served by a friendly family.

★Yasmin MIDDLE EASTERN $$
(Map p198; www.facebook.com/yasmin123.86; Jln Pantai Cenang, Pantai Cenang; mains RM22-49; ⊙noon-midnight; ❄🔊) Langkawi is home to heaps of Middle Eastern restaurants and this Syrian place is one of the best. Expect friendly staff, slightly less fluorescent lighting than its competitors, and a reassuringly short menu that ranges from meze to grilled dishes, with the freshly baked flatbreads a highlight.

Kasbah INTERNATIONAL $$
(Map p198; ☎011-1215 8946; www.kasbah.my; Pantai Cenang; mains RM8-38; ⊙9am-11pm; 🖉) A relaxed, friendly cafe housed in a spacious, open-sided wooden structure constructed and furnished by the artistic owners using recycled materials. Reggae, hammocks, books and games attract a crowd of happy travellers, as does the menu of decent coffee, breakfasts, salads, burgers and sandwiches – as well as meat-free options – and recommended daily Malaysian specials.

Red Tomato INTERNATIONAL $$
(Map p198; ☎04-955 4055; www.redtomato restaurant.com.my; Jln Pantai Cenang, Pantai Cenang; mains RM20-30; ⊙9am-11.30pm) Red Tomato is run by expats who crank out some of the best pizzas on Pulau Langkawi. It's also a popular breakfast spot; options include eggs cooked how you like them and served with homemade bread.

Orkid Ria CHINESE $$
(Map p198; ☎04-955 4128; 1225 Jln Pantai Cenang, Pantai Cenang; mains RM35-55; ⊙noon-3pm & 6-11pm) This is the place to go to on Pantai Cenang for Chinese-style seafood. Fat shrimp, fish and crabs are plucked straight from tanks out front, but they don't come cheap.

Putumayo ASIAN $$
(Map p198; ☎04-953 2233; 1584 Jln Pantai Cenang, Pantai Cenang; mains RM30-45; ⊙1-11.30pm) At Putumayo the cuisine ranges from across Asia, looping from Malaysia through Thailand to China with fresh fish and seafood (including prawns the size of your hand) priced by weight. Set amid a beautiful open-air courtyard, with excellent service (the waiter even folds your napkin on your lap).

Nam INTERNATIONAL $$$
(Map p198; ☎04-955 3643; Bon Ton Resort, Pantai Cenang; mains RM50-70; ⊙noon-11pm; 🖉) At Bon Ton resort (p202), Nam boasts a well-executed menu of fusion food, from chargrilled rack of lamb with roast pumpkin, mint salad, hummus and tomato jam, to a nine-dish sampler of Nonya cuisine. There are plenty of veggie options, and at night the setting amid Bon Ton's jungle grounds is superb. Reservations are recommended during peak season (December to January).

Pantai Tengah & Around

★La Chocolatine FRENCH $$
(Map p198; ☎04-955 8891; 3 Jln Teluk Baru, Pantai Tengah; mains RM12-40; ⊙9am-7pm Sat-Thu; ❄🔊) This sophisticated, air-conditioned snack stop serves excellent French desserts – croissants, tarts and eclairs – as well as light salads, sandwiches, quiches and crepes. Beverage choices include coffees, teas and hot chocolate.

LANGKAWI'S ROVING NIGHT MARKET

Local food can be tricky to find on Langkawi. Fortunately, for fans of Malay eats there's a rotating *pasar malam* (night market) held at various points across the island. It's a great chance to indulge in cheap, take-home meals and snacks, and is held from about 6pm to 10pm at the following locations:

Monday Jalan Makam Mahsuri Lama (Map p194; Jln Makam Mahsuri Lama; mains RM3-6; ⊙6-11pm Mon), in the centre of the island, not far from MARDI Agro Technology Park.

Tuesday Kedawang (Map p194; Jln Kedawang; mains RM3-6; ⊙6-11pm Tue), just east of the airport.

Wednesday & Saturday Kuah (Map p194; Lencongan Putra 3; mains RM3-6; ⊙6-11pm Wed & Sat), opposite Masjid Al-Hana; this is the largest market.

Thursday Bohor Tempoyak (Map p198; Jln Bohor Tempoyak, Pantai Cenang; mains RM3-6; ⊙6-11pm Thu), at the northern end of Pantai Cenang.

Friday Padang Lalang (Map p194; Jln Teluk Yu, Padang Lalang; mains RM3-6; ⊙6-11pm Fri), at the roundabout near Pantai Pasir Hitam.

Sunday Padang Matsirat (Map p194; Jln Lapangan Terbang; mains RM4-7; ⊙6-11pm Sun), near the roundabout just north of the airport.

Istanbul
TURKISH $$
(Map p198; ☑04-955 2100; hungry_monkey@hotmail.com; Jln Pantai Cenang, Pantai Tengah; mains RM29-59; ⊙noon-midnight; 🛜) Istanbul serves a brief menu of familiar but hearty and delicious Turkish dishes, including İskender kebap, smothered in a rich tomato sauce and served with a thick homemade yoghurt. The folks behind Istanbul also run a Turkish grocery store opposite Pantai Tengah.

fatCUPID
INTERNATIONAL $$
(Map p198; ☑04-955 3010; www.fatcupid.com.my; 2273 Jln Teluk Baru, Pantai Tengah; mains RM25-48; ⊙8am-2pm & 5-10.30pm) The bar and restaurant at La Pari-Pari (p203) serves Western breakfasts, sandwiches, burgers and Nonya dishes including laksa, as well as a good selection of wine and inventive cocktails.

Melayu
MALAYSIAN $$
(Map p198; ☑04-955 3775; Jln Teluk Baru, Pantai Tengah; mains RM18-25; ⊙7.30am-11pm; ✸) The comfortable dining room, pleasant outdoor seating area and efficient service here belie the reasonable prices. It's a good place to go for authentic Malaysian food in the evening, since most of Pulau Langkawi's local restaurants are lunchtime buffets.

Alcohol isn't served, but you can bring your own for no charge.

Unkaizan
JAPANESE $$$
(Map p198; ☑04-955 4118; www.unkaizan.com; 395 Jln Teluk Baru, Pantai Tengah; mains RM40-60; ⊙6-11pm Thu-Tue; ✸) Unkaizan serves lauded Japanese food, with seating in a cosy bungalow and on an open patio. The menu spans much that Japan is known for, but don't forget to ask for the specials board, which often includes dishes made with imported Japanese seafood. Reservations are recommended.

Elsewhere on the Island

★Siti Fatimah
MALAYSIAN $
(Map p194; ☑04-955 2754; Jln Kampung Tok Senik, Kawasan Mata Air; mains from RM5; ⊙7am-4.30pm Thu-Tue) This is possibly Langkawi's most famous destination for Malay food – and it lives up to its reputation. Come mid-morning, dozens of rich curries, grilled fish, dips, stir-fries and other Malay-style dishes are laid out in a self-service buffet. The flavours are strong and the prices low. It's located on Jln Kampung Tok Senik; most taxi drivers know the place.

★Selera Akmal
MALAYSIAN $
(Map p194; ☑012-594 4638; www.facebook.com/seleraakmal; 12 Jln Lapangan Terbang, Padang Matsirat; mains from RM3; ⊙8am-5pm Sat-Thu) This is where locals go for *nasi campur*. Serve yourself from trays holding dishes such as rich rendang, fiery *sambal,* a coconut milk curry with chunks of pineapple, grilled fish, and a generous selection of vegetable sides.

Gallo Nero
ITALIAN $$
(Map p194; ☑04-952 3555; www.facebook.com/GalloLangkawi; 19 Bandar Padang Matsirat, Pa-

dang Matsirat; 3-course lunch RM38, mains RM35-42; ☺noon-3pm & 6.30-10.30pm Tue-Sun; ✤) A cheesy cartoon logo and Disney wall art contrast with the serious Italian food at this local staple. Come for handsome and hearty dishes, many using milk from local buffalos, such as buffalo ricotta gnocchi with toasted almonds and raisins.

Scarborough Fish & Chips   INTERNATIONAL $$
(Map p194; ☑012-352 2236; 1388 Jln Tanjung Rhu, Tanjung Rhu; mains RM35-50; ☺10am-10pm) The fish and chips here are passable, but honestly it's more about the location – a quiet, sandy stretch of Tanjung Rhu that encourages making an afternoon of your meal. A few other English-inspired dishes and beers are also available.

🍷 Drinking & Nightlife

Langkawi's duty-free status makes it one of the cheapest places to buy booze in Malaysia, and alcohol at many restaurants and hotels is half the mainland price. There are some decent beach-style bars along Pantai Cenang, including some informal candlelit and deckchair affairs that pop up on the sand as the sun goes down. The bar scene is pretty laid-back, and those looking to party hard may be disappointed.

★ Yellow Café   BAR
(Map p198; ☑012-459 3190; www.facebook.com/yellowbeach.cafe; Pantai Cenang; ☺noon-1am Wed-Mon; 🛜) The best bar on Pantai Cenang has a mellow soundtrack, shaded seating and beanbags on the sand. Cocktails from RM20.

Nest Rooftop   BAR
(Map p198; ☑017-462 0241; www.nestrooftop.com; 5th fl, Royal Agate Beach Resort, 1659 Jln Pantai Cenang, Pantai Cenang; ☺7-11.30am & 5-11pm) One of the best bars on Pantai Cenang, Nest doesn't sell alcohol. However, you can buy a bottle from a duty-free shop in the area, take it to the 5th floor of Royal Agate Beach Resort and, for RM20, Nest will provide glassware and ice (mixers cost extra but the views are free).
Check its Facebook page for weekly events.

Thirstday   BAR
(Map p198; 1225 Jln Pantai Cenang, Pantai Cenang; ☺3pm-1am) Slightly more sophisticated than the average beachside beer bar, Thirstday boasts an open-air deck with uninterrupted sunset views and thoughtful mini champagne buckets for your beer.

Kalut Bar   BAR
(Map p198; 2 Jln Pantai Cenang; ☺noon-1am) Sink into an umbrella-shaded beanbag on this beach bar in the middle of Pantai Cenang. A bassy soundtrack of house and pop animates the place by day, while events from live music to fire dancing take place on some nights. Happy hour (5pm to 6pm) has two-for-one drinks offers.

Smiling Buffalo   CAFE
(Map p198; www.facebook.com/Smilingbuffalocafe; 965 Kuala Cenang, Pantai Cenang; ☺8am-6pm) Good coffee and freshly pressed juices are served in shady grounds at this idyllic, friendly cafe, north of Pantai Cenang. Smiling Buffalo also offers great burgers, desserts and brunches.

Cliff   BAR
(Map p198; ☑04-953 3228; www.theclifflangkawi.com; 63 & 40 Jln Pantai Cenang, Pantai Cenang; ☺noon-11pm) Perched on a wave-lashed rocky outcrop between Pantai Cenang and Pantai Tengah, this is an exhilarating spot for a sundowner. Expect a full bar, a good wine selection, and cocktails a class above those mixed on the beach below (from RM18).

The largely Malaysian dinner menu includes whole baked fish, plus Western dishes such as pistachio-crusted salmon (mains RM65 to RM80).

La Sal   COCKTAIL BAR
(Map p198; www.casadelmar-langkawi.com; Casa del Mar, Jln Pantai Cenang, Pantai Cenang; ☺11am-11.30pm) This open-air restaurant and cocktail bar has some creative drinks – who fancies a five-spiced poached apple and cinnamon mojito? Tom yum martini, anyone? Come evening, tables in the sand and torchlight make La Sal a sexy sunset drink destination (cocktails start at RM29).

Charlie's Bar & Grill   BAR
(Map p194; www.langkawiyachtclub.com; Jln Pantai Dato Syed Omar, Langkawi Yacht Club Hotel, Kuah; ☺9am-midnight) Located at the Langkawi Yacht Club Hotel, this is a friendly, unpretentious place that functions equally well as a bar or restaurant (mains RM26 to RM48).

🛍 Shopping

Duty-free shopping in Langkawi is a big draw for Malaysians, who flock here to stock up on cooking utensils, suitcases, liquor and chocolate. But unless you're planning to pick up a new set of fancy dinner plates you are unlikely to be wildly excited by the duty-free shops; the greatest conglomeration of these is at Kuah jetty and at the southern end of Pantai Cenang, near Underwater World.

Atma Alam Batik Art Village ARTS & CRAFTS

(Map p194; ☑04-955 2615; www.atmaalam.com; Bandar Padang Matsirat, Padang Matsirat; ☺10am-6pm) This is a huge handicrafts complex with an emphasis on batik. Visitors can paint and take home their own swatch of batik for RM30. Atma Alam is located in Padang Matsirat, not far from the airport; most taxi drivers are familiar with it.

Zon Duty Free
Shopping Centre SHOPPING CENTRE

(Map p198; www.zon.com.my; Jln Pantai Cenang, Pantai Cenang; ☺11am-9pm) A large duty-free shopping centre.

Kompleks Kraf Langkawi ARTS & CRAFTS

(Langkawi Craft Complex; Map p194; ☑04-959 1913; www.kraftangan.gov.my; Jln Teluk Yu, Pantai Pasir Hitam; ☺10am-6pm) Watch demonstrations of traditional crafts and buy any traditional Malaysian product or craft you can imagine at this enormous handicrafts centre. There are also a couple of on-site exhibitions devoted to local legends and wedding ceremonies, and a craft museum. The complex is located in the far north of Pulau Langkawi, close to Pantai Pasir Hitam.

❶ Information

Naturally Langkawi (www.naturallylangkawi.my) A comprehensive source of island information.

INTERNET ACCESS

While most hotels and many cafes offer wi-fi, the connection can be weak or limited to the reception area, especially in the more jungly parts of the island. Internet cafes are few and far between.

MEDICAL SERVICES

Langkawi Hospital (Map p194; ☑04-966 3333; http://hlangkawi.moh.gov.my; Jln Bukit Teguh; ☺24hr) Located just west of Kuah, off the 112 road to the airport.

❶ FERRY WARNING

During the wet season, from July to September, you may want to shelve any notions of taking the ferry to Langkawi, particularly from Penang. At this time of year the seas are typically very rough and the ferry ride can be a terrifying and quite literally vomit-inducing experience.

MONEY

The only banks are at Kuah and Telaga Harbour Park, but there are ATMs at **Cenang Mall** (Map p198; Jln Pantai Cenang), the jetty and the airport. There are a few **money changers** (Map p198; 16 Jln Pantai Cenang; ☺10am-10pm) at Pantai Cenang.

TOURIST INFORMATION

Tourism Malaysia (Map p194; ☑04-966 7789; www.malaysia.travel; Jln Persiaran Putra, Kuah; ☺9am-5pm) This office is next to the mosque in Kuah town, and offers comprehensive information on the whole island. There are two other offices, one located opposite the ferry terminal entrance at Kuah jetty, and one in the airport arrivals hall (open until 10pm).

❶ Getting There & Away

AIR

Langkawi International Airport (Map p194; ☑04-955 1311; www.langkawiairport.com) is located in the west of the island near Padang Matsirat. It's well stocked with ATMs, currency-exchange booths, car-rental agencies, travel agencies and a Tourism Malaysia office. More than a dozen airlines connect Langkawi with domestic destinations (George Town, Johor Bahru, Kuala Lumpur) and others overseas (Singapore and Chinese cities).

BOAT

All passenger ferries operate from the busy terminal at **Kuah Jetty** (Map p194; Kuah). **Langkawi Ferry Service** (LFS; Map p194; ☑04-966 9439; www.langkawi-ferry.com) – for the Langkawi–Penang route – and Tropical Charters (p200) service the destinations below.

DESTINATION	PRICE (RM, ADULT/ CHILD)	DURATION	FREQUENCY
George Town	60/45	2¾ hrs	10.30am & 3pm
Ko Lipe (Thailand)	105/95	1½ hrs	9.30am & 9.45am
Kuala Kedah	23/17	1¾ hrs	every 1½hr, 7.30am-7pm
Kuala Perlis	18/13	1¼ hrs	every 1½hr, 7.30am-7pm
Satun (Thailand)	35/28	1¼ hrs	9.30am & 5.15pm

❶ Getting Around

TO/FROM THE AIRPORT/JETTY

Fixed taxi fares from the airport include Kuah jetty (RM30), Pantai Cenang or Pantai Kok

(RM25), Tanjung Rhu (RM36) and Teluk Datai (RM60). Buy a coupon at the desk before leaving the airport terminal and use it to pay the driver. The taxi fare from the jetty to Pantai Cenang is RM30.

BICYCLE
Many places rent bikes for RM15 per day.

CAR & MOTORCYCLE
Cars can be rented cheaply and touts from the travel agencies at the Kuah jetty will assail you upon arrival. Rates are around RM70 to RM100 per day, but drop with bargaining.

The easiest way to get around is to hire a motorbike for around RM35 per day. You can do a leisurely circuit of the island (70km) in a day. The main roads are excellent, and outside Kuah it's very pleasant and easy riding. Motorbikes can be hired at stands all over the island.

T Shoppe (Map p198; ☑ 04-955 5552; Jln Pantai Cenang, Pantai Cenang) offers car and motorbike rentals as well as air tickets and the usual boat trips and snorkelling excursions. It has another branch in Kuah.

TAXI
As there is no public transport in Langkawi, taxis are the main way of getting around. Fares are relatively high (RM15 between Pantai Cenang and Pantai Tengah, regardless of the pick-up/drop-off points), so it can be worthwhile renting your own vehicle. Ride-sharing apps like GrabCar function on the island, though fares are usually only a couple of ringgit less than standard taxis. There are taxi stands at the airport, Kuah jetty, **Pantai Cenang** (Map p198; Jln Pantai Cenang) and **Cenang Mall** (Map p198; Jln Pantai Cenang), and **Pantai Tengah** (Map p198; Jln Teluk Baru), at the Frangipani hotel. There are fixed rates for all destinations – displayed at the stand – and no taxi should use a meter. It's also possible to hire a taxi for four hours for RM120.

Alor Setar
☑ 04

Most travellers use the capital of Kedah, formerly known as Alor Star, as a jumping-off point to Langkawi or southern Malaysia. But it's worth lingering long enough to admire its architectural treasures: Alor Setar's impressive buildings include Masjid Zahir, one of the most beautiful mosques in Malaysia; towering Menara Alor Setar; and a stately clock tower nearby.

Alor Setar is generally a welcoming place for foreign visitors, though it's rooted in a conservative mindset built on a fairly strict interpretation of Islam and reverence for the local monarchy.

ⓘ GETTING TO THAILAND: PULAU LANGKAWI TO SATUN & KO LIPE

Getting to the border There are two daily ferries from Kuah to Satun on the Thai mainland (one-way adult/child RM35/28, 1¼ hours, 9.30am and 5.15pm), and also between Langkawi and the Thai island of Ko Lipe (one-way adult/child from RM105/95, 1½ hours, 9.30am and 9.45am). Ferry availability may lessen during the month of Ramadan, so be sure to check timings and routes.

At the border You'll get stamped out of Malaysia at immigration at the ferry terminal then get stamped into Thailand when you arrive at the ferry terminal in Satun. Most visitors can get a Thai visa for 15 days or more on arrival.

Moving on From Satun there are more bus and boat connections. From Ko Lipe there are onward services available to as far as Ko Lanta.

⊙ Sights

Impressive buildings front the *padang*, the grassy town square. From here you can admire views of Masjid Zahir, the **clock tower** (Jln Sultan Muhammad Jiwa) and Menara Alor Setar.

Masjid Zahir
MOSQUE

(Jln Kampung Perak; ⊙7am-7pm) **FREE** The Kedah state mosque instantly impresses with its richly decorated arches and five broad domes, which represent the pillars of Islam. Built in 1912, Moorish-style Masjid Zahir is one of the oldest and loveliest mosques in Malaysia. It is also the site of a cemetery for Kedah warriors who fought the Siamese in 1821.

Modestly dressed visitors may enter; both sexes should be covered from shoulders to knees and women are advised to bring a headscarf.

Menara Alor Setar
TOWER

(Alor Setar Tower; ☑ 04-720 2234; www.menara alorsetar.com.my/en; Lr Darul Aman; adult/child RM18/12; ⊙9am-midnight) If the Petronas Towers in KL isn't enough for you, the second-tallest tower in the country is Menara Alor Setar, which at 165.5m is by far the tallest structure in town. A glass-sided lift will take you to the observation deck for

LANGKAWI, KEDAH & PERLIS ALOR SETAR

good views of Alor Setar and the surrounding countryside.

Mahathir's Birthplace
MUSEUM

(Rumah Kelahiran Mahathir; ☑04-772 1795; 18 Lg Kilang Ais; ⊙10am-5pm Tue-Thu, Sat & Sun, 10am-noon & 3-5pm Fri) **FREE** Dr Mahathir Mohamad, Malaysia's seventh and longest-serving prime minister, was born the youngest of nine children in Alor Setar in 1925. Rumah Kelahiran Mahathir, his childhood home, is now preserved as a small but worthwhile museum, containing family effects, photos and the politician's old bicycle. Aside from providing an insight into Mahathir's early life, the museum is an interesting example of a traditional Malaysian house.

Galeri Sultan Abdul Halim
MUSEUM

(Jln Sultan Muhammad Jiwa; adult/child RM5/2; ⊙10am-5pm Sun-Thu) The former High Court, erected in 1922, is today a museum dedicated to Abdul Halim Mu'adzam Shah, twice Malaysia's head of state, the Yang Di Pertuan Agong. Inside you'll find photos and an exhaustive collection of memorabilia from the sultan's life, with everything from golf visors to Rolls-Royces and even His Majesty's old mobile phones on display.

Balai Nobat
HISTORIC BUILDING

(Padang Court) Built in 1906, this is a striking octagonal tower topped by an onion-shaped dome. It's the repository of the *nobat* (royal orchestra), principally composed of percussion instruments; the drums in this orchestra are said to have been a gift from the sultan of Melaka in the 15th century. It isn't open to the public, and the instruments are brought out only on ceremonial occasions such as royal weddings.

Balai Besar
HISTORIC BUILDING

(Great Hall; Jln Sultan Muhammad Jiwa) This open-sided structure was built in 1896 and is still used by the sultan of Kedah for royal and state ceremonies, though it is not open to the public. Supported on tall pillars topped with Victorian iron lacework, the building also shows Thai influences in its decoration.

Wat Nikrodharam
BUDDHIST TEMPLE

(Jln Stadium) **FREE** Although Alor Setar has weathered periods of Thai rule over the years, its main Buddhist community is Chinese in heritage. Thus the presence of this cross-cultural wat (Buddhist temple): typically Thai in structure yet scattered with Chinese Buddhist saints of importance to the Chinese donors who funded the construction of the complex. The wat is located between Telok Wanjah and Jln Stadium, close to the roundabout.

Muzium Diraja Kedah
MUSEUM

(Royal Museum; Padang Court, Jln Raya; ⊙9am-5pm Sat-Thu, 9am-12.30pm & 2.30-5pm Fri) **FREE** Now a museum, these connected structures with creaking wooden floorboards formerly served as the royal palace for the sultan and other members of the family from 1856. Among the royal paraphernalia on display is memorabilia from the historic joint wedding in 1904 of the five children (two princes and three princesses) of the 26th sultan of Kedah – the festivities lasted 90 days.

Muzium Negeri
MUSEUM

(Kedah State Museum; ☑04-733 1162; Lr Darul Aman; ⊙9am-5pm Sat-Thu, 9am-12.30pm & 2.30-5pm Fri) **FREE** The State Museum is 2km north of the main square. The collection includes early Chinese porcelain, information on the archaeological finds at the former Hindu/Buddhist trade centre of Lembah Bujang in the southern part of the state, and dioramas of royal and rural life in Kedah. A taxi from the town centre costs RM10.

🛏 Sleeping

Comfort Motel
HOTEL $

(☑04-734 4866; 2C Jln Kampung Perak; r incl breakfast RM45; P❄) This is a good-value, Chinese-style budget hotel, located in a renovated wooden house across from Masjid Zahir (p209). The rooms are tidy and come equipped with TV and air-con, but are otherwise bare and share bathrooms.

Fuller Hotel
HOTEL $$

(☑04-733 3999; www.fuller.com.my/alorsetar; 10 Jln Pintu Sepuluh, 1 Kompleks Perniagaan; r RM118-210; P❄🛜) Smart, contemporary and convenient, Fuller is a great midrange catch. The rooms are functional and the hotel is a brief walk to Alor Setar's handful of attractions, shopping and lots of food.

New Regent
HOTEL $$

(☑04-731 5000; regentnew@gmail.com; 1536 Jln Sultan Badlishah; r from RM120, ste RM256, all incl breakfast; ❄🛜) A makeover at this long-standing hotel has left the lobby area looking relatively contemporary and jazzy. Though the rooms don't quite match up, they are clean and well-equipped.

Alor Setar

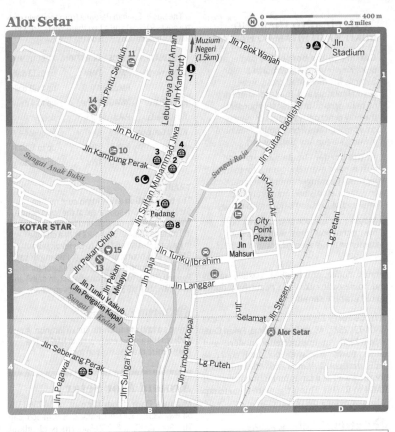

0 — 400 m
0 — 0.2 miles

KOTAR STAR

LANGKAWI, KEDAH & PERLIS ALOR SETAR

Alor Setar

Sights
1	Balai Besar	B2
2	Balai Nobat	B2
3	Clock Tower	B2
4	Galeri Sultan Abdul Halim	B2
5	Mahathir's Birthplace	A4
6	Masjid Zahir	B2
7	Menara Alor Setar	B1
8	Muzium Diraja Kedah	B3
9	Wat Nikrodharam	D1

Sleeping
10	Comfort Motel	B2
11	Fuller Hotel	B1
12	New Regent	C2

Eating
13	Caffe Diem	A3
14	Nasi Lemak Ong	A1

Drinking & Nightlife
15	Terrace Forty Eight	B3

Eating & Drinking

Nasi Lemak Ong MALAYSIAN $
(📞012-498 3660; ground fl, 24 Jln Putra; mains RM5-12; ⏰10.30am-3.30pm Thu-Tue; ✳️🍽️) This efficient, family-run canteen is the most popular *nasi lemak* place in Alor Setar. At the counter, select your rice and choice of accompaniments from the wide array of dishes laid out, including rich, spicy *sambal,* dried anchovies, curried prawns or mutton, and various vegetable dishes. Worth the queue.

Caffe Diem CAFE $$
(📞04-730 9328; 44 Jln Penjara Lama; mains RM14-16; ⏰noon-midnight; ✳️🛜) Alor Setar's answer to a hipster cafe is this quirky, friendly place

---

ⓘ GETTING TO THAILAND: BUKIT KAYU HITAM TO HAT YAI

Getting to the border The border at Bukit Kayu Hitam, 48km north of Alor Setar, is the main road crossing between Malaysia and Thailand. There are no taxis or local buses at this border; the only practical way to cross here is on a through bus from points elsewhere in Malaysia (eg Alor Setar or KL).

At the border The Malaysian border post is open every day from 6am to midnight. All passengers must disembark to clear customs and immigration (both Thai and Malaysian) before reboarding.

Moving on The lack of local transport means that you'll most likely pass this border on a bus already bound for Hat Yai.

---

serving coffee, sandwiches, pastas, salads and homemade cakes in a beautifully done-up old Chinese shophouse.

Terrace Forty Eight BAR
(☑04-731 2527; 48 Jln Penjara Lama, Pekan Cina; ☺5pm-2am) An unexpectedly modern and rather flashy bar with polished concrete walls, draught Guinness and other imported booze as well as a tapas menu (items around RM14 to RM18). This is the place to go to tap into Alor Setar's party scene.

ⓘ Getting There & Away

AIR

Alor Setar Airport (Sultan Abdul Halim Airport; ☑04-714 6876) is 11km north of town, just off the Lebuhraya. **AirAsia** (www.airasia. com; Level 1, Sultan Abdul Halim Airport; ☺7am-8pm), **Firefly** (☑04-714 3911; www. fireflyz.com.my; Main Terminal, Sultan Abdul Halim Airport; ☺7am-8pm), **Malaysia Airlines** (☑1300-883 000; www.malaysiaairlines.com; Sultan Abdul Halim Airport; ☺7am-8pm) and **Malindo Air** (☑04-714 4881; www.malindoair. com; Sultan Abdul Halim Airport; ☺7am-9pm) offer daily flights to KL (KLIA and Subang airports; from around RM100, one hour).

BUS

The main bus terminal, **Shahab Perdana** (Lr Bahiyah), is 4km north of the town centre. A local bus links Shahab Perdana and Kuala Kedah (RM3, one hour, frequent departures from 7am to 10pm), passing through the town centre on the way. There is a **bus stop** (Jln Langgar) near the taxi stand on Jln Tunku Ibrahim.

The bus to Shahab Perdana from the town centre costs RM1.30 and a taxi there costs around RM10. Destinations include the following:

DESTINATION	PRICE	DURATION	FREQUENCY
Butterworth	RM11	1½hr	up to 13 daily
Ipoh	RM28	4hr	up to 11 daily
Kota Bharu	RM40	7-8hr	up to 4 daily
Kuala Kedah	RM3	1hr	hourly
Kuala Lumpur	RM45	6½-7hr	frequent
Melaka	RM56	8¼hr	up to 11 daily
Singapore	RM80	12hr	up to 4 daily

TRAIN

The **train station** (www.ktmb.com.my; Jln Stesyen) is 850m southeast of the town centre. There is one daily northbound train to Hat Yai in Thailand (RM40, 3½ hours with a change in Padang Besar) and one to Bangkok (about RM110, 18½ hours, also through Padang Besar), and southbound trains to Tasik Gelugor for Penang (RM18 to RM22, one hour, two daily) and KL (RM70 to RM93, five hours, seven daily).

ⓘ Getting Around

There's a **taxi stand** on Jln Tunku Ibrahim. A taxi to/from the airport costs around RM25. The town centre is accessible on foot.

Around Alor Setar

Muzium Padi (Paddy Museum; ☑04-735 1315; off Hwy K351; adult/child RM5/2; ☺9am-5pm Sat-Thu, 9am-12.30pm & 2.30-5pm Fri) is all about Kedah's main crop: rice. It's located 10km northwest of Alor Setar amid green rice paddies; a taxi costs RM25. The complex, which has a distinctly socialist, utopian feel (some of its murals were made by North Korean artists), is supposed to emulate the gunny sacks used by rice farmers. And if you're *really* into rice, you'll love the exhaustive exhibits inside.

The main event is a top-floor, rotating observation deck that looks out onto a mural of the surrounding rice fields; the gimmick pays homage to Gunung Keriang, a nearby limestone hill that, according to local folklore, is also supposed to rotate.

Kuala Kedah

☑04 / POP 20,000

This busy fishing village, 11km from Alor Setar, is little more than a departure point for boats to Langkawi. Ferries leave for the island approximately every hour between 7am and 7pm (adult/child RM23/17). A taxi to Kuala Kedah from Alor Setar costs RM20; hourly buses (RM3, one hour) also make the run between 7am and 10pm.

Kota Kuala Kedah (www.jmm.gov.my; Jln Marina Harbour; ⊙9am-6pm), completed in 1780, is a fort opposite Kuala Kedah town on the far bank of Sungai Kedah, a 10-minute taxi ride from the ferry terminal. It was once used as a base by the Portuguese in Melaka and was later a bastion of Malay independence against the Siamese until finally falling to the invaders in 1821. On the well-kept site there is also a museum providing background on the history of the fort and Kedah state. Look out for Meriam Badak Berendam (the Wallowing Rhino), a cannon believed to be the abode of the fortress's guardian spirit.

PERLIS

Perlis is Malaysia's smallest state. It doesn't tend to register on most travellers' radars except as a transit point to Thailand or Langkawi (via Kuala Perlis). Even Malays tend to regard it as essentially a rice-producing pocket along the Thai border. Though it isn't an area that's particularly heavy on sites of interest to tourists, it can be a kick just to hang out with the locals and improve your Bahasa Malaysia (because English definitely isn't widely spoken). Otherwise, small but beautiful Taman Negeri Perlis (p214) is worth exploring.

History

Perlis was originally part of Kedah, though it variously fell under Thai and Acehnese sovereignty. After the Siamese conquered Kedah in 1821, the sultan of Kedah made unsuccessful attempts to regain his territory until, in 1842, he agreed to Siamese terms. The sultan's position was restored, but Perlis became a separate principality with its own raja.

As with Kedah, power was transferred from the Thais to the British under the 1909 Anglo-Siamese Treaty, and a British Resident was installed at Arau. During the Japanese occupation in WWII, Perlis was 'returned' to Thailand, and then after the war it was again under British rule until it became part of the Malayan Union, and then the Federation of Malaya in 1957.

Kangar
⌨ 04 / POP 54,300

Kangar is the capital of Malaysia's smallest state, Perlis. This workaday town isn't home to any standout attractions, but it's a common way station for overland travel between Malaysia and Thailand.

⊙ Sights

Muzium Kota Kayang   MUSEUM
(✆04-977 0027; Al-Marhum Kayang; ⊙10am-5pm) FREE Around 7km southwest of Kangar, the small but impressive Muzium Kota Kayang houses displays on local history, including neolithic tools, royal regalia and ceramics. There are some real treasures here and facilities are surprisingly modern, with clear English descriptions. The museum is attractively located on a plot of land backed by limestone cliffs and shallow caves, as well as the modest mausoleums of two 16th-century sultans of Kedah. You'll need to catch a taxi from Kangar to get here (RM12).

⨳ Sleeping

Kangar Hotel   HOTEL $
(✆04-976 7225; kangarhotel@ymail.com; 16 Jln Penjara; r RM90; ❋🛜) This hotel is located above a KFC, with Christmas-coloured rooms that are spacious if frumpy. An acceptable crash pad for a night.

ⓘ GETTING TO THAILAND: KANGAR TO HAT YAI

Getting to the border There are frequent daily buses from Kangar to Padang Besar (RM4.20), stopping at a bus stop by a roundabout about 500m from the border.

At the border The Malaysian border post is open every day from 6am to 10pm. Few people walk the more than 2km of no-man's land between the Thai and Malaysian sides of the border. Motorcyclists shuttle pedestrian travellers back and forth for less than RM5 each way. For train passengers, customs and immigration are dealt with at Padang Besar station.

Moving on Once in Thailand there are frequent buses to Hat Yai, 60km away (44B). There are trains at 10.30am and 6.40pm connecting Padang Besar and Hat Yai (RM6 to RM13, 50 minutes).

TAMAN NEGERI PERLIS

Taman Negeri Perlis (Perlis State Park; ☑ 04-976 5966; Wang Kelian; adult/child RM2/1; ⊙ 7am-6pm), the small state park in the northwest of Perlis, runs for 36km along the Thai border. It comprises the Nakawan Range of limestone hills and the Mata Ayer and Wang Mu Forest Reserves, but the main draw for visitors is the vast system of **caves**. To visit them you must hire a guide (RM50), which can be arranged at the park's visitor centre. There is no public transport to the park and a taxi from Kangar costs RM50.

This is a remote, wild-feeling place. A winding mountain road leads from Kaki Bukit to the tiny border village of Wang Kelian, 3km from the park's visitor centre. There is very rustic, basic accommodation available, booked through the visitor centre, in the form of wooden chalets (RM50) and dorm beds (RM10) – there is no restaurant but staff can prepare food.

The park is the country's only semideciduous forest and is rich in wildlife; this is the only habitat in Malaysia for the stump-tailed macaque. White-handed gibbons and a rich array of birds can also be found here. In the evening, as the sky glows orange with the setting sun, the forest's residents make their presence known with a crescendo of squawks and rustling leaves.

Hotel Ban Cheong   HOTEL **$**
(☑ 04-976 1184; 79 Jln Kangar; r RM65; ❖ ☎) This long-standing Chinese hotel in the town centre has basic rooms. They're in need of updating, but it's an acceptable budget option for an overnight stay.

Hotel Sri Garden   HOTEL **$$**
(☑ 04-977 3188; 96 Persiaran Jubli Emas; r incl breakfast RM118-180; ❖ ☎) Standard Malaysian midranger with capable, if somewhat musty, rooms.

❶ Getting There & Away

BUS

The **long-distance bus station** (Jln Bukit Lagi) is on the southern edge of town. Departures include the following:

DESTINA-TION	PRICE (RM)	DURATION (HR)	FREQUENCY
Alor Setar	5-10	1¼	frequent
Butterworth	20	3	frequent
Ipoh	30	6, via Butterworth	2 daily
Kota Bharu	42-44	10	3 daily
Kuala Lumpur	50-54	7½	4 daily
Melaka	61	10-12	4 daily
Singapore	95	13	4 daily

Regular buses to Padang Besar (RM4.20, one hour) via Kaki Bukit leave from the **local bus station** (Jln Tun Abdul Razak) beneath the Store shopping mall on Jln Tun Abdul Razak. The bus waits 15 minutes before doing the return route from Padang Besar to Kangar. There are also buses from Kangar's local bus station to Alor Setar (RM6, about every two hours from 6.15am to 8pm) and there's a taxi rank here – drivers can take you to Padang Besar (RM36), Alor Setar (RM50) and Taman Negeri Perlis (RM50).

Kuala Perlis, about 10km southwest of Kangar, is a departure point for Pulau Langkawi. From Kangar, the pier can be reached by bus (RM3) or taxi (RM18), and ferries to Langkawi (adult/child RM18/13) leave approximately every 1½ hours from 7.30am to 7pm. From Kuala Perlis, there are buses to a number of destinations across Malaysia, including Kuala Lumpur.

Around Kangar

Gua Kelam (Cave of Darkness; Kaki Bukit; adult/child RM1/50 sen; ⊙ 8am-5.30pm Sun-Fri, to 6pm Sat) is a 370m-long cavern that was gouged out in the tin-mining days. Access is along a rickety gangway above a river that runs through the cave and emerges at a popular swimming spot in an attractive landscaped park, with a backdrop of craggy limestone hills. Gua Kelam is 1km from Kaki Bukit; the bus from Kangar to Padang Besar passes close to the entrance as it does a U-turn on the way back out of the one-street town.

Melaka

🎵 06 / POP 872,900

Includes ➡

Melaka City 217
Ayer Keroh 235
Alor Gajah 236

Best Places to Eat

➡ Salud Tapas (p229)

➡ Baboon House (p230)

➡ Navy Cafe (p229)

➡ Kocik Kitchen (p230)

➡ Seeds Garden (p229)

➡ Bulldog (p231)

Best Places to Stay

➡ 1825 Gallery Hotel (p228)

➡ 45 Lekiu (p227)

➡ Nomaps (p226)

➡ Rucksack Caratel (p228)

➡ Majestic Malacca (p228)

➡ Wayfarer Guest House (p227)

Why Go?

This compact Malaysian state's catchphrase – 'Don't mess with Melaka' – sums up its confident attitude. Recent years have seen Melaka capitalise on its illustrious history and assert itself as one of Malaysia's most irresistible tourist draws.

In the 15th century, Melaka was one of Southeast Asia's greatest trading ports. Over time it lost favour to Singapore, but this slowdown in trade protected much of the ancient architecture of the state capital, Melaka City, from falling foul of development. The historic centre was crowned a Unesco World Heritage Site in 2008, kick-starting a decade of renewal. Modern Melaka swaggers once more, with visitors pouring in to experience the bustling weekend night market, heritage architecture and famously glitzy trishaws.

The rest of the state is a patchwork of forests, farmland and often deserted beaches. There's a generous scattering of family-friendly attractions in the smaller towns of Alor Gajah and Ayer Keroh.

When to Go
Melaka

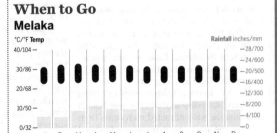

Jan & Feb Chinese New Year brings chaos and colour to the hot and dry months.

Apr–Jul Milder temperatures and festivals galore.

Oct–Dec Book ahead to see Deepavali and Christmas celebrations.

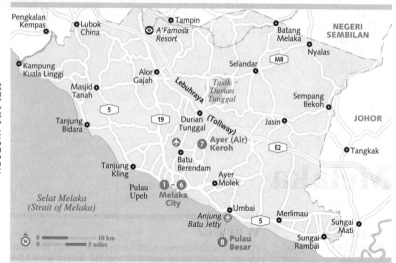

Melaka Highlights

1 Eating in Melaka City (p228) Feasting on Peranakan curries, Portuguese seafood, Indian banana leaf spreads and good coffee.

2 Chinatown (p222) Discovering galleries, craft workshops, historic temples and heritage architecture.

3 Jonker Walk Night Market (p233) Experiencing the razzle-dazzle and street food of Melaka City's weekend night market.

4 Trishaws (p235) Going for a spin around Melaka City's historic centre in one of these kitschy contraptions with music set to nationality.

5 Baba & Nyonya Heritage Museum (p222) Embracing nostalgia at this atmospheric museum in a gorgeously decorated old home.

6 Villa Sentosa (p223) Discovering the delightful Malay village of Kampung Morten and learning about one family's history.

7 Melaka Botanical Garden (p235) Going for a gentle hike or swinging through the trees like Tarzan in Ayer Keroh.

8 Pulau Besar (p236) Getting off the beaten track on this tranquil pilgrimage island.

History

The modern city-state of Melaka bloomed from a simple 14th-century fishing village founded by Parameswara, a Hindu prince or pirate (take your pick) from Sumatra. According to legend, Parameswara was inspired to build Melaka after seeing a plucky mouse deer fend off a dog attack.

Melaka's location halfway between China and India, with easy access to the spice islands of Indonesia, soon attracted merchants from all over the East and it became a favoured port. In 1405, the Chinese Muslim Admiral Cheng Ho (Zheng He; 鄭和) arrived in Melaka bearing gifts from the Ming emperor and the promise of protection from Siamese enemies. Chinese settlers followed. They mixed with the local Malays and became known as Baba-Nonya, Peranakan or Straits Chinese. By the time of Parameswara's death in 1414,

Melaka was a powerful trading state. Its position was consolidated by the state's adoption of Islam in the mid-15th century.

In 1509 the Portuguese came seeking spice wealth and in 1511 Alfonso de Albuquerque forcibly took the city. Under the Portuguese, the fortress of A'Famosa was constructed. While Portuguese cannons could easily conquer Melaka, they could not force Muslim merchants from Arabia and India to continue trading there. Other ports in the area, such as Islamic Demak on Java, grew to overshadow Melaka and its prominence ebbed.

Suffering attacks from neighbouring Johor and Negeri Sembilan, as well as from the Islamic power of Aceh in Sumatra, Melaka declined further. The city passed into Dutch hands after an eight-month siege in 1641, leading to about 150 years of Dutch rule. Melaka again became the centre for peninsular trade, but the Dutch directed more energy into their possessions in Indonesia.

When the French occupied Holland in 1795, the British (as allies of the Dutch) temporarily assumed administration of the Dutch colonies. In 1824 Melaka was permanently ceded to the British.

Melaka, together with Penang and Singapore, formed the Straits Settlements, the three British territories that were the bases for later expansion into the peninsula. However, under British rule Melaka was eclipsed by other Straits Settlements and then superseded by the rapidly growing commercial importance of Singapore. Apart from a brief upturn in the early 20th century when rubber was an important crop, Melaka returned again to being a quiet backwater, patiently awaiting its renaissance as a tourist drawcard, which duly arrived when Melaka City gained its Unesco World Heritage listing in 2008.

A number of mega projects are set to transform the historic city on the ever-expanding mass of reclaimed land offshore in Selat Melaka (the Strait of Melaka). Due to open in the first half of 2020 is Harbour City, a huge development comprising a four-storey water park, a six-level shopping mall and three hotels, all set within a building shaped like a vast cruise ship, on the artificial island of Pulau Melaka. One of the hotels will have cruise-themed rooms. Exactly how all of this will fit in with Melaka's unique heritage is yet to be seen.

Melaka City

📍 06 / POP 484,900

The peacock of Malaysian cities, Melaka City preens with its wealth of colourful trishaws, home-grown galleries and crimson colonial buildings. The city's historic centre achieved Unesco World Heritage status in 2008 and since then Melaka City's tourism industry has developed at breakneck pace. Old shophouses and mansions have enjoyed makeovers as galleries and hotels and Melaka City's kaleidoscope of architectural styles – spanning Peranakan, Portuguese, Dutch and British elements – is well preserved. Tourism has boomed, particularly on weekends when the vibrant Jonker Walk Night Market (p233) provides music, shopping and street-food galore, but you'll share the experience elbow-to-elbow with other travellers.

Inevitably, a strong whiff of commercialism has accompanied this success. However,

it's easy to feel the town's old magic (and get a seat at popular restaurants) on quiet weekdays. Melaka City, as it has for centuries, continues to exude tolerance and welcomes cultural exchange.

⊙ Sights

⊙ Historic Town Centre

Striking crimson-painted buildings and a multitude of museums dominate the historic centre. Many of the museums are small, with a niche focus and an uninspiring diorama format. Start with more developed attractions like Stadthuys and the Maritime Museum complex.

★**Stadthuys**   HISTORIC BUILDING
(Map p218; 📞 06-282 6526; Dutch Sq; foreign/local visitor RM10/4; ⊙ 9am-5.30pm Sat-Thu, 9am-12.15pm & 2.45-5.30pm Fri) This former town hall and governor's residence dates to the 1650s and is believed to be the oldest Dutch building in the East. Erected after the Dutch captured Melaka in 1641, it's a reproduction of the former Stadhuis (town hall) of the Frisian town of Hoorn in the Netherlands. Today it's a museum complex exhibiting colourful artefacts like record-breaking trishaws and bird-shaped longboats; the **History & Ethnography Museum** is the highlight.

Admission covers all the small museums within the complex. There is no fee for

---

WORTH A TRIP

MELAKA'S FLOATING MOSQUE

Especially beautiful at morning or dusk, gold-domed **Masjid Selat Melaka** (off Jln Baiduri 8; ⊙ 7am-7pm) overlooks the Strait of Melaka from its shoreside perch on an artificial island a short taxi or bicycle ride from central Melaka. Completed in 2006, the mosque's grand archways are panelled with stained glass. When water levels are high, it appears to float. To enter, non-Muslim visitors need to dress modestly and heed the 'no shoe' signs. Women must bring a scarf or use a rental shawl to cover their head.

There are few attractions nearby and taxis don't always ply this part of town. If you don't have your own wheels, ask a taxi driver for a return trip (RM15 each way, plus waiting time).

Central Melaka City

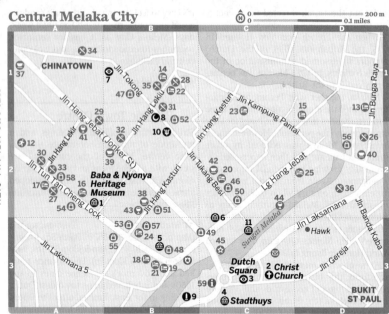

MELAKA MELAKA CITY

guided tours, which take place at 10.30am and 2.30pm on Saturdays and Sundays.

For in-depth acquaintance with Melaka past and present, peruse the **Governor's House**, **Democratic Government Museum**, a **Literature Museum** focusing on Malaysian writers, **Cheng Ho Gallery** and the **Education Museum**.

★**Dutch Square** SQUARE

(Map p218; Jln Gereja) The focal point of the Unesco Heritage zone, this attractive and elegant square is surrounded by Dutch-era buildings that have been painted crimson, shady trees and a mass of kitschly decorated trishaws waiting for customers. Take a moment to admire the pretty fountain erected in 1904 in memory of Queen Victoria and decorated with four bas-relief images of the monarch.

★**Christ Church** CHURCH

(Map p218; 06-284 8804; Jln Gereja; ⊙9am-4.30pm) **FREE** Built in 1753 from laterite bricks brought from Zeeland in Holland, this eye-catching cherry-pink church is one of the most photographed and imposing landmarks in Melaka. Inside, find Dutch and Armenian tombstones in the floor and 15m-long ceiling beams, each one cut from a single tree. A service in English is held here every Sunday at 8.30am.

Maritime Museum & Naval Museum MUSEUM

(Map p220; 06-283 0926; Jln Merdeka; adult/child RM10/6; ⊙9am-5.30pm Mon-Thu & Sat-Sun, 9am-12.15pm & 2.45-5.30pm Fri) Embark on a voyage through Melaka's maritime history at these linked museums. The most enjoyable of the Maritime Museum's three sections (one ticket covers them all) is housed in a re-creation of *Flor de la Mar,* a Portuguese ship that sank off Melaka's coast. The fun of posing on the deck and clambering between floors eclipses the displays and dioramas.

The Maritime Museum continues in the building next door (follow the signs) with exhibits featuring local vessels, including the striking *kepala burung* (a boat carved like a feathered bird), plus an assortment of nautical devices. Across the road from here, the Naval Museum has uniforms and informative displays, but the highlight is an atrium packed with boats and a helicopter.

St Paul's Church RUINS

(Map p220; Jln Kota; ⊙24hr) **FREE** The evocative and sublime ruin of St Paul's Church crowns the summit of Bukit St Paul overlooking central Melaka. Steep stairs from Jln Kota or Jln Chang Koon Cheng lead up to this faded sanctuary, originally built by a Portuguese captain in 1521. The church was regularly visited by St Francis Xavier, whose

Central Melaka City

◎ **Top Sights**
1 Baba & Nyonya Heritage
   Museum..............................A2
2 Christ Church..........................C3
3 Dutch Square C3
4 Stadthuys C3

◎ **Sights**
5 8 Heeren Street.....................B3
6 Cheng Ho Cultural Museum...............C2
7 Cheng Hoon Teng Temple.................B1
8 Masjid Kampung Kling..................B1
9 Melaka Malay Sultanate Water
   Wheel B3
10 Sri Poyatha Venayagar Moorthi
   Temple.................................B2
11 Zheng He Duo Yun Xuan....................C3

⊕ **Activities, Courses & Tours**
   Old Melaka Heritage Tour..........(see 59)
12 Puri Spa A2

🛏 **Sleeping**
13 1825 Gallery Hotel....................D1
14 45 Lekiu B1
15 Bridge Loft D1
16 Cafe 1511 Guesthouse..................A2
17 Courtyard@Heeren......................A2
18 Gingerflower...........................B3
19 Heeren House..........................B3
   Hotel Puri.......................(see 12)
20 Layang-Layang........................C2
21 Nomaps B3
22 Opposite Place.........................B1
23 Rooftop Guesthouse...................C1
24 Stables................................B3
25 Wayfarer Guest House.................D2

🍴 **Eating**
26 13 Hibiscus Vintage Art Cafe...............D2
27 Baboon House.........................A2

   Cafe 1511 ....(see 16)
28 Eat at 18.............................B1
29 Jonker 88 ....A1
30 Kocik Kitchen.........................A2
31 Low Yong Moh B1
32 Navy Cafe............................B2
33 Salud Tapas...........................A2
34 Seeds Garden A1
35 Shui Xian Vegetarian.................B1
36 Street Kitchen........................D2

🍷 **Drinking & Nightlife**
37 Backlane Coffee......................A1
38 Calanthe Art Cafe....................B2
39 Daily Fix.............................B2
40 Discovery Cafe & Guest House..........D2
41 Geographér Cafe A2
42 Kaya Kaya Cafe......................C2
43 Me & Mrs Jones.....................B2
44 Reggae on the River..................C2

🎭 **Entertainment**
45 Hard Rock Cafe.......................C3

🛍 **Shopping**
46 Clay House............................C2
47 Hueman Studio.........................B1
48 Joe's Design...........................B3
49 Jonker Walk Night Market...............C3
50 Orangutan House......................C2
51 Puri Padi.............................B2
52 RazKashmir Crafts B1
53 Red Handicrafts.......................B3
54 Sixty 3 Heritage......................A2
55 Tham Siew Inn Artist Gallery...............B3
56 Trash & Treasure.....................D2
57 Umyang Batik........................B3
58 Wah Aik Shoemaker...................A2

ℹ **Information**
59 Tourism Malaysia C3

marble statue – minus his right hand and a few toes – stands in front of the ruin.

St Francis' Institution Melaka SCHOOL
(Map p220; Jln Merdeka; ⊗8.30am-5pm) Originally founded in 1880 and once named St Mary's School, this charming, red-roofed Roman Catholic school is worth a visit to explore its pleasant stained-glass-illuminated chapel and elegant heritage architecture. The school is generally open from the morning, but ask the guard at the gate if it's OK to visit and he should let you in.

Melaka Malay Sultanate Water Wheel MONUMENT
(Map p218; Jln Merdeka) In 2006, work on the Menara Taming Sari revolving tower uncovered another part of the city's fortress walls. The revolving tower was relocated further inland; the remains of the fortress walls were reconstructed and are now home to the 13m-high Melaka Malay Sultanate Water Wheel replica. The original wheel would have been used to channel the river waters for the large number of traders swarming Melaka during the 15th and 16th centuries.

Menara Taming Sari VIEWPOINT
(Map p220; ☑06-288 1100; www.menaratamingsari.com; Jln Merdeka; adult/child RM23/15; ⊗10am-11pm) Melaka's revolving viewing deck looks worryingly like a theme-park ride without the seat belts. Luckily, this is a leisurely thrill ride and one with air-con. The UFO-shaped

MELAKA

Melaka City

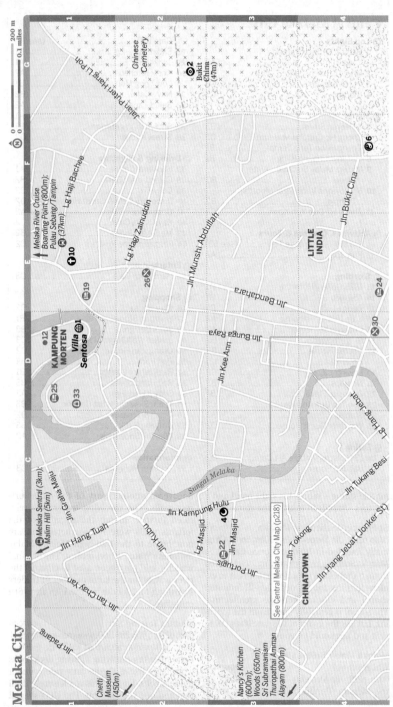

200 m
0.1 miles

Chinese Cemetery

Bukit Cina (47m) ☉2

☉6

Jalan Puteri Hang Li Poh

LITTLE INDIA

Jln Bukit Cina

Melaka River Cruise
Boarding Point (800m);
Pulau Sebang/Tampin
(37km) ⊞

Lg Haji Bachee

Lg Haji Zainuddin

✚10

Jln Munshi Abdullah

☒26

⊞19

Jln Bendahara

⊞24

☒30

Jln Bunga Raya

Villa Sentosa ⊞1
●12
KAMPUNG MORTEN

Jln Kee Ann

⊞25
⊞33

Sungai Melaka

Lg Hang Jebat

Jln Graha Maju

Melaka Sentral (3km);
Malim Hill (5km)

Jln Hang Tuah

Jln Kubu

Jln Kampung Hulu

Lg Masjid

☉4
Jln Masjid

Jln Tukang Besi

See Central Melaka City Map (p218)

Jln Tokong

⊞22
Jln Portugis

CHINATOWN

Jln Hang Jebat (Jonker St)

Jln Tan Chay Yan

Jln Padang

Chetti Museum
(450m)

Nancy's Kitchen
(600m);
Woods (650m);
Sri Subramaniam
Thuropathai Amman
Alayam (800m)

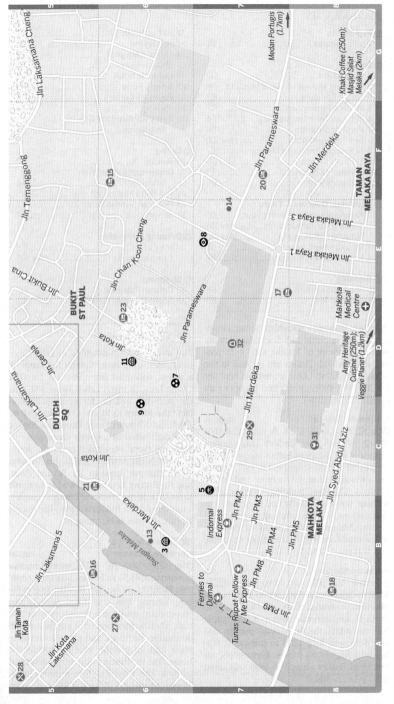

Melaka City

⊚ **Top Sights**
1 Villa Sentosa...D1

⊚ **Sights**
2 Bukit China... G2
3 Maritime Museum & Naval Museum... B6
4 Masjid Kampung Hulu..........................B3
5 Menara Taming Sari..............................C7
6 Poh San Teng Temple............................F4
7 Porta de Santiago................................. D6
   Sky Tower Malacca.................... (see 33)
8 St Francis' Institution Melaka..............E7
9 St Paul's Church.................................. C6
10 St Peter's Church.................................. E1
11 Sultanate Palace D6

⊕ **Activities, Courses & Tours**
12 Kampung Morten Walking Tour...........D1
   Kristang Culinary Journey...........(see 19)
   Malacca Night Cycling............... (see 22)
13 Melaka River Cruise............................. B6
14 Nonya Culinary Journey.......................E7

⊜ **Sleeping**
15 Apa Kaba Home & Stay.........................F6
16 Casa Del Rio.. B5

17 Hatten Hotel... E7
18 Holiday Inn..B8
19 Majestic Malacca..................................E1
20 Melaka House F7
21 Quayside Hotel....................................C5
22 Ringo's Foyer..B3
23 Rucksack Caratel...................................D6
24 Sterling... E4
25 Swiss-Garden Hotel &
   Residences D1

⊗ **Eating**
26 Bulldog E2
27 Green House Vegetarian
   Restaurant A6
28 Pak Putra Restaurant..........................A5
29 Restoran Nyonya Suan.........................C7
30 Selvam D4

⊚ **Drinking & Nightlife**
31 Mixx...C8
   Pampas Sky Bar ....(see 33)

⊙ **Shopping**
32 Dataran Pahlawan...............................D7
33 Shore Shopping Gallery.......................D1

chamber atop this 80m-high tower slowly rotates as it ascends and descends, allowing panoramic views of Melaka City, with binoculars provided. Tickets are on sale in the adjacent building. Other attractions here are the 3D Mini Rider (RM5) and bumper cars (adult/child RM10/5).

Sultanate Palace MUSEUM
(Map p220; ☎06-282 6526; Jln Kota; adult/child RM5/2; ⊗9am-5.30pm Tue-Sun) This wooden replica of the palace of Sultan Mansur Shah, who ruled Melaka from 1456 to 1477, houses an open-air cultural museum and lovely gardens. The fine buildings were crafted without the use of nails and closely follow descriptions of the original palace from *Sejarah Melayu* (Malay Annals), a chronicle of the establishment of the Malay sultanate and 600 years of Malay history.

Porta de Santiago RUINS
(A'Famosa; Map p220; Jln Kota; ⊗24hr) FREE Most visitors pause for a photo here before hiking to the ruined church on Bukit St Paul. Porta de Santiago was built as a Portuguese fortress in 1511; the British took over in 1641 and destroyed it in 1806 to prevent it falling into Napoleon's hands. Fortunately, Sir Stamford Raffles arrived in 1810 and saved what remains today.

⊙ **'Chinatown'**

The so-called 'Chinatown' is Melaka City's most interesting area, though the name is a recent, colloquial invention. Jln Tun Tan Cheng Lock, formerly called Heeren St, was the preferred address for wealthy Peranakan (also known as Straits Chinese) traders. Jln Hang Jebat, formerly known as Jonker St, is dominated by souvenir shops and restaurants; every weekend it hosts the Jonker Walk Night Market (p233). Jln Tokong, which changes name to Jln Tukang Emas and Jln Tukang Besi as you head from north to south, is home to several Chinese temples, a mosque and an Indian temple – the reason it is also known as Harmony St.

★ **Baba & Nyonya Heritage Museum** MUSEUM
(Map p218; ☎06-282 1273; www.babanyonyamuseum.com; 48-50 Jln Tun Tan Cheng Lock; adult/child RM16/11; ⊗10am-5pm Mon-Thu, to 6pm Fri-Sun) Touring this traditional Baba-Nonya (Peranakan) townhouse transports you to a time when women peered at guests through decorative partitions and every social situation had its specific location within the house. The captivating museum is arranged to look like a typical 19th-century Baba-Nonya residence. Tour guides (an extra

RM4; every half-hour) enliven the setting with their arch sense of humour.

Cheng Hoon Teng Temple TEMPLE

(Qing Yun Ting or Green Clouds Temple; Map p218; ☑06-282 9343; www.chenghoonteng.org.my; 25 Jln Tokong; ⊙7am-7pm) FREE Malaysia's oldest still-operating Chinese temple, constructed in 1673, remains a central place of worship for the Buddhist and Taoist communities here. It's also a testament to the perseverance of the local Chinese community which funded its restoration. Traditional methods were used throughout, from the ornate roof ceramics to the painted tigers by the door. Though the temple is dedicated to Kuan Yin, the goddess of mercy, it is also a multifaith temple, with Buddhist, Taoist and Confucian elements and effigies.

Masjid Kampung Kling MOSQUE

(Map p218; cnr Jln Hang Lekiu & Jln Tukang Emas) FREE Originally dating back to 1748, the 19th-century rebuild of the mosque you see today mingles several styles. Its multi-tiered *meru* roof (a stacked form similar to that seen in Balinese Hindu architecture) owes its inspiration to Hindu temples, the Moorish watchtower minaret is typical of early mosques in Sumatra, while English and Dutch tiles bedeck its interior. Admission times vary; dress modestly and, if you're female, bring a scarf.

Sri Poyatha Venayagar Moorthi Temple HINDU TEMPLE

(Map p218; Jln Tukang Emas) FREE One of the first Hindu temples built in Malaysia, this temple was constructed in 1781 on a plot donated by the religiously tolerant Dutch and dedicated to the Hindu deity Venayagar. The building adds a dash of Indian colour and spiritual variety to 'Harmony St'.

Masjid Kampung Hulu MOSQUE

(Map p220; cnr Jln Masjid & Jln Kampung Hulu) The oldest functioning mosque in Malaysia was, surprisingly, commissioned by the Dutch in 1728. The mosque is made up of predominantly Javanese architecture with a multi-tiered roof in place of the standard dome (at the time of construction, domes and minarets had not yet come into fashion). It's not particularly well set up for visitors, but this Chinatown icon is worth admiring from outside.

8 Heeren Street HISTORIC BUILDING

(Map p218; www.badanwarisanmalaysia.org/visit-us/no-8-heeren-street; 8 Jln Tun Tan Cheng Lock; ⊙11am-4pm) FREE This 18th-century, Dutch-period residential house was restored as a model conservation project. A guide is on hand to explain the features and history behind this airy two-storey building. Entry is free, but donations are appreciated. Opening hours can be spotty.

Zheng He Duo Yun Xuan GALLERY

(Map p218; ☑06-282 6966; 42A & 44A Lg Hang Jebat; ⊙9.30am-6pm) FREE A Shanghai-based auction house has funded this impressive gallery split between two large converted warehouses facing the Melaka River and entered from the path running alongside the water. Exhibitions (at which some of the works are for sale) change roughly every three weeks and focus mainly on Chinese arts and culture.

Cheng Ho Cultural Museum MUSEUM

(Map p218; ☑06-283 1135; www.chengho.org/museum; 51 Lg Hang Jebat; adult/child RM20/10; ⊙9am-6pm) The impressive exploits of Chinese-Muslim seafarer Cheng Ho (Zheng He) are celebrated through this museum's dioramas and maritime miscellany. The Ming admiral's tremendous voyages make for interesting reading, though the level of detail in this multi-floor museum wearies after a while. Still, it's a good excuse to wander through a Chinese mansion, complete with swaying lanterns and furnishings embossed with mother-of-pearl.

◉ North of the City Centre

★ Villa Sentosa HISTORIC BUILDING

(Peaceful Villa; Map p220; ☑06-282 3988; Jln Kampung Morten; entry by donation; ⊙hours vary, usually 9am-1pm & 2-6pm) The highlight of visiting the charming Malay village of Kampung Morten (p225) is this living museum within a 1920s *kampung* (village) house. Visitors (or rather, guests) are welcomed by a member of the household who points out period objects, including photographs of family members, Ming dynasty ceramics and a century-old Quran. You're unlikely to leave without a photo op on plush velvet furniture or striking the gong a few times for luck.

Sky Tower Malacca VIEWPOINT

(Map p220; ☑06-288 3833; www.skytower.theshoremelaka.com; 193 Pinggiran @ Sungai Melaka, Jln Persisiran Bunga Raya; adult/child RM25/18; ⊙10.30am-9.30pm Sun-Thu, to 10.30pm Fri & Sat) Starting on the 43rd floor of the Shore complex and going up to the building's roof, this is – at 153m – Melaka City's highest viewpoint. The panorama of the city is impressive and there are added thrills in the form of a vertigo-inducing glass-floor balcony over the edge where you can have your fear-filled face snapped for posterity.

Bukit China
CEMETERY

(Map p220; Jln Puteri Hang Li Poh) More than 12,500 graves, including about 20 Muslim tombs, cover the 25 grassy hectares of serene 'Chinese Hill'. In the middle of the 15th century, the sultan of Melaka married the Ming emperor's daughter in a move to seal relations with China. She brought with her a vast retinue, including 500 handmaidens, who settled around Bukit China. It has been a Chinese area ever since.

Since the time of British rule, there have been several attempts to acquire Bukit China for road widening, land reclamation or development purposes. Fortunately, Cheng Hoon Teng Temple (p223), with strong community support, has thwarted these attempts.

At the base of the hill is **Poh San Teng Temple** (⊙ 7am-6pm). 'Precious Hill Temple' was built around 1795 and is dedicated to the guardian deity Tua Pek Kong. To the right of the temple is King's Well, a 15th-century well built by Sultan Mansur Shah.

St Peter's Church
CHURCH

(Map p220; ☑ 06-282 2950; 166 Jln Bendahara; ⊙ 8am-1pm Mon, 6.30am-3pm Tue-Fri, 8am-1pm & 4-7pm Sat, 8am-1pm Sun) **FREE** This is the oldest functioning Roman Catholic church in Malaysia, built in 1710 by descendants of early Portuguese settlers. It's quite an elegant picture in its repainted state, while the church bell is the oldest object in the house of worship and was cast in Goa in 1608. The Latin words *Tu es Petrus* ('You are Peter') are above the apse.

◉ Kampung Chetti

As well as the Peranakan community, Melaka City also has a small contingent of Chetti – Straits-born Indians, offspring of the Indian traders who intermarried with Malay women. Arriving in the 1400s, the Chetties are regarded as older than the Chinese-Malay Peranakan community.

Their traditional village, Kampung Chetti, lies west of Jln Gajah Berang, about 1km northwest of Chinatown; look for the archway with elephant sculptures opposite where Jln Gajah Berang meets Jln Kampong Empat. The best time to visit this colourful neighbourhood is during Hindu festivals such as the Mariamman Festival (Pesta Datuk Charchar) in late April or early May.

Chetti Museum
MUSEUM

(☑ 06-281 1289; Jln Gajah Berang; adult/child RM2/1; ⊙ 9am-1pm & 2-5pm Tue-Sun) This small museum is a community effort with a collection of artefacts, including antique *cendol* (shaved-ice dessert with green noodles, syrups, fruit and coconut milk) makers and embroidered wedding garb. There are excellent English-language explanations about the Chetti language and rites of passage, plus news clippings about local efforts to preserve Chetti heritage.

Sri Subramaniam Thuropathai Amman Alayam
TEMPLE

(Jln Gajah Berang, Kampung Chetti; ⊙ 7.30am-10pm) **FREE** A huge *gopuram* (tower), as elaborate and pink as a tiered wedding cake, erupts from this temple. Few visitors come here, but if you shed your shoes you can marvel at exterior statues of Surya with his chariot pulled by seven horses, and at a rainbow of enamelled decorations inside.

◉ Little India

East of Chinatown on the opposite side of the river is the surprisingly plain Little India. While it's not nearly as charming as the historic centre or Chinatown, this busy area along Jln Bendahara and Jln Temenggong is a worthwhile place to soak up some Indian sensations and grab a banana-leaf meal.

🏃 Activities

Reflexology centres are plentiful in Chinatown. A half-hour foot massage costs from RM25, but it's often worth paying a few extra ringgit for a quality experience.

Puri Spa
SPA

(Map p218; ☑ 06-282 5588; www.hotelpuri.com; Hotel Puri, 118 Jln Tun Tan Cheng Lock; ⊙ 10am-7pm) Set in a sensual garden, this spa isn't a walk-in like Jonker St's casual reflexology outlets. The reward for booking ahead is the menu of treatments, including steams, scrubs, facials and milk baths. Aromatherapy foot treatments (45 minutes) start at RM68, a 60-minute scalp massage and hair treatment is RM128, while a 60-minute exfoliating and moisturising body wrap is RM188.

🍽 Courses

Kristang Culinary Journey
COOKING

(Map p220; ☑ 06-289 8000; www.majesticmalacca. com; Majestic Malacca Hotel, 188 Jln Bunga Raya; 1st person RM380, subsequent people RM290) Learn about each ingredient and the history of each Kristang (Portuguese-Eurasian) dish with one of the chefs (usually chef Melba, who does most of the cooking at Majestic Malacca Hotel). Book one week in advance. There's no minimum number, but there's a maximum of four people. This activity includes a market trip, cooking class and lunch.

Nancy's Kitchen COOKING
(✑06-283 6099; www.eatatnancyskit.com; 13 Jln KL 3/8, Taman Kota Laksamana Seksyen 3; per person RM180) Nancy of this near-legendary Peranakan restaurant teaches cookery classes by request. Reserve well in advance.

Nonya Culinary Journey COOKING
(Map p220; ✑Hotel Equatorial 06-282 8333; Seri Nyonya Restaurant, Hotel Equatorial, Jln Parameswara; per person RM150) These two-hour cooking classes include a set lunch and a certificate of completion. You'll cook three Peranakan (Nonya) dishes, including specialities such as *ayam pong teh* (miso soy chicken) and *udang lemak nenas* (prawns with pineapple and spicy coconut), hands-on with the chef. Advanced booking is required. Times are 10am to noon (with lunch) or 2pm to 4pm (with dinner).

☞ Tours

Old Melaka Heritage Tour WALKING
(Map p218; Tourism Malaysia, Jln Merdeka; ⊙9am Tue, Thu & Sat) FREE Lasting around 2½ hours, this guided walk sets off from Tourism Malaysia's office beside Dutch Sq and takes in the key sights of the Unesco Heritage area, including Bukit St Paul and Chinatown.

Malacca Night Cycling CYCLING
(Map p220; ✑016-668 8898; 46A Jln Portugis; per person RM35) Operating out of Ringo's Foyer (p226), these guided cycling tours through Melaka City will test your trishaw-dodging skills. It's more pleasant to tour the city in the evening, when the temperature drops. Tours leave by arrangement at 8.30pm and last 90 minutes (or longer, if you like), generally on a weekday. Call a day or two in advance to book.

Kampung Morten Walking Tour WALKING
(Map p220; Jln Kampung Morten; ⊙4pm Mon, Wed & Fri) FREE Protected by a bend in the Melaka River, Kampung Morten is a charming village of 85 homes, including 52 in traditional Melakan style. These free guided tours leave from Villa Sentosa (p223); as long as you don't arrive at the same time as a tour bus, walking around is a relaxing experience and you'll meet plenty of welcoming people.

SUNGAI MELAKA & CHINATOWN STREET ART

Some efforts have been made by the Melaka authorities to create pleasant walkways alongside Sungai Melaka (Melaka River) between Chinatown and Kampung Morten. Along the route you'll pass many colourful and creative murals on building walls. Images include those of Melaka's founder Parameswara and Ming dynasty princess Hang Li Po. The alley leading to the river at the end of Jln Tukang Besi in Chinatown looks like a child's picture book come to life, while on the corner of Jln Hang Kasturi and Jln Kampung Pantai you'll find horses galloping up the street in the style of classical Chinese painting. For some real wildlife, look out for the huge monitor lizards seeking shade under the boardwalk!

Melaka River Cruise CRUISE
(Map p220; ✑06-286 5468, 06-281 4322; www.melakarivercruise.my; Jln Merdeka; adult/child RM23/10; ⊙9am-11.30pm) The most convenient place to board this 40-minute riverboat cruise along Sungai Melaka is at the quay near the Maritime Museum (p218). Cruises go 9km upriver past Kampung Morten and old *godown* (river warehouses) with a recorded narration explaining the riverfront's history. Kids under the age of two go free.

Eco Bike Tour CYCLING
(✑019-652 5029; www.melakaonbike.com; half-day per person RM100) Explore the fascinating landscape around Melaka City with Alias on his three-hour bike tour (minimum two people) through 20km of oil-palm and rubber-tree plantations and *kampung* communities. Book at least three days in advance and flag your level of fitness. Pick-ups are from your accommodation. The day trip is RM180 per person (minimum four people).

★ Festivals & Events

Melaka City celebrates all the major Malaysian holidays, including Chinese New Year, but the city's significant Christian population means that holidays such as Christmas and Easter are also important here.

Masimugam Festival RELIGIOUS
(Jln Tukang Emas; ⊙Feb) A Melakan version of Thaipusam, just as gory but without the crowds, takes place shortly after Chinese New Year. A procession heads from

Sri Poyatha Venayagar Moorthi Temple in Chinatown to Kampong Cheng, about 15km outside Melaka City.

Melaka Historical City Day   CULTURAL
(⊙ Apr) There's a public holiday on 15 April to celebrate the founding of Melaka.

Vesak Day Parade   RELIGIOUS
(⊙ May) Vesak Day celebrates the birth, enlightenment and death of Buddha on the first full moon of the fourth month of the Chinese calendar. It's marked in Melaka City with a large and colourful parade that goes along various streets, including Jln Tun Tan Cheng Lock in Chinatown.

Festa San Juan   RELIGIOUS
(Medan Portugis; ⊙ late Jun) The Eurasian community celebrates this festival by lighting candles in the Portuguese Settlement.

Dragon Boat Festival   CULTURAL
(⊙ Jun/Jul) This Chinese festival (known by the Chinese as Duanwu Jie) is marked by a dragon-boat race on Sungai Melaka (Melaka River). It commemorates the death by drowning of 3rd-century BC Chinese poet and statesman, Qu Yuan.

Festa Santa Cruz   RELIGIOUS
(⊙ mid-Sep) This festival honours a miraculous cross with Catholics conducting a candlelight procession to Santa Cruz Chapel on Malim Hill, about 7km north of central Melaka City.

Melaka Art & Performance Festival   ART
(www.melakafestival.com; Bukit St Paul; ⊙ Nov) This performance, arts and film fest draws artists from around the world to liven up Bukit St Paul and Melaka City's historical sites for three days in late November.

Medan Portugis Christmas Lights   CHRISTMAS
(Medan Portugis; ⊙ Dec) Melakans descend on Medan Portugis (Portuguese Square) to view the brightly decorated homes.

🛌 Sleeping

The accommodation scene here is ever-changing, with new places popping up as frequently as others wind down. The quality is the best it's been in years; as well as hotels and hostels across different price ranges, there's a good range of rental properties in characterful heritage buildings. Chinatown is the best area to be based in or near, although it can get busy and noisy, particularly at weekends. From hostels to top-end hotels, rates rise at weekends.

🏠 'Chinatown'

★ Nomaps   HOSTEL $
(Map p218; ☎ 06-283 8311; www.thenomaps.com; 11 Jln Tun Tan Cheng Lock; dm R70-100, d from RM150, with shared bathroom RM250, all incl breakfast; P ❄ @ 🛜) This is a step up for Melaka's hostel options. The attractive street art of Kenji Chai decorates the walls of this otherwise minimalist flashpackers in a key Chinatown location. Six- and four-bed dorms are tiny but have colourful duvets and quality mattresses. Free laundry and a comfy TV room are other pluses.

Layang-Layang   GUESTHOUSE $
(Map p218; ☎ 06-292 2722; www.layanglayang melaka.com; 24-26 Jln Tukang Besi; r from RM93; ❄ 🛜) An arty boho vibe in the common areas and a tranquil, whitewashed courtyard give this budget 20-room guesthouse an edge. Guests can rent bikes for a bargain RM5 a day, too. The street the guesthouse is on was formerly known as 'Blacksmith' Street, while the building itself once served as an opium den and brothel.

Cafe 1511 Guesthouse   GUESTHOUSE $
(Map p218; ☎ 06-286 0150; 52 Jln Tun Tan Cheng Lock; s/d with shared bathroom incl breakfast from RM60/90, weekend s/d incl breakfast from RM70/100; @ 🛜) As well as operating a very charming cafe on the ground floor, this old Peranakan mansion right in the heart of town has six small, simple, very clean rooms for overnight stays. The place has an old-style feeling accompanied by the music of a water fountain in the light well that extends from the restaurant below.

Ringo's Foyer   GUESTHOUSE $
(Map p220; ☎ 016-668 8898, 06-281 6393; www. ringosfoyer.com; 46A Jln Portugis; dm/d/q incl breakfast from RM38/80/140; ❄ 🛜) The friendly owners do a great job of keeping the atmosphere sociable here, particularly in the rooftop cafe and hang-out areas. Beds in the 18-bed dorm are pod-style, allowing reasonable privacy. With bike rental, free lockers, laundry (RM5 per kilo) and guitars, this place has everything a weary backpacker could want.

Rooftop Guesthouse   HOSTEL $
(Map p218; ☎ 012-327 7746, 012-380 7211; rooftopguesthouse@yahoo.com; 39 Jln Kampung Pantai; dm RM93, dm/d/tr with shared bathroom RM25/63/84; ❄) This hostel is simple but hits the spot with decent air-con, a choice of dorm room or private accommodation, and a bird's-eye view from the roof terrace, plus free tea and coffee in the kitchen.

★**Wayfarer Guest House** GUESTHOUSE **$$**
(Map p218; ☎06-281 9469; www.wayfarermelaka.
com; 104 Lorong Hang Jebat; r RM132-222; ❄️🌐) Situated by the river, this welcoming Hakka-family-run guesthouse is set up in a former rubber trading house, with seven charming wood-floored rooms. The riverview rooms – 1 and 6 – are the most popular, but come in at a bit of a premium (worth it). Prices rise by around RM40 to RM50 at the weekend.

★**Hotel Puri** HOTEL **$$**
(Map p218; ☎06-282 5588; www.hotelpuri.com; 118 Jln Tun Tan Cheng Lock; d/tr/q/f from RM188/310/380/430, all incl breakfast; ❄️@🌐) Why merely tour one of Melaka's heritage buildings when you can stay overnight in one? Inhabiting a superbly renovated 1822 Peranakan mansion, this hotel has an elaborate lobby with beautiful old cane and inlaid furniture, opening to a lush courtyard garden with a fountain. Rooms have crisp sheets, shuttered windows and a regal crimson-and-white colour scheme.

Bridge Loft RENTAL HOUSE **$$**
(Map p218; ☎012-681 2719; www.thebridgeloft.com; 5 Lg Jambatan; house RM180-380; ❄️@🌐) One of the more affordable house-rental options in Melaka City is Bridge Loft, which rents out rooms in three cosy shophouses steps from the Melaka River. Each is simply but tastefully furnished and sleeps between two and six people. You can grab breakfast in the cute cafe beneath unit number 5.

Gingerflower BOUTIQUE HOTEL **$$**
(Map p218; ☎06-288 1331; www.gingerflowerboutiquehotel.com; 13 Jln Tun Tan Cheng Lock; d incl breakfast from RM210; ❄️🌐) Rooms are rather small, but period fittings and immaculate housekeeping make this restored 13-room Peranakan townhouse a very pleasant place to stay. It's a few paces from the Jonker St hubbub and well placed for gallery and museum visits along Jln Tun Tan Cheng Lock.

Courtyard@Heeren BOUTIQUE HOTEL **$$**
(Map p218; ☎06-281 0088; www.courtyardatheeren.com; 91 Jln Tun Tan Cheng Lock; d & tw RM200, ste RM300, all incl breakfast; ❄️🌐) Professionally run with great service, this welcoming choice has each room decorated with an individual touch, with light and bright decor paired with antique wood furniture. Some rooms have minimalist stained-glass details, modern takes on Chinese latticework or luxuriant drapes; windows face onto an interior courtyard. Rates increase at weekends by at least RM60, depending on the type of room.

Heeren House GUESTHOUSE **$$**
(Map p218; ☎06-281 4241; www.heerenhouse.com; 1 Jln Tun Tan Cheng Lock; s/d/q incl breakfast from RM139/159/269; ❄️🌐) The traditional furnishings of this prime-location hotel have a nostalgic air, while the family-run vibe and hearty breakfasts infuse the place with a homely feel. The six airy and clean rooms in this former warehouse largely overlook the river. Not all rooms pick up the wi-fi signal from the lobby. The hotel also has a good cafe.

★**45 Lekiu** RENTAL HOUSE **$$$**
(Map p218; ☎016-274 9686, 012-698 4917; www.45lekiu.com; 45 Jln Hang Lekiu; weekdays/weekends RM1299/1499; ❄️🌐🏊) Sleeping four, this gorgeously restored shophouse has kept the big old beams and original exposed brickwork but has been updated with stylish contemporary decor. Highlights include a bougainvillea-filled courtyard with a dipping pool and a roof terrace overlooking the city; cooking facilities are available.

The same company also rents the similar luxe restorations **Stables** (Map p218; ☎012-698 4917, 016-274 9686; www.thestablemalacca.com; D Jln Hang Kasturi; r weekdays/weekends RM380/480; ❄️🌐) and **Opposite Place** (Map p218; ☎016-274 9686, 012-698 4917; www.opposite-place.com; 18 Jln Hang Lekiu; r weekday from RM499-599, weekend from 599-699, incl breakfast; ❄️🌐).

Casa Del Rio HOTEL **$$$**
(Map p220; ☎06-289 6888; www.casadelrio-melaka.com; 88 Jln Kota Laksmana; r/ste incl breakfast from RM665/1574; ❄️@🌐🏊) With a fabulous location right on the river and steps from Chinatown, Casa Del Rio has palatial architecture that blends Portuguese/Mediterranean with Malaysian for a result that's airy and grand. Rooms are massive, with bathrooms fit for a Portuguese princess, and river-view rooms capture the feel of Asia and Venice combined.

🛏️ Jalan Merdeka & Around

Quayside Hotel HOTEL **$$**
(Map p220; ☎06-284 1001; www.quaysidehotel.com.my; 1 Jln Merdeka; tw/d from RM132/169, ste 285-395, all incl breakfast; ❄️@🌐) Occupying an airy, former customs warehouse in a key location, Quayside combines contemporary style with great value. Rooms are spacious and modern, with wooden floors and big beds; the best suites and rooms have balconies or river views, while the cheapest offer city views. Breakfast is served in the attached Halia Inc restaurant.

Holiday Inn
HOTEL $$

(Map p222; ☑ 06-285 9000; www.holidayinnmelaka. com; Jln Syed Abdul Aziz; r from RM348; ⊞❄@ ☎☒) Holiday Inn promises chain-brand reliability and comfort if not the most snazzy ambience. The generously sized rooms are not the most charming you'll find in town, but they are modern and comfortable enough, the staff is keen to assist and it's value for money.

Sterling
HOTEL $$

(Map p220; ☑ 06-283 1188; www.thesterling.com. my; 43 Jln Temenggong; r from RM250; ⊞❄☎) You may need to shield your eyes against this blinding-white behemoth of a hotel. Though billed as colonial-style, with rooms named after British icons like Winston Churchill and Brighton Beach, the spacious rooms are more business-Ikea-chic than awash in history. The bathrooms gleam and there are great views from the rooftop restaurant.

Hatten Hotel
HOTEL $$

(Map p220; ☑ 06-286 9696; www.hattenhotel. com; Hatten Square, Jln Merdeka; r from RM238; ⊞❄☎☒) A marbled reception area with velvet sofas and a chandelier promises much, but the cheapest rooms have windows onto internal air wells so you'll need to spend a bit more for a view of the city or the strait. There's a large pool on the 12th floor and sweeping views from Alto Sky Lounge on the 22nd floor.

🏘 Little India to Bukit China

Apa Kaba Home & Stay
GUESTHOUSE $

(Map p220; ☑ 012-798 1232, 06-283 8196; www.apa-kaba.com; 28 Kg Banda Kaba; d with shared bathroom RM52-82, tw/tr with shared bathroom from RM52/71, all incl breakfast; ❄☎) This tranquil homestay has a low-key *kampung* setting, but is within walking distance of central Melaka City. The 1912 building is a mishmash of Malay and Chinese styles. Its seven rooms (the more expensive have air-con) are arranged around the reception on the ground floor. Completing the picture are a large garden with mango trees and a house cat.

Melaka House
GUESTHOUSE $

(Map p220; ☑ 012-588 6000, 012-639 6820; 52 Jln Parameswara; dm/d/tw RM40/68/68, entire house RM788; ☎) This lovely place in an old traditional home is very good value and away from the crowds. There's a kitchen with free coffee, a decent lounge area, and the double rooms are simple but comfy. The owners are a mine of information and it's only a 15-minute walk into the heritage district.

★ Rucksack Caratel
BOUTIQUE HOTEL $

(Map p220; ☑ 06-292 2107; www.therucksackgroup. com; 107 Jln Banda Kaba; r incl breakfast from RM90; ⊞☎☒) There's a fun flashpacker vibe at this great budget choice. The cheapest rooms are in mock 'caravans' on the ground floor, each given a famous star's name and decorated with their portrait. Pricier rooms offer king-sized beds and views of the neighbouring lush gardens of Sultanate Palace (p222).

If it's full, ask after Rucksack's excellent Jonker Wing accommodation on nearby Jln Laksamana.

★ 1825 Gallery Hotel
BOUTIQUE HOTEL $$

(Map p218; ☑ 06-288 2868; www.1825galleryhotel. com; 27-31 Jln Bunga Raya; r from RM151; ❄☎) Three shophouses built in 1825 have been combined to create this classy hotel. Original features such as lofty ceilings, brick walls and wood beams harmonise with contemporary art, reclaimed-wood furniture and a waterfall splashing into a fish-filled pond in the lobby. Opt for a river suite with balcony overlooking the Melaka River, or check the view you'll be getting.

★ Majestic Malacca
BOUTIQUE HOTEL $$$

(Map p220; ☑ 06-289 8000; www.majesticmalacca. com; 188 Jln Bunga Raya; r incl breakfast from RM568; ❄@☎☒) Claw-foot tubs and polished four-poster beds are just some of the trappings at this regal hotel. The bar, library and dining areas groan with nostalgia (think ornate Peranakan screens and gleaming teak furniture), while a small pool and richly endowed spa area add to the opulent feel. It's mere steps from Kampung Morten and a five-minute walk to Little India.

Swiss-Garden Hotel & Residences
HOTEL $$$

(Map p220; ☑ 06-288 3131; www.swissgarden.com; T2, The Shore @ Melaka River, Jln Persisiran Bunga Raya; r/ste from RM700/1170; ⊞❄@☎☒) Swiss-Garden occupies part of the swanky Shore development. Rooms are slickly designed and spacious with all the amenities you could wish for. It also manages some of the residency units in the attached apartment block; both the hotel and the units have access to a large central pool and gym facilities.

🍴 Eating

Peranakan cuisine is Melaka City's most famous type of cooking. It's also known as Nonya (or Nyonya), an affectionate term for a Peranakan wife (often the family chef). You'll also find Portuguese Eurasian food, Indian, Chinese and more.

✕ 'Chinatown' & Around

★ Navy Cafe INTERNATIONAL $
(Map p218; www.facebook.com/navycafe; 5 Jln Hang Lekiu; mains from RM8; ⊙9am-6pm; 🛜) A lovely place for a scrambled egg breakfast, smoothie bowl or moreish lunch, the food at this small cafe is tops. Dishes regularly change, but stewed white fish with Japanese tofu, salmon and egg *donburi* and savoury chicken burger, along with sandwiches and salads, are all a hit. Wash it all down with an iced coffee.

★ Seeds Garden VEGETARIAN $
(Map p218; ☑ 017-363 9626; www.seedsgarden. com.my; 60 Jln Tokong; mains RM13-15; ⊙11.30am-3.30pm & 6-9pm Thu-Tue; 🍴) Among the spate of veggie restaurants that appear to be blooming across Melaka, this quiet and civilised nook is certainly the trendiest looking. With just two rooms, this good-looking little sanctuary is perfect for a bowl of pumpkin soup, baked mushroom salad or a vegan pizza.

Nancy's Kitchen MALAYSIAN $
(☎ 06-283 6099; www.eatatnancyskit.com; 13 Jln KL 3/8, Taman Kota Laksamana; mains from RM10; ⊙11am-5pm Sun-Mon & Wed-Thu, to 9pm Fri & Sat) The Peranakan (Nonya) cuisine here has a dedicated following, but service can be a bit curt and a wait is inevitable at weekends. However, many consider it worth it for the juicy pork fried with bean curd or signature candlenut chicken dish – simmered in a nutty sauce, fragrant with lemongrass. Buy some *kuih* (sticky-rice sweets) on your way out.

Low Yong Moh CHINESE $
(Map p218; ☑ 06-282 1235; 32 Jln Tukang Emas; dim sum RM2.50-4; ⊙5.30am-noon Wed-Mon) Famous across Melaka for its large and well-stuffed *pao* (steamed pork buns; also known as *bao*), this place is Chinatown's biggest breakfast treat. With high ceilings, plenty of fans running and a view of Masjid Kampung Kling (p223), the atmosphere oozes charm. It's usually packed with talkative, newspaper-reading locals by around 7am. Food offerings thin out by 11am, so arrive early.

Shui Xian Vegetarian CHINESE $
(Map p218; ☑ 012-635 8052; 43 Jln Hang Lekiu; mains RM3-6; ⊙7.30am-2.30pm Mon-Sat; 🍴) In a city where vegetable dishes so often arrive strewn with shrimp or pork, vegetarians can breathe a sigh of relief here. With bamboo sprouting out front, this no-frills canteen whips up mock meat versions of *char kway teow* (broad noodles, clams and eggs fried in

chilli and black bean sauce), laksa and even 'chicken' rice balls. The name means 'Water Immortal' vegetarian restaurant.

Pak Putra Restaurant PAKISTANI $
(Map p220; ☑ 012-601 5876; 58 Jln Kota Laksamana 4; mains RM10-12; ⊙5.30pm-1am, closed alternate Mon; 🍴) Scarlet tikka chickens rotate hypnotically on skewers, luring diners to this excellent Pakistani restaurant. With aromatic vegetarian dishes, seafood and piquant curries, there's no shortage of choice (try the garlic chilli chicken). The unchallenged highlights are oven-puffed naan bread and chicken fresh from the clay tandoor. Portions are generous, but you may need to queue.

Green House Vegetarian Restaurant VEGETARIAN $
(Map p220; ☑ 011-1073 1188; www.facebook.com/greenhousemalacca; 4 Jln Kota Laksamana 1; mains RM10; ⊙11.30am-3.30pm & 5.30-9.30pm; 🍴) This restaurant serves tasty vegetarian versions of traditional meat dishes such as Hong Kong roasted goose and *char siew*. If you don't fancy mock-meat dishes, there are plenty of other dishes that can be cooked just to your liking, such as a mixed vegetables curry, Hokkien noodles or hot and spicy noodles.

Cafe 1511 CAFE $
(Map p218; ☑ 06-286 0150; 52 Jln Tun Tan Cheng Lock; mains from RM6; ⊙9am-5pm Mon-Wed & Fri-Sun) This charming, relaxing and heritage-feel cafe has round marble-top tables and a fan-cooled ambience. The room itself once served as the servants quarters of the building that now houses the Baba & Nyonya Heritage Museum (p222) next door. The cafe serves a menu of Nonya dishes and international bites. Accommodation is available here at Cafe 1511 Guesthouse (p226).

Jonker 88 DESSERTS $
(Map p218; 88 Jln Hang Jebat; mains RM6-10.50; ⊙11am-10pm Tue-Thu, to 11pm Fri & Sat, to 9pm Sun) Slurp-worthy laksa and decent Peranakan fare are served at this efficient and busy canteen. But the highlight is its *cendol*, which comes in a fabulous selection of flavours and toppings.

★ Salud Tapas SPANISH $$
(Map p218; ☑ 06-282 9881; www.facebook.com/saludtapas; 94 Jln Tun Tan Cheng Lock; tapas/mains from RM15.50/48; ⊙2pm-midnight Wed-Thu, 1pm-midnight Fri-Sun, 3pm-midnight Mon; 🛜) This tapas bar is very authentic and its inner courtyard is a cooling place to sip a sangria. It helps that the chef is Spanish, and imports

MELAKA MELAKA CITY

DON'T MISS

JONKER WALK'S HAWKER CRAWL

The best reason for elbowing your way through the crowds that descend on Jonker Walk Night Market (p233) is to graze on its lip-smacking range of local hawker food. Look out for the following treats.

Kuih nonya Coconut milk and sticky-rice sweets, too colourful to resist.

Dodol Jellies made from the seaweed agar agar in *gula melaka* (palm sugar), pandan and durian flavours.

Fried quail eggs A skewer of little eggs, laden with curry or sweetcorn, cooked on a griddle.

Pineapple tarts Buttery pastries with a chewy jam filling.

Popiah Spring rolls without the crunch, stuffed with shredded veggies, prawns, garlic and more.

Watermelon slushies Whole watermelons are punctured with two big holes; the contents mushed up with an electric whisk and ice.

ingredients and recipes from back home; the open kitchen is a winning ingredient too. Nibble tapas and a platter of *ibérico* ham or splurge on a full meal such as paella.

The restaurant serves drinks till 1am and there's a bar open upstairs at the weekend.

★**Kocik Kitchen**　　　　　PERANAKAN $$
(Map p218; ☑016-929 6605; 100 Jln Tun Tan Cheng Lock; mains RM20-30; ☺11am-6.30pm Mon, Tue & Thu, 11am-10pm Fri & Sat, 11am-7.30pm Sun) This unassuming but lovely little restaurant is making waves in Melaka. Try the creamy *lemak nenas* prawns, swimming in fragrant coconut milk with fresh chunks of pineapple, but don't forget the lovely Nonya *cendol*. The set lunch (RM12 to RM15) is a bargain. Booking up front is advised.

★**Baboon House**　　　　　BURGERS $$
(Map p218; ☑012-938 6013; 89 Jln Tun Tan Cheng Lock; burgers RM15; ☺10am-5pm Mon & Wed-Sun; 🐱) If gourmet burgers, such as Greek-style spicy lamb or the signature Baboon pork belly, sound like a pleasant change from taste bud–searing Indian or Peranakan cuisine, make a beeline to Baboon House for a memorable meal. The food and setting – in a time-worn shophouse with a plant-filled courtyard and light wells – is delightful, hence the unending popularity and plaudits.

Eat at 18　　　　　INTERNATIONAL $$
(Map p218; ☑06-281 4679; www.eat18.com; 18 Jln Hang Lekiu; breakfast from RM16, mains from RM25; ☺8.30am-6pm Wed-Mon) This charming cafe/restaurant – behind a tangle of vegetation – is a welcome option for a bowl of nourishing mushroom soup, a Cajun chicken burger, beef stew or for starting your morning off

on the right foot with delicious pancakes or French toast. When you're done admiring the brickwork, try to work out the cryptic wrought-iron code on the wall.

✗ Jalan Merdeka & Around

★**Veggie Planet**　　　　　VEGETARIAN $
(☑06-292 2819; www.veggieplanet.my; 41 & 43 Jln Melaka Raya 8; mains from RM8; ☺9am-10pm; 🐱) The emphasis is on crisp, fresh, organic ingredients and a wholesome bent that makes dining here a detox joy. It's very popular, so you may need to wait. The flavour-packed Nonya curry ramen (RM15) is superb and worth getting in line for, but the entire menu is a rewarding culinary experience.

Restoran Nyonya Suan　　　　　MALAYSIAN $$
(Map p220; ☑06-286 4252; www.nyonyasuan.com; 1336D Jln Merdeka; mains RM17-30; ☺11.30am-2.30pm & 5.30-9.30pm) A feast of fiery Peranakan specialities are served at this large and pleasant restaurant, with *ikan gerang asam* (fish in a spicy tamarind sauce) and chicken rendang raising the temperature. A couple of swaying lanterns and some stained-glass panelling set the scene while you await your towering *cendol*. Nyonya Suan has another branch on Jln Tokong (Jonker Walk).

Amy Heritage Cuisine　　　　　PERANAKAN $$
(☑06-286 8819; 75 Jln Melaka Raya 24; mains RM22-28; ☺noon-2.30pm & 6-9pm Tue-Sun) Amy Heritage Cuisine dishes up delectable food in a no-frills restaurant, 1km southeast of Dutch Sq. Melt-in-the-mouth candlenut chicken, spicy asam fish and *kangkung belacan* (spinach flavoured with shrimp and chilli) make this perennially busy place worth booking ahead.

✕ Little India to Bukit China

★ Bulldog
MALAYSIAN $

(Map p220; ☑ 019-655 2373; www.facebook.com/bulldogmalacca; 145 Jln Bendahara; mains RM10-15; ⊙ 6.30am-9pm Mon, 11.30am-2pm & 6.30-9pm Tue-Thu, to 10.30pm Fri, to 12.30am Sat; ☏) Specialising in Peranakan cuisine, Bulldog is a contemporary space that serves excellent food with a spicy edge. Don't miss the chilli-paste-slavered aubergine, *otak otak* (fish-paste patties) or the Nonya *pai tee* (crispy 'top hats' filled with cooked turnip, with omelette and fried shallots). Live music sets toes tapping every Saturday night from 9.30pm to 12.30am.

13 Hibiscus Vintage Art Cafe
MALAYSIAN $

(Map p218; ☑ 011-1073 1188; www.facebook.com/13hibiscus; 13 Jln Bunga Raya; mains RM7; ⊙ 9am-5pm Sat & Sun; ☏) For its quirky retro decor alone, which includes giant letters from an old cinema hung on the wall plus engaging street art, this weekend-only cafe is well worth a visit. It serves dishes such as *nasi lemak* (rice boiled in coconut milk, served with fried *ikan bilis,* peanuts and a curry dish) and *nonya laksa* (noodles in spicy coconut broth).

Upstairs is a rental apartment sleeping up to five people (weekdays/weekends RM380/550); it also has another two-person apartment (weekdays/weekends RM280/400) for rent nearby with a view of Sungai Melaka.

Selvam
INDIAN $

(Map p220; ☑ 06-281 9223; 2 Jln Temenggong; mains RM5-11; ⊙ 7am-10pm; ☏) One of Melaka's great bargains, this well-loved banana-leaf restaurant has helpful and efficient staff. Generous servings of aromatic chicken biryani are eclipsed by the vegetarian offerings, in particular the Friday-afternoon veggie special. Selvam is also an excellent stop for a breakfast *dosa* (paper-thin rice-and-lentil crepes) or *idli* (savoury, soft, fermented-rice-and-lentil cakes).

Street Kitchen
FUSION $$

(Map p218; ☑ 017-329 8331; www.facebook.com/thestreetkitchenmlk; 47 Jln Laksamana; mains RM10-22; ⊙ 5pm-2am Wed-Mon) Dishes such as sweet-and-sour pomfret, homemade popcorn chicken and Thai-style spaghetti are among the Asian-fusion dishes that this youthful and friendly operation turns out. With seats beside the Melaka River, it's also a great spot to sip one of the tropical mocktails or juices.

☕ Drinking & Nightlife

Unlike much of Malaysia, there is no shortage of spots to cool down with a beer in Melaka City. On Friday, Saturday and Sunday nights, Jonker Walk Night Market (p233) in Chinatown closes Jln Hang Jebat to traffic and the bars along the lane become a mini street party with live music and tables spilling beyond the sidewalks.

★ Daily Fix
CAFE

(Map p218; ☑ 06-283 4858; www.facebook.com/thedailyfixcafe; 55 Jln Hang Jebat; ⊙ 9am-11.30pm; ☏) You may have to grab a number and join fastidious Instagrammers waiting patiently for a spot in this retro-styled cafe, located behind a Chinatown souvenir shop. Most of Daily Fix's fans arrive for the impressive brunches (RM18 to RM29), such as banana French toast and eggs Benedict. The signature rose latte, sprinkled with petals, tastes as good as it looks.

★ Pampas Sky Bar
BAR

(Map p220; ☑ 017-707 2731; www.pampas.com.my; Level 41, The Shore Shopping Gallery, 193 Pinggiran @ Sungai Melaka, Jln Persisiran Bunga Raya; ⊙ 4pm-1am Sun-Thu, until 2am Fri & Sat) The views of Melaka from the 41st floor of the Shore complex are impressive, but this bar and steakhouse restaurant goes one further with a leafy outdoor area to relax in and enjoy a cocktail or beer. If dining, it's worth reserving ahead for a good table either alfresco or for a window table with a view.

Backlane Coffee
CAFE

(Map p218; ☑ 06-282 0542; www.facebook.com/Backlane-Coffee-574343952693116; 129 Jln Hang Jebat; ⊙ 9am-midnight; ☏) This ace chill-out space is an ideal retreat from all the tourist and karaoke craziness at this end of Jonker Walk Night Market. There's a good range of coffee, tea and other beverages as well as a tempting range of professionally made cakes.

Calanthe Art Cafe
COFFEE

(13 States Coffee; Map p218; ☑ 06-292 2960; http://calanthe.letseat.at; 11 Jln Hang Kasturi; ⊙ 9am-11pm Sun-Wed, to midnight Fri & Sat; ☏) Fancy a full-bodied Johor or classic Perak white? Sip a coffee inspired by your favourite Malaysian state at this perky place. The coffee is excellent, and it's worth dropping by simply to gaze at this temple to retro decor: you won't be the only customer photographing its vinyl-adorned walls or the fish tank framed by a vintage TV.

Geographér Cafe
BAR

(Map p218; ☑06-281 6813; www.geographer.com.my; 83 Jln Hang Jebat; ⊙10am-1am Sun-Thu, from 9am Fri & Sat; 🛜) A swinging soundtrack of jazz and classic pop keeps the beers flowing at this traveller magnet on the corner of Jonker St. It's a well-ventilated cafe-bar, strewn with greenery and managed by helpful staff. This is a great place for breakfast: try a black Malacca coffee (RM4.50) if you need help waking up.

Khaki Coffee
CAFE

(☑06-281 9276; www.khakicoffeebar.com; 632 Jln Melaka Raya 10; ⊙10am-6pm) Serving superb coffee and featuring a different bean each week, this lovely cafe is tucked away out of the action. The baristas really know their stuff, enjoy their work and are super helpful. The tiramisu, crème brûlée and panna cotta are worth shelling out for.

Reggae on the River
BAR

(Map p218; 88 Lg Hang Jebat; ⊙5.30pm-2am Thu-Tue, 8.30pm-2am Wed) You'll want to grab a seat out front by the boardwalk overlooking the river to maximise what this no-nonsense waterside bolt-hole has to offer. Beer is inexpensive and the chilled reggae soundtrack is just what the doctor ordered. Sit back and watch the night boats glide by.

Kaya Kaya Cafe
CAFE

(Map p218; ☑06-281 4089; www.facebook.com/kayakayacafelol; 32 Jln Tukang Besi; ⊙8am-6pm; 🛜) Good spot if you're hankering for an early morning coffee or a spot of breakfast: try the yummy Melaka Elvis banana pancakes with peanut butter and chocolate sauce. The bare brick walls, street art and retro, mismatched furniture all add to the hipster vibe.

Woods
CAFE

(☑016-622 7770; www.facebook.com/thewoods bookstore; 35 Jln Gajah Berang; ⊙11am-8pm Thu-Sat & Mon-Tue, to 6pm Sun; 🛜) Located near Kampung Chetti, this charmingly rustic cafe and secondhand bookshop is worth searching out. The owner takes his time making his hand-dripped coffee and herbal teas.

Me & Mrs Jones
PUB

(Map p218; ☑016-234 4292; 3 Jln Hang Kastu-ri; ⊙7pm-midnight Tue-Sun) This cosy pub is staunchly unhip and all the more enjoyable for it, especially for older visitors. At weekends there's live blues and rock, often with retired co-owner Mr Tan leading an open jam session. Relax into the easygoing atmosphere and grab a beer or juice (long menus are not the Joneses' style).

Mixx
CLUB

(Map p220; ☑016-621 5577; www.mixx.com.my; 2nd fl, Mahkota Arcade, Jln Syed Abdul Aziz; ⊙5pm-3am Wed-Sat) In a city with few nightclubs, Mixx dominates the scene with Paradox, a laser-lit, warehouse-style venue where international DJs spin techno and electronica; the wine bar S-19 (open 5pm to 1am Wednesday to Saturday) has live music. Cover for men only (RM35) on Wednesday, Friday and Saturday for Paradox includes one drink.

Discovery Cafe & Guest House
CAFE

(Map p218; ☑06-292 5606, 012-683 5606; www.discovery-malacca.com; 3 Jln Bunga Raya) Owner Bob Teng offers nearly everything that caters to travellers' needs here, from budget rooms (from RM50), bicycle and scooter rental to bus tickets, all manner of Melaka tours and cafe food. At the very least drop by for a beer, which gets cheaper with each subsequent order. There's live music most nights and the nearby riverside setting is pleasant.

☆ Entertainment

Encore Melaka
THEATRE

(☑06-270 7777; www.encore-melaka.com; 3 Jalan KSB; from RM148; ⊙shows 5.30pm & 8.30pm Mon-Sat, 2.30pm & 5.30pm Sun) This 70-minute performance may be designed with a mainland Chinese audience in mind, but it's a colourful and entertaining theatrical experience exploring the history of Melaka in a state-of-the-art piece of architecture built around a stage with revolving platforms. There's a two-tier pricing structure for local and foreign visitors; prices in the peak season go up by RM20.

Hard Rock Cafe
LIVE MUSIC

(Map p218; ☑06-292 5188; www.hardrock.com/cafes/melaka; 28 Lg Hang Jebat; ⊙11.30am-1am, until 2am Fri & Sat) Occupying a prominent position next to the Melaka River at the heart of Chinatown, it's hard to ignore this global franchise's presence. If you're coming to listen to the live music, it kicks off at around 9.30pm daily with a break on Monday.

🛍 Shopping

Chinatown's shopping spans antiques and contemporary art through to elaborate Chinese papercuts, novelty flip-flops (thongs) and key-rings. Best buys include Peranakan beaded shoes and clogs, Southeast Asian and Indian clothing, Chinese *cheongsam* (*qipao*), handmade tiles and ink stamps, woodblock-printed T-shirts and jewellery. Many shops double as art-and-craft studios where you can glimpse a painter or silversmith busy at work.

★ Red Handicrafts ARTS & CRAFTS
(Map p218; 30C Jln Hang Kasturi; ⊙10am-6pm Thu-Tue) Ray Tan draws Japanese- and Chinese-inspired designs that range from flowing organic patterns to quirky cartoons. Watch him hand-print your favourite onto a 100% cotton T-shirt or peruse his intricate paper-cutting art. Also for sale are colourful handmade Chinese lions, children's toys, tiger slippers and lovely lanterns.

★ Tham Siew Inn Artist Gallery ART
(Map p218; ☑06-281 2112; www.thamsiewinn.com; 49 Jln Tun Tan Teng Lock; ⊙10am-6pm Thu-Tue) Vibrant watercolours of sunsets, street scenes and temples fill this lovely art gallery spanning the entire length of a shophouse along with its inner courtyard garden. Also here, the artist's son carves traditional Chinese stone seals to your choice of design and is a very able artist in his own right.

★ Jonker Walk Night Market MARKET
(Map p218; Jln Hang Jebat; ⊙6-11pm Fri-Sun) Food hawkers, trinket sellers and fortune-tellers line Jln Hang Jebat for Melaka City's weekly extravaganza of street food and shopping. The street closes to traffic, shops stay open late and a party atmosphere prevails. Graze on barbecued quail eggs and *kuih* as you squeeze between souvenir and T-shirt stalls, pausing to watch the occasional Chinese karaoke performance.

Orangutan House ART
(Map p218; ☑06-282 6872; www.absolutearts.com/charlescham; 59 Lg Hang Jebat; ⊙10am-6pm) It's impossible to miss the giant orangutan mural above artist Charles Cham's gallery and T-shirt store. His colourful, primitive-style paintings sell for US$525 upwards, while his cheeky range of T-shirts (RM40 to RM45) are a more affordable, wearable art for all. Designs range from Chinese astrology animals to uplifting slogans and 'play safe' banners above condoms.

Sixty 3 Heritage CLOTHING
(Map p218; ☑06-282 6222; www.facebook.com/sixty3heritage; 63 Jln Tun Tan Cheng Lock; ⊙9am-6pm Mon-Thu, to 7pm Fri-Sun) If you need a figure-hugging *qipao*, a colourfully patterned Nonya *kebaya* (blouse), sarong, batik clothing or an elegant man's shirt, this shop has an eye-catching selection. There are several other branches in town.

Trash & Treasure MARKET
(Map p218; ☑012-298 3834; 3 Jln Bunga Raya; ⊙10am-5pm Sat & Sun) It's great fun rooting around this excellent flea market in a riverside warehouse behind Discovery Cafe. All kinds of gifts and collectables are on offer, from vintage signs and bicycles to handmade jewellery, art and old magazines. The vibe is very relaxed, but it's best to turn up around 11.30am as some vendors don't open early.

Clay House ARTS & CRAFTS
(Map p218; ☑06-292 6916; 18 Jln Tukang Besi; ⊙10am-6pm Thu-Tue) This lovely shop displays a delightful galaxy of perforated pottery tea-light holders, bowls and ornaments, made here by clay craftsman Leong Chee Hsiung. For RM60 he will teach you how to make your own pot and post the finished product back to you in a month's time.

Shore Shopping Gallery MALL
(Map p220; www.theshoreshoppinggallery.com; 193 Pinggiran @ Sungai Melaka, Jln Persisiran Bunga Raya; ⊙10am-10pm) Anchored by upmarket Singaporean department store Tangs, this mall is a pleasant spot for a browse of around 100 shops and restaurants over four floors as well as several other attractions, including an aquarium and the Sky Tower (p223) viewing platform.

Umyang Batik CLOTHING
(Map p218; ☑06-292 6569; 6 Jln Hang Kasturi) The cat-and-mouse designs on Ha Mi Seon's hand-painted, batik-print T-shirts and other clothing are undeniably cute. It's a great place to pick up something for a child to wear and she uses all-natural colours for her dyes.

Puri Padi HOMEWARES
(Map p218; ☑06-283 2116; 16 Jln Hang Kasturi) One of the more sophisticated gift shops in Chinatown, Puri Padi stocks everything you could need to turn your home into an old-world Asian oasis, from stone Buddha heads and batik wall hangings to carved wood and pottery ornaments.

RazKashmir Crafts FASHION & ACCESSORIES
(Map p218; www.facebook.com/razkashmir; 12 Jln Tukang Emas; ⊙10am-7pm) This little boutique is packed floor-to-ceiling with authentic Kashmiri crafts, jewellery, rugs and clothing. Peruse embroidered cotton tunics, enamelled teapots and attention-seizing labradorite pendants among the glittering shelves. The enthusiastic, welcoming owner is just as pleased to share cultural insights as he is to make a sale.

Joe's Design
JEWELLERY

(Map p218; ☑06-281 2960; www.facebook.com/joedesignhandcrafted; 6 Jln Tun Tan Cheng Lock; ☺10am-5pm) Owl-shaped ornaments, iridescent floral necklaces and beautifully curled copper-wire creations are some of the stock at this lovely craft-jewellery shop owned by amiable jewellery designer Joe Ng.

Hueman Studio
ART

(Map p218; ☑06-288 1795; www.huemanstudio.blogspot.com; 9 Jln Tokong; ☺10.30am-6pm) Woodblock prints, many with themes such as astrology and calligraphy, take centre stage in this art studio gift shop. Portable souvenirs include hand-painted rosewood jewellery (from RM16), buffalo-horn pendants (RM45) and more.

Wah Aik Shoemaker
SHOES

(Map p218; ☑06-284 9726; www.wahaikshoemakermelaka.webs.com; 92 Jln Tun Tan Cheng Lock; ☺9.30am-5.30pm) The three Yeo brothers continue the shoemaking tradition begun by their grandfather. Their beaded Peranakan shoes are considered Melaka's finest and begin at a steep but merited RM350. The most unusual souvenirs are tiny bound-feet shoes (from RM95).

Dataran Pahlawan
MALL

(Map p220; ☑06-281 2898; www.dataranpahlawan.com; Jln Merdeka; ☺10am-10pm) Melaka's largest mall has a collection of upscale designer

---

❶ GETTING TO INDONESIA: MELAKA TO DUMAI

Getting to the border High-speed Indomal Express (Map p220; ☑019-665 7055, 06-286 2506; G35, Jln PM2, Plaza Mahkota) ferries make the trip from Melaka to **Dumai** (Map p220; Jln Merdeka) in Sumatra daily at 10am (one-way/return RM110/170, two hours; child tickets half price). The quay is walking distance or a short taxi ride from most hotels and guesthouses. Tickets are available at **Tunas Rupat Follow Me Express** (Map p220; ☑06-283 2516, 06-283 2506; www.tunasrupat.com; G-29, Jln PM10, Plaza Mahkota) near the wharf.

At the border Citizens of most countries can obtain a 30-day visa on arrival (US$35).

Moving on Dumai is on Sumatra's east coast and is a 10-hour bus ride from Bukittinggi.

---

shops and restaurants in the western half and an underground craft-and-souvenir market in the eastern portion, which is beneath a grassy square where events are held and which is pleasant to stroll at night.

❶ Information

Pretty much every hotel and guesthouse has wi-fi, as do many restaurants and cafes.

There are plenty of ATMs at shopping malls but fewer in Chinatown.

Mahkota Medical Centre (Map p220; ☑06-285 2999, emergency 06-285 2991; www.mahkotamedical.com; 3 Jln Merdeka; ☺24hr) A private hospital offering a full range of services including accident and emergency treatment.

Post Office (Map p218; Jln Laksamana; ☺8.30am-5pm Mon-Fri, to 1pm Sat)

Tourist Police (Map p218; ☑06-282 2222, 06-281 4803; Lg Hang Jebat; ☺24hr) Available by phone around the clock.

❶ Getting There & Away

Melaka City is 149km south from Kuala Lumpur, 220km northwest from Johor Bahru and 80km southeast from Port Dickson.

AIR

Melaka International Airport (☑06-317 5860; Lapangan Terbang Batu Berendam) is 12km north of Melaka City. Malindo Air (www.malindoair.com) offers daily flights from Melaka to Penang and Pekanbaru (Indonesia).

BUS

Melaka Sentral (☑06-288 1321; www.melakasentral.com.my; Jln Sentral), the huge, modern long-distance bus station, is 5km north of the city. Luggage deposit is RM2 per bag. You'll also find an ATM and restaurants here.

A medley of privately run bus companies make checking timetables a Herculean feat; scout popular routes at www.expressbusmalaysia.com/coach-from-melaka or book ahead (not a bad idea on busy weekends or if you have a plane to catch) on www.busonlineticket.com. You can also buy bus tickets in advance at Discovery Cafe (p232) in downtown Melaka City – there's a small commission, dependent on the ticket fare.

TAXI

At Melaka Sentral, follow the signs to the taxi booking kiosk to ensure you receive standard rates. Indicative long-distance fares are Johor Bahru (RM272), Mersing (RM300) and Kuala Lumpur (RM184).

TRAIN

The closest train station is inconveniently located for travellers to Melaka. Known as **Pulau Sebang/Tampin Station** (☑06-441 1034), the railway stop is 39km north of the city. Taxis from Melaka to the station cost around RM80. Alternatively, there's a half-hourly bus from Melaka Sentral (RM5, 1½ hours).

There are three daily KTM Komuter (www.ktmb.com.my) services from Pulau Sebang/Tampin to Kuala Lumpur (RM25, two hours) and Ipoh (RM50, four hours), and more services if you connect in Seremban (RM15, 30 minutes, at least three daily). At least one daily service reaches Butterworth (RM75, seven hours), which is handy for Penang. For Johor Bahru, travel via Gemas (RM18, 35 minutes, three daily).

❶ Getting Around

Melaka City is compact enough and pretty easy to get around on foot, especially in the heritage areas. You can rent a bike for between RM5 and RM10 per day from guesthouses.

A useful service is bus 17, running every 15 minutes from Melaka Sentral to the centre of town (Dutch Sq), past the huge Mahkota Parade shopping complex, to Taman Melaka Raya and on to Medan Portugis (per ride RM2). You can find local bus route information at www.panoramamelaka.com.my/routes.

Melaka City's streets can be seen by trishaw – rates are supposedly fixed at RM40 per hour, but you'll still have to bargain. A one-way trip within town should cost roughly RM20.

Taxis should cost around RM10 to RM15 for a trip anywhere around town (and less than RM20 between Melaka Sentral and the centre of town). The **Grab** (www.grab.com/my/taxi) app is in common use in Melaka for ride-sharing or calling your nearest Grab taxi.

If you're driving to Melaka City, park your car by displaying a coupon in the front window (RM5 per day), which can be bought at supermarkets and some shops (ask your hotel where the nearest one is). Saturdays and Sundays are free. Avoid driving around Melaka to avoid the confusing one-way system.

Car-hire prices begin at around RM110 per day. Try **Hawk** (Map p218; ☑ 06-283 7878; www.hawkrentacar.com.my; 34 Jln Laksamana; ⏰8am-5.30pm Mon-Fri, to 1pm Sat) in the centre of town.

Ayer Keroh

☑ 06 / POP 37,700

Ayer Keroh (also spelt Air Keroh) has a handful of kid-friendly attractions that are largely deserted on weekdays. Some feel a little contrived, but there's no denying this area, about 13km northeast of Melaka City, makes for a fine family day trip.

HELLO KITSCHY

The sun goes down, the lights go on. First you hear a distant blare of honking, hip-hop or techno. Then, suddenly, a convoy of three-wheeled vehicles is careening your way in a blur of fairy lights and soft toys. Melaka City's trishaws are the glitziest you'll see anywhere in Malaysia, decorated with paraphernalia from papier-mâché models of colonial buildings to Disney princesses, Hello Kitty and wide-eyed Minions. Music is selected according to nationality. Local opinion is divided over whether these blinged-up trishaws help save the historic mode of transport or hideously distort it. But it's hard to imagine a trip to Melaka City without at least one ride. And it's impossible not to laugh when tourist groups hire them en masse, forming a carnivalesque, cycle-powered conga line.

◉ Sights & Activities

Melaka Botanical Garden PARK
(Taman Botanikal Melaka; ☑06-231 4343; Lr Ayer Keroh) FREE A good place for an easy ramble, this lush green enclave is part jungle and part landscaped park with paved trails along which you can walk, cycle or ride an electric buggy – both the buggies and bikes can be rented at the entrance. The garden is also the base for the fun zip-line and tree-climbing adventure course, Skytrex Melaka.

Skytrex Melaka AMUSEMENT PARK
(☑018-909 5679; www.skytrex-adventure.com; Melaka Botanical Garden, Lr Ayer Keroh; RM55-65; ⏰9am-3pm) There are two adventurous circuits strung between the trees to be tackled here – you'll get to do some climbing, zip lining and generally get to be like Tarzan; there's also a course for kids. Bookings for time slots between 9am and 3pm should be made online and it's a good idea to pay the extra RM20 for gloves and water.

Melaka Wonderland WATER PARK
(☑06-231 3333; www.melakawonderland.com.my; off Lr Ayer Keroh; adult/child RM47/40.50, with Melaka Bird Park RM65.20/53.30; ⏰11am-7pm Tue-Fri, 9am-7pm Sat & Sun) When it gets too steamy in Melaka, this water park, which is close to **Melaka Bird Park** (☑06-233 0330; off Lr Ayer Keroh; adult/child RM23.70/17.80, with Melaka Wonderland RM65.20/53.30; ⏰9am-6pm), is a great spot to cool off and have some fun

PULAU BESAR

Said to resemble a pregnant woman lying on her back in the sea, this small, placid island, 10km off the southeast coast of Melaka, was once a retreat for Muslim mystics. Pilgrims still arrive to seek out Pulau Besar's meditation caves and the graves of prominent Islamic teachers, such as the 15th-century Islamic preacher **Sultan Al Ariffin Syeikh Ismail**.

The main reason for other visitors to come here is to do some jungle hiking or lounge on palm-shaded beaches. Do note that amenities are few and some areas of the shore are scattered with as many cola bottles as coconut shells. If you're planning to hit the sand, modest attire (slip a T-shirt over your bathing suit) is recommended for women.

The basic **D'Puteri Kurnia Resort** (☑06-295 5899, 019-602 4099; www.dputerikurnia resort.wordpress.com; Pulau Besar; tent/r/chalet from RM60/70/180; ❈ ❋), less than 1km north of the boat jetty, is the island's sole accommodation option. It's possible to camp, stay in a simple fan-cooled or air-con room, or rent a chalet that sleeps up to four. The cafe here serves meals throughout the day.

Exploring Pulau Besar is best done as a full- or half-day excursion from Melaka City. Boats (return trip adult/child RM15/11, 15 minutes) depart from **Anjung Batu** (☑06-261 0492; Merlimau) jetty every two to three hours from 8am (last boat returns at 7pm). The last boat from the jetty leaves at 8.30pm, so you'll need to be spending the night on the island if you take that one. Inclement weather can disrupt schedules, so check ahead with **Tourism Malaysia** (Map p218; www.tourismmalaysia.gov.my; Jln Kota; ⊙9am-5pm) in Melaka City or call the jetty. Children aged one to four years of age travel return for RM4.

For Anjung Batu, take buses 6A, 6B or 17 from Melaka Sentral towards Merlimau and ask to be let off at Anjung Batu jetty (RM2.50). The jetty is a 15-minute walk from the bus stop. Taxis from central Melaka City to Anjung Batu should cost around RM40.

with the kids. There are plenty of different slides to slosh down – try the Tornado Chaser, Kamikaze Racer, Big Wave Pool or Adventure Island.

ℹ Getting There & Away

Bus 19 from Melaka Sentral (p234; RM2, 40 minutes) stops at both the **zoo** (☑06-232 4054; www.melakazoo.com; Lr Ayer Keroh; adult/child RM23.70/17.80; ⊙9am-6pm, night zoo 8-11pm Fri & Sat; ℗) and **Taman Mini Malaysia** (☑06-234 9988; www.pknm.gov.my; Lr Ayer Keroh; adult/child RM24/18; ⊙9am-6pm; ℗). A taxi to the area will cost around RM45.

Ayer Keroh's attractions are all clustered on either side of a main highway. Having your own wheels – either a car or scooter – will make it far easier to travel between each one as they are fairly spread out. Bicycles (RM5 per hour) can be rented at the entrance to Melaka Botanical Garden (p235).

Alor Gajah

☑06 / POP 21,300

The main draw of Alor Gajah, 24km north of Melaka City, is the nearby resort **A'Famosa** (☑06-552 0888; www.afamosa.com; Jln Kemus; water park adult/child RM33/30, golf course weekday/weekend RM118/198; ⊙11am-7pm Mon, Wed & Fri, 9am-7pm Sat & Sun), with its fun water park

which is excellent for families. The countryside town itself, 6km from the resort and just off the highway to Kuala Lumpur, has a small museum, some gaily painted shophouses and the striking blue-roofed mosque **Masjid Al-Rasyidin Daerah** – but little else of great interest.

✖ Eating

Nasi Ayam Nadia   MALAYSIAN $
(Jln Datuk Md Zin; meals RM5; ⊙9.30am-2.30pm Mon-Sat) If you're passing through Alor Gajah around lunchtime, you won't fail to miss the crowd at this chicken-rice stall close to the bus station. Nadia's delicious take on the dish peps it up with a sweet chilli sauce.

ℹ Getting There & Away

Many Melaka–Kuala Lumpur buses stop in Alor Gajah so it's possible to pause here between the two cities if you're willing to change buses.

Buses to **Alor Gajah Sentral** (Jln Datuk Md Zin) from Melaka Sentral (RM3, one hour) run roughly hourly during the day. A taxi from Alor Gajah to A'Famosa costs around RM30.

A'Famosa is huge so is best visited with your own set of wheels. Otherwise, Transnational runs direct buses here from Melaka Sentral (p234) and Kuala Lumpur International Airport; see www.afamosa.com for details.

Johor

📍 06, 07 / POP 3.5 MILLION

Includes ➡

Johor Bahru	238
Muar	244
Mersing	246
Seribuat Archipelago	248
Endau-Rompin National Park	250

Best Places to Eat

➡ 434 Kopi House (p245)

➡ The Replacement (p242)

Best Places to Stay

➡ Rimba Resort (p249)

➡ Replacement Lodge (p239)

➡ Rawa Island Resort (p249)

➡ Mirage Island Resort (p248)

➡ Legoland Hotel (p241)

Why Go?

Malaysia's most populous state is a growing economic power player. Most travel itineraries skip it, but those who do choose to stop will be rewarded with the blissful solitude of its postcard-perfect islands and wild jungles, while getting access to a taste of authentic Malaysian culture and character not easily found in bigger tourist hotspots.

The top draw is the ridiculously gorgeous white-sand islands of the Seribuat Archipelago, where you'll find world-class diving, lost-beach trails and plenty of relaxation time with a fraction of Tioman's crowds. Inland, Endau-Rompin National Park offers rich flora, elusive fauna and swashbuckling action in a more pristine setting than the more famous Taman Negara.

And then there's the lively capital Johor Bahru, with its religious sites, museums and a heritage district, that plays sister-city to neighbouring Singapore.

When to Go
Johor Bahru

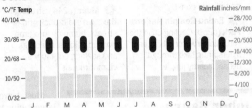

Nov–Feb The monsoon season brings bargains, rain and jungle leeches. Surfers head to Rawa for rollers.

Mar–May Visibility in Seribuat's already translucent waters is at its best for diving and snorkelling.

Jun & Jul Expect high temperatures everywhere and lots of sunshine.

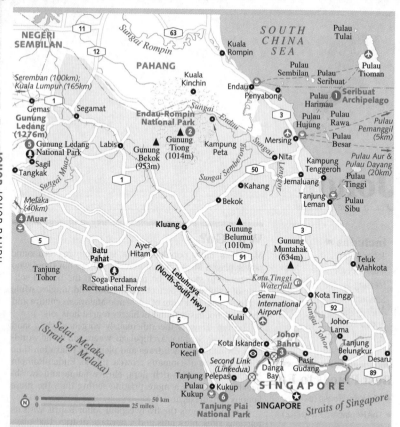

Johor Highlights

1 Seriluat Archipelago
(p248) Swimming, diving, snorkelling and beach bumming to the max on the islands in the azure waters off the east coast.

2 Endau-Rompin National Park (p250) Cooling off in the sensational waterfalls after a perspiring hike through dense, steamy jungle.

3 Johor Bahru (p238)
Discovering the city's historic backstreets, ornate temples and imposing mosque architecture.

4 Muar (p244) Strolling the town's laid-back grid of streets, bumping into time-warped colonial buildings and seeking out Muar's vibrant murals.

5 Gunung Ledang (p245)
Sweating your way to the top of Johor's highest peak.

6 Tanjung Piai National Park (p246) Taking the road less travelled to the mangrove swamps of this off-the-beaten-track park on the southernmost point of mainland Asia.

Johor Bahru

📍 07 / POP 1,448,000

Johor's capital city of Johor Bahru (JB for short) has been repaved and replanted and is well on the way to rebranding itself, after years of being habitually criticised as a dirty, chaotic border town.

Most travellers skip southern Malaysia's largest city, but for intrepid souls there's a handful of worthwhile museums, temples and mosques, shopping and party zones. If that ain't your thing, JB also has a Legoland, where 'everything is awesome'.

As one of the five 'economic zones' of the Iskandar development project, which will radically change southern Malaysia over the next decade, JB is in for one hell of a make-over yet. The 720-hectare Danga Bay area, 5km from the Causeway, is poised to be a financial and commercial centre. Work on the development began in 2006 and is expected to be completed in 2025. For now, Danga Bay is a sprawl of construction.

⊙ Sights

Arulmigu Sri Rajakaliamman HINDU TEMPLE
(Glass Temple; 22 Lorong 1; RM10; ⊙1-5pm) Step through the looking glass into this wonderland of a temple built from mirrors, glass and metal – not a single inch of the vaulted roof or wall has been left unadorned. The temple is dedicated to Kali, known as the goddess of time, change, power and destruction.

Chinese Heritage Museum MUSEUM
(⊘07-224 9633; 42 Jln Ibrahim; adult/child RM6/3; ⊙9am-5pm Tue-Sun) Well-displayed exhibits chronicling the history of Chinese immigrants in this part of the Malay peninsula are the highlight of this three-storey museum. Learn how the Cantonese brought their carpentry skills to this area, while the Hakkas traded in Chinese medicines and the Hainanese kick-started a trend in coffee shops, which lasts to this day. There's good English signage.

Heritage District ARCHITECTURE
Wandering around the characterful heritage area between Jln Ibrahim and Jln Ungku Puan is a high point of any visit to Johor Bahru. Walk past colourful old shophouses filled with barbers, Ayurvedic salons, sari shops, gorgeous temples, a few modern-art galleries and old-style, as well as trendy, cafes and restaurants.

Johor Bahru Old Chinese Temple TAOIST TEMPLE
(Roufo Gumiao; Jln Trus; ⊙7am-5pm) FREE Once the centre of JB's Chinese immigrant community, and used by five different ethnic groups to worship five different Chinese gods, this small but atmospheric temple is more than 130 years old. Little remains of its original masonry after major renovations in 1995, but it does house some genuine antiques. In the first lunar month of every year, the temple organises a *chingay*, a procession through the city honouring the five deities.

Sultan Abu Bakar Mosque MOSQUE
(Jln Abu Bakar) FREE The stunning whitewashed walls and blue-tiled roof of this Victorian-inspired mosque speak of a mix of architectural influences. Built between 1892 and 1900, it is quite rightly hailed as one of the most magnificent mosques in the area. At the time of research it was undergoing long-term renovation with no confirmed completion date – so for now the mosque cannot be entered, but you can visit the grounds and admire the exterior.

Arulmigu Rajamariamman Devasthanam HINDU TEMPLE
(⊘07-223 3989; www.rajamariammanjb.com; 1A Jln Ungku Puan; ⊙7am-9pm) FREE This beautiful Hindu temple, with ornate carvings, devotional artwork and a tall, brightly painted *gopuram* (tower) entranceway, is the heart of JB's Hindu community. Photos are allowed, but be respectful of devotees.

Royal Abu Bakar Museum MUSEUM
(⊘07-223 0555; 107 Jln Tun Dr Ismail; US$7, converted to ringgit; ⊙9am-5pm Sat-Thu) The marvellous Istana Besar, once the Johor royal family's principal palace, was flung up in Victorian style by Anglophile sultan Abu Bakar in 1866. It was opened as a museum to the public in 1990, displaying the incredible wealth of the sultans to the hoi polloi in over 60,000 pieces. It's now the finest museum of its kind in Malaysia with beautifully manicured 53-hectare palace grounds (free entry); an extensive upgrade of the museum saw it shut for many years.

Bangunan Sultan Ibrahim ARCHITECTURE
(Jln Bukit Timbalan, State Secretariat Bldg; ⊙Tue-Sat) Sitting magnificently atop Bukit Timbalan, the imposing Bangunan Sultan Ibrahim is a mighty melange of colonial pomp, Islamic motifs and indigenous design. Completed in 1942, the city landmark was employed as a fortress by the Japanese as they prepared to attack Singapore. Visitors are not allowed to enter, although you can take pictures from the road. The building looks brilliant at night, when it's illuminated.

🛏 Sleeping

Grand Jade Hotel HOTEL
(⊘07-222 0118; www.thejade.com.my; 15R & 15S Jln Bukit Meldrum; r incl breakfast RM130-220; ᴾ ❋ 🛜) This smart place may seem stranded on the far side of the flyovers immediately east of central JB, but it's a short walk to the action and prices are good. The website paints a more classic picture than what you find, but rooms are comfortable, service is quiet and congenial and there's a space or two for cars out front.

Replacement Lodge HOSTEL $$
(⊘012-547 7885; www.themerkgroup.com/the replacement; 33–34 Jln Dhoby; tw/d incl breakfast RM135/160; ❋ 🛜) This very small lodge (with

Johor Bahru

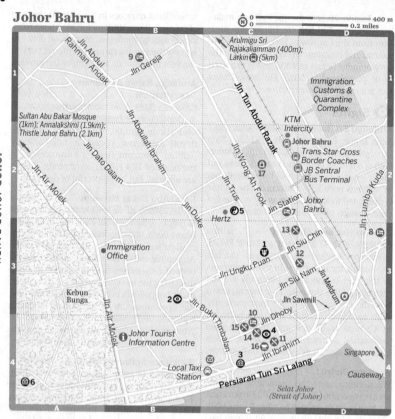

Johor Bahru

◎ **Sights**
1 Arulmigu Rajamariamman
  Devasthanam C3
2 Bangunan Sultan Ibrahim B3
3 Chinese Heritage Museum C4
4 Heritage District C4
5 Johor Bahru Old Chinese Temple C2
6 Royal Abu Bakar Museum A4

🛏 **Sleeping**
7 Citrus Hotel C2
8 Grand Jade Hotel D3
9 Hilton DoubleTree B1
10 Replacement Lodge C4

🍽 **Eating**
  Go Noodle House ....(see 17)
11 Hiap Joo Bakery & Biscuit Factory C4
12 Kam Long Fishhead Curry D3
13 Medan Selera Meldrum Walk C3
14 The Replacement C4
15 Restoran Reaz Corner C4

🍸 **Drinking & Nightlife**
16 Chaiwalla & Co. C4

🛍 **Shopping**
17 Johor Bahru City Square C2

only three rooms) enjoys a superb location in the old heritage area of Johor Bahru. With Nordic-inspired interiors (whitewashed walls, pale wooden furnishings and sporadic pot plants), rooms are light-filled and comfy. Its location near a mosque can make for an early morning wake-up call.

Thistle Johor Bahru HOTEL $$

(📞 07-222 9234; www.thistle.com; Jln Sungai Chat; d from RM300; 🅿 ❄ @ 🛜 🏊) Overlooking the Strait of Johor, the rooms at the ageing Thistle could do with a makeover – though refurbishment is planned – but the lovely pool and airy ambience still make it a good option. The location, near Danga Bay, is a little out of the way – you'll pay around RM7 for a taxi back into the city.

The Thistle is about 4km from the town centre, just off Jln Lingkaran Dalam, the main road.

Citrus Hotel
HOTEL **$$**

(☑07-222 2888; www.citrushoteljb.com; 16 Jln Station; d/tr RM129/209; ❈@🖥) Rooms are small but clean with white walls and bright accents of green and orange – citrusy indeed. Breakfasts are tasty, staff are helpful and the location, just next to Johor Bahru City Square, couldn't be better. Check on the hotel website for offers.

Hilton DoubleTree
BUSINESS HOTEL **$$$**

(☑07-268 6868; www.doubletree3.hilton.com; 12 Jln Ngee Heng; d RM400; P❈@🖥☷) While it lacks the intimacy of the small boutiques in town, the DoubleTree does deliver business-class comfort with well-tailored ample rooms, several restaurants and a 13th-floor pool and bar terrace that gives you a bird's-eye view of the city. Big savings can be found online. Front desk and waiting staff are first-rate.

Hotel Jen Puteri Harbour
HOTEL **$$$**

(☑07-560 8888; www.hoteljen.com/johor/puteri harbour; Persiaran Puteri Selatan, Puteri Harbour, Nusajaya; d RM480; P❈@🖥☷; 🚊LM1) This contemporary 283-room hotel provides decent, wallet-friendly accommodation for those visiting nearby Legoland and Puteri Harbour attractions. Facilities are clean and modern, plus there's a small gym, a spa, three rooftop pools, and good restaurants and bars. Harbour rooms have a pleasant outlook over the water and for those with kids the Hello Kitty–themed rooms are fun.

 Eating

The streets of JB sizzle with some of the country's best food, including local specialities *ikan bakar* (grilled fish), *mee rebus* (yellow noodles with potato-based gravy) and the famous laksa. The smoky **Medan Selera Meldrum Walk** (Meldrum Walk; meals from RM3; ⏱5pm-late) is a good place to start. For European-style fare head to Jln Dhoby and the Heritage District, malls and upper midrange hotels.

Go Noodle House
NOODLES **$**

(有間麵館; Level 6, Johor Bahru City Sq, 108 Jln Wong Ah Fook; mains from RM10; ⏱10.30am-9.30pm; 🕾) This neat, well-run, steaming, modern noodle house packs in the diners for fast servings of the filling stuff, with an ample menu of all sorts including wonton, fish balls, pork belly slices, fried shallots, frogs – you name it – and loads of chilli that you can ladle in for just the right degree of scorchiness. Queues can get long. Cash only.

Restoran Reaz Corner
INDIAN **$**

(www.facebook.com/pg/restoranreazcorner; 24A Jln Dhoby, cnr Jln Duke; RM3-12.50; ⏱24hr) You can't go wrong with the yellow rice topped with spicy chicken curry at this clean, open-air, often-packed and long-standing curry joint that's open round the clock. The very refreshing and smooth ginger tea is an unforgettable accompaniment. If you're here for breakfast, it's hard to pass up the lovely flaky roti.

Hiap Joo Bakery & Biscuit Factory
BAKERY **$**

(13 Jln Tan Hiok Nee; buns/cake from RM3.50/5; ⏱7am-5.30pm) For over 80 years this little bakery has prepared delicious buns, cakes and biscuits in a charcoal oven just as the founder had done in his native Hainan,

JOHOR JOHOR BAHRU

WORTH A TRIP

LEGOLAND!

Got kids? Asia's first **Legoland** (☑07-597 8888; www.legoland.com.my; Medini, Nusajaya; adult/child RM188/150, waterpark adult/child RM122/103, combined ticket adult/child RM235/188; ⏱10am-6pm) offers over 70 rides and attractions, plus a waterpark that can be visited separately or as part of a package. Nearly everything is hands-on, and it's not just about the bricks. Expect to crawl around, pull yourself up a tower with ropes, ride a dragon-coaster and shoot lasers at mummies. The centrepiece is Miniland, where you'll find miniature Lego versions of regional landmarks, such as the Petronas Towers and Singapore's Merlion.

Complete your Legoland experience with a night or two at **Legoland Hotel** (☑07-597 8888; www.legoland.com.my/legoland-hotel/hotel; 7 Jln Legoland, Bandar Medini Iskandar; r RM850; P❈🖥☷; 🚊LM1). From the giant Lego playground in the lobby, to the themed rooms (such as Pirate and Ninjago), the fun is in the detail – from figurine swapping with staff, to the in-room treasure hunt. Rooms sleep up to five, with bunk beds and pull-out trundle beds for kids.

Located 19km from JB; buses to Legoland depart JB Sentral and Larkin Sentral bus terminals, or catch a taxi for RM50.

China. Join the queue spilling out the bright blue door for the famous spongy banana cake – not too sweet and slightly smoky – sold in lots of five or 10 (RM5/10).

Annalakshmi INDIAN $
(☑ 013-753 1377; 19 Jln Dapat; meals by donation; ⊙ 11am-3pm Mon-Sat; ☑) An authentic vegetarian Indian restaurant run by volunteers of the Temple of Fine Arts, with the motto 'eat what you want and give as you feel'. Meals are set and change daily.

★ The Replacement INTERNATIONAL $$
(www.themerkgroup.com/thereplacement; 33 Jln Dhoby; mains from RM27; ⊙ 10am-6pm Mon-Thu, 9am-11pm Fri-Sun; ☎) With a fantastic brunch menu, this good-looking, elegant but minimalist restaurant is overseen by attentive staff serving a host of trendy lunchers, brunchers, diners and people photographing their food. The breakfast platter is just the thing to kick-start your Johor Bahru day; alternatively there's a tasty array of burgers, fish and chips, rice, noodles and *baozi* (steamed buns).

Kam Long Fishhead Curry SEAFOOD $$
(74 Jln Wong Ah Fook; curry from RM20; ⊙ 8am-4pm) The lunch line snakes up the road so if you want to get a taste of this seriously addictive, mildly spicy fish curry, aim to get here before 11am. There's only one dish on the menu, but you can choose from fish head or tail; the head is best, dished up with bean-curd skin, okra, tomatoes and cabbage.

Olive INDIAN $$
(☑ 07-509 6617; 11 & 12 lower ground fl, Puteri Harbour, Nusajaya; mains RM12-35; ⊙ 11am-11pm; ☎; ☐ LM1) One of several international restaurants overlooking Puteri Harbour, Olive is a good choice to enjoy Indian cuisine, cooking up a wonderfully tender Lahori *seekh* (lamb kebab with cinnamon, mace, nutmeg and green cardamom), a tasty prawn biryani, and lots of vegetarian options. The daily lunch (RM30) and dinner (RM35) buffets from 6.45pm on Friday and Saturday nights are popular.

> ### ⓘ SAFE TRAVEL
> Although travelling in Johor Bahru is generally safe, visitors should be alert to motorcycle-riding bag-snatchers. If you experience troubles, call the **police** (☑ 07-223 2222; Jln Meldrum).

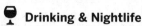

⚲ Drinking & Nightlife

SkyBar COCKTAIL BAR
(☑ 07-560 8888; www.hoteljen.com/johor/puteri harbour/taste/bars/skybar-restaurant; Persiaran Puteri Selatan, Puteri Harbour; ⊙ noon-midnight; ☎) For delectable views over the harbour and across the waters to Singapore, stop by the ambient restaurant/bar SkyBar. As the sun sets, sip a cocktail or a chilled glass of white wine at a table by the infinity pool. The dress code is smart casual.

Chaiwalla & Co. CAFE
(☑ 012-735 3572; www.facebook.com/chaiwalla. co; Lot 2810, Jln Tan Hiok Nee; ⊙ 11am-midnight Sun-Thu, to 1am Fri & Sat; ☎) Elevating the usual *chai walla* (tea seller) stall, this drinks cafe has made its home in a trendy, all-black, double-storey shipping container, with industrial-styled interiors and lush hanging-garden wall. You can grab a decent cup of hot coffee; however, the speciality of the house is iced beverages, including Vietnamese coffee, Thai milk tea and build-your-own smoothies, plus brownies and muffins.

Zon BAR
(www.zon.com.my; 88 Jln Ibrahim Sultan, Zon Ferry Terminal; ⊙ noon-3am, individual bar hrs vary) Two words: duty-free booze. About eight bars and clubs, including Texas Pub, Avenue Zon and The Geoventure restaurant/bar, surround the courtyard of this happening spot.

⛒ Shopping

The mall is where it's at. Expect decent food courts, blaring air-con and plenty of visiting Singaporeans looking for deals. Top malls include **Johor Bahru City Square** (www.citysqjb.com; 108 Jln Wong Ah Fook; ⊙ 10am-10pm), **KSL City Mall** (☑ 07-288 2930; www.kslcity.com.my; 33 Jln Seladang; ⊙ 10am-10pm), **Johor Premium Outlets** (☑ 07-661 8888; www.premiumoutlets.com.my; Indahpura, Kulai; ⊙ 10am-10pm) and **AEON Tebrau City Shopping Centre** (☑ 07-352 2220; www.aeonretail.com.my; 1 Jln Desa Tebrau; ⊙ 10am-10pm; ⛟), JB's biggest shopping centre.

ⓘ Information

ATMs and banks are everywhere in the central areas. Money changers infest Jln Wong Ah Fook, and have competitive rates.
Immigration Office (☑ 07-224 4255, 07-233 8400; www.imi.gov.my; Jln Air Molek;

ⓘ GETTING TO INDONESIA: JOHOR BAHRU TO BATAM & BINTAN (RIAU ISLANDS)

Getting to the border Fifteen ferries depart daily for Batam Centre (one way RM69, 1½ hours), six ferries depart daily for Harbour Bay (one way RM71, 1½ hours) on Batam Island, while three ferries depart daily for Tanjung Pinang on Bintan Island (one way RM86, 2½ hours), part of Indonesia's Riau Islands. Ferries depart from the **Berjaya Waterfront Ferry Terminal** (☑07-221 1677; www.berjayawaterfront.com.my; 88 Jln Ibrahim Sultan, Zon Ferry Terminal), which is served by several buses from downtown Johor Bahru.

At the border You'll be charged a RM10 seaport tax, RM2 insurance and RM3 fuel surcharge (total RM15) on top of your ticket price and stamped out of Malaysia before you board the boat in JB.

Moving on Trans Batam BRT (bus rapid transit) is the local public transport, with links connecting the port towns of Batam Centre, Nagoya and Sekupang. Metered taxis and Grab (p244) online taxis are the primary ways to get around Pulau Batam. From the main town of Nagoya, a taxi to the airport is around 130,000Rp.

From Sekupang port, Dumai Express runs mainland Sumatra ferries daily to both Tanjung Buton (240,000Rp, four to five hours) and Dumai (400,000Rp, seven hours); a minibus links to Pekanbaru (around three hours).

Batam Jet has a boat at 7pm from Sekupang to Dumai (400,000Rp, eight hours). You'll also need to pay 10,000Rp for a boarding pass.

Hang Nadim Airport is located on the eastern side of Pulau Batam, with flights to Jakarta and other destinations in Indonesia.

⊘8am-5pm Sun-Wed, to 3.30pm Thu) For visa extensions.

Post Office (☑07-224 2545; www.pos.com. my; JKR 2521, Jln Dato Onn; ⊘8.30am-5.30pm Sun-Thu, to 1pm Sat)

Johor Tourist Information Centre (☑07-224 4133; www.malaysia.travel; Jln Air Molek; ⊘10am-10pm) Look out for the counter at JB Sentral, right after you pass through immigration from Singapore.

ⓘ Getting There & Away

AIR

JB is served by **Senai International Airport** (☑07-599 4500; www.senaiairport.com), 32km northwest of JB. Prices are much lower to/from here than Singapore.

Senai International Airport is linked to the city centre by regular shuttle buses (RM8, 45 minutes) that run from the bus station at Kotaraya 2 Terminal. White AA1 Causeway Link buses (RM8, 45 minutes) run from the airport to JB Sentral.

A taxi between the airport and JB is RM45 to RM50, taking 30 to 45 minutes depending on traffic.

BUS

Larkin Sentral (Larkin Bus Terminal; Jln Garuda) is about 5km north of town and is the main terminal for long-distance buses departing to greater Malaysia.

DESTINATION	PRICE	DURATION
Butterworth	RM65-75	9hr
Kuala Lumpur	RM35	4½hr
Kuala Terengganu	RM48.40	9hr
Kuantan	RM29	6hr
Melaka	RM21	3hr
Mersing	RM13	2½hr
Muar	RM17	3hr

JB Sentral Bus Terminal (Jln Jim Quee) is located beside JB Sentral Railway, and serves local and regional buses as well as buses to and from Singapore.

TAXI

JB's long-distance taxi station is at Larkin Sentral, 5km north of town, from where specially licensed **taxis to Singapore** (Larkin Sentral, Jln Garuda) leave, costing RM80 per taxi, or RM20 if shared. Unlicensed taxis leave for Singapore from outside JB Sentral.

TRAIN

Daily express trains on **KTM Intercity** (☑03-2267 1200; www.ktmb.com.my; JB Sentral) leave from JB Sentral station. You'll have to catch the rather old, slow, single-track line to Gemas, before boarding the new fast train ETS service, which runs all the way to Padang Besar. ETS operates as part of KTM Intercity so tickets can be purchased at the KTM counter. The line passes through Tampin (for Melaka), Seremban,

ⓘ GETTING TO SINGAPORE

Getting to the border At JB Sentral you can clear immigration and travel across the Causeway to Singapore. All buses and taxis stop at Malaysian immigration. You'll need to disembark from your vehicle with your luggage (and ticket), clear immigration and re-board.

By bus from central JB, board at JB Sentral Bus Terminal after clearing Malaysian immigration just before the Causeway – you can buy your tickets on board. There are also frequent buses between JB's Larkin Sentral, 5km north of the city, and Singapore's Queen St bus station. **Causeway Link** (www.causewaylink.com.my; from JB/Singapore RM3.40/S$3.50; ⊙4am-11pm) is the most convenient and fastest service: the CW2 (from JB/Singapore RM3.40/S$3.50) runs to Queen St while the CW1 (from JB/Singapore RM1.90/S$1.50) runs to Kranji MRT station; both buses operate from around 4am to 11pm. **Trans Star Cross Border Coaches** (☑03-2010 5199; www.transtar.travel/cross-border-services) also run between Johor Bahru CIQ and Singapore's Changi Airport, departing every one to two hours from 5am to 9.15pm and embarking in the Terminal 2 coach area. Have the exact fare (RM10/S$9) ready for boarding, as no change is given.

Specially licensed taxis depart from Larkin Sentral, with trips to Singapore's Orchard Rd or Queen St terminal costing S$48 per taxi. Local city taxis cannot cross the Causeway. The taxis outside JB Sentral are technically pirate taxis but can be used as a last resort.

KTM (p243) has a service called **Shuttle Tebrau** with trains (RM5) between JB Sentral and Woodlands in Singapore, running every few hours from 5am to 10.30pm. Note that this only gets you as far as Woodlands – then you need to change to the Singapore metro system for the hour-long journey to the centre.

After clearing immigration, you can walk across the Causeway from Johor Bahru to Singapore if you want to; in the reverse direction, the partial lack of a pavement at the end as you approach Johor Bahru can be a deterrent, but it's still doable with care. This is sometimes a faster option than a bus over the jammed Causeway, but take a sunhat.

At the border Buses stop at Singapore immigration; you will need to clear immigration with your luggage, before getting back on board for the last leg to Queen St bus station, Kranji MRT or Changi Airport. There are tourism information offices and money exchanges at the border.

Moving on At Queen St there are buses, taxis and an MRT (light rail) system that can take you almost anywhere you need to go in the city. If taking the shuttle train, you'll go through passport checks and switch to the Singapore metro system at Woodlands.

KL Sentral, Tapah Rd (for Cameron Highlands), Ipoh, Taiping and Butterworth. Ekspres Rakyat Timuran, known as the 'Jungle Train', runs daily to Tumpat; you can board this service for Jerantut (for Taman Negara) and Kuala Lipis.

ⓘ Getting Around

BUS

Local buses operate from several stops around town, the most convenient being the stop in front of Public Bank on Jln Wong Ah Fook. From Larkin Sentral (p243) bus station, bus 39 goes into central JB (RM1.80).

CAR

Car hire in JB is considerably cheaper than in Singapore, but check that the hire firm allows cars to enter Singapore. Many rental companies have cars for hire at Senai International Airport (p243). **Hertz** (☑07-223 7520; www.hertz.com; Lot S15 & 15a, Podium 1, Menara Ansar, 65 Jln Trus; ⊙8am-6pm Mon-Sat) has an office in town and at the airport.

TAXI

Taxis in JB have meters, and drivers are legally required to use them although many drivers will try to negotiate fares. Flagfall is RM3, with an average trip costing RM10. There is a **taxi rank** (Jln Dato Onn) in front of the Post Office (p243). **Grab** (www.grab.com/my/taxi) is the cheapest way to get about town by taxi or ride-sharing.

Muar

☑06 / POP 357,000

A good-looking spot on the river, with plenty of heritage architecture and an infectiously languorous mood, the royal town of Muar (once known as Bandar Maharani, or 'Empress Town') was historically a very important commercial centre. So important in fact, that it had its own rail system, known as Muar State Railways, running from 1889 to 1925.

With each road in its central core painted a certain colour, Muar is very pretty and well worth spending a day or two exploring. It was also voted the cleanest city in the Asean region in 2018. Most of the heritage buildings are handily inscribed with their year of construction.

Central Chinatown sees most of the action, showing off its handsome pre-war architecture, temples and a handful of good restaurants and Chinese teahouses. Muar makes for an intriguing and rewarding off-the-beaten-track stop between Melaka and Johor Bahru.

◎ Sights

The graceful, colourful and compact **colonial district** at the heart of town by the river and immediately west of the Sultan Ismail Bridge turns up many buildings of note and outstanding heritage value. Walk around the area and look out for the former **Royal Customs and Excise Building** (Jln Maharani), the **high school** (Jln Meriam), the astonishing **Masjid Jamek Sultan Ibrahim Muar** (Jln Petri), the **Sultan Abu Bakar Building** (Jln Peteri) and the courthouse. It's also worth wandering the multihued grid of streets at the heart of Muar, pausing to admire the old Chinese shophouses, many of which fuse Chinese and European motifs. Check out the mouldering, fenced-off, bombastic classical **colonial building** on the corner of Jln Majidi and Jln Othman.

Keep an eye out for old Chinese **guildhalls**, usually from southern Chinese provinces; one example is the colourful and imposing **Chiang Chuan Association Building** (漳泉公會) on Jln Ali, in between Jln Haji Abu and Jln Sayang. Today, it's also home to a *nasi lemak* restaurant called Miss Coco Rice.

'The Loving Sisters' PUBLIC ART
(Jln Arab) Look out for this terrific black and white mural of two sisters on the side of a building by the roundabout as Jln Arab meeets Jln Bakri. The 12m-high painting was created by Russian artist Julia Volchkova.

Tanjung Emas Park PARK
(Jln Peteri; ⊗24hr) This pleasant riverside park is well worth a stroll for views of sunset, or early in the morning.

Chinese Opera Mural PUBLIC ART
(Jln Ali) Tucked away behind the four-storey Kwong Siu Building on Jln Ali (between Jln Sisi and Jln Sayang) are some blue-painted buildings, one of which is decorated with a superbly colourful mural of a Chinese opera actress, painted by an artist called Huang Zhongwei.

🛏 Sleeping & Eating

Muar doesn't have a great selection of hotels. **Muarar Hotel 99** (⊉06-953 9799; http://muararhotel.com.my; Jln Abdullah; d RM95; ❉ 🛜) offers comfortable rooms that are reasonably priced. **Streetview Hotel** (⊉06-953 7088; www.riverviewhotel.com.my/streetview; 11-13 Jln Ali; d RM105-124, ste RM169; ❉ 🛜) is a sound choice for comfort, helpful staff at the front desk and a location in the heart of the colonial district.

Muar is known for its Nonya-style *otak otak* (fish cakes) and satay breakfasts. *Mee bandung* – a spicy bowl of noodles in a shrimp and beef sauce – was also invented here. You'll find hawker stalls on Jln Haji Abu just off Jln Ali, while there's no shortage of Chinese teahouses. For fast food, head to **Wetex Parade** (69 Jln Ali; ⊗10am-10pm).

434 Kopi House CAFE $
(121 Jln Maharani; mains from RM7.50; ⊗8am-5.30pm) Running since 1953, busy 434 Kopi is the best cafe in town, its marble-topped tables overlooked by a large copy of the *Mona Lisa*. Delicious coffee (brewed from Malaysia Liberica Elephant beans and other varieties) is served in dainty cups, but there's also fruit and herbal teas, shakes, and a menu of Malay dishes.

Wah San CHINESE $
(華山; 69a Jln Abdullah; mains from RM4; ⊗7.30am-4.30pm Sat-Thu) This place – named after the famous Taoist mountain Hua Shan in China's Shaanxi Province – looks like it's

> **WORTH A TRIP**
>
> ### GUNUNG LEDANG NATIONAL PARK
>
> According to legend, the highest mountain in Johor is the home of Puteri Gunung Ledang, a mythical princess whose presence is said to permeate the jungle slopes. Climbing Gunung Ledang (also called Mt Ophir; 1276m) is a very demanding – yet rewarding – two-day return trip from the National Park Office at **Gunung Ledang National Park** (⊉07-266 1301; www.johorparks.gov.my/en; Jln Muar; admission RM3, hiking fee RM23, camp site RM10, dm RM25, chalet from RM75) to the summit. Consider a side trip to the Puteri Waterfalls, which feature a cool bathing pool. The route is dangerous in parts; mandatory guides cost RM140 per day.

been going forever and is best known for its *mee bandung*, a shallow bowl of noodles served in a spicy sauce of shrimp, onion, beef and egg. The dish was created in, and is most associated with, Muar.

ℹ Information

Several banks in town, including **HSBC** (15 Jln Peteri; ⊙ ATM 24hr), have ATMs that take international cards.

The Chinese-owned **Ruyi Travel** (☑ 06-951 6161; 8 Jln Perdana 12) offers tours of Muar led by locals.

ℹ Getting There & Away

Regular buses to JB (RM20, 2½ hours), Singapore (RM60, three hours) and KL (RM18, 2½ hours) depart from the **Muar long-distance bus station** (104 Jln Maharani) by the river. Buses to/from Melaka (RM6, one hour), and Gunung Ledang/Segamat (RM5, one hour) operate from the **local bus station** (Jln Petri). The taxi rank is just to the right of the bus station; a taxi to Melaka costs around RM80.

Mersing

☑ 07 / POP 70,000

This busy, compact fishing town on the east Johor coast is the principal gateway to Pulau Tioman. It has most of what travellers passing through on their way to the islands might need: OK sleeping options, shops, restaurants, cold beers and even a laundry. You probably won't want to linger as there are few sights and Mersing is by and large a functional transit town, though the Mersing River is enlivened by colourful fishing boats and views from the hilltop **Masjid Jamek Bandar Mersing** (Jln Masjid) are rewarding.

☞ Tours

Several places around the port work as booking offices for islands in the Seribuat Archipelago and Tioman Island, and can arrange packages. Enquire near the ferry terminal.

Pure Value Travel Agency   TOURS
(☑ 019-7534 250; 33 Plaza D'Jeti, Jln Abu Bakar; ⊙ 9am-5pm) This small operator by the ferry dock offers day trips to Endau-Rompin for RM200 per person (minimum four people). Overnight trips start at RM350 per person.

🛏 Sleeping

You may end up spending a night or two in Mersing waiting for ferries (due to weather or tides).

Avoid arriving during Chinese New Year and other holiday periods, when midrange hotels can be booked solid. Note there isn't much accommodation available at the top end.

Sweet Hotel   HOTEL $
(☑ 07-799 2228; www.mersingsweethotel.com; 5 Jln Jemaluang; d RM90; P ❀ 🛜) Serviceable for a night or two, this modest hotel has simple but very affordable rooms, with parking out front and a 24-hour restaurant pretty much right next door. It's a short walk from the bus station.

Zeeadam Backpackers   HOSTEL $
(☑ 019-740 3456; 1C-1 Jln Abu Bakar; dm RM20, tw RM50; 🛜) The only true backpacker place in town, the Zeeadam has just two dorm rooms, sleeping 10 people on ultrafirm beds, and a twin with terrace. There's a little TV and a hangout area at this second-storey spot that is short on charm but long on value.

OFF THE BEATEN TRACK

EXPLORE MORE OF JOHOR

Johor encompasses over 19,000 sq km of palm plantations, jungle, mountain tops, city, village, sea, mangrove and forest settings, and there's plenty of off-track adventures to be had. Here are some top spots to veer off the tourist trail. Accommodation and tourist infrastructure in these areas is limited; look for homestays or small hotels in larger nearby villages.

Tanjung Piai National Park Just 90km south of Johor Bahru city centre, this national park protects shorebirds and mangrove swamps. Tourism is only just taking hold, but it has a small visitor centre, boardwalks and a jetty.

Soga Perdana Recreational Forest Head out from Batu Pahat to visit this small forest that's popular with local birders.

Sungai Bantang Recreational Forest Accessed from Bekok, this green zone is known for its waterfalls and waterways. There are some camp sites.

Kota Tinggi Hop out of town to visit a *kampung* (village) known for its royal tombs, check out a wonderful cascading waterfall or just revel in seeing something new.

Mersing

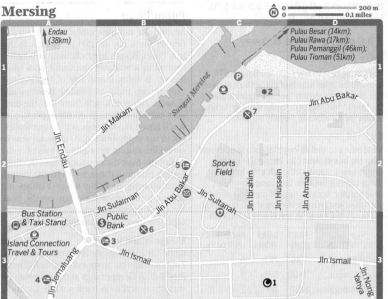

Endau
(38km)

Pulau Besar (14km);
Pulau Rawa (17km);
Pulau Pemanggil (46km);
Pulau Tioman (51km)

Sungai Mersing

Jln Makam

Jln Endau

Jln Abu Bakar

Sports
Field

Jln Sulaiman

Jln Abu Bakar

Jln Sultanah

Jln Ibrahim

Jln Hussein

Jln Ahmad

Public
Bank

Bus Station
& Taxi Stand

Island Connection
Travel & Tours

Jln Ismail

Jln Ismail

Jln Norig
Yahya

Jln Jemaluang

Hotel Embassy
HOTEL **$**

(☏ 07-799 3545; 2 Jln Ismail; r RM65; ❀ ☎) A decent choice compared with other cheapies in town, this is a reasonable place to clean up and return to reality after bumming it on island beaches. All rooms are huge and bright, with cable TV, gusty air-con and attached bathrooms.

🍴 Eating

Mersing has a decent, if rather limited, choice of restaurants. There are a couple of food courts serving typical Malaysian hawker food near the entrance to the ferry terminal.

Mersing Harbour Centre
HAWKER **$**

(Jln Abu Bakar; dishes RM3-8; ⊙ 5am-10pm) As well as housing a collection of stalls selling hawker food, this centre opposite the ferry terminal is where you go to book ferry tickets and resorts on Tioman as well as to pay the marine park entrance fee.

Loke Tien Yuen Restaurant
CHINESE **$**

(55 Jln Abu Bakar; mains RM8-20; ⊙ 12.30-3pm & 6.45-8.30pm Sat-Wed; ❀) Mersing's oldest Chinese restaurant is one of the friendliest and busiest places in town. You may have to wait for a marble table to enjoy deliciously prepared prawn and pork dishes. The speciality, whole

Mersing

◎ Sights
1 Masjid Jamek Bandar Mersing..........C3

✪ Activities, Courses & Tours
2 Pure Value Travel Agency.................. C1

🛏 Sleeping
3 Hotel Embassy B3
4 Sweet Hotel A3
5 Zeeadam Backpackers....................B2

🍴 Eating
6 Loke Tien Yuen Restaurant...............B3
7 Mersing Harbour Centre...................C1

steamed fish that you'll see all the locals eating isn't on the English menu, so ask your server.

ℹ Information

Mersing is a pretty safe town, but with so many travellers passing through en route to Pulau Tioman, the usual warnings about pickpockets and keeping an eye on your belongings apply.

There are several banks with ATMs along and near Jln Ismail including **Public Bank** (21-22 Jln Sulaiman; ⊙ ATM 24hr), which has a 24-hour ATM that accepts MasterCard, Maestro, Cirrus, Visa and Plus.

Police (☏ 07-799 2222; Jln Sultanah)

Post Office (Jln Abu Bakar; ⊘ 8.30am-5.30pm Mon-Thu, to 1pm Sat)

❶ Getting There & Away

BOAT

You can connect by **ferry** (Jln Abu Bakar) to Tioman and the other islands of the Seribuat Archipelago. Buy tickets and pay the marine park entrance fee (adult/child RM30/15) at the Mersing Harbour Centre (p247) opposite the jetty entrance.

BUS

Most buses as well as long-distance taxis depart from the **bus station** (Jln Terminal) near the bridge over the river, although a few long-distance buses leave from bus-company offices near the pier. Some buses will drop you off at the pier when you arrive in Mersing if you ask nicely. For buses to Cherating, travel first to Kuantan.

DESTINATION	PRICE (RM)	DURA- TION	FREQUENCY (PER DAY)
Johor Bahru	17.80	2½hr	6
Kuala Lumpur	38.30	5½hr	5
Kuala Terengganu	37.60	9hr	2
Kuantan	18.20	5hr	7
Melaka	25.10	4hr	3
Singapore	48	3hr	2
Penang	80	10hr	1

TAXI

Long-distance taxis depart from the bus station. Destinations and costs (per car) include:
➡ Johor Bahru (RM250)
➡ Kuantan (RM300)
➡ Tanjong Gemok (RM60)
➡ Pekan (RM200)
➡ Tanjung Leman, for boats to Sibu Island (RM100)

Seribuat Archipelago

☑ 07

The Seribuat Archipelago, off the east coast of Johor, is a constellation of some of Malaysia's most beautiful islands. Of the cluster of 64 islands, most people only know of Pulau Tioman (p253), the largest, which is actually a part of Pahang. This leaves the rest of the archipelago as far less-visited dots of tranquillity.

Divers can expect to see excellent coral and an array of marine life, from butterfly fish and parrotfish to barracuda, giant clams and more. The waters around the archipelago are frequently whipped into foam during the monsoon (November to February), so ferry services can be patchy, especially during the high monsoon (November and December).

Pulau Besar

Around 30 minutes offshore by boat and perfect for a day or two of serious lounging, Pulau Besar's long white-sand beach is fronted by a veritable swimming pool when the sea is calm. If you tire of vegging out, explore the trails to hidden beaches and through plenty of jungle. Note that the coral isn't great and there is no dive operator, so you'll have to spend your water time frolicking in the sandy-bottomed turquoise seas or snorkelling along the scattered bits of reef.

Resorts have their own speedboats, which usually charge in the region of RM100 return from Mersing to Pulau Besar. Visitors not staying at the resorts can hop on the boat, but check there's a return boat the same day, otherwise you'll need to stay overnight.

Mirage Island Resort   RESORT $$
(☑ 07-799 2334; www.mirageislandresort.com.my; 2 night package r per person incl transfers & all meals RM420-880) Cheaper digs at this 10-room resort are in stylish A-frames while the more expensive options are in huge, louvred wood bungalows – all exuding a tropical-colonial charm. The staff are young and fun, and there's a bar and pool table in the restaurant area. A barbecue dinner is also available for RM22 extra. Prices include return speedboat voyage to Mersing.

Aseania Resort   RESORT $$
(☑ 03-6211 1055; www.aseaniapulaubesar.com; chalets incl breakfast from RM300; ❋ ❀) Rooms are big and clean enough, with dark-wood interiors. The service is stellar and the jungle pool, surrounded by a stylish wooden deck, is a shady alternative to the beach; there's a decent bar, too. Sunsets are, of course, superb.

Pulau Sibu

Aside from Tioman Island, this cluster of several islands (**Pulau Sibu Besar**, **Pulau Sibu Kukus**, **Pulau Sibu Tengah**, **Pulau Tengah** and **Pulau Sibu Hujung**) is the most popular destination in the archipelago – particularly with expat families living in Singapore. The main attractions are good diving, even better beaches and a great choice of beachside resorts for the ultimate getaway.

Some boats for Pulau Sibu leave from Mersing, but others depart from the jetty at Tanjung Leman around 65km south of town. There are no public boats so you'll have to organise transport (around RM100 return, usually included in package prices) with your resort – each resort arranges its own boats.

★Rimba Resort   RESORT $$

(📞012-710 6855; www.resortmalaysia.com; Pulau Sibu Besar; chalet per person incl meals s/d/tr from RM400/300/285, child RM120-165) Welcome to a super-chilled-out beachy paradise, with 21 comfy thatched chalets overlooking Pulau Sibu Besar's best swimming and snorkelling beach. The spacious digs are stylish with canopy mosquito nets, cushion-clad lounging spaces and sunken semi-open-air bathrooms. There's a choice of sea-view or family chalets and Island suites. The cheapest chalets have no hot-water shower.

Guests from the other resorts are often lured here by the lovely white beach and loungeable deck bar. There's a dive centre and massage hut, and the staff are lovely. Boats all leave from Tanjung Leman jetty and cost RM100 return.

Sea Gypsy Village Resort   RESORT $$

(📞07-229 8642; www.siburesort.com; Pulau Sibu Besar; A-frames per person d or tw RM245) ⚡ This resort is one of the best, most affordable places to relax with kids in Malaysia. Special children's meals are served throughout the day, there's a fun kids' club, a mini-playground and even an ingenious worm-composting system for ecofriendly nappy disposal. On the northeast coast, the beach here is better suited to playing in the waves than swimming. No wi-fi.

Batu Batu   RESORT $$$

(📞07-228 8000, 017-755 0672; www.batubatu.com. my; Pulau Tengah; d incl breakfast & transfers from RM780; ❄@🛜🏊) ⚡ This upscale eco-resort on Pulau Tengah offers 22 private villas on a shimmering coral-sand island. It also runs a turtle sanctuary and takes volunteers (who pay for lodging), rents out all sorts of watercraft and has a PADI dive centre.

Pulau Rawa

Edged by a fine white-sand beach, and luring bands of sunseekers, surfers and snorkellers, the tiny island of Rawa pokes out of the sea 16km from Mersing. Its resorts arrange transport for guests, to and from the jetty at the south of the island.

★Alang's Rawa Resort   RESORT $$$

(📞07-798 0579; www.alangsrawa.com; 2 nights per person incl meals & transfers from RM690) Cheerful white huts with sky-blue shutters line the best part of the beach: the destination for a perfect do-nothing escape. Service is nonexistent – but in this setting, who cares?

There are 14 rooms, including beachfront A-frames with hammocks, a beach house with balconies and hut rooms by the jungle. Wi-fi available in the restaurant.

Rawa Island Resort   RESORT $$$

(📞07-799 1204; www.rawaislandresort.com; full board per person 2 nights s/d from RM1780/2296; ❄@) The island's main resort has basic, ageing beachfront and hillside chalets, bungalows and villas, but you'll be outdoors all the time so it's fine as a bed for the night. This is a lively, family-style heaven with paddleboats and a trampoline, while the beach is divine. There's a restaurant, dive centre and a wide range of facilities and activities.

Pulau Aur, Pulau Dayang & Pulau Pemanggil

These three islands are so far from the mainland (three to six hours by boat, depending on the vessel and the weather) that you'll need to devote a few days to make it worth the trip. In fact, you may not be able to get here at all outside of weekends and holidays, when the resorts run boats to pick up groups of Singaporean divers.

Sixty-five kilometres from the mainland, Pulau Aur has crystal-clear azure water, fantastic coral and a few wrecks off its coast, with the smaller island of Dayang sitting in sapphire waters just to the north.

Fifty kilometres east of Mersing, beautiful Pulau Pemanggil supports a very sparse

WORTH A TRIP

PULAU TINGGI

About 10km northeast of Pulau Sibu Besar, jungle-clad Tinggi is an impressive sight when seen from a distance – it's an extinct volcano with a 600m-high cone that creates a dreamy silhouette. Most resorts offer day trips around the island, which include excellent snorkelling and a trek to a beautiful waterfall.

The island supports three village populations: Kampung Tanjung Balang, Kampung Pasir Panjang and Kampung Sebirah Besar. The main place to stay is the **Tad Marine Resort** (📞012-908 9929, 03-8023 9009; www.tadmarineresort. com; Kampung Pasir Panjang, Pulau Tinggi; per person incl meals s/tw/tr from RM465/330/300; ❄🏊) offering a variety of garden- and sea-view chalets alongside a lovely white-sand beach.

population. Needless to say, the water and views are stunning.

You will need to book your room or package first and then check boat times with your accommodation provider. It is not possible to visit the islands on a regular ferry from the mainland. During the monsoon months, expect considerable disruption to the sailing schedule.

Gilligan's Lodge & Retreat CHALET $$
(☑012-998 0057; www.aurislandresort.com; Pulau Aur; 2/3 nights RM528/998, 1 night d RM250-320; ❄☎) Gilligan's is tucked away on a small sandy bay in the north of the island, scenically located opposite Pulau Dayang. With air-con rooms, restaurant, beach bar and terrific diving opportunities, it makes a quiet, secluded base and the views are gorgeous. Packages are available or you can just pay for the room, but in either case the ferry ticket from Mersing is extra.

Dayang Blues Resort RESORT $$$
(☑in Singapore 65-6536 6532; www.dayangnow.com; from S$400; ❄) About 300 beds are available at this resort, north across the channel from Pulau Aur. Dayang Blues Resort is located on the scenic beach on the south of the island in Kampung Pasir Pulih. Diving packages are available.

Endau-Rompin National Park

The forest here dates back over 248 million years, to the Permian Triassic period – this is a pristine, waterfall-laden jungle teeming with animals, waterfalls and knockout views. Straddling the Johor–Pahang border, the 870-sq-km park is the second-largest on the peninsula after the much more developed and accessible Taman Negara (p273). Not nearly as many visitors venture to Endau-Rompin, so there is far less hiking traffic but, as there are few trails, exploration is limited. What you can see, however, is really quite spectacular.

The park's lowland forests are among the last in Peninsular Malaysia and have been identified as harbouring unique varieties of plant life, including enormous umbrella palms with their characteristic fan-shaped leaves, and *Livinstona endanensis,* a species of palm with serrated circular leaves.

Herds of elephants are sometimes spotted near Kampung Peta around sunset. The park's birds include red jungle fowl, the black hornbill and the grey wagtail, while king fishers can be spied around the river. You may well see gibbons moving about in the trees.

The majority of travellers arrive on tours arranged by private operators but it's just as easy (and less expensive) to organise a trip through the park itself, though you will need to book in advance. First contact the **Johor National Parks Corporation** (☑07-266 1301; www.johorparks.gov.my/en; Level 1, Dato' Muhamad Salleh Perang Bldg, Kota Iskandar, Nusajaya, Johor Bahru; ⊙8am-1pm & 2-5pm Mon-Sat), or the individual park entrance office: the Endau-Rompin Peta Office or the Endau-Rompin Selai Office. Make sure you take your passport along as you will need it to register.

Note that most of Endau-Rompin is closed during the monsoon season (November to February), but with surfaces becoming so slippery, squelchy and treacherous, that's not a great time to visit anyway.

Guides
For reasons of safety, the Johor National Parks Corporation insists that you hire a guide to explore the park. Guides can be engaged for around RM100 per day at the park headquarters at Kampung Peta, or at the Selai office, and are usually Orang Asli who come from the nearby villages and who have grown up in these jungles. Note that their English skills may not be that good. A conservation fee (RM20) is also required. Most people spend around three days exploring the park.

◉ Sights & Activities

🏃 Kampung Peta Entrance
The park office and lodging is right next to a charming Orang Asli village whose residents often give demonstrations on local games (mostly puzzles – get ready to use your brain) and animal-trapping techniques. It's a lush setting a short walk from the river. To go on walks you'll need to first take a scenic boat trip (RM150 for up to 10 people, around 45 minutes) upriver – keep an eye out for wildlife as you go. From the boat drop-off, it's about a half-hour walk to **Kuala Jasin base camp**, from where all the trails lead. To organise A-frame lodging and activities from this entrance, call the Endau-Rompin Peta Office.

Upeh Guling Falls HIKING
The main trail in the park follows the Sungai Jasin from Kuala Jasin base camp. An easy, one-day, mostly flat walk with a few river crossings through pristine jungle takes you to these multitiered falls. There's a nice leech-free picnic spot on a rock facing the falls.

Endau-Rompin National Park

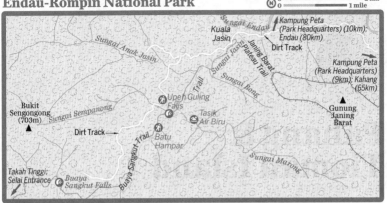

Batu Hampar   HIKING

It's a 40-minute hike from the Upeh Gul-ing Falls to the flat rocks and camp site of Batu Hampar, from where it's about a chal-lenging 4km uphill slog over several ridges from Batu Hampar to the the top of the falls (a 40m drop) at Buaya Sangkut. The path is quite faint – only attempt this hike with a guide.

Tasik Air Biru   SWIMMING

On the way back from one- or two-day treks, most people stop for a swim at this bright blue, clear and refreshing swimming hole, a few minutes' walk from Kuala Jasin base camp.

Kampung Selai Entrance

Selai – the western entrance to the park – has far fewer facilities than Kampung Peta and, notably, you need to bring your own food. Treks from **Lubuk Tapah base camp** in the west of the park follow the Sungai Selai to explore the many waterfalls along the river. To organise a trip from this en-trance directly through the park, call the Endau-Rompin Selai Office.

About a 1½-hour walk from base camp up a steep hill you'll reach the tall, single-drop **Takah Berangin Falls** where you can plop in for a dip and some body pummelling from the rapids. Thirty minutes on from here are the tall and slender **Takah Pandan Falls** where you can dive into a much calmer pool (around 2m deep).

From base camp at the park's office, trek about 1½ hours along a good trail to the roaring, low-slung **Takah Tinggi Falls**. You'll cross a few suspension bridges en route.

Sleeping & Eating

There are fan dorms and decent bunga-lows available in Kampung Peta (dorm bed RM25, bungalow RM100 to RM150) and simple A-frames at Kuala Jasin. Tents can also be rented from Kampung Peta for RM40 per night. Make sure you take ade-quate mosquito repellent.

At Selai, simple chalet accommodation (from RM60) is available at Lubuk Tapah base camp.

You can camp at designated sites for RM5 per night per person.

Kampung Peta has a canteen where three good Malaysian-style meals per day (includ-ing a packed lunch if you're hiking) cost RM37. There's no canteen at Selai but there are simple cooking facilities.

Getting There & Away

Unless you have your own 4WD, getting to Endau-Rompin means either booking a tour in Mersing (try Pure Value; p246) or making arrangements independently through the park itself.

To go by yourself, for Kampung Peta first take a bus to Kahang and ask to be let off at the park office. Call the **Endau-Rompin Peta Office** (☑ 07-888 2812; jnpc@johor.gov.my; 11 Jln Bawal 1, Kahang; ⊙ 8am-5pm) in advance to charter one of the park's 4WDs with a driver (RM370) from here. It's a 56km ride through palm-oil plantations to Kampung Peta.

For Selai take a train to Kampung Bekok station, or take a bus to Bekok. Call the **Endau-Rompin Selai Office** (☑ 07-922 2875; jnpc@johor.gov.my; 8, Jln Satria 1, Taman Berjaya, Bekok) in advance to arrange a 4WD (RM120) pickup for the 45-minute drive over a rough road to base camp.

Pahang & Tioman Island

🌏 09 / POP 1.6 MILLION

Includes ➡

Pulau Tioman	253
Pekan	262
Kuantan	263
Cherating	268
Temerloh & Around	270
Jerantut	272
Taman Negara	273
Kuala Lipis	279
Raub	280

Best Places to Eat

➡ Coastal Store (p266)

➡ Tjantek Art Bistro (p267)

➡ Seri Mutiara Restaurant (p278)

➡ ABCD Restaurant (p258)

➡ Jalan Lebai Ali Food Street (p266)

Best Places to Stay

➡ Swiss Cottage Resort (p257)

➡ Rainbow Chalets (p259)

➡ Mutiara Taman Negara Resort (p277)

➡ Residence Inn (p270)

➡ 1511 Coconut Grove (p259)

Why Go?

For many visitors, a journey to Peninsular Malaysia's largest state begins and ends on the enchanted isle of Tioman. Between its exhilarating diving, brilliant beaches, vegetation-choked jungle treks and spirited villages, its tropical-island allure is impossible to resist.

Pahang's other big ticket – the primordial jungles of Taman Negara – lies tucked up in the state's north. Its virgin tracts of rainforest, home to a howling, twittering, trumpeting (and occasionally roaring) rabble of elusive wildlife, offer a direct connection with nature as nature intended it: wild, unrelenting, raw.

Between these big acts, you'll find reggae beach parties on the surf-bum sands of Cherating, royal splendour and noble palaces in riverside Pekan, a fine crop of colonial architecture in Kuala Lipis, abandoned tin mines in the hills of Sungai Lembing and a culinary adventure or two in the restaurants and cafes of Kuantan.

When to Go
Endau

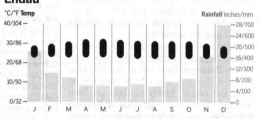

Jan–Apr The weather is at its warmest and driest. Crowds are at their peak.

May–Dec Prepare to sweat: the thermometer hovers between 21°C and 32°C, and humidity exceeds 82%.

Nov–Feb Monsoon season. Some places close, the surf is up in Cherating and discounts abound.

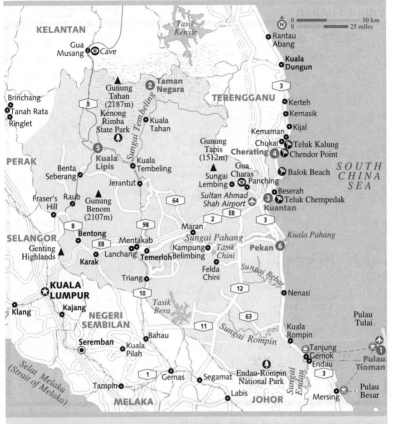

Pahang & Tioman Island Highlights

1 Pulau Tioman (p253)
Village hopping, diving, snorkelling, jungle hiking and sunset watching.

2 Taman Negara (p273)
Hiking into the primeval heart of this deep, dark and undeniably adventurous national park.

3 Kuantan (p263)
Enjoying some of the best food in Pahang with day trips to nearby beaches, caves and old tin mining towns.

4 Cherating (p268)
Taking an evening firefly trip along the dark river, with the luminous bugs floating on the breeze towards your boat.

5 Kuala Lipis (p279)
Exploring the heritage buildings of this charming and laid-back riverside town.

6 Pekan (p262) Admiring the regal architecture, old palaces and traditional *kampung* (village) houses of this town at the mouth of the Pahang River.

PULAU TIOMAN

🎵 09 / POP 3000

Sitting like an emerald dragon guarding the translucent waters of the South China Sea, Tioman Island offers every possible shade of paradise. There are cascading waterfalls, rigorous jungle hikes that take you past hibiscus blooms under an evergreen canopy, and a wide range of laid-back villages facing idyllic beaches. And then there's the gorgeous sea of greens, blues and chartreuse swirls that beckons you to paddle, snorkel, dive and sail.

At 20km long and 11km wide, the island is so spacious that your ideal holiday spot is surely here somewhere. Tekek, Tioman's largest village and its administrative centre, is where ferries arrive from Mersing (in Johor) and Tanjung Gemok (in Pahang), but

other beachside villages and resorts are a short water taxi ride or drive away. Despite its popularity, Tioman retains an unspoiled feel, with pristine wilderness and friendly, authentic village life, rounded off with terrific jungle-hiking options.

A stretch of road runs along the western side of the island from Selesa Tioman Hotel past Berjaya Tioman Resort to the northern end of Tekek, where it narrows to allow only motorbikes or bicycles to continue to the northern end of Kampung Air Batang (p257) (better known as ABC). Another 9km winding road links the southern end of Tekek with the dozy east coast idyll of Kampung Juara (p257). For walkers, there are road-jungle trail combos that connect most of the west coast, all the way from Kampung Salang (p257) to Kampung Genting (p257).

Tekek is Tioman's largest village and its administrative centre. The airport is here, as is the island's only cash machine. Bear in mind that everything stocked in shops on Tioman is shipped from the mainland and tends to be expensive (except beer and tobacco as this is a duty-free zone), so stock up on essentials before you arrive.

◉ Sights & Activities

Water Sports

The underwater world around the island offers some of the best (and most accessible) diving and snorkelling in Malaysia. It's also one of the few places in the country where you have a good chance of seeing pods of dolphins. The season runs from February to November, out of the monsoon months.

There are plenty of excellent dive centres on Tioman, and Open Water Diver (OWD) certification courses are priced competitively. Expect to pay about RM1100 to RM1200 for a four-day PADI (Professional Association of Diving Instructors) OWD course and RM120 to RM130 for fun dives. Discover dives (beginner dives that do not require precertification and include basic instruction), cost RM200 to RM250 for a half-day course. SSI (Scuba Schools International) courses can also be found. Schools are dotted around the island, clustering mainly in ABC, Tekek, Salang, Paya and Juara. The dive schools in Paya cater mainly to Chinese visitors.

There is good snorkelling off the rocky points on the west coast of the island, particularly those just north of ABC, but the best snorkelling is around nearby Pulau Tulai, better known as Coral Island. Snorkelling equipment for hire is easy to find (masks and snorkels are typically RM15 per day) at many places on the island. Snorkelling trips with boat transfers cost RM40 to RM100.

For freediving, contact **Freedive Tioman** (☑ 011-2358 0667; www.facebook.com/pg/freedive tioman; Swiss Cottage Resort, Kampung Tekek; 1-/2-day course RM450/900; ⊗ 8am-6pm).

Above water you may wish to try your hand at kayaking, paddleboarding or surfing (this is best during the monsoon season). Kayaks and boards can be rented from hotels and beachside operations for around RM25 for two hours. A round-trip island boat tour costs about RM150.

Marine Park
Information Centre   NATURE CENTRE
(☑ 09-414 1595; www.dmpm.nre.gov.my; Tekek; ⊗ 8am-1pm & 2-5pm Mon-Fri, to 12.15pm & 2.45-5pm Sat) FREE With coral displays, short videos and plenty of information on marine flora and fauna, this centre, north of Tekek Airport, is a worthwhile stop particularly for divers and snorkellers as well as anyone wishing to discover more about Tioman's natural environment.

★ **B&J**   DIVING
(☑ 09-419 1218; www.divetioman.com; Kampung Air Batang) This PADI 5-Star Dive Centre with its own pool offers DSAT (Diving Science and Technology) and IANTD (International Association of Nitrox and Technical Divers) courses, along with Open Water Diver courses (RM1100), discover scuba dives from the beach (RM200) as well as technical dives (from RM400), two-day freediving courses (RM1000) and wreck dives (RM800).

Blue Heaven Divers   DIVING
(☑ 013-338 0893; www.blueheavendivers.com; from RM90) Run by Japanese couple Aki and Aiko, this diving outfit in ABC is a popular choice as a smaller operation for SSI (Scuba Schools International) and PADI courses, offering a high degree of safety and professionalism with a dependable team of instructors. Fun dives start at RM90 for a beach dive, while a half-day scuba diving intro course is RM200.

DiveAsia   DIVING
(☑ 09-419 5017; www.diveasia.com.my; Kampung Salang; from RM150) This Salang-based dive school has a professional and friendly dive crew who relate well to their students. The

PAHANG & TIOMAN ISLAND PULAU TIOMAN

LOCAL KNOWLEDGE

TIOMAN'S TOP DIVE SITES

The leeward side of Tioman offers a remarkable variety of killer dive and snorkel sites, while the east coast's offerings are more limited. Most dives have a maximum depth of 30m.

Renggis Island Good for snorkelling and beginner dives, this spot just off the Berjaya Resort pier on the west shore has blacktip reef sharks, turtles and lionfish.

Tiger & Labas Heading off Labas Island, advanced divers can spot reef fish, rays and schools of barracuda and jackfish at Tiger Reef.

Coral Island Head out for stunning soft coral, reef fish and an occasional pufferfish. This is a top half-day boat excursion for snorkellers.

Cebeh Island Offers diving in depths of between 5m and 30m, as well as volcanic caves and tunnels. Visibility is good; expect to see a lot of sea fans as well as pufferfish, parrotfish, angelfish and maybe barracudas.

Experienced divers won't want to miss two famous WWII-era wreck sites 45 nautical miles north of Tioman: HMS *Repulse* and HMS *Prince of Wales*. Both sites are astounding for their historical significance and wide array of marine life. They're challenging – best suited for those with more than a few dives under their belts – but you don't need certification aside from your open water. Also ask about diving the KM *Sipadan* sunk at the Sawadee dive site in 2012 to create an artificial reef.

full range of PADI courses is offered, from those targeted at first-timers to night dives, wreck dives, advanced open water, deep dives, underwater photography and more.

Ray's Dive Adventures
DIVING

(☑019-330 8062; www.raysdive.com; ABC) A popular and reliable dive outfit, Ray and his team in ABC offer the full range of PADI courses, and there are various other dive packages and trips as well. Accommodation can also be arranged.

Hiking

Jungle-swathed Tioman offers plenty of excellent hikes to keep the intrepid land-lubber exhausted and happy. You'll see more wildlife than in most of Malaysia's national parks, including black giant squirrels, long-tailed macaques, brush-tailed porcupines and – if you're out with a torch at dawn or dusk and incredibly lucky – the endangered, nocturnal *binturong* (bear cat). Also look out for huge monitor lizards: there are two types, one which lives on land and the other which is amphibious.

While you can easily take on most hikes by yourself, guided jungle trips (arranged through your accommodation) give you a curated look at the island's unique flora and fauna, and cost around RM100 for a half-day. If you're setting out on foot, be wary of

entering the jungle after around 4.30pm, as it's easy to get lost in the dark.

Tekek to Juara Jungle Walk
HIKING

This 7km hike offers an excellent feel for the richness of Tioman's spectacular interior, with the added bonus of finishing at beautiful Juara. While the walk isn't too strenuous, parts of it are steep, and hiking in tropical heat can be taxing, so take water (though you'll be in the shade).

ABC to Salang Trail
HIKING

This 3.5km trail, connecting ABC to Salang, runs inland from the coast leading past lovely beaches. The hike takes around two and a half to three hours; the trail is pretty hard going as it isn't well marked – follow the black electricity cables. To set off, hike up from Bamboo Hill Chalets at the northern end of ABC bay.

Tekek to Berjaya Tioman Resort Hike
HIKING

An easy and enjoyable 30-minute hike heads south from Tekek to Berjaya Tioman Resort (p261), either by the road or by rock-hopping around the headland at low tide. From there you can walk alongside the golf course; just before the telecommunications tower there is a trail to the deserted beach of Bunut. You can continue from the resort to Kampung Paya.

Berjaya Tioman Resort to Kampung Paya Walk
HIKING

From Berjaya Tioman Resort, the road leads to Selesa Tioman Hotel before continuing over the headland to Kampung Paya. Follow the black electricity cables and concrete posts supporting them (the posts are inscribed with the name 'Paya'). At the south end of Kampung Paya, the 40-minute trail from Paya to Genting is easy enough to follow.

Other Activities

Genting is the home of renowned Malaysian batik artist Suhadi Mahadi, who runs traditional batik-making classes at his **arts and crafts centre** (☑019-692 2409; suzilabatik @gmail.com; Kampung Genting) just south of the jetty.

Juara Turtle Project
VOLUNTEERING

(☑09-419 3244; www.juaraturtleproject.com; Mentawak beach, Kampung Juara; tour RM10, dm RM120; ⊙10am-5pm) 🐾 This voluntourism operation works to protect declining sea-turtle populations by collecting eggs and moving them to a hatchery, and patrolling the beaches for

---

ℹ️ TRAIL SAFETY

Don't let Tioman's laid-back vibe fool you into forgetting you're in the jungle.

➡ Carry enough water. Many a day tripper has learned too late the folly of heading out with insufficient fluids.

➡ Rethink your hiking plans if it's been raining. Especially during monsoon season, when nearly every trail becomes unpleasantly muddy at best and impossible to follow at worst.

➡ Take a headlamp or torch. Necessary if you think there's even the slightest chance you'll be out past sundown.

➡ Tell someone where you are going and when you expect to be back.

➡ Try to avoid trekking solo.

➡ Watch for snakes. Don't freak out, but there are 25 snake species on Tioman, including the king cobra and reticulated python. Closed shoes are a wise choice.

CHOOSING A SLICE OF PARADISE

The hardest part of your Tioman adventure may well be deciding where to go. The major options are, counterclockwise from north to south:

Kampung Salang The most backpacker-esque of Tioman's *kampung*. Come to snorkel off nearby Coral Island, join a dive class or stay for the beach parties.

ABC (Kampung Air Batang) North of Kampung Tekek and slightly more upscale than Salang, ABC has a good choice of budget restaurants and accommodation. Though the beach isn't all that spectacular, it's pleasant in parts and sunsets are frequently lovely.

Kampung Tekek Tioman's commercial hub is a good central location from which to explore the rest of the island, but it's not such a great place to stay.

Kampung Paya The moderately priced resorts here on the east coast south of Kampung Tekek, offering all-inclusive packages, make Paya popular with Chinese and Singaporean tourists and the organised-tour set looking to snorkel off Paya beach.

Kampung Genting The beach here on the southwest coast is fairly built up, but is surrounded by a local village with an appealing *kampung* atmosphere.

Kampung Nipah Offering a serene beach, rugged and isolated Nipah on the south coast is the way to go for those wanting to leave the world behind (the village lacks internet and mobile-phone access).

Kampung Mukut This traditional *kampung* may be one of the prettiest towns on the island, and the beach is lovely. Find it on the south coast, east of Kampung Nipah.

Kampung Juara This east-coast village has the best surfing beach in Tioman and enough restaurants and accommodation to make it well worth the trip. The beachfront bungalows offer blissful views and the all-important sunrise.

poachers and predators. Anyone can tour the facility to learn more about the area's turtles, which nest here from February to October, with public releases June through November.

Volunteers (accepted March to October) get basic dorm accommodation and full board. When you're not working on patrols and participating in information seminars, activities including sea kayaking, treks and cooking classes. There's a minimum four-night stay in dorm accommodation.

🛏 Sleeping & Eating

All villages and beaches with accommodation on Tioman's west coast are serviced by regular ferries from Mersing and Tanjung Gemok. To get to Juara, take a ferry to Tekek, then jump in a taxi to get over the cross-island road.

Budget accommodation largely comprises small wooden chalets, typically with a bathroom, fan and mosquito net. More expensive rooms have air-con and hot showers. Most operations have larger family rooms for those with children. Larger places and resorts have all kinds of activities for guests, from diving to trekking, batik painting and round-island trips.

🛏 Tekek

All accommodation options lie close to each other on the excellent southern beach.

Dine on Malaysian dishes at **Delima** (Tekek; mains RM7-10) or Chinese food at **Chinese Sarang Seafood** (☑ 013-706 6484; Tekek; mains RM20; ⊙ 10am-3pm & 6-11pm), which also serves beers.

Cheers Chalet & Souvenir CHALET $
(☑ 09-419 1425, 013-931 1425; cheersteo@yahoo.com; Kampung Tekek; s&d with shared bathroom RM60, r RM130-200; ❄ 🛜) If you don't mind skipping beach views, this is a fine budget option, with some of the cheapest rooms in this section of the island. The gardens are lovely and it's only a short walk away from the water.

★ **Swiss Cottage Resort** BOUTIQUE HOTEL $$
(☑ 017-704 1773; www.swiss-cottage-tioman.com; Kampung Tekek; r RM180-260; ❄ 🛜) The small number of rooms gives this place a boutique feel and this friendly resort is operated by creative folk who invest effort in their rooms. The ones to nab are the sea-view chalets (RM220) with bamboo and wood interiors, or the bungalows (RM260) with elegant

Asian furniture and roomy balconies. Other options are nestled in a shady garden.

Coral Reef Tioman
HOTEL $$

(☑ 09-419 1868, 013-357 8326; www.coralreef tioman.com; Kampung Tekek; d RM130-220, f RM350-450; ❈ ☏) Adik and Hasnizah's simple beachfront hotel has rooms with individually crafted stonework, raised platform beds, air-con and colour TVs – some face the sea, as does the property's restaurant serving Western and local food. The cheapest rooms have a garden view. Ask after the package deals that are available.

★ Tioman Cabana
INTERNATIONAL $$

(☑ 013-717 6677; www.tiomancabana.com; Kampung Tekek; mains RM22-35; ◷ 9am-3pm & 7-10.30pm; ☏) This castaway-chic restaurant with bed and breakfast rooms (RM150 to RM280) is right on the beach, steps from the lapping waves. On the menu are excellent homemade burgers and local dishes, and there's a very chilled vibe. You can bring your own alcohol and expect jamming sessions late into the night.

🛏 Air Batang (ABC)

Walkable from Tekek along the walkway around the headland but also with its own jetty, ABC has a great choice of budget restaurants and accommodation, with a pleasant stretch of beach in the north and loads of dive operators.

Mokhtar's Place
BUNGALOW $

(☑ 019-704 8299; www.facebook.com/Mokhtar Place; Kampung Air Batang/ABC; s & d with fan RM40-60, d with air-con from RM160; ❈ ☏) Great budget value, old-timer Mokhtar's has a cluster of 16 bungalows along the beach south of town featuring little patios and mozzie nets. If the wind's just right, you can catch a cooling ocean breeze at night. Snorkelling gear can be rented from the front desk; wi-fi can be a bit patchy.

Bamboo Hill Chalets
BUNGALOW $$

(☑ 09-419 1339; www.bamboohillchalets.com; ABC; r RM130-380; @ ☏) These six well-kept chalets are in a stupendous location, perched quietly on rocks on the northern end of the beach at ABC, surrounded by bougainvillea and humming cicadas alongside a waterfall and pool. Service is very friendly and helpful. The chalets are almost always full, so call ahead or book well in advance before hauling your stuff here.

Nazri's Place
GUESTHOUSE $$

(☑ 017-490 1384; www.nazrisplace.net; Kampung Air Batang/ABC; d&tw RM60-200, f RM200-300; ❈ ☏) Located at the far southern end of the beach where some of ABC's best sand can be found, this long-standing stalwart has clean rooms and a wide range of accommodation. The no-nonsense A-frames with fan and shared toilet are the simplest and cheapest, while the range goes up to the air-con deluxe family rooms that have breakfast included.

The restaurant is right on the water and serves an excellent seafood barbecue.

Tioman House
HOTEL $$

(☑ 09-419 1021; tiomanhouse@yahoo.com; Kampung Air Batang/ABC; tr/f RM170/250; ❈) Located at ABC's north end, this place offers eight air-con chalets painted a happy yellow and featuring modern hotel decor.

Tioman Dive Resort
HOTEL $$

(☑ 09-419 5555, 09-419 1218; www.divetioman. com; Kampung Air Batang/ABC; d & tw/tr/q from RM270/320/380; ❈ @ ☏) All the rooms at this comfortable diver-oriented resort have flat-screen TVs, air-con, safes, coffee-makers and other touches worthy of a three-star hotel. The lack of waterfront views is a bit of a downer, but the beach is only steps away. The wi-fi can be patchy. Prices rise a bit on Fridays and Saturdays.

ABCD Restaurant
MALAYSIAN $

(ABC; mains RM10-20; ◷ breakfast, lunch & dinner; ☏) This restaurant (part of ABC Chalets) at the north end of the beach is packed most nights with travellers who flock to enjoy ABCD's BBQ special (RM20), a tantalising array of freshly caught fish, prawn or squid. For less adventurous eaters, chicken will have to do. It's a good choice for breakfast, too.

Sunset Corner
INTERNATIONAL $$

(☑ 016-704 0088; ABC; pizza from RM16; ◷ 2pm-late) The last spot before the stairs leading south, Sunset serves beer, booze, milkshakes and deservedly popular pizza. The wildly popular happy hour is from 5pm to 7pm.

🛏 Salang

With a more isolated feel than Tekek or ABC, Salang has more of a party vibe than elsewhere on the island. A very wide and inviting white-sand beach is just south of the jetty and is good for swimming. Several dive operators are here, too.

Ella's Place
CHALET $

(☎ 09-419 5004, 014-844 8610; Kampung Salang; fan/air-con chalets RM60-100/150-200; ❄ ⊛ 🛜) There's usually a lounge-able patch of sand at this cute-as-a-button family-run place at the quiet northern end of Salang beach. There are 10 clean bungalows (some with air-con) and a small cafe. The owners can rustle together a boat if you want to head to ABC, Tekek or elsewhere.

Salang Indah Resort
RESORT $$

(☎ 09-419 5015; www.salangindahtioman.com; Salang; fan tw RM60, air-con r RM100-250, f RM240-380; ⊛ 🛜) The expanse of bungalows seemingly sprawls forever at this resort complex. Most rooms aren't in tip-top condition, but if you look at several you'll probably find one to your liking. The top choice is the sunset-view family chalets on stilts over the rocks and the sea. There's a good restaurant here, too.

Salang Dream
MALAYSIAN $

(Kampung Salang; mains from RM10; ⊗ 11am-4pm & 7-11pm) This open place not far from the jetty is flushed with the sea breeze, serving decent seafood, with tables out front on the sand and barbecues in the evening.

🛏 Juara

The only place to stay on the east coast, Juara has a gorgeous pair of beaches and enough restaurants and accommodation to make it well worth the trip. To get here, take a taxi from Tekek (RM70 one-way for two people).

★ Bushman
CHALET $

(☎ 09-419 3109; bushmanchalets@outlook.my; Barok beach, Kampung Juara; r RM100-150; ⊛ 🛜) Nabbing one of Bushman's eight varnished wood bungalows, with their inviting wicker-furnished terraces, is like winning the Juara lottery – reserve in advance! The location is right up against the boulder outcrop at the southern end of Barok beach.

Bushman's deservedly popular **cafe** (mains from RM15; ⊗ 8.30am-3pm & 7-9pm Sat-Thu, to 11.30am & 7-9pm Fri; 🛜) is a wondrously languorous place to chill out and chomp on pizza and banana pancakes.

★ Rainbow Chalets
CHALET $$

(☎ 012-989 8572; rainbow.chalets1980@gmail.com; Barok beach, Kampung Juara; s&d with fan RM70, d/tr/q RM120/150/170; ⊛ 🛜) Eight colourful bungalows await you at this friendly place. All come with wooden porches that are decorated with shells and coral, and pro-

vide direct access to the beach and glorious views of the South China Sea. Wi-fi is available in the front area.

★ 1511 Coconut Grove
BUNGALOW $$

(☎ 010-766 4089; Juara; d/q incl breakfast RM298/500) Escape the crowds to this plot on the far south side of Juara just before the turtle sanctuary, where boutique beach bungalows have ceiling fans, thatched roofs and gorgeous balconies that look out to sea. Hardwood floors mix with South China Sea touches to create a classic mishmash of styles. The on-site restaurant is recommended.

Mutiara Resort
BUNGALOW $$

(☎ 09-419 3161/76; www.juaramutiararesort.blogspot.co.uk; Juara; s/tw/q/tr chalets RM80-100/160/160/180, villa RM220; ⊛ 🛜) Just south of the jetty, this place has lots of options and high standards, with some rooms on the beach and others in a garden on the far side of the road.

Beach Shack Tioman
CHALET $$

(☎ 019-989 1093; beachshacktioman@gmail.com; Mentawak beach, Kampung Juara; A-frame RM55-70, r RM160-190; ⊛ 🛜) For a lovely perspective on the beach, ideally grab one of the sweet top-floor rooms in the double-storey chalets right on the sand at this friendly operation. Those on a budget can opt for the few A-frames set back from the beach that just might catch an ocean breeze.

The rustic beachside Driftwood Cafe (open 8am to 2pm and 6.30pm to 9.30pm) is the spot to connect to wi-fi and other travellers.

The Barat Tioman
RESORT $$$

(☎ 09-419 3288; www.barattioman.com; Mentawak beach, Kampung Juara; r/f/chalet/villa with breakfast from R280/320/420/860; ❄ ⊛ 🛜) This new resort of concrete rooms, chalets and luxurious villas sticks out from the low-key village surroundings, but does provide a previously unavailable level of comfort on this side of the island. The sea-view restaurant and bar are excellent and there are good facilities including water-sports activities, diving and a pool. Round-island boat tours are offered.

Santai Bistro
MALAYSIAN $

(☎ 010-705 8496; Barok beach, Kampung Juara; mains RM7-25; ⊗ 8.30am-3pm & 7-10pm) This bar-restaurant right next to the jetty in Juara plays classic rock and serves good-enough sambal prawns, spicy Thai tom yum soups, vegetable salads and fish and chips. The beers are cold and the sea views hypnotising.

Paya

The short, wide, white-sand beach is jam-packed with resorts and a few restaurants, food shacks and dive schools.

The **Aman Tioman Beach Resort** (☑ 09-419 7788; www.amantioman.com; Kampung Paya; s/d/tr/q from RM440/440/500/590; ✳ 🤶) was still expanding when we visited, with 135 rooms planned but just 32 open (with a partial sea view). A pool was in the works, so the resort was still finding its feet at time of inspection, though rooms were of course very clean and fresh. Dive and snorkelling packages are available.

Genting

Genting caters mostly to the weekend crowds from Singapore and Kuala Lumpur, but its surrounding local village gives it a touch of authenticity.

Sun Beach Resort (☑ 07-799 4918; www.sunbeachresort.com.my; Genting; fan s/d/tr/q from RM88/88/88/128, air-con s/d/tr/q from RM128/128/138/148, ste RM338-638; ✳) has plenty of oceanfront chalets ranging from simple rooms to deluxe family suites (featuring minibar, jacuzzi and pantry) and a decent restaurant. It focuses on full board three- or four-day package tours (which are the only option at weekends and public holidays when individual nights are not available).

Nipah

Blissful, isolated Nipah is the place to come to hang in a hammock, snorkel or hike in the jungle. Nipah's hotels can arrange pickup from the ferry stop in Genting for RM30 each way.

Bersatu Nipah Chalets　　　　HOTEL $
(☑ 07-797 0091; bersatunipah_tioman@yahoo.com; Kampung Nipah; r with fan/air-con RM60/90; ✳) This clean beachfront longhouse has great service (from the amiable Jalil and Amy) and an excellent riverside restaurant with dishes such as freshly caught fish (priced by weight) and calamari fritters. Jalil also runs a free river cruise for guests.

The Nipah Chalet　　　　BUNGALOW $
(☑ 019-735 7853; Kampung Nipah; bungalow from RM70) Young, friendly host Abbas runs these rustic bungalows on stilts by the water's edge. They sit so close to the beach that the sound of waves lapping at the stairs will soothe you to sleep.

Mukut

Located on the southern tip of Tioman, Mukut may be the loveliest – and perhaps loneliest – *kampung* on the island. The pretty village, with its traditional homes and flower-lined paths, is fringed by a gorgeous beach.

Mukut Coral Chalets (☑ 019-984 0369; Mukut; chalet/f RM150/180; ✳ 🤶) has eight village-style chalets (all with air-con and hot water, some with TV), set in a marvellous location not far from Mukut's jetty. There's a sea-view restaurant serving Chinese and Western food. Wi-fi is only available in the restaurant.

Tioman's Resorts

Tioman resorts have exclusive beaches, pools, restaurants and private jetties. Your best bet for booking most resorts is going through travel aggregators (skip the all-inclusives if you have access to a nearby village for meals). Note that many of these resorts offer amazing deals (up to 50% off listed price) during the monsoon season (November to February).

★**Melina Beach Resort**　　RESORT $$
(☑ 09-419 7080; www.melinabeachresort.com; Genting; chalets for 4-8 people incl breakfast RM200-495) Melina is located on a remote beach with photogenic boulders and white sand. Each sleeping option is different, creatively designed from wood, thatch and Plexiglas to create a certain Crusoe chic; the most spacious rooms are the lovely beachfront chalets with large decks outside for a full-on sea view.

★**Tunamaya Resort**　　RESORT $$
(☑ 07-798 8108; www.tunamayaresort.com; Kampung Mukut; r per person from RM388; ✳ 🤶 ✳) The 54-villa Tunamaya overlooks white-sand beaches and provides high-quality amenities including an infinity pool, a plunge pool, spa, a bar with beers from around the world, games room and a whole range of activities, including batik painting, island tours, diving, hiking and alfresco movie nights.

Panuba Inn Resort　　RESORT $$
(☑ 09-419 1424; www.panubainnresort.com; ABC; fan d/tw from RM75, air-con r RM115-215; ✳) Peaceful Panuba Inn, located over the headland from ABC, clusters around its own jetty and restaurant with 30 chalets built on a hill

overlooking the bay. All rooms face the sea and range from simple fan affairs to chalets with hot shower, air-con, fridge and coffee. Check the website for good value full-board packages. The resort organises round-island boat trips.

Berjaya Tioman Resort RESORT $$
(☑09-419 1000; www.berjayahotel.com/tioman; r from RM200; ❄@🛜🏊) Easily accessible from Tekek, the four-star and sprawling Berjaya is the biggest resort on Tioman, with 268 rooms. For those seeking a resort experience on a budget, this is the best spot on the island. Accommodation ranges from chalets and suites to entire villas, not to mention standout attractions including tennis, a kids' playground and an arcade.

Paya Beach Spa & Dive Resort RESORT $$
(☑07-799 1432; www.payabeach.com; Paya; r RM169, bungalow RM229-449; ❄🛜🏊) Spacious chalets are linked by wooden bridges over a lily pond along with tidy, air-con standard rooms in the lodge at a decent price, plus a restaurant, full holistic spa, dive centre, lounge, bicycle hire and a range of activities, including archery and yoga. Check the website for details of good-value packages.

🍷 Drinking & Nightlife

B&J Beach Bar BAR
(ABC) Part of B&J Dive Centre (p255), this popular beachside bar in ABC always attracts a crowd with reasonable prices and fun bar staff.

Hallo Bar BAR
(ABC; ⊙6pm to late) On the far side of the path from Nazri's II and towards the northern end of the beach at ABC, this tiny but popular open beach bar offers a three-beers-for-RM12 happy hour from 5pm to 8pm.

ℹ Information

Tioman's sole ATM (Tekek; ⊙24hr) is on the exterior wall of BSN (Bank Simpanan Nasional) across from Tekek's airport and takes international cards. It's been known to occasionally run dry, so consider withdrawing extra cash in Mersing. There's a money changer at the airport.

There's a small post office (Tekek) in BSN (Bank Simpanan Nasional) opposite the airport in Tekek.

The island's sole clinic is Tekek Clinic (Klinik Kesihatan Tekek; ☑09-419 1880; Tekek; ⊙8am-1pm & 2-5pm Mon-Thu, to 12.15pm & 2.45-5pm Fri).

ℹ Getting There & Away

AIR
There are no scheduled flights to Tekek Airport (Tekek). To enquire about a private air charter here contact SAS Air (☑03-7847 2007, 013-627 2473; www.sassb.com.my) based at Subang Airport in Kuala Lumpur.

BOAT
Ferries (Map p247; ☑014-988 4281; https://tiomanferryticket.com; 38 Jln Jeti; return RM70; ⊙10am-6pm Mon-Sat, 11am-6pm Sun) from Mersing tend only to run early in the morning and are very much dependent on the tides. Several operators run boats, including Island Connection (Map p247; ☑014-988 4281; https://tiomanferryticket.com; 38 Jln Jeti; return RM70; ⊙10am-6pm Mon-Sat, 11am-6pm Sun), but only Gemilang/Bluewater Express (☑09-413 1363; Tanjong Gemok Ferry Terimnal; one-way/return RM35/70) has services from Mersing and Tanjung Gemok – you can go from one port and return to another which can be useful depending on your travel plans.

If you have a car, the safest option is to leave it at the car park near the jetty in Mersing, which charges around RM7 per day.

An alternative jumping-off point for Pulau Tioman is Tanjung Gemok (p262), 35km north of Mersing. As well as Gemilang/Bluewater Express, other ferry companies here include Dragon Star Shipping (☑09-413 1177; www.dragonstarshipping.com.my; Tanjong Gemok Ferry Terminal; return RM70) and Cataferry (☑09-4131 1445; www.cataferry.com; Tanjong Gemok Ferry Terminal; return around RM70).

Note that at either port you will need to pay a Tioman Marine Park Conservation fee (adult/child RM30/15) before travelling to the island.

ℹ Getting Around
Typical sea-taxi fares from Tekek:
➡ ABC/Panuba (RM25)
➡ Genting (RM50)
➡ Nipah (RM120)
➡ Mukut (RM150)
➡ Paya Beach (RM35)
➡ Salang (RM35)

Some sea taxis have a two-person minimum so you'll need to pay for two if solo. Otherwise you can hop on the boat to and from the mainland to move between Salang and Genting and stops in between, but you'll be at the mercy of the timetable. Most hotels can arrange boat charter. Expect to pay around RM600 for a full day on a boat, and expect waters to be far rougher on the Juara side of Tioman.

If you have the time, you can certainly explore some of the island on foot. Bicycles can be hired at guesthouses on all the main beaches (per hour/day RM5/30), and scooters (per hour/day RM15/40) are a good bet for trips to Juara. You may find a local willing to take you on the back of their scooter to Juara for around RM25.

Taxis from Tekek to Juara cost around RM70.

THE COAST

Tanjung Gemok

There's no reason to hang around Tanjung Gemok, but should you need accommodation **Hotel Jeti Tanjung Gemok** (☑09-413 1449; 1/2 Jln Sri Tanjung, Tanjong Gemok; s/tw RM86/108; ✽) has clean, modern rooms, some without windows.

Sanwa Express (☑013-646 5773; Tanjung Gemok Ferry Terminal; one-way RM30.90) runs daily direct buses (RM30.90) from Kuala Lumpur's Terminal Bersepadu Selatan bus station (p102) at 4am, 9am, 3pm and 11pm and from **Tanjung Gemok ferry terminal** (Endau) at 8.30am, 12.30pm and 6pm.

Pekan

☑09 / POP 104,000

The seat of the Pahang sultanate, Pekan has a regal air and is uncommonly scenic with its wide clean streets, spacious *padang* (field or grassy area) and many grand buildings surrounded by expansive pristine lawns, as well as an impressive polo field and several noble palaces that are slowly disintegrating beneath a combination of fierce sun and heavy rain.

Look out for the abandoned and much forlorn **Istana Leban Tunggal** (Lg Taman Mesra 1), a wood and stone palace built in 1935. With unusual twin yellow cupolas, it's quite a picture. The historic **Royal Pahang Polo Club** (Jln Padang Polo) is located next to **Istana Abu Bakar**, the grandiose and imposing sultan's palace. The magnificently restored, snow-white **Sultan Abdullah Mosque** (Jln Sultan Ahmad; ◷ 9.30am-5pm Tue-Thu, Sat & Sun, to 12.15pm & 2.45-5pm Fri) dates to 1929 and is fronted by a photogenic rectangle of water.

Drop by the **Museum Sultan Abu Bakar** (Jln Sultan Ahmad; admission RM1; ◷ 9.30am-5pm Tue-Thu, Sat & Sun, 9am-12.15pm & 2.45-5pm Fri) to view exhibits largely about the Pahang royal family, with other displays featuring weapons, pottery (including Chinese porcelain and Arab ceramics unearthed on Pulau Tioman) and exhibits on wildlife in Pahang.

Galeri Pengangkutan Air (Jln Sultan Ahmad; ◷ 9.30am-5pm Tue-Thu, Sat & Sun, 9am-12.15pm & 2.45-5pm Fri) FREE displays traditional Malaysian watercraft – look out for the fabulously carved craft with the head of a mythical beast.

🛏 Sleeping & Eating

Restaurants are not in short supply in the centre of Pekan. A few restaurants, **food stalls** (snacks from RM5) and **fruit stalls** can be found in the grid of streets between the *padang* and Sungai Pahang and along the riverfront at Jln Sultan Ahmad.

Chief's Rest House   HISTORIC HOTEL $
(☑09-422 6941; Jln Istana Permai; dm RM30-40, d RM55-70; ✽) This c 1929 colonial wooden building exudes atmosphere and style, and is reason enough to stop in Pekan. All rooms have wood floors, towering ceilings, TV and air-con. It's nearly 1km from the bus terminal, so let the driver know that you want to get off near the rest house. The absence of wi-fi is a bit of a let-down, though.

Ancasa Royale Pekan Pahang   HOTEL $$
(www.ancasahotels.com; Jln Pekan-Kuantan; r from RM220, ste from RM480; P✽🛜🏊) This hotel overlooks the Pahang River and is a very good choice. It may not be at the heart of town as it's located on the far side of the bridge, but it's a winner for comfort and class, with spacious, contemporary and well-equipped rooms, a restaurant and an outdoor pool.

Kedai Kopi Tien Lock   CHINESE $
(5 Jln Sultan Ahmad) Run by the Gan family for over a century, this friendly old-timer is a classic old Chinese *chashi* (茶室) – tearoom – which can supply a cup of tea or coffee or a refreshing and filling bowl of noodle soup (RM5.50). It's located at the heart of Pekan, with busy Jln Sultan Ahmad beyond.

ℹ Information

CIMB Islamic Bank (Jln Rompin Lama; ◷ 6am-midnight) Has an ATM that accepts foreign cards.
Klinik Kesihatan Bandar Pekan (☑09-421 1710; Jln Sultan Abu Bakar; ◷ 8am-4.30pm Mon-Fri)
Police Station (☑09-422 1222)
Post Office (Jln Sultan Mahmud; ◷ 8.30am-5.30pm Mon-Fri, to 1pm Sat)

ℹ Getting There & Away

Buses leave from **Terminal Bas Pekan** (Jln Engku Muda Mansor). Rapid Kuantan bus 400

Pekan

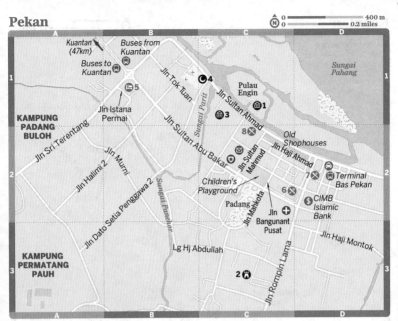

(RM4, one hour) leaves from here every half an hour for Kuantan; other buses run to Kuala Rompin (RM8.20, two hours), Chini Village (RM6, 1½ hours) and Mersing (RM15). Long-distance buses run to Kuala Terengganu (RM24), Kuala Lipis (RM28.60) and Kuala Lumpur (RM30). Buses **to Kuantan** (Jln Sultan Abu Bakar) and **from Kuantan** (Jln Sultan Abu Bakar) also leave from Jln Sultan Abu Bakar.

The **taxi station** (Jln Sultan Ahmad) is at the bus station. A taxi to/from Kuantan costs RM60; to Tasik Chini it's RM60.

Kuantan

📞 09 / POP 354,400

Most travellers pause briefly in Pahang's capital and Malaysia's second-biggest port to break up longish bus trips. This is a shame; while the city isn't especially geared towards tourism, it is definitely interesting enough to warrant a day or two's exploration, even just to make the most of the coast's best eating opportunities. The nearby sands of Teluk Chempedak offer upmarket resort accommodation and beach views.

👁 Sights & Activities

⭐ **Pahang Art Museum**   MUSEUM
(📞010-924 7134; www.pahangartmuseum.com; Jln Masjid; adult/child RM4/free; ⏰9.30am-5pm Mon-

Pekan

👁 Sights
1 Galeri Pengangkutan Air.................C1
2 Istana Leban Tunggal.....................C3
3 Museum Sultan Abu Bakar.............C1
4 Sultan Abdullah Mosque Museum....C1

🛌 Sleeping
5 Chief's Rest House.........................B1

🍴 Eating
6 Food Stalls....................................C2
7 Fruit Stalls....................................D2
8 Kedai Kopi Tien Lock......................C2

Thu, to 12.15pm & 2.45-5pm Fri) This museum's collection is housed in an attractive colonial-era building just north of the Padang (Jln Mahkota). The focus is on the state's culture, history and art. Look out for contemporary ceramics by Mohd Roslan Ahmad, sculptures by Raja Shahanman and an exhibition on Orang Asli, Malaysia's indigenous people.

Masjid Sultan Ahmad Shah   MOSQUE
(State Mosque; 📞014-840 3802; Jln Masjid) The east coast's most impressive and imposing mosque presides regally over the Padang. At night it's a magical sight with its illuminated spires and turrets contrasting against the dark sky.

Kuantan

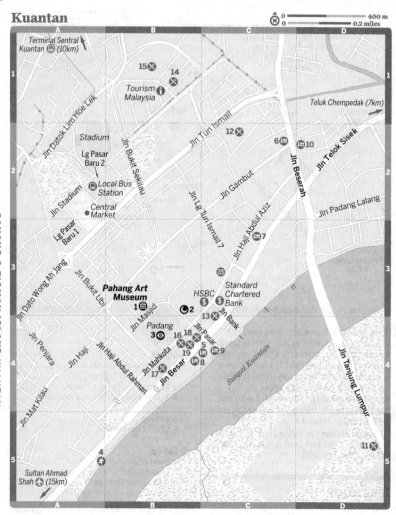

PAHANG & TIOMAN ISLAND KUANTAN

Beserah Beach
BEACH

This long beach is a lovely place to catch the sunrise and watch large crabs scuttling at high speed over the sands in the twilight. There are several accommodation options here, making it a pleasant alternative to staying in Kuantan. Take the regular bus 600 or 602 (RM2) from Kuantan's local bus station (p267).

River Cruises
CRUISE

(☎019-743 1988; Jln Tanah Putih; adult/child from RM21/15) Ninety-minute river cruises (adult/child RM42/30) run five times daily from the jetty to the mouth of Sungai Kuantan, passing fishing villages and mangrove

swamps before returning to town. Cheaper trips head either to the river mouth or just visit the mangroves, with the first departing at 9am and the last at 6pm. Firefly trips are also offered (adult/child RM50/40).

🛏 Sleeping

Hotel Kosma
HOTEL $

(☎09-516 2214; www.kosma.com.my/hotel/index.html; 59 Jln Haji Abdul Aziz; s&d RM60, tr RM75, q RM95-100; ✳@🛜) Among the better of the budget choices, the ageing Kosma lacks the boutique vibe of some of the newer midpriced hotels but is centrally located and affordable.

Kuantan

◎ Top Sights
1 Pahang Art Museum B3

◎ Sights
2 Masjid Sultan Ahmad Shah B3
3 Padang B4

⊙ Activities, Courses & Tours
4 River Cruises A5

⊙ Sleeping
5 Classic Hotel C4
6 Grand Darulmakmur Hotel C2
7 Hotel Kosma C3
8 Hotel Sentral Kuantan B4

9 Mega View Hotel C4
10 Signature Hotel D2

⊗ Eating
Akob Patin House .... (see 8)
11 Ana Ikan Bakar Petai D5
12 Berjaya Megamall C2
13 Coastal Store C4
14 Dubuyo B1
15 East Coast Mall B1
16 Jalan Lebai Ali Food Street B4
17 Kula Cakes B4
18 Pickers Cafe B4
19 Tjantek Art Bistro B4

★ **Hotel Sentral Kuantan** BOUTIQUE HOTEL **$$**
(☑ 09-565 9999; www.hotelsentralkuantan.com.my; 45 Jln Besar; r incl breakfast RM128-168; ❄ 🛜) This centrally located boutique hotel has a slick lounge downstairs with very helpful staff – with chromed-out styling over six floors, while the lift announces each floor in a very posh British accent. Standard rooms are a bit small, but deluxe rooms feature floor-to-ceiling views of the riverway. Breakfast includes continental choices.

★ **Classic Hotel** BOUTIQUE HOTEL **$$**
(☑ 09-516 4599; 7 Bangunan LKNP, Jln Besar; r RM100-170; ❄ 🛜) All rooms (ask for a river view) are spacious and clean, with large bathrooms and all the mod cons. Central location, ample Malay-style breakfasts and considerate staff make this a top pick. The cheapest room is RM90 with no breakfast.

Signature Hotel BOUTIQUE HOTEL **$$**
(☑ 09-513 2919; signaturehotel2012@gmail.com; 41 Jln Beserah; s RM98, d RM138-158; ❄ @ 🛜) With friendly lobby staff and cool modern lines, this is a solid entrant in the lower mid-range tier. The rooms can be pretty small, but feature a neat design, contemporary trimmings and flat-screen TVs.

Grand Darulmakmur Hotel HOTEL **$$**
(☑ 09-511 8888; www.gdmhotel.com.my; Lots 5 & 10, Lg Gambut, off Jln Beserah; r incl breakfast from RM225-360, ste RM390-855; ❄ @ 🛜 🏊) This smart 204-room four-star hotel has spacious rooms, a choice of four restaurants, a fitness centre, sauna and an awesome garden pool. The best views range out from the 12-storey block's 50 rooms, while the majority of rooms are in the lower five-floor podium block. There's also a three-unit penthouse at RM6500.

Mega View Hotel BUSINESS HOTEL **$$**
(☑ 09-517 1888; Lot 567, Jln Besar; d RM146-179, q RM207-278, studio RM127; ❄ 🛜) This business hotel has professional service and designer studios with funky murals and padded bedheads. Its 21st-century-take-on-art-deco feel puts it a step up from the crowd in the midrange category.

Hyatt Regency Kuantan RESORT **$$**
(☑ 09-518 1234; www.kuantan.regency.hyatt.com; Teluk Chempedak; r from RM340; ❄ @ 🛜 🏊) This spacious, breezy and effortlessly luxurious 301-room resort has very amenable staff, lovely views and a solid list of amenities (including two pools, a large choice of restaurants, three tennis courts, a spa and a children's play area). Rooms and suites have been extensively refurbished and come with a balcony or patio. There's a decent beachfront bar for twilight cocktails.

Swiss Garden Resort & Spa RESORT **$$$**
(☑ 09-548 8288; www.swissgarden.com/hotels/sgrk; Balok Beach; r inc breakfast RM668-937, studio/f/ste RM937/1205/2163; ❄ 🏊) If you prefer to be by the beach, this 304-room resort with spa is a good option up the coast on Balok Beach outside Kuantan. It's no newcomer so is a bit tired in places, but many of the rooms have been refurbished and come with a balcony, while the restaurant is a good choice for dinner with live music.

✕ Eating

Kuantan's most distinctive dish is *patin* (silver catfish). A very good selection of hip and appealing restaurants and cafes can be found along Jln Besar near the river. **Berjaya Megamall** (☑ 09-508 3936; Jln Tun Ismail; ⊙ 10am-10pm) and **East Coast Mall**

GUA CHARAS & SUNGAI LEMBING

Located 26km north of Kuantan, the limestone karst containing **Gua Charas** (Charas Caves/Charah Caves; admission RM2; ⏱9am-5pm) towers high above the surrounding palm plantations. The caves owe their fame to a Thai Buddhist monk who came to meditate here about 50 years ago. It's a steep climb up a stairway to the caves' entrance.

The colossal and very deep **Sleeping Buddha Cave** (Wofo Dong; RM2) is decorated with small altars to Guanyin, Puxian and other Bodhisattvas leading to the sleeping Buddha, a rather modest cement effort at the rear.

To many visitors, the cave is more mesmerising for its vast sense of scale than for its Buddhist statuary. Back at the entrance, continue up the steps to the cave above, which is an entirely different affair, open at both ends and so illuminated with sunlight, caressed with a refreshing breeze and looking out onto views of the surrounding land.

It's best to drive here if you have a car (parking is RM3), or take the Sungai Lembing-bound bus 500 (RM4, one hour, every 20 to 30 minutes) from the local bus station (p267) and disembark at the small village of Panching, just past the sign reading 'Gua Charas 4km'. From the bus stop in Panching it's a hot 4km walk each way, but you may be able to get someone in Panching to give you a lift on the back of a motorcycle.

Whether driving or coming by bus, consider carrying on to **Sungai Lembing** in the hills to explore the informative regional **museum** (☑09-541 2378; Jln Muzium; RM5; ⏱9am-5pm Mon-Thu, to 12.15pm & 2.45-5pm Fri) (RM2) that covers the history of local tin mining to the collapse of the industry in 1986, or head up the road for a claustrophobic tour of the abandoned **tin mines** (☑09-541 2738; Sungai Lembing; adult/child RM30/15; ⏱9am-12.45pm & 2-6pm Mon-Thu, to 12.15pm & 2.45-6pm Fri, to 6pm Sat & Sun).

There are a couple of accommodation options and a decent restaurant or two if you want to spend some time here. **Kuantan Waffle Station**, located obliquely opposite the *padang* and near the big tree, serves tasty waffles while **Country View Inn** just down the road on Jln Sungai Lembing has comfortable rooms.

(☑09-565 8600; www.eastcoastmall.com.my; Jln Putra Sq; mains from RM10; ⏱10am-10pm) have everything from Starbucks to Malay-style food courts. There's also a good selection of cheap restaurants and stalls around the local bus station (p267).

★**Coastal Store** CAFE $
(☑09-531 6595; 4E Jln Besar; mains from RM6; ⏱noon-midnight Tue-Thu, Sat & Sun, from 2.30pm Fri; ☏) Shame about the late start here, but Coastal Store is a gem, littered with books, second-hand vinyl, CDs and surfboarding paraphernalia. There are only two main dishes – Coastal chicken rice and Coastal beef noodles (the latter a killer bowl, the whole nine yards) – but it's the easygoing vibe you're here for and some excellent coffee.

★**Jalan Lebai Ali Food Street** MARKET $
(Jln Leban Ali; mains from RM4; ⏱6pm-2am) This fun, vibrant and often packed sit-down street market kicks off in the evenings just south of the floodlit Padang (p263). Find everything from spaghetti, to beef and lamb burgers, burritos, *nasi lemak* and much more, served from a dozen or so food trucks.

Dubuyo KOREAN $
(☑09-531 6671; www.dubuyo.com; GF-13 & 13A, Parkson Kuantan City Mall, Jln Putra Square 6; mains from RM12; ⏱10am-10pm) Located in Parkson Kuantan City Mall, this restaurant has all manner of tasty Korean goodies, from *mandu* (dumplings) to *bibimbap* (rice bowls), *jajanmyeon* (noodles in black bean sauce), *pajeon* (pancakes), *namyeon* noodles, *bulgogi* (grilled marinated beef) and more, served in a colourful setting with a K-pop soundtrack. It has good value meal sets, too.

Pickers Cafe CAFE $
(☑014-824 1102; 32 Jln Besar; mains from RM2; ⏱7am to 7pm) Located in an old shophouse along Jln Besar, friendly Pickers is a decent cafe and spot for Vietnamese coffee and buns in the morning or *roti* or *nasi lemak* for lunch. On the shelves are vintage toys, vinyl, a small library and other odds and ends as well as collectable curios.

Kula Cakes BAKERY $
(☑017-971 1396; 96 Jln Besar; from RM8.50; ⏱1-9pm Tue-Thu, to 10pm Fri & Sat, 11am-7pm Sun) There always seems to be a line outside this

small cake shop for the mango cheesecake, which is lovely but a rather brief reward if the queue has been overwhelming. So double up on your order, or go for the pavlova or chocolate cake, too.

Akob Patin House
MALAYSIAN $
(Lg Haji Abdul Rahman 1; mains RM8-20; ⊙ 8.30am-6pm Mon-Sat) Fancy trying *patin* (silver catfish), the local delicacy? Both wild-caught and cheaper farmed *patin* in a *tempoyak* (fermented durian sambal) sauce are part of a buffet with other Malay-style meat and vegetable dishes. The friendly staff can help explain what's what.

★Tjantek Art Bistro
INTERNATIONAL $$
(☑ 019-917 2021; www.tjantek.blogspot.com; 46 Jln Besar; mains RM18-45; ⊙ 5pm-1am Mon-Sat) With soft lighting, a jumble of antiques, odds and ends, curios and vintage paintings, and an enticing choice of tables, this superb, eclectic and very elegant place is stuffed with charm and romantic appeal. The menu is also excellent: you can't go wrong with the *spaghetti aglio tuna cili padi*, a delightfully spicy dish, or the delicious lemon butter salmon.

★Ana Ikan Bakar Petai
SEAFOOD $$
(Tanjong Lumpur; mains RM20-40; ⊙ lunch & dinner) If it's authentic you're after, look no further than this huge open-air seafood restaurant across the river on the island of Tanjong Lumpur. On any given evening Malaysian families flock here to feast on a plethora of traditional Malay seafood dishes.

ℹ Information

Lots of banks (many with 24-hour ATMs), including **HSBC** (1 Jln Mahkota; ⊙ ATM 24hr) and **Standard Chartered Bank** (1-3 Jln Haji Abdul Aziz; ⊙ ATM 24hr), are on or near the aptly named Jln Bank.

Post Office (☑ 09-517 9108; Jln Haji Abdul Aziz; ⊙ 8.30am-5.30pm Mon-Fri, to 1pm Sat)

Tourism Malaysia (☑ 09-567 7112; Lot 7 & 9 Tingkat Bawah, ICT Hub, Jln Putra Square 4; ⊙ 8am-1pm & 2-5pm Mon-Thu, 8am-12.15pm & 2.45-5pm Fri) Staff aren't much help but there are plenty of brochures to help you find your way.

ℹ Getting There & Away

AIR

Sultan Ahmad Shah Airport (☑ 09-531 2123; www.malaysiaairports.com.my) is 17km west of the city centre; a taxi here costs RM35. Malaysia Airlines (p607) has several daily direct flights to Kuala Lumpur International Airport (KLIA) with plenty of onward connections from there. Firefly

(p607) has two daily flights to/from Subang Airport in Kuala Lumpur and four weekly flights to Singapore.

BUS

Long-distance buses leave from **Terminal Sentral Kuantan** (TSK; Jln Pintasan Kuantan), about 20 minutes from the city centre (taxi RM20). The ticket offices, food court and left luggage centre (RM2 per piece) are on the 2nd floor of the building.

Head to the **local bus station** (Hentian Bas Bandar Kuantan; 2704 Jln Stadium) for services to nearby destinations, including bus 400 to Pekan (RM4, every 20 to 30 minutes, one hour), buses 600 and 602 to Balok Beach (RM4, every hour, 20 minutes), via Beserah Beach (RM2, 15 minutes), bus 200 to Teluk Chempedak (RM2, every 20 to 30 minutes, 20 minutes) and bus 500 to Sungai Lembing (RM4, every 20 to 30 minutes, one hour).

DESTINATION	PRICE	DURATION
Butterworth	RM56	8½hr
Jerantut	RM17	3½hr
Kota Bharu	RM30	6hr
Kuala Lipis	RM28	6hr
Kuala Lumpur	RM24	4hr
Kuala Terengganu	RM20	4hr
Melaka	RM27	6hr
Mersing	RM34	3hr
Singapore	RM48	6hr
Temerloh	RM20	2hr

To get to Teluk Chempedak, take bus 200 from in front of Kuantan's Berjaya Megamall (p265) (RM2, 30 minutes) or from the local bus station. A taxi between the two towns costs around RM25.

CAR

Hawk (☑ 09-538 5055; www.hawkrentacar.com.my; Sultan Ahmad Shah Airport)

TAXI

Ask your hotel to order a long-distance taxi or grab one from in front of Terminal Sentral Kuantan or **Central Market** (Pasar Besar; 3 Jln Tun Ismail). Approximate costs (per car):

➜ Cherating (RM60 to RM70)
➜ Jerantut (RM320)
➜ Johor Bahru (RM450)
➜ Kuala Lumpur (RM315)
➜ Kuala Terengganu (RM250)
➜ Mersing (RM295)
➜ Pekan (RM60)
➜ Tanjung Gemok (RM250)
➜ Temerloh (RM175)

Prices may vary, and bargaining is possible.

Cherating

🎵 09 / POP 300

With a sweeping white beach bordered by coconut palms, this small village of guesthouses and shops is a very popular spot for surfing, windsurfing and general beach-front slacking. Outside of the surf season, Cherating can be dead quiet, which only adds to the appeal, with the occasional sound of a guitar strumming between the rustling palms or the heavy thud of a falling coconut.

◉ Sights & Activities

Cherating's bay has a long sandy shelf, making this a peaceful spot for swimming most of the year. Watch out for jellyfish in June and July. Surfing is popular during the monsoon months, when the surf shops open.

The beach isn't great for snorkelling but places all around town offer half-day snorkelling tours for around RM60 to the aptly named Coral Island.

The most popular activities are the amazing firefly tours that head upriver after sunset and the turtle-watching tours.

Surfing

Malaysia experiences some of its best surfing waves here during monsoon season, from late October to the end of March, and things get busy in Cherating. In town, a point break rolls across the bay, with up to 2m waves and rides that last 400m. Rent a car in Kuantan to find more spots north of here.

Kam's Surf Shack　　　WATER SPORTS
(📞09-581 9134, 018-974 7187; Cherating Beach; ⊙9am-10pm) This beachside surf shop rents boards, organises lessons and doubles as a cafe and bar, while also providing accommodation (fan/air-con room RM80/150). You can rent kayaks (per hour/day RM40/100) or kitesurfing gear for RM150 (experienced riders only); lessons cost RM300. Windsurf

---

LOCAL KNOWLEDGE

BATIK COURSE

Batik-making (canvas drawing with local dyes) is a Cherating speciality. **Limbong Art** (Tie Dye Never Die; 📞019-939 9870; www.facebook.com/dolegomo; Main Rd; course from RM30; ⊙10am-10pm) offers courses where you can make your own batik handkerchief or sarong.

---

rentals are RM80, while a class costs RM150. Paddleboards are RM50/100 for an hour/half-day and surfboards are RM40/70 per half-/full-day.

Cherating Point Surf School　　SURFING
(📞012-933 7590; www.cheratingpoint.com; Matahari Holiday Huts, Jln Kampung Cherating; ⊙Oct-Mar) Only open during monsoon season, this popular surf shack offers 1½-hour surf classes (RM120 to RM140 for small groups, or from RM190 for one-to-one), and rents boards (half/full day RM45/75). Accommodation/surf packages are also available with lodgings at **Matahari Holiday Huts** (📞017-924 7465; d without/with bathroom RM30/60, tr RM80, r/q with air-con RM80/150; ❄️📶🛜).

Wildlife Viewing

Several places around town run river mangrove tours, firefly tours, turtle watching (April to September), releasing baby turtles into the sea, nature walks and other activities. The firefly and turtle-oriented activities are particularly fascinating and a real hit with kids.

Turtle Sanctuary　　ANIMAL SANCTUARY
(📞09-581 9087; Bukit Cherating; ⊙9.30am-4.30pm Tue-Sun) FREE The animal-friendly but small turtle sanctuary next to Club Med has a few basins with baby and rehabilitating green turtles, and can offer information about the laying and hatching periods. For the full turtle experience, join one of the tours to release hatchlings.

★Hafiz's Cherating Activities　　BOATING
(📞017-978 9256; www.hafizcheratingactivities.blogspot.com; tours from RM30) These nighttime firefly boat tours along the mangroves upriver are a Cherating activity par excellence. Hafiz is a long-time firefly enthusiast and self-made expert at Cherating Activities. Tours leave at around 7.30pm and are introduced with a detailed talk. Don't put on mosquito repellent, otherwise the fireflies (actually a kind of beetle) won't settle on you.

Dinbadger Services　　OUTDOORS
(📞09-581 9355) Owner Din offers a variety of activities, including river trips (RM30), animal-friendly baby turtle releasing (RM35), turtle watching (RM70, April to October), firefly tours (RM30, 7.45pm and 9pm) and jungle trekking and waterfall hikes (RM180, March to October). Din can also sort out taxis to Kuantan.

Cheratin

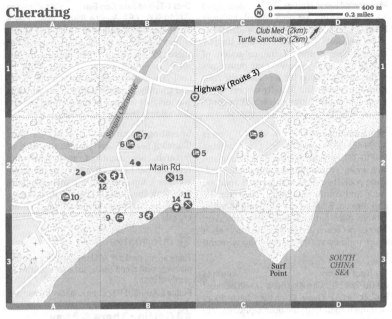

Club Med (2km);
Turtle Sanctuary (2km)

Highway (Route 3)

Main Rd

Surf
Point

SOUTH
CHINA
SEA

Cherating

Activities, Courses & Tours
Cherating Point Surf School	(see 6)
1 Dinbadger Services	B2
2 Hafiz's Cherating Activities	A2
3 Kam's Surf Shack	B3
4 Limbong Art	B2

Sleeping
5 Ku Mimi Cablet	C2
6 Matahari Holiday Huts	B2
7 Maznah's Guest House	B2
8 Residence Inn	C2
9 Tanjung Beach	B3
10 Tanjung Inn	A2

Eating
11 Don't Tell Mama Eco Bar	B2
12 Nabill Café	B2
13 Ombok Surf Cafe	B2

Drinking & Nightlife
14 Cherating Beach Bar	B2

Sleeping

Budget digs tend to fill up with surfers during the monsoon (November through January), and midrange places tend to fill up on the weekends year round. Book in advance.

★Ku Mimi Cablet
CHALET $

(☑019-927 3871; https://kumimicablet.business. site; r fan/air-con from RM60/90; ❄️🛜) Cablet is a blend of the words 'cabin' and 'chalet' and that's just what you'll find at this sweet place located a short walk from the main road. The white-washed wood chalets with attached bathrooms are simple and clean, while converted shipping containers are the cabins. Pluses are a shared kitchen, cool central hang-out and a hospitable owner.

Tanjung Inn
BUNGALOW $

(☑09-581 9081; www.tanjunginn.com; tents RM70, r with fan RM100-130, r with air-con RM180-425, villa RM384-1400; ❄️🛜) This L-shaped plot offers wooden bungalows with decks set around a lovely grassy area near the road. All bungalows have hot showers, and there's an excellent lending library. There's another section with rather weary looking safari-style tents over mattresses on wooden palates around a pond for those who prefer to glamp and another choice of rooms near the beach.

Maznah's Guest House
BUNGALOW $

(☑09-581 9307; s/d with shared bathroom RM30/35, r RM50-70, r with air-con RM120-150, all incl breakfast; ❋☎) Spirited kids happily chase chickens around the collection of sturdy and good-value wooden bungalows at this sleepy spot on the far side of the road from the beach. The friendly owners speak English and a delicious *nasi lemak* or continental breakfast is served for breakfast.

★ Residence Inn
HOTEL $$

(☑09-581 9333; www.ric.my; r incl breakfast RM240-320; ❋☎☒) Surrounding a large and welcoming swimming pool and smaller paddling pool, the rooms at this resort are good value and comfortable, with flat-screen TV and air-con. Staff are friendly, and there's a football pitch out back and a downstairs bar. There's no beach access, but the sands are a short walk away. Try to avoid the weekend as it's busy.

Tanjung Beach
CHALET $$

(☑017-249 3711; Cherating Beach; r with breakfast RM250; ❋☎) These 12 chalets have doors that open right onto the beach, pitched ceilings and clean lines.

Club Med
RESORT $$$

(☑09-581 9133; www.clubmed.com.sg; all-incl package from RM550; P❋☎☒) Crafted to look like a particularly beautiful Malaysian *kampung* with wooden buildings on stilts, this resort comes fully equipped with its own stretch of beach, lawns, international restaurants, nightclub, kids club, nearby turtle sanctuary and sports facilities. It's about 2km north of town. Note you will be stopped at the gate and refused entry unless you're a guest.

✕ Eating & Drinking

Ombok Surf Cafe
CAFE $

(☑09-581 9275; mains from RM8; ☺11am-5pm; ☎) Doubling as a surf school when the monsoon winds blow and run by seasoned surfer staff, this enjoyable spot is a great choice for breakfast, brunch or lunch served on paint-splattered tables. The menu includes dishes such as avocado salad, tuna cheese toasties or fish and chips, or you can just sit back with a coffee or smoothie.

Nabill Café
MALAYSIAN $

(mains RM6-9; ☺6pm-midnight Tue-Sun) Eat where the locals do and save a handful of ringgit. Choose your fresh seafood then watch it get grilled in a delicious spicy sambal.

Don't Tell Mama Eco Bar
INTERNATIONAL $$

(☑010-900 5663; Ranting Resort; mains RM25-55; ☺6pm-late Wed-Mon) ✎ Don't Tell Mama is best known for its legendary burgers but there are plenty of other options on the menu including vegetarian ones. With its cool beachside shack set-up, reggae music and friendly service it's easy to see why this is a top spot to relax in the evening, but the downside is the aggressive dogs.

Cherating Beach Bar
BAR

(Cherating Beach; ☺3pm-late) At the time of research, this beachfront option was being rebuilt closer to the action, but its predecessor was a fun spot and the main drinking hub, with the pace picking up after sunset, complemented by good cocktails and a lively crowd.

❶ Information

There are no banks or ATMs in Cherating and few places accept credit cards, so be sure to bring plenty of cash.

Police (☑09-581 9322; Jln Kuantan-Kemaman)

❶ Getting There & Away

Whether travelling from the north or south by long-distance bus, you'll first arrive at Terminal Sentral Kuantan (p267). From there take bus 303 to Kuantan's local bus station (p267; RM2, 30 minutes) and transfer to bus 600 to Batok (RM4, 40 minutes), followed by bus 604 to Cherating Lama (Old Cherating; RM2, 20 minutes); ask the driver to let you know when to get off.

It's simpler and speedier to take a taxi from Kuantan (RM60, 45 minutes).

From Kuala Lumpur, it's best to get a direct bus to Kemaman and ask to be dropped off at Cherating Lama.

For taxis from Cherating call Dinbadger Services (p268). Owner Din charges RM70 for a taxi to Kuantan. Taxis to resorts outside town cost about RM30.

THE INTERIOR

Temerloh & Around
☑09 / POP 159,000

An old town on the banks of the enormous Sungai Pahang, Temerloh has hints of colonial style and a colourful Sunday market. As the main city of central Pahang, it principally serves as a transport hub, so most people are just passing through.

TASIK CHINI

Tasik Chini (Lake Chini) is a series of 12 lakes linked by vegetation-clogged channels. It's one of Pahang's natural flood retention basins, but environmentalists long ago criticised the increasing threat to the area as a result of decades of uncontrolled mining and logging. Dam construction over 20 years ago seriously impacted the lotus flowers that once filled the lake waters in summer and though this situation was alleviated, floodwaters in 2014 killed off a lot of the flowers. A lotus flower replanting program is under way, but the results are patchy and it could take many more years for the flower population to fully recover.

Tasik Chini's shores are inhabited by the Jakun people, an Orang Asli tribe of Melayu Asli origin, and the surrounding jungle hills are some of the least-visited trekking areas in the country, still hiding tigers and elephants amid glorious waterfalls and caves.

Nestled in flower-filled and extremely quiet Kampung Gumum, the rustic but clean longhouse rooms (with fan, mosquito nets and shared bathrooms) at **Rajan Jones Guest House** (☑016-771 4509, 017-913 5089; www.facebook.com/rajanjones.chini; Kampung Gumum; r per person incl breakfast & dinner RM40; ℗) make for a simple but fun base camp for jungle and lake adventures. Breakfast and dinner served lakeside are included in the price, and for just an extra RM5, lunch with tea is thrown in, too.

The comfortable and magnificently landscaped **Lake Chini Resort** (☑09-468 8088; Lake Chini; campsite per tent RM5, dm incl breakfast RM25, r incl breakfast RM130-300; ℗❄🛜) has good rooms facing the lake and an on-site restaurant. The 10-bed dorms are neat and often filled with student groups. Staff at the resort can arrange all activities for you, including boating tours of the lake waters. There's a camp site here as well.

Tasik Chini is easily accessed if you have your own set of wheels. Both accommodation options can arrange transfers. Otherwise take a bus to Kampung Chini from either Kuantan (RM9.80, two hours) or Pekan (RM8.90, 1½ hours) and then hire a private car for the remaining 7.5km to Kampung Gunum for about RM30. You can get a taxi from either Pekan or Kuantan for around RM125.

The closest main sight is the National Elephant Conservation Centre, 33km west of Temerloh.

☉ Sights

National Elephant Conservation Centre　　WILDLIFE RESERVE
(☑013-931 9650; www.wildlife.gov.my; Kuala Gandah, Lanchang; entry by donation; ☉8am-1pm & 2.30-4.30pm Sat-Thu, 8am-12.30pm & 2.30-4.30pm Fri) This is the base for the Department of Wildlife and National Parks' Elephant Relocation Team, which helps capture rogue elephants from across Southeast Asia and relocate them to other suitable habitats throughout the peninsula. A round-trip taxi ride from Temerloh costs RM120.

After registering, you can observe elephants (behind an electric fence) on a small interpretive trail from 10am to noon; shortly after is a chance to see and feed young elephants. An educational video is shown at 1pm and 1.30pm; visitors can see adult elephants from 2pm and later on the young elephants are bathed; the young elephant

bathing is popular and is restricted to 100 people, with a charge for a guide (RM50) and RM10/5 per adult/child (you need to register as well to book your place). Most of the elephants at the centre are work elephants from Myanmar, India and Thailand. Mounting evidence suggests elephant interactions present various animal welfare issues, and some visitors may find elements at the centre distressing.

The town of Lanchang is west of Mentakab and about 150km east of Kuala Lumpur. Most people visit on tours from Kuala Lumpur, Jerantut, Cherating and other tourist hubs on the peninsula.

⌘ Sleeping & Eating

Green Park Hotel　　HOTEL $$
(☑09-296 3333; www.greenpark.com.my; 1 Jln Terkukur, off Jln Merbah; s RM113, d RM118-180, tw RM153, f RM145; ℗❄🛜) This tall hotel towers over the town and offers clean, pretty rooms with hot showers and coffee- and tea-making facilities, as well bathrooms with bath. The rooms are rather plain, but are

comfortable enough and very good value. They are in two blocks: the taller tower with lift and a lower block (without lift). Staff are friendly.

ℹ Getting There & Away

The bus station is in the centre of the new town, which is full of shops and restaurants and just a few minutes' walk from the old town. The train station (currently not operating) is 12km away at Mentakab, a thriving satellite of Temerloh with a bustling nightly market.

Jerantut

✓ 09 / POP 90,000

Sleepy Jerantut is the gateway to Taman Negara and an access point for the 'jungle railway' connecting with Kota Bharu in the north. If you have to spend a night here before heading into the jungle, it's a pleasant enough place to wander around and has good accommodation and places to eat.

🛏 Sleeping & Eating

Wau Hotel HOTEL $
(✓ 09-260 2255; www.wauhotels.com; K1 Pusat Perniagaan Sungai Jan; d RM78-154, tr RM99, ste RM180; P❄🛜) This 16-room hotel has helpful staff and the best accommodation in town, but it's a 15-minute walk (or RM10 taxi ride) from the centre, making it less appealing for travellers without their own wheels. The hotel has clean and neat rooms, cheery halls decorated in yellow, peach and red, and deluxe rooms with flat-screen TVs.

Sakura Castle Inn HOTEL $
(✓ 09-266 9664, 09-266 9663; www.sakuracastle inn.blogspot.com; S1-2, Jln Bomba; r RM70-110; ❄🛜) This is one of the better inexpensive places to stay, offering clean, comfortable rooms all with TVs, hot water and air-con. The cheapest rooms don't have exterior windows. There's usually a promotional rate in force than knocks RM10 off the price.

Town Inn Hotel HOTEL $
(✓ 09-266 6811; www.towninn-hotel.com; Jln Tahan, Lot 3748; d/tr/q RM55/70/80; P❄@🛜) The bright clean rooms with pink bed spreads and flat-screen TVs are a big step up from the backpacker-oriented places – they're clean and well maintained, while service is friendly. Wi-fi is, like everywhere, a bit hit-and-miss.

Hotel Firdaus HOTEL $
(✓ 09-266 1409; www.facebook.com/hfjerantut; 2-5 Jln Kuantan; s/d/f RM38/55/90; ❄🛜) This hotel has clean rooms (mostly with no windows) that are reasonably priced. Throw in its brightly decorated ground-floor cafe Kopi Chantek and bakery Dania Cakes Corner and it's an ok choice.

★ **Gypsy Garden** INTERNATIONAL $
(✓ 016-460 4798; www.facebook.com/gypsy. smokedngrill.3; Pejabat Pos Lama, Jln Besar; mains from RM10; ⏰ 6.30am-11pm) Run by charming Abid and Zubidah (with their delightful young son cavorting about), this adorable cafe occupies a large greenhouse-like building tacked onto Jerantut's old post office. The menu is fairly short but includes delicious traditional Malay dishes, pasta, homemade pizza and French fries. The quirkiness continues to the garden terrace and a tiny gypsy caravan (used for barbecues).

During the day from 11am you can order takeaway food. It's also a good idea to make a reservation for dinner as the cafe has limited seating.

ℹ Information

A few banks can change cash (change money before heading into Taman Negara). The ATMs dry up sometimes so it's best to get money before reaching Jerantut.

CIMB Bank (Jln Tahan; ⏰ 9.15am-4.30pm Mon-Thu, to 4pm Fri) Has an ATM that accepts most foreign cards.

Police (✓ 09-266 2222; Jln Besar)

Post Office (Jln Bomba; ⏰ 8.30am-5.30pm Mon-Fri, to 1pm Sat)

ℹ Getting There & Away

BUS

All buses arrive and depart from **Jerantut Bus Station** (120 Jln Bandar Baru).

DESTINATION	PRICE	DURATION
Kuala Lipis	RM5	1½hr
Kuala Lumpur (Pekeliling)	RM20	4hr
Kuantan	RM17	3hr
Temerloh	RM6.20	1hr

Public buses go to the jetty at Kuala Tembeling for boats to Taman Negara (RM4, 45 minutes) usually every hour from 10.30am to 3.30pm. The schedule is unreliable and doesn't coincide with boat departures.

Jerantut

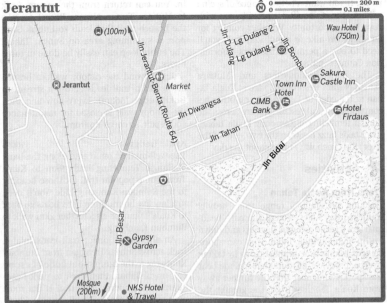

N 0 ———————————— 200 m
  0 ———————————— 0.1 miles

NKS Hotel & Travel (☑ 09-266 4488; www.
taman-negara-nks.com; 21-22 Jln Besar, Bandar
Lama; ⏱ 7.30am-6pm; ☏) arranges minibuses
and buses to a variety of destinations, including
Tembeling jetty (RM10), Kuala Lumpur (RM40),
Kuala Besut (RM70) and Cameron Highlands
(RM60). Buses leave from outside the agency's
cafe. NKS can also arrange a river trip to the
national park from the jetty in Kuala Tembeling
(RM45). If you want to skip the riverboat, take
one of the agency's minibuses directly from
Kuala Tahan for Taman Negara (RM25, 8am and
sometimes 4.30pm).

TAXI

Fares from the **Jerantut Bus Station taxi
stand** (☑ 09-266 2088; Jerantut Bus
Station) are:

➜ Cherating (RM240)

➜ Kampung Kuala Tahan (RM80)

➜ Kuala Lipis (RM65)

➜ Kuala Lumpur (RM200)

➜ Kuala Tembeling (RM30)

➜ Kuantan (RM220)

➜ Mersing and Tanjung Gemok (R550)

➜ Temerloh (RM60)

A surcharge of RM30 is enforced after 3pm.

TRAIN

Jerantut train station is on the Tumpat–
Gemas line (also known as the East Line or 'jungle railway'). Going north the 4.44am train stops

at Kuala Lipis and Gua Musang before arriving at
Wakaf Baharu close to Kota Bharu (RM25, eight
hours). Going south the 2.13am sleeper train
heads to Johor Bahru (seat/sleeper RM30/36,
10 hours), where you can transfer to either the
shuttle train or bus to Singapore.

For an up-to-date timetable and list of fares,
consult KTM (p607).

Taman Negara

☑ 09

Malaysia's oldest, largest and most popular national park straddles the borders of
Pahang, Kelantan and Terengganu in an area
spanning a colossal 4343 sq km: welcome
to Malaysia's greatest swath of continuous
lowland dipterocarp rainforest. Since 1939,
Taman Negara (which means national park
in Bahasa Malaysia) has been a haven for
an astonishing range of tropical flora and a
vast variety of wildlife, including elephants,
tigers, leopards, tapirs and flying squirrels.

The more time you put into a visit to
Taman Negara, the more you'll get out of
it. Though they're feasible, fleeting visits
only scratch the surface; however, you can
spend several days exploring and encounter little wildlife apart from birds. It's well
worth considering an overnight trek or at
least a long boat trip up one of the park's

rivers. If you want a better chance of seeing wildlife, the hides (RM1) provide you with your best opportunity. Whether coming for an afternoon hike or a multiday trek, you'll need to buy a permit at the Park Information Counter (p278).

The park headquarters and Mutiara Taman Negara Resort (p277) are at Kuala Tahan at the edge of Taman Negara; other accommodation and restaurants are across the Sungai Tembeling at Kampung Kuala Tahan. River taxis buzz between the two sides of the river (RM1 each way) throughout the day.

🏃 Activities

Treks from Kuala Tahan

Trekking possibilities range from heavily trafficked day hikes around the park headquarters to nine arduous days up and down 2187m-high Gunung Tahan. You can shorten your hiking time in most cases by taking riverboat services or tours that include boat transport. Remember that the further away from Kuala Tahan you go, the greater the chance of spotting wildlife.

Trails within the vicinity of park headquarters are along raised boardwalks, signposted and marked with approximate walking times; enquire at the Park Information Counter for details on other routes and pick up the useful trail map *Taman Negara Kuala Tahan* (RM5). The office also sells the book *Taman Negara: A Guide to the Park* (RM25), which is highly informative.

★ Canopy Walk & Around   HIKING

(adult/child RM5/3; ⊙9am-3pm Sat-Thu, to noon Fri) Taman Negara's most popular hike is to the canopy walk, a 500m bridge suspended between huge trees and around 45m above the forest floor. The easy-to-follow boardwalk starts east of the park headquarters and leads along Sungai Tembeling to the turnoff to the canopy walk, 30 minutes away. Get here early for the best birding and wildlife watching.

This is an excellent way to get a glimpse of the canopy, which is made up of the upper branches of various very tall tree species, including *merawan* and *meranti*. You need to keep a distance of 10m between walkers on the walkway; most of the main tree stations along the route are staffed by park rangers. There is a toilet near the end of the walkway, at ground level. On the way to the canopy walk a steep trail leads to Bukit Teresik (344m), which can be tied

in. You can return from the canopy walk to Mutiara Taman Negara Resort or take the branch trail that leads to Lubok Simpon, a swimming area on Sungai Tahan. The entire loop can easily be done in three hours.

Just beyond the canopy walk, a branch of the main trail leads across a stream to Bukit Indah (563m). Every now and then the canopy walk is closed for maintenance and repair, so check up front.

Kuala Trenggan   HIKING

The well-marked main trail along the bank of Sungai Tembeling leads 9km to Kuala Trenggan, a popular trail for those heading to the Bumbun Kumbang hide. You'll need to allow five hours. From here, boats go back to Kuala Tahan, or it's a further 2km walk to Bumbun Kumbang.

An alternative longer trail leads inland, back across Sungai Trenggan from Bumbun Kumbang to the camp site at Lubok Lesong on Sungai Tahan, then back to park headquarters (six hours). This trail is flat most of the way and crosses small streams. Check with park headquarters for river levels.

Lata Berkoh   HIKING

North from park headquarters, it's a two-hour jungle hike to Lata Berkoh, a set of cascading rapids on Sungai Tahan; many visitors take a boat there (return RM240 for four). The trail passes Lubok Simpon and Bumbun Tabing, and ultimately leads up to Gunung Tahan.

There is one river crossing before you reach the falls, which can be treacherous if the water is high. Do not attempt the river crossing in high water – you should hail one of the boat operators waiting on the opposite side to ferry you across. Look out for kingfishers and fish eagles. Before heading out to Lata Berkoh, check with park headquarters as a guide may be compulsory.

Kuala Keniam   HIKING

The trail from Kuala Trenggan to Kuala Keniam is a popular day hike. It's normally done by chartering a boat to Kuala Keniam and then walking back to Kuala Trenggan (six hours). The trail is quite taxing and hilly in parts, and passes a series of limestone caves.

This walk can be combined with one of the Kuala Tahan–Kuala Trenggan trails to form a two-day trip, staying overnight in Trenggan Lodge or at Bumbun Kumbang. It is also possible to walk from Kuala Keniam

Taman Negara

0 — 10 km
0 — 5 miles

Map labels:

KELANTAN

Four Steps Waterfall

Gunung Tahan

Gunung Tahan (2187m)

Gunung Ulu Kechau (1945m)

Gunung Gedung (2065m)

Sungai Tekai

Sungai Keniam

Sungai Perkai

Sungai Trenggan

Kuala Perkai

Kuala Keniam

Kuala Keniam

Gunung Pantat Lesong (1641m)

Sungai Melantai

Sungai Tahan

Bukit Luas (578m)

Gunung Raja

Sungai Tembeling

Sungai Tenor

Lata Berkoh

Bukit Indah (563m)

Kuala Trenggan

Kuala Trenggan

Bukit Hulu Ketir (773m)

Rentis Tenor

Bukit Teresik (344m)

Bukit Indah

Bukit Teresik

Nusa Holiday Village

Sungai Atok

Bukit Guling Gendang (569m)

Canopy Walk & Around

Kuala Tahan

PAHANG

Kuala Atok; Kuala Tembeling (60km)

to the lodge at **Kuala Perkai**, an easy two-hour walk.

Gunung Tahan
TREKKING

Should you wish to conquer Gunung Tahan (2187m), the highest peak in Peninsular Malaysia and 55km from park headquarters, it takes nine days at a steady pace, although it can be done in seven. A guide is compulsory (RM1200 for seven days plus RM75 for each day thereafter). There are no shelters so you have to be fully equipped.

Rentis Tenor
TREKKING

From Kuala Tahan, this four-day trek takes you to remote corners of the park where you are more likely to see wildlife. The 35km circuit is steep and difficult so hiring a guide is important, if not essential.

Fishing

Anglers will find the park a real paradise. Almost 500 species of fish live in the teeming river waters, including the superb fighting fish known in India as *mahseer* and here as *kelah*.

Rivers where you are permitted to fish include Sungai Keniam (north of Kuala Trenggan) and the remote Sungai Sepia. Simple **fishing camp sites** are scattered through the park and can be booked at the Park Information Counter. The best fishing months are February, March, July and August. Fishing permits are RM10; rods can be hired across the river for between RM20 and RM30 per day. A boat to Sungai Keniam costs around RM450 return for a minimum of three people, while a five-day return trip to Sungai Sepia will cost around RM4000.

River Bus & Boat Trips

At either Mutiara Taman Negara Resort or the boat operators at Kuala Tahan's jetty, you can enquire about trips along the river to the following destinations. Departures are on request and there's often a minimum number of passengers.

GEAR HIRE & LEECHES

Leeches are everywhere inside the park (but are rarely found in Kampung Kuala Tahan). Wearing boots with gaiters or long socks tucked over your trousers and doused in DEET will make hiking more pleasant.

You can hire camping, hiking and fishing gear at several places in Kuala Tahan and also at Mutiara Taman Negara Resort (p277). Approximate asking prices per day:

➡ sleeping bag RM10

➡ rucksack RM30

➡ tent RM10 to RM25

➡ fishing rod RM30

➡ sleeping pad RM8 to RM10

➡ stove RM8

➡ boots RM8

DESTINATION	PRICE PER BOAT	DURATION
Bunbun Yong	RM120	20min
Canopy Walkway	RM100	15min
Gua Telinga	RM120	30min
Kuala Kenian	RM450	60-90min
Kuala Tembeling	RM200	180min
Lata Berkoh	RM200	45min

☞ Tours

There is a wide variety of thematic tours offered by nearly every hotel and a few independent operators in town. You can do some activities easily on your own but for longer treks, or if you really want to learn about the jungle, a tour is the way to go.

Good options are night jungle trips, on foot or by four-wheel drive (RM25 to RM45), a boat trip to the rapids at Lata Berkok via the *kelah* fish sanctuary (RM200), and motorboating through Class I rapids (RM40 to RM80).

Inside Taman Negara are around nine villages of the Batek, a subgroup of the indigenous people of the peninsular known collectively as Orang Asli. On tours to their settlements (around RM80), tribal elders give a general overview of life there and you'll learn how to use a long blowpipe and start a fire. While local guides insist that these tours provide essential

income for the Orang Asli, most of your tour money will go to the tour company. A handicraft purchase in the village will help spread the wealth.

🛌 Sleeping

Kampung Kuala Tahan, directly across the river from park headquarters and Mutiara Resort, is where most of Taman Negara's lodging, restaurants and shops are found. There are a handful of secluded places just 10 minutes' walk south and north of Kampung Kuala Tahan that are worth checking out if you are looking for a little more tranquillity.

🛌 Kampung Kuala Tahan

I Am Wild Travellers   HOSTEL $
(☎016-665 7844; www.pahangoutdoor.com; Kampung Kuala Tahan; dm R25-30; ✳🕸) This hostel by the road down to the river overlooks the water and is close to the jetty, with rooms that are simply furnished and with views into the park; the more expensive rooms have beds rather than bunk beds. There's free tea and coffee, beer (RM10 to 13) and an outdoor lounge area also with river views.

Mahseer Chalet   BUNGALOW $
(☎019-383 2633; www.facebook.com/Mahseer Chalet; Kampung Kuala Tahan; dm incl breakfast RM30, r from RM100; ✳🕸) This clutch of jungle bungalows occupies a quiet part of the village above the river. The rooms and bungalows are well maintained and there's a restaurant on site serving breakfast and dinner. Cats patrol the grounds and there's a cool vibe that's wide-grinning friendly.

Yellow Guesthouse   GUESTHOUSE $
(☎017-946 3357; myusofth@gmail.com; Kuala Tahan; d/tr/q RM80/100/120; ✳@🕸) Up and over the top of the hill (behind the school), this friendly and simple guesthouse consists of a single-storey house and a two-storey building that are cleaner and in slightly better shape than many of the others. All rooms have hot showers and private balconies.

Xcape Resort   RESORT $$
(☎09-266 1111, 09-267 1111; www.xcapetaman negara.com; Kuala Tahan; dm RM30, r RM240; @🕸🏊) With a pool, this resort has comfortable enough but simple chalets and good value four- to eight-person air-con dorms

on a large 1.6-hectare plot in Kuala Tahan. Wi-fi is only good in the reception area, but staff are helpful. Breakfast can be provided at extra cost.

★**Mutiara Taman Negara Resort** RESORT $$$
(☑09-266 3500, in KL 03-2782 2222; www.mutiara hotels.com; Kampung Kuala Tahan; camp site RM10, dm/chalet/ste/bungalow incl breakfast RM100/450/650/1500; ⊖❄☎) Conveniently located right at park headquarters, this eco-minded resort spreads over a large area of riverfront property. There are simple dorm rooms that sleep eight and come with air-con; a small bungalow and 'chalet' cabins with dramatic lighting, rustic roofs and gorgeously modern showers; plus a grassy camping area with its own kitchen section.

The best part is you're in the park proper – with right-out-your-door access to afternoon hikes. That said, if you want to get across to town for dinner (the food here is great but pricey), you'll need to shell out the RM1 fee for the crossing. As you walk up the steps to the resort, note the marker indicating the high water line during the floods of January 1971.

🛏 South of Kampung Kuala Tahan

Several peaceful places lie removed from the action just off the main Kampung Kuala Tahan–Jerantut road south of Kampung Kuala Tahan.

Park Lodge BUNGALOW $
(☑019-733 1661; Kuala Tahan; bungalow RM70) The setting below a verdant hill 500m south of town is tranquil and idyllic, in a small and green patch, secluded at the end of the track. There are just six fan-cooled back-to-basics bungalows, making this a welcome and particularly quiet retreat way beyond the action.

Holiday View Inn HOTEL $$
(☑012-952 9069; www.viewinn.com.my; 500m south of Kuala Tahan; r RM140, q RM170; P ❄) This hillside offering has clean, high-ceilinged rooms with tile floors and plenty of air-con. Views are rather obscured by foliage, but the setting is quiet. However, there's no common area and the dividing door between rooms means you can hear what's going on in the next room. There are just four rooms.

🛏 North of Kampung Kuala Tahan

Nusa Holiday Village HOTEL $
(☑09-266 2369; www.tamannegara-nusaholiday. com.my; dm RM30, r RM160-180, f RM280; ❄) About a 15-minute boat ride upriver from park headquarters, Nusa Holiday Village offers more of a 'jungle camp' feel than other places, a sense reinforced by the isolation. There's a choice of serviceable dorms, garden-view chalets, river-view houses and spacious cottages for families. Packages are offered.

Mat Leon Village BUNGALOW $
(☑013-998 9517; www.matleon.net/about-us; dm with fan RM15, bungalow with fan RM80-100, bungalow with air-con & breakfast RM180-240; ❄) This spot has a supreme forest location with river views, a good restaurant and free boat pick-up from Kampung Kuala Tahan (7am to 9.45am). On foot it's about 15 minutes from Kuala Tahan past Durian Chalet for around 350m to the sign; follow the forest path for 200m and the bungalows are on the far side of a small stream.

🛏 Kuala Perkai & Kuala Keniam

Kuala Keniam Lodge (about an hour's boat ride upstream from Kuala Trenggan) and Kuala Perkai (a further two hours' walk past Kuala Keniam) are both officially closed and do not offer lodging; however, people still do camp there. If you're camping at either of these places, bring your own tent.

🍴 Eating

Floating barge restaurants line the rocky shore of Kampung Kuala Tahan, most selling cheap basic noodle and rice meals plus bland Western fare. All are open from morning until late, though most take rest breaks between 2pm and 4pm. The best and most dependable cuisine by a long chalk is available from Mutiara Taman Negara Resort, which serves everything from breakfast to dinner.

Family Restaurant MALAYSIAN $
(Kuala Tahan; mains RM6-15; ⊗8.30am-10.30pm) This floating restaurant serves a dish called *kerabu*, finely diced meat and vegetables with a light lemongrass sauce that's got way more local cred than the standard banana pancakes. It also serves banana pancakes.

Note the restaurant usually closes for a siesta between 2pm and 4pm.

Mama Chop ASIAN $
(Kampung Kuala Tahan; mains from RM3, set meals RM8-35; ⊙7.30am-10pm; 🖉) In a nice change from other floating restaurants, Mama serves Asian food including freshly made *roti* and *naan* breads and vegetarian meals as well as good claypot dishes, but it's still a pretty simple set-up. Note the restaurant usually closes for a siesta between 2pm and 4pm.

⭐**Seri Mutiara Restaurant** INTERNATIONAL $$
(Mutiara Taman Negara Resort; RM25-50; ⊙7am-11pm; 🖃) The excellent restaurant at the resort is open to nonguests and serves a fantastic range of foods, from local dishes such as satay (RM26) to salads, sandwiches, burgers and pizza. The buffet dinner (RM50) is a great option if you're hungry. It also serves a good range of alcoholic drinks including wine and cocktails.

❶ Information

EMERGENCY
Police (🖉09-266 6721; Kuala Tahan) Located 300m up from Teresek View Motel.

MEDICAL SERVICES
Klinik Kesihatan (Community Clinic; 🖉09-266 7468; Kuala Tahan; ⊙24hr) Next to Agoh Chalets in Kuala Tahan, opposite the school.

TOURIST INFORMATION
There is no tourist information office in Kuala Tahan, though most accommodation options can provide tips.

Danz Travel & Adventures (🖉013-655 4789, 09-266 3036; www.danzecoresort.com; Kuala Tahan; ⊙8am-10pm; 🖃) Occupying a prime position at the heart of Kuala Tahan, this busy outfit provides information on onward transport including its own boat transfers back to Jerantut. It's also, like most other seemingly independent tourist information providers in Kuala Tahan, primarily aimed at getting you to sign up for tours and activities.

Park Information Counter (🖉09-266 4152, 09-266 1122; tnp@wildlife.gov.my; Mutiara Taman Negara Resort; park entrance/camping/camera/canopy/hides/fishing RM1/1/5/5/5/10; ⊙8am-10pm Sun-Thu, to noon & 3-10pm Fri) You need to come to this office 100m north of Mutiara Taman Negara Resort's reception to register your name and nationality so staff can keep track of who is in the park; you also need to purchase an assortment of permits before heading off into the trees, including a photography permit (even if you are using a mobile phone camera). It's worth grabbing the leaflet and map *Taman Negara Kuala Tahan* (free). The office also sells the excellent book *Taman Negara: A Guide to the Park* (RM25), a well-produced and comprehensive introduction to the park and its fauna and flora.

❶ Getting There & Away

A recommended option is to head to Taman Negara by minibus or taxi from Jerantut and return by boat. Driving to Kuala Tahan is also feasible for those with hire cars. The bold of spirit can access the park on foot.

It's a straightforward and fast drive from Jerantut along the 1508 road to Kuala Tahan. Parking in Kuala Tahan is plentiful. From Jerantut, take road 64 east out of town, cross the Pahang River bridge and take the first left north (the 1508).

BOAT
The 60km boat trip from Kuala Tembeling (18km north of Jerantut) to Kuala Tahan is a beautiful journey and a highlight for many visitors. The boat ride is three hours to the park and two hours in the other direction.

Boats (one-way RM45) depart daily from Kuala Tembeling at 2pm. Extra boats are laid on during the busy season, and service can be irregular from November to February. Boats are run by NKS (p273), Danz Travel & Adventures and **Han Travel** (Map p62; 🖉03-2031 0899; www.han.travel; Ground fl, Bangunan Mariamman, Jln Hang Kasturi, Chinatown, Kuala Lumpur; LRT Pasar Seni). On the return journey, boats leave Kuala Tahan at around 8.30am.

At the Kuala Tembeling Jetty you will find tourist offices and a National Parks Information Office where you can purchase passes.

BUS
Minibus services go directly from several tourist destinations around Malaysia to Kampung Kuala Tahan. Han Travel, NKS and Danz Travel & Adventures run several useful private services, including daily buses from Kuala Tahan to Jerantut (RM25), Cameron Highlands (RM95), Kuala

---

❶ MOSQUITOES

To prevent mosquito-borne illnesses, such as malaria, the best precaution is to avoid being bitten. Wear light long-sleeved clothes and cover up with DEET. Mosquitoes generally bite between 6am and 9am and then again between 6pm and 9pm. Malaria meds are recommended by international travel clinics for the park.

Besut, for the Perhentians (RM100), Kota Bharu (RM140), Kuantan (RM90) and Penang (RM140). These minibuses can also drop you off en route anywhere in between.

WALKING

You can walk into or out of the park at the entrance at Sungai Relau via Merapoh, at the Pahang–Kelantan border. The trail from Merapoh joins the Gunung Tahan trail (p275), adding another two days to the Gunung Tahan trek. Guides are compulsory and can be hired in Merapoh to take you in. Popular and reputable travel guide Zeck, from Zeck's Traveller's Inn (p286) in Kota Bharu, can arrange a trip into the park from Kelantan that will definitely take you well off the beaten path. Other entrances to Taman Negara exist at Kuala Koh in Kelantan and Tanjung Mentong in Terengganu.

Kuala Lipis

09 / POP 20,000

Situated at the confluence of the Lipis and Jelai rivers, Kuala Lipis is a bustling little town with a charming colonial-era centre filled with Chinese shophouses. A large percentage of the population is Chinese or Indian, and their common language is English so it's easy to chat with them and find your way around.

Lipis was a gold-mining centre long before the British arrived in 1887, but the town's heyday began in 1898 when it became the capital of Pahang. Grand colonial buildings date from this period, and trade increased when the railway came through in 1924. In 1957 the capital shifted to Kuantan and Kuala Lipis went into decline. The somewhat less charming 'New Town' is across the river from the old centre.

It's best known as a launching pad for visits to the nearby Kenong Rimba State Park (p280), but Kuala Lipis also draws people for its delightful colonial-era architecture and welcoming character.

Sights

A very pleasant walk starts on the road uphill behind Lipis Centrepoint Complex. You will soon pass **Istana Hinggap** on your right; keep going uphill and the road forks. Take either branch and you will be led to a series of colonial-era houses, some in the process of being reclaimed by jungle.

Other buildings of note in town include **Clifford School**, the **Lipis District Administration Building** (Jln Utama Kecau) and **Pahang Club**. The post office is also a heritage building, as is the train station, dating to 1926.

A taxi around town for an hour of sightseeing costs around RM25. This can also be done on foot, though you'll need about half a day to do the walk.

Night Market   MARKET

If you're in town on Friday evening, be sure to visit the night market in the parking lot next to the bus station. It extends until about noon the next day.

Activities

Appu's Jungle Treks   HIKING

(09-312 2619, 017-947 1520, 09-312 3142; jungleappu@yahoo.com or jungleappu@hotmail.com; Jln Besar; from RM80) Appu has been running one- to six-day treks of Kenong Rimba State Park for decades. Tours cost RM80 per person per day for a minimum of four people, plus RM150 for the van and boat trip to and from Jeti Tanjung Kiara (there's a different rate for less than four people).

Hutan Lipur Terenggun Park   HIKING

(7am-6pm) For an afternoon romp, grab a taxi 7km out of town to the small 23-hectare Hutan Lipur Terenggun Park, which features a little lake and a few hiking tracks.

Empang Jaleh   SWIMMING

Take a side trip to this lake and waterfall 14km west of Kuala Lipis. From here, you could also stage a climb of 2187m-high Gunung Tahan (p275).

Sleeping & Eating

There are busy and popular food stalls on either side of the northern end of the overhead walkway crossing Jln Pekeliling.

Lipis Plaza Hotel   HOTEL $

(09-312 5521; www.lipisplaza.com; 6 Komplek Taipan, Jln Benta Lipis; d RM130-180, ste RM240-480; P*) This large hotel has decent and large, if somewhat bland, rooms that come with flat-screen TVs and rather wobbly wi-fi, but staff are courteous and the breakfast is good. Rooms at the rear look out onto the jungle greenery of Bukit Residen, while rooms at the front have small balconies. Regular discounts make the hotel a good value choice.

Centrepoint Hotel & Apartments   HOTEL $

(09-312 2688; www.centrepointhotel.com.my; Jln Pekeliling, 5th fl, Lipis Centrepoint; economy s/d RM48/50, deluxe d from RM108;*) You could film a horror movie in this rather bizarre high-rise complex, but once you get through

KENONG RIMBA STATE PARK

A far less visited alternative to Taman Negara, this sprawling area of lowland forest rises to the limestone foothills bordering Taman Negara itself. The 120-sq-km forest park can be explored on one- to six-day jungle treks organised from Kuala Lipis. Sightings of big mammals are rare but expect to see monkeys, wild boar, squirrels, civets and possibly nocturnal tapir; this is also a prime destination for bird-watching. The park is home to the Batek people, an Orang Asli tribe.

Visitors need to acquire a permit issued by the Kuala Lipis District Forest Office, but usually acquired through your guide. Guides are compulsory for entry to the park and can be arranged in Kuala Lipis. Appu of Appu's Jungle Treks (p279) in Kuala Lipis does expeditions. Park entry is RM50 per person.

You will need to take a torch, insect repellent, a thin sleeping bag, decent walking shoes, a raincoat or poncho and a first aid kit. After rain, leeches are pretty much a fact of life, so consider taking high socks impregnated with insect repellent, with your trouser legs tucked into them.

the front door of this hotel, things change for the better. Economy rooms are on the 7th floor and are slightly aged, while the deluxe options on the main floor (5th floor) are worth the upgrade.

Residence Rest House   HISTORIC HOTEL **$**
(☑ 09-312 2788; r RM60-150; ❄) This huge, homey colonial hilltop mansion once housed the British Resident. Rooms are massive, with floral wallpaper and big windows, but the whole place is rather done in, with old paintwork and mismatched furniture. The restaurant opens for dinner, with live music; a taxi to town costs RM7 or you can walk up the corkscrewing road.

Follow the road from across the KFC outlet that leads uphill behind Lipis Plaza.

❶ Information

There are a few banks with ATMs on Jln Besar.

The **post office** (Jln Besar; ❂ 8.30am-5.30pm Mon-Fri, to 1pm Sat) is a very short walk southeast of the train station.

❶ Getting There & Away

Buses run from the **bus station** (☑ 09-312 5055) in New Town across Jelai River to Kuala Lumpur (RM14, 4½ hours), Kuantan (RM29, six hours), Temerloh (RM17, one hour), Raub (RM6.30, 1½ hours), Jerantut (RM6.50, 40 minutes) and Gua Musang (RM16, 1½ hours), from where you can catch onward buses to Kota Bharu.

The line from the **train station** (Jln Besar) forms part of the jungle railway, with trains from Tumpat running through Wakaf Baharu to Kuala Lipis and continuing to Jerantut; for Kuala Lumpur, change at Gemas.

Taxis leave from the bus station. Approximate costs:

➡ Gua Musang (RM140)
➡ Jerantut (RM80)
➡ Kuala Lumpur (RM250)
➡ Kuala Tahan (RM170)
➡ Kuantan (RM350)
➡ Raub (RM80)
➡ Temerloh (RM140)

Raub

☑ 09 / POP 92,000

Raub is Malay for 'scoop' or a 'handful', which makes sense as this town was built around a gold mine in the waning days of British Malaya. It's a pretty and quiet small town rarely visited by international tourists, with a measure of colonial-era charm and architecture along with a decent selection of restaurants.

Raub's Bukit Koman gold mine is a source of controversy, and multiple large-scale protests have been mounted in the past by both Malaysian environmentalists and locals who claim to have been directly affected by cyanide used in a mining process called 'cyanide leach mining'. For the casual visitor, there should be no danger from a short stay in Raub.

The negative impact of the area's other two major industries – palm oil and timber – are more noticeable. Trucks carrying timber roll through town with noisy regularity, and much of what was once jungle outside of Raub has been transformed into oil palm plantations.

◉ Sights

Like nearby Kuala Lipis, Raub also has some colonial-era architecture and a more traditional *kampung* (village) on the outskirts. Standing together, there is a small **Hindu temple** and a Chinese Buddhist **Guanyin Temple** (Kuan Yin Temple; Jln Lipis) located just 1km west of the bus terminal on the road to Kuala Lipis, just after a small Methodist church.

Raub is also a great base for exploring the nearby **Sungai Pasu Recreation Centre**, **Jeram Besu Rapids, Fraser's Hill** and **Bukit Telaga Waterfalls**. Expect to pay around RM150 for a taxi to these sights.

🛏 Sleeping & Eating

Hotel Tai Tong   HOTEL $
(☑09-356 1053; Jln Dato Abdullah; s/d/tr/q RM40/45/55/60; ❄🔊) This is one of the better budget places that are located across from the bus station (find it 100m south of the bus station). All rooms have a TV and hot shower. The friendly manager went to university in the US.

Grandview Hotel Raub   HOTEL $$
(☑09-355 6500; www.grandviewhotel.com.my; off Jln Lipis; d/tr/q from RM95/120/165; P❄🔊) This is one of the better choices in Raub. The rooms are comfortable, the staff are pleasant and there's a decent Buddhist vegetarian restaurant right next door.

Sun Yuen Cheong   CAFE $
(25 Jln Tun Razak; snacks RM2-5; ⊘6am-5pm) This traditional, family-run Chinese-Malaysian coffee shop is bursting with customers from the early hours every morning.

Restoran Ratha Raub   INDIAN, MALAYSIAN $$
(☑09-356 1651; 82 Jln Tun Razak; mains from RM12; ⊘6.30am-9.30pm) What brings people here is Ratha's Kari Kepala Ikan Raub (fish-head curry, small portion RM55), served fresh in a metal tureen of fiery curry, green chilli, string beans, local eggplant and a special variant of light tofu that's been puffed with air – and, of course, the tender meat from the split head of a large red snapper.

Restoran Sentosa   CHINESE $$
(Jln Padang; mains RM10-30; ⊘dinner) Sentosa specialises in whole fish prepared in Chinese fashion and served in a variety of ways – hotpot and grilled are quite popular. The building – a 100-year-old round pavilion with stained-glass windows and a lovely blue country facade 50m west of the bus station – is alone worth a visit. It charges by the pound, so meals can get pricey.

ⓘ Information

There are several banks in town (some even sell gold), including an **HSBC** (Jln Tun Razak; ⊘24hr ATM) with an ATM that accepts foreign cards.

ⓘ Getting There & Away

Raub's **bus station** is on Jln Dato Abdullah at the heart of things. A number of companies, including Transnasional (p608), run several buses daily between Raub and Kuala Lumpur's Pekeliling Station (from RM9, four hours), Kuantan (RM22.90, four hours), Kuala Lipis (RM5.20, 1 hour) and Temerloh (RM10.10).

Taxi drivers tend to congregate at the bus station, offering rides to destinations all around Pahang. A taxi to Kuala Lumpur will cost RM200 and to Kuala Lipis RM70.

PAHANG & TIOMAN ISLAND RAUB

Peninsular Malaysia's Northeast

Includes ➡
Kota Bharu 283
Pulau Perhentian . . . 293
Pulau Redang 301
Pulau Kapas 304
Kuala Terengganu. . . 305
North of
Kuala Terengganu. . . .312
South of
Kuala Terengganu. . . .312

Best Places to Eat

➡ Santai (p299)

➡ Kedai Kopi Ambassador (p289)

➡ Four Seasons (p289)

➡ Mandalica Empire (p298)

➡ Restoran Golden Dragon (p310)

Best Places to Stay

➡ BuBu Resort (p298)

➡ D'Lagoon Chalet (p299)

➡ Rose House Dabong (p293)

➡ Terrapuri Heritage Village (p312)

➡ Kapas Turtle Valley (p305)

➡ Gem Island Resort & Spa (p305)

Why Go?

Picturesque palm-fringed beaches and bucolic *kampung* (villages) abound on peninsular Malaysia's northeast coast, but what brings folks back to the region time and again are the tantalising tropical islands offshore. 'Paradise' barely does these gems justice, though that'll likely be the word that comes to mind when you first lay eyes on the white sands and azure waters of Pulau Perhentian, Pulau Redang or Pulau Kapas. Snorkellers and divers revel in these crystal-clear waters featuring colourful coral gardens and myriad fishes.

For a change of pace and scene, the regional hubs of Kota Bharu and Kuala Terengganu have retained their Malay heritage and feature lively Chinatown districts, as well as an excellent selection of eating spots. Nature lovers will want to spend time exploring the national parks protecting the remaining pockets of rainforest and best accessed along the famous jungle railway.

When to Go
Kuala Terengganu

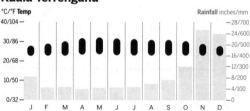

Apr & May Island resorts have opened after the monsoon though visitor numbers are yet to peak.

Jun–Aug Drier weather and calm seas make summer a great time to visit the islands.

Nov–Feb Monsoonal rains. Most island resorts are closed, but discounts are available elsewhere.

KELANTAN

Malaysia's northeasternmost state is often considered to be a waypoint between Thailand and the white-sand beaches of Pulau Perhentian, Redang or Kapas. Those who don't linger miss out experiencing a stronghold of traditional Malay culture and one of Southeast Asia's great buffer zones, combining a distinctive blend of Malay, Chinese, Indian and Thai cultures.

Ride the jungle railway inland to feast on blue rice and spot siamang gibbons, or join the bustle at Kota Bharu's markets and Chinatown. Kelantan is one of Malaysia's most conservative regions, and the state has been ruled by the Islamic Party of Malaysia (PAS) since 1990. It is one of only two states left under PAS rule after the 2018 elections. PAS has made ongoing attempts to introduce strict sharia laws, but this has been continually overruled by the federal government. Despite the conservative political environment, the Kelantanese are friendly and welcoming to visitors.

Kota Bharu

📞 09 / POP 314,900

The northernmost major city in Malaysia is also one of its most devoutly Muslim and it is deeply grounded in traditional Malay heritage. Kota Bharu has all the energy of a mid-sized city with the compact feel and friendly vibe of a small town. There are excellent markets and ample opportunities to taste superb local cuisine. There is also a good spread of accommodation options from backpacker hostels to business hotels. This is a logical overnight stop between Thailand and the resort islands of neighbouring Terengganu: Perhentian and Redang.

Kota Bharu is the gateway for exploring the geography and culture of Kelantan. Many traditional Malay villages and colourful Thai Buddhist temples are within day-tripping distance, and local crafts, cuisine and culture can be found while strolling in the city itself. For exploring the interior, the enticing jungle railway passes by Kota Bharu's doorstep.

◉ Sights

Gathered around Padang Merdeka is a cluster of museums. Spend a leisurely day exploring them and you'll be well on your way to becoming a semi-expert in Malay history and culture. Nearby are good restaurants and shopping opportunities. If you've only got half a day, your priority should be Istana Jahar and Istana Batu.

Istana Jahar   MUSEUM
(Royal Ceremonies Museum; 📞 09-748 2266; www.muzium.kelantan.gov.my; Jln Istana; adult/child RM4/2; ⊗ 8.30am-4.45pm Sat-Wed, to 3.30pm Thu) Kota Bharu's best museum focuses on Kelantanese ritual and crafts. It's housed in a beautiful chocolate brown building that dates back to 1887 and is easily one of the most attractive traditional buildings in the city.

The collection here includes detailed descriptions of batik-weaving, the elaborate ceremonies of coming-of-age circumcision, wedding nights and funerary rights.

Gelanggang Seni   CULTURAL CENTRE
(Cultural Centre; 📞 03-744 3124; Jln Mahmud; ⊗ 3.30-5.30pm Mon, Wed, Sat & 9-11pm Sat Feb-Sep) **FREE** Local cultural events, including *gasing uri* (top-spinning), *silat* (a Malay martial art), kite-making, drumming and shadow-puppet shows are held regularly at Gelanggang Seni. The events are kid-friendly and all are free.

Note, it's closed from October to end of January and during Ramadan. Check with the tourist information centre (p290) for the latest timetable.

Muzium Islam   MUSEUM
(Islamic Museum; Jln Sultan; ⊗ 8.30am-4.45pm Sat-Wed, to 3.30pm Thu) **FREE** Muzium Islam occupies an old villa once known as Serambi Mekah (Verandah to Mecca) – a reference to its days as Kelantan's first school of Islamic instruction. Nowadays it displays a small collection of photographs and artefacts relating to the history of Islam in the state.

Muzium Negeri Kelanta   MUSEUM
(State Museum; 📞 09-748 2266; Jln Hospital; adult/child RM4/2; ⊗ 8.30am-4.45pm Sat-Wed, to 3.30pm Thu) Next to the tourist information centre, this is the official state museum. The exhibits on Kelantan's history and culture are interesting, but the accompanying signage can be poor.

Kampung Kraftangan   ARTS CENTRE
(Handicraft Village; Jln Hilir Kota; village admission free, museum adult/child RM4/2; ⊗ museum 8.30am-4.45pm Sat-Thu) This handicraft market, a touristy affair opposite Istana Batu (p286), has a one-room museum with displays of woodcarving, batik-making and other crafts.

Peninsular Malaysia's Northeast Highlights

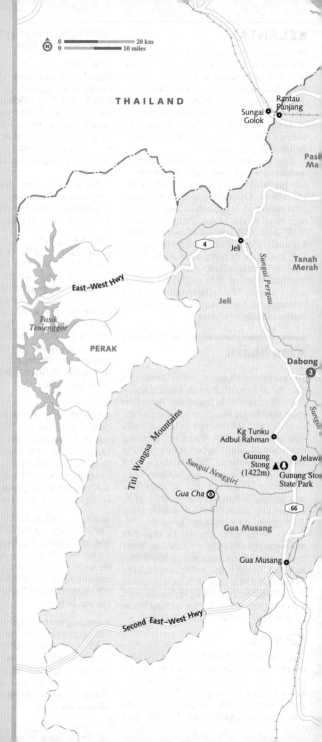

1 Kota Bharu (p283) Discovering Malay culture and history at the museums before sampling the tasty offerings at street stalls, markets and restaurants.

2 Pulau Perhentian Kecil (p293) Savouring barbecued seafood and chilled wine on a beach as the moon rises over the South China Sea.

3 Dabong (p293) Catching the jungle railway into Kelantan's interior to explore traditional Dabong and Gunung Stong National Park.

4 Tumpat (p292) Visiting the colourful Thai temples in the northern borderlands.

5 Pulau Redang (p301) Basking in the sun on a picture-perfect tropical island beach.

6 KT's Chinatown (p307) Imbibing the tastes, culture and history of Kuala Terengganu's most vibrant district.

7 Pulau Kapas (p304) Snorkelling, chilling and beachcombing in a budget-friendly tropical paradise.

8 Penarik Firefly Sanctuary (p312) Taking a night-time boat tour through ghostly mangroves and being surrounded by fireflies.

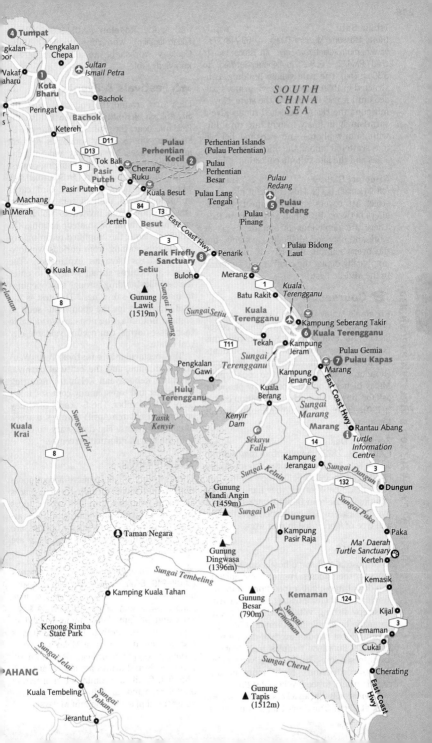

Istana Batu — MUSEUM

(Royal Museum, Muzium Diraja; ☎09-748 7737; www.muzium.kelantan.gov.my; Jln Istana; adult/child RM4/2; ◎8.30am-4.45pm Sat-Wed, to 3.30pm Thu) The pale yellow building, constructed in 1939, was the crown prince's palace until it was donated to the state. Now a museum, the richly furnished rooms give a surprisingly intimate insight into royal life, with family photos and personal belongings scattered among the fine china, chintzy sofas and the late sultan's collection of hats.

Streetart Gallery — PUBLIC ART

(off Jln Ismail) FREE This colourful display of street art covers several connecting back alleys between Jln Ismail and Jln Dato Pati. There are depictions of smiling locals at work and play and idyllic jungle scenes, but the overwhelming majority of the murals graphically depict the conflict and suffering in the Middle East.

Courses

Roselan's Malay Cookery Workshop — COOKING

(☎012-909 6068; Jln Sultan Ibrahim; per person RM135) The ever-cheerful Roselan runs this popular Malay cookery workshop. Students are invited to a middle-class Malay home (Roselan's own) and taught to cook typical Malay dishes. Contact Roselan by phone or ask for him at the tourist information centre (p290). There is a minimum group size of two people.

Zecsman Design — ART

(☎012-929 2822; www.facebook.com/zecsman; Jln Hilir Kota, Kampung Kraftangan; courses half day RM50-70, full day RM150; ◎10am-5pm Sat-Thu) Buy ready-made batik or try your hand at batik painting at Zecsman Design's tutored four- to five-hour classes. The cost depends on the size and type of fabric used in your work.

Tours

Most hostels and some hotels can organise tours for their guests. Possible tours include two-day, three-night expeditions into the jungle around Gua Musang, and boat trips to sleepy fishing villages where silk kites are made by candlelight (around RM85 per person). Most popular are half-day tours of Tumpat's Buddhist temples including detours to see kite-, batik- and silver-making (RM60 per person). Night tours include river journeys to see fireflies (RM25).

Pawi at KB Backpackers Lodge (p288), Zeck at Zeck's Travellers Inn, and freelance tour guide Roselan (☎012-909 6068; Jln Sultan Ibrahim), who runs Roselan's Malay Cookery Workshop, are all reputable and knowledgeable.

Festivals & Events

Each year around the end of August, the city holds a bird-singing contest at Padang Perdana near the Sultan Muhammad IV Stadium, where Malay songbirds perform in ornate cages. Most Friday and Saturday mornings there's also a bird-singing contest at the bird-singing field (Jln Sri Cemerlang), where locals hang decorative bird cages up on long poles, then sit back and listen. Travellers are often invited to watch and even provide a bit of amateur judging. On a different note, the amplified recordings of bird tweets coming from curious windowless buildings have an explanation. The tweets and chirps attract swiftlets to enter the cave-like building through tiny openings to make a bird-saliva nest. The nest is the vital ingredient for the eponymous soup so popular in China. The nests are so valuable that these 'farms' can occupy valuable city real estate.

The spectacular kite festival (Pesta Wau) is held in June, and the cultural carnival (Karnival Kebudayaan Kelantan), featuring drumming and top-spinning contests, takes place in September. The Sultan's Birthday celebration (March/April) involves a week of cultural events. The dates vary, so check with the tourist information centre.

Sleeping

There's plenty of inexpensive accommodation around town, including a few places aimed at overland travellers where tours and onward transport can easily be arranged. Mid-range and luxury options are aimed at business travellers and there are interesting homestays out of town.

Zeck's Travellers Inn — HOMESTAY $

(☎019-946 6655; www.zecktravellers.blogspot.my; 7088-F Jln Sri Cemerlang; dm/s/d from RM15/25/40, r with air-con RM45-70; ❀@☎) Zeck and Miriam Zaki's home, located in a peaceful nook north of the city centre, is a great way to experience Malaysian *kampung* (village) life in the heart of Kota Bharu. Light meals and drinks are always at hand. The Zaki family are a mine of information on Kelantan and can help you with your ongoing travel plans throughout Malaysia.

Kota Bharu

N 0 — 400 m
0 — 0.2 miles

Kota Bharu

◎ Sights
1 Gelanggang Seni	B3
2 Istana Batu	A1
3 Istana Jahar	A1
4 Kampung Kraftangan	B1
5 Muzium Islam	A1
6 Muzium Negeri Kelanta	B3
7 Streetart Gallery	B2

⊕ Activities, Courses & Tours
8 Roselan	B3
9 Roselan's Malay Cookery Workshop	B3
Zecsman Design	(see 4)

⊟ Sleeping
10 G Home Hotel	A1
11 Grand Riverview Hotel	A2
12 Hotel Perdana	B3
13 KB Backpackers Lodge	B2
14 My Place Guest House	C1
15 Room @ Zishi	B1
16 Zeck's Travellers Inn	D1

⊗ Eating
17 Four Seasons	D1
18 Kedai Kopi Ambassador	C1
Kedai Kopi White House	(see 3)
19 Medan Selera Kebun Sultan Food Court	C1
20 Muhibah Bakery & Cafe	B1
21 Nasi Air Hideng Pok Sen Food Court	B2
22 Night Market	B1
23 Restoran Capital	A1
24 Shan Sri Dewi Restaurant	C2
25 Sun Two	A2
26 Westlake Eating House	C1

⊖ Drinking & Nightlife
27 Arnold Cycling Cafe	C1
28 Only One	A2
29 Restoran Golden City	C2

⊞ Shopping
30 Bazaar Buluh Kubu	B1
31 Central Market	B1

Zeck also helps to arrange tours to local sights as well as into Taman Negara through the park's far-less trafficked Kelantan entrance, and also to Gunung Stong State Park.

Room @ Zishi
GUESTHOUSE $

(☑ 012-921 8103; theroom.zishi@hotmail.com; 67 Jln Pintu Pong; r without/with window RM88/108, f RM168; ✳ 🛜) Located opposite Kota Bharu's central market, this well-run guesthouse features stylish decor. Rooms are furnished simply, and the shared downstairs area has a cool relaxation space with lots of throw cushions and shag pile carpet, as well as free tea, coffee and snacks.

A key card system to the building guarantees security.

My Place Guest House
HOSTEL $

(☑ 013-9011 463; myplacekb@yahoo.com; Jln Pintu Pong; s RM25, d without/with air-con RM39/55, all incl breakfast; ✳ 🛜) Just a short stroll from Chinatown, My Place Guest House is a welcoming and friendly spot. Retro posters including the Beatles and Che Guevara punctuate the eclectically furnished interior, and the rooms are simple but clean. The common bathroom (no hot water) is downstairs.

KB Backpackers Lodge
HOSTEL $

(☑ 019-944 5222; www.facebook.com/kbbackpackerslodge; 2879-D, Section 12, Taman Laksmana, Jln Mahmood; dm RM30/35, s RM45-70, d RM55-85; ✳ 🛜) Dorms and rooms are simple and clean and come with a fruit breakfast. The air-conditioner in the dormitory is switched on from 10pm to 10am, while guests in the other rooms can use their air-conditioner anytime. There's a basic kitchen for guest use and local guided tours can be arranged here.

Owner Pawi has a wealth of local information and is also a bicycling enthusiast. He organises bike trips (on- and off-road) and rents bicycles (RM15 to RM30 per day) to guests.

Min House Camp
HOMESTAY $

(☑ 013-922 5440; www.minkem.com; Lot 1287, Kg Pulau, Kubang Kerian; dm RM20, s/d from RM30/50, r with air-con & bathroom from RM140; ✳ @ 🛜) Around 6km from central Kota Bharu, Min House Camp has a huge open-sided dining deck overlooking the river. Accommodation ranges from basic huts through to rooms and apartments suitable for groups and families. There's a strong emphasis on experiencing authentic Malay culture with opportunities for after-dark firefly cruises, handicraft workshops, and playing traditional games and sports.

Note that the property is alcohol-free and popular with large school groups.

★ Pasir Belanda Homestay
HOMESTAY $$

(☑ 09-747 7046; www.pasirbelanda.com; Jln PCB, Pantai Cahaya Bulan; d RM182-215; ✳ 🛜 ≋) Pasir Belanda Homestay, around 4km from the centre of Kota Bharu, is one of Kelantan's choicest options. Three sizes of traditional Malay homes have been decked out with crisp bed linen and modern amenities. Relax under your *kampung* (village)-style awning or in the swimming pool overlooking the river. On-site activities include cooking classes and workshops on batik and kite decoration.

Hotel Perdana
HOTEL $$

(☑ 09-745 8888; www.hotelperdanakotabharu.com; Jln Mahmud; d incl breakfast from RM275; ✳ 🛜 ≋) The Moorish-accented Hotel Perdana is hands down the flashiest accommodation in town. The lobby has colourful examples of *wau bulan* (Malaysian kites), while the rooms are spacious and stylish. Additional services include a well-equipped gym, huge swimming pool, three restaurants (all alcohol-free) and two coffee shops.

G Home Hotel
HOTEL $$

(☑ 09-747 2219; www.ghomehotel.my; Pelangi Mall, Jln Post Office Lama; s/d from RM60/100, river view r RM149; ✳ 🛜) G Home may well be Kota Bharu's most colourful hotel. Rooms are decked out in a fetching shade of lime green, and bathrooms combine brown and white tiles. Some cheaper rooms are definitely compact, but the family rooms feature a river view. The location is great with several waterfront restaurants nearby.

The entrance is on the river side, not the road side.

Grand Riverview Hotel
HOTEL $$

(☑ 09-743 9988; www.grv.com.my; 9 Jln Post Office Lama; r/ste from RM228/2376; ✳ @ 🛜 ≋) This huge hotel offers a good standard of room at reasonable prices; seasonal promotions will shave up to 50% off the published rates. Some rooms have fine views over the river, and all have king-sized beds and big bathrooms with both showers and baths. The in-house restaurants (one Malay, one Chinese) aren't great and there's no alcohol.

✕ Eating

One of the great things about Kota Bharu is how well (and cheaply) you can eat without ever setting foot in a restaurant. A notable option is the Night Market, which is packed with hawker stalls. Other options for traditional Malay food are limited, and your best bet is to head to the Chinese restaurants and food courts along Jln Kebun Sultan.

★**Kedai Kopi Ambassador** ASIAN $
(Jln Kebun Sultan; mains RM4-6; ☺8am-2pm, 5pm-1am) Just inside the red archway entrance to Chinatown, the flaming woks and beer advertising of this outdoor restaurant draws in the crowds on balmy evenings. Choose from Thai, Malay or Chinese; each style has its own chef and cooking stall. A more limited offering is available in the mornings.

If all the tables are occupied, try the similar Kow Lun Restoran next door.

Muhibah Bakery & Cafe CAFE $
(☑016-922 2735; http://muhibahbakery.business. site; Jln Pintu Pong; cakes RM5-7; ☺9am-10pm) This lovely bakery has wicked cakes, iced desserts, sticky doughnuts and decent coffee. Stop by for a green tea frappé, pandan sponge cake, or a chocolate and cashew doughnut for a midafternoon treat.

Sun Two INTERNATIONAL $
(☑09-746 2225; 782-A Jln Temenggong; mains RM6-18; ☺noon-10pm Thu-Tue; ☏) The welcome is friendly and food delicious at this brightly decorated place that has been in business since 1946. Sample Chinese, Malay and popular Western-style food including soups and steamboats, chicken chop, and fish and chips.

Restoran Capital MALAYSIAN $
(234 Jln Post Office Lama; mains RM4-7; ☺7am-1pm) For a favourite local breakfast, get here before 9am when the excellent *nasi kerabu* (blue rice with coconut, fish and spices) often sells out. Nutty-flavoured rice combines with a variety of subtle Kelantanese curries, and optional extras include eggs and crunchy crackers.

It's also a top spot for an iced coffee or other snacks like *popiah* (fresh spring rolls) from the other stallholders filling the heritage space. On Friday and Saturday they also offer laksa.

Kedai Kopi White House CAFE $
(1329-L Jln Sultan Zainab; snacks from RM3; ☺7am-1pm) For a very local experience, pop into this old-school Chinese coffee shop for a tea or coffee while you're exploring Kota Bharu's museum precinct (mornings only). The ambience is straight from decades past,

and a lazy brunch of runny boiled eggs, crisp toast and homemade *kaya* (coconut jam) should definitely be considered.

Nasi Air Hideng Pok Sen
Food Court MALAYSIAN $
(Jln Padang Garong; mains from RM4; ☺8am-5pm) The open-sided, fan-cooled, but still steamy Nasi Air Hideng Pok Sen Food Court has several small stalls serving Malay specialities and a self-serve buffet.

Westlake Eating House CHINESE $
(Jln Kebun Sultan; mains RM5-16; ☺11am-8pm; ☑) Don't let the plain decor fool you. Westlake Eating House serves some of the tastiest Chinese fare in Eastern Malaysia. Dig into the likes of braised pork ribs, roast duck, fish in spicy sauce and stir-fried vegetables.

Night Market MALAYSIAN $
(Jln Parit Dalam; mains RM3-5; ☺5-9pm) The most popular spot for the best Malay food in town is this night market. Specialities include *ayam percik* (marinated chicken on bamboo skewers) and *nasi kerabu* (blue rice with coconut, fish and spices), squid-on-a-stick and *murtabak* (pan-fried flat bread with your choice of a filling that can range from minced meat to bananas).

Say *suka pedas* ('I like it hot') to eat as the locals do.

Shan Sri Dewi Restaurant INDIAN $
(☑09-746 2592; www.facebook.com/shansridewi; 4213-F Jln Kebun Sultan; mains RM5-10.50; ☺7am-9pm; ☑) As popular with locals as it is with tourists, this mint-green, fan-cooled place serves authentic curries on a banana leaf and a delicious, lurid-yellow mango lassi. It also serves a terrific *roti canai* (flaky flatbread served with curry), which is available in the morning and evening.

Medan Selera Kebun
Sultan Food Court CHINESE $
(Jln Kebun Sultan; mains from RM5; ☺noon-11pm) This bustling, fan-cooled Chinatown food court, which opens late in a town that closes early, offers dishes like claypot chicken rice and *kway teow* (rice-flour noodles), as well as ice-cold beer. Vegetarians are specifically catered for at Stall 21.

Four Seasons CHINESE $$
(www.fourseasonsrestaurant.com.my; 5670 Jln Sri Cemerlang; mains RM16-45; ☺noon-2.30pm & 6-10pm) The Four Seasons is packed nightly with locals enjoying seafood dishes like braised sea cucumber, claypot prawns and

PENINSULAR MALAYSIA'S NORTHEAST KOTA BHARU

dried cuttlefish with mango salad. The house speciality, deep-fried soft-shell crab, should only set you back about RM50 for two people.

🍷 Drinking & Nightlife

★ Only One
BAR

(Weyig Restaurant; ☑ 011-1111 5253; Jln Sultan Zainab; beer small/large bottle RM11/20, wine from RM72 a bottle, mains RM6-13; ⊙6pm-1am) This is one of the few bars that serves wine (Spanish and Australian) to accompany surprisingly good Thai and Western food. The open-sided design makes it a great place to wait out a downpour, and there's a big screen for watching sport. Come for a snack or a full meal. There are several beer and cider brands to choose from.

★ Arnold Cycling Cafe
CAFE

(☑ 09-744 6088; 260 Tingkat Bawan, off Jln Kebun Sultan; coffee RM5-13, sandwich RM12; ⊙9am-midnight; 🛜) The cycling part of this contemporary-styled cafe refers to some of the decoration, which also includes bare-branched trees and suspended coffee-bean sacks. It's a very pleasant place to refresh on the city's best espresso coffee, check your emails, and ponder the creamy cakes or healthy sandwiches.

Restoran Golden City
PUB

(☑ 010-801 9993; 3950-G Jln Padang Garong; Happy hour pints RM19-24; ⊙4pm-midnight Sun-Fri; 🛜) A cold pint of draught beer goes down very nicely at this centrally located combination of pub and sports bar especially during happy hour from 4pm to 9pm. It serves Guinness, Tiger, Kilkenny and Heineken on tap, plus bottled beer, and a limited menu of Western and Asian mains.

🛍 Shopping

Kota Bharu is a centre for Malay crafts. Batik, *kain songket* (traditional handwoven fabric with gold threads), silverware, wood-carving and kite-making factories and shops are dotted around town.

One of the best places to see handicrafts is on the road north to Pantai Cahaya Bulan. There are a number of workshops stretched out along the road to the beach.

Central Market
MARKET

(Pasar Besar Siti Khadijah; Jln Hulu; ⊙7am-6pm) One of the most colourful and active markets in Malaysia, this market is at its busiest first thing in the morning. Downstairs is the fresh produce section, while upstairs are stalls selling spices, brassware and batik. Also on the 1st floor is a tasty array of food stalls that are a top spot for breakfast or lunch.

Bazaar Buluh Kubu
ARTS & CRAFTS

(Jln Hulu; ⊙8am-6pm Sat-Thu) Located near Central Market, Bazaar Buluh Kubu is the place to purchase the local handicrafts such as batik, traditional Malay clothing and jewellery that the residents here buy.

ℹ Information

Central Post Office (☑ 09-741 2677; 15670 Jln Sultan Ibrahim; ⊙8.30am-5pm Sun-Thu)

HSBC Bank (Jln Padang Garong; ⊙10am-3pm Sat-Wed, 9.30-11.30am Thu) Centrally located with ATM.

Kelantan Tourist Information Centre (☑ 09-748 5534; www.facebook.com/tic.kelantan; Jln Sultan Ibrahim; ⊙8am-5pm Sun-Wed, to 3.30pm Thu, to 1.30pm Fri & Sat) Information on homestays, tours and transport.

Maybank (Jln Pintu Pong; 10am-7pm Sat-Thu) Has an ATM.

Police Station (☑ 09-748 5522; Jln Sultan Ibrahim)

ℹ Getting There & Away

AIR

Daily or weekly flights to major domestic destinations, such as Penang, Kota Kinabalu and KL, depart from **Sultan Ismail Petra Airport** (☑ 09-773 7400; www.malaysiaairports.com. my; Sultan Ismail Petra Airport Darul Naim). A number of airlines have offices inside the airport.

AirAsia (p607) To/from Kuala Lumpur, Kota Kinabalu, Johor Bahru and Kuching.

Firefly (p607) To/from Kuala Lumpur, Penang and Johor Bahru.

Malindo Air (p608) To/from Kuala Lumpur, Melaka, Ipoh and Penang.

Malaysia Airlines (p607) To/from Kuala Lumpur.

BUS

Local buses and Transnasional express buses operate from the **Central Bus Station** (☑ 09-747 5971, 09-747 4330; Jln Padang Garong). Other express and long-distance buses leave from the **Interstate Bus Terminal** (Terminal Bas Kota Bharu; Jln Datuk Wan Halim) near Tesco; a taxi from this bus station to the centre of town is around RM15.

Most regional buses leave from the Central Bus Station. Destinations include Wakaf Baharu (buses 19 and 27, RM2), Rantau Panjang (bus 29, RM5.10) and Tumpat (bus 19 and 43, RM4).

For the Perhentian Islands there are regular departures from the Central Bus Station be-

> **ⓘ GETTING TO THAILAND: KOTA BHARU TO SUNGAI KOLOK**
>
> **Getting to the borders** The Thailand border is at Rantau Panjang; bus 29 (RM5.10, 1½ hours) departs half-hourly from Kota Bharu's Central Bus Station. Taxis, also departing from the Central Bus Station, cost around RM50 and take 45 minutes.
>
> There's another border crossing at Pengkalan Kubor, on the coast, but transport links on the Thai side aren't as good and crossing here can be dodgy during periods of sectarian violence in southern Thailand. Enquire at the tourist information centre before using this crossing. During the day a large car ferry (RM1 for pedestrians) crosses the river to busy Tak Bai in Thailand. From Kota Bharu, take bus 27 or 43 (RM4.50) from the Central Bus Station.
>
> **At the borders** From Rantau Panjang you can walk across the border to Sungai Kolok, where you can arrange ongoing transport to Bangkok.
>
> **Moving on** There are four buses daily to Bangkok's southern bus terminal (707B to 1414B, 17 to 20 hours). Two daily trains (11.30am and 2.20pm, 20 to 22 hours) connect Sungai Kolok with Bangkok. There are also hourly minibuses (200B, four hours) from Sungai Kolok to Hat Yai.

tween 6am and 6.30pm to Kuala Besut (bus 639, RM6, around two hours).

Long-Distance Buses from Kota Bharu

DESTINATION	PRICE (RM)	DURATION (APPROX)
Alor Setar	39	7hr
Butterworth	38	7hr
Gua Musang	18	4hr
Ipoh	37	6hr
Kuala Lumpur	45	7hr
Kuala Terengganu	17	3hr
Kuantan	34	6hr
Lumut	44	7hr
Melaka	57	8hr
Johor Bahru (for Singapore)	65	10hr

CAR
Hire cars from **Hawk** (☑ 013-924 2455; www.hawkrentacarkelantan.blogspot.co.uk; Sultan Ismail Petra Airport) at the airport.

TAXI
The **taxi stand** (☑ 09-744 7104; Jln Hilir Pasar) is on the southern side of the Central Bus Station. Avoid the unlicenced cab drivers who will pester you around town, and take an official taxi as these are cheaper and safer.

For early morning trains, take a taxi to Wakaf Baharu (RM25, 20 minutes). Taxis can be arranged the night before at your accommodation. A taxi to Kuala Besut for boats to the Perhentian Islands is around RM75.

TRAIN
The nearest railway station is **Wakaf Baharu** (☑ 09-719 6986; Jln Stesen, Wakaf Baharu),

around 10km west of Kota Bharu; it can be reached by local buses 19 or 17 (RM2, 45 minutes) or by taxi (RM25, 20 minutes).

Destinations on what is sometimes called the **jungle railway** (KTM Berhad; ☑ 03-2267 1200; www.ktmb.com.my) include Dabong (from RM5, 3½ hours), Jerantut (RM31, 8½ hours) and Johor Bahru (RM49, 18 hours). For Kuala Lumpur you'll need to change lines at Gemas.

Check with the tourist information centre for printed timetables. Or see Keretapi Tanah Melayu (p607; KTM) for the latest times and fares.

ⓘ Getting Around

Sultan Ismail Petra Airport is 10km outside Kota Bharu's centre. Bus 9 (RM3, 20 minutes) leaves hourly from the main bus station. Taxis are RM35/30 heading to/coming from the airport.

Trishaws are not as common as they once were; you may find them around Central Market. Prices are negotiable but expect to pay around RM5 and upwards for a short journey of up to 1km.

Around Kota Bharu

Pantai Cahaya Bulan

Kota Bharu's main beach was once known as Pantai Cinta Berahi, or the Beach of Passionate Love. In keeping with Islamic sensibilities, it's now known as Pantai Cahaya Bulan or Moonlight Beach. Most people call it 'PCB'. Erosion events have seen the installation of a concrete breakwater, but PCB's sandy sprawl is still worth considering for a seafood lunch.

The road leading to PCB is quite pretty, especially by bicycle, and there are batik shops and workshops along the way. To get here by public transport, take bus 10 (RM2) from behind Kampung Kraftangan (p283) in Kota Bharu. Buses also leave from the Central Bus Station.

Tumpat's Temples

Located to the north of Kota Bharu, the Tumpat district is Malaysia's culturally diverse hinterland, neither wholly Malay nor Thai, with a dash of Chinese culture thrown in. Tumpat is a major agricultural area with picture-postcard villages fringed by a lush green sea of rice paddies. Bordering Thailand, the Thai influence is conspicuous with numerous colourful Thai temples rising above the trees. Tumpat town is also the end or beginning of the jungle railway (p291) line that stretches along the spine of Peninsular Malaysia to Johor Bahru.

Numerous Buddhist temples, such as the fascinating Wat Phothivihan, with its extraordinary reclining Buddha statue, are found scattered throughout the region. **Wesak Day** (a celebration of Buddha's life, usually held in April or May) is a good time to visit the district's temples.

The following sights are best visited as part of a tour organised by your hostel or at Kota Bharu's Kelantan Tourist Information Centre (p290). Most tours include four or five temples. Directions are given here for doing it by bus and foot for those up to the challenge.

Supposedly one of the largest Buddhist temples in Southeast Asia, **Wat Phothivihan** has a 40m-long reclining Buddha statue, which was erected in 1973. There are some smaller shrines within the grounds, as well as a canteen and a rest house for use by devotees, for a donation. Take bus 19 or 27 from Kota Bharu to Chabang Empat. Get off at the crossroads and turn left (southwest). Walk 3.5km along this road until you reach Kampung Jambu and the reclining Buddha (about one hour).

At Chabang Empat, if you turn north at the traffic light in front of the police station, you will come to **Wat Kok Seraya** after about 1km, which houses a modest standing female Buddha. While the temple's architecture is Thai, the female Buddha has Chinese features, which is probably attributable to most Buddhists here being of Chinese origin. You can get here on bus 19; continue past Chabang Empat and ask the driver to let you off.

Around 4km north of Chabang Empat near the village of Kampung Bukit Tanah is **Wat Maisuwankiri**. A richly decorated dragon boat surrounded by murky water constitutes the 'floating temple'. Unfortunately the sheer number of malnourished and sickly dogs here may be a distressing sight for some visitors. The bus from Kota Bharu's Central Bus Station (p290) to Pengkalan Kubor (around 30 minutes) stops outside the temple. Further north towards Tumpat is **Wat Pikulthong**, which houses an impressive gold mosaic standing Buddha.

Also worth a look is **Wat Matchinmaram** with its magnificent 50m-high seated Buddha (more Chinese than Thai), allegedly the largest of its type in Asia. Just across the road from here is **Sala Pattivetaya**, a Thai temple and village complex dotted with colourful statues. They are located about 2km south of Tumpat.

Around Kota Bharu

DABONG

Lined with flowers, trees and a mixture of old- and new-style *kampung* (village) houses, attractive Dabong is an excellent exploration base. The town has restaurants, shops and guesthouses and an excellent Wednesday market. The best place to stay is **Rose House Dabong** (☑ 019-960 6789; www.facebook.com/Rose.House.Dabong; Dabong; r RM70-100; ✳ 🛜), a five-minute walk from the train station. Ask for Abang Din when you book.

There are several caves in the limestone outcrops a few kilometres southeast of Dabong; **Gua Ikan** (Fish Cave) is the most accessible, but the most impressive is **Stepping Stone Cave**, a narrow 30m corridor through a limestone wall that leads to a hidden grotto and on to **Kris Cave**. These last two should not be attempted by those who experience claustrophobia.

About 15km from Dabong is **Gunung Stong State Park**. Named for the 1422m-high Gunung Stong, the park offers amazing hiking, swimming and trekking. Next to the mountain, the park's star attractions are its waterfalls, located a 20-minute climb past the park's derelict resort (in the future this resort may be reinstated). A further 45 minutes of climbing brings you to the top of the falls and a camp site, from which you can make longer excursions to the mountain's summit and the upper falls. Keep an eye out, and an ear open, for siamang gibbons in the treetops above the resort. Most tour companies divide the trek into three checkpoints. A combination of jungle mist and mountain fog can make for hazy conditions, but on good days you get the sense you're climbing over clouds humming with the calls of animals in the jungle below.

It is possible to explore the area via a tour organised in Kota Bharu, or just head down yourself and hire a taxi from Dabong train station. However, to get the most out of a visit, it's strongly recommended you contact the experienced and well-regarded **Bukhari 'Bob' Mat** (☑ WhatsApp 019-979 1099; www.kelantanature.blogspot.com; Jelawang) in Jelawang. With excellent English skills and boundless enthusiasm for the area, Bob leads caving, hiking and rafting tours, and has also launched river tubing on automotive tyre tubes. He is also the contact for **Jlawe Lodging House** (☑ 019-979 1099; bobtg6084@ gmail.com; Jelawang; r RM35-80; ✳), around 10 minutes' walk from the entrance to Gunung Stong State Park.

The jungle railway links Kota Bharu to Dabong (RM5, 3½ hours) daily with both local and express trains. If you catch the express train the fare is higher (RM17) and the ride quicker (2½ hours).

TERENGGANU

Terengganu has arguably some of Malaysia's best tropical beaches to laze about on and the clearest of sapphire waters to dive into. These idyllic beaches are found on the postcard-perfect islands of Perhentian, Redang and Kapas. With so many amazing beaches and island resorts to choose from, Terengganu's mainland is seen by many travellers as a mere pass-through to paradise. Travellers who take the time to explore between paradise-hops will find the entire state is rich in traditional culture, cuisine and scenery.

This region of Malaysia is fairly isolated geographically from the rest of the country and hasn't experience the large influxes of Indians and Chinese. Traditional activities such as kite flying, top spinning, *songket* (silk or cotton brocade) weaving and batik printing are alive and well in Terengganu.

Pulau Perhentian

☑ 09 / POP 2000

The Perhentian islands are well developed with resorts and yet still have refreshing, crystal-clear waters that are perfect for swimming, diving and snorkelling. There are hiking trails through jungles that are home to leaf monkeys, and numerous crescent beaches with shimmering white sand.

Pulau Perhentian comprises several islands, two of which are large and developed for tourism. These two major islands in the group are Kecil ('Small'), popular with the younger backpacker crowd, and Besar ('Large'). Perhentian Besar has slightly higher standards of accommodation, a slightly more packaged-group ambience, and attracts families. Both are traffic-free and share a laid-back islander vibe. Speedboats can take you out to five smaller

Pulau Perhentian

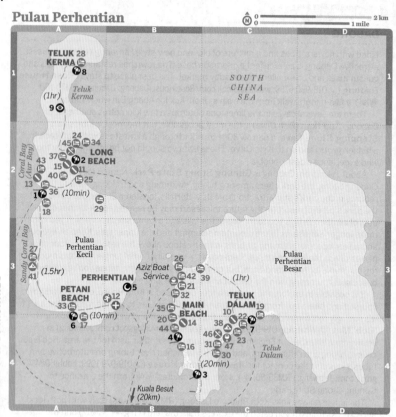

islands for day trips. With relatively shallow and calm waters, great visibility and largely gentle currents, the Perhentian islands are an ideal place to snorkel or learn to dive.

Sights & Activities

Wind Turbines
WINDMILL

(Pulau Perhentian Kecil) This pair of wind turbines can be reached either by the hiking path between Long Beach and Teluk Kerma or by a water taxi that will drop you off at a set of steep stairs leading up the cliff face. The views across the islands are the reward for the effort of getting here.

Masjid A R Rahman
Pulau Perhentian
MOSQUE

(Kampung Pasir Hantu, Pulau Perhentian Kecil) This attractive mosque, built over the water, makes an impression as you arrive at the island's main village. If you go inside, you should be respectfully dressed.

Diving & Snorkelling

There are coral reefs off both islands and around nearby uninhabited islands. There's good snorkelling off the northern end of Long Beach on Kecil, and the point in front of Coral View Island Resort (p297) on Besar. You can also swim out to an easily accessible coral reef in front of Tuna Bay Island Resort (p297) on Besar.

Most guesthouses organise snorkelling trips for around RM40 per person (minimum two people). Highlights include Turtle Point at the northern end of Main Beach (p296), and Shark Point on Besar's southwestern tip.

For scuba divers, competition between many dive centres keeps prices keen. At the time of research, a PADI open-water course cost around RM1000. Most operators also run day trips to Pulau Lang Tengah and Pulau Redang.

Recommended operators:

Angel Diver (017-358 3567; www.angel-diver.com; Long Beach, Pulau Perhentian Kecil)

Pulau Perhentian

⊙ Sights

1	Coral Bay	A2
2	Long Beach	A2
3	Love Beach	B4
4	Main Beach	B4
5	Masjid A R Rahman Pulau Perhentian	B3
6	Petani Beach	A4
7	Teluk Dalam	C4
8	Teluk Kerma	A1
9	Wind Turbines	A1

⊙ Activities, Courses & Tours

10	Alu Alu Divers	C4
11	Angel Diver	A2
12	Blue Temple Conservation	B3
	Flora Bay Divers	(see 31)
	Leisure Divers	(see 19)
	Panorama Divers	(see 37)
	Pro Diver's World	(see 26)
13	Quiver Dive Team	A2
14	Seahorse	B4
15	Turtle Bay Divers	A2

⊙ Sleeping

16	Abdul's Chalets	B4
17	Alunan Boutique Resort	A4
18	Amelia Cafe Chalet	A2
19	Arwana Perhentian Resort	C3
20	Ayumni House	B4
21	Barat Perhentian Beach Resort	B3
22	Bayu Dive Lodge	C4
23	B'First Chalet	C4
24	BuBu Resort	A2
25	BuBu Villa	A2
26	Coral View Island Resort	B3
27	Crocodile Rock Villas	A3
28	D'Lagoon Chalet & Restaurant	A1
29	D'Rock Garden Resort	A2
30	EcoMarine Perhentian Island Resort	C4
31	Flora Bay Resort	C4
32	Mama's Chalet	B3
33	Mari Mari Beach Bar & Resort	A3
34	Mimpi	A2
35	New Cocohut & Cozy Chalet	B3
36	Ombak Dive Resort	A2
37	Panorama Chalet	A2
38	Perhentian Cabana Cafe & Campsite	C4
39	Perhentian Island Resort	B3
	Perhentian Tivoli Inn	(see 40)
40	Perhentian Tropicana Inn	A2
41	RainForest Camping	A3
42	The Reef Chalets	B3
43	Shari-la Island Resort	A2
44	Tuna Bay Island Resort	B4

⊗ Eating

45	Awatif Cafe	A2
46	Mandalica Empire	C4
	Santai	(see 24)
	World Cafe	(see 25)

⊙ Drinking & Nightlife

47	Jimmy's Bar	C4

Flora Bay Divers (☏ 09-691 1661; www.florabay divers.com; Teluk Dalam, Pulau Perhentian Besar)

Leisure Divers (☏ 019-980 5977; www.diving perhentian.com.my; Teluk Dalam, Pulau Perhentian Besar; open-water course RM1100)

Panorama Divers (☏ 019-960 8630; www. panoramaperhentianisland.com; Long Beach, Pulau Perhentian Kecil; 3-dive package from RM390, PADI open-water course plus accommodation from RM990)

Pro Diver's World (☏ 09-691 1705; www. prodiversworld.com; Coral View Resort, Pulau Perhentian Besar; Boat dive RM90, PADI open-water dive course RM1250)

Quiver Dive Team (☏ 012-213 8885; www. quiver-perhentian.com; Pulau Perhentian Kecil)

Seahorse (☏ WhatsApp 019-984 1181; www.sea horsediver.com; Long Beach, Pulau Perhentian Kecil)

Turtle Bay Divers (☏ 019-333 6647, 019-913 6647; www.turtlebaydivers.com; Long Beach, Pulau Perhentian Kecil; discover scuba dive RM200, open-water course RM990) Also has an office at Mama's Place on Pulau Perhentian Besar.

Hiking

There's plenty of hiking on both islands. Some tracks can get washed out in heavy rains, so use common sense. Hot and humid is the norm, so bring plenty of water, and don't hike at night without a torch (flashlight).

On Besar, a long and hilly track (around one hour, 2.5km) cuts from north to south from close to Perhentian Island Resort (p298) to Teluk Dalam (p296). The hike over the hill from Love Beach (p296) to Teluk Dalam (around 800m, 20 minutes) is also pretty steep and rugged.

On Kecil partly paved and signposted track over the hill between Long Beach (p296) and Coral Bay (p296) is an easy 15-minute walk (around 1km). In the middle you can branch out south down a paved track to **Kampung Pasir Hantu** (around one hour, 3.2km) which continues around to **Petani Beach** (Pulau Perhentian Kecil) looping back to Coral Bay (one hour, 3km). The west coast section between Coral Bay and Petani Beach is a lovely shaded walk with glimpses of the ocean; keep an eye out for

FINDING THE RIGHT BEACH

Your biggest dilemma on the Perhentians may well be choosing the right beach as your base. A narrow strait separates Perhentian Besar from Perhentian Kecil, so hopping between the two is just a matter of hopping onto a water taxi (RM15 to RM20).

Main Beach (Pulau Perhentian Besar) Besar's main beach stretches along the west coast of the island to the southern tip, interrupted by several rocky headlands – you can walk around them on short trails, otherwise take a water taxi. The white sand here is almost as lovely as Long Beach on Kecil. As a general rule the sand, swimming and snorkelling improves as you head north.

Teluk Dalam (Pulau Perhentian Besar) The big island's 'southern bite', this circular bay has a white-sand beach and accommodation in all budget ranges. There are good snorkelling spots on the bay's western edge, and a few good restaurants, though note that most are alcohol-free. It's easier to take a water taxi than to walk here.

Love Beach (Pulau Perhentian Besar) This secluded beach at the south of the island can be reached by a steep and rugged track (around 800m, 20 minutes) from Teluk Dalam.

Long Beach (Pulau Perhentian Kecil) This attractive stretch of sand offers umbrella-shaded lounges and the most party-ish vibe on the Perhentians. Those looking for a natural paradise might find this to be a little overdeveloped. There can be crowds, and sadly petty crime (keep an eye on your belongings on the beach) as well as noise from the nightlife.

Coral Bay (Pulau Perhentian Kecil) Dead-coral-strewn Coral Beach is aptly named. A construction boom has diminished the quaintness of this once-quiet spot but it's perfect for those wanting to stay within easy walking distance of Long Beach's party vibe without being in the midst of it.

From Coral Beach you can also easily access several other sandy beaches heading south along the walking track that leads to Perhentian Village.

Teluk Kerma (Pulau Perhentian Kecil) Home to a single accommodation option (p299), this small but lovely bay is peaceful and quiet. There's great diving and snorkelling and a few equally isolated beaches within walking distance. It's an hour's hike or a two-minute water taxi ride (RM10) to your nearest neighbour (Long Beach).

huge monitor lizards and local birdlife. Hiking the rugged and exposed 3km path that runs between Long Beach and Teluk Kerma takes around one hour, during which you'll pass the island's wind turbines (p294).

🛏️ Sleeping & Eating

🛏️ Besar

The big island's two main bases are Main Beach and Teluk Dalam. Both are more family-oriented than backpacker-oriented Kecil and both offer a good range of accommodation to suit all budgets, with Teluk Dalam more budget-focused.

MAIN BEACH

⭐ **Barat Perhentian Beach Resort** RESORT **$$**
(📞 09-691 1288; www.baratperhentian.com; Main Beach, Pulau Perhentian Besar; r RM220-450; ❄️📶) Located at the northern end of Main Beach, with its own pier and good snorkel-

ling close by, this modern resort comprises lovely wooden chalets with verandahs. There's a good range of rooms from ones with bunk beds to those with sea views.

It also has an excellent restaurant with a wide selection of Asian and international dishes, a seafood BBQ, plus beer and wine.

The Reef Chalets RESORT **$$**
(📞 013-981 6762, 09-691 1762; www.thereef perhentian.com; Main Beach, Pulau Perhentian Besar; chalet RM140-385; ❄️📶) This family-owned resort offers a wide range of pleasant wooden chalets set back from the beach and surrounding a beautifully maintained jungle garden. Occasionally visitors include acrobatic dusky leaf monkeys (langurs), birds and bats. Many chalets have sea views; the cheapest are fan-cooled, the more expensive have air-conditioning.

The friendly owners rent out kayaks and snorkelling equipment and can help you plan your stay.

Abdul's Chalets
RESORT $$

(☑ 019-912 7303; www.abdulchalet.com; Main Beach, Pulau Perhentian Besar; r RM200-280; ❄ ⑤) The once-humble Abdul's continues to upgrade, and options range from garden-view bungalows at the lower end of the price range to sea-view family rooms at the higher end. The dining deck, where freshly caught fish and a variety of Malay and international dishes are served, is alcohol-free. There's a handy minimart for snacks and soft drinks.

The adjacent beach is safe and family friendly.

Mama's Chalet
BUNGALOW $$

(☑ 013-984 0232,019-985 3359; www.mamaschalet. com.my; Main Beach, Pulau Perhentian Besar; bungalow RM110-180, f RM380; ❄ ⑤) This established property has 45 bungalows on the beach. All are comfortable, spacious and clean, and the more expensive ones have sea views and air-conditioning. Mama's also has an alcohol-free restaurant serving local dishes. Helpful manager Aziz has a boat service (p302) to Pulau Lang Tengah and Pulau Redang.

Tuna Bay Island Resort
RESORT $$

(☑ 09-690 2902; www.tunabay.com.my; Main Beach, Pulau Perhentian Besar; d/tr/f from RM290/370/580; ❄ @ ⑤) These bungalows occupy a lovely stretch of palm-shaded white sand, with more bungalows set in the pretty gardens or facing the jungle behind. Swim on a vibrant coral reef just offshore, or relax in the cocktail bar with a Long Island iced tea or cappuccino.

For dinner, Tuna Bay serves seafood BBQs featuring prawn, squid, barracuda and snapper, plus a large range of western and Asian dishes as well as cocktails, beer and wine.

New Cocohut & Cozy Chalet
BUNGALOW $$

(☑ 09-691 1810; www.perhentianislandcocohut. com; Main Beach, Pulau Perhentian Besar; r RM290-440; ❄ ⑤) New Cocohut has a good choice of rooms including beachside bungalows and a two-storey longhouse, which has some great views from the balcony. The cheapest rooms are in the rear and closest to the generator. Cocohut manages the adjacent property, Cozy Chalet, which has a collection of wooden bungalows ascending the hillside.

The relaxed and friendly restaurant at New Cocohut has a seaview deck, and serves barbecued seafood, cold beer and wine.

Coral View Island Resort
RESORT $$

(☑ 09-697 4943; http://coralviewislandresort. my; Main Beach, Pulau Perhentian Besar; r/ste from RM150/950; ❄ @ ⑤ ☒) Coral View has a great location at the northern end of Main Beach – the best end for swimming and snorkelling. Rooms range from fan-cooled, two-bed bungalows to lavish sea-view villas with their own private pool. The resort also has an alcohol-free restaurant serving Asian and international dishes as well as shops and a quiet beach at its northern edge.

Ayumni House
RESORT $$

(☑ 019-4364463,09-6911680; www./d-ayumnihouse. blogspot.com; Main Beach, Pulau Perhentian Besar; dm RM50, fan/air-con r RM120/180; ❄ ⑤) This pretty wooden house rises over a series of low-slung, teak bungalows. It's popular with domestic tourists and those seeking a budget backpacker vibe. Owner Ms Lee is a fount of information, and can arrange ongoing travel all over Southeast Asia. She also has a shop, laundry service and a kitchen for those who have brought their own food.

TELUK DALAM

EcoMarine Perhentian Island Resort
RESORT $

(☑ 013-396 2245, 011-1083 4729; www.ecomarine perhentian.com; Teluk Dalam, Pulau Perhentian Besar; dm/r RM57/185-220; ❄) Located at the southwest end of Teluk Dalam, EcoMarine offers a variety of budget accommodation and package deals. There's also an air-conditioned dorm with a hot shower as well as comfortable rooms in air-con concrete bungalows facing the beach. The small restaurant is alcohol-free.

B'First Chalet
RESORT $

(☑ 019-915 9871; Teluk Dalam, Pulau Perhentian Besar; fan/air-con r RM60/100; ❄) The Azman family runs this small resort and restaurant on the eastern edge of the beach. The fan-cooled bungalows are comfortable and have two beds; air-con bungalows have a double bed and a single. Showers are cold. The restaurant serves Malaysian food and a seafood barbecue every night, and also has a beach-side bar with music, cocktails and cold beer.

Perhentian Cabana Cafe & Campsite
CAMPGROUND $

(☑ 013-970 5319; cabanacampsite@smart.com; Teluk Dalam, Pulau Perhentian Besar; RM15 per person) Nylon tents under a tarp provide some of the cheapest accommodation on the island.

Bayu Dive Lodge
BUNGALOW $$

(☑ 09-691 1650; www.bayudivelodge.com; Teluk Dalam, Pulau Perhentian Besar; fan/air-con r

RM120/215-330; ❄) A collection of smartly furnished, dark-brown bungalows is situated around a beautifully manicured garden courtyard. All rooms are comfortable, with the more expensive ones having air-con and hot showers. The alcohol-free restaurant serves wraps, burgers, pizzas and Asian dishes. **Alu Alu Divers** (www.alualudivers.com) operates from here.

Arwana Perhentian Resort   RESORT $$
(☎ 09-778 0888; www.arwanaperhentian.com.my; Teluk Dalam, Pulau Perhentian Besar; d RM160-390, f RM295-425; ❄ 🛜 🏊) This huge resort occupies the eastern flank of Teluk Dalam and has a swath of narrow beach frontage plus a huge pool. The cheaper 'standard' rooms are a bit small; more expensive ones are decently furnished, some with balconies. Most comfortable are the beachside bungalows. Facilities include a snooker room, karaoke room and a dive centre.

Flora Bay Resort   RESORT $$
(☎ 09-691 1666; www.florabayresort.com; Teluk Dalam, Pulau Perhentian Besar; r RM70-210; ❄ @ 🛜) Flora Bay has a variety of options facing the beach or set back in the forest. There are fan-cooled huts with a hill view and 'deluxe' air-con beach bungalows. A somewhat neglected extension of Flora Bay Resort, with a smaller range of identical bungalows, is a little further east along the beach. An alcohol-free restaurant is near the reception area. Wi-fi is charged at RM12 for two days.

Mandalica Empire   CAFE $
(Teluk Dalam, Pulau Perhentian Besar; drinks RM5-10, snacks RM6-12; ⏱7am-11pm) Halim and Aida run a casual cafe (with some very basic tent and hut accommodation) right on the beach. There are fresh juices, including a legendary mango shake (RM9), amazing roti (banana and chocolate) and an evening seafood barbecue.

Jimmy's Bar   BAR
(Teluk Dalam, Pulau Perhentian Besar; can of beer RM10; ⏱6pm-late) This friendly pop-up stall is one of only two places selling beer and other drinks on this beach.

TELUK PAUH

Perhentian Island Resort   RESORT $$$
(☎ 09-691 1111; www.perhentianislandresort.net; Teluk Pauh, Pulau Perhentian Besar; r RM560-730; ❄ @ 🛜 🏊) This semiluxurious option overlooks perhaps the best beach on the islands –

a sweeping half-moon bay with good coral (and turtle viewing) around the points on either side. There's a huddle of comfortable bungalows and an alcohol-free restaurant serving international and Malay dishes. There are seasonal discounts and a bewildering array of three-day/two-night packages.

🛏 Kecil

Long Beach (p296) offers a variety of accommodation from flimsy nylon tents and barebones backpacker hostels to luxe upmarket resorts. Coral Bay (p296) has a good variety of accommodation, also in all budget brackets. The more isolated Petani Beach (p295) offers an upmarket resort.

LONG BEACH

Panorama Chalet   RESORT $$
(☎ 019-960 8630; www.panoramaperhentianisland. com; Long Beach, Pulau Perhentian Kecil; dm RM50, r RM150-230; ❄ 🛜) A favourite with divers and snorkellers, Panorama is set back a short way from the sand in party central, Long Beach. Rooms range from fan-cooled doubles to air-conditioned chalets. The family room has two queen-sized beds, near-wraparound windows and a balcony. Electricity is available from noon to 4pm and from 6.30pm to 7.30am.

D'Rock Garden Resort   RESORT $$
(☎ 09-8922 2667, 013-928 9619; drockgarden@ gmail.com; Long Beach, Pulau Perhentian Kecil; d without/with bath RM80/180, r with air-con from RM250; ❄ 🛜) Steep steps running up the southern end of Long Beach will get you to this vertiginous place on the rocks. Cheaper rooms are fan-cooled, and only the deluxe ones have hot showers. The position of the huts (even the cheaper ones) overlooking the long sweep of Long Beach is fabulous.

★ BuBu Resort   RESORT $$$
(☎ 03-2142 6688; www.buburesort.com; Long Beach, Pulau Perhentian Kecil; r from RM500; ❄ 🛜) Located at the northern end of the bay, this top-end option offers 38 rooms in a modern, three-storey setting overlooking Long Beach. All rooms face the beach and offer air-con and hot showers. Views are best from the top floor; request a room here. There's a quality restaurant in *palapa* style (open-sided with thatched roof) and a bar.

Mimpi   RESORT $$$
(☎ 09-697 7777; www.mimpiperhentian.com; Long Beach, Pulau Perhentian Kecil; hill-view/sea-view

VOLUNTEERING ON THE EAST COAST ISLANDS

Pulau Perhentian and Pulau Lang Tengah have marine-focused volunteer projects. See www.facebook.com/perhentianturtleproject and www.ecoteer.com for more details.

Blue Temple Conservation (www.divescover.com/dive-center/blue-temple-conservation/17390; Pulau Perhentian Kecil; 1/2 weeks US$520/1300) Combines diving and assisting with the sustainable management of the islands' marine resources. Volunteer activities include beach-cleaning and educating snorkelling groups about why hand-feeding fish is harmful to the marine ecosystem. Costs include all meals, transfers and accommodation in the funky village house at Blue Temple on Perhentian Kecil. A seven-day PADI open-water course costs US$785.

Perhentian Turtle Project (www.perhentianturtleproject.org; Main Beach, Pulau Perhentian Besar; 2/3 weeks £621/782) The UK-based Perhentian Turtle Project is focused on supporting the islands' sea turtle population. Activities include snorkelling trips to identify and catalogue turtles, night beach patrols, and educating locals and visitors. See the website for how travellers can play their part with cameras and Instagram. Volunteer programs include meals and transfers, and accommodation is near Main Beach (p296) on Perhentian Besar.

Lang Tengah Turtle Watch (www.langtengahturtlewatch.org; Turtle Bay; per 2 weeks US$530) Lang Tengah Turtle Watch works to safeguard the island's population of nesting turtles (mostly green turtles). Volunteers assist with tasks such as beach patrols, egg collection and data maintenance, with the bonus of observing turtles come ashore to lay their eggs (April to October) and hatchlings emerge around 100 days later. Programs are a minimum of two weeks and include basic accommodation and meals.

r RM600/700, ste RM1900; ❋🛜❄) This three-storey, modern resort right at the foot of Long Beach jetty features a lift, ramps and a seawater swimming pool. Rooms are plush and stylishly furnished. There is an on-site dive centre, pool, spa and a multicuisine restaurant (no alcohol).

BuBu Villa RESORT $$$
(☏09-6911333; www.buburesort.com; Long Beach, Pulau Perhentian Kecil; villa from RM800; ❋🛜) The 18 villas here are possibly the most high-end option on the Perhentian islands. The air-conditioned units have private terraces, hot showers and huge, comfortable beds. The decor is chic and sophisticated, on-site spa and yoga services are available, and Word Cafe serves excellent food. Room prices include breakfast for two. Low-season discounts are available.

Awatif Cafe CAFE $
(Long Beach, Pulau Perhentian Kecil; breakfast RM8-12, mains RM10-30; ⊙7.30am-10.30pm) Awatif is a good, inexpensive choice for breakfast: juice, lassi, muesli, pancakes and eggs are available. Red umbrellas shade tables set right on the beach or you can sit on the fan-cooled deck. There are vegetarian options on the extensive lunch and dinner menu, featuring tacos, burgers and numerous Asian dishes.

★**Santai** BISTRO $$
(www.buburesort.com/santai-restaurant; BuBu Resort, Long Beach, Pulau Perhentian Kecil; mains RM25-70; ⊙noon-10.30pm) With a similar menu as World Cafe, BuBu's Santai restaurant offers laid-back views that may see you opting for a second beer or cocktail before your candlelit dinner kicks off. Lighter dishes like burgers and wraps are complemented by more sophisticated European and Asian fare including rack of lamb or grilled prawns. There's also a popular nightly barbecue.

World Cafe INTERNATIONAL $$
(www.buburesort.com/the-world-cafe; BuBu Villa, Long Beach, Pulau Perhentian Kecil; mains RM30-80; ⊙noon-10.30pm; 🛜) One of the top choices on Long Beach is this open-sided restaurant cooled by a sea breeze and jazz vibes. Cocktails, fresh juices and smoothies, and a decent selection of beers are all on offer, and the menu features good pasta and salads, and a nightly seafood barbecue. Try the smoked-salmon sandwich combined with a chilled coconut juice.

TELUK KERMA

★**D'Lagoon Chalet & Restaurant** RESORT $
(☏019-985 7089; www.dlagoon.my; Teluk Kerma, Pulau Perhentian Kecil; camp site RM15, dm RM25, r RM70-220, mains RM8-15; ⊙restaurant

7.45am-4pm & 7-10.30pm; ✴🛜) Family-run D'Lagoon is the sole property on a tranquil bay, Teluk Kerma, with fine coral a short swim from the beach. Accommodation ranges from camping and a longhouse with dorm beds to simple stilt chalets. Activities include snorkelling, jungle hikes to remote beaches, and a 200m flying fox.

The restaurant serves decent international and Malay food. Take a water taxi to reach here, otherwise it's an hour's hike from the Long Beach jetty. Free wi-fi is available in the restaurant in the evenings.

CORAL BAY & AROUND

RainForest Camping   CAMPGROUND $

(📞019-902 4902; www.facebook.com/rainforest campingperhentianislandmalaysia; Kampung Pasir Karang, Pulau Perhentian Kecil; camping RM51) Simple tents resting on bamboo decks sit in a shady (and bug-infested) rainforest glade. Shared toilets and bathrooms are rudimentary, but the real attractions here are the small, uncrowded beach, good snorkelling and the chilled vibe of the attached cafe.

The semibright lights of Coral Bay are a 15-minute walk away north along the coast.

Amelia Cafe Chalet   RESORT $

(📞09-414 4895; Coral Bay, Pulau Perhentian Kecil; fan/air-con r RM90/120; ✴🛜) Fronted by a popular restaurant and a well-stocked general store, Amelia's pastel-painted bungalows are bright and clean, with tiny verandahs and basic bedding.

Perhentian Tropicana Inn   BUNGALOW $

(📞09-691 8888; www.perhentiantropicana.com; Coral Bay, Pulau Perhentian Kecil; fan r RM290, air-con r from RM500; ✴🛜) This resort's bungalows are found on the saddle of land between Coral Bay and Long Beach. Standard rooms have double beds with fans and cold

showers, and the more expensive, but still plain, rooms feature air-conditioning. At the rear of the property is the related **Perhentian Tivoli Inn** (www.perhentiantivoli.com; dm RM30, d fan-only RM180; ✴🛜) featuring dorm accommodation. Management makes cash advances on Visa and MasterCard.

Crocodile Rock Villas   VILLAS $$

(www.crocodilerockvillas.com; Kampung Pasir Karang, Pulau Perhentian Kecil; tent/villa from RM250/315; ⊙restaurant 9-11am & 6.30-10pm; ✴🛜) Crocodile Rock is a luxe option nestled in the rainforest about a 15- to 20-minute walk south of Coral Beach. Glampers will swoon over their spacious safari-tents, while flashpackers are just as well served by the timber-clad chalets, raised on stilts and with sea-facing balconies. An excellent restaurant serving Malay and international cuisine rounds out the package.

Shari-la Island Resort   RESORT $$

(📞09-691 1500; www.shari-la.com; Coral Bay, Pulau Perhentian Kecil; r RM290-350, ste RM430; ✴@🛜) Situated at Coral Bay's northern end, and sprawling into the jungle, this place offers a surprisingly nice package. A-frame bungalows feature spacious wooden decks, and suites have satellite-equipped TVs and full bathrooms. Most bungalows are equipped with solar-powered hot showers, and Shari-la has its own secluded beach. It is one of the few Coral Bay places with 24-hour electricity.

The on-site restaurant serving Malay, Thai and international dishes is also good.

Ombak Dive Resort   RESORT $$

(📞09-691 1021; www.ombak.my; Coral Bay, Pulau Perhentian Kecil; dm without/with breakfast RM40/70, fan/air-con r RM275/375; ✴🛜) Ombak provides modern digs in Bali-inspired rooms on Coral Bay. Beds are comfortable, bathrooms are tiny and management are very helpful. Credit cards are accepted and cash

---

KUALA BESUT

The transport gateway to one of Malaysia's best-known island paradises is a lovely seaside town, but most visitors only spend an hour or two here.

The restaurants and coffee shops are all located around the jetty (where you can rent snorkelling equipment for use on the islands). The town's few hotels are also scattered around the jetty. A good one is **T'Lodge** (📞09-697 8777; Perkedaian 2 Tingkat 'Merpati' MDB, Jln Besar, Kuala Besut; d from RM99; ✴🛜), featuring large comfortable rooms with private bathrooms. It's near the jetty and about a 500m walk from the **bus station**.

A bus from Kota Bharu is RM6 (two hours), a taxi around RM75 (1½ hours). The bus from Kuala Terengganu is RM13, and a taxi around RM130; both take around two hours. There is at least one daily bus from Kuala Lumpur (RM45, nine hours). Many travel agents run minibus services to Kuala Besut from tourist hotspots around Malaysia.

advances are possible. A big draw is the excellent sand-floor, casual, international-cuisine restaurant with house-made bakery items. Divers get good package deals, including free dorm accommodation.

PETANI BEACH

Mari Mari Beach Bar & Resort   RESORT $

(☑ 017-938 1501; Petani Beach, Pulau Perhentian Kecil; r RM80-150) Look no further if you're after a more remote Perhentians stay. Mari Mari is constructed solely of recycled and salvaged material, and there's a Robinson Crusoe vibe to the simple beach huts with shared bathrooms and the more private tree houses with rustic en suites. The attached beach bar and restaurant accentuate the laid-back island mood.

Alunan Boutique Resort   RESORT $$$

(☑ 016-448 8297; www.alunanresort.com; Petani Beach, Pulau Perhentian Kecil; r/ste from RM500/950; ❄🔊) Alunan's array of sleek designer pavilions cascade down a rocky, forested hillside to a compact cove. Translating to 'Waves' in Malay, the more remote southern coast location on Petani Beach is a quieter alternative to other parts of the island.

Complementing the stylish rooms and suites are a dive centre, tour desk and Bayu restaurant. Note that water taxi fares will add up if you wish to head around to other beaches for alternative eating and drinking opportunities.

❶ Information

The conservation fee (adult/child RM30/15) for entering the marine park around Pulau Perhentian is payable at the jetty in Kuala Besut.

INTERNET ACCESS

Free wi-fi is ubiquitous on both islands at accommodation and restaurants. Don't expect it to be fast or available outside the common areas.

If you're planning on using your own smartphone, Celcom has the best 3G broadband coverage in the islands.

MEDICAL FACILITIES

Klinik Kesihatan (☑ 09-691 1733; Kampung Pasir Hantu, Pulau Perhentian Kecil; ⊙ 8am-9pm Sun-Thu) The only medical facility on the islands. The clinic is closed on Friday and Saturday, but emergency service is available. Dive operators and some of the bigger resorts can offer first aid if needed.

MONEY

There are no banks or ATMs on the islands. If you run out of money, several resorts on both islands accept payment and offer cash advances on credit or bank cards linked with Visa and MasterCard with a surcharge of between 5% and 10%. There are even fewer places willing to exchange major international currencies for ringgit.

TELEPHONE SERVICES

Mobile phone numbers for resorts may change from one season to the next, and some have no phone at all. Check websites for the latest details.

❶ Getting There & Away

Speedboats run several times a day between Kuala Besut and the Perhentians (return trip adult/child RM70/35, 30 to 40 minutes) from 8.30am to 5.30pm. Tickets are sold by travel agents around Kuala Besut. The boats will drop you off at any of the beaches. Expect delays or cancellations if the weather is bad or if there aren't enough passengers.

In the other direction, speedboats depart from the islands daily at 8am, noon and 4pm. Let your guesthouse owner know a day before you plan on leaving so they can arrange a pick-up. If the water is rough or tides are low, you may be ferried from the beach on a small boat to your mainland-bound craft; you'll have to pay around RM5 for this.

❶ Getting Around

While there are some trails around the islands, the easiest way to go from beach to beach or island to island is by boat. From island to island, the trip costs around RM15 to RM30, and a jaunt from one beach to another on the same island usually costs RM10 to RM15. There's a minimum requirement of two passengers (so double the rate if you're a solo passenger). Prices double after sunset.

Pulau Redang

Featuring stunning white-sand beaches backed by lush green jungle, Pulau Redang lies within a **protected marine park** and has excellent dive sites and snorkelling reefs. Unfortunately, it can be difficult, and potentially more expensive, to visit independently, rather than as part of a package tour. Some packages tend to be regimented affairs with arrival lectures and set times for meals, snorkelling and 'leisure'. These packages are aimed at groups of young Malaysians and weekending Singaporeans and so holiday periods can be crowded.

Pulau Redang shuts down from the start of November for the monsoon season and reopens at the start of March; the best time to visit is from mid-March to late September. There is a conservation fee (adult/child RM30/15) for entering the marine park,

PULAU LANG TENGAH

Tiny, idyllic Pulau Lang Tengah lies roughly halfway between Pulau Redang and Pulau Perhentian off the northeast coast of Peninsular Malaysia. With only three resorts to choose from, this patch of paradise is much quieter and less developed than its better-known neighbouring islands. The diving and snorkelling is excellent here, with numerous pristine sites and a healthy fish and turtle population. There is much less physical damage to coral here than is evident at the more well-touristed islands. This lesser-known gem also features beautiful white-sand beaches, particularly on its western shore, crystal-clear waters and a lush, pristine jungle.

Similar to nearby Pulau Redang (p301), almost everyone who comes here is on a package deal that includes boat transport, water activities and meals. Check the internet for discounted packages.

D'Coconut Lagoon (☑03-4252 6686; www.dcoconutlagoon.com; r RM280-740; ❄️📶📶), the island's best accommodation, has two separate areas, joined by a forest track, each with its own private beach, restaurant, bar and swimming pool. Comfy rooms and bungalows have fridges, TVs and other modern conveniences. There's an on-site dive centre plus waters sports equipment to hire. Package deals are available.

Nurul Boat Services (☑019-929 9587; www.boattoredang.com; Merang jetty; per person RM80) has four boats depart daily from Merang jetty to Pulau Lang Tengah at 8am, 10am, 1pm and 3pm. Return boats leave the island at 9am, 11am, 1pm and 4pm, and there's also an 11am departure from Pulau Lang Tengah to Pulau Redang.

Aziz from Mama's Chalet (p297) runs **Aziz Boat Service** (☑013-984 0232; abdul azizcheabdullah@gmail.com; Main Beach, Pulau Perhentian Besar; RM500) from Pulau Perhentian (any resort) to Pulau Lang Tengah and Pulau Redang (one hour). Minimum cost is RM500. For more than two people the per person cost reduces.

usually payable as you catch the boat from Merang or Kuala Terengganu.

🛏 Sleeping & Eating

Accommodation on Pulau Redang needs to be arranged in advance. Tour companies sell packages for all the resorts, and several of the resorts have offices in Kuala Terengganu. Where rates given here are for a room including breakfast, expect to pay extra for activities and transfer to/from the island.

Off-peak rates (usually March and October) attract significant discounts. Weekday (Sunday to Wednesday) rates are cheaper than weekends (Thursday to Saturday).

Some places only sell packages that include activities. Unless otherwise stated, package prices given in this section are for three days and two nights and are per person, based on twin-sharing, and include boat transfer from Merang, all meals and two snorkelling trips. Promotional packages are frequently offered; check resort websites in advance.

🛏 Teluk Kalong

Wisana Village   BUNGALOW $$
(☑012-629 7875; www.wisanaredang.com; Teluk Kalong Kecil, Pulau Redang; s/d full board per night from RM345/490; ❄️📶) With a private beach, Wisana Village is one of Redang's most alluring places to stay. Accommodation ranges from comfortable rooms to deluxe bungalows, all infused with an Asian design aesthetic. In contrast to other resorts, occupancy is limited to just 36 guests. Relaxation is maximised in the chic guest lounge and Wisana's cafe with views of nearby Pulau Kerengga.

Accommodation on a per night basis is available. Note this is a dry resort (no alcohol for sale), but you can bring your own supplies.

🛏 Teluk Dalam

Teluk Dalam is in the north of the island, near a village with local restaurants.

Taaras Beach & Spa Resort   RESORT $$$
(☑09-221 3997; www.thetaaras.com; Teluk Dalam, Pulau Redang; r incl breakfast from RM661; ❄️📶📶) One of Redang's most luxurious resorts, Taaras offers beachside bungalows and hillside apartments set in delightful, landscaped gardens. Pride of place goes to the simply gorgeous private beach. The two on-site restaurants, Asian All Day Dining

and Beach Brasserie, are complemented by the casual Bayu Bar. Packages include breakfast and dinner (plus boat transfers).

Pasir Panjang

Most of the smaller resorts are built on a beautiful stretch of white-sand beach known as Pasir Panjang (Long Beach), on the east coast of the island.

Coral Redang Island Resort   RESORT $$

(☑09-630 7110; www.coralredang.com.my; Pasir Panjang, Pulau Redang; s/d incl breakfast RM330/390; 🅿🛜🍴) Located towards the northern end of the beach, this 31-room resort has a dive centre attached. A wide variety of snorkelling/diving packages is on offer (see the website). Even if you're not staying here, it's worth considering the Matahari restaurant or a drink at the resort's poolside Chicak Bar, which are open to nonguests.

Redang Bay Resort   RESORT $$

(☑09-620 3200; www.redangbay.com.my; Pasir Panjang, Pulau Redang; 3-day, 2-night package dm/d per person from RM268/388; 🅿🛜🍴) Located at the southern end of the beach, this rather characterless resort has a mix of concrete block-style accommodation and bungalows. Rooms are neat and clean, if a little spartan. The karaoke lounge is open till all hours and there's a 'beach disco' on weekends, so don't come looking for a quiet island retreat.

Redang Holiday Beach Villa   BUNGALOW $$

(☑09-624 5500; www.redangholiday.com; Pasir Panjang, Pulau Redang; 3-day, 2-night package per person from RM400; 🅿🛜) Located at the northern tip of the beach is this series of duplex bungalows climbing the rocks (bungalows S13 and S14 have the best outlooks). Larger bungalows sleep up to eight.

Redang Beach Resort   RESORT $$$

(☑09-623 8188; www.redang.com.my; Pasir Panjang, Pulau Redang; d inc breakfast from RM435; 🅿@) Comprising a collection of modern double-storey bungalows and with a five-star PADI dive centre, shops plus a beach disco, this place may be a bit intense if you are looking for a quiet escape. The resort's two-night/three-day snorkelling/diving package (per person RM559) includes all meals, boat transfer equipment and activities.

Redang Pelangi Resort   RESORT $$$

(☑09-624 2158; www.redangpelangi.com; Pasir Panjang, Pulau Redang; 3-day, 2-night package per person from RM406; 🅿🛜) This is a casual resort that offers fairly simple and basic two- and four-bed wooden bungalows. There's an on-site dive centre, a couple of shops, and a beachfront bar that usually has live music and decent happy hour prices most nights.

South of Pasir Panjang

The bay directly south of Pasir Panjang has an excellent white-sand beach.

Redang Reef Resort   RESORT $$$

(☑09-622 6181; www.redangreefresort.com.my; Pasir Panjang, Pulau Redang; 3-day, 2-night package per person from RM425; 🅿🛜) This resort on the headland has a great location, though you'll get your feet wet going to and fro at high tide. The two-storey wooden bungalows are very basic but popular with student groups. The better bungalows on the rocks are more secluded and have fantastic bay views. The resort also has a tiny private beach and a dive centre.

Laguna Redang Island Resort   RESORT $$$

(☑09-630 7888; www.lagunaredang.com.my; Pasir Panjang, Pulau Redang; r incl breakfast RM610-970, ste from RM1040; 🅿🛜🍴) Redang's biggest resort – a vast 400-room complex – dominates this beach. It has luxurious sea-view suites with balconies, two restaurants, a dive centre and live music from Friday to Wednesday. Buildings are in traditional Malay style, but it definitely has a big-hotel vibe. From 5.30pm, a food court also operates. Check the website for good-value diving/snorkelling package deals.

🛈 Getting There & Away

Nearly all visitors to Redang come on packages that include a boat transfer to the island. Independent travellers can get a ride on one of the resort-destined boats (adult/child RM55/30 one-way), but in the high season (April to September) room-only deals may be scarce. The conservation fee (adult/child RM30/15) is usually added to the ferry price at the jetty.

Nurul Boat Services (☑019-929 9587; www.boattoredang.com; Merang Jetty, Merang) is one of several companies that has speedboats departing from Merang jetty. Daily boats depart from here for Redang (30 minutes, adult/child RM55/30) at 8am, 9.30am, 10.30am, 1pm and 3pm. Return boats leave Redang at 9am, 11am, 1pm and 4pm. There's also an 11am departure from Redang to Lang Tengah (per person RM80). Taxis from Merang jetty can take you to Kuala Terrengganu town or airport (RM60, 40 to 45 minutes).

Sejahtera Ferry Services (📞016-416 0338; Shah Bandar Jetty; adult/child RM55/30) runs ferries from **Shah Bandar Ferry Terminal** (Ferry to Pulau Redang; Jln Sultan Zainal Abidin), conveniently located in downtown Kuala Terengganu. These are slower and less frequent (1½ hours, per adult/child RM55/30), but avoid the taxi fare to/from Merang. Ferries run at 9am (for Pasir Panjang), and 10.30am and 3pm (for Kampung jetty). Return journeys run at 7am and 1pm (from Kampung jetty), and 11am (from Pasir Panjang). These can be booked at the jetty and may be arranged via your resort. It's also possible to transfer between Pulau Redang and Pulau Perhentian with Aziz Boat Service (p302).

Pulau Kapas

📞09

Just 15 minutes by speedboat from the mainland, Pulau Kapas is the most accessible of the East Coast resort islands and is the perfect place to chill out for a few days. Try to visit during the week, as this small island with beautiful beaches can become overrun with day trippers on holidays and long weekends. In the unlikely event that even Kapas seems too large, tiny **Pulau Gemia** (home to a single resort) lies just 800m off the north coast. Although there are a couple of mid-range options, Pulau Kapas enjoys a budget-traveller vibe and has some of the cheapest island resorts in Malaysia with back-to-basic dorms and campgrounds. Most resorts can arrange snorkelling and diving trips.

Pulau Kapas and Pulau Gemia usually shut down during the monsoon season (November to March), when the seas are rough.

🏃 Activities

Kapas is a snorkelling paradise, with the best coral to be found off the less accessible beaches on the northern end of the island and around tiny Pulau Gemia. The most impressive sites are best reached on a boat trip. North of Gemia, a sunken WWII Japanese landing craft, now carpeted in coral, is a popular dive site.

Aqua-Sport Divers   DIVING
(📞019-983 5879; www.aquasportdiver.com.my; Pulau Kapas; snorkelling RM40, 1/2 dives incl equipment RM130/240, open-water course RM1400; ⊙9am-5pm) This is the only dive outfit on Kapas. It offers trips out to the Japanese wreck, snorkelling and a four-day PADI open-water course.

🛏 Sleeping & Eating

All accommodation on Pulau Kapas is concentrated on three small beaches on the west coast. Though most travellers visit on all-inclusive package tours, it's possible to find a place to stay, especially on weekdays.

Several of the resorts have restaurants and bars, but many visitors also bring their own supplies and simply picnic on the beach.

Long Sha Campsite   CAMPGROUND $
(📞017-965 2968; Pulau Kapas; tent per person RM15) Expect flimsy tents right on the beach with shared facilities including a camp kitchen. It's basic, cheap and popular. Staff – look for someone splayed out in a hammock – can organise snorkelling and boat trips.

Captain's Longhouse   HOSTEL $
(www.facebook.com/Captains-Longhouse-3525131 48480371/; Pulau Kapas; camping/dm/r from RM25/50/100) Surrounded by trees and centred on a longhouse at the southernmost tip of the bay, Captain's is rustic, chilled and comfortable. Guests can enjoy art-covered walls, dorm beds bedecked in colourful batik blankets and mosquito nets, and a front porch with hammocks, chairs and an out-of-tune piano.

For campers, tents can be provided on the beach or under cover. There are discounts for stays of more than one day.

Pak Ya Seaview Chalet & Restoran   RESORT $
(📞019-960 3130; Pulau Kapas; r RM90; ⊙restaurant 8am-4.30pm, 8-11.30pm) Located just north of the jetty, Pak Ya offers seven basic, fan-cooled A-frame bungalows with small sea-facing porches right on the beach. Pak Ya also rents kayaks and snorkelling gear, and has a beachfront restaurant (mains RM8-12).

Ombak Kapas Resort   RESORT $
(📞017-985 9600, 019-951 4771; www.ombakkapas. com; Pulau Kapas; r without/with air-con RM110/170; ❄) Ombak Kapas Resort has rooms ranging from simple fan-cooled affairs to air-conditioned bungalows. There's a well-stocked store, kayaking and snorkelling gear for hire, and an attractive beachfront restaurant.

KBC   HOSTEL $
(Kapas Beach Chalet; 📞019-343 5606; hans. keune@gmail.com; Pulau Kapas; dm RM35, r RM80-200; ⊙restaurant 8am-3.30pm, 7-9.30pm; ❄) This laid-back spot offers decent, eight-bed, mixed dorms and a range of other rooms, with air-con and attached bathrooms at the pricier end of the scale. There's a great social

vibe, courtesy of the breezy beachfront restaurant serving excellent Malay, Thai and international dishes.

There's a two-night minimum stay, and confusingly two KBCs. This place started as the restaurant to the original KBC business that still operates next door.

★ Kapas Turtle Valley   RESORT $$
(☑ 013-354 3650; www.kapasturtlevalley.com; Pulau Kapas; bungalow incl activities for min 2 nights RM240; ☺ open Mar–mid-Oct; ☎) Hidden in a rocky nook on the island's southern end, Kapas Turtle Valley has eight bungalows – all furnished with colourful local batik – and sits above a white-sand beach that's perfect for swimming, lounging and snorkelling. There's an excellent on-site restaurant with a daily-changing menu, cold beer, wine and good coffee. Dutch expat hosts Peter and Sylvia are very welcoming.

Kayaks and snorkelling gear are free for guests. Meals cost extra – expect to pay around RM30 to RM45.

Qimi Private Bay   RESORT $$
(☑ 017-917 5744; www.facebook.com/QimiChalet; Pulau Kapas; fan/air-con d RM100-130/200-250) Qimi offers comfortable hillside bungalows with excellent sea views and private bathrooms. It also has rustic and cheaper bungalows that lack the hillside elevation, an exceptionally relaxed and friendly family-owned restaurant, and the opportunity to go snorkelling, kayaking and beachcombing on Qimi's sandy private cove. Triple and quad rooms are available.

Kapas Coral Beach   RESORT $$
(☑ 09-618 1976; www.pulaukapas.com; Pulau Kapas; r without/with air-con RM130/180-280; ❄) What this place lacks in character it makes up for in spacious bungalows (all have one double bed and a single bed), TVs, air-conditioning and hot showers. It's located north of the jetty.

★ Gem Island Resort & Spa   RESORT $$$
(☑ 09-688 2505; www.gemisland.com.my; Pulau Gemia; villa RM400-540, ste RM640-950; ❄@☎☎) Located on Pulau Gemia, 800m north of Pulau Kapas, this resort offers breezy bungalows set right over the edge of a reef – watch schools of fish and black-tipped reef sharks cruise by from your balcony. There are a couple of small private beaches, but note the coral starts a few steps from the beach; much better for snorkelling than swimming.

The spa offers the usual pampering services, and all-inclusive package deals are available. The restaurant captures the sea breeze and the quality of the food matches the magical views.

Koko Kitchen   ASIAN, INTERNATIONAL $
(Pulau Kapas; mains RM16-30; ☺ 8am-10pm, closed Wednesday) Koko gets good reviews from campers for its small but changing menu of Asian and international dishes. You can also get a beer here, and it even has budget dorm beds and tents behind the restaurant.

❶ Information
Pulau Kapas enjoys free wireless internet courtesy of www.terengganuwifi.com. Just log on and register. The transmitter is on the jetty so you may have to leave your room and sit on the beach.

❶ Getting There & Away
Buses and taxis connect Marang (p312), the jumping-off point on the mainland for the islands, with Kuala Terengganu. Several speedboat companies operate to Pulau Kapas but all keep the same timetable. Speedboats (adult/child RM40/20 return) depart from Marang's main jetty at 9am, 11am, 1pm, 3pm and 5pm, with returns half an hour later from Pulau Kapas. **Suria Link Boat Service** (☑ 019-983 9454, 09-618 3754; www.kapassurialink.com; Marang Tourist Jetty; adult/child RM40/20 return; ☺ 9am-5.30pm) will continue to Pulau Gemia if requested.

Taxis are usually waiting at the jetty in Marang as all boats arrive at about the same time. If you want to be certain of finding a taxi you can book one in Kuala Terengganu before you depart for the island or ask your island accommodation or boat-service companies to arrange a taxi.

The following boat companies can also book accommodation on the island.

MGH Boat Service (☑ 016-922 5454, 09-618 3166; Marang Tourist Jetty; adult/child RM40/20 return)

Suria Link Boat Service (☑ 019-983 9454, 09-618 3754; www.kapassurialink.com; Marang Tourist Jetty; adult/child RM40/20 return; ☺ 9am-5.30pm)

Kuala Terengganu
☑ 09 / POP 285,100

Kuala Terengganu is the capital of Terengganu. It occupies a promontory jutting into the South China Sea and is flanked by the estuary of Sungai Terengganu. The city is a microcosm of Malaysia's economic history: fishing village strikes oil and rapid modernity ensues. In just a few years this once sleepy town has been inextricably altered. Land reclamation and development

Kuala Terengganu

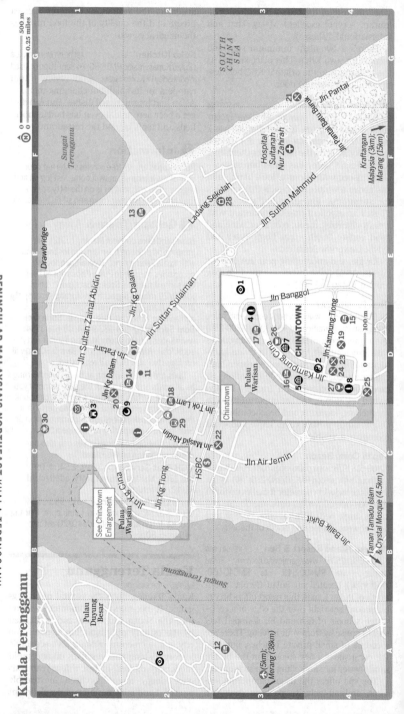

Kuala Terengganu

⊙ Sights

1 Central Market E3
2 Ho Ann Kiong D4
3 Istana Maziah C1
4 Pasar Payang Alley D3
5 Perakanan Photo Gallery D3
6 Pulau Duyung A2
7 Teck Soon Heritage House D3
8 Turtle Alley D4
9 Zainal Abidin Mosque C2

◔ Activities, Courses & Tours

10 Heritage One Stop Travel & Tours D2
11 Ping Anchorage D2

⊟ Sleeping

12 Awi's Yellow House A3
13 Hotel Grand Continental E2
14 Hotel YT Midtown D2
15 Jen's Homestay D4
16 KT Chinatown Lodge D3
17 Suite 18 Boutique Hotel D3
18 Uncle Homestay D2

⊗ Eating

19 Chinatown Hawker Centre D4

20 MD Curry House D1
21 Pantai Batu Buruk Night Market G3
22 Pertama Steak & Sushi House C3
23 Restoran Golden Dragon D4
24 Restoran Keong Kee D4
25 Town City Food Court D4

⊙ Drinking & Nightlife

26 Star Anise D3
27 Vinum Exchange D4

⊖ Shopping

28 Wanisma Craft & Trading F3

⊙ Transport

Heritage Buses .... (see 29)
29 Main Bus Station C2
MARA Liner .... (see 29)
Sani Express .... (see 29)
Sejahtera Ferry Services .... (see 30)
30 Shah Bandar Ferry Terminal C1
SP Bumi .... (see 29)
Transnasional .... (see 29)

of the waterfront has seen the creation of attractive parks and parades plus a modern harbour that has one of Asia's biggest drawbridges. Despite the rapid modernisation Kuala Terengganu retains plenty of charm. Here you'll find one of eastern Peninsular Malaysia's prettiest and most interesting Chinatowns, and old *kampong*-style stilthouses can still be found just across the river. With seafood-heavy local cuisine and good transport links, it's definitely worth spending a day or two in Kuala Terengganu in between the islands and jungles.

⊙ Sights

⊙ Chinatown

Centred on Jln Kampung Cina (also known as Jln Bandar), this compact area features heritage buildings and temples, as well as buildings and alleys jazzed up with contemporary and quirky street art. Gentrification is in full swing with cafes, bars and gift shops opening up, but sleepy hardware shops and traditional Chinese medicinal herb shops can also be found.

Worth seeking out are **Turtle Alley** (off Jln Kampung Cina), with mosaics telling the story of Kuala Terengganu's now-endangered turtles, and **Pasar Payang Alley** (Memory Lane; off Jln Kampung Cina), which commemorates local Chinese community leaders and famous Malays. Pick up the *Chinatown Heritage Trail* brochure at the tourist information office (p311).

Ho Ann Kiong   TAOIST TEMPLE

(Jln Kampung Cina; ⊙7.30am-7pm) **FREE** One of Chinatown's most attractive buildings, this compact and colourful riot of red and gold architecture and decor dates back to 1796. It was extensively rebuilt in 1801 and again in 2010 after a devastating fire. Explore the 'wishing tree' behind the temple that is slowly engulfing an old building, and admire the wonderful stone carvings, both inside and outside the temple.

Central Market   MARKET

(Pasar Payang; cnr Jln Kampung Cina & Jln Sultan Zainal Abidin; ⊙6am-5pm) The Central Market is a lively place to sample tasty local snacks, sniff a durian and purchase other fresh fruit. The floor above the fish section has a wide collection of batik and *kain songket* (traditional handwoven fabric). Many stalls don't operate on Fridays.

Teck Soon Heritage House   HISTORIC BUILDING

(☏09-622 1464; 73 Jln Kampung Cina; ⊙10.30am-3pm Sat-Thu) **FREE** This handsomely painted Chinatown shophouse originally belonging to the Teck Soon trading company is now an interesting museum focusing on the history of Chinese Peranakan culture in Kuala Terengganu.

Perakanan Photo Gallery   GALLERY

(Jln Kampung Cina; ⊙9am-5pm) **FREE** A compact display of interesting B&W photos telling the story of Kuala Terengganu's Chinatown history.

◉ Elsewhere in Kuala Terengganu

Kompleks Muzium Negeri Terengganu   MUSEUM

(Terengganu State Museum; ☑09-632 1200; http://museum.terengganu.gov.my; Bukit 20566 Darul Iman, Kuala Terengganu; adult/child RM15/10; ⊙9am-5pm Sat-Thu) Located around 6km west of the city centre, the traditional houses that front the museum's spacious grounds are worth the price of admission. Exhibits range from the historically interesting (a Jawi – traditional Malay text – inscription that essentially dates the arrival of Islam to the nation) to threadbare taxidermy. English signage is sparse.

To get here, catch Heritage Bus (p311) C-02 from the main bus station (RM1). A taxi will cost around RM10.

Masjid Tengku Tengah Zaharah   MOSQUE

(off Jln Kuantan-Kuala Terengganu) **FREE** The most famous religious structure in the state is the Floating Mosque, located 4.5km southeast of Kuala Terengganu. It's not really floating, just set on an artificial island, but its white, traditional Moorish design shimmers in the daylight and is warmly enchanting as the sun sets. Bus 13 from Kuala Terengganu's main bus station will drop you outside (RM2).

Taman Tamadu Islam   PARK

(☑09-627 8888; www.tti.com.my; Pulau Wan Man; Zone A free, Zone B adult/child RM22/16; ⊙10am-7pm Mon-Thu, 9am-7pm Fri-Sun) Touted as the world's first 'Islamic civilisation park'. Taman Tamadu Islam is divided into two zones. Zone A is free to the public and houses the **Crystal Mosque** (Pulau Wan Man). Zone B, for which there is an admission charge, features a series of miniature models of famous Islamic landmarks from across the world. There's Jerusalem's Dome of the Rock, Agra's Taj Mahal and Mecca's Masjid al-Haram among others.

The park is located 2.5km west of central Kuala Terengganu. Heritage Bus C-02 runs here (RM1) and a taxi costs around RM15. Dining river cruises spend around one hour exploring the nearby waterways, but regular departures can be dependent on the number of other visitors in the park.

Zainal Abidin Mosque   MOSQUE

(Jln Masjid Abidin) **FREE** The gleaming Zainal Abidin mosque dominates the city centre. The interior is relatively austere, but enlivened by sunlight streaming through nine domes and a framework of delicate latticed windows. Non-Muslims can enter if dressed conservatively.

Pulau Duyung   ISLAND

This is the largest island in the estuary. It is changing fast, with modern housing estates being built on reclaimed land, but there is still a sizeable presence of old wooden houses and a village lifestyle. Fishing boats are built here, using mostly age-old techniques and tools, and visitors are welcome to look around. Note that of the original 30 or so boat-building yards, only three remain on the island, and fewer and fewer younger people are learning the trade.

LIVING HISTORY: BIDONG ISLAND

As the Vietnam War came to an end, millions of Vietnamese citizens decided to take to the high seas rather than face communist rule in newly reunified Vietnam. Dubbed 'boat people' by the international community – the first time this now-common and poignant phrase was coined – many of these refugees wound up in Malaysia. In 1978, Bidong, a tiny island off the coast of Terengganu, was designated a refugee camp. For the next two decades, Bidong served as a temporary home and transit point for tens of thousands of refugees, who endured unsanitary living conditions in shelters made from salvaged materials. At one point, the tiny island held 40,000 people, making it the most densely populated place on the planet. The camp was closed in 1990 and Bidong has since returned to a pristine state. Small groups occasionally visit Bidong for day trips (there is no accommodation on the island); divers in particular are drawn to the fantastic coral landscapes surrounding Bidong.

Trips to Bidong can be arranged through Ping Anchorage (p309) in Kuala Terengganu.

To see boat building head to Awi's Yellow House, which sits between two boat yards. You can catch a ferry (RM1) from the jetty behind Central Market to Pulau Duyung, but there's only one ferry a day and the timing varies. Most ferries from this dock head for Sebarang Takir on the north bank of Sungai Terengganu. A taxi from downtown Kuala Terengganu to Pulau Duyung will cost RM20 (each way), and a bus from the main bus station costs RM1.

Istana Maziah — PALACE

(Jln Masjid Abidin) On the eastern flank of the hill near the Central Market is the sultan's palace. It's built in colonial-era style, but renovations have given the structure a blocky feel. The palace is closed to the public, except for some ceremonial occasions.

👉 Tours

Popular tours include day trips to Tasik Kenyir and packages to Pulau Redang. Going in groups reduces individual rates.

Ping Anchorage — TOURS

(☎09-626 2020; www.pinganchorage.com.my; 77A Jln Sultan Sulaiman; ⊙8.30am-5.30pm) This long-running tour company organises numerous tours around Terengganu, including day trips to Tasik Kenyir and Sungai Terengganu. The latter takes in Pulau Duyung (p308), the mangroves and a stop at the tiny village of Kampung Jeram, with its exotic fruit trees and Chinese temple. Ping also manages Terrapuri Heritage Village (p312) in Penarik, and can arrange tours to the islands.

The office has a museum, a shop called Terradala that sells local crafts, and a pleasant cafe serving espresso coffee, cakes and sandwiches.

Heritage One Stop Travel & Tours — TOURS

(☎09-631 6468; Jln Sultan Sulaiman, T009, Blok Teratai, Taman Sri Kolam; ⊙9am-5pm Sat-Thu) Offers tours to the islands, the jungles and around Kuala Terengganu. The office is located on the ground floor (and around the back) of a housing complex on Jln Sultan Sulaiman.

🛏 Sleeping

★**KT Chinatown Lodge** — GUESTHOUSE $

(☎013-931 6192, 09-622 1938; lawlorenz@gmail.com; 113 Jln Kampung Cina; s RM75, d RM98-108; ❋🛜) Located in the heart of Chinatown this three-storey guesthouse has spotless rooms and a friendly welcome. The cheapest rooms have no windows, but all include

multichannel TV, private bathrooms and aircon. Retro photos of Chinatown reinforce the heritage ambience. Owner Lorenz is an excellent source of information on the city, and downstairs there's a decent cafe for an inexpensive breakfast.

Awi's Yellow House — GUESTHOUSE $

(☑WhatsApp 017-984 0337; Pulau Duyung; dm/r/bungalow RM20/40/120) Awi's is what Terengganu once was: a gathering of rustic, wooden stilt-houses built over the tidal Sungai Terengganu. The smell of fish paste, salt and chilli, the sound of lapping waters, and nights that stick to you like a wet kiss; Awi's will immerse you in the old Terengganu *kampung* way of life.

Awi's attracts artists and travellers from all over. From the ferry dock or Pulau Duyung bus stop, it's a short but circuitous walk to Awi's; ask a local for directions.

Uncle Homestay — HOSTEL $

(☎014-609 9585; 77A Jln Tok Lam; r without/with bathroom RM50/70; ❋🛜) This budget hotel is handy for the bus station. Rooms are prosaic (and mostly windowless), but the shared bathrooms are clean and well kept. Spacious, shared areas make it a good option for the thrifty traveller.

Suite 18 Boutique Hotel — HOTEL $$

(☎09-631 2288; www.facebook.com/Suite18BoutiqueHotel; 65 Jln Kampung Cina; dm/tw/d from RM45/108/148; ❋🛜) This contemporary hotel, while not exactly boutique, is certainly stylish, with polished concrete and exposed bricks. Rooms feature TVs and there are affordable dorm bunks on the top floor. Nice additions include a courtyard with artificial grass and bicycle rental (RM10 for two hours).

Jen's Homestay — APARTMENT $$

(☎019-957 8368; www.jenhomestay.weebly.com; 8-12 Pangsapuri Kampung Tiong, Jln Kampung Tiong; r from RM115; ♿❋🛜) Jen's Homestay has four rental apartments in this highrise building, each with three bedrooms, a shared lounge, and balconies with washing machine and sweeping views across the river or towards the ocean. The entire apartment can be rented, or rent them just by the bedroom (the more expensive rooms have a private bathroom).

Hotel Grand Continental — HOTEL $$

(☎09-625 1888; www.grandcontinental-kt.com; Jln Sultan Zainal Abidin; d RM180-220, ste RM700-950; ❋🛜🏊) This high-rise has spacious and comfortable rooms, some with harbour views. There's a swimming pool on the 3rd floor, a dry (as in no alcohol) restaurant in the lobby, and location-wise, you're well placed near the town centre (taxi RM10) and the beach. It's worthwhile for a comfortable overnight stay.

Hotel YT Midtown
HOTEL $$

(📞 09-623 5288; www.hotelytmidtown.com.my; 30 Jln Tok Lam; r incl breakfast RM116-195; ❄ @ 🛜) This big, modern hotel in the centre of town has neat, good-value rooms that come with a TV, mini fridge and kettle. On the higher floors, the deluxe rooms are particularly comfortable and offer good views. There's a cafe on the 1st floor.

🍴 Eating

Fish plays a big role in local cuisine, but the real local speciality is *kerepok* (a grey concoction of deep-fried fish paste and sago, usually moulded into sausages). Some restaurants in Chinatown serve local spins on Peranakan (Straits Chinese) cuisine including Terengganu laksa, a version of the Malay noodle classic.

Town City Food Court
HAWKER $

(Jln Kampung Cina; mains RM5-10; ⊗ 11am-9pm) Pull up a plastic chair under the whirling fans for cheap Malay, Thai and Chinese hawker favourites and the best selection of cold beer in Kuala Terengganu.

Pantai Batu Buruk Night Market
MARKET $

(Jln Pantai Batu Buruk; mains from RM3; ⊗ 3-7pm Friday) The aroma from charcoal grills wafts over Pantai Batu Buruk every Friday night. It's very popular. If you are taking a taxi here on a Friday evening, expect to get caught in a traffic jam!

Chinatown Hawker Centre
HAWKER $

(off Jln Kampung Tiong; mains RM2-6; ⊗ 7am-11pm) Chinatown's outdoor hawker centre is divided into Chinese and Malay sections. You can get a chilled beer here and there's a small morning craft and produce market here, too – well worth visiting for takeaway foods.

MD Curry House
MALAY, INDIAN $

(Jln Kampung Dalam; mains RM6-9; ⊗ 7.30am-2.30pm & 5.30-9pm) Sometimes you just need a curry, and you need it served on a banana leaf by friendly locals. MD covers all the bases.

⭐ Restoran Golden Dragon
CHINESE $$

(📞 09-622 3039; 198 Jln Kampung Cina; mains RM10-28; ⊗ 11.30am-2.30pm & 5-11pm, closed every 2nd Mon) This restaurant is constantly packed. There's ice-cold beer aplenty and one of the finest Chinese seafood menus in town. Fresh fish, squid and prawns are charged by weight and steamed or fried with your choice of sauce. Recommended are the sambal squid and fried grouper with Thai sauce.

Restoran Keong Kee
CHINESE $$

(200-202 Jln Kampung Cina; mains RM10-21; ⊗ 7.30am-10pm, closed every 2nd Wed; ❄) Keong Kee specialises in claypot dishes that come in three sizes and which feature pork, chicken, prawns or tofu in various tasty sauces. There are also sizzling prawn dishes and freshly fried fish at market prices. Add this to a decent variety of bottled beers and you have another excellent choice in Chinatown for lunch or dinner.

Pertama Steak & Sushi House
JAPANESE $$

(www.facebook.com/pertama808; 2A Jln Air Jernih; mains from RM12; ⊗ noon-10pm) Excellent Japanese fare is served at this alcohol-free place just south of the town centre. Sashimi and sushi are well prepared and super fresh, and robust bowls of rice and noodles are savoury antidotes to the often sweet local Malay food. Generous bento boxes offer a bit of everything, and salads, pasta and steak quell yearnings for international flavours.

🍷 Drinking & Nightlife

⭐ Vinum Exchange
BAR

(www.facebook.com/thevinumXchange; 221 Jln Kampung Cina; ⊗ 11am-11pm) Equal parts cafe, bar, restaurant and wine shop, Vinum Exchange is a game changer for Kuala Terengganu. The stylish interior features a great selection of international wine and spirits lining one wall. Other drinking options include espresso, beer and cider. The food, which ranges from bar snacks through to excellent Malay, Chinese and international meals, also deserves a mention.

Star Anise
CAFE

(www.facebook.com/staranisekt; 82 Jln Kampung Cina; coffee RM6-10; ⊗ noon-midnight; 🛜) One of Kuala Terengganu's best coffee joints, Star Anise extracts a fine espresso and concocts several flavoured variations of coffee for those with a sweet tooth. Secure a table in the front and admire the display of gifts and local souvenirs including organic honey, or retire for conversation and blueberry cheesecake or chicken pie in the lounge at the back.

🛍 Shopping

Batik and *kain songket* cloth are particularly good buys in Kuala Terengganu. Check out the Central Market (p307) near the river.

Wanisma Craft & Trading ARTS & CRAFTS
(📞09-622 3311; Ladang Sekolah; ⊙9.30am-6.30pm) Batik and local brassware can be purchased at this shop where you can also view artisans at work. Check with the tourist information office before heading there, as nearby real estate development may necessitate a change in location at some point.

Kraftangan Malaysia ARTS & CRAFTS
(📞09-622 6458; off Jln Marwar 1; ⊙9am-5pm Sun-Thu) Located about 4.5km south of town, this outlet sells high-quality *kain songket* costing as much as RM12,000 for 2.5 sq metres. There's also a tiny 'Songket Heritage' Exhibition showing varying designs. Bus 13 (RM2) will take you here from the main bus station.

ℹ Information

You'll find plenty of banks, such as **HSBC** (📞09-622 3100; 57 Jln Sultan Ismail), on Jln Sultan Ismail. Most of these banks have ATMs that accept international cards.

Hospital Sultanah Nur Zahirah (📞09-621 2121; http://hsnzkt.moh.gov.my; Jln Sultan Mahmud) Has English-speaking staff and offers a good standard of care.

Post Office (📞09-630 1844; Jln Sultan Zainal Abidin; ⊙8.30am-5.30pm Sun-Thu, 8.30am-1pm Sat)

Tourism Malaysia Office (📞09-630 9093; www.tourism.gov.my; Unit 11, Jln Kampung Daik; ⊙8am-5pm Sun-Wed, to 3.30pm Thu) Good maps and English-language brochures.

Tourist Information Office (📞09-622 1553; www.beautifulterengganu.com; Jln Sultan Zainal Abidin; ⊙9am-5pm Sat-Thu) Closed for renovations at the time of research. Due to open by the time this edition goes to press, expect this handy office to provide maps, brochures and up-to-date information on cultural activities in Kuala Terengganu.

ℹ Getting There & Away

AIR
Sultan Mahmud Airport (📞09-667 3666; www.malaysiaairports.com.my; Jln Lapangan Terbang) is around 11km north of the city centre. AirAsia (p607) and Malaysia Airlines (p607) have services to/from KLIA, while Firefly (p607) and Malindo Air (p608) connect with SkyPark Subang Terminal (also known as

Sultan Abdul Aziz Shah Airport) closer to Kuala Lumpur. AirAsia flies three times a week to/from Johor Bahru.

BUS
The **main bus station** (Jln Masjid Abidin) is the terminus for local buses and long-distance express buses. Express bus companies at the station include **Transnasional** (📞09-622 2700; www.transnasional.com.my; Jln Syed Hussein), **MARA Liner** (📞09-622 2097; www.maraliner group.my; Jln Syed Hussein), **Sani Express** (📞09-622 2717; www.saniexpress.com.my; Jln Syed Hussein) and **SP Bumi** (📞09-623 7789; www.spbumi.com.my; Jln Syed Hussein).

Buses from Kuala Terengganu

DESTINATION	PRICE (RM)	DURATION (APPROX)
Dungun	8.70	1.5hr
Johor Bahru (for Singapore)	48.40	9hr
Kota Bharu	15.80	3hr
Kuala Besut (for Pulau Perhentian)	13	2hr
Kuala Lumpur	43.80	8hr
Kuantan	9	5hr
Melaka	48	8hr
Merang (for Pulau Redang)	8	1.5hr
Penang	51	9hr
Rantau Abang	7	1hr

TAXI
Kuala Terengganu's **main taxi stand** (Jln Syed Hussein) is near the main bus station, but taxis can be found throughout the city. Destinations include Marang (RM30), Kota Bharu (RM200), Kuala Besut (RM130), Rantau Abang (RM100), Merang (RM60) and Tasik Kenyir (RM180 return).

ℹ Getting Around

Local buses leave from the main bus station. The two routes taken by the whimsical **Heritage Buses** (Jln Masjid Abidin; per person RM1-3; ⊙9am-6pm route CO-1, 9am-11.30pm route CO-2) stop here, too. Timings for Heritage Buses are every 1½ hours starting at 9am, but these services are handy for getting to the Muzium (p308) and Taman Tamadu Islam (p308) (route C-02, RM1).

Taxis to any point in town cost a minimum of RM10. A taxi to the airport, which is around 11km north of the city, costs around RM35.

Bicycle rickshaws are a dying mode of transport in Kuala Terengganu, but you may be able to spot some around the Central Market. Prices are highly negotiable.

North of Kuala Terengganu

Merang

✏ 09 / POP 3300

Merang is the gateway and closest point on the mainland coast to the island resorts of Pulau Redang (p301) and Pulau Lang Tengah (p302), plus the excellent diving spots off **Pulau Bidong**. Speedboats run regularly between the islands and this river port. Merang should not be confused with Marang (p312; the ferry terminus for boats to Pulau Kapas), which lies to the south of Kuala Terengganu.

The sleepy fishing village of Merang has little to offer travellers beyond the jetty and harbour on the banks of Sungai Merang with its colourful fishing boats and mangroves. The windswept but attractive palm-fringed beaches to the east of the harbour are worth a stroll if you find you have to spend some time waiting for ferry connections.

Kembara Resort (☎ 09-653 1770; http://kembararesort.tripod.com; 474 Pantai Peranginan Merang; dm RM35, d RM130-160; ❄ 🛜) is an inexpensive and friendly place, with simple bungalows that are popular with the student crowd. There are organised activities and a common kitchen. Follow the signs from the main road.

Local buses run from the main bus station in Kuala Terengganu to Merang (RM5, 1½ hours). Taxis from Kuala Terengganu and Sultan Mahmud Airport (p311) cost RM60 per car. Allow 40 to 45 minutes. Coming from the north is more difficult and it is easiest to go south as far as Kuala Terengganu and then backtrack.

Penarik

✏ 09 / POP 600

With its windswept beach and population of fishers and farmers, the village of Penarik is as lovely a spot for a taste of coastal Malaysian culture as you could wish for. Just offshore, the islands of Perhentian, Lang Tengah and Redang appear tantalisingly close. But for something truly magical, stick around until the sun goes down and charter a boat to take you down the Penarik river for a journey through the **Penarik Firefly Sanctuary**. On certain nights, but the darker the better, you'll be treated to a most unusual sight: thousands of fireflies blinking in near-perfect synchronisation. This synchronised flashing pattern is unique

to the area, and entomologists suspect it is associated with mating behaviour. The night-time boat trip through the ghostly and ethereal mangrove forest is an unforgettable experience.

For somewhere special to stay, the manicured grounds of **Terrapuri Heritage Village** (☎ 09-624 5020; www.terrapuri.com; houses min 2 nights RM600-1200; ❄ 🛜) resemble a film set about the lives of sultans of yore. Meaning 'Land of Palaces', Terrapuri is equal parts conservation and restoration museum, and resort. The resort features 29 classically furnished antique houses painstakingly restored and is laid out to resemble a Terengganu palace c 1850 (though all are fully equipped with modern amenities).

The land on which Terrapuri sits is equally regal, flanked by the South China Sea (with stunning views of Pulau Perhentian, Lang Tengah and other islands) on one side, and the Setiu Wetland mangrove river on the other. By night, the flashing of fireflies is reflected in Terrapuri's long swimming pool, and during the summer months visitors may see green turtles laying their eggs on the sandy shore. Terrapuri offers delicious traditional meals (breakfast RM45, lunch RM65, dinner RM75) and many activities.

A wide range of activities is offered at the resort, including excursions into local villages and boat trips to the **Firefly Sanctuary** (☾ after sunset) and outlying islands. Nonguests can book these same activities through Ping Anchorage (p309). From Kuala Terengganu, a Firefly Sanctuary tour with Ping costs RM200 per person (dependent on group size and minimum of two people) including dinner and transport. Buses from Kuala Terengganu to Kuala Besut will drop you off at the Kampung Penarik mosque in Penarik for RM6. From the other direction, buses from Kota Bharu to Kuala Terengganu are RM17. Taxis from either city are also available.

South of Kuala Terengganu

Marang

✏ 09 / POP 21,400

Marang is a sizeable fishing village on the mouth of Sungai Marang. It is also the jumping-off point for ferries to Pulau Kapas. It's a little overdeveloped around the highway, but down by the harbour you will discover its charms. Hundreds of colourful fishing boats bob in the clear harbour waters or recline on mudbanks if the tide is out. There is a colourful daily **market** (Jln Pasar Lama; ⊙6am-5pm) behind the jetty. Pick up some bananas to munch on while waiting for your boat to Pulau Kapas.

If you are in town on Sunday be sure to check out the excellent **Sunday Market**, which starts at 3pm near the jetty. There are a few decent hotels and restaurants plus several relaxed *kedai kopi* (coffee shops) and **food stalls** (Jln Kampung Paya; snacks RM4-8) just north of the jetty.

🛏 Sleeping & Eating

Hotel Pelangi
HOTEL $$

(☑09-618 2033; www.hotelpelangi.my; Jln Pasar Lama; s/d inc breakfast RM80/100; ❄ 🕏) Brightly painted and with a harbourside location, Hotel Pelangi is a comfortable option that's convenient if you'd like to stay near the jetty for boats to Pulau Kapas (p304) and the bustling Marang Market. Rooms are simple but clean and well maintained and more than OK for an overnight stay. Meals are available in the pleasant Coral Cafe downstairs.

❶ Getting There & Away

Buses connect Marang with Kuala Terengganu (RM2.50, 30 minutes). The first bus leaves at 6.45am and subsequent departures are every hour between 8am and 5pm. A taxi from Kuala Terengganu to Marang jetty costs RM30 one-way. Usually there are taxis waiting for boats arriving from Pulau Kapas for the return journey to Kuala Terengganu. To be certain there is a taxi for when you arrive at the jetty, you can arrange for a Kuala Terengganu-based taxi to meet you at the Marang jetty. Alternatively, get your accommodation on the island to book one for you before you leave.

It is sometimes possible to flag down buses travelling to Kuala Terengganu (RM4) and Dungun/Rantau Abang (RM7/5), but often these services are express buses and will not always stop in Marang. The main bus stop is near the traffic roundabout on the main road (Route 3, the East Coast Highway), in front of the Sultanah Nur Zahirah mosque.

Speedboats (adult/child RM40/20 return) depart from Marang's main jetty at 9am, 11am,

1pm, 3pm and 5pm, with returns half an hour later from Kapas. Suria Link Boat Service (p305) will continue to Pulau Gemia if requested.

For travel further afield, such as to Kuala Lumpur or Cherating, the most straightforward option is to return to Kuala Terengganu and catch an express bus from there.

Tasik Kenyir

The construction of Kenyir Dam in 1985 flooded some 2600 sq km of jungle, creating Southeast Asia's largest artificial lake. Today Tasik Kenyir (Lake Kenyir) and its 340 islands constitute one of Terengganu's most popular inland tourism destinations. However, the children's water park, and special islands dedicated to contrived displays of orchids and butterflies, have somewhat diminished the remote appeal of the area.

Factor in poor public transport links and the fact that some attractions are only available to groups, and the area is best visited by independent travellers on a tour from Kuala Terengganu. At the time of research the sole accommodation option here, **Lake Kenyir Resort** (☑09-666 8888; www.lakekenyir.com; Kuala Berang; ❄ 🕏 🐾), was closed.

Despite the area's increasing development, boating on the lake is still enjoyable, but it's best to avoid weekends and public holidays when the serenity can often be ambushed.

There is a small **tourist information office** (☑09-626 7788; Pengkalan Gawi; ⊙9am-5pm) near the jetty in Pengkalan Gawi, the lake's main access point. It can supply maps and brochures, but it only books tours and activities for groups.

The main access point is the jetty at Pengkalan Gawi on the lake's northern shore. A taxi from Kuala Terengganu is expensive, costing around RM1400, and it can be expensive arranging boat transport once you reach the jetty at Pengkalan Gawi. Your best bet is to book an all-inclusive package or day trip with Ping Anchorage (p309) in Kuala Terengganu (around RM295 per person, dependent on group size and minimum of two people).

Sabah

POP 3.87 MILLION

Includes ➡

Kota Kinabalu 316

Mt Kinabalu & Kinabalu National Park 332

Northwest Coast 341

Sandakan 346

Sepilok 351

Sungai Kinabatangan 358

Danum Valley Conservation Area .. 365

Semporna 367

Tawau 376

Beaufort Division ... 385

Pulau Labuan 388

Best Places to Eat

➡ Kam Ling Seafood (p378)

➡ Sakura Seafood Restaurant (p364)

➡ Restaurant Seafood Sim Sim 88 (p350)

➡ A-Square Night Market (p325)

Best Places to Stay

➡ Bike & Tours B&B (p364)

➡ Scuba Junkie Mabul Beach Resort (p373)

➡ Tampat Do Aman (p343)

➡ Orou Sapulot (p385)

Why Go?

Sabah occupies a relatively small chunk of the world's third-largest island, Borneo, yet what a punch it packs: the treasure of turquoise-fringed desert islands with coral reefs swarming with marine biodiversity; trekkers' paradise Mt Kinabalu reaching 4095m into the clouds; and jungles pulsing with a menagerie of bug-eyed tarsiers, gibbons, pythons, clouded leopards and huge crocs. Around 55% of Sabah is forest, and protected areas such as the Maliau Basin and the Danum Valley Conservation Area are more accessible than ever.

Getting from one of Sabah's highlights to the next is eminently doable, while as a former British colony, English is commonly spoken here, making it extremely traveller friendly. Whether it's coffee-shop haunting in Kota Kinabalu, watching baby orangutans learning to climb at Sepilok, beach flopping on the northern Tip of Borneo, or searching for pygmy elephants near Tawau, your time here will feel like five holidays condensed into one.

When to Go
Kota Kinabalu

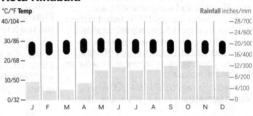

Jan–Apr Dry, pleasant weather, good for trekking; also vibrant celebrations for Chinese New Year.

Mar–Oct Arguably the best time for spotting orangutans in the wild.

Apr–Dec Best time for diving, with excellent visibility in July and August.

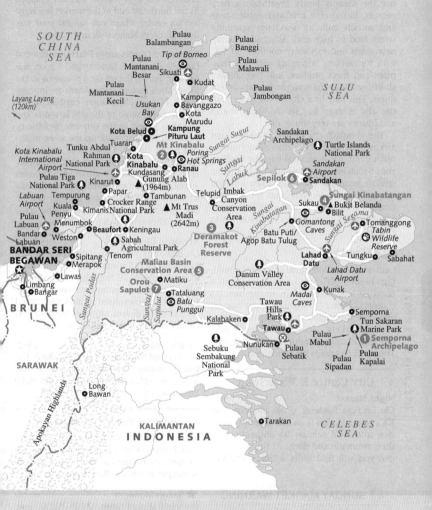

Sabah Highlights

1 **Semporna Archipelago** (p369) Diving among sea turtles and sharks along multicoloured reefs.

2 **Mt Kinabalu** (p332) Trekking up Borneo's highest mountain for the ultimate sunrise.

3 **Deramakot Forest Reserve** (p357) Looking for leopard cats, civets and deer on night safaris.

4 **Sungai Kinabatangan** (p358) Spotting monkeys, orangutans and giant crocs on boat rides along the mighty river.

5 **Maliau Basin** (p380) Trekking to waterfalls through virgin rainforest in Borneo's 'Lost World'.

6 **Sepilok** (p351) Getting up close and personal with rescued orangutans and sun bears.

7 **Orou Sapulot** (p385) Exploring primary jungle and the Batu Punggul rock formations with the Murut people.

KOTA KINABALU

📞 088 / POP 309,900

In busy Kota Kinabalu (KK) you'll soon notice the friendly locals, breathtaking fiery sunsets, blossoming arts and music scene and a rich culinary spectrum spanning street food to high end. Alongside swanky new malls and expensive condos, old KK, with its markets brimming with sea creatures and fresh produce, and busy fishers shuttling about the waterfront, happily endures. This may be a city on the move with the 21st century, but its old-world charm and history are very much alive.

The compact city centre is easy to get around, but most of the city's attractions lie further out. KK is an ideal base for booking your Sabah adventure, whether it be diving, wildlife watching or Mt Kinabalu trekking (though if you have your heart set on a particular experience, book ahead). Believe us, KK will soon grow on you once you get to know it.

◎ Sights

Central KK is a dense grid of concrete buildings nestled between the waterfront and a range of low, forested hills to the east. It's compact, walkable (when not too humid) and easy to navigate – most of the restaurants, markets, accommodation, tourist offices and tour operators are located here. Transport terminals bookend the city.

◎ City Centre & Waterfront

Night Market MARKET
(Jln Tun Fuad Stephens; ⊗ late afternoon-11pm) KK's Night Market is an unmissable immersion into local culture. It's authentic, bustling, aromatic and noisy. At the southwest end you will find stalls selling everything

---

❶ SUNDAY MARKET WARNING

On Sundays a lively Chinese **street fair** (Jln Gaya; ⊗ 6am-noon Sun) takes over a section of Jln Gaya. It's vividly chaotic, with stalls cheek by jowl hawking batik sarongs, fruit, goldfish, wild honey and antiques.

Animal-lovers may prefer to avoid the market area where Jln Gaya intersects Beach St. Overheating, thick-furred Persian kittens and gasping puppies in mesh cages are likely to distress.

---

from *belacan* (fermented shrimp paste) to snake beans. Towards the waterfront are the fish stalls: row upon row of bug-eyed bream, tuna, tiger prawns and red snapper. At the northeast end of the market is a huge hawker centre where you can eat your way through every Malay dish in the book.

Signal Hill Observatory Platform VIEWPOINT
(Jln Bukit Bendera; ⊗ 8am-midnight) Up on Signal Hill, among the art deco mansions at the city-centre's eastern edge, there's an unmissable UFO-like observation pavilion. Come here to make sense of the city layout below. The view is best as the sun sets over the islands. To reach it, walk up the steps at the end of Lg Dewan. Other steps are behind **Lucy's Homestay** (Backpacker's Lodge; 📞 088-261495; backpackerkk@yahoo.com; lot 25, Lg Dewan, Australia Pl; dm/s/d with shared bathroom incl breakfast RM25/52/62; 🖥️), passing the huge banyan tree, to reach the road that you follow to the tower. Otherwise, catch a cab (RM15).

Atkinson Clock Tower LANDMARK
(Jln Balai Polis) The modest timepiece at the foot of Signal Hill is one of the only structures to survive the Allied bombing of Jesselton in 1945. It's a square, 15.7m-high wooden structure that was completed in 1905 and named after the first district officer of the town, FG Atkinson, who died of malaria aged 28.

Central Market MARKET
(Jln Tun Fuad Stephens; ⊗ 5.30am-6.30pm) The Central Market is a bustling spot for people watching, with locals going about their daily business as they shop for fresh produce.

◎ Beyond the City Centre

Most of KK's best attractions, such as museums, culture villages and orchid gardens, are located beyond the city centre, and it's well worth putting in the effort to check them out.

⭐ **Sabah Museum** MUSEUM
(Kompleks Muzium Sabah; 📞 088-253199; www.museum.sabah.gov.my; Jln Muzium; RM15; ⊗ 9am-5pm; 🅿️) About 2km south of the city centre, this museum provides an excellent introduction to Sabah's indigenous cultures, with displays focusing on the traditional attire, festivals, customs and crafts of the Dusun, Murut, Rungus, Bajau and other Sabah peoples. Try your hand at playing traditional musical instruments, marvel at the fine embroidery and learn about past headhunting practices of the Murut and

KK'S ART SCENE

KK is buzzing with festivals and gigs; you just need to keep an eye out for them. While the free and widely available monthly glossy magazine *Sabah* lists upcoming events, it's also worth checking out SPArKS' (Society of Performing Arts Kota Kinabalu) website (www. sparks.org.my). SPArKS works with the US Embassy to bring world-famous acts to play gigs in intimate venues, as well as organising the hugely popular Jazz Festival (http:// kkjazzfest.com) in June or July, and the KK Arts Festival, which also runs through June and July.

Look out, too, for the quirky street market, **Tamutamu**, which is part arts and crafts, part eclectic gathering, with artists, musos and tarot readers, on the third Sunday of every month from 10am to 5pm. Enquire at Biru Biru restaurant (p324).

Kadazan-Dusun. Upstairs are the centuries-old Chinese ceramics retrieved from the *Jade Dragon* wreck, circa CE 1300, in 2013.

The adjoining **Heritage Village** has traditional tribal dwellings, including Kadazan bamboo houses and a Chinese farmhouse, all nicely set on a lily-pad lake.

Next door, the **Science & Education Centre** has an informative exhibition on the petroleum industry, from drilling to refining and processing.

Hold on to your ticket: it also includes entry to the nearby Museum of Islamic Civilisation (p319).

Mari Mari Cultural Village   MUSEUM
(☑ 088-260501; www.marimariculturalvillage.com; Jln Kiansom; adult/child RM175/155; ⊙ tours at 10am & 2pm; 🎏) With its three-hour tours, Mari Mari showcases various traditional homes of Sabahan ethnic communities – the Bajau, Lundayeh, Murut, Rungus and Dusun – all of which are built by descendants of the tribes they represent. Along the way you'll get the chance to see blowpipe making, tattooing, fire-starting and an insight into the mystical belief systems of each of these groups, as well as culinary nibbles from each tribe! It's touristy, sure, but good fun, especially for families.

A short dance recital is also included in the visit. The village is a 20- to 30-minute drive east of KK and transport to/from your hotel can be arranged when booking. There is also a small waterfall – **Kiansom Waterfall** – about 400m beyond the cultural village, which is easily accessible by private transport or on foot. The area around the cascade lends itself well to swimming and it's a great place to cool off after a visit to Mari Mari.

Sabah Art Gallery   GALLERY
(14 Jln Shantung; adult/6-12yr RM15/8; ⊙ 9am-5pm) The first 'green' building in Sabah has outdoor sculpture displays and hosts contemporary art exhibitions by the likes of Francis Cheong and Awang Fadilah Bin Haji Hussein on its three floors.

Kota Kinabalu
Wetland Centre   BIRD SANCTUARY
(☑ 088-246955; www.sabahwetlands.org; Jln Bukit Bendera Upper, Likas District; adult/child RM15/10; ⊙ 8am-6pm Tue-Sun; 🅿) This centre features 1.4km of wooden walkways passing through a 24-hectare mangrove swamp, where you can expect to see scuttling fiddler and mangrove crabs, mud lobsters, mudskippers, skinks, turtles, water monitors and mangrove slugs. For many the big attraction is a stunning variety of migratory birds. To get here, take the bus towards Likas from the bus stations in front of City Hall or Wawasan Plaza, to Likas Sq. A taxi from KK costs around RM15; a Grab ride no more than RM10.

Orchid De Villa   FARM
(☑ 088-380611; www.orchid-de-villa.com.my; Jln Kiansom, Kampung Kawakaan; ⊙ 8am-5pm; 🅿) If you're crazy about flora, head to this farm, located about 20km from central KK, along the road to Penampang. The farm specialises in rare Bornean orchids, hybrid orchids, cacti and herbal plants, and provides all of the five-star hotels in the region with flower arrangements. At last count there were 300 different kinds of orchids.

City Mosque   MOSQUE
(off Jln Tun Fuad Stephens; ⊙ hours vary; 🚌 5A) Built in classical style, this mosque is far more attractive than the **State Mosque** (Jln Tunku Abdul Rahman; ⊙ hours vary) in both setting and design. Completed in 2000 it can hold up to 12,000 worshippers. It can be entered by non-Muslims outside regular prayer times, but there's not much worth seeing inside. It's about 5km north of the centre. To get here, take bus 5A towards UMS (University of Malaysia Sabah, RM2).

Kota Kinabalu

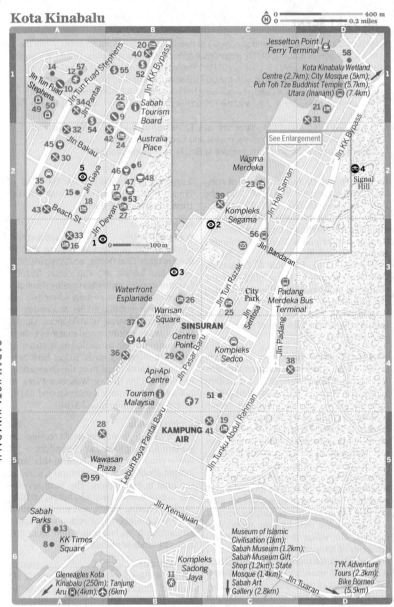

SABAH KOTA KINABALU

Ask the conductor to drop you off after the Tanjung Lipat roundabout.

Monsopiad Cultural Village MUSEUM
(☑ 088-774337; www.monsopiad.com; Kampong Kuai/Kandazon, Penampang; adult/7-12yr RM55/25; ☺ 9am-5pm) Monsopiad is named after a legendary warrior and headhunter. The highlight of this tacky but fun place is the House of Skulls, which supposedly contains the ancient crania of Monsopiad's unfortunate enemies, as well as artefacts illustrating native rituals from the time when the *bobolian* (priest) was the most important figure

Kota Kinabalu

⊙ Sights
1	Atkinson Clock Tower	A3
2	Central Market	C3
3	Night Market	B3
4	Signal Hill Observatory Platform	D2
5	Sunday Market	A2

⊙ Activities, Courses & Tours
6	Adventure Alternative Borneo	B2
7	Amazing Borneo	B4
8	Borneo Adventure	A6
9	Borneo Divers	B1
10	Borneo Dream	A1
11	Borneo Nature Tours	B6
12	Diverse Borneo	A1
13	Downbelow Marine & Wildlife Adventures	A6
14	Only in Borneo	A1
	River Junkie	(see 10)
	Riverbug/Traverse Tours	(see 14)
	Scuba Junkie KK	(see 57)
	Seaventures	(see 10)
15	Sticky Rice Travel	A2
	Sutera Sanctuary Lodges	(see 14)

⊙ Sleeping
16	Akinabalu Hostel	A3
17	Borneo Backpackers	B2
18	Bunk	A2
19	Hilton Hotel Kinabalu	C5
20	Hotel Eden 54	B1
21	Hotel Grandis	D1
22	Hotel Sixty3	B1
23	Hyatt Regency Kota Kinabalu	C2
24	Jesselton Hotel	B2
25	Kooler Inn	C3
26	Le Méridien Kota Kinabalu	B3
27	Lucy's Homestay	B2

⊙ Eating
28	A-Square Night Market	A5
	Biru Biru	(see 17)
29	Centre Point Food Court	B4
30	Chilli Vanilla	A2
31	Grazie Ristorante	D1
32	Kedai Kopi Fatt Kee	A2
33	Kedai Kopi Yee Fung	A3
34	Little Italy	A1
35	Milimewa Superstore	A2
36	Mother India	B4
	Night Market	(see 3)
37	Sakagura Japanese Restaurant	B4
38	Sri Latha Curry House	C4
39	Todak Waterfront	C2
40	Tong Hing Supermarket	B1
41	Welcome Seafood Restaurant	C5
42	Yu Kee Bah Kut Teh	B2
43	Yuit Cheong	A2

⊙ Drinking & Nightlife
44	BED	B4
45	El Centro	A2
46	Fruto	B2
47	Nook Cafe	B2
48	October Coffee House	B2

⊙ Shopping
49	Borneo Shop	A1
50	Sabah Batik & Craft	A1

⊙ Information
51	Cleansway Laundry	C4
52	HSBC	B1
53	Laundry@25	B2
54	Maybank	A1
55	Standard Chartered Bank	B1

⊙ Transport
56	City Park Bus Terminal	C3
57	GogoSabah	A1
58	Ticketing Hall	D1
59	Wawasan Plaza Bus Terminal	A5

SABAH KOTA KINABALU

in the community. The quality of your experience depends on the guide you get. The village is 16km from KK; taxis from KK cost around RM50.

To get here independently, take bus 13 from central KK to Donggongon (RM2), where you can catch a minivan to the cultural village (RM1).

Museum of Islamic Civilisation MUSEUM
(☎088-538234; Jln Menteri; RM15; ◉9am-5pm Sat-Thu; 🅿) This collection of historical objects from all over the Islamic world is very engaging. Look out for replica mosques from Melaka and Sandakan, ornate krises from Java and Bali, curved Sulu swords, an 18th-century Persian Quran stand and Indonesian wooden caskets engraved with Quranic verses. The Malaysian history section, by contrast, is wordy and rather dry.

To get here, catch bus 13 (RM1) along Jln Tunku Abdul Rahman and alight just before the mosque.

**Puh Toh Tze
Buddhist Temple** BUDDHIST TEMPLE
(Mile/Batu 5.5; ◉8am-5pm) This impressive temple features a stone staircase-pavilion flanked by 10 Chinese deities leading up to a main temple complex dominated by Kwan Yin, Goddess of Mercy. A Chinese-style reclining Buddha rests inside. The temple is

on a small hill west of the main highway junction north. You can get here by taking the Jln Tuaran bus or, more easily, get a Grab ride of hire a taxi; a round trip shouldn't be more than RM45.

Tanjung Aru
BEACH

This pretty sweep of sand begins around the Shangri-La's Tanjung Aru Resort and stretches south to the airport. Tanjung Aru is a locals' beach, full of picnic spots and swoony-eyed couples. Food stalls are plentiful, most closing up come dark. We would advise against swimming here; the water may look pretty, and some locals may tell you it's fine, but others claim it's tainted by run-off from KK and nearby water villages.

🏃 Activities & Tours

There are many tour companies based in KK, offering anything from multiday jungle treks and day-trip dives in the Tunku Abdul Rahman National Park to treks up Mt Kinabalu, cultural immersion and white-water rafting on the Padas River. Wisma Sabah on Jln Haji Saman is where many operators are based. **Sabah Tourism Board** (p327) runs free walking tours of KK thrice weekly.

★ Sticky Rice Travel
ADVENTURE

(☑088-251654; www.stickyricetravel.com; 3rd fl, 134 Jln Gaya; ⊕9am-6pm) 🗡 *National Geographic* prefers this outfit for a reason; it's organised, original in its choice of tours and has excellent, knowledgeable guides. Responsible community-based tourism – expect adventure, culture and something very different. Sticky Rice will tailor your experience around your interests, fitness and budget. The Maliau Basin, Sapulot, Crocker Range Park and Tabin Wildlife Reserve are among the destinations offered.

★ Top Peak Travel
OUTDOORS

(☑088-251254; https://toppeaktravel.com; 2nd fl, lot 1, block H, Lg Pusat Komercil 88/1 88 Marketplace; ⊕9am-5pm) 🗡 Outstanding operator with close ties to local communities, offering off-the-beaten-track Sabah adventures as well as the greatest hits. Signature tours include the five-day, four-night Long Pasia jungle adventure (RM1995), the five-day, four-night Salt Trail trek (RM1020), half-day cooking classes with a local family near KK (RM200) and multiday trekking and camping at the Kawang Forest Reserve near KK. Minimum two people per adventure.

★ TYK Adventure Tours
TREKKING

(☑088-232821; https://tykadventuretours.com; 2nd flr, block E, Jln Damai; 5-day, 4-night Salt Trail per person RM2200, 2-day, 1-night Sandakan Death March RM1200) Outstanding trekking specialist Tham Yau Kong organises multiday adventures in the Crocker Range, including the Salt Trail, ascents of Mt Trusmadi (RM2200) and much more. Together with renowned historian Lynette Silver, he also runs Sandakan Death March treks that trace the final journey of the Australian and British POWs – hike or bike just two days or the whole thing.

★ Adventure Alternative Borneo
ADVENTURE

(☑019-872 6355; www.adventurealternative.com; Lg Dewan; ⊕9am-6pm) 🗡 Sustainable and ethical travel are key to this British-owned company, a pioneer that launched the first-ever tours into Deramakot Forest Reserve. Runs multiday wildlife-spotting and trekking adventures to Maliau Basin, Imbak Canyon and Danum Valley, elephant spotting near Tawau and cultural immersion in Sapulot, as well as seriously off-the-beaten-track adventure with the Penan in deep, dark Sarawak.

Borneo Divers
DIVING

(☑088-222226; www.borneodivers.info; Head Office 9th fl, Menara Jubili, 53 Jln Gaya; day trip to Mamutik incl 3 dives RM330; ⊕9am-6pm) The original dive outfit, and still one of the best, thanks to its high safety standards, quality equipment, excellent PADI teachers and divemasters. It has a lovely resort (p374) on Mabul island. Recommended.

Scuba Junkie KK
DIVING

(☑088-255816; www.scubajunkiekk.com; ground fl, lot G7, Wisma Sabah, Jln Haji Saman; 2 dives KK Marine Park RM270; ⊕9am-6pm) 🗡 An ecologically progressive dive outfit, ploughing part of its profits into its turtle hatchery and rehab centre, as well as employing a shark conservationist and an environmentalist. SJ tends to attract a younger, Western crowd. Great vibe, friendly instructors. Its KK office organises dives/snorkelling in Tunku Abdul Rahman National Park, as well as off Pulau Tiga and Snake Island.

Seaventures
DIVING

(☑017-811 6020, 088-251669; http://seaventuresdive.com; suite 305, 3rd fl, Wisma Sabah, Jln Tun Fuad Stephens; 4-day, 3-night package incl meals & transfers to island & airport RM3360) Based out of its funky blue/orange oil rig (p375) next to Mabul island, this is a well-regarded outfit with a full range of diving courses available, professional divemasters and its own house reef. Three-night minimum stay in a standard room to guarantee a Sipadan permit. Two-night minimum stay in dorms (Sipadan permit not guaranteed).

Diverse Borneo   OUTDOORS
(☑016-826 8547; www.diverse-borneo.com; lot G30, ground fl, Wisma Sabah, Jln Tun Razak; day trip incl 3 dives to Tunku Abdul Rahman National Park RM275) One of the top diving operators in KK, Diverse Borneo also offers land adventures, from trekking in the Kawang Forest Reserve not far from KK, to abseiling down waterfalls.

Bike Borneo   CYCLING
(☑Mon-Fri 088-484734, WhatsApp 012-833 0106; www.bikeborneo.com; lot 11, block C, 2nd flr, City Mall, Jln Lintas; 1-day tours from RM300; ☉8.30am-5.30pm) Bike Borneo runs its mountain-biking activities largely out of Tuaran. Packages include a one-day ride in the vicinity of town that crosses three swinging bridges, and a four-day cycling adventure across the foothills of Mt Kinabalu. Groups are small, with a maximum of six people. Bikes are well maintained, guides experienced. City Mall is about 6km east of central KK.

Riverbug/Traverse Tours   ADVENTURE
(☑088-260501; www.riverbug.asia/sabah; lot 227, 2nd fl, Wisma Sabah, Jln Tun Fuad Stephens; ☉8am-5pm Mon-Fri, 9am-1pm Sat) ✐ An excellent and forward-thinking operator that makes admirable efforts to engage in sustainable travel practices. Particularly popular for its adrenaline-packed white-water rafting trips down the Padas River from Beaufort (RM235), as well as more sedate half-day floats down the Kiulu River (RM190).

Downbelow Marine & Wildlife Adventures   DIVING
(☑012-866 1935; www.divedownbelow.com; lot 67 & 68, 5th fl, KK Times Sq; diving day trip to Manukan per person RM380; ☉9am-6pm) A well-respected dive outfit, with an office in KK and a PADI centre on Pulau Gaya and Pulau Manukan. Can arrange all kinds of travel packages across Borneo.

Amazing Borneo   OUTDOORS
(☑088-448409; www.amazingborneo.com; L1.39 1st fl, Star City North Complex, Jln Asia City; 2-day, 1-night Mt Kinabalu climb per person from RM1500; ☉9am-5pm) This large tour agency works with numerous operators across Sabah and

COOKING COURSE

Equator Adventure Tours (☑014-550 4429; www.facebook.com/equator.tours; Dsoka Restaurant, Jln Pengalat-Lok Kawi Hwy, Papar; per person RM240 (min 2 persons); ☉9am-6pm) runs the Hajah Halimah Traditional Cooking course, giving you the chance to get savvy with Malaysian cuisine in an authentic environment. You'll be picked up at 9am from your hotel and spirited to the wet market for ingredients, then learn how to make two memorable dishes at Dsoka Restaurant (22km south of KK in Papar).

Sarawak and can set you up with most popular adventures, from multiday Kinabatangan River stays and trips to Danum Valley, to Mt Kinabalu climbs. Booking your Mt Kinabalu climb couldn't be easier – its website tells you how many slots are available and for which dates.

Borneo Dream   DIVING
(☑088-811 8149; www.borneodream.com; G27 Wisma Sabah, Jln Tun Fuad Stephens; day trip incl 3 dives in Tunku Abdul Rahman National Park RM310; ☉9am-6pm) Operating out of Kota Kinabalu and at the Gaya Island Resort (p331) on Pulau Gaya, this outfit has a good name and can take you diving on a try-dive excursion, or take you through your PADI paces to become an Open Water diver.

Borneo Nature Tours   HIKING
(☑088-267637; www.borneonaturetours.com; lot 10, ground fl, block D, Kompleks Sadong Jaya; 5-day, 4-night all-inclusive tour of Maliau Basin per person in 2- or 3-person group RM5230) Yayasan Sabah runs tours to the Maliau Basin through its subsidiary, Borneo Nature Tours. These five-day adventures comprise flights from KK to Tawau, and then, once in the park, overnighting at three different camps – Agathis, Nepenthes and Ginseng. Each day you'll trek between five to seven hours over at-times-challenging terrain.

River Junkie   RAFTING
(☑088-255816, 017-601 2145; www.river-junkie.com; ground fl, lot 105, Wisma Sabah, Jln Haji Saman) Diving operator Scuba Junkie's affiliated river-rafting outfit comes highly recommended by travellers. It specialises in white-water rafting expeditions on Padas River (full day, grade III to IV rapids, RM250 per person) and family-friendly Kiulu River

(half-day, grade I to II, RM200 per person). Leisurely boat tours and proboscis monkey spotting in the Klias wetlands also offered. Bookings normally require 24 hours' advance notice.

Only in Borneo WILDLIFE WATCHING
(088-262507, WhatsApp 019-840 0402; www.oibtours.com; Wisma Sabah, ground fl, lot G13, Jln Tun Fuad Stephens; Klias wetlands tour RM170; 9am-5pm Mon-Fri, to 2pm Sat & Sun) An offshoot of Traverse Tours, this reputable operator specialises in half-day boat trips in the Klias wetlands, in search of proboscis monkeys and fireflies (tours typically run from 1.30pm to 9.30pm). Snorkelling and diving off Sepanggar and Mantanani islands also offered, along with day trips to the Poring hot springs (p340).

Borneo Adventure TOURS
(088-486800; www.borneoadventure.com; block E-27-3A, Signature Office, KK Times Sq; 9am-6pm) Award-winning Sarawak-based company with professional staff, imaginative sightseeing, multiday activity itineraries that combine the best of wildlife watching and cultural immersion, and a genuine interest in local people and the environment. Get in touch if you're heading to the Maliau Basin.

Borneo Authentic TOURS
(088-773066; www.borneo-authentic.com; lot 3, 1st fl, Putatan Point, Jln JKR Putatan; 8am-5pm Mon-Fri) A friendly operation offering a variety of package tours, including day-trip cruises on the Sungai Klias and combos that include visiting Pulau Tiga Resort on Pulau Tiga with Sungai Klias, as well as diving and cycling options. Located in Putatan, about 11km south of central KK.

Borneo Eco Tours OUTDOORS
(088-438300; www.borneoecotours.com; Pusat Perindustrian Kolombong Jaya, Mile 5.5 Jln Kolombong; 5-day, 4-night Maliau Basin trek per person RM5230; 9am-6pm) Arranges tours throughout Malaysian Borneo to Danum Valley, Mt Kinabalu, the Crocker Range and Maliau Basin, as well as a community-based program at Camp Lemaing (near Mt Kinabalu). Its office is about 6km northeast of the city centre.

Sutera Sanctuary Lodges TREKKING
(088-287887; www.suterasanctuarylodges.com.my; ground fl, lot G15, Wisma Sabah, Jln Haji Saman; 9am-5.30pm Mon-Fri, to 1pm Sat) Sutera runs

a lot of the tourism activities in Sabah, and has a monopoly on accommodation within Kinabalu National Park, as well as permits for trekking up Mt Kinabalu.

Sleeping

Hostels and cool cafes congregate on Lg Dewan, aka Backpacker Street, and along Jln Gaya. KK's midrange and budget options have been augmented by a proliferation of room- and apartment-sharing services. On the fringes of KK and further out there are several glitzy resorts.

Bunk HOSTEL $
(017-972 9128; http://the-bunk-hostel.kota-kinabalu-hotels.com/en; 113 Jln Gaya; dm R35;) Head up the steep stairs in the cosy little bar and you find yourself in a vast space with 33 bunks connected by metal walkways and scaffolding. Each comes with privacy curtains, creating a quiet pod into which to retreat. Lots of excursions on offer, too.

Akinabalu Hostel HOSTEL $
(088-272188; www.akinabaluyh.com; 133 Jln Gaya; dm/d/tr from RM25/65/95;) Jolly hostel with a welcoming common area, plant-filled space with water feature and bold, crimson-and-lime-green rooms. Some have natural light, while others face the corridor. It's worth splurging RM10 extra on air-con. The staff are friendly and helpful.

Borneo Backpackers HOSTEL $
(088-234009; www.borneobackpackers.com; 24 Lg Dewan; dm/s/d incl breakfast from RM30/60/80;) Turquoise and chic with Hoi An lanterns, choice art, wood floors and an excellent cafe (p324) down below firing up Asian fusion cuisine, this is one of KK's best backpacker haunts. Dorms and rooms are immaculate, (most) with art-stencilled walls, a balcony and reading room to chill in, and constantly whirring fans.

★Hotel Sixty3 HOTEL $$
(088-212663; www.hotelsixty3.com; 63 Jln Gaya; r/f/ste from RM281/442/668;) This fabulous award-winning hotel has an international feel in its 100 rooms, with glossy floors, evocative black-and-white photos of Kota Kinabalu and Sabah on the walls, subtle downlighting, flat-screen TVs, a smoke-free policy and refillable glass bottles for drinking water. Stylish, fresh and sustainable. There's no restaurant, but there are plenty of options in the neighbourhood.

Kooler Inn HOTEL **$$**

(📋 088-215551; www.hotelkoolerinn.com; 8 Jln Tugu; r RM115-148, f RM198; ❄️ 📶) Friendly staff preside over snug, well-appointed, spotless rooms that are within handy walking distance of most central attractions. The windowless doubles are a little claustrophobic; it's worth paying extra for a room with a window.

Hotel Eden 54 BOUTIQUE HOTEL **$$**

(📋 088-266054; www.eden54.com; 54 Jln Gaya; s/d/f RM109/139/239; ❄️ 📶) This compact, friendly hotel has plenty of boutique flair, with stylish rooms decked in chocolate drapes, glass-topped desks, contemporary bedsteads and burgundy or peacock-green walls. The communal kitchen area behind the lounge is a boon for flashpackers. Avoid windowless rooms, however, and note there are steep stairs to negotiate.

Jesselton Hotel HISTORIC HOTEL **$$**

(📋 088-223333; www.jesseltonhotel.com; 69 Jln Gaya; r/ste from RM215/515; ❄️ 📶) KK's first post-WWII hotel is plush and charming with its pink marble lobby, Persian carpets and baby grand piano. A colonial theme runs through to the rooms: Rungus bed runners, dark-wood panelling, sketches of local botany above the beds and small but marble-heavy bathrooms. The soundproofing could be better, but if you're after colonial character, this central hotel has it.

Shangri-La's Tanjung Aru Resort & Spa RESORT **$$$**

(STAR; 📋 088-327888; www.shangri-la.com/kota kinabalu/tanjungaruresort; Tanjung Aru; r from RM1500; 🅿️ ❄️ 📶 🏊) Located in the Tanjung Aru area, about 3km south of the city centre, this is one of the finest hotels in Sabah. There are beautifully stylish rooms with huge baths, comfy-as-cloud beds, sea-view balconies looking out over manicured, flower-filled gardens, spa treatments, a chic breakfast bar, plus lashings of water sports available.

Hilton Hotel Kinabalu HOTEL **$$$**

(📋 088-356000; www.kotakinabalu.hilton.com; Jln Tunku Abdul Rahman; r/ste from RM680/1210; ❄️ @ 📶 🏊) Smart and sleek, the Hilton has many modern touches. Rooms are straightforward international style with sumptuous beds, big TV and neutral colour scheme. There are big buffet breakfasts, multicuisine restaurants and a coffee shop that discounts its delicious cakes by 50% after 5pm. The rooftop pool is pure delight; next to it is the overchilled bar and grill.

Hotel Grandis HOTEL **$$$**

(📋 088-522888; www.hotelgrandis.com; Grandis Hotels & Resorts, Suria Sabah Shopping Mall 1, Jln Tun Fuad Stephens; r/f/ste from RM750/1100/1600; ❄️ @ 📶 🏊) Attached to the Suriah Sabah Shopping Mall, this four-star hotel is unfailingly clean and stylish. Standard rooms are huge, while family suites are large enough to tenpin bowl in. The last word in style, rooms have bath, plush modern fittings, downlighting and flat-screen TV. Sea-view rooms have soaring vistas of the waterfront.

Hyatt Regency Kota Kinabalu HOTEL **$$$**

(📋 088-221234; www.hyatt.com; Jln Datuk Salleh Sulong; r from RM680; 🅿️ ❄️ 📶 🏊) Built in 1967, the Hyatt looks decidedly dated from the outside, but inside it's a marble oasis of soaring ceilings, dark-wood chic and an inviting open-plan restaurant and lounge in the lobby. Low-lit rooms are huge, stylish affairs with all the mod cons: flat-screen TV, rain shower, fine linen. Be sure to ask for discounts outside of peak season.

Shangri-La's Rasa Ria Resort RESORT **$$$**

(📋 088-792888; www.shangri-la.com; Pantai Dalit; r incl breakfast from RM780; 🅿️ ❄️ @ 📶 🏊) Occupying a fine stretch of peach-hued dunes about 45 minutes' drive north of KK's airport, this beautiful resort has its own 18-hole golf course, several fine restaurants, a lovely pool (plus a great kids' pool with a twirly slide) and a relaxing spa. One of its best features is the small nature sanctuary.

Le Méridien Kota Kinabalu HOTEL **$$$**

(📋 088-322222; www.lemeridienkotakinabalu.com; Jln Tun Fuad Stephens; r/ste from RM640/1290; 🅿️ ❄️ 📶 🏊) Four-star comfort with a glass-and-wood-accented lobby and soothing lighting seguing blue to pink. Rooms are less inventive with international, somewhat anonymous decor, and flat-screen cable TVs and floor-to-ceiling windows (that don't open), but perks include six restaurants and a large rooftop pool. Avoid rooms with no view. Best prices online.

🍴 Eating

KK's eating scene is the best in Borneo and diverse enough to refresh the noodle-jaded palate. Besides the ubiquitous Chinese *kedai kopi* (coffee shops) and Malay halal restaurants, there are fusion restaurants, sushi, Italian, superb seafood, night markets and a trendy container market. Several speciality coffee shops, too.

★ Sri Latha Curry House INDIAN $
(☏088-253669; 28 Jln Berjaya; mains RM7-12; ☺7am-5pm; 🖉) Particularly good for its veggie thalis, this unassuming spot serves its spread of Indian dishes on banana leaves in a busy, cafeteria-like setting. Get here early at lunchtime to get a seat.

Kedai Kopi Yee Fung MALAYSIAN $
(☏088-312042; 127 Jln Gaya; laksa RM9; ☺6.30am-6pm) By far the best place in town to try authentic laksa, this place gets totally packed during lunchtime. You'll be directed to your plastic seat with military precision; slurp up your bowl of laksa and be on your way if you're here during the busiest times: this is not the place for a quiet tête-à-tête.

Yuit Cheong MALAYSIAN $
(☏088-252744; http://yc.weebly.com; 50 Jln Pantai; satay 10 skewers RM8; ☺6am-7pm Mon-Sat, 7am-7pm Sun) Though this *kopitiam* (coffee shop) has moved around during its long history, it's still going strong after more than 100 years in business and is KK's oldest coffee shop. It's renowned for its toast with *kaya* (coconut jam) and at noon the satay stall kicks off by the entrance, serving sizzling skewers of fragrant beef and chicken satay to a packed house.

Biru Biru FUSION $
(☏016-923 7258; www.facebook.com/birubirucafe; 24 Lg Dewan; mains RM11-19; ☺11am-midnight) Below Borneo Backpackers (p322) this blue joint with parasols and bikes on the wall features dishes such as *ikan basung,* poke bowls, fried mackerel with spicy sambal, vegetarian quesadillas and waffles with sweet toppings. Try the Lihing rice wine (aka, rocket fuel) or stick to the beer, fruit juices and cocktails. It's easy to fall in love with this place.

Yu Kee Bah Kut Teh CHINESE $
(☏088-221192; 74 Jln Gaya; mains RM8-11; ☺2-11pm) Expect brisk service at this bustling plastic-chair joint where tables are spread out onto the pavement and the chopsticks clack. The buffet counter bubbles with noodles and glistens with sauce-laden pork. That's right, Cantonese-style pork, in herbal soup, fatty pork ribs...every which way you can. It's hot, crowded and delicious.

MAKAN: KK-STYLE

KK's melting pot of cultures has fostered a lively dining scene that differentiates itself from the rest of Malaysia. KK's essential *makan* (food) experiences include the following:

Sayur manis Also known as 'Sabah veggie', this bright-green jungle fern can be found at any Chinese restaurant worth its salt. It's best served fried with garlic, or mixed with fermented shrimp paste. The *sayur manis* plant is a perennial and can grow about 3m high. It is harvested year round, so it tends to be very fresh.

Filipino barbecue Located at the north end of the KK Night Market, the Filipino Barbecue Market is the best place in town for grilled seafood at unbeatable prices. A similar market can be found at the Todak Waterfront just to the north. Hunker down at one of the crowded tables and point to your prey. On the shared tables are a basin (to wash your hands) and a small plate to prepare your dipping sauce (mix up the chilli sauce, soy sauce, salt and fresh lime for your own special concoction). Figure around RM15 to RM20 for a gut-busting meal.

Hinava Perhaps the most popular indigenous appetiser, colourful *hinava* is raw fish pickled with fresh lime juice, *chilli padi,* sliced shallots and grated ginger. The melange of tangy tastes masks the fishy smell quite well. The best place to try *hinava* is A-Square Night Market (p325); you'll find it, along with other indigenous Sabah foods, at the Punya Sadap stall.

Roti canai The ubiquitous *roti canai,* a flaky flat bread fried on a skillet, is served from dawn till dusk at any Indian Muslim *kedai kopi* (coffee shop) around town. Although the dish may appear simple, there's actually a lot of skill that goes into preparing the perfect platter. The cook must carefully and continuously flip the dough (à la pizza chef) to create its signature flakiness. *Roti canai* is almost always served with sauce, usually dhal or another curry made from either chicken or fish.

KK'S HAWKER CENTRES & FOOD COURTS

As in any Southeast Asian city, the best food in KK is the street food and hawker stalls. If you're worried about sanitation, you really shouldn't be, but assuage your fears by looking for popular stalls, especially those frequented by families.

Night Market (Jln Tun Fuad Stephens; dishes RM8-30, satay RM1.50; ⊙5-11pm) and **Todak Waterfront** (Jln Tun Fuad Stephens; mains RM8-20; ⊙5-10pm) These night markets are the best, cheapest and most interesting places in KK for barbecued squid, chicken hearts on sticks, fish and a vast selection of other delicious seafood cooked right before your eyes.

A-Square Night Market (Jln Tun Fuad Stephens; dishes from RM5; ⊙5-11pm) Undecided about what you'd like for dinner? Here you have over 30 containers and stalls to choose from, including Devil Laksa, Filipino barbecue, Chinese-style grilled seafood, gourmet hot dogs, Malay desserts, indigenous Sabah specialities, *hinava* (raw fish with lime and chilli), wild ferns and pickled bamboo shoots.

Centre Point Food Court (basement, Centre Point Shopping Mall, Jln Raya Pantai Baru; mains from RM4; ⊙9am-9.30pm; 🖉) Your ringgit will go a long way at this popular and varied basement food court in the Centre Point Mall. There are Malay, Chinese and Indian options, as well as drink and dessert specialists.

Kedai Kopi Fatt Kee CHINESE $
(28 Jln Bakau; mains from RM8; ⊙noon-10pm Mon-Sat) The woks are always flamin' and sizzlin' at this popular Cantonese joint below Ang's Hotel. Look out for sweet-and-sour shrimp, jungle fern, and oyster-sauce chicken wings.

★**Sakagura Japanese Restaurant** JAPANESE $$
(🖉088-273604; www.facebook.com/sakagurakk; G-23 & G-25, ground fl, Oceanus Waterfront Mall, Jln Tun Fuad Stephens; mains from RM20; ⊙11.30am-3pm & 5-10pm) A chorus of welcomes greets you as you walk into this minimalist Japanese place and a joyful call-and-response from the staff conveys your order to the chef. Choose from bento boxes, sashimi spreads and more. Good sake selection, too.

★**Chilli Vanilla** FUSION $$
(🖉088-238098; 35 Jln Haji Saman; mains RM19-35; ⊙10am-10.30pm Mon-Sat, 5-10.30pm Sun; 🖝) This cosy bijou cafe is run by a Hungarian chef and is a real fave with travellers thanks to its central location. The well-thought-out menu makes an eclectic voyage through goulash, smoked duck salad, Moroccan lamb stew, chilli-chocolate braised beef, excellent pasta and gourmet burgers. Wine is available by the glass or bottle.

Mother India INDIAN $$
(🖉088-276136; ground fl, lot G-40A, Oceanus Waterfront Mall, Jln Tun Fuad Stephens; mains RM20-55; ⊙11am-3pm & 5.30-10pm; 🖉) The enticing aromas lead you into this beautifully decorated restaurant accented with ochre and golden tones, pendant lighting and carved screens. With attentive staff, sparkling white china and linen napkins, Mother India is a cut above the rest. The food is Mughal-style Indian, with rich, creamy sauces accompanying the main ingredients, be they vegetables, fish, prawns, mutton or chicken.

Little Italy ITALIAN $$
(🖉088-232231; http://littleitaly-kk.com; ground fl, Hotel Capital, 23 Jln Haji Saman; mains RM20-38; ⊙10am-11pm Mon-Thu, to 11.30pm Fri-Sun; 🖉) This popular restaurant fairly buzzes with an army of bandanna-wrapped staff waiting on your every need. Good homemade pasta, great pizzas, Roman statues and, above all, consistency when it comes to cooking. Italian coffee, cold beer, wine by the glass? Check, check, check.

Welcome Seafood Restaurant SEAFOOD $$
(🖉012-805 2680; lot G, 18 Kompleks Asia City, Jln Asia City; per 100g RM6-40; ⊙noon-midnight) The crowded tables and queues of hungry patrons ready to pounce on any vacant seat speak volumes for the popularity of this place after sunset. If you want to experience the pleasure of choosing your live prey from its fish-tank confines, marrying it to a delicious sauce and feasting upon it, but without the crowds, then come for lunch.

Alu-Alu Kitchen SEAFOOD $$
(🖉088-230842; www.alualukitchen.com; Lg Mangga 1, Jln Kolombong; mains RM9-48; ⊙10am-3pm & 6-10pm) 🖝 This restaurant wears its stripes in the tastiness of its food, and the fact it gets its seafood from sustainable

sources. Alu-Alu excels in taking the Chinese seafood concept to new levels, with dishes such as lightly breaded fish chunks doused in a mouth-watering buttermilk sauce, or simmered amid diced chillies. A taxi/Grab ride from the centre should cost RM20/10.

Grazie Ristorante ITALIAN $$
(☎ 019-821 6936; http://grazierestaurantkk.wixsite.com/grazie; 3-36, 3rd fl, Suria Sabah Shopping Mall; mains RM25-73; ⏰ noon-10pm) Delightful Italian cuisine in a stylish restaurant with deep-red walls and an alfresco terrace with sea views. Dishes span homemade ravioli stuffed with fish and prawns to spaghetti bolognese, seafood risotto, heavenly thin-crust pizza and melt-in-the-mouth panna cotta. Beer and wine available.

Self-Catering

There is a variety of places to stock up on picnic items and hiking snacks, including the centrally located **Milimewa Superstore** (Jln Haji Saman; ⏰ 9.30am-9.30pm) and **Tong Hing Supermarket** (55 Jln Gaya; ⏰ 8am-10.30pm), the best such store in KK.

Drinking & Nightlife

There's a cluster of bars and a booming nightclub around the Waterfront Esplanade, with a few more options in the city centre. Don't expect craft beer, though. The coffee scene has become progressively good, with specialist coffee shops clustered along Lg Dewan, aka Backpacker Street.

★**October Coffee House** COFFEE
(☎ 088-277396; www.facebook.com/10October CoffeeHouse; Lg Dewan; ⏰ 10.30am-midnight; 🎵) Adding more appeal to backpacker street Lg Dewan, October is welcoming with a wood-accented interior and cosy mezzanine,

arguably the best coffee in town, herbal teas, French toast, juices and cakes. The food's as good as the coffee: interesting sandwiches include pastrami and kimchi.

Nook Cafe COFFEE
(☎ 088-275834; www.facebook.com/nookcafekk; 19 Jln Dewan; ⏰ 8am-11pm Thu-Tue; 🎵) 🍴 There's much to like about this cavernous coffee shop, strewn with rattan and bamboo furniture: the quality of the beans, a chilled environment in which to tap on your laptop, a tranquil covered garden out back, and great French toast and homemade Scotch eggs. It also promotes metal and bamboo straws and reusable coffee cups.

El Centro BAR
(☎ 014-862 3877; www.facebook.com/ElCentroKK; 32 Jln Haji Saman; ⏰ 5pm-midnight Tue-Sun) El Centro is understandably popular – it's friendly, its Tex-Med dishes and lamb pizza are good and it makes for a nice spot to meet other travellers. It has cool tunes and a laid-back vibe, and also hosts impromptu quiz nights, costume parties and live-music shows.

Fruto JUICE BAR
(☎ 088-212659; www.facebook.com/frutojuicebar; 12C Lg Dewan; ⏰ 10am-10pm Mon-Sat, 8am-9pm Sun) You know a city is undergoing gentrification when it acquires a 'lifestyle juice bar'. And as these places go, it's a very good one: you can power up on green-vegetable concoctions, or indulge your sweet tooth without worrying that your juice has been adulterated with sugar or ice. Our only quibble is the disposable plastic cups.

BED CLUB
(☎ 088-251901; www.facebook.com/BEDKK; Waterfront Esplanade; entry Fri & Sat incl drink RM20; ⏰ 8pm-2am, until 3am Fri & Sat) KK's largest club thunders with pop, gyrating Filipino musicians and shrill teenagers, and features guest DJs nightly. It's overcrowded and cheesy, but if you're looking for a party, this is it. Bands play from 9pm.

Shopping

KK has several uber-shiny malls chock-full of designer brands, but in terms of Borneo-specific purchases, we recommend a couple of speciality bookshops and a craft store in Wisma Merdeka that sells locally made gifts. The majority of gift shops sell mass-produced tat from China or the Philippines

SABAH KOTA KINABALU

ℹ️ **TANJUNG ARU**

In the early evening head to Tanjung Aru at the south end of town near the airport for sunset cocktails and light snacks along the ocean edge. The area has three beaches – First Beach offers up a few restaurants, Second Beach has steamy local stalls and several food trucks, and Third Beach is a great place to bring a picnic as there are no establishments along the sand. A taxi to Tanjung Aru costs RM20, or you can take bus 16, 16A or city bus 2 (RM2) from Wawasan Plaza.

and Balinese masks in the guise of 'made in Borneo'.

Sabah Museum Gift Shop   BOOKS
(Jln Muzium; ⊙9am-5pm) Across from the Sabah Museum, this place sells books on all things Borneo – from field guides to birds, fish and mammals to WWII history, indigenous culture and first-hand accounts of life in colonial British Sabah – check out the trilogy by Agnes Keith.

Sabah Batik & Craft   GIFTS & SOUVENIRS
(Wisma Merdeka, ground fl, Jln Tun Razak; ⊙10am-8pm) 🖉 If you're looking to support Sabah-made craftspeople, there is no better place in KK to buy containers, baskets, backpacks and other Murut and Dusun crafts, all expertly woven from natural fibres.

Borneo Shop   BOOKS
(☑088-538689; shop 26, ground fl, Wisma Merdeka Phase 2, Jln Haji Saman; ⊙10am-8pm) There's a wealth of wildlife and flora books here, all focused on Borneo.

ⓘ Information

EMERGENCIES
Ambulance ☑088-218166, 999
Fire ☑994
Police ☑088-253555, 999, Jln Balai Polis

IMMIGRATION
Immigration Office (Pejabat Imigresen; ☑088-488700; Kompleks Persekutuan Pentadbiran Kerajaan, Jln UMS; ⊙7am-1pm & 2-5.30pm Mon-Fri) In an office complex near the Universiti Malaysia Sabah (UMS), 9km north of town.

LAUNDRY
Cleansway Laundry (Asia City, Jln Singgahmata; wash/dry from RM8/4; ⊙24hr)
Laundry@25 (25 Lg Dewan; 1 load from RM6; ⊙8am-10pm)

MEDICAL SERVICES
Jesselton Medical Centre (☑088-366399; http://jmc.my; Jalan Metro 2, Metro Town Off, Jalan Lintas; ⊙24hr) Excellent private medical centre.
Gleneagles Kota Kinabalu (☑088-518911; http://gleneagleskk.com.my; Riverson@Sembulan, block A-1, Lg Riverson@Sembulan; ⊙24hr) Borneo's best private hospital, with emergency care and doctors from Singapore.

MONEY
Central KK is chock-a-block with 24-hour ATMs.
HSBC (56 Jln Gaya)

Maybank (9 Jln Pantai)
Standard Chartered Bank (20 Jln Haji Saman)

POST
Main Post Office (Jln Tun Razak; ⊙8am-5pm Mon-Sat) Western Union cheques and money orders can be cashed here.

TOURIST INFORMATION
Free maps of central KK and Sabah are available at almost every hostel or hotel.
Sabah Parks (☑088-523500, 088-486430; www.sabahparks.org.my; 1st-5th fl, lot 45 & 46, block H, Signature Office, KK Times Sq; ⊙8am-1pm & 2-4.30pm Mon-Thu, 8-11.30am & 2-4.30pm Fri, 8am-12.50pm Sat) Source of information on the state's parks.
Sabah Tourism Board (☑088-212121; www. sabahtourism.com; 51 Jln Gaya; ⊙8am-5pm Mon-Fri, 9am-4pm Sat, Sun & holidays) Housed in the historic post office building, KK's tourist office has plenty of brochures, maps and knowledgeable staff keen to help you with advice tailored around your needs. Its website is equally worth a visit. It runs free walking tours of KK three times weekly; double-check meeting times.
Tourism Malaysia (☑088-248698; www. tourism.gov.my; ground fl, Api-Api Centre, Jln Pasar Baru; ⊙8am-4.30pm Mon-Thu, 8am-noon & 1.30-4.30pm Fri) A few interesting brochures on sights in Peninsular Malaysia.

ⓘ Getting There & Away

AIR
KK is well served by Malaysia Airlines (www. malaysiaairlines.com) and AirAsia (www.airasia. com), which have international flights to/from Brunei, Shenzhen, Jakarta, Manila, Singapore and Taipei. Within Malaysia, flights go to/from Johor Bahru, Kuala Lumpur and Penang in Peninsular Malaysia, and Kuching, Labuan, Lawas, Miri, Kudat, Sandakan, Lahad Datu and Tawau in Borneo. Jetstar (www.jetstar.com) and Tiger Airways (www.tigerairways.com) offer flights to Singapore.

BOAT
Passenger boats connect KK to Pulau Labuan (adult 1st/economy class RM41/36, child 1st/economy class RM28/23, 3½ hours) twice daily at 8am and 1.30pm, with onward service to Brunei.

Speedboats link **Jesselton Point** (Jln Haji Saman) with the islands of Tunku Abdul Rahman National Park, while ferries connect Jesselton Point with Pulau Labuan. Tickets can be bought at the Jesselton Point **ticketing hall** (Jesselton Point Ferry Terminal; ⊙8am-6pm).

All passengers must pay an adult/child RM3.82/1.91 terminal fee for ferries departing from KK.

BUS

Several different stations around KK serve a variety of out-of-town destinations. There is a daily bus to Brunei.

In general, land transport heading east departs from **Inanam Bus Station** (Jln Undan) at Inanam, 9km north of the city, while those heading north on the west coast leave from **Padang Merdeka Bus Terminal** (Merdeka Field; Jln Tunku Abdul Rahman). Those heading south on the west coast leave from both Padang Merdeka and **Wawasan Plaza**, while the latter is being redeveloped. BSB services leave from the **City Park Bus Terminal** (Jln Haji Saman).

Local buses (RM2) departing from Wawasan Plaza can take you to Inanam if you don't want to splurge on the RM20 taxi or RM10 (or so) Grab ride. Have your lodgings call ahead to the bus station to book your seat in advance. Same-day bookings are usually fine, though weekends are busier than weekdays. It's always good to ring ahead because sometimes transport will be halted due to flooding caused by heavy rains.

TAXI

Share taxis operate from the Padang Merdeka Bus Terminal. Several share taxis do a daily run between KK and Ranau, passing the entrance road to the Kinabalu National Park office. The fare to Ranau or Kinabalu National Park is RM30 per person, or you can charter a taxi for RM120 per car (four passengers). Note that a normal city taxi will charge around RM350 to RM400 for a charter (return journey plus waiting time).

Download Grab, Malaysia's answer to Uber, for cheaper rides (roughly half a taxi fare).

ⓘ Getting Around

TO/FROM THE AIRPORT

Kota Kinabalu International Airport (KKIA; www.kotakinabaluairport.com; Jln Putatan, Tanjung Aru) is in Tanjung Aru, 7km south of central KK and takes around 25 to 40 minutes to reach by taxi or bus.

Airport shuttle buses (adult/child RM5/3) leave Padang Merdeka station every 45 minutes to an hour between 7.30am and 7.15pm daily. From the airport to the city, buses depart from 8am until 8.30pm. It's usually 45 minutes between services but some gaps are longer.

Taxis heading from terminals into the city operate on a voucher system (RM30) sold at a

MAIN DESTINATIONS & FARES FROM KOTA KINABALU

The following bus and minivan transport information was provided to us by the Sabah Tourism Board (p327) and should be used as an estimate only. Transport times can fluctuate due to weather, prices may change and the transport authority has been known to alter departure points.

DESTINATION	PRICE	DURATION	TERMINAL	DEPARTURES
Bandar Seri Begawan (Brunei)	RM100	8½hr	City Park Bus Terminal	8am
Beaufort	RM15	2hr	Padang Merdeka	7am-5pm (frequent)
Keningau	RM10-20	2hr	Padang Merdeka	7am, 8am, 10am, 1.30pm, 2.30pm, 4pm
Kota Belud	RM10	1hr	Padang Merdeka	6am-6pm (frequent)
Kuala Penyu	RM20	2hr	Segama Bridge	8-11am (hourly)
Kudat	RM25	3hr	Padang Merdeka	6am-6pm (frequent)
Lahad Datu	RM52	8hr	Inanam	7am, 9am, noon, 7pm, 8pm
Lawas (Sarawak)	RM25	4hr	City Park Bus Terminal	8am
Mt Kinabalu National Park	RM15-20	2hr	Inanam & Padang Merdeka	7am-8pm (very frequent)
Ranau	RM20	2hr	Padang Merdeka	7am-5pm
Sandakan	RM43	6hr	Inanam	7am-8pm (frequent)
Semporna	RM75	9hr	Inanam	7.30am, 8.30am, 2pm, 7.15pm & 7.30pm
Tawau	RM71.50	9-10hr	Inanam	7.30am, 8am, 10am, 12.30pm, 4pm & 8pm
Tawau via Keningau	RM61	7hr	Padang Merdeka	6.30am & noon
Tenom	RM20	3hr	Padang Merdeka	8am, noon, 2.30pm & 4pm

RIDING THE BORNEO RAILS

The Sabah State Railway is a 134km single track that stretches from **Tanjung Aru Station** (Jln Kepayan), 5km south of central KK, to Tenom (p384), up in the coffee-growing hills. Completed in 1906 it was used to transport tobacco to Jesselton (now KK), but was almost completely destroyed during WWII.

You have two options when it comes to riding the rails. One is to have a tourist-only, step-back-in-time experience aboard the twice-weekly **North Borneo Railway** (www.suteraharbour.com; Jln Putatan, Tanjung Aru; per person RM380), complete with vintage locomotive, scenic stops and tiffin lunch, from Tanjung Aru to the market town of Papar (RM380; book ahead in KK). The other is to ride two rickety local commuter trains – all open doorways, furnishings distressed to the point of being inconsolable – for a tiny fraction of the price (less than RM8 in total), either from Tanjung Aru to Beaufort (p385) or, even better, from Beaufort to Tenom, passing through the wonderfully scenic Padas Gorge and watching the rushing white water against the backdrop of dense jungle and lush countryside through your window. It's possible to ride all the way from Tanjung Aru to Tenom in one day: catch the 7.45am from Tanjung Aru and then the 1.30pm from Beaufort, overnighting in Tenom and returning the following day.

taxi desk on the terminal's ground floor. Taxis heading to the airport should also charge RM30 if you catch one in the city centre. Grab rides should cost no more than RM20.

CAR & MOTORCYCLE

Major car-rental agencies have counters on the 1st floor of the airport and branch offices elsewhere in town. Small cars start at around RM100 to RM160 per day and most agencies can arrange chauffeured vehicles as well.

Borneo Express (☑ 016-886 0793, in Sandakan 016-886 0789; http://borneocar.com; lot 1-L01 C4, Kota Kinabalu International Airport)

Extra Rent A Car (☑ 088-251529, 088-218160; www.e-erac-online.com; lot 31, 1st fl, Likas Sq Commercial Centre, Jln Istiadat, Likas)

Kinabalu Heritage Tours & Car Rental (☑ 088-318311; www.sabahborneotours.com; block F, Tanjung Aru Plaza; ⊙ 9am-6pm)

GogoSabah (☑ 012-838 5566, 088-276796; www.gogosabah.com; lot G4, ground fl, Wisma Sabah, Jln Haji Saman; ⊙ 9am-6pm Mon-Sat) Yamaha FZ150 and Honda Future motorbikes for hire, as well as 125cc scooters.

MINBUS

Minibuses operate from several stops, including Padang Merdeka Bus Terminal, Wawasan Plaza and the car park outside Milimewa Superstore (near the intersection of Jln Haji Saman and Beach St). They circulate the city looking for passengers. Since most destinations in the city are within walking distance, it's unlikely that you'll need to catch a minibus, although they're handy for getting to the airport or to KK Times Sq. Most destinations within the city cost RM4 to RM6.

TAXI

Expect to pay a minimum of RM15 for a ride in the city centre (even a short trip!). Taxis can be found throughout the city and at all bus stations and shopping centres. There's a **stand** (near cnr Jln Haji Saman & Beach St) by Milimewa Supermarket and **another** 200m southwest of City Park. For cheaper rides download the Grab app.

TUNKU ABDUL RAHMAN NATIONAL PARK

Whenever you enjoy a sunset off KK, the view tends to be improved by the five jungly humps of Manukan, Gaya, Sapi, Mamutik and Sulug islands. These swaths of sand, plus the reefs and cerulean waters in between them, make up **Tunku Abdul Rahman National Park** (www.sabahparks.org.my; adult/child RM10/6), covering a total area of just over 49 sq km (two-thirds of which is water). Only a short boat ride from KK, the islands are individually quite pretty, but in an effort to accommodate the ever-increasing tourist flow (especially large numbers of Chinese), barbecue stalls and restaurants now crowd the beaches. On weekends the islands can get *very* crowded, but on weekdays you can easily find some serenity. Snorkelling and diving are the islands' big draws.

❶ Getting There & Away

Your first step is to head to the ticketing hall at Jesselton Point Ferry Terminal (commonly known as 'The Jetty' to locals and taxi drivers)

ℹ THE SABAH LOOP

A decent sealed road makes a frowning arc from KK to Tawau, passing Mt Kinabalu, Sepilok, Sandakan, Lahad Datu and Semporna (the gateway to Sipadan) along the way. The same can be said of the other half of the loop (going back to KK from Tawau via Keningau). It passes right by the entrance of the formerly elusive Maliau Basin, and is a much quicker way of driving from Tawau to KK (seven hours versus 10 to 12 hours) as well as a stupendously scenic drive through primary and secondary forest (once you get past the palm-oil plantations, that is).

in KK. Counters one to 11 are operators of boats to Mamutik, Manukan and Sapi islands. To reach Pulau Sulug or Pulau Gaya you either have to charter a boat or go with a diving outfit. Choose your company, your tour (one, two or three islands), activity (snorkelling, parasailing, sea walking etc) and then sign up for that company's next departure. Take a seat in the waiting area until the staff indicate it's time to depart. Usually they try to remain on schedule, but they may wait 15 minutes or so to see if they can attract more passengers.

Boats to the park leave from 8am to 4pm. The last boats leave the islands for KK around 5pm. Service is every 30 minutes, but on slower days this can be every hour.

Boats also run from Sutera Harbour – more convenient for those staying near Tanjung Aru (or for those wanting to reach Pulau Gaya). Return fares to Mamutik, Manukan and Sapi hover around adult/child three to 12 years RM23/18. You can also buy two-/three-island passes for adult RM33/43, child three to 12 years RM23/28.

The set fee to charter a boat privately to one/two/three islands is RM250/350/450, but this can be negotiated.

A terminal fee of adult/child RM7.63/3.82 plus 6% GST is added to all boat journeys, as well as an entrance fee to the national park (adult/child RM10/6), paid when you purchase your ticket (if you are chartering a boat, this should be included).

Pulau Manukan

Though this dugong-shaped island may not lay claim to a beach as beautiful as Sapi, beneath its waters you'll find far richer coral, and therefore more marine life, attracting snorkellers and divers. Currents tend to be strong on the north and west sides of the island, which affects visibility, as do the crowds

in the water and the trash that gets washed in from elsewhere. It is the second-largest island in the group, with its 20 hectares largely covered in dense vegetation. There's a good beach with coral reefs off the southern and eastern shores, a walking trail around the perimeter and a network of nature trails – if you want to thoroughly explore all of the above it shouldn't take more than two hours, and you don't need to be particularly fit.

Manukan Island Resort (☎017-833 5022; www.manukan.com; Pulau Manukan; r from RM991; ✳ ☎ ☎ ☎) has the only non-camping accommodation on the island. It comprises a restaurant, swimming pool, tennis courts and 20 dark-wood villas, all overlooking the South China Sea and decked out in tasteful Bali-chic style.

Pulau Mamutik

Mamutik is the smallest island in Tunku Abdul Rahman National Park, a mere 300m end to end. A sandy 200m beach runs up and down the east coast, but beware of razor-sharp coral beneath the water that can cut your feet. Visibility can sometimes be poor due to strong waves, but on a still day the snorkelling is OK. There's a nice, short walking trail that ends on a cliff overlooking the water. Better still, Pulau Mamutik picks up a small portion of the day-tripper footfall, so if you're here during the week, it will be mercifully quiet.

Borneo Divers (p320) has its diving academy here, and the shallow reefs, largely intact coral and calm, clear waters make this a good place to do your PADI diving course. Camping (RM40 per tent) is available, with basic Sabah Parks facilities – bring your own mosquito repellent. You'll also find a small store-restaurant-snorkel-rental place, barbecue stalls, resting pavilions, gift shop and public toilets. The last boat back to Jesselton Point is at 4pm.

Pulau Sapi

The tiny sibling to Pulau Gaya, separated by a 200m channel, attracts huge loads of day trippers to its lovely beach and can get overwhelmed on weekends. There are lifeguards keeping vigil on the beach, and clearly defined areas for swimming. The deep turquoise waters between Pulau Sapi and Pulau Gaya, where the reef drops off, hides decent amounts of sea life and makes for good snorkelling. Other fun things to do include spotting monitor lizards (corralled behind a fenced area next to the main entrance) and flying between Pulau Sapi and Gaya on a zip line.

Beachside activities include walking under the sea with **Borneo Sea Walking** (Sapi dock, Pulau Sapi; 30-min sea walk RM250; ⊙8.30am-3pm), snorkelling with equipment rented from **Seasport** (Sapi dock, Pulau Sapi; fins, mask & snorkel per day RM15; ⊙8am-4pm) (though drifts of trash in the water can make the experience far from idyllic), and flying over the water on the **Coral Flyer zip line** (☑011-2984 2023; www.coralflyer.com; Sapi dock, Pualu Sapi; adult/child RM86/45; ⊙10am-3.30pm). Alternatively you can explore the trails through Sapi's forest; it takes about 45 minutes to walk around the island.

Sabah Parks runs a basic outfitted campsite (RM40 per tent) with musty tents and basic toilet facilities. There's a large barbecue area, popular with day trippers, and a small snack kiosk. The last boat back is at 4pm.

Pulau Gaya

☑088

With an area of about 15 sq km, Pulau Gaya is the Goliath of KK's offshore islands, rising to an elevation of 300m. It's also the closest to KK and covered in virtually undisturbed coastal dipterocarp forest, bisected by several worthwhile walking trails.

For most visitors Gaya's raison d'être is its three diving resorts on the east side of the island, as well as its impressive underwater topography. All three island resorts offer diving courses, and Downbelow (p321) has a diving academy on the west side of the island.

The bays on the east end are filled with bustling water villages, inhabited by Filipino immigrants (legal and otherwise) who live in cramped houses built on stilts in the shallow water. Mosques, schools and simple shops are also built on stilts.

Regular boats don't run to Pulau Gaya. The diving-resort packages include speedboat transfers; otherwise you can charter a boat from Jesselton Point for around RM200.

🛏 Sleeping

★**Gaya Island Resort**   RESORT $$$
(☑KL 03-2783 1000; www.gayaislandresort.com; Pulau Gaya; villas from RM1640; ❄🛜🏊) Around

100 beautifully finished villas set in either lush jungle foliage, atmospheric mangroves, or looking out on the greens and blues of the sea. This is a beautiful spot to fish, snorkel, dive, kayak, practise yoga, go on a sunset cruise or take a relaxing spa at the treatment centre. On-site dive school offers a range of courses.

Gayana Marine Resort   RESORT $$$
(☑088-380390; www.echoresorts.com/gayana; Pulau Gaya; villas from RM1226; ❄🛜🏊) 🍴 Fifty-two stunning villas stuffed with modern amenities and island-chic touches make up posh Gayana. The Bakau (mangrove) Villa overlooks a tangled, flooded forest, while the Palm Villa's deceptive simplicity masks steps that lead into the warm heart of Tunku Abdul Rahman's protected waters. Minimum two-night stay mid-July through August.

Bunga Raya Island Resort   RESORT $$$
(☑088-380390; http://bungarayaresort.com; Pulau Gaya; villas from RM1316; ❄🛜🏊) Well-spaced villas with mod cons from satellite TVs to safe-deposit boxes, iPod docks and Bose sound systems are spread around this tasty resort. The deep plunge pool overlooks the beach, while the romantic Treehouse, reached by a private walkway, perches over a jacuzzi, lounge and its own natural jungle pool. Minimum two-night stay mid-July through August.

Pulau Sulug

Shaped like a cartoon speech bubble, 8-hectare Pulau Sulug is the least visited of the Tunku Abdul Rahman island group, probably because it's the furthest from KK. It only has one beach, on a spit of land extending from its eastern shore, and calm, clear waters for snorkelling. If you want a quiet getaway, Sulug is a decent choice, but you'll have to charter a boat to get here (at least RM250) as the regular boats don't stop at the island. Coming here with a diving outfit is fantastic, as Sulug's two main diving sites attract exciting pelagic life, such as turtles, barracuda and octopus.

NORTHWESTERN SABAH

The northern edge of Sabah manages to compact, into a relatively small space, much of the geographic and cultural minutiae that makes Borneo so special. The ocean?

SABAH PULAU GAYA

Lapping at miles of sandy beach, sky blue to stormy grey, and concealing superlative dive sites. The people? Kadazan–Dusun, Rungus, rice farmers, mountain hunters, ship builders and deep-sea fishers. And then, of course, 'the' mountain: Gunung Kinabalu, or Mt Kinabalu, the focal point of the island's altitude, trekkers, folklore and spiritual energy. For generations the people of Sabah have been drawn to the mountain; don't be surprised when you fall under its spell, too.

Mt Kinabalu & Kinabalu National Park

Gunung Kinabalu, as it is known in Malay, is the highest mountain on the world's third-largest island. It is also the highest point between the Himalayas and New Guinea. Rising almost twice as high as its Crocker Range neighbours, and culminating in a crown of wild granite spires, it is a sight to behold. March to August (dry season) is considered to be the best time to climb.

The 4095m Mt Kinabalu may not be a Himalayan sky-poker, but Malaysia's first Unesco World Heritage Site is a major drawcard, attracting thousands of climbers every year. The climb, by no means an easy jaunt, is essentially a long walk up a very steep hill, through jungle then barren moonscapes, with a little scrambling thrown in for good measure. On a clear day you can see the Philippines from the summit; often, though, the mountain is wreathed in cloud.

History

The 15-million-year-old mountain's name is derived from the Kadazan Dusun tribe's phrase 'Aki Nabalu', meaning the resting place of the souls of the departed. Although it is commonly believed that local tribesmen climbed Kinabalu many years earlier, it was Sir Hugh Low, the British colonial secretary on Pulau Labuan, who recorded the first official ascent of Mt Kinabalu in 1851. Today Kinabalu's tallest peak is named after him; thus Borneo's highest point is ironically known as Low's Peak.

In those days the difficulty of climbing Mt Kinabalu lay not in the ascent, but in getting through the jungle at the mountain's base. Finding willing local porters was another tricky matter – the tribesmen who accompanied Low believed the spirits of the dead inhabited the mountain. Low was therefore obliged to protect the party by supplying a large basket of quartz crystals and teeth, as was the custom back then. During the subsequent years, the spirit-appeasement ceremonies became more and more elaborate, so that by the 1920s they had come to include loud prayers, gunshots and the sacrifice of seven eggs and seven white chickens. You have to wonder at what point explorers started thinking the locals might be taking the mickey...These days, the elaborate chicken dances are no more, though climbing the mountain can still feel like a rite of passage.

On 5 June 2015, an earthquake measuring 6.0 on the Richter scale struck Mt Kinabalu. Massive landslides and huge rockfalls followed. Even one of the famous 'Donkey's Ears' rock formations snapped off. The strongest quake to affect Malaysia since 1976, it lasted 30 seconds and tragically took the lives of 18 people, many of them students from Singapore. There were 137 people stranded on the mountain but later rescued. That first evening alone three massive aftershocks were felt, and by 23 June, 90 had been felt as far away as Kota Kinabalu.

Geology

Many visitors to Borneo assume Mt Kinabalu is a volcano, but the mountain is actually a huge granite dome that rose from the depths below some nine million years ago. In geological terms Mt Kinabalu is still young. Little erosion has occurred on the exposed granite rock faces around the summit, though the effects of glaciers that used to cover much of the mountain can be detected by striations on the rock. There's no longer a snowline and the glaciers have disappeared, but at times ice forms in the rock pools near the summit.

Orientation & Information

Kinabalu National Park headquarters is 88km by road northeast of KK and set in gardens with a magnificent view of the mountain. At 1588m the climate is refreshingly cool compared to the coast – the average temperatures are 20°C in the day and 13°C at night. The hike to the summit is difficult.

On the morning of your arrival, pay your park entry fee, present your lodging reservation slip to the Sutera Sanctuary Lodges office to receive your official room assignment, and check in at the visitors centre to pay your registration/permit and guide fees. Advance accommodation bookings are *essential* if you plan on climbing the mountain.

Permits, Fees & Guides

A park fee, climbing permit, insurance and a guide fee are *mandatory* if you intend to climb Mt Kinabalu. All permits and guides must be arranged at the **Sabah Parks office** (Climbers Registration Office; Kinabalu Park headquarters; ⏱ 7am-7pm), which is next door to the Sutera Sanctuary Lodges office, immediately on your right after you pass through the main gate of the park. Pay all fees at park headquarters before you climb and don't ponder an 'unofficial' climb as permits (laminated cards worn on a string necklace) are scrupulously checked at two points you cannot avoid passing on the way up the mountain. Virtually every tour operator in KK can hook you up with a trip to the mountain; solo travellers are often charged around RM1400. It's possible, and a little cheaper, to do it on your own – but plan ahead. Packages are obviously easier.

All visitors entering the park are required to pay a **park entrance fee**: RM15 for adults and RM10 for children under 18 (Malaysians pay RM3 and RM1 respectively). A **climbing permit** costs RM200/80 for adults/children, while Malaysian nationals pay RM50/30. **Climbing insurance** costs a flat rate of RM7 per person. **Guide fees** for the summit trek cost RM230 for a group of one to five people.

Your guide will be assigned to you on the morning you begin your hike. If you ask, the park staff will try to attach individual travellers to a group so that guide fees can be shared. Couples can expect to be given their own guide. Guides are mostly Kadazan, from a village nearby, and many of them have travelled to the summit several hundred times. Try to ask for a guide who speaks English – he or she (usually he) might point out a few interesting specimens of plant life. The path up the mountain is pretty straightforward, and the guides walk behind the slowest member of the group, so think of them as safety supervisors rather than trailblazers.

All this does not include at least RM1069 for dorm and board, or RM2000 for private room and board, on the mountain at Laban Rata. With said lodging, plus buses or taxis to the park, you're looking at spending over RM1700 for the common two-day, one-night trip to the mountain.

Optional extra fees include the shuttle bus (RM34, one-way) from the park office to the Timpohon Gate, a climbing certificate (RM10) and a porter (RM160 per return trip to the summit, or RM130 to/from Laban Rata), who can be hired to carry a maximum load of 10kg.

If you need a helicopter lift off the mountain for emergency reasons, the going rate is around RM6000.

Equipment & Clothing

No special equipment is required to successfully summit the mountain, though a head torch is strongly advised for the predawn jaunt to the top – you'll need your hands free to climb the ropes on the summit. Expect freezing temperatures near the summit, as well as strong winds and the occasional rainstorm. Don't forget a water bottle, which can be refilled at unfiltered (but potable) tanks en route. The average temperature range at Kinabalu National Park is 15°C to 24°C. Along the Timpohon (the summit trail) it's about 6°C to 14°C, and can sometimes drop to as low as 2°C.

The Climb to the Summit

This schedule assumes you're doing a two-day, one-night ascent of the mountain, since hikers are no longer allowed to attempt a one-day ascent and descent (no matter how

KINABALU PACKING LIST

- ☐ Head torch (with spare batteries)
- ☐ Comfortable hiking shoes
- ☐ Whistle
- ☐ Energy food (Dextrasol tablets, sweets, chocolate, energy bars)
- ☐ Wool socks and athletic socks
- ☐ Hiking shorts or breathable pants
- ☐ Three T-shirts (made of quick-dry synthetic material)
- ☐ Fleece jacket
- ☐ Lightweight shell jacket, poncho, or rain jacket
- ☐ Fleece or wool hat
- ☐ Gloves
- ☐ Hand towel
- ☐ Water bottle
- ☐ Sunscreen
- ☐ Sunglasses
- ☐ Insect repellent
- ☐ Camera
- ☐ Money
- ☐ Earplugs for dorms

fit they are!). You'll want to check in at park headquarters at around 9am (7am at the latest for *via ferrata* participants) to pay your park fees, grab your guide and start the ascent (four to six hours) to Laban Rata (3272m), where you'll spend the night before the summit climb. On the following day you'll start scrambling to the top at about 2.30am in order to reach the summit for a breathtaking sunrise over Borneo.

A climb up Kinabalu is only advised for those in adequate physical condition. The trek is tough, and *every step you take* will be uphill. You will negotiate several obstacles along the way, including slippery stones, heavy humidity, frigid winds and slow-paced trekkers. Mountain Torq compares the experience to squeezing five days of hiking into a 38-hour trek.

There is now only one trail option leading up the mountain – the Timpohon Trail (the trailhead is an hour's walk, or short park shuttle ride, from the entrance to Kinabalu National Park). The Mesilau Trail was badly damaged in the 2015 earthquake and is closed for good. If you are participating in Mountain Torq's *via ferrata,* you are required to reach Laban Rata in time for your safety briefing at 4pm.

As you journey up to the summit, you'll happen upon signboards showing your progress – there's a marker every 500m. There are also rest shelters *(pondok)* at regular intervals, with basic toilets and tanks of unfiltered (but potable) drinking water. The walking times we give are conservative estimates. Don't be surprised if you move at a slightly speedier pace, and certainly don't be discouraged if you take longer – everyone's quest for the summit is different.

Timpohon Gate to Layang Layang

'Why am I sweating this much *already*?'

> ### ⓘ CLIMBING SPACES
>
> The Amazing Borneo (p321) website provides an easy way of checking how many spaces are left to climb Mt Kinabalu on any given day, and of booking the whole thing online. If you have no reservation for a night on the mountain at Laban Rata, go to the Sutera office and wait for a last-minute cancellation; you will be informed if there is space in one of the huts.

The trip to the summit officially starts at the Timpohon Gate (1866m) and from there it's an 8.7km march to the summit. There is a small toilet located 700m before the Timpohon Gate and a convenience shop at the gate itself for impulse snack and beverage purchases.

After a short, deceptive descent, the trail leads up steep stairs through the dense forest and continues winding up and up for the rest of the trip. There's a charming waterfall, **Carson's Falls**, beside the track shortly after the start, and the forest can be alive with birds and squirrels in the morning. Five *pondok* (shelters) are spaced at intervals of 15 to 35 minutes between Timpohon Gate and Layang Layang and it's about three hours to the Layang Layang (2621m) rest stop. Near **Pondok Lowii** (2286m), the trail follows an open ridge giving great views over the valleys and up to the peaks.

Layang Layang to Pondok Paka

This part of the climb can be the most difficult for some – especially around the 4.5km marker. You've definitely made some headway, but there's still a long trek to go – no light at the end of the jungly tunnel quite yet. It takes about 1¾ hours to reach **Pondok Paka** (3053m), the seventh shelter on the trail, 5.5km from the start.

Pondok Paka to Laban Rata

Also known as the 'can't I pay someone to finish this for me?' phase, this part of the climb is where beleaguered hikers get a second wind as the treeline ends and the summit starts to feel closer. At the end of this leg you'll reach **Laban Rata** (3272m), your home sweet home on the mountain. Take a good look at the slender signpost announcing your arrival – it's the propeller of the helicopter once used to hoist the construction materials to build the elaborate rest station. This leg takes around 45 minutes.

Laban Rata to Sayat-Sayat Hut

It's 2am and your alarm just went off. Is this a dream? Nope. You're about to climb the last part of the mountain in order to reach the summit before sunrise.

Most people set off at around 2.45am, and it's worth heading out at this time even if you're in great shape (don't forget your torch). The one-hour climb to **Sayat-Sayat** hut (3668m) involves a lot of hiker traffic

Mt Kinabalu Summit Trail

4003m
Victoria Peak
(4094m) ▲

St Andrews
▲ Peak (4052m)

Ugly Sister
Peak
(4032m)

Alexandra   Low's Peak
Peak (4003m)   (4095m) ▲

Ulu Sungai Penataran

St John's   8km•
Peak (4091m)   Donkey
                         Ears
75km•   7km•   (4055m) ▲
Kinabalu   Sayat-Sayat Hut
South   6.5km•   (3668m)
(4032m) ▲   •Gunting

6km• Pendant Hut (3323m)
Laban Rata Resthouse (3272m)   Burlington Hut
Helipad   (3270m)
Waras Hut (3243m)   Pondok Paka
Paka Cave•   (3053m)
         5.5km• •Helipad
         5km•   Pondok Villosa
                 (2942m)

Mesilau
(4km) →

•4.5km

4km• Layang Layang
      Staff Quarters (2621m)
•3.5km
      Pondok Mempening
      (2518m)
•3km
2km• •2.5km
      Pondok
      Lowii (2286m)
1.5km• Pondok
        Ubah (2059m)

Sungai Kolopis

Sungai Liwagu

Sleeping
Shelter

Vegetation Zones
Bare Rock
Mixed Dipterocarp Forest
Rainforest

1km•
Carson's   Pondok
Falls   Kandis (1981m)
            Timpohon
Power   Gate (1866m)
Station
Bukit Ular Park Headquarters
Trail →   (4km)

and the crossing of the sheer Panar Laban rock face. There is little vegetation, except where overhangs provide some respite from the wind. It is one of the toughest parts of the climb, especially in the cold and dark of the predawn hours. Note that on some particularly steep sections, you have to haul yourself up specially strung ropes (gloves essential).

Sayat-Sayat Hut to Summit

After checking in at Sayat-Sayat, the crowd of hikers begins to thin as stronger walkers forge ahead and slower adventurers pause for sips from their water bottles. Despite the stunning surroundings, the last stretch of

the summit ascent is the steepest and hardest part of the climb.

From just beyond Sayat-Sayat, the **summit** looks deceptively close and, though it's just over 1km, the last burst will take between one to three hours, depending on your stamina. You might even see shattered climbers crawling on hands and knees as they reach out for the top of Borneo.

The Summit

This is it – the million-dollar moment. Don't forget the sunrise can be glimpsed from anywhere on the mountain. In the predawn, teeth chatter and hikers huddle together for warmth, as it's practically freezing at the top. The summit warms up quickly as the sun starts its own ascent between 5.45am and 6.20am, and the weary suddenly smile; the climb is now a distant memory, the trek down an afterthought.

Consider signing up with Mountain Torq to climb back to Laban Rata along the world's highest *via ferrata,* in which case you have to start heading down at 6am in order to meet your guide at 6.30am at the 7.5km mark. The Low's Peak Circuit *via ferrata* takes four to five hours to complete.

The Journey Back to the Bottom

You'll probably leave the summit at around 7.30am and you should aim to leave Laban Rata no later than 12.30pm. The gruelling descent back down to Timpohon Gate from Laban Rata takes between three and four hours. The weather can close in very quickly and the granite is slippery even when dry. During rainstorms the downward trek feels like walking through a river. Slower walkers often find that their legs hurt more the day after – quicker paces lighten the constant pounding as legs negotiate each descending step. If you participated in the *via ferrata* you will be absolutely knackered during your descent and will stumble into Timpohon Gate just before sunset (around 6pm to 6.30pm).

A 1st-class certificate can be purchased for RM10 by those who complete the climb;

2nd-class certificates are issued for making it to Laban Rata. These can be collected at the park office.

Walks Around the Base

It's well worth spending a day exploring the marked trails around park headquarters – if you have time, it may be better to do it before you climb the mountain, as chances are you won't really feel like it afterwards. There are 10 trails and lookouts, though three of the trails – Bukit Ular, Liwagu and Mountain View – were closed at research time and may or may not reopen.

The base trails interconnect with one another, so you can spend the day, or indeed days, walking at a leisurely pace through the beautiful forest, spotting interesting plants, plenty of birds and, if you're lucky, the occasional mammal. When it rains, watch out for slippery paths and legions of leeches.

At 11am each day a guided walk (per person RM5) starts from the Sabah Parks Office (p333) and lasts for one to two hours. The knowledgeable guide points out flowers, plants, birds and insects along the way. If you set out from KK early enough, it's possible to arrive at the park in time for the guided walk.

Many of the plants found on the mountain are cultivated in the Botanical Garden (p340) behind the visitors centre. Guided tours of the garden depart at 9am, noon and 3pm and cost RM5.

VIA FERRATA

Mountain Torq (📞 088-268126; www.mountaintorq.com; Kinabalu Park headquarters; Low's Peak Circuit RM2050, Walk the Torq RM1830) has dramatically changed the Kinabalu climbing experience by creating an intricate system of rungs and rails crowning the mountain's summit. Known as *via ferrata* (literally 'iron road' in Italian), this alternative style of mountaineering has been a big hit in Europe for the last century and is starting to take Asia by storm. Mountain Torq is Asia's first *via ferrata* system, and, according to the *Guinness Book of World Records,* it's the highest 'iron road' in the world.

After ascending Kinabalu in the traditional fashion, participants use the network of rungs, pallets and cables to return to Laban Rata along the mountain's dramatic granite walls. Mountain Torq's star attraction, the **Low's Peak Circuit** (minimum age 17), is a four- to five-hour scramble down metres upon metres of sheer rock face. This route starts at 3766m, passing a variety of obstacles before linking up to the Walk the Torq path for the last part of the journey. The route's threadlike tightropes and swinging planks will have you convinced that the course designers are sadistic, but that's what makes it such fun – testing your limits without putting your safety in jeopardy. Your guide may encourage you to lean back for the photo shoots, with nothing between you and the abyss but your safety belt and harness. Those who don't want their heart leaping out of their chest should try the **Walk the Torq** (minimum age 10) route. This two- to three-hour escapade is an exciting initiation into the world of *via ferrata,* offering dramatic mountain vistas with a few less knee-shaking moments. No matter which course you tackle, you'll undoubtedly think that the dramatic vertical drops are nothing short of exhilarating.

FLORA & FAUNA OF MT KINABALU

Mt Kinabalu is a botanical paradise, designated a Centre of Plant Diversity as well as a Unesco-listed World Heritage Site. The altitudinal range of habitats supports a wide range of flora, and over half the species growing above 900m are unique to the area.

Among the more spectacular flowers are orchids, rhododendrons and the insectivorous *nepenthes* (pitcher plant). Around park headquarters, there's dipterocarp rainforest. Creepers, ferns and orchids cling to the trunks and branches of forest giants, while fungi feed on the forest floor. Between 900m and 1800m there are oaks, laurels and chestnuts, while higher up there's dense rhododendron forest. On the windswept slopes above Laban Rata, vegetation is stunted, with *sayat-sayat* a common shrub. The mountain's uppermost slopes are bare of plant life.

Deer and monkeys are no longer common around park headquarters, but you can see squirrels, including the handsome Prevost's squirrel and the mountain ground squirrel. Tree shrews can sometimes be seen raiding rubbish bins. Common birds are Bornean treepies, fantails, bulbuls, sunbirds and laughing thrushes, while birds seen only at higher altitudes are the Kinabalu friendly warbler, the mountain blackeye and the mountain blackbird. Other wildlife includes colourful butterflies and the huge green moon moth.

🛏 Sleeping

🛏 Laban Rata (On The Mountain)

Camping is not allowed on the mountain, and thus access to the summit is limited by access to the huts on the mountain at Laban Rata (3272m); only 135 climbing permits are issued daily. Accommodation *must* be booked in advance, the earlier the better, because without a prior accommodation booking, you may not climb. In order to have any hope of clear weather when you reach the summit you must arrive around dawn, and the only way to do this is by spending a night at Laban Rata.

Sutera Sanctuary Lodges (p322) in Kota Kinabalu operates almost all of the accommodation at Laban Rata, and space is limited. Bookings can be made online (easiest done via the Amazing Borneo (p321) website), in person or over the phone.

The most common sleeping option is the non-heated dormitory (bedding included) in the **Laban Rata Resthouse** (http://sutera sanctuarylodges.com.my; Laban Rata; dm/tw incl 3 meals RM1069/2000). If you need privacy, three heated twin shares are available. Three meals are included in the price. **Waras Hut** acts as the dorm spillover.

The other option at Laban Rata is **Pendant Hut** (☑088-268126; www.mountaintorq. com; Laban Rata; r incl via ferrata RM850-4000), which is owned and operated by **Mountain Torq**. All guests sleeping at Pendant Hut take two of three meals at Sutera's cafeteria, and are required to participate in (or at least pay for) the *via ferrata* circuit. Pendant Hut is slightly more basic (there's no heat, though climbers sleep in uberwarm sleeping bags), but there's more chance of a last-minute space than at the Laban Rata Resthouse.

🛏 Park Headquarters (At the Base) & Around

Sleeping options located at the base of the mountain, operated by **Sutera Sanctuary Lodges** (www.suterasanctuarylodges.com; Kinabalu Park headquarters; ⊙8.30am-4.30pm Mon-Sat, to 12.30pm Sun), range from spacious suites to bare-bones bunks. They're expensive compared to numerous sleeping spots just outside the park entrance and in the nearby village of Kundasang.

Grace Hostel HOSTEL $$
(dm incl breakfast RM150) Clean, comfortable, 20-bed hostel (choose between four- and six-bed dorms) with fireplace and drink-making area.

Rock Hostel HOSTEL $$
(tw incl breakfast RM250) Small, clean twin rooms that share common bathrooms. There is an inviting common lounge.

Hill Lodge CABIN $$$
(cabins incl breakfast RM896) These semi-detached cabins are a good option for those who can't face a night in the hostel or in a twin with a share bathroom. They're clean and comfortable, with private bathrooms.

Kinabalu National Park Headquarters & Trails

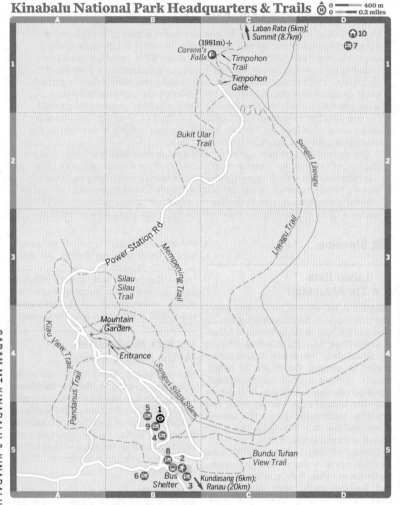

Kinabalu National Park Headquarters & Trails

◉ Sights
1 Botanical Garden B5

✛ Activities, Courses & Tours
2 Mountain Torq B5

🛏 Sleeping
3 D'Villa Rina Ria Lodge........................... B5
4 Grace Hostel B5
5 Hill Lodge... B5
6 J Residence.. B5
7 Laban Rata Resthouse D1
8 Liwagu Suites.. B5

9 Nepenthes Lodge B5
  Peak Lodge ....(see 4)
10 Pendant Hut D1
  Rock Hostel ....(see 4)

✕ Eating
  Liwagu Restaurant............................(see 8)
  Restoran Kinabalu Balsam ....(see 8)

ℹ Information
  Sabah Parks Office ....(see 2)
  Sutera Sanctuary Lodges................(see 2)

Liwagu Suites HOTEL **$$$**
(ste incl breakfast RM1037; 🖵) These four split-level suites with rain showers can be found in the Liwagu Building. While they sleep up to four people, they're best for couples as they contain only one mezzanine bedroom and one living room.

Nepenthes Lodge LODGE **$$$**
(unit incl breakfast RM1509) These attached two-storey units fall somewhere between hotel rooms and private lodges. They have two bedrooms (one with a twin bed, one with a queen) and verandahs offering limited mountain views.

Peak Lodge LODGE **$$$**
(cabins incl breakfast RM1886) These semi-detached cabins have two bedrooms (one with a bunk bed and one with two twin beds), pleasant sitting rooms, fireplaces and nice views from their verandahs.

✕ Eating

✕ Laban Rata (On The Mountain)

At Laban Rata the cafeteria-style restaurant in the Laban Rata Resthouse (p337) has a simple menu and also offers buffet meals. Most hikers staying at Laban Rata have three meals (dinner, breakfast and lunch) included in their accommodation packages. It is no longer possible to negotiate a price reduction if you plan on bringing your own food. Buffet meals can also be purchased individually – dinner costs RM75, breakfast RM55 and lunch RM45. A small counter in the dining area sells an assortment of items, including soft drinks, chocolate, pain relievers and postcards.

✕ Park Headquarters (At the Base)

In addition to a small shop selling snacks, ice creams and drinks at the park's main office, there are two nearby restaurants. Most lodgings outside the park entrance have attached restaurants.

Restoran Kinabalu Balsam CAFETERIA **$**
(Kinabalu Park headquarters; dishes RM5-15, buffet breakfast/lunch/dinner RM40/55/65; ⊙ 6.30am-10pm Mon-Fri, to 11pm weekends) The cheaper and more popular of the two options in the park is this canteen-style spot directly below the park visitors centre. It offers basic but decent Malaysian, Chinese and Western dishes at reasonable prices. There is also a small but well-stocked shop in Balsam selling tinned and dried foods, chocolate, beer, spirits, cigarettes, T-shirts, bread, eggs and margarine.

Liwagu Restaurant CAFETERIA **$$**
(Kinabalu Park headquarters; dishes RM10-30; ⊙ 8am-10pm Mon-Fri, to 11pm weekends) This pleasant cafe serves a huge range of dishes, including noodles, rice, fresh fruit juices, seafood standards and an 'American breakfast'.

ⓘ Getting There & Away

It is highly advised that summit seekers check in at the park headquarters by 9am, which means if you're coming from KK, you should plan to leave no later than 7am, or consider spending the night somewhere near the base of the mountain.

BUS
Express buses (RM30) leave KK from the Inanam bus station every hour on the hour from 7am to 10am and at 12.30pm, 2pm and 8pm and leave at the same times in the reverse direction. Alternatively take a Ranau-bound minivan (RM25) from central KK at Padang Merdeka bus terminal, asking the driver to drop you at a **bus shelter** (Jln Kota Belud – Ranau) outside the gate at Kinabalu National Park. Minivans leave when full and run from early morning till around 2pm. We recommend leaving by 7am at the very latest for the two-hour trip.

Express buses and minivans travelling between KK and Ranau (and Sandakan) pass the park turn-off, 100m uphill from the park entrance. From Sandakan express buses leave at 6.30am, 7am, 9am, 12.30pm, 2pm and 8pm (RM 40, 4½ hours), ideal if you're not looking to hike until the following day.

4WD
Share 4WDs park just outside of the park gates and leave when full for KK (RM200 per 4WD) and Sandakan (RM500). Each 4WD can hold around four to five passengers, and they can be chartered by individuals.

TAXI
Shared taxis leave KK from Inanam and Padang Merdeka bus stations (RM30 per person, RM120 per vehicle).

Around Mt Kinabalu

There are several spots surrounding Mt Kinabalu that are also worth exploring, including Poring Hot Springs and **Ranau**. The

SABAH AROUND MT KINABALU

latter, a collection of concrete shop blocks on the road between KK and Sandakan, hosts a busy Saturday **night market** (off Jln Kembar Pekan; ⊙ 4pm-late Sat), and it's a bus hub, but otherwise there's little here to detain you.

◉ Sights & Activities

Kundasang War Memorial
MEMORIAL

(Kota Kinabalu–Ranau Hwy, Kundasang; adult/child RM10/1; ⊙ 8.30am-5pm) At Kundasang, beside the KK–Ranau Hwy, 10km east of Kinabalu National Park headquarters, is this poignant memorial conceived in 1961. It commemorates the Australian and British prisoners who died on the infamous Sandakan Death Marches and at the Sandakan and Ranau POW camps, as well as those from Borneo who died while assisting the prisoners. Four modest gardens individually represent the Australians, the British and the people of Borneo, plus a colonnaded Contemplation Garden.

In the Contemplation Garden is a list of the deceased and at the back of this garden there is a stunning vista of Mt Kinabalu.

Botanical Garden
GARDENS

(Kinabalu National Park; adult/under 18 RM15/10; ⊙ 9am-1pm & 2.30-4pm) Many of the plants found on Mt Kinabalu and in Kinabalu National Park are cultivated in the Botanical Garden, north of the visitors centre. Guided tours of the garden depart at 9am, noon and 3pm and cost RM5.

Sabah Tea Garden
PLANTATION

(☑ 088-440882; www.sabahtea.com.my; KM17, Jln Ranau–Sandakan; admission free, guided tour RM14, with set lunch RM44; ⊙ 8am-4.30pm) A pretty tea plantation huddles in the mountains near Ranau, producing the famous Sabah Tea. Contact the garden to arrange tours of both the plantation and surrounding rainforest and river valleys. Overnight packages (room/cottage RM140/280, camping per person RM30) are available in a cosy bungalow, a traditional longhouse or campsite. Also offers tours of the facilities coupled with a trip for a fish foot massage (RM120). It gets pretty nippy at night, so take a sweater if staying overnight.

Pialungan Sandakan-Ranau Death March Memorial
MEMORIAL

(Tambunanan–Tawau road; RM3; ⊙ 8am-5pm) In 1945 Sabah-occupying Japanese sent 641 British and 1793 Australian POWs on a series of forced marches from Sandakan

to Ranau. Only six – all Australians – survived by escaping and being cared for by locals. The rest perished from illness, hard labour and harsh living conditions, or were killed outright by their captors. The memorial stone names the 183 men who were killed at this last camp, beside a bend in the Kagibangan river below. It's 6km south of Ranau.

Poring Hot Springs
HOT SPRINGS

(Poring Hot Springs; adult/child incl Kinabalu National Park RM15/10; ⊙ entrance gate 7am-5pm, park until 8pm, Butterfly Garden & Canopy Walk closed Mon) The more pleasant part of the legacy of the Japanese invasion of Borneo during WWII, Poring Hot Springs consists of a dozen-or-so small pools and tubs, fed with hot sulphurous water from an underground spring. It's a great place for a soak after trekking up Mt Kinabalu, especially if you don't mind smelling like a rotten egg afterwards.

For our ringgit, the highlight of Poring Hot Springs is actually way above the springs: a **canopy walkway** (RM15; ⊙ 9am-4pm Tue-Sun) that consists of a series of walkways suspended from trees, up to 40m above the jungle floor, providing unique views of the surrounding forest. Get there early if you want to see birds or other wildlife. A tropical garden, **butterfly farm** (adult/child RM5/3; ⊙ 9am-4pm Tue-Sun) and **orchid garden** (adult/child RM10/5; ⊙ 9am-4pm) are also part of the Poring complex. Rafflesia sometimes bloom in the area; look out for signs in the visitors centre and along the road.

⌂ Sleeping

There are midrange and budget places to stay outside the park, most on the road between the park headquarters and Kundasang (6km east of the park's main entrance), as well as in Kundasang proper.

J Residence
BUNGALOW $

(☑ 012-869 6969; www.jresidence.com; Jln Kota Belud – Ranau; r/tr RM88/99, villa RM480; ☎) Just 300m from Kinabalu National Park's entrance, this tasteful accommodation clinging to the mountainside is redolent with the scent of surrounding pine trees – fresh and peaceful. Eight rooms with wood floors, balcony and bathroom, plus tasteful linen and soaring views. Note the prices listed are weekday prices; add an additional 40% at the weekend.

Kundasang Guesthouse
GUESTHOUSE $$

(☑017-831 8797; www.kundasangguesthouse.com; Jln Kundasang Lauluan, Kundasang; r/f from RM160/220; ❋🛜) This smart brick guesthouse with great views of Mt Kinabalu from its terraces sits in a quiet cul-de-sac in Kundasang village. Most of the spotless rooms and units are geared towards families and there are barbecue facilities for those who feel like cooking. Small restaurant, too.

Mesilau Atamis
HOMESTAY $$

(☑019-580 2474, 013-886 2474; Mesilau; r from RM370) The trademark signing says that it's 'The coldest and highest homestay village in Malaysia',. This organisation has nine different households you can stay in, with cultural activities included in the price of an overnight stay. You need your own wheels to get up there, but the views are worth it.

D'Villa Rina Ria Lodge
LODGE $$

(☑011-601 6936, 088-889282; www.dvillalodge.com.my; Km 53, Jln Tinompok; dm/d/q RM30/120/220; 🛜) Close to the Kinabalu National Park entrance, with 'traveller magnet' tattooed across its open restaurant and spartan yet balconied rooms with jaw-dropping valley views. This is a great one-stop shop – literally. Stock up on everything from batteries to chocolate, and socks to ponchos here. Rooms are basic with yellow walls, cosy quilts and piping-hot showers.

❶ Getting There & Around

Kinabalu National Park operates a minibus service between the headquarters and Poring for RM25 – it leaves the park headquarters (p339) at noon.

KK round-trip buses stop in Ranau (RM25 to RM30, two hours) from 7am to 8pm. Minibuses operate from a blue-roofed shelter in Ranau, servicing the nearby attractions (park headquarters, Poring etc) for RM5. Several buses daily head to Keningau (RM20, three hours) via Tambuan, and several minibuses serve Sandakan (RM30, four hours) throughout the morning.

Northwest Coast

The northwest coast of Sabah is criminally underexplored. The A1 runs north from KK to Kudat and the Tip of Borneo past wide headlands, rice paddies and hidden beaches. This is a good area for renting a car or motorbike – the roads are pretty level, and public transport links aren't reliable for getting off the main road.

Tuaran

☑088 / POP 3300

Tuaran, 33km from KK, is a bustling little town with tree-lined boulevard-style streets and the distinctive nine-storey **Ling Sang Pagoda**, its approaches dominated by vividly painted guardian deities. There's little point stopping in the town itself unless you happen to pass through on a market day (Tuaran is likely named for the Malay word *tawaran,* or 'sale', reflecting its history as a trading post), but the surrounding area conceals a few cool sights. You'll see signs for **Mengkabong Water Village**, a Bajau stilt village built over an estuary, but development and pollution have diminished this spot's charms. If you're on your way to Mt Kinabalu and have time to kill, there's a mildly quirky **museum** (The Upside Down House; ☑088-260263; www.upsidedownhouse.com.my; Kampong Telibong, Batu 21, Jln Telibong Tamparuli; Upside Down House adult/child RM19/5, 3D Wonders Museum adult/child RM35/15, combo ticket adult/child RM48/19; ⏰7am-7pm; P♿) just outside Tuaran.

All buses north from KK pass through Tuaran, and minivans shuttle regularly to and from KK (RM6 to RM10, 30 minutes). Minivans to Mengkabong are less frequent and cost RM2. Regular minivans go from Tuaran to Kota Belud (around RM15, 30 minutes).

Kota Belud

☑088 / POP 8500

This bustling town makes for a useful stopover en route to Mantanani or Kudat. Other than the gold mosque on the hill, and the presence of cows blithely wandering the streets, the town's Sunday *tamu* (market) – a congested, colourful melee of vendors, hagglers and hawkers – is definitely worth your camera's time.

Once a year in October, Kota Belud hosts the famous **Tamu Besar**, the biggest market organised in Sabah. The highlight is a procession of fully caparisoned Bajau horsemen from the nearby villages, decked out, along with their steeds, in vivid, multicoloured satin 'armour' and embroidered barding. The best way to experience this commercial event is to come not expecting to buy anything – soak up the convivial, occasionally manic atmosphere, and enjoy a good meal at the lovely food stalls.

Most people visit Kota Belud as a day trip from KK, since you can make it there and back with plenty of time for the market.

There's very little reason to stay in Kota Belud, but if for some unlikely reason you get stranded here, there are several low-key hotels.

🏃 Activities

⭐ Bigfin Divers
DIVING

(📱 012-389 0424; www.bigfindivers.com; Kampung Mengkabar, Kota Belud; 2 dives RM280, PADI 4-day Open Water course RM1150) This excellent outfit offers PADI courses and diving on a nearby reef within the 'coral triangle', a reef so large it's not yet been charted. If you're looking to dive for several days, it has camping spots (two nights' camping and six dives RM800) and en-suite rooms (two nights and six dives RM920). Access is by boat only.

Mayne Point has huge granite boulders, while Ella's Garden is coral-rich and bursting with squid, cuttlefish, nurse and leopard sharks, stingrays, barracuda and – if you're here between April and June – whale sharks. Dive sites, including a downed WWII Japanese tanker, are close by, so you waste little time getting there, and on a clear day as you ascend from the depths you can clearly see Mt Kinabalu in the distance. April to June are the best months for diving here.

ℹ️ Getting There & Away

Minivans and share taxis gather in front of Pasar Besar, the old market. Most of these serve the Kota Belud–KK route (RM10, two hours) or Kudat (RM20, two hours), departing from 7am to 5pm. To get to Kinabalu National Park, take any minibus going to Ranau; all pass the park entrance (RM20, 1½ hours).

Kudat

📱 088 / POP 32,400

With its sunburnt buildings, fishing boats on the bay and slow tropical pace, Kudat may grow on you. Believe it or not, sleepy Kudat used to be an important trading post and capital of Borneo back in the late 19th century. You may notice some of the streets have Chinese names, harking back to the British administration's request to the Chinese to come and run its coconut plantations. Many of their descendants are still here today, along with a warm cast of Bajau, Rungus and Filipino.

Kudat town's impressive **Fuk Tek Kung Temple** (Jln Ibrahim Arshad; ⊙ hours vary) by the main square is worth a look, or you might visit the photogenic (and odiferous) **Tamu Kudat** (Jln Lintas; ⊙ 6am-2pm Tue & Wed), a market selling tropical fruits, dried fish and edible seaweed. For travellers without their own wheels, Kudat is just the jumping-off point for visiting the Tip of Borneo, but once the ferry service to the Philippines commences, the town may become more popular.

There are several unmemorable hotels in central Kudat, but nothing that'll get your heart racing.

ℹ️ Getting There & Away

There are twice-weekly flights with Malaysia Airlines from Kudat to Kota Kinabalu (40 minutes) and Sandakan (50 minutes) from **Kudat Airport** (Jln Bawah).

The **bus station** (Jln Ibrahim Arshad) is in Kudat Plaza in the western part of town, very close to the Ria Hotel. Destinations include KK (RM25, three hours, twice daily), Kota Belud (RM15, 1½ hours, twice daily) and Sandakan (RM60, eight hours, one daily). Minivans and jeeps also operate from here; a ride to KK in a full van will cost around RM50.

Tip of Borneo

📱 088 / POP UNDER 3000

Sabah's northernmost headland, at the end of a wide bay 40km from Kudat, is known as Tanjung Sipang Mengayu, or the Tip of Borneo. Magellan reputedly landed here for 42 days during his 16th-century round-the-world voyage. Once a wild promontory, this windswept viewpoint where the cliffs meet the sea is dominated by a large, truncated globe monument. But the monument is not what you come for. You come for the surreal, punch-drunk sunsets, for some of Borneo's loveliest beaches (that you'll likely have all to yourself), for Malaysia's best surfing, for lazy hours spent watching Rungus kids kicking a football in between bamboo-and-thatch houses, and for clear, starry nights undimmed by nonexistent streetlights. Even though visitors have been coming here for years, most of the time you'll still feel as if you've stumbled upon a well-kept secret.

◎ Sights & Activities

Between November and February there's great surfing off Kosohui Beach. There's good diving off the coast, too. On land, you can go jungle trekking, hammocking (sleep overnight in the jungle), or do a jungle survival course in the Tampat Do Aman nature reserve. The local Rungus villages are interesting to explore on foot or on wheels, and locals are very friendly.

Kudat Turtle
Conservation Society   WILDLIFE RESERVE
(☑013-839 7860; www.ktcsborneo.com; Kampung
Bavang Jamal; conservation fee RM15) 🏊 Run
by Roland, the Kudat Turtle Conservation
Society is based at the south end of the
Bavang Jamal beach. There's an education
centre nearby and it's possible to assist
the society on night vigils at local beaches
to protect the eggs of green and hawksbill
turtles.

Rungus Museum   MUSEUM
(Jln Marang Parang, Tampat Do Aman; RM5; ⊙9am-
5pm) At the Tampat Do Aman guesthouse
(p343), this worthwhile museum aims to
preserve traditional Rungus culture, with
detailed displays on marriage and funeral
rites, the Rungus language, gongs in traditional music and the role of the *bobohizan*
(female elder).

Tampat Do Aman
Nature Reserve   NATURE RESERVE
(Jln Marang Parang) Part of the 2.4-hectare
property of Tampat Do Aman, this small
nature reserve, across the road from the
eponymous jungle camp, has several walking trails and a watchtower for looking out
over the dense forest. Good for spotting civets, monkeys and other wildlife. Tampat Do
Aman owner Howard holds jungle survival
courses here.

★ Borneo Biostation   DIVING
(☑010-803 7310; www.borneobiostation.com; Jln
Bak Bak; 2 dives from RM280) This excellent,
highly experienced diving outfit runs excursions into the Banggi Strait, seeking out
the best wall, drift, wreck and reef dives
off Pulau Banggi and the surrounding islands, as well as off the Tip of Borneo. Full
range of PADI courses offered and you
can stay on site in comfortable, spacious,
air-conditioned chalets (two-person chalet
RM260 to RM320).

Blue Fin Diving   DIVING
(☑012-826 1662; Pantai Kosohui; 1 dive RM150,
2 dives RM250; ⊙8am-5pm) Reputable operator offering a range of dive options and
courses. Also has surfboards for rent (RM30
per hour); surfing lessons cost RM80 per
hour. Blue Fin also acts as custodian of
the community-owned bamboo huts and
Rungus longhouse next door (room with/
without air-conditioning RM150/120), just
steps away from the lovely Kosohui Beach.

SURF'S UP

Surfing is beginning to take off on the
west coast of Sabah, thanks to swells
produced by the South West and North
East monsoons – November to February being the best time to catch a glassy
wave. The top spot is the northern Tip of
Borneo, where the beautiful white-sand
beaches and turquoise water are not
the only pull – when the conditions are
right, there's very clean surf with glassy
lefts and rights, perfect peels, and faces
varying in size from 2ft to 9ft. Also
there's no bad-tempered, overcrowded
line-up – but for the odd local, the waves
are yours and board hire is easy.

For surf lessons and board rental,
check out Blue Fin Diving.

🛏 Sleeping

Tampat Do Aman   GUESTHOUSE $
(☑013-880 8395; http://tampatdoaman.com; Jln
Marang Parang; r from RM50, chalet/family chalet
RM175/220; 🐱) 🏊 With its maze of jungle
walkways, atmospheric Rungus longhouse
rooms, fan-cooled chalets and bamboo
huts overlooking hibiscus-rich gardens,
this is a fine place to stay. Owner Howard
and his Rungus wife pour the profits into
local initiatives like school building and
nature conservation, and numerous ecofriendly practises abound. There's an on-site
museum and wildlife reserve, and the food
is terrific. Recommended.

Tip of Borneo Lodge   RESORT $$
(Tommy's Place; ☑013-811 2315, 088-493468;
http://tipofborneoresort.com; Pantai Kosohui; r
with/without air-con from RM150/100, villas RM280;
❄🐱) 🏊 With its welcoming cafe, this is a
good place to stay right near the actual Tip
of Borneo. The older cabins are fan cooled,
and there's a row of appealing cabins with
terraces and air-conditioning for up to four
people. The villas on the hill have widescreen
views, huge beds and flat-screen cable TV.

★ Hibiscus Beach Retreat   BUNGALOW $$$
(☑019-895 0704; www.hibiscusbeachretreat.com;
Jln Marang Parang; 2-person bungalows incl breakfast RM575-625) Perched on a hill overlooking a
beautiful 1.5km swath of sand lapped by teal-
green sea, these two bijou one-bedroom caba-
nas, Treetops and Clifftop, have high thatch
roofs, fan-only rooms, self-catering facilities,

sundeck with loungers and contemporary art. Order a fresh fruit breakfast, snorkel, then kick back, watch the sunset and prepare for the barbecue, cooked by a local chef.

⭐ **Hibiscus Villa Borneo** VILLA $$$
(☑ 019-895 0704; www.hibiscusvillaborneo.com; Jln Marang Parang; per night from RM1100; ❄ 🛜 🏊) With its infinity pool, dark-wood floors, moody subdued lighting and exquisitely chosen furniture, this fine three-bedroom villa on a private beach leaps straight from the pages of a glossy interiors magazine. It's both a wonderful place to disconnect and an excellent base for active pursuits – from stand-up paddleboarding to diving and snorkelling.

🍴 Eating

The Secret Place Cafe MALAYSIAN $
(☑ 010-414 5291; secretplaceborneo@gmail.com; Pantai Bavang Jamal; mains RM7-10; ⊘ 8.30am-9.30pm) This family-run joint on Bavang Jamal Beach is popular for its nasi goreng, fresh fish, chicken wings and barbecued food. Whatever's been caught finds its way to the grill. There are hammocks to lounge in and drink up the sea view. You can even rent a tent (single/double RM40/50) and owner Roby is planning to add guest rooms.

Tip Top Restaurant INTERNATIONAL $$
(☑ 013-880 8395; http://tampatdoaman.com. my/tip-top-restaurant-tip-of-borneo-kudat-sabah/; Pantai Kosuhui; mains RM9-18; ⊘ 8am-8pm; 🛜) Just steps from the beach, with terrific food ranging from *hinava* (local take on ceviche) to swordfish steak, curries, cheesecake, sweet-and-sour chicken, breakfast, carrot cake and fresh juices. Complement your dinner or beer with killer sunsets on the outdoor decked area. Run by the excellent Tampat Do Aman, Tip Top doubles as the local nightspot.

❶ Getting There & Away

The Tip of Borneo is around 30km from Kudat. There's no public transport, so you'll need to negotiate a taxi from Kudat (around RM100) or drive yourself along the newly paved road. Some accommodation places offer free transfers, provided you notify them in advance.

Island Getaways

The scattering of gem-like islands lying off Sabah's northwest coast will appeal mainly to divers.

Pulau Mantanani

The 3km-long **Pulau Mantanani Besar** (Big Mantanani Island) and **Pulau Mantanani Kecil** (Little Mantanani Island) are two little flecks of land fringed by bleach-blond sand and ringed by a halo of colourful coral, about 25km off the coast of northwest Sabah (about 40km northwest of Kota Belud). Dugongs are spotted here from time to time, as is the rare Scops owl. The islanders, commonly referred to as Bajau sea gypsies, have clashed with the government because of their opposition to resorts buying up land for development.

The two islands are not the peaceful idyll they once were, with large groups of tourists coming here on day trips, particularly on weekends. Stay on the island, however, and it's still a chance to cut free of the outside world for a few days. You can night kayak and night dive here, bird-watch or take a sunset cruise.

Mari Mari Backpackers Lodge (☑ 088-260501; www.riverbug.asia; Pulau Mantanani; dm RM250, tw per person RM310; 🛜) has simple but welcoming raised stilt chalets *(sulaps)* around a white-sand beach. **GreenHouse Lodge** (☑ 012-455 9402; Pulau Mantanani; r per person RM450) – dedicated to sustainable living and bursting forth from a riot of greenery, a minute's walk from Pulau Mantanani's loveliest beach – is the kind of place that travellers find themselves reluctant to leave, largely due to the warmth of hosts Fred and SP. Excellent meals, good snorkelling and crimson-and-gold sunsets on your doorstep. Two-night minimum stay includes transfers from KK.

Boat transfers from Kota Belud are included in the package price of staying at the lodges. Transport from KK also arranged.

Pulau Banggi

If you want to fall off the map, head to Pulau Banggi, 40km northeast of Kudat where the Sulu and South China Seas meet. The Banggi people, known locally for their unusual tribal tree houses, are Sabah's smallest indigenous group, and speak a unique non-Bornean dialect. The island itself is unimpressive, with a trash-strewn main fishing settlement and beach and little else. However, you can negotiate with fishers to take you to the stunning, nearby Pulau Maliangin, a small island that really is a postcard-esque slice of sand, tropical trees and clear water – the snorkelling is excellent here, but you have to bring your own gear. Further out, and pricier to reach, is Pulau Balambangan, another beautiful island with 12 impressive caves, one of which you can explore.

Firmly in the 'coral triangle', one of the most biodiverse submarine habitats on earth, the diving around Pulau Banggi and neighbouring Pulau Maliangin, Pulau Malawali, Pulau Panukaran, and Pulau Balak is superb, but be warned: due to its proximity to the Balabic Straight Corridor, the currents are a challenge, so most dives are only for experienced drift divers. There are wreck dives, 20m to 50m down, and you'll possibly see whale sharks, turtles, dolphins and a colourful mix of coral from gorgonian fans to staghorns and bubble. Amid this are batfish, clownfish, squid and moray eels. Keep an eye out too for dugongs, thanks to the presence of the island's mangroves and seagrasses. Borneo Biostation (p343) runs highly recommended dives here from its resort on the Tip of Borneo.

There are two official lodging options in the main settlement of Karakit: **Bonggi Resort** (seriously below par) and the basic but clean **Hotel Karakit** (☑ 011-1601 3156; r RM80; ☒). For a much better time, go with one of the locals offering a homestay experience for around RM60 to RM70 per night once you step off the boat.

Kudat Express (☑ 088-328118; Jln Wan Siak; one way 1st class/economy RM18/15) runs a twice-daily ferry between Kudat and the main settlement on Pulau Banggi. It departs Kudat's pier (near the Shell station) at around 8.30am and 1pm daily. In the reverse direction it leaves Pulau Banggi daily at around 7.15am and 3pm. Departure times are subject to change; check locally.

Layang Layang

This turquoise-haloed coral atoll, 300km northwest of KK, is actually artificial, constructed for the Malaysian Navy and debated among scubaholics as one of the top-10 dive sites in the world. However, what lies beneath what is now an exclusive diving resort could only have been created by nature: Technicolor reefs teeming with gorgonian fans, excellent visibility and impossibly steep walls down to 2000m. Beyond the macro fish found in its 20m-deep lagoon – seahorses, pipefish, cuttlefish and batfish – large pelagics to the outer walls include

hammerhead, grey reef, leopard, thresher, silvertip and whale sharks, as well as orcas, dolphins, mantas and devil rays.

Keep in mind that there is no decompression chamber at Layang Layang, so don't press your luck while underwater. The resort only provides air – no nitrox.

The island's location offers absolute isolation; the only way to get here is by plane from Kota Kinabalu.

The only accommodation on the island, **Avillion Layang Layang** (☑ in Kuala Lumpur 03-2730 9941; www.avillionlayanglayang.com; 6-day, 5-night all-inclusive package, twin share per person from US$1500; ☒ ☒) is all about diving. The five daily meals – that's right, five – are scheduled around the dive times. The standard rooms are very comfortable, with aircon, TV, private verandahs and hot-water showers. The all-inclusive packages include accommodation, food, 12 boat dives and tank usage.

The resort operates its own Antonov 26 aircraft, which flies every Tuesday, Thursday, Friday and Sunday between KK and Layang Layang (though MASWings is due to take over once contracts are finalised). The flight over from KK in this bare-bones Russian prop plane is a big part of the adventure. The return flight costs US$460, which is not included in the accommodation-food-dive package.

EASTERN SABAH

Eastern Sabah takes nearly everything that is wonderful about the rest of Borneo and condenses it into a richly packed microcosm of the island, consisting of equal parts adventure, wildlife, undersea exploration and flat-out fun. Let's tick off some of the natural wonders of this relatively tiny corner of the island: the rescued orangutans and sun bears of Sepilok; the chocolate-coloured crocodile highway of the Sungai Kinabatangan, with pot-bellied proboscis monkeys perched in the trees above; forest canopies that reach for the sky in the Danum Valley and Tabin; plunging sea walls rainbow-spattered with tropical marine life in the Semporna Archipelago; a forest as old as human civilisation in the Maliau Basin; cycling adventures all over Sabah from a Lahad Datu launch pad; and leopard cats and civets prowling the night forest in the newly protected reserves of Deramakot and Imbak Canyon. Did we pique your interest?

Sandakan

☑ 089 / POP 276,800

Looking out across the teal-blue Bay of Sandakan, dotted with fishing trawlers, to distant isles, it's easy to visualise the remarkable past of the former capital of British Borneo, with its exotic cast of foreign interests – German traders, Dutch and Chinese planters, Arab and Indian traders, and pearl divers. Sadly it was razed to the ground during WWII by the British in an attempt to shake off the grip of the invading Japanese. After the war a roaring timber trade blossomed here, with wood from Borneo exported all over the world. Today this little city is buzzing again with the success of the palm-oil industry and the busy, compact city centre retains little of its former colonial romance.

As well as being a gateway to the Sungai Kinabatangan and Sepilok, Sabah's second city is dotted with religious relics, colonial mansions and haunting mementoes of WWII.

⊙ Sights

Central Sandakan is where you'll find numerous historic attractions, and history buffs will appreciate the *Sandakan Heritage Trail* brochure available at hotels and tour agencies. The city centre, where you'll find most hotels, banks and local transport, consists of a few blocks squashed between the waterfront and a steep escarpment from where you can look out over the bay, Teluk Sandakan.

★**Agnes Keith House**   MUSEUM
(☑089-221140; www.museum.sabah.gov.my; Jln Istana; RM15; ⊙9am-5pm) This atmospheric two-storey colonial villa, Newlands, tells the story of American writer Agnes Keith and her British husband Harry, the Conservator of Forests in North Borneo. They lived in Sandakan from 1934 to 1952 and spent three years in Japanese internment camps during WWII. The house was immortalised by Keith in her award-winning, funny and engaging portrayal of colonial life in *Land Below the Wind*.

To get here, take the Tangga Seribu (100 Steps) to Jln Istana.

This is the second incarnation of their abode, with the original destroyed during the war. Newlands has been immaculately restored, its polished wooden floors gleaming and period furniture in place. Photos of the family and of Sandakan in the 1930s and artefacts such as brass gongs, Chinese stoneware jars, Penan blowpipes and woven Murut backpacks add to the atmosphere.

Sandakan Memorial Park   HISTORIC SITE
(http://sandakandeathmarch.com; Jln Taman Rimba; ⊙9am-5pm) A beautiful rainforest garden marks the site of a Japanese POW camp and starting point for the infamous WWII 'death marches' to Ranau. Of the 1793 Australian and 641 British troops originally imprisoned here, the only survivors by July 1945 were six Australian escapees. A concrete water tank and a few rusting machines from the British agricultural station that became a prison comprise the only physical remains. A pavilion recounts the horrors and heroism and includes photographs and survivor accounts.

Download the app, Sandakan, to learn more about the camp, the privations endured (particularly by Australians, seen as troublemakers by the Japanese), the horrific diet and the locals who saved and hid the six surviving Australians.

To reach the park, take any Batu 8 (or higher-numbered) bus from the local bus station on the waterfront in the city centre (RM1.50). Get off at the 'Taman Rimba' signpost and walk down Jln Rimba. A taxi from the city centre costs about RM80 return with one hour waiting time; two Grab rides work out cheaper.

Chinese Cemetery   CEMETERY
(Lg Istana; ⊙24hr) Sandakan's Chinese Cemetery is huge. As you wander along the cemetery, you'll notice the graves become older and more decrepit – many have been claimed by the jungle. You will also see some charnel houses that accommodate the important members of Sandakan's major Chinese clans. Just before the cemetery entrance, on a hillock, is a **memorial** to the 30 Chinese victims of the Sandakan Massacre on 27 May 1945 – mostly community leaders who were part of the underground movement.

Puu Jih Syh Temple   BUDDHIST TEMPLE
(off Jln Leila; ⊙hours vary) Wrapped in the usual firework display of reds, golds and twining dragons, festooned with lanterns illuminating the grounds like a swarm of fireflies, this is one of the finest Chinese temples in Sabah. It's about 4km west of the centre. Take a bus to Tanah Merah and ask for directions. A taxi shouldn't cost more than RM10 one way, but don't be surprised if cabbies try to charge RM25 for a round trip plus waiting at the temple.

Japanese Cemetery   CEMETERY
(Lg Istana; ☉ 24hr) A poignant piece of Sandakan's ethnic puzzle, this cemetery was founded in the 1890s by Kinoshita Kuni, known as the successful madam-manager of Sandakan's lucrative 'Brothel 8'. Today's cemetery is small, but at one time there were hundreds of prostitutes buried here. A monument to the fallen Japanese soldiers of WWII was erected in the cemetery in 1989. To get here climb the Tangga Seribu to Lg Istana and turn right, following signs to the cemetery.

St Michael's & All Angels Church   CHURCH
(Jln Puncak (Church Rd); ☉ hours vary) One of the very few surviving pre-WWII buildings, this pretty stone church (1893) sits as a relic of colonial times and a monument to Christian worship on a hillside high above Sandakan. Its construction reportedly involved prisoner labourers dragging huge slabs of local granite across the Bornean jungle. Notice its stunning stained-glass windows, donated by Australians to commemorate the 60th anniversary of the end of WWII.

 Tours

It is possible to visit many of the attractions around Sandakan independently, but if you want to stay at the river lodges on the Kinabatangan, you'll need to book before arriving. It's advisable to do so in Sandakan or in KK. Sandakan has plenty of tour operators offering packages to Sepilok and the Gomantong Caves. Hotels in Sandakan can also book tours.

★**Uncle Tan**   WILDLIFE WATCHING
(☎ 089-535784, 016-824 4749; www.uncletan.com; Labuk Sq, block A, lot 1, 1st fl, Mile 9, Jln Labuk; ☉ 9am-5pm) Booking office for off-the-beaten-track jungle adventures on the Kinabatangan with original operator Uncle Tan.

**Sepilok Tropical
Wildlife Adventure**   WILDLIFE WATCHING
(☎ 089-271077; www.stwadventure.com; 13 Lebuh Tiga; ☉ 9am-6pm) This mid-priced tour specialist is connected to Sepilok Jungle Resort (p355) and Bilit Adventure Lodge (p361) on the Sungai Kinabatangan.

SABAH SANDAKAN

THE SANDAKAN DEATH MARCHES

Sandakan was the site of a Japanese prisoner-of-war camp during WWII, and in September 1944, 1793 Australian and 641 British troops were interned here. What is not widely known is that more Australians died here than during the building of the infamous Burma Railway.

Early in the war, food and conditions were bearable and the death rate stood at around three per month. As the Allies closed in, however, it became clear to the officers in command that they didn't have enough staff to guard against a rebellion in the camps. They decided to cut the prisoners' rations to weaken them, causing disease to spread and the death rate to rise.

It was also decided to move the prisoners inland – 250km through the jungle to Ranau, on a route originally cut by locals to hamper the Japanese invaders, passing mainly through uninhabited, inhospitable terrain. On 28 January 1945, 470 prisoners set off; 313 made it to Ranau. On the second march, 570 started from Sandakan; just 118 reached Ranau. The 537 prisoners on the third march were the last men in the camp.

Conditions on the marches were deplorable: most men had no boots, rations were less than minimal and many men fell by the wayside. The Japanese brutally disposed of any prisoners who couldn't walk. Once in Ranau the surviving prisoners were put to work carrying 20kg sacks of rice over hilly country to Paginatan, 40km away. Disease, starvation and executions took a horrendous toll, and by the end of July 1945 there were no prisoners left in Ranau. The only survivors from the 2400 at Sandakan were six Australians who escaped, either from Ranau or during the marches.

As a final bitter irony, it emerged postwar that a rescue attempt had been planned for early 1945, but intelligence at the time had suggested there were no prisoners left at the camp.

You can trace the men's final journey on foot with KK-based TYK Adventure Tours (p320), run by a local trekking veteran and an Australian historian. Choose from a two-day, one-night taster, or hike the whole thing in 10 to 11 days.

Sandakan

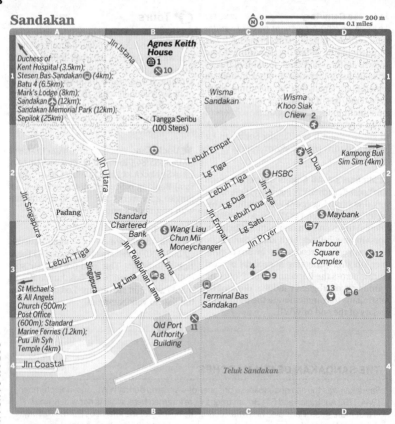

N 0 —————————— 200 m
0 —————————— 0.1 miles

Duchess of
Kent Hospital (3.5km);
Stesen Bas Sandakan (4km);
Batu 4 (6.5km);
Mark's Lodge (8km);
Sandakan (12km);
Sandakan Memorial Park (12km);
Sepilok (25km)

Agnes Keith House 1
10

Tangga Seribu
(100 Steps)

Wisma
Sandakan

Wisma
Khoo Siak
Chiew 2

Kampong Buli
Sim Sim (4km)

Lebuh Empat
Lg Tiga
Lebuh Tiga
Lg Dua
Lebuh Dua
Lg Satu

HSBC
Jln Dua
3
Jln Tiga

Maybank
7

Jln Utara

Padang

Standard
Chartered
Bank

Wang Liau
Chun Mii
Moneychanger

Jln Empat
Jln Lima

Jln Pryer
5
4
9

Harbour
Square
Complex

12

Jln Singapura

Lebuh Tiga

Jln Singapura

Jln Pelabuhan Lama

Lg Lima

8

13
6

St Michael's
& All Angels
Church (500m);
Post Office
(600m); Standard
Marine Ferries (1.2km);
Puu Jih Syh
Temple (4km)

Terminal Bas
Sandakan

11
Old Port
Authority
Building

Jln Coastal

Teluk Sandakan

Sandakan

◉ Top Sights
1 Agnes Keith House.................................B1

⊙ Activities, Courses & Tours
2 Crystal Quest..D1
3 Sepilok Tropical Wildlife Adventure D2
4 SI Tours C3

⊜ Sleeping
5 Borneo Sandakan Backpackers............C3
6 Four Points by Sheraton Sandakan......D3
7 Harbourside Backpackers D3

8 Nak Hotel B3
9 Sandakan Backpackers Hostel.............C3

⊗ Eating
Ba Lin Roof Garden ....(see 8)
10 English Tea House & Restaurant...........B1
11 Harbour Bistro Cafe B4
San Da Gen Kopitiam ....(see 8)
12 Sandakan Central Market.....................D3

⊖ Drinking & Nightlife
13 Best Brew D3

SI Tours   TOURS
(☎089-213502; www.sitoursborneo.com; lot 59,
block HS-5, Sandakan Harbour Sq Phase 2; ⊗9am-
6pm) This full-service agency operates Abai
Jungle Lodge (p363) and Kinabatangan
River Lodge and runs overnight turtle-
spotting trips to the Sandakan Archipelago.

🛏 Sleeping

If you're only passing through Sandakan
to see the orangutans, it's better to stay at
Sepilok itself. Sandakan has several excellent budget hostels and a few upscale, midrange options in the city centre, as well as
a few more hotels scattered throughout the
outlying neighbourhoods.

★**Sandakan Backpackers Hostel** HOSTEL $
(🖉089-211213; www.sandakanbackpackershostel.
com; lot 109, Harbour Sq; dm/d/f RM33/70/138;
❄🛜) Decorated with murals by the former
owner and former guests, this friendly and
clean hostel has rooms with sea views and
a rooftop area with even more watery vistas.
It's close to the waterfront restaurants and
some of the staff go beyond the call of duty
to make guests feel welcome. Note that the
front door is locked at 11pm.

Harbourside Backpackers HOSTEL $
(🖉089-217072;www.harboursidebackpackers.com;
Harbour Sq, 1st fl, lot 43, block HS-4; dm/s/d
RM35/65/75; ❄@🛜) Right near the waterfront, this hostel gets a lot of love from the
backpacker contingent for its cleanliness
and the helpfulness of its staff. The cosy
common area and guest kitchen is where
folks congregate to discuss their next adventure – on the Kinabatangan, Turtle Island or
beyond.

Borneo Sandakan Backpackers HOSTEL $
(🖉089-215754; www.borneosandakan.com; 1st fl,
54 Harbour Sq; dm/s/d RM30/60/75; ❄🛜) This
superclean, welcoming hostel has warm
orange walls, air-con in every room and a
lobby with a flat-screen TV. It also serves up
a decent, complimentary breakfast (eggs).
There are six rooms and two well-sized
dorms (though some rooms lack windows).
It has a relaxed vibe and helpful staff who
are also qualified guides and run a number
of tours.

★**Four Points by**
Sheraton Sandakan LUXURY HOTEL $$
(🖉089-244888; www.fourpointssandakan.com;
Harbour Sq, Jln Pryer; r incl breakfast from RM260;
❄🛜❄) The infinity pool on the 13th floor
looks out over the waterfront, while the
spacious rooms are blessed with wonderful
views and feature down pillows, flat-screen
TV, desk and minibar. The old B&W photos
of Sandakan add charm. The Eatery Restau-
rant has arguably the best buffet breakfast
in Sabah, while Best Brew (p350) serves
cocktails in front of the big screen.

Nak Hotel HOTEL $$
(🖉089-272988; www.nakhotel.com; Jln Pelabuhan
Lama; s/d/ste incl breakfast from RM98/138/198;
❄🛜) We like Nak for its quirky lobby of
oxblood walls, Chinese lanterns, giant bird
cages and Oriental vases. Rooms aren't large
but they are stylish, with retro elements and
functional en suites. On the ground floor is

an excellent *kopitiam* . Best of all, however,
one of the city's finest eateries, the Ba Lin
(p350), perches on the rooftop.

✖ Eating

For an authentic Malay meal, head to the
waterfront by Harbour Sq. There are several decent international restaurants in the
city centre. The best seafood is found in the
Sim Sim stilt village, and the best *bah kut
teh* (pork-rib soup with hints of garlic and
Chinese five-spice) in Tanah Merah. There
are clusters of good restaurants in Bandar
Indah and Bandar Utara.

Rock Paper Scissors Cafe CAFE $
(🖉089-232733; www.facebook.com/rockpaper
scissorscafe; Prima Sq, Mile 4, lot 169, ground fl,
block 18A; breakfast from RM12; ⏱7.30am-8pm;
❄🛜) Driving to/from Sepilok and in need
of a caffeine pick-up? Look no further:
at this cute cafe you just input your order
electronically and your double espresso and
kaya (coconut-cream jam spread on bread)
toast arrive at your table.

Good Taste Bah Kut Teh CHINESE $
(🖉089-615899; lot 5, block D, Bandar Nam Tung,
Tanah Mera; mains from RM5; ⏱8am-2pm &
6-9pm) *Bah kut teh* literally means 'meat,
bone, tea', and in much of Malaysia you can
expect pork (and pork innards) in a fragrant
herbal soup. Good Taste does it the Sandakan way, serving the likes of cuttlefish *bah
kut teh* and prawn *bah kut teh,* though
the traditional belly pork, simmered in an
earthy, rich, dark broth, is tops.

Harbour Bistro Cafe INTERNATIONAL $
(waterfront; mains RM8-30; ⏱2pm-2am; 🖉)
Regarded by many as the best of the gaggle of casual eateries that line the waterfront, the Harbour Bistro menu lists plenty
of Asian options using beef, chicken and
local seafood, plus there are Western-style
mains such as fish and chips, and steaks.
Vegetarians will find plenty of options, but
be wary of the addition of dried shrimp.

Sandakan Central Market HAWKER $
(Jln Dua; mains RM1-8; ⏱7am-3pm) Located in
what looks like a multistorey car park, this
is the best spot in town for cheap eats and
food stalls. Upstairs you'll find strictly halal
food stalls, with a mix of Chinese, Malay,
Indonesian and Filipino stalls. Hours given
for the food stalls are a bit flexible, but by
3pm most are empty.

SABAH SANDAKAN

★ Ai Xin   VEGETARIAN $$

(☑ 089-232121; Bandar Indah; mains RM16-29; ⊙ 11am-10pm Tue-Sun; ✳ ☑) ✐ Black sesame bean curd, braised shiitake mushrooms with yam, laksa with handmade noodles and tender steamed dumplings, bursting forth with crunchy, fresh vegetables from the restaurant's own organic farm, are just some of the treats on the menu here. Great care is taken both with presentation and flavour. Outstanding.

★ Restaurant Seafood
Sim Sim 88   SEAFOOD $$

(Sim Sim 88; dishes RM10-20; ⊙ 7.30am-9.30pm) Located in the heart of the stilt village of **Kampong Buli Sim Sim** (Jln Buli Sim Sim), 3km east of the centre, this large, breezy terrace strung with fairy lights is a terrific bet for creatures of the deep. Come for seafood noodles, grilled baby squid, deep-fried *sui kao* (dumplings) filled with seafood and century egg and more. Pick your fresh fish for steaming.

★ Ba Lin Roof Garden   INTERNATIONAL $$

(☑ 089-272988; www.nakhotel.com; 18th fl, Nak Hotel, Jln Pelabuhan Lama; mains RM24-45; ⊙ 7.30am-1am, happy hour 2-8pm; ✳ 🖥) A hidden treat at the top of the Nak Hotel, this stylish restaurant/bar has retro paper light shades, wicker swing-chairs, and swallow-you-up couches. Eat on the pot-plant-shaded verandah or up on the rooftop. The menu runs the gamut from pizza, pastas, marinated NZ lamb and grass-fed Angus steaks to a wealth of fresh juices and original cocktails (RM20 to RM25).

San Da Gen Kopitiam   MALAYSIAN $$

(☑ 089-238988; Lebuh Dua; mains RM16-29; ⊙ 8am-5pm; ✳ 🖥) Bedecked with vintage posters, this bright cafe serves upmarket takes on *kopitiam* food: slipper lobster *nasi lemak,* a kick-ass tom yum with river prawns, laksa and also such breakfast delights as salted egg lava French toast. Good place to lurk with a laptop, too.

English Tea House & Restaurant   BRITISH $$$

(☑ 088-448631; www.englishteahouse.org; Jln Istana; mains RM17.50-73; ⊙ 10am-9pm) More English than a Graham Greene novel, this beautiful stucco-pillared villa, with its manicured croquet lawn, bay views and wicker chairs parked under a giant mango tree, is great for the ambience, as well as high tea. English standards, such as shepherd's pie and fish and chips, tend to disappoint, however, and service slows down when the tour groups arrive.

Drinking & Nightlife

Out of the centre, Bandar Indah (Mile 4 or Batu 4) and Bandar Utara are where you'll find more local bars and decent coffee shops.

★ Urban Cafe   COFFEE

(☑ 089-238426; www.facebook.com/urbancafe sandakan; Lg Ave 5 Bandar Utama IJM, lot 151, ground fl, block G; ⊙ noon-9pm; 🖥) A favourite with young, laptop-toting locals and coffee fiends, this cafe is well worth the detour to Bandar Utama. There are cosy couches to lounge around on, an impressive array of hot and cold coffee beverages and even a single-origin ice drip – all the rage in Japan, we hear. Occasional hip foodie events held here.

Best Brew   SPORTS BAR

(☑ 089-244602; www.fourpointssandakan.com; Four Points by Sheraton Sandakan, Harbour Sq, Jln Pryer; ⊙ 5pm-midnight Sun-Thu, to 2am Fri & Sat) This cosy harbour-view bar in Sandakan's top hotel features a few international beers, wine and decent cocktails as well as excellent snacks. There's a pool table and darts and it's ideal for watching the game on the big screen.

ℹ Information

Duchess of Kent Hospital (☑ 089-248600; http://hdok.moh.gov.my; Batu 2/Mile 2, Jln Utara; ⊙ 8am-10pm) Overstretched public hospital; go to KK if you need serious medical treatment.

HSBC (Lebuh Tiga)

Maybank (Jln Pryer; ⊙ 9am-5pm Mon-Fri)

Main Post Office (Pejabat Pos; ☑ 089-210594; Jln Leila; ⊙ 8.30am-5pm Mon-Fri, to 12.30pm Sat)

Police (☑ 089-221251; Lebuh Empat)

Standard Chartered Bank (Lebuh Tiga)

Wang Liau Chun Mii Moneychanger (23 Lebuh Tiga; ⊙ 8.30am-4.30pm)

ℹ Getting There & Away

AIR

From **Sandakan Airport** (Jln Airport), Malaysia Airlines/MASwings (www.malaysiaairlines.com) has several flights per day to/from KK and KL, two per day to/from Tawau and twice-weekly flights (Thursday and Saturday) to Kudat. AirAsia (www.airasia.com) operates direct daily flights to/from KL and KK.

BOAT

Standard Marine Ferries (☑ 089-216996; block G, lot 1, 1st fl, Bandar Ramai-Ramai Jln Leila) links Sandakan with Zamboanga (economy/cabin RM280/300) on the Philippine island of Mindanao. Ferries depart **Sandakan harbour** (Jln Batu Sapi, Kg Bokara) at 6pm every Friday, arriving at 4pm the next day (22 hours). There are currently no ferries to Jolo because of insurgency problems.

Because of lawlessness, including kidnappings of foreign nationals, and Islamist insurgency, Western embassies warn against travel to or through Zamboanga, so check local conditions before you sail. Travellers we spoke to said you don't need an onward ticket to enter the Philippines, however the Filipino government says otherwise, so it may be wise to have one.

BUS

Buses and minibuses to KK, Lahad Datu, Semporna and Tawau leave from the **long-distance bus station** (Jln Lintas Utara) in a large car park at Batu 2.5, 4km north of town. Most express buses to KK (RM43, six to seven hours) leave between 6.30am and 2pm, with several evening departures between 5pm and 8pm. All pass the turn-off to Kinabalu National Park headquarters.

Buses depart half-hourly for Lahad Datu (RM22, three hours) and Tawau (RM42, six hours) between 6.30am and 10.30am. There are also buses to Semporna (RM42, six hours) at 7.30am and 2pm. If you miss them, head to Lahad Datu then catch a frequent minibus to Semporna.

Minibuses depart throughout the morning from Batu 2.5 for Ranau (RM30, four hours) and Lahad Datu (some of those continuing to Tawau). Minibuses for Sukau (RM15) leave from a lot behind Centre Point Mall in town.

Getting Around

TO/FROM THE AIRPORT
The airport is 11km from the city centre. Batu 7 Airport bus (RM2) stops on the main road about 500m from the terminal. A coupon taxi to the town centre costs RM30, while a Grab ride will set you back around RM15.

BUS

Terminal Bas Sandakan (Minibus Stand; Jln Pryer), behind the Centre Point Mall, is Sandakan's minibus terminal. Buses run from 6am to 6pm on the main road to the north, Jln Utara. Buses display a sign indicating how far from town they go, eg Batu 2.5 (the long-distance bus station, RM1.50), Batu 14 (the turn-off to Sepilok) and Batu 32 (the end of the line on the KK–Semporna Hwy). Fares range from RM2 to RM5.

To reach the long-distance bus station, you can also catch a local bus (RM1.50) from the **local bus station** (Minibus Stand; Jln Pryer) at the waterfront; the journey takes about 20 min-

utes. The same bus returns when full from the bus station for the city centre.

CAR

Borneo Express (016-886 0789; http://borneocar.com; lot GL 08 (A), ground fl, terminal bldg, Sandakan Airport) has an office at Sandakan Airport, as does **Sandakan Car Rental** (019-823 7050, 016-815 0029; http://sandakancarrental.com; Jln Letat Jaya, block J, lot 8). Having your own wheels does make it easier to get to Sandakan's more-spread-out neighbourhoods. Colour-coded parking spaces in the city centre require you to purchase scratch-off parking vouchers from corner shops and 7-Elevens.

TAXI

Short journeys around town should cost RM15. It's about RM20 to Bandar Indah and RM50 to Sepilok. A taxi from the long-distance bus station to town (or vice versa) will cost RM20. Around half the price of taxi rides are rides with Grab, Sabah's answer to Uber; download the app.

Sepilok

A visit to the world's most famous place to see orangutans in their natural habitat is all the more compelling thanks to the outdoor nursery for orangutan youngsters in the same complex, and the nearby Sun Bear Conservation Centre and Rainforest Discovery Centre. In addition, the Labuk Bay Proboscis Monkey Sanctuary is only a short drive away.

What makes Sepilok Orangutan Rehabilitation Centre (SORC) work so well as a destination is its organisation, special-needs-friendly paths, transport links and the fact that, with the exception of the Labuk Bay Proboscis Monkey Sanctuary, the other sights here are all within walking distance. There are also some beautiful places to stay on the edge of the jungle.

Sights

★**Sepilok Orangutan Rehabilitation Centre** ANIMAL SANCTUARY
(SORC; 089-531189, emergency 089-531180; www.wildlife.sabah.gov.my; Jln Sepilok; adult/5-17yr RM30/15, camera fee RM10; 9am-noon & 2-4pm) Around 25km north of Sandakan, and covering 40 sq km of the Kabili-Sepilok Forest Reserve, this inspiring, world-famous centre welcomes orphaned and injured orangutans for rehabilitation before returning them to forest life. In

2018 we were told there were around 200 living in the reserve, many more than the website suggests, though only a few are regular visitors to the feeding platform. At the **outdoor nursery**, a short walk from the feeding platform, you can watch orphaned youngsters at play.

The youngsters you'll be charmed by are between six and nine years old, and in either the air-conditioned or fan-cooled viewing stalls you can sit and watch them play and practise their swinging – just one of the skills they'll need to stay alive should they return to what's left of their rainforest home. Try to get here early in the morning before they are fed and become sleepy.

➡ **Platform Feeding**

Feedings at the platforms are at 10am and 3pm, and last 30 to 50 minutes. Tickets are valid for one day, so you can see two feedings with the same ticket. Watching the trees begin to shake, the ropes vibrating, the first swatch of orange shifting through the branches, is a moment you'll never forget.

Also worth noting is that only around two to four of the population will feed at any one time. During fruiting season, few will turn up, if any at all, since there's plenty to eat in the forest. The larger males almost never congregate here. In order to get a good spot for your camera or kids, get here 20 minutes before feeding time. The morning feeding is always more crowded with Homo sapiens, as this is when more tour groups visit, so if you want a quieter experience, try the afternoon. Don't bring any containers of insect repellent into the reserve, as these are highly toxic to the apes and other wildlife. Spray yourself before entering, and put on plenty of sunblock.

➡ **Nature Education Centre**

A worthwhile 20-minute video about Sepilok's work is shown six times daily (9am, 10.30am, 11am, noon, 2.10pm and 3.30pm) in the auditorium opposite reception. Strangely the impact of palm-oil plantations, which have supplanted much of the orangutan's habitat, is not specifically mentioned.

★**Borneo Sun Bear Conservation Centre** ANIMAL SANCTUARY (BSBCC; ☑ 089-534491; www.bsbcc.org.my; Jln Sepilok; adult/12-17 yr/under 12 yr RM30/15/free; ⊙ 9am-3.30pm) 🌿 The wonderful BSBCC provides care to rescued sun bears (44 bears at the time of writing), the world's second-most endangered bear. The centre has full access for the disabled, and it's possible to see the bears foraging, climbing and sunning themselves in the forest from two elevated walkways and viewing platforms. There are also telescopes set up for a closer look. The gift shop screens an educational video on BSBCC and its valuable work.

Named for the golden bracelet of fur around their necks, the sun bears' Rorschach-like pattern is never duplicated, varying as they do in colour from cream to orange. At a maximum of 150cm and 60kg in weight, they are little larger than Paddington and are the smallest of the world's bears. Sun bears are found throughout Southeast Asia, in eastern India, southern China, Myanmar, Laos, Vietnam and Borneo, usually at an altitude of around 2700m. An average male sun bear needs at least 39 sq km of forest to find sufficient food. They're excellent climbers, equipped with long claws to scale high trees in search of beehives. As they'll rip a cavity in the trunk to get to their honey, they create a safe place for hornbills and

---

🛈 WATCH YOUR BELONGINGS!

Be warned, when visiting the Sepilok Orangutan Rehabilitation Centre, it's better to leave valuables in your coach, car or locker (available on request) before entering the orangutan feeding area, for certain members of their population are renowned for their collecting habits. They're not fussy – Leica cameras and Ray-Ban sunglasses will suffice. One ape in particular (with a distinguished black face) usually singles out a female member of the audience and makes a beeline, only to cross the divide between the arboreal to the viewing area. He may get attached to you, literally, and has been known to occasionally bite. If he gets too close, move away and alert a member of staff.

If you're extremely lucky you might spot C.I.D, a fully flanged large male and resident king of this particular jungle, though he's only seen once or twice a year. To learn more about these orangutans so you can identify them by name, check out www.orangutan-appeal.org.uk/about-us/meet-the-orangutans.

THE WILD MAN OF BORNEO & HOW TO HELP HIM

The term 'orangutan' literally means 'man of the wild', or 'jungle man' – a testament to the local reverence for these great ginger apes. Traditionally, orangutans were never hunted like other creatures in the rainforest. In fact Borneo's indigenous people used to worship their skulls in the same fashion as they did the heads taken from enemy tribesmen. Orangutans are the only species of great ape found outside Africa. A mature male is an impressive creature with an arm span of 2.25m, and can weigh up to 144kg. Dominant males also have distinctive wide cheek pads to reinforce their alpha status.

It was once said that an orangutan could swing from tree to tree from one side of Borneo to the other without touching the ground. Sadly this is no longer the case, and hunting and habitat destruction continue to take their toll; it's estimated 104,000 of the animals exist in the wild.

If you'd like to get involved with the work of the Sepilok Orangutan Rehabilitation Centre, contact **Sepilok Orangutan Appeal UK** (www.orangutan-appeal.org.uk), a UK-based charity. The Appeal's orangutan adoption scheme is a particular hit with visitors: for £36.75 a year, you can sponsor a ginger bundle of fun and receive updates on its progress. See the Appeal's website for details. If you're really taken with the place, Sepilok has one of the most popular overseas volunteer programs in Malaysia. Apply through **Travellers Worldwide** (www.travellersworldwide.com). The cost of an eight-week volunteer package, including accommodation, meals and a number of excursions, is £3295.

other birds to nest at a later date. They also control the forest's destructive population of termites, which are a critical part of the bears' diet.

Across Asia the sun bear is caught and slaughtered for meat and Chinese medicine. In countries such as China and Vietnam, the poor beasts are strapped in tiny cages and hooked to IVs that pump bile from their gallbladders. Thankfully this does not happen in Sabah, though the bears are still under enormous threat from habitat loss. Animals donated to the centre are first checked for diseases they may have caught as humans' pets, before being transferred to the training pen. A new arrival will learn to socialise, climb, build nests and forage before its eventual release into the wild.

It's possible to donate to help with feeding and veterinary costs and to 'adopt' a bear. If you wish to volunteer as a keeper, it costs RM8180 for a month, or RM4368 for two weeks, including accommodation and meals. See the website for details.

Rainforest Discovery Centre NATURE RESERVE (RDC; ☏089-533780; www.forest.sabah.gov.my/rdc; off Jln Sepilok; adult/5-17yr RM15/7; ☺ticket counter 8am-5pm, night walk 6-8pm Mon-Fri) The RDC, about 1.5km from SORC, offers an engaging education in tropical flora and fauna. Outside the exhibit hall filled with child-friendly displays, a botanical garden presents samples of tropical plants. There's a gentle 1km lakeside walking trail, and a series of eight canopy

towers connected by walkways to give you a bird's-eye view of the rooftops of the trees. During the highly recommended night walks (RM30) you may spot tarsiers, slow loris, civets, flying squirrels and other night critters.

It's best to get there either at 8am or 4pm, as wildlife tends to hibernate during the sweltering hours in the middle of the day. It takes around 1½ hours to walk the trails and climb the towers. Although it doesn't correspond with the best bird and wildlife spotting times, it is still a good place to while away time between feedings at the SORC.

Paddleboats (RM5) are available to ride around the inviting lake near the centre's entrance. As for the trails, the 20km-return Kabili Trail requires a Forest Reserve Entry Permit (available at the RDC ticket office; plenty of water to be carried and plenty of stamina required). There are three shelters along the trail. You don't need a guide, but they can be arranged for RM100.

Labuk Bay Proboscis
Monkey Sanctuary ANIMAL SANCTUARY

(☏089-672133; www.proboscis.cc; Labuk Bay; adult/child RM60/30, camera & video RM10; ☺8am-6pm) A local palm-plantation owner has created a private proboscis monkey sanctuary, attracting the floppy-conked locals with sugar-free pancakes at 9.30am and 2.30pm feedings at Platform A, and 11.30am and 4.30pm at Platform B, 1km away. An estimated 300 wild monkeys live in the 6-sq-km reserve. The proboscis monkeys are enticed

SABAH SEPILOK

Sepilok

Sepilok

◉ Top Sights
1 Borneo Sun Bear Conservation
   Centre B3
2 Sepilok Orangutan Rehabilitation
   Centre A3

◉ Sights
3 Rainforest Discovery Centre A2

◔ Sleeping
4 Paganakan Dii A1
5 Sepilok B&B A2
6 Sepilok Forest Edge Resort B3
7 Sepilok Jungle Resort B3
8 Sepilok Nature Resort A3

◍ Eating
   Kafeteria Sepilok .... (see 2)
   Lake Bistro & Bar .... (see 8)
9 Mama Wati's B3

onto the main viewing platform, which may put you off if you're looking for a more ecologically minded experience. Come here by shuttle from Sandakan or drive yourself.

Proboscis monkeys *(Nasalis larvatus)* are found only on Borneo, although if you take a close look at them, you'd swear you've spotted one in the corner of a dodgy bar. Named for their long bulbous noses, proboscis monkeys are potbellied and red-faced, and males are constantly, unmistakably... aroused. With the arrival of Europeans, Malays nicknamed the proboscis *monyet belanda* (Dutch monkey). Also keep an eye out for the delicately featured silver leaf langurs with their orange-coloured babies.

Food and accommodation are provided at the sanctuary's Nipah Resort (p354).

🛏 Sleeping

If you've come to the Sandakan area for the wild creatures of Sepilok, do yourself a favour and stay near the apes and bears. The lodgings here range from simple guesthouse dorms to sumptuous dark-wood chalets. Most accommodation options are scattered along Jln Sepilok, the 2.5km-long access road to the rehabilitation centre.

★ Sepilok Nature Resort   RESORT $$
(☏089-674999; http://sepilok.com; Jln Sepilok; r RM320; ❄️🛜) Beside an ornamental pond, this beautiful wood-accented hotel is a study in comfort, with mature rubber plants shading its two-tiered central lodge, and carriage lamps casting their glow on its welcoming lounge and restaurant. Chalets are roomy with sumptuous bathrooms, huge beds and private balconies. The cuisine, coffee and waterfront setting at the resort's Lake Bistro & Bar are exquisite.

Nipah Resort   RESORT $$
(☏089-672133; www.labuikbay.com.my; Labuk Bay; dm/r/f RM35/180/550, all incl breakfast; ❄️🛜) This accommodation is at Labuk Bay Proboscis Monkey Sanctuary, on the edge of the palm-oil plantations that surround the sanctuary. The resort comprises a fan-cooled dorm and a collection of air-con bungalows that are simply adorned, airy and inviting in a tropical-chic way. Guests can also venture out on mangrove treks into the surrounding jungle and night treks with guides.

Paganakan Dii   BOUTIQUE HOTEL $$
(☏012-885 1005, 012-868 1005; www.paganakandii. com; Mile 14, Jln Labuk; dm RM32, 2- & 4-person bungalows RM162-190, all incl breakfast; ❄️🛜) Popular with families wanting a taste of nature, with hammocks at every turn, brick-and-wood bungalows with balconies and nicely crafted furniture, wood floors and step-in showers. Make sure you ask for one with a view of the lake and mountains (RM28 extra). Same owner as Sandakan's Nak Hotel

(p349). Three daily transfers to Sepilok are included; trips to Labuk Bay arranged.

Sepilok Jungle Resort RESORT $$
(✆089-533031; www.sepilokjungleresort.com; Jln Rambutan; dm RM43, r with/without air-con from RM140/90, all incl breakfast; P❋🤚🛜❄) Rooms are tile-floored with desk, bathroom, TV and fan or air-con. All are adequate, though many are in need of refurbishment. Similarly, the complimentary breakfast is not quite up to scratch, but the restaurant's seafood and local vegetables and fruits are excellent. The resort's best features are the large pool and its proximity to the Orangutan Rehabilitation Centre.

There are extensive bird-filled gardens, a boardwalk over a fish-stocked pond and a peculiar tendency to paint concrete to look like saw logs.

Sepilok B&B HOSTEL $$
(✆089-534050; www.sepilokbednbreakfast.com. my; Jln Fabia; camping RM20, dm with fan/air-con RM40/50, d with air-con RM140-200; ❋🛜) Located about 400m from the Rainforest Discovery Centre, this place has a relaxed hostel vibe. Bamboo-walled dorms are spartan but clean and comfortable and supplied with fresh linen. Pitta Lodge has self-catering facilities for families. Camping here is better in March and April when there's less rain. Wi-fi is available only in reception/restaurant and the eight rooms of Hornbill Lodge.

Sepilok Forest Edge Resort RESORT $$$
(✆089-533190; www.sepilokforestedgeresort. com; Jln Rambutan; dm RM50, chalets RM325-700; ❋🛜❄) Set within manicured lawns, this stunning accommodation is choking on plants and flowers and has chalets fit for a colonial explorer, with polished-wood floors, choice art and private balcony with wrought-iron chairs. There are also dorms located in a pretty longhouse, **Labuk Longhouse B&B**, plus a tiny relaxing pool/spa.

✗ Eating

Mama Wati's MALAYSIAN $
(Jln Sepilok; mains RM8; ⊙6am-8pm) Friendly Mama Wati's is set up in a ramshackle contrivance beside the road just outside the SORC entrance. There's usually a gaggle of guides and drivers here having a smoke or a dish of noodles. Snacks include fried bananas, and in addition to the inexpensive rice and noodle dishes there are cold drinks and ice creams.

Kafeteria Sepilok CAFE $
(Jln Sepilok; snacks & mains RM8-12; ⊙7.30am-4pm, kitchen closes at 3.30pm; ❋) Beside the entrance to SORC is this oasis of a cafe with hot and cold drinks, ice creams, sandwiches and hot meals.

★ Lake Bistro & Bar INTERNATIONAL $$
(✆089-674999; Sepilok Nature Resort, Jln Sepilok; mains RM20-30; ⊙7am-10pm) This open-sided restaurant makes the most of its lakeside setting with the dark tropical timbers complementing the lush garden and carriage lighting. Pan-Asian dishes of beef, chicken and seafood, pasta, burgers and more feature on the excellent menu. Pizzas are available after 6pm. Add the professional service, good coffee, juices, cocktails, beer and wine and you have Sepilok's best restaurant.

❶ Information

Sepilok is located at 'Batu 14' – 14 miles (23km) from Sandakan.

It's best to get money in Sandakan, and there are two ATMs in Sandakan Airport, en route if driving. Money can be changed at resorts for a poor exchange rate.

❶ Getting There & Away

BUS
A shuttle bus (RM4) runs between Sandakan's local bus station (p351; departing 9.30am, 11.30am, 2pm and 5pm) and Sepilok (departing 6.30am, 10.30am, 12.30pm and 4pm).

A private shuttle is operated by the Labuk Bay Proboscis Monkey Sanctuary (RM20 per person one way). It departs Hotel Sandakan at 9.30am, arrives at Sepilok 40 to 45 minutes later, then departs Sepilok at 10.30am to arrive at Labuk Bay in time for the feeding at Platform B (11.30am). The scheduled transfer from Labuk Bay Proboscis Monkey Sanctuary back to Sandakan is at 3pm (so you could catch a second feeding at Platform A (2.30pm). Note there is a cafe at Labuk Bay. If you wish to head back to Sandakan earlier, however, you can pay RM80 per person.

If coming from KK, board a Sandakan-bound bus and ask the driver to let you off at 'Batu 14' (RM43). You will pay the full fare, even though Sandakan is 23km away.

TAXI
If you are coming directly from Sandakan, a taxi should cost no more than RM50 (RM40 from the airport). If you want one to wait and return you to Sandakan, you're looking at RM120. Taxi 'pirates', as they're known, wait at Batu 14 to give tourists a ride into Sepilok. It's RM3 per person

for a lift. Travellers spending the night can arrange a lift with their accommodation if they book ahead of time.

Sandakan Archipelago

While everyone knows about the Semporna Archipelago, fewer visitors head to the Sandakan Archipelago, off the coast of its namesake port. The archipelago is made up of a number of large islands such as Libaran and Berhala, while Selingan, Bakungan Kecil and Gulisan islands comprise the Turtle Islands National Park. The last three all have turtle hatcheries, but the only one you can visit is Selingan. Libaran has its own private turtle hatchery. Further out is Pulau Lankayan, home to a high-end diving resort.

Pulau Berhala

Once a leper colony and used by the Japanese as a civilian internment centre and POW camp during WWII, Pulau Berhala is supremely serene, and an exemplar of a rare genre: a lovely tropical island hardly touched by tourists.

Sandstone cliffs rise above the Sulu Sea, hemming in quiet patches of dusty, sandy prettiness. The vibe is so sleepy it's narcoleptic, an atmosphere accentuated by two quiet water villages on the north side of the island, inhabited by fishing families, loads of migrating birds (their presence is heaviest in October and November) and...well, OK, there's not a lot else, except some very big rocks.

But, oh, what rocks. Rock climbers grade the formations here F5a – F6b, which is jargon for a mix of slow sloping walls and vertical cliff faces. There are no longer any formal rock-climbing tours here, but adventurous and experienced climbers could try negotiating a boat ride there and back from the mainland.

Pulau Selingan

The only island in the Turtle Islands National Park with visitor-accessible hatcheries, Pulau Selingan used to have a mixed reputation with regards to turtle tours. However, recent reports suggest that the former circus of gawping visitors watching a mother hawksbill or green turtle shuffling up the beach and laying her eggs has become much more considerate of the reptiles' needs, with

smaller numbers and stricter regulation on how close you get. For your part, please don't shine lights in the hatching mother's eyes in pursuit of a photo, don't use flash, nor allow any of your party to touch hatchlings – however cute they are – as they are released from their 50-day incubation. You may have to wait a while for the mothers to come, but come they will, often late in the night. When not turtle watching, you can snorkel off the pretty white-sand beach; there's snorkel gear for rent at the lodge.

Accommodation on the small island consists of three wooden bungalows, each divided into six air-conditioned rooms. They're a five-minute walk from the two turtle hatcheries and near an observation tower. Two-day, one-night packages typically cost RM650 to RM800 per person.

To organise a trip here, book through **Crystal Quest** (☑089-212711; cquest1996@gmail.com; Jln Buli Sim-Sim; boat transfer from Sandakan, accommodation & dinner on Selingan Island RM850, camera fee RM10, entrance fee RM60; ☺9am-5pm), or SI Tours (p348), which does combo tours – one night on Selingan and one night in Abai village on the Kinabatangan River.

Pulau Lankayan

A sand-haloed, jungly speck far out at sea, Pulau Lankayan isn't just photogenic, it's desktop-screen-saver material. Water isn't supposed to be this clear, nor sand this sugary white. But Lankayan's main attractions lie amid the reefs and wrecks of its underwater landscape. More often than not, honeymooners combine celebrations of their big day with exploration of the island's 14 dive sites, rich in leopard sharks, stingrays, giant groupers, harlequin ghost pipefish, parrotfish and other creatures of the deep. Pulau Lankayan is also a turtle nesting ground, with hatcheries around the island and sightings pretty much guaranteed both above and beneath the waves.

Lankayan Island Resort (☑089-673999, 088-238113; http://lankayan-island.com; Pulau Lankayan; 3-day, 2-night package diver/non-diver RM2574/2069; ❄) is a popular spot for diving romantics that's also heavily involved in turtle conservation. There are a couple of dozen cabins dotted along the sand where the jungle meets the sea, decked out in flowing, light linens and deep tropical hardwood accents. Speedboat transfers from Sandakan are included in your accommodation.

IMBAK CANYON CONSERVATION AREA

Comprising around 300 sq km of primary and secondary rainforest deep in the heart of Sabah, the Imbak Canyon Conservation Area contains the canyon itself – a 25km-long corridor of pristine rainforest, hemmed in on three sides by immense sandstone cliffs. Initial exploration of this self-contained ecosystem suggests that it's one of the most biodiverse areas in Borneo, with its dipterocarp and heath forests sheltering a wealth of animal life, including pygmy elephants, clouded leopards, orangutans, proboscis monkeys and more than 250 species of birds, including all eight species of hornbill.

You can only come to Imbak Canyon as part of a package with a licensed operator. Recommended operators that run trips into Imbak Canyon include Borneo Adventure (p322) and Adventure Alternative Borneo (p320). A four-day, three-night package typically costs around RM4866 per person, based on two people sharing. Bike & Tours B&B (p364) runs cycling tours of the canyon. If you come with Adventure Alternative Borneo, you can combine your trip with a stay at the nearby Deramakot Forest Reserve.

The jumping-off point for Imbak Canyon is the small town of Telupid, 134km west of Sandakan. You are driven here from Kota Kinabalu (five to six hours) or Sandakan (around four hours) and in Telupid you meet your guide and switch to a 4WD to tackle the unpaved plantation roads and rough dirt tracks. From Telupid the journey takes around two hours.

Pulau Libaran

POP UNDER 4000

This large island has a fishing village on one side and mangrove-fringed beaches, where sea turtles are often spotted, on the other. In 2013 a turtle hatchery was set up on Pulau Libaran in cooperation between Sabah Wildlife Department and Alexander Yee, manager of Narsalis Larvatus tours. Narsalis Larvatus, in turn, works with the villagers of Pulau Libaran, who alert it to the presence of any laying turtles so that the eggs can be collected and kept safe in the hatchery. Visitors to the resort can attend the release of baby turtles – a life-affirming experience, and a much more intimate one than on neighbouring Pulau Selingan.

There's only one place to stay here: **Walai Penyu Resort** (☑in Kota Kinabalu 088-260263; www.walaipenyuresort.com; Pulau Libaran; 2-day, 1-night package RM516; ✳), comprising a clutch of safari tents, right near the turtle hatchery. Run by Narsalis Larvatus tours, this secluded spot on Pulau Libaran consists of a handful of fan-cooled safari tents with twin beds inside, and out-doorsy bathroom facilities. The meals are excellent, and when you're not learning about turtle conservation or attending the release of baby turtles, you can paddle a sea kayak through mangroves, or chill on the beach. Speedboat transfers from the Sandakan yacht-club jetty are included in the package prices.

Deramakot Forest Reserve

Covering 555 sq km, the Deramakot Forest Reserve has been a success story of sustainable logging, with the strategic felling of tropical hardwoods coexisting alongside conservation efforts that protect some of Borneo's most vulnerable animal species. The reserve has been open to the public since 2012 and has gained in popularity. Around 260 bird species and numerous mammals call this dense lowland forest home, including the rhinoceros hornbill, fluffy crested hornbill, the shy clouded leopard and all of Borneo's smaller wild cats. In the mornings you might hear the lilting call of the gibbon and see sleek simian shapes move through the forest canopy. In the afternoons orangutans rise from their naps and go foraging, while the cover of darkness brings out sambar deer and diminutive mouse deer, civets, giant flying squirrels, wild boars, leopard cats, clouded leopards and bats. Given the reserve's limited visitor capacity, you'll never encounter crowds.

The only way to enter the reserve is by organised tour. Adventure Alternative Borneo (p320) was the pioneer, and it still does most of the tours in the reserve, though several other operators now also work with Sabah Parks.

The main activity in the reserve is a wildlife drive in open-top safari vehicles along the 32km logging road that leads to the

Sungai Kinabatangan and smaller, adjoining logging roads. There are three wildlife drives per day, with a high likelihood of spotting Borneo's impressive mammals and varied birdlife. The best time to spot wildlife tends to be from July to September, though seasons are changing.

Visitors are accommodated in two chalets, each consisting of three spacious, tiled en-suite rooms with air-con. There are also two hostel buildings, each with two four-bed dorms and a two-bed dorm; all are en suite. Book your tour well in advance from July to September, when both visitors and biology students converge on the reserve.

Sungai Kinabatangan

The Kinabatangan River is Sabah's longest: 560km of chocolatey-brown water, coiling like the serpents that swim its length far into the Bornean interior. Riverine forest creeps alongside the water, swarming with wildlife that is being squeezed for habitat by the ever-encroaching palm-oil plantations. Lodges are tastefully scattered along the banks, while homestay programs feature in several villages.

Dozens of boats putter along the banks offering tourists the opportunity to have a close encounter with a wild friend. This is the only place in Sabah where you can find a concentration of 10 primates, including orangutan, Bornean gibbon, long-tailed and short-tailed macaque, three kinds of leaf monkey, western tarsier, slow loris and proboscis monkey. Add to this eight different kinds of hornbill, herds of pygmy elephants, crocs, wild boars and perhaps – if you're super lucky – a clouded leopard.

◉ Sights

★ Agop Batu Tulug   CAVE
(☑ 089-565145;   http://museum.sabah.gov.my; admission adult/under 12yr RM15/free; ◷ 9am-5pm) This hill, 2km north of the Batuh Putih bridge, features three caves housing the ancestors of local Orang Sungai (People of the River). Because the Kinabatangan has a habit of frequently flooding, the final resting place of the dead has traditionally been located in cave complexes. Nine-hundred-year-old ironwood coffins are interred in the Batu Tulug caves with spears, knives, gongs, bells and Chinese curios, making the hill one of the most important archaeological sites in Sabah.

Steep wooden staircases snake up the 40m hill to the caves. Of the three caves, two are open to the public. Agop Lintanga, the larger cave, has the largest coffin collection, though they are unadorned, suggesting they were used for interring the bodies of common people. Smaller Agop Sawat, accessible from the lookout on top of the hill, has five carved log coffins, decorated with ox heads – more elaborate coffins reserved for chieftains. From the viewpoint you'll be rewarded with a 360-degree view of palm-oil plantations encroaching on the secondary forest and the Kinabatangan River.

Halfway to the top, a small museum details the history of cave burials in the Kinabatangan area and showcases some funereal objects found in the caves, as well as a splendid example of an ornate ironwood coffin.

The easiest way to get here is to include the caves in your package tour of the Kinabatangan. If you've got your own vehicle, look for signs indicating the turn-off to the Batu Caves, 18km south of the Sukau junction.

Gomantong Caves   CAVE
(☑ 089-230189; www.sabah.gov.my/jhl; Gomantong Hill, Lower Kinabatangan; adult/child RM30/15, camera/video RM30/50; ◷ 8am-1pm & 2-5pm Sat-Thu, 8-11.30am & 2-5pm Fri) Imagine a cathedral-like inner chamber shot with splinters of sunlight and a cave floor swarming with cockroaches that crunch underfoot, and you have the Gomantong Caves. The smell has a presence of its own, thanks to the ubiquity of bird and bat guano, and you'll want covered shoes, a raincoat and a hat, but the only cave open to visitors, Simud Hitam, is magnificent. The turn-off to Gomantong is well signposted en route to Sukau; most tours include a stop here.

A standard visit involves a trot counter-clockwise along the raised boardwalk that loops around the vast chamber. Besides cockroaches, you may spot mud crabs, giant centipedes, scorpions, plus lots of swiftlets and bats that occasionally fall to the cave floor and provide nourishment for the scuttling creatures that dwell in swiftlet and bat excrement. If you happen to be outside the cave entrance at around 6pm, you will see an impressive vortex of bats streaming out in search of food (unless it's raining, in which case they tend to stay in).

The majority of visitors to Gomantong come as part of an add-on to their Kinabatangan tour package. If you're driving the caves are reachable via 5km of paved road, around 22km northeast of Bilit and 27km northeast of Sukau.

Due to dwindling swiftlet bird populations, the caves are closed over certain periods, so check before planning your visit.

Kinabatangan Orangutan Conservation Project (KOCP)   RESEARCH CENTRE

(HUTAN; ☎ 088-413293; www.hutan.org.my; Sukau) Inside Sukau village this conservation camp, run in partnership with a French NGO, is dedicated to studying and protecting the orangutan. It also establishes environmental-education programs, reforestation initiatives and an elephant-conservation project in the Sukau-Bilit area. It's not open to casual visitors, but staff may be willing to hire out guides for tracking wild orangutans; contact them well in advance.

Bukit Belanda   HILL

(Bilit) Bukit Belanda – Dutch Hill – is a 420m hill located behind the village of Bilit. The land is owned by the citizens of Bilit, who, despite pressures from logging companies, have not opened the hill to the timber industry, preferring to maintain it as a haven for wildlife. Hike to the top early in the morning, before it gets hot, where you'll be rewarded by lovely views of Sungai Kinabatangan and, if you're lucky, glimpses of local wildlife.

🏃 Activities

Wildlife Riverboat Cruises

A wildlife cruise down the Kinabatangan is unforgettable. In the late afternoon and early morning, binocular-toting enthusiasts have a chance of spotting nest-building orangutans, nosy proboscis monkeys, shy silver leaf and maroon langurs, basking monitor lizards and chattering long-tailed and pig-tailed macaques. The reason so many animals are here though is depressing – the expansion of palm-oil plantations has driven local wildlife to the riverbank. The animals simply have nowhere else to live. Add to this that the Green Belt rule, established to ensure a safe corridor of cover next to the river for animals to pass by new plantations, is being regularly broken by farmers who want to maximise every inch of their land, and it's even more concerning.

Mammals can be seen all year, moving around in small groups. Colourful birds are a huge draw: all eight varieties of Borneo's hornbills, plus brightly coloured pittas, kingfishers and, if you're lucky, a Storm's stork or the bizarre Oriental darter nest in the forests hugging the Kinabatangan. Avian wildlife is more numerous and varied during rainier months (usually October to late March), which coincides with northern-hemisphere migrations. Though friendly for birds, the rainy season isn't accommodating for humans. Flooding has been a problem of late and a couple of lodges will sometimes shut their doors when conditions are severe.

The success rate of animal spotting largely depends on luck and the local knowledge of your guide. In the late afternoon you'll be looking for proboscis monkeys and crocs. You may veer off the Kinabatangan and explore its narrow tributaries. River cruises by night are even more dramatic, with the sky a silent theatre of electric-yellow lightning, or a jeweller's cloth of glittering gems, then set out into the crow-black mass of the Kinabatangan River. Your life and the

SABAH SUNGAI KINABATANGAN

THE BUSINESS OF BIRD NESTS

The Gomantong Caves are Sabah's most famous source of swiftlet nests, used for one of the most revered dishes of the traditional Chinese culinary oeuvre: the eponymous bird's nest soup, made from dried swiftlet spit, which when added to the broth dissolves and becomes gelatinous.

There are two types of soupworthy bird nests: black and white. The white nests are more valuable and Gomantong has a lot of them. A kilogram of white swiftlet spit can bring in over US$4000 (as witnessed in swiftlet nest-selling shops in KK), making nest-grabbing a popular profession, despite the perilous task of shimmying up bamboo poles.

In the last few years visiting the caves has been restricted due to dwindling bird populations (cash-hungry locals were taking the nests before the newborn birds had enough time to mature). Today the caves operate on a four-month cycle, with closings at the beginning of the term to discourage nest hunters. It's worth asking around before planning your visit – often the caves are empty or off-limits to visitors. The four-month cycles are strictly enforced to encourage a more sustainable practice of harvesting.

success of the cruise is in the hands of your multitasking driver, who scopes the trees with his torch while driving. You'll possibly see sleeping stork kingfishers with their eyes open, pygmy elephants in the river, pythons coiled in trees, civet cats, egrets hanging like phantom pods from branches, buffy fish owls, flatheaded cats and the eyes of crocodiles glinting redly in torchlight, as they emerge like periscopes to slyly chart your progress.

River tours should always be included in lodge package rates. If you prefer to explore independently, contact local homestay programs, which will be able to hook you up with a boat operator. Or ask about renting a boat in Sukau – everyone in the village is connected to the tourism industry either directly or through family and friends, and someone will be able to find you a captain. Another option: just before the entrance to Sukau village is a yellow sign that says 'Di sini ada boat servis' (Boat service here) – different river pilots hang out here throughout the day. Whatever way you choose to find a boat and a guide, expect to pay at least RM100 for a two-hour river cruise on a boat that can hold up to six people (ie you can split the cost with friends).

Hiking

Depending on the location of your lodge, some companies offer short hikes (one to three hours) through the jungle. Night hikes are some of the best fun to be had on the Kinabatangan – there's something magical about being plunged into the intense, cavernlike darkness of the jungle at night. Head torches should be carried in your hand rather than on your head – all manner of creatures tend to be attracted to light sources.

Sleeping & Eating

Bilit has the greatest concentration of river lodges and homestays, followed by Sukau. More isolated accommodation (upriver or in Abai) can increase the chances of wildlife spotting. Book the river lodges in advance. In Kinabatangan lingo, a 'three-day, two-night' stint usually involves two boat cruises daily (at dawn and dusk) and jungle walks. Many packages include transfer prices from Sandakan.

Accommodation is almost always packaged with meals, which tend to be varied and of good quality. Alcohol costs extra.

Sukau

Tiny Sukau village sits on the river across from massive stone cliffs seemingly lifted from a Chinese silk-scroll painting. It's more low key than Bilit, with accommodation geared towards the shoestring end of the market.

Sukau Greenview B&B   B&B $
(089-565266, 013-869 6922; www.sukaugreen view.net; waterfront, Sukau; 2-day, 1-night packages per person incl breakfast dm/r RM335/360) Run by friendly locals, this lime-green wooden affair has snug, fan-cooled dorms and basic rooms. There's also a pleasant cafe looking out on the river. Greenview runs special elephant-sighting trips priced at RM250 per person (minimum two).

Kinabatangan Riverside Lodge   LODGE $$
(089-213502; www.sitours.com; Sukau; 2-day, 1-night packages incl visit to Sepilok's Sun Bear Conservation Centre & Orangutan Nursery from RM550;) Come here to fall gently asleep in a series of luxury chalets, adrift in simple white sheets and polished wood floors, all connected by a series of shady raised walkways through the jungle. A looping nature trail is out the back and an adorable dining area abounds with stuffed monkeys, faux foliage and traditional instruments. It's managed by SI Tours.

Proboscis Lodge Bukit Melapi   LODGE $$
(088-240584; www.sdclodges.com; Sukau; 2-day, 1-night packages tw share per person RM780;) Based on a promontory that saw a battle between local Orang Sungai (People of the River) and the Japanese in WWII, this lodge's fruit-luxuriant grounds are popular with sweet-toothed elephants. There's a games room and pleasant lounge, while rooms are huge with river-facing balcony, cable TV, bathroom, and comfy beds. Frequent hornbill sightings. Staff are super friendly.

The two-day, one-night packages include three meals, one river cruise and a pick-up from the Lapit jetty.

★ **Sukau Rainforest Lodge**   LODGE $$$
(088-438300; www.sukau.com; Sukau; 3-day, 2-night packages RM1625;) One of *National Geographic*'s 'Top 30 Lodges in the World', this is the most upscale place on the river. It has beautifully appointed split-level rooms with wood and terrazzo floors, rain shower, lounge area and mosquito nets. There's a fine restaurant, an on-site natural-

ist who gives wildlife talks and night walks, plus a welcome plunge pool to cool off in. Romantic.

Bilit

The most populous of the Sungai Kinabatangan villages, Bilit is framed by palm-oil plantations and jungle-clad hills. The lion's share of Sungai Kinabatangan's upmarket jungle lodges are dotted along the riverbanks here.

Borneo Natural
Sakau Bilit Resort RESORT $$
(☎017-972 9128; www.amazingborneo.com; Bilit; 3-day, 2-night package incl all meals, dm/chalet per person from RM500/780; ❋ 🛜) On the western edge of Bilit, this newish jungle lodge is all soaring ceilings in the airy dining area, while the cosy air-con chalets come with four-poster beds and rain showers (the deluxe ones are more spacious and have terraces overlooking a pond). Large, luxurious bunks are de rigueur in the dorm. River cruises and jungle walks offered.

Myne Resort RESORT $$
(☎089-223366; www.myne.com.my; Bilit; 3-day, 2-night package ex Sandakan in longhouse/chalet RM1107/1160; ❋ 🛜) Situated on a sweeping river bend, Myne has an open, breezy reception, games room and restaurant festooned with lifeguard rings, vaguely reminiscent of a wooden ship. Hillside chalets are beautiful, with river-facing balcony, polished-wood floors, comfy beds, flat-screen cable TV and hot showers. Packages include river cruises and jungle walks. Extra activities include nocturnal walks and cruises. Reachable by road.

Nature Lodge Kinabatangan LODGE $$
(☎088-230534; www.naturelodgekinabatangan.com; Bilit; 3-day, 2-night stay incl 4 boat rides & all meals dm/chalet RM470/700; ❋) 🌱 Welcoming staff await in this fine eco-conscious lodge, run by River Junkie and divided into the Civet Wing dorm-style huts and the Agamid Wing with twin-bed chalets with high ceilings and wood floors. The food is tasty and the guides are top-notch. The activity schedule is fantastic: the three-day, two-night packages include four boat tours and one guided hike.

Last Frontier Resort RESORT $$
(☎017-629 3363, 016-676 5922; www.thelastfrontierresort.com; Bilit; 3-day, 2-night package RM750; ❋ 🛜) Maybe they should rename this place the Last Breath Resort after the torturously

steep hill you have to ascend to reach the place. Your reward, however, is a serene view of the floodplain and a sense of absolute escape with four boutique-style rooms with dark-wood beds and oxblood-hued linen. Package price includes two river cruises and one ridge trek.

Kinabatangan Jungle Camp LODGE $$
(☎017-228 0299, 089-533190; www.kinabatanganjunglecamp.com; Bilit; 3-day, 2-night package RM580) This secluded, earth-friendly retreat on a river bend caters to birders and serious nature junkies. Facilities are functional, with the focus on quality wildlife spotting over soft, comfortable accommodation, with fan-only rather than air-con rooms. Packages include three meals, two boat rides, guiding and transfers. The owners also run the Labuk B&B in Sepilok.

Bilit Rainforest Lodge LODGE $$$
(☎088-448409; http://bilitrainforestlodge.com; Bilit; 2-day, 1-night package incl meals RM840; ❋ 🛜) Rainforest has 24 rooms with stained-wood floors, balcony complete with hammock, armoire and bathroom. Although it's comparatively bland compared with some of the competition, the service is warm and the grounds are large. There's also a handsome central building with a nice bar come evening. Additional cruises cost RM120 per person.

Bilit Adventure Lodge LODGE $$$
(☎089-271077; www.stwadventure.com; Bilit; 2-day, 1-night package from RM998, with air-con RM1100; ❋) Built over a decade ago, this cosy lodge has 16 air-con and eight fan rooms. It feels authentic with its river-bar cafe and bamboo-accented rooms with colourful quilts. The fan-only rooms are less impressive. Set in 4 hectares of untamed wilderness across the river from Bilit, the lodge's lights are kept low at night to encourage the presence of wildlife.

Abai & Elsewhere on the River

Tiny Abai sits on a peninsula on the Sungai Kinabatangan, connected by a tenuous land bridge to dry land. This is as downriver as you can stay without hitting the sea.

Tungog Rainforest Eco Camp CABIN $
(☎089-551070; www.mescot.org; per night incl 3 meals RM95, river cruises per boat RM95 or per person RM40 (minimum 3)) 🌱 This eco camp faces a pretty oxbow lake by the Kinabatangan River. Luxurious it isn't – expect

DON'T MISS

HOMESTAYS ON THE KINABATANGAN

Homestay programs are popping up with increasing frequency in Sukau, Bilit and other villages, giving tourists a chance to stay with local Orang Sungai (People of the River) and inject money almost directly into local economies. Please note the contacts we provide are for local homestay program coordinators who will place you with individual families.

The villagers of **Abai** love hosting guests and chatting with you; expect to be asked to participate in the local village volleyball matches! A homestay is best arranged through Adventure Alternative Borneo (p320) in Kota Kinabalu, which maintains direct contact with the villagers. A typical two-night package includes meals, guided village walk and jungle walk, one day and night river cruise, plus boat from Sandakan and room and meals.

In **Sukau**, **Bali Kito Homestay** (☑ 013-869 9026; http://sukauhomestay.com; waterfront, Sukau; 3-day, 2-night package for 4 people RM680 per person, 1 night incl 2 meals RM60) can connect you with several different families and hook you up with cultural programs, fishing trips, opportunities to work on traditional farms, treks, wildlife cruises and other fun. A special walk-in rate of RM30 is also available if you just rock up at the village (meals are RM10 each). A four-person three-day, two-night package that includes meals, four river cruises, transport to and from Sandakan and a visit to the Gomantong Caves costs RM650 per person, but different packages can be arranged for smaller groups.

Homestays in **Bilit** are on a rotation system of nine households so they all get a fair crack of the whip. The dwellings we visited were all fiercely house-proud with mattresses on clean floors (expect squat loos). You can just turn up here or look for the official 'Homestay Malaysia' sign. Three-day, two-night rates, which include river cruises and trekking, cost RM840 per person.

Near **Batu Puti** (the village adjacent to the Batu Tulug caves), **Miso Walai Homestay** (☑ 089-551070, 019-582 5214, 012-889 5379; www.mescot.org; Jln Sandi, Batu Putih; r RM70) is one of the oldest, best-run community ecotourism initiatives in the area and works with the excellent KOPEL, a village co-operative managed and run by the local people themselves. We've had really glowing reports from travellers who have stayed and worked here on the volunteer program planting trees. You'll be encouraged to learn to cook, and take part in village sports and farming as part of the experience. By dint of its location, this homestay also happens to be outside the tourist crush in Sukau and Bilit, so your chances of spotting wildlife are much better.

When staying in a homestay, it is important to act as a guest in someone's home. Privacy will be reduced, and you may be expected to help with chores, cooking, cleaning etc (this depends on the family you stay with). Men and women should dress modestly and couples will want to avoid overt displays of affection, which locals tend to frown on. English may not be widely spoken. The experience is a different one, which many visitors absolutely love, but it's certainly not everyone's cup of tea. That said, we strongly encourage giving homestays a shot if you haven't done so before.

wooden shelters with mattress, fragrant sheets and pillows, plus a mosquito net and shared bathrooms; however, the immersion in nature and chance to put something back by planting trees is magical. Given there's no other camps for miles, you have the wildlife to yourself.

★ **Tanjung Bulat Jungle Camp** LODGE $$ (☑ 016-812 0704; www.oxbowlakeborneo.simple site.com; Tanjung Bulat; 3-day, 2-night package incl all meals RM470) Located on the bank of an oxbow lake, far from any village, this wonderful place is great for wildlife spot-

ting. Digs are simple: six twin rooms with bug netting, flushing toilets and rainwater bucket showers. Owner/guide Afiq is a treasure trove of nature-related knowledge and great with kids, too. Arrange pick-up in advance, as it entails two boat rides.

Activities include boat cruises, with the oxbow lake made magic by night with silvery fish leaping out of the water, jungle walks and the 'Borneo Big Five' – a day-long trip down the Kinabatangan River, almost as far as the sea if need be, in search of the orangutan, pygmy elephant, proboscis monkey, rhinoceros hornbill and crocodile. Boat pick-ups from Deramakot Forest Reserve (p357) can be arranged.

One of the advantages of Tanjung Bulat is its location in a namesake 220-hectare swath of protected secondary forest. The lodge is actively involved in the reforestation program and welcomes volunteers.

Uncle Tan's Jungle Camp — LODGE $$

(☏089-535784, 016-824 4749; www.uncletan. com; 2-day, 1-night packages from RM350, 3-day, 2-night packages from RM480) Uncle Tan was one of the earliest environmentalists working along the Kinabatangan. This is *not* the Hilton: accommodation consists of raised, open huts with mattresses; bring mosquito net. Expect bags of enthusiasm from the great staff, knowledgeable guides and a warm atmosphere. Due to its isolated location in a wetland in the midst of the rainforest, animal sightings are high.

Abai Jungle Lodge — LODGE $$$

(☏089-213502, 013-883 5841; www.sitoursborneo. com; Abai; 3-day, 2-night packages incl visit to Sepilok's Sun Bear Conservation Centre & Orangutan Nursery from US$518) Managed by SI Tours (p348), ecofriendly Abai Jungle Lodge sits 37km downstream from Sukau as the river emerges from secondary forest. Rooms are comfortable fan-only affairs with polished wooden floors, and dinner may feature river prawns, fish and veggies. The wildlife here is terrific, and Abai's guides go all out to find what you're looking for.

❶ Getting There & Away

Transfers are usually arranged with your lodging as part of your package. You can save by arriving independently, although it's hardly worth the hassle or delays. Don't get on Birantihanti buses – they stop any time someone wants to get on or off, which can quadruple travelling time.

BUS & MINIBUS

From KK, board a Tawau- or Lahad Datu-bound bus and ask the driver to let you off at 'Sukau Junction', also known as 'Meeting Point', the turn-off road to reach Sukau. If you are on a Sandakan-bound bus, ask your driver to stop at the Tawau–Sandakan junction – it's called 'Batu 32' or 'Checkpoint' (sometimes it's known as Sandakan Mile 32).

From Sepilok or Sandakan, expect to pay around RM20 to reach 'Batu 32', and around RM35 if you're on a Sandakan–Tawau bus and want to alight at 'Meeting Point'.

Arrange in advance with your Sepilok accommodation to be picked up from these drop-off points. The alternative is expensive taxis.

A minibus ride to 'Meeting Point' from Lahad Datu costs RM25. When buying your bus tickets, remember to tell the vendor where you want to get off so you don't get overcharged.

CAR

If you are driving from Sandakan, note that the petrol station just before the Kinabatangan junction (not the Sukau junction) is the last place to fill up before arriving at the river. The road to Sukau and the turn-off to Bilit are both paved, though they are rather potholed and bumpy.

Lahad Datu

☏089 / POP 27,900

If you linger in Lahad Datu, and hook up with Bike & Tours (p364), you can learn to cook the Borneo way, dive and snorkel the local reef and shipwreck without the Semporna/ Mabul crowds, or go mountain biking up and down Mt Silam for scenic views of Darvel Bay. It's a far cry from the first glance of this little coastal town, which appears to have a lively produce market, dry-goods market, sun-scorched buildings and very little else. Travellers who breeze through en route to Tabin Wildlife Park and Danum Valley, arriving on early morning flights from KK and spirited away immediately, are missing out. Lahad Datu's location, roughly halfway between Semporna and Sungai Kinabatangan, makes it an ideal place to fly into from KK if you're looking to commune both with sea creatures and orangutans.

🏃 Activities & Tours

Tabin Wildlife Holidays — WILDLIFE WATCHING

(☏088-267266; www.tabinwildlife.com.my; lot GL02, arrival concourse, Lahad Datu Airport; ⊙7.30am-5pm Mon-Fri, to 4.30pm Sat & Sun) Book your stay at the Tabin Wildlife Resort (p367) here and get your entry permit. If driving yourself to Tabin Wildlife Reserve, enquire about package discounts.

Borneo Nature Tours — TREKKING

(☏089-880207; www.borneonaturetours.com; lot 20, block 3, Fajar Centre; ⊙9am-5pm) Borneo Nature Tours, which runs the Borneo Rainforest Lodge (BRL), has an office in the upper part of town – known as Taman Fajar, or Fajar Centre. Make sure you enter the correct office – some tourists book their

Danum Valley expedition with the wrong company.

🛏 Sleeping

House 11   GUESTHOUSE $
(☑089-881007; lot 11, Taman Panji, Jln Panji; r RM90; ❄🤖) While not quite a hostel, this wallet-friendly budget spot gets high marks for its clean private rooms (some windowless), the helpfulness of its staff and nice little touches such as being given cakes as a treat. Walking distance from a cluster of shops and restaurants.

★Bike & Tours B&B   B&B $$
(☑017-293 6376, 017-864 2016; www.bikeandtours. com; lot 62, Taman Hap Heng, Batu 1 1/4, Jln Segama; r with/without bathroom from RM260/160, f RM325 all incl breakfast; ❄🤖🏊) Winning applause for its cycling excursions in the area, and the quality of its accommodation, B&T is run by friendly Swiss/Malay couple Itisha and Simon. The four rooms are cool affairs with laminate floors and fresh linen. There's a dipping pool in the garden, great breakfast, fantastic candlelit dinners (RM70) and a complimentary pick-up from the bus station/airport.

B&T is all about introducing you to secret spots around Lahad Datu and mindfulness in nature – taking your time on two wheels to get to know the locals and the environment around you. It also organises diving and snorkelling day trips with an enthusiastic one-man show, Dominic. Highly recommended.

Bay Hotel   HOTEL $$
(☑089-882801; block O, lot 1 & 2, 7b Jln Pantai; s/d from RM100/110; ❄🤖) Fresh rooms with flat-screen TV, swish decor, bathroom and air-con, plus a pleasant cafe downstairs serving Western food, make this a good waterfront option. Wi-fi comes and goes like a stray cat.

Hotel De Leon   HOTEL $$
(☑089-881222; www.sabahhotels.com; Darvel Bay Commercial Centre, Jln Pantai; r/ste from RM148/188; ❄🤖) While not the five-star experience touted on its website, Lahud Datu's plushest option has a chic, baroque-accented lobby and restaurant, and air-conditioned rooms. Perfect for those needing a night of comfort after the bush. As for the wi-fi speed, we've encountered faster snails.

🍴 Eating

Ah Seng Chicken Rice   CHICKEN $
(☑089-880 089; Sedco Bldg, Jln Kimbang; mains RM6; ⏰7.30am-3pm) This unassuming spot gets Hainanese chicken rice just right. The chicken, simmered in broth, is melt-in-your-mouth tender, the broth zings with ginger and the chicken and rice are served with a punchy chilli-and-garlic sauce.

Rumpun Selera   INDIAN $
(www.facebook.com/RumpunSeleraLahadDatu; Jln Perdana 1, Bandar Sri Perdana; mains RM7-15; ⏰8am-11pm; ☑) Besides a full buffet of curries and other Indian-Malay dishes, this unassuming joint makes the flakiest, softest *roti canai* in town.

Dovist   CHINESE $
(☑089-889033; Lg Fajar 4, Fajar Centre; mains from RM7; ⏰6am-11.30pm) A respectable spot for a substantial meal of Chinese-style seafood dishes. Around the corner from the Danum Valley Field Centre.

★Sakura Seafood Restaurant   SEAFOOD $$
(☑089-885622; block J, Bahagian Sedco Baru, Jln Pantai Baru; mains RM9-17; ⏰11am-11pm) Sakura doesn't look like much at first glance – a few plastic tables and chairs scattered under an awning. But then the food arrives: succulent butter prawns in a creamy sauce, crispy, tender, delicately spiced softshell crab, crunchy and garlicky *sayur manis,* steamed fish with ginger...flawless.

ℹ Getting There & Away

AIR
Malaysia Airlines operates four daily flights to Lahad Datu from KK. The **airport** (Jln Tun Hussein Onn) is in the upper part of town, near Fajar Centre. You must take the first flight of the day (departing KK at 6.10am) if you don't want an overnight layover in town before heading to the Danum Valley.

BUS
Express buses on the KK–Tawau route stop at **Lahad Datu bus station** (Lg Fajar 10) at the Shell station (Fajar Centre) behind the Danum Valley Field Centre in the upper part of town. Other buses and minivans leave from a **vacant lot** (Jln Bunga Raya) near Tabin Lodge in the lower part of town. There are frequent departures for Sandakan (RM25, 2½ hours), Sukau (RM25, two hours), Semporna (RM22 to RM25, two hours) and Tawau (RM20, 2½ hours).

Danum Valley Conservation Area

Comprising 440 sq km of central Sabah, the Danum Valley Conservation Area is home to a mind-blowing spectrum of creatures: orangutans, tarsiers, sambar deer, bearded pigs, flying squirrels, king cobras, proboscis monkeys, red-leaf monkeys, gibbons and pygmy elephants, though you'd be lucky to spot most of them. The area is also known for its medium-sized cats, with the beautifully marked clouded leopard spotted on night drives, as well as the flat-headed cat, marbled cat, leopard cat and cartoon-like bay cat. This almost impenetrable arboreal fortress is watered by Sungai Segama and shaded by 70m-high old-growth trees and 1093m-high Mt Danum. Recognised as one of the world's most complex ecosystems, a new species of plant is found by scientists here every week. Your alarm clock is the dawn chorus of gibbons, the chainsaw drone of cicadas is the soundtrack for breathless afternoons, and the shrill of crickets is your bedtime cue.

This pristine primary forest is currently under the protection of Yayasan Sabah logging concession (www.ysnet.org.my), a semigovernmental organisation tasked with both protecting and utilising the forest resources of Sabah. They say that at any given time, there are more than 100 scientists doing research in the Danum Valley. See the website of South East Asia Rainforest Research (www.searrp.org) for more information on research occurring in the valley.

Activities

Both the Borneo Rainforest Lodge and the Danum Valley Field Centre offer a variety of jungle-related activities. Only the lodge has official nature guides. There are no professionally trained guides at the field centre – only rangers who can show you the trails if you just turn up (RM30 per hour) – but book with a tour company and it will provide you with one. We recommend Sticky Rice Travel (p320).

Sunrise Watching

Getting out of bed while it's still dark and your clock reads 4.45am is no fun; the jungle is as quiet as a cemetery, the air shivery cold. But driving through the forest to a vertiginously high wooden watchtower, climbing to its top and waiting for the sun to appear over the mist- and forest-shrouded hills below make it all worthwhile. As the first cicadas wake, and with the melodic call of the gibbon reaching out of the mist-veiled jungle, you feel like a privileged voyeur witnessing a sacred, primal moment. Then slowly the fireworks begin as a sliver of sun appears over the distant forest ridge, the sky seguing through ruby to salmon, orange to vermilion. Priceless. It can be chilly, so bring a sweater! The dawn drive is not included in tour packages and costs RM160 (which can be split between four people).

Trekking in the Valley

The main activities at the Borneo Rainforest Lodge (BRL) and the Danum Valley Field Centre (DVFC) are walks on more than 50km of marked, meandering trails. BRL has 12 trails, while the DVFC only has three or four open to the general public – the rest are strictly for researchers. You can't hike the trails without a guide, lest you get lost in the rainforest and your mortal remains are never seen again. The average group is about six to eight people, and fitness will vary considerably – if you're in a troupe of superheroes and get left behind, don't be afraid to ask the guide to slow down. Depending on the zeal of your group, you might walk as much as 16km or more in one day over a series of short walks or one long and short walk (excluding night walks). Remember you're in the jungle and clambering over roots and fallen trees is hard work, so don't push yourself unnecessarily.

At the BRL take advantage of the well-trained guides who can point out things you would never see on your own. The **Coffincliff Trail** is a good way to start your exploration and get your bearings. It climbs for 3km to a cliff where the remains

> **DANUM KIT LIST**
>
> We strongly recommend leech socks (especially if there's been rain), a stash of energy sweets, insect repellent, plasters for blisters, a strong torch and, if you're looking for that front-cover shot of a rhinoceros hornbill in flight, a powerful zoom lens. Sneakers are fine in dry weather; hiking boots, though heavier, provide better support in slippery conditions.

of some Kadazan–Dusun coffins can be seen (although the provenance of the coffins is unclear). After reaching a fairly eye-popping panoramic viewpoint 100m further up the way, you can either return the way you came or detour around the back of the cliffs to descend via scenic **Fairy Falls** and **Serpent Falls**, a pair of 15m-high waterfalls that are good for a quick dip.

The **Danum, Elephant** and **Segama Trails** all follow various sections of the Danum Valley and are mostly flat trails offering good chances for wildlife spotting. All can be done in an hour or two. The **Hornbill** and **East Trails** have a few hills, but are still relatively easy, with similarly good chances for wildlife sightings. Finally, if you just need a quick breath of fresh air after a meal, the **Nature Trail** is a short plankwalk near the lodge that allows you to walk into the forest unmolested by leeches.

Around the field centre, it's about a two-hour hike to the **Tembaling Falls**, a cool slice of tropical Edenic beauty. A more strenuous, four-hour trek gets you to the immensely rewarding **Sungai Purut** falls, a series of seven-tiered pools that are fed by waters that drop 20m from the nearby mountains. The **Coffin Trail**, across the suspension bridge, is a 30-minute walk to a large rocky overhang, beneath which are a few 500-year-old ironwood coffins, some still containing the mortal remains of Dusun people. There's a short nature-trail loop next to the field centre, with well-labelled plants, that you can tackle by yourself.

At the centre you'll also take **night walks**. These tend to be hour-long or so, and give you the chance to see mostly creepy crawlies – a remarkable assortment of spiders, grasshoppers and stick insects. If you're very lucky, you might spot chameleons, bug-eyed tarsiers, various serpents – vine snakes, pit vipers – and curious sambar deer.

Bird-watching
Bird-watchers from around the world come to see a variety of rainforest species, including the great argus pheasant, crested fireback pheasant, blue-headed pitta, Bornean bristlehead and several species of hornbill, among many others. If you're serious about birding, it may be best to stay at the Borneo Rainforest Lodge. The canopy walkway here is ideal for bird-watching, and some of the guides are particularly knowledgeable about birds. The access road to the lodge is also a good spot for birding, as is, frankly, your porch.

Canopy Walkway
Most of the action in a tropical rainforest happens up in the canopy, which can be frustrating for earthbound humans. The Borneo Rainforest Lodge's 107m-long, 27m-high canopy walkway gives mere mortals a means of glimpsing life high up in the canopy. The swinging bridges traverse a nice section of forest, with several fine *mengaris* and *majau* trees on either side. Bird-watchers often come here at dawn in hope of checking a few species off their master lists. Even if you're not a keen birder, it's worth rolling out of bed early to see the sun come up over the forest from the canopy walkway – when there's a bit of mist around, the effect is quite magical. The walkway is located on the access road, a 10-minute walk from the lodge. You need to be a guest at the BRL to access the walkway.

Night Drives
Night drives are one of the surest ways to see some of the valley's 'night shift'. Expect to see one or two species of giant flying squirrels, sambar deer, civets, porcupines and possibly even leopard cats. Lucky sightings could include elephants and slow loris.

Night drives (RM160, up to eight people) leave the Borneo Rainforest Lodge and Danum Valley Field Centre most evenings. The best trips are the extended night drives from BRL, which depart at about 8.30pm and return at 1am or 2am. Things you'll be glad you brought: light waterproof jacket, binoculars and a powerful torch. It can be cold, too, so bring another layer.

Sleeping & Eating
Danum Valley Field Centre LODGE $$
(DVFC; ☎088-881688, 089-841101; dinisiah. cemd@gmail.com; Danum Valley Conservation Area; dm RM95, resthouse r RM200, camping per person RM80, VIP chalet RM390; ☺closed over Christmas & New Year; ❄) ✎ An outpost for scientists and researchers, the field centre also welcomes wildlife enthusiasts. Accommodation is organised into four categories: hostel, resthouse, VIP and camping. We recommend the resthouse, with basic clean rooms, ceiling fans and twin beds, located by the canteen. The simple hostel is about a seven-minute walk from the canteen, and consists of two longhouse-style gender-segregated rooms.

Towels are provided for the cold-water showers. Electricity is only on from 7am to 11pm; dorms tend to get hot and stuffy. The VIP chalets come with air-con. Walks start from the canteen, so if you're staying in the dorms you'll constantly be walking between the two. If you want to camp, you can lay your sleeping kit (no tent needed) out on the walkways – bug spray recommended!

Guests take their meals in the cafeteria-style canteen (veggie friendly). Near the camp is a clear stretch of shallow river in which to cool off.

★**Borneo Rainforest Lodge**   RESORT $$$
(BRL; ☑089-880207, 088-267637; www.borneo naturetours.com; Danum Valley Conservation Area; d standard/deluxe 3-day & 2-night package per person RM3496/3590; ✳@) Set beside the Danum River, Borneo Rainforest Lodge is for Indiana Jones types with healthy wallets – adventure combined with luxury, if you will. If you can afford to splash out on one of the lovely 31 en-suite chalets – the deluxe ones have private balcony with hot tub overlooking the jungle – you won't be disappointed. Bird-watching's a speciality here.

There are talks on wildlife and conservation, knowledgeable wildlife guides, slide shows, raised wooden walkways and a romantic outside terrace.

ℹ Information

There's snail-slow wi-fi at the Danum Valley Field Centre reception and if you have any local SIM card, you should get a strong-enough signal to use data as long as the telecommunications tower is functioning.

ℹ Getting There & Away

The Danum Valley is only accessible by authorised private vehicle. Borneo Rainforest Lodge guests depart from the lodge office in Lahad Datu at 9am, arriving by lunchtime. If you do not want to spend the night in Lahad Datu, take the 6.10am Malaysia Airlines flight from KK.

Tourists staying at the Danum Valley Field Centre either come in a private vehicle provided by their tour company, or they must board one of two jungle-bound vans that leave the booking office in Lahad Datu at 3.30pm on Mondays, Wednesdays and Fridays. Transport is around RM100 per person each way. Vans return to Lahad Datu from the field centre at 8.30am.

Tabin Wildlife Reserve

About an hour's drive from Lahad Datu, this 1120-sq-km reserve consists mainly of lowland dipterocarp forest with mangrove areas – most of it is technically secondary forest, but that doesn't seem to trouble the wildlife or visitors. The stars here are the elephants and primates – gibbons, red-leaf monkeys and macaques, plus a lot of orang-utans. Rescued orangutans from Sepilok are released here, so you've got a pretty good chance of spotting some.

Mammals that you'd be very lucky to see include the shy clouded leopard, tarsier, slow loris and porcupine. Sadly you're unlikely to see the Sumatran rhino; the only two remaining specimens are kept away from visitors. Birdlife is particularly abundant, with a staggering 253 species recorded here, including all eight of the hornbill family, from rhino through to helmeted, and some naturalists come for the frogs and toads alone: the nocturnal croaking chorus consists of 71 species.

Tabin has a number of mud volcanoes and salt licks where animals and birds gather for their precious minerals, and you can watch them, cameras poised, from viewing towers. Dawn forest walks and dawn safaris are better for bird spotting, while afternoon hikes and night walks and drives improve your chances of seeing the animal life.

There are eight hiking trails around the Tabin Wildlife Resort, varying in difficulty and in length from 400m to 2.8km. Three trails lead directly from the resort, including the Gibbon Trail (2.8km), which snakes its way to the pretty Lipa Waterfall, where you can take a refreshing dip. The Elephant Trail (2.2km) takes you from the Wildlife Department office near the resort to Lipad mud volcano to see the belching mud pits and improve your complexion by giving yourself a natural facial. Trails may only be tackled with a guide.

Tabin Wildlife Resort (☑in Lahad Datu 088-267266; www.tabinwildlife.com.my; Tabin Wildlife Reserve; 2-day, 1-night package incl meals from RM1590; ✳🛜) is an attractive retreat with a clutch of upscale, pricey chalets with polished wooden floors and shady terraces overlooking the creek in the heart of the Tabin Wildlife Reserve. All meals are included, as are two guided walks, a night safari drive and transport to/from Lahad Datu.

Semporna

☑088 / POP 62,600
The main reason to come to Semporna is to get yourself over to the Semporna Archipelago, a short boat journey away. The dive companies are all conveniently located in the same area, and many have a dive centre

at the resorts on Mabul Island. If you've booked your dive and stay from KK already, you'll be picked up from the airport by your respective tour company and spirited straight to Semporna's port to take you to your end destination, so there's no need to stay a night here.

You won't be using up your camera's memory card in the town of Semporna, which, except for its mosque, is not immediately captivating. There's a trash-strewn wet market and some pretty stilted, over-the-water hotels, but little reason to extend a stay beyond dumping your bags and chatting with dive-company staff – they'll soon have you salivating over the archipelago.

Sights & Activities

Scuba is the town's lifeline, and there's no shortage of places to sign up for it. If you have your heart set on diving at Sipadan, book up to three months in advance in peak season (July and August) and several weeks in advance the rest of the year. Only 120 permits are issued daily, and not all diving operators go to Sipadan.

Mosque
MOSQUE

(waterfront; ⊘ hours vary) Dominating the waterfront with its elegant golden cupola and soaring minarets, this sky-blue mosque is probably the best-looking thing in Semporna, especially when silhouetted against the sunset.

Sleeping

Cube Bed Station
HOSTEL $

(☑ 089-781999; http://cbshostel.com.my; lot B10, Semporna seafront; dm/r from RM68/188; ❋ 🛜) At first glance this place exudes urban chic, which is much needed in Semporna: a graffiti-scrawled yet inviting common area, private rooms that are all exposed brick and grained wood, cute reading lights in the dorm 'cubes' that offer greater privacy than bunks. Some downsides, though: air-con is off from 9am to 5pm, so rooms get stuffy, and service is inconsistent.

Aloha Capsule Hostel
HOSTEL $

(☑ 016-924 9594; www.facebook.com/alohasabah; lot A8, Semporna seafront; dm/r RM58/480; ❋ 🛜) Likely to appeal to *Star Trek* fans (but less to folks suffering from claustrophobia), these futuristic pods, lit with neon, look like something you crawl into, only to emerge from your cryogenic slumber some 3000 years later. There are sockets inside to charge your

electronic gear and twin pods for couples. Less-than-perfect sound insulation means involuntary eavesdropping.

Scuba Junkie Dive Lodge
HOSTEL $

(☑ 089-785372; www.scuba-junkie.com; block B 36, 458 Semporna seafront; diver or snorkeller/non-diver dm RM25/50, r without bathroom RM80/180, r with bathroom RM110/220; ❋ 🛜) With its walls peppered with underwater shots of marine life, clean bathrooms and a variety of air-con rooms to choose from, this a sure bet. It's handily opposite Scuba Junkie's office (p372), but the rooms themselves are tired and unmemorable, staff seem disinterested and wi-fi is patchy outside the lobby.

★ Kuree Hut
GUESTHOUSE $$

(☑ 089-782251; lot 8, Bandar Baru, 1st fl, block B; r/f RM135/215; ❋ 🛜) This guesthouse, a short walk from the waterfront, is inside a busy apartment block. Rooms are spotless and furnished either with a bunk bed or bunk bed and single bed (for families). A generous American-style breakfast is served every morning and the welcoming staff make a huge difference – from giving useful local tips to booking Tawau transfers.

Holiday Dive Inn
HOTEL $$

(☑ 089-919148; www.holidaydiveinn.com; lot A5-A7, Semporna seafront; r/tr from RM103/165; ❋ 🛜) This 24-room, fully air-conditioned hotel has spotless accommodation featuring a bright colour scheme, fresh bathrooms, TVs and some rooms with balcony. It's affiliated with Sipadan Scuba (p372) nearby. There's also a nice sundowner roof lounge. Avoid the windowless rooms, though.

Dragon Inn
HOTEL $$

(Rumah Rehat Naga; ☑ 089-781088; www.dragoninnfloating.com.my; 1 Jln Kastam, Semporna Ocean Tourism Centre; dm RM45, r incl breakfast from RM122, f RM170-190; ❋ 🛜) Arriving at Dragon Inn, built on stilts and connected by a long boardwalk over bottle-green water, the first thing you see is a taxidermied giant grouper outside the lobby. Rooms are simple, with wood floors, TV and bathroom, and in need of renovation. There's also a peaceful shaded cafe in which to watch the harbour life buzzing by.

Eating

Various Malay-Indian joints and Chinese restaurants specialising in seafood line the 'Semporna Seafront'. A number of these seafood restaurants have been implicated in cooking seafood illegally gathered in Tun Sakaran Marine Park. If you want to sample *nasi lemak* (rice boiled in coconut milk, served with fried *ikan bilis,* peanuts and a curry dish) or *korchung* (rice dumplings), Semporna is well known for these two dishes.

Restoran Bismillah   MALAYSIAN $
(☑ 016-939 3375; Taman Bandar Semporna; mains from RM5; ☺ 24hr) This reliable stalwart caters to night owls and insomniacs, with fried noodle dishes, seafood rice and all manner of variations on the *roti canai.* Wednesday and Sunday are biryani days.

Restoran Al-Thaufika   MALAYSIAN $
(Taman Bandar Semporna; mains RM3-6; ☺ 8am-9pm) This unassuming place is always a good bet for such Indian-Malaysian standards as *roti kosong* (crispy, flaky roti with curry to dip it in), *murtabak* (filled roti) and *roti cobra* (roti topped with dhal, veggies, chicken and fried egg). Wash it down with a fresh fruit juice.

★ Fat Mom's   SEAFOOD $$
(Semporna seafront; mains RM16-48; ☺ 5-10pm) Let's be clear about this: Fat Mom's is Semporna's go-to place for some of the tastiest, freshest seafood around – so fresh that your dinner might be glowering at you from the fish tanks. The squid is wonderfully tender, the fish melts in your mouth and *sayur belacan* greens pack a crunchy punch. But continents may drift before you get served.

❶ Information

Maybank (☑ 089-784852; Jln Jakarullah; ☺ 9.15am-4.30pm)

❶ Getting There & Away

AIR
The nearest airport to Semporna, served by flights from KK and KL, is **Tawau Airport** (off A5), roughly 83km from town. A taxi from Tawau Airport to Semporna (1½ hours) costs RM100, while Semporna–Tawau buses (RM20, two hours) will stop at the airport if you ask the driver nicely. Buses that don't stop at the airport will let you off at Mile 28, a few (unshaded) kilometres from the terminal.

Remember that flying less than 24 hours after diving can cause serious health issues, even death.

BUS
The '**terminal** (Jln Hospital)' is vaguely around the Milimewa supermarket, not too far from the mosque. All buses run from early morning until 4pm (except to Kota Kinabalu) and leave when full. Buses to Kota Kinabalu (RM55 to RM75, nine hours), via Lahad Datu, leave at 7.30am and 7pm. Buses also go to Lahad Datu (RM30, 2½ hours), Sandakan (RM45, 5½ hours) and Tawau (RM25, two hours).

If you're arriving in Semporna by bus, leave the bus drop-off area and head towards the mosque's minaret. This is the way to the waterfront. Follow the grid of concrete streets to the right until you reach 'Semporna Seafront' – home to the diving outfitters, each stacked one next to the other in a competitive clump.

Semporna Archipelago

The stunning sapphire waters and emerald isles of the Semporna Archipelago, home to Bajau sea gypsies in Crayola-coloured boats, are plucked from your most vivid dreams of tropical paradise. Of course few visitors come this way for the islands – rather, it is the ocean and the lure of what lies beneath its surface. This is first and foremost a diving destination – one of the best in the world.

The Semporna Islands are loosely divided into two geographical sections: the northern islands, protected as **Tun Sakaran Marine Park**, and the southern islands. Both areas have desirable diving – Sipadan is located in the southern region, as is Pulau Mabul and Pulau Kapalai. Sibuans belong to the northern area, while Pulau Mataking is just outside the marine reserve. If you are based in Semporna, you'll have a greater chance of diving both areas, although Tun Sakaran now suffers from an influx of mass tourism, and most people are happy to stick with Sipadan and its neighbours.

🏊 Activities

In local speak 'Semporna' means perfect, but there is only one island in the glittering Semporna Archipelago that deserves this title. Miniature-sized **Sipadan**, aka Pulau Sipidan, 36km off the southeast coast, is perfection – turquoise water lapping sugar-fine sand, backed by a lush forest of palm trees and strangler figs. The island sits atop a pinnacle of rock and prompted world-famous diver Jacques Cousteau to describe it as 'an untouched piece of art'. A virtual motorway of marine life passes around you on any given day, including parrotfish, batfish, octopus and cuttlefish changing colour like underwater disco lights, reef sharks, lionfish, and clownfish. Pelagic visitors include hammerhead and whale sharks and regular

SABAH SEMPORNA ARCHIPELAGO

Semporna

SABAH SEMPORNA ARCHIPELAGO

200 m
0.1 miles

Semporna Seafront

Jln Simunul

Jln Tawau–Semporna

Maybank $

Bus & Minibus Terminal

Jln Hospital

Tawau (107 km)

Semporna

◎ Sights

1 Mosque.. A2

● Activities, Courses & Tours

2 Big John Scuba................................E3
3 Billabong Scuba D3
4 Scuba Junkie D3
5 Sipadan Scuba D3
6 Uncle Chang's.................................. D3

⊜ Sleeping

7 Aloha Capsule Hostel D2
8 Cube Bed Station D2
9 Dragon Inn..E2
10 Holiday Dive Inn.............................. D2
11 Kuree Hut B3
12 Scuba Junkie Dive Lodge D3

⊗ Eating

13 Fat Mom's.. D2
14 Restoran Al-Thaufika......................... D3
15 Restoran Bismillah........................... C3

visits from majestic manta and eagle rays. And we haven't even gotten to the reef itself – staghorn, black and seawhip corals, barrel sponges and filigree coral fans all looking as if they've been dipped in funhouse paint.

Roughly a dozen delineated dive sites orbit the island, the most famous being **Barracuda Point**, where chevron and blacktail barracuda merge to form impenetrable walls of undulating fish. Reef sharks, attracted to the strong current here, almost always swing by to say hello. **South Point** hosts large pelagics such as hammerhead and thresher sharks and manta rays, as well as bumphead parrotfish. Expect the current to be strong here. The west side of the island features walls that tumble down to an impossibly deep 2000m – words can't do the sight of this justice. The walls are best appreciated from out in the blue on a clear afternoon.

Although Sipadan outshines its neighbouring sites, there are other reefs in the marine park that are well worth exploring. The macro-diving around **Pulau Mabul** is world famous, and on any given day you can expect to see blue-ringed octopus, bobtail squid, boxer and orangutan crabs and cardinal fish. In fact the term 'muck diving' was invented here. The submerged sites around **Pulau Kapalai**, **Pulau Mataking** and **Pulau Sibuan** are also of note.

It's unlikely you can rock up in Semporna and chance upon an operator willing to take you to Sipadan the following day, because you'll have to do an orientation dive on Pulau Mabul first. And if you're here in the peak months of July and August, or the Christmas period, and haven't booked in advance, you're likely to have a wait. Groups need to book many weeks in advance to get a shot at Sipadan.

The government issues 120 passes (RM148.40) to Sipadan each day (this number includes divers and snorkellers). Each dive company is issued a predetermined number of passes per day and each operator has a unique way of 'awarding' tickets – some companies place their divers in a permit lottery, others promise a day at Sipadan after a day (or two) of diving at Pulau Mabul and Pulau Kapalai. No matter which operator you choose, you will be required to do a non-Sipadan intro dive unless you are a divemaster who has logged a dive in the last six months. Permits to Sipadan are issued by day (and not by dive), so make sure you are getting at least three dives in your package.

A three-dive day trip costs between RM750 and RM850 (some operators include park fees, other don't – be sure to ask), and equipment rental (full gear) comes to about RM60 per day. Cameras and dive computers (around RM100 per day) are also available for rent at most dive centres. Top-end resorts on Pulau Mabul and Pulau Kapalai offer all-inclusive package holidays (plus a fee for equipment rental).

Although most of the diving in the area is 'fun diving', Open Water certifications are available, and advanced coursework is popular for those wanting to take things to the next level. Diving at Sipadan is geared towards divers with an Advanced Open Water certificate (currents and thermoclines can be strong), but Open Water divers should not have any problems (they just can't go as deep as advanced divers). A three-day Open Water course will set you back at least RM1000. Advanced Open Water courses (two days) cost around RM700.

Several dive operators are based at their respective resorts, while others have shopfronts and offices in Semporna and/or KK.

Diving Operators

Numerous operators offer diving in the Semporna Archipelago; not all take divers to Sipadan and not all are reputable. Also beware of any operator that tolerates or even encourages the breaking off of coral and hassling marine life – when found out, they tend to get shamed by responsible operators.

SABAH SEMPORNA ARCHIPELAGO

SNORKELLING IN SEMPORNA

Many non-divers wonder if they should visit Semporna. Of course you should! If you're travelling in a group (or as a couple) where some dive and some don't, the Semporna islands are a lot of fun – dive and snorkelling trips are timed so groups either go together or leave and come back at similar times. If you're on your own and only want to snorkel, it's still great, but not as world class as the diving experience, and a bit pricey relative to the rest of Malaysia – snorkel trips cost around RM180, and you also have to factor in the relatively high cost of accommodation here and the price of getting out to the islands. Then again you still have a good chance of seeing stingrays, sea turtles and all sorts of other macro marine wildlife in the midst of a tropical archipelago, so really, who's complaining?

Other operators fall into two categories: those attached to high-end resorts, with quality gear and professional divemasters, and the more backpacker-friendly operations where you can expect worn and sometimes faulty equipment, hit-and-miss divemasters and large groups per divemaster. Basically you get what you paid for. Particularly recommended operators include the following:

Borneo Divers (p320) Longest-operating diving outfit in Sabah. High safety standards, quality equipment, excellent PADI teachers and divemasters. Luxurious diving lodge on Pulau Mabul.

Scuba Junkie (☑089-785372; www.scuba-junkie.com; lot 36, block B, Semporna seafront; 2 dives RM258, discover scuba 2 dives RM354; ☺9am-6pm) ✎ Highly committed to marine conservation, excellent divemasters, ideal for divers of all abilities, full range of diving courses, comfortable private rooms, plus a dorm on Pulau Mabul.

Seaventures (p320) Purpose-built sea rig with its own house reef next to Pulau Mabul, professional divemasters and full range of diving courses. Three-night minimum stay in private room (not dorm) to guarantee Sipadan pass.

Sipadan Scuba (☑089-781788, 012-813 1688; www.sipadanscuba.com; lot 28, block E, Semporna seafront; 3-dive package off Sibuan RM260, 2-day & 1-night package incl 3 Sipadan dives, accommo-dation, transfer & equipment RM1000) Reliable Semporna-based outfit with over 20 years of experience. Dives Sipadan and Tun Sakaran Marine Park. Some staff more engaged than others.

Sipadan Water Village (☑010-932 5783, 089-784227, 089-950023, 089-751777; www.swvresort.com; Pulau Mabul; 4-day, 3-night package incl all meals & 2 dives daily RM2895) Recommended outfit attached to high-end Pulau Mabul resort.

SMART (☑088-486389; www.sipadan-mabul.com.my; Pulau Mabul; 6-day, 5-night dive package per diver tw share from US$1443 incl 2 dives daily) Another recommended outfit on Pulau Mabul that serves two high-end resorts.

The following operators cater to the budget end of the market:

Big John Scuba (BJ Scuba; ☑089-785399; www.bigjohnscuba.com; Jln Causeway unit 4/5; 3-dive package RM350) Specialises in muck diving off Pulau Mabul and Pulau Kapalai, plus Sipadan trips. Basic guesthouse on Pulau Mabul, but consistently good diving experiences.

Billabong Scuba (☑089-781866; www.billabongscuba.com; lot 28, 1st fl, block E, Semporna seafront; 2 dives Mabul RM275, 3 dives Sipadan RM848) Large groups per diving instructor, worn diving equipment, basic accommodation on Pulau Mabul but fun atmosphere.

Uncle Chang's (Borneo Jungle River Island Tours; ☑017-897 0002, 089-781002; www.ucsipadan.com; 36 Semporna seafront; 3 dives Sipadan RM750, 3 dives Mabul RM350) Snorkelling and diving day trips to Pulau Mataking (RM200), diving at Sipadan, Pulau Mabul and Pulau Kapalai. Basic accommodation on Pulau Mabul and divemasters ranging from enthusiastic to indifferent.

✨ Festivals & Events

Regatta Lepa   CULTURAL
(☺mid-Apr) Traditionally the so-called Bajau sea gypsies only set foot on mainland Borneo once a year; for the rest of the time they lived on small islets or their boats. Today the old cycle of annual return is celebrated and marked by the regatta *lepa*. For visitors the highlight of the festival is the *lepa*-decorating (boat-decorating) contest held between Bajau families.

Their already rainbow-coloured boats are further decked out in streamers, flags (known as *tapi),* bunting, ceremonial umbrellas (which symbolise protection from the omnipresent sun and rain that beats down on the ocean) and *sambulayang,* gorgeously decorated sails passed down within Bajau clans. Violin, cymbal and drum music, plus 'sea sports' competitions such as duck catching and boat tug-of-war, punctuate the entire affair. Check www.sabah tourism.com/events/regatta-lepa-semporna for details.

🛏 Sleeping & Eating

From opulent bungalows to ragtag sea shanties, the archipelago offers a variety of accommodation catering to all budgets, with most clustered on Mabul Island (Sipadan's closest neighbour). No one is allowed to stay on Sipadan. Prices rise in August and September. Non-divers are charged at different rates than divers.

Divers and snorkellers can opt to stay in Semporna, but that only makes sense if you're looking to dive in the Tun Sakaran Marine Park. For diving around Pulau Mabul, Pulau Kapalai and Sipadan, it's much better to stay on Pulau Mabul.

At almost all of the accommodation options, you're tied to a schedule of three to five set meals broken up by roughly three diving (or snorkelling) trips per day. Meals are included, with drinks extra, although tea and coffee are often gratis. High-end resorts have their own bars and restaurants.

🛏 Pulau Mabul

A small island that you can circumnavigate on foot in around half an hour, Pulau Mabul is home to world-class muck diving and speedboat trips to the legendary underwater world of Sipadan, famous for its fiery sunsets. On the other hand, there's a stark contrast between the manicured resort grounds and the squalor of the two pungent villages: the smaller one is home to the stateless Bajau sea gypsies, and the larger, mixed Malay-Bajau one has stilt houses connected by rickety boardwalks overlooking a trash-swamped beach.

Two worlds coexist side by side. In one, tanned bodies emerge from beneath the waves after hours of communing with sharks, turtles and massive shoals of reef fish, and head for their resort bar. In the other, salt-worn, woodcarved tombstones of the cemetery rest beneath the palms, and Bajau children paddle their tiny boats

between the colourful houseboats and the squalid driftwood shacks on stilts.

Uncle Chang's
GUESTHOUSE $

(☑ 089-781002, 017-895 0002; www.ucsipadan. com; Malay village, Pulau Mabul; dm RM75, d without/with air-con RM90/110; ❄) Shipwrecked amid the stilted weaveworld of the Malay village, Chang's is all banana-yellow basic rattan-walled rooms in small chalets, a lively threadbare communal deck with occasional jam sessions and a happy, sociable vibe (when the staff aren't ignoring you). Seven Sipadan permits daily, though the diving guides are hit and miss. Meals are basic. Non-divers add RM100 to accommodation price.

★Scuba Junkie
Mabul Beach Resort
RESORT $$

(☑ 089-785372; www.scuba-junkie.com; Pulau Mabul; 2-day, 1-night package incl all meals & 6 dives dm/r from RM661/708; ❄🛜) 🐾 The most eco-conscious of all Pulau Mabul's lodges, this place attracts a younger international crowd. Superfresh chalets come with porches and bathrooms, dorms are airy and of a good size, plus there's a welcoming central gazebo that houses the restaurant, and a lively bar upstairs where Scuba Junkie does presentations on its many eco-marine causes. Seven Sipadan slots daily.

Divers (but not snorkellers) who book with Scuba Junkie get a 25% discount on packages.

Scuba Junkie is involved in turtle conservation (with on-site hatchery), shark conservation and community education and outreach. It organises beach cleanups and invites Bajau ladies to come and sell crafts that don't involve endangered marine creatures. Rainwater is collected for showers and buffet meals don't serve fish or seafood (due to it being caught using unsustainable fishing practices).

Sipadan Dive Centre
RESORT $$

(SDC; ☑ 010-947 8888, in Kota Kinabalu 088-240584; www.sdclodges.com; Malay village, Pulau Mabul; dm/r RM135/190, 2 dives RM260; ❄) Simple rainbow-coloured huts with attached bathroom, Caribbean-blue walls, fresh linen, and a dive outfit – and less-cramped quarters than other budget places thanks to its spacious grassy compound – make this a solid budget pick. Friendly management, too, with occasional barbecue feasts cooked up for groups. Despite the name, it doesn't offer Sipadan dives, only dives around Pulau Mabul and Pulau Kapalai.

Scuba Jeff
LODGE $$

(☎089-781566, 019-585 5125; www.scubajeff sipadan.com; Malay village, Pulau Mabul; 3-day, 2-night package incl all meals & 5 dives RM915; ☎) Jeff's is a fan-only affair at the end of the world's most rickety boardwalk. There's a breezy open deck offering sea views, plus lively bar with welcoming staff. That's the good stuff. The less good? Forgettable wooden box rooms, less-than-clean bed linen, and indifferent diving instructors, some unqualified. Boat transfer from Semporna costs RM100. Seven Sipadan permits daily.

Billabong Scuba Backpackers
GUESTHOUSE $$

(☎in Semporna 089-781866; www.billabongscuba. com; Malay village, Pulau Mabul; r with fan/aircon RM90/120, chalets with/without sea view RM180/150, 3 dives at Sipadan RM848; ☀) Select from a choice of grotty old rooms and dorm, faded chalets and newer chalets with ox-blood walls, which are built right out to sea. The food doesn't get rave reviews, the scuba equipment is ill-maintained and while some of the dive guides really know their thing, the rest seem bored and uncaring. Seven Sipadan permits daily.

★ Borneo Divers Mabul Resort
RESORT $$$

(☎in Kota Kinabalu 088-222226; www.borneodivers. info; Pulau Mabul; 3-days, 2-nights incl transfer, food & dives per diver/non-diver RM1800/1440; ☀☎☀) ✔ With flower-filled lawns, this charming accommodation has lovely chalets with wood floors and boutique accents, clustered around the pool. The restaurant is terrific, the lounge open and comfy and the staff ever-friendly. Is involved in turtle conservation and offers 14 Sipadan permits daily.

Runs one of the archipelago's best dive centres; Borneo Divers introduced Cousteau to Sipadan back in '89.

Mabul Water Bungalow
RESORT $$$

(☎088-486389; www.mabulwaterbungalows.com; Pulau Mabul; 3-day, 2-night package per diver/ non-diver from US$1323/807; ☀☎) Idyllically lapped by turquoise water, these Balinese-style stilted bungalows with their peaked roofs, fine interiors and palm-fronted porches are exquisite. Diving packages include three dives daily and the 14 daily Sipadan permits are shared with its sister hotel. There's also a decent restaurant here, though if you're a day visitor, you're charged a cheeky RM10 to walk around the resort.

Sipadan-Mabul Resort
RESORT $$$

(SMART; ☎in Kota Kinabalu 088-486389; www. sipadanmabulresort.com; Pulau Mabul; 6-day, 5-night package per diver/non-diver tw share from US$1443/1058; ☀☎☀) Winking with fairy lights and drowning in greenery, this resort has a welcoming restaurant, glossed wood floors and a well-stocked shop. Bungalows are tastefully finished with art, private balcony and fresh linen. The stand-alone bungalows cost an extra RM112 per night, but benefit from private alfresco showers. The

---

SIPADAN SECURITY

If staying on Pulau Mabul you'll inevitably notice the presence of black-clad armed police patrolling the beach. Arriving at Sipadan after your first dive you'll no doubt also double take at the dozen-or-so members of the Malaysian military stationed in a little hut with machine guns while you're diving. Try not to be alarmed; they're here for your safety and as a powerful deterrent.

Since 2000 when the notorious Abu Sayyaf group abducted 21 people in Sipadan, there have been regular attacks on and kidnappings of tourists and locals. In 2018 four Filipino gunmen were shot dead by the coast guard in Lahad Datu waters. A night time curfew was advised for residents of Sandakan, Tawau, Lahad Datu and Semporna (it is now lifted).

Covering 1400km of the east coast of Sabah from Kudat to Tawau, Esscom (Eastern Sabah Security Command) claims to know of 14 kidnap-for-ransom groups from the southern Philippines, four of which have carried out kidnappings on Sabah's east coast.

So is it safe in the archipelago? With the proactively beefed-up police numbers on the islands, the kidnappers have had to become more opportunistic – typically snatching people off boats – but they continue to be active in the region. Always check the latest security warnings with your home country's travel advisories.

14 daily Sipadan permits are shared with Mabul Water Bungalow.

Seaventures Dive Resort RESORT $$$
(☑ in Kota Kinabalu 088-261669; www.seaventures dive.com; Pulau Mabul; 4-day, 3-night dive package per person tw share from RM3360; ✸) Moored beside Pulau Mabul, this orange and polar-blue former oil rig accommodation platform is for serious divers. The dive centre is terrific, as are the comfortable rooms and restaurant. It sits on its own house reef, which is ideal for beginners and muck divers, and Sipadan permits are guaranteed with a three-night stay in a private room (but not dorm).

Sipadan Water Village Resort RESORT $$$
(☑ in Tawau 089-751777; www.swvresort.com; Pulau Mabul; 4-day, 3-night package diver/non-diver RM2895/3505; ✸) Set in a horseshoe design with a decent restaurant at the centre, these 42 stilted chalets perched on the turquoise water are connected by wooden walkways. Expect fresh, inviting rooms with bathroom and unblemished views of the Celebes Sea. Be prepared to be lulled to sleep by the lap of the waves.

🏝 Pulau Kapalai

Set on stilts on the shallow sandbanks of the Ligitan reefs, this is one of the best macro dive sites in the world – on any given day you'll see blue-ringed octopus, bobtail squid, cardinal fish and orangutan crabs. Although commonly referred to as an island, Pulau Kapalai is a small, sloping reef, approximately 15m deep, ringed with two dozen dive sites. The five wrecks on the sandy plateau below the reef attract giant stingrays, massive potato groupers and schools of barracuda and jackfish, as well as different species of shrimp and spider crabs. Standout dive sites include **Mid-Reef**, with its pygmy seahorses, **Gurnard Point** (expect lots of morays, flying gurnard and giant frogfish) and **Mandarin Alley**, which attracts the rare Mandarin fish, stonefish and harlequin ghost pipefish.

★ Kapalai Resort RESORT $$$
(☑ 088-316011; http://sipadan-kapalai.com; Pulau Kapalai; 4-day, 3-night package from RM2790; ✸) This sumptuous stilted water village sits on its own private sandbar on the Ligitan reefs and has beautiful, wood-accented rooms with finely chosen decor that look over the crystal-clear water. There's a long, thin, powdery sandbar you can sunbathe on and snorkel from, and most dive sites are reachable via a short speedboat ride or by swimming off the jetty.

🏝 Pulau Mataking

Furthest from Semporna of all the islands in the Tun Sakaran Marine Park, Pulau Mataking is essentially a sandbar, with two little patches of green bookending a dusty tadpole tail of white sand. This sandy escape has some beautiful diving – the house reef provides some of the best underwater adventure outside Sipadan for divers and snorkellers alike, with plenty of clownfish and schools of yellow snapper. A deliberately sunk wooden cargo boat has become an artificial reef, attracting plenty of sea life and doubling as an actual post office for divers. At the southern end of the island, angelfish, moorish idols and ribbon eels weave their way in and out of the Garden of Eden, while D'Wall, at Pulau Mataking's north end, is a spectacular drift dive, visited by eagle and cownose rays, grey reef sharks and the occasional whale shark and manta.

★ Mataking Island Resort RESORT $$$
(☑ 089-770022, 089-786045; www.mataking.com; Pulau Mataking; 2-day, 1-night package for divers/non-divers from RM1415/1215; ✸ @) 🏊 As the only resort on leaf-shaped Pulau Mataking, this hotel is something special. With its deluxe villas, some with private balcony, and attractive lounge, spa, bar and restaurant, it's a cut above much of the archipelago's competition. The resort also employs a full-time marine-biologist team and manages a green and hawksbill turtle hatchery. Seven Sipadan places daily.

🏝 Pulau Pom Pom

About an hour by boat from Semporna, and near the Tun Sakaran Marine Park, this pear-shaped idyll with its azure water and white sand is a more attractive option than Pulau Mabul for those who want to dive and beach flop. With only two resorts on the island, it's far less crowded here; in fact, many come to get married and explore the underwater treasures as a secondary pursuit. The diving is decent, and the reef that has been damaged by past destructive fishing practises, such as dynamiting, is now being restored through the work of a marine conservation agency that's based on the island.

Pom Pom Island Resort
RESORT $$$

(☑089-781918; www.pompomisland.com; Pulau Pom Pom; s/d from RM1000/1500; ✳🛜) This resort has a range of tasteful rooms, from garden chalets and beach villas to dreamy stilted water cabanas, and resident turtles looking for a swimming date. There's also a solid dive school here, popular with honeymooners. Good muck diving around the island, but the house reef sustains damage from bad fishing practises.

ⓘ Information

Consider stocking up on supplies (sunscreen, mosquito repellent etc) before making your way into the archipelago. Top-end resorts have small convenience stores with inflated prices. Pulau Mabul has shack shops selling basic foodstuffs, and a small pharmacy.

The closest **decompression chamber** (☑DAN (Divers Alert Network) 088-212 9242; Pangkalan TLDM, Semporna) is at the Semporna Naval Base.

ⓘ Getting There & Away

Your accommodation will arrange any transport needs from Semporna or Tawau Airport (sometimes included, sometimes for an extra fee – ask!).

All transport to the archipelago goes through Semporna. Most boats depart in the morning. That means if you arrive in Semporna in the afternoon, you will be required to spend the night in town. Higher-end diving lodges include boat transfer in package prices; budget ones typically do not.

Tawau

☑089 / POP 113,800

Sabah's third city, Tawau, may not be the most picturesque of places, despite its position beside the Celebes Sea and proximity to the Semporna Archipelago, but its dining scene features Sabah's best seafood and if you're flying to and from Tawau to dive Sipadan, it's a more pleasant place to overnight than Semporna. Poor Tawau was bombed by the British in 1944 to force out the invading Japanese army, which is why it's not an architect's delight today, but on the upside, it's the gateway to the awesome Tawau Hills Park (p379), the launch pad for spotting pygmy elephants on a private plan-

tation and is the starting point for one of the most scenic long-distance drives in Sabah.

Tawau is Sabah's border crossing with Kalimantan and the only place where foreigners can get a visa to enter Indonesia.

◉ Sights & Activities

Bukit Gemok Forest Reserve NATURE RESERVE
(Jln Tawau-Keningau; adult/child RM5/1; ⊙8am-5pm) About 10km from Tawau's centre, this reserve is great for a day visit, the jungle filled with chattering monkeys and popular with local picnickers. About an hour's hiking will bring you to the **Titian Selara canopy walkway**, which, at 231m in length, offers terrific views of Tawau and the countryside. There are seven huts along the way for walkers to rest and relax. A one-way taxi to the park costs RM35 – make sure your driver waits for you.

★ **Softwoods Plantation** WILDLIFE WATCHING
(off Jln Tawau-Kalabakan) 🐾 This eucalyptus plantation is actively involved in the conservation of three groups of pygmy elephants (around 80 in total) that roam its 660-sq-km territory. Come here with **1StopBorneo Wildlife** (☑phone & WhatsApp 012-824 8052) and go looking for elephants on an exhilarating drive in the back of a pick-up truck – one in the afternoon and one early in the morning.

🛏 Sleeping

There's a clutch of good-value midrange accommodation in central Tawau, near the waterfront. Budget accommodation tends to be pretty dire.

Eden Boutique Hotel
HOTEL $

(Jln Masjid, Fajar Complex, lot 4; r/f RM78/108; ℗✳🛜) A short walk from the city centre's excellent dining, this intimate, welcoming option is all snug rooms with hardwood floors, excellent wi-fi connections and cable TV. It offers an airport shuttle, too, making this an ideal post-diving overnighter. Parking costs RM5 per day.

City Garden Hotel
HOTEL $

(☑089-769991; https://citygardenhotel.net/index.html; Jln Chen Fook; r/tr RM99/149; ℗✳🛜) Though no gardens are in evidence, this is one of Tawau's best options: spotless rooms in light, almost-Scandi woods, with desks and powerful showers, plus an excellent city-centre location opposite Tawau's best seafood restaurants.

Tawau

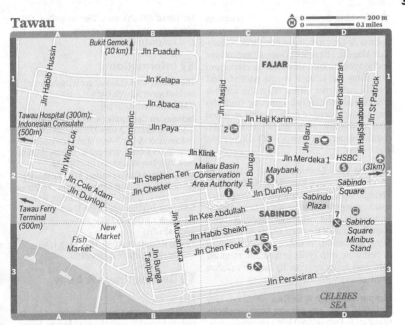

N 0 _____ 200 m
0 _____ 0.1 miles

ROOMS
HOTEL $$

(📞089-916333; Jln Kubota, Kubota Sq, lot 4, block F; r RM138-190; P❄️📶) Not central, but ideal if you have to overnight in Tawau after diving, ROOMS is a small, squeaky-clean hotel with large, comfy beds and helpful staff. Kubota Sq – the surrounding area – has numerous restaurants and ATMs.

Shervinton Executive
Boutique Hotel
HOTEL $$

(📞089-770000; www.shervintonhotel.com; Jln Bunga; r from RM104; ❄️📶) The name's a bit of a misnomer, but the Shervington does have the kind of lobby that would get Liberace excited, with its kitsch mirrored front desk festooned with fairy lights. There's a rooftop bar and the staff are eager to please, but the rooms are tired and worn and wi-fi is intermittent.

🍴 Eating & Drinking

Tawau is particularly well known for its terrific seafood (mostly found in casual restaurants near the waterfront). There are cheap Chinese *kedai kopi* (coffee shops) along Jln Bunga and Jln Budi; most open around 7am and close about 10pm.

Yassin Curry House
INDIAN $

(📞089-754802; Sabindo Sq; mains from RM5; 🕐24hr) Open around the clock, this curry

Tawau

🛏️ **Sleeping**
1 City Garden Hotel C3
2 Eden Boutique Hotel C2
3 Shervinton Executive Boutique
   Hotel... C2

🍴 **Eating**
4 Good View Seafood............................. C3
5 Kam Ling Seafood................................ C3
6 Sabindo Hawker Centre C3
7 Yassin Curry House D3

🍷 **Drinking & Nightlife**
8 Simple Sandwich & Coffee D2

joint serves night owls, or anyone else who likes their *roti canai* flaky and not greasy. There's alfresco seating with a big screen for watching football, and air-conditioned seating inside where you may devour your biryani or curry in peace.

Sabindo Hawker Centre
HAWKER $

(Jln Persisiran; dishes from RM5; 🕐11am-10pm) Between Jln Chen Fook and Jln Persisiran there's a clutch of stalls and low-key alfresco dining options that serve inexpensive dishes, from Malaysian standards to Indonesian *gado gado*. See where the crowds are and pull up a plastic chair.

★**Kam Ling Seafood** SEAFOOD **$$**
(☑ 019-883 2511; www.facebook.com/KamLing
Seafood; Jln Chen Fook; mains from RM19; ⊙ 11am-
10pm Mon-Sat, 1-10pm Sun) One of Tawau's best
seafood restaurants, this Chinese emporium
with shiny fish tanks is always packed. Find
a table and order either from the specials
scrawled above the fish tanks, or from the
menu: black pepper crab, freshly steamed
catch-of-the-day with garlic and ginger,
clams, lobster, sea snails – it's all present
and correct.

★**Good View Seafood** SEAFOOD **$$**
(Jln Chen Fook; mains from RM19; ⊙ 11am-10pm)
Though some locals complain about consistency, we find the seafood here almost
impeccable. The extensive menu features
such delights as steamed clams with garlic,
kung pao squid, 'drunken' prawns cooked
in rice wine with chilli, grilled and steamed
fish, and crunchy, punchy *sayur belacan*
(wild greens with shrimp paste).

Simple Sandwich & Coffee CAFE
(☑ 089-747743; www.facebook.com/simplecafe
tawau; off Jln Perbandaran) With cheerfully mis-
translated slogans on walls, this is central
Tawau's best coffee shop. Full range of coffee
drinks, including frappés, and if you go for
an espresso, you'll get a potent, slightly bitter hit of Sabah's own Tenom coffee. Other
offerings include smoothies, chicken rice
and spaghetti dishes.

ⓘ Information

The website www.etawau.com is useful for all
sorts of general tourist info.
HSBC (Jln Perbandaran)
Indonesian Consulate (Konsulat Republik
Indonesia Tawau; ☑ 089-772052; Jln Sinn Onn;
⊙ 8am-noon & 1 or 2-4pm Mon-Fri, closed
Indonesian & Malaysian public holidays) Come
here to get an Indonesian tourist visa.
Maliau Basin Conservation Area Authority
(☑ 089-759214; http://maliaubasin.org/about-
mbca; 2nd fl, UMNO Bldg, Jln Dunlop; ⊙ 9am-
5pm Mon-Fri) Has info on the Maliau Basin.
Maybank (☑ 089-762333; Jln Dunlop; ⊙ 8am-
5pm Mon-Fri)
Tawau Hospital (☑ 089-773533; Jln Utara;
⊙ 24hr) Basic medical services.

ⓘ Getting There & Away

AIR
From Tawau Airport there are numerous flights
daily to KK and KL with Malaysia Airlines (www.
malaysiaairlines.com) and AirAsia (www.airasia.
com). MASwings (www.maswings.com.my) flies
to Sandakan daily and thrice-weekly to Tarakan,
Indonesia.

TAWAU TREATS

Thanks to Tawau's proximity to Indonesia and large population of Indonesians, Filipinos,
Bajau and Hakka Chinese, the town has developed some worthwhile culinary specialities.
All of the following can be found in almost any of Tawau's *kedai kopi* (coffee shops) and
in the Sabindo Hawker Centre.

Mee Jawa Javanese-style noodles; the Javanese take on Asia's ubiquitous noodle soup.
This version comes with a yellowish broth swimming with bean sprouts, groundnuts,
bean curd, fish balls, the occasional prawn and sometimes (interestingly) sweet potato,
plus the usual garlic, shallots, chillies and shrimp paste.

Gado Gado A deliciously simple Indonesian speciality: vegetable salad with prawn
crackers and peanut sauce. The glory of *gado* is the variations of the standard recipe –
every cook and hawker puts a different spin on it.

Nasi Kuning Rice cooked with coconut milk and turmeric, hence the English translation
of the name: 'yellow rice'. In Tawau it is often wrapped and served in a banana leaf with
deep-fried fish and eaten on special occasions.

Soto Makassar Oh yes! Soto (also spelled 'coto' and pronounced 'cho-to') Makassar
is buffalo/beef soup from southern Sulawesi, Indonesia. The dark broth is made incredibly rich by the addition of buffalo/cow blood, and enriched by a plethora of some
40 spices, plus beef heart, liver, tripe and brain. If you have a weak stomach, ignore
those ingredients and trust us: this stuff is *delicious*, like liquid essence of beef spiced
with all the wonderful herbs and spices of Southeast Asia.

ⓘ GETTING TO INDONESIA: TAWAU TO TARAKAN

Getting to the border Tawau is the only crossing point with Kalimantan where foreigners can get a visa to enter Indonesia. The local Indonesian Consulate (p378) is known for being fast and efficient – many travellers are in and out in an hour. The consulate is in Wisma Fuji, on Jln Sinn Onn. Flag down a taxi (RM15) and ask the driver to drop you in front of the consulate.

Visa applications are processed between 9.30am and 2pm Monday to Friday. You technically need to either provide proof of onward travel or a credit card, which consulate staff will make a copy of. A 60-day tourist visa will cost RM205 and require two passport photos. Bank on spending at least one night in town before shipping off to Indonesia, and bring extra cash to the consulate, as there are no ATMs nearby.

A number of ferry companies, including Tawindo Express and Indomaya Express, make the three- to four-hour trip to Tarakan (RM140, 11.30am Monday, Wednesday and Friday, 10.30am Tuesday, Thursday and Saturday) and the one-hour trip to Nunukan (RM65, 9am and 2pm daily); times are subject to change. We recommend showing up at least an hour before departure to get a ticket; less than that is cutting it fine. A taxi ride to the ferry terminal costs RM10. MASWings (www.maswings.com.my) flies from Tawau to Tarakan (RM292) on Monday, Thursday and Saturday.

At the border Blue minibuses in Tarakan can get you around the city for Rp3000. Expect to pay around Rp20,000 to get to the airport.

Moving on Ferry company Pelni (www.pelni.co.id) has boats from Tarakan to Balikpapan and the Sulawesi ports of Toli-Toli, Pare-Pare and Makassar.

BOAT

The large **Tawau Ferry Terminal** (Jln Utara) serves Tarakan and Nunukan, Kalimantan. Get your Indonesian visa before you set sail.

BUS

Minivans to Sandakan (RM45, five hours, roughly hourly between 7am and 2pm), Lahad Datu (RM20, three hours) and Semporna (RM25, two hours) depart from the **Sabindo Sq minibus stand** (off Jln Dunlop).

Express buses to Kota Kinabalu – via Lahad Datu and Ranau (RM71, 10 hours, depart 8am and 8pm) or via Keningau (RM60, seven hours, depart 9.30am and 1.30pm) along the new, shorter, scenic road – leave from the **Sri Indah Regional Bus Terminal** (Bandar Sri Indah; off A5), 17km east of town.

CAR & MOTORCYCLE

If you're driving the wonderfully scenic paved road from Tawau to Keningau that passes through picturesque, mist-wreathed primary forest, fill up on petrol in Tawau. Your last chance is a Petronas petrol station 53km northwest of the city. After that, the next one is near Sook, 252km away.

ⓘ Getting Around

Tawau Airport A shuttle bus (RM10) from the airport to the local bus station in Tawau's centre leaves six times daily. A taxi costs around RM50. The airport is 35km from town along the main highway to Semporna and Sandakan. Some accommodation places in Tawau and Semporna offer transfers.

Tawau Hills Park

Hemmed in by agriculture and human habitation, this 280-sq-km nature reserve comprises lowland rainforest, with jungle-clad hills rising dramatically from the surrounding plain. The **park** (admission RM10) was gazetted in 1979 to protect the water catchment for settlements in the area, but not before most of the accessible rainforest had been logged. Some of the remaining forest clings to steep-sided ridges that rise to 1310m Mt Magdalena.

Tawau Hills is a user-friendly alternative to the Maliau Basin or Danum Valley. There are trails for hikers of all abilities and the park is excellent for bird-watching and night walks. One trail leads along the Sungai Tawau for 2.5km to Bukit Gelas Falls, which, when not swarmed with school groups and tourists, are perfectly picturesque and fine for a dip. Another track leads 3.2km to a tepid sulphur spring – locals believe the ubat kulit (skin medication) water has medicinal properties. Alternatively you can always take a quick 30-minute walk to Bombalai Hill (530m) to the south – the views from here are quite rewarding. Another reason for coming here is to see what was formerly the world's tallest tropical tree (88m); a 900m trail leads to a newly found 96m-tall tree (the second tallest tropical tree in Asia).

Longer trails lead to the three main hills; only Mt Lucia is accessible without a guide and there's a hostel on its slopes.

Accommodation at **Tawau Hills Park** (☑ 089-768719; Tawau Hills Park; r/chalet RM30/ 290; ❋) consists of a chalet for up to six people and spartan, spotless four-bed dorms. It's well worth staying here overnight to go birding at sunset and dawn, and frog and snake spotting by the creek at night. Book ahead with Adventure Alternative Borneo (p320) to combine a stay at Tawau Hills with elephant spotting at the nearby Softwoods Plantation (p376).

Tawau Hills is 28km northwest of Tawau. A taxi will cost around RM40; a Grab ride is around RM20.

Maliau Basin Conservation Area

This pocket of primeval wilderness tells the same untouched story it did millennia ago. Encircled by insurmountable cliffs in southwestern Sabah, the Maliau Basin Conservation Area (MBCA), known very appropriately as 'Sabah's Lost World', is something special.

The basin, a 25km-wide bowl-shaped depression of rainforest, was unnoticed by the world until a pilot almost crashed into the walls that hem it off in 1947, and is the single best place in Borneo to experience old-growth tropical rainforest. More than that, it is one of the world's great reserves of biodiversity, a dense knot of almost unbelievable genetic richness – more than 2000 types of fauna and flora are found here, with more awaiting discovery. It wasn't until 1988 that an expedition into the basin found a self-contained ecosystem of 12 types of forest and tremendous waterfalls. Maliau Basin attracts a small number of adventurous, hardy trekkers and naturalists per year.

🏃 Activities

Trekking

Several treks are possible in the basin, ranging from short nature walks around **Agathis Research Station** to the multiday slog to the rim of the basin via **Strike Ridge Camp**. The vast majority of visitors undertake a five-day, four-night loop through the southern section of the basin that we'll call the Maliau Loop. Shorter packages restrict visitors to just a taste of Maliau Basin around the Maliau Basin Studies Centre and Agathis Camp.

The Maliau Loop trek will likely be the most memorable hike of your Borneo experience. It vies with the Salt Trail (p382) for the title of Sabah's toughest trek. It takes in wide swaths of diverse rainforest and four of the basin's waterfalls: **Takob Falls**, **Giluk Falls**, the stupendous, seven-tiered **Maliau Falls** and **Ginseng Falls**. It's not for novices: there are several strenuous, steep hill climbs, rivers to ford and stretches of dense forest that require machete use. You'll be trekking around 7km per day (six to eight hours). Do not attempt the trek unless you are in excellent shape (adventure-tour operators insist that your travel insurance policy covers a helicopter evacuation and a fitness certificate from your doctor).

Wildlife Watching

The density of the old-growth forest is striking, and as it is more remote than the Danum Valley, the preserved wildlife is even better. Eighty species of mammals (and counting) have been recorded here, including clouded leopard, Sumatran rhino, Malayan sun bear, pygmy elephant, Bornean gibbon, red- and grey-leaf monkeys and banteng.

That said, you will be in dense primary forest, where wildlife is not easy to spot. You may walk away without seeing anything (unlikely) except for some of Borneo's most ancient trees, though the night drives around Maliau Basin Studies Centre (MBSC) give you a good opportunity to spot nocturnal mammals. During treks you'll be looking out for langurs, gibbons, birds, frogs and reptiles.

A canopy walkway stretches near the MBSC, and it is pretty astounding to walk its length amid rainforest canopy that has never felt a human cut. Bird-watchers tend to go up there at dawn.

Guided Tours

There are two ways to get to Maliau Basin: with a trusted trekking operator or on your own. The former is by far the easier option and you won't save much money by trying to do it independently. Among those that run treks here, we recommend Sticky Rice Travel (p320) and Borneo Nature Tours (p321), both of which offer four-day, three-night all-inclusive tours of the Maliau for around RM2900, or five-day, four-night options for around RM5100 per person for two to three people.

Your tour operator will supply a forest ranger, guide and porters to carry your food. A porter to carry your gear costs RM100 per day for a maximum of 12kg, with up to an additional 6kg costing RM100 per porter. You'll be in charge of your day pack, camera, leech socks, walking clothes and dry kit for the evening. You should also bring mosquito repellent, swimming outfit, powerful torch, sunscreen, poncho, sleeping sheet, a towel and energy sweets.

🛏 Sleeping & Eating

At the **Maliau Basin Studies Centre** (Maliau Basin), accommodation varies in standard from the upscale (VIP House/deluxe/standard RM1400/540/410) and regular resthouse rooms (from RM300 to RM350), to dorm beds (RM95) and camping in your own tent (RM40). There are also seven official research stations dotted around the basin. Visitors tend to stay at Agathis, Ginseng and Nephenthes, where accommodation consists either of basic bunk rooms or stretcher hammocks.

ℹ Information

Shell Maliau Basin Reception (Jln Tawau-Keningau; ⊙9am-5pm) Pay your park entry fee at the entrance to the reserve and consult the information centre (if it's open) on the Maliau Basin wildlife and trekking trails.

Otherwise there's ample info on the conservation area at the Maliau Basin Studies Centre.

ℹ Getting There & Away

BUS
Buses running between Tawau and KK can drop you off at the park entrance. Not that it helps you much, since you need a permit and a guide to do anything in the protected area.

CAR & MOTORCYCLE
It's possible to drive yourself to the park via the sealed road that runs between Keningau and Tawau, passing by the entrance to the reserve; it's a two-hour drive from Tawau and a five-hour drive from KK via Keningau. A beautifully paved 30km road leads from the entrance all the way to the Maliau Basin Studies Centre, the Maliau Basin headquarters, past the Agathis Research Station, around 20km from the entrance. For anything beyond that, however, you need a 4WD.

4WD & VAN
Operators that run tours into the Maliau Basin include 4WD transport in the price of the packages, with pick-up from KK or Tawau. If you've prearranged with the Maliau Basin Conservation Area Authority (p378) in Tawau, that office may get a minivan to take you to the park entrance for RM700. In the park, rangers can arrange vans to take you back to Tawau or Keningau for a similar price.

SOUTHWESTERN SABAH

The Crocker Range is the rugged backbone of southwestern Sabah, separating coastal lowlands from the wild tracts of jungle in the east, and offering Sabah's toughest trekking challenges. White-sand beaches scallop the shores from KK down to the border,

ℹ INDEPENDENT EXPEDITIONS TO THE MALIAU BASIN

It's best to first contact the Maliau Basin Conservation Area Authority (p378) in Tawau if you want to go to the basin under your own steam. You may need to show up to the office in person, as this is not a tourism body accustomed to dealing with visitors.

To get into the park you need to pay an administration fee (RM50), a vehicle entry fee (RM5 per vehicle), a trekking fee (RM150) and, if you stay overnight, a conservation fee (RM20). If you plan to hike you *must* hire a guide, which costs RM150 per day. Breakfast, lunch and dinner can be taken in the guest camps for RM195. You can also arrange meals while trekking; this requires a porter (RM100, maximum 12kg per porter, up to an additional 6kg RM100 per porter) and costs RM390 for breakfast/lunch/dinner. If you want to cook for yourself, bring your own supplies and rent utensils from the park authorities for RM50 per day. Night safaris cost RM160, and night walks (lasting about an hour) RM40.

Ideally, if you're not buying a package tour, we advise prearranging your tour with the office in Tawau, now only 2½ hours away from the basin thanks to the new road.

passing the turbid rivers of the Beaufort Division, home of Borneo's best white-water rafting. Offshore you'll find Pulau Tiga, forever etched in the collective consciousness as the genesis site for the reality show *Survivor*, and Pulau Labuan, centre of the region's oil industry and the transfer point for ferries heading to Sarawak and Brunei.

Interior Sabah

Sabah's interior constitutes some of the state's wildest territory, and the best place for accessing this largely unexplored hinterland is the southwest.

The landscape is dominated by the Crocker Range – home to one of Borneo's toughest treks – which rises near coffee-growing Tenom in the south and runs north to Mt Kinabalu. The range forms a formidable barrier to the interior and dominates the eastern skyline from Kota Kinabalu down to Sipitang. Once across the Crocker Range, you descend into the green valley of the Sungai Pegalan, which runs from the bustling market hub of Keningau in the south to Ranau in the north. The heart of the Pegalan Valley is Tambunan – Sabah's rice bowl – a good place to delve into traditional Murut culture. An even better place to do so is Batu Punggul, near the Kalimantan border. Near Tambunan you'll find Mt Trusmadi, Sabah's most challenging peak ascent.

Crocker Range National Park

Cutting through the Crocker Range National Park is part of a century-old trail used by the Murut, who carried jungle goods through the mountains and down to the coast to trade for salt. The **Salt Trail** (☑088-553500; www.sabahparks.org.my/index.php/salt-trail-crp), at 34km long, is Sabah's most demanding trek, complete with chest-high river crossings and navigation through primary forest. A guide is absolutely essential.

There are two KK-based operators that offer this trek: TYK Adventure Tours (p320) and Top Peak (p320). Treks tend to be five days and four nights, going from Tikolod to Inobong via the indigenous villages of Kionop, Buayan and Terian. The guided treks cost from RM1200 per person and require considerable physical fitness. Expect numerous steep ascents and descents (the highest and lowest points of the hike are 1320m and 220m, respectively), wildlife-

spotting opportunities, mud, leeches and a tremendous sense of achievement. You'll be overnighting in basic accommodation in villages along the way; bring own sleeping bag and sleeping mat and make sure your rucksack is waterproof.

Tambunan

☑ 087 / POP UNDER 5000

Nestled among the green curves of the Crocker hills, Tambunan, about 81km south of KK, is Sabah's rice basket. The region was the last stronghold of Mat Salleh, who became a folk hero for rebelling against the British in the late 19th century. Sadly Salleh later blew his reputation by negotiating a truce, which so outraged his own people that he was forced to flee to the Tambunan plain, where he was eventually killed. The Dusan people who live here are renowned for their fierce fighting against the Japanese during WWII and past headhunting practises.

◎ Sights & Activities

To make the most of Tambunan, we recommend coming here with Top Peak, which has a good relationship with the local community. Two-day, one-night packages typically include a hike up **Mt Wakid** (Kampong Sunsuran), rice planting with the locals in the rice paddies surrounding the village, quad biking and a local homestay.

Tambunan Rafflesia Reserve NATURE RESERVE (☑088-898500; Jln KK–Tambunan; admission RM5; ⊙8am-3pm) Near the top of the Crocker Range, next to the main highway, 20km north of Tambunan, this park is devoted to the world's largest flower. The Rafflesia Rangers can guide you into the jungle reserve for the day for RM100. Keningau-bound buses will stop here if you ask, but getting back to Tambunan will require hitching on the highway. A round-trip taxi from Tambunan costs RM120, which includes waiting time. Call ahead to make sure the reserve is open.

The rafflesia is a parasitic plant that grows hidden within the stems of jungle vines until it bursts into bloom, at which point it eerily resembles the monster plant from *Little Shop of Horrors*. It emits a stench of rotting flesh, mimicking a newly dead animal, to attract carrion flies that help with pollination. The large bulbous flowers can be up to 1m in diameter. The 12-or-so species of rafflesia here are found only in

Borneo and Sumatra; several species are unique to Sabah, but as they only bloom for a few days, it's hard to predict when you'll be able to see one. Check with rangers at what stage the blooms are, as by day four they tend to be blackening and wilting.

Mahua Waterfall
WATERFALL

(Air Terjun Mahua; Jln Tambunan–Ranau; adult/child RM10/6) Around 26km northeast of Tambunan, this gorgeous 17m-high waterfall plunges into a deep pool below, perfect for a refreshing dip. There's a spartan hostel on site (dorm/room RM30/70) if you wish to stay the night, and a basic restaurant. Tambunan–Ranau buses can drop you at the turn-off, from where it's a 5km walk.

Dusun Museum
MUSEUM

(Kampung Sunsuron; RM5; ⊙9am-5pm) Well worth a peek, this museum showcasing traditional Dusun culture is located inside a traditional bamboo dwelling. Inside you'll find antique Chinese stoneware jars, woven containers for hunting and gathering, weaponry, agricultural implements, boldly decorated conical hats and foodstuffs being smoked over the hearth. In the corner of the main room, check out the loft: that's where all the young women used to be ushered during harvest festivals – to keep them out of reach of drunk menfolk.

Sunsuron Guritom
MONUMENT

(House of Skull; Kampung Sunsuron) Partially eroded by the elements, the stone skull topping this squat stone container, resembling a postbox, gives a clue as to its past use. Back in Sunsuron's headhunting days, the Dusun warriors would display the severed heads of the vanquished on top of the box before interring them inside and bringing out the remains to strike fear into the hearts of visitors to the village.

🛏 Sleeping & Eating

There are several homestays in Kampung Sunsuron, on the outskirts of Tambunan. A room for two people, including all meals, typically costs around RM60.

Homestays provide simple meals. In central Tambunan there are several Malaysian and Chinese restaurants, as well as a decent pizza place. If you're driving from KK, stop at **Mee Sup Pipin I** (☑016-830 2088; Penampang; mains RM3-5; ⊙8am-6pm) on the way for a traditional noodle-soup breakfast.

LONG PASIA

Home to the Lundayeh people, this remote **village** (Long Pasia, Ulu Padas; 5-day, 4-night trip RM1995, minimum 2 people) lies deep in the jungle in southwestern Sabah, within trekking distance of both the Sarawak and Kalimantan borders. Top Peak (p320) offers multiday cultural immersion: exploring rivers, caves, mountains and waterfalls, learning about plant medicine and jungle survival skills from your guide and staying in a traditional Lundayeh longhouse.

This is a unique experience and as off the beaten track as it's possible to get in Sabah. Trip costs include experienced jungle guide and 4WD transport to and from KK.

Gunung Alab Substation
LODGE $

(☑019-870 0162; Jln KK–Tambunan; r/f RM50/120) At 1800m above sea level, high up in montane forest en route from KK to Tambunan, this lodge is surrounded by humongous pitcher plants and a wealth of orchids. It makes for a tranquil escape from the city and the heat. It's just off the main road; the turn-off is opposite the only restaurant between KK and Tambunan.

ℹ Getting There & Away

Regular minivans ply the roads between Tambunan and KK (RM10, 1½ hours), Ranau (RM15, two hours), Keningau (RM10, one hour) and Tenom (RM20, two hours). KK–Tenom express buses also pass through, though you may have to ask the driver to stop. The **minivan shelter** (Jln Datuk Gibon) is in the middle of Tambunan town. Minivans to KK pass the entrance to the rafflesia reserve; you'll usually be charged for the whole trip to KK.

Mt Trusmadi

About 20km southeast of Tambunan town is the dramatic Mt Trusmadi, Sabah's second-highest peak, rising to 2642m. The views from the top are not the otherworldly splendour you get on a good day on Mt Kinabalu, but when the morning sky is clear, you do get cracking views of the taller mountain. Trekking Mt Trusmadi is a much tougher physical challenge than Mt Kinabalu and more difficult to arrange. Independent

SABAH INTERIOR SABAH

trekkers must be well equipped and bring their own provisions to the mountain.

There are two trails up the mountain: one from the main entrance near Tambunan and the other from Kampong Sinua, near Keningau. Whichever way you tackle it, it's a steep, relentless climb from the base to the summit. The easiest way to do it is to arrange the trek through TYK Adventure Tours (p320) or Amazing Borneo (p321).

On the Tambunan side, there are two places to stay: Mirad-Irad Riverside camp (RM20) at base camp and SFD New Rest House (RM100) halfway up the mountain. On the Sinua side, it's an overnighter at the Tainiskon Base Camp (RM20) and then camping on the second night (bring tent, four-season sleeping bag and sleeping mat). Bring winter clothes, as it gets cold towards the summit, and be prepared for a steep, muddy slog, whichever trail you take.

You have to obtain permits to climb the mountain from the Forestry Department, either in **Tambunan** (Jabatan Perhutanan; ☑ 087-774691, 089-660811; Jln Mondowoi, Tambunan; ⊙ 8am-5pm Mon-Fri) or Keningau. If you go with a tour agency, it does it for you.

If you tackle the mountain from the Tambunan side, you get picked up from KK and taken to Tambunan to meet your guide before proceeding to the starting point, 1500m above sea level, by 4WD. If you hike from Kampong Sinua, you're picked up from KK and taken to the village via Keningau.

Keningau

☑ 087 / POP 190,000

If you have a bent for the bucolic, you'll probably want to skip Keningau – this busy service town has a touch of urban sprawl about it, and most visitors only pass through to pick up transport, use an ATM or stock up on supplies. As far as attractions go, you might check out **Taipaek-gung**, a colourful Chinese temple in the middle of town, or the large **tamu** (market), held every Thursday, that showcases the wares of the local Dusun population.

If you do have to sleepover, **Hotel Juta** (☑ 087-337888; www.sabah.com.my/juta; Lg Milimewa 2; s/d from RM128/133; ⏰ 🛜) has business-like, international-style rooms with clean bathrooms, fresh linen and mismatched furniture.

There are eight daily express buses to/from KK (RM15, two hours) and four to/from Tenom (RM10, one hour). These buses stop at the Bumiputra Express stop on the main road, across from the Shell station. Minivans operate from several places in town, including the car park next to the market, across the street from the Petronas petrol station; they all leave when full. There are services to/from KK (RM50, two hours), Ranau (RM30, three hours) via Tambunan, and also Tenom (RM12, one hour). A couple of daily buses from KK to Tawau (RM40, five hours) pass through Keningau, taking the scenic road south.

Keningau is the starting point for the epic, scenic 343km drive to Tawau that passes through largely virgin primary forest. If driving, fill up in Keningau – there's another petrol station near Sook, 39km south, but it's not always reliable. The next petrol station after that, near Tawau, is 290km from Keningau.

Tenom

☑ 087 / POP 5000

That coffee you've been drinking in coffee shops around Sabah? The *kopi susu* (coffee with condensed milk) over ice that's been tiding you over on the hot, sultry days? Tenom Kopi, a lower-altitude robusta bean with a slightly bitter aftertaste, found all over Sabah, is grown in the verdant hills around Tenom, a pretty town bisected by a meandering river. Tenom has a warrior past, with the Murut chief Ontoros Antanom involved in uprisings against the British in 1915. There are several coffee factories in town, the most well known of which is **Fatt Choi** (☑ 087-735230; https://fccoffee.com; Jln Tenom Lama; ⊙ by appointment), where you can do tastings. If you like the look of the place, Fatt Choi's owners also have a clutch of **cabins** (☑ 087-735230; https://fccoffee.com; Jln Tenom Lama; f RM90-180; 🖼) in a lofty hilltop location that make for an ideal retreat from Tenom's bustle.

About 15km northeast of Tenom and originally set up as an orchid centre, the vast **Sabah Agriculture Park** (Taman Pertanian Sabah; ☑ 087-737952; www.sabah.net.my/agripark; adult/6-13yr RM25/10; ⊙ 9am-5.30pm Tue-Sun) has become a major research facility and tourist attraction, building up superb collections of rare plants such as hoyas, and developing new techniques for use in agriculture, agroforestry and domestic cultivation. Take a minivan from Tenom to Lagud Seberang (RM5). Tell the driver you're going to Taman Pertanian. The park entrance is

BATU PUNGGUL

This is as remote as it gets in Sabah. Not far from the Kalimantan border, Batu Punggul is a jungle-topped limestone outcrop riddled with caves, towering nearly 200m above Sungai Sapulot. This is deep in Murut country and the stone formation was one of several sites sacred to these people. Batu Punggul and the adjacent Batu Tinahas are traditionally believed to be longhouses that gradually transformed into stone. The view from the upper reaches of Batu Punggul may be the best in Sabah – in every direction is deep jungle, knifelike limestone outcrops and, if you are lucky, swinging orangutans. It can be difficult and expensive to get here, but this is a beautiful part of Sabah that few tourists visit, and it offers a chance to rub shoulders with the jungle Murut.

The only feasible way to get here is with a responsible tour operator. A two- to three-night adventure with **Orou Sapulot** (☑016-311 0056; www.orousapulot.com; 4-day, 3-night per person for a group of 4 RM1493) encompasses **Romol Eco Village**, a Murut longhouse homestay; the **Pungiton Caves**, an extensive cavern system with underground rivers; an **eco-camp** by Pungiton located on a riverbank; and finally a sweat-inducing climb up Batu Punggul followed by a rapid shoot downriver all the way to the Kalimantan border in a motorised canoe. The prices here are estimated rates that take in all/some of the activities mentioned above. To share costs, bigger groups are best, but if you're a solo visitor, ask when booking if there are other groups to join. In KK Adventure Alternative Borneo (p320) and Sticky Rice Travel (p320) are Orou Sapulot's preferred booking agencies.

1km off the main road. A taxi from Tenom costs around RM90.

Coffee and plants aside, Tenom is also the south end of the Sabah State Railway and a great place to kick off a cheap-as-chips, scenic train journey.

ⓘ Getting There & Away

From the **train station** (Stesen Keretapi Tenom; Jln Pasar Baru Tenom), two trains daily run down to Beaufort (RM2.20) at 7.30am and 1pm Monday to Saturday and 7.30am and 12.30pm Sunday. It's a wonderfully picturesque route through the Padas Gorge and lush countryside, even if the trains are seriously on the ramshackle side.

Shared taxis to Keningau (RM12) and KK (RM30) depart from the side of the football field when full between 7am and 5pm.

Beaufort Division

This shield-shaped peninsula, popping out from Sabah's southwestern coast, is a marshy plain marked with curling rivers and fringed by golden sand. Visitors with tight travel schedules should consider doing a wildlife river cruise at Weston or Klias if they don't have time to reach Sungai Kinabatangan. Yes, the Kinabatangan is better, but packs of proboscis monkeys can still be spotted here and it's only a half-day trip from KK or Tempurung. The latter has one of Borneo's loveliest beaches and is a good

jumping-off point for visiting the former site of *Survivor* on Pulau Tiga. For something more adrenalin packed, book in KK a white-water rafting trip on Sungai Padas and catch Borneo's most scenic railway stretch en route from Beaufort.

Beaufort

☑087 / POP 12,600

Born as a timber town, Beaufort has reinvented itself with the proliferation of palm-oil plantations. A suitable pit stop for tourists travelling between Sabah and Sarawak, this sleepy town is the gateway to white-water rapids on the **Sungai Padas** and the monkey-filled Klias and Garama areas. It's also the departure point for the wonderfully scenic, if ramshackle, railway to Sabah's coffee capital of Tenom. The Sungai Padas divides Beaufort into two sections: the aptly named Old Town with its weathered structures, and New Town, a collection of modern shophouses on flood-phobic stilts. During WWII Beaufort was the site of a major skirmish between the Japanese and Australians.

⦿ Sights & Activities

Memorial Stone   MEMORIAL
(Jln Tugu) There's a small monument to Private Thomas Leslie Starcevich, an Australian WWII veteran. In 1945 Starcevich

single-handedly overwhelmed a Japanese machine-gun position, for which he received the Victoria Cross, the British military's highest decoration. The stone is at the bottom of a small embankment and is marked by brown signs and an arch.

Rafting

White-water rafting enthusiasts can book a trip on the Sungai Padas with Riverbug (p321), the premier operator in the area. A day trip starts in KK at 5.20am, involves a two-hour drive to Beaufort then a two-hour scenic train ride to Pangi village, from where you ride eight separate grade III and IV rapids over 9km of the muddy-brown Padas to its base in Rayoh village, where you have lunch. Riverbug delivers you back to KK for 6pm, dog-tired but fully exhilarated!

Scuba Junkie's affiliated river-rafting outfit, River Junkie (p321), also comes highly recommended by travellers, and offers exactly the same package (RM250); the two companies work together and pool passengers if necessary. All trips include transfers by van, and normally require 24 hours' advance notice.

🛌 Sleeping & Eating

There's really no need to spend the night here but if you must then try the unexciting **River Park Hotel** (☑ 087-223333; Jln Sipitang-Beaufort; r from RM140; 🅿 ☀ 🛜).

If you're stopping in town for a bite, make sure you try a pomelo (football-sized citrus fruit) and local *mee* Beaufort (Beaufort noodles) – both are locally famous. Opposite the train station, **Wei Hiong** (Jln Padas Utama; mains RM7-12; ☺ 7am-7pm) serves fluffy *char siu* buns (RM2.50), *mee sup* (noodle soup topped with pork), Singapore-style mee goreng and Chinese BBQ pork.

❶ Getting There & Away

BUS

Express buses operate from near the old train station at the south end of Jln Masjid (the ticket booth is opposite the station). There are departures at 9am, 1pm, 2.15pm and 5pm for KK (RM15, 1½ hours). There are departures at 9.10am, 10.30am, 1.45pm and 6.20pm for Sipitang (RM25, 1½ hours). The KK to Lawas express bus passes through Beaufort at around 3pm; the trip from Beaufort to Lawas costs RM30 and takes 1¾ hours.

MINIVAN

Minivans operate from a stop across from the mosque, at the north end of Jln Masjid. There are frequent departures for KK (RM20, two hours) and less-frequent departures for Sipitang (RM30, 1½ hours), Lawas (RM40, 1¾ hours) and Kuala Penyu (RM15, until around 2.30pm, one hour). There are plenty of minivans to Menumbok (for Labuan) until early afternoon (RM15, one hour).

TAXI

Taxis depart from the stand outside the train station, at the south end of Jln Padas Utama. Charter rates include KK (RM120), Kuala Penyu (RM100), Sipitang (RM100), Menumbok (RM100) and Lawas (RM120).

TRAIN

Beaufort train station (Jln Padas Utama) is the departure point for the wonderfully scenic train to Tenom (RM3, two hours). The train departs twice daily (7.50am and 1.30pm Monday to Saturday, 7.50am and 1pm Sunday). From Tenom the Beaufort train departs at 7.30am and 1pm Monday to Saturday and 7.30am and 12.30pm Sunday. Everyone has to alight and change trains at Halogilat station, halfway along, as trains reconnect and disconnect here.

In the other direction, twice-daily trains run to Tanjung Aru, near KK, at 5am and 11am (RM4.70, 2¼ hours).

Tempurung

☑ 088

If you've been disappointed by the trash-strewn state of beaches in Borneo, seek out this quiet, bucolic beach setting 10km northwest of Kuala Penyu. Quiet back roads meander past several beach retreats that sit in glorious isolation, facing Sabah's loveliest beach.

🛌 Sleeping

⭐ **Naga Puri** RESORT $$ (☑ 016-880 2357; https://nagapuri.com; Pantai Tempurung; dm/f RM85/125, chalet RM155; ☀ 🛜) Owner Max makes his guests feel extremely welcome at this rustic spot right by the sea. Rooms are simple and come with mosquito nets (with the exception of the dorm), and if you want to visit Pulau Tiga, go scuba diving, or search for proboscis monkeys and fireflies in the Klias mangroves, that can be arranged. KK airport pick-up offered.

SUNGAI KLIAS

The tea-brown Sungai Klias looks somewhat similar to the mighty Kinabatangan, offering short-stay visitors a chance to spend an evening in the jungle cavorting with proboscis monkeys. There are several companies offering two-hour river cruises and the river has become quite crowded with numerous boats, though the natural spectacles are still compelling. We recommend Borneo Authentic (p322), the first operator to set up shop in the region. Trips include a large buffet dinner and a short night walk to view the swarms of fireflies that light up the evening sky like Christmas lights. Cruises start at dusk (around 5pm), when the sweltering heat starts to burn off and animals emerge for some post-siesta prowling.

Visitors can make their own way to the row of private jetties 20km west of Beaufort, but most people sign up for a hassle-free half-day trip from KK (which ends up being cheaper since you're sharing transport) or from one of the lodges in Tempurung.

Tempurung Golden Beach Resort
RESORT $$

(☑019-810 6829; www.tempuronggoldenbeach resort.com; Pantai Tempurung; f RM250) Consisting of a clutch of spacious, bamboo-accented rooms, this small, family-run resort is ideal for disconnecting and engaging in such pursuits as sea kayaking and sunset watching from the hammock. Day trips to Pulau Tiga and firefly-watching trips amid the mangroves of the Klias River are on offer.

Tempurung Seaside Lodge
LODGE $$

(☑088-773066; www.borneotempurung.com; Pantai Tempurung; 2-day, 1-night package per person from RM170, minimum 2 people; 🛜) 🌿 Set along the quiet coastal waters of the South China Sea, the serene Tempurung Seaside Lodge is the perfect place for hermits who seek a pinch of style. Friendly management, decent food and some of the most psychedelic sunsets in Borneo. Rustic, bamboo-accented rooms – family, twin and double – are scattered around the lovely grounds. Pick-up from KK offered (RM80).

❶ Getting There & Away

Borneo Express runs buses from KK (departing from Wawasan Plaza) at 6.45am, 10am and 12.30pm daily. Ask the driver to let you off at the junction with the large Kuala Penyu sign. The bus will turn left (south) to head towards Menumbok; you want to go right (north) in the direction of Kuala Penyu. It's possible to prearrange pick-up from the turn-off with the lodges. Buses pass the junction at 9.30am and 3.30pm heading back to KK.

If you're driving, take a left at the junction; the Google maps app is really useful for finding these isolated lodges.

Weston

☑088 / POP UNDER 500

The little village of Weston, a street full of wooden houses clustered around a gold-domed mosque, is the remotest of the three jumping-off points for firefly- and proboscis monkey–spotting in the wetlands. Conservation efforts have brought groups of curious proboscis monkeys into the tidal marshlands, which are shaded by towering nipa palms and copses of mangroves. As the tide rolls in and out, entire swaths of jungle are submerged and revealed. Monkeys, monitor lizards, otters and mud skippers flash through the aquatic undergrowth, and as the sun sets, clouds of flying foxes (ie *big* bats) flap in with the darkness and the air is lit up with hundreds of firefly sparks.

In the village itself, look out for the Che Hwa Schoolhouse, the oldest wooden school building in Borneo and a fine example of antique Chinese architecture.

You need your own wheels to come to Weston (or else come as part of a tour) as there's no public transport. KK-based Top Peak (p320) runs sensitive tours of the mangroves by working directly with the villagers of Weston and contributing to the little community. The other tour company to run tours in these wetlands is Weston Wetland and is not recommended because it runs trips with large groups.

Pulau Tiga National Park

The name Pulau Tiga actually means 'three islands' – the scrubby islet is part of a small chain created during an eruption of mud volcanoes in the late 1890s. More than

100 years later, in 2001, the island had its 15 minutes of fame when it played host to the smash-hit reality TV series *Survivor,* so is commonly referred to now as 'Survivor Island'. TV junkies still stop by for a look-see, although the 'tribal council' was destroyed in a storm and the debris was cleared after it turned into a home for venomous snakes. Whether you come here on a day trip or opt to stay, it's still a great place for relaxing on the gorgeous beach, hiking in the forest and taking a cooling dip in burping mud pits at the centre of the island.

Pulau Kalampunian Damit is famous for the sea snakes (up to 150 per day) that come ashore to mate, hence the island's nickname, Snake Island. Enigmatically the snakes are never seen on nearby Pulau Tiga. Pulau Tiga Resort runs boat trips to the island (RM60 per person), with a stop en route for snorkelling for RM30 extra. You can also dive off the island for RM100 per dive, or RM200 for a fun dive for those with no scuba experience. KK-based outfits such as Scuba Junkie KK (p320) and Downbelow (p321) run day trips here also.

🛏 Sleeping

Sabah Parks
LODGE $

(☑ 088-211881; www.sabahparks.org.my; Pulau Tiga; r from RM80) Sabah Parks runs basic lodging (a four-person chalet and two modest cabins) on the island for less-than-affluent survivalists. It's next to Pulau Tiga Resort, about 100m from where 'tribal council' was once held (sadly, tiki torches no longer line the way). Facilities are limited, though a cooking area is provided. Book through the KK Sabah Parks (p327) office.

Pulau Tiga Resort
RESORT $$$

(Survivor Lodge; ☑ 088-240584; www.sdclodges. com; Pulau Tiga; 2-day, 1-night package per person from Kuala Penyu RM420-460; ❀) Built to house the production crew for the first series of *Survivor,* the lodge has accommodation in two types of chalets with double beds and air-con. The beach-facing grounds offer amazing views of the sunset, while a map is available should you want to track down the beach where the Pagong Tribe lived (called Pagong-Pagong Beach).

❶ Getting There & Away

From Kuala Penyu the boat ride takes about 20 minutes; there are no public boats and boat cost is typically included in the package price.

If staying in the Sabah Parks facilities, contact it in advance about boat transfers. You can try showing up in Kuala Penyu and asking if you can board one of the day's boats out to the island, though we don't recommend this option as priority is given to resort guests with bookings.

Naga Puri (p386) and Tempurung Golden Beach Resort (p387) in nearby Tempurung run day trips to Pulau Tiga on request.

Pulau Labuan

☑ 087 / POP 54,800

Originally a pestilential swamp, Labuan lies 115km southwest of KK and only 50km northeast of BSB (Brunei) and if it were a school student, the report card would read, 'failed to live up to expectations'. The Sultan of Brunei ceded Labuan to the British in 1846 and it remained part of the empire for 115 years, during which time it was distinguished by a failed coal industry and the Pollyanna-like optimism of some British officials, who believed that Labuan might become the next Singapore.

The Japanese held the island for three years during WWII and it was here that the Japanese forces surrendered at the end of the war, and the officers responsible for the death marches from Sandakan were tried.

Bandar Labuan is the main town and the transit point for ferries linking Kota Kinabalu and Brunei. Duty-free shopping and ample booze make it a favourite destination for Bruneians.

◉ Sights & Activities

Labuan's main settlement is light on character, but has a couple of passable attractions.

Labuan Museum
MUSEUM

(☑ 087-414135; 364 Jln Dewan; ⊙ 9am-5pm) **FREE** This museum provides a good (if dry) introduction to the island's history and culture, from precolonial days through British and Japanese occupation, WWII and the establishment of Labuan as an independent federal territory – a lot of history and turbulence for a tiny island. Upstairs are displays on the different ethnic groups that have made the island home.

Labuan Marine Museum
MUSEUM

(☑ 087-414462, 087-452927; Jln Tanjung Purun; ⊙ 10am-5pm) **FREE** On the coast just east of the centre, the Labuan International Sea Sports Complex houses a decent little museum with a good shell collection and

Bandar Labuan

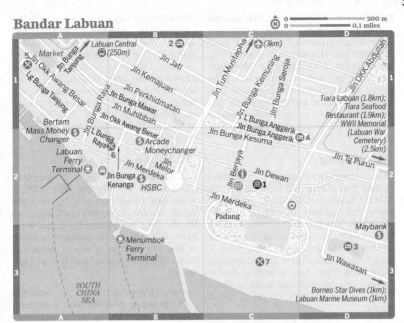

displays of local marine life. Head upstairs to find a 12.8m-long skeleton of an Indian fin whale.

Around Pulau Labuan

Labuan Marine Park   NATIONAL PARK

Pulau Kuraman, Pulau Rusukan Kecil and Pulau Rusukan Besar are uninhabited islands lying southwest of Labuan that are now protected by the federal government. The beaches are pristine, but dynamite fishing has destroyed much of the coral. You can hire boats from the jetty at the Labuan International Sea Sports Complex to explore the marine park. A day's charter costs around RM600 per group of six people.

If you want to dive here, enquire at Borneo Star Dives.

WWII Memorial
(Labuan War Cemetery)   CEMETERY

(Jln Tanjung Batu) A dignified expanse of lawn with row upon row of headstones dedicated to the nearly 4000 Commonwealth servicemen, mostly Australian and British, who lost their lives in Borneo during WWII. The cemetery is near the golf course, about 2km east of town. A **Peace Park** on the west side of the island at Layang Layangan commemorates the place of Japanese surrender and has a Japanese war memorial.

Bandar Labuan

⊙ Sights
1   Labuan Museum.......................................C2

⊜ Sleeping
2   Expo Hotel...B1
3   Grand Dorsett Labuan........................D3
4   Mariner Hotel.......................................D2

⊗ Eating
5   Restoran Selera Farizah......................A1
6   Restoran Sharifah.................................B2
7   Tambayan at Kainang.........................C3

Labuan Bird Park   WILDLIFE RESERVE

(☎ 087-463544; Jln Tanjung Kubong; adult/child/under 5yr RM4/1/free; ⊙ 10am-5pm, closed Fri) This pretty park offers refuge to a wide range of species (580, apparently) in three geodesic domes, and a swath of rainforest. The birds look a little bored, but healthy. The park is located at the north end of the island, a 20-minute taxi ride from town.

Diving

Labuan is famous for its **wreck diving**, with no fewer than four major shipwrecks off the coast (two from WWII and two from the 1980s). The only dive outfit operating here is **Borneo Star Dives** (☎ 087-429278; star divers2005@yahoo.com; Labuan International Sea

Sports Complex, Jln Tanjung Purun; dive packages from RM335 (minimum 3 divers)), which does island-hopping tours and can take you to all four sites. Note that only the 'Cement Wreck' is suitable for novice divers; the 'Blue Water Wreck' (in our opinion, the most impressive of the bunch) requires advanced Open Water certification, and the 'American' and 'Australian' wrecks are only recommended for those with a wreck-diving course under their belt.

🛏 Sleeping

Labuan Homestay Program HOMESTAY $
(📋 Bukit Kuda 013-851 1907, Patau Patau 2 016-824 6193, Sungai Labu 016-804 1147; www.tourism.gov.my/niche/homestay; 1/2 days incl full board RM80/160) This excellent service matches visitors with a friendly local in one of three villages around the island: Patau Patau 2, Kampong Sungai Labu and Kampong Bukit Kuda. If you want to be near Bandar Labuan, ask for accommodation at Patau Patau 2 – it's a charming stilt village out on the bay.

If you want to enrol in the program, book at least a few days in advance.

Tiara Labuan RESORT $$
(📋 087-414300; www.tiaralabuan.com; Jln Tanjung Batu; r/ste incl breakfast from RM300/450; ❄ 🛜 🏊) Pulau Labuan's favourite hotel is a cut above the rest with its cobalt-blue outdoor pool nestled in manicured gardens at Tanjung Batu. There's a good Asian fusion restaurant, courtyard bar and handy shuttles to whisk you around the island, plus large and very alluring wood-signatured rooms with bed runners, snow-white linen, spotless bathrooms and recessed lighting.

Expo Hotel HOTEL $$
(📋 087-422588; Jati Shophouse Phase 1, Jln Tun Mustapha; r from RM110; ❄ 🛜) While considerably less grand than its name suggests it might be, Expo is clean, central, good value for money and will do in a pinch as an overnighter. The decor is unlikely to make your social media posts, though.

Mariner Hotel HOTEL $$
(📋 087-418822; mhlabuan@streamyx.com; U0468 Jln Tanjung Purun; s/d RM130/150; ❄ @ 🛜) Mariner's rooms are recently renovated and spacious, with laminate floors, psychedelic art on the walls, fridges and clean bathrooms. Decent breakfast.

Grand Dorsett Labuan HOTEL $$$
(📋 087-422000; www.granddorsett.com/labuan; 462 Jln Merdeka; r/ste from RM445/735; ❄ @ 🛜 🏊) One of the most luxurious hotels in town, Dorsett is palatial, with a columned marble lobby, outdoor pool, pleasant carpeted rooms in neutral creams and beiges, and with balcony views over the city or harbour, plus friendly staff. Breakfast buffet, packed with fresh fruit and pastry, is tip-top.

Eating

Restoran Sharifah MALAYSIAN $
(📋 087-425498; Jln Merdeka; mains RM2-9; ☺ 7am-9pm) Handily opposite the ferry terminal, Sharifah fills up with locals who come for the flaky roti prepared a dozen ways, *murtabak* filled with sardines, chicken or beef and an array of noodle dishes and rice with curry. Fill your boots for just a few ringgit.

Restoran Selera Farizah MALAYSIAN $
(Lg Bunga Tanjung; meals from RM4; ☺ 8am-9pm) If you prefer a Muslim *kedai kopi* (coffee shop), you could try this place, which serves roti, curries and *nasi campur*, with a rapt local audience watching pro wrestling videos.

★ Tambayan at Kainang FILIPINO $$
(📋 014-371 7778; www.facebook.com/tambayanbh; Times Sq, off Jln Merdeka; mains RM10-30; ☺ 8am-11pm) Behind a facade of bamboo and greenery, this Filipino joint is primarily a temple to pork, and we love its crispy *lechon kawali* (pork loin), *adobo* (pork slow-cooked in soy sauce and vinegar) and *dinuguan* (pork simmered in a gravy of pig blood, chilli, garlic and vinegar). Stir-fried jungle greens, spicy chicken wings and grilled fish make worthy accompaniments.

Tiara Seafood Restaurant SEAFOOD $$
(📋 087-581801; Tiara Labuan, Jln Tanjung Batu; mains RM18-28; ☺ 10.30am-2.30pm & 6-10pm) Tiara Labuan's Chinese restaurant has good reports for its seafood (though scallops and mussels are imported and cooked from frozen). For the freshest stuff, pick your dinner from the tanks, choose a preparation method, *et voila!* Standouts include grilled local fish (RM75 to RM110 per 1kg), chilli crab (RM85 per 1kg) and salt-and-pepper squid. Efficient service and oblique sea views.

ℹ Information

Arcade Moneychanger (📞 087-412545; 168 Jln OKK Awang Besar; ⊙ 9am-6pm Mon-Sat)

Bertam Mass Money Changer (Jln Bunga Raya; ⊙ 9am-6pm Mon-Sat)

HSBC (📞 087-422610; 189 Jln Merdeka; ⊙ 9.30am-4pm Mon-Fri)

Maybank (Financial Park)

Police Station (Jln OKK Abdullah)

Post Office (Jln Berjaya; ⊙ 8am-4.30pm Mon-Fri, to noon Sat)

Tourist Information Centre (📞 087-423445; www.labuantourism.my; cnr Jln Dewan & Jln Berjaya; ⊙ 8am-5pm Mon-Fri, 9am-3pm Sat)

ℹ Getting There & Away

AIR

From **Labuan Airport** (Jln Tun Mustapha), Malaysia Airlines (www.malaysiaairlines.com) has flights to/from KK (30 minutes), KL (2½ hours) and Miri (45 minutes). AirAsia (www.airasia.com) flies to/from KL twice daily most days for onward connections.

BOAT

Kota Kinabalu Passenger ferries (business class RM31 to RM44, economy class RM26 to RM39, 3¼ hours) depart KK for Pulau Labuan from Monday to Saturday at 8am and 1.30pm (3pm Sundays). In the opposite direction, they depart the **Labuan Ferry Terminal** (Jln Merdeka) for KK from Monday to Saturday at 8am and 1pm, and 10.30am and 3pm on Sundays.

Sarawak There are ferries to Limbang (two hours, RM17 to RM31) and Lawas (2¼ hours, RM18 to RM33) in Sarawak's Limbang Division.

Brunei Ferries depart Labuan's **Menumbok Ferry Terminal** (Jln Merdeka) for the Bruneian

---

ℹ GETTING TO BRUNEI: BANDAR LABUAN TO BANDAR SERI BEGAWAN

Getting to the border Ferries depart Bandar Labuan for the Bruneian port of Muara (RM40, 1¼ hours) daily at 9am, 1.30pm, 3.30pm and 4pm.

At the border In Brunei most visitors are granted a visa on arrival for free, although Australians and Chinese must pay a fee.

Moving on You'll be dropped at Serasa Ferry Terminal; from here buses 37 or 39 can take you to central Bandar Seri Begawan (B$1, one hour). Express buses (B$2) to BSB are supposed to coincide with the ferry arrivals. A taxi should cost around B$30; a Dart ride around half that.

---

port of Muara (RM40, 1¼ hours) four times daily.

ℹ Getting Around

MINIBUS

Labuan has a good minibus network based on a six-zone system. Minibuses depart from the **Labuan central bus station** (Jln Tan Mustapha). Their numbers are clearly painted on the front, and fares range from 50 sen for a short trip to RM2.50 for a trip to the top of the island. Services are generally more frequent before sunset.

TAXI

Taxis are plentiful and there's a **stand** on Jln Merdeka next to the local ferry terminal. The base rate is RM15 for short journeys, with most destinations costing around RM20.

Sarawak

Includes ➡

Kuching 393
Bako National Park . . . 414
Kubah National
Park 421
Sibu 430
Batang Rejang 434
Bintulu 438
Miri 446
Gunung Mulu
National Park 453
Kelabit Highlands . . . 459
Limbang Division . . . 465

Best Places to Eat

➡ Madli's Restaurant (p449)

➡ Top Spot Food Court (p407)

➡ Summit Café (p449)

➡ Lepau (p407)

➡ Choon Hui (p406)

Best Places to Stay

➡ Batik Boutique Hotel (p405)

➡ Kurakura Homestay (p421)

➡ Village House (p418)

➡ Garden Bungalows (p457)

➡ Labang Longhouse
Guesthouse (p460)

Why Go?

Sarawak makes access to Borneo's natural wonders and cultural riches a breeze. From Kuching, the island's most dynamic city, pristine rainforests – where you can spot orangutans, proboscis monkeys, crocodiles and the world's largest flower, the rafflesia – can be visited on day trips, with time in the evening for a tasty meal and a drink by the waterfront. More adventurous travellers can take a 'flying coffin' riverboat up the 'Amazon of Borneo', the Batang Rejang, on their way east to hike from longhouse to longhouse in the cool environs of the Kelabit Highlands, or to the spectacular bat caves and extraordinary rock formations of Gunung Mulu National Park. For the best chance of seeing an orangutan in the wild, venture to the Batang Ai region. Everywhere you go, you'll encounter the warmth, unforced friendliness and sense of humour that make the people of Malaysia's most culturally diverse state such delightful hosts.

When to Go
Kuching

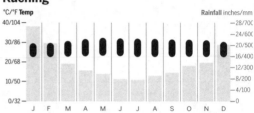

Jul Local bands and international artists jam at Kuching's Rainforest World Music Festival.

Jul–Sep It's tourist high season, so book flights and treks early, especially for smaller upcountry towns.

Nov–Jan Rough seas can make coastal boat travel difficult or impossible.

History

After a century of rule by the 'white rajas' and four years of Japanese occupation, Sarawak became a British Crown colony in 1946. At the urging of the British parliament, the territory joined the Malay Peninsula, Sabah and Singapore to form Malaysia in 1963 (Singapore withdrew two years later). At about the same time, neighbouring Indonesia, under the leftist leadership of President Soekarno, laid claim to all of Borneo, including Sarawak, launching a military campaign known as the Konfrontasi (1962–66). Tens of thousands of troops from the UK, Australia and New Zealand were deployed to secure Sarawak's border with Kalimantan.

The appointment of Adenan Satem as chief minister of Sarawak in 2014 marked the end of the 13-year tenure of Abdul Taib Mahmud. Frequently accused of corruption, and with a personal fortune estimated at US$15 billion, Taib is now the Sarawak state governor.

Unfortunately, Satem died in office in 2017, but throughout his tenure he brought a degree of optimism to the people of Sarawak, and expressed a determination to protect the state's forests from further oil-palm plantations and fight illegal logging and timber-industry corruption.

He was also an advocate of increasing the share of revenue Sarawak receives from oil and gas production within its territory. In 2018 this was pegged at only 5% of the total revenue state-owned Petronas derives from Sarawak's reserves, but negotiations were continuing with Malaysia's new federal government to increase this percentage. Also in 2018, Petros was formed as a Sarawak-based company focused on exploration for and development of new oil and gas fields. For these new fields, 100% of profits will be retained by Sarawak.

KUCHING

📞 082 / POP 618,000

It's easy to see why Raja Brooke chose this spot for his capital. Hugging the curves of the languid Sungai Sarawak, Kuching was an ideal trading post between other Asian sea ports and Borneo's interior. It's still a gateway to both jungle and sea, and Kuching's proximity to national parks makes it the ideal base for day trips to wild coastal and rainforest destinations.

Sarawak's sophisticated capital also merges cultures, crafts and cuisines, and the city's energetic collage of bustling streets and narrow alleys lined with carpenter shops, cafes and bars is best explored on foot. Attractions include time-capsule museums, Chinese temples decorated with dragons, a weekend market, heritage shophouses, and a riverfront esplanade that's perfect for a warm-evening stroll and a delicious meal. For history buffs, galleries, museums and walking tours present the thrilling stories of the Brooke family, white rajas of Sarawak from 1841 to 1946.

◉ Sights

The main attraction here is the city itself. Leave plenty of time to explore the lanes and alleys and soak up the relaxed vibe and charming street frontages of Jln Carpenter (Old Chinatown), Jln India, Jln Padungan (New Chinatown) and the Waterfront Promenade.

◉ Waterfront Promenade

The south bank of Sungai Sarawak has been turned into a promenade with paved walkways, grass and trees, and food stalls. It's a fine place for a stroll any time a cool breeze blows off the river, especially at sunset. In the evening the waterfront is ablaze with colourful fairy lights and full of couples and families eating snacks as *tambang* (small passenger ferries) glide past with their glowing lanterns. The water level is kept constant by a downstream barrage.

★**Darul Hana Bridge** BRIDGE
(Jambatan Darul Hana; Kuching Waterfront; ⏰6am-midnight) Opened in late 2017 to link the northern and southern parts of Kuching, the city's spectacular new pedestrian bridge (335m) is constructed to resemble the letter 'S' (for Sarawak), and the two towers are designed to look like the hornbill-inspired structures of traditional Bidayuh bamboo bridges. Two spacious viewing decks provide the best locations for taking in sprawling riverfront views.

From the northern end of the bridge a new riverfront esplanade continues east past the Sarawak State Assembly to provide pedestrian access to Fort Margherita and its Brooke Gallery.

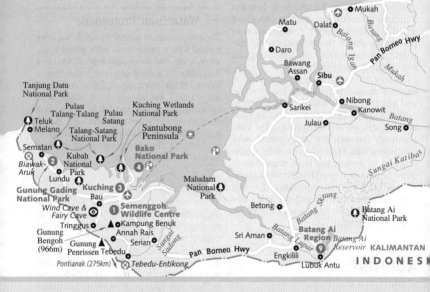

383

SOUTH
CHINA
SEA

0 ————————— 50 km
0 ————————— 25 miles

Mukah
Matu   Dalat
Daro
Bawang
Assan   Sibu
Nibong
Sarikei   Kanowit
Julau   Batang
Song

Batang Igan   Pan Borneo Hwy
Mukah

Sungai Katibas

Tanjung Datu
National Park
Pulau
Talang-Talang   Pulau
Teluk   Satang
Melano   Kuching Wetlands
Talang-Satang   National Park
Sematan   National Park   Santubong
Peninsula
Biawak-   2   Kubah   Bako
Aruk   National   National Park
Lundu   Park
Gunung Gading
National Park   Kuching   3
Bau   Maludam
Wind Cave &   1   National
Fairy Cave   Semenggoh   Park
Tringgus   Wildlife Centre   Betong
Kampung Benuk
Gunung   Annah Rais   Batang Ai
Bengoh   Serian   Sri Aman   National Park
(966m)   Gunung   Sungai   Batang Ai
Penrissen   Tebedu   Sadong   Batang Ai   Region   Reservoir   KALIMANTAN
Pontianak (275km)   Tebedu-Entikong   Pan Borneo Hwy
Engkilili   INDONESI
Lubuk Antu

Batang Skrang   Batang Lupar

Sarawak Highlights

1 Semenggoh Wildlife Centre (p420) Seeing orangutans swing through the canopy.

2 Gunung Gading National Park (p425) Spotting the

elusive rafflesia, the world's largest flower.

3 Kuching (p393) Strolling the waterfront promenade.

4 Bako National Park (p414) Getting a chance to

spot endangered proboscis monkeys.

5 Batang Rejang (p434) Watching the jungle glide by as you make your way along 'Borneo's Amazon'.

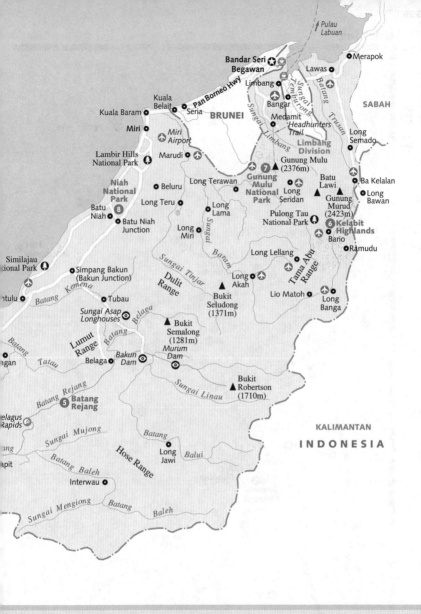

6 Kelabit Highlands (p459)
Experiencing longhouse life and Kelabit hospitality in friendly Bario.

7 Gunung Mulu National Park (p453) Ascending

Gunung Mulu, Borneo's highest peak, or exploring caves in Sarawak's best nature park.

8 Niah National Park (p443) Entering a netherworld

of stalactites and bats in the caves.

9 Batang Ai Region (p429)
Negotiating the Red Ape Trail for a good chance of seeing orangutans in the wild.

Kuching

KAMPUNG LINTANG

23
PETRA JAYA

7

Sungai Sarawak

25

Fort Margherita
4

Darul Hana Bridge
3

Lebuh Jawa

Jln Gambier
67
16
Old Court House Complex
27
5 9

Jln India
Indian Mosque Ln

Main Bazaar
51
38
60
92
78
43
Jln China
OLD CHINATOWN

Jln Market
73
95

19

Jln Khoo Hun Yeang

84
26
13
Jln Carpenter
35

96

Jln Mosque (Jln Masjid)

Jln Barrack

45
65 14
82

12

Padang Merdeka

Jln Pearl

29

Jln Wayang

8

Jln Temple

Jln Padungan

Jln Green Hill

Jln P Ramlee

24
17

Jln Tun Abang Haji Openg

22

Art Museum
1

McDougall

6
Sarawak Museum

Jln Tabuan

Medan Niaga Satok (6km)
Jln Satok

21

Jln Reservoir

Reservoir Park

32
71

Jln Were

28

Jln Taman Budaya

Jln Tun Abang Haji Openg

Lorong Park

Sarawak General Hospital (1km);
Kuching Sentral (8km)

See Enlargement

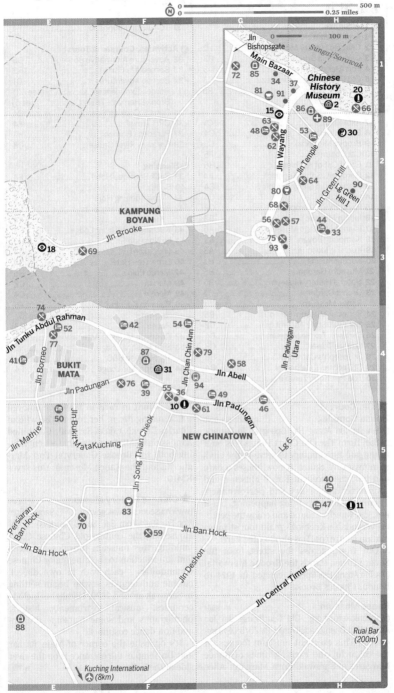

0   500 m
0   0.25 miles

Jln Bishopsgate

Jln
Bishopsgate
Main Bazaar
72   85
      34   37
81   91
15
      63
48   62   53
      80
      68
56   75   57
      93

Chinese History Museum
20
2   66
89
86
30
44   33
90
Jln Green Hill
Lg Green Hill 1
Jln Temple
Jln Wayang
64

Sungai Sarawak

KAMPUNG BOYAN
Jln Brooke
18   69

74
Jln Tunku Abdul Rahman
52
77
41
BUKIT MATA
Jln Borneo
Jln Padungan
76   39
50
Jln Mathies
Jln Bukit Mata Kuching
Jln Song Thian Cheok
83
70
59
Persiaran Ban Hock
Jln Ban Hock

42
87
31
54
79
Jln Chan Chin Ann
58
94   Jln Abell
55   36
10   61
Jln Padungan
49
46

NEW CHINATOWN

Jln Padungan Utara
Lg 6

40
47   11

Jln Ban Hock
Jln Deshon

Jln Central Timur

Ruai Bar (200m)

88

Kuching International ✈ (8km)

Kuching

◎ **Top Sights**
1 Art Museum B5
2 Chinese History Museum H1
3 Darul Hana Bridge C3
4 Fort Margherita D3
5 Old Court House Complex C3
6 Sarawak Museum B5

◎ **Sights**
7 Astana C1
8 Bishop's House C4
9 Brooke Memorial C3
10 Cat Column F5
11 Great Cat of Kuching H6
12 Gurdwara Sahib Kuching A4
13 Hiang Thian Siang Temple C4
14 Hin Ho Bio C4
15 Hong San Si Temple G2
16 Indian Mosque B3
17 Islamic Heritage Museum A5
18 Kampung Boyan E3
19 Kuching Mosque A3
20 Kucing Kucing H1
21 Museum Garden B5
22 Natural History Museum B5
23 Orchid Garden C1
   Ranee Museum .... (see 5)
24 Sarawak Museum Campus B5
25 Sarawak State Assembly D2
26 Sarawak Textile Museum B4
27 Square Tower C3
28 St Joseph's Cathedral B6
29 St Thomas's Cathedral B4
30 Tua Pek Kong Temple H2

31 Tun Jugah Foundation F4

◎ **Activities, Courses & Tours**
32 Adventure Alternative Borneo D6
33 Borneo à la Carte H3
34 Borneo Adventure G1
   Borneo Experiences .... (see 53)
   Brooke Heritage Trails .... (see 5)
35 Bumbu Cooking School C4
36 CPH Travel F4
37 Paradesa Borneo H1
38 Sarawak River Cruise C3

◎ **Sleeping**
39 Batik Boutique Hotel F4
40 Beds H5
41 Hilton Kuching Hotel E4
42 Hotel Grand Margherita
   Kuching F4
43 Kuching Waterfront Lodge C3
44 Le Nomade H3
45 lima.tujoh C4
46 Lime Tree Hotel G4
47 Marco Polo's H6
48 Marian G2
49 Meritin G4
50 Pullman Kuching E5
   Radioman .... (see 37)
51 Ranee C3
52 Riverside Majestic Astana Wing E4
53 Singgahsana Lodge H2
   Threehouse B&B .... (see 45)
54 Woodpecker Lodge F4

★ Old Court House Complex
HISTORIC BUILDING

(btwn Jln Tun Abang Haji Openg & Jln Barrack; ⊙8am-11pm) The Old Court House was built in the late 19th century to serve as the city's administrative centre. It now houses a **cafe** and **bar**, the excellent Ranee Museum and several venues for **art and performance**. There's usually something happening, but if not, just wander around and enjoy the peaceful verandahs. Kuching's main tourist information centre (p411) is also located here.

Out front, across the street from the Square Tower, stands the **Brooke Memorial** (Jln Tun Abang Haji Openg), erected in 1924 to honour Charles Brooke.

Ranee Museum
MUSEUM

(www.brooketrust.org; Old Courthouse, Jln Tun Abang Haji Openg; adult/child RM20/5; ⊙9am-4.45pm) This excellent museum focuses on the colourful and exciting times of Ranee Margaret of Sarawak. Born Margaret Alice Lili de Windt in Paris in 1849, she enjoyed a fascinating life in her role as the wife of Charles Brooke, raja of Sarawak. Combined admission (RM30) is available when visiting both the Brooke Gallery at Fort Margherita and the Ranee Museum; this saves RM10.

★ Chinese History Museum
MUSEUM

(www.museum.sarawak.gov.my; ⊙9am-4.45pm Mon-Fri, 10am-4pm Sat, Sun & holidays) **FREE** Housed in the century-old Chinese Court building, this museum provides an excellent introduction to the nine major Chinese communities – each with its own dialect, cuisine and temples – who began settling in Sarawak around 1830. Highlights include ceramics, musical instruments, historic photographs and some fearsome dragon- and lion-dance costumes.

It's opposite the corner of Main Bazaar and Jln Temple; the entrance is on the river side of the building.

⊗ Eating

55	21 Bistro	F4
56	Bla Bla Bla	G3
57	Cha Bo	G3
58	Chong Choon Cafe	G4
59	Choon Hui	F6
60	Commons	C3
61	Everrise Supermarket	G5
62	Fig Tree Cafe	G2
63	Granary	G2
64	Green Hill Corner	H2
65	Indah House	C4
66	James Brooke Bistro & Cafe	H1
67	Jubilee Restaurant	B3
68	Junk	G2
69	Kampung Boyan Hawker Centres	E3
70	Lepau	E6
	lima.tujoh	(see 45)
71	Lok Lok	D6
72	Maria Kek Lapis	G1
73	Open-Air Market	B3
74	Riverside Hawker Stalls	E4
75	Ting & Ting	G3
76	Top Spot Food Court	F4
77	Tribal Stove	E4
78	Yang Choon Tai Hawker Centre	C3
79	Zhun San Yen Vegetarian Food Centre	G4
	Zinc	(see 32)

⊙ Drinking & Nightlife

	Barber	(see 57)

80	Bear Garden	G2
81	Black Bean Coffee & Tea Company	G1
82	Drunken Monkey	C4
83	Monkee Bar	F6
	Sky Lounge	(see 52)

⊚ Shopping

	Fabriko	(see 85)
84	Juliana Native Handwork	C3
85	Main Bazaar	G1
	Mohamed Yahia & Sons	(see 61)
86	Museum Cafe & Shop	H1
	Nelson's Gallery	(see 86)
87	Popular Book Co	F4
88	Tanoti	E7
	UD Siburan Jaya	(see 85)

ⓘ Information

89	Klinik Chan	H2
	Mohamed Yahia & Sons	(see 61)
90	Mr Clean	H2
91	My Express Laundry Service	G1
92	Visitors Information Centre	C3

ⓘ Transport

93	An Hui Motor	G3
94	Bus Asia	G4
95	Bus to Bako National Park	A3
96	City Public Link	A4
	Sarawak Transport Company	(see 96)
	Saujana Bus Station	(see 96)

Square Tower   HISTORIC BUILDING
(Main Bazaar) Along with Fort Margherita (p402), the Square Tower, built in 1879, once guarded the river against marauders. Over the past century the structure – still emblazoned with Sarawak's Brooke-era coat-of-arms – has served as a prison, a mess and a dance hall. Currently, it hosts a dinner-only **restaurant**.

⊙ Old Chinatown

Lined with evocative colonial-era shophouses and home to several vibrantly coloured Chinese temples, Jln Carpenter is the heart of Kuching's Old Chinatown.

Hong San Si Temple   TEMPLE
(Say Ong Kong; cnr Jln Wayang & Jln Carpenter; ⊙6am-6pm) **FREE** Thought to date to around 1840, this fine Hokkien Chinese temple with intricate rooftop dragons was fully restored in 2004. There's a big

celebration here in April, when a long procession of floats, lion and dragon dancers and others winds its way through town following the altar of Kong Teck Choon Ong, the temple's deity.

Sarawak Textile Museum   MUSEUM
(Muzium Tekstil Sarawak; www.museum.sarawak.gov.my; Jln Tun Abang Haji Openg; ⊙9am-4.45pm Mon-Fri, 10am-4pm Sat, Sun & holidays) **FREE** Housed in a 'colonial Baroque'–style building constructed in 1909, this museum displays some superb examples of traditional Sarawakian textiles, including Malay *songket* (gold brocade cloth), as well as the hats, mats, belts, basketwork, beadwork, silver work, bark work, bangles and ceremonial headdresses created by the Iban, Bidayuh, Penan and other Dayak groups. Dioramas recreate the sartorial exuberance of Orang Ulu, Malay, Chinese and Indian weddings. Explanatory panels shed light on materials and techniques.

Tua Pek Kong Temple TAOIST SITE
(Jln Padungan) Tua Pek Kong, atop the red wedding-cake structure on Jln Padungan at the end of Main Bazaar, is the most popular temple in town for Chinese residents.

Hiang Thian Siang Temple TEMPLE
(Sang Ti Miao Temple; btwn 12 & 14 Jln Carpenter) FREE This temple, rebuilt shortly after the fire of 1884, serves the Teochew congregation as a shrine to Shang Di (the Emperor of Heaven). On the 15th day of the **Hungry Ghosts Festival** (mid-August or early September) offerings of food, prayer, incense and paper money are made to appease the spirits, and then burned in a dramatic bonfire.

Hin Ho Bio TEMPLE
(36 Jln Carpenter; ⊙ 6am-5pm) FREE It's easy to miss this temple, tucked away on the roof of the Kuching Hainan Association. Go up the staircase to the top floor and you'll come to a vivid little Chinese shrine, **Hin Ho Bio** (Temple of the Queen of Heaven), with rooftop views of Jln Carpenter.

⊙ Jalan India Area

Once Kuching's main shopping area for imported textiles, brassware and household goods, pedestrianised Jln India – essentially the western continuation of Jln Carpenter – remains an exuberant commercial thoroughfare. The shops along the eastern section are mostly Chinese owned; those to the west are run by Indian Muslims with roots in Tamil Nadu. It's *the* place to come in Kuching for cheap textiles.

Indian Mosque MOSQUE
(www.museum.sarawak.gov.my; Indian Mosque Lane; ⊙ 6am-8.30pm except during prayers) FREE Turn off Jln India (between No 37 and No 39A) or waterfront Jln Gambier (between No 24 and No 25A) onto tiny **Indian Mosque Lane** (Lg Sempit) and you enter another world. About halfway along, surrounded by houses and spice shops, stands Kuching's oldest mosque, a modest structure built of *belian* (ironwood) in 1863 by Muslim traders from Tamil Nadu.

Notable for its simplicity, it is an island of peace and cooling shade in the middle of Kuching's commercial hullabaloo. There's usually someone sitting outside the mosque keeping an eye on things. If you would like to go inside, ask permission and they will probably offer to show you around. Women will be given a long cloak and headscarf to wear.

⊙ Museum Precinct & Around

The museums in the area just south of Padang Merdeka (Independence Sq) contain a first-rate collection of cultural artefacts that no one interested in Borneo's peoples and habitats should miss.

Facing the east side of Padang Merdeka and its monumental **kapok tree**, the Anglican **St Thomas's Cathedral** (www.stthomascathedralkuching.org; Jln Tun Abang Haji Openg; ⊙ 8.30am-6pm Mon-Sat, to 7pm Sun) FREE has a mid-20th-century look and,

---

SARAWAK MUSEUM COMPLEX

At research time, construction was under way on a new **Sarawak Museum Complex** (https://museum.sarawak.gov.my; Jln Tun Abang Haji Openg; 10am-7pm Mon-Thu, Sat & Sun, to 11pm Fri) set for completion in 2021. The modern five-storey building will bring the city's archaeology, ethnology, zoology and history collections under one roof, and include state-of-the art interactive displays.

It is envisaged that some of the most interesting ethnographic exhibitions displayed at the old **Sarawak Museum** (https://museum.sarawak.gov.my; Jln Tun Abang Haji Openg; ⊙ 10am-7pm Mon-Thu, Sat & Sun, to 11pm Fri) FREE will be reinstalled here. The Sarawak Museum was established in 1891 by Charles Brooke as a place to exhibit indigenous handicrafts and wildlife specimens, many collected by naturalist Alfred Russel Wallace in the 1850s. A highlight of the historic building are the two colonial cannons protecting the entrance.

Some exhibits may be relocated to the new building from the **Islamic Heritage Museum** (Jln P Ramlee; ⊙ 9am-4.45pm Mon-Fri, 10am-3.45pm Sat, Sun & holidays) FREE. Offering a pretty good introduction to Malay-Muslim culture and its long ties with the Muslim heartland far to the west, the museum's current displays range from Bornean-Malay architecture, musical instruments and woodcarvings to Arabic calligraphy and astrolabes of the sort that helped Arab mariners travel this far east.

KUCHING KITTIES

It's just a coincidence that in Bahasa Malaysia, Kuching means 'cat' (spelled *kucing*), but the city has milked the homonym for all it's worth, branding Sarawak's capital 'Cat City' and erecting a number of marvellously kitschy cat statues to beautify the urban landscape.

Perhaps the nicest of the statues is **Kucing Kucing** (Waterfront Promenade), Gaye Porter's life-size bronze sculpture of playful felines cavorting on the lawn outside the James Brooke Bistro & Cafe (p408). On a roundabout, the **Cat Column** (cnr Jln Padungan & Jln Chan Chin Ann) features four cats around the bottom and four hibiscus flowers near the top – the latter are just below the cat-adorned shield of the South Kuching municipality. You also won't miss the **Great Cat of Kuching** (Jln Padungan) a 2.5m-high white pussycat with blue eyes and wire whiskers perched on a traffic island just outside the Chinese ceremonial gate.

Located 8km north of the centre, the **Cat Museum** (www.dbku.sarawak.gov.my; Jln Semariang, Bukit Siol; camera/video RM4/5; ⊙9am-5pm; 🚌K15) **FREE** features hundreds of entertaining, surprising and bizarre feline figurines – some the size of a cow, others tiny – alongside detailed presentations on 'Cats in Malay Society' and 'Cats in Chinese Art'. By the time you reach the exhibits on 'Cats in Stamps' and 'Cats in Film' (in which Bond villain Blofeld's mog features), you may feel it's all getting a little silly.

---

inside, a bright-red barrel-vaulted ceiling. At the top of the hill, on the other side of the Parish Centre, stands the **Bishop's House**, Kuching's oldest building (constructed in 1849) with admirable solidness by a German shipwright.

Museum Garden (Jln Tun Abang Haji Openg; ⊙9am-4.45pm Mon-Fri, 10am-4pm Sat, Sun & holidays) stretches south from the hill, leading past flowers and fountains to a white-and-gold column called the **Heroes' Monument**. South of the garden is **St Joseph's Cathedral** (Museum Garden, Jln Tun Abang Haji Openg) – built as a church in 1969 and granted cathedral status in 1976, this Roman Catholic cathedral is notable for its impressive *belian* (ironwood) roof.

West of Padang Merdeka is the Sikh temple **Gurdwara Sahib Kuching** (Jln P Ramlee) and **Kuching Mosque** (Jln Market), which was the state mosque until a larger one was built in 1990 at Petra Jaya – its gold domes are particularly beautiful at sunset.

★**Art Museum**　　　　　　　　　MUSEUM
(www.museum.sarawak.gov.my; Jln Tun Abang Haji Openg; ⊙9am-4.45pm Mon-Fri, 10am-4pm Sat, Sun & holidays) **FREE** This museum features an exhibit called Urang Sarawak, which deftly and succinctly describes the people and culture of the region, especially indigenous lifestyles and traditional mythology, historical periods such as the Brooke era and World War II, as well as contemporary Sarawak. Other exhibits feature prehistoric archaeology, including important finds from the Niah Caves, and Chinese ceramics.

Natural History Museum　　　　MUSEUM
(www.museum.sarawak.gov.my; Jln Tun Abang Haji Openg) This building, built in 1908 and adorned with Rajah Brooke's birdwing butterfly, so named by famous naturalist Alfred Russel Wallace, is currently being used to store zoological and archaeological specimens (including finds excavated in Niah). It's not open to the public, but researchers and students can apply for access to the collections.

◉ New Chinatown

Built starting in the 1920s, initially with money from the rubber boom, Kuching's liveliest commercial thoroughfare stretches 1.5km along Jln Padungan from Jln Tunku Abdul Rahman to the Great Cat of Kuching. It's lined with Chinese-owned businesses and noodle shops and a growing number of cafes, bars and restaurants. Covered arcades make it a fine place for a rainy-day stroll.

Tun Jugah Foundation　　　　MUSEUM
(☎082-239672; www.tunjugahfoundation.org.my; 4th fl, Tun Jugah Tower, 18 Jln Tunku Abdul Rahman; ⊙9am-noon & 1-4pm Mon-Fri) **FREE** The textile gallery and museum of this charitable foundation, which aims to promote and preserve Iban culture, has excellent exhibits on Iban *ikat* (tie-dyed yarn fabric) and *sungkit* (gold brocade) weaving, as well as bead work. Iban women come here to make traditional textiles using hand looms.

North Bank of the River

To get to Sungai Sarawak's northern bank, take a *tambang* (river ferry; RM1) from one of the docks along the Waterfront Promenade. An alternative is to use the Darul Hana pedestrian bridge (p393), which crosses the river to near the Sarawak State Assembly.

★ Fort Margherita   MUSEUM
(Brooke Gallery; www.brookemuseums.org; Kampung Boyan; adult/child RM20/5; ⊙ 9am-4.45pm) Built by Charles Brooke in 1879 and named after his wife, Ranee Margaret, this compact hilltop fortress long protected Kuching against surprise attack by pirates. Inside, the Brooke Gallery illustrates the remarkable story of the white rajas of Sarawak with fascinating artefacts and story boards. You can also explore the ramparts for excellent views of the Kuching waterfront. Combined admission (RM30) is available when visiting both the Brooke Gallery at Fort Margherita and the Ranee Museum; this saves RM10.

Astana   HISTORIC BUILDING
(Jln Taman Budaya; ⊙ closed to public) Built by Charles Brooke in 1869, the Astana (a local word meaning 'palace') – conveniently labelled in giant white letters – and its manicured gardens still serve as the home of the governor of Sarawak. The best views of the complex are actually from the south (city centre) bank of the river, so it's not really worth taking a *tambang* across or using Kuching's new bridge.

Kampung Boyan   AREA
This sedate, old-time Malay *kampung* (village), filled with joyously colourful houses and a profusion of flowering plants, is a world away from the glitz and bustle of downtown Kuching, to which it's connected by boat (RM1). The waterfront area has two roofed hawker centres as well as other Malay-style eateries.

Sarawak State Assembly   NOTABLE BUILDING
(Dewan Undangan Negeri, Petra Jaya) On the north bank of Sungai Sarawak and inaugurated in 2009, the iconic home of the State Assembly is an imposing structure whose soaring golden roof is said to resemble either a *payung* (umbrella) or a *terendak* (Melanau sunhat). The best views of the building (not open to the public) are from the Waterfront Promenade and Jln Bishopsgate. A waterfront esplanade below the building links with the city's spectacular Darul Hana footbridge.

Orchid Garden   GARDENS
(Jln Astana Lot; ⊙ 9.30am-6pm Tue-Sun) FREE Sarawak's state flower, the Normah orchid, is just one of the 82 species growing in these peaceful gardens and greenhouse nursery. Other Borneo orchids to look out for are lady's slippers, identifiable by their distinct, insect-trapping pouches.

To get here from the city centre, cross the Darul Hana footbridge to Pengakalan Sapi on the north bank (next to the Sarawak State Assembly building) and then walk a short distance up the hill.

Elsewhere in Kuching

Medan Niaga Satok   MARKET
(Satok Weekend Market; Jln Matang Jaya; ⊙ 5.30am-7.30pm; 🚌 K7) Kuching's biggest and liveliest market is 9km west of the city centre. It's open every day, but the main event is the larger weekend market that begins around midday on Saturday, when folk, some from rural longhouses, arrive with fruit, vegetables, fish and spices.

The air is heady with the aromas of fresh coriander, ginger, herbs and jungle ferns, which are displayed among piles of bananas, mangoes, custard apples and obscure jungle fruit. If you smell something overpoweringly sickly-sweet and pungent, chances are it's a durian. Vendors are friendly and many are happy to tell you about their wares, which are often divided into quantities worth RM1 or RM2.

Kuching North City Hall   NOTABLE BUILDING
(DBKU; Jln Semariang, Bukit Siol; 🚌 K15) Situated 8km north of the city centre is the hilltop Kuching North City Hall (known by its Malay abbreviation, DBKU), a landmark prestige project – some say it looks like a UFO – inaugurated in 1993. It houses the local council, as well as the Cat Museum (p401) on the ground floor.

If you're going to the Santubong Peninsula by car, you can stop here on the way.

Activities

Sarawak River Cruise   CRUISE
(📞 082-240366; www.sarawakrivercruise.com; waterfront jetty; adult/child RM65/32; ⊙ 5.30-7.30pm) This is a very pleasant way to segue from afternoon to evening, as 90 minutes of cruising takes in more than 30 cultural and historical landmarks. Drinks and snacks are available for purchase and the cruise includes an informative commentary.

Bumbu Cooking School

COOKING

(☑019-879 1050; http://bumbucookingclass.
weebly.com; 57 Jln Carpenter; per person RM150;
☺9am-1pm & 2.30-6.30pm) Raised in a Bidayuh
village, Joseph teaches the secrets of cooking
with fresh, organic rainforest ingredients.
At the market you'll learn how to spot top-
quality jungle ferns; back in the kitchen
you'll prepare this crunchy delicacy, along
with a main dish, and a dessert that's served
in a *pandan*-leaf basket you'll weave yourself. Maximum 10 participants.

The small shop that serves as the entrance
to the cooking school is like a mini-museum
full of pieces Joseph has collected: blowpipes, rattan baskets (one designed to be
used as a baby carrier), a rice mill, and ceremonial blankets and masks from Iban and
Orang Ulu longhouses.

🖙 Tours

Brooke Heritage Trails

HISTORY

(www.brookegallery.org; Ranee Museum, Old Courthouse; per person RM100; ☺9am Sat) These
three-hour guided tours through the city's
historic buildings explore Malay settlement
in the 1830s; the coming of the Europeans,
Chinese and Indians from the 1840s to the
1880s; and the development of the Sarawak
nation state during the time of the 'white
rajas' and the Brooke family. All transport,
and entry to Fort Margherita and the Ranee
Museum (p398) included.

Backyard Tour

TOURS

(☑Abbie 011-1584 1448, Dawson 016-537 1128;
www.mybackyardtour.com) Excellent day trips
and two- and three-day excursions focusing
on village visits and nature with an emphasis
on more authentic and off-the-beaten-track
destinations around Kuching. Accommodation options include traditional homestays.

Paradesa Borneo

CYCLING

(One Wayang Tours; ☑082-238801; www.paradesa
borneo.com; 1 Jln Wayang) Specialises in bike
tours, offering city tours (from RM122) and
off-road mountain biking (from RM228).
Sign up for the Kampung Sunset ride to sample lots of great hawker food along the way.

Borneo Experiences

TOURS

(☑082-429239; www.borneoexperiences.com;
ground fl, 1 Jln Temple; ☺10am-7pm Mon-Sat, may
also open Sun) The travel agency at Singgahsana Lodge (p404) runs trips to a remote
Bidayuh 'village in the clouds' – only accessible by jungle trekking – and an Iban

longhouse in the Batang Ai area. Also offers
cycling tours and departures exploring the
Kuching wetlands or Tanjung Datu National
Park. Consistently gets excellent reviews
from travellers. Ask about plans for oceanfront glamping north of Lundu.

Adventure Alternative Borneo

ADVENTURE

(☑082-248000, WhatsApp 019-892 9627; www.
adventurealternativeborneo.com; Lot 37 Jln Tabuan;
☺9am-5pm Mon-Sat) 🖉 Offers ethical and
sustainable trips that combine 'culture,
nature and adventure'. Can help you design
and coordinate an itinerary for independent
travel to remote areas, including the Penan
villages of the Upper Baram. Also offers
jungle trips on ATV 4WD motorcycles and
excellent tours from Kuching combining
trekking, jungle camps and staying at the
Iban longhouse of Tuba.

Borneo à la Carte

TOURS

(☑082-234126; www.borneoalacarte.com; Le Cafe
Rouge, 3 Jln Green Hill; ☺9am-6pm) 🖉 A Kuching-
based agency offering innovative, tailor-made
trips, mainly for a French-speaking clientele,
to indigenous communities that other agencies don't cover. The company is known for
having very reasonable prices and sharing
receipts equitably with local communities.

Rucksack Rainforest Kayaking

TOURS

(Borneo Trek & Kayak Adventure; ☑WhatsApp 013-
804 8338; www.rainforestkayaking.com; packages
per person from RM198) Specialises in fully
catered river trips including transport to/
from Kuching. Bookings can be made via
tour agencies in the city and include hotel
pick-ups and drop-offs.

Borneo Adventure

TOURS

(☑082-245175; www.borneoadventure.com; 55
Main Bazaar; ☺9am-6pm Mon-Sat) Award-
winning company that sets the standard for
high-end Borneo tours and is the leader in
cooperative projects benefiting Sarawak's
indigenous peoples. Known for its excellent
guides. Highlights include excellent multiday trips exploring the Batang Ai region and
the spectacular Tanjung Datu National Park.

🎆 Festivals & Events

Chinese New Year

NEW YEAR

(☺late Jan/early Feb) The main festivities are
along Jln Padungan.

Rainforest Fringe

CULTURAL

(www.rainforestfringe.com; ☺Jul) Running for
10 days in the lead-up to the Rainforest

World Music Festival in mid-July, this cultural celebration including music, art, film, food and photography was inaugurated in 2017. Many of the exhibitions and installations are held in Kuching's Old Courthouse complex.

★ **Kuching Festival**   FOOD & DRINK
(https://sarawaktourism.com/event/kuching-festival; Kuching City South Council, Jln Padungan; ⊙ 5-11pm for 1 month late Jul-Aug) A huge food extravaganza with hundreds of stalls selling a whole range of meals and snacks – from Mongolian barbecue to Vietnamese spring rolls and deep-fried ice cream. Held in the park in front of the Kuching City South Council (the blue, teepee-shaped building just east of Jln Padungan, on the other side of the roundabout). Also music and cultural performances.

★ **Rainforest World Music Festival**   MUSIC
(www.rwmf.net; 1/3-day pass adult RM146/387, child RM76/189; ⊙ Jul/Aug) This three-day gathering, one of the world's great music festivals, is held in the Sarawak Cultural Village. International artists, who usually perform music that is traditional in their country, hold informal workshops in the longhouses in the afternoon, while the main performances are held on the main stage at night. Accommodation gets booked out well in advance.

Mooncake Festival   FAIR
(⊙ Sep/early Oct) Musical performances and food stalls selling Chinese food, drink and, of course, mooncakes take over Jln Carpenter.

What About Kuching   CULTURAL
(✆ 082-414326; www.aboutkuching.com; ⊙ Oct) Launched in 2017, this month-long celebration of cultural, art and musical events showcases Kuching. Past events have included a waterfront jazz festival, urban sketching sessions and local street art. Events are held across the city.

🛏 Sleeping

Kuching's accommodation options range from international-standard suites with high-rise views to windowless, musty cells deep inside converted Chinese shophouses. The majority of guesthouse rooms under RM50 have shared bathrooms; prices almost always include a very simple breakfast of the toast-and-jam variety. Rates at some guesthouses rise in July, especially during the Rainforest World Music Festival.

★ **Singgahsana Lodge**   GUESTHOUSE $
(✆ 082-429277; www.singgahsana.com; 1 Jln Temple; incl breakfast dm RM29, d RM109-129; ❋ @ 🛜) Setting the Kuching standard for backpacker digs, this hugely popular guesthouse, decked out with stylish Sarawakian crafts, has an unbeatable location, a great chill-out lobby and a sociable rooftop bar. Free bicycle hire is available to guests. Dorms have 10 beds and lockers.

Woodpecker Lodge   HOSTEL $
(✆ 019-665 2420, 082-523729; www.facebook.com/woodpeckerlodgekuching; 2nd & 3rd fl, 264 Jln Chan Chin Ann; dm/s/d RM20/49/60; ❋ 🛜) Tucked away in a side street near the river in New Chinatown, Woodpecker Lodge features a variety of room options with modern decor, plenty of information for travel in Kuching and beyond, and the soothing presence of a couple of fluffy cats. The roof terrace is a good place to kick back and relax.

lima.tujoh   GUESTHOUSE $
(✆ 082-231382; www.facebook.com/pg/limatujoh57; 57 Jln China; s/d/tr RM60/95/120; ☺ ❋ 🛜) Stylish and compact rooms feature at this welcoming spot above the hip cafe (p406) of the same name. Location-wise, you're in a laneway in the absolute heart of Old Chinatown, and it's just a short stroll to excellent eating and drinking and the after-dark bustle of Kuching's riverfront.

Kuching Waterfront Lodge   HOTEL $
(✆ 082-231111; www.kuchingwaterfrontlodge.com; 15 Main Bazaar; s/d incl breakfast from RM60/90; ❋ 🛜) In an atmospheric old shopfront, this lodge has a variety of rooms, some with windows and some without, so you should definitely look at a few. Thought has gone into the decoration and colour scheme, and for a budget hotel this place exudes tropical character.

Marco Polo's   GUESTHOUSE $
(✆ 082-246679, Samuel Tan 019-888 8505; www.marcopolokuching.com; 1st fl, 236 Jln Padungan; incl breakfast dm RM27, d/tr/f without bathroom RM62/90/115; ❋ 🛜) A well-run, comfortable place with a breezy verandah and a cosy living room. The breakfast of fresh fruit, banana fritters and muffins is a popular bonus. Only some rooms have windows. Owner Sam is happy to give travel advice and sometimes brings guests to the market. Situated about 15 minutes' walk (1.5km) from the waterfront; entrance is around the corner.

Radioman
HOSTEL **$**

(☑082-248816, 082-238801; www.facebook.com/theradiomanheritage; 1 Jln Wayang; incl breakfast dm RM205, d with shared bathroom RM62-65; ✳️🛜) This central, self-styled 'heritage hostel' occupies a century-old shophouse once used for radio repairs. The building still has the original ceilings, floors and fiendishly steep stairs and has been thoughtfully redecorated. There's a 12-bed mixed dorm and a four-bed female dorm. Dorms and private rooms share a shower and toilet.

Threehouse B&B
GUESTHOUSE **$**

(☑082-423499; www.threehousebnb.com; 51 Jln China; incl breakfast dm/s/d RM20/40/60; 🛜) A spotless, family-friendly guesthouse in a great Old Chinatown location that is warm and welcoming – everything a guesthouse should be. The nine rooms are spaced over three creaky wooden floors and share a bright-red colour scheme. Amenities include a common room with TV, DVDs and books, a laundry service and a kitchen.

Beds
GUESTHOUSE **$**

(☑082-424229; 229 Jln Padungan; dm RM25, s/d without bathroom RM48/58; ✳️@🛜) This guesthouse has attracted a loyal following thanks to comfy couches in the lobby, a well-equipped kitchen you can cook in and 12 spotless rooms, nine with windows. Dorm rooms have six metal bunks of generous proportions. Located in New Chinatown, about 15 minutes' walk (1.5km) from Main Bazaar.

Le Nomade
HOSTEL **$**

(☑082-523442; www.lenomadehostel.com; 3 Jln Green Hill; dm incl breakfast RM22, d RM75, s/d with shared bathroom RM33/70; ✳️@🛜) There's a buzzing backpacker vibe at this relaxed, Iban-run place – guests often hang out in the lounge area with the friendly management. Breakfast times are flexible to suit late risers and there's a kitchen that guests can use. Of the 12 rooms, most have windows (the others make do with exhaust fans).

★Batik Boutique Hotel
BOUTIQUE HOTEL **$$**

(☑082-422845; www.batikboutiquehotel.com; 38 Jln Padungan; d incl breakfast RM300; ✳️🛜) A superb location, classy design and super-friendly staff make this an excellent choice. The swirling batik used on the hotel's facade is continued in the lobby and the 15 spacious, colour-coordinated rooms.

Riverside Majestic Astana Wing
HOTEL **$$**

(☑082-247777; www.riversidemajestic.com; Jln Tunku Abdul Rahman; d from RM153; 🚭✳️🛜🏊) The Riverside Majestic is one of Kuching's older hotels, but the addition of the new Astana Wing means it's again a great place to stay. Rooms are modern and spacious, bathrooms feature rain showerheads, and there's a rooftop bar on the 17th floor. When booking, ask for a room with river views – one of the best vistas in Kuching.

Marian
BOUTIQUE HOTEL **$$**

(☑082-252777; www.themarian.com.my; Jln Wayang; r incl breakfast RM160-260; ✳️@🛜🏊) Delightfully different, the Marian occupies a mansion once owned by a Chinese merchant before it became a convent attached to nearby St Thomas's Cathedral (p400). Great care has been taken to preserve the building's long and varied historical legacy while providing modern comforts. The 40 rooms are divided into several categories, reflecting the highly individual nature of the design.

Meritin
HOTEL **$$**

(☑082-550800; www.meritinhotel.com; Lot 315, Jln Padungan; d/f/ste from RM148/238/318; ✳️🛜) Modern and spacious rooms feature at this hotel, opened in 2017. The decor blends clean, neutral tones with subtle nods to a traditional Asian design aesthetic, and the location in New Chinatown means that snacking and dining opportunities abound. The cheapest rooms do not have windows.

Lime Tree Hotel
HOTEL **$$**

(☑082-414600; www.limetreehotel.com.my; Lot 317, Jln Abell; d incl breakfast RM158-218; ✳️@🛜) Dashes of lime green – a pillow, a bar of soap, a staff member's tie, the lobby's Cafe Sublime – accent every room of this well-run boutique hotel. (The family who owns it also owns a lime orchard.) The 50 non-smoking rooms are sleek and minimalist. The rooftop bar has river views and a good selection of meals, including vegan and vegetarian options.

Pullman Kuching
HOTEL **$$**

(☑082-222888; www.pullmankuching.com; 1A Jln Mathies, Bukit Mata; d from RM260; ✳️@🛜🏊) The 23-storey Pullman stands on a hill, towering over its neighbours. The vast white lobby is so grandiose that the rooms – in subdued tones of aquamarine, brown, white and green – feel small by comparison. The focus is on business travellers. Online rates are often cheaper than those shown here.

Hotel Grand Margherita Kuching HOTEL $$

(📞 082-423111; www.grandmargherita.com; Jln Tunku Abdul Rahman; d incl breakfast from RM160; ❄@🅟🛜🏊) On a fine piece of riverfront real estate, this place will spoil you with a bright, modern lobby, 288 very comfortable rooms, and amenities such as a fitness centre, a river-view swimming pool and a spa.

★ Ranee BOUTIQUE HOTEL $$$

(📞 082-258833; www.theranee.com; 6 & 7 Main Bazaar; d incl breakfast RM298-465; ❄@🛜) This riverfront property, housed in an old shop-house that was completely rebuilt after a fire, has an urban-resort feel. All 24 rooms are different, with plenty of design touches (the odd striped wall or globe-like lamp), high ceilings, hardwood floors and huge bathrooms with sleek indirect lighting.

Hilton Kuching Hotel HOTEL $$$

(📞 082-233888; www.hilton.com; cnr Jln Tunku Abdul Rahman & Jln Borneo; d RM405-485, ste RM755-790; ❄@🛜🏊) The Hilton has spacious, international-standard rooms in shades of cream, beige and maroon and all the amenities you'd expect from this class of hotel. The best of the rooms have excellent views of the river; others look out onto the city and rooftops of Old Chinatown. This hotel boasts the biggest and best swimming pool in Kuching.

🍴 Eating

Kuching is the ideal place to explore the entire range of Sarawak-style cooking. You can pick and choose from a variety of Chinese and Malay hawker stalls, while Jln Padungan is home to some of the city's best noodle houses. There's also an expanding range of stylish and cosmopolitan Western eateries.

Borneo's luckiest visitors start the day with a breakfast of *Sarawak laksa*, a tangy noodle soup made with coconut milk, lemon grass, sour tamarind and fiery *sambal belacan* (shrimp-paste sauce), with fresh calamansi lime juice squeezed on top. Unbelievably *lazat* ('delicious' in Bahasa Malaysia).

★ Choon Hui MALAYSIAN $

(📞 082-893709; 34 Jln Ban Hock; laksa RM7-10; ⏰7-11am Tue-Sun) This old-school *kopitiam* (coffee shop) makes the most delicious laksa in town. There's also a stall here selling excellent *popia* (a kind of spring roll made with peanuts, radish and carrot; RM3). The place can get crowded, especially at weekends.

lima.tujoh CAFE $

(📞082-231382; www.facebook.com/limatujoh57; 57 Jln China; snacks & mains RM10-20; ⏰10am-6pm Tue-Sun; 🛜🅟) 🐾 Friendly cats Ginger and Serai (aka 'Lemon Grass') are feline hosts at this cool cafe, while their human underlings serve up excellent *nasi lemak* (rice boiled in coconut milk), a good selection of beer, cakes and Vietnamese-style coffee. Occasional gigs and performances are held in the stylish interior studded with retro paraphernalia – check Facebook for listings – and there's good-value accommodation (p404) upstairs.

Indah House CAFE $

(📞082-231382; www.facebook.com/IndahHouse Kuching; 38 Jln China; snacks RM6-11; 🅟) 🐾 A one-stop blend of cool neighbourhood cafe, cooking-class venue and hip art space, Indah is one of Kuching's best cafes. Menu highlights include tasty *roti canai* wraps and Western-style sandwiches. A concise selection of vegan and vegetarian menu items combines with good coffee, juices and teas. It can also arrange tours in and around Kuching, and longhouse and homestay visits.

Fig Tree Cafe MALAYSIAN $

(📞012-855 5536; www.facebook.com/TheFigTree Cafe; 29 Jln Wayang; mains RM6-10; ⏰10.30am-8.30pm Tue-Sun; ❄🅟) This innovative cafe features Malay-Chinese dishes served with flair and enthusiasm. There are plenty of vegetarian choices, and vegan options are available. The adventurous should try the *lui cha* (rice and vegetables accompanied by a deep-green soup of Sarawak herbs). Carnivores can opt for the *kacangma* (rice-wine chicken). Also available: waffles, smoothies and a glowing green-tea cheesecake.

Lok Lok MALAYSIAN $

(7D Jln Ban Hock; mains RM6.50-9, lok lok RM2.50-3; ⏰6pm-3am) This popular nocturnal eatery specialises in *lok lok* (skewers, eg of fish, prawn, cuttlefish or bean curd; RM2.50 to RM3) that are boiled or deep-fried and eaten with sweet, sweet-and-sour, *belacan* (fermented prawn paste) or satay sauce. Also serves *rojak* (a mixed-vegetable dish with a thick shrimp-based sauce) and traditional mains such as curry chicken. Ideal for a late meal.

Chong Choon Cafe HAWKER $

(Lot 121, Section 3, Jln Abell; mains RM6-7; ⏰7-11am Wed-Mon) Under a large verandah cooled by a fleet of helicopter fans, this cafe serves some of Kuching's best Sarawak laksa. There are also stalls selling other local favourites.

Arrive early to avoid the inevitable packed house from around 8.30am.

Jubilee Restaurant   INDIAN $
(49 Jln India; mains RM6-11; ⊙ 6.30am-5.30pm) A fixture in the heart of Kuching's Indian Muslim district since 1974. Halal specialities include *nasi biryani* (rice with chicken, beef or lamb; RM9 to RM12) and *roti canai* (flatbread with egg and/or cheese; RM1 to RM3).

Yang Choon Tai Hawker Centre   CHINESE $
(23 Jln Carpenter; mains RM4-8; ⊙ 4am-midnight) Six food stalls, run by members of the Teochew Chinese community, serve up an eclectic assortment of native bites, including rice porridge with pork (3am to 9am), *kolo mee* (flash-boiled egg noodles; available from 6am to 2pm), super fish soup (3pm to 10pm) and – the most popular stall – pork satay (from 2pm).

Zhun San Yen
Vegetarian Food Centre   VEGETARIAN $
(Lot 165, Jln Chan Chin Ann; mains RM4-6; ⊙ 8am-4.30pm Mon-Fri, 9am-5pm Sat; ✿🖬) A meat-free buffet lunch of Chinese-style curries, priced by weight, is served from 11am to 2pm (RM2.50 per 100g). When the buffet is over, you can order from a menu of dishes such as ginger 'chicken' (made with a soy-based meat substitute).

Riverside Hawker Stalls   HAWKER $
(Waterfront Promenade; mains RM5-10; ⊙ 6pm-late) What could be better than an evening constitutional along the river, followed by a fresh fruit juice and a few sticks of satay?

Maria Kek Lapis   MALAYSIAN $
(🖉 012-886 3337; 4 Jln Bishopgate; with butter RM15-25, with margarine RM10; ⊙ 8am-5pm) Sells over 40 varieties of *kek lapis* (a colourful layered cake made with wheat flour, egg, prodigious quantities of butter or margarine, and flavourings such as melon, blueberry or *pandan* leaves).

Since *kek lapis* are prepared one layer at a time and each layer – there can be 30 or more – takes five or six minutes to bake, a single cake can take up to five hours from start to finish.

Kampung Boyan Hawker Centres   HAWKER $
(Kampung Boyan; mains RM3-6; ⊙ 11.30am-11pm or midnight) Reached by *tambang* (ferries; RM1) from the Waterfront Promenade, Kampung Boyan's two tent-roofed hawker centres offer cheap, tasty Malay dishes and romantic views across the river.

Open-Air Market   HAWKER $
(Tower Market; Jln Khoo Hun Yeang; mains RM3-8; ⊙ most stalls 6am-4pm, Chinese seafood 3pm-4am) Cheap, tasty dishes to look for include laksa, Chinese-style *mee sapi* (beef noodle soup), red *kolo mee* (noodles with pork and a sweet barbecue sauce), tomato *kueh tiaw* (a fried rice-noodle dish) and shaved-ice desserts (ask for 'ABC' at stall 17). The Chinese seafood stalls that open in the afternoon are on the side facing the river.

Green Hill Corner   MALAYSIAN $
(cnr Jln Temple & Jln Green Hill; meals RM3-8; ⊙ 7am-10.30pm Mon-Sat, to noon Sun) Look behind the green, Milo-sponsored awnings for the half-a-dozen stalls that crank out porridge, laksa, and chicken, rice and noodle dishes. Popular with locals, especially Kuching's legions of tour guides. The *kaya* toast with runny boiled eggs is a great way to start the day.

★Lepau   MALAYSIAN $$
(🖂 082-242160; www.facebook.com/lepaurestaurant; Persiaran Ban Hock; mains RM15-25; ⊙ 10.30am-2pm & 5.30-11pm; 🖉) 🍴 Organic and free-range ingredients feature at this buzzy restaurant showcasing the cuisine of Sarawak's indigenous Iban and Bidayuh people. The open kitchen encourages a breezy informality, as loyal Kuching locals and in-the-know visitors enjoy dishes like *ayam pansuh* (chicken steamed in bamboo) and prawn *umai* (marinated raw seafood). Weekends are very popular, so booking ahead is recommended.

★Top Spot Food Court   SEAFOOD $$
(Jln Padungan; fish per kg RM30-75, vegetable dishes RM8-14; ⊙ noon-11pm) A perennial favourite among local foodies, this neon-lit courtyard and its half-dozen humming seafooderies sits, rather improbably, on the roof of a concrete parking garage – look for the giant backlit lobster sign. Grilled white pomfret is a particular delicacy. **Ling Loong Seafood** and the **Bukit Mata Seafood Centre** are especially good.

Granary   INTERNATIONAL $$
(🖂 WhatsApp 011-2508 9321; www.thegranary.my; 23 Jln Wayang; mains lunch RM14-26, dinner RM24-62; ⊙ 11am-11pm) Housed in an old granary that has been renovated with minimalist flair, this breezy restaurant serves up burgers, pizzas and pasta, plus some pricier meat options. Check the specials board and pencil in happy hour (noon to 8pm) for good deals on cocktails, beer and spirits. Brunch (11am

SINIAWAN NIGHT MARKET

Held along the heritage main street of Siniawan – a former mining town established in 1840 – **Siniawan Night Market** (www.facebook.com/pg/heritage oldtown; Siniawan; ⏱ 6-10pm Fri-Sun) is an excellent evening detour from Kuching. Weekends see the town's atmospheric row of 19th-century wooden shophouses transformed with street-food stalls illuminated by Chinese lanterns. A few locals like to get dressed up as cowboys and sing karaoke.

Visits to the night market are offered by Kuching travel agencies from around RM100 per person. By Grab it's around RM35. It's worth negotiating with your driver to wait for you, as transport back to Kuching can sometimes be difficult to secure.

to 5pm Saturday and Sunday) is fast becoming a Kuching institution.

Check the website for regular quiz nights and occasional Saturday-afternoon arts-and-crafts markets held here.

Junk ITALIAN **$$**
(📞 082-259450; 80 Jln Wayang; mains RM28-70; ⏱ 6-10.45pm, bar to 2am, closed Tue; 🛜) Filled to the brim with antiques, this is the middle of a complex of restaurants and bars – each with different names housed in three 1920s shophouses. The Junk has a busy kitchen and the food here is very good. Pasta mains cost RM30 to RM40, pizzas are RM30 to RM45; other mains include Fisherman's Basket (RM40) and rib-eye steak (RM70). Portions are generous.

Stretching either side, and part of the same business, are the Barber (p409) (with a great bar out the back), **Junk Bar** (karaoke), the **Wayang** (live music 10pm Friday and Saturday), **Cha Bo** (Jln Wayang; mains RM18-28; ⏱ 5pm-midnight Mon-Fri, 5pm-2am Sat & Sun) (Thai) and **Bla Bla Bla** (📞 082-233944; 27 Jln Tabuan; mains RM25-42; ⏱ 6-11.30pm Wed-Mon) (Chinese fusion).

James Brooke Bistro & Cafe INTERNATIONAL **$$**
(📞 082-412120; Waterfront Promenade; mains RM10-39; ⏱ 10.30am-10.30pm, for drinks only to midnight) This place gets consistently good reviews for cuisine, service and lovely river views. Local dishes such as Sarawak laksa

(RM12) and its own invention, uniquely flavoursome wild Borneo laksa (RM12), are great value and tasty. Other signature dishes include butter chicken and, perhaps surprisingly, beef stroganoff. Also available are cooling juices (try the calamansi), beer and cocktails. Opposite Jln Temple.

Tribal Stove MALAYSIAN **$$**
(📞 082-234873; 10 Jln Borneo; mains RM15-20; ⏱ 11.30am-10.30pm Mon-Sat; ❄🛜📖) This laid-back restaurant serving delicious Sarawak food is decorated with photos of Bario, the highland 'capital'. Although it no longer specialises in Kelabit food, you'll find plenty of vegetarian options and several local dishes such as grilled fish with banana beans, Sarawak laksa and pineapple curry.

21 Bistro FUSION **$$**
(64 Jln Padungan; mains RM25-80; ⏱ 4pm-2am or later Mon-Sat, food to 11pm) This lively bar-restaurant has a range of draught and bottled beers plus wine and cocktails. Also available are decent Western, Asian and fusion dishes such as pasta, grilled meats (New Zealand lamb and steaks) and seafood. A live band injects a bit of atmosphere.

Commons CAFE **$$**
(📞 082-417601; www.facebook.com/CommonsKch; Old Courthouse, Jln Tun Abang Haji Openg; mains RM20-34; ⏱ 10am-11pm; ❄🛜) A popular all-day haunt for both locals and visitors, Commons features mains including excellent pasta, burgers and Asian dishes, and a very tempting array of freshly baked cakes. Wine and beer are available, and newspapers, board games and hip retro furniture are all distractions while you partner an iced coffee with salted-caramel cheesecake. Outdoor seating enjoys heritage-courtyard views.

Zinc MEDITERRANEAN **$$$**
(📞 WhatsApp 011-3690 6675; www.facebook.com/ZincKuching; 38 Jln Tabuan; mains RM38-78; ⏱ 6pm-1am Mon-Sat) Zinc features a selection of imported ingredients: Spanish Iberico ham, French cheeses and Canadian lobster, plus imported wines that aren't all that common elsewhere in Borneo. Naturally, the finest imported ingredients aren't cheap, but you don't come to Zinc unless you're prepared to splurge. Live music and DJs may feature later in the week.

Self-Catering

Ting & Ting (30A Jln Tabuan; ⏱ 9am-9pm, closed Sun & holidays) offers a good selection of wine, snack food and chocolate. Handy for New Chinatown is **Everrise Supermarket** (Jln Pandungan; ☉9.30am-9.30pm).

🍷 Drinking & Nightlife

Popular bars can be found in Old Chinatown and along Jln Carpenter, and trendy restaurant-bars on Jln Tabuan and Jln Padungan.

★Ruai Bar
BAR

(282 Jln Padungan; ☉4am-2am Mon-Thu, to 3am Fri & Sat) This self-styled 'Modern Dayak' bar features a mash-up of modern and indigenous design, and there's occasional live music – including metal and local hip hop – at weekends. Beers are cheap and cold, and more adventurous imbibers can sample *tuak* (rice wine) and more potent *langkau* infused with flavours like cinnamon and vanilla. The place really gets jumping around 9pm.

★Drunken Monkey
BAR

(☎082-242048; 68 Jln Carpenter; ☉2pm-2am) This bar attracts a relaxed crowd of tourists and local professionals. Although it's a bar only, you'll find menus from several nearby restaurants scattered about, and a variety of food can be delivered to your table. Drinks include draught Guinness (RM19 per pint), a decent range of imported wines and a whole page of whiskies.

Barber
BAR

(☎082-242961; www.facebook.com/thebarberkch; Jln Wayang; mains RM18-35; ☉5pm-late Wed-Mon) The designers of this repurposed barber's salon made use of the original tiled floor, the mirrors and even old hairdryers to create a suitably hip hang-out for Kuching's in-crowd. Serves a menu of burgers and American-diner-style food and a good selection of desserts (RM16). Beyond the diner, out the back is a stylish and popular bar.

Black Bean Coffee & Tea Company
CAFE

(Jln Carpenter; drinks RM3-6; ☉9am-6pm Mon-Sat; 🛜) The aroma of freshly ground coffee assaults the senses at this tiny shop, believed by many to purvey Kuching's finest brews. Specialities, roasted daily, include Arabica, Liberica and Robusta coffees grown in Java, Sumatra and, of course, Sarawak. Also serves oolong and green teas from Taiwan. Has just three tables. Decaf not available.

Bear Garden
BAR

(☎082-233787; www.facebook.com/BearGardenKch; 66 Jln Wayang; ☉5pm-2am) Formerly known as the Tiger Garden – look for the neon sign – the corner-located Bear Garden is a good spot for the first (well-priced) beer of the evening before kicking on to other nearby spots. Outdoor seating creates a sociable atmosphere, and 50% of the bar's profits assist NGO the Orangutan Project's efforts in animal welfare and conservation.

Sky Lounge
ROOFTOP BAR

(17th fl, Riverside Majestic Hotel, Jln Tunku Abdul Rahman) Every emerging Southeast Asian city needs a decent rooftop bar, and the ritzy Sky Lounge provides superb river views as sleepy afternoons slowly merge through dusk into languid tropical evenings. Secure a table near the huge windows and enjoy happy-hour cocktails and beers (5.30pm to 7.30pm) as *sampan* (small ferries) make their way lazily across the Sungai Sarawak.

Monkee Bar
BAR

(Jln Song Thian Cheok; beer RM7-13, spirit & mixer RM13; ☉3pm-2am; 🛜) At Monkee Bar, 50% of profits go to the Orangutan Project, a wildlife-conservation NGO that works at Matang Wildlife Centre (p423). If the idea of 'drinking for conservation' doesn't entice you, the prices might: Monkee Bar has some of the cheapest drinks in town. It's a smoky joint with a young, local crowd interspersed with volunteers enjoying downtime from cage cleaning.

🛍 Shopping

Kuching has the best shopping on the island for collectors and cultural enthusiasts. Don't expect many bargains, but don't be afraid to negotiate either. Quality varies as much as price, and dubiously 'aged' items are common, so be sure to spend some time browsing to familiarise yourself with what's on offer.

Most of Kuching's shops are closed on Sunday.

★Museum Cafe & Shop
ARTS & CRAFTS

(☎082-232492; www.facebook.com/sarawak museumshopandcafe; 96 Main Bazaar; ☉7am-6pm Sun-Thu, 9am-5pm Fri & Sat) Local textiles, organic soaps and an excellent selection of books on Sarawak's history and culture are all good reasons to visit this combination of gallery, gift shop and cafe. Come for the all-day breakfast and good coffee and stay to admire (and maybe purchase) the striking artworks by Kuching-born Ramsay Ong Liang Thong.

Juliana Native Handwork
ARTS & CRAFTS

(☎082-230144, 016-809 5415; ground fl, Sarawak Textile Museum, Jln Tun Abang Haji Openg; ☉9am-

4.30pm) As well as her own Bidayuh bead-work pieces – most of which have been displayed in an exhibition in Singapore – Juliana sells quality rattan mats made by Penan artists (RM780) and *pua kumba* Iban woven cloths. Her intricate, 50cm-long beaded table runners (RM680) take her three months to complete.

Tanoti ARTS & CRAFTS
(☑ 082-239277; www.tanoticrafts.com; Tanoti House, 56 Jln Tabuan; ☉ 8am-5.30pm, closed public holidays) The group of women at Tanoti are the only people to practise a distinct Sarawakian form of *songket* weaving, a way of creating embroidered fabrics. Visitors are welcome to visit the workshop and see the weaving, but call first to make arrangements. There's a small number of pieces for sale in the gallery shop.

UD Siburan Jaya FOOD
(66 Main Bazaar; ☉ 8.30am-9pm Mon-Sat, 9.30am-5pm Sun) Down the back of this souvenir shop you can find an excellent selection of Sarawakian specialities such as pepper (black and white), laksa paste, sambal, Bario rice and even *tuak* (rice wine).

Main Bazaar ARTS & CRAFTS
(☉ some shops closed Sun) The row of old shop-houses facing the Waterfront Promenade is chock-full of handicrafts shops, some outfitted like art galleries, others with more of a 'garage sale' appeal, and yet others (especially along the Main Bazaar's western section) stocking little more than kitschy-cute cat souvenirs.

Handmade items worth seeing (if not purchasing) – many from the highlands of Kalimantan – include hand-woven textiles and baskets, masks, drums, brass gongs, statues (up to 2m high), beaded headdresses, swords, spears, painted shields and cannons from Brunei. At many places, staff enjoy explaining the origin and use of each item.

Mohamed Yahia & Sons BOOKS
(☑ 082-416928; basement, Sarawak Plaza, Jln Tunku Abdul Rahman; ☉ 10am-9pm) Specialises in English-language books on Borneo, the history of Sarawak and natural history. Also carries Sarawak maps and a few travel guides. Doubles as a **money changer** (basement, Sarawak Plaza, Jln Tunku Abdul Rahman; ☉ 10am-9pm).

Fabriko CLOTHING
(☑ 082-422233; www.fabriko.com.my; 56 Main Bazaar; ☉ 9am-5pm Mon-Sat) This fine little boutique has a well-chosen selection of made-in-Sarawak fabrics and clothing in

both traditional and modern Orang Ulu–inspired designs, including silk sarongs and men's batik shirts.

Nelson's Gallery ART
(54 Main Bazaar; ☉ 9am-5pm) Upstairs, artist Narong Daun patiently creates vibrant jungle-themed batik paintings on silk.

Popular Book Co BOOKS
(Level 3, Tun Jugah Shopping Centre, 18 Jln Tunku Abdul Rahman; ☉ 10am-9.30pm) A capacious modern bookshop with a big selection of English titles, including works by local authors.

❶ Information

EMBASSIES & CONSULATES
Australian Honorary Consulate (☑ 082-230777; https://dfat.gov.au; Level 2, Taman Sri Sarawak Mall, Jln Tunku Abdul Rahman; ☉ 10am-5pm Mon-Fri)
British Honorary Consulate (☑ 082-250950; www.british-consulate.net; The English Language Centre, Fortune Land Business Centre, Jln Rock; ☉ 9am-5pm Mon-Fri)
Bruneian Consulate (☑ 082-417616; Riverbank Suites & Commercial Towers, Jln Tunku Abdul Rahman; ☉ 8.30am-12.30pm & 1.30-4.30pm Mon-Fri)
Indonesian Consulate (☑ 082-460734; 21 Jln Stutong; ☉ 9am-5pm Mon-Fri)

EMERGENCIES
Police, Ambulance & Fire (☑ 999)

LAUNDRY
Most hotels have pricey laundry services with per-piece rates, but some guesthouses let you do your washing for just RM5 to RM10 per load, including drying.
Mr Clean (☑ 082-246424; www.facebook.com/mr.cleankuching; 9 Jln Green Hill; per kilogram RM6; ☉ 8am-6pm)
My Express Laundry Service (Jln Wayang; 10kg cold/warm/hot RM5/6/7, dryer per 25min RM5; ☉ 24hr)

MEDICAL SERVICES
Kuching has decent and affordable medical facilities, so it's no surprise that 'medical tourism', especially from Indonesia, is on the rise. For minor ailments, guesthouses and hotels can refer you to a general practitioner, who may be willing to make a house call.
Klinik Chan (☑ 082-240307; 98 Main Bazaar; ☉ 8am-noon & 2-5pm Mon-Fri, 9am-noon Sat, Sun & holidays)
Normah Medical Specialist Centre (☑ 082-440055, emergency 082-311999; www.normah.com.my; 937 Jln Tun Abdul Rahman, Petra Jaya;

⊘emergency 24hr, clinics 8.30am-4.30pm
Mon-Fri, to 1pm Sat; 🖵1)

Sarawak General Hospital (Hospital Umum
Sarawak; 🖉082-276666; http://hus.moh.gov.
my; Jln Hospital; ⊘24hr)

Timberland Medical Centre (🖉082-234466,
emergency 082-234991; www.timberland
medical.com; Jln Rock, mile 2½; ⊘emergency
24hr)

MONEY

The majority of Kuching's banks and ATMs are on
Jln Tunku Abdul Rahman. If you need to change
cash or traveller's cheques, money changers are
a better bet than banks, which often aren't keen
on handling cash or US$100 bills.

POLICE

Central Police Station (Balai Polis Sentral;
🖉082-244444; 2 Jln Khoo Hun Yeang; ⊘24hr)

Tourist Police (🖉082-250522; Waterfront
Promenade; ⊘8am-midnight)

POST

Main Post Office (Jln Tun Abang Haji Openg;
⊘8am-4.30pm Mon-Fri, to noon Sat) An
impressive colonnaded structure built in 1931
still serves as the main post office.

SAFE TRAVEL

There are occasional incidents of bag snatch-
ing by motorbike-mounted thieves. Exercise
reasonable caution when walking along deserted
stretches of road (eg Jln Reservoir and Jln
Tabuan), especially after dark.

TOURIST INFORMATION

Visitors Information Centre (🖉082-410942,
082-410944; www.sarawaktourism.com; Old
Courthouse, Jln Tun Abang Haji Openg; ⊘9am-
6pm Mon-Fri, to 3pm Sat & Sun) Conveniently
located in Kuching's Old Courthouse complex,
with helpful staff offering good city maps, bus
schedules and national-park information.

National Park Office (🖉082-248088; https://
ebooking.sarawak.gov.my; Jln Setia Raja, Sama
Jaya Nature Reserve; ⊘8am-5pm Mon-Fri)
Located 9km southeast of Kuching Waterfront
at the time of writing, but a move to the Old
Courthouse was being considered. Check at
Kuching's visitor centre for the latest. To reach
this Sama Jaya location, catch bus K1 (RM1.50)
from near the open-air market. By Grab it's
around RM15. National-park accommodation
bookings can also be made online.

VISAS

Visa Department (Bahagian Visa; 🖉082-
245661; www.imi.gov.my; 2nd fl, Bangunan
Sultan Iskandar, Kompleks Pejabat Persekutuan, cnr Jln Tun Razak & Jln Simpang Tiga;
⊘8am-5pm Mon-Thu, 8-11.45am & 2.15-5pm
Fri) Situated in a 17-storey federal office build-

ing about 3km south of the centre (along Jln
Tabuan). Served by City Public Link buses K8
or K11, which run every half-hour or so. A taxi
from the centre costs around RM15.

❶ Getting There & Away

AIR

Kuching International Airport (www.kuching
airportonline.com), 11km south of the city centre, has direct air links with Singapore, Johor
Bahru (the Malaysian city across the causeway
from Singapore), Kuala Lumpur (KL), Penang,
Kota Kinabalu (KK), Bandar Seri Begawan
(BSB) and Pontianak. There are also direct
flights to Shenzhen in southern China.

MASwings, a subsidiary of Malaysia Airlines, is
basically Malaysian Borneo's very own domestic
airline. Flights link its hubs in Miri and Kuching
with 14 destinations around Sarawak, including
the lowland cities of Sibu, Bintulu, Limbang and
Lawas and the upland destinations of Gunung
Mulu National Park, Bario and Ba Kelalan.

The airport has three departure halls: 'Domestic Departures' for flights within Sarawak;
'Domestic Departures (Outside Sarawak)' for
travel to other parts of Malaysia; and 'International Departures'.

Inside the terminal, there's a **Tourist Information Centre** (Arrivals level, Kuching International Airport; ⊘8am-5pm Mon-Fri) next to
the luggage carousels and customs. Foreign
currency can be exchanged at the **CIMB Bank
counter** (Arrivals level, Kuching International
Airport; ⊘7.30am-7.30pm), but rates are poor.
Among the ATMs is one in front of McDonald's.
For ticketing issues, drop by the **Malaysian
Airlines & MASwings office** (www.malaysia
airlines.com; departure level, Kuching International Airport; ⊘5am-8pm).

BOAT

Ekspress Bahagia (🖉016-800 5891, 016-889
3013, Kuching 082-412246, Sibu 084-319228;
Jln Pelabuhan, Pending Industrial Estate; 1 way
RM55; ⊘departs Kuching 8.30am & departs
Sibu 11.30am) runs a daily express ferry from
Kuching's Express Wharf, 6km east of the centre, to Sibu (RM55, five hours). It's a good idea
to book a day ahead. A taxi from town to the
wharf costs RM30. By Grab it's around RM15.

BUS

Every half-hour or so from about 6am to
6.30pm, various buses run by **City Public Link**
(🖉082-239178) (eg K9) and STC (eg 3A, 4B,
6 and 2) link central Kuching's **Saujana Bus
Station** (Jln Masjid & Jln P Ramlee) with Kuching
Sentral, the Regional Express Bus Terminal
(RM2). Saujana's ticket windows can point you
to the next departure. A taxi to Kuching Sentral

from the centre costs RM35 (25 minutes). By Grab the fare is around RM15.

Kuching Sentral

This massive **bus terminal and shopping mall** (cnr Jln Penrissen & Jln Airport) handles most of Kuching's medium-haul routes and all of its long-haul ones. Situated about 10km south of the centre, it's also known as Six-and-a-Half-Mile Bus Station. Amenities include electronic departure boards and cafes offering wi-fi. Book your ticket at a company counter, then pay at counter 2 or 3 (marked 'Cashier/Boarding Pass'). Before boarding, show your ticket to the staff at the check-in desk.

To Central Sarawak

From 6.30am to 10.30pm, a dozen companies send buses at least hourly along Sarawak's northern coast to Miri (RM100, 14½ hours), with stops at Sibu (RM50 to RM60, 7½ hours), Bintulu (RM80, 11½ hours), Batu Niah Junction (jumping-off point for Niah National Park) and Lambir Hills National Park. **Bus Asia** (☑ 082-411111; www.busasia.my; cnr Jln Abell & Jln Chan Chin Ann; ☺7am-10pm), for instance, has seven departures a day, the first at 8am, the last at 10pm. Unlike its competitors, the

company has a city-centre office and, from Monday to Saturday, runs shuttle buses out to Kuching Sentral. Luxurious 'VIP buses', eg those run by **Asia Star** (☑ 082-610111; Kuching Central Bus Station), have just three seats across (28 in total), and some come with on-board toilets, and yet they cost a mere RM10 to RM20 more than regular coaches. To get to Brunei, Limbang or Sabah, you have to change buses in Miri.

To Western Sarawak

Buses are also available to the Semenggoh Wildlife Centre, Bako National Park, Kubah National Park and the Matang Wildlife Sanctuary, all of which stop in town at or near Saujana Bus Station, and to Lundu (including the Wind Cave and Fairy Cave), whose buses use Kuching Sentral. The visitor centre (p411) in the Old Courthouse is an excellent source of up-to-date bus details for these destinations.

TAXI

For some destinations, the only transport option – other than taking a tour – is chartering a taxi through your hotel or guesthouse or via a company such as Kuching City Radio Taxi. Hiring a red-and-yellow cab for an eight-hour day should cost about RM300 to RM350, with the price depending in part on distance; unofficial taxis may charge less. If you'd like your driver to wait at your destination and then take you back to town, count on paying about RM35 per hour of waiting time.

Sample taxi fares from Kuching (prices are 50% higher at night):

DESTINATION	PRICE (RM)
Annah Rais Longhouse	90 one way
Bako Bazaar (Bako National Park)	65 one way
Express Wharf (ferry to Sibu)	30 one way
Fairy Cave (with Wind Cave)	200 return incl wait
Kubah National Park	65 one way
Matang Wildlife Centre	70 one way
Santubong Peninsula Resorts	90 one way
Sarawak Cultural Village	90 one way
Semenggoh Wildlife Centre	160 return incl 1hr wait

ⓘ Getting Around

Almost all of Kuching's attractions are within easy walking distance of each other, so taxis or buses are only really needed to reach the airport, Kuching Sentral (the long-haul bus terminal), the Express Wharf for the ferry to Sibu and the Cat Museum.

TO/FROM THE AIRPORT

The red-and-yellow taxi fare from the airport into Kuching is fixed at RM26 (RM39 for late-night arrivals), including luggage; a larger *teksi eksekutiv* (executive taxi), painted blue, costs RM43 (RM64 late night). Coupons are sold inside the terminal next to the car-rental counters.

By Grab it's around RM15. Specify the Arrivals area when you book a Grab driver so that it's easy for them to find you at the busy airport.

BICYCLE

On Jln Carpenter, basic bicycle shops can be found at Nos 83, 88 and 96. Borneo Experiences (p403) can rent out bicycles for RM50 per day including helmet and lock.

BOAT

Bow-steered wooden boats known as *tambang*, powered by an outboard motor, shuttle passengers back and forth across Sungai Sarawak, linking jetties along the Waterfront Promenade with destinations such as Kampung Boyan (for Fort Margherita) and the Astana. The fare for Sarawak's cheapest cruise is RM1 (more from 10pm to 6am); pay as you disembark. If a *tambang* isn't tied up when you arrive at a dock, just wait and one will usually materialise fairly soon.

BUS

Handling local and short-haul routes, Saujana Bus Station is situated in the city centre on the dead-end street that links Jln Market with the Kuching Mosque. Three companies use the bus station, including City Public Link and the **Sarawak Transport Company** (STC; ☑ 082-233579; Jln P Ramlee).

CAR & MOTORCYCLE

Not many tourists rent cars in Sarawak: road signage isn't great, road maps are poor, and picking up a vehicle in one city and dropping it off in another incurs hefty fees. That said, having your own car can be unbelievably convenient.

Before driving off, make sure the car you've been assigned is in good shape mechanically and has all the requisite safety equipment (eg seat belts). Some companies rent out vehicles that have seen better days.

Half-a-dozen car-rental agencies have desks in the arrivals hall of Kuching Airport:

AMI Car Rental (☑ 082-427221, 082-579679; www.amicarrental.com; Arrivals level, Kuching International Airport)

Golden System (☑ 016-888 3359; www.gocar.com.my; Counter 5, ground fl, Arrivals level, Kuching International Airport)

Hertz (☑ 082-450740; www.hertz.com; ground fl, Kuching International Airport)

Hornbill Tours & Car Rental (☑ 082-457948; hornbill.car.rental@gmail.com; counter 4, Kuching International Airport)

Renting a motorcycle can be a great way to visit Kuching-area sights – provided you know how to ride, your rain gear is up to scratch and you manage to find your way despite the poor signage.

An Hui Motor (☑ 082-240508, 016-886 3328; 29 Jln Tabuan; ⊗ 8am-6pm Mon-Sat, to 10.30am Sun)

TAXI

Kuching has two kinds of taxi: the traditional red-and-yellow kind, and larger, more comfortable – usually pricier – executive taxis (*teksi eksekutiv*), which are painted blue.

The ride-sharing app Grab is also very popular, and fares are usually just over half of traditional taxi fares.

Taxis can be hailed on the street, found at taxi ranks (of which the city centre has quite a few, eg at larger hotels) or ordered by phone 24 hours a day from the following:

ABC Radio Call Service (☑ 016-861 1611, 082-611611)

Kuching City Radio Taxi (☑ 082-480000, 082-348898)

Kuching taxis are required to use meters; however, most won't. Overcharging is not common because there is an active agreement on what to charge for all the popular destinations (including waiting times). Be aware that fares go up by 50% from midnight to 6am.

One-way taxi fares from central Kuching:
* Cat Museum (North Kuching): RM35
* Indonesian consulate: RM30
* Kuching Sentral (long-distance bus terminal): RM35
* Visa Department: RM15

WESTERN SARAWAK

Western Sarawak offers a dazzling array of natural sights and indigenous cultures, including a number of accessible longhouses, sandy beaches and rainforests, as well as the chance to see rainforest inhabitants – including proboscis monkeys and orangutans – up close.

While much of the region can be conveniently visited as a day trip from Kuching, the only way to get to many nature sites is to rent a car, hire a taxi or join a tour. The following exceptions have public bus access: Bako National Park, Semenggoh Wildlife Centre, Kubah National Park, Matang Wildlife Centre and, somewhat less conveniently, the Wind Cave and the Fairy Cave.

Around Kuching

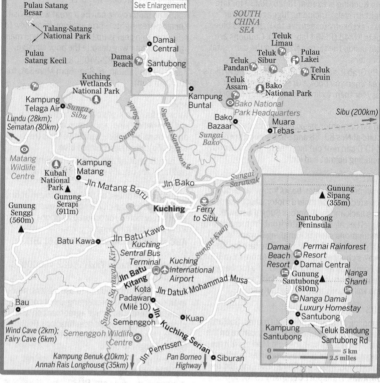

Bako National Park

Occupying a jagged peninsula jutting into the South China Sea, Sarawak's oldest national park (🗗 Bako terminal 082-370434; www.sarawakforestry.com; adult/child RM20/7; ⊙ park office 8am-5pm) is just 37km northeast of downtown Kuching but feels worlds away. Bako is notable for its incredible biodiversity, which encompasses everything from orchids and pitcher plants to proboscis monkeys and bearded pigs. The park is one of the best places in Borneo to observe these endemics up close.

The coastline of the 27-sq-km peninsula consists of secluded beaches and bays interspersed with wind-sculpted cliffs, forests and stretches of tangled mangroves. The interior of the park features distinct ecosystems, including classic lowland rainforest (mixed dipterocarp forest) and *kerangas* (heath forest), streams and waterfalls. Hiking trails traverse the central sandstone plateau and connect with several of the beaches.

Bako is an easy day trip from Kuching, but it's best to stay a night or two to fully experience the wild beauty and have the best chance of seeing wildlife.

💿 Sights & Activities

Interpretation Centre   MUSEUM
(Bako National Park HQ; ⊙ 7.30am-5pm) **FREE**
Offers an old-fashioned introduction to the park's seven distinct ecosystems and an exposition on the codependent relationship between nepenthes (pitcher plants) and ants.

Wildlife Watching

Scientists estimate that Bako is home to 37 species of mammal, including silver-leaf monkeys, palm squirrels and nocturnal creatures such as the mouse deer, civet and colugo (flying lemur); 24 reptile species, among them the common water monitor, which can reach a length of over 1m; and about 190 kinds of bird, some of them migratory.

Jungle creatures are easiest to spot shortly after sunrise and right before sunset, so for the best wildlife watching you'll have to stay over. Surprisingly, the area around park HQ is a particularly good place to see animals, including reddish-brown proboscis monkeys, whose pot-bellied stomachs are filled with bacteria that help them derive nutrients from almost-indigestible vegetation. You often hear them as they crash through the branches long before you see a flash of fur – or a male's pendulous nose flopping as he munches on tender young leaves.

The monkeys, who show little fear of, or interest in, humans, can often be found on branches above the park's visitor cabins, around the mangrove boardwalk between the jetty and park HQ, in the trees along Teluk Assam Beach near park HQ, along the Teluk Paku Trail, where they forage in the trees lining the cliff, and along the Teluk Delima Trail.

The muddy floors of mangrove forests are home to an assortment of creatures, including hermit crabs, fiddler crabs and mudskippers (fish that spend much of their time skipping around atop the tidal mud under mangrove trees).

Bornean bearded pigs, striking-looking creatures that hang around near the cafeteria and cabins with their piglets, are easy to spot.

Jungle Walks

Bako's 17 trails are suitable for all levels of fitness and motivation, with routes ranging from short strolls to strenuous all-day treks to the far end of the peninsula. It's easy to find your way around because trails are colour-coded and clearly marked with stripes of paint. Plan your route before starting out and aim to be back at park HQ before dark (by 6pm at the latest). It's possible to hire a boat to one of the far beaches and then hike back, or to hike to one of the beaches and arrange for a boat to meet you there.

Park staff are happy to help you plan your visit, provide updates on trail conditions and tides, help with boat hire and provision you with a B&W map that has details on each of the park's hiking options. A billboard near the Interpretation Centre lists conservative time estimates for each trail. Even if you know your route, advise staff of where you'll be going and make a note in the Guest Movement Register Book; sign back in when you return.

Take adequate water, a sunhat and sunscreen, as the *kerangas* (a distinctive vegetation zone of Borneo) has precious little shade for long stretches. Sun-sensitive folks should consider lightweight long-sleeved shirts and trousers. Insect repellent is also a good idea.

Lintang Trail   HIKING
If you have only one day in Bako, try to get an early start and take the Lintang Trail (5.8km, 3½ to four hours return). It traverses a range of vegetation and climbs the sandstone escarpment up to the *kerangas,* where you'll find some grand views and many pitcher plants (especially along the trail's northeastern segment).

Teluk Pandan Kecil Trail   HIKING
One of the park's most popular trails is the 2.6km path to **Teluk Pandan Kecil**, a gorgeous sandy beach surrounded by spectacular sandstone formations. The trail climbs through the forest before emerging onto an open plateau covered in scrub. Pitcher plants can be seen on the trail down to the beach.

On the way to Teluk Pandan Kecil it's possible to make a 30-minute detour to a viewpoint overlooking **Teluk Pandan Besar**, an attractive stretch of sand accessible only by boat.

Around the point from (northwest of) Teluk Pandan Kecil is the famous **Bako Sea Stack**, an islet that looks like a cobra rearing its head. To get close enough for a photo, though, you'll have to hire a boat (from park HQ; RM35/70 one way/return for up to five people).

Teluk Tajor Trail   HIKING
A 3.5km trail leads across scrub, past Tajor Waterfall (where you can have a dip) and on to Tajor Beach, where it's possible to camp.

Boat Trips   BOATING
(Bako Tourist Boat Association; per boat for up to 5 people 1 way/return to Teluk Paku RM18/36, to Teluk Pandan Kecil RM35/70, to Teluk Tajor RM105/210) Catching a boat ride to or from one of the park's beaches is a good way to avoid retracing your steps on a hike. Arrangements can be made at the Koperasi Warisan Pelancongan Bako Berhad (p417) counter at park HQ, although skippers sometimes pass by the more popular beaches looking for tired hikers who might be tempted by a lift back.

Going out on the water is also the best way to view the unique sandstone sea stacks

SARAWAK BAKO NATIONAL PARK

off Bako's coast, and the only way to get close enough to photograph them. Look out for sea snakes, sometimes visible in the water.

Night Walk
WILDLIFE WATCHING

(per person RM10; ⊘8pm) The best way to see creatures that are out and about at night – spiders, fireflies, cicadas, frogs, anemones, owls and the like – is to take a night walk led by a park ranger trained in spotting creatures that city slickers would walk right by. These 1½- to two-hour night walks are not to be missed. Bring a torch.

Swimming

At Bako it used to be popular to combine rainforest tramping, which quickly gets hot and sweaty, with a refreshing dip in the South China Sea. However, ever since a large saltwater crocodile was spotted on the sand of a popular beach, swimming has not been allowed, and signs in the park specifically warn against the activity. To keep away the sandflies on the beach, use mozzie repellent.

Tours

Park HQ does not have enough permanent staff to accompany individual visitors, so if you'd like to hike with a **licensed guide** (☑Sabariman 019-469 2570; riman1978@gmail. com; Bako Bazaar; per group per hour/day RM35/120), enquire at the boat terminal at Bako Bazaar. The park is very strict about allowing only certified guides: unlicensed guides and the groups they're with are forced to leave.

🛏 Sleeping & Eating

Bako's accommodation is basic and in need of minor renovations but well run and adequately equipped.

Accommodation often fills up, especially from May to September, so book ahead. Some travel agencies reserve rooms that they release a week ahead if their packages remain unsold, and individual travellers also sometimes cancel, so week-before and last-minute vacancies are common. There's a RM10 key deposit; unlocked storage (free) is available at reception.

Cooking is not allowed in park accommodation. Meals and snacks are served at the **Kerangas Cafe** (Canteen; meals RM8-12; ⊘7.30am-10.30pm). The nearest grocery shop is in **Bako Bazaar**.

Forest Lodge Type 5
CABIN $

(☑Bako Terminal 082-370434, Kuching 082-248088; http://ebooking.sarawak.gov.my; r RM100) 'Type 5' accommodation is in either two-room wooden lodges (three single beds in each) with a shared bathroom, or a newer concrete terraced block (four single beds in each) with attached bathrooms. All are fan cooled only.

Forest Hostel
HOSTEL $

(☑Bako terminal 082-370434, Kuching 082-248088; http://ebooking.sarawak.gov.my; dm RM15, q RM40) Built of wood, the old hostel buildings are scuffed and dented but perfectly serviceable. Rooms have four single-storey beds lined up in a row, fridges and wall-mounted fans. Bring your own towel.

Forest Lodge Type 6
CABIN $

(☑Bako Terminal 082-370434, Kuching 082-248088; http://ebooking.sarawak.gov.my; d RM50, 2-room cabins RM75) Each rustic, two-bed room has a wood-plank floor, a private bathroom, a fridge and a fan.

ℹ CHEEKY MACAQUES

That sign at Bako National Park's campground – 'Naughty monkeys around – watch out!' – is not a joke. The long-tailed macaques that hang about the park HQ are great to watch, but they're mischievous and cunning. Thanks to tourists who insist on offering them food (please don't!), they can become aggressive if they suspect you to be carrying something edible, and will make running leaps at anything they think they can carry off. Keep the doors and windows of your room closed, zip your bags, and don't leave valuables, food or drink – or anything in a plastic bag (known by macaques to be the preferred human repository for edibles) – unattended, especially on beaches or cabin verandahs.

It's wise to leave the monkeys in peace – the males can be aggressive, and once you've seen a macaque tear open a drink can with his teeth you'll be happy that you didn't mess with them. Rangers advise against looking a macaque in the eye (he'll think you're about to attack) or screaming (if he knows you're scared, he'll be more aggressive). Monkeys are not a problem after dark.

Camping
CAMPGROUND $

(✓ Bako Terminal 082-370434, Kuching 082-248088; http://ebooking.sarawak.gov.my; per person RM5) To avoid falling prey to raiding monkeys, tents can be set up at park HQ's fenced-in camping zone only after 6pm and must be taken down again early in the morning. You can also pitch your tent at Tajor (p415), 3.5km from park HQ.

Forest Lodge Type 4
BUNGALOW $$

(✓ Bako Terminal 082-370434, Kuching 082-248088; http://ebooking.sarawak.gov.my; d RM150, cabin RM225; ❄) There are just two cabins each with two rooms each containing three single beds. Rooms have attached bathrooms and are air conditioned.

❶ Getting There & Away

Getting to the park by public transport is a cinch. First, take one of the hourly buses from Kuching to Bako Bazaar, then hop on a motorboat to Teluk Assam jetty, about 400m along a wooden boardwalk from park HQ.

Kuching travel agencies charge from RM360 per person for a tour, including the boat ride.

BOAT
Boat transfers to Bako park HQ from Bako Terminal (at Bako Bazaar) are managed by **Koperasi Warisan Pelancongan Bako Berhad** (Bako Boat Transfers; ✓ 011-2509 5070, 011-2513 2711; ⊙ 7.30am-4pm), which has a counter at the terminal and at park HQ. The 20-minute journey from the terminal to the park costs RM30 per person (private hire is RM150 – in case you don't want to wait around for a boat to collect enough passengers). From May to September transfers are usually every hour from 8am to 4pm (ask at the counter for the day's schedule). The last boat back from Bako is at 4pm.

When the tide is low, boats may not be able to approach the jetty at Teluk Assam, so you may have to wade ashore. Skippers may insist on an early-afternoon return time to beat a late-afternoon low tide – but bold outboard jockeys have been known to make the trip back to Bako Bazaar even at the lowest of tides.

From late November to February or March, the sea is often rough and scheduled boat trips may be less frequent.

BUS
Bus 1 (1 way RM4) leaves from 6 Jln Khoo Hun Yeang in Kuching, across the street from the food stalls of the open-air market. Departures from Kuching are every hour from 7am to 5pm, and from Bako Bazaar every hour from 6.30am to (usually) 5.30pm. If you miss the last bus, ask

around the village for a minibus or private car (RM65) to Kuching.

In Kuching, bus 1 also picks up passengers at stops along the waterfront, on the river side of the street; motion to the driver to stop. These stops include bus shelters on Jln Gambier across the street from the Brooke Memorial; across the street from 15 Main Bazaar, next to the Chinese Museum; on Jln Tunku Abdul Rahman next to the 7-Eleven in the Riverside Suites; and on Jln Abell in front of Alliance Bank, a block northwest of the Lime Tree Hotel.

TAXI
A cab from Kuching to Bako Bazaar (45 minutes) costs RM65. By Grab it's around RM40, but you may struggle to find return transport.

Santubong Peninsula
✓ 082

Like Bako National Park 8km to the east, the Santubong Peninsula (also known as Damai) is a 10km-long finger of land jutting into the South China Sea. It was declared a national park in 2007. With some decent sandy strips and a couple of resorts, Santubong is the best place in Sarawak for a lazy, pampered beach holiday. It's a popular getaway for Kuching residents, and being only about 20km from the city it makes for a good day trip or overnight excursion.

The main drawcards here are the beaches, a golf course, rainforest hikes, and the Sarawak Cultural Village, which showcases traditional lifestyles and plays host to the annual Rainforest World Music Festival (p404). The peninsula is also known for a collection of rock carvings within its forested interior that are estimated to be up to 1000 years old.

⊙ Sights & Activities

Sarawak Cultural Village
MUSEUM

(SCV; ✓ 082-846411; www.scv.com.my; Damai Central; adult/child RM60/30; ⊙ 9am-4.45pm) This living museum centres on seven traditional dwellings, including three tribal longhouses, a Penan hut, a Malay town house, a Melanau tall house and a Chinese farmhouse. It may sound contrived, but the SCV is highly esteemed by locals for its role in keeping their cultures and traditions alive.

At 11.30am and 4pm daily, a cultural show presents traditional music and dance. The lively Melanau entry involves whirling women and clacking bamboo poles, while the Orang Ulu dance features a blowpipe hunter.

The dwellings are (supposed to be) staffed by members of the ethnic group they represent. Signage, however, is poor, so if you don't ask questions of the 'locals' – who demonstrate crafts – the subtle differences in architecture, cuisine, dress and music between the various groups may not be apparent. At the Penan hut you can try a blowpipe, while the Malay house offers top spinning.

It may be possible to book **workshops** in handicrafts (eg bead making), music and dance – contact the SCV in advance. If you're planning to get married, you can choose to tie the knot here with a colourful Iban, Bidayuh, Orang Ulu or Malay ceremony.

Hotels and tour agencies in Kuching offer packages (RM250 per person, minimum two), but it's easy enough to get here by shuttle bus or private taxi. The SCV is located at Damai junction.

Permai Rainforest Resort BEACH
(☑ 082-846490; www.permairainforest.com; Damai Beach; adult/child RM8/5; ⊙ 7am-7pm) The day rate at this bungalow complex is a real bargain. In addition to a safe, fine-sand beach with changing facilities, the resort offers a variety of leisure and adventure activities, including a high-ropes course (per person RM65), a perfectly vertical climbing wall (RM50), sea kayaking (three hours RM85) and a bird-watching tower (RM30).

Damai Central Beach BEACH
`FREE` A beach with showers, lockers and places to eat. Situated across the parking lot from Sarawak Cultural Village.

Jungle Walks HIKING
Several trails lead into the jungle interior of the peninsula. One, a challenging route with red trail markings, ascends towering **Gunung Santubong** (810m); the last bit is pretty steep, with steps and rope ladders, so it takes about three hours up and two hours down. The trail can be picked up at Bukit Puteri on the road to Damai Central.

Another trail, an easy-to-moderate circular walk (3km, two hours) with blue markings, passes by a pretty waterfall.

Damai Beach Golf Course GOLF
(☑ 082-846088; www.damaigolf.com; Jln Santubong; weekday/weekend from RM60/148) An 18-hole course designed by the legendary Arnold Palmer.

☞ Tours

Coastal areas west and east of the Santubong Peninsula are home to a variety of wildlife. Oft-spotted species include endangered Irrawaddy dolphins, dragonflies, proboscis monkeys, estuarine crocodiles and all manner of birds.

Resorts on the peninsula, and guesthouses and tour agencies in Kuching, can make arrangements.

🛏 Sleeping

BB Bunkers HOSTEL $
(☑ 082-846835; www.facebook.com/BBBunkers; Damai Central; dm RM50-80; ❄ 🛜) Situated a few metres from Damai Central Beach in the Damai Central Mall, this hostel has the peninsula's only dorm beds. The industrial-type space is subdivided by curtains, creating not-so-private spaces for one to three beds, either twins or queens. Secure storage is available. Rates are higher at weekends.

★ Village House GUESTHOUSE $$
(☑ 082-846166, WhatsApp 016-860 9389; www.villagehouse.com.my; Lot 634, Kampung Santubong; incl breakfast dm RM123, d RM334-627; ❄ 🛜) Tucked away in the quiet Malay village of Santubong, this place exudes serenity. Rooms with *belian* (ironwood) floors and four-poster beds are arranged around a gorgeous pool framed by frangipani trees. A well-stocked bar and a menu of local dishes (mains RM18 to RM60) mean there's really no reason to leave. Try the superb eight-course tasting menu (RM198 per person).

Located off Jln Pantai Puteri. A scheduled shuttle service to/from Kuching is available.

Nanga Shanti HOMESTAY $$
(☑ WhatsApp 011-2517 7108; www.nangashanti.weebly.com; d/bungalows incl breakfast RM150/250; ⊙ Apr-Sep; ❄) ✦ This unique beachside dwelling, located on the wild and undeveloped eastern side of the Santubong Peninsula, is reachable only via a 30-minute boat ride from Kampung Buntal (RM50 return) or a two-hour hike. Accommodation is in a four-room wooden longhouse or three stand-alone A-frame bungalows. Solar panels provide 24-hour electricity and water comes (filtered) from a mountain stream.

The homestay is run by a French couple who built it themselves using recycled materials where possible; the time and care that went into the construction are evident in the design details, such as the dining room's

OFF THE BEATEN TRACK

KUCHING WETLANDS NATIONAL PARK

The only way to see the majestic mangroves of 66-sq-km **Kuching Wetlands National Park** (https://sarawaktourism.com/attraction/kuching-wetland-national-park) is by boat. About 15km northwest of Kuching, the park has no office, just low-lying islands and saline waterways lined with salt-resistant trees that provide food and shelter for proboscis monkeys, silver-leaf monkeys, fireflies, estuarine crocodiles, amphibious fish called mudskippers, and countless varieties of fish and prawns. Nearby open water is one of the finest places in Sarawak to spot snub-nosed Irrawaddy dolphins.

The morning (about 9am) is the best time to see the dolphins, while late-afternoon cruises are optimal for sighting a flash of reddish-brown fur as proboscis monkeys leap from tree to tree in search of the tenderest, tastiest young leaves. Sunset on the water is magical – and unbelievably romantic, especially if your guide points out an api-api tree (a 'firefly tree', surrounded by swirling green points of light). After dark, by holding a torch up at eye level, you can often spot the reflections of animalian eyes, including – if you're lucky – a crocodile.

Kuching-based CPH Travel (p428) offer tours here. Packages include hotel transfers.

atap (thatched) roof and the glass bottles used in some of the walls. Activities include walking or kayaking to a nearby beach. Lunch and dinner cost RM14 to RM45. Two-night minimum stay; no children under 12.

Permai Rainforest Resort BUNGALOW $$
(☎ 082-846490, 082-846487; www.permairainforest.com; Damai Beach; incl breakfast 6-bed cabins with fan/air-con RM480/510, tree houses RM385, camping per person not incl breakfast RM10; @ 🛜) This lushly forested bungalow complex, on a beach-adjacent hillside, hosts macaques and silver-leaf monkeys in addition to paying guests. Accommodation ranges from rustic, simply furnished cabins to air-con wooden bungalows towering 6m off the ground. Offers plenty of outdoor activities. Prices drop from Sunday to Thursday.

Nanga Damai Luxury Homestay HOMESTAY $$
(☎ WhatsApp 019-887 1017; www.nangadamai.com; Jln Sultan Tengah, Kampung Santubong; incl breakfast dm/tw RM80/160, d RM220-250; ❄ @ 🛜) A beautiful garden with glimpses of jungle wildlife, friendly family dogs, hospitable owners, an 8m kidney-shaped pool and bright, comfortable rooms all make it easy to meet the two-night minimum stay. A delicious breakfast on the breezy verandah is included. Recent additions include a private waterfall swimming hole and a spacious yoga room. Not suitable for children under 14.

Good-value 'Nomad' rooms downstairs are more simple and share a bathroom.

Damai Beach Resort RESORT $$
(☎ 082-846999; www.damaibeachresort.com; Teluk Bandung, Kampung Santubong; d incl breakfast from RM240; ❄ @ 🛜 🏊) This 252-room resort offers a huge range of activities and amenities, including boat excursions, sea kayaking and even an 18-hole golf course (p418) designed by Arnold Palmer. Although in some areas the hotel falls short of four-star expectations, it's a reasonable option for families looking for a convenient beach location and a decent pool. Check online for solid discounts.

🍴 Eating

Food Court HAWKER $
(Damai Central; mains RM5-9; ⊙8am-10pm) A convenient food court with 10 stalls selling noodles, fried rice and cold drinks, as well as a stall selling excellent *roti canai* (flaky flat bread; RM3 to RM45).

Escobar Bar & Grill INTERNATIONAL $$
(☎ 082-846039; www.facebook.com/escobarDC; Damai Central; mains Asian RM14-17, Western RM20-27; ⊙noon-midnight) A casual eatery on the waterfront with breezy outdoor seating, Escobar offers plenty of fresh seafood options accompanied by rice or noodles, as well as pizzas, pastas and burgers. Try the tasty Mexican chicken salad with a pretty decent margarita. A can of beer costs RM11, a bottle of wine RM88.

Lim Hock Ann Seafood SEAFOOD $$
(Kampung Buntal; mains RM9-20, fish per kg RM46-74; ⊙11am-2pm & 5-10pm, closed lunch Mon) A sprawling, open-air shed on stilts with a wide-plank floor and a tin roof, this classic Chinese-style seafood restaurant is in Kampung Buntal, a fishing village 11km southeast of Damai Central (on the east coast

of the base of the peninsula). The freshly landed fish is superb and the beer's always frosty. Try the tasty oyster omelette.

❶ Getting There & Away

MINIBUS
Kuching is linked to the Santubong Peninsula (RM3.50, 45 minutes) by the slow K15 bus from Saujana Bus Station and minibuses operated by **Damai Shuttle** (☑ 082-423111; www.grand margherita.com/facilities-services; 1-way adult/child RM20/10).

Damai Shuttle has departures from Kuching's Grand Margherita Hotel to Damai Beach and Sarawak Cultural Village four times a day (9.15am, 10.15am, 12.15pm and 2.15pm). Shuttles from Damai to Kuching leave Sarawak Cultural Village at 11.15am, 1.15pm, 3.15pm and 5.15pm.

TAXI
A cab from Kuching to Damai Central costs RM90 (about 30 minutes), or about RM100 (45 minutes) from the airport. By Grab it's around RM50.

Semenggoh Wildlife Centre

One of the best places in the world to see semiwild orangutans in their natural rainforest habitat, swinging from trees and scurrying up vines, **Semenggoh Wildlife Centre** (☑ 082-618325; www.sarawakforestry.com; Jln Puncak Borneo; adult/child RM10/5; ⊗ 8-10am & 2-4pm, feeding 9am & 3pm) is home to 28 orangutans who often (literally) swing by park HQ to dine on bananas and coconuts. There's no guarantee that orangutans will show up, but even when there's plenty of fruit in the forest the chances are excellent.

Hour-long feedings are held in the rainforest a few hundred metres from park HQ. When the sessions look as though they're over, rangers sometimes try to shoo visitors away (especially groups, whose guides are in any case eager to get back to Kuching), but orangutans often turn up at park HQ, so don't rush off straight away if everything seems quiet.

For safety reasons, visitors are asked to stay at least 5m from the orangutans – the animals can be unpredictable – and are advised to keep a tight grip on their backpacks, water bottles and cameras because orangutans have been known to snatch things in search of something yummy. To avoid annoying – or even angering – the orang-utans, do not point at them with anything that looks like a gun (such as a walking stick or camera tripod); do not scream or make sudden moves; and, when you take pictures, do not use a flash.

Rangers keep an eye out and radio back with news of the approach of Semenggoh's dominant male orangutan, Ritchie, who is easily recognised by his cheek flanges. If he decides to stop by, his food must be ready for him when he arrives to avoid provoking his wrath.

Semenggoh has two trails that pass through primary rainforest: the Masing Trail (Main Trail; red trail markings; 30 minutes), which links the HQ with the highway; and the Brooke's Pool Trail (yellow and red trail markings), a 2km loop from HQ, but they are not normally open to the public because it is important to limit the orangutans' contact with humans.

❶ Getting There & Away

Buses provide reliable public transport from Kuching's Saujana Bus Station to the park gate (RM4, 45 minutes), which is 1.3km down the hill from park HQ.

City Public Link bus K6 (RM4.30) departs Kuching at 7.20am and 1pm, and Semenggoh at 11.05am and 4pm.

A taxi from Kuching costs around RM70 one way or RM160 return, including one hour of waiting time.

Tours are organised by Kuching guesthouses and tour agencies.

Annah Rais Longhouse

Although this Bidayuh longhouse village has been on the tourist circuit for decades, it's still a good place to get a sense of what a longhouse is and experience longhouse life. It's possible to visit as a day guest and eat a meal here or stay overnight in one of the several homestays.

The 500 or so residents of **Annah Rais** (adult/student RM8/4) are as keen as the rest of us to enjoy the comforts of modern life – they do love their mobile phones and 3G internet access – but they've made a conscious decision to preserve their traditional architecture and the social interaction it engenders. They've also decided that welcoming tourists is a good way to earn a living without moving to the city, something most young people in the area end up doing.

WORTH A TRIP

KAMPUNG BENUK

This quiet, flowery Bidayuh village, where the loudest sound is often the crowing of a cock, attracted lots of tourists back when the road ended here. These days it gets relatively few visitors, despite being a pleasant place to spend a few hours. The traditional longhouse (Lg 5; RM8) is still home to a few families, though most villagers now live in attractive modern houses. In the *barok* (ritual hall) hang about a dozen head-hunted skulls, bone white but tinged with green, hanging from the rafters.

There's no accommodation in Kampung Benuk itself, however in the surrounding rural hinterland, and only accessible by boat, is the excellent **Kurakura Homestay** (☑ WhatsApp 012-892 0051; www.kurakura.asia; Kampung Semadang; per person incl meals for 2 nights RM325; ▦) Run by Norwegian-born Lars and his Bidayuh wife, Liza, this super-friendly, sustainable jungle homestay occupies a wooden house built on land that once belonged to Liza's grandfather. Meals are prepared using homegrown vegetables, fruit and herbs, and possible activities include hiking and kayaking. Situated about 30 minutes by boat from Kampung Semadang. Rates include transport to and from Kuching.

⊙ Sights

Longhouse Verandah   HOUSE
Once you've paid your entrance fee you're free to explore Annah Rais' three longhouses (**Kupo Saba**, **Kupo Terekan** and, across the river, **Kupo Sijo**).

The most important feature of a Bidayuh longhouse is the *awah* (a long, covered common verandah with a springy bamboo floor that's used for socialising and celebrations). Along one side a long row of doors leads to each family's private *bilik* (apartment). Parallel to the *awah* is the *tanju* (an open-air verandah).

Headhouse   HOUSE
(adult/child RM8/4) Whereas the Iban traditionally hung head-hunted heads outside each family's *bilik*, the Bidayuh grouped theirs together in the community's *panggah* or *baruk* (communal meeting hall). The heads are no longer believed to protect the village – these days the people of Annah Rais are almost all Anglican (and the Bidayuh of Kalimantan are mainly Catholic) – but about a dozen smoke-blackened human skulls still have pride of place in the headhouse, suspended near an 18th-century Dutch cannon.

⤴ Sleeping

Half-a-dozen families run homestays with shared bathrooms, either in one of the three longhouses or in an adjacent detached house. Standard rates, agreed upon by the community, are RM298 per person for accommodation and delicious Bidayuh board. It's also possible to arrange a package including activities such as hiking, rafting, fishing, (mock) blowgun hunting, soaking in a natural hot spring and a dance performance.

Akam Ganja   HOMESTAY $$
(☑ 010-984 3821; winniejagig@gmail.com; per person incl meals RM298) Akam, a retired forestry official, and his wife, Winnie, an English teacher, run a welcoming homestay at their comfortable detached house on the riverbank.

❶ Getting There & Away

Annah Rais is about 55km south of Kuching. A taxi from Kuching costs around RM90 one way (about 90 minutes).

A variety of Kuching guesthouses offer four-hour tours to Annah Rais (from RM125).

Kubah National Park

Mixed dipterocarp forest, among the lushest and most threatened habitats in Borneo, is front and centre at this 22-sq-km **national park** (☑ 082-845033; www.sarawakforestry.com; incl Matang Wildlife Centre adult/child RM20/7; ⊙ 8am-5pm), which more than lives up to its clunky motto, 'the home of palms and frogs'. Scientists have found here an amazing 98 species of palm, out of 213 species known to live in Sarawak; and they have identified 61 species of frog and toad out of Borneo's more than 190 species. The list includes the aptly named (but oddly shaped) horned frog and a flying frog that can glide from tree to tree thanks to the webbing between its toes. The forest is also home to a wide variety of orchids.

Kubah's trails offer a good degree of shade, making the park ideal for the sun averse. And when you're hot and sweaty from walking you can cool off under a crystal-clear waterfall.

◉ Sights & Activities

Rainforest Trails

When you pay your entry fee you'll receive a hand-coloured schematic map of the park's six interconnected **trails** (☑park HQ 082-845033; www.sarawakforestry.com). They're well marked, so a guide isn't necessary. The park has about half-a-dozen rain shelters – keep an eye out for them so you'll know where to run in case of a downpour.

The **Selang Trail** (40 minutes to 60 minutes; trail-marked in yellow), linking the **Main Trail** (white trail markers) with the **Rayu Trail** (orange trail markers), passes by the **Selang Viewpoint**. Offshore you can see the turtle sanctuary of Pulau Satang.

The concrete-paved **Summit Road** (closed to nonofficial traffic), also known as the Gunung Serapi Summit Trail, runs along the park's southeastern edge from park HQ right up to the top of Kubah's highest peak, **Gunung Serapi** (911m), which holds aloft a TV and telecom tower; on foot, it's 3½ hours up and a bit less coming down. As you ascend, notice that the mix of trees and plants (including pitcher plants and ferns) changes with the elevation. The summit is often shrouded in mist, but near the top there's a viewing platform. When it's clear, there are stupendous views all the way from Tanjung Datu National Park on the Indonesian border (to the northwest) to Gunung Santubong and Kuching (to the east).

The **Waterfall Trail** (3km or 1½ hours from HQ one way; trail-marked from the Summit Rd in blue) passes by wild durian trees and *belian* (ironwood) trees. The latter, an incredibly durable – and valuable, and thus endangered – tropical hardwood, was traditionally used in longhouse construction. As you would expect, this trail ends at a waterfall and a natural swimming pool. Some visitors combine the Selang Trail and the Waterfall Trail to create a circuit that takes four to six hours.

The **Rayu Trail** (3.8km or three to 3½ hours) leads to Matang Wildlife Centre (p423). Walked in the direction of Kubah HQ to Matang, the trail is mainly downhill.

Frog Pond

Situated 300m above sea level and about a half-hour's walk from park HQ, this artificial

pool (☑park HQ 082-845033; www.sarawakforestry.com) provides a breeding ground for numerous frog species. The delicate amphibians are especially active at night, particularly when it's raining hard (during the day most prefer to hide in a hole in a tree), though their remarkable chorus begins about an hour before nightfall.

A track recorded at Kubah entitled 'Dusk at the Frog Pond' was voted the winner in a 2014 competition to find the most beautiful sound in the world.

Palm Garden

In this labelled **garden** (☑park HQ 082-845033; www.sarawakforestry.com), near park HQ on the Main Trail, you'll find examples of the 98 species of palm growing in the park.

🛏 Sleeping & Eating

While there are usually vacancies, even at weekends, in the park's accommodation, it can fill up on public and school holidays. It's always a good idea to book ahead.

All accommodation options have fully equipped kitchens, including fridge, toaster and stove, but there's nowhere to buy food, so bring all you need.

Forest Lodge Type 5   CABIN $
(☑082-370422, Kuching 082-248088; http://ebooking.sarawak.gov.my; 10-bed cabins RM150) These attractive cabins have a living room with couch, chairs and dining table, and three bedrooms with a total of 10 beds. Fan cooled.

Forest Hostel   HOSTEL $
(☑082-370422, Kuching 082-248088; http://ebooking.sarawak.gov.my; dm RM15) A comfortable, homely hostel with three small rooms containing four beds. Fan cooled.

Forest Lodge Type 4   CABIN $$
(☑082-370422, Kuching 082-248088; http://ebooking.sarawak.gov.my; 6-bed cabins RM225; ❋) Two-storey, all-wood cabins that come with a balcony, a sitting room, a two-bed room and a four-bed room.

❶ Getting There & Away

Kubah National Park is 22km northwest of Kuching. A taxi from Kuching costs RM65/130 one way/return. Your taxi driver may charge around RM35 per hour of waiting.

From Kuching's Saujana Bus Station, bus K21 to the Politeknik stops on the main road 400m from park HQ, next to the Kubah Family Park (RM4, one hour). Departures from Kuching are at 8am, 11am, 2pm and 5pm, and from the main road (opposite the turn-off for Kubah) at 6.30am, 9.30am, 12.30pm and 3.30pm (be there at 3pm; the bus sometimes leaves early).

Matang Wildlife Centre

Situated at the western edge of Kubah National Park, the **Matang Wildlife Centre** (☑ 082-374869; www.sarawakforestry.com; incl Kubah National Park adult/child RM20/7; ⊗ 8am-5pm, animal enclosure trail 8.30am-3.30pm) has had remarkable success rehabilitating rainforest animals rescued from captivity, especially orangutans. The highly professional staff do their best to provide their abused charges with natural living conditions on a limited budget, but there's no denying that the centre looks like a low-budget zoo plopped down in the jungle. Because of the centre's unique role, it's home to endangered animals that you're unlikely to see anywhere else in Sarawak.

Some of the creatures at the Matang Wildlife Centre were orphaned, some were confiscated and others were surrendered by the public. Unless they're needed as evidence in court, or lack the necessary survival skills, all are released as soon as possible.

Many of the centre's caged animals are fed from 9am to 10am. Orangutan life-skills training sessions are usually from 8am to 11am and 2pm to 4pm.

⊙ Sights & Activities

Interpretation Centre   MUSEUM
(⊗ 8am-1pm & 2-5pm Mon-Thu, 8-11.30am & 2-5pm Fri) **FREE** In the gazebo-like administrative building, the centre is a good introduction to Matang and its residents. Most of the display panels provide information on orangutan rehabilitation.

Trails   HIKING
(⊗ animal enclosure trail 8.30am-3.30pm) The **Animal Enclosure Trail** takes visitors through the jungle past animals' cages. If they've got time, rangers are happy to guide visitors around. Pitcher plants can be seen on the 15-minute **Special Trail** loop.

The **Rayu Trail**, a 3.8km (three to 3½ hour) uphill hike to Kubah National Park (p421), is best done in the opposite direction unless you desire a hot and sweaty uphill workout. The starting/finishing point is near the park accommodation.

Orangutan Project   VOLUNTEERING
(☑ Leo Biddle/WhatsApp 013-845 6531; www. projectorangutan.com; 2 weeks incl food & lodging UK£1280) 🖉 For details on volunteering – nothing glamorous; this is hard physical labour – contact the Orangutan Project. In keeping with best practice, volunteers have zero direct contact with orangutans because proximity to people (except a handful of trained staff) will set back their rehabilitation by habituating them to humans. Placements are two or four weeks.

🛏 Sleeping & Eating

Matang's accommodation options, which include a **hostel** (☑ 082-374869, Kuching 082-248088; http://ebooking.sarawak.gov.my; dm/r RM15/40) and a simple **forest hut** (☑ 082-374869, Kuching 082-248088; http://ebooking. sarawak.gov.my; per person RM5), are basic and rustic. Although there's usually no shortage of space, it's best to book in advance so that staff are expecting you and can make sure the room is ready.

There's nowhere to buy food in the park, so bring your own. Cooking is forbidden inside park accommodation, but an electric kettle is available on request and there are barbecue pits outside (but no utensils).

Type 5 Forest Lodge   CABIN **$$**
(☑ 082-374869, Kuching 082-248088; http:// ebooking.sarawak.gov.my; r/cabins RM100/150; ❄) The two cabins each sleep eight (there are two double beds in each room), and have attached bathrooms and air-con.

ⓘ Getting There & Away

Matang is about 33km northwest of Kuching. By the most direct road, it's 8km from Kubah National Park HQ. There is no public transport.

A taxi from Kuching costs RM70/140 one way/ return and up to RM35 per hour waiting time.

Bau & Around

About 26km southwest of Kuching, the one-time gold-mining town of Bau is a good access point for two interesting cave systems and some Bidayuh villages. The town is relatively easily reached by public transport from Kuching, but all-inclusive day tours are also available from the city's travel agencies.

⊙ Sights & Activities

Wind Cave   CAVE
(Gua Angin; ☑ 082-765472; adult/child RM5/2; ⊗ 8.30am-4.30pm) Situated 5km southwest of Bau, Wind Cave is essentially a network of underground streams. Unlit boardwalks

TRINGGUS & GUNUNG BENGOH

Inland from Bau, most of the population is Bidayuh. Unlike their distant relations on the eastern side of the Bengoh (Bungo) Range – that is, in the area around Padawan and Annah Rais – the Bau Bidayuh have never lived in longhouses. The area's Bidayuh speak a number of distinct dialects.

Tour agencies in Kuching can arrange treks into the valleys around **Gunung Bengoh** (966m) – including the fabled **Hidden Valley** (aka Lost World) – from the Bau side or the Padawan side.

Borneo Experiences' (p403) Village in the Clouds departures trek to the remote and very traditional Bidayuh community of Semban, where a few elderly women still sport brass ankle bracelets.

A three-day, two-night trip, including transport, food and a guide, costs around RM1100 per person, depending on group numbers (minimum two people). Trips depart from Kuching.

in the form of a figure eight run through the caves, allowing you to wander along the three main passages (total length: 560m), with chittering bats (both fruit and insect eating) swooping overhead. In January and February the cave may close if the water level is too high. It's best to bring your own torch (flashlight).

Torches are available for rent (RM3) – if you get a feeble one, ask to exchange it. No food is sold at the reserve itself, though there's a drinks stand. Near HQ, 300m from the cave entrance, you can cool off with a refreshing swim in Sungai Sarawak Kanan.

Fairy Cave CAVE
(Gua Pari Pari; adult/child RM5/2; ⊙8.30am-4pm) About 9km southwest of Bau, Fairy Cave – almost the size of a football pitch and as high as it is wide – is an extraordinary chamber whose entrance is 30m above the ground in the side of a cliff; access is by staircase. Outside, trees grow out of the sheer rock face at impossible angles. Inside, fanciful rock formations, covered with moss, give the cavern an other-worldly aspect, as do the ferns straining to absorb every photon they can.

Cliff faces near Fairy Cave, many rated 6a to 7a according to the UK technical grading system, are popular with members of Kuching's rock-climbing community.

Serikin Weekend Market MARKET
(Pasar Serikin; Kampung Serikin; ⊙6am-4pm Sat, to 3pm Sun) Vendors from Kalimantan (Indonesia) cross the mountains on motorbikes to sell fruit, electronics, handicrafts, rattan furniture and clothes at this sprawling market, which occupies most of the otherwise quiet border town of Serikin. The lack of a customs post here means there's a free flow of cheap Indonesian produce; Kuchingites often come in search of bargains. Serikin is 20km southeast of Bau; a taxi from Kuching is around RM100. From Bau, catch bus 3 or 3A (RM3.20) at 9am, 11am or 3pm.

Caving

Many of Sarawak's limestone hills are as filled with holes as a Swiss cheese. Boardwalks let you stroll around inside the Wind Cave, the Fairy Cave and the caverns of Niah National Park and Gunung Mulu National Park, but to get off the beaten track you need an experienced guide – someone just like UK-born James, who runs **Kuching Caving** (☑012-886 2347; www.kuchingcaving. com). He knows more than almost anyone about the 467 cave entrances that have been found within two hours of Kuching, the longest of which is 11km. For an all-day caving trip, prices start at RM350 per person (minimum two).

ⓘ Getting There & Away

Bau is 43km southwest of Kuching. The town is linked to Kuching's Saujana Bus Station (RM5, 1½ hours) by bus 2 (every 20 minutes from 6.20am to 6pm). A taxi from Kuching costs around RM90 (50 minutes).

Lundu

☑082
The pleasant town of Lundu, an overgrown fishing village about 55km west of Kuching, is the gateway to Gunung Gading National Park.

The road north out of town leads not only to Gunung Gading but also to two beaches that are popular with Kuchingites at weekends and on holidays. Romantic, coconut-palm-fringed **Pantai Pandan**, 11km north of Lundu, is one of Sarawak's nicest beaches (despite the sandflies), with a gentle gradient that's perfect for kids. A few huts sell food and drinks. For beachfront accommodation, **Pantai Siar**, 8km north of Lundu, is home to several small resorts that appeal mainly to domestic travellers and a few savvy Kuching expats.

🛏 Sleeping

Lundu Gading Hotel   HOTEL **$**
(☑ 082-735199; 174 Lundu Bazaar; d RM70; ❄) It may not be the most stylish hotel in Sarawak, but Lundu's only hostelry – whose rooms sport blue-tile floors and big windows – provides more than adequate lodgings. Ask for one of the newer rooms. Situated diagonally across the street from the RHB Bank; look for the red Chinese lanterns framing the hotel's lobby.

Retreat   RESORT **$$**
(☑ 082-453027; www.sbeu.org.my; Pantai Siar; cabins incl breakfast Sun-Fri from RM119, incl breakfast & dinner Sat from RM229; ❄ 🛜 🏊) Owned by the Sarawak Bank Employees Union, this is the ideal place to mix chilling on the beach with workers' solidarity. The grassy, family-friendly campus has 38 comfortable rooms, including 21 cabins, and gets enthusiastic reviews from travellers. Day use of the pool costs RM15/5 per adult/child; the beach itself is free. Situated 8km from Lundu.

🍴 Eating

Pusat Penjaja Gading Lundu   HAWKER **$**
(Lundu Hawker Centre; Jln Stunggang Malayu Baru; mains RM4-6; ⊙ 7am-5pm) Above the fruit-and-vegetable market is a hawker centre with 26 Chinese and Malay food stalls. The Malay buffet at stalls 4 and 5 includes delicious fresh crab as well as other local seafood like spicy calamari. Around RM8 to RM10 will provide you with an overflowing plate.

Happy Seafood Centre   SEAFOOD **$**
(☑ 014-691 8577; Jln Blacksmith; mains RM5-15; ⊙ 7.30am-9pm Tue-Sun) Lundu's location at the edge of Sungai Stamin and just a few kilometres from the ocean makes for delicious fresh fish from both river and sea. This informal eatery is a great place to sample it, as well as local jungle vegetables like *midin* (fern). Also serves chicken and pork. Located opposite the bus station.

ℹ Getting There & Away

City Public Link runs bus K26 (RM12), which links Kuching Sentral long-haul bus station with Lundu (RM12, 1½ hours); departures from Kuching are at 7.45am, 10am, 1.30pm and 4pm. Buses from Lundu leave at 7.30am, 10.30am, 1.30am and 4.30pm.

Buses run from Lundu to Sematan (RM5) at 9.30am, 11.30am, 3.30pm and 5.30pm.

At Lundu's bus station it's possible to hire a private car to take you to Gunung Gading National Park (around RM10 per person) or Sematan (about R35 one way).

Gunung Gading National Park

The best place in Sarawak to see the world's largest flower, the renowned Rafflesia, **Gunung Gading National Park** (☑ 082-735144; www.sarawakforestry.com; adult/child RM20/7; ⊙ 8am-5pm) makes a fine day trip from Kuching. Its old-growth rainforest covers the slopes of four mountains *(gunung)* – Gading, Lundu, Perigi and Sebuloh – and is traversed by **hiking trails**. The park features the incredible biodiversity of lowland mixed dipterocarp forest; dipterocarp trees are particularly valuable for timber and thus especially vulnerable to clear-cutting.

The star attraction at 41-sq-km Gunung Gading is the *Rafflesia tuan-mudae*, a species that's endemic to Sarawak. Up to 75cm in diameter, they flower pretty much year-round but unpredictably, and each flower lasts no more than five days, so to see one you'll need some luck. To find out if a rafflesia is in bloom – something that happens here only about 25 times a year – contact the park or call the National Park Booking Office on 082-248088.

👁 Sights & Activities

A variety of well-marked, often steep trails lead through the lush jungle. Park signs give one-way hike times. Except when instructed otherwise by a ranger, keep to the trails to avoid crushing rafflesia buds underfoot.

Don't count on seeing many animals, as most species found here are nocturnal and wisely prefer the park's upper reaches, safely away from nearby villages.

Since these hikes must be done in one day (camping is permitted only at park HQ), you might want to arrive the day before to facilitate an early-morning start. Sign in at park HQ before setting off.

SEMATAN

The quiet fishing town of Sematan is Sarawak's westernmost town. Most travellers who pass through are on their way to Tanjung Datu National Park, usually accessible by boat but now increasingly reached via a road that links Sematan to the village of Teluk Melano.

A grassy north–south **promenade** lines the waterfront, where a concrete **pier** affords wonderful views of the mouth of the river, its sandbanks and the very blue, very clear South China Sea. The deserted beaches of **Teluk Pugu**, a narrow spit of land across the mouth of the Sematan River from Sematan's jetty, can be reached by boat (around RM40 return).

At the northern end of the row of stores facing the waterfront, check out the shop called **Teck Hunt** (the furthest west of the waterfront stores), which hasn't changed in over a century. Built of *belian* (ironwood), it still has wooden shutters instead of windows.

The sands of shallow **Pantai Sematan**, clean and lined with coconut palms, stretch along the coast northwest of town. The beach is home to several resorts that fill up with Kuchingites at the weekends.

The nearby forested mountains are in Kalimantan, but the border at Biawak is not usually crossed by travellers. Road conditions on the Indonesian side are very poor, and you'll definitely need to arrange an Indonesian visa in advance if you're heading this way.

Accommodation options include a basic **hotel** (☑ 011-2025 1078; 162 Sematan Bazaar; d RM60; ✱) and a few simple homestays. **Sam Chai Seafood** (☑ 013-803 4892; Sematan waterfront; mains RM3-6; ⊙ 7am-7pm) A simple seafront *kopitiam* (coffee shop) serving delicious seafood *mee* (noodles) with fresh prawns (RM7).

Sematan is 107km northwest of Kuching, 25km northwest of Lundu and 30km (by sea) from Tanjung Datu National Park. Buses link Kuching Sentral long-distance bus station with Lundu (RM12), and depart Lundu for Sematan (RM5) at 9.30am, 11.30am, 3pm and 5.30pm. An unofficial taxi from Lundu bus station costs about RM35 one way.

Interpretation Centre MUSEUM
(Gunung Gading National Park HQ; ⊙ 8am-5pm) FREE The well-presented displays provide detailed information on the rafflesia, a parasitic plant with buds the size of cabbages and flowers with diameters up to 68cm. The centre also highlights the dangers posed to this critically endangered species, and efforts aimed at protecting it.

Rafflesia Loop Trail WALKING
(per hour for group of up to 10 RM30) This 620m-long plank walk, which begins 50m down the slope from park HQ, goes through a stretch of forest that rafflesias find especially convivial. If the flower happens to be close to the trail, it's possible to go alone, but since most of the blooms are off the path, finding them requires a ranger or guide.

When the flowers are out, the local freelance (licensed) guide who usually takes groups is likely to already be at the park; if not, the office can give her a call.

Circular Route HIKING
For views of the South China Sea, you can take a circuit that incorporates the **Viewpoint Trail** (follow the red-and-yellow stripes painted on trees), the **Lintang Trail** (red stripes) and the **Reservoir Trail** (a cement stairway).

Gunung Gading HIKING
Hiking up Gunung Gading (906m) takes seven to eight hours return, but don't expect panoramic views on the way up: the trail is thickly forested, so you'll see mainly the bottom of the rainforest canopy. Only once you reach the summit, where the British army cleared the jungle to make a camp during the Konfrontasi, are you rewarded with views.

At **Batu Berkubu** (10 to 12 hours return; trail marked in red and blue) you can see a communist hideout from the same period.

Waterfalls SWIMMING
Three lovely cascades are easily accessible along the **Main Trail** (marked in red and white). You can take a dip at **Waterfall 1**, **Waterfall 7** (1.5km from park HQ) and the **swimming hole**, fed by a crystal-clear mountain stream, at the beginning of the Rafflesia Loop Trail. For safety reasons, swimming is not allowed at Waterfall 3.

🛏 Sleeping

The busiest times are weekends, school holidays and when a rafflesia is blooming, but even at quieter times park staff prefer advance bookings.

Hostel   HOSTEL **$**
(✆ 082-735144, Kuching 082-248088; http://ebooking.sarawak.gov.my; Gunung Gading National Park HQ; dm/r with shared bathroom RM15/40) The hostel has four fan rooms, each with four beds (bunks). There's a kitchen with cooking utensils and a barbecue pit for cooking.

Camping   CAMPGROUND **$**
(✆ 082-735144, Kuching 082-248088; http://ebooking.sarawak.gov.my; Gunung Gading National Park HQ; per person RM5) The campground has a toilet and shower block and barbecue pits.

Forest Lodges   CABIN **$$**
(✆ 082-735144, Kuching 082-248088; http://ebooking.sarawak.gov.my; Gunung Gading National Park HQ; cabins RM150; ❄) Each three-bedroom cabin has one master bedroom with air-con and a double bed, while the other two rooms make do with single beds and a fan. There's a shared kitchen with cooking utensils and a dining area.

ℹ Getting There & Away

Gunung Gading National Park is 85km northwest of Kuching.

Bus K26 (RM12), departing at 7.45am, 10am, 1.30pm and 4pm, links Kuching Sentral long-distance bus station with Lundu. From there you'll have to walk north 2.5km to the park or hire an unofficial taxi (about RM10).

A tour from Kuching costs from around RM250 per person including lunch (minimum two people). Groups could consider hiring a taxi for around RM300 including waiting time.

Tanjung Datu National Park

Occupying a remote, rugged peninsula at Sarawak's far northwestern tip, this 14-sq-km **national park** (✆ emergency-only satellite phone 87077673978; www.sarawakforestry.com; adult RM20) features endangered mixed dipterocarp rainforest, jungle trails that hear few footfalls, crystal-clear seas, unspoilt coral reefs and near-pristine white-sand beaches on which endangered turtles – the green turtle and olive ridley turtle – occasionally lay their eggs. Few visitors make the effort and brave the expense to travel out here, but those who do often come away enchanted.

A road links Sematan with the village of Teluk Melano, but for the foreseeable future Tanjung Datu National Park will remain one of Sarawak's more off-the-radar destinations. Because of the costs of independent transport, including pricey boat hire, Tanjung Datu is often best visited on an organised trip.

🏃 Activities

Park Trails   WALKING
The park has four trails, including the **Teluk Melano Trail** from the Malay fishing village of Teluk Melano (a demanding 3.7km), linked to Sematan by boat; and the **Belian Trail** (2km), which goes to the summit of 542m-high **Gunung Melano** (2km, one hour) and affords breathtaking views of the coastlines of Indonesia and Malaysia.

To spot nocturnal animals, you can take a **night walk** on your own or with a ranger.

Snorkelling   SNORKELLING
Snorkelling (but not scuba diving) is allowed in certain areas; details are available at park HQ. Bring your own equipment. Please don't touch the easily damaged coral, but bring water shoes just in case (the coral can be sharp).

🛏 Sleeping & Eating

For details of homestays in Teluk Melano, a steep three-hour walk from park HQ, contact the National Park Booking Office in Kuching on 082-248088, or ask around at the Sematan jetty.

There's no food at the park, so buy all you need in Sematan before getting the boat or heading north to Teluk Melano. Cooking equipment can be rented for RM11 a day; cooking gas costs RM6.

Guest Rooms   CABIN **$**
(✆ Kuching 082-248088; http://ebooking.sarawak.gov.my; d with shared bathroom RM42) These four basic rooms, each with two single beds, share bathrooms and a kitchen.

Shelters   HUT **$**
(✆ Kuching 082-248088; http://ebooking.sarawak.gov.my; per person RM5) These open-sided huts are as basic as they come, but the location – almost on the beach, looking out at the sea – makes a night here pretty special. The park can provide bedding and mosquito nets (RM16).

❶ Getting There & Away

Following the opening of a sealed road linking Sematan to the village of Teluk Melano just south of the park, it's now slightly easier to reach Tanjung Datu independently.

Sematan is linked by bus to Kuching via Lundu. From Sematan, motorcycle transport (around RM10) is sometimes available 30km northwest to the village of Teluk Melano. Options from Teluk Melano to the park include a boat (RM150) or a trek through the jungle of around three hours.

Alternatively, a boat directly from Sematan to the park is around RM450 to RM500 one way. To hire a motorboat (one to 1½ hours) for up to seven people, ask at Sematan jetty or contact **Mr Minhat** (☏ 013-567 9593).

Finally, weather and waves permitting, locals often (but not necessarily every day) head from Teluk Melano to Sematan early in the morning, returning in the early afternoon (around 2pm or 3pm). If you join them, expect to pay around RM45 per person one way. Sea conditions are generally good from February or March to October. From October to February, rough seas make Tanjung Datu more or less inaccessible.

Walking from Sematan to Teluk Melano – the only other way to get there – takes a full day.

Talang-Satang National Park

Sarawak's first **marine park** (www.sarawak forestry.com), established in 1999 to protect four species of endangered turtle, consists of the coastline and waters around four islands: the two **Pulau Satang**, known as *besar* (big) and *kecil* (small), which are 16km west of the Santubong Peninsula; and, 45km to the northwest, the two **Pulau Talang-Talang**, also *besar* and *kecil*, situated 8km due north of Pantai Sematan.

Snorkelling and diving are permitted, but only within certain dewsignated areas, and divers must be accompanied by an approved guide.

Pulau Satang can be visited with Kuching travel agencies; Pulau Talang-Talang can only be accessed by participants in the park's Sea Turtle Volunteer Programme.

Once every four or five years, female turtles (primarily green turtles but occasionally hawksbill turtles, olive ridley turtles and leatherback turtles) swim vast distances – sometimes thousands of kilometres – to lay their eggs on the same beach where they themselves hatched. Of every 20 turtles that come ashore in Sarawak to lay eggs, 19 do so on a beach in 19.4-sq-km Talang-Satang National Park. But of the 10,000 eggs a female turtle may lay over the course of her life, which can last 100 years, only one in a thousand is likely to survive into adulthood. To increase these odds, park staff patrol the beaches every night during the egg-laying season (mainly June and July, with fewer turtle arrivals in August and a handful in April, May and September) and either transfer the eggs to guarded hatcheries or post guards to watch over them in situ.

Pulau Satang

The larger of Pulau Satang's two islands, 1-sq-km **Pulau Satang Besar**, 14km northwest of Telaga Air, is the only island that is partially open to visitors. Groups are allowed to land, but swimming is forbidden within the core protected zone (anywhere within a 2km radius of the island's highest point).

The island has a fine beach and dorm accommodation with generator-powered electricity. Overnight visitors can sometimes watch fragile eggs being moved from the beach to a hatchery and, possibly, witness baby turtles being released into the wild.

Visiting Pulau Satang is usually only possible from April to September.

CPH Travel (☏ 082-243708; www.cphtravel. com.my; 70 Jln Padungan; ⊘ office 8.30am-5pm Mon-Fri, to noon Sat) offers day trips (RM285) and overnight stays (RM720) on the island.

Pulau Talang-Talang

The two Pulau Talang-Talang, accessible from Sematan, are not open to the general public; visitors are only allowed within 2.8km of Pulau Talang Besar, Pulau Talang Kecil, Pulau Satang Kecil or the Ara-Banun Wildlife Sanctuary by special arrangement with Sarawak Forestry. Such permission is normally only granted to bona fide researchers, students, conservation organisations, and people participating in the **Sea Turtle Volunteer Programme** (www.sarawakforestry. com/sea-turtle-conservation-program; 4 days & 3 nights RM2500-3800; ⊘ Jun-Sep). With this program, paying volunteers can stay on Pulau Talang-Talang Besar and help the staff of the Turtle Conservation Station patrol beaches, transfer eggs to the hatchery and even release hatchlings. For details, contact the National Park Booking Office in Kuching on 082-248088. Booking is through Kuching-based agencies such as Borneo Adventure (p403) and CPH Travel.

Batang Ai Region

Ask anyone in Kuching where to find old-time longhouses – that is, those least impacted by modern life – and the answer is almost always the same: Batang Ai, many of whose settlements can only be reached by boat.

Batang Ai is also the best place in Sarawak to have a chance of seeing truly wild orangutans. Sightings are not guaranteed, of course, but they're not rare either: a female orangutan was recently seen just 90 minutes' trek from lodge accommodation.

This remote region, about 250km (4½ hours by road) southeast of Kuching, can only be visited through organised departures with Kuching-based tour companies. Whistle-stop overnight visits are available, but to truly experience Iban culture amid stunning river and jungle landscapes, and have a decent chance of seeing orangutans in the wild, a minimum of two nights' stay is recommended.

◉ Sights & Activities

Batang Ai National Park NATIONAL PARK
(☑ National Park Booking Office in Kuching 082-248088; www.sarawakforestry.com; RM20) Batang Ai National Park's dipterocarp rainforests have the highest density of wild orangutans in central Borneo and are also home to gibbons, langurs and hornbills. Managed with the help of an Iban community cooperative, the park has various forest trails (ranging from an easy 1.8km walk to a strenuous 8.2km hike), but you must go with a guide. The only way to reach the park is by boat from Batang Ai jetty (two hours); there's no food or accommodation available.

The 240-sq-km park is part of a vast contiguous area of protected rainforest that includes the Batang Ai Reservoir (24 sq km) and Sarawak's Lanjak Entimau Wildlife Sanctuary (1688 sq km) as well as protected areas across the border in Kalimantan (Indonesia).

Hiking

Hikes range from easygoing strolls along the Delok River and its tributaries to the difficult five-day, four-night **Red Ape Trail** (☑ 082-245175; www.borneoadventure.com; per person RM2170) pioneered by Kuching-based Borneo Adventure. Other moderate trails range from one to three hours, often ending with lunch and a swim at the Enseluai Waterfall. These moderate treks are accessible to travellers of average fitness and, according to local guides, offer a fifty-fifty chance of seeing orangutans in the wild. At the least, many orangutan nests will definitely be spotted.

🛏 Sleeping

★ **Nanga Sumpa** LODGE **$$**
(☑ 082-245175; www.borneoadventure.com; 3 days & 2 nights per person from RM1130) The flagship Batang Ai accommodation for Borneo Adventure, Nanga Sumpa features surprisingly stylish rooms – some with private bathroom – wooden verandahs, and a common space with perfect river views. Shared meals are substantial and tasty, and the lodge's guides are very knowledgeable about the area. The lodge is linked by swing bridge to an Iban longhouse where the residents are welcoming hosts.

Lubok Kasai CABIN **$$**
(☑ 082-245175; www.borneoadventure.com; 3 days & 2 nights per person incl meals RM1800) This simple riverside cabin has three rooms and a spacious wooden verandah that's an excellent place to relax after jungle trekking. Packages include a three-day, two-night option incorporating one night's stay at Nanga Sumpa lodge, and a more adventurous four-day, three-night trip (RM2170 per person) staying solely at Lubok Kasai.

Aiman Batang Ai
Resort & Retreat RESORT **$$$**
(☑ 019-336 8033; www.aimanbatangai.com; ☺ 3 days & 2 nights incl meals RM1680; ❀✿⬆◈) With an elevated location above Batang Ai lake, this very comfortable resort is a popular inclusion for visitors after a few days roughing it in more basic accommodation in the jungle. Rooms and suites are lined with honey-toned timber and enlivened by colourful Iban design motifs. The resort is most often booked as part of tour packages.

❶ Getting There & Away

From Kuching it's a four- to five-hour drive to the jetty at Batang Ai lake, from where longboats cross the lake and continue along the spectacular river system for up to another two hours.

Trips to Batang Ai can be booked through Kuching-based tour companies. Borneo Adventure has been particularly instrumental in developing excellent accommodation and activities in the area.

CENTRAL SARAWAK

Stretching from Sibu, on the lower Batang Rejang, upriver to Kapit and northeastward along the coast to Bintulu and Miri, Sarawak's midsection offers some great river journeys, fine national parks and modern urban conveniences.

Sibu

📱 084 / POP 162,700

Gateway to the Batang Rejang, Sibu has grown rich from trade with Sarawak's interior since James Brooke's time. Offering some of Sarawak's best food – local seafood is especially well priced – the 'swan city' is a good place to spend a day or two before or after a boat trip into Borneo's wild interior. Visit in July for one of the state's best cultural festivals, or explore one of Sarawak's most interesting regional museums year-round.

Situated 60km upriver from the open sea, Sibu is Sarawak's most Chinese city. Two-thirds of locals trace their roots to China, and many of them are descendants of migrants who came from Foochow (Fujian or Fuzhou) province in the early years of the 20th century. The city was twice destroyed by fire, in 1889 and 1928. Much of Sibu's modern-day wealth can be traced to the timber trade, which began in the early 1930s.

⊙ Sights

Strolling around the city centre is a good way to get a feel for Sibu's fast-beating commercial pulse. Drop by the Visitors Information Centre (p432) for a brochure covering the **Sibu Heritage Trail**.

Features of architectural interest include the old **shophouses** along Jln Tukang Besi near the Visitors Information Centre and the old **Rex Cinema** (Jln Ramin), where art deco meets shophouse functionality.

Sibu's mascot is the swan, an ancient Chinese symbol of good fortune and health. Keep an eye out for statues as you wander around town.

★ **Sibu Heritage Centre**   MUSEUM
(Jln Central; ⊙ 9am-5pm, closed Mon & public holidays) FREE Housed in an airy, circular municipal complex built in 1960, this excellent museum explores the captivating history of Sarawak and Sibu. Panels, rich in evocative photographs, take a look at the various Chinese dialect groups and other ethnic groups, Sarawak's communist insurgency (1965–90),

Sibu's Christian (including Methodist) traditions, and local opposition to Sarawak's incorporation into Malaysia in 1963.

Don't miss the photo of a 1940s street dentist – it's painful just to look at.

Tua Pek Kong Temple   TAOIST TEMPLE
(Jln Temple; ⊙ 6.30am-8pm) FREE A modest wooden structure existed on the site of this colourful riverfront Taoist temple as far back as 1871; it was rebuilt in 1897 but badly damaged by Allied bombs in 1942.

For panoramic views over the town and the muddy Batang Rejang, climb the seven-storey **Kuan Yin Pagoda**, built in 1987; the best time is sunset, when a swirl of swiftlets buzzes around the tower at eye level. Ask for the key at the ground-floor desk.

The temple grounds feature exquisite stone carvings, shady trees and places to sit and catch the breeze as the river traffic beetles past. Anchored outside the temple and visible from the pagoda are 'floating supermarkets': boats used to transport supplies to upriver longhouses.

Bawang Assan Longhouse Village   VILLAGE
An Iban village one hour downstream from Sibu (by road the trip takes just 40 minutes), Bawang Assan has nine 'hybrid' longhouses (longhouses that combine traditional and 21st-century elements).

Rejang Esplanade   PARK
(Jln Maju) One of Sibu's 22 community parks – most donated by Chinese clan associations – this pleasant strip of riverfront grass affords views of the wide, muddy river and its motley procession of fishing boats, tugs, timber-laden barges and 'flying coffin' express boats.

Lau King Howe Memorial Museum   MUSEUM
(📱 084-350080; www.lkhhmm.org; Jln Pulau; ⊙ 9am-5pm Tue-Sun) One glance at this rather bizarre medical museum's exhibits and you'll be glad saving your life never required the application of early-20th-century drills, saws and stainless-steel clamps. Another highlight is an exhibit on the evolution of local nurses' uniforms that some visitors may find kinky. The museum is named after Lau King Howe, a pastor from Hokkien, China, who settled in Sibu in 1916 and helped fund hospitals and medical services in the area.

☞ Tours

Greatown Travel   TOURS
(📱 084-219243, 084-211243; www.greatown.com; No 6, 1st fl, Lg Chew Siik Hiong 1A) A well-regarded

tour company offering longhouse visits to Bawang Assan and around Sarikei, as well as trips to the 'Melanau heartland' around Mukah. Staff are happy to create an itinerary based on your interests and budget. The office is about 1km northeast of the centre along Jln Hardin Walk.

Great Holiday Travel TOURS
(☑ 084-348196, WhatsApp 012-890 8035; www.ghtborneo.com; No 23, 1st fl, Pusat Pedada, Jln Pedada; ⊙ 8am-5pm Mon-Fri, to 1pm Sat) Based out near the long-distance bus station, this outfit can organise half-day walking tours of Sibu, visits to Bawang Assan Longhouse (half-day tour RM150, overnight stay RM330) and two-day trips up to the Kapit area, usually with an overnight stay at Rumah Jandok. Reasonably priced.

⚡ Festivals & Events

Borneo Cultural Festival PERFORMING ARTS
(www.sarawaktourism.com/event/borneo-cultural-festival; ⊙ Jul) A 10-day festival of food, music and dance representing Central Sarawak's Chinese, Iban, Bidayuh, Orang Ulu and Malay-Melanau culture and traditions. The sights, sounds and tastes of the festival sprawl over Sibu's centrally located Town Sq. Performances are all free of charge.

🛏 Sleeping

Sibu has dozens of hotels, so there's no shortage of beds. Some of the ultra-budget places (those charging less than RM35 a room) are of a very low standard and double as brothels.

★ **Zuhra Hotel** HOTEL $
(☑ 084-310711; www.zuhrahotel.com.my; 1st fl, 103 Jln Kampung Nyabor; r RM75-115; ❄ 🛜) Excellent value in Sibu, the Zuhra features simple but spotless rooms, and a top location a short walk from the city's night market. The friendly team at reception love a good chat, especially if you ask them the best places to eat around town. Just the ticket when you're preparing to head upriver for a few days.

Li Hua Hotel HOTEL $
(☑ 084-324000; www.lihuahotel.com.my; cnr Jln Maju & Jln Teo Chong Loh; s/d/ste from RM47/61/141; ❄ @ 🛜) Sibu's best-value hotel has 68 spotless, tile-floor rooms spread out over nine storeys and staff that are professional and friendly. It's especially convenient if you're arriving or leaving by boat. Light sleepers should avoid the rooms above the

karaoke bars on Jln Teo Chong Loh that blare out music late into the night.

River Park Hotel HOTEL $
(☑ 084-316688; 51-53 Jln Maju; d RM50-65; ❄ 🛜) A friendly, well-run, 30-room budget hotel in a convenient riverside location. The cheapest rooms don't have windows and are best avoided.

Premier Hotel HOTEL $$
(☑ 084-323222; www.premierh.com.my; Jln Kampung Nyabor; s/d incl breakfast from RM221/264; ❄ 🛜) This popular hotel offers 189 spacious rooms in an excellent downtown location. Rates can be significantly cheaper through online booking sites. Check out floors seven and eight for rooms renovated in 2018.

Tanahmas Hotel HOTEL $$
(☑ 084-333188; www.tanahmas.com.my; s/d from RM300/330; ❄ @ 🛜 🏊) As comfortable as it is central, with large, bright rooms, a small fitness centre and an open-air pool. Eating opportunities include an air-conditioned downstairs cafe, and plenty of food stalls and local eateries are also close by. Located off Jln Kampung Nyabor.

RH Hotel BUSINESS HOTEL $$$
(☑ 084-365888; www.rhhotels.com.my; Jln Kampung Nyabor; r/ste from RM400/800; ❄ 🛜 🏊) With more than 200 rooms, the RH Hotel is Sibu's most impressive place to stay. Expect a hefty discount on the rates listed here and excellent views of Sibu's riverine sprawl. Facilities include a bar and a couple of restaurants, and the hotel is linked by a skybridge to a nearby mall. Sibu's excellent night market is very close.

🍴 Eating

Sibu is famous for Foochow-style Chinese cuisine, such as the city's signature dish, *kampua mee* (thin noodle strands soaked in pork fat and served with a side of roast pork or mince), and *kompia* (mini sesame bagels filled with pork). The city's night market is regarded as one of Sarawak's best.

Night Market HAWKER $
(Pasar Malam; Jln Market; ⊙ 5-11pm or midnight) Chinese stalls (selling pork and rice, steamed buns etc) are at the western end of the lot, while Malay stalls (with superb satay and barbecue chicken) are to the northeast. There are also a few Iban-run places. Look for the stall selling quite possibly Southeast Asia's

best doughnuts (just RM1 for five). Welcome to the best night market in Sarawak.

Youtiao Stand
HAWKER $

(27 Jln Maju; doughnuts 40 sen, youtiao RM1; ☺6am-7pm) A street stall selling freshly made doughnuts and *youtiao* (fried Chinese churros) – perfect to bring on an upriver boat trip. Follow your nose to its location in front of the Nasi Ayam Malaya cafe.

Kopitiam
CAFE $

(Jln Maju; mains RM3.30-6; ☺6am-4pm) Several old-time *kopitiam* (coffee shops) can be found along Jln Maju. In the morning, locals gather to dine on Foochow specialities, read Chinese newspapers and chat, making for a typical Sarawakian scene.

Sibu Central Market
HAWKER $

(Pasar Sentral Sibu; Jln Channel; mains RM3-7; ☺food stalls 3am-midnight) Malaysia's largest fruit-and-veg market has more than 1000 stalls. Upstairs, Chinese-, Malay- and Iban-run food stalls serve up local specialities, including porridge, *kampua mee* and *kompia*. Most of the noodle stalls close around noon.

★ Payung Café
MALAYSIAN $$

(☑016-890 6061; 20F Jln Lanang; mains RM8-19; ☺10am-11pm Mon-Sat, 5.30-11pm Sun) At this delightful cafe diners feast on healthy local food such as mushroom rolls, spicy *otak-otak* barbecued fish, deliciously fresh herb salad and generous servings of the volcano-like Mulu ice cream. There's no re-used oil, deep frying or MSG. Drinks include fresh-pineapple-and-ginger soda (very refreshing) and local Sibu coffee.

Ark
ASIAN $$

(407 Rejang Esplanade; mains RM18-35; ☺11am-10pm; ✻) Nudging the Rejang Esplanade, the Ark has an air-con interior plus outdoor seating upstairs, and is the perfect place to watch the river drift by with a cold beer or a wine. Chinese, Malaysian and Thai dishes of seafood, pork, chicken and tofu grace the extensive menu. Try the delicious *sambal sotong* (chilli squid) with a frosty Anchor beer.

Café Café
ASIAN $$

(☑084-328101; 8 Jln Chew Geok Lin; mains RM19-36, set lunch RM12.90-19.90; ☺noon-4pm & 6-11pm Tue-Sun) Café Café serves decent Southeast Asian fare, including Nonya-style chicken, Thai curries and Chinese noodles. There are daily specials and inventive desserts such as salted-caramel-apple-crisp cheesecake and

Reese's-peanut-butter-chocolate cheesecake. With decor that mixes Balinese, Chinese and Western elements, this is a sophisticated urban dining spot. The Vietnamese-style drip coffee is a good way to ease into a sultry Sibu afternoon.

New Capitol Restaurant
CHINESE $$

(☑084-326066; 46 Jln Kampung Nyabor; mains RM12-40; ☺11am-2pm & 5-9pm; ✻) A classy, old-school Chinese restaurant that locals flock to. Foochow specialities include sea-cucumber soup (RM10) and white pomfret (RM70 to RM80 for a portion to share).

🍷 Drinking & Nightlife

Queen
BAR

(12 Jln Chew Geok Lin; beer from RM15, cocktails RM25-38; ☺6pm-12.30am Tue-Sun) Decked out like a Victorian sitting room, this dimly lit bar features plush couches and overstuffed wing chairs in black and burgundy velvet. Happy-hour prices until 10pm. Occasionally there are live-music sessions or a karaoke machine is cranked up.

🛍 Shopping

Sibu Heritage Handicrafts
ARTS & CRAFTS

(☑084-333353; ground fl, Sibu Heritage Centre, Jln Central; ☺8am-6pm) This great little store is so packed full of Kayan and Iban beads, Penan rattan baskets and Melinau and Kayan handicrafts that it's difficult to move around. Hidden behind the vintage photographs of Queen Elizabeth and her family in the shop window is a chaotic treasure trove. The more time you spend here the more you're likely to unearth.

ℹ Information

Main Post Office (☑084-337700; Jln Kampung Nyabor; ☺8am-4.30pm Mon-Fri, to 12.30pm Sat) Sibu's main post office.

Rejang Medical Centre (☑084-323333; www.rejang.com.my; 29 Jln Pedada; ☺emergency 24hr) Has 24-hour emergency services, including an ambulance. Situated about 1.5km east of the city centre.

Sibu General Hospital (☑084-343333; www.hsibu.moh.gov.my; Jln Ulu Oya, Km 5½; ☺24hr) Situated 8km east of the centre, towards the airport.

Terazone IT Centre (Level 4, Wisma Sanyan, 1 Jln Sanyan; per hour RM3; ☺10am-9.45pm)

Visitors Information Centre (☑084-340980; www.sarawaktourism.com; Sublot 3a & 3b, Sibu Heritage Centre, Jln Central; ☺8am-5pm Mon-Fri, closed public holidays) Well worth a

Sibu

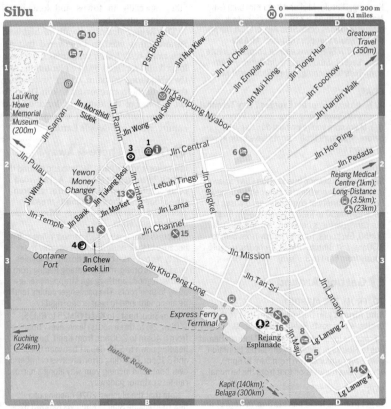

Sibu

◉ Top Sights
1 Sibu Heritage Centre	B2

◉ Sights
2 Rejang Esplanade	C4
3 Rex Cinema	B2
4 Tua Pek Kong Temple	A3

⌂ Sleeping
5 Li Hua Hotel	D4
6 Premier Hotel	C2
7 RH Hotel	A1
8 River Park Hotel	D4
9 Tanahmas Hotel	C2
10 Zuhra Hotel	A1

⊗ Eating
Ark	(see 8)
11 Café Café	B3
12 Kopitiam	C4
New Capitol Restaurant	(see 6)
13 Night Market	B2
14 Payung Café	D4
15 Sibu Central Market	B3
16 Youtiao Stand	C4

◉ Drinking & Nightlife
Queen	(see 11)

⌂ Shopping
Sibu Heritage Handicrafts	(see 1)

stop. Has friendly and informative staff, plenty of maps, bus and ferry schedules, and brochures on travel around Sarawak.

Yewon Money Changer (8 Jln Tukang Besi; ⊙9.30am-5pm Mon-Sat, 2-4pm Sun) Changes cash. Look for the gold-on-red sign.

ⓘ Getting There & Away

AIR

MASwings (☑084-307888, ext 2; www. maswings.com.my; Sibu Airport, Jln Durin; ⊙6am-8.30pm) has inexpensive services to

Kuching, Bintulu, Miri and Kota Kinabalu (KK), **Malaysia Airlines** (✈ 084-307799; www. malaysiaairlines.com; Sibu Airport, Jln Durin) flies to Kuala Lumpur (KL), and **AirAsia** (✈ 084-307808; www.airasia.com; Departure Area, Level 1, Sibu Airport, Jln Durin; ⊘ 7am-8pm) flies to Kuching, Johor Bahru and KL.

BOAT

All boats leave from the **Express Ferry Terminal** (Terminal Penumpang Sibu; Jln Kho Peng Long; 📶). Make sure you're on board 15 minutes before departure time – boats have been known to depart early.

BUS

Sibu's **long-distance bus station** (Jln Pahlawan) is about 3.5km northeast of the centre along Jln Pedada. A variety of companies send buses to Kuching (RM50 to RM60, seven to eight hours, regular departures between 7am and 4am), Miri (RM50, 6½ hours, roughly hourly from 6am to 3.30am) and Bintulu (RM27, 3¼ hours, roughly hourly from 6am to 3.30am).

🛈 Getting Around

TO/FROM THE AIRPORT

Sibu Airport (Jln Durin) is 23km east of the centre; a taxi costs RM45 (35 minutes).

From the local bus station, the Panduan Hemat bus to Sibu Jaya passes by the airport junction (RM3, every hour or two from 6am to 6pm), which is five minutes on foot from the terminal.

BUS

To get from the **local bus station**, in front of the Express Ferry Terminal, to the long-distance bus station, take Lanang Bus 21 (RM2.50, 15 minutes, once or twice an hour 6.30am to 5.15pm).

TAXI

Taxis (✈ 084-320773, 084-315440, 084-313658) can be ordered 24 hours a day. Taking a taxi from the city centre to the long-distance bus station costs RM25. By Grab it's around RM12.

Batang Rejang

A trip up the tan, churning waters of 640km-long Batang Rejang (Rejang River) – the 'Amazon of Borneo' – is one of Southeast Asia's great river journeys. Express ferries barrel through the currents, eddies and whirlpools, the pilots expertly dodging angular black boulders half-hidden in the roiling waters. Though the area is no longer the jungle-lined wilderness it was in the days before Malaysian independence, it retains a frontier, *ulu-ulu* (upriver, back-of-beyond)

vibe, especially in towns and longhouses accessible only by boat.

The Rejang drains a swath of highland Sarawak that used to be covered in pristine rainforest. Today, vast areas have been logged and replaced by tree plantations and the ubiquitous oil palm, or are underwater thanks to the controversial Bakun Dam. To get a sense of the extent of logging, road building, inundation and oil-palm monoculture, check out Google Earth.

🛈 Getting There & Away

The major transport arteries into and around the Batang Rejang region are rivers. A gravel road connects Bintulu with Belaga, and at research time a road from Kapit to Kanowit (already connected to Sarawak's highway network) was nearing completion.

Express river boats – nicknamed 'flying coffins' because of their design, not necessarily their safety record – run by half a dozen companies head up the broad, muddy Batang Rejang from Sibu with goods and luggage strapped precariously to their roofs. The passenger cabins tend to be air-conditioned to near-arctic frigidity.

From Sibu, boats to Kapit (RM25 to RM35, 140km, 2½ to three hours) leave every hour from 5.45am to 2.30pm; from Kapit, boats heading down to Sibu depart between 6.40am and 3.15pm. Boarding often involves clambering over boats and inching your way along a narrow, rail-less exterior gangway.

Note that the planned 2020 opening of a new road linking Sibu to Kapit via Kanowit may reduce the frequency of boats along the Batang Rejang. Contact Daniel Levoh (p437) in Belaga or the Sibu visitor centre (p432) for the latest information.

🛈 Getting Around

Boats can navigate the perilous Pelagus Rapids, between Kapit and Belaga, only when the water level is high enough – these days, this is determined mainly by how much water is released from the Bakun Dam.

If the water level at the Pelagus Rapids (32km upriver from Kapit) is high enough, one 77-seat **express boat** (✈ 013-806 1333) a day sometimes goes all the way to Belaga, 155km upriver from Kapit, stopping at various longhouses along the way. At the time of writing, however, this schedule was intermittent at best, and an overnight stay in Kapit was needed.

Heading upriver, departures are at 5.45am from Sibu (RM85, 11 hours) and at 9.30am from Kapit (RM55, 4½ hours). Coming downriver, the boat leaves Belaga at about 7.30am. When the river is too low, the only way to get to Belaga is overland via Bintulu.

When the water level in the Batang Rejang is too low for boats to make the trip upriver from Kapit, Belaga-based Daniel Levoh can arrange to collect you in his own small boat at Punan Bah longhouse – about halfway between Kapit and Belaga and the last stop before the Pelagus Rapids, which larger boats are unable to pass. He can take you to see the longhouse before continuing upriver to Belaga, with lunch on the way (RM500 for up to four people). The trip can also be done in reverse, from Belaga to Kapit.

Kapit

📋 084 / POP 16,000

The main upriver settlement on the Batang Rejang, Kapit is a bustling trading and transport centre dating back to the days of the 'white rajas'. Kapit's lively markets reveal its importance as a trading hub for the surrounding longhouse communities. The main activities here include wandering the docks and markets to see what is being traded, and to visit Fort Sylvia, which dates back to 1880. A number of nearby longhouses can also be visited by road or river, but it can be difficult for independent travellers to just turn up and find a good local guide.

Fans of Redmond O'Hanlon's *Into the Heart of Borneo* may remember Kapit as the starting point of the author's adventures. Kapit retains a frontier vibe and is just the place to begin your own adventure up the Batang Baleh.

⊙ Sights

Fort Sylvia   MUSEUM
(Jln Kubu; ⊙10am-noon & 2-5pm, closed Mon & public holidays) FREE Built by Charles Brooke in 1880 to take control of the Upper Rejang, this wooden fort – built of *belian* (ironwood) – was renamed in 1925 to honour Ranee Sylvia, wife of Charles Vyner Brooke.

The exhibits inside offer a good introduction to the traditional lifestyles of the indigenous groups of the Batang Rejang and include evocative colonial-era photographs. Also on show is the peace jar presented during the historic 1924 peacemaking ceremony between previously warring Iban, Kayan and Kenyah groups.

Waterfront   PORT
Kapit's waterfront is lined with ferries, barges, longboats and floating docks, all swarming with people. Porters carry impossibly heavy or unwieldy loads – you may witness 15 egg crates stacked in a swaying pile – up the steep steps and ramps as boats are unloaded.

Pasar Teresang   MARKET
(Jln Penghulu Gerinang; ⊙5.30am-6pm) Some of the goods unloaded at the waterfront end up in this colourful covered market. It's a chatty, noisy hive of grassroots commerce, with a galaxy of unfamiliar edibles that grow in the jungle, as well as handicrafts. Orang Ulu people sell fried treats and steamed buns.

🎎 Festivals & Events

Baleh-Kapit Raft Safari   SPORTS
(https://sarawaktourism.com/event/baleh-kapit-raft-safari/; ⊙Apr) A challenging two-day race recreating the experience of Iban and Orang Ulu people rafting downstream to bring their jungle produce to Kapit. For details, check with the Resident's Office (p436) in Kapit or Sibu's visitor centre (p432).

🛌 Sleeping

New Rejang Inn   HOTEL $
(📋084-796700, 084-796600; www.facebook.com/newrejanginn; 104 Jln Teo Chow Beng; d RM98; ❄️🛜) A welcoming and well-run hotel whose 15 spotless, good-sized rooms come with comfortable mattresses, hot water, TV, phone and mini fridge. Easily the best-value accommodation in town. A discount of RM10 on the rack rates is often there for the asking. The friendly Chinese owners have plenty of tips about eating in Kapit, onward travel and staying in local longhouses.

Hiap Chiong Hotel   HOTEL $
(📋084-796314; 33 Jln Temenggong Jugah; d RM55-70; ❄️🛜) Not much to look at from the outside, the Hiap Chiong has 15 passably clean rooms with outdated furniture and tiny flatscreen TVs. Cash only. A sign on the door proclaims 'No Chicken or Durian'. You have been warned.

🍴 Eating

Famous Bakery   BAKERY $
(22 Jln Teo Chow Beng; pastries RM1-3.50; ⊙5.30am-6pm) Freshly baked Chinese and Western-style pastries, cakes, mini pizzas and other easy-to-pack day-trip picnic fare or on-the-river snacks for the boat trip to Belaga. Don't miss the unique sausage-and-bun

Kapit

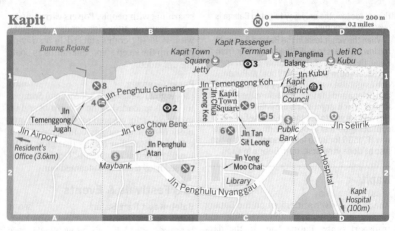

Kapit

⊙ Sights
1	Fort Sylvia	D1
2	Pasar Teresang	B1
3	Waterfront	C1

⊑ Sleeping
4	Hiap Chiong Hotel	A1
5	New Rejang Inn	C1

⊗ Eating
6	Famous Bakery	C2
7	Gelanggang Kenyalang	B2
8	Night Market	A1
9	Soon Kit Café	C1

satay on a stick or the 'Mexican Peanut' bun. Sheer culinary genius.

Soon Kit Café   CHINESE $
(13 Jln Tan Sit Liong; mains RM4-8; ⊙5am-6pm) An old-time *kopitiam* (coffee shop) with laksa (RM7) in the morning and excellent nasi goreng (fried rice; RM5) and cheap cold beer (RM3 to RM5). Push the boat out with the special laksa (RM9), topped with omelette and shredded chicken.

Night Market   MALAYSIAN $
(mains RM3-6; ⊙5-11pm or midnight) Delicious satay and barbecue chicken are the highlights of this night market.

Gelanggang Kenyalang   HAWKER $
(mains from RM3.50; ⊙6am-5pm) An indoor food court off Jln Penghulu Nyanggau with Malay and Chinese stalls. A good, if gloomy, place for breakfast laksa or *roti canai* (flaky flat bread).

⊙ Information

Kapit Hospital (☎084-796333; Jln Hospital; ⊙24hr)

Maybank (73C Jln Penghulu Atan; ⊙9.15am-4pm or 4.30pm Mon-Fri)

Police Station (Jln Selirik)

Post Office (Jln Teo Chow Beng; ⊙8am-4.30pm Mon-Fri, to 12.30pm Sat)

Public Bank (64 Jln Panglima Balang; ⊙9am-4pm Mon-Fri)

A permit for upriver travel takes just a few minutes to issue at the **Resident's Office** (☎084-796230; www.kapit.sarawak.gov.my; 9th fl, Kompleks Kerajaan Negeri Bahagian Kapit, Jln Bleteh; ⊙8am-1pm & 2-5pm Mon-Thu, 8-11.45am & 2.15-5pm Fri). Staff cannot provide information on visiting longhouses. The office is 3.6km west of the centre; to get there, take a minibus from the southeastern corner of Pasar Teresang. Ask the lobby guards for help catching a ride back to town (offer to pay the driver). Drivers will charge around RM20, including waiting time, if you wish to charter your own van.

⊙ Getting There & Away

BOAT
Express boats to Sibu (RM25 to RM35, 2½ to three hours, once or twice an hour) depart between 6.40am and 3.15pm from the **Kapit Passenger Terminal** (Jln Panglima Balang; ☎), which has a pleasant verandah cafe with breezy river views. Purchase tickets next door inside the Petronas petrol station.

    Water levels permitting (for details, call Daniel Levoh (p437) in Belaga), an express boat heads upriver to Belaga (RM55, 4½ hours) from the **Kapit Town Square jetty**, two blocks downriver from the Kapit Passenger Terminal, once a day at about 9.30am. Be on board by 9.15am.

One express boat a day heads up the Batang Baleh, going as far as the Iban longhouse of Rumah Penghulu Jampi. It departs from Kapit at about 10am and from Rumah Penghulu Jampi at 12.30pm.

Private longboats heading to longhouses that are accessible only by river can be found at **Jeti RC Kubu** (Jln Kubu).

MINIBUS
A small road network around Kapit, unconnected to the outside world, links the town to a number of longhouses. Minibuses that ply these byways congregate at Kapit Town Sq.

Belaga
📞 086 / POP 36,100

By the time you pull into Belaga after the long cruise up the Batang Rejang, you may feel as though you've arrived in the very heart of Borneo. It certainly feels remote – in reality, you're only about 100km (as the crow flies) from the coastal city of Bintulu. Belaga is the main trading bazaar and administrative centre along the upper Rejang. There's not much to do in town except soak up the frontier vibe. However, nearby rivers are home to quite a few Orang Ulu (primarily Kayan and Kenyah) longhouses, and guides in Belaga can help with visits.

The boat from Kapit drops you at the bottom of a steep set of concrete steps leading up to the small town centre. All the town's facilities are found in just a couple of blocks.

◎ Sights & Activities

To get a feel for the pace of local life, wander among the two-storey shophouses of the compact, mostly Chinese town centre, or stroll through the manicured park – complete with basketball and tennis courts – between Main Bazaar and the river. Along the riverfront, a wooden bridge leads downstream to **Kampung Melayu Belaga**, Belaga's Malay quarter, whose wooden homes are built on stilts.

The main reason travellers visit Belaga is to venture up a jungle stream in search of hidden longhouses and secret waterfalls. Possible destinations include the following:

Dong Daah A Kayan longhouse 10 minutes upriver by boat from Belaga.

Lirong Amo A Kayan longhouse a 30-minute walk from Belaga.

Long Liten A huge old Kejaman longhouse a way upriver.

Long Segaham A Kejaman longhouse situated some way upriver.

Sekapan Panjang A traditional, all-wood Sekapan longhouse 30 minutes downstream by boat from Belaga.

Sihan A Penan settlement a two-hour walk from the other bank of the Batang Rejang.

Before you can share shots of *tuak* (the local 'firewater' alcohol) with the longhouse headman, however, you'll need to find a guide. A good package should include a boat ride, jungle trekking, a waterfall swim, a night walk and activities such as cooking and fruit harvesting.

Daniel Levoh TOURS
(📞086-461198, WhatsApp 013-848 6351; www.facebook.com/oranguluhomestay; Jln Teh Ah Kiong) A Kayan former school headmaster, Daniel is friendly and knowledgeable. Possible excursions include walking to Sihan, a Penan settlement across the river, and stopping at a waterfall (unguided; RM65 for the boat and a gift for the longhouse; Daniel will call ahead). Daniel can also arrange private transport around Belaga and Bintulu and other longhouse visits.

Hamdani TOURS
(📞WhatsApp 019-886 5770) Former guide Hamdini may be able to help arrange longhouse visits.

🛏 Sleeping & Eating
Belaga's accommodation stretches to a rustic but friendly travellers' guesthouse and a scattering of fairly grim budget hotels.

There are several simple cafes serving Chinese and Malay dishes around Main Bazaar.

Daniel Levoh's Guesthouse GUESTHOUSE $
(📞086-461198, WhatsApp 013-848 6351; www.facebook.com/oranguluhomestay; Jln Teh Ah Kiong; dm RM20, d with shared bathroom RM40; 🛜) The four simple rooms sharing a bathroom are on the 2nd floor, opening off a large open verandah decorated with a traditional Kayan mural. Owner Daniel is happy to share stories of longhouse life and his wife, Florence, is equally welcoming. Each of the rooms is named after one of their children; all have names beginning with the letter R.

Syarikat Kim Guan Huat Trading MALAYSIAN $
(Jln Teh Ah Kiong; mains RM4-6; ⊙6am-5pm) Sharing signage with an electronics shop next door, this friendly Chinese-owned *kopitiam* (coffee shop) is Belaga's best place for breakfast before a jungle hike or onward

travel. The *wantan sup* (wonton soup) and laksa are both very good, and the owners have created a colourful ambience with lots of bright hues.

Crystal Cafe
MALAYSIAN $

(Jln Temenggong Matu; mains RM3.50-8; ☺7am-7pm) Owned by an Iban-Kenyah family, Crystal Cafe is a good bet for a simple meal of mee goreng (fried noodles; RM4), laksa Sarawak (RM5), *nasi lemak ayam* (chicken with rice cooked in coconut milk; RM6) or *nasi ayam penyet* (smashed fried chicken with rice and sambal; RM8).

Night Market
HAWKER $

(mains RM4-12; ☺3.30-10pm) An outdoor food court a block behind Main Bazaar with six stalls selling Kayan, Kenyah and Malay food. Look for Robina's stall selling delicious ginger chicken (RM6).

ⓘ Information

The town's only ATM is often out of order; bring plenty of cash. Several places to stay have wi-fi.

ⓘ Getting There & Away

When the express boat (p434) is running, it's possible to visit Belaga without backtracking, cruising the Batang Rejang in one direction and taking the logging road to/from Bintulu in the other.

UPRIVER FROM BELAGA

About 40km upstream from Belaga, the Batang Rejang divides into several rivers, including the mighty Batang Balui, which wends and winds almost all the way up to the Kalimantan border. Just below this junction, the controversial **Bakun Dam** generates electricity and provides locals with a place to catch fish, which they come down to the dam to sell on Wednesday and Saturday mornings. Belaga-based guides can arrange visits to area longhouses. The 15 longhouses in Sungai Asap are new – built to rehouse the communities displaced by flooding due to the dam – but traditional in style. There are plans to develop tourism around the lake formed by the Bakun Dam, which is larger than Singapore in surface area, but these projects have stalled in recent years.

The dam is 40km (two hours) by road from Belaga.

BOAT

If the water levels at the Pelagus Rapids (32km upriver from Kapit) are high enough, you can take an express boat to Kapit (RM55, 4½ hours), usually departing at about 7.30am. To find out if the boat is running, call tour guide Daniel Levoh (p437). When the river is too low, the only way to get out of Belaga is by 4WD to Bintulu.

LAND

A bone-jarring (and, in the rain, fiendishly slippery) logging road connects Belaga with Bintulu (160km). The first two hours of the four-hour journey see you traverse jungle and hills, and for the last two hours the route follows the 125km-long paved road from the Bakun Dam.

4WD Toyota Land Cruisers link Belaga with Bintulu (RM50 per person, RM400 for the whole vehicle, around four hours) on most days, with departures from Belaga at about 7.30am and from Bintulu in the early afternoon (between noon and 2pm). In Belaga, vehicles to Bintulu usually congregate in front of Main Bazaar. To arrange a vehicle from Bintulu, call Daniel Levoh.

If you're coming from Miri or Batu Niah Junction or heading up that way (ie northeast), you can arrange to be picked up or dropped off at Simpang Bakun (Bakun Junction), which is on the inland (old) highway 53km northeast of Bintulu and 159km southwest of Miri. Frequent buses pass by the junction. If you're travelling from Belaga all the way through to Miri, count on a travelling day of around eight hours.

Bintulu

⏺086 / POP 189,000

Fifty years ago Bintulu was a small fishing village with a population of 5000; now, thanks to its offshore natural-gas fields, it's a booming industrial town and Sarawak's most important centre for the production of liquefied natural gas (LNG) and fertiliser.

Most travellers who pass through Bintulu, roughly midway between Sibu and Miri (about 200km from each), plan to visit Similajau National Park or travel overland to or from Belaga. A handful of good restaurants, decent accommodation and an interesting riverside area also make the town worth a stop.

Tua Pek Kong (Main Bazaar; ☺7am-6pm) FREE, a classic Chinese temple, adds vibrant colour to the rather drab city centre.

🛏 Sleeping

There are quite a few budget hotels, some on the seedy side, on and near Jln Keppel, its southern continuation, Jln Abang Galau, and parallel Jln Masjid. These are best avoided by paying a bit more at a midrange hotel. Recent openings include higher-end places where good online discounts are commonplace.

★ **Velton Inn**   HOTEL $

(📞 086-351530; www.facebook.com/theveltoninn; Lot 3530 BDA Shahida Commercial Centre; s/d from RM60/70; 🚐❄🛜) After a few nights upriver, the Velton's cool, spacious air-con rooms could be just what you need to recharge your travel batteries. Opened in 2017, the Velton Inn also features slick bathrooms with excellent rainforest showers, and a modern cafe downstairs whips up coffees of every persuasion. It's at the edge of downtown Bintulu, with plenty of eating places nearby.

The cheapest double rooms have no windows.

Riverfront Inn   HOTEL $

(📞 086-333111; riverfrontinn@hotmail.com; 256 Taman Sri Dang; s/d from R78/83; ❄🛜) A long-standing favourite with business and leisure visitors alike, the Riverfront is low-key but has a touch of class. Try to get a deluxe room (RM115) overlooking the river – the view is pure Borneo. Downstairs is an air-conditioned cafe renowned for serving some of Bintulu's best Sarawak laksa.

Kintown Inn   HOTEL $

(📞 086-333666; ktowninn@ymail.com; 93 Jln Keppel; r from RM75; ❄🛜) The carpeted rooms in this centrally located hotel, though small and rather musty, are a reasonable option for those on a budget who aren't put off by a bit of well-worn patina. Lots of good eating is available nearby.

Kemena Plaza Hotel   HOTEL $$

(📞 086-335111; www.kemenahotelgroup.com; 116 Jln Abang Galau; d/ste incl breakfast from RM180/300; ❄🛜🏊) Renovations in 2016 have refreshed the hotel's 162 rooms, which are spacious with wooden floors, neutral colours and small bathrooms; rooms on upper floors overlook the river. The highlight is a rooftop swimming pool and sun terrace, with spectacular views of the town and river and the ocean beyond. Downstairs is an incongruous Irish pub with ill-defined opening hours.

Kemena's Bintulu mini-empire also includes two other hotels in the city's expanding suburbs north of the more atmospheric older section near the river.

🍴 Eating & Drinking

Famous Mama   MALAYSIAN $

(10 Jln Somerville; mains RM5-12; 🍴) Famous Mama does Mamak (halal Indian-Malay) cuisine and is a popular place for quick, cheap *nasi kandar* (rice served with side dishes of different curries) and *roti canai* (flaky flat bread).

Ban Kee Café   SEAFOOD $

(📞 012-876 5558; mains RM7-15; ⊙7am-11pm) An atmospheric Chinese seafood specialist with seating in a semicovered outdoor courtyard, selling fresh fish and seafood (per kilogram RM40 to RM80), breakfast noodles and laksa. Excellent pork belly and a decent selection of frosty beers are other tasty distractions. Located off Jln Abang Galau.

Popular Corner Food Centre   HAWKER $

(50 BDA Shahida Commercial Centre, Jln Abang Galau; mains RM7-12; ⊙6am-5pm) If you've ever wanted to try fresh frog porridge (RM14), this is the place to come. Less-adventurous diners can choose from one of eight stalls selling dim sum and fresh seafood.

Night Market   MALAYSIAN $

(Pasar Malam; mains RM3-6; ⊙4-10pm) A good place to pick up snacks, fresh fruit and Malay favourites such as satay and *nasi lemak* (rice boiled in coconut milk, served with fried *ikan bilis* (small, dried sardines or anchovies), peanuts and a curry dish). A hearty feed will set you back around RM5. Located off Jln Abang Galau.

Pasar Utama   HAWKER $

(New Market; Main Bazaar; mains RM3-6; ⊙7am-4pm) Malay and Chinese food stalls fill the upper floor of this blue-coloured fruit-and-vegetable market. The cone-shaped roofs of Pasar Utama and the next-door **Pasar Tamu** (Bintulu Market; Main Bazaar; ⊙7am-6pm) wet market represent *terendak*, the traditional headwear of the Melanau tribe.

Chef   BAKERY $

(📞 086-312964; 97 Jln Abang Galau; cakes from RM1; ⊙8.30am-9pm) Makes Chinese-inflected baked goods, including sweet and savoury bread rolls, sandwiches, pastries and surprisingly tasty Belgian chocolate cake. Ideal fare for a picnic lunch.

Rooftop Bar   ROOFTOP BAR

(📞 086-311113; www.goldenbayhotel.my; GoldenBay Hotel, Jln Tun Razak; ⊙4pm-midnight) It wins no prizes for an original name, but the bar at

Bintulu

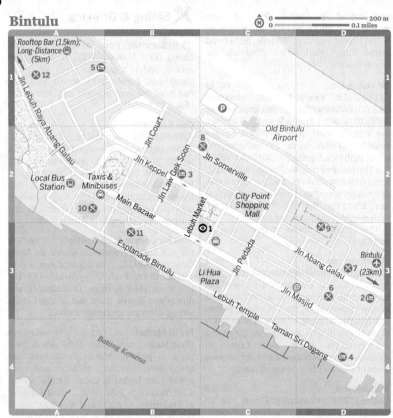

Rooftop Bar (1.5km);
Long-Distance (5km)

Bintulu

◉ Sights
1 Tua Pek Kong.....................................C3

🛏 Sleeping
2 Kemena Plaza Hotel..........................D3
3 Kintown Inn.......................................B2
4 Riverfront Inn....................................D4
5 Velton Inn...A1

🍴 Eating
6 Ban Kee Café....................................D3
7 Chef..D3
8 Famous Mama...................................C2
9 Night Market.....................................D3
10 Pasar Tamu......................................A2
11 Pasar Utama.....................................B3
12 Popular Corner Food Centre..............A1

the new GoldenBay Hotel is the best place in town to combine sunset views of the South China Sea with vistas of Bintulu's impetuous sprawl. Happy-hour prices kick in around

6pm and the hotel is about RM5 by Grab from the Bintulu riverfront.

🛈 Getting There & Away

To arrange transport by 4WD Toyota Land Cruiser from Bintulu to Belaga (per person RM50, four hours) on some pretty rough logging roads, call Daniel Levoh (p437). Departures are generally in the early afternoon (between noon and 2pm).

AIR

AirAsia (www.airasia.com; Bintulu Airport, Jln Bintulu; ⊙6am-6.30pm) and **Malaysia Airlines** (☑086-331349; www.malaysiaairlines.com; Bintulu Airport, Jln Bintulu; ⊙9am-6pm Mon-Sat) have direct flights to Kuching and Kuala Lumpur. **MASwings** (☑086-331349; www.maswings.com.my; Bintulu Airport, Jln Bintulu; ⊙7am-7pm) flies to Kota Kinabalu, Miri, Mukah, Sibu and Kuching.

A taxi to/from the airport, which is 23km from the centre by road, costs RM40. A Grab booking will set you back around RM30.

BUS

The long-distance bus station is at Medan Jaya, 5km northeast of the centre (aka Bintulu Town); a taxi costs RM15 and Grab around RM10. About a dozen companies have buses approximately hourly to the following.

Kuching (RM75, 11 hours) via Sibu (RM27, four hours), 6am to midnight.

Miri (RM25, four hours) via Batu Niah Junction (RM20, 2¾ hours), 6am to 9.30pm.

❶ Getting Around

Local buses (Main Bazaar) are stationed at the western end of the Main Bazaar.

Find taxis along **Lebuh Temple** (☑086-332009; Lebuh Temple; ⊙4am-7pm), and at the **western end** of the Main Bazaar. Grab is available in Bintulu for cheaper fares.

Similajau National Park

An easy 30km northeast of Bintulu, **Similajau National Park** (☑Miri office 085-434184, Park office 086-489003; www.sarawakforestry.com; Kuala Likau; adult/child RM20/7; ⊙park office 8am-1pm & 2-5pm Sat-Thu, 8-11.45am & 2.15-5pm Fri) is a fine little coastal park with golden-sand beaches, good walking trails and simple accommodation. Occupying a narrow, 30km strip along the South China Sea, its 90 sq km encompasses littoral habitats such as mangroves, *kerangas* (heath forest) and mixed dipterocarp forest (classic lowland tropical rainforest). Four species of dolphin, including Irrawaddy dolphins, can sometimes be spotted out at sea, and green turtles occasionally trundle ashore to lay their eggs along Turtle Beach II and Golden Beach. The park is also home to gibbons, long-tailed macaques, mouse deer, barking deer and wild boars.

Bintuluans flock to Similajau (especially the beaches) at weekends and on public holidays, but the park is gloriously deserted on weekdays.

◉ Sights & Activities

Interpretation Centre   NATURE CENTRE
(⊙8am-5pm) **FREE** Similajau's Interpretation Centre offers modern and interactive exhibits covering the park's flora, fauna and natural history. In front of the centre, don't miss the impressive skeleton of a Cuvier's beaked whale that washed up on the shores of the park in 2017.

Hiking Trails   HIKING
(☑086-489003; Similajau National Park) Similajau's beautiful forest trails are easy to follow and clearly marked, so a guide isn't necessary, though it's possible to hire one (call in advance) for RM30 per hour (RM40 per hour for a night walk). Before setting off remember to sign in at park HQ and pick up the simple but useful trail map. Bring plenty of drinking water.

The gently undulating **Main Trail** (Coastal Trail) parallels the coast, starting at the suspension bridge that crosses Sungai Likau and ending at **Golden Beach** (10km, four hours one way). The trail passes by rocky headlands, small bays and **Turtle Beach I** (6.5km, 2½ hours) and **Turtle Beach II** (7km, three hours). For a view back along the coast towards Bintulu and its natural-gas installations, head to the **View Point** (1.3km from HQ, 40 minutes).

Branching off to the right after crossing the suspension bridge, a 1.7km Circular Trail passes through brilliant estuarine mangroves and mixed dipterocarp forest.

Boat Trips   BOATING
(☑086-489003; www.sarawakforestry.com; Similajau National Park; boat for up to 5 people to Turtle Beach 1 way/return RM180/230, to Golden Beach 1 way/return RM220/280; ⊙office 8am-5pm) To avoid retracing your steps on a hike, one option is to arrange a ride in the park boat to one of the beaches and walk back. The boat, with space for five passengers, can be hired for one-way or return trips. Sea conditions are often rough later in the day, so it's best to head out before 8am.

Options include a return trip to the rocky island of **Batu Mandi** (RM150), or making a 30-minute stop at the island before continuing on to **Golden Beach** to hike back from there (RM420). It's also possible to arrange a **night river cruise** (RM150) to see the crocs (reserve during office hours).

---

❶ BEWARE CROCODILES

Similajau's waterways are prime crocodile habitat, so don't swim or wade in the rivers or near river mouths and be careful when walking near riverbanks, especially early or late in the day.

Swimming is forbidden at the two Turtle Beaches and at Golden Beach because of dangerous undertows.

🛏 Sleeping & Eating

Similajau's rustic overnight options, just 100m from the beach, sometimes fill up at weekends. Choose between basic **camping** (☑ 086-489003; www.sarawakforestry.com; Similajau National Park; per person RM5), a **hostel** (☑ 086-489003; www.sarawakforestry.com; Similajau National Park; dm RM15), six simple but comfortable **cabins** (☑ 019-861 0998, 086-489003; www.sarawakforestry.com; Similajau National Park; r RM100, 2-room units RM150; ❄) and the self-contained, air-conditioned **Rest House** (☑ 086-489003; www.sarawakforestry.com; Similajau National Park; 2-room units RM300; ❄) with its own living room and verandah.

Cooking is not allowed in the park cabins or hostel, but there are designated sites for barbecuing. A **cafeteria** (mains RM5-13; ☉ 7.30am-8.30pm; 🖉) serves simple rice and noodle dishes and can prepare packed lunches.

LONGHOUSE VISITS

Many of the indigenous people of the Batang Rejang basin, both Iban and members of Orang Ulu groups such as the Kenyah, Kayan and Punan, still live in longhouses. While most longhouses aren't as traditional as travellers may envision, visiting one can be a great way to interact with some of Sarawak's indigenous people.

Based on geography, Kapit and Belaga *should* be good bases from which to set out to explore longhouses along the upper Batang Rejang and its tributaries. Unfortunately, travellers may face two types of difficulty.

First, visiting longhouses without an invitation or a guide is becoming more complicated as traditional norms, according to which visitors are always welcome, have given way to more 'modern' (that is, commercial) ideas. But it is not only about commercialism; travellers who turn up unannounced may inadvertently cause offence – for example, by entering a longhouse during a period of mourning. In such cases the headman may ask for payment as a fine.

Second, it can be difficult to find a guide in Kapit to take you, and if you do, the guide may demand inflated prices and/or provide services that aren't up to standard. For instance, visitors may be dropped off at a longhouse with nothing to do and no way to communicate with the residents until they're picked up the next day.

If you're flexible and have some time to spend in the area, you may well be lucky enough to be invited by locals to their longhouse. It's also worth enquiring at the New Rejang Inn (p435) in Kapit or with Daniel Levoh (p437) in Belaga. Both have good contacts in the area. Otherwise, the best option is to make arrangements through one of the tour agencies based in Sibu.

A few communities around Kapit are accustomed to independent travellers, and charge between RM20 and RM50 for a day visit or RM70 to RM100 per person if you stay overnight, including meals. The headman may also expect a tip, and if you plan to stay overnight, you should also bring a gift. Remember that there may not be much to do at a longhouse, especially if there aren't any English speakers around.

Longhouses you may consider visiting:

Rumah Bundong One of the area's few remaining traditional Iban longhouses. Situated on Sungai Kapit a 45-minute (10km) drive from Kapit.

Rumah Jandok A traditional longhouse on Sungai Yong with quite a few English speakers, situated down the Batang Rejang from Kapit. The longhouse is one hour by road from Kapit and charges RM40 for a visit, plus RM15 for the headman and RM15 for taking photos of the skulls.

To arrange land transport, ask the car and van drivers in Kapit outside Pasar Teresang (on Jln Teo Chow Beng). Alternatively, you could try joining the locals in the service-taxi minivans that hang out around Kapit Town Sq (at the corner of Jln Teo Chow Beng and Jln Chua Leong Kee) and at Pasar Teresang (on Jln Teo Chow Beng).

To get to longhouses accessible only by river, head to Jeti RC Kubu (p437), the jetty facing Fort Sylvia, and negotiate for a longboat. These can be expensive – imagine how much fuel the outboard slurps as the boat powers its way upstream.

ℹ Getting There & Away

The HQ of Similajau National Park is about 30km northeast of Bintulu, 9km off the coastal road to Miri.

Count on paying around RM70 one way to hire a taxi from Bintulu (there is no public bus). To get back to Bintulu, you can pre-arrange a pick-up time or ask HQ staff to help you call for a taxi. From Bintulu to Similajau is around RM40 with a Grab driver.

Niah National Park

The vast limestone caverns of 31-sq-km **Niah National Park** (☑085-737454, 085-737450; www.sarawakforestry.com; adult/child RM20/7; ⊙park office 8am-5pm) are among Borneo's most famous and impressive natural attractions. At the heart of the park is the Great Cave, one of the largest caverns in the world.

Niah's caves have provided groundbreaking insights into human life on Borneo way back when the island was still connected to mainland Southeast Asia. In 1958 archaeologists discovered the 40,000-year-old skull of an anatomically modern human, the oldest remains of a *Homo sapiens* discovered in Southeast Asia. Rock paintings and several small canoe-like coffins ('death ships') indicate that the site was used as a burial ground much more recently. Travellers who have been (or are going) to Gunung Mulu National Park may feel caved out at the thought of Niah, but for anyone with even a passing interest in human prehistory it is not to be missed.

◉ Sights & Activities

Despite the historical significance of the site, Niah has not been overly developed for tourists. It's possible to visit the caves without a guide and during the week you may have the place to yourself. Some of the artefacts found at Niah are kept in Kuching; others (a handful) are in the park's own museum.

Great Cave
CAVE
(park entry adult/child RM20/7; ⊙park office 8am-5pm) A raised boardwalk leads 3.1km (3½ to four hours return) through swampy old-growth rainforest to the mouth of the Great Cave, a vast cavern approximately 2km long, up to 250m across and up to 60m high. Inside, the trail splits to go around a

massive central pillar, but both branches finish at the same point, so it's impossible to get lost if you stick to the boardwalk. The stairs and handrails are usually covered with guano, and can be slippery.

The rock formations are spectacular and ominous by turns, and you may find yourself thinking of Jules Verne's *Journey to the Centre of the Earth*. When the sun hits certain overhead vents, the cave is penetrated by dramatic rays of other-worldly light. When you're halfway through the dark passage known as Gan Kira (Moon Cave), try turning off your torch to enjoy the experience of pure, soupy blackness.

Painted Cave
CAVE
(park entry adult/child RM20/7; ⊙park office 8am-5pm) After passing through the part of the Great Cave known as Gan Kira, you emerge into the forest and a section of boardwalk before arriving at the Painted Cave, famed for its ancient red-hematite drawings depicting jungle animals, human figures and the souls of the dead being taken to the afterlife by boat. It can be tricky to make out the images, as many have faded to indistinct scrawls along a narrow 30m strip at the back of the cave.

To return, retrace your steps, taking the stairs up to your left to close the loop in the Great Cave.

Niah
Archaeology Museum
MUSEUM
(motor launch per person RM1, 5.30-7.30pm RM1.50; ⊙9am-4.45pm Tue-Fri, 10am-4pm Sat & Sun) Across the river from park HQ, this museum has displays on Niah's geology, ecology and prehistoric archaeology, including an original burial canoe that's at least 1200 years old, a reproduction of the Painted Cave, a case featuring swiftlets' nests, and a replica of the 40,000-year-old 'Deep Skull' discovered in 1958.

To get to the museum, cross Sungai Niah by motor launch. Torches – essential if you want to go any distance into the caves – can be rented at the museum (RM5).

Bukit Kasut
WALKING
This 45-minute trail, part of a boardwalk through freshwater swamp forest, leads to the summit of **Bukit Kasut** (205m). In the wet season it can get muddy and treacherously slippery.

NIAH'S BATS & SWIFTLETS

The chorus of high-pitched squawking you'll hear as you enter the Great Cave (p443) is not the sound of bats; rather, it is Niah's resident swiftlets; further in, you'll detect the squeaking of bats. At one time some 470,000 bats and four million swiftlets called Niah home. Current numbers are not known, but the walls of the caves are no longer thick with bats and there are fewer birds' nests to harvest.

Several species of swiftlet nest on the cave walls. The most common by far is the glossy swiftlet, whose nest is made of vegetation and is therefore of no use in making soup. For obvious reasons, the species whose nests are edible (those that are made of salivary excretions that are considered by some to be a great delicacy) are far less abundant and can only be seen in the remotest corners of the cavern. Several types of bat also roost in the cave, but not in dense colonies as at Gunung Mulu National Park.

Traditionally, the Penan are custodians and collectors of the nests, while the Iban have the rights to the cave's other commodity, bat and bird guano, which is highly valued as fertiliser. During the harvesting season (August to March), nest collectors can be seen on towering bamboo structures wedged against the cave roof.

The best time to see the cave's winged wildlife is at dusk (5.30pm to 6.45pm) during the 'changeover', when the swiftlets stream back to their nests and the bats come swirling out for the night's feeding. If you decide to stick around, let staff at the park HQ's registration counter know and make sure you either get back to the boat by 7.30pm or coordinate a later pick-up time with the skipper.

🛏 Sleeping & Eating

Bookings for park-run accommodation can be made at park HQ (p443) (in person or by phone), online, or through one of the **National Park Booking Offices** (☑ Kuching 082-248088, Miri 085-434184). Lodges and rooms often fill up on Chinese, Malay and public holidays.

Batu Niah town, 4km from park HQ (or 3km by the walking path), has a couple of basic hotels.

Cooking is prohibited in park accommodation, but you can, except at the hostel, boil water to make instant noodles.

Rumah Patrick Libau
Homestay   HOMESTAY **$**
(☑ Asan 014-596 2757; Niah National Park; per person incl meals RM90; 📶) The traditional, 100-door Iban longhouse Rumah Patrick Libau, which is home to about 400 people, operates an informal homestay program. Accommodation is basic, but the longhouse has wi-fi and 24-hour electricity. To get here, take the signposted turn off the main trail that leads to the caves. Villagers often sit at the junction selling cold drinks and souvenirs.

Hostel   HOSTEL **$**
(Niah National Park HQ; r RM40, towel rental RM6) Each basic hostel room has space for up to four people.

Campground   CAMPGROUND **$**
(Niah National Park HQ; per person RM5) Camping is permitted near park HQ.

Forest Lodges   CABIN **$$**
(Niah National Park HQ; q with fan RM100, d/q with air-con RM150/250) The park has six rustic two-room cabins with attached bathrooms; each room can sleep up to four people. Two additional, more expensive air-con units each have two rooms with twin beds.

ℹ Getting There & Away

Niah National Park is about 115km southwest of Miri and 122km northeast of Bintulu and can be visited as a day trip from either city.

Park HQ is 15km north of **Batu Niah Junction**, a major transport hub on the inland (old) Miri–Bintulu highway. This makes getting to the park by public transport a tad tricky.

BUS
All long-haul buses linking Miri's Pujut Bus Terminal with Bintulu, Sibu and Kuching stop at Batu Niah Junction, but the only way to get from the junction to the park is to hire an unofficial taxi. The price should be RM35 to RM40, but you'll have to nose around the junction to find one. A good place to check is the bench in front of Shen Yang Trading, at the corner of Ngu's Garden Food Court. National-park staff (or, after hours, park security personnel) can help arrange a car back to the junction.

From Batu Niah Junction, buses head to Miri (RM12, 1¾ hours) from about 8am to 1am and to

Bintulu (RM20, two hours) from about 8am to 10.30pm. Other well-served destinations include Sibu (RM40, five to six hours) and Kuching (RM80, 12 hours). Kiosks representing various companies can be found at both ends of the building directly across the highway from Batu Niah Food Court Centre.

TAXI

From Miri, a taxi to Niah costs around RM180 one way or RM300 return, including waiting time.

It is also worth considering hiring a car or motorbike in Miri for the day. Rental-car availability in Miri can be limited, so try to book a few days ahead.

Lambir Hills National Park

The 69-sq-km **Lambir Hills National Park** (☑085-471609; www.sarawakforestry.com; Jln Miri-Bintulu; adult/child RM20/7; ⊙8am-5pm, last entry 4pm) shelters dozens of jungle waterfalls, plenty of cool pools where you can take a dip, and a network of walking trails through mixed dipterocarp and *kerangas* forests. A perennial favourite among locals and an important centre of scientific research, Lambir Hills makes a great day or overnight trip out of Miri.

The park encompasses a range of low sandstone hills with an extraordinary variety of plants and animals. Studies of a 52-hectare research plot found an amazing 1200 tree species. Fauna include clouded leopards, barking deer, pangolins, tarsiers, five varieties of civet, 10 bat species and 50 other kinds of mammals, though you are unlikely to see many of them around park HQ. Lambir Hills is also home to an unbelievable 237 species of bird, among them eight kinds of hornbill, and 24 species of frog – and more are being found all the time.

🏃 Activities

Lambir Hills' interconnected, colour-coded trails branch off four primary routes and lead to 14 destinations – rangers, based in the park HQ building, can supply you with a map and are happy to make suggestions. Make sure you get back to HQ before 5pm – unless you're heading out for a night walk, that is, in which case you need to coordinate with park staff. Hiring a guide (optional) costs RM30 per hour for up to five people.

From HQ, the **Main Trail** follows a small river, Sungai Liam, past two attractive

waterfalls to the 25m-high **Latak Waterfall** (1km, 15 to 20 minutes one way), which has a picnic area, changing rooms and a refreshing, sandy pool suitable for swimming. It can get pretty crowded at weekends and on holidays.

You're likely to enjoy more natural tranquillity along the path to **Tengkorong Waterfall**, a somewhat strenuous 6km walk (one way) from park HQ.

There are wonderful views from the top of **Bukit Pantu**, a 3.6km (one way) walk from HQ that is a good option for those on a day trip.

Another more challenging trail, steep in places, goes to the summit of **Bukit Lambir** (465m; 7km one way from HQ), which also affords fine views. Keep an eye out for changes in the vegetation, including wild orchids, as the elevation rises.

🛏 Sleeping & Eating

Cabins   CABIN $

(☑085-471609; https://ebooking.sarawak.gov.my; Jln Miri-Bintulu; r with air-con RM150, r with fan & shared bathroom RM75) The park has reasonably comfortable two-room cabins; the old ones are wooden, the newer ones made of concrete. Fan rooms (classified as Forest Lodge 6) have two beds, while air-con rooms (Forest Lodge 5) have three beds and attached bathrooms.

Camping   CAMPGROUND $

(☑085-471609; https://ebooking.sarawak.gov.my; Jln Miri-Bintulu; per person RM5) Camping is permitted near the park HQ.

Canteen   CAFETERIA $

(Jln Miri-Bintulu; mains RM4-6; ⊙8am-5pm) The park's canteen serves simple rice and noodle dishes. If you are staying in the park and would like to eat an evening meal at the canteen, inform staff in advance. May close early.

ℹ Getting There & Away

Park HQ is 32km south of Miri on the inland (old) highway to Bintulu.

All buses that link Miri's Pujut Bus Terminal with Bintulu, Sibu and Kuching pass by here – just ask the driver to stop. The fare from Miri is RM12. There's a bus stand on the main road by the turn-off for the park, from where you can flag down a bus to Miri for the return journey.

A taxi from Miri costs RM60 one way (RM120 to RM140 return, including two hours' waiting time).

Miri

085 / POP 358,000

Miri, Sarawak's second city, is a thriving oil town that is vibrant and modern. Thanks to the offshore oil, there are plenty of service industries and money sloshing around, so the eating is good, the broad avenues are brightly lit, and there's plenty to do when it's raining.

Miri serves as a major transport hub, so if you're travelling to/from Brunei, Sabah, the Kelabit Highlands or the national parks of Gunung Mulu, Niah or Lambir Hills, chances are you'll pass this way. The city's friendly guesthouses are a great place to meet other travellers, and the new Marina Parkcity area offers modern cafes, restaurants and bars.

Miri lies on a narrow coastal plain between the South China Sea and a series of low, crumbly hills that were once covered in oil derricks. The population is about 40% Dayak (mainly Iban), 30% Chinese and 18% Malay.

⊙ Sights

Miri isn't big on historical sites – it was pretty much destroyed during WWII – but it's not an unattractive city. A walk around the centre is a good way to get a feel for the local vibe. Streets worth a wander include (from north to south) Jln North Yu Seng, Jln South Yu Seng, Jln Maju and Jln High St.

Saberkas Weekend Market   MARKET

(Jln Miri Pujut; ⊙4-11pm Thu-Sat, 8am-noon Sun) At Saberkas, one of the most colourful and friendly markets in Sarawak, vendors are more than happy to answer questions about their produce, which includes tropical fruits and vegetables, barbecue chicken, satay and handicrafts. The market is about 3km northeast of the centre outside the Saberkas Commercial Centre. A taxi costs RM20, and by Grab it's around RM10; there's no bus.

Miri City Fan   PARK

(Jln Kipas; ⊙24hr) An attractive open, landscaped park with Chinese- and Malay-style gardens and ponds that is a popular spot for walking and jogging. The complex also comprises a library, an indoor stadium and an Olympic-size public swimming pool (RM2).

Petroleum Museum   MUSEUM

(082-244232; www.museum.sarawak.gov.my; Bukit Tenaga; ⊙9am-4.45pm Tue-Fri, 10am-4pm Sat & Sun; ⓘ) FREE The Petroleum Museum sits atop **Canada Hill**, a low ridge 2km southeast of the town centre that was the site of

Malaysia's first oil well, the **Grand Old Lady**, drilled in 1910. Appropriately, the old derrick stands right outside the museum, whose interactive exhibits, some designed for kids, are a good introduction to the hugely lucrative industry that has so enriched Miri.

The hill itself is a popular exercise spot, and it's worth coming here at sunset for the views across town to the South China Sea.

Tua Pek Kong Temple   TEMPLE

(Jln Bendahara; ⊙8am-6pm) FREE Miri's oldest Chinese temple (founded in 1913) is a good spot to watch the river traffic float by. During the week-long celebration of Chinese New Year, virtually the whole of this area, including Jln China, is taken over by a lively street fair with plenty of red lanterns and gold foil.

San Ching Tian Temple   TAOIST TEMPLE

(Jln Krokop 9; ⊙8am-6pm) FREE One of the largest Taoist temples in Southeast Asia, San Ching Tian was built in 2000. Set in a peaceful courtyard with soothing wind chimes, the temple features intricate dragon reliefs brought from China and majestic figures of the Three Pure Ones. Situated in the suburban neighbourhood of Krokop, 3km northeast of Miri town centre. A taxi costs RM20; Grab around RM10.

⚡ Activities

Although the waters off Miri are better known for drilling than diving, the area – much of it part of the Miri-Sibuti Coral Reef Marine Park – has some excellent 7m- to 30m-deep scuba sites, including old oil platforms teeming with fish and assorted trawler and freighter wrecks. Water visibility is at its best from March to September.

The corals here are in good condition and the water unpolluted, despite the proximity of heavy industry. When visibility is good you might see giant cuttlefish, whale sharks and sting rays.

Coco Dive   DIVING

(085-417053; www.divemiri.com; Lot 2117, Block 9, Jln Miri Pujut; dives/PADI courses from RM400/1050) A well-regarded dive company with a fat program of dive packages and PADI-certification courses. Gets rave reviews for its friendly, professional staff and solid equipment.

⚐ Tours

1Stop Borneo   MOUNTAIN BIKING

(Shavez/WhatsApp 012-824 8052; www.1stop borneo.org) Contact the friendly Shavez to arrange three-night, four-day mountain-biking adventures commencing in the town of Marudi, 90 minutes from Miri. Rides traverse rural and forest tracks on old logging roads, with full-board accommodation in village longhouses. Costs depend on activities and how much guiding is involved; reckon on around RM500 to RM600 per person for a group of two.

Happy Trails Borneo Tours TOURS
(☑ 085-433511; www.happytrailsasia.com; Unit 2.06B, 2nd fl, Wisama Pelita Tunku, Jln Padang; ☺ 9am-5pm Mon-Sat) Well-established tour agency offering trips exploring Mulu and the Headhunters' Trail as well as longer departures incorporating Brunei, Sabah or the rest of Sarawak.

Borneo Trekkers TREKKING
(☑ WhatsApp 012-872 9159; www.borneotrekkers. blogspot.com) Guide Willie Kajan specialises in treks to Mulu along the Headhunters' Trail with the possibility of beginning or ending with a night at a longhouse in Limbang. Can also arrange treks in the Kelabit Highlands and runs special orchid-viewing tours in April and October.

Borneo Tropical Adventure TREKKING
(☑ 085-419337; www.borneotropicaladventures. com; Lot 906, Shop 12, ground fl, Soon Hup Tower, Jln Merbau; ☺ 9am-6pm) Veteran Miri-based company offering packages including the Headhunters' Trail from Gunung Mulu National Park (five days, from RM1840) as well as longhouse visits and multiday Borneo-wide tours. Also an agent for MASwings.

🎊 Festivals & Events

Borneo Jazz MUSIC
(www.jazzborneo.com; Coco Cabana, Marina Bay; adult/child pass 1 day RM124/64, 2 days RM254/124, 3 days RM334/164; ☺ 2nd weekend May) An outdoor jazz festival held over three nights that features an eclectic ensemble of international talent. Prices quoted are for online pre-sale tickets, conveniently available until the day before the festival kicks off.

🛌 Sleeping

Miri has a few good backpackers' guesthouses, but if you're on a tight budget, choose your bed carefully – at the cheapie dives catering to oil-rig roustabouts (on and east of Jln South Yu Seng), many of the dreary rooms are windowless and musty. Newer options are much better value.

★ La Mirina Boutique Inn GUESTHOUSE $
(☑ WhatsApp 012-830 3556; Lot 1955, ground fl, Marina Sq 2, Marina Parkcity; d RM79-99, f RM108-118; ❄ 🛜) Located in the Marina Parkcity area, a modern district packed with bars, cafes and restaurants, La Mirina's trendy rooms are very good value. If you're willing to forgo a central location – and downtown Miri is only RM5 by Grab – then La Mirina is a relaxing option before or after onward travel or a sojourn at the Mulu caves.

Coco House GUESTHOUSE $
(☑ 085-417051; www.cocohouse.com.my; Lot 2117, Block 9, Jln Miri Pujut; incl breakfast dm/s/d RM30/55/90; ❄ @ 🛜) Coco House has bright, modern dorms with pod-like bunks and small but functional private rooms with splashes of colour. The spotless bathrooms have rain shower heads, and there's a comfy common area with books, board games, DVDs and a microwave for heating food. The roof terrace has a barbecue for communal dining.

My Homestay GUESTHOUSE $
(☑ 085-429091; http://staymyhomestay.blogspot. com; Lot 1091, Jln Merpati; dm incl breakfast RM39, d RM59-99; ❄ @ 🛜) A friendly place in a good location, My Homestay has a spacious balcony with comfy chairs overlooking the bustling street below. Most rooms, though clean and colourful, are windowless and a little stuffy. Prices are higher at weekends. Car rental can be arranged.

Next Room Guesthouse GUESTHOUSE $
(☑ 085-322090, 085-411422; www.facebook.com/ nextroomhomestay8; 1st & 2nd fl, Lot 637, Jln North Yu Seng; incl breakfast dm RM32, d RM85-95, d with shared bathroom RM60-65; ❄ @ 🛜) In the heart of Miri's dining and drinking district, this cosy establishment offers 13 rooms, a small kitchen, a DVD lounge and a great rooftop sundeck. Dorm rooms are pretty packed, with 10 beds. Light sleepers, be warned: the nightclub across the street pumps out music until 2am. Prices are higher at weekends.

★ Kingwood Boutique Hotel BOUTIQUE HOTEL $$
(☑ 085-415888; www.kingwoodmiri.com.my; Lot 826, Jln North Yu Seng; r/ste from RM160/400; ❄ 🛜) Following a thorough makeover in 2017, the Kingwood is easily the most comfortable place to stay in Miri. Rooms and suites blend modern and heritage decor, walk-in showers are quite possibly Miri's biggest, and a cosmopolitan cool envelops

Miri

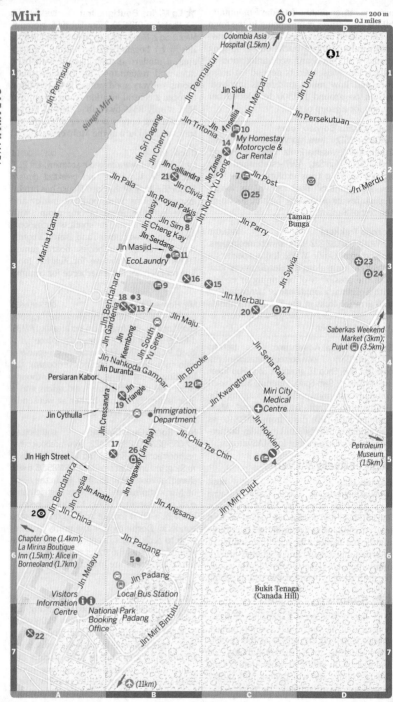

0 — 200 m
0 — 0.1 miles

Colombia Asia Hospital (1.5km)

Jln Peninsula

Sungai Miri

Jln Permaisuri

Jln Sida

Jln Merpati

Jln Unus

Jln Persekutuan

Jln Tritonia

Jln Sri Dagang

Jln Cherry

Jln Arsellia

10

My Homestay Motorcycle & Car Rental

Jln Calliandra

Jln Clivia

21

Jln North Yu Seng

Jln Zinnia

14

7 Jln Post

Jln Merdu

Jln Pala

Jln Royal Pakis

25

Jln Daisy

Jln Sim

8

Taman Bunga

Jln Cheng Kay

Jln Serdang

Jln Parry

Jln Masjid

11

EcoLaundry

Jln Sylvia

23

24

Marina Utama

9

16

15

Jln Bendahara

18 3

13

Jln Merbau

20

27

Jln Gardenia

Jln Maju

Jln Keembong

Jln South Yu Seng

Jln Nahkoda Gampar

Jln Brooke

Saberkas Weekend Market (3km); Pujut (3.5km)

Jln Duranta

Persiaran Kabor

19

Jln Triangle

12

Jln Setia Raja

Jln Kwangtung

Miri City Medical Centre

Jln Cressandra

Jln Cythulla

Immigration Department

Jln Chia Tze Chin

Jln Hokkien

6 4

Petroleum Museum (1.5km)

Jln High Street

17

26

Jln Kingsway (Jln Raja)

Jln Bendahara

Jln Cassia

Jln Anatto

2

Jln China

Jln Angsana

Jln Miri Pujut

Chapter One (1.4km); La Mirina Boutique Inn (1.5km): Alice in Borneoland (1.7km)

Jln Melayu

Jln Padang

5

Bukit Tenaga (Canada Hill)

Jln Padang

Visitors Information Centre

Local Bus Station

National Park Booking Office

Padang

Jln Miri Bintulu

22

(11km)

Miri

◎ **Sights**
1 Miri City Fan.. D1
2 Tua Pek Kong Temple A6

➊ **Activities, Courses & Tours**
3 Borneo Tropical Adventure B3
4 Coco Dive C5
5 Happy Trails Borneo Tours....................B6
  Megalanes East Bowling Alley ..... (see 24)

🛏 **Sleeping**
6 Coco House.. C5
7 Imperial Hotel C2
8 Kingwood Boutique Hotel B3
9 Mega Hotel B3
10 My Homestay..C2
11 Next Room Guesthouse B3
12 Nova Hotel...B4

🍴 **Eating**
13 Khan's Islamic Restaurant B3
14 Madli's Restaurant C2

15 Meng Chai Seafood C3
16 Ming Cafe.. B3
17 Miri Central Market................................ B5
18 Nok & Net.. B3
19 Persiaran Kabor B4
20 Rainforest Cafe C3
21 Sau Pau Cafe B2
22 Summit Café A7

🍷 **Drinking & Nightlife**
  Ming Cafe... (see 16)

🎭 **Entertainment**
23 Golden Screen Cinema Bintang
  Megamall D3

🛍 **Shopping**
24 Bintang Plaza D3
25 Imperial Mall...C2
26 Miri Central Superstore B5
27 Miri Handicraft Centre C3
  Popular Book Store ....(see 24)

the entire property. Excellent breakfasts are served in the ground-floor restaurant, but surrounding streets are packed with good places to eat.

Nova Hotel HOTEL $$
(☏ 085-322555; www.facebook.com/novahotelmiri; Lot 1016, Jln Brooke; r RM110-138; ☀❄🛜) Room dimensions tend towards the cosy and compact, but regular specials and openness to negotiation make this a good-value place. Launched in 2016, the Nova is a few blocks from Miri's best eating and drinking spots, making for a convenient and hassle-free time in the city. Maybe they could cut down on the kitschy towel art, though.

Imperial Hotel HOTEL $$
(☏ 085-431133; www.imperial.com.my; Jln Post; d incl breakfast RM165-194; ❄🛜🏊) The city centre's poshest multistorey hotel has business and fitness centres, restaurants, a sauna and a swimming pool. Try to book a more modern room in the new Imperial Palace wing, opened in 2017.

Mega Hotel HOTEL $$
(☏ 085-432432; www.megahotel.com.my; Lot 907, Jln Merbau; r incl breakfast RM138-200; ❄@🛜🏊) Don't judge a hotel by its tacky lobby – the 239 rooms here, spread over 16 storeys, are comfortable and spacious, if a bit old-fashioned. Amenities include a fitness centre (7th floor) and a 30m pool with sea views and a jacuzzi (4th floor). Book directly with the hotel to secure the best rates.

🍴 Eating

★ Madli's Restaurant MALAYSIAN $
(☏ 085-426615; www.facebook.com/madlis restaurant; Lot 1088, ground fl, Block 9, Jln Merpati; mains RM6-24; ⊙8am-midnight Sun-Thu, to 1am Fri & Sat; ❄) A long-running family business that started off as a satay stall in the 1970s; read the history on the wall above the kitchen. Madli's is open on two sides for ventilation and is spotlessly clean. As well as lip-smackingly good chicken-fillet and Australian-beef satay (RM1.30 per stick), the menu includes Malaysian dishes like *nasi lemak* and kampung fried rice.

★ Summit Café MALAYSIAN $
(☏ WhatsApp 019-885 3920; Lot 1245, Centre Point Commercial Centre, Jln Melayu; meals RM7-15; ⊙7am-4pm Mon-Sat; ❄) If you've never tried Kelabit cuisine, this place will open up whole new worlds for your taste buds. Queue up and choose from the colourful array of 'jungle food' laid out at the counter, including *dure* (fried jungle leaf), minced tapioca leaves, and *labo senutuk* (wild boar). The best selection is available before 11.30am – once the food runs out it closes.

Nok & Net THAI $
(227 Jln Maju; mains RM9-15; ⊙10am-10pm; ❄) Authentic Thai flavours shine at this place, opened in 2018. Once the staff have dragged themselves away from watching Thai soap operas on their smartphones, get ready to be served excellent *pad Thai*, spicy pork

ribs, and salads and dishes with the zingy flavours of Isaan (northeastern Thailand). A tasty alternative after your 10th bowl of *kolo mee* noodles.

Sau Pau Cafe
BAKERY **$**

(www.facebook.com/saupaucafemiri; Jln Calliandra; snacks RM1.50-2.50; ☉7am-6.30pm) Steamed *bao* buns and delicious egg tarts are perfect reasons to hunt out this neighbourhood bakery. A recommended combo is an iced coffee with a couple of buttermilk buns. Follow your nose and look for the big '2185' screen-printed on the cafe's bamboo blinds. Freshly baked goodies emerge warm from the oven around 9.30am and 1.30pm.

Persiaran Kabor
CHINESE **$**

(Persiaran Kabor, btwn Jln Duranta & Jln Cythulla; mains RM3-4.50; ☉6am-6pm) Come mid-morning this atmospheric covered court-yard, known locally as Old Folks' St, is full of men of a certain vintage, who congregate to drink coffee, read the paper and play chess (the Chinese Chess Association is located in one of the shop lots). The surrounding coffee shops sell the usual rice and noodle dishes.

Khan's Islamic Restaurant
INDIAN **$**

(☑WhatsApp 011-855 3450; 229 Jln Maju; mains RM6-12; ☉6.30am-9pm; 🖋) This simple can-teen is one of Miri's best North Indian eat-eries, serving up mouth-watering tandoori chicken (RM12), naan bread and mango lassi (RM5) as well as a variety of curries and many vegetarian dishes.

Miri Central Market
HAWKER **$**

(Pasar Pusat Miri; Jln Brooke; mains RM2-6; ☉24hr, most stalls 6am-noon) Of the Chinese-food pur-veyors selling *kari ayam* (chicken curry), porridge and the usual rice and noodle dishes, stall 6 (open 3.30am to 10am) is par-ticularly popular. Stall 20 serves up vegetar-ian fare.

Ming Cafe
INTERNATIONAL **$$**

(☑085-422797; cnr Jln North Yu Seng & Jln Merbau; mains RM5-40; ☉10am-2am) This very popular cafe-bar serves excellent food in a relaxed casual, open-sided restaurant. There's an indoor air-conditioned section, but the pot plants and fans keep the outdoor section comfortable and make it a great place to socialise. The menu features Chinese and Malay dishes, pizzas (from RM19) and burg-ers (RM6 to RM40), plus particularly good Indian fare.

Meng Chai Seafood
SEAFOOD **$$**

(☑085-413648; 11A Jln Merbau; meals from RM25; ☉4pm-midnight) Discerning locals crowd this first-rate eatery, housed in two unassuming adjacent buildings. There's no menu – make your selection from the fishy candidates lined up on ice, decide how you would like it cooked and order any accompaniments such as rice or *midin* (fern). Seawater tanks hold live clams and prawns. Servings of fish are priced by weight.

Rainforest Cafe
CHINESE **$$**

(☑085-426967; 49 Jln Brooke; mains RM10-30; ☉10.30am-2pm & 5-11pm) Often packed with families tucking into a banquet of shared dishes, this breezy, open-air eatery special-ises in Chinese-style dishes such as 'braised rainforest bean curd', 'crispy roasted chicken' and 'pork leg Philippine style'.

🍷 Drinking & Nightlife

★Ming Cafe
BAR

(☑085-422797; www.facebook.com/mingcafe borneo; cnr Jln North Yu Seng & Jln Merbau; ☉10am-2am) This ever-busy corner bar stocks 25 imported bottled beers and has several on tap, including Paulaner wheat beer. The drinks menu also lists Australian and New Zealand wines and several pages of cocktails. Fresh juices and shakes cost RM5 to RM10, and wine by the glass is RM15. Expect a mixed crowd of local and expat drinkers and diners.

Alice in Borneoland
BAR

(☑085-324650; www.facebook.com/AliceinBorneo land; Lot 2003, ground fl, Marina Sq, Marina Park-city; ☉5pm-3am) The hippest – and often the loudest – venue in Miri's Marina Parkcity neighbourhood, Alice in Borneoland alter-nates between a cool spot for an evening drink and a happening venue for everything from local hip hop to Dayak heavy metal. Check Facebook to see what's scheduled and make the short RM6 Grab journey from cen-tral Miri to this interesting area.

Chapter One
CAFE

(☑085-680691; www.facebook.com/ChapterOne CafeMiri; Lot 2288, Jalan MS2/1, Marina Sq, Marina Parkcity; ☉10am-11.30pm) Lined with book-cases and channelling a cool and cosmopoli-tan ambience, Chapter One is the best of the more modern and stylish cafes taking hold in Miri's new Marina Parkcity neighbour-hood. A huge selection of coffees and teas creates havoc for the indecisive customer, and it's a good place to meet the locals over a wedge of green-tea cheesecake.

🛍 Shopping

Imperial Mall SHOPPING CENTRE
(Jln North Yu Seng) With several clothes shops and a useful supermarket in the basement, this is a good place to stock up on supplies before a trek. Linked by a skybridge, the adjacent Permaisuri Imperial City Mall features a rooftop cinema complex, a food court, and Korean and Japanese eateries.

Miri Handicraft Centre ARTS & CRAFTS
(cnr Jln Brooke & Jln Merbau; ⊙9am-6pm) Re-opened in an interesting modern building in 2018, this centre showcases stalls selling colourful bags, baskets, sarongs, textiles etc made by Iban, Kelabit, Kenyah, Kayan, Lun Bawang, Chinese and Malay artisans.

Miri Central Superstore SHOES
(998 Jln Raja; ⊙8am-6pm) Sells rubber 'kampung shoes' (RM6 to RM10), which are perfect for jungle hikes.

Bintang Plaza MALL
(Jln Miri Pujut; ⊙10am-10pm) A modern, multi-storey, air-con mall with shops specialising in computers and cameras on the 3rd floor. Rainy-day entertainment comes in the form of **Megalanes East Bowling Alley** (3rd fl, Bintang Plaza; per game RM7-9, shoes RM3; ⊙9am-11.45pm) and a **cinema** (www.gsc.com.my; 4th fl, Bintang Plaza; adult RM8-12, child RM7).

Popular Book Store BOOKS
(2nd fl, Bintang Plaza, Jln Miri Pujut; ⊙10am-10pm) A mega-bookshop with a large selection of English books, and Lonely Planet titles in English and Chinese.

ℹ Information

For some great tips and an outline of local history, see Miri's unofficial website: www.miriresortcity.com.

ATMs can be found at the airport and all over the city centre.

LAUNDRY

EcoLaundry (☑085-414266; 638 Jln North Yu Seng; per kg RM6; ⊙7am-6pm Mon-Sat, to 5pm Sun) Free pick-up and delivery within the town centre.

MEDICAL SERVICES

It's a good idea to stock up on first-aid supplies before heading inland to Gunung Mulu National Park or the Kelabit Highlands, where medical services are scarce.

Colombia Asia Hospital (☑085-437755; www.columbiaasia.com; Lot 1035-1039, Jln Bulan Sabit; ⊙24hr) A 35-bed private hospital with a 24-hour accident-and-emergency ward and a 24-hour ambulance. Situated about 3km northeast of the city centre.

Miri City Medical Centre (☑085-426622; 916-920 Jln Hokkien; ⊙emergency 24hr) Has an ambulance service, a 24-hour accident-and-emergency department and various private clinics. Located in the city centre.

POST

Main Post Office (☑085-433423; Jln Post; ⊙8am-4.30pm Mon-Fri, to 12.30pm Sat)

TOURIST INFORMATION

National Park Booking Office (☑085-434184; www.sarawakforestry.com; 452 Jln Melayu; ⊙8am-5pm Mon-Fri) Inside the Visitors Information Centre. Has details on Sarawak's national parks and can book beds and rooms at Niah, Lambir Hills and Similajau (but not Gunung Mulu).

Visitors Information Centre (☑085-434181; www.sarawaktourism.com; 452 Jln Melayu; ⊙8am-5pm Mon-Fri, 9am-3pm Sat, Sun & public holidays) The helpful staff can provide city maps and information on accommodation in and around Miri, including the national parks.

VISAS

Immigration Department (Jabatan Imigresen; ☑085-442112; www.imi.gov.my; 2nd fl, Yulan Plaza, cnr Jln Kingsway & Jln Brooke; ⊙7.30am-5.30pm Mon-Thu, 8am-12.15pm & 2.45-5.30pm Fri) For visa extensions.

🚌 Getting There & Away

Miri is 212km northeast of Bintulu and 36km southwest of the Brunei border.

AIR

Miri's **airport** (www.miriairport.com; Jln Airport) is 10km south of the town centre and is served by **AirAsia** (☑600 85 8888; www.airasia.com; ground fl, Miri Airport, Jln Airport; ⊙7.30am-8.30pm), **Malaysia Airlines** (☑085-414155; www.malaysiaairlines.com; Lot No 10635, Airport Commercial Centre, Jln Airport) and **MASwings** (☑085-423500; www.maswings.com.my; ground fl, Miri Airport, Jln Airport; ⊙6am-9pm).

There is a separate check-in area for MASwings 'Rural Air Service', which includes flights to Bario. If you are flying on a Twin Otter plane you'll be asked to weigh yourself on giant scales while holding your carry-on.

Destinations in Sarawak from Miri include Kuching, Sibu, Bintulu, Bario, Limbang and Gunung Mulu National Park, and several smaller highland communities with MASwings. Further

ℹ GETTING TO BRUNEI: MIRI TO BANDAR SERI BEGAWAN (BSB)

Getting to the border The only company that's allowed to take passengers from Miri's Pujut Bus Terminal to destinations inside Brunei is **PHLS Express** (☑in Brunei +673 277 1668, in Miri 085-438301; www.phls38.com; Pujut Bus Terminal), which sends buses to BSB (RM65, three hours) via Kuala Belait (RM50) and Seria (RM50) at 8.15am and 3.45pm. Tickets are sold at the Bintang Jaya counter. Another option for travel between BSB and Miri is a private transfer (which may be shared with other travellers) run by Mr Ah Pau (RM70 per person, three hours). Call Ah Pau on 016-807 2893 (Malaysian mobile) or 866 8109 (Brunei mobile). Departures from Miri are generally at 9am or 10am but may be earlier; departures from BSB to Miri are usually at 1pm or 2pm.

At the border Border formalities are usually quick, and for most nationalities Bruneian visas are free, but the process can slow down buses. If you're eventually headed overland to Sabah, make sure you have enough pages in your passport for 10 new chops (stamps).

Moving on Brunei's Serasa Ferry Terminal, 20km northeast of BSB, is linked by ferry with Pulau Labuan, from where boats go to Kota Kinabalu in Sabah. Several buses a day go from BSB to Sarawak's Limbang Division and destinations in Sabah.

afield there are regular flights to Kuala Lumpur, Kota Kinabalu and Singapore.

BUS

Long-distance buses use the **Pujut Bus Terminal** (Jln Miri Bypass), about 4km northeast of the centre.

About once an hour, buses head to Kuching (RM80 to RM90, 12 to 14 hours, departures from 7.15am to 8.30pm) via the inland (old) Miri–Bintulu highway, with stops at Lambir Hills National Park, Batu Niah Junction (access point for Niah National Park; RM12, 1½ hours), Bintulu (RM25, 3½ hours) and Sibu (RM50, seven to eight hours). This route is highly competitive, and the spacious 'VIP' buses are worth the extra spend. Companies include **Bintang Jaya** (☑ Kuching 082-531133, Miri 085-432178; www.bintangjayaexpress.com) and Miri Transport Company.

Bintang Jaya also has services northeast to Limbang (RM45, four hours), Lawas (RM75, six hours) and Kota Kinabalu (KK; RM90, 10 hours). Buses leave Miri at 8.45am; departures from KK are at 7.30am. Borneo Express serves the same destinations at 7.45am; departures from KK are also at 7.45am. With both these companies, getting off in Brunei is not allowed.

ℹ Getting Around

TO/FROM THE AIRPORT

A taxi from the airport to the city centre (15 minutes, in traffic 25 minutes) costs RM26; a *kupon teksi* (taxi coupon) can be purchased at the taxi desk just outside the baggage-claim area (next to the car-rental desks). If you're heading from town to the airport, the fare is RM25. A Grab fare from the city to the airport is around RM15.

BUS

Local bus transport in Miri is handled by three companies: Miri City Bus, **Miri Transport Company** (MTC; ☑in Kuching 082-531161, in Miri 085-434161; www.mtcmiri.com; Pujut Bus Terminal) and Miri Belait Transport. The **local bus station** (Jln Padang), next to the Visitors Information Centre, has schedules posted. Fares start at RM1; most lines run from 7am to about 6pm.

Buses 20 and 33A link the local bus station with Pujut Bus Terminal (RM2 to RM3, hourly until 6.30pm).

CAR

Most of Miri's guesthouses are happy to organise private transport to area destinations such as Lambir Hills National Park (RM130 return) and Niah National Park (RM300 return).

Self-drive car rental begins at around RM120 per day. Note that the availability of rental cars can be surprisingly limited and booking ahead is recommended.

FT Car Rental (☑085-438415; www.ftcarrental. com; Terminal Bldg, Miri Airport, Jln Airport)

Golden System Car Rental (☑085-613359, WhatsApp 012-874 1200; www.gocar.com.my; counter 3, ground fl, Miri Airport, Jln Airport)

Hertz (☑ 085-614740; www.hertz.com; arrivals hall, Miri Airport, Jln Airport; ⊘8am-5pm Mon-Sat)

Kong Teck Car Rental (☑ 085-617767; www. kongteck.com.my; arrivals concourse, Miri Airport, Jln Airport)

My Homestay Motorcycle & Car Rental (☑085-429091; http://staymyhomestay. blogspot.com; Jln Merpati)

TAXI

Taxi ranks are sprinkled around the city centre: **Jln Padang**, **Jln South Yu Seng**, **Jln Brooke**. A short cab ride around downtown is RM15 to RM20, while a ride from the centre to the Pujut Bus Terminal costs RM25. Taxis run by the **Miri Taxi Association** (☏085-432277; ☺24hr) can be summoned by phone 24 hours a day. Grab is available around Miri and costs are usually around half of regular taxi fares.

NORTHEASTERN SARAWAK

Sarawak's rugged northeastern corner hides some of Borneo's best gems for adventurous travellers.

Gunung Mulu National Park

Also known as the Gunung Mulu World Heritage Area, this **park** (Gunung Mulu World Heritage Area; ☏085-792300; www.mulupark.com; 5-day pass adult/child RM30/10; ☺HQ office 8am-5pm) is one of the most majestic and thrilling nature destinations anywhere in Southeast Asia.

Few national parks anywhere in the world pack so many natural marvels into such a small area. Home to caves of mind-boggling proportions, other-worldly geological phenomena such as the Pinnacles, and brilliant old-growth tropical rainforest (the park has 17 vegetation zones), this is truly one of the world's wonders.

Among the remarkable features in the 529-sq-km park are its two highest peaks, Gunung Mulu (2376m) and Gunung Api (1710m). In between are rugged karst mountains, deep gorges with crystal-clear rivers, and a unique mosaic of habitats supporting fascinating and incredibly diverse wildlife. Gunung Mulu's most famous hiking attractions are the **Pinnacles**, a forest of razor-sharp limestone spires, and the **Headhunters' Trail**, an old tribal warpath down to Limbang.

◉ Sights & Activities

When you register at park HQ you'll receive a park map to help you plan your activities. HQ staff are generally helpful in planning itineraries and accommodating special interests.

The park's website and the brochures available at HQ have details of tours and activities. Note that some cave tours and treks may be booked out well in advance.

Mulu Discovery Centre   MUSEUM
(park HQ; ☺8am-6pm) FREE Offers a very accessible introduction to the park as a 'biodiversity hot spot' and to its extraordinary geology. Situated in the HQ building between the park office and Café Mulu (if it's raining you can pass through the cafe to the centre to avoid getting wet).

Mandara Spa   SPA
(☏085-792388; www.mandaraspa.com; Mulu Marriot Resort & Spa; 50/80min massage RM115/155; ☺10am-9pm) The spa and massage services at the Marriot (p458) are just the ticket, especially after exploring Mulu's adventure caves.

Activities Without Guides

Visitors are not allowed to go inside any of the caves without a qualified guide, but you can take a number of jungle walks unaccompanied so long as you inform the park office (or, when it's closed, someone across the path in the park security building). The trails are well marked and interconnected, so by using the park's map it's easy to join them up to create your own route.

Paku Valley Loop   WALKING
An 8km loop through the forest that runs alongside the Melinau River to the Paku Waterfall (3km), where it's possible to swim. The walk takes five to six hours at an easy pace. No guide is necessary.

Botanical Heritage Trail   WALKING
This easy 1.5km boardwalk loop has information panels on general plant evolution but not much information on the numerous fascinating plants it passes as it winds through the rainforest.

Tree Top Tower   BIRD-WATCHING
FREE The best times to spot feathered friends at this 30m-high bird hide are early morning (5am to 9am) or late afternoon and early evening (4pm to 8pm). Reserve a time slot and pick up the key (deposit RM50) at park HQ or, after 4.30pm, from park security (across the boardwalk from the park office). Situated about 500m from park HQ.

Guided Forest Walks

Garden of Eden Valley Walk   WALKING
(per person RM120; ☺9.30am-5pm) This memorable day hike takes you through 2km-long Deer Cave (p454) to a seemingly enchanted

enclosed valley. There's a certain amount of walking on bat guano, scrambling over slippery rocks and wading through streams (rubber shoes are best; sandals are not suitable), but emerging into lush green forest surrounded by limestone is a fine reward.

A jungle trail leads up to a waterfall and rock pools that are perfect for swimming. Since the only way into – and out of – the garden of Eden is through Deer Cave, you'll need to retrace your steps through the cave to the bat observatory, where the walk ends in time to watch the bat exodus at dusk.

The price includes a packed lunch and afternoon tea.

Night Walk
WALKING
(per person RM22; ⊙ 7pm or 7.30pm) This 1½- to two-hour walk wends its way through alluvial forest. Creatures you're likely to see – after the guide points them out – include tree frogs just 1cm long, enormous spiders, vine snakes that are a dead ringer for a vine, and stick insects (phasmids), extraordinary creatures up to 30cm long that look like they've been assembled from pencils and toothpicks.

If you put your torch (bring one!) up to eye level and shine it into the foliage, the eyes of spiders and other creatures will reflect brightly back. Don't wear insect repellent or you risk repelling some of the insects you're trying to see. Mosquitoes are not a problem.

If you order dinner at Café Mulu (p458) before heading out, you can pick it up when you return (make sure you're back before 9.30pm). Eateries outside the park stay open later.

You can take the night-walk trail on your own, without a guide, after 8pm – make sure you inform either the park office or, when it's closed, someone in the park-security pavilion. Between 5pm and 8pm you can design your own night walk by taking trails the guided group isn't using.

Mulu Canopy Skywalk
WALKING
(per person RM42; ⊙ 7am, 8.30am, 10am, 10.30am, 1pm & 2pm) Mulu's 480m-long skywalk, unforgettably anchored to a series of huge trees, has excellent signage and is one of the best in Southeast Asia. Often gets booked out early; for a specific time slot, reserve as soon as you've got your flight.

Climbing into the canopy is the only way to see what a tropical rainforest is all about, because most of the flora and fauna do their thing high in the trees, not down on the ground, where less than 2% of the forest's total sunlight is available. Your guide can help point out the nuances of the surrounding forest, including traditional medicine plants that are still gathered and used in the nearby Penan settlement.

Show Caves
Mulu's 'show caves' (the park's name for caves that can be visited without specialised training or equipment) are its most popular attraction and for good reason: they are, quite simply, awesome.

Deer Cave & Lang Cave
CAVE
(per person RM35; ⊙ tours 2pm & 2.30pm) A 3km walk through the rainforest takes you to these adjacent caverns. Deer Cave – over 2km long and 174m high – is the world's largest cave passage open to the public, while Lang Cave – more understated in its proportions – contains interesting stalactites and stalagmites. Be sure to stay on for the 'bat exodus' at dusk.

Deer Cave is home to 2 to 3 million bats, belonging to 12 species (more than in any other single cave in the world), who cling to the roof in a seething black mass as they gear up for their evening prowl. Every day between 4pm and 6pm (unless it's raining), millions of bats exit the cave in spiralling, twirling clouds that look a bit like swarms of cartoon bees. It's an awe-inspiring sight when viewed from the park's **bat observatory**, a kind of amphitheatre outside the cave. The bats' corkscrew trajectory is designed to foil the dinner plans of bat hawks perched on the surrounding cliffs.

The record is silent on who did the calculations or how, but it's said that Deer Cave's bats devour 30 tons of mosquitoes every night. If it's raining the bats usually stay home because echolocation (the way they find prey) is not very good at homing in on flying insects amid an onslaught of raindrops.

Count on getting back to park HQ at around 7pm; bring a torch for the walk back.

Wind Cave & Clearwater Cave
CAVE
(per person incl boat ride RM67; ⊙ tours 8.45am & 9.15am) Wind Cave, named for the cool breezes blowing through it, has several chambers, including the cathedral-like King's Chamber, filled with dreamlike forests of stalagmites and columns. There's a sweaty 200-step climb up to Clearwater Cave and the subterranean river there. The cave itself is vast: more than 200km of passages have been surveyed so far.

ADVENTURE CAVES

Cave routes that require special equipment and a degree of caving (spelunking) experience are known here as 'adventure caves'. Rosters for the seven half- or full-day options fill up early, so reserve well ahead. Groups are limited to eight participants. Heavy rains can cause caves to flood.

Caving routes are graded beginner, intermediate and advanced; guides determine each visitor's suitability based on their previous caving experience. If you have no background in spelunking, you will be required to do an intermediate route before moving on to an advanced one. Minimum ages are 12 for intermediate and 16 for advanced. Fees include a helmet and a headlamp; bring closed shoes, a first-aid kit and clothes you won't mind getting dirty.

Keep in mind that adventure caving is not for everyone, and halfway into a cave passage is not the best time to discover that you suffer from claustrophobia, fear the dark or simply don't like slithering in the mud with all sorts of unknown creepy-crawlies.

Sarawak Chamber (per person RM310; ⊙6.30am) A demanding 10- to 15-hour adventure.

Clearwater Connection (per person RM225) Six hours, including underground rivers and scrambling; for more experienced cavers.

Racer Cave (per person RM165) Climbing and rope sections; for intermediate cavers.

After visiting the caves you can take a dip in the refreshing waters of a sandy swimming spot.

Tours include a stop at the riverside village of **Batu Bungan**, a Penan settlement set up by the government as part of a campaign to discourage their nomadic lifestyle. Locals sell trinkets and handicrafts.

The cave tour takes about four hours, leaving time for another cave visit in the afternoon.

Langang Cave   CAVE
(per person incl boat RM65; ⊙tour 2pm) Langang Cave can be visited on the park's Fast Lane tour, which passes extraordinary stalactites and stalagmites. Keep an eye out for blue racer snakes and the fibrous mineral formation 'moonmilk' – known to scientists as Lublinite – which is created when bacteria break down calcite, the main component of limestone. Don't touch it – it's very fragile.

Getting to the cave requires a 20-minute boat ride followed by a 1km walk to the cave entrance. The whole tour lasts three hours.

Trekking & Climbing
Mulu offers some of the best and most accessible jungle trekking in Borneo. The forest here is in excellent condition and there are routes for every level of fitness and skill.

Expect rain, leeches, slippery and treacherous conditions, and a very hot workout – carry lots of water. Guides are required for overnights. Book well ahead, and bring a first-aid kit and a torch.

Pinnacles   TREKKING
(per person RM423; ⊙3-day treks Tue-Thu & Fri-Sun) An incredible formation of 45m-high stone spires, the Pinnacles protrudes from the forested flanks of Gunung Api. Getting there involves a boat ride and, between two overnights at the park's camp 5 (p457), an unrelentingly steep 2.4km ascent. Coming down is just as taxing, so by the time you stagger back to camp, the cool, clear river may look pretty enticing.

Bring shoes that will give you traction on sharp and slippery rocks, and bedding (many people find that a sleeping-bag liner or sarong is sufficient). If you book the tour through the park, you'll also need to bring enough food for six meals; it's worth buying supplies in Miri, as the park shop sells only a limited selection of instant noodles and canned food. You can buy a packed lunch from the park cafe for the first day, and it may be possible to buy fried rice (RM10) from staff at camp 5, but don't count on it.

On the way to camp 5 on day one you can stop off at Wind Cave and Clearwater Cave for a fee of RM30 (if you don't want to see the caves and you're in a group with others who do, you'll need to wait for them). From the boat drop-off point it's an 8km hike to camp 5 along an easy trail (though be prepared for leeches).

Since both nights are spent at camp 5, you only need to carry a day pack on the Pinnacles climb on day two, but be sure to bring plenty of water – at least 2L – in two separate containers (one bottle will be left halfway up to pick up on the way down), as well as snacks and oral rehydration salts. If it's raining heavily, the guide may deem it necessary to cancel the climb, in which case you will be refunded RM80.

Right from the get-go the trail up to the Pinnacles is steep and rocky. There's plenty of clambering on all fours, and the rocks are sharp. The final 400m section involves some serious climbing and use of ladders – most of them little more than spaced-out metal brackets drilled into the rock, requiring a steady nerve and good balance to avoid falling onto the spikes below. The Pinnacles themselves are only visible from the very top. Factoring in the humidity, the climb is an intense experience, but most people find it rewarding. What's more, the trail passes through some gorgeous jungle and there are beautiful views of the valley below – if you dare look up from the track to admire them.

It's possible to continue along the Headhunters' Trail on day three instead of returning to HQ.

Gunung Mulu Summit   TREKKING

(per person for 3-8 people RM650) The climb to the summit of Gunung Mulu (2376m) – described by one satisfied ascendee as 'gruelling' and, near the top, 'treacherous' – is a classic Borneo adventure. If you're very fit and looking for a challenge, this 24km, three-day, four-night trek may be for you. The climb must be booked at least a month ahead.

Bring proper hiking shoes, a sleeping bag (Camp 4 can get quite chilly, often dropping below 15ºC), a sleeping pad (unless you don't mind sleeping on wooden boards), rain gear and enough food for four days. The camps along the way have very basic cooking equipment, including a gas stove. Bring water-purification tablets if you're wary of drinking the rainwater collected at shelters en route.

Near the summit you may spend much of your time inside clouds; a fleece jacket is the best way to ward off the damp and cold.

GUIDES, RESERVATIONS & FEES

For almost all of the caves, walks and treks in Gunung Mulu National Park, visitors must be accompanied by a guide licensed by Sarawak Forestry; guides are generally supplied by the park or an adventure-tour agency (such as those based in Kuching, Miri or Limbang). Tours and activities booked directly through the park are cheaper and are often booked up well in advance; agencies charge considerably more but also supply extras, such as meals, and can often offer more flexibility when it comes to advance booking.

If you've got your heart set on adventure caving, or on trekking to the Pinnacles or up to the summit of Gunung Mulu, advance reservations – by phone or email (enquiries@ mulupark.com) – are a must. They're doubly important if you're coming in July, August or September, when some routes are booked out several months ahead, and they're essential if your travel dates are not flexible. If this is your situation, don't buy your air tickets until your trek or caving dates are confirmed.

That's not to say a last-minute trip to Mulu is impossible. The park may be able to reassign guides to accommodate you, so it's worth getting in touch. And if you can spend a week or so hanging out at the park (this usually means staying in a basic guesthouse outside the park's boundaries, as in-park accommodation is in very short supply), trekking and caving slots do sometimes open up.

The park's own trekking and caving guides are well trained and speak good English, but there are only about 15 of them. Some travellers hire a freelance guide unattached to a tour agency, usually from a nearby village. Despite being licensed by Sarawak Forestry (they wouldn't be allowed to operate in the park if they weren't), such guides' nature knowledge and English skills vary widely, from excellent to barely sufficient. In addition, they may lack safety training and equipment (such as two-way radios, which the park supplies to all of its own guides) and, perhaps most importantly, are unlikely to have proper insurance, a factor that could be crucial if a helicopter evacuation is necessary.

A caving group must consist of at least four participants (including the guide) so that if someone is injured, one person can stay with them and the other two can head out of the cave together to seek help.

Park prices for caving and treks are on a straight per-person basis (minimum three people).

Trekkers report having been visited by rats at Camp 3 and by squirrels who were 'keen on noodles' at Camp 4. The steep trail – which is slippery when wet – passes through limestone and sandstone forest. Fauna you might see on the way include gibbons, wild boar and (possibly) sun bears.

Reaching the summit involves leaving Camp 4 at 3am to arrive at the top in time to see the spectacular sunrise.

Headhunters' Trail
TREKKING

The physically undemanding Headhunters' Trail runs from the park's camp 5 for 11km in the direction of Limbang and is an overland alternative to flying in or out of Mulu. The park does not offer guided trips along this trail, but several private tour operators do, and it's also (theoretically) possible to trek it without a guide.

This backdoor route from Mulu to Limbang takes two days and one night and can be done in either direction, although most people start at the park. After climbing the Pinnacles (p455), it's possible to walk the Headhunters' Trail (unguided) on day three instead of returning to park HQ.

From camp 5, the Headhunters' Trail runs through the forest to Kuala Terikan, from where you'll need to take a boat to Medamit, linked by road with Limbang. If you plan to do this trip without a guide, you must arrange road and river transport ahead of time – Borneo Touch Ecotour (p466) can organise a boat and van in either direction for about RM500. If you're starting in Limbang, remember to contact the park to reserve sleeping space at camp 5.

The route is named after the Kayan war parties that used to make their way up the Sungai Melinau from the Baram area to the Melinau Gorge, then dragged their canoes overland to the Sungai Terikan to raid the peoples of the Limbang region. New roads mean that the trail is no longer much used, making it more likely that you'll spot wildlife along the way.

🛏 Sleeping

Accommodation options range from five-star luxury to extremely basic digs. Camping is not permitted at park HQ (p453), but you can pitch a tent at some of the guesthouses outside the park. If you find that accommodation within the park is fully booked, don't panic. There's always a bed of some kind available at one of the informal homestays just outside the park gates.

🛏 Inside the National Park

Park HQ, a lovely spot set amid rainforest and tropical gardens, has 24-hour electricity and tap water that's safe to drink. All private rooms have attached bathrooms. Rooms can be cancelled up to 48 hours ahead without penalty, which is why space sometimes opens up late in the game; phone for last-minute availability.

Hostel
HOSTEL $

(☑ 085-792300; www.mulupark.com; dm incl breakfast RM50) All 20 beds are in a clean, spacious dormitory-style room with ceiling fans.

★ Garden Bungalows
BUNGALOW $$

(☑ 085-792300; www.mulupark.com; s/d/tr incl breakfast RM255/304/344; ❄ 🛜) These eight spacious units, the park's most luxurious accommodation, are light and modern and have their own private verandahs.

Longhouse Rooms
GUESTHOUSE $$

(☑ 085-792300; www.mulupark.com; d/tr/q incl breakfast RM225/278/320; ❄) There are eight of these rooms across two wooden buildings. Rooms in Longhouse 1 have a double bed and three singles, while Longhouse 2 features four single beds per room.

Camp 5
HUT $$

(☑ park HQ 085-792300; www.mulupark.com; per person incl boat ride RM204) This basic wooden 'forest hostel' or large hut is divided into four dorms with sleeping platforms and mats, a kitchen (with gas for cooking and boiled water for drinking) and bathrooms with showers. Space is limited to 50 people; reserve at the park office. Most people find it's warm enough here without a sleeping bag (a sarong will do).

If you're doing the Pinnacles or Headhunters' Trail treks you'll spend a night at camp 5 whether you book through the park or a tour operator; the tariff will already be included in your fee.

🛏 Outside the National Park

Several budget places, unaffiliated with the park, are located just across the bridge from park HQ, along the banks of the Melinau River. Reservations are not necessary, so if you don't mind very basic accommodation you can fly up without worrying about room availability.

Mulu Village
HOMESTAY $

(☑ WhatsApp 017-743 4763; www.facebook.com/
muluvillage; s/d incl breakfast RM 50/100) Located
around 3km from the park entrance, well-
run Mulu Village has basic but decent accommodation, and offers a big list of services
and excursions. Bike hire is RM5 per day,
and friendly owners Brenda and James can
arrange trekking, jungle-cooking classes and
longhouse visits. Information and assistance
on tackling the Pinnacles (p455) and the
Headhunters' Trail (p457) are also available.

Mulu River Lodge
HOSTEL $

(Edward Nyipa Homestay; ☑ 012-852 7471; dm/d/q
incl breakfast RM35/70/140) Has 30 beds, most
in a giant, non-bunk dorm room equipped
with clean showers and toilets at one end.
Electricity flows from 5pm to midnight. It's
one of the few guesthouses outside the park,
if not the only one, with a proper septic system. Just a two-minute walk from park HQ,
its Sweetwater restaurant supplies simple
meals and beer.

D'Cave Homestay
HOMESTAY $

(☑ Dina/WhatsApp 012-872 9752; www.facebook.
com/DCaveMuluNationalPark; incl breakfast dm
RM35, d without bathroom RM80) A very friendly,
rather ramshackle place with beds crammed
into small rooms and basic, outdoor bathrooms. Owner Dina cooks buffet-style lunches
(RM15) and dinners (RM18), and her partner
Robert is a licensed guide. There's always
boiled water for water-bottle refills. Situated
between the airport and the turning for the
park – about a 10-minute walk from each.

Mulu Backpackers
GUESTHOUSE $

(☑ Helen 011-1407 5006, Peter 011-3524 1007;
mulubackpackers@gmail.com; dm/d incl breakfast
RM35/80) Mulu Backpackers, situated just
past the airport, occupies a picturesque spot
by the river but is a 15-minute walk from the
park. There's a pleasant, sheltered outdoor
dining area with views of the water and
electricity from 6pm to 6am. The 11 beds
are arranged in a large, barn-like space with
randomly positioned partition walls.

Rainforest Lodge
CABIN $$

(☑ 085-792300; www.mulupark.com; s/d incl
breakfast RM268/312; ❄) Expanded and new-
ly built throughout 2017 and 2018, Mulu's
Rainforest Lodge offers a variety of config-
urations, including some family rooms with
two single beds and a double bed. Bath-
rooms are spacious and light; the private
balconies are best enjoyed at dusk.

Mulu Marriott Resort & Spa
RESORT $$$

(☑ 085-792388; www.marriott.com; d/ste incl
breakfast from RM485/890; ❄ 🗚 🗐 🗐) Situated
3km from park HQ, this 101-room complex
has been designed and decorated in a way
that is both stylish and sympathetic to its
jungle surroundings. Rooms come with all
the amenities you would expect from a five-
star resort and have balconies overlooking
the forest or river.

The Balinese-style swimming pool is a real
draw after a sweaty day of caving and hiking. The resort also has its own jetty for river
trips that bypass park HQ and go straight to
the caves (trips are booked through the hotel
for much more than the park tours). Wi-fi is
available in the bar area only.

🍴 Eating

A handful of tiny shops sells a very limited
selection of food items, such as instant noodles. Most food is flown in, which explains
why prices are slightly higher than on
the coast.

Cooking is not allowed at any park
accommodation except Camps 1, 3, 4 and 5.

Good Luck Cave'fe Mulu
MALAYSIAN $

(mains RM8-12; ⏲ 11.30am-3pm & 5pm-midnight,
kitchen closes 9.15pm) The Good Luck 'Cave'fe'
Mulu (geddit?) is located right outside the
park gates and stays open later than the
park cafe, making it a good dinner option
if you come back late from a night walk.
Serves noodle and fried-rice dishes. A beer
costs RM9. Also good for transport to the
airport (RM5).

Café Mulu
INTERNATIONAL $$

(mains RM12-21; ⏲ 7.30am-8.30pm) This cafe-
restaurant serves excellent breakfasts (eggs,
pancakes, muesli), and lunch and dinner
with a few Western items, Indian curries
and local dishes including Mulu laksa and
umai (Sarawak sushi). A beer costs RM13
and wine is available. Staff are happy to
prepare packed lunches. The nasi goreng
mamak (spicy fried rice) really goes down a
treat after a day's adventuring.

ℹ Information

For sums over RM100, the park accepts Visa
and MasterCard. In the past, staff could do cash
withdrawals of RM100 to RM300 (one trans-
action per day) for a 2% fee, but at the time of
writing this service was not available.

As there's no ATM in Mulu it's vital to bring
enough cash to cover your expenses.

The shop and cafe area at park HQ has an excruciatingly slow and unreliable wi-fi connection (RM5 per day).

The clinic in the nearby village of Batu Bungan is staffed by a doctor and has a dispensary.

❶ Getting There & Away

Unless you hike in via the Headhunters' Trail, the only way to get to Mulu is by **MASwings** (☎085-206900; www.maswings.com.my; ground fl, Mulu Airport; ☉8.30am-5pm) plane. From July to September, book a few weeks ahead if possible.

MASwings flies 68-seat ATR 72-500 turboprops to Miri (10.15am and 2.40pm daily), Kuching (1.10pm Monday, Wednesday, Thursday and Saturday; 2.15pm Tuesday, Friday and Sunday) and Kota Kinabalu (2.40pm Monday, Tuesday, Wednesday, Thursday, Saturday and Sunday, via Miri; 12.25pm Tuesday, Friday and Sunday).

❶ Getting Around

Park HQ is a walkable 1.5km from the airport. Minibuses and SUVs run by **Melinau Transportation** (☎012-871 1372, 012-852 6065; per person RM5) and other minibuses meet incoming flights at the airport; transport to park HQ and the adjacent guesthouses costs RM5 per person.

It's possible to hire local longboats for excursions to destinations such as the government-built Penan longhouse village of Long Iman (RM95 per person return, minimum three people) and the nearby Ba Desai Waterfall swimming spot, 40 minutes away by river.

Kelabit Highlands

☎085

Nestled in Sarawak's remote northeastern corner, the mountains and rainforests of the Kelabit (keh-*lah*-bit) Highlands are sandwiched between Gunung Mulu National Park and the Indonesian state of East Kalimantan. The area is home to the Kelabits, an Orang Ulu group who number only about 6500. Also here are the Penan people, a seminomadic group whose members have not fared well in modern Malaysia as their traditional forest lands have been cleared away from under them.

The main activity here, other than enjoying the clean, cool mountain air, is hiking from longhouse to longhouse on old forest trails to witness and experience traditional lifestyles and meet the locals. Unfortunately, logging roads are continuously encroaching and swaths of the highlands' primary forest have already succumbed to the chainsaw.

Bario

POP 1200

The 'capital' of the highlands, Bario consists of about a dozen 'villages' – each with its own church – spread over a beautiful valley, much of it given over to growing the renowned local rice. Some of the appeal lies in the mountain climate (the valley is 1500m above sea level) and the splendid isolation (the only access is by air and torturous 4WD track), but above all it's the hospitality of the Kelabit people that will win you over. Travellers can find themselves extending their stays in Bario by days, weeks or more. Since late 2017 Bario has had 24-hour electricity courtesy of a new solar-energy farm.

Before the Konfrontasi, Bario consisted of only one small longhouse, but in 1963 residents of longhouses near the frontier fled raids by Indonesian troops and settled here for safety, and the community has slowly expanded ever since.

◉ Sights & Activities

The Bario area offers plenty of opportunities for jungle exploration even if you're not a hardcore hiker. The nearby forests are a great place to spot pitcher plants, butterflies and even hornbills – and are an excellent place for tiger leeches to spot you. Most guesthouses are happy to pack picnic lunches. The fee for a local guide is RM150 per day.

Bario Asal Longhouse　　　　HOUSE
(RM5) This all-wood, 22-door longhouse has the traditional Kelabit layout. On the *dapur* (enclosed front verandah) each family has a hearth, while on the other side of the family units is the *tawa'*, a wide back verandah – essentially an enclosed hall over 100m long – used for weddings, funerals and celebrations, and decorated with historical family photos.

A few of the older residents still have earlobes that hang almost down to their shoulders, created by a lifetime of wearing heavy brass earrings. If you'd like a picture, it's good form to chat with them (they may offer you something to drink) and only then ask if they'd be willing to be photographed. Afterwards you might want to leave a small tip.

Bario Asal has 24-hour electricity (evenings only during dry spells) thanks to a microhydro project salvaged from a larger government-funded project that functioned for just 45 minutes after it was switched on in 1999 (it had been designed to operate on a much bigger river).

Junglebluesdream Art Gallery GALLERY
(☑ WhatsApp 019-8901797; www.junglebluesdream.
weebly.com; Ulung Palang longhouse; ⊙ 9am-6pm)
Many of artist Stephen Baya's paintings
have traditional Kelabit motifs. In April
2013 his colourful illustrations of the Kelabit
legend of Tuked Rini were featured at the
Museum of Archaeology and Anthropology
in Cambridge, England. Stephen also works
from here in his studio.

Community House CULTURAL CENTRE
This handsome multilevel wooden building – topped with a colourful carved hornbill – is used as the focus for the Bario Food &
Cultural Festival. Throughout the rest of the
year there are occasional displays and photographic exhibitions about Kelabit culture.

Tom Harrisson Monument MEMORIAL
Shaped like a *sapé* (a traditional stringed
instrument), this stainless-steel monument
commemorates the March 1945 parachute
drop into Bario by British and Australian
troops under the command of Major Tom
Harrisson. Their goal – achieved with great
success – was to enlist the help of locals to
fight the Japanese. The statue is across the
first bridge heading west from the airport.

After the war Harrisson stayed on in Borneo and was curator of the Sarawak Museum
(p400) from 1947 to 1966. During this time,
he and his wife Barbara began excavating
the Niah caves, leading to the discovery of
a 40,000-year-old human skull. For the life
story of this colourful and controversial
character, see *The Most Offending Soul
Alive*, a biography by Judith M Heimann.

Kayaking KAYAKING
(☑ text messages or WhatsApp 019-807 1640;
roachas@hotmail.com; per kayak from RM60, guide
& transport from RM200) A typical day trip with
guide Stu Roach involves a morning paddle upriver in inflatable kayaks, a barbecue
lunch on a sandy river beach and an easy
return trip downstream in the afternoon.
Transport to the start point close to Pa Umur
village is included. Can also arrange camping trips in hammocks or tents. Advance
booking preferred.

Prayer Mountain HIKING
From Bario Asal Longhouse (p459) it's a
steep, slippery, two-hour ascent up to the
summit of Prayer Mountain, which has
a cross erected in 1973, thickets of pitcher
plants and amazing views of the Bario valley
and of the mixed Penan and Kelabit hamlet

of Arur Dalan, with its three defunct wind
turbines. Two-thirds of the way up is an
extremely rustic church.

At the base is a multidenominational
prayer house.

🎉 Festivals & Events

Bario Food & Cultural Festival FOOD & DRINK
(Pesta Nukenen Bario; www.facebook.com/pages/
bariofoodfestival; ⊙ Jul/Aug) Visitors flock to
Bario for this three-day festival celebrating traditional Kelabit food cultivation and
cooking techniques. Delicacies on offer
include plump wiggling grubs known as
kelatang, river snails (*akep*), wild spinach,
asparagus, ginger and plenty of Bario pineapples. Music, dance and art are also important aspects of the festival. Flights and
accommodation are full to capacity; book
ahead if possible.

🛏 Sleeping

Bario's various component villages are home
to 19 guesthouses. Air-con isn't necessary
up here, and almost all rooms have shared
bathroom facilities.

There is usually no need to book ahead as
there's ample availability.

🛏 Bario

Libal Paradise GUESTHOUSE $
(☑ WhatsApp 019-807 1640; roachas@hotmail.com;
per person incl meals RM90) 🌿 Surrounded by
a verdant fruit and vegetable garden where
you can pick your own pineapples, this sus-
tainably run farm offers accommodation in
two neat wooden cabins, each occupying its
own idyllic spot in the greenery. From the
airport terminal, walk east along the road
that parallels the runway. Prefers text mes-
saging to email for contact.

Nancy & Harriss GUESTHOUSE $
(Hill View Lodge; ☑ 019-858 5850; nancyharriss@
yahoo.com; per person incl meals RM80) This
rambling place has seven guest rooms,
a lovely verandah, a library-equipped
lounge and endearingly tacky floor cov-
erings. Situated 250m along a dirt track
south of the main road. Prices include airport transfer.

**★ Labang Longhouse
Guesthouse** GUESTHOUSE $$
(☑ WhatsApp 019-815 5453; www.labanglonghouse.
com; per person incl meals RM120) This 16-room,
longhouse-style guesthouse with valley

DON'T MISS

BARIO'S MYSTERIOUS MEGALITHS

Hidden deep in the jungle around Bario are scores of mysterious megaliths. The **Cultured Rainforest Project** (www.arch.cam.ac.uk/research/projects/crp-home1) involved a study of these sites as part of an investigation into how the people of the area interact with the rainforest.

The Kelabits believe in marking the landscape in order to establish rights over it, and these sites are viewed as spiritually significant. The markers include *perupan* (large mounds made from thousands of stones from the riverbed), believed to have been built by rich men and women without heirs to bury their possessions and avoid fights breaking out over inheritance.

Pa' Umor From Bario it's a 1½-hour walk to Pa' Umor, and another 15 minutes to Arur Bilit Farm, home to **Batu Narit**, an impressive stone carving featuring a human in a spread-eagled position among its designs.

Take the log bridge across the small river to reach **Batu Ipak**. According to legend, this stone formation was created when an angry warrior named Upai Semering pulled out his *parang* (machete) and took a wrathful swing at the rock, cutting it in two.

This circuit should take four or five hours – maybe a tad longer if your guide is a good storyteller.

Pa' Lungan The trail from Bario to Pa' Lungan is walkable without a guide. About halfway along you'll see **Batu Arit**, a large stone featuring bird carvings and humanoid figures with heart-shaped faces.

At Pa' Lungan is **Batu Ritung**, a 2m stone table (probably a burial site, although no one is sure). Also near Pa' Lungan is **Perupun**, a huge pile of stones of a type assembled to bury the valuables of the dead who had no descendants to receive their belongings.

If you've got a bit more time, you could consider basing yourself for a day or two in Pa' Lungan, believed by many to produce the very best Bario rice.

views is full of evocative photographs, each with a story that owners Lucy and David Labang will happily relate. Look forward to excellent food on the shared verandah and the opportunity to learn about the history and culture of the Kelabit Highlands. Lian, Lucy and David's friendly son, picks up guests at the airport.

Tarawe Lodge   GUESTHOUSE **$$**
(☑ Lian/WhatsApp 013-845 1213; liantarawe@ yahoo.com; per person with/without meals RM50/110, self-contained cottages RM180) Located near Bario's police station, Tarawe Lodge is run by the friendly Lian Tarawe. Accommodation includes a shared long-house room, double rooms and a simple garden cottage with two single beds and a compact kitchen. A larger inside kitchen can be used by all guests, and Lian is a very experienced guide who can arrange various treks around the region.

Junglebluesdream   GUESTHOUSE **$$**
(☑ WhatsApp 019-890 1797; www.jungleblues dream.weebly.com; Ulung Palang Longhouse; per person incl meals RM100) Owned by artist and

one-time guide Stephen Baya, a Bario native, and his friendly Danish wife, Tine, this super-welcoming lodge (and art gallery) has four mural-decorated rooms, good-quality beds and quilts, a library of books on local culture and wildlife, and fantastic Kelabit food. Guests can consult Stephen's extraordinary hand-drawn town and trekking maps. Free airport pick-up.

Tuan Guesthouse   GUESTHOUSE **$$**
(☑ WhatsApp 019-486 9141; anndrew@pacificwest. com; Bario Asal Longhouse; per person incl meals RM120) Something different for Bario, Tuan Guesthouse features five rooms adjacent to the Bario Asal Longhouse. Spacious bathrooms are shared, there's a modern kitchen, and the lounge room has high cathedral ceilings and stylish, cosmopolitan decor. A deck offers excellent rice-paddy views. Welcoming host Andrew has returned to Bario to retire after working in the oil and gas industry.

Bario Valley Homestay   HOMESTAY **$$**
(☑ Bulan/WhatsApp 019-467 4112; bariovalley homestay@gmail.com; Bario Asal Longhouse; per person incl meals RM120) Located in the

Bario Asal Longhouse (p459), Bario Valley Homestay is run by the very friendly Bulan. Expect excellent food, a personally guided visit of the longhouse, and the opportunity to explore the region. Day tours include a visit to a nearby eco-farm and waterfall, and the chance to collect wild forest vegetables.

Bario Asal Longhouse HOMESTAY $$

(✔ WhatsApp 011-2508 1114; www.facebook.com/SinahRangHomestayAndHandicraft; per person incl meals RM90) There are various homestays in this traditional longhouse, including a six-room guesthouse at **Sinah Rang Lemulun**. Staying at Bario Asal – which is home to 22 families – is a great way to experience longhouse living. Also available here are various 'farmstay' packages offering different rural experiences. Airport transfers are RM30.

Ngimat Ayu's House GUESTHOUSE $$

(✔ WhatsApp 013-840 6187; engimat_scott@yahoo.com; per person incl meals RM125) This spacious, two-storey family home has five comfortable rooms and paddy-field views from its broad verandahs. Situated on a slope 200m east of the yellow public library. Rates include airport transfer. Bikes are for rent from friendly owner Scott.

🛏 Pa'Lungan

Batu Ritung Lodge GUESTHOUSE $

(✔ WhatsApp 019-805 2119; www.baturitunglodge.blogspot.my; per person incl meals RM90) 'Aunty' Saupang is a welcoming host at her two-storey wooden lodge built on stilts over a pond, with views of the mountains and paddy fields beyond. Plenty of space for larger groups. Meals are cooked using fresh jungle produce. She's often staying with family in Kuching but with at least a week's notice is happy to return to Pa' Lungan.

HIRING A GUIDE: THE PRACTICALITIES

With very few exceptions, the only way to explore the Kelabit Highlands is to hire a local guide. Fortunately, this could hardly be easier. Any of the guesthouses in Bario can organise a wide variety of short walks and longer treks led by guides they know and rely on. Some of the best guides for longer treks live in Pa' Lungan, an easy walk from Bario. If you link up with other travellers in Bario or Miri, the cost of a guide can be shared.

Although there's a growing shortage of guides, in general it's no problem to just turn up in Bario and make arrangements after you arrive, especially if you don't mind hanging out for a day or two in Bario. If you're in a hurry, though, or your trip coincides with the prime tourism months of July and August, consider making arrangements with your guesthouse or guide in advance by email or phone.

The going rate for guides is around RM150 per day for either a Bario-based day trip or a longer trek. Some itineraries involve either river trips (highly recommended if the water is high enough) or travel by 4WD – naturally, these significantly increase the cost. The going rate for a porter is around RM120 a day, usually a mandatory inclusion in case a lead guide gets injured or sick.

If you're connecting the dots between rural longhouses, expect to pay around RM90 for a night's sleep plus three meals (you can opt out of lunch and save around RM15). Gifts are not obligatory, but the people who live in remote longhouses are appreciative if, after you drink tea or coffee with them, you offer RM15 to cover the costs.

If your route requires that you camp in the forest, expect to pay approximately RM120 per night; in addition, you may be asked to supply food, which is provided for both you and your guide when you stay in a longhouse. Equipment for jungle camping (eg sleeping bag, hammock, mozzie net and bed roll) cannot be purchased in Bario, so it's a good idea to bring your own, though Bario Asal Longhouse may be able to rent it out.

If you're trekking in one direction only (eg Bario to Ba Kelalan), you will need to hire a porter and continue paying the guide and porter's fee while they return home through the jungle (in this scenario, it would take them two days to trek from Ba Kelalan back to Bario). This is so that the guide does not have to spend a night alone in the forest.

Detailed topographical maps of Sarawak exist, but it's nearly impossible to get hold of them.

David & Jenni Homestay

HOMESTAY $

(☑ WhatsApp 019-844 7814; per person incl meals RM90) Operated by experienced guide David Atu and his wife Jenni, this basic but comfortable lodge has five rooms and a verandah that's perfect for watching Pa'Lungan's passing traffic of water buffaloes.

✕ Eating & Drinking

Most guesthouses offer full board – almost always tasty local cuisine – but Bario also has several modest eateries. Pasar Bario, the town's yellow-painted commercial centre, is home to a few basic cafes selling mainly generic fried noodle and rice dishes, though Kelabit food can sometimes be special ordered.

Finding a beer in Bario can be a bit of a challenge. This is a very evangelical town – you're as likely to hear Christian country music as the sound of the *sapé* (traditional stringed instrument) – so most establishments do not serve alcohol, and those that do keep it hidden. Please be discreet.

🛍 Shopping

Persutuan Ibu Tunggal

ARTS & CRAFTS

(⊙ 8am-5pm Mon-Sat) Profits from this cafe and arts-and-crafts shop support single-mother families in the Kelabit Highlands. It's a good place for coffee and cake and to buy local handicrafts and tasty food items. Don't leave town without picking up a jar of *jem nanas* (pineapple jam). Also has mountain bikes available for rent.

Nearby cafes and food stalls are good for a simple lunch or dinner.

Renai Cafe

FOOD & DRINKS

(⊙ 9am-8pm) A general store with packaged noodles, drinks and some grocery items.

ℹ Information

INTERNET ACCESS

Wi-fi is limited to community access at **Pusat Internet** (Wifi Komuniti; registration RM5; ⊙ 8am-5pm). As most guesthouse owners use WhatsApp over the internet for communication, getting responses from them can take a few days.

MEDICAL SERVICES

Klinik Kesihatan Bario (☑ 085-786404, out-of-hours emergencies 013-837 1996; ⊙ 8am-1pm & 2-5pm Mon-Thu, 8-11.45am & 2.15-5pm Fri, emergency 24hr) Located at the Airport Rd intersection, Bario's innovative, ecologically sustainable rural health clinic, powered by solar energy, has one doctor, two paramedics, a dispensary (small pharmacy), and a helicopter on standby.

MONEY

At research time there were no banks, ATMs or credit-card facilities in the Kelabit Highlands, so bring plenty of small-denomination banknotes for accommodation, food and guides, plus some extra in case you get stranded.

TELEPHONE

The only Malaysian mobile-phone company to have up here is Celcom and even that is limited to voice and text services.

USEFUL WEBSITES

The Bario Experience (www.barioexperience.com) is kept (mainly) up-to-date with the latest info on Bario.

ℹ Getting There & Away

AIR

Bario Airport (☑ 013-835 9009) is linked with Miri twice a day by Twin Otters operated by MASwings (p608). Weather, especially high winds, sometimes causes delays and cancellations. For flight updates, or if you're having a problem making a flight out of Bario, just ring the friendly staff at the airport. MASwings also has one flight a week (on Thursday) to/from Ba Kelalan.

Twin Otters have strict weight limits – so much so that checked baggage is limited to 10kg and hand luggage to 5kg; passengers themselves are weighed on a giant scale along with their hand luggage when they check in.

The airport is about a 30-minute walk south of the shophouses, but you're bound to be offered a lift on arrival. As you'll notice, the people of Bario treat the air link to Miri almost like their own private airline and love dropping by to meet flights and hang out with arriving or departing friends.

4WD

The overland trip between Bario and Miri, possible only by 4WD (around RM150 per person), takes 12 hours at the very least and sometimes a lot more, the determining factors being the weather and the condition of the rough logging roads and their old wooden bridges. When things get ugly, vehicles travel in convoy so that when one gets stuck the others can push or winch it out. Don't say you weren't warned.

ℹ Getting Around

In Bario 4WD vehicles can be hired for around RM300 a day including driver and petrol; guesthouses can make arrangements.

SALT, RICE & PINEAPPLES

One of Bario's celebrated local ingredients is salt, produced at the **main tudtu** under an hour's walk from Pa' Umor. Mineral-rich saline water is put in giant vats over a roaring fire until all that's left is high-iodine salt that goes perfectly with local specialities such as deer and wild boar. This traditional production technique is beginning to die out, but in Bario you can still purchase salt made the old way – look for a sausage-shaped 20cm-long leaf (RM20).

Bario is famous throughout Malaysia for two other cooking ingredients: Bario rice, whose grains are smaller and more aromatic than lowland varieties, and sweeter-than-sweet pineapples, which are free of the pucker-inducing acidity of their coastal cousins. Outside the Kelabit Highlands, 1kg of Bario rice can cost RM18, and Bario pineapples are usually unavailable at any price.

Motorbikes (RM70 per day) can be rented from Bario Valley Homestay (p461).

Mountain bikes can be hired at guesthouses, in **Arur Dalan village** (☑ 011-1937 8337; Arur Dalan; per day RM35), and in Bario town for RM35 per day. The terrain around Bario's component villages is largely flat and a bike is a good way to get around.

Trekking in the Kelabit Highlands

The temperate highlands along Sarawak's far eastern border with Indonesia offer some of the best jungle trekking in Borneo, taking in farming villages, rugged peaks and supremely remote Kenyah, Penan and Kelabit settlements. Most trails traverse a variety of primary and secondary forest, as well as an increasing number of logged areas. Treks from Bario range from easy overnight excursions to nearby longhouses to week-long slogs over the border into the wilds of Kalimantan.

While the highlands are certainly cooler than Borneo's coastal regions, it's still hard work trekking up here and you should be in fairly good shape to consider a multiday trek. Be prepared to encounter leeches – many trails are literally crawling with them. Bring extra cell-phone and camera batteries, as charging may not be possible.

With so many trails in the area, there's ample scope for custom routes and creative planning beyond the most well-known routes.

BARIO TO BA KELALAN

The three- to four-day trek from Bario to Ba Kelalan covers a variety of terrain, including paddy fields and primary rainforest – some of it on the Indonesian side of the frontier – and gives a good overview of the Kelabit Highlands.

The first day is an easy walk from Bario to Pa' Lungan (p462). If you find a guide to take you from Pa' Lungan it's possible to do this first day alone. The path follows an open trail for an hour and then continues through the jungle along what used to be the only route between the two villages. With a logging road now connecting Bario with Pa' Lungan, the jungle trail is less used and not as clear as it once was. Check with locals before setting out or walk along the road. Alternative options for linking Bario to Pa' Lungan are a bumpy 4WD journey (around 90 minutes), or combining a boat ride with a one-hour hike.

From Pa' Lungan there are two possible routes to Ba Kelalan. The first involves a night at a jungle shelter at **Long Rebpun** – your guide will find edible jungle mushrooms and ferns to cook for dinner – and on to Ba Kelalan (via Kalimantan) the following day. The alternative route is via the jungle shelter at **Long Pa Diit** and the Kalimantan village of **Tanjung Karya** (where it's possible to spend the night at a homestay).

To avoid doubling back, you can trek from Bario to Ba Kelalan and then fly or take a 4WD down to the coast. Remember, though, that you'll have to pay the guide for the two days it will take them to walk back to Bario. It's possible to do the trek in either direction, but finding a guide is much easier in Bario or Pa' Lungan than in Ba Kelalan.

BATU LAWI

If you were sitting on the left side of the plane from Miri to Bario, you probably caught a glimpse of the two massive limestone spires known as Batu Lawi, the taller of which soars to 2040m. During WWII they were used as a landmark for parachute drops.

While an ascent of the higher of the two rock formations, known as the 'male peak', is only for expert technical rock climbers, ascending the lower 'female peak' – described by one veteran trekker as 'awe-inspiring' – is possible for fit trekkers without special skills. It's a tough, four- or five-day return trip from Bario. Be prepared to spend the second day passing through areas that have been impacted by logging. Only a handful of guides are experienced enough to tackle Batu Lawi.

GUNUNG MURUD

Sarawak's highest mountain (2423m), part of 598-sq-km **Pulong Tau National Park**, is just begging to be climbed, but very few travellers make the effort to put the trip together. Since 1985, evangelical Christians in the area have made annual pilgrimages up the mountain for prayer meetings.

Gunung Murud is linked by trails with both Ba Kelalan and Bario. From Bario, the more common starting point, a typical return trip takes six or seven days. You can also walk from Bario via Gunung Murud to Ba Kelalan (five days one way), but as you approach Ba Kelalan you'll have to walk along a depressing logging road. This is only an adventure for the fittest of the fittest.

A rough logging road links the base of Gunung Murud with the lowland town of Lawas (five to eight hours by 4WD).

Ba Kelalan

Known for its rice, organic vegetables and apples, the Lun Bawang town of Ba Kelalan is a popular destination for treks from Bario.

The village is built on a hillside in an attractive valley; when the paddy fields are flooded, the effect of the mirror-like surface reflecting the surrounding mountains is spectacular. This is a deeply religious community: at the head of the large grassy playing field that acts as the town square sits the Borneo Evangelical Mission church, with Sunday services that last most of the day. The church seems incongruously large for such a small town, but at times it's filled to bursting with worshippers who come to Ba Kelalan to climb nearby **Gunung Murud** (2423m), known to some as prayer mountain.

Ba Kelalan is also one of Sarawak's best spots for for bird-watching. Twitchers come here to spot ruddy cuckoo doves, oriental bay owls and broadbills.

🛏 Sleeping & Eating

Juliasang Homestay   HOMESTAY $
(incl meals per person RM80) A large family house in the village's grassy main square opposite the church. Electricity from 6pm to 11pm only.

Ponook Santai Café   MALAYSIAN $
(mains RM4.50-7; ⊘7pm-midnight) Opposite the airport (on the other side of the runway from the terminal building), this relaxed cafe has chicken rice as its speciality. One of the cafe's main draws seems to be the large flat-screen TV, which tends to show Discovery Channel documentaries at full volume.

ⓘ Getting There & Away

The only way to get from Ba Kelalan to Bario is on foot, a hike that takes three to four days. A rough, 125km logging road links Ba Kelalan with Lawas (RM70 to RM80 per person by 4WD, seven hours, daily).

It's possible to get from Ba Kelalan to Long Bawan in Kalimantan by motorbike.

MASwings (www.maswings.com.my) flies Twin Otters from Ba Kelalan to Lawas and Miri three times a week. There's also a weekly flight on Thursday to/from Bario.

Limbang Division

🗐 085 / POP 41,000

Shaped like a crab claw, the Limbang Division slices Brunei in two. Tourism is underdeveloped in these parts, but Bruneians love popping across the border to find shopping bargains, including cheap beer smuggled in from duty-free Pulau Labuan.

The bustling river port of Limbang is something of a backwater, but you may find yourself here before or after taking the Headhunters' Trail to or from Gunung Mulu National Park.

ⓘ CROSSING INTO INDONESIA

Thanks to an agreement between the Indonesian and Malaysian foreign ministries, it's possible for highland residents and tourists to cross from Ba Kelalan into Kalimantan on a trek to Bario (or vice versa), but you must bring your passport (it won't be stamped) and explain your plans. The immigration checkpoint outside Ba Kelalan is not an official border crossing and doesn't issue visas on arrival. If you want to continue your journey into Indonesia, you'll need to get a visa in advance.

Malaysian ringgits (RM) are very popular in this remote part of Kalimantan, but US dollars are not.

The area, snatched from the sultan of Brunei by Charles Brooke in 1890, was claimed by Brunei up until the territorial dispute was settled in 2009.

Sights & Activities

Limbang's old town stretches inland from riverfront Jln Wong Tsap En (formerly Main Bazaar) and south along the riverbank, following a pleasant esplanade. Across the river is a traditional Malay village, which can be reached by regular *sampan* (small boats; RM1) leaving from the riverfront.

Possible activities around Limbang include canoeing in the Limpaki Wetlands, where proboscis monkeys can sometimes be seen, and a self-spa at the Maritam Mud Spring, 39km outside town.

Limbang Regional Museum MUSEUM
(www.museum.sarawak.gov.my; Jln Kubu; ⊙9am-4.30pm Tue-Fri, 10am-4.30pm Sat & Sun) This small museum features well-presented exhibits on Limbang Division's archaeology, culture and crafts, including Chinese ceramic jars that were a symbol of status and wealth for Orang Ulu communities. It's housed in a Charles Brooke–era fort originally built in 1897 and rebuilt (after a fire) in 1991. Located on the riverbank, about 1km south of the centre.

Bukit Mas Nature Reserve NATURE RESERVE
A pleasant and easygoing 45-minute trail negotiates a meandering route through this riverside nature reserve near the town's regional museum.

Borneo Touch Ecotour TREKKING
(☑WhatsApp 013-844 3861; www.walk2mulu.com) Run by the dynamic Mr Lim, this local company offers highly recommended treks along the Headhunters' Trail (p457) to or from Gunung Mulu National Park (five days and four nights including the Pinnacles costs RM1040 per person for a minimum of three people).

Can provide basic lodgings in Limbang (RM30 per person) and arrange for luggage to be sent by air cargo (RM70) so that you don't need to carry it on the trek. Advance booking recommended.

A half-day trip to the Limpaki Wetlands including transport and two hours' canoeing costs RM60 per person (minimum three people).

Sleeping

Prime Hotel HOTEL $
(☑085-217 8888; Lot 1122, Jln Buangsiol; s/d from RM50/75; ❀🤖) Limbang's best budget hotel is in close proximity to decent restaurants. Rooms are relatively spartan, but the strength of the air-con and wi-fi makes it perfectly fine for a night.

Bookings for boats to Pulau Labuan in Sabah can also be made here.

Purnama Hotel HOTEL $$
(☑085-216700; www.purnamalimbang.com; Jln Buangsiol; r incl breakfast from RM105; ❀🤖) Ensconced in Limbang's tallest building (12 storeys), this uninspiring hotel – ornamented with rainbow-hued balconies and 218 spacious but aesthetically challenged rooms that come with big views and small bathrooms.

Eating

Limbang Food Court FOOD HALL $
(Jln Buangsiol; mains RM6-10; ⊙10am-11pm) This outdoor food court features 40 stalls handily divided into a Malay side and a Chinese side. It's a breezy and cool spot to be after dark with the friendly Limbang locals.

Musbee Cafe MALAYSIAN, THAI $
(☑085-210987; Pekan Limbang; ⊙12.30-11pm; ☑) Fairy lights and brightly coloured walls lift Musbee above Limbang's dining pack. The menu, introducing a few Thai flavours, is also a little different. Try the spicy *ayam kerabu* chicken salad and choose between river views or local variety shows on the cafe's multiple big-screen TVs.

Diyana Cafe INDONESIAN $
(☑019-486 3342; Jln Wong Tsap Eng; mains RM6-15; ⊙6am-11.30pm) A buzzing little place with pavement tables and views of the river that serves up tasty Indonesian fare, including *nasi lalapan* (rice, vegetables and tofu served with a spicy sambal sauce).

Pusat Penjaja Medan Bangkita MARKET $
(Jln Bangkita; ⊙6am-5pm) Bisaya, Lun Bawang and Iban stallholders sell jungle edibles, sausage-shaped Ba Kelalan salt and a dozen kinds of upland rice. The larger weekly *tamu* (market) takes place all day Thursday and until noon on Friday.

Night Market HAWKER $
(Jln Bangkita; mains RM3-7; ⊙3-9pm) Stalls selling quick, flavoursome bites such as *kolo mee* (noodles cooked with pork lard; RM6),

wonton mee (noodles with dumplings; RM6) and fresh juices (RM4) are a popular nightly snacking option. Nearby stalls sell everything from camouflage gear and knock-off sportswear through to handy dry bags ideal for jungle trekking.

ℹ Information

Sun City Cybercafe (1st fl, cnr Jln Bangkita & Jln Tarap; per hour RM2.50; ⏰ 8.30am-midnight) A haven for gamers.

ℹ Getting There & Around

AIR

Limbang's small **airport** (Jln Rangau) is 7km south of the centre. A taxi into town costs RM20. **MASwings** (☎ 085-211086; www. maswings.com.my; Limbang Airport, Jln Rangau; ⏰ 6.30am-5.50pm) has two flights per day to/from Miri. As there are too few taxis to meet flights, your driver may take other passengers in the same car (but still charge you the full rate).

BOAT

Express ferries from Limbang's immigration hall to Pulau Labuan (RM50, two hours, 2.30pm Tuesday, Thursday, Friday, Saturday and Sunday) are run by **Express Pertama Limbang** (RM50). Tickets are sold at the jetty or bookings can be made at the Prime Hotel (p466) in Limbang. Departures from Pulau Labuan to Limbang are at 9.30am Monday, Wednesday, Friday, Saturday and Sunday.

Royal Limbang (☎ 013-882 3736) departs Limbang around 8am, returning from Pulau Labuan around 1.30pm.

BUS

Bintang Jaya (☎ 085-211178; www.bintang jayaexpress.com; Jln Bangkita) sends daily buses to Miri (RM45) at 1.45pm, and to Lawas (RM30) and Kota Kinabalu (KK; RM50) at 12.45pm. Buy tickets for Bintang Jaya at the tiny **convenience store** (Jln Bangkita) near the auto-repair shops on Jln Bangkita.

A spot in a seven-seater unlicensed van to Miri costs RM50, departing from the tiny **old bus station** (Jln Wayang) at the eastern end of Jln Wayang, two blocks inland from the river.

The only company that can drop you off inside Brunei is **Jesselton Express** (PHLS; ☎ +673-714-5735, Brunei +673-714-5734, Kota Kinabalu 016-836 0009, Lawas 016-832-6722, Limbang 016-855 0222; www.sipitangexpress.com.my), which has daily buses to Bandar Seri Begawan (BSB; RM20) at 3pm; and to Bangar (Brunei), Lawas (RM30, two hours) and KK (RM50) at 9.30am. Tickets are sold at **Wan Wan Cafe & Restaurant** (Jln Bangkita; ⏰ 6am-10pm). Heading to Limbang, a bus departs from BSB every day at 8am.

Note that departure times are liable to change. Check with Mr Lim at Borneo Touch Ecotour for the latest.

TAXI & MINIBUS

Minibuses and red-and-yellow taxis hang out at the **Stesen Teksi** (☎ 085-213781; Jln Wong Tsap En; ⏰ 5am-6pm or later), on the waterfront. If you're heading towards BSB, one-way travel to the Kuala Lurah crossing costs RM70. From there, public buses run to BSB until 5.30pm. If you're coming from BSB, taxis wait on the Malaysian side of the Kuala Lurah crossing.

Brunei Darussalam

🔊 673 / POP 422,678 / AREA 5765 SQ KM

Includes ➡

Bandar Seri
Begawan 470

Tutong & Belait
Districts 482

Jalan Labi 482

Seria 483

Temburong District...483

Bangar 484

Batang Duri 485

Ulu Temburong
National Park 485

Best Places to Eat

➡ Kaizen Sushi (p478)

➡ Pasar Malam Gadong (p476)

➡ Rack & Brew (p478)

➡ Pondok Sari Wangi (p477)

➡ Thiam Hock Restaurant (p478)

➡ Nasi Katok Corner (p476)

Best Places to Stay

➡ Ulu Ulu Resort (p486)

➡ Brunei Hotel (p476)

➡ Sumbiling Eco Village (p485)

➡ Home Stay Nur Rahim Kampong Ayer (p476)

➡ Qing Yun Resthouse (p476)

Why Go?

The tiny sultanate of Brunei is just a remnant of a naval empire that once ruled all of Borneo and part of the present-day Philippines. Nevertheless this quiet darussalam (Arabic for 'abode of peace') has the largest oilfields in Southeast Asia (though they're due to run dry in 30 years).

Look beneath the surface of this tightly regulated sultanate and you'll see the wisely conserved wildness of its natural environment. Thanks to the money generated by the oilfields, Brunei hasn't turned its rainforests into palm-oil plantations. Old-growth, primary forest abounds, especially in verdant Ulu Temburong National Park.

However, the introduction of a strict interpretation of sharia law in April 2019 has prompted global criticism and concern. Under the new legislation, adultery and homosexual acts are punishable by death by stoning, and theft is punishable by the amputation of limbs. As the world struggles to come to terms with Brunei's new direction, the future of tourism is uncertain.

When to Go
Bandar Seri Begawan

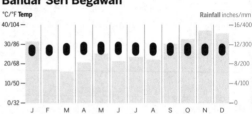

Oct–Dec The rainiest, ever so slightly coolest, months of the year.

Feb & Mar The driest months. National Day is celebrated on 23 February.

May & Jun The sultan opens his palace to visitors for three days after Ramadan.

Pulau
Labuan (35km);
Menumbok,
Sabah (45km)

0 — 20 km
0 — 10 miles

SOUTH
CHINA
SEA

Brunei Bay

Pantai
Muara

Pantai
Meragang

Bukit
Shahbandar
(103m)

Serasa

Pulau Muara
Besar

Jerudong Park
Playground

Brunei
International
Airport

7 Diving

Pulau
Selirong

Sundar

Lawas
(Sarawak)
(15km)

BANDAR
SERI BEGAWAN

2

3 Kampong
Ayer

BRUNEI-MUARA

Kampung
Parit

6 Sungai
Brunei

TEMBURONG

Pantai Seri
Kenangan

Tutong

Sinaut

Limbang

Labu

Trusan

Bukit Peradayan
(410m)

Pan Borneo Hwy

Kampung
Abang

Limau Manis

Bangar

Kampung
Telisai

Kuala Lurah

Bukit
Patoi
(310m)

Peradayan
Forest
Reserve

Layong

Lamunin

Trans Borneo Hwy

LIMBANG
DIVISION

Sumbiling
Eco Village

Kuala
Baram (40km);
Miri (60km)

Lumut

Kampung
Sungai Liang

Tasek
Merimbun

4

Sungai Terasan

LIMBANG DIVISION

Seria

Forestry
Museum

Sungai Liang
Forest Recreation
Park

Kampung
Merimbun

TUTONG

Batang
Duri

Ulu Temburong
National Park

1

Kampung
Badas

Luagan Lalak
Recreation Park

Bukit Belalong
(913m)

Kuala
Balai

Sungai
Damit

Jln Labi

Labi

BELAIT

Sungai Tutong

Sungai Limbang

5 Jalan Labi

Bukit Teraja
(442m)

Kampung
Sukang

SARAWAK
INDONESIA

Bukit Pagon
(1850m)

Kampung
Melilas

Marudi

Gunung Mulu
National Park

Brunei Darussalam Highlights

1 Ulu Temburong National Park (p485) Climbing high into the rainforest canopy and cooling off in a jungle stream.

2 Bandar Seri Begawan (p470) Visiting a mosque or museum and exploring the restaurants and coffee shops.

3 Kampong Ayer (p470) Taking a water taxi to this charming water village and learning about Brunei's heritage.

4 Sumbiling Eco Village (p485) Experiencing the Iban culture and camping overnight in the jungles of Temburong District.

5 Jalan Labi (p482) Visiting traditional longhouses and

exploring a watery nature reserve.

6 Sungai Brunei (p475) Spotting proboscis monkeys and glimpsing royal palaces from a water taxi.

7 Diving (p475) Exploring the reefs and wrecks of Brunei's unspoilt dive sites off Serasa Beach.

BANDAR SERI BEGAWAN

POP 422,700

Cities built on oil money tend to be flashy, ostentatious places, but with the exception of a palace you can't enter most of the time, a couple of enormous mosques and one wedding cake of a hotel, Bandar (as the capital is known, or just BSB) is a very understated place. Urban life pretty much revolves around two pastimes: shopping and eating – there is virtually no nightlife (though an enduring love of karaoke). BSB does have a few good museums and the biggest water village in the world, providing a little slice of vintage Malay life.

BSB's city centre is on the north bank of Sungai Brunei at a spot – 12km upriver from Brunei Bay – that's sheltered from both storms and tsunamis. During the Japanese occupation, the city centre – known until 1970 as Brunei Town – was severely damaged by Allied bombing.

◉ Sights

All of central BSB is within easy walking or boating distance of the Omar Ali Saifuddien Mosque, but unless you don't mind pounding the streets for hours under the tropical sun, you'll need to take buses or taxis, or rent a car to get to sights east, north and west of the centre.

◉ Central BSB

Omar Ali Saifuddien Mosque   MOSQUE
(Jln Stoney; ⊘ interior 8.30am-noon, 1.30-3pm & 4.30-5.30pm Sat-Wed, exterior compound 8am-8.30pm daily except prayer times) Completed in 1958 Masjid Omar Ali Saifuddien – named after the 28th Sultan of Brunei (the late father of the current sultan) – is surrounded by an artificial lagoon that serves as a reflecting pool. This being Brunei, the interior is pretty lavish. The floor and walls are made from the finest Italian marble, the chandeliers were crafted in England and the luxurious carpets were flown in from Saudi Arabia. A 3.5-million-piece glass mosaic overlaying real gold leaf covers the main dome.

The mosque's 52m-high minaret makes it the tallest building in central BSB, and woe betide anyone who tries to outdo it – apparently the nearby Islamic Bank of Brunei building originally exceeded this height and so had the top storey removed by order of the sultan. The ceremonial stone boat sitting in the lagoon is a replica of a 16th-century *mahligai* (royal barge) where Quran-reading competitions were once held.

Come evening the grounds surrounding the mosque are basically the happening centre of city life in Bandar. Folks come for prayer, then stroll along the waterfront, around the illuminated fountain and the baobab trees, or promenade along the pedestrian bridge across the Kedayan River.

★ Royal Regalia Museum   MUSEUM
(Jln Sultan; ⊘ 9am-5pm Sun-Thu, 9-11.30am & 2.30-5pm Fri, 9.45am-5pm Sat, last entry 4.30pm) `FREE`
When called upon to present a gift to the sultan of Brunei, you must inevitably confront the question: what do you give a man who has everything? At this entertaining museum you'll see how heads of state have solved this conundrum. Look out for a solid silver model of Angkor Wat (Cambodia), Nazca Lines–shaped silver pins (Peru) and a model of the Grand Mosque of Mecca made of precious metals and stones (Saudi Arabia).

Family photos and explanatory texts offer a good overview of the life of the sultan, who is himself depicted in myriad forms (including a hologram) from childhood through military service at Sandhurst to his lavish wedding and sporty adult life.

Also on display are the chariot used during the sultan's 1992 silver-jubilee procession (the chariot is accompanied by an army of traditionally dressed headless mannequins representing those present on the day) and a second chariot used for the 1968 coronation.

Kampong Ayer   VILLAGE
Home to around 30,000 people, Kampong Ayer consists of 42 contiguous stilt villages built along the banks of the Sungai Brunei (Brunei River). A century ago, half of Brunei's Malay population lived here, and even today many Bruneians still prefer the lifestyle of the water village to residency on dry land. The village has its own schools, mosques, police stations and fire brigade.

Founded at least 1000 years ago, the village is considered the largest stilt settlement in the world. When Venetian scholar Antonio Pigafetta visited Kampong Ayer in 1521, he dubbed it the 'Venice of the East', which is, as descriptions go, a bit ambitious. The timber houses, painted sun-bleached shades of green, blue, pink and yellow, have not been done up for tourists, so while it's far from squalid, be prepared for rubbish that, at low tide, carpets the intertidal mud under the banisterless boardwalks, some with missing planks.

In some places smart new houses have been constructed – these sturdy buildings look better equipped to survive the monsoon storms that have been known to cause flimsier wooden structures in the village to collapse.

If you look to the main roads on the banks opposite the village, you'll see luxury cars lined up on the shoulder of the road; many of these cars belong to water village residents. That said, Kampong Ayer is also home to a sizeable population of the undocumented immigrants who constitute Brunei's underclass.

The villages on the river's north bank (the same side as the city centre) used to cover a much larger area, but many have been razed as part of plans to spruce up the waterfront area around the Omar Ali Saifuddien Mosque. To get to these villages, follow the plank walks that lead west (parallel to the river) from the Yayasan Complex, itself built on the site of a one-time water village.

The water villages used to be the epicentre of traditional industries, such as silversmithing, goldsmithing, the weaving of fine cloth and boat making. Boat making is still something you can see easily, but to find the weavers you need to go with an operator who can arrange a demonstration in advance.

To get across the river, flag down a water taxi (B$1).

Kampong Ayer Cultural & Tourism Gallery GALLERY
(south bank, Kampong Ayer; ⊙9am-5pm Sat-Thu, 9-11.30am & 2.30-5pm Fri) FREE A good place to start a visit to Kampong Ayer – and get acquainted with Brunei's pre-oil culture – is the Cultural & Tourism Gallery, directly across the river from Sungai Kianggeh (the stream at the eastern edge of the city centre). Opened in 2009 this riverfront complex focuses on the history, lifestyle and crafts of the Kampong Ayer people. A square, glass-enclosed viewing tower offers panoramic views of the scene below.

Tiang Yun Dian Chinese Temple TEMPLE
(Jln Kianggeh; ⊙hours vary) Colourful Tiang Yun Dian (Temple of Flying Clouds), built in the 1960s, is the oldest Chinese temple in BSB and open during the day and evening for worshippers and visitors alike.

⊙ East of Central BSB

Malay Technology Museum MUSEUM
(Muzium Teknologi Melayu; Jln Muzium Teknologi Melayu; ⊙9am-5pm Sun-Thu, 9-11.30am & 2.30-5pm Fri, 9.45am-5pm Sat, last entry 30min before closing; P; 🚌39) FREE This absorbing museum focuses on the traditional lifestyle and artisanship of Brunei's ethnic groups. Peek into the bamboo dwellings of

BRUNEI DARUSSALAM BANDAR SERI BEGAWAN

INSIDE THE SULTAN'S PALACE

If shaking hands with royalty is your thing, and you happen to be in Brunei for the Hari Raya Aidil Fitri festivities at the end of Ramadan, be sure to call in on the sultan at Istana Nurul Iman (p473), his 1788-room primary residence. In keeping with the local tradition of hosting an open house, during which guests are welcomed into the home and plied with a buffet of curries, dried fruit and cake, the royal family receives members of the public at his palace in morning and afternoon sessions for three days. There is no need for an invitation; simply turn up and join the queue (arriving early means a shorter wait). Bruneians will be dressed in their best clothes, some in outfits made especially for the occasion using brightly patterned materials, so wear something modest and reasonably smart.

After piling your plate high with a selection of curries and making multiple trips to the cake table at the free banquet, you'll have to join a gender-segregated queue for the initial waiting area, where seats are provided and Hari Raya pop songs are played on a loop on the big screen to keep the crowds entertained. You may have to wait for up to three hours before you pass through a magnificent banquet hall, where you will sit and wait again (for around an hour) before being ushered along a marble walkway beneath a sinuous wooden ceiling to one of the royal reception rooms, with crystal 'tears' dangling from the ceiling and Quran verses imprinted on the rich green upholstery. There you will shake hands with the sultan (if you are a man) or the queen (if you are a woman), who receive guests in separate rooms, along with other members of the royal family. Each visitor is given a goody box on the way out, containing a cake and a Hari Raya greeting card with a photo of the sultan.

If your moment with the sultan or queen feels all too fleeting, bear in mind that they will greet up to 50,000 people a day during the festivities.

Bandar Seri Begawan

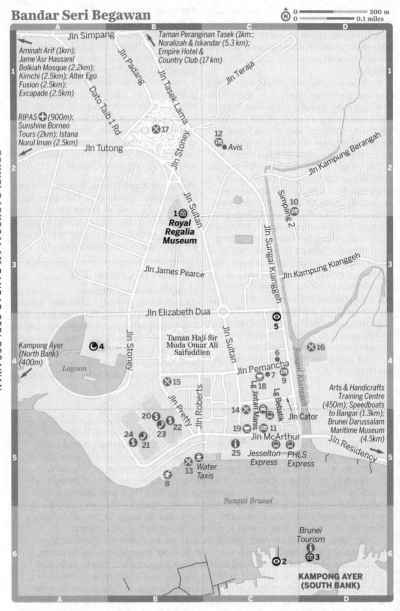

a re-created Malay water village, peer into a Murut longhouse with weaponry on the walls, and observe the blowpipe-making technique of the nomadic Penan. Learn about traditional livelihoods, from fishing and farming to trampling sago pith and boat making, and explore the crafts still practised in Brunei's water villages, from silversmithing and goldsmithing to weaving fine cloth.

Brunei Museum MUSEUM
(Jln Kota Batu; ⊙9am-5pm Sat-Thu, 9-11.30am & 2.30-5pm Fri, last entry 30min before closing; Ⓟ; ⊞39) FREE Brunei's national museum, with

Bandar Seri Begawan

⊙ Top Sights
1 Royal Regalia Museum B2

⊙ Sights
2 Kampong Ayer C6
3 Kampong Ayer Cultural &
    Tourism Gallery D6
4 Omar Ali Saifuddien Mosque A4
5 Tiang Yun Dian Chinese Temple C4

⊙ Activities, Courses & Tours
6 Borneo Guide C4
7 Freme Travel Services C4
8 Water-Taxi Cruise B5

⊙ Sleeping
9 Brunei Hotel C4
10 Capital Residence Suites C2
11 Joy Rest Station C5
    Qing Yun Resthouse .... (see 11)
12 Radisson Hotel C2

⊗ Eating
As-Salihah .... (see 6)
13 Kaizen Sushi B5
14 Nasi Katok Corner C5
15 Seri Damai Restaurant B4
16 Tamu Kianggeh D4
17 Tamu Selera B2

⊖ Drinking & Nightlife
18 Another C4
19 Piccolo Café C5

⊙ Information
20 BIBD B5
21 DST B5
22 Isman Money Changer B5
23 Progresif B5
24 RHB B5
25 Tourist Information Centre C5

BRUNEI DARUSSALAM BANDAR SERI BEGAWAN

its Islamic-art gallery, exhibits depicting Brunei's role in Southeast Asian history from the arrival of the Spanish and Portuguese in the 16th century, and natural-history gallery, is a decent place to blow an hour of your time. It is situated 4.5km east of central BSB along the coastal road, at Kota Batu. At research time the museum was closed for ongoing renovations.

The oldest pieces here are ceramics from Iran and Central Asia and blown glass from Egypt and the Levant dating from the 9th and 10th centuries, as well as manuscripts of the Quran, tiny Qurans the size of a matchbox and gold jewellery. Don't miss the collection of Brunei's famous ceremonial cannons, known as *bedil,* some with barrels shaped like dragon heads. It wasn't oil but these bronze-cast weapons that were once the source of the sultanate's wealth and power.

Brunei Darussalam
Maritime Museum   MUSEUM
(Muzium Maritim; Simpang 482, Jln Kota Batu; ⊙9am-5pm Sun-Thu, 9-11.30am & 2.30-5pm Fri, 9.45am-5pm Sat, last entry 30min before closing; P; ☐39) FREE The impressive skeleton of a ship, lined with ceramic vessels, greets you as you step into the main hall inside this gleaming, ship-like building at Kota Batu, 5km east of the city centre. On display are some of the 13,261 artefacts excavated from the country's most important shipwreck, discovered by divers in 1997. The ship is believed to have sailed from China in the late 15th or early 16th centuries before being struck by stormy weather as it approached Brunei.

⊙ North & West of Central BSB

Jame'Asr Hassanil Bolkiah Mosque MOSQUE (Sultan Hassanal Bolkiah Hwy, Kampung Kiarong; ⊙8am-noon, 2-3pm & 5-6pm Mon-Wed & Sat, 10.45am-noon, 2-3pm & 5-6pm Sun; P; ☐1) Built in 1992 to celebrate the 25th year of the current sultan's reign, Brunei's largest mosque and its four terrazzo-tiled minarets dominate their surroundings. It's impossible to miss as you head towards Gadong, about 3km from the city centre. It's certainly an impressive building – because the sultan is his dynasty's 29th ruler, the complex is adorned with 29 golden domes. At night the mosque is lit up like a gold flame.

The interior more than matches the mosque's lavish exterior. The sheer volume in itself is remarkable, not to mention the myriad woven rugs scattered across the men's prayer hall.

Look out for the sultan's own personal escalator at his private entrance to the mosque.

Istana Nurul Iman PALACE (Palace of the Light of Faith; Jln Istana Nurul Iman; ☐42) The sultan's official residence, the world's largest residential palace, is more than four times the size of the Palace of Versailles. It has 1788 rooms, air-conditioned stables for the sultan's polo ponies, gold door handles and 257 bathrooms. The palace is open to the public only during the three-day Hari Raya Aidil Fitri festivities (p471) at the end of Ramadan. The best way to check it out on the other 362 days of the year is to take a water-taxi cruise (p475).

WORTH A TRIP

JERUDONG

For much of the 1990s the sultan's younger brother and Brunei's then finance minister, Prince Jefri, was renowned for the extravagance of both his personal and public spending. The legacy of the latter lives on in the neighbourhood of Jerudong, an area so enveloped with Las Vegas–style bling that there is even a roundabout adorned with a giant replica diamond ring.

Amid the rows of mansions lie the **Jerudong Park Polo Club** (the sultan himself is a keen polo player) and Jerudong Park Medical Centre (p479).

Back in the golden days, a concert hall hosted free shows by the likes of Whitney Houston and Michael Jackson, the latter to celebrate the sultan's 50th birthday in 1996. But in 1997 the party came to a halt when Prince Jefri (dubbed the Playboy Prince) was accused by the Brunei government of embezzling billions of dollars of state funds. After a long dispute involving a series of court cases, Prince Jefri now seems to have been welcomed back into the fold.

Nowhere sums up the legacy of Prince Jefri more than **Jerudong Park Playground** (www.jerudongpark.com.bn; Jerudong; adult/child to 12yr B\$20/10; ⊙ 4-11pm Wed, 3-11.30pm Fri, 10.30am-11.30pm Sat & Sun; 🚶; 🚌 55), a rather tame amusement park. It's a great place to bring kids, but despite a facelift the park continues to feel underused and rather empty. In its 1990s heyday this B\$1 billion attraction was the pride of Brunei, and the only major modern amusement park in Southeast Asia. Bruneians who were teenagers then have fond memories of the rides – all of them free – which included a roller coaster. Although the new attractions may be no match for the golden days, the place still evokes a feeling of nostalgia.

The Empire Hotel & Country Club (p476), commissioned by Prince Jefri at a cost of US\$1.1 billion, is worth a visit if only to gawp at the cavernous, glass atrium and US\$500,000 lamp made of gold and Baccarat crystal in the lobby. For B\$25 you can use the seafront swimming-pool complex, and the hotel also has eight restaurants, including the overpriced and disappointing **Pantai** (📞 241 8888; www.theempirehotel.com/categories/dining; Beachfront, level 1, Empire Hotel & Country Club, Jerudong; buffet adult/child B\$50/26; ⊙ 6-10pm daily, lunch buffet Sat). The resort even has its own three-screen cinema (p479).

Jerudong, which lies 20km northwest of BSB, is difficult to explore without private transport, although the 57 bus from the city centre will take you as far as the Empire Hotel.

Designed by Filipino architect Leandro Locsin, the palace mixes elements of Malay (the vaulted roofs) and Islamic (the arches and gold domes) design with the sweep and oversized grandeur of a 200,000-sq-metre airport terminal. Nonetheless it's relatively attractive from a distance or when illuminated in the evening.

The crystal teardrops in the royal reception room, sinuous wooden ceilings above covered walkways, and the glass ceiling features of the grand banquet hall are the work of Khuan Chew, responsible for Dubai's Burj Al Arab.

Istana is located 3km southwest of the town centre.

Taman Peranginan Tasek　　　PARK
(Tasek Recreational Park; Jln Tasek Lama; ⊙ 6am-6pm Sun-Thu, 6-11am & 2-6pm Fri; 🅿) If you need a reminder that just beyond BSB's air-conditioned malls lies the Bornean jungle, this city park, with its background chorus of buzzing, chirping and rustling rainforest sounds, should do it. Well-marked paths lead to waterfalls, picnic areas and a hilltop *menara* (tower) offering views of the city and encroaching greenery. There are rougher jungle trails for longer walks (wear proper shoes). The park is 2km north of the city centre.

◉ Muara

Peranginan Pantai Muara　　　BEACH
(Muara Beach Recreational Park; Jln Pantai Muara; ⊙ 6am-6pm; 🅿; 🚌 38) Muara Beach Recreational Park is a popular weekend retreat. It's pretty, but like many beaches in Borneo, it's littered with driftwood and other flotsam that comes in with the tide. Quiet during the week, it has picnic tables and a children's playground. A plaque commemorates the nearby Australian amphibious landings of 10 June 1945. The beach lies just past Muara town, 27km from central BSB. Take bus 38 to Jln Pelempong, from where it is a 500m walk.

🏃 Activities

Diving

Brunei's burgeoning dive scene has the advantage of having some decent dive operators without the downside of crowds.

There are several interesting wrecks – some dating back to WWII – as well as plenty of undamaged reef here, including patches that are largely unexplored. On most of the shipwrecks and all the coral dive sites there is colourful hard and soft coral, such as large gorgonian fans and wide table corals. Marine life you are likely to see includes cuttlefish, octopus, morays, porcupine fish, giant puffers and perhaps a sea snake or two.

The best time to dive is between March and October; from May to mid-July the conditions are often ideal.

Recommended operators are **Poni Divers** (📞 277 1778; www.ponidivers.com; Kompleks Sukan Air Serasa, Simpang 287, Pantai Serasa; 2 fun dives B$200; ⊙9am-5pm) – Brunei's largest dive centre, which offers a full range of PADI certification courses, recreational dives and various water sports – and the well-regarded **Oceanic Quest Company** (📞 277 1190; www. oceanicquest.com; No 6, Simpang 46, Jln Perusahaan, Kampong Serasa; 4-day, 3-night full board incl 6 boat dives B$500).

Cruises

Water-Taxi Cruise   BOATING

(1hr B$30-40) The best way to see BSB's water villages and the sultan's fabled palace, Istana Nurul Iman (p473), is from a water taxi, which can be chartered along the waterfront for about B$30 to B$40 (a bit of negotiating will occur, but at least you know the locals can't claim the petrol is expensive).

Finding a boat won't be a problem, as the boat operator will have spotted you before you spot them. After you admire the palace's backyard, your skipper can take you further upriver into the mangroves to see proboscis monkeys. Head out in the late afternoon if you can; the monkeys are easiest to spot around sunset.

👉 Tours

A number of local agencies offer tours of BSB and trips to nature sites around the sultanate, including Ulu Temburong National Park (p485) and the mangroves of Pulau Selirong (p485), 45 minutes by boat from the city. Some also offer night safaris where you can spot proboscis monkeys, crocs and fireflies.

★ Borneo Guide   TOURS

(📞 242 6923, 718 7138; www.borneoguide.com; unit 204, Kiaw Lian Bldg, Jln Pemancha; ⊙9am-5pm Mon-Thu, 9am-noon & 2-5pm Fri, 9am-1pm Sat & Sun) Excellent service, good prices and a variety of packages around Brunei and Borneo available. A day trip to Ulu Temburong National Park costs B$135 per person from BSB. Also offers overnight trips to Temburong with accommodation at Sumbiling Eco Village (p485) just outside the park (two days and one night from B$185). The office serves as a useful tourist information centre.

Sunshine Borneo Tours   TOURS

(📞 244 6812; www.bruneiborneo.com; No 2 Simpang 146, Jln Kiarong; ⊙8am-5pm Mon-Thu & Sat, 8am-noon & 2-5pm Fri) Has a range of tour packages in Brunei and Borneo, with bird-watching, river cruises, water-village tours and city night tours. Trips to Ulu Temburong National Park start at B$165 for a day trip and from B$330 for two days and one night with accommodation at the Ulu Ulu Resort (p486). The office is 3km west of the city centre.

Intrepid Tours   TOURS

(📞 222 1685; www.bruneibay.net/intrepidtours; Kampung Sungai Belukut, Simpang 912, Jln Kota Batu; ⊙9am-5pm Mon-Thu, 9am-noon & 2-5pm Fri, 9am-1pm Sat & Sun) Offers a range of day tours and multiday packages, including trips to Ulu Temburong National Park (day trips from B$185 per person, minimum two), dawn tours of Pulau Selirong (from B$90 per person), fishing tours and diving trips.

Freme Travel Services   TOURS

(📞 223 4277; www.freme.com; 4th fl, office 403B, Wisma Jaya, Jln Pemancha; ⊙9am-5pm Mon-Thu, 9am-noon & 2-5pm Fri, 9am-1pm Sat & Sun) A bit corporate, but Freme has plenty of tour options, as befits one of Brunei's largest travel agencies. Freme also has its own lodge close to Ulu Temburong National Park and prices start from B$130 for a day trip and B$240 for an overnight trip that covers the park's highlights.

🛏 Sleeping

Several decent budget guesthouses have opened in the city centre, in Gadong and elsewhere. There are several upscale hotels in the centre, while the rest are spread along Jln Gadong, west of the centre, and clustered around the airport. Room-sharing services are a massive boon for budget travellers, since hosts are often happy to drive them around. For homestays in village areas contact Borneo Guide.

Joy Rest Station GUESTHOUSE $
(📞 8900638; https://joydowntownreststation.weebly. com; No. 9 1F McArthur Bldg, Jln McArthur; s/d from B$20/30; ❄ 🛜) Good budget accommodation used to be as rare as hen's teeth in BSB, so this centrally located, waterfront guesthouse is a welcome addition. The sparsely decorated rooms are unlikely to thrill you, but the staff are friendly and there's a tonne of helpful sightseeing info on the wall of the lounge.

Home Stay Nur Rahim Kampong Ayer HOMESTAY $
(📞 879 2977, 888 1037; 6b Kampong Ayer, Burong Pingai Ayer; r B$30) If you wish to experience traditional water-village life, stay at this Malay stilt house, run by a friendly local family. Rooms are simple, but clean and come with clunky, prehistoric TVs. Meals available on request.

Qing Yun Resthouse GUESTHOUSE $
(📞 873 5503; 3F, McArthur Bldg, Jalan McArthur; s/d from B$40/47; ❄ 🛜) Some of the rooms here may lack natural light and the decor is a bit Any Hotel, Anywhere, but the location is hard to beat, as are the prices. Rooms are business-style with desks, TVs and fridges, and there are other branches in Gadong and near the airport. Great value.

★ **Brunei Hotel** HOTEL $$
(📞 224 4828; www.thebruneihotel.com; 95 Jln Pemancha; r/ste incl breakfast from B$110/210; ❄ @ 🛜) A chic, dare we say hip, hotel with clean lines, monochromatic colour schemes, geometric patterns and a general up-to-date style that is pretty unexpected in the sultanate. There's a decent breakfast buffet thrown into the deal, served in the downstairs **Choices Cafe**.

Capital Residence Suites HOTEL $$
(📞 222 0067; www.capitalresidencesuites.com; Simpang 2, Kampong Berangan; d/ste incl breakfast B$97/323; ❄ 🛜) This good-value, rather bland hotel is lifted by friendly, helpful staff and a free shuttle service (9am to 9pm) that transports guests all around BSB city and to the beaches and attractions beyond. The spacious suites are like small apartments with sofas, kitchen and washing machine. Standard rooms, though comfortably furnished, are a little cramped, with tiny bathrooms.

Empire Hotel & Country Club RESORT $$$
(📞 241 8888; www.theempirehotel.com; Lebuhraya Muara-Tutong, Jerudong; r/ste from B$270/980, villa from B$2200; 🅿 ❄ @ 🛜 ≋) Pharaonic in its proportions and opulence, this 522-room extravaganza was commissioned by Prince

Jefri as lodging for the royal family guests and transformed into an upscale resort. Behold the US$500,000 crystal camel! The Emperor Suite where Michael Jackson lived comes with own pool and even the cheapest rooms have remote-control everything, hand-woven carpets, gold-plated power points and enormous marble bathrooms.

Other famous hotel guests have included Bill Clinton and Pamela Anderson.

Radisson Hotel BUSINESS HOTEL $$$
(📞 224 4272; www.radisson.com/brunei; Jln Tasek Lama; d/ste B$417/797; ❄ @ 🛜 ≋) This Radisson chain hotel, on the edge of the city centre, flies the flag for international standards. The sparkling lobby exudes comfort and wealth, as do the business-class rooms. Amenities include a pool, a fitness centre, a spa and two restaurants. Guests enjoy a free shuttle to Gadong and the city centre thrice daily.

Rizqun International Hotel LUXURY HOTEL $$$
(📞 242 3000; www.rizquninternational.com; Simpang 137, Abdul Razak Complex; r/ste incl breakfast from B$320/700; ❄ 🛜 ≋) The Rizqun is more sophisticated than you'd expect for something attached to a shopping mall and has all the usual business-class amenities on hand, including a gym and a decent outdoor pool. The opulent lobby is pure Brunei, with marble, wood and stained glass, and the 7th-floor lounge has great views of the Jame'Asr Hassanil Bolkiah Mosque.

✕ Eating

The dining scene is international and varied. In the city centre, restaurants can be found along the waterfront and on Jln Sultan. Other foodie enclaves include Gadong and Kiulap, a short drive/bus ride from the waterfront.

★ **Pasar Malam Gadong** MARKET $
(Gadong Night Market; off Jln Pasar Gadong; dishes from B$1; 🕓 4-10pm; 🚌 1) Thanks to its authentic local snacks and dishes (grilled things on skewers, rice topped with chicken and sambal inside a banana leaf etc), this is Brunei's most popular night market. Unfortunately it's more geared to takeaway customers, so there are only a few picnic tables at which to sit. Situated 3km northwest of the city centre.

After about 7pm the only way back to town is by taxi (B$15 until 10pm, then B$20).

Nasi Katok Corner BRUNEIAN $
(Seri Mama Express; cnr Jln Sultan & Jln Cator; nasi katok B$1; 🕓 24hr) Locals queue at night for a cheap snack of *nasi kotok* at this tiny

AMBUYAT – GUMMY, GLUEY & GLUTINOUS

Remember that kid in kindergarten who used to eat craft glue? Well, *ambuyat,* Brunei's unofficial national dish, comes pretty darn close. It's a gelatinous, porridge-like goo made from the pith of the sago tree, which is ground to a powder, mixed with water and eaten with a variety of flavourful sauces.

To eat *ambuyat* you'll be given a special pair of chopsticks called *chandas* that are attached at the top (don't snap them in two!) to make it easier to twirl up the tenacious mucous. Once you've scooped up a bite-sized quantity, dunk it into the sauce. After your *ambuyat* is sufficiently drenched, place the glob of dripping, quivering, translucent muci-lage in your mouth and swallow – don't chew, just let it glide down your throat.

The best place to try it is at one of the branches of Aminah Arif (p478).

shopfront. Rice, sambal and a piece of hot and spicy/barbecue/honey mustard/black pepper chicken (or fishball or tofu) are placed in a paper cone, you hand over a dollar and off you go.

Although always open, this corner hole-in-the-wall only comes alive after 4pm. By 5pm there are cars double parked outside and plastic bags bursting with *nasi katok* cones are hauled away.

Soto Pabo
NOODLES $

(☑ 868 6388; www.facebook.com/sotopabo; Simpang 228, Kampong Pintu Malim, Jln Sultan Bolkiah; mains B$2.50-4.50; ☉ 9am-10.30pm Sat-Thu, 9-11.30am & 2-10.30pm Fri) Overlooking the water a little way across the bridge to the water villages, Soto Pabo is locally renowned for one of Brunei's iconic dishes: noodles in broth, topped with chicken or beef, chilli and herbs. (Here you can try the tendon and tripe version, too!) Catch a boat taxi (B$1) from the centre.

As-Salihah
INDONESIAN $

(Jln Pemancha; mains B$3-6; ☉ 11am-9pm Sat-Thu, 11am-noon & 2-9pm Fri) Overlook the laminated floor and the sticky table tops and tuck into some good, inexpensive Indonesian dishes, such as grilled fish with sambal, mee goreng (fried noodles) and *gado gado* (blanched vegetables with tofu) for the noncarnivorous diners.

Pondok Sari Wangi
INDONESIAN $

(☑ 244 5403; block A, No 12-13, Abdul Razak Complex, Jln Gadong; mains B$5.50-7; ☉ 10am-10pm Sat-Thu, 10am-noon & 2-10pm Fri) Located in Gadong, Pondok Sari Wangi is a beloved Bandar institution. The extensive menu includes a variety of tasty noodle and rice dishes, stir-fries and curries. *Nasi ayam bakar sari wang* (grilled chicken and rice) is one of the signature dishes. Fish fillet in pepper sauce and the old favourite, *daging rendang* (beef curry), also feature.

It's in a separate block, north of the Mall.

Noralizah & Iskandar
INDIAN $

(☑ 867 5781; www.facebook.com/pages/Noralizah-Iskandar/228873527126802; 15 ground fl, Kompleks Awang Hj Ibrahim, Jln Berakas; mains B$3.50-6.80; ☉ 7.45am-9pm Sat-Thu, 7.45-11am & 2.30-9pm Fri; ☑) This busy spot is all about the roti. The full *roti kosong* set is a flaky, buttery roti topped with potato and spiced dhal, tangy pickled vegetables, corned sardines and corned beef. *Roti bom,* filled with condensed milk, is a buttery, saccharine hit to the taste buds, while *murtabak* comes stuffed with ground lamb. Located near the airport.

Tamu Kianggeh
HAWKER $

(Kianggeh market; Jln Sungai Kianggeh; mains from B$1; ☉ 5am-5pm Sat-Thu, 5am-noon & 2-5pm Fri) The food stalls here serve Brunei's cheapest meals, including *nasi katok* (plain rice, a piece of fried or curried chicken and sambal; B$1) and *nasi lemak* (rice cooked in coconut milk and served with chicken, egg and cucumber slices; B$1). Many stalls are closed by 4pm.

Tamu Selera
HAWKER $

(cnr Jln Tasek Lama & Jln Stoney; mains B$2-7; ☉ 5pm-midnight) At this bustling, makeshift hawker centre, set in a shady park, diners eat excellent, cheap Malaysian and Indonesian dishes under colourful tarps and ceiling fans. Options include fresh seafood, satay, fried chicken – particularly *ayam penyet* (Indonesian fried chicken with sambal) – *ambuyat* (thick, starchy porridge), rice and noodle dishes and iced drinks. Situated 1km north of the waterfront.

★ Alter Ego Fusion
FUSION $$

(☑ 223 0388; www.facebook.com/alteregofoods; unit No 2 & 3, block E, ground fl, lot 5788, Kampong Kiulap; mains B$10.50-23; ☉ 10am-10pm Sat-Thu, 10am-noon & 2-10pm Fri; ☀☎) It's hard to pin down Alter Ego, except to say that it's one of BSB's most creative offerings, served in an equally impressive space that looks like the coffee shop of your dreams crossed with a jazz bar. Expect falafel, Mandarin short ribs, French onion soup and blackened chicken, and be sorely tempted by the salted caramel eclairs.

★ **Rack & Brew**   CAFE **$$**
(🖉 245 7886; www.facebook.com/rackandbrew; unit 9, block H, 1st & 2nd fl, Abdul Raak Complex, Gadong; mains B$8-13; ⊙9am-11pm Sat-Thu, 9am-noon & 2-11pm Fri; 🌦 🛜) 'Coffee is always a good idea' announces a poster on the wall of this funky cafe, and we concur. It's good coffee, too; locals come here for the caffeine hit and the epic breakfasts, from soft-shell crab florentine and salmon avo smash to French toast.

★ **Kaizen Sushi**   JAPANESE **$$**
(Kompleks Yayasan Sultan Haji Hassanal Bolkiah, Jln McArthur; mains B$6-17; ⊙11am-2.30pm & 6-10.30pm) All clean lines and bamboo accents, the minimalist interior of this waterfront restaurant focuses your attention on the food. The menu is extensive, from the imaginative sushi rolls and sashimi sets to noodles and teriyaki meats, but everything, from the teriyaki skewers to tobiko roe popping on your tongue, is competently prepared and bursting with flavour. Great fruit juices, too.

Excapade   JAPANESE **$$**
(🖉 244 3012; Regent Sq, Gadong; mains B$5-15; ⊙11am-10pm Sat-Thu, 11am-noon & 2-10pm Fri) This excellent Japanese restaurant has an extensive menu of sushi, tempura, gyoza, teppanyaki and rice and noodle dishes. Expertly prepared and presented dishes, attentive staff and decidedly Japanese decorations complete the picture. Well, almost: no Asahi or sake here.

Seri Damai Restaurant   PAKISTANI **$$**
(Rice & Grill; 🖉 222 5397; ground fl, 144A Jln Pemancha; mains B$4-18; ⊙9am-10pm Thu-Sat, 9am-11.30am & 2-10pm Fri; 🌦 🖉) This friendly, family-run Pakistani restaurant with an all-out green colour scheme, wedding-style chair covers and plenty of satin serves up some of the best biryanis, curries, naan breads and lassis in town. There is a good variety of vegetarian as well as meat and seafood dishes available. At B$6 the set menus are good value.

Kimchi   KOREAN **$$**
(🖉 222 2233; www.facebook.com/KimchiRestaurant.brunei; unit 19, block B, Regent Sq, Kiulap; mains B$7-30; ⊙11am-10.30pm Sun-Thu, 2-10.30pm Fri; 🅿) Korean restaurants are ubiquitous in BSB,

and Kimchi is arguably the best in town. The titular *kimchi* (fermented cabbage) is one of a cluster of tiny dishes served with every main, the *tteok* (rice cakes) come drowned in a spicy, rich sauce, and the marinated assorted meats and *sotong* (squid) destined for the barbecue really make your palate sing.

Aminah Arif   BRUNEIAN **$$**
(🖉 223 6198; www.aminaharif.com.bn; unit 2-3, block B, Rahman Bldg, Simpang 88, Kiulap; mains B$5-28, set meals for 2 from B$22; ⊙7am-10pm Sat-Thu, 7am-noon & 2-10pm Fri; 🌦 🖉) Aminah Arif is synonymous with *ambuyat*, Brunei's signature dish, served with hot sauce for dipping and an accompaniment of meat, fish and vegetable dishes. If you're up for a generous serving of wiggly white goo, this is a good spot to do it. Meals can be washed down with iced *kasturi ping* (lime juice).

There are five branches of Aminah Arif in town; this one – located in Kiulap, about 3km northwest of the waterfront – is the most central.

Thiam Hock Restaurant   CHINESE **$$$**
(🖉 244 1679; 5 Yong Siong Hai Bldg, Gadong; mains from B$10-30; ⊙10.30am-10pm Sat-Thu, 10.30am-noon & 2-10pm Fri) This long-standing Chinese restaurant used to be famous for its curry fish head, but these days locals come for the less challenging fare, such as the delicious butter prawns and a range of pork dishes. Thiam Hock is by the river on the block behind the Mall in Gadong.

🍷 Drinking & Nightlife

The sale and public consumption of alcohol is banned, though visitors can import some and it's unofficially found in Chinese restaurants and some hotels. Speciality coffee shops are on the rise, and decent espresso is readily available. Locals are fond of the *air batu campur* or ABC (ice, little green noodles, grass jelly, sago pearls and red beans).

★ **Roasted Sip**   COFFEE
(🖉 261 0850; www.roastedsip.com; unit 3, ground flr, Blk D, Simpang 508, Jerudong Complex, Jln Jerudong; ⊙7am-10pm Mon-Thu, 7-11.30am & 2-11pm Fri, to 11pm Sat & Sun; 🛜) Everything a mini-temple to the bean should be, this coffee roastery draws Bruneians from BSB all the way to Jerudong. There's a good mix of coffees here from Brazil, Guatemala, Mexico and Ethiopia, prepared using V60, Chemex or Aeropress and served against a backdrop of bare brick wall and glossy bean photography.

Kapra Coffee
COFFEE

(🖉 234 2850; http://kapracoffee.com; unit 26, ground fl, block C, Simpang 440, Jln Muara; ☺ 7am-7pm Sun-Thu, 7am-noon & 2-7pm Fri) If you're Muara bound, or just in need of a good caffeine fix, swing by this coffee roastery. Go for piccolo latte, espresso or affogato and perch at the large communal table. There's a range of iced coffees also, including the espresso tonic (double espresso over ice and tonic water) – refreshing or a step too far? You decide!

Piccolo Café
CAFE

(🖉 224 1558; www.facebook.com/piccolocafebn; lot 11, Jln McArthur; ☺ 7.30am-11pm Mon-Wed, 7.30am-1am Thu & Sat, 7.30-11.30am & 2pm-1am Fri, 9.30am-11pm Sun; 🛜) This cafe serves up lavender lattes (an original, if not completely delicious, drink) as well as more conventional coffees, teas and smoothies and a range of sandwiches, wraps, waffles and a few lunchtime mains, including garlic and cumin chicken and pasta with seared prawns.

Another
CAFE

(🖉 222 3012; G8, ground fl, Wisma Jaya, Jln Pemancha; ☺ 7am-7pm Mon-Thu & Sat; 🛜) There's an industrial chicness to the corrugated metal walls, polished concrete floors and distressed furniture. Coffee lovers (even the fussy ones) should be more than satisfied by the aromatic brews served here, and there is a tempting selection of pastries, cakes (chocolate brownies and Dutch apple pie) and sandwiches. There's another branch in Kiulap, open daily.

☆ Entertainment

Locals often head to Gadong for a night out, which in Brunei usually amounts to dinner and perhaps a movie (censored so that even the kissing scenes are cut). Based on the enthusiasm locals have for Gadong, you might conclude that the area is a seething nightlife zone, though it's just some air-con shopping malls and commercial streets.

For cinematic distractions there are a couple of multiplexes: **Mall Cineplex** (🖉 242 2455; www.themallcineplex.com; 3rd fl, The Mall, Gadong; adult B$4-10, child B$3-6; ☺ 11am-midnight) and **Empire Cinema** (🖉 261 0001; www.times cineplex.com; Empire Hotel & Country Club, Jerudong; adult B$4-8, child B$3-8; ☺ 11am-2am).

🛍 Shopping

Dewan Sumbangsih Mulia
ARTS & CRAFTS

(Jln Industri Beribi; ☺ 6am-6pm) A wallet-friendly spot for those looking to buy genuine local crafts, this place combines a craft market with some cheapo food stalls. Head upstairs for finely woven cloth or browse the ground-level stalls for bamboo fish traps and intricately woven containers made by the Murut, Iban and Kedayan people.

Arts & Handicrafts
Training Centre
ARTS & CRAFTS

(🖉 224 0676; Jln Residency; ☺ 8am-5pm Sat-Thu, 8-11.30am & 2-5pm Fri) Sells silverwork, carved wood items, ornamental silver cannons (B$1000) and gong sets (B$1400), hand-made, embroidered shirts (B$897) and *sinjang* (embroidered cloth traditionally worn by local men around their waist), made by the centre's students and graduates. The *jong sarat* (hand-woven cloth made from gold and silver threads) is gorgeous. The centre is on the river, 600m east of Sungai Kianggeh.

The Mall
SHOPPING CENTRE

(Simpang 137, Gadong; ☺ 10am-10pm) Sure, BSB's much-touted shopping mall is sleek, and the ceiling mural of a Royal Brunei Airlines plane careering across the sky is an interesting touch, but here you'll find a collection of local and international-brand outlets, a useful supermarket, an inexpensive food court and an eight-screen cineplex (the most popular cinema in Brunei!).

ℹ Information

EMERGENCY

Ambulance	🖉 991
Fire Brigade	🖉 995
Police	🖉 993

INTERNET ACCESS

Free wi-fi is ubiquitous in most hotels and guesthouses and becoming increasingly available in restaurants and cafes.

MEDIA

Keep an eye out for the free **Borneo Insider's Guide** (www.borneoinsidersguide.com), a glossy magazine published four times a year.

MEDICAL SERVICES

Jerudong Park Medical Centre (🖉 261 1433; www.jpmc.com.bn; Tutong–Muara Hwy; ☺ 24hr) Private hospital with high medical standards. It's your best bet if you're a visitor, especially since services cost only marginally more than at the public hospital.

RIPAS Hospital (🖉 224 2424; www.moh.gov. bn; Jln Putera Al-Muhtadee Billah; ☺ 24hr) Brunei's public hospital, with modern facilities but slow emergency services.

MONEY

Banks and international ATMs are sprinkled around the city centre, especially along Jln McArthur and Jln Sultan. The airport has an ATM.

BIBD (basement, Yayasan Complex, Jln McArthur) Handy ATM in the basement of Block A of the Yayasan Complex.

Isman Money Changer (shop G14, ground fl, block B, Yayasan Complex, Jln Pretty; ⊘10am-8pm Sat-Thu, 10am-noon & 2-8pm Fri) Changes cash. Just off the central atrium.

RHB (Yayasan Complex, Jln McArthur) Has a 24-hour ATM; on the west side of Block D, Yayasan Complex.

POST

Menglait Post Office (Jln Menglait; ⊘8am-4.30pm Mon-Thu & Sat, 8-11.30am & 2-4.30pm Fri) The most central post office now that the city-centre branch has closed.

TELEPHONE

You can buy SIM cards for the two main mobile-phone networks at the airport or at DST and Progresif stores around the city. The following branches are centrally located: **DST** (Yayasan Complex, Jln McArthur; ⊘9am-4pm Mon-Thu & Sat, 9am-noon & 2.30-4pm Fri); **Progresif** (Yayasan Complex, Jln McArthur; ⊘9am-5pm Mon-Thu & Sat, 9-11.30am & 2-5pm Fri, 10am-5pm Sun).

TOURIST INFORMATION

Tourist Information (ground fl, arrival hall, Brunei International Airport; ⊘9am-5pm) Kiosk at the airport.

Tourist Information Centre (Pusat Maklumat Pelacong; www.tourismbrunei.com; Old Customs House, Jln McArthur; ⊘9am-5pm Sat-Thu, 9-11.30am & 2.30-5pm Fri) Helpful office by the waterfront.

ⓘ Getting There & Away

AIR

There are flights from **Brunei International Airport** (⊘233 1747; www.civil-aviation.gov.bn; Lebuhraya Sultan Hassanal Bolkiah) to Malaysia, the Philippines, Hong Kong, Thailand, Indonesia, Australia, China, Dubai, Korea and Singapore.

BOAT

While the state-of-the-art Sultan Haji Omar Ali Saifuddien Bridge links Muara and Temburong, another option is by speedboat (B\$7, 45 minutes, at least hourly from 6am to at least 4.30pm – later on Sundays). The **dock** (Jln Residency) is near the Sungai Kebun bridge, about 1.5km southeast of the centre.

BUS

BSB's carbon-monoxide-choked **bus terminal** (Jln Cator) is on the ground floor of a multistorey parking complex two blocks north of the waterfront. It is used by domestic lines, including those to Muara, Seria, Tutong and Kuala Lurah, but not to Sabah or Sarawak. Schematic signs next to each numbered berth show the route of each line.

A **Jesselton Express** (⊘BSB 714 5734, Kota Kinabalu 016-830 009; www.sipitangexpress. com.my; Jln McArthur) departs from the waterfront at 8am daily for Kota Kinabalu (B\$45, 8½ hours), stopping in Limbang, Bangar, Lawas and various towns in Sabah.

The **PHLS Express** (⊘277 1668; www.phls38. com; Jln McArthur) leaves BSB waterfront (near Sungai Kianggeh) at 7am and 1pm and stops in Tutong (B\$5), Seria (B\$6) and Kuala Belait (B\$6) en route to Miri, Sarawak.

ⓘ Getting Around

TO/FROM THE AIRPORT

Brunei International Airport About 8km north of central BSB, linked to the city centre, including the bus terminal on Jln Cator, by buses 23,

---

ⓘ GETTING TO SARAWAK: BANDAR SERI BEGAWAN TO MIRI

Getting to the border The once-daily PHLS Express (p452) links BSB with Miri (B\$20 from BSB, RM50 from Miri, 3½ hours). Departures from BSB's waterfront are at 7am and from Miri's Pujut Bus Terminal at 8.30am. Tickets are sold on board but can also be booked online through www.easybook.com or a local operator such as Borneo Guide (p475). Another option for travel between BSB and Miri is a private transfer (which may be shared with other travellers) run by Ah Pau (B\$25/100 or RM70/300 per person/car, three hours). Call Ah Pau on 016-807 2893 (Malaysian mobile) or 866 8109 (Brunei mobile). Departures from BSB are usually at 1pm or 2pm; departures from Miri are generally at 9am or 10am, but may be earlier.

At the border The border is open from 6am until midnight. Most travellers to Malaysia are granted a 30- or 60-day visa on arrival.

Moving on The bus will leave you at Miri's Pujut Bus Terminal, a 4km taxi ride from the city centre.

24, 34 and 38 (B$1) until about 5.30pm. A cab to/from the airport costs B$25; pay at the taxi counter. Some hotels offer airport pick-up.

BUS

Brunei's limited public bus system, run by a variety of companies, is somewhat erratic, at least to the uninitiated, so getting around by public transport takes effort. Buses (B$1) operate daily from 6.30am to about 6pm; after that, your options are taking a cab or hoofing it. If you're heading out of town and will need to catch a bus back, ask the driver if and when they're coming back and what time the last bus back is.

Finding stops can be a challenge – some are marked by black-and-white-striped uprights or a shelter, others by a yellow triangle painted on the pavement, and yet others by no discernible symbol. Fortunately numbers are prominently displayed on each 20- or 40-passenger bus.

The bus station lacks an information office or a ticket counter, though there is a schematic route map that, while it's hard to decipher, explains what buses (routes are numbered) go where. It may be best to ask about transport options at your hotel before heading to the bus station.

Useful bus routes include:

Airport 23, 24, 34, Express
Brunei Museum, Malay Technology Museum, Maritime Museum 39
Empire Hotel, Jerudong 57, 58
Gadong 1, 20, 23
Istana Nurul Iman 44-49, 56
Jame'Asr Hassanil Bolkiah Mosque 1, 20
Kiulap 20, 23
Serasa Ferry Terminal 33, Express

CAR

Brunei has Southeast Asia's cheapest petrol (cheaper per litre than bottled water). If you're driving a car (eg a rental) with Malaysian plates and are not a Brunei resident, you'll be taken to a special pump to pay more (this is to prevent smuggling).

Hiring a car is the best way to explore both BSB and Brunei's hinterland. Parking is plentiful and driving conditions are very good. Rental prices start at about B$75 a day. Surcharges may apply if the car is taken into Sarawak. Most agencies will bring the car to your hotel and pick it up when you've finished, and drivers can also be arranged, though this could add B$100 to the daily cost. The main roads are in good condition, but some back roads require a 4WD.

Indera En Voy Transportation (☑ 873 1621; www.ievbrunei.com.bn; Simpang 209, block A, unit 2, Jln Utama Berakas, Lambak Kanan; ⊙8am-5pm Mon-Sat) Local rental company with competitive rates. Near airport.

ⓘ **GETTING TO SABAH: BANDAR SERI BEGAWAN TO KOTA KINABALU**

Getting to the border At 8am daily a Jesselton Express bus runs to Kota Kinabalu (B$45, 8½ hours) via Limbang, Bangar, Lawas and various towns in Sabah. A travel agent will charge B$48 at most.

If you miss the bus in BSB Take a B$1 water taxi to Temburong ferry terminal and a B$7 ferry ride (45 minutes) to Bangar. If you get to Bangar before the bus (about 10.30am) and there are seats available, hop on and pay B$25 for the run to KK (six to seven hours). If you are planning to visit Temburong district before heading to Sabah, you can also just catch the bus from Bangar.

At the border The border is open 6am to midnight. Make sure you have your passport ready because you'll be stopping at a whopping eight checkpoints. As long as your ID is in order you'll be fine – the trip is tedious rather than dodgy.

Moving on The same long-distance bus heads to KK and drops you off close to the main stretches of hotels and restaurants.

Avis (☑ 222 7100; www.avis.com; Radisson Hotel, Jln Tasek Lama 2203; ⊙8am-noon & 1.30-5pm Mon-Thu, 8am-noon & 2-5pm Fri, 8am-noon & 1.30-4pm Sat, 9am-noon & 1.30-3pm Sun) Also has an office at the **airport** (☑ 233 3298; arrival hall, Brunei International Airport; ⊙8.30am-5.30pm).

Hertz (☑ 872 6000; www.hertz.com; arrival hall, Brunei International Airport; ⊙8am-5pm)

TAXI & DART

Taxis are a convenient way of exploring BSB – if you can find one, that is, as there are only about 50 in the country. There is no centralised taxi dispatcher, and it's difficult or impossible to flag down a cab on the street. Hotels can provide drivers' mobile-phone numbers. Most taxis have yellow tops; a few serving the airport are all white.

BSB's only proper **taxi rank** is two blocks north of the waterfront, at the bus terminal on Jln Cator.

Some taxis use meters, although many drivers will just try to negotiate a fare with you. Fares go up by 50% after 10pm; the charge for an hour of wait time is B$30 to B$35. Sample day-time taxi fares from the city centre include the Brunei Museum (B$25), Gadong (B$15), the airport (B$20 to B$25), the Serasa Ferry Terminal in Muara (B$40), the Empire Hotel & Country Club (B$35) and the Jerudong Park Playground (B$35).

Download the Dart app if you have a smartphone and you get access to Brunei's answer to Uber, meaning prices are more competitive than taxis.

WATER TAXI

If your destination is near the river, water taxis – the same little motorboats that ferry people to and from Kampung Ayer – are a good way of getting there. You can hail a water taxi anywhere on the waterfront a boat can dock, as well as along Venice-esque Sungai Kianggeh. Crossing straight across the river is supposed to cost B$1 per person; diagonal crossings and tours of Kampung Ayer cost more.

TUTONG & BELAIT DISTRICTS

Most travellers merely pass through the districts of Tutong and Belait, west of BSB, en route to Miri in Sarawak, but there are a few worthwhile attractions here, from beaches and monuments to the oil industry, to Iban longhouses deep in the interior.

Tutong

POP 20,000

About halfway between Seria and BSB lies Tutong, the main town in central Brunei. The town itself is neat and unremarkable, but the area is famous in Brunei for two things: pitcher plants and sand. Locals cook a variety of dishes in the insect-catching sacs of the area's six species of pitcher plants on special occasions, while some of the sand near Tutong is so white that Bruneians take pictures with it, pretending it's snow (have your fun any way you can, Brunei). You can see *pasir putih* (white sand) in patches along the side of the Pan Borneo Hwy.

◉ Sights

Pantai Seri Kenangan BEACH
(Pantai Tutong; Jln Kuala Tutong) Set on a spit of land, with the South China Sea on one side and Sungai Tutong on the other, this casuarina-lined beach is arguably the best in Brunei, meaning powdery white sand only lightly sprinkled with plastic, and warm water to paddle in. Sandflies can be a problem around sunset, so be sure to bring repellent. The beach is 2km west of Tutong town.

Tasek Merimbun Heritage Park LAKE
Tasek Merimbun is Brunei's largest lake and supports ample birdlife. Near the lake there's a small visitor centre that isn't always open. When it is you can learn all about the birds and animals that call the nature reserve home. The boardwalk offers great views of the watery expanse. You need a car to get out there.

❶ Getting There & Away

The PHLS express buses that link BSB with Seria, Kuala Belait and Miri stop at the **bus station** (Jln Enchi Awang). Departures west to Seria, Kuala Belait and Miri are at 8am and 2pm, and east to BSB at 10.45am and 6.15pm (arrive 15 minutes early as times are approximate and the bus doesn't wait).

Jalan Labi

POP UNDER 2000

A few kilometres after you enter Belait district (coming from Tutong and BSB), a road – Jalan Labi – branches inland (south) to Labi and beyond, taking you through some prime forest areas. Fully paved, it leads to a number of Iban longhouses. Temburong District aside, this is your best opportunity for cultural immersion, best organised through Borneo Guide (p475); turning up on spec doesn't really work. You can explore the small wetland reserve on your own, though.

◉ Sights

Luagan Lalak Recreation Park NATURE RESERVE
(Jln Labi; ⊙24hr) If you're craving peace and serenity this is the place to find it: a trident of wooden walkways extend across alluvial freshwater swamp, with tufts of greenery dotted like islands in mirror-like water. It's a beautiful spot for picnicking, bird-watching or meditating. Locals come here for illegal fishing. Following Jln Labi down from the main highway, the park is 20km before Labi (look for the sign). There is no public transport here.

Labi Longhouses NOTABLE BUILDING
Labi is a small Iban settlement about 40km south of the coastal road with four longhouses: Rampayoh, Mendaram Besar, Mendaram Kecil and, at the end of the track, Teraja. How much of a longhouse you are able to see if you go without a guide will depend on whether there's an English speaker there to show you around. The cost of such a tour might be B$3 per person. To visit Teraja longhouse, register at the police station nearby.

These longhouses are a mix of the modern and the traditional: you will see women weaving baskets, though nowadays they may be plastic rather than rattan, and the longhouses have 24-hour electricity. Outside, among the fruit trees and clucking chickens, there is a rustic shelter for a row of gleaming cars.

Borneo Guide runs day trips from BSB, with a local lunch arranged. Contact it, or talk to longhouse inhabitants directly, about overnight stays and jungle treks.

Forestry Museum MUSEUM
(Simpang 50, Jln Labi, Sungai Liang; ⊙ 8am-12.15pm & 1.30-4.30pm, closed Fri & Sun) FREE The Forestry Museum is a small, simple place with seriously thorough information about the local forest. Exhibits detail the history of logging and conservation in the area, with labelled examples of more than 50 types of wood found here, along with taxidermic examples of the resident wildlife – sadly it's the closest you're likely to come to seeing a clouded leopard in Borneo. It's located down the Simpang 50 turnoff (on the right as you head towards Labi).

Waterfalls WATERFALL
In the jungle beyond the Teraja longhouse, there are around 40 waterfalls. You can enlist a guide from the longhouse to take you to two falls that are within an hour's hike: the stunning 70m Wasai Beluloh, and the smaller Wasai Teraja, with a deep plunge pool for swimming.

ⓘ Getting There & Away

There's no public transport, but it's a beautiful 54km drive from the main highway, through jungle and past fruit plantations, to the Teraja longhouse at the end of the road.

Seria

POP 30,000

Spread out along the coast between Tutong and Kuala Belait, low-density Seria is where the viscous black blood (oil) flows through Brunei's veins. It's great place to educate yourself about the industry.

ⓞ Sights

Oil & Gas Discovery Centre MUSEUM
(☑ 337 7200; www.ogdcbrunei.com; off Jln Tengah; adult/child 5-17yr B$16/8; ⊙ 8.30am-noon & 1.30-5pm Mon-Thu & Sat, 8.30am-11.30am & 2.30-5pm Fri, 9.30am-noon & 1.30-6pm Sun; ⓓ) Puts an 'edutainment' spin on the oil industry, with hands-on exhibits aimed largely at kids. Occasional themed temporary exhibitions, too. About 700m northwest of Seria town centre.

Billionth Barrel Monument MONUMENT
(off Jln Tengah) Commemorates (you guessed it) the billionth barrel of crude oil produced at the Seria field, a landmark reached in 1991. Copper panels leading up to the monument depict oil-related scenes – one of them features what looks like a giant lizard or possibly an alien.

🛏 Sleeping & Eating

Roomz Hotel HOTEL $$
(☑ 322 3223; www.roomz.com.bn; lot 1, No 1, Jln Sultan Omar Ali; s/d incl breakfast B$100/130; ❇ 🛜) A handy four blocks from the Oil & Gas Discovery Centre, this sleek hotel is a good bet for spotless, tiled rooms with little desks, balconies and sea views. Rooms can be rented by the hour (!). The place is easy to find – it's the tallest building in town, situated two blocks northwest of the bus station.

Kaizen Sushi JAPANESE $$
(☑ 322 2662; No 26, 1st fl, Jln Sultan Omar Ali; mains B$6-18; ⊙ 11am-2.30pm & 5.30-10pm Sun-Thu, 10am-noon & 5.30-10pm Fri) The Seria outpost of one of BSB's best restaurants, Kaizen delights with its extensive selection of Japanese dishes. Special treats include toro (fatty tuna) sashimi, oysters grilled with enoki mushrooms, and seared giant scallops with a tangy, spicy sauce.

ⓘ Getting There & Away

Frequent purple minibuses depart from the **bus station** (Jln Bunga Pinang) for Kuala Belait (B$1). The PHLS express to Miri (B$15) goes through Kuala Belait at 9am and 3pm, and to BSB (B$6) via Tutong at 9.45am and 5.15pm (arrive 15 minutes early as times are approximate and the bus doesn't wait).

TEMBURONG DISTRICT

Brunei's 1288-sq-km Temburong District is physically separated from the rest of the nation by Sarawak's Limbang division, and happens to contain one of the best preserved tracts of primary rainforest in all of Borneo. The main draw is the brilliant Ulu Temburong National Park.

For now at least, the journey from BSB to Bangar, the district capital, is an exhilarating speedboat ride: you roar down Sungai Brunei, slap through the nipa-palm-lined waterways and then tilt and weave through mangroves into the mouth of Sungai Temburong.

Bangar

POP 27,300

If little Bangar were any more soporific, it would be in a coma. Perched on the banks of Sungai Temburong, it's the gateway to Temburong District, and everyone seems to go to sleep at around 8pm. You can use Bangar as a base for visiting Ulu Temburong National Park – provided you make arrangements with Ulu Ulu Resort (p486). If you don't have time to visit Ulu Temburong, the nearby Bukit Patoi Recreational Park gives you a quicker taste of the jungle.

◉ Sights

Bukit Patoi Recreational Park NATURE RESERVE
(Taman Rekreasi Bukit Patoi) Within the protected **Peradayan Forest Reserve**, this recreational park offers the chance of a 2km (one way) hike to the top of **Bukit Patoi** (310m). The well-marked trail, through pristine jungle, begins at the picnic tables and toilet block at the park entrance, about 15km southeast of Bangar (towards Lawas). It's best organised through a BSB tour company. To get here from BSB ask around for an unofficial taxi (about B$30 return). Bring plenty of water.

Once you reach the peak, enjoy the views then turn around and come back down – in theory it is possible to continue on to Bukit Peradayan (410m), but the path is poorly maintained. Up-to-date trail information is available from tour companies in BSB.

If you want to explore the Bruneian rainforest without the logistics and expense of a trip further upriver, Peradayan Forest Reserve makes a good alternative that can easily be done as a day trip from BSB.

🛏 Sleeping

Lukat Intan Guesthouse GUESTHOUSE $
(☑ 522 1078, 864 3766; No 18, Simpang 59, Jln Kampong Menengah, Kampong Sungai Tanit; r incl breakfast B$55; [P][❄]) Run by a friendly couple, Lukat offers spic-and-span rooms and personable service. They're happy to give free rides to Bangar jetty. Call for directions.

Youth Hostel HOSTEL $
(Pusat Belia; ☑ 522 1694; Jln Bangar Puni-Ujong; dm B$10; ⊙ office staffed 7.30am-4.30pm, closed Fri & Sat; [❄]) This basic hostel is in a bright-orange building about 50m, and across the road (walk under the road bridge), from the Bangar ferry terminal. The sex-segregated dorms, each with six beds (bunks), are clean and have air-con. The office is upstairs.

Stoneville Hotel HOTEL $$
(☑ 522 2252; stonevillehotel@yahoo.com; 1532 Kampong Sungai Tanam; r from B$85; [❄][🛜]) Bangar's first (and only) hotel is a modern if modest establishment with simple, clean, comfortable rooms with TV and cable channels. In the lobby the restaurant is open for breakfast, lunch and dinner. It is about 500m northwest of the ferry terminal, along the road running parallel to the river's west bank.

✗ Eating

The small shopping mall beyond the row of shops northwest of Bangar ferry terminal has a **food court** (1st fl, Kompleks Utami Bumiputera, Jln Pekan Bangar; mains B$1-3; ⊙ 6am or 7am-8pm, closed noon-2pm Fri). A handful of restaurants serving good Malay and Chinese food can be found in the rows of shops also northwest of the ferry terminal. There is also an outdoor **produce market** (Jln Pekan Bangar; ⊙ 8am-4pm) beside the highway just west of the bridge and ferry terminal.

Afsara Restaurant BRUNEIAN $
(☑ 522 1338; Lg Pekan Bangar 3; mains B$2-4; ⊙ 7am-8pm Sun-Thu, 7am-noon & 2-7pm Fri; [🍴]) The pick of Bangar eateries, Afsara is responsible for excellent *roti kosong* – flaky without being greasy – with a dhal and a curry to dip it into, as well as *murtabak* (filled roti) and an assortment of fried-noodle dishes.

RR Max Cafe MALAYSIAN $
(Lg Pekan Bangar 3; mains B$1-3; ⊙ 7.30am-8pm) This cafe north of the jetty has inexpensive meals, such as *nasi katok* (B$1) and egg (B$3) or tuna (B$2.50) sandwiches and fresh fruit juice (B$3.50). The owners are also very helpful with travellers new to Bangar.

🛍 Shopping

Nadi Utama Minimart DEPARTMENT STORE
(Jln Pekan Bangar, Kompleks Utama Bumiputera; ⊙ 8am-8pm) Sells rubber shoes ideal for jungle walks; larger sizes may not be available.

ℹ Information

Some of the accommodation places offer wi-fi access. Otherwise it helps to have a smartphone with local SIM card.

BIBD (Jln Pekan Bangar 2; ⊙ 8.45am-3.45pm Mon-Thu, 8.45-11am & 2.30-4pm Fri, 8.45-11.15am Sat) The only bank in town has two ATMs that accept foreign cards.

Chop Hock Guan Minimarket (Lg Pekan Bangar 3; ⊙ 8am-8pm) Exchanges Malaysian ringgits for Brunei dollars.

ⓘ Getting There & Away

BOAT
By far the fastest way to and from BSB is by speedboat (B$7, 45 minutes, hourly from 6.30am to 5.15pm). Bangar's ferry terminal, Terminal Perahu Dan Penumpang, is on the western bank of the river, just south of the road bridge.

Boats depart at a scheduled time or when they're full, whichever comes first. When you get to the ticket counters, check which company's boat will be the next to leave and then pay and add your name and passport number to the passenger list.

BUS
Buses run by **Jesselton** (📞717 7755, 719 3835, in BSB 718 3838; www.sipitangexpress.com. my; Jln Pekan Bangar) pick up passengers heading towards Limbang and BSB (B$10, two hours) in the early afternoon; its bus to KK (B$25, six hours) via Lawas (B$10, three hours) passes through town at about 10am (it can be up to an hour late). Buses stop on Jln Labu, just across the bridge on the west side of the river, beside the produce market.

CAR & MOTORCYCLE
The Sultan Haji Omar Ali Saifuddien Bridge opened in 2020, linking Temburong District with Muara. Asia's longest bridge makes it possible to drive from Muara to Bangar in about 40 minutes.

TAXI
Bangar doesn't have official taxis, but it's usually not too difficult to hire a car if you ask around under the rain awning in front of the ferry terminal. Drivers may not speak much English. Possible destinations include Lawas (B$50), Limbang in Malaysia (about B$40) and the Peradayan Forest Reserve (Bukit Patoi; about B$30 return).

Taxis do not wait on the Malaysian side of the border, so make sure your transport goes all the way to Limbang.

Batang Duri
POP UNDER 500

Batang Duri, 12km south of Bangar, is the jumping-off point for longboat rides to Ulu Temburong National Park. As you head south the sealed road passes Malay settlements, then Murut (Lun Bawang) hamlets and finally a few modern Iban longhouses. It's definitely worth staying here overnight, or even for a few days, to delve into local Iban culture and do some serious jungle trekking.

There is no public transport here. Tour companies include transport to and from ecolodges in tour package prices.

PULAU SELIRONG RECREATIONAL PARK
At the northern tip of Temburong District lies this 25-sq-km mangrove-forested island reachable only by boat (45 minutes from BSB). Intrepid Tours (p475) runs half-day guided trips for around B$100 per person. Two kilometres of elevated walkways lead through the mangroves, which are the untamed habitat of proboscis monkeys and flying lemurs – if you're lucky you might spot one gliding down from the trees. **Pulau Selirong** is also known as Mosquito Island; bring repellent.

At certain times the tide levels are such that it is not possible to access the island.

🛏 Sleeping

⭐ **Sumbiling Eco Village** CABIN $$$
(📞718 7138, 242 6923; www.borneoguide.com/eco village; Kampong Sumbiling Lama, Jln Batang Duri; per person day trips from US$115, 2-day, 1-night incl meals & guided hikes from US$148) 🍴 If you're looking for Brunei's version of a jungle camp with basic amenities and a chilled-out atmosphere, come to Sumbiling. This ecofriendly rustic camp in a beautiful riverside location offers tasty Iban cuisine and accommodation in bamboo huts or tents, which have beds, mosquito nets and fans. Sumbiling is run by Borneo Guide (p475) in cooperation with the local Iban community.

When you're not lounging in a hammock, there are plenty of outdoor activities on hand (to be booked in advance), including visits to nearby Ulu Temburong National Park, jungle overnights, inner tubing on the river, night walks and dawn hikes to a lofty viewpoint to watch the morning mist rise from the jungle.

Sumbiling is situated a few minutes downstream from Batang Duri. Prices include transport from Bangar jetty.

Ulu Temburong National Park

Ulu Temburong National Park, located in the heart of a 500-sq-km area of pristine rainforest covering most of southern Temburong, is a highlight of a visit to Brunei. It's odd that a small country such as Brunei should contain such a sizeable chunk of true untamed wilderness. Only about 1 sq km of the park is accessible to tourists, who are only admitted as part of guided-tour packages. To protect it, the rest is off-limits to everyone except scientists, who flock here from around the world. Permitted activities include a canopy walk, some short jungle walks and swimming in the cool mountain waters of Sungai Temburong.

Ulu Temburong's forests are teeming with life, including as many as 400 kinds of butterfly. The best times to spot birds and animals are around sunrise and sunset, but you're much more likely to hear hornbills and Bornean gibbons than to see them.

🏃 Activities

Aluminium Walkway
WALKING

Ulu Temburong National Park's main attraction is a delicate aluminium walkway, its base accessed via some 800 steps. Secured by guy wires, it brings you level with the jungle canopy, up to 60m above the forest floor. From the walkway, jungle-clad hills and valleys stretch to the horizon – this is what the rainforest in neighbouring Malaysia looked like before rampant illegal deforestation.

In primary rainforests only limited vegetation can grow on the ground because so little light penetrates, but up in the canopy all manner of life proliferates. Unfortunately there are no explanatory signs along the walkway, but a good guide will explain the importance of the canopy ecosystem and point out the huge variety of organisms that can live on a single tree: orchids, bird's-nest ferns and other epiphytes, ants and myriad other insects, amphibians, snakes and a huge selection of birds.

The trail up to the canopy walk begins near the confluence of Sungai Belalong and Sungai Temburong. It's a short, steep, sweaty walk. If you stay overnight at Ulu Ulu Resort you can do the canopy walk at sunrise or sunset, when birds and animals are most likely to be around.

Waterfall
SWIMMING

At this waterfall, 500m from the park headquarters, you can stand in a pool and 2cm- to 4cm-long catfish will nibble on the dry skin on your feet, giving you a gentle, ticklish pedicure. Your guide will lead you a couple of hundred metres up the creek to reach it. Another, smaller waterfall nearby has a deep pool perfect for swimming.

🛏 Sleeping

⭐ Ulu Ulu Resort
LODGE $$$

(📞244 1791; www.uluuluresort.com; Ulu Temburong National Park; per person 2-day, 1-night incl meals dm/s/d B$275/330/660; ❄) The only accommodation inside the park is an upscale riverside lodge, constructed entirely of hardwood, with some rooms built to resemble 1920s Malaysian-style chalets. Standard rooms are dormitory style with shared bathrooms. Prices include transfers from Bangar, meals and activities. Guests at the resort have a 4.30am wake-up call to see sunrise at the canopy walk, an unforgettable experience.

In Malay, *ulu* (as in Ulu Temburong) means 'upriver' and *ulu ulu* means, essentially, 'back of beyond'. The park's wildness and lack of established trails rule out the possibility of unguided walks, so resort activities are restricted to an easygoing timetable of kayaking and river swimming during the day and a guided night walk.

ℹ Getting There & Away

The only way to visit the park is by booking a tour. While you can reach Bangar under your own steam, to get into the park itself you need to engage the services of one of several BSB-based agencies.

One of Ulu Temburong National Park's charms is that the only way to get there is by *temuai* (shallow-draft Iban longboat). The trip upriver from Batang Duri (organised as part of a guided tour) is challenging even for experienced skippers: submerged boulders and logs have to be dodged, hanging vines must be evaded and the outboard must be taken out of the water at exactly the right moment when shooting the rapids.

The journey takes between 25 and 45 minutes, depending on river conditions. When it rains the water level can quickly rise by up to 2m, but if the river is low you might have to get out and push (wear waterproof shoes).

SURVIVAL GUIDE

ℹ Directory A–Z

CURRENCY
Brunei dollar (B$)

EATING PRICE RANGES
The following price ranges refer to a main course.

$ less than B$6

$$ B$6–16

$$$ more than B$16

EMERGENCY

Ambulance	991
Police	993
Fire	995
Search & Rescue	998

LEGAL MATTERS

In May 2014 Brunei began phasing in a new criminal code based on sharia law. Offences in this first phase became punishable with a fine, imprisonment or both. Prayer for Muslims on Fridays became compulsory and, consequently, all businesses and restaurants tend to be shut between noon and 2pm. In April 2019 plans to introduce more severe penalties, including the severing of limbs for theft and stoning to death for adultery, were implemented despite global criticism. Make sure you're up to date on Brunei's laws in order to ensure you're on the right side of them.

LGBTIQ+ TRAVELLERS

Homosexual acts are illegal in Brunei and punishable by death. Visitors to Brunei best err on the side of caution and not openly advertise their sexual orientation.

POST

The Brunei postal service (www.post.gov.bn) is generally reliable and reasonably efficient. BSB no longer has a central post office, though there's a post office in several outlying neighbourhoods.

Brunei postal tariffs for a postcard/letter weighing 20g:
➡ Brunei Darussalam – B$0.20
➡ Singapore, Malaysia, Australia and New Zealand – B$0.30
➡ Rest of the world – B$0.50

PUBLIC HOLIDAYS

Brunei shares major public holidays with Malaysia. Holidays specific to Brunei include **Brunei National Day** (23 February), **Royal Brunei Armed Forces Day** (31 May) and the **Sultan of Brunei's Birthday** (15 July).

SLEEPING PRICE RANGES

The following price ranges refer to a double room with bathroom. Unless otherwise stated, breakfast is included in the price.
$ less than B$60
$$ B$60–150
$$$ more than B$150

TELEPHONE

Inexpensive prepaid SIM cards are readily available. If you bring your own phone, make sure it

RAMADAN RULES

Brunei is a religious, majority-Muslim country that takes Ramadan seriously. Under laws introduced in 2014, all eating, drinking and smoking in public is illegal during daylight hours for the month of Ramadan. During the day, cafes and restaurants are open for takeaway only (bring food and drinks back to your hotel to consume).

If you're visiting during the holiest month of the Islamic year, it's a particularly good idea to dress conservatively: men and women should cover their shoulders and wear clothes reaching below the knees. Museums close early (at 3pm Saturday to Thursday and noon on Friday) and other businesses may also operate for shorter hours. Mosques are closed to non-Muslim visitors for the whole month.

can handle 900/1800MHz and is not locked. There are no area codes within Brunei.

TIME

Brunei is eight hours ahead of Greenwich Mean Time (GMT/UTC+8). Brunei does not observe daylight-saving time.

TOURIST INFORMATION

Brunei Tourism (220 0874; www.brunei tourism.travel; Kampong Ayer Cultural & Tourism Gallery; ⊙9am-12.15pm & 1.30-4.30pm Mon-Thu & Sat, 9-11.30am & 2-4.30pm Fri) A useful website, containing information on transport, business hours, accommodation, tour agencies and more.

VISAS

Travellers from the US, UK, European Union, Switzerland and Norway are granted a 90-day visa-free stay. Travellers from New Zealand, Singapore, South Korea and Malaysia, among others, receive 30 days. Japanese and Canadians get 14 free days. Chinese can apply for a 14-day single-entry visa (B$20). Australians can apply for the following visas upon arrival: 72-hour transit (B$5), 30-day single entry (B$20) or multiple entry (B$30).

WOMEN TRAVELLERS

Loose-fitting clothes that cover the shoulders and the knees are culturally appropriate in this area.

Singapore

🎵 65 / POP 5.6 MILLION

Includes ➡

Sights............	489
Activities..........	517
Courses..........	520
Tours.............	520
Festivals & Events..	520
Sleeping...........	531
Eating............	536
Drinking & Nightlife..........	546
Entertainment......	552
Shopping.........	553
Survival Guide......	556

Best Places to Eat

➡ Odette (p537)

➡ Burnt Ends (p540)

➡ National Kitchen by Violet Oon (p537)

➡ Gluttons Bay (p536)

➡ A Noodle Story (p538)

Best Places to Stay

➡ Fullerton Bay Hotel (p532)

➡ Raffles Hotel (p532)

➡ Parkroyal on Pickering (p534)

➡ Six Senses Duxton (p534)

➡ Ritz-Carlton Millenia Singapore (p532)

Why Go?

Capitalising on its melting pot of cultures, Singapore has become one of Asia's hit-list destinations – an ambitious, ever-evolving wonder of sci-fi architecture in billion-dollar gardens, of masterpieces in colonial palaces, and single-origin coffee in flouncy heritage shophouses. From cult-status Aussie chefs to fashion-forward local designers, some of the world's hottest creatives have set up shop on these steamy streets, turning the Little Red Dot into a booming hub for all things hip and innovative.

Don't think, though, that the Singapore of old has been entirely swept aside: there's still a spicy broth of Chinese, Malay, Indian and Peranakan traditions, smoky temples, raucous wet markets, and sleepy islands reached by bumboat. Sure, it might be clean, rich and a stickler for rules, but dig a little deeper and you'll uncover a Singapore far more complex than you ever imagined.

When to Go
Singapore

°C/°F **Temp**   **Rainfall** inches/mm

| J | F | M | A | M | J | J | A | S | O | N | D |

Jan/Feb Catch Chinese New Year fireworks, dragon parades and markets.

May Bag some grin-inducing bargains at the Great Singapore Sale in late May.

Sep Fans flocking to the F1 night race means accommodation is scarce and expensive.

History

Chinese traders en route to India had plied the waters around what is now Singapore from at least the 5th century CE, though the records of Chinese sailors as early as the 3rd century refer to an island called Pu Luo Chung, a name reputedly derived from the Malay Pulau Ujong, meaning 'island at the end'.

Landing on its shores in 1819 was Sir Stamford Raffles. Then lieutenant general of Java, Raffles deemed the muddy island an ideal spot for a new British-controlled entrepôt to counter Dutch power in the region. Signing a treaty with the Sultan of Johor and *temenggong* (senior judge), Raffles acquired the use of Singapore in exchange for modest annual allowances to Sultan Hussein and the judge. This exchange ended with a cash buyout of the pair in 1824 and the transfer of Singapore's ownership to Britain's East India Company.

Large waves of immigration soon washed over the free port, driven by thrifty merchants keen to avoid the high tariffs at the competing, Dutch-controlled port of Melaka. Despite a massive fall in rubber prices in 1920, Singapore's prosperity continued, the population soared and millionaires were made almost overnight.

Crashing the party on 15 February 1942 was General Yamashita Tomoyuki and his thinly stretched army, who caught the British rulers by surprise and swiftly wrested control from them, renaming the island 'Syonan' (Light of the South) and interning or executing countless locals, Europeans and Allied POWs. Though the British regained power in 1945, the occupation had eroded Singapore's innate trust in the British empire's protective embrace. New political forces were at work and the road to independence was paved.

If one person can be considered responsible for the position Singapore finds itself in today, it is Lee Kuan Yew (1923–2015), the first prime minister of Singapore. This third-generation Straits-born Chinese was named Harry Lee, and brought up to be, in his own words, 'the equal of any Englishman'. His education at the elite Raffles Institution and Cambridge University equipped him well to deal with both colonial power and political opposition when Singapore took control of its own destiny in the 1960s.

The early years were not easy. Race riots in 1964 and ejection from the Malay Federation in 1965 made Lee's task even harder. Lee used tax incentives and strict new labour laws to attract foreign investment. This, combined with huge resources poured into developing an English-language education system that produced a competent workforce, saw Singapore's economy rapidly industrialise, securing the road to today's affluent, role-model nation.

Lee Kuan Yew's son, Lee Hsien Loong, who was deputy Prime Minister and Defence Minister under Goh Chok Tong, took over the top job unopposed in 2004. The 2015 elections were fiercely contested; for the first time in history the opposition parties stood in every seat. Hot topics included the failing economy, 'worsening' public transport, the high cost of living and immigration issues. Mr Lee called the election a year early, possibly in the hope of capitalising on the national pride stirred up during the nation's 50th birthday celebrations. This also coincided with the death of Singapore's founding father Lee Kuan Yew, in March. The election was a landslide win for the People's Action Party (PAP), who gained 70% of the votes. Mr Lee secured the party's 15th consecutive election victory in 2020.

◉ Sights

◉ Colonial District, the Quays & Marina Bay

The Colonial District brims with iconic heritage architecture and must-see museums. Straddling the river are the eateries, bars and nightspots of Boat Quay, Clarke Quay and Robertson Quay. Further east, the river spills into attention-seeking Marina Bay, home to Marina Bay Sands and Gardens by the Bay.

★ **Gardens by the Bay**   GARDENS
(Map p492; ☑ 6420 6848; www.gardensbythebay.com.sg; 18 Marina Gardens Dr; gardens free, conservatories adult/child under 13yr S$28/15, OCBC Skyway adult/child under 13yr S$8/5; ⊙ 5am-2am, conservatories & OCBC Skyway 9am-9pm, last ticket sale 8pm; Ⓜ Bayfront) Singapore's 21st-century botanic garden is a S$1 billion, 101-hectare fantasy land of space-age biodomes, high-tech Supertrees and whimsical sculptures. The Flower Dome replicates the dry Mediterranean climates found across the world, while the even more astounding Cloud Forest is a tropical montane affair, complete with waterfall. Connecting two of the Supertrees is the OCBC Skyway, with knockout views of the gardens, city and South China Sea. At 7.45pm and 8.45pm, the Supertrees twinkle and glow for the spectacular Garden Rhapsody show.

SINGAPORE SIGHTS

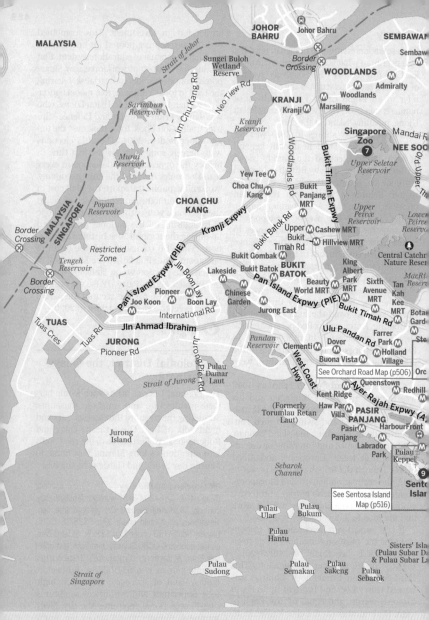

Singapore Highlights

1 **Gardens by the Bay** (p489) Scaling Supertrees and a glass-enclosed mountain.

2 **National Gallery Singapore** (p495) Touring

exhibitions at the jewel in the crown of Singapore's art scene.

3 **National Museum of Singapore** (p496) Reliving Singaporean history at this multisensory museum.

4 **Little India** (p501) Exploring this vibrant ethnic enclave.

5 **Chinatown** (p499) Wining and dining in this hot-spot heritage 'hood.

Pulau
Seletar

Yishun
YISHUN Ⓜ

atib Ⓜ

Pulau
Punggol
Barat

Pulau
Punggol
Timor

Seletar
Airport

Punggol Point

Pulau
Ubin

Noordin Ⓜ
Beach

Mamam Ⓜ
Beach

Pulau
Tekong
Kechil

JL KAYU

Punggol Ⓜ

Ⓜ **Pulau Ubin**

Pulau
Tekong

er Seletar
eservoir

PUNGGOL

Pulau
Serangoon

Changi
Point

Ⓜ Sengkang

Yio Chu
Kang

HOUGANG

Buangkok Ⓜ

Pulau Ubin
Ferry Terminal

Changi Point
Ferry Terminal

g Mo Kio Ⓜ

Hougang Ⓜ

**PASIR
RIS**

Pulau
Ketam

Changi
Golf Club

CHANGI

Changi
Beach Park

Ang Mo Kio Ave 3

Pasir Ris
Park

Mo Kio Ave 1

SERANGOON

Lorong
Chuan

Kovan Ⓜ

**TAMPINES
RIS**

TAMPINES

Pasir
Ris

LOYANG Ⓜ

Ⓜ Singapore Changi Airport

rymount Ⓜ

Ⓜ Ⓜ Bishan

Ⓜ Serangoon

Tampines Ⓜ

Simei Ⓜ

**Upper Changi
East Rd**

Changi Airport Ⓜ

ddell Ⓜ **TOA
PAYOH**

**PAYA
LEBAR**

Bedok
Reservoir

SIMEI Ⓜ

Expo Ⓜ

See Little India &
Kampong Glam
Map (p504)

Potong Ⓜ
Pasir

**KIM
CHUAN**

BEDOK

Tanah Ⓜ
Merah

Aljunied Ⓜ

Little Ⓜ ④
India

Little India Ⓜ

Ⓜ Ⓜ
Eunos

Kembangan Ⓜ

vton Ⓜ

Ⓜ Lavender

Paya
Lebar

**JOO CHIAT
(KATONG)**

GEYLANG

③ **National Museum of Singapore**

ong Ⓜ
hru

② **National Gallery
Singapore**

See Eastern Singapore
Map (p510)

⑤

See Colonial District, the Quays & Marina Bay Map (p492)

hinatown Ⓜ

① **Gardens by the Bay**

See Chinatown & the CBD Map (p500)

au
ni

Lazarus Island
(Pulau Sakijang
Pelepah)

*Strait of
Singapore*

Kusu Island
(Pulau Tembakul)

St John's
Island

Ⓝ 0 —————— 5 km
0 —————— 2 miles

Seletar Expwy (SLE)

Central Expwy

Tampines Expwy (TPE)

Punggol Rd

Tampines Rd

Simei Ave

Loyang Rd

Xilin Ave

Changi Coast Rd

⑥ **Pulau Ubin** (p509)
Catching a bumboat to this
bicycle-friendly rustic
island.

⑦ **Singapore Zoo** (p511)
Hanging out at one of

the world's most inviting,
enlightening animal
sanctuaries.

⑧ **Tiong Bahru** (p503)
Exploring this low-rise, art
deco-styled neighbourhood.

⑨ **Sentosa Island** (p515)
Enjoying the island's
world-class theme parks,
amusements and clean
beaches.

Colonial District, the Quays & Marina Bay

SINGAPORE

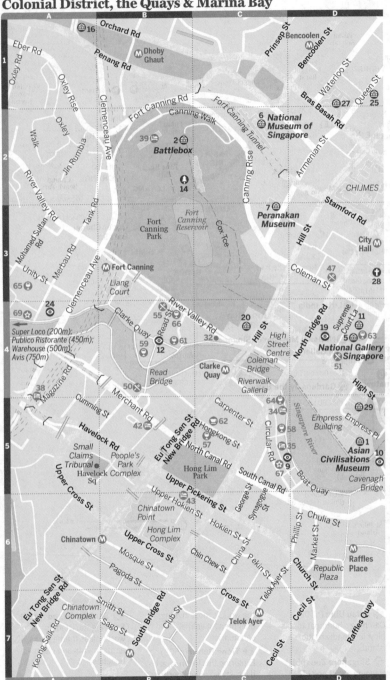

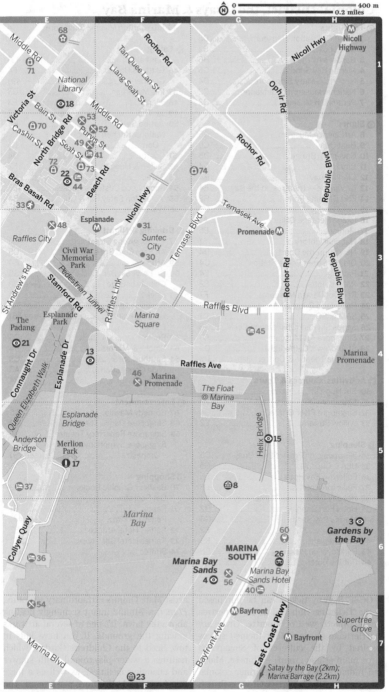

Colonial District, the Quays & Marina Bay

◉ Top Sights
1 Asian Civilisations Museum D5
2 Battlebox B2
3 Gardens by the Bay H6
4 Marina Bay Sands G6
5 National Gallery Singapore D4
6 National Museum of Singapore C2
7 Peranakan Museum C3

◉ Sights
8 ArtScience Museum G5
9 Boat Quay C5
10 Cavenagh Bridge D5
11 City Hall D4
12 Clarke Quay B4
13 Esplanade – Theatres on the Bay E4
14 Fort Canning Park B2
15 Helix Bridge G5
16 Istana Heritage Gallery A1
17 Merlion E5
18 National Library E1
19 New Supreme Court D4
20 Old Hill Street Police Station C4
21 Padang E4
22 Raffles Hotel E2
23 Red Dot Design Museum F7
24 Robertson Quay A4
25 SAM at 8Q D1
26 Sands SkyPark Observation Deck G6
27 Singapore Art Museum D1
28 St Andrew's Cathedral D3
29 Victoria Theatre & Concert Hall D5

◉ Activities, Courses & Tours
30 SIA Hop-On F3
31 Singapore Ducktours F3
32 Singapore River Cruise C4
33 Willow Stream E2

◉ Sleeping
34 5Footway.Inn Project Boat Quay C5
35 BEAT. Capsules C5
36 Fullerton Bay Hotel E6
37 Fullerton Hotel E5
38 Holiday Inn Express Clarke Quay A4
39 Hotel Fort Canning B2
40 Marina Bay Sands G6
41 Naumi E2
42 Park Regis B5
43 Parkroyal on Pickering B6
44 Raffles Hotel E2

45 Ritz-Carlton Millenia Singapore G4

◉ Eating
Garibaldi .... (see 49)
46 Gluttons Bay F4
Gunther's .... (see 49)
47 Inle Myanmar D3
48 Jaan E3
49 Jai Thai E2
50 Jumbo Seafood B4
National Kitchen by Violet
Oon .... (see 11)
51 Odette D4
52 Salted & Hung E2
53 Saveur E2
54 Super Loco Customs House E7
55 Violet Oon Satay Bar & Grill B4
56 Waku Ghin G6

◉ Drinking & Nightlife
57 28 HongKong Street C5
58 Ah Sam Cold Drink Stall C5
59 Attica B4
60 CÉ LA VI SkyBar G6
Chihuly Lounge .... (see 45)
61 Fleek B4
Headquarters by the Council ...... (see 34)
Landing Point .... (see 36)
Lantern .... (see 36)
62 Ronin C5
63 Smoke & Mirrors D4
64 Southbridge C5
65 Wine Connection A3
66 Zouk B4

◉ Entertainment
67 Comedy Masala C5
68 Singapore Dance Theatre E1
69 Singapore Repertory Theatre A4
Singapore Symphony
Orchestra .... (see 29)

◉ Shopping
70 Basheer Graphic Books E2
Cat Socrates .... (see 70)
71 Kapok E1
Peninsula Plaza .... (see 47)
72 Raffles Hotel Arcade E2
73 Raffles Hotel Gift Shop E2
74 Suntec City G2

OCBC Skyway tickets can be purchased at the Ticketing Hub and at the Supertree Grove. Directly west of Supertree Grove are the Heritage Gardens, four themed spaces inspired by the cultures of Singapore's three main ethnic groups – Chinese, Malay and Indian – as well as its former colonial ruler. South of the Supertree Grove is British artist Marc Quinn's extraordinary sculpture, *Planet,* a 7-tonne infant seemingly floating above the lawn. It's one of several artworks gracing the grounds. If you have kids in tow, head to the Children's Garden, which features a water playground (with shower and changing facilities), as well as a huge tree house and adventure playground. The

Visitor Centres offer stroller hire (S$2), lockers (S$2 to S$4 depending on size) and audio guides (S$4), or if you prefer, jump on the outdoor gardens tour shuttle bus (adult/child under 13 years S$8/3) for a whiz around the garden to an audio commentary. Regular shuttle buses (9am to 9pm, first Monday of the month from 12.30pm; unlimited rides S$3) run between Dragonfly Bridge at Bayfront MRT and the domed conservatories.

★**National Gallery Singapore**   GALLERY
(Map p492; ☎6271 7000; www.nationalgallery.sg; St Andrew's Rd; adult/child S$20/15; ☺10am-7pm Sat-Thu, to 9pm Fri; P; MCity Hall) Connected by a striking aluminium and glass canopy, Singapore's historic City Hall (Map p492; 1 St Andrew's Rd; MCity Hall) and Old Supreme Court buildings now form the city's breathtaking National Gallery. Its world-class collection of 19th-century and modern Southeast Asian art is housed in two major spaces, the DBS Singapore Gallery and the UOB Southeast Asia Gallery. The former delivers a comprehensive overview of Singaporean art from the 19th century to today, while the latter focuses on the greater Southeast Asian region.

Beyond them, the Singtel Special Exhibition Gallery is the setting for temporary exhibitions, which include major collaborations with some of the world's highest-profile art museums. Young culture vultures shouldn't miss the National Gallery's Keppel Centre for Art Education, which delivers innovative, multisensory art experiences for kids.

The S$530 million National Gallery is a befitting home for what is one of the world's most important surveys of colonial and post-colonial Southeast Asian art. Among its many treasures are pieces by Singaporean greats Cheong Soo Pieng, Liu Kang, Chua Mia Tee and Georgette Chen, as well as works from luminaries such as Indonesia's Raden Saleh, the Philippines' Fernando Cueto Amorsolo and Imelda Cajipe-Endaya, and Myanmar's U Ba Nyan.

Home to a string of good eateries and a gift shop stocked with specially commissioned art books, design pieces and prints, the complex also runs daily guided tours, artist talks, lectures and workshops.

★**Asian Civilisations Museum**   MUSEUM
(Map p492; ☎6332 7798; www.acm.org.sg; 1 Empress Pl; adult/student/child under 6yr S$20/15/ free, 7-9pm Fri half price; ☺10am-7pm Sat-Thu, to

SINGAPORE IN ...

Two Days

Take a riverside stroll at the Quays for a jaw-dropping panorama of brazen skyscrapers and refined colonial buildings. Dive into the **Asian Civilisations Museum** or keep walking to the **National Museum of Singapore**, the **Peranakan Museum** or the **National Gallery Singapore**. After lunch at **National Kitchen by Violet Oon** move on to touristy Chinatown to seek out the **Buddha Tooth Relic Temple** and the **Thian Hock Keng Temple**. Head up **Pinnacle@Duxton** for a bird's-eye view of the city skyline. Grab an early dinner at **Ding Dong**, then catch a taxi to the fantastic **Night Safari**, where you have a date with a cast of majestic and curious creatures. Start day two in spicy Little India, home to riotously colourful **Sri Veeramakaliamman Temple**. Lunch at **Lagnaa Barefoot Dining**, then escape the afternoon heat in the air-conditioned comfort of **Orchard Rd's malls**. Grab dinner at **Satay by the Bay** then catch the light-show spectacular at **Gardens by the Bay**.

Four Days

Surround yourself with lush greenery in the World Heritage–listed Singapore **Botanic Gardens** then lunch at Michelin-starred **Candlenut**. For an afternoon of pure, unadulterated fun head to Singapore's pleasure island, Sentosa, home to movie theme park **Universal Studios** and the spectacular **SEA Aquarium**. Or just lounge on the beach, enjoying drinks at the **Tanjong Beach Club** and Greek eats at **Mykonos on the Bay**. Come day four, reflect at **Changi Museum & Chapel** before catching a bumboat to **Pulau Ubin** for a jungle cycle. While out in eastern Singapore treat yourself to a marine feast at **No Signboard Seafood**. Finally end your night at trendy rooftop bar **Smoke & Mirrors**, atop the **National Gallery Singapore**.

9pm Fri; M Raffles Place, City Hall) This remarkable museum houses the region's most comprehensive collection of pan-Asian treasures. Its galleries explore the history, cultures and religions of Southeast Asia, China, the Asian subcontinent and Islamic west Asia. Having completed a radical transformation in 2015, the galleries are now curated to emphasise the cross-cultural connections developed through Singapore's history as a port city. The Tang Shipwreck exhibition showcases over 500 pieces of recovered booty – look out for the Chinese bronze mirrors, one of which is over 2000 years old.

The museum occupies the stately Empress Place Building. Designed by British architect John Frederick Adolphus McNair and built using Indian convict labour in 1865, it originally housed the colonial government offices. Note the elegant fusion of Palladian classicism and tropical touches, among them timber louvered shutters and a wide, shaded porch.

★ **Battlebox**   MUSEUM
(Map p492; ☑ 6338 6133; www.battlebox.com.sg; 2 Cox Tce; adult/child S$18/9, not suitable for children below 8 years; ⊘ tours 1.30pm, 2.45pm & 4pm Mon, 9.45am, 11am, 1.30pm, 2.45pm & 4pm Tue-Sun; M Dhoby Ghaut) Take a tour through the Battlebox Museum, the former command post of the British during WWII, and get lost in the eerie and deathly quiet 26-room underground complex. War veterans and Britain's Imperial War Museum helped recreate the authentic bunker environs; life-size models re-enact the fateful surrender to the Japanese on 15 February 1942. Japanese Morse codes are still etched on the walls. Note that due to the tour length and underground location, the museum is recommended for children over eight years old.

Enthusiasts can also join the Of Graves, Guns & Battles tour (adult/child S$32/15), which includes Fort Canning Hill, every Monday and Thursday at 2pm (except public holidays).

★ **National Museum of Singapore** MUSEUM
(Map p492; ☑ 6332 3659; www.nationalmuseum.sg; 93 Stamford Rd; adult/child S$15/10; ⊘ 10am-7pm, last admission 6.30pm; P ; M Dhoby Ghaut, Bencoolen) Imaginative and immersive, Singapore's National Museum is good enough to warrant two visits. At once cutting edge and classical, the space ditches staid exhibits for lively multimedia galleries that bring Singapore's jam-packed biography to vivid

life. It's a colourful, intimate journey, spanning ancient Malay royalty, wartime occupation, nation-building, food and fashion. Look out for interactive artwork *GoHead/GoStan: Panorama Singapura,* which offers an audiovisual trip through the city-state's many periods. Free guided tours are offered daily; check the website for times.

★ **Peranakan Museum**   MUSEUM
(Map p492; ☑ 6332 7591; www.peranakanmuseum.org.sg; 39 Armenian St; adult/child under 7yr S$10/6, 7-9pm Fri half price; ⊘ 10am-7pm, to 9pm Fri; M City Hall, Bras Basah) This is the best spot to explore the rich heritage of the Peranakans (Straits Chinese descendants). Thematic galleries cover various aspects of Peranakan culture, from the traditional 12-day wedding ceremony to crafts, spirituality and feasting. Look out for intricately detailed ceremonial costumes and beadwork, beautifully carved wedding beds and rare dining porcelain. An especially curious example of Peranakan fusion culture is a pair of Victorian bell jars in which statues of Christ and the Madonna are adorned with Chinese-style flowers and vines.

The museum shop stocks embroidered bags, Peranakan-style *kebayas* (traditional blouse dresses) and ceramics, and books spanning Peranakan history, food and architecture.

Raffles Hotel   NOTABLE BUILDING
(Map p492; ☑ 6337 1886; www.rafflessingapore.com; 1 Beach Rd; M City Hall, Esplanade) Although its resplendent lobby is only accessible to hotel guests, Singapore's most iconic slumber palace is worth a quick visit for its magnificent ivory frontage, famous Sikh doorman and lush, hushed tropical grounds. The hotel started life in 1887 as a modest 10-room bungalow fronting the beach (long gone thanks to land reclamation).

St Andrew's Cathedral   CHURCH
(Map p492; ☑ 6337 6104; www.cathedral.org.sg; 11 St Andrew's Rd; ⊘ 9am-5pm; P ; M City Hall) Funded by Scottish merchants and built by Indian convicts, this wedding cake of a cathedral stands in stark contrast to the glass and steel surrounding it. Completed in 1838 but torn down and rebuilt in its present form in 1862 after lightning damage, it's one of Singapore's finest surviving examples of English Gothic architecture. Interesting details include the tropics-friendly *porte-cochère* (carriage porch) entrance – designed

MARINA BAY SANDS

Love it or hate it, it's hard not to admire the sheer audacity of Singapore's S\$5.7 billion Marina Bay Sands. Perched on the southern bank of Marina Bay, the sprawling hotel, casino, theatre, exhibition centre, mall and museum is the work of Israeli-born architect Moshe Safdie. Star of the show is **Marina Bay Sands** (Map p492; ☑ 6688 8888; www. marinabaysands.com; 10 Bayfront Ave; r from S\$550; P ✻ @ 🛜 🛋; M Bayfront) hotel, its three 55-storey towers inspired by propped-up playing cards and connected by a cantilevered, 1.2-hectare SkyPark.

The SkyPark offers one gob-smacking panorama. Its world-famous infinity pool is off-limits to non-hotel guests, but the **Observation Deck** (Map p492; ☑ 6688 8826; www. marinabaysands.com/sands-skypark; Level 57, Marina Bay Sands Hotel Tower 3, 10 Bayfront Ave; adult/child under 13yr S\$23/17; ☉ 9.30am-10pm Mon-Thu, to 11pm Fri-Sun; M Bayfront) is open to all. Information plaques point out the landmarks below, which include Gardens by the Bay, grand colonial buildings and the sprawl beyond. The deck is completely exposed, so use sunscreen and wear a hat, and avoid heading up on wet days. A better value option is the adjoining **CÉ LA VI SkyBar** (Map p492; ☑ 6508 2188; www.sg.celavi.com; Level 57, Marina Bay Sands Hotel Tower 3, 10 Bayfront Ave; admission S\$20, redeemable on food or drinks; ☉ noon-late; M Bayfront), where for a similar price as the Observation Deck you can enjoy a cocktail served up with the amazing view.

Marina Bay Sands' attention-seeking tendencies extend to the nightly **Spectra** (☑ 6688 8868; www.marinabaysands.com; Event Plaza, Promenade, Marina Bay Sands; ☉ 8pm & 9pm Sun-Thu, 8pm, 9pm & 10pm Fri & Sat; M Bayfront) FREE, a 15-minute extravaganza of interweaving lasers, water screens, fountain jets and video projections set to a pumping soundtrack. While its 'journey as a multicultural society into the cosmopolitan city theme' is a little hard to follow, there's no denying the technical brilliance of the show. The best views are had from the city side of Marina Bay.

Back at ground level check out the **ArtScience Museum** (Map p492; ☑ 6688 8826; www.marinabaysands.com; Marina Bay Sands, 6 Bayfront Ave, Marina Bay; adult/child under 13yr from S\$17/12; ☉ 10am-7pm, last admission 6pm; M Bayfront). Also designed by Safdie and looking like a giant white lotus, the lily pond–framed building hosts major international travelling exhibitions across a wide range of topics. Expect anything from explorations of deep-sea creatures to retrospectives of world-famous industrial designers.

to shelter passengers – and the colourful stained glass adorning the western wall.

Fort Canning Park
PARK

(Map p492; ☑ 1800 471 7300; www.nparks.gov. sg; bounded by Hill St, Canning Rise, Clemenceau Ave & River Valley Rd; M Dhoby Ghaut, Clarke Quay, Fort Canning) When Raffles rolled into Singapore, locals steered clear of Fort Canning Hill, then called Bukit Larangan (Forbidden Hill) out of respect for the sacred shrine of Sultan Iskandar Shah, ancient Singapura's last ruler. Today, the hill is better known as Fort Canning Park, a lush retreat from the hot streets below. Take a stroll in the shade of truly enormous trees, amble through the spice garden or ponder Singapore's wartime defeat at the Battlebox Museum, the former command post of the British during WWII.

Red Dot Design Museum
MUSEUM

(Map p492; ☑ 6514 0111; www.museum.red-dot.sg; 11 Marina Blvd; S\$6; ☉ 10am-8pm Mon-Thu, to 11pm Fri-Sun; M Bayfront, Downtown) After bidding farewell to its former bright red Chinatown location, the Red Dot Museum's new home is sleek, modern and smack on the banks of Marina Bay. The museum showcases winning design pieces from the international Red Dot Awards: Design Concept. The exhibition is continuously being updated and is well worth a gawk. Find unique gifts at the onsite design store.

Marina Barrage
PARK

(☑ 6514 5959; www.pub.gov.sg/marinabarrage; 8 Marina Gardens Dr; ☉ 24hr; 🚍 400, M Bayfront) Singaporean ingenuity in action, Marina Barrage is both a flood-control dam of the Marina Channel and a gorgeous park with commanding skyline views. The on-site

Sustainable Singapore Gallery (9am to 6pm Wednesday to Monday), includes fascinating photos and archival footage of the Singapore River before its extreme makeover, as well as a nifty working model of the Marina Barrage itself. The park's lawn is dotted with locals flying their colourful kites.

SAM at 8Q   MUSEUM

(Map p492; ☑ 6589 9580; www.singaporeart museum.sg; 8 Queen St; adult/child under 6yr S$6/free, 6-9pm Fri free; ☺ 10am-7pm Sat-Thu, to 9pm Fri; Ⓜ Bras Basah, Bencoolen) The younger sibling of the **Singapore Art Museum** (SAM; Map p492; 71 Bras Basah Rd; Ⓜ Bras Basah, Bencoolen), which is undergoing a significant revamp until 2021, is named after its address. Snoop around four floors of contemporary art, from quirky

installations and video art to mixed-media statements. Last entry is 45 minutes before closing time.

National Library   LIBRARY

(Map p492; ☑ 6332 3255; www.nlb.gov.sg; 100 Victoria St; ☺ 10am-9pm; Ⓟ; Ⓜ Bugis, Bras Basah, City Hall) Designed by Malaysian architect and ecologist Ken Yeang, this white, curvaceous brains trust is home to numerous facilities, including a reference library, lending library and drama centre. For visitors, the real draws are the display of beautiful maps of Asia on level 10 (some dating back to the 16th century), and the library's program of free exhibitions. If you have little ones in tow, head to the forest-themed children's library in the basement for some storytime R&R.

QUAYS OF THE CITY

The stretch of riverfront that separates the Colonial District from the CBD is known as the Quays. The Singapore River – once a thriving entryway for bumboats bearing cargo into the godown (warehouses) that lined the riverside – now connects the three quays together. A walk along them offers an eye-opening view of the changes that have impacted Singapore's trade through the years: from the dirt and grit of the once-filthy waterways to the gleaming steel and glass of today's financial district.

Boat Quay (Map p492; Ⓜ Raffles Place, Clarke Quay) Closest to the former harbour, Boat Quay was once Singapore's centre of commerce, and remained an important economic area into the 1960s. By the mid-1980s, many of the shophouses were in ruins, business having shifted to high-tech cargo centres elsewhere on the island. Declared a conservation zone by the government, the area became a major entertainment district filled with touristy bars, shops and menu-clutching touts luring the masses into their waterside restaurants. Discerning punters ditch these for the growing number of clued-in cafes and drinking dens dotting the streets behind the main strip, among them coffee peddler Ronin (p547) and 'speakeasy' cocktail bars 28 HongKong Street (p546) and Ah Sam Cold Drink Stall (p546).

Clarke Quay (Map p492; Ⓜ Clarke Quay, Fort Canning) Named after Singapore's second colonial governor, Sir Andrew Clarke, this is the busiest and most popular of the three quays, its plethora of bars, restaurants and clubs, including legendary mega-club Zouk (p547), pulling in the pleasure seekers every night of the week. How much time you spend in Clarke Quay really depends upon your personal taste in aesthetics. If pastel hues, Dr Seuss–style design and lad-and-ladette hang-outs are your schtick, you'll be well in your element. Fans of understated cool, however, should steer well clear.

Robertson Quay (Map p492; Ⓜ Clarke Quay, Fort Canning) At the furthest reach of the river, Robertson Quay was once used for the storage of goods. Now some of the old godown have found new purposes as bars and members-only party places. The vibe here is more 'grown up' than Clarke Quay, attracting a 30-plus crowd generally more interested in wining, dining and conversation than getting hammered to Top 40 hits. Perch up at alfresco **Super Loco** (☑ 6235 8900; www.super-loco.com; 01-13, 60 Robertson Quay; tacos S$8-12, quesadillas S$14-16; ☺ 5-10.30pm Mon-Thu, to 11pm Fri, 10am-3.30pm & 5-11pm Sat, to 10pm Sun; Ⓜ Fort Canning) and **Publico Ristorante** (☑ 6826 5040; www.publico. sg; InterContinental Hotel, 1 Nanson Rd; mains S$21-42; ☺ 4-11pm Mon-Thu, to midnight Fri, 1pm-midnight Sat, 11am-11pm Sun; Ⓜ Fort Canning) and enjoy watching the riverside traffic walk by, refreshing drink in hand.

Chinatown & the CBD

While Singapore's Chinatown may be a tamer version of its former self, its temples, heritage centre, and booming restaurant and bar scene make the trip there worthwhile. The CBD is best known for its stunning, ever-evolving skyline: rooftop bars jostle with old-school temples, all set against the financial heart that funds Singapore.

★ Baba House   MUSEUM

(Map p500; ☑ 6227 5731; http://babahouse.nus. edu.sg; 157 Neil Rd; S$10, children must be 12yrs & above; ⊙1hr tour 10am Tue-Fri, self-guided tour 1.30pm, 2.15pm, 3.15pm & 4pm Sat; Ⓜ Outram Park) Baba House is one of Singapore's best-preserved Peranakan heritage homes. Built in the 1890s, this beautiful blue three-storey building was donated to the National University of Singapore (NUS) by a member of the family that used to live here. The NUS then set about renovating it so that it best matched how it would have looked in 1928 when, according to the family, Baba House was at its most resplendent. The only way in is on a guided/self-guided tour; bookings are essential.

★ Buddha Tooth Relic Temple   BUDDHIST TEMPLE

(Map p500; ☑ 6220 0220; www.btrts.org.sg; 288 South Bridge Rd; ⊙7am-7pm, relic viewing 9am-6pm; Ⓜ Chinatown) FREE Consecrated in 2008, this hulking, five-storey Buddhist temple is home to what is reputedly a tooth of the Buddha, discovered in a collapsed stupa (Buddhist relic structure) in Mrauk U, Myanmar. While its authenticity is debated, the relic enjoys VIP status inside a 320kg solid-gold stupa in a dazzlingly ornate 4th-floor room. More religious relics await at the 3rd-floor Buddhism museum, while the peaceful rooftop garden features a huge prayer wheel inside a 10,000 Buddha Pavilion.

★ Chinatown Heritage Centre   MUSEUM

(Map p500; ☑ 6224 3928; www.chinatownheritage centre.com.sg; 48 Pagoda St; adult S$15, child under 13/7yr S$11/free; ⊙9am-8pm, closed 1st Mon of month; Ⓜ Chinatown) Delve into Chinatown's gritty, cacophonous backstory at the immersive Chinatown Heritage Centre. Occupying several levels of a converted shophouse, its interactive exhibitions shed light on numerous historical chapters, from the treacherous journey of Singapore's early Chinese immigrants to the development of

MURAL ART

Spanning 44m, **Thian Hock Keng Mural** (Map p500; www.yipyc.com; Amoy St, rear wall of Thian Hock Keng Temple, 158 Telok Ayer St; Ⓜ Telok Ayer), painted by Singaporean artist Yip Yew Chong (accountant by weekday, artist by weekend), tells the story of Singapore's early Hokkien immigrants. Start from the right end and follow the immigrants' story, from leaving China to arriving in Singapore, and the sacrifices, hardships and joys they experienced along the way. Discover the mural's hidden secrets via the LocoMole app: instructions are to the mural's far left.

This isn't the artist's only mural; others can be found all over the island from Changi Village to Tiong Bahru to the National Museum of Singapore, and Yip is still going! Make sure to check his website for locations, and for even more fun, check him out on Instagram (@yip yewchong) to see how fans interact with these Singaporean heritage scenes.

local clan associations to the district's notorious opium dens. It's an evocative place, digging well beneath modern Chinatown's touristy veneer.

Thian Hock Keng Temple   TAOIST TEMPLE

(Map p500; ☑ 6423 4616; www.thianhockkeng.com. sg; 158 Telok Ayer St; ⊙7.30am-5.30pm; Ⓜ Telok Ayer) FREE Surprisingly, Chinatown's oldest and most important Hokkien temple is often a haven of tranquillity. Built between 1839 and 1842, it's a beautiful place, and was once the favourite landing point of Chinese sailors, before land reclamation pushed the sea far down the road. Typically, the temple's design features are richly symbolic: the stone lions at the entrance ward off evil spirits, while the painted depiction of phoenixes and peonies in the central hall symbolise peace and good tidings respectively.

Pinnacle@Duxton   VIEWPOINT

(Map p500; ☑ 8683 7760; www.pinnacleduxton. com.sg; Block 1G, 1 Cantonment Rd; 50th-fl sky-bridge S$6; ⊙9am-9pm; Ⓜ Outram Park) For killer city views at a bargain S$6, head to the 50th-floor rooftop of Pinnacle@Duxton, the world's largest public housing complex. Skybridges connecting the seven

Chinatown & the CBD

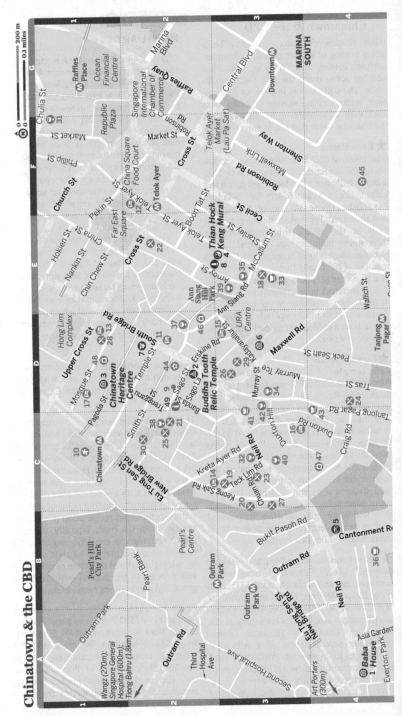

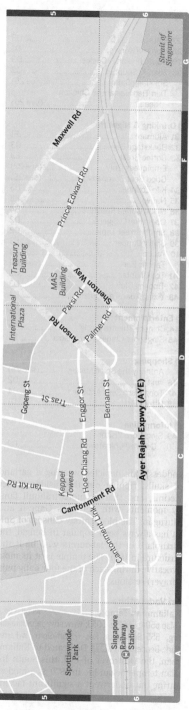

towers provide a 360-degree sweep of city, port and sea. Find the 'blink or you'll miss it' ticket booth at level one, Block G, hand over your cash and register your Ez-Link transport card, before taking the lift up to the 50th floor, where you'll tap your card at the gate – stand inside the turnstile before tapping.

Singapore City Gallery MUSEUM
(Map p500; ☑6321 8321; www.ura.gov.sg/city gallery; URA Centre, 45 Maxwell Rd; ⊙9am-5pm Mon-Sat; Ⓜ Chinatown, Tanjong Pagar) FREE See into Singapore's future at this interactive city-planning exhibition, which provides compelling insight into the government's resolute policies of land reclamation, high-rise housing and meticulous urban planning.

Art Porters GALLERY
(☑6909 0468; www.artporters.com; 64 Spottiswoode Park Rd; ⊙10.30am-7pm Tue-Sun; Ⓜ Outram Park) Located in a cute-as-a-button shophouse, the ethos of this art gallery is to share happiness with art. It exhibits contemporary artworks by local and international artists in many mediums, including sculpture, painting, photography, digital animation and drawing. Outside, you'll find the heritage mural 'provision shop' by Yip Yew Chong (p499), on the side wall of 8 Spottiswoode Park Rd.

⊙ Little India

Little India is Singapore trapped in its gritty past – it's frenetic, messy and fun. Spice traders spill their wares across its five-foot ways and Indian labourers swarm into the area each weekend.

★**Indian Heritage Centre** MUSEUM
(Map p504; ☑6291 1601; www.indianheritage.org.sg; 5 Campbell Lane; adult/child under 6yr S$6/free; ⊙10am-7pm Tue-Thu, to 8pm Fri & Sat, to 4pm Sun; Ⓜ Little India, Jalan Besar) Delve into the origins and heritage of Singapore's Indian community at this S$12 million state-of-the-art museum. Divided into five themes, its hundreds of historical and cultural artefacts, maps, archival footage and multimedia displays explore everything from early interactions between South Asia and Southeast Asia to Indian cultural traditions and the contributions of Indian Singaporeans to the development of the island nation. Among the more extraordinary objects is a

SINGAPORE SIGHTS

Chinatown & the CBD

◎ Top Sights
1 Baba House A4
2 Buddha Tooth Relic Temple D2
3 Chinatown Heritage Centre D1
4 Thian Hock Keng Mural E3

◎ Sights
5 Pinnacle@Duxton B4
6 Singapore City Gallery D3
7 Sri Mariamman Temple D2
8 Thian Hock Keng Temple E3

⊕ Activities, Courses & Tours
9 Food Playground D2
  Mr Lim Foot Reflexology .... (see 10)
10 People's Park Complex C1

⊟ Sleeping
11 Adler Hostel D2
12 Amoy F2
13 Beary Best Hostel D1
14 Hotel 1929 .... C2
15 Scarlet D3
16 Six Senses Duxton C3
17 Wink Hostel D1

⊗ Eating
18 A Noodle Story E3
19 Burnt Ends C3
20 Butcher Boy C3
21 Chinatown Complex C2
22 Ding Dong E2
23 Esquina C3
24 Ginza Tendon Itsuki D4
  Hong Kong Soya Sauce
    Chicken Rice & Noodle .... (see 25)
  Lad & Dad .... (see 29)
25 Lian He Ben Ji Claypot Rice C2
26 Maxwell Food Centre D3

27 Meta C3
28 Momma Kong's D1
29 Rojak, Popiah & Cockle D3
30 Shen Xi Soup C2
  Shi Xiang Satay .... (see 25)
  Tian Tian Hainanese Chicken
    Rice .... (see 26)

◎ Drinking & Nightlife
31 Altimate F1
32 Backstage Bar C3
33 Coffee Break E3
  Employees Only .... (see 22)
  Good Beer Company .... (see 25)
34 Kilo Lounge D3
35 Native E3
36 Nylon Coffee Roasters B4
37 Operation Dagger D2
38 Smith Street Taps C2
39 Spiffy Dapper E3
40 Taboo C3
  Tantric Bar .... (see 32)
41 Tea Chapter C3
42 Tippling Club D3
43 Yixing Xuan Teahouse C4

✪ Entertainment
44 Chinese Theatre Circle D2
45 Singapore Chinese Orchestra F4

⊕ Shopping
  Anthony the Spice Maker .... (see 25)
46 innit D2
47 Tong Mern Sern Antiques C4
48 Utterly Art D1

⊕ Information
49 Singapore Visitor
  Centre@Chinatown D2

19th-century Chettinad doorway, intricately adorned with 5000 minute carvings.

Inspired by the *baoli* (Indian stepped well), the museum's architecture is equally intriguing. As night falls, the building's translucent facade transforms into a giant tapestry of sorts, showcasing the richly coloured mural behind it.

Alongside the main galleries, the centre also houses a rooftop garden, activity spaces and a visitor centre.

Sri Veeramakaliamman
Temple   HINDU TEMPLE
(Map p504; ☑6295 4538; www.sriveeramakaliamman.com; 141 Serangoon Rd; ⏰5.30am-12.30pm & 4-9.30pm; Ⓜ Little India, Jalan Besar) **FREE** Little India's most colourful, visually stunning temple is dedicated to the ferocious

goddess Kali, depicted wearing a garland of skulls, ripping out the insides of her victims, and sharing more tranquil family moments with her sons Ganesh and Murugan. The bloodthirsty consort of Shiva has always been popular in Bengal, the birthplace of the labourers who built the structure in 1881. The temple is at its most evocative during each of the four daily puja (prayer) sessions.

Sri Vadapathira
Kaliamman Temple   HINDU TEMPLE
(Map p504; ☑6298 5053; www.srivadapathirakali.org; 555 Serangoon Rd; ⏰6am-9pm; Ⓜ Farrer Park, Bendemeer) **FREE** Dedicated to Kaliamman, the Destroyer of Evil, this South Indian temple began life in 1870 as a modest shrine but underwent a significant facelift

in 1969 to transform it into the beauty standing today. The carvings here – particularly on the *vimana* (domed structure within the temple) – are among the best temple artwork you'll see anywhere in Singapore.

Abdul Gafoor Mosque   MOSQUE

(Map p504; ☎6295 4209; www.facebook.com/masjidabdulgafoor; 41 Dunlop St; ⊙10am-noon & 2-4pm Sat-Thu, 2.30-4pm Fri; Ⓜ Rochor, Jalan Besar) **FREE** Completed in 1910, the Abdul Gafoor Mosque serves up a storybook fusion of Moorish, South Indian and Victorian architectural styles. Look out for the elab-

orate sundial crowning its main entrance, each of its 25 rays decorated with Arabic calligraphy denoting the names of 25 prophets. The sundial is the only one of its kind in the world.

Sri Srinivasa Perumal Temple   HINDU TEMPLE

(Map p504; ☎6298 5771; www.sspt.org.sg; 397 Serangoon Rd; ⊙6am-noon & 6-9pm Sun & Mon, 5.30am-12.30pm & 5.30-9.30pm Sat; Ⓜ Farrer Park, Bendemeer) **FREE** Dedicated to Vishnu, this temple dates from 1855, but the striking, 20m-tall *gopuram* (tower) is a S$300,000 1966 add-on. Inside are statues of Vishnu, Lakshmi and Andal, and Vishnu's

SINGAPORE SIGHTS

WORTH A TRIP

A LAZY MORNING IN TIONG BAHRU

For a taste of both old and new Singapore spend a late weekend morning in Tiong Bahru, three stops from Raffles Place on the East–West (green) MRT line or walkable south of Chinatown. More than just hip boutiques, bars and cafes, this low-rise neighbourhood was Singapore's first public-housing estate, and its walk-up, art deco apartments now make for unexpected architectural treats.

Start at the **Tiong Bahru Market & Food Centre** (83 Seng Poh Rd; dishes from S$3; ⊙6am-late, stall hours vary; Ⓟ; Ⓜ Tiong Bahru), which remains staunchly old-school, right down to its orange-hued exterior, the neighbourhood's original shade. Whet your appetite exploring the wet market, then head upstairs to the hawker centre for *shui kueh* (steamed rice cake with diced preserved radish) at **Jian Bo Shui Kueh** (www.jianboshuikueh.com; 02-05 Tiong Bahru Market & Food Centre, 83 Seng Poh Rd; 5 shui kueh S$2.50; ⊙5.30am-10pm; Ⓜ Tiong Bahru).

Tiong Bahru's trendiest strip is Yong Siak St. Here you'll find **BooksActually** (☎6222 9195; www.booksactually.com; 9 Yong Siak St; ⊙10am-8pm Tue-Sat, to 6pm Mon & Sun; Ⓜ Tiong Bahru), Singapore's coolest independent bookstore, with often unexpected choices of fiction and nonfiction, including some interesting titles on Singapore. For beautiful children's books, check out **Woods in the Books** (☎6222 9980; www.woodsinthebooks.sg; 3 Yong Siak St; ⊙10am-7pm Tue-Fri, to 8pm Sat, to 6pm Sun; Ⓜ Tiong Bahru), three doors down. **Nana & Bird** (www.nanaandbird.com; 1M Yong Siak St; ⊙noon-7pm Mon-Fri, from 11am Sat & Sun; Ⓜ Tiong Bahru) is a sound spot for fresh independent fashion and accessories for women, with labels including Singapore designers Aijek and Rye, and international up-and-comers like N12H and Cassey Gan. Drop into **40 Hands** (☎6225 8545; www.40handscoffee.com; 01-12, 78 Yong Siak St; ⊙7am-7pm Mon-Fri, from 7.30am Sat & Sun; Ⓜ Tiong Bahru) for a killer caffeine rush. Pimped with geometric murals, it's one of the city's top coffee spots – not surprising, given the owner hails from coffee-obsessed Australia. The brunch menu here is legendary.

Lovers of a good bake off will be in heaven. Star French baker Gontran Cherrier stakes his claim at **Tiong Bahru Bakery** (☎6220 3430; www.tiongbahrubakery.com; 01-70, 56 Eng Hoon St; pastries S$2.20-4.60, sandwiches S$5.30-12; ⊙8am-8pm; Ⓜ Tiong Bahru), a cool, contemporary bakery and cafe. Faultless pastries include flaky *kouign amanns* (Breton-style pastry), while savouries include salubrious sandwiches exploding with prime ingredients. Squaring up is ex-lawyer-turned-baker Vanessa Kenchington with her passion project **Plain Vanilla Bakery** (☎8363 7614; www.plainvanillabakery.com; 1D Yong Siak St; cupcakes from S$4.20; ⊙8am-7pm Mon-Sat, 9am-6pm Sun; Ⓜ Tiong Bahru) – come here for ridiculously moist, utterly scrumptious cupcakes in flavours such as Earl Grey lavender and strawberry white chocolate.

To reach Tiong Bahru catch the MRT to Tiong Bahru station, walk east along Tiong Bahru Rd for 700m, then turn right into Seng Poh Rd.

Little India & Kampong Glam

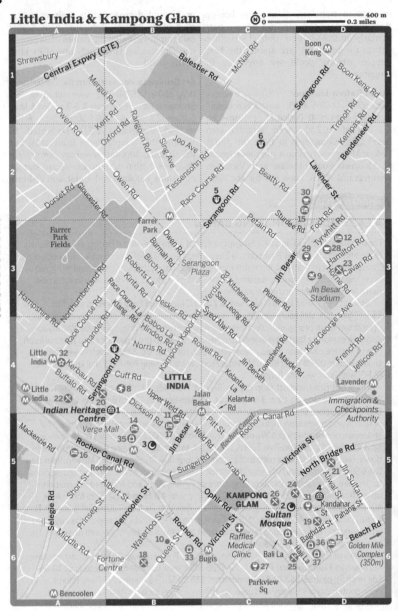

bird-mount Garuda. The temple is the starting point for a colourful, wince-inducing street parade during the Thaipusam festival: to show their devotion, many participants pierce their bodies with hooks and skewers.

Kampong Glam

The former home of the local sultan, Kampong Glam is an eclectic mix of Islamic stores and eateries, hipster bars and boutiques.

Little India & Kampong Glam

◉ Top Sights
1 Indian Heritage Centre............................B4
2 Sultan Mosque C5

◉ Sights
3 Abdul Gafoor Mosque B5
4 Malay Heritage Centre D5
5 Sri Srinivasa Perumal Temple C2
6 Sri Vadapathira Kaliamman Temple C2
7 Sri Veeramakaliamman Temple...........B4

◎ Activities, Courses & Tours
8 Amrita Ayurveda & Yoga.......................B4
9 Jalan Besar Swimming Complex..........D3
10 Trishaw Uncle B6

◎ Sleeping
11 Bunc B5
12 Dream Lodge..D3
13 Five Stones Hostel................................D6
   Great Madras ....(see 14)
14 InnCrowd B5
15 Kam Leng Hotel D2
16 Village Hotel Albert Court A5
17 Wanderlust...B5

◎ Eating
18 Ah Heng Curry Chicken Bee Hoon
   Mee B6
   Ar Rahman Royal Prata...............(see 22)
19 Cicheti..D6
   Komala Vilas................................(see 20)

20 Lagnaa Barefoot Dining A4
21 Nan Hwa Chong Fish-Head
   Steamboat Corner............................D5
   New Rong Liang Ge
   Cantonese Roast Duck
   Double Boiled Soup..................(see 18)
   QS269 Food House ....(see 18)
22 Tekka Centre A4
23 Two Bakers D3
24 Warong Nasi Pariaman C5
25 Windowsill Pies C6
26 Zam Zam...C5

◎ Drinking & Nightlife
27 Atlas...C6
28 Chye Seng Huat Hardware....................D3
29 Druggists..D3
30 Liberty Coffee D2
31 Maison Ikkoku The Art of
   Mixology D5

◎ Entertainment
   BluJaz Café ....(see 25)
32 Wild Rice...A4

◎ Shopping
33 Bugis Street Market B6
34 Haji Lane C6
35 Rugged Gentlemen Shoppe B5
36 Sifr Aromatics D6
37 Supermama D6

★**Sultan Mosque** MOSQUE
(Map p504; ☑6293 4405; www.sultanmosque.
sg; 3 Muscat St; ☉10am-noon & 2-4pm Sat-Thu,
2.30-4pm Fri; M Bugis) FREE Seemingly pulled
from the pages of the *Arabian Nights*, Singapore's largest mosque is nothing short of
enchanting, designed in the Saracenic style
and topped by a golden dome. It was originally built in 1825 with the aid of a grant
from Raffles and the East India Company,
after Raffles' treaty with the sultan of Singapore allowed the Malay leader to retain
sovereignty over the area. In 1928, the original mosque was replaced by the present
magnificent building, designed by an Irish
architect.

Non-Muslims are asked to refrain from
entering the prayer hall at any time, and all
visitors are expected to be dressed suitably
(cloaks are available at the entrance). Pointing cameras at people during prayer time is
never appropriate.

Malay Heritage Centre MUSEUM
(Map p504; ☑6391 0450; www.malayheritage.org.
sg; 85 Sultan Gate; adult/child under 6yr $6/free;

☉10am-6pm Tue-Sun; M Bugis) The Kampong
Glam area is the historic seat of Malay
royalty, resident here before the arrival
of Raffles, and the *istana* (palace) on this
site was built for the last sultan of Singapore, Ali Iskandar Shah, between 1836
and 1843. It's now a museum, its galleries
exploring Malay-Singaporean culture and
history, from the early migration of traders
to Kampong Glam to the development of
Malay-Singaporean film, theatre, music and
publishing.

Free guided tours run at 2pm Tuesday,
Thursday and Saturday.

◉ Orchard Road

Orchard Rd offers a seemingly endless row
of malls. For a slice of history, take a stroll
along Emerald Hill Rd, a heritage strip lined
with pretty Peranakan houses.

★**Emerald Hill Road** ARCHITECTURE
(Map p506; Emerald Hill Rd; M Somerset) Take
time out from your shopping to wander up
frangipani-scented Emerald Hill Rd, graced

Orchard Road

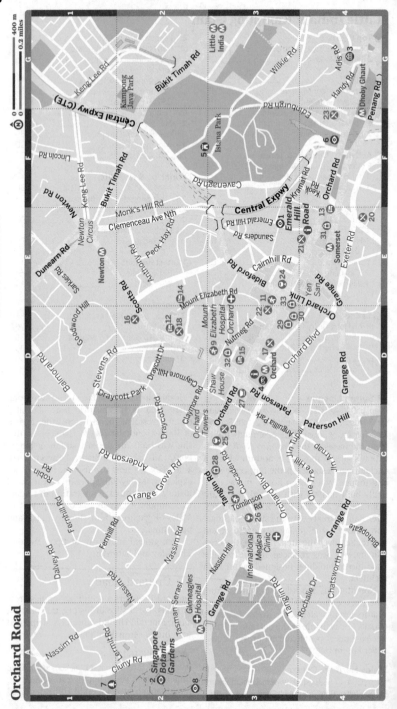

Orchard Road

◎ Top Sights
1 Emerald Hill Road E3
2 Singapore Botanic Gardens A2

◎ Sights
3 Cathay Gallery G4
4 ION Sky D3
5 Istana F2
6 Istana Entrance Gateway F4
7 Rainforest A1
8 Swan Lake A2

◎ Activities, Courses & Tours
9 Damai Spa D3
10 Remède Spa C3
11 Spa Esprit E3

◎ Sleeping
12 Goodwood Park Hotel D2
13 Hotel Jen Orchardgateway E4
14 Quincy E2
15 Singapore Marriott D3
St Regis .... (see 10)

◎ Eating
16 Buona Terra D2
Din Tai Fung .... (see 11)
17 Food Republic D3

18 Gordon Grill D2
19 Iggy's C3
20 Killiney Kopitiam E4
Paradise Dynasty .... (see 4)
21 Signs A Taste Of Vietnam Pho E4
Takashimaya Food Village .... (see 30)
22 Tambuah Mas D3
23 Tim Ho Wan F4

◎ Drinking & Nightlife
24 Bar Canary E3
25 Horse's Mouth C3
26 Manhattan B3
Other Room .... (see 15)
27 Privé D3
TWG Tea .... (see 4)

◎ Entertainment
SISTIC .... (see 4)

◎ Shopping
28 Antiques of the Orient C3
ION Orchard Mall .... (see 4)
29 Kinokuniya D3
30 Ngee Ann City D3
31 Orchardgateway E4
32 Pedder On Scotts D3
33 Takashimaya E3

with some of Singapore's finest terrace houses. Special mentions go to No 56 (one of the earliest buildings here, built in 1902), No 39 to 45 (unusually wide frontages and a grand Chinese-style entrance gate), and No 120 to 130 (art deco features dating from around 1925). At the Orchard Rd end of the hill is a cluster of popular bars housed in fetching shophouse renovations.

Istana Heritage Gallery   MUSEUM
(Map p492; ☑6904 4289; www.istana.gov.sg; Istana Park, 35 Orchard Rd; ⊙10am-6pm, closed Wed; Ⓜ Dhoby Ghaut) FREE If your visit to Singapore doesn't coincide with one of the five days per year the **Istana** (Map p506; www.istana.gov.sg; Orchard Rd; grounds/palace S$2/4; ⊙8.30am-6pm Chinese New Year Labour Day, National Day, Diwali & Hari Raya Puasa (Eid-ul Fitr); Ⓜ Dhoby Ghaut) opens to the public (or you don't have time to spend hours queuing on one of those days), you can now take a peek behind the formidable **gates** (Map p506; www.istana.gov.sg; Orchard Rd; Ⓜ Dhoby Ghaut) at this informative museum. Discover the building's history, peruse the guest book, marvel at opulent state gifts and even sit for a picture-perfect moment in front of a life-sized backdrop of the East Drawing Room.

Cathay Gallery   MUSEUM
(Map p506; www.thecathaygallery.com.sg; 02-16 The Cathay, 2 Handy Rd; ⊙11am-7pm Mon-Sat; Ⓜ Dhoby Ghaut, Bencoolen) FREE Film and nostalgia buffs will appreciate this pocket-sized silver-screen museum, housed in Singapore's first high-rise building. The displays trace the history of the Loke family, early pioneers in film production and distribution in Singapore and founders of the Cathay Organisation. Highlights include old movie posters, cameras and programs that capture the golden age of local cinema.

◎ Dempsey Hill & the Botanic Gardens

★ **Singapore Botanic Gardens**   GARDENS
(Map p506; ☑1800 471 7300; www.nparks.gov.sg/sbg; 1 Cluny Rd; ⊙5am-midnight; ℗; ☐7, 75, 77, 105, 106, 123, 174, Ⓜ Botanic Gardens) FREE Singapore's 74-hectare botanic wonderland is a Unesco World Heritage Site and one of the city's most arresting attractions. Established in 1860, it's a tropical Valhalla peppered with glassy lakes, rolling lawns and themed gardens. The site is home to the **National Orchid Garden** (adult/child under

12yr S\$5/free; ⊙8.30am-7pm, last entry 6pm), as well as a rare patch of dense **primeval rainforest** (Map p506, the latter home to over 300 species of vegetation, over half of which are now (sadly) considered rare in Singapore.

The National Orchid Garden itself is the legacy of an orchid-breeding program that began in 1928, and its 3 hectares house over 1000 species and 2000 hybrids. Of these, around 600 are on display – the largest showcase of tropical orchids on Earth. Located next to the National Orchid Garden is the 1-hectare **Ginger Garden**, with over 250 members of the Zingiberaceae family. The garden's newest addition, the **Learning Forest**, guides visitors on a network of boardwalks and elevated walkways through different habitats, including swampy wetlands and rainforest canopies. Children will love exploring the interactive **Jacob Ballas Children's Garden** (⊙8am-7pm Tue-Sun, last entry 6.30pm), complete with water-play feature and forest adventure playground. Enjoy swan spotting at **Swan Lake** (Map p506), where along with the large bronze swan sculpture you might also see the real mute white swans imported all the way from the Netherlands. Free, themed guided tours of the Botanic Gardens run on Saturday, while the Symphony Lake makes a romantic setting for seasonal opera performances – check the website.

⊙ Eastern Singapore

Geylang is an incongruous combo of temples, mosques, brothels and cult-status local eating places. East Coast Park is perfect for cycling and picnics by the beach, while nearby Joo Chiat (Katong) is steeped in Peranakan culture. At the extreme tip of the island, you'll find moving exhibits at Changi Museum and Chapel and bumboats (motorised sampans) to Pulau Ubin.

★**Peranakan Terrace Houses**   AREA
(Map p510; Koon Seng Rd & Joo Chiat Pl; ☐10, 14, 16, 32) Just off Joo Chiat Rd, Koon Seng Rd and Joo Chiat Pl feature Singapore's most extraordinary Peranakan terrace houses, joyously decorated with stucco dragons, birds, crabs and brilliantly glazed tiles. *Pintu pagar* (swinging doors) at the front of the houses are a typical feature, allowing cross breezes while retaining privacy. Those on Koon Seng Rd are located between Joo Chiat and Tembeling Rds, while those on Joo Chiat Pl run between Everitt and Mangis Rds.

East Coast Park   PARK
(Map p510; ☑1800 471 7300; www.nparks.gov.sg; P; ☐36, 43, 48, 196, 197, 401) This 15km stretch of seafront park is where Singaporeans come to swim, windsurf, wakeboard, kayak, picnic, bicycle, in-line skate, skateboard, and – of course – eat. You'll find swaying coconut palms, patches of bushland, a lagoon, sea-sports clubs, and some excellent eating options.

Renting a bike, enjoying the sea breezes, watching the veritable city of container ships out in the strait, and capping it all off with a beachfront meal is one of the most pleasant ways to spend a Singapore afternoon.

East Coast Park starts at the end of Tanjong Katong Rd in Joo Chiat (Katong) and ends at the National Sailing Centre in Bedok, which is actually closer to the Tanah Merah MRT station. It's connected to Changi Beach Park by the Coastal Park Connector Network (PCN), a 15km park connector running along Changi Coast Rd, beside the airport runway. At the western end of the park, the bicycle track continues right through to Joo Chiat, ending at the Kallang River.

CHANGI MUSEUM & CHAPEL

The **Changi Museum & Chapel** (☑6214 2451; www.changimuseum.sg; 1000 Upper Changi Rd N; ⊙9.30am-5pm, last entry 4.30pm; P; ☐2) FREE commemorates the WWII Allied POWs who suffered horrific treatment at the hands of the invading Japanese. The museum includes replicas of the famous Changi Murals painted by POW Stanley Warren in the old POW hospital and a replica of the original Changi Chapel.

The museum was shifted from its original Changi prison site in 2001 when Singapore Prisons reclaimed the land to expand its operations. Former POWs, veterans and historians will feel the loss of the actual site most keenly, but to the architects' credit, the understated design of the current building is well suited to its dual role as a shrine and history museum.

The easiest and fastest way to get here is by taxi (\$S25).

PULAU UBIN

It may be just a 10-minute bumboat (motorised sampan) ride from Changi Village, but Pulau Ubin seems worlds apart from mainland Singapore and is the perfect city getaway for those who love the outdoors, particularly cycling. This unkempt jungle of an island offers a forest full of weird and wonderful creatures, dusty village streets and the chance yo indulge in a seafood feast at the water's edge. Set aside a full day if you can. It takes a couple of hours just to get here and, once you arrive, you won't want to be rushed.

Half the fun of exploring Ubin's sights is finding them. At the far east you can park your bike to explore **Chek Jawa Wetlands** (☑1800 471 7300; www.nparks.gov.sg; ⊘8.30am-6pm) **FREE**, with a 1km coastal boardwalk and 20m-high viewing tower. You'll find wildlife in abundance here; keep your eyes peeled for crabs in the water, Oriental Pied Hornbills flying by or small wild pigs in the forest. To the west you'll find the **Ketam Mountain Bike Park** (☑1800 471 7300; www.nparks.gov.sg) and some great viewing points over the disused quarries. On the way is the quirky **German Girl Shrine** (near Ketam Quarry); legend has it that the young daughter of a German coffee plantation manager was running away from British troops who had come to arrest her parents during WWI and fell fatally into the quarry behind her house. Somewhere along the way, this daughter of a Roman Catholic family became a Taoist deity, whose help some Chinese believers seek for good health and lottery numbers.

There are plenty of places in Pulau Ubin Village that rent perfectly adequate bikes for the day. Cheapest and fairest of the lot is Shop 31, which rents bikes for S$7 to S$15, and helmets for S$2. Uncle also has a number of fancier bikes for the more serious peddler for S$38. Vendors should throw in a basket and a bike lock if you ask. Most offer a range of tandems, as well as bikes with child seats. An alternative to cycling is a kayaking tour of the island's waterways with **Adventures by Asian Detours** (☑6733 2282; http://adventures.asiandetours.com; 34 Pulau Ubin; tours adult/child 7-12yr from S$85/63).

The only place to have a meal is in Pulau Ubin Village. Get off the boat and turn left. There are half a dozen or so places here – a good choice is **Season Live Seafood** (☑6542 7627; 59E Pulau Ubin; dishes S$4-25, crab per kg from S$60; ⊘11am-6pm, closed Tue), a no-frills, waterfront eatery serving a repertoire of classics including butter prawns, fried squid and sambal sweet potato leaf.

To reach the island first head to Tanah Merah MRT Station, where you'll then need to hop on bus 2 (30 minutes) to the terminus bus stop at Changi Point Ferry Terminal. From here it's a 10-minute chug-along bumboat (motorised sampan) ride to Pulau Ubin Ferry Terminal (one-way S$3, bicycle surcharge S$2). The small wooden boats seat 12 passengers, and only leave when full, but you rarely have to wait long. No tickets are issued. You just pay the boat-hand once you're on board.

From central Singapore, catch bus 36, 48 or 196 to Marine Parade Rd, then walk south one block to East Coast Parkway (ECP), crossing it to East Coast Park via one of the pedestrian underpasses.

Geylang Serai Market
MARKET

(Pasar Geylang Serai; Map p510; 1 Geylang Serai; ⊘8am-10pm; Ⓜ Paya Lebar) Suitably inspired by *kampong* architecture, this bustling market lies at the heart of Singapore's Malay community. The ground floor is crammed with stalls selling everything from tropical fruits and spices to halal meats and Malay CDs. Upstairs, cheap, colourful Islamic fashion hobnobs with a popular hawker centre.

Lined with great Malay and Indian stalls, the hawker centre is a good spot for a fix of *pisang goreng* (banana fritters) and *bandung* (milk with rose-cordial syrup).

Katong Antique House
MUSEUM

(Map p510; ☑6345 8544; 208 East Coast Rd; 45min tour S$15; ⊘by appointment; ☐10, 12, 14, 32, 40) Part shop, part museum, the Katong Antique House is a labour of love for owner Peter Wee, a fourth-generation Baba Peranakan. A noted expert on Peranakan history and culture, Peter will happily regale you with tales as you browse an intriguing collection of Peranakan antiques, artefacts and other objets d'art.

Eastern Singapore

N
0   1 km
0   0.5 miles

Bedok South Ave

New Upper Changi Rd

Bedok

Bedok Rd

East Coast Rd

East Coast Pkwy (ECP)

Siglap Rd

East Coast Park

Siglap Rd

Marine Vista

Siglap Rd

Frankel Ave

Siglap Canal

6

Kembangan

Strait of Singapore

JOO CHIAT (KATONG)

Telok Kurau Rd

East Coast Rd

Marine Parade Rd

Jln Eunos

Still Rd

17

Eunos

Joo Chiat Tce

Joo Chiat Pl

10 4

Koon Seng Rd

Changi Rd

Joo Chiat Rd

15 12

Tembeling Rd

Marine Parade Rd

Carpmael Rd

9

8

16

Sims Ave

Onan Rd

5

Peranakan Terrace Houses

14

3

Brooke Rd

Marshall Rd

Amber Rd

Pan-Island Expwy

Ceylon Rd

Haig Rd

Paya Lebar Rd

Paya Lebar

Joo Chiat Rd

Dunman Rd

Tanjong Katong Rd

Goodman Rd

Mountbatten Rd

GEYLANG SERAI

Guillemard Rd

Broadrick Rd

East Coast Park

Geylang Rd

Arthur Rd

Aljunied

Sims Ave

Fort Rd

Katong Park

Mountbatten

Aljunied Rd

13

East Coast Pkwy (ECP)

Mountbatten Rd

Mountbatten Rd

KALLANG

Lor 3

Lor 1

Kallang

National Stadium Blvd

Stadium Rd

Geylang River

Kallang River

Marina Bay Golf Course

Eastern Singapore

◎ **Top Sights**
1 Peranakan Terrace Houses D2

◎ **Sights**
2 East Coast Park E3
3 Geylang Serai Market D2
4 Katong Antique House E3

◎ **Activities, Courses & Tours**
5 Betel Box: The Real Singapore
   Tours...D2
6 Cookery Magic.......................................F1
7 Singapore Wake Park G3

◎ **Sleeping**
Betel Box ....(see 5)
8 Hotel Indigo...D3

◎ **Eating**
9 328 Katong Laksa.................................D3
10 Chin Mee Chin Confectionery E3
11 East Coast Lagoon Food Village G3
12 Long Phung..D2
13 No Signboard Seafood..........................B2
14 Roland Restaurant.................................D3
15 Smokey's BBQ D2

◎ **Drinking & Nightlife**
16 Cider Pit D2

◎ **Entertainment**
17 Necessary Stage....................................E3

◎ **Shopping**
Kim Choo Kueh Chang ....(see 9)
Rumah Bebe ....(see 9)

◎ Northern & Central Singapore

From treetop walks in MacRitchie Reservoir to the hiking and biking trails of Chestnut Park, there's plenty to keep lovers of the outdoors busy. If hiking isn't your thing, seek out grand temples and the Singapore Zoo, **Night Safari** (✆6269 3411; www.wrs.com. sg; 80 Mandai Lake Rd; adult/child under 13yr/3yr S\$47/31/free; ◎7.15pm-midnight; ⟨▪⟩; ⟨🚌138) and **River Safari** (✆6269 3411; www.wrs.com.sg; 80 Mandai Lake Rd; adult/child under 13yr/3yr S\$32/21/free; ◎10am-7pm; ⟨▪⟩; ⟨🚌138).

★**Singapore Zoo**   ZOO
(✆6269 3411; www.wrs.com.sg; 80 Mandai Lake Rd; adult/child under 13/3yr S\$33/22/free; ◎8.30am-6pm; ⟨▪⟩; ⟨🚌138) The line between zoo and botanic oasis blurs at this pulse-slowing sweep of spacious, naturalistic enclosures and interactive attractions. Get up close to orang-utans, dodge Malaysian flying foxes, even snoop around a replica African village. Then there's *that* setting: 26 soothing hectares on a lush peninsula jutting out into the waters of the Upper Seletar Reservoir.

There are over 2800 residents here, and as zoos go, the enclosures are among the world's most comfortable. Among the highlights is the **Jungle Breakfast with Wildlife** (✆6269 3411; www.wrs.com.sg; Ah Meng Restaurant, Singapore Zoo, 80 Mandai Lake Rd; adult/child under 12yr/6yr S\$35/25/free; ◎9-10.30am; ⟨🚌138), a morning buffet enjoyed in the company of orang-utans. Close encounters with free-roaming ring-tailed lemurs, lories and tree-hugging sloths await at the giant Fragile Forest biodome, or spy on shameless, red-bummed baboons doing things that Singaporeans still get arrested for at the evocative Great Rift Valley exhibit. If you have kids in tow, let them go wild at **Rainforest Kidzworld** (✆6269 3411; www.wrs.com.sg; Singapore Zoo, 80 Mandai Lake Rd; carousel/pony rides per person S\$4/6; ◎9am-6pm; ⟨🚌138), a wonderland of slides, swings, pony rides and farmyard animals happy for a feed. There's even a dedicated wet area, with swimwear available for purchase if you didn't bring your own.

The zoo prides itself on fostering respect for nature, and works together with other like-minded institutions on conservation projects both locally and regionally. One stain on its otherwise admirable record is the elephant and other animal shows it still puts on. Although elephant rides were stopped in 2014, shows involving elephants, which are criticised by animal-welfare experts for being harmful to the animals, still take place here.

Singapore Zoo tickets purchased online are subject to a 5% discount or enjoy further discounts by purchasing a multipark ticket, which includes the River Safari, Night Safari and Jurong Bird Park (p513).

To get here catch bus 138 from the Ang Mo Kio MRT station.

★**Former Ford Factory**   MUSEUM
(✆6462 6724; www.nas.gov.sg; 351 Upper Bukit Timah Rd; adult/child under 6yr S\$3/free; ◎9am-5.30pm, from noon Sun; ⟨P⟩; ⟨🚌67, 75, 170, 961) The former Ford Motors assembly plant is best remembered as the place where the British surrendered Singapore to the Japanese on 15 February 1942. It's now home to an exhibition that charts Singapore's descent into

war, the three dark years of Japanese occupation and Singapore's recovery and path to independence. This sombre story is told through audio interviews, news reels and clippings, photographs, diaries and harrowing personal accounts.

Catch the MRT to Beauty World Station (take exit B) and board bus 67, 75, 170, 961, alight three stops later at After Old Jurong Rd and walk a further 150m up the road.

Lian Shan Shuang Lin Monastery TEMPLE
(Siong Lim Temple; ☑ 6259 6924; www.shuanglin. sg; 184 Jln Toa Payoh; ⊙ 8am-5pm; P; Ⓜ Toa Payoh) FREE This breathtaking monastery was established in 1898 and inspired by the Xi Chang Shi temple in Fuzhou, China. Two majestic gates frame the entrance, while further to the right is a seven-storey pagoda adorned with carvings. Inside the complex, shaded pathways lead from bonsai-filled courtyards to the monastery's three main halls, of which the Mahavira Hall is the most spectacular.

★**MacRitchie Reservoir** NATURE RESERVE
(☑ 1800 471 7300; www.nparks.gov.sg; Lornie Rd; P; ⬚ 130, 132, 162, 166, 167, 980) FREE MacRitchie Reservoir makes for a calming, evocative jungle escape. Walking trails skirt the water's edge and snake through the mature secondary rainforest spotted with long-tailed macaques and huge monitor lizards. You can rent kayaks at the **Paddle Lodge** (☑ 6258 0057; www.scf.org.sg; per hr from S$15; ⊙ 9am-noon & 2-6pm), but the highlight is the excellent 11km walking trail – and its various well-signposted offshoots. Aim for the **TreeTop Walk** (⊙ 9am-5pm Tue-Sun), the highlight of which is traversing a 250m-long suspension bridge, perched 25m up in the forest canopy.

Trails then continue through the forest and around the reservoir, sometimes on dirt tracks, sometimes on wooden boardwalks. It takes three to four hours to complete the main circuit. From the service centre (which has changing facilities and a small cafe), near where the bus drops you off, start walking off to your right (anticlockwise around the lake) and you'll soon reach the Paddle Lodge. TreeTop Walk is around 3.5km beyond this.

Chestnut Park PARK
(☑ 1800 471 7300; www.nparks.gov.sg; Chestnut Ave; ⊙ 7am-7pm; P; ⬚ 700, 966) FREE Set over 81 hectares, making it Singapore's largest

nature park, it has 8.2km of bike trails ranging from beginner to hell-bent crazy. Two skill parks are also available for bikers to practise their moves; those who prefer to use their feet are also catered for with designated hiking trails – running adjacent to the bike trails, they're separated from them by a barrier. Bring water, sunscreen and mosquito repellent.

With the closest bus stop 2km away, it's not the easiest place to get to. A taxi from the city will cost approximately S$16. Mountain bikes can be hired at the entrance (per hour from S$15).

Kong Meng San Phor Kark See Monastery MONASTERY
(☑ 6849 5300; www.kmspks.org; 88 Bright Hill Rd; ⊙ gate 6am-10pm, halls 8am-4pm; P; ⬚ 52, 410) FREE Take a few hours to explore the Kong Meng San Phor Kark See Monastery, Singapore's largest (12 buildings) and most stunning. 'Don't speak unless it improves the silence' is the creed here, the resultant quiet a surreal counterpart to dragon-topped pagodas, shrines, plazas and lawns linked by Escher-like staircases. On the premises is a large columbarium and several different halls devoted to various guises of the Buddha.

Bukit Timah Nature Reserve NATURE RESERVE
(☑ 1800 471 7300; www.nparks.gov.sg; Hindhede Dr; ⊙ 7am-7pm; P; Ⓜ Beauty World) FREE Singapore's steamy Bukit Timah Nature Reserve is a 163-hectare tract of primary rainforest clinging to Singapore's highest peak, Bukit Timah (163m). The reserve supposedly holds more tree species than the entire North American continent, and its unbroken forest canopy shelters what remains of Singapore's native wildlife, including long-tailed macaques (monkeys), pythons and dozens of bird species. The visitor centre (8am to 5.30pm) showcases the area's flora and fauna, including two Sumatran tigers who once roamed Singapore.

Also, keep in mind that the steep paths are sweaty work, so take plenty of water, smother yourself in mosquito repellent, and don't feed the monkeys no matter how politely they ask.

◎ West & Southwest Singapore

Leaving Singapore's downtown area, you'll see the concrete jungle give way to thriving green jungles. Museum and gallery-hopping, wildlife-viewing and walks are the drawcards in west and southwest Singapore. Hit the Southern Ridges in the early morning or head to Sungei Buloh Wetland Reserve to spot kingfishers and crocs before retiring to the air-conditioned cool of a gallery, or a shady perch in Jurong Bird Park.

★ **Southern Ridges**   PARK
(✆1800 471 7300; www.nparks.gov.sg; ⊘24hr; ℗; Ⓜ Pasir Panjang) Made up of a series of parks and hills connecting Kent Ridge Park to Mt Faber and the Labrador Nature Reserve, the Southern Ridges will have you trekking through the jungle without ever really leaving the city. The entire route spans 10km; the best stretch is from Kent Ridge Park to Mt Faber. Not only is it relatively easy, this 4km section offers forest-canopy walkways, lofty skyline vistas and the chance to cross the spectacular Henderson Waves, an undulating pedestrian bridge suspended 36m above the ground.

Alight from the MRT at Pasir Panjang station, from where Kent Ridge Park is a steep but manageable 800m walk up Pepys Rd. At the top of the hill is the small yet fascinating **Reflections at Bukit Chandu** (✆6375 2510; www.nhb.gov.sg; 31K Pepys Rd; ⊘9am-5.30pm Tue-Sun; ℗; Ⓜ Pasir Panjang) FREE war museum. Directly beyond is **Kent Ridge Park** (✆1800 471 7300; www.nparks.gov.sg; Vigilante Dr; ⊘24hr; ℗; Ⓜ Pasir Panjang) and its short forest-canopy walk. The idyllic leafy shade of Kent Ridge quickly gives way to the themed gardens and prototype glasshouses of **HortPark** (✆1800 471 7300; www.nparks.gov.sg; 33 Hyderabad Rd; ⊘6am-10pm; ℗; Ⓜ Labrador Park). The park is especially family-friendly with its playground, drinking fountains and nursery-cafe.

Cross the leaf-like Alexander Arch bridge from HortPark to the impressive Forest Walk, offering eye-level views of the jungle canopy covering Telok Blangah Hill. The walkway eventually leads to **Telok Blangah Hill Park** (✆1800 471 7300; www.nparks.gov.sg; Telok Blangah Green; ⊘24hr; ℗; 🚌124, 131, 145, 175,195), with its beautiful floral displays, and further along to the sculptural Henderson Waves bridge. The pointed towers you can see rising above the forest canopy form part of the Daniel Libeskind-designed luxury residential complex, Reflections at Keppel Bay.

It's a short but rather steep climb up the final 550m to the summit of **Mt Faber** (✆1800 471 7300; www.nparks.gov.sg; Mt Faber Rd; ⊘24hr; ℗; 🚌Mt Faber), with fine city views awaiting (skip the average restaurants). The **cable car** (✆6377 9688; www.onefabergroup.com; adult/child return S$33/22; ⊘8.45am-9.30pm; Ⓜ Harbour-Front) connecting Mt Faber to HarbourFront

mall and MRT, and on to Sentosa Island is exorbitantly priced (adult/child return S$33/22) – consider grabbing a taxi instead (expect to pay around S$7 to HarbourFront).

Jurong Bird Park   BIRD SANCTUARY
(✆6269 3411; www.wrs.com.sg; 2 Jurong Hill; adult/child under 13/2yr S$30/20/free; ⊘8.30am-6pm; ℗🚻; 🚌194) Home to some 400 species of feathered friends – including spectacular macaws – Jurong is a great place for young kids. Highlights include the wonderful Lory Loft forest enclosure, where you can feed colourful lories and lorikeets, and the interactive High Flyers (11am and 3pm) and Kings of the Skies (10am and 4pm). We must note, however, that some birds are made to perform for humans, which is discouraged by animal-welfare groups.

Young ones can splash about at the Birdz of Play (open 11am to 5.30pm weekdays, 9am to 5.30pm weekends), a wet and dry play area with a shop selling swimwear. There's a guided tram to cart you around the park when energy levels are low. Jurong Bird Park tickets purchased online are subject to a 5% discount, or enjoy further discounts by purchasing a multipark ticket, which includes the Singapore Zoo (p511), River Safari (p511) and Night Safari (p511).

To reach here catch the 194 bus from Boon Lay MRT station.

NUS Museum   MUSEUM
(✆6516 8817; www.museum.nus.edu.sg; National University of Singapore, 50 Kent Ridge Cres; ⊘10am-6pm Tue-Sat; ℗; 🚌96) FREE Located on the verdant campus of the National University of Singapore (NUS), this museum is one of the city's lesser-known cultural delights. Ancient Chinese ceramics and bronzes, as well as archaeological fragments found in Singapore, dominate the ground-floor Lee Kong Chian Collection; one floor up, the South and Southeast Asian Gallery showcases paintings, sculpture and textiles from the region. The Ng Eng Teng Collection is dedicated to Ng Eng Teng (1934–2001), Singapore's foremost modern artist, best known for his figurative sculptures.

To get here catch the 96 bus from Clementi MRT station.

Lee Kong Chian Natural History Museum   MUSEUM
(✆6601 3333; http://lkcnhm.nus.edu.sg; 2 Conservatory Dr; adult/child under 13yr S$21/13; ⊘10am-7pm Tue-Sun; ℗; 🚌96) What looks like a giant rock bursting with greenery

SINGAPORE SIGHTS

GILLMAN BARRACKS

Where soldiers once stomped, curators now roam. Built in 1936 as a British military encampment, **Gillman Barracks** (www.gillmanbarracks.com; 9 Lock Rd; ⊙11am-7pm Tue-Sun; P; MLabrador Park) **FREE** is now a rambling art outpost with 11 commercial galleries studding the verdant grounds. It's a civilised way to spend a few hours, browsing free temporary exhibitions of painting, sculpture and photography from some of the world's most coveted creatives.

Among the galleries is New York's **Sundaram Tagore** (☑6694 3378; www.sundaram tagore.com; 01-05, 5 Lock Rd, Gillman Barracks; ⊙11am-7pm Tue-Sat; MLabrador Park) **FREE**, whose stable of artists includes award-winning photographers Edward Burtynsky and Annie Leibovitz. Across the street, Italy's **Partners & Mucciaccia** (☑6694 3777; www. partnersandmucciaccia.net; 02-10, 6 Lock Rd, Gillman Barracks; ⊙noon-7pm Tue-Fri, from 11am Sat, 11am-6pm Sun; P; MLabrador Park) **FREE** profiles mostly modern and contemporary Italian artists, with the odd retrospective featuring the likes of Marc Chagall and Pablo Picasso. Next door, **Chan + Hori Contemporary** (☑6338 1962; www.chanhori.com; 02-09, Block 6, Lock Rd, Gillman Barracks; ⊙11am-7pm Tue-Sun; MLabrador Park) **FREE** showcases mostly contemporary, emerging Singaporean talent.

Plan ahead and book a table at Gillman's **Naked Finn** (☑6694 0807; www.nakedfinn. com; 39 Malan Rd, Gillman Barracks; mains S$30-78; ⊙noon-2.30pm Tue-Sat, 6-9pm Tue-Thu, to 9.30pm Fri & Sat; MLabrador Park), a hip restaurant and cocktail joint with an ever-changing menu of phenomenally fresh seafood (if you're there for lunch don't pass up the lobster roll). If you don't have a booking, try your luck – walk-ins are welcome, but space is limited.

If heading there on the MRT, alight at Labrador Park station and walk north up Alexandra Rd for 800m; the entry to Gillman Barracks is on your right. A one-way taxi fare from the CBD is around S$12.

is actually Singapore's high-tech, child-friendly natural history museum. The main Biodiversity Gallery delves into the origin of life using a stimulating combo of fossils, taxidermy and interactive displays. Hard to miss are Prince, Apollonia and Twinky: three 150-million-year-old Diplodocid sauropod dinosaur skeletons, two with their original skulls. Upstairs, the Heritage Gallery explores the collection's 19th-century origins, with an interesting section on Singapore's geology to boot.

Labrador Nature Reserve   PARK
(☑1800 471 7300; www.nparks.gov.sg; Labrador Villa Rd; ⊙24hr; P; MLabrador Park) Combining forest trails rich in birdlife and a beachfront park, Labrador Park is also scattered with evocative British war relics, only rediscovered in the 1980s. Look out for old gun emplacements mounted on moss-covered concrete casements, as well as for the remains of the entrance to the old fort that once stood guard on this hill. The reserve's hilly terrain sweeps down to the shore, where expansive lawns, shade and the sound of lapping waves invite a lazy picnic.

Sungei Buloh Wetland Reserve   WILDLIFE RESERVE
(☑6794 1401; www.nparks.gov.sg; 60 Kranji Way; ⊙7am-7pm; P; ☐925) Sungei Buloh's 202 hectares of mangroves, mudflats, ponds and secondary rainforest are a bird-watcher's paradise, with migratory birds including egrets, sandpipers and plovers joining locals such as herons, bitterns, coucals and kingfishers. The reserve is also a good spot to see monitor lizards, mudskippers, crabs and – if you're very lucky – an estuarine crocodile. Free guided tours run every Saturday at 9.30am; registration required via the website.

The reserve is one of the few remaining mangrove areas in Singapore, and its lush, tranquil walking trails – which include a Migratory Bird Trail (1.9km) and a Coastal Trail (1.3km) – are dotted with bird-viewing huts and lookouts. Also on-site is a visitor centre complete with mangrove exhibition gallery (open 8.30am to 5.30pm), shedding light on the reserve's wildlife and botany. To get here, catch bus 925 from Kranji MRT station and alight at Kranji Reservoir Car Park B, directly opposite the reserve's entrance on Kranji Way. On Sunday, bus 925C also stops at the reserve's other entrance on Neo Tiew

Cres. Alternatively the **Kranji Countryside Express** (www.kranjicountryside.com; Kranji MRT station; per round trip S$3; ⊗8.30am-5.45pm; Ⓜ Kranji) runs daily from Kranji MRT.

Kranji War Memorial   MEMORIAL
(☑ 6269 6158; www.cwgc.org; 9 Woodlands Rd; ⊗8am-6.30pm; Ⓟ; 🚇 Kranji) 𝗙𝗥𝗘𝗘 The austere white structures and rolling hillside of the Kranji War Memorial contain the WWII graves of thousands of Allied troops. Headstones, many of which are inscribed simply with the words: 'a soldier of the 1939–1945 war', are lined in neat rows across manicured lawns. Walls are etched with the names of over 24,000 men and women who lost their lives in Southeast Asia, and registers are available for inspection. There is no wheelchair access.

◉ Sentosa Island

Connected to the 'mainland' by a causeway, Sentosa is essentially one giant Pleasure Island. It's packed with rides, activities and shows, most of which cost extra, so it's very easy for a family to rack up a huge bill in one day spent here (and that's not counting visits to the casino). The beaches are completely free and very popular with locals and tourists alike.

Sentosa Island charges a small entry fee, based on the form of transport you take. If you walk across from VivoCity, you pay nothing. If you ride the Sentosa Express monorail, it's S$4, which you can pay using cash or your EZ-Link card. Ride the cable car and the entrance fee is included in the price of your cable-car ticket.

★ Fort Siloso   MUSEUM
(Map p516; ☑ 6736 8672; www.sentosa.com.sg; Siloso Point, Siloso Rd; ⊗10am-6pm; 👍; 🚇 Silo-

so Point) 𝗙𝗥𝗘𝗘 Dating from the 1880s, when Sentosa was called Pulau Blakang Mati (Malay for 'the island behind which lies death'), this British coastal fort was famously useless during the Japanese invasion of 1942. Documentaries, artefacts, animatronics and recreated historical scenes take visitors through the fort's history, and the underground tunnels are fun to explore. The Surrender Chambers bring to life two pivotal moments in Singapore's history: the surrender of the British to the Japanese in 1942, and then the reverse in 1945.

SEA Aquarium   AQUARIUM
(Map p516; ☑ 6577 8888; www.rwsentosa.com; Resorts World, 8 Sentosa Gateway; adult/child under 13yr S$39/29; ⊗10am-7pm; Ⓟ; 🚇 Waterfront) You'll be gawking at more than 800 species of aquatic creature at Singapore's impressive, sprawling aquarium. The state-of-the-art complex recreates 49 aquatic habitats found between Southeast Asia, Australia and Africa. The Open Ocean habitat is especially spectacular, its 36m-long, 8.3m-high viewing panel one of the world's largest. The complex is also home to an interactive, family-friendly exhibition exploring the history of the maritime Silk Route.

★ Universal Studios   AMUSEMENT PARK
(Map p516; ☑ 6577 8888; www.rwsentosa.com; Resorts World, 8 Sentosa Gateway; adult/child under 13yr S$76/56; ⊗10am-7pm; 🚇 Waterfront) Universal Studios is the top draw at Resorts World. Shops, shows, restaurants, rides and roller coasters are all neatly packaged into fantasy-world themes based on blockbuster Hollywood films. Top attractions include Transformers: The Ride, a next-generation thrill ride deploying 3D animation, and Battlestar Galactica: Human vs Cylon,

SENTOSA BEACHES

Squint hard enough and Sentosa's trio of beaches could pass for a Thai island paradise. The most popular of the three is **Siloso Beach** (www.sentosa.com.sg; Ⓟ; 🚇 Beach). A quick walk from Beach monorail station, it's jam-packed with activities, eateries and bars. Further east is **Palawan Beach** (www.sentosa.com.sg; Ⓟ 👍; 🚇 Palawan Beach) , home also to the extremely popular **KidZania** (☑1800 653 6888; www.kidzania.com. sg; 01-01/02 Palawan Kidz City, 31 Beach View; adult/child under 18yr S$58/35; ⊗10am-6pm; 🚇 Beach). Continue east and you'll reach **Tanjong Beach** (www.sentosa.com.sg; Ⓟ; 🚇 Tanjong Beach) where eye-candy crowds perfect their beach-volleyball moves or simply flirt by the bar. Despite the disconcerting number of cargo ships out at sea, the water at all three beaches is monitored by the National Environment Agency and deemed safe for swimming. To reach Palawan and Tanjong Beaches, catch Sentosa's free beach tram.

Sentosa Island

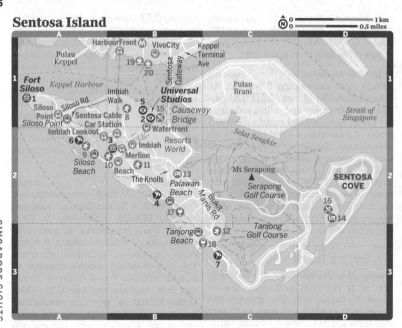

Sentosa Island

◎ Top Sights
1 Fort Siloso		A1
2 Universal Studios		B1

◎ Sights
3 Images of Singapore Live		B2
4 Palawan Beach		B2
5 SEA Aquarium		B1
6 Siloso Beach		A2
7 Tanjong Beach		C3

◎ Activities, Courses & Tours
8 Adventure Cove Waterpark		B1
9 AJ Hackett Bungy		A2
10 iFly		B2
11 KidZania		B2
MegaAdventure		(see 6)
12 Sentosa Golf Club		C3
Skyline Luge Sentosa		(see 10)
Wave House		(see 6)

◎ Sleeping
13 Capella Singapore		B2
14 W Singapore – Sentosa Cove		D2

◎ Eating
Knolls		(see 13)
15 Malaysian Food Street		B1
16 Mykonos on the Bay		D2

◎ Drinking & Nightlife
17 FOC Sentosa		B2
18 Tanjong Beach Club		C3

◎ Transport
19 BatamFast		B1
20 Singapore Cruise Centre @ HarbourFront		B1

the world's tallest duelling roller coasters. Opening times are subject to slight variations across the year, so always check the website before heading in.

Images of Singapore Live   MUSEUM
(Map p516; ☑6715 4000; www.imagesofsinga-porelive.com; 40 Imbiah Rd; adult/child under 13yr S$42/32; ⊙10am-6pm, to 7.30pm Sat & Sun; ⊠Imbiah) Using actors, immersive exhibi-

tions and dramatic light-and-sound effects, Images of Singapore Live resuscitates the nation's history, from humble Malay fishing village to bustling colonial port and beyond. Kids will especially love the Spirit of Singapore Boat Ride, a trippy, high-tech journey that feels just a little *Avatar*. Tickets include entry to Madame Tussauds and are S$10 cheaper when purchased online.

🏃 Activities

Golf

Sentosa Golf Club
GOLF

(Map p516; ☑ 6275 0022; www.sentosagolf.com; 27 Bukit Manis Rd; green & buggy fees per round S$400-540; ⊙ 7am-9pm; 🚌 B) A luxury golf club with two of the best championship courses in Asia. However, as a nonmember you can only play if you possess a certain handicap; check website for details. Rental of clubs (S$86) and shoes (S$10) is available.

Champions Golf
GOLF

(☑ 6463 0332; www.championsgolf.co; 60 Fairway Dr; per round from S$45, trolley/buggy hire from S$6/20; ⊙ 7am-10pm, last tee off 6pm; Ⓜ Sixth Ave) In land-sparse Singapore a golf game can set you back upwards of a few hundred dollars, so a round at Champions' lush nine holes is an absolute bargain. Perfect your swing at the driving range before kitting yourself out at the pro shop, and post-round you can enjoy cold beer and a bite to eat at on-site restaurant Picotin Express (☑ 6877 1191; www.picotin.com.sg; 60 Fairways Dr; mains S$20-36, pizzas S$18-28; ⊙ 7am-11pm, to 1am Fri & Sat; Ⓜ Sixth Ave).

Adventure Sports

iFly
ADVENTURE SPORTS

(Map p516; ☑ 6571 0000; www.iflysingapore.com; 43 Siloso Beach Walk; 1/2 skydives S$89/119; ⊙ 9am-9.30pm, from 11am Wed; 🚌 Beach) If you fancy free-falling from 3660m to 914m without leaping out of a plane, leap into this indoor-skydiving centre. The price includes an hour's instruction followed by a short but thrilling skydive in a vertical wind chamber. Divers must be at least seven years old. Tickets purchased two days in advance for off-peak times are significantly cheaper. See the website for details.

Skyline Luge Sentosa
ADVENTURE SPORTS

(Map p516; ☑ 6274 0472; www.skylineluge.com; 45 Siloso Beach Walk; luge & skyride combo from S$24; ⊙ 10am-9.30pm; 🚌 Beach (Siloso Beach), 🚠 Imbiah Station) Hop onto your luge (think go-cart meets toboggan) and race family and friends around hairpin bends and along bone-shaking straights carved through the forest (mandatory helmets are provided). Young kids will love this. Those with heart conditions or bad backs won't. You'll find entrances at Imbiah Lookout and Siloso Beach.

MegaAdventure
ADVENTURE SPORTS

(Map p516; ☑ 3163 4394; www.sg.megaadventure.com; 10A Siloso Beach Walk; ⊙ 11am-7pm; 🚌 Beach)

This multi-activity playground will really get your adrenaline pumping. MegaZip, the 450m-long, 75m-tall zip-line (S$50), is the highlight and runs from Imbiah Lookout to a tiny island off Siloso Beach (p515). Alternatively, conquer the 15m drop in the Mega-Jump (S$25) or feel like a harnessed Tarzan while you scramble through high-ropes adventure course MegaClimb ($45).

AJ Hackett Bungy
BUNGEE JUMPING

(Map p516; ☑ 6911 3070; www.ajhackett.com/sentosa; 30 Siloso Beach Walk; bungy S$199, swing S$79, skybridge S$16; ⊙ 1-7pm, to 8pm Fri-Sun; 🚌 Siloso Beach) The famous New Zealand bungee company has now set up shop on Palawan Beach on Sentosa, complete with a 47m platform to hurtle yourself off should the desire grab you. There's also a giant swing, and a sky bridge for those who'd just like to look.

Spas & Massage

★ Remède Spa
SPA

(Map p506; ☑ 6506 6896; www.remedespasingapore.com; St Regis Hotel, 29 Tanglin Rd; massage from S$105; ⊙ 9am-11pm; Ⓜ Orchard) Reputed to have the best masseurs in town, the St Regis Hotel's in-house spa is also home to the award-winning Pedi:Mani:Cure Studio by renowned pedicurist Bastien Gonzalez. Remède's wet lounge – a marbled wonderland of steam room, sauna, ice fountains and spa baths – is a perfect prelude to standout treatments like the warm jade stone massage ($300).

Damai Spa
SPA

(Map p506; ☑ 6416 7156; www.hyatt.com/corporate/spas/Damai-Spa/en/home.html; Grand Hyatt, 10 Scotts Rd; 30min facial from S$160, 1hr massage from S$195; ⊙ 10am-10pm; Ⓜ Orchard) Ladies who lunch swear that the facials at the Grand Hyatt's spa are the best in town. The extensive list of options includes custom treatments based on your skin type (from S$160), the opulence facial using botanical brighteners and vitamin C serum (S$350), and anti-ageing treatments using high-tech serums and oxygen (from S$350).

Willow Stream
SPA

(Map p492; ☑ 6431 5600; www.willowstream.com/singapore; Level 6, Fairmont Hotel, 80 Bras Basah Rd; treatments from S$148; ⊙ 7am-10pm, treatments from 9am; Ⓜ City Hall, Esplanade) Spoil yourself silly at this lavish spa, complete with Jacuzzis, plunge pools, rooms that puff aromatic steam and staff who will slather good stuff on your face before pushing, prodding and

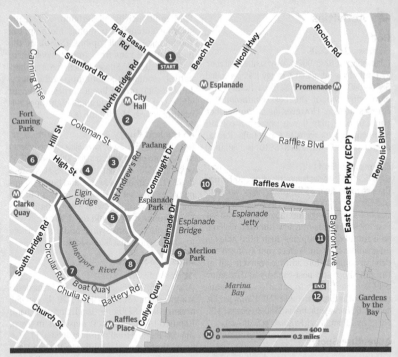

City Walk
Colonial to Cutting Edge

START RAFFLES HOTEL
END MARINA BAY SANDS
LENGTH 4KM; FOUR TO FIVE HOURS

Start at **1** **Raffles Hotel** (p496), taking in the magnificent ivory frontage, colonial arcades and tropical gardens. Head out along North Bridge Rd and turn left into elegant **2** **St Andrew's Cathedral** (p496), used as an emergency hospital during WWII. Heading south down St Andrew's Rd you'll pass City Hall and the Old Supreme Court, two colonial dames that house the **3** **National Gallery Singapore** (p495). Behind it, along Parliament Pl, is the **4** **New Supreme Court**), a sci-fi statement co-designed by Sir Norman Foster's company Foster + Partners. Return to the St Andrew's Rd corner, and look below where it curves to the left, where the **5** **Victoria Theatre & Concert Hall** (p552) stands, one of Singapore's first Victorian Revivalist buildings. Before it is the original Raffles statue, which once stood at the Padang. Hang a right to walk along the northern bank of the Singapore River,

one of the best spots to take in the CBD's powerhouse towers. They're significantly taller than the multicoloured **6** **Old Hill St Police Station** on the corner of Hill St, proclaimed a 'skyscraper' upon completion in 1934. The building houses several high-end art galleries. Cross Elgin Bridge and head down to **7** **Boat Quay** (p498), its riverfront shophouses now home to bars, restaurants and snap-happy tourists. Look out for the area's great sculptures, including Fernando Botero's *Bird* and Salvador Dalí's *Homage to Newton*. Following the river further east you'll pass **8** **Cavenagh Bridge**, constructed in Scotland and reassembled in Singapore in 1869. Soaring beside it is the mighty Fullerton Hotel, Singapore's general post office until 1996. Take a 'wacky' photo with the famous **9** **Merlion statue**, then head north along the Esplanade Bridge towards **10** **Esplanade – Theatres on the Bay** (p552). Continue east along Marina Promenade to the **11** **Helix Bridge**, where the impressive views of the Singapore skyline are upstaged by those from the Sands SkyPark atop **12** **Marina Bay Sands** (p546).

kneading the kinks out of your jet-lagged (or shopped-out) body. There's also an in-house salon covering everything from hair and waxing to manicures and pedicures.

Spa Esprit SPA
(Map p506; ☑ 6479 0070; www.spa-esprit.com; 03-19 Wheelock Place, 501 Orchard Rd; massage from S$59; ⊗ 10am-9pm; M Somerset) Hip, friendly Spa Esprit is an apothecary and spa in one. Freshly picked ingredients and Certified Pure Therapeutic Grade (CPTG) essential oils are the stars here, deployed in everything from the 'ultra replenishing' facial (S$180) to the qi-restoring 'tui na massage' (S$128) and the blockbuster 'back to balance' body massage (S$235).

Nimble & Knead SPA
(☑ 6438 3933; www.nimbleknead.com; 01-28, 66 Eng Watt St; 60min massage from S$76, 90min facials from S$169; ⊗ 11am-10pm; M Tiong Bahru) When you need a massage, head to this funky spa tucked inside a shophouse. Get lost in the maze of shipping containers (it's any wonder how they got them through the door) before settling in for some serious relaxation. Nimble fingers will work out every knot, kink and ache, while the list of facial and body treatments will have you feeling like new.

Amrita Ayurveda & Yoga MASSAGE
(Map p504; ☑ 6299 0642; www.amrita.sg; 11 Upper Dickson Rd; 30min massage from S$35; ⊗ 9am-9pm Mon-Sat, to 3pm Sun; M Little India, Jalan Besar) If Little India's hyperactive energy leaves you frazzled, revive the Indian way with an Ayurvedic (traditional Indian medicine) massage at this modest, friendly place. Treatments include the highly popular Abhyangam (synchronised massage using medicated oils) and the deeply relaxing Shirodhara (warm oil poured over the forehead). Yoga classes are also on offer.

People's Park Complex MASSAGE
(Map p500; www.peoplesparkcomplex.sg; 1 Park Cres; ⊗ 9am-10pm, shop hours vary; M Chinatown) Heady with the scent of Tiger balm, Singapore's oldest mall is well known for its cheap massage joints. Our favourite is **Mr Lim Foot Reflexology** (Map p500; ☑ 6327 4498; 03-54 & 03-78 People's Park Complex, 1 Park Cres; 20min foot reflexology S$10; ⊗ 10.30am-10pm; M Chinatown), where you'll queue with regulars awaiting a robust rubdown. Feeling adventurous? Try one of the fish-pond foot spas, where schools of fish nibble the dead skin right off your feet.

Swimming

Jurong East Swimming Complex SWIMMING
(☑ 6563 5052; 21 Jurong East St 31; weekdays/weekends S$2/2.60; ⊗ 8am-9.30pm Tue, Thu, Fri & Sun, from 6.30am Wed & Sat; M Chinese Garden) This impressive complex includes a massive wave pool, a bubble-jet spa bath, a lazy river, a wading pool, and a tower of three intertwining water slides. If it's just laps you're after, head to the Olympic-size pool. The complex gets very busy, especially at weekends. From Chinese Garden MRT station, walk northwest along Boon Lay Way and turn right into Jurong East St 31.

Jalan Besar Swimming Complex SWIMMING
(Map p504; ☑ 6293 9058; 100 Tyrwhitt Rd; weekdays/weekends S$1.30/1.70; ⊗ 8am-9.30pm Thu-Tue, 2.30-9.30pm Wed; M Farrer Park, Lavender) An outdoor swimming complex in hipster enclave Jalan Besar. Facilities include a 50m competition pool and a 25m teaching pool.

Water Sports

Singapore Wake Park WATER SPORTS
(Map p510; ☑ 6636 4266; www.singaporewakepark. com; 1206A East Coast Parkway; weekday/weekend 1hr from S$32/42; ⊗ 11am-9pm, from 9am Sat & Sun; ☐ 31, 36, 43, 47, 48, 196, 197, 401) What better way to cool off than by strapping on a wakeboard, a kneeboard or waterskis and getting dragged around a lagoon on the end of a cable? It's best to visit weekday mornings, when there's hardly anyone there. There's also a breezy on-site cafe, which serves decent meals and cold beers.

From central Singapore, catch bus 196 to Marina Parade Rd, then walk south one block to East Coast Parkway (ECP), crossing to East Coast Park via one of the pedestrian underpasses.

Adventure Cove Waterpark WATER PARK
(☑ 6577 8888; www.rwsentosa.com; Resorts World, 8 Sentosa Gateway; adult/child under 13yr S$38/30; ⊗ 10am-6pm; ☐ Waterfront) Despite its rides being better suited to kids and families, adult thrill-seekers will appreciate the Riptide Rocket (Southeast Asia's first hydro-magnetic coaster), Pipeline Plunge and Bluwater Bay, a wave pool with serious gusto.

Dolphin Island, charged separately, allows visitors to interact with Indo-Pacific dolphins in a pool. Captive-dolphin swims have been criticised by animal-welfare groups, who say that captivity is debilitating and stressful for the animals, and that this is exacerbated by human interaction.

Wave House
SURFING

(☑6238 1196; www.wavehousesentosa.com; 36 Siloso Beach Walk; from S$30; ⊙11.30am-9.30pm, from 10.30am Sat & Sun; 🚌 Siloso Beach) Two specially designed wave pools allow surfer types to practise their gashes and cutbacks at ever-popular Wave House. The noncurling Double Flowrider (one-hour session S$35) is good for beginners, while the 3m FlowBarrel (30-minute session from S$30, closed Tuesdays and Thursdays) is more challenging. Wave House also includes beachside eating and drinking options.

Courses

Food Playground
COOKING

(Map p500; ☑9452 3669; www.foodplayground.com.sg; 24A Sago St; 3hr class from S$119; ⊙9.30am-12.30pm Mon-Fri; Ⓜ Chinatown) You've been gorging on Singapore's famous food, so why not learn to make it? This fantastic hands-on cooking school explores Singapore's multicultural make-up and sees you cook up classic dishes like laksa, *nasi lemak* (coconut rice) and Hainanese chicken rice. Courses usually run for three hours and can be tailored for budding cooks with dietary restrictions.

Cookery Magic
COOKING

(Map p510; ☑9665 6831; www.cookerymagic.com; 117 Fidelio St; 3hr classes from S$110; Ⓜ Kembangan) Ruqxana conducts standout cooking classes in her own home so you can take the tastes of Asia home with you. Options span numerous regional cuisines, including Chinese, Malay, Indian, Peranakan and Eurasian. She also conducts classes in a century-old *kampong* (village) home on the bucolic island of Pulau Ubin, as well as cooking classes for kids.

Palate Sensations Cooking School
COOKING

(☑6478 9746; www.palatesensations.com; 01-03 Chromos, 10 Biopolis Rd; courses from S$130; ⊙by appointment; Ⓜ Buona Vista) Novices and serious foodies head here to hone their skills with top-notch chefs. Standard courses run for three hours and are wonderfully hands-on, with anything from Thai favourites to Southern Indian cuisine and French designer pastries. For a true Singaporean culinary adventure, sign up for the tourist class to learn how to perfect local favourites like chicken rice and laksa.

Tours

Betel Box: The Real Singapore Tours
TOURS

(Map p510; ☑6247 7340; www.betelboxtours.com; 200 Joo Chiat Rd; S$60-100; Ⓜ Paya Lebar) Insider tours led by Tony Tan and the team at **Betel Box hostel** (Map p510; dm S$20-25, d S$80; @ 🛜). Choose from culture and heritage walks, city kick scootering or food odysseys through the historic Joo Chiat (Katong), Kampong Glam or Chinatown neighbourhoods. If you're looking for a walk on the wild side, join the Friday night tour through the red-light district in Geylang.

Singapore River Cruise
BOATING

(Map p492; ☑6336 6111; www.rivercruise.com.sg; bumboat river cruise adult/child S$25/15; Ⓜ Clarke Quay) This outfit runs 40-minute bumboat tours of the Singapore River and Marina Bay. Boats depart about every 15 minutes from various locations, including Clarke Quay, Boat Quay and Marina Bay. A cheaper option is to catch one of the company's river taxis – commuter boats running a similar route on weekdays; see the website for stops and times.

Note that river-taxi payment is by NETS or EZ-Link transport card only.

Singapore Ducktours
BOATING

(Map p492; ☑6338 6877; www.ducktours.com.sg; 01-330 Suntec City, 3 Temasek Blvd; adult/child under 13yr S$43/33; ⊙10am-6pm; Ⓜ Esplanade, Promenade) An informative, kid-friendly, one-hour romp in the 'Wacky Duck', a remodelled WWII amphibious Vietnamese war craft. The route traverses land and water, with a focus on Marina Bay and the Colonial District. You'll find the ticket kiosk and departure point in Tower 5 of **Suntec City** (Map p492; ☑6266 1502; www.sunteccity.com.sg; 3 Temasek Blvd; ⊙10am-10pm; 🛜; Ⓜ Promenade, Esplanade), directly facing the Nicoll Hwy. Tours depart hourly, on the hour.

Festivals & Events

With so many cultures and religions, there is an astounding number of colourful celebrations in Singapore. Some have fixed dates, but Hindus, Muslims and Chinese follow a lunar calendar that varies annually. Check out www.visitsingapore.com for exact dates and full event listings.

St Jerome's Laneway Festival
MUSIC

(http://singapore.lanewayfestival.com; ⊙Jan) Uber-hip one-day music fest featuring top-tier indie acts from around the globe.

(Continued on page 531)

AUGUSTINE BIN JUMAT / SHUTTERSTOCK ©

The Mega-Diversity Region

Home to thousands of natural species (with more being discovered all the time), Malaysia, Singapore and Brunei are a dream come true for budding David Attenboroughs. Tropical flora and fauna is so abundant that this region is a 'mega-diversity' hot spot. You don't need to venture deep into the jungle to see wildlife either.

Contents
➡ Jungle Life
➡ Aquatic Life
➡ Natural Wonders
➡ Diverse Ecosystems

Above Taman Rekreasi Gunung Lang (p129), Ipoh

Jungle Life

The region's lush natural habitats, from steamy rainforests to tidal mangroves, teem with mammals, birds, amphibians, reptiles and insects, many of them found nowhere else on earth. Although vast areas of old growth forest have been cleared, a few magnificent stands remain, mostly protected within reserves and parks.

Apes & Monkeys

Orangutans, Asia's only great apes, are at the top of many visitors' lists. Researchers estimate that the number of orangutans left on Borneo stands at between 70,000 and 100,000, a population that has declined by 50% since 1999. Captive orangutans can be viewed at Sabah's Sepilok Orangutan Rehabilitation Centre, the Semenggoh Wildlife Rehabilitation Centre in Sarawak, and Singapore Zoo.

The male proboscis monkey is an improbable-looking creature with a pendulous nose and bulbous belly; females and youngsters are more daintily built, with quaint, upturned noses. A beautiful langur (leaf monkey) is the silvered leaf monkey, whose fur is frosted with grey tips. Macaques are the stocky, aggressive monkeys that solicit snacks from tourists at temples and nature reserves. If you are carrying food, watch out for daring raids and be wary of bites – remember these are wild animals and rabies is a potential hazard.

Tailless and shy gibbons live in the trees, where they feed on fruits such as figs. Their raucous hooting – one of the most distinctive sounds of the Malaysian jungle – helps them establish territories and find mates.

Wild Cats

Species of leopard including the black panther and the rare clouded leopard are found in Malaysia, as well as smaller species of wild cats, including the bay cat, a specialised fish-eater, and the leopard cat, which is a bit larger than a domestic cat but with spotted fur.

The exact population of Malayan tigers is unknown but considered by WWF to be no more than 340, the vast majority of which are found in the jungles of Pahang, Perak, Terengganu and Kelantan.

1. Proboscis monkey 2. Clouded leopard 3. Mother and baby orangutan

1. Malayan tapir 2. Bornean pygmy elephant 3. Rhinoceros hornbill 4. Fruit bat (flying fox)

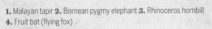

CHRISTIAN EDELMANN/SHUTTERSTOCK ©

Elephants, Rhinos & Tapirs

Around 1500 pygmy elephants live in northeastern Borneo, the largest population roaming the forests around Sungai Kinabatangan. It's thought they've lived on the island for at least 18,000 years.

If you're very lucky you may spot wild Asian elephants in Taman Negara. The animal is endangered with WWF reckoning the population across the region of being between 38,000 to 51,000.

Sadly, according a Danish study published in 2015, the Sumatran rhinoceroses, which previously had been found in isolated areas of Sabah and Endau-Rompin National Park on the peninsula, is now considered extinct in the wild in Malaysia. None have been sighted since 2007.

Similarly under threat from habitat loss is the Malayan tapir, a long-nosed creature with black and white body hair. They can also be found living in Taman Negara.

Birds & Bats

Well over a 1000 species of birds can be spotted in this part of the world. The most easily recognisable species in Malaysia are the various types of hornbill, of which the rhinoceros hornbill is the most flashy. Other birds that easily catch the eye include the brightly coloured kingfishers, pitas and trogons as well as the spectacularly named racket-tailed drongo.

The region has more than 100 species of bat, most of which are tiny, insectivorous species that live in caves and under eaves and bark. Fruit bats (flying foxes) are only distantly related to insectivorous bats; unlike them they have well-developed eyes and do not navigate by echolocation.

Aquatic Life

In the region's rivers, lakes and and oceans, you'll find a mind-boggling variety of corals, fish and aquatic life. The seas around islands and atolls, including Sipadan, the Perhentians, Tioman and specks off the northeast coast of Sabah, offer some of the finest diving in the world.

Coral Kingdoms

Amid thriving coral – sea fans can grow to 3km – and a wealth of sponges, divers often encounter shimmering schools of jacks, bumphead parrotfish and barracudas, and find themselves making the acquaintance of green turtles, dolphins, manta rays and several species of shark.

Know Your Turtle

Of the world's seven species of turtle, four are native to Malaysia. The hawksbill and the green turtle both have nesting areas within Sabah's Turtle Islands National Park. Both these species, along with the olive ridley and giant leatherback, also swim in the waters off Peninsular Malaysia's east coast. Here there are beaches which are established turtle rookeries where you may chance upon expectant mother turtles dragging themselves above the high-tide line to bury their eggs.

1. Scuba diver, Pulau Bidong (p312) 2. Orange-spotted spinefoot fish near Pulau Redang (p301) 3. Green sea turtle, Sipadan (p3

TOP DIVE SITES

Sipadan Legendary for its deep wall dives, Sipadan is a favoured hangout of turtles, sharks and open-ocean fish.

Layang Layang A deep-ocean island famed for its pristine coral and 2000m drop-off.

Pulau Perhentian Coral reefs surround both main islands and some you can even wade out to.

Pulau Redang Corals, green and hawksbill turtles and a rainbow of tropical fish.

Pulau Tioman One of the few places where you stand a good chance of seeing pods of dolphins.

afflesia flower **2.** Rajah Brooke's birdwing **3.** Bats in Deer Cave

Natural Wonders

Record-breaking plants, geological gems and remarkable creatures big and small are among the multiple natural wonders within the mega diversity region of Malaysia, Singapore and Brunei.

Rafflesia

A parasite that lacks roots, stems and leaves, this botanical wonder grows up to 1m in diameter. Rafflesias bloom for just three to five days before turning into a ring of black slime. Taman Negara, Cameron Highlands, Royal Belum State Park and the parks of Malaysian Borneo are the places to view these extraordinary specimens.

Deer Cave

Found in Gunung Mulu National Park, the world's largest cave passage open to the public is over 2km in length and 174m in height. It's home to anything between two and three million bats belonging to more than 12 species who cling to the roof in a seething black mass as they gear up for the evening prowl.

Rainbow Toad

Rediscovered in the jungles of western Sarawak in 2011, after having been thought extinct for almost 90 years, the Sambas stream toad or Bornean rainbow toad, has long limbs and a pebbly back covered with bright red, green, yellow and purple warts. Also endemic of Borneo is the *Microhyla nepenthicola*, the world's tiniest frog no bigger than the size of a pea.

Rajah Brooke's Birdwing

Malaysia's national butterfly was discovered on Borneo in 1855 by the explorer and naturalist Alfred Russel Wallace. He named this black and iridescent-green winged beauty after James Brooke, the White Raja of Sarawak at the time. It can be found also on Peninsular Malaysia at below altitudes of 800m and often around hot-spring areas.

Mt Kinabalu (p3.

Diverse Ecosystems

Dense tropical jungle is not the only type of natural habitat you'll encounter in the region. Head to the mountains and coastal regions to see different types of flora and fauna.

Mangroves

These remarkable coastal trees have developed extraordinary ways to deal with an ever-changing mix of salt and fresh water. Uncounted marine organisms and nearly every commercially important seafood species find sanctuary and nursery sites among the mangrove's muddy roots. They also fix loose coastal soil, protecting against erosion and tsunamis. You'll see them on Pulau Langkawi, Bako National Park, Kuching Wetland National Park and Brunei's Temburong District.

Mt Kinabalu

A huge granite dome that formed some nine million years ago, Malaysia's highest mountain is botanical paradise. Over half of the species growing above 900m are unique to the area and include oaks, laurels, chestnuts and a dense rhododendron forest. Elsewhere in the park are many varieties of orchids and insect-eating pitcher plants.

Kerangas

These heath forests, whose name in Iban means 'land that cannot grow rice,' are composed of small, densely packed trees. They also support the world's greatest variety of pitcher plants (nepenthes), which trap insects in chambers full of enzyme-rich fluid and then digest them. There are patches in Sarawak's Bako National Park and Sabah's Maliau Basin Conservation Area.

(Continued from page 520)

Chinese New Year CULTURAL
(⊘ Feb) Dragon dances, parades and wishes of '*gong xi fa cai*' ('I hope that you gain lots of money') mark the start of the Chinese New Year.

Chingay CULTURAL
(www.chingay.org.sg; ⊘ Feb) Singapore's biggest and brightest street parade is held over two nights during the first weekend of Chinese New Year.

Singapore International Jazz Festival MUSIC
(www.sing-jazz.com; Marina Bay Sands; ⊘ Apr) The three-day 'Sing Jazz' presents known and emerging jazz talent from around the world.

Affordable Art Fair ART
(☑ 6220 5682; www.affordableartfair.com/singapore; F1 Pit Building; ⊘ Apr & Nov) A biannual expo with over 75 local and international exhibitors showcasing art (priced between S$100 and S$15,000) from hundreds of artists.

**Singapore International
Festival of Arts** CULTURAL
(https://sifa.sg; ⊘ mid-May–early Jun) A world-class event offering drama, film, dance, literary and visual art curated by Gaurav Kripalani, who was previously the artistic director at the Singapore Repertory Theatre.

Singapore Food Festival FOOD & DRINK
(www.yoursingapore.com; ⊘ Jul) A two-week celebration of all things edible and Singaporean. Events take place across the city and include tastings, pop-up restaurants and cooking workshops.

Great Singapore Sale SHOPPING
(www.greatsingaporesale.com.sg; ⊘ early Jun–mid-Aug) Eight credit-crunching weeks of sales across the city. For the best bargains, raid the racks during the first week.

Singapore National Day PARADE
(www.ndp.org.sg; ⊘ 9 Aug) A nationalistic frenzy of military and civilian parades, air-force fly-bys and fireworks. Tickets are snapped up well in advance.

Beerfest Asia BEER
(www.beerfestasia.com; ⊘ Aug or Sep) Held over four days, Asia's biggest beer event pours more than 600 types of brews from international heavyweights and craft microbreweries. Events include DJs, live music and a beer-pong tournament.

Hungry Ghost Festival CULTURAL
(⊘ Aug or Sep) Fires, food offerings and Chinese opera honour roaming spirits at this traditional festival.

Singapore Night Festival CULTURAL
(www.nightfestival.sg; ⊘ Aug) Spectacular light projections, plus interactive installations, performance art, cabaret, comedy and more.

Singapore Formula One Grand Prix SPORTS
(www.singaporegp.sg; ⊘ Sep) The F1 night race screams around Marina Bay. Off-track happenings include major international music acts. Book accommodation months in advance.

Deepavali RELIGIOUS
(⊘ Oct or Nov) Rama's victory over the demon king Ravana is celebrated during the 'Festival of Lights'. Little India is ablaze with lights for a month, culminating in a huge street party on the eve of the holiday.

🛏 Sleeping

Staying in Singapore is expensive, especially in the CBD and around shoppers paradise Orchard Rd, however more modest and budget friendly digs are available in the surrounding areas of Little India and Chinatown. Prices all over the island skyrocket during September's F1 night race so you should book early if visiting during that time. Accommodation options range from simple, shared backpacker dorms to some of the most historical and luxurious sleep spots in Asia.

🛏 Colonial District, the Quays & Marina Bay

⭐ **BEAT. Capsules** HOSTEL $
(Map p492; ☑ 6816 6960; www.beathostel.co; 50A Boat Quay; s/q capsules from S$50/60; ✱ @ 🖥; Ⓜ Clarke Quay, Raffles Place) Smack bang on the Singapore River, BEAT. Capsules is located right in the action. The sleek single and queen capsules offer underbed storage, folding workstation, hanging rack, power points and roll-down privacy screen. The best bit, however, is the views – straight over to Parliament and the skyline beyond.

There is a female-only dorm available.

5Footway.Inn Project Boat Quay HOSTEL $
(Map p492; ☑ 6557 2769; www.5footwayinn.com; 76 Boat Quay; dm from S$36, s from S$70, tw&d from S$90, tr from S$110, q from S$136; ✱ @ 🖥; Ⓜ Clarke Quay, Raffles Place) Right on Boat Quay, the whitewashed dorms come in one-,

two-, three- and four-bed configurations, and though rooms are small (superior rooms have windows), they're modern and comfortable, with wooden bunks and handy bedside power sockets and lights. Bathrooms are modern, reception operates round-the-clock, the walls are adorned with art and the chic breakfast lounge comes with an amazing river view.

Hotel Fort Canning · HOTEL $$

(Map p492; ☑6559 6770; www.hfcsingapore.com; 11 Canning Walk; r from S$330; ⏸☀@🛜🏊; Ⓜ Dhoby Ghaut) What was once British military headquarters is now a luxury hideaway surrounded by Fort Canning Park. While we love the mineral-water-filled swimming pools, exceptional gym and complimentary evening aperitifs and canapés, the rooms are the star attraction. These gorgeous retreats are graced with high ceilings, parquetry flooring, soothing botanical colours, Nespresso coffee machine and Jim Thompson silk bedhead.

Holiday Inn Express Clarke Quay · HOTEL $$

(Map p492; ☑6589 8000; www.hiexpress.com; 2 Magazine Rd; r from S$250; ⏸☀@🛜🏊; Ⓜ Clarke Quay) This smart hotel delivers modern, earthy-hued rooms with high ceilings, massive floor-to-ceiling windows and comfortable beds with both soft and firm pillows. Small bathrooms come with decent-size showers. Best of all is the rooftop garden, home to a tiny gym and impressive glass-sided pool with spectacular city views. The hotel's self-service laundry room is a handy touch.

Discounted online rates can see rooms offered for under S$230.

Park Regis · HOTEL $$

(Map p492; ☑6818 8888; www.parkregissingapore. com; 23 Merchant Rd; r from S$260; ⏸☀@🛜🏊; Ⓜ Clarke Quay, Chinatown) This affable place has light-filled rooms that are smallish but modern, with window seating and warm, citrus accents. The gym is petite but adequate, and overlooks the hotel's terrace pool, which comes with a cascading waterfall feature and semisubmerged sun-loungers. Staff are helpful, and the hotel is an easy

---

ⓘ **BOOKING ON THE FLY**

If you arrive in Singapore without a hotel booking, don't despair. The Singapore Visitors Centre @ Orchard (p559) works with hotels in the local area and can help visitors get the best available rates.

---

walk from both the quays and Chinatown. Entrance is from New Market Rd.

Raffles Hotel · HISTORIC HOTEL $$$

(Map p492; ☑6337 1886; www.rafflessingapore. com; 1 Beach Rd; ☀@🛜🏊; Ⓜ City Hall, Esplanade) The grand old dame of Singapore has seen many a famous visitor in her time, from Somerset Maugham to Michael Jackson. It's a beautiful place of white colonial architecture, lush pockets of green, and historic bars.

★ Fullerton Bay Hotel · HOTEL $$$

(Map p492; ☑6333 8388; www.fullertonhotels. com; 80 Collyer Quay; r from S$600; ⏸☀@🛜🏊; Ⓜ Raffles Place) The Fullerton Hotel's contemporary sibling flanks Marina Bay. It's a light-filled, heavenly scented, deco-inspired number. Rooms are suitably plush, with high ceilings, wood and marble flooring, and warm, subdued hues. Recharge courtesy of the in-room Nespresso machine and lather up with Bottega Veneta toiletries; glass panels in the marble bathrooms look into the room and at Marina Bay and beyond.

★ Ritz-Carlton Millenia Singapore · HOTEL $$$

(Map p492; ☑6337 8888; www.ritzcarlton.com/sin gapore; 7 Raffles Ave; r from S$550; ⏸☀@🛜🏊; Ⓜ Promenade) No expense was spared, no feng shui geomancer went unconsulted and no animals were harmed in the building of this luxe establishment. Its spacious rooms are light, plush and beige, with good-sized work spaces, high-end linen and unimpaired city or Marina Bay views. The hotel's multi-million-dollar art collection features works by Hockney, Warhol, Stella and Chihuly; collect a guide from the concierge desk.

★ Warehouse · BOUTIQUE HOTEL $$$

(☑6828 0000; www.thewarehousehotel.com; 320 Havelock Rd; r from S$360; ⏸☀🛜🏊; 🚌51, 64, 123, 186, Ⓜ Fort Canning) If the location on the main road makes you think twice about booking this hotel, stop thinking and just book! Touted as one of the hottest openings in Singapore in years, the Warehouse quietly screams super trendy. With its industrial-chic interiors, the river-view infinity pool and its luxurious, muted-toned hotel rooms, you might never want to leave.

Fullerton Hotel · HOTEL $$$

(Map p492; ☑6733 8888; www.fullertonhotels.com; 1 Fullerton Sq; r from S$460; ⏸☀@🛜🏊; Ⓜ Raffles Place) Occupying what was once Singapore's magnificent, Palladian-style general post office, the grand old Fullerton offers classically elegant rooms in muted tones. Entry-level rooms look 'out' into the inner atrium, so consider upgrading to one of the much more inspiring river- or bay-view rooms. A river-and-skyline backdrop awaits at the 25m terrace pool, the hotel's alfresco jewel.

Naumi BOUTIQUE HOTEL $$$

(Map p492; ☑ 6403 6000; www.naumihotel.com; 41 Seah St; r from S$420; ☀@☎☒; Ⓜ City Hall, Esplanade) Slinky Naumi comes with commissioned artwork, playful quotes and a rooftop infinity pool with skyline views. Standard rooms are relatively small but cleverly configured, with 400-thread-count Egyptian-cotton bed linen, Nespresso machine and complimentary minibar. Shower panels turn opaque at the flick of a switch, with a dramatically lit, stand-alone 'beauty bar' (bathroom counter) in the room itself. Ninth-floor rooms have city views.

🛏 Chinatown & the CBD

⭐ **Adler Hostel** HOSTEL $

(Map p500; ☑ 6226 0173; www.adlerhostel.com; 259 South Bridge Rd; cabin s/d S$55/100; ☀@☎; Ⓜ Chinatown) Hostelling reaches sophisticated new heights at this self-proclaimed 'poshtel'. Chinese antiques grace the tranquil lobby lounge, and fresh towels and feather-down duvets and pillows the premium beds. Airy, air-con dorms consist of custom-made cabins, each with lockable storage and curtains that can be drawn for privacy. Some even feature king-size beds for couples. Book around three weeks ahead for the best rates.

⭐ **COO** HOSTEL $

(☑ 6221 5060; www.staycoo.com; 259 Outram Rd; dm from S$44; ☀@☎; Ⓜ Outram Park) Looking more like a funky dance club with its graphic artwork, neon lighting and cage walls, this self-proclaimed 'sociatel' is all about everything social – social media, socialising – you get the drift. A great place to make new friends and Snapchat about it, dorms come in four-, six- or eight-bed configurations. Super-clean and super-comfy, there's a bistro on-site and free bike rental.

Wink Hostel HOSTEL $

(Map p500; ☑ 6222 2940; www.winkhostel.com; 8A Mosque St; pod s/d S$45/81; ☺7am-11pm, self check-in 11pm-7am; ☀@☎; Ⓜ Chinatown) Located in a restored shophouse in the heart of Chinatown, flashbacker favourite Wink merges hostel and capsule-hotel concepts.

Instead of bunks, dorms feature private, soundproof 'pods', each with comfortable mattress, coloured mood lighting, adjacent locker and enough room to sit up in. Communal bathrooms feature rain-shower heads, while the in-house kitchenette, laundry and lounge areas crank up the homey factor.

Beary Best Hostel HOSTEL $

(Map p500; ☑ 6222 4957; www.bearybesthostel.com; 16 Upper Cross St; dm from S$22; ☀@☎; Ⓜ Chinatown) In a restored heritage building just steps from Chinatown MRT, this fun, brightly coloured affair offers clean dorms, comfy beds and good-sized lockers. Bathrooms are unisex or ladies only, and there's also free daily walking tours, a beary nice touch. Staff are super helpful and if you've a teddy needing a new home, they'll happily take him in.

Hotel 1929 BOUTIQUE HOTEL $$

(Map p500; ☑ 6347 1929; www.hotel1929.com; 50 Keong Saik Rd; r from S$130; ☀☎; Ⓜ Outram Park, Chinatown) Occupying a whitewashed heritage building, Hotel 1929 sits on up-and-coming Keong Saik Rd. Rooms are tight, but good use is made of limited space, and interiors are cheerily festooned with vintage designer furniture (look out for reproduction Eames and Jacobsen pieces) and Technicolor mosaic bathrooms. Rooftop suites spice things up with private, clawed-foot bathtub-graced verandahs.

Wangz BOUTIQUE HOTEL $$

(☑ 6595 1388; www.wangzhotel.com; 231 Outram Rd; r from S$280; ℗☀@☎; Ⓜ Outram Park) Curvaceous, metallic Wangz is a winner. A quick walk from Tiong Bahru's heritage architecture and hip hang-outs, its 41 rooms are smart and modern, accented with contemporary local art, sublimely comfortable beds, iPod docking stations and sleek bathrooms. Further perks include complimentary nonalcoholic minibar beverages, in-house gym, handy smartphone and a rooftop lounge serving well-mixed drinks, all topped off with sterling service.

Scarlet BOUTIQUE HOTEL $$

(Map p500; ☑ 6511 3333; www.thescarlethotel.com; 33 Erskine Rd; r from S$240; ☀@☎; Ⓜ China-town, Telok Ayer) Dark, luscious Scarlet offers great service and svelte rooms just around the corner from drinking hot spots Ann Siang Rd and Club St. In opulent jewel colour schemes – sapphire blues and ruby reds – the chic rooms feature silky wallpaper and dark Oriental furniture. There are also five plush suites to tempt you; the 'lavish' boasts a Hästens bed valued at S$38,500!

⭐ **Six Senses Duxton** BOUTIQUE HOTEL $$$
(Map p500; ☑ 6914 1428; www.sixsenses.com; 83 Duxton Rd; r from S$510; ❄ 🖥; Ⓜ Tanjong Pagar) Making a dramatic departure from Six Senses' usual beachside locations, Six Senses Duxton is the brand's first foray into inner city jungle. Acclaimed British designer Anouska Hempel has worked her magic on the row of heritage shophouses that comprise the hotel, fusing Chinese, Malay and European elements into an opulent masterpiece. The turn-down service plus double-glazed windows ensure a blissful sleep.

The larger Six Senses Maxwell, just steps away, has undergone a major refurbishment and now has an outdoor lap pool for guests of both hotels.

Amoy BOUTIQUE HOTEL $$$
(Map p500; ☑ 6580 2888; www.stayfareast.com; 76 Telok Ayer St; s/d S$280/360; ❄ @ 🖥; Ⓜ Telok Ayer) Not many hotels are accessed through a historic Chinese temple, but the Amoy is no ordinary slumber pad. History inspires this contemporary belle, from the lobby feature wall displaying old Singaporean Chinese surnames to custom-made opium beds in the cleverly configured 'Cosy Single' rooms. Plush doubles include Ming-style porcelain basins, and all rooms please with designer bathroom, Nespresso machine and complimentary minibar.

Parkroyal on Pickering HOTEL $$$
(Map p492; ☑ 6809 8888; www.parkroyalhotels.com; 3 Upper Pickering St; r from S$420; 🅿 ❄ @ 🖥 ♨; Ⓜ Chinatown) Dramatic, cascading gardens, bird-cage cabanas right on the infinity pool, and a striking design evocative of terraced paddy fields: this outstanding hotel is the work of local architecture firm Woha, which designed everything down to the wastepaper baskets. Rooms are light, crisp and contemporary, with natural wood and soothing green hues, high ceilings and heavenly mattresses.

📟 Little India & Kampong Glam

⭐ **Dream Lodge** HOSTEL $
(Map p504; ☑ 6816 1036; www.dreamlodge.sg; 172 Tyrwhitt Rd; pod from S$53; ❄ @; Ⓜ Bendemeer, Farrer Park, Lavender) This popular hostel is spick and span, with comfy beds in a pod formation and super-helpful staff. The location is quiet but hip (you'll find decent coffeeshops and

bars just steps away), just moments from three MRT stations and hyperactive Little India. Choose from 12- to 14-bed mixed dorms, or six-bed female-only dorms. Motivational wall quotes will keep you inspired.

InnCrowd HOSTEL $
(Map p504; ☑ 6296 9169; www.the-inncrowd.com; 73 Dunlop St; dm/d/tr from S$20/59/79; ❄ @ 🖥; Ⓜ Rochor, Jalan Besar) Wildly popular, the InnCrowd is ground zero for Singapore's backpackers. Located right in the heart of Little India, the highlight of this fairly basic hostel is the free kick-scooter city tours (6pm Tuesday, Thursday and Sunday), a social and fun way to discover Singapore. Staff are very helpful and there are board games, DVDs and a laundry. Balcony rooms get noisy – request a room without one.

Bunc HOSTEL $
(Map p504; ☑ 6262 2862; www.bunchostel.com; 15 Upper Weld Rd; dm from S$28, d S$100; ❄ @ 🖥; Ⓜ Rochor, Jalan Besar) Just steps away from the bustle of Little India, Bunc is the coolest flashpacker hostel in town. A concrete floor, art installations and monochromatic colour scheme give the spacious lobby a hip, boutique feel. Dorms – in four-, six-, eight-, 12- and 16-bed configurations – offer both single and double beds. Starting to look a little tired but still good value.

Five Stones Hostel HOSTEL $
(Map p504; ☑ 6535 5607; www.fivestoneshostel.com; 285 Beach Rd; dm from S$28, tw/d S$95/105; ❄ @ 🖥; Ⓜ Bugis, Nicoll Hwy) This upbeat, no-shoes hostel comes with polished-concrete floors and both Wii and DVDs in the common lounge, plus complimentary use of washing machines and dryers. While not all dorms have windows, all feature steel-frame bunks, personal power sockets and lamps, and bright, mood-lifting murals depicting local themes. There's an all-female floor, plus private rooms with bunks or a queen-size bed.

Kam Leng Hotel BOUTIQUE HOTEL $
(Map p504; ☑ 6239 9399; www.kamleng.com; 383 Jln Besar; r from S$95; ❄ 🖥; Ⓜ Bendemeer, Farrer Park) Heritage gets a modern makeover at Kam Leng, a revamped retro hotel in the rising Jalan Besar district. Common areas are studiously raw, with distressed walls, faded Chinese signage, colourful wall tiles and modernist furniture. Rooms are tiny and simple yet cool, with old-school terrazzo flooring and pastel accents. A word of warning: rooms facing Jln Besar can get rather noisy.

★ **Wanderlust** BOUTIQUE HOTEL **$$**
(Map p504; ☑ 6396 3322; www.wanderlusthotel.
com; 2 Dickson Rd; r from S$210; 🅰️@🛜;
Ⓜ Rochor, Jalan Besar) Wanderlust delivers
wow factor with its insanely imaginative ac-
commodation, ranging from seriously bright
Pantone-coloured rooms to calm comic-
book 'mono' rooms, to those with themes in-
cluding 'Tree' and 'Space'. Take some time to
chillax on the rooftop garden, complete with
rainbow Jacuzzi, guarded by a herd of tiny
elephants. Early bookings and online deals
deliver great rates.

Village Hotel Albert Court HOTEL **$$**
(Map p504; ☑ 6339 3939; www.stayfareast.com;
180 Albert St; r from S$280; 🅰️@🛜; Ⓜ Rochor,
Little India) A short walk south of Little India
is this colonial-era hotel, in a shophouse
redevelopment that now shoots up eight
storeys. Rooms are classic and spacious,
with carved wooden furniture, smallish
but spotless bathrooms, and a choice of fan
or air-con. Service is top-notch and there's
wi-fi throughout. You'll find the best deals
online.

Great Madras HOSTEL **$$**
(Map p504; ☑ 6914 1515; www.thegreatmadras.
com; 28 Madras St; private dm $155, ste from
S$222; 🅰️🛜🏊; Ⓜ Little India) An Instagram-
mer's heaven, this art deco gem in the heart
of Little India is pimped out in pastel col-
ours, bright wallpapers and an amazing
lobby level mural of Singapore. Rooms
are clean and hip, and the more expensive
come with their own bathroom. All hostel
rooms have king-sized beds and doors for
privacy. Mixed and all-female dorms are
available.

Orchard Road

★ **Lloyd's Inn** BOUTIQUE HOTEL **$$**
(☑ 6737 7309; www.lloydsinn.com; 2 Lloyd Rd; r
from S$180; 🅰️🛜; Ⓜ Somerset) A short stroll
from Orchard Rd is where you'll find this
spread-out, minimalist boutique hotel. Eight
types of rooms each engage with nature in
different ways, and higher-end rooms have
outdoor bathtubs. Guests can cool down
in the dipping pool (not deep enough for a
proper swim) or enjoy dusk on the rooftop
terrace. It's insanely popular so book early.

The giant neighbourhood wall map in
the lobby, paired with the downloadable
walking guide, will have you navigating the
streets like a local in no time.

★ **Goodwood Park Hotel** HOTEL **$$$**
(Map p506; ☑ 6737 7411; www.goodwoodparkhotel.
com; 22 Scotts Rd; r from S$360; 🅿️🅰️@🛜🏊;
Ⓜ Orchard) Dating back to 1900, this wonder-
ful heritage hotel with gracious service feels
like an elegant, old-world retreat: the kind of
place you just want to hang out in, sinking
into a plush sofa with a good book. Deluxe
rooms in the main building are impressively
spacious; rooms in the newer wing are ren-
ovated but smaller. There are two beautiful
swimming pools.

St Regis HOTEL **$$$**
(Map p506; ☑ 6506 6888; www.stregissingapore.
com; 29 Tanglin Rd; d from S$520; 🅿️🅰️@🛜🏊;
Ⓜ Orchard) One of the swankiest additions to
Orchard Rd's five-star hotel scene, St Regis
doesn't disappoint: from its striking facade
to its classic, French-inspired decadence and
impeccable service. Rooms are enormous,
with lavish textiles, tasteful art and marble
bathrooms with free-standing soaking tubs.

SINGAPORE SLEEPING

STUCK AT THE AIRPORT

If you're only in Singapore for a short time or have a long wait between connections, try
the **Ambassador Transit Hotel** (☑ Terminal 2: 6542 8122, Terminal 3: 6507 9788; www.
harilelahospitality.com; Terminals 2 & 3 Departures, Changi Airport; s/d/tr from S$100/110/145;
🅰️@🛜; Ⓜ Changi Airport). Rates are for the first six hours and each additional hour block
thereafter is around S$25; rooms don't have windows and there are budget singles
(S$60, each subsequent hour S$20) with shared bathrooms. Both branches offer gym
access for an extra S$28 charge.

The only swish option at Changi Airport is the **Crowne Plaza** (☑ 6823 5300; www.ihg.
com; 75 Airport Blvd; r from S$300; 🅿️🅰️@🛜🏊; Ⓜ Changi Airport). It's a svelte, business-
oriented place with an in-house spa and lush, palm-studded pool. A skybridge connects
the hotel to Terminal 3, with Terminals 1 and 2 accessible by SkyTrain and Terminal 4
connected by bus with Terminal 2. Unfortunately, the lack of competition means hiked-
up prices; always check online for deals.

Each room comes with 24-hour butler service to boot.

Hotel Jen Orchardgateway   HOTEL $$$
(Map p506; ☑6708 8888; www.hoteljen.com; 10-01, 277 Orchard Rd; r from S$360; P✳@🛜🏊; MSomerset) Shopaholics will love this fresh, 502-room pad, right above **Orchardgateway** (Map p506; ☑6513 4633; www.orchardgateway.sg; 277 & 218 Orchard Rd; ⊙10.30am-10.30pm; MSomerset) mall and connected to two other malls and Somerset MRT. Rooms are simple yet stylish, with calming hues and sleep-coaxing beds. Twenty-first-century touches include phone-charging lockers and a PressReader app with free access to thousands of online publications. The star attraction, however, is the rooftop pool, with its gorgeous skyline views.

Quincy   BOUTIQUE HOTEL $$$
(Map p506; ☑6738 5888; www.stayfareast.com; 22 Mount Elizabeth Rd; r from S$330; P✳@🛜🏊; MOrchard) Smart, slimline Quincy offers svelte, Armani-chic rooms, with light-grey walls and high ceilings with fetching back-lighting. TVs are flat, mattresses soft, and charcoal-tiled bathrooms stocked with fancy Le Labo Santal 33 toiletries. Minibars are complimentary, breakfast is included, as are the all-day light refreshments and evening cocktails; you might never want to leave. The glass-enclosed balcony pool is utterly inviting.

🛏 Eastern Singapore

★Hotel Indigo   HOTEL $$
(Map p510; ☑6723 7022; www.hotelindigo.com; 86 East Coast Rd; r from $220; P✳@🛜🏊; 🚌10,14,16, 32) If it's all in the detail, then this Peranakan-inspired hotel has nailed it. Taking inspiration from the traditional Singaporean neighbourhood that surrounds it, each nook and cranny is bursting with nostalgic memorabilia: from street scene murals to old-school sweets, Peranakan-inspired tiles to carrom-board coffee tables. Book a premier room with bathtub and enjoy your soak with a view.

Don't miss taking a dip in the 25m-long infinity pool with a panoramic vista of the Joo Chiat (Katong) and beyond.

🛏 West & Southwest Singapore

Villa Samadhi   BOUTIQUE HOTEL $$$
(☑6274 5674; www.villasamadhi.com.sg; 20 Labrador Villa Rd; r from S$360, villas from S$920; P✳🛜; MLabrador Park) Hankering for a dose of Old-World nostalgia and glamour? Villa Samadhi, housed in a tastefully restored former British officers' quarters, gives guests the ultimate colonial Singaporean experience. Surrounded by lush jungle, the hotel's lofty ceilings, teak furnishings, mood lighting and creaking floorboards add to the charm, but it's the luxurious touches, including evening cocktails and sherry, that seal the deal.

🛏 Sentosa Island

★Capella Singapore   RESORT $$$
(Map p516; ☑6377 8888; www.capellahotels.com/singapore; 1 The Knolls; r/villas from S$920/1380; P✳@🛜🏊; 🚌Imbiah) Capella is one of Singapore's A-list slumber numbers, a seductive melange of colonial and contemporary architecture, an elegant spa, restaurants, a bar and three cascading swimming pools in lush, landscaped gardens. The beautifully appointed rooms are spacious and chic, with king-size beds, earthy, subdued hues, and striking contemporary bathrooms. The villas are even more decadent: each has its own plunge pool.

★W Singapore – Sentosa Cove   HOTEL $$$
(Map p516; ☑6808 7288; www.wsingaporesentosacove.com; 21 Ocean Way; r/ste from S$580/1100; P✳@🛜🏊; 🚌B) At one of Singapore's hottest slumber spots, rooms are playful, whimsical and spacious, with a choice of mood lighting, botanical motifs and good-size bathrooms. Of the 10 room categories, the spa-themed Away Rooms are especially fabulous, each with its own private plunge pool. The hotel's huge, 24-hour pool is one of Singapore's best, complete with wet bar and underwater speakers.

🍴 Eating

Singaporeans are obsessed with *makan* (food), from talking incessantly about their last meal, to feverishly photographing, critiquing and posting about it online. It's hardly surprising – food is one of Singapore's greatest drawcards, the nation's melting pot of cultures creating one of the world's most diverse, drool-inducing culinary landscapes.

🍴 Colonial District, the Quays & Marina Bay

★Gluttons Bay   HAWKER $
(Map p492; www.makansutra.com; 01-15 Esplanade Mall, 8 Raffles Ave; dishes from S$4.50; ⊙5pm-2am Mon-Thu, to 3am Fri & Sat, 4pm-1am Sun; MEsplanade, City Hall) Selected by the *Makansutra Food Guide*, this row of alfresco

SINGAPORE'S MINI-THAILAND & MYANMAR

If you're pining for some authentic Thai cuisine, you've just hit the jackpot. The **Golden Mile Complex** (www.goldenmilecomplex.sg; 5001 Beach Rd; dishes from S$3.50; ⊘10am-10pm, some eateries 24hr; Ⓜ Bugis, Nicoll Hwy) is Singapore's mini Thailand, full of Thai shops, grocers, butchers and eateries. The signs are in Thai, the customers are mostly Thai, and the food, clustered on the ground floor, is 100% magnificent, like-mother-makes Thai.

Peninsula Plaza (Map p492; www.peninsulaplaza.com.sg; 111 North Bridge Rd; ⊘8am-10pm; Ⓜ City Hall), is a sepia-toned 1980s hangover now unofficially known as Singapore's 'little Burma'. A legion of Burmese businesses can be found here, from visa and travel agencies to cluttered tailors and minimarts, stalls selling sweet Burmese tea, and even betel nut stands peddling folded leaves of the mild stimulant. The air is heady with the smell of spicy cooking, wafting from the string of simple eateries serving up authentic Burmese grub. The most accessible of these is basement restaurant **Inle Myanmar** (Map p492; ✆6333 5438; www.inlemyanmar.com.sg; B1-07 (A/B) Peninsula Plaza, 111 North Bridge Rd; dishes S$8-25; ⊘11am-10pm; ☎; Ⓜ City Hall), a bright, upbeat space serving classics like *mohinga*, a delicate, sweet-and-sour noodle soup of fish broth, hard-boiled eggs, fishcake and crunchy chickpea fritters.

hawker stalls is a great place to start your Singapore food odyssey. Get indecisive over classics like oyster omelette, satay, barbecue stingray and carrot cake (opt for the black version). Its central, bayside location makes it a huge hit, so head in early or late to avoid the frustrating hunt for a table.

Satay by the Bay   HAWKER $

(✆6538 9956; www.sataybythebay.com.sg; Gardens by the Bay, 18 Marina Gardens Dr; dishes from S$4; ⊘stall hours vary, drinks stall 24hr; Ⓜ Bayfront) Gardens by the Bay's own hawker centre has an enviable location, alongside Marina Bay and far from the roar of city traffic. Especially evocative at night, it's known for its satay, best devoured under open skies on the spacious wooden deck. The bulk of the food stalls are open 11am to 10.30pm.

★ National Kitchen
by Violet Oon   PERANAKAN $$

(Map p492; ✆9834 9935; www.violetoon.com; 02-01 National Gallery Singapore, 1 St Andrew's Rd; dishes S$15-42; ⊘noon-2.30pm & 6-9.30pm, high tea 3-4.30pm; Ⓜ City Hall) Chef Violet Oon is a national treasure, much loved for her faithful Peranakan dishes – so much so that she was chosen to open her latest venture inside Singapore's showcase National Gallery (p495). Feast on made-from-scratch beauties like sweet, spicy *kueh pie ti* (pastry cups stuffed with prawns and yam beans), dry laksa and beef *rendang*. Bookings two weeks in advance essential.

True to its name, the restaurant also touches on Singapore's other culinary traditions, from Indian and Eurasian to Hainanese. The high tea offers a wonderful sampling of Violet's signature flavours – the perfect afternoon break. There are several other branches in town, including one at **Clarke Quay** (Map p492; ✆9834 9935; www.violetoon.com; 01-18, 3B River Valley Rd; dishes S$15-50; ⊘6-10.30pm; Ⓜ Clarke Quay, Fort Canning) – the National Gallery outlet is the best, though.

Super Loco Customs House   MEXICAN $$

(Map p492; ✆6532 2090; www.super-loco.com/customshouse; 01-04 Customs House, 70 Collyer Quay; dishes S$8-38, set lunch from S$35; ⊘noon-3pm & 5-10.30pm Mon-Thu, noon-11pm Fri, 5-11pm Sat; ☎; Ⓜ Raffles Place, Downtown) With a perfect harbourside location and twinkling string lights, this Mexican restaurant injects a laid-back vibe into Singapore's super-corporate CBD. Tacos are the house speciality and the *de baja* with crispy fish and chilli mango salsa is a winner; wash it down with a margarita (choose from eight flavours!) while admiring the in-your-face Marina Bay Sands view.

★ Odette   FRENCH $$$

(Map p492; ✆6385 0498; www.odetterestaurant.com; 01-04 National Gallery Singapore, 1 St Andrew's Rd; lunch from S$128, dinner from S$268; ⊘noon-1.30pm Tue-Sat, 7-9pm Mon-Sat; ☎; Ⓜ City Hall) Cementing its place in the upper echelons of Singapore's saturated fine-dining scene, this modern French restaurant keeps people talking with its newly minted two Michelin stars. With former Jaan (p538) chef Julien Royer at the helm, menus are guided by the seasons and expertly crafted. The space is visually stunning, with a soft colour palette and floating aerial installation by local artist Dawn Ng.

★ Waku Ghin
JAPANESE $$$

(Map p492; ☑6688 8507; www.tetsuyas.com/singapore; L2-01 Shoppes at Marina Bay Sands, 2 Bayfront Ave, access via lift A or B; degustation S$450, bar dishes S$20-60; ⊗5.30pm & 8pm seatings, bar 5.30-11.45pm; Ⓜ Bayfront) The refinement and exquisiteness of the 10-course degustation menu by acclaimed chef Tetsuya Wakuda is nothing short of breathtaking. Using only the freshest ingredients, the modern Japanese-European repertoire changes daily, though the signature marinated Botan shrimp topped with sea urchin and Oscietra caviar remains a permanent showstopper. The newly awarded two Michelin stars has only added to this elusive restaurant's appeal.

If your pockets don't run deep enough to cover the full degustation menu's price tag, head to the Waku Ghin bar (no reservation needed) where you can sip a sublime cocktail and order from a range of decadent tapas-style bar bites.

Jumbo Seafood
CHINESE $$$

(Map p492; ☑6532 3435; www.jumboseafood.com.sg; 01-01/02 Riverside Point, 30 Merchant Rd; dishes from S$15, chilli crab per kg around S$88; ⊗noon-2.15pm & 6-11.15pm; Ⓜ Clarke Quay) If you're lusting after chilli crab – and you should be – this is a good place to indulge.

The gravy is sweet and nutty, with just the right amount of chilli. Just make sure you order some *mantou* (fried buns) to soak it up. While all of Jumbo's outlets have the dish down to an art, this one has the best riverside location.

One kilo of crab (or 1.5kg if you're especially hungry) should be enough for two. Book ahead if heading in later in the week.

Jaan
EUROPEAN $$$

(Map p492; ☑6837 3322; www.jaan.com.sg; Level 70, Swissôtel The Stamford, 2 Stamford Rd; lunch/dinner set menus from S$98/268; ⊗noon-2.30pm & 7-10.30pm Mon-Sat; ☑; Ⓜ City Hall, Esplanade) Seventy floors above the city, chic and intimate Jaan is home to British chef Kirk Westaway, sous chef to his predecessor French chef Julien Royer. Since taking the reins, Westaway has dazzled diners with his artisanal cuisine and added a Michelin star to his accolades. Menu changes seasonally, flavours are revelatory and presentation utterly theatrical. Always book ahead, and request a window seat.

✗ Chinatown & the CBD

★ A Noodle Story
NOODLES $

(Map p500; ☑9027 6289; www.anoodlestorydotcom.wordpress.com; 01-39 Amoy Street Food Centre, cnr Amoy & Telok Ayer Sts; noodles S$8-15; ⊗11.15am-2.30pm & 5.30-7.30pm Mon-Fri, 10.30am-1.30pm Sat; Ⓜ Telok Ayer) With a snaking line and proffered apology that 'we may sell out earlier than

---

THE ART OF HIGH TEA

A long, slow session of high tea is not only a civilised antidote to Singapore's high speed and higher temperatures, it's the perfect midafternoon recharge. While most luxury hotels are in on the act, not all high teas are created equal.

Singapore's best high tea is arguably at the **Landing Point** (Map p492; ☑6333 8388; www.fullertonhotels.com; Fullerton Bay Hotel, 80 Collyer Quay; high tea per adult/child under 12yr S$48/24; ⊗9am-midnight Sun-Thu, to 1am Fri & Sat, high tea 3-5.30pm Mon-Fri, noon-2pm & 3-5pm Sat & Sun; ☎; Ⓜ Raffles Place), the plush, waterfront lounge inside the Fullerton Bay Hotel. Style up and head in on an empty stomach. Blue-ribbon TWG teas are a fine match for luxe bites, like melt-in-your-mouth Boston lobster tarts, sesame buns filled with duck *rilette* (similar to pâté) and scandalously rich, salted-caramel-filled dark-chocolate tarts.

The Landing Point's most serious competitor is the Ritz-Carlton's **Chihuly Lounge** (Map p492; ☑6434 5288; www.ritzcarlton.com/en/hotels/singapore; Ritz-Carlton Millenia Singapore, 7 Raffles Ave; high tea from S$49; ⊗9am-1am, high tea weekday noon-5pm, weekend 2.30-5pm; ☎; Ⓜ Promenade), whose eight-course version includes an equally sublime array of bites, from moreish smoked salmon and sauerkraut sandwiches to champagne sorbet with macaron crumb. Aptly, the light-filled lounge is graced with an original Dale Chihuly glass sculpture.

High tea at either establishment should be booked well ahead (at least two days for weekdays, a week or two for weekends).

LOCAL KNOWLEDGE

PURVIS STREET FOOD OUTLETS

In the heart of the Colonial District, Purvis St packs it in with a whole heap of restaurants, many of them excellent. Those with deep pockets will want to splash out on Italian at **Garibaldi** (Map p492; ☑6837 1468; www.garibaldi.com.sg; 01-02, 36 Purvis St; mains S$28-88, set lunch from S$39; ☺noon-2.30pm & 6.30-10.30pm; MCity Hall, Esplanade) or French at **Gunther's** (Map p492; ☑6338 8955; www.gunthers.com.sg; 01-03, 36 Purvis St; set lunch S$38, mains S$25-140, degustation from S$148; ☺noon-2.30pm & 6.30-10pm Mon-Fri, 6.30-10pm Sat; MCity Hall, Esplanade), while carnivores will love **Salted & Hung** (Map p492; ☑6358 3130; www.saltedandhung.com.sg; 12 Purvis St; dishes S$16-72, chef's feed me menu S$75, set lunch from S$25; ☺11.30am-2.30pm & 6-10pm Tue-Fri, 11.30am-3.30pm Sat & Sun, 6-10pm Sat; ☎; MCity Hall, Esplanade) for nose-to-tail dining. You can shovel in Thai food at **Jai Thai** (Map p492; ☑6336 6908; www.jai-thai.com; 27 Purvis St; dishes S$6-14; ☺11.30am-3pm & 6-9.30pm; MCity Hall, Esplanade), and the French fare at **Saveur** (Map p492; ☑6333 3121; www.saveur.sg; 01-04, 5 Purvis St; mains S$17-27, set lunch/dinner S$22.90/29.90; ☺noon-9.30pm; MCity Hall, Esplanade) is both tasty and filling, and surprisingly cheap for this area.

stipulated timing' on the facade, this one-dish-only stall is a magnet for Singapore foodies. The object of desire is Singapore-style ramen created by two young chefs, Gwern Khoo and Ben Tham. It's Japanese ramen meets wanton *mee* (noodles): pure bliss in a bowl topped with a crispy potato-wrapped prawn.

★**Chinatown Complex**   HAWKER $
(Map p500; 335 Smith St; dishes from S$1.50; ☺stall hours vary; MChinatown) Leave Smith St's revamped 'Chinatown Food Street' to the out-of-towners and join old-timers and foodies at this nearby labyrinth, now home to Michelin-starred Hong Kong Soya Sauce Chicken Rice & Noodle. You decide if the two-hour wait is worth it. Other standouts include mixed claypot rice at Lian He Ben Ji Claypot Rice (p540) and the rich, nutty satay at **Shi Xiang Satay** (Map p500; 02-79 Chinatown Complex, 335 Smith St; 10 sticks S$6; ☺4-9pm Fri-Wed; MChinatown).

For a little TLC, opt for Ten Tonic Ginseng Chicken Soup at **Shen Xi Soup** (Map p500; www.shenxisoup.com; 02-06, Chinatown Complex, 335 Smith St; soups S$2.80-6.80; ☺noon-2.30pm & 5-8.30pm; MChinatown). After 6.30pm head over to Smith Street Taps (p548) and **Good Beer Company** (☑9430 2750; www.facebook.com/goodbeersg; 01-23 Savourworld, 2 Science Park Dr; ☺4-11pm Mon-Thu, to 11.45pm Fri & Sat; MKent Ridge) for craft and premium beers on tap – not what you'd expect in a hawkers centre!

Stalls are open from early in the morning, with lunchtime and 5pm to 7pm being the busiest hours. Most places shut by 8pm, however a few remain open till after 10pm.

★**Hong Kong Soya Sauce Chicken Rice & Noodle**   HAWKER $
(Hawker Chan Soya Sauce Chicken Rice & Noodle; Map p500; www.facebook.com/hawkerchanSG; 02-126 Chinatown Complex, 335 Smith St; dishes S$2-3; ☺10.30am-3.30pm Thu-Tue; MChinatown) With its newly bestowed Michelin star, this humble hawker stall has been thrust into the culinary spotlight. The line forms hours before Mr Chan Hon Meng opens for business, and waiting times can reach two hours. Standout dishes are the tender soy sauce chicken and the caramelised *pork char siew* ordered with rice or perfectly cooked noodles. Worth the wait? You bet.

Ah Chiang's   CHINESE $
(☑6557 0084; www.facebook.com/ahchiang porridgesg; 01-38, 65 Tiong Poh Rd; porridge S$5-6; ☺6am-11pm; MOutram Park) Join gossiping uncles and Gen-Y hipsters for a little Cantonese soul food at Ah Chiang's. The star turn at this retro corner *kopitiam* (coffeeshop) is fragrant, charcoal-fired congee (a rice-based porridge). While it's all soul-coaxingly good, don't go past the raw sliced fish, delectably drizzled with sesame oil. Do not lick the bowl.

★**Maxwell Food Centre**   HAWKER $
(Map p500; cnr Maxwell & South Bridge Rds; dishes S$2.50-12; ☺8am-2am, stall hours vary; ☎; MChinatown) One of Chinatown's most accessible hawker centres, Maxwell is a solid spot to savour some of the city's street-food staples. While stalls slip in and out of favour with Singapore's fickle diners, enduring favourites include **Tian Tian Hainanese**

Chicken Rice (Map p500; 01-10 Maxwell Food Centre, cnr Maxwell & South Bridge Rds; chicken rice from S$3.50; ⊙10am-8pm Tue-Sun; Ⓜ Chinatown) and **Rojak, Popiah & Cockle** (Map p500; 01-56 Maxwell Food Centre, cnr Maxwell & South Bridge Rds; popiah S$1.50, rojak S$3-8; ⊙10am-10pm; Ⓜ Chinatown), as well as new favourite British fare **Lad & Dad** (Map p500; ☑9247 7385; www.facebook.com/ladanddadsg; 01-79 Maxwell Food Centre, cnr Maxwell & South Bridge Rds; dishes S$4-12; ⊙11.30am-2.30pm & 5.30-9pm Mon-Fri; Ⓜ Chinatown).

Lian He Ben Ji Claypot Rice HAWKER $$
(Map p500; ☑6227 2470; 02-198/199 Chinatown Complex, 335 Smith St; dishes S$2.50-5, claypot rice S$5-20; ⊙4.30-10.30pm Fri-Wed; Ⓜ Chinatown) The most popular claypot rice stall in Chinatown Complex (p539), and the only one cooking over charcoal stoves. Get the mixed claypot rice, which comes with Chinese sausage, pork and chicken. Pair it with deep-green vegetables with oyster sauce, sprinkled with fried shallots for crunch and extra sweetness. Expect to wait around 45 minutes, as each pot is cooked from scratch.

Ding Dong SOUTHEAST ASIAN $$
(Map p500; ☑6557 0189; www.dingdong.com.sg; 01-02, 115 Amoy St; dishes S$14-38; ⊙noon-3pm & 6pm-midnight Mon-Sat; Ⓜ Telok Ayer) From the kitschy vintage posters to the meticulous cocktails to the wow-oh-wow modern takes on Southeast Asian flavours, it's all about attention to detail at this iconic Asian fusion restaurant. Book a table and drool over *char siew* pork belly with caramalised pineapple, duck dumplings wtih roasted duck *consommé* and baby bok choy or the moreish Ding Dong Scotch egg.

Good-value options include a weekday two-/three-course set lunch (S$29/37) and 'feed me' menus (S$78) for indecisive gourmets.

Ginza Tendon Itsuki JAPANESE $$
(Map p500; ☑6221 6678; www.tendon-itsuki.sg; 101 Tanjong Pagar Rd; mains S$12.90-13.90; ⊙11.30am-2.30pm & 5.30-10pm; ☑; Ⓜ Tanjong Pagar) Life's few certainties include taxes, death and a queue outside this dedicated *tendon* (tempura served on rice) eatery. Patience is rewarded with cries of *irrashaimase!* (welcome) and generous bowls of Japanese comfort grub. Both the tempura and rice are cooked to perfection, drizzled in sweet and sticky soy sauce, and served with *chawanmushi* (Japanese egg

custard), miso soup and pickled vegetables. A cash-only bargain.

Tip: avoid the longest queues by heading in by noon or 7pm.

★**Burnt Ends** BARBECUE $$$
(Map p500; ☑6224 3933; www.burntends.com.sg; 20 Teck Lim Rd; dishes S$8-45; ⊙6-11pm Tue-Thu, 11.45am-2pm & 6-11pm Fri & Sat; Ⓜ Chinatown, Outram Park) The best seats at this mod-Oz hot spot are at the counter, which offers a prime view of chef Dave Pynt and his 4-tonne, wood-fired ovens and custom grills. The affable Aussie cut his teeth under Spanish charcoal deity Victor Arguinzoniz (Asador Etxebarri), an education echoed in pulled pork shoulder in homemade brioche, and beef marmalade and pickles on chargrilled sourdough.

Butcher Boy FUSION $$$
(Map p500; ☑6221 6833; www.butcherboy.com.sg; 31 Keong Siak Rd; mains S$24-42; ⊙noon-3pm Wed, Thu & Fri, 6-10.30pm Sun-Thu, to 11pm Fri & Sat, bar 5pm-late; Ⓜ Chinatown, Outram Park) Meat lovers will love the Asian-inspired creations by chef-owner Andrew Walsh, formerly of tapas haven **Esquina** (Map p500; ☑6222 1616; www.esquina.com.sg; 16 Jiak Chuan Rd; mains S$24-34; ⊙noon-2pm Tue-Sat & 6-10pm Mon-Sat; Ⓜ Outram Park, Chinatown), in this dimly lit shophouse grill and bar. Perfectly charred, the tender black Angus rib eye is not to be missed, and the masala roasted cauliflower has vegetarians swooning. The good vibes keep on rolling with wickedly strong cocktails.

Meta FRENCH $$$
(Map p500; ☑6513 0898; www.metarestaurant.sg; 9 Keong Saik Rd; set lunch/dinner from S$58/118; ⊙noon-2pm Tue-Fri, 6-11pm Mon-Sat; ☑; Ⓜ Chinatown, Outram Park) It's all about French food with a delicate Asian twist at this sleek, one Michelin star restaurant in trendy Keong Saik Rd. The open kitchen runs nearly the length of this very long and narrow space, with the high stools positioned so guests have front-row seats as chefs create delectable masterpieces. The evolutionary menu changes with the seasons.

Momma Kong's SEAFOOD $$$
(Map p500; ☑6225 2722; www.mommakongs.com; 34 Mosque St; crab dishes S$50, set menu for 2 from S$132; ⊙5-11pm Mon-Fri, from 11am Sat & Sun; Ⓜ Chinatown) Small, funky Momma Kong's is run by two young brothers and a cousin obsessed with crab. While the compact menu features numerous finger-licking, MSG-free

crab classics, opt for the phenomenal chilli crab, its kick and nongelatinous gravy unmatched in this town. One serve of crab and four giant, fresh *mantou* (Chinese bread buns) should happily feed two stomachs.

Unlike many other chilli-crab joints, you'll find fixed prices, which means no unpleasant surprises when it's payment time. Book two days ahead (three days for Friday and Saturday) or take a chance and head in late.

✖ Little India & Kampong Glam

★ **Zam Zam** MALAYSIAN $
(Map p504; ☑ 6298 6320; www.zamzamsingapore. com; 697-699 North Bridge Rd; murtabak from S$5; ◷ 7am-11pm; Ⓜ Bugis) These guys have been here since 1908, so they know what they're doing. Tenure hasn't bred complacency, though – the touts still try to herd customers in off the street, while frenetic chefs inside whip up delicious *murtabak*, the restaurant's speciality savoury pancakes, filled with succulent mutton, chicken, beef, venison or even sardines. Servings are epic, so order a medium between two.

Komala Vilas SOUTH INDIAN $
(Map p504; ☑ 6293 6980; www.komalavilas. com.sg; 76-78 Serangoon Rd; dishes S$2.40-9; ◷ 7am-10.30pm; ⟟; Ⓜ Little India) This prime-position branch of the Komala Vilas chain is extremely popular due to the wallet-friendly, authentic dishes and generous portions. The wafer thin *dosa* (paper-thin lentil-flour pancake) is legendary – order the meal and enjoy it served with three vegetable curries and condiments. Complete your feast with a cup of warm masala tea, served in a traditional metal cup.

QS269 Food House HAWKER $
(Map p504; Block 269B, Queen St; dishes from S$2.50; ◷ stall hours vary; Ⓜ Bugis) This is not so much a 'food house' as a loud, crowded undercover laneway lined with cult-status stalls. Work up a sweat with a bowl of award-winning coconut-curry noodle soup from **Ah Heng** (Map p504; www.facebook.com/AhHengChickenCurryNoodles; 01-236 QS269 Food House, Block 269B, Queen St; soup S$4.50-6.50; ◷ 9.30am-10pm; Ⓜ Bugis) or join the queue at **New Rong Liang Ge** (Map p504; 01-235 QS269 Food House, Block 269B, Queen St; dishes from S$2.50; ◷ 9am-8pm, closed 1st Wed of the month; Ⓜ Bugis), with succulent roast-duck dishes that draw foodies from across the city. The laneway is down the side of the building.

TEKKA CENTRE

Little India's most famous hawker centre, the **Tekka Centre** (Map p504; cnr Serangoon & Buffalo Rds; dishes S$3-10; ◷ 7am-11pm, stall hours vary; Ⓟ ⟟; Ⓜ Little India) has stalls serving the Hainanese chicken rice and nasi goreng (Indonesian fried rice) you can find in other food centres across Singapore, but it focuses on Indian food too, which means plenty of biryani and tandoor offerings and mutton curries galore. Well worth seeking out is **Ah-Rahman Royal Prata** (Map p504; 01-248 Tekka Centre, cnr Serangoon & Buffalo Rds; murtabak S$5-8; ◷ 7am-10pm Tue-Sun; Ⓜ Little India), which serves even better *murtabak* (stuffed savoury pancake) than those you'll find at *murtabak* masters Zam Zam (p541) – really, they are impossibly good – and watching the chef mould, flip and fill them is like witnessing an artist at work.

Each stall keeps different opening times, but most are generally open from around 8am to 8pm, but often later.

Warong Nasi Pariaman MALAYSIAN, INDONESIAN $
(Map p504; ☑ 6292 2374; www.pariaman.com.sg; 736-738 North Bridge Rd; dishes from S$3; ◷ 7.30am-8pm; Ⓜ Bugis) This no-frills corner *nasi padang* (rice with curries) stall is the stuff of legend. Top choices include the delicate *rendang* beef, *ayam bakar* (grilled chicken with coconut sauce) and spicy sambal goreng (long beans, tempeh and fried bean curd). Get here by 11am to avoid the lunch hordes and by 5pm for the dinner queue.

And be warned: most of it sells out well before closing time.

Two Bakers BAKERY $
(Map p504; ☑ 6293 0329; www.two-bakers.com; 88 Horne Rd; pastries & cakes S$6.50-9; ◷ 9am-6pm Mon, Wed, Thu & Sun, 10am-10pm Fri & Sat; Ⓜ Bendemeer, Lavender) The bakers at this light, contemporary bakery-cafe earned their stripes at Paris' Cordon Bleu. The result? Irresistible sweet treats and countless broken diets. Which tart to choose: crowd-favourite *yuzu* (Japanese citrus fruit) lemon or the tea-infused *Hojicha* Crepecake with numerous layers of crepes filled with *hojicha* (Japanese green tea) cream and *azuki* beans? What the hell: order both!

Also on offer is a delectable brunch menu (till 3pm), as well as a raft of mains – the bacon mac and cheese with five-cheese mornay sauce is hard to resist.

★ Lagnaa Barefoot Dining INDIAN $$

(Map p504; ☑ 6296 1215; www.lagnaa.com; 6 Upper Dickson Rd; dishes S$8-22; ⊙ 11.30am-10.30pm; 🕿; Ⓜ Little India) You can choose your level of spice at friendly Lagnaa: level three denotes standard spiciness, level four significant spiciness, and anything above admirable bravery. Whatever you opt for, you're in for finger-licking-good homestyle cooking from both ends of Mother India, devoured at Western seating downstairs or on floor cushions upstairs. If you're indecisive, order chef Kaesavan's famous Threadfin fish curry.

★ Cicheti ITALIAN $$

(Map p504; ☑ 6292 5012; www.cicheti.com; 52 Kandahar St; pizzas S$18-25, mains S$22-56; ⊙ noon-2.30pm & 6.30-10.30pm Mon-Fri, 6-10.30pm Sat; Ⓜ Bugis, Nicoll Hwy) Cool-kid Cicheti is a slick, friendly, buzzing scene of young-gun pizzaioli, chic diners and seductive, contemporary Italian dishes made with hand-picked market produce. Tuck into beautifully charred woodfired pizzas, made-from-scratch pasta and standouts like *polpette di carne* (slow-cooked meatballs). Book early in the week if heading in on a Friday or Saturday night.

Nan Hwa Chong Fish-Head Steamboat Corner CHINESE $$

(Map p504; ☑ 6297 9319; www.facebook.com/nanhwachong; 812-816 North Bridge Rd; fish steamboats from S$20; ⊙ 4pm-1am; Ⓜ Bugis, Lavender) If you only try fish-head steamboat once, do it at this noisy, open-fronted veteran. Cooked on charcoal, the large pot of fish heads is brought to you in a steaming broth spiked with *tee po* (dried flat sole fish). One pot is enough for three or four people, and can stretch to more with rice and side dishes.

There are several fish types to choose from; the grouper is the most popular with locals.

✕ Orchard Road

Killiney Kopitiam CAFE $

(Map p506; ☑ 6734 3910; www.killiney-kopitiam.com; 67 Killiney Rd; dishes S$1-7; ⊙ 6am-11pm, to 6pm Tue & Sun; Ⓜ Somerset) Start the day the old-school way at this veteran coffee joint, pimped with endearingly lame laminated jokes. Order a strong *kopi* (coffee), a serve of *kaya* (coconut jam) toast and a side of soft-boiled egg. Crack open the egg, add a dash

of soy sauce and white pepper, then dip your *kaya* toast in it.

Post-breakfast, chow down on bargain staples like curry chicken, laksa or seafood fried rice.

Signs A Taste Of Vietnam Pho VIETNAMESE $

(Map p506; B1-07 Midpoint Orchard, 220 Orchard Rd; dishes S$5-8; ⊙ 11am-9pm; Ⓜ Somerset) Bowls of flavoursome broth and Vietnamese spring rolls bursting with freshness are the signature dishes at this no-frills eatery, and it's the owners, deaf couple Anthony and Angela, you'll find dishing up the goods. Enter with a smile and Anthony will quickly have you ticking boxes on the menu. Portions are generous.

★ Paradise Dynasty CHINESE $$

(Map p506; www.paradisegroup.com.sg; 04-12A ION Orchard, 2 Orchard Turn; dishes S$5-20; ⊙ 11am-9.30pm, from 10.30am Sat & Sun; Ⓜ Orchard) Preened staffers in headsets whisk you into this svelte dumpling den, passing a glassed-in kitchen where Chinese chefs stretch their noodles and steam their buns. Skip the novelty-flavoured *xiao long bao* (soup dumplings) for the original version, which arguably beats those of legendary competitor Din Tai Fung (Map p506; ☑ 6836 8336; www.dintaifung.com.sg; B1-03 Paragon, 290 Orchard Rd; buns S$2, dumplings S$5-16; ⊙ 11am-10pm, from 10am Sat & Sun; Ⓜ Somerset). Beyond these, standouts include *la mian* (hand-pulled noodles) with buttery, braised pork belly.

Tim Ho Wan DIM SUM $$

(Map p506; ☑ 6251 2000; www.timhowan.com; 01-29 Plaza Singapura, 68 Orchard Rd; dishes S$4-7; ⊙ 10am-10pm, from 9am Sat & Sun; Ⓜ Dhoby Ghaut) Hong Kong's Michelin-starred dim-sum seller is steaming in Singapore, with the same Mong Kok queues (head in after 8.30pm) and tick-the-boxes order form. While nothing compares to the original (the Singapore branches need to import many ingredients), the recipes are the same and the results still pretty spectacular. Must-trys include the sugary buns with barbecue pork and the perky prawn dumplings.

Tambuah Mas INDONESIAN $$

(Map p506; ☑ 6733 2220; www.tambuahmas.com.sg; B1-44 Paragon, 290 Orchard Rd; mains S$8-29; ⊙ 11am-10pm; 🕿; Ⓜ Somerset) Hiding shyly in a corner of Paragon's food-packed basement, Tambuah Mas is where Indonesian expats head for a taste of home. Bright, modern and good value for Orchard Rd, it proudly makes

FOOD COURT FAVOURITES

Burrow into the basement of most malls on Orchard Rd and you'll find a food court with stall upon stall selling cheap, freshly cooked dishes from all over the world. These are the best two stalls:

Takashimaya Food Village (Map p506; ☑ 6506 0458; www.takashimaya.com.sg; B2 Takashimaya Department Store, Ngee Ann City, 391 Orchard Rd; dishes S$4-17; ☺10am-9.30pm; ☎; Ⓜ Orchard) Slick, sprawling and heavenly scented, Takashimaya's basement food hall serves up a *Who's Who* of Japanese, Korean and other Asian culinary classics. Look out for *soon kueh* (steamed dumplings stuffed with bamboo shoots, *bangkwang* (dried mushroom, carrot and dried prawn), and don't miss a fragrant bowl of noodles from the Tsuru-koshi stand.

Food Republic (Map p506; www.foodrepublic.com.sg; Level 4, Wisma Atria, 435 Orchard Rd; dishes S$5-15; ☺10am-10pm; ☎; Ⓜ Orchard) OK, so this one is not actually in the basement, but the formula remains the same – lip-smacking food, a plethora of choices and democratic prices. Food Republic offers traditional hawker classics, as well as Korean, Japanese, Indian, Thai and Indonesian. Muck in with the rest of the crowd for seats before joining the longest queues. Roving 'aunties' push around trolleys filled with drinks and dim sum.

much of what it serves from scratch, a fact evident in what could possibly be Singapore's best beef *rendang*. No reservations, so arrive early if dining Thursday to Saturday.

★ **Buona Terra** ITALIAN $$$
(Map p506; ☑ 6733 0209; www.buonaterra.com. sg; 29 Scotts Rd; 3-/5-course lunch S$48/128, 4-/6-course dinner S$128/168; ☺noon-2.30pm & 6.30-10.30pm Mon-Fri, 6.30-10.30pm Sat; ☎; Ⓜ Newton) This intimate, linen-lined Italian is one of Singapore's unsung glories. In the kitchen is young Lombard chef Denis Lucchi, who turns exceptional ingredients into elegant, modern dishes, like seared duck liver with poached peach, amaretti crumble and Vin Santo ice cream. Lucchi's right-hand man is Emilian sommelier Gabriele Rizzardi, whose wine list, though expensive, is extraordinary.

★ **Iggy's** FUSION $$$
(Map p506; ☑ 6732 2234; www.iggys.com.sg; Level 3, Hilton Hotel, 581 Orchard Rd; set lunch/dinner from S$85/195; ☺7-9.30pm, plus noon-1.30pm Thu-Sat; ☑; Ⓜ Orchard) Iggy's refined, sleek design promises something special, and with a large picture window drawing your eye to the magic happening in the kitchen, you can take a peek. Head chef Aitor Jeronimo Orive delivers with his ever-changing, highly seasonal, creative fusion dishes. Superlatives extend to the wine list, one of the city's finest.

Gordon Grill INTERNATIONAL $$$
(Map p506; ☑ 6730 1744; www.goodwoodparkhotel. com; Goodwood Park Hotel, 22 Scotts Rd; mains S$44-62; ☺noon-2.30pm & 7-10.30pm; ☎; Ⓜ Orchard) With its old-world charm – complete with

crisp linens – and its famed steaks, Gordon Grill, housed inside a colonial-era hotel (p535), is a step back in time compared with ultramodern Orchard Rd. It's as much an experience as it is a meal, so this is perhaps the best place for splashing out on the wagyu beef, ordered by weight, cut at your table and cooked to your specifications.

✕ Dempsey Hill & the Botanic Gardens

Samy's Curry Restaurant INDIAN $$
(☑ 6472 2080; info@samyscurry.com; Block 25, Dempsey Rd; mains S$5-21; ☺11am-3pm & 6-10pm, closed Tue; ☑; ☐7, 75, 77, 105, 106, 123, 174) A Dempsey institution, Samy's opened in 1950 and has been in this particular spot since the 1980s. Its location is charming and the food is as outstanding as it has always been, plus this is one of the least pretentious restaurants in Dempsey. You can order either from the menu or from the food display counter; the fish head curry is outstanding.

2am: dessertbar DESSERTS $$
(☑ 6291 9727; www.2amdessertbar.com; 21A Lorong Liput; dishes S$15-24; ☺3pm-2am Tue-Fri, from 2pm Sat & Sun; Ⓜ Holland Village) Posh desserts with wine and cocktail pairings are the deal at this swanky hideout. While the menu includes savoury grub like pork sliders and mac and cheese, you're here for Janice Wong's sweet showstoppers, from chocolate tart to cassis plum bombe with elderflower yoghurt foam, Choya (Japanese plum liqueur) granita, *yuzu* (Japanese citrus fruit) pearls and rubies. Book ahead for Thursday to Saturday night.

★ **Candlenut**   PERANAKAN $$$

(☑ in Singapore 1800 304 2288; www.como
dempsey.sg; Block 17A, Dempsey Rd; mains S$20-
32; ⏱ noon-2.30pm & 6-9.30pm, to 10.30pm Fri &
Sat; 🚌 7, 75, 77, 105, 106, 123, 174) The first and
only Peranakan restaurant with a Michelin
star, Candlenut is where Singaporeans head
to impress out-of-towners. Chef Malcolm
Lee does not churn out any old Straits Chinese
dishes; instead, he elevates them to new cu-
linary heights. Most are amazing, but some
are a little lost in translation. The jury is still
out on whether Nonya would approve.

★ **Chopsuey**   CHINESE $$$

(☑ 6708 9288; www.chopsueycafe.com; 01-23,
Block 10, Dempsey Rd; dumplings S$7-15, mains
S$12-46; ⏱ 11.30am-10.30pm, from 10.30am Sat &
Sun; 🚌 7, 75, 77, 105, 106, 123, 174) Swirling ceiling fans, crackly 1930s tunes and ladies on
rattan chairs – Chopsuey has colonial chic
down pat. It serves revamped versions of
retro American-Chinese dishes, but the real
highlight is the lunchtime yum cha; standouts include grilled pork and coconut salad,
crispy lobster wantons, and *san choy pau*
(minced meat in lettuce cups). The marble
bar is perfect for solo diners.

Dempsey Cookhouse & Bar   BISTRO $$$

(☑ in Singapore 1800 304 5588; www.como
dempsey.sg; Block 17D, Dempsey Rd; mains $19-67;
⏱ noon-2.30pm & 6-10pm, to 11pm Fri & Sat; 🚌 7,
75, 77, 105, 106, 123, 174) Visually stunning with
a white-and-black colour scheme, a soaring
ceiling dotted with oversized lantern lights,
and touches of tropical greenery, there is a
definite buzz in this restaurant opened by
one of New York's most celebrated chefs,
Jean-Georges Vongerichten. Skip the sig-
nature egg caviar and opt for the creamy

OFF THE BEATEN TRACK

THE OVAL @ SELETAR AEROSPACE PARK

The recently redeveloped Seletar Aero-
space Park is now home to a number
of cafes and restaurants, including
Wildseed (☑ 6262 1063; www.the
summerhouse.sg; 3 Park Lane; ⏱ 9am-11pm,
to 1am Fri & Sat; 🚌 117), many ensconced
in grand colonial houses. There's an
airport-themed playground for little ones
and a view of the runway at the adjoining
airport. To get here catch bus 117 from
the Khatib MRT station.

---

burrata (Italian semi-soft cheese) with lemon
jam, followed by the spice-crusted snapper.

✗ Eastern Singapore

★ **328 Katong Laksa**   MALAYSIAN $

(Map p510; ☑ 9732 8163; www.328katonglaksa.
com; 51 East Coast Rd; laksa S$5.50-7.50; ⏱ 10am-
10pm; 🚌 10, 12, 14, 32) For a bargain foodie high,
hit this cult-status corner shop. The star is
the namesake laksa: thin rice noodles in a
light curry broth made with coconut milk
and coriander, and topped with shrimps and
cockles. Order a side of *otah* (spiced mack-
erel cake grilled in a banana leaf) and wash
it down with a cooling glass of lime juice.

East Coast Lagoon Food Village   HAWKER $

(Map p510; 1220 East Coast Parkway; dishes from
S$3; ⏱ 10.30am-11pm; 🚌 36, 43, 47, 48, 196, 197,
401) There are few hawker centres with
a better location. Tramp barefoot off the
beach, find a table (note the table number
for when you order), then trawl the stalls for
staples such as satay, laksa, stingray and the
uniquely Singaporean *satay bee hoon* (rice
noodles in a chilli-based peanut sauce). Not
all stalls are open during the day – it's best
to visit between 5pm and 8pm.

Chin Mee Chin Confectionery   BAKERY $

(Map p510; ☑ 6345 0419; 204 East Coast Rd; kaya
toast & coffee from S$2; ⏱ 8.30am-3.30pm Tue-
Sun; 🚌 10, 12, 14, 32) A nostalgia trip for many
older Singaporeans, old-style bakeries such as
Chin Mee Chin are a dying breed, with their
geometric floors, wooden chairs and indus-
trious aunties pouring *kopi* (coffee). One of
the few Singaporean breakfast joints that still
makes its own *kaya* (coconut jam), it's also a
good spot to pick up some pastries to go.

★ **No Signboard Seafood**   SEAFOOD $$

(Map p510; ☑ 6842 3415; www.nosignboardseafood.
com; 414 Geylang Rd; dishes S$15-60, crab per kg
from S$80; ⏱ 11am-1am; Ⓜ Aljunied) Madam Ong
Kim Hoi famously started out with an un-
named hawker stall (hence 'No Signboard'),
but the popularity of her seafood made her a
rich woman, with four restaurants and counting. Principally famous for its white-pepper
crab, No Signboard also dishes up delightful
lobster, abalone and less familiar dishes such
as bullfrog.

Long Phung   VIETNAMESE $$

(Map p510; ☑ 9105 8519; 159 Joo Chiat Rd; dishes
S$7-23; ⏱ noon-10pm; Ⓜ Paya Lebar) Yellow plas-
tic chairs, easy-wipe tables and staff shouting

out orders: down-to-earth Long Phung serves up some of Singapore's best Vietnamese food. The *pho* (noodle soup) is simply gorgeous, its fragrant broth featuring just the right amount of sweetness. There's also a mouth-watering choice of real-deal classics, including mango salad and the popular *sò huyêt xào satê* (cockles with satay). Cash only.

Roland Restaurant SEAFOOD **$$**
(Map p510; ☑ 6440 8205; www.rolandrestaurant. com.sg; 06-750 Block 89, Marine Parade Central, Deck J, multistorey carpark; dishes S$12-60, crab per kg from S$73; ◷ 11.30am-2.15pm & 6-10.15pm; ☒ 36, 48, 196, 197) According to Roland, it was his mum, Mrs Lim, who invented Singapore's iconic chilli crab back in the 1950s. Decades on, Roland has his own giant restaurant, with a chilli crab that lures former prime minister Goh Chok Tong on National Day. The crabs are fleshy and sweet and the gravy milder than many of its competitors: good news if you're not a big spice fan.

Smokey's BBQ AMERICAN **$$**
(Map p510; ☑ 6345 6914; www.smokeysbbq.com.sg; 73 Joo Chiat Pl; mains S$19-65; ◷ 3-11pm, from 11am Sat & Sun; ☏; Ⓜ Paya Lebar) You'll be longing for sweet home Alabama at this breezy, all-American barbecue legend. Californian owner Rob makes all the dry rubs using secret recipes and the meats are smoked using hickory and mesquite woodchips straight from the USA. Start with the spicy buffalo wings with blue-cheese dipping sauce, then stick to slow-roasted, smoked meats such as ridiculously tender, fall-off-the-bone ribs.

✖ West & Southwest Singapore

★ Timbre+ HAWKER **$**
(☑ 6252 2545; www.timbreplus.sg; JTC LaunchPad@ one-north, 73A Ayer Rajah Cres; dishes from S$3; ◷ 6am-midnight Mon-Thu, to 1am Fri & Sat, 11am-10pm Sun, stall hours vary; Ⓜ One North) Welcome to the new generation of hawker centres. With over 30 food outlets, Timbre+ has it all: artwork-covered shipping containers, Airstream trailer food trucks, craft beer and live music nightly. But it's the food that draws the crowds: a mixture of traditional and New Age. Head here in the late afternoon before the old-school hawker stalls shut at 6pm.

★ Tamarind Hill THAI **$$$**
(☑ 6278 6364; www.tamarindrestaurants.com; 30 Labrador Villa Rd; mains S$18-59; ◷ noon-2.30pm Mon-Sat, 11.30am-3pm Sun, 6.30-9.45pm Sun-Thu, to 10.30pm Fri & Sat; ☏; Ⓜ Labrador Park) In a

MELLBEN SEAFOOD

When it comes to chart-topping crab, no shortage of locals will direct you to **Mellben Seafood** (☑ 6285 6762; 01-1222, 232 Ang Mo Kio Ave 3; dishes from S$11-22, crab per kg from S$75; ◷ 5-10pm; Ⓜ Braddell), a modern, hawker-style set-up at the bottom of a nondescript block. Signature dishes are claypot crab *bee hoon* (rice vermicelli noodles), butter crab and the ever-famous chilli crab. The crabs here yield gorgeous chunks of sweet, fresh meat; order a male unless you like roe.

Arrive before 5.30pm or after 8.30pm to avoid the longest queues; midweek is also quieter. Service can sometimes be slow, so come with a little patience.

colonial bungalow in Labrador Park, Tamarind Hill sets an elegant scene for exceptional Thai. The highlight is the Sunday brunch (S$60; noon to 3pm), a buffet of beautiful cold dishes and salads plus as many dishes from the à la carte menu as you like (the sautéed squid is sublime). Book ahead.

✖ Sentosa Island

Malaysian Food Street HAWKER **$**
(Map p516; www.rwsentosa.com; Level 1, Waterfront, Resorts World, 8 Sentosa Gateway; dishes S$2-11; ◷ 11am-9pm, 9am-10pm Fri-Sun; ☒ Waterfront) With its faux-Malaysian streetscape, this indoor hawker centre beside Universal Studios feels a bit Disney. Thankfully, there's nothing fake about the food, cooked by some of Malaysia's best hawker vendors.

Mykonos on the Bay GREEK **$$**
(Map p516; ☑ 6334 3818; www.mykonosonthebay. com; 01-10 Quayside Isle, 31 Ocean Way; tapas S$9-26, mains S$26-43; ◷ 6-10.30pm Mon-Wed, noon-2.30pm & 6-10.30pm Thu & Fri, noon-10.30pm Sat & Sun; ☑; ☒ B) At Sentosa Cove, this slick, marina-flanking taverna serves up Hellenic flavours that could make your *papou* weep. Sit alfresco and tuck into perfectly charred, marinated octopus, pan-fried Graviera cheese and house-made *giaourtlou* (spicy lamb sausage). Book ahead if you plan to come later in the week.

★ Knolls EUROPEAN **$$$**
(Map p516; ☑ 6591 5046; www.capellahotels.com/ singapore; Capella, 1 The Knolls; mains S$24-59, Sun brunch from S$148; ◷ 7am-11pm; ☒ Imbiah) Free-flowing-alcohol Sunday brunch is huge

in Singapore, and this posh, secluded spot – complete with strutting peacocks and roaming band – serves one of the best (12.30pm to 3pm). Style up and join the fabulous for scrumptious buffet fare like freshly shucked oysters, sizzling skewers straight from the live grills, fine-cut meats, mountains of cheese and don't forget to leave room for the delectable dessert bites.

Drinking & Nightlife

You'll find many of Singapore's hottest bars in Chinatown, especially on Club St and Ann Siang Rd, Duxton Hill, and up-and-coming Keong Saik Rd. Chinatown's Neil Rd is home to a handful of swinging gay venues. Other popular drinking spots include bohemian-spirited Kampong Glam, heritage-listed Emerald Hill Rd (just off Orchard Rd), leafy expat enclave Dempsey, and hyper-touristy Boat and Clarke Quays.

Bars generally open around 5pm until at least midnight Sunday to Thursday, and through to 2am or 3am on Friday and Saturday.

Colonial District, the Quays & Marina Bay

★ **28 HongKong Street**　　COCKTAIL BAR
(Map p492; www.28hks.com; 28 Hongkong St; ⊙5.30pm-1am Mon-Thu, to 3am Fri & Sat; Ⓜ Clarke Quay) Softly lit 28HKS plays hide and seek inside an unmarked 1960s shophouse. Slip inside and into a slinky scene of cosy booths and passionate mixologists turning grog into greatness. Marked with their alcohol strength, cocktails are seamless and sublime, among them the fruity '93 'til Infinity' with pisco, pineapple, lime and cypress. House-barreled classics, hard-to-find beers and lip-smacking grub seal the deal.

Email findus@28hks.com for reservations.

★ **Smoke & Mirrors**　　BAR
(Map p492; ☑9234 8122; www.smokeandmirrors.com.sg; 06-01 National Gallery Singapore, 1 St Andrew's Rd; ⊙3pm-1am Mon-Thu, to 2am Fri, noon-2am Sat, to 1am Sun; Ⓜ City Hall) Oozing style, this rooftop bar offers one of the best views of Singapore. Perched on the top of the National Gallery, the vista looks out over the **Padang** (Map p492; Ⓜ City Hall, Esplanade) to **Marina Bay Sands** (Map p492; www.marinabaysands.com; 10 Bayfront Ave, Marina Bay; Ⓟ; Ⓜ Bayfront) and is flanked by skyscrapers on either side. Arrive before sunset so you can sit, drink in hand, and watch the city transition from day to night. Book ahead.

If you can't tear yourself away for dinner, there are some tasty treats on the bar menu; most are surprisingly reasonably priced for the location.

Ah Sam Cold Drink Stall　　COCKTAIL BAR
(Map p492; ☑6535 0838; www.facebook.com/AhSamColdDrinkStall; 60A Boat Quay; ⊙6pm-midnight Mon-Thu, to 2am Fri & Sat; Ⓜ Clarke Quay, Raffles Place) Get that in-the-know glow at this sneaky cocktail den, perched above the tacky Boat Quay pubs. Adorned with vintage Hong Kong posters and feeling more like a private party than a bar, Ah Sam specialises in Asian mixology. Simply tell the bartender your preferences, and watch them twist, shake and torch up clever creations.

They mightn't be the strongest drinks in town, but they beat the tourist dross downstairs hands down.

Lantern　　BAR
(Map p492; ☑6333 8388; www.fullertonhotels.com; Fullerton Bay Hotel, 80 Collyer Quay; ⊙8am-1am Sun-Thu, to 2am Fri & Sat; Ⓜ Raffles Place) It may be lacking in height (it's dwarfed by the surrounding CBD buildings) and serve its drinks in plastic glasses (scandalous!), but Lantern remains a magical spot for a

---

CLUB RULES

Zouk (Map p492; ☑ 6738 2988; www.zoukclub.com; 3C River Valley Rd; women/men from S$30/35 redeemable for drinks; ⊗ Zouk 10pm-4am Fri, Sat & Wed, Phuture 10pm-3am Wed & Fri, to 2am Thu, to 4am Sat, Red Tail 6-11pm Sun-Tue & Thu, 7pm-3am Wed & Fri, to 4am Sat, Capital 10pm-2am Thu, to 3am Fri, to 4am Sat; Ⓜ Clarke Quay, Fort Canning) remains the city's best-known club, and its annual **ZoukOut** (www.zoukout.com; ⊗ Dec), a massive dance party held each December, attracts 40,000 revellers and A-list DJs. Hot spots include sky-high beat-pumping **Altimate** (Map p500; ☑ 6438 0410; www.1-altitude.com; Level 61, 1 Raffles Pl; admission incl 1 drink S$30; ⊗ 10pm-4am Fri & Sat; Ⓜ Raffles Place) and shrine to hip-hop **Fleek** (Map p492; ☑ 8808 0854; www.facebook.com/FleekSG; 01-10, 3C River Valley Rd; ⊗ 6pm-4am Wed-Sat; Ⓜ Clarke Quay, Fort Canning). Dance clubs proliferate around the Quays area, among them **Attica** (Map p492; ☑ 6333 9973; www.attica.com.sg; 01-03 Clarke Quay, 3A River Valley Rd; ⊗ 10pm-late Wed-Sat; Ⓜ Clarke Quay, Fort Canning) and hidden, techno-pumping **Headquarters by the Council** (Map p492; ☑ 8125 8880; www.facebook.com/headquarters; Level 2, 66 Boat Quay; ⊗ 6pm-3am Wed-Fri, 10pm-4am Sat; Ⓜ Clarke Quay). Beyond this, check out **Super O** (www.superO.sg), which runs top-notch pop-up dance parties, usually towards the end of the year. For updated listings, hit www.timeout.com/singapore/music-nightlife.

sophisticated evening toast. Why? There are the flickering lanterns, the shimmering, glass-sided pool – for Fullerton Bay Hotel (p532) guests only – and the romantic views over Marina Bay.

To avoid disappointment, consider booking a table two to three days ahead, especially on weekends.

Ronin
CAFE
(Map p492; http://ronin.sg; 17 Hongkong St; ⊗ 8am-6pm; Ⓜ Clarke Quay, Raffles Place) Ronin hides its talents behind a dark, tinted-glass door. Walk through and the Brutalist combo of grey concrete, exposed plumbing and low-slung lamps might leave you expecting some tough-talking interrogation. Thankfully, the only thing you'll get slapped with is smooth Australian Genovese coffee – wellness lovers try the 'dirty matcha'. Simple food options include homemade granola and gourmet panini. Cash only.

Wine Connection
WINE BAR
(Map p492; ☑ 6235 5466; www.wineconnection.com.sg; 01-19/20 Robertson Walk, 11 Unity St; ⊗ 11.30am-2am Mon-Thu, to 3am Fri & Sat, to 11pm Sun; 🛈; Ⓜ Fort Canning) Oenophiles love this savvy wine store and bar at Robertson Quay. The team works closely with winemakers across the world, which means no intermediary. They have an interesting wine list and very palatable prices: glasses from S$7 and bottles as low as S$30. Edibles include decent salads and tartines, not to mention top-notch cheeses from their fabulously stinky, next-door Cheese Bar.

Southbridge
BAR
(Map p492; ☑ 6877 6965; www.southbridge.sg; Level 5, 80 Boat Quay; ⊗ 5pm-midnight; Ⓜ Clarke Quay) Rising above the glut of mediocre Boat Quay bars, this discerning rooftop hang-out delivers a panorama guaranteed to loosen jaws. Scan skyline and river with a 'lust, caution' cocktail (Sichuan pepper-infused gin, Cynar, lemon and soda), or taste test an interesting selection of spirits that include Zacapa Solera 23 rum and Nikka Coffey gin. Entry is via the back alley off South Bridge Rd.

Chinatown & the CBD

★ Operation Dagger
COCKTAIL BAR
(Map p500; ☑ 6438 4057; www.operationdagger.com; 7 Ann Siang Hill; ⊗ 6pm-late Tue-Sat; Ⓜ Chinatown, Telok Ayer) From the cloud-like light sculpture to the boundary-pushing cocktails, extraordinary is the keyword here. To encourage experimentation, libations are described by flavour, not spirit, the latter shelved in uniform, apothecary-like bottles. Sample the sesame-infused Gomashio, or the textural surprise of the Hot & Cold. Head up the hill where Club St and Ann Siang Hill meet; a symbol shows the way.

★ Nylon Coffee Roasters
CAFE
(Map p500; ☑ 6220 2330; www.nyloncoffee.sg; 01-40, 4 Everton Park; ⊗ 8.30am-5.30pm Mon & Wed-Fri, 9am-6pm Sat & Sun; Ⓜ Outram Park, Tanjong Pagar) Hidden away in the Everton Park public housing complex, this pocket-sized, standing-room-only cafe and roastery has an epic reputation for phenomenal seasonal

LOCAL KNOWLEDGE

HIDDEN HANGS

In an area where hidden opium and gambling dens once reigned, crafty mixologists are now king. You won't find any signboards leading the way, though – you'll need to follow the clues down alleys, up staircases, even past a fortune teller. Amoy St is where to start: head up above Wanton restaurant to be seduced by the flavours of Southeast Asia at **Native** (Map p500; ☎ 8869 6520; www.tribenative.com; 52A Amoy St; ⊗ 6pm-midnight Mon-Sat; M Telok Ayer), where locally foraged ingredients are paired with spirits distilled from the region. Next, head across the road to hunt for the Dapper Coffee signboard and slink up to the **Spiffy Dapper** (Map p500; ☎ 8742 8908; www.spiffydapper.com; 73 Amoy St; ⊗ 5pm-late Mon-Fri, from 6pm Sat & Sun; M Telok Ayer) on the 2nd floor. Alternatively, head further down the street towards Telok Ayer MRT and look out for the neon pink 'pyschic' sign, behind which you'll be welcomed into **Employees Only** (Map p500; http://employeesonlysg.com; 112 Amoy St; ⊗ 5pm-1am Mon-Fri, to 2am Sat, 6pm-1am Sun; M Telok Ayer), the local outpost of the famous New York City cocktail bar.

blends and impressive single origins. At the helm is a personable, gung-ho crew of coffee fanatics, chatting away with customers about their latest coffee-sourcing trip abroad (they deal directly with the farmers).

While the espresso is outstanding, try the 'clever dripper', which shows off the more subtle notes in your cup of Joe.

★ Tippling Club
COCKTAIL BAR
(Map p500; ☎ 6475 2217; www.tipplingclub.com; 38 Tanjong Pagar Rd; ⊗ noon-midnight Mon-Fri, from 6pm Sat; M Tanjong Pagar) Tippling Club propels mixology to dizzying heights, with a technique and creativity that could turn a teetotaller into a born-again soak. Sample the Dreams & Desires menu before ordering by chewing your way through alcohol-infused gummy bears, which give a hint of what's to come. Our pick is the champagne-based Beauty, served with a cherry sorbet lipstick.

Kilo Lounge
CLUB
(Map p500; ☎ 9824 9747; www.kilokitchen.com; 21 Tanjong Pagar Rd; ⊗ 5.30pm-midnight Wed, to 3am Thu & Fri, 9.30pm-4am Sat; M Tanjong Pagar, Chinatown) Known as one of Singapore's best clubs, Kilo Lounge is not to be missed for those who love letting loose. You'll have to search around to find the door (hint: check the graffiti-covered back laneway). Inside, this warehouse-esque club serves up killer cocktails and house/techno acts, which quickly fill the sprawling dance floor to capacity.

Tea Chapter
TEAHOUSE
(Map p500; ☎ 6226 1175; www.teachapter.com; 9-11 Neil Rd; ⊗ teahouse 11am-9pm Sun-Thu, to 10.30pm Fri & Sat, shop 10.30am-9pm Sun-Thu, to 10.30pm Fri & Sat; M Chinatown) Queen

Elizabeth and Prince Philip dropped by this tranquil teahouse in 1989, and for S$10 you can sit at the table they sipped at. A minimum charge of S$8 per person will get you a heavenly pot of loose-leaf tea, prepared with traditional precision. The selection is excellent and the adjoining shop sells tea and a selection of beautiful tea sets.

Want to take your tea tasting to a new level? Book a tea appreciation package (from S$70 for two people), either the 'fragrance and aroma' or 'shades of tea', and become a tea master.

Coffee Break
COFFEE
(Map p500; www.facebook.com/coffeebreakamoystreet; 02-78 Amoy Street Food Centre, cnr Amoy & Telok Ayer Sts; ⊗ 7.30am-2.30pm Mon-Fri; M Telok Ayer) Operated by a sister and brother team who took the reins from their grandfather, this humble drink stall has a menu that reads more like it's from a hipster cafe. Sea-salt caramel lattes and melon milk tea anyone? Make no mistake, it's still good old Singaporean *kopi* (coffee) – with a twist. Toast spreads have also been given an overhaul – try the black sesame.

Smith Street Taps
CRAFT BEER
(Map p500; ☎ 9430 2750; www.facebook.com/smithstreettaps; 02-62 Chinatown Complex, 335 Smith St; ⊗ 6.30-10.30pm Tue-Thu, 5-11pm Fri, 2-10.30pm Sat; M Chinatown) Head to this hawker-centre stall for a top selection of ever-changing craft and premium draught beers from around the world. A few food stalls stay open around this back section of the hawkers market, creating a local hidden-bar buzz. Tuck into a plate of smoky skewers from Shi Xiang Satay (p539) with your brew. Last call 15 minutes before closing.

Sister stall the **Good Beer Company** (Map p500; 🎵 9430 2750; www.facebook.com/smithstreettaps; 02-58 Chinatown Complex, 335 Smith St; ⊗ 6.30-10.30pm Mon-Sat; Ⓜ Chinatown) sells bottled suds.

Yixing Xuan Teahouse TEAHOUSE
(Mapp500; 🎵 62246961; www.yixingxuan-teahouse. com; 78 Tanjong Pagar Rd; ⊗ 10am-8pm Mon-Sat, to 7pm Sun; Ⓜ Tanjong Pagar) Banker-turned-tea-purveyor Vincent Low is the man behind this venture, happily educating visitors about Chinese tea and the art of tea drinking. To immerse yourself more deeply, book a 45-minute tea appreciation workshop with tastings (S$30; if there's less than five participants, a S$5 surcharge per person will apply).

🍷 **Little India & Kampong Glam**

⭐ **Atlas** BAR
(Map p504; 🎵 6396 4466; www.atlasbar.sg; Lobby, Parkview Sq, 600 North Bridge Rd; ⊗ 10am-1am Mon-Thu, to 2am Fri, 3pm-2am Sat; Ⓜ Bugis) Straight out of 1920s Manhattan, this cocktail lounge is an art deco–inspired extravaganza, adorned with ornate bronze ceilings and low-lit plush lounge seating,

and a drinks menu filled with decadent champagnes, curated cocktails and some mean martinis. However, it's the 12m-high gin wall, displaying over 1000 labels, that really makes a statement – make sure you ask for a tour.

Night-time bookings are essential; however, if you arrive before 6pm, you should still be able to nab a table. Doors open in the morning for coffees, and European-inspired bites are served throughout the day and well into the night. The afternoon tea (3pm to 5pm, from S$52) is also worth stopping in for. Dress to impress; no shorts or slippers after 5pm.

⭐ **Chye Seng Huat Hardware** CAFE
(CSHH Coffee Bar; Map p504; 🎵 6396 0609; www. cshhcoffee.com; 150 Tyrwhitt Rd; ⊗ 9am-10pm Tue-Thu & Sun, to midnight Fri & Sat; Ⓜ Bendemeer, Farrer Park, Lavender) An art deco former hardware store provides the setting and name for Singapore's coolest cafe and roastery, its third-wave offerings including on-tap Nitro Cold Brew, a creamy, malty, black coffee infused with nitrogen. Get your coffee geek on at one of the education sessions (from S$25); see www.papapalheta.com for details.

SINGAPORE DRINKING & NIGHTLIFE

LGBTIQ+ SINGAPORE

Although public debate around LGBTIQ+ rights is increasing, homosexual acts remain technically illegal. Despite this, a small but thriving LGBTIQ+ scene exists, centred mostly on Neil Rd in Chinatown. Bars and clubs aside, annual events include the Love & Pride Film Festival (dates vary), July's Pink Dot (pinkdot.sg) solidarity gathering in Hong Lim Park (note that as of 2017 this gathering is only open to Singaporean citizens and permanent residents, so police recommend all others stay away) and August pride festival IndigNation (https://indignationsg.wordpress.com). For more info on what's on, check out www.travelgayasia.com, www.pluguide.com and www.utopia-asia.com.

Backstage Bar (Map p500; 🎵 6423 9232; www.homeofthebluespin.com; 80 Neil Rd; ⊗ 8pm-3am Sun-Fri, to 4am Sat; Ⓜ Outram Park, Chinatown) Chinatown's veteran gay bar has found new life in a converted Neil Rd shophouse, complete with snug alfresco courtyard and a splash of Broadway posters. Very friendly, it's a top spot to chat, flirt or just sit back and people watch. Entry is via the side alley.

Tantric Bar (Map p500; 🎵 6423 9232; www.homeofthebluespin.com; 78 Neil Rd; ⊗ 8pm-3am Sun-Fri, to 4am Sat; Ⓜ Outram Park, Chinatown) Two indoor bars and two alfresco palm-fringed courtyards is what you get at Singapore's best-loved gay drinking hole. Especially heaving on Friday and Saturday nights, it's a hit with preened locals and eager expats and out-of-towners, who schmooze and cruise to Kylie, Gaga and Katy Perry chart-toppers.

Taboo (Map p500; 🎵 6225 6256; www.taboo.sg; 65 Neil Rd; ⊗ 8pm-2am Wed & Thu, 10pm-3am Fri, to 4am Sat; Ⓜ Outram Park, Chinatown) Conquer the dance floor at what remains the favourite gay club in town. Expect the requisite line-up of shirtless gyrators, doting straight women and regular racy-themed nights. The dance floor goes ballistic from midnight and the beats bump till the wee hours of the morning.

Maison Ikkoku The Art of Mixology
COCKTAIL BAR

(Map p504; ☑ 6294 0078; www.ethanleslieleong.com; Level 2, 20 Kandahar St; ☺ bar 6pm-1am Sun-Thu, to 2am Fri & Sat; ☎; Ⓜ Bugis) Pimped with modern, industrial finishes and flushes of greenery, Maison Ikkoku The Art of Mixology is where real magic happens. There's no menu, so let the bartenders know what you like – a request for something sour might land you a tart, hot combo of spicy gin, grape, lemon and Japanese-chilli threads. Not cheap, but worth it.

Druggists
BEER HALL

(Map p504; ☑ 6341 5967; www.facebook.com/DruggistsSG; 119 Tyrwhitt Rd; ☺ 4pm-midnight Mon-Thu, to 2am Fri & Sat, 2-10pm Sun; Ⓜ Bendemeer, Farrer Park, Lavender) Druggists is indeed addictive for beer aficionados. Its 23 taps pour a rotating selection of craft brews from cognoscenti favourites like Denmark's Mikkeller and the Netherlands' De Molen. The week's beers are scribbled on the blackboard, with the option of 250mL or 500mL pours. Sud-friendly grub is also available, though the place is better for drinking than for eating.

A pared-back combo of trippy, vintage floor tiles, traditional wooden *kopitiam* (coffeeshop) chairs and marble-top tables, the space occupies the ground floor of the Singapore Chinese Druggists Association.

Liberty Coffee
CAFE

(Map p504; ☑ 6926 7600; www.libertycoffee.sg; 387 Jln Besar; ☺ 10am-6pm Tue-Fri, to 8pm Sat; Ⓜ Farrer Park, Bendemeer) After years of supplying beans to some of the island's best coffeeshops, Singapore's home-grown coffee roaster Liberty Coffee has finally opened a coffee bar to showcase its brewing skills. Don't expect a run-of-the-mill cup of joe; here its signature nutty Speakeasy and chocolatey Goliath blends take centre stage along with a multitude of brewing apparatus.

🍸 Orchard Road

★Manhattan
BAR

(Map p506; ☑ 6725 3377; www.regenthotels.com/en/Singapore; Level 2, Regent, 1 Cuscaden Rd; ☺ 5pm-1am, to 2am Fri & Sat, noon-3pm Sun; Ⓜ Orchard) Step back in time to the golden age of fine drinking at this handsome *Mad Men*–esque bar, where long-forgotten cocktails come back to life. Grouped by eras of New York, the drinks menu is ever changing; however, waistcoated bartenders are only too happy to guide you. Sunday brings freshly shucked oysters, and an adults-only cocktail brunch (S$150) with make your own bloody Marys.

★Other Room
BAR

(Map p506; ☑ 6100 7778; www.theotherroom.com.sg; 01-05 Singapore Marriott, 320 Orchard Rd; ☺ 6pm-3am, to 4am Fri-Sun; Ⓜ Orchard) You'll find this hidden drinking house, a throwback to a bygone era, behind a secret door in the Singapore Marriott (Map p506; ☑ 6735 5800; www.singaporemarriott.com; 320 Orchard Rd; r from S$490; 🅿 ❄ @ ☎ ☒; Ⓜ Orchard) lobby – ring the doorbell for entry. Peruse the 50-page drinks menu and settle in for a night to remember. Award-winning mixologist Dario Knox takes spirits seriously; the American oak-barrel-aged spirits in different finishings are where to begin.

Bar Canary
BAR

(Map p506; ☑ 6603 8855; www.parkhotelgroup.com/orchard; Level 4, Park Hotel Orchard, 270 Orchard Rd, entry on Bideford Rd; ☺ noon-1am, to 2am Fri & Sat; ☎; Ⓜ Somerset) Canary-yellow sofas, artificial turf and the sound of humming traffic and screeching birds – this alfresco bar hovers high above frenetic Orchard Rd. It's fab for an evening tipple, with well-positioned fans. Book at least a week ahead for its Wednesday Girls' Night Out: S$55, plus tax, for free-flow champagne, house pours and selected cocktails from 7pm to 9pm.

Horse's Mouth
BAR

(Map p506; ☑ 8188 0900; www.horsesmouthbar.com; B1-39 Forum Shopping Mall, 583 Orchard Rd; ☺ 6pm-midnight, to 1am Fri & Sat; Ⓜ Orchard) As discreet as bars come, this hidden Japanese izakaya-inspired watering hole is accessed through a ground floor black door or via the better-lit Uma Uma Ramen restaurant above (at 01-41). Inside, discover slick, inventive cocktails and a long list of sake and whisky. Perch at the bar, chat with the friendly bartenders and watch delectable concoctions come to fruition.

TWG Tea
TEAHOUSE

(Map p506; ☑ 6735 1837; www.twgtea.com; 02-21 ION Orchard, 2 Orchard Rd; ☺ 10am-10pm; ☎; Ⓜ Orchard) Posh tea purveyor TWG sells more than 800 single-estate teas and blends from around the world, from English breakfast to Rolls Royce varieties like 24-carat-gold-coated Grand Golden Yin Zhen. Edibles include tea-infused macarons (the *bain de roses* is divine), ice cream and sorbet. It also has an all-day dining menu available.

Privé   CAFE

(Map p506; ✉ 6776 0777; www.theprivegroup.com.sg; 01-K1 Wheelock Place, 501 Orchard Rd; ⊘ 9am-1am; Ⓜ Orchard) With its pedestrian sidewalk location and terraced seating, this Parisian style cafe is the perfect ringside spot to watch the masses strutting up and down Orchard Rd. Serving decent cafe fare, plus soups, pastas and all-day breakfasts, Privé has a good cocktail and wine list and more than 15 whiskys. Happy hour is 5pm to 8pm; book for the best seats.

Dempsey Hill & the Botanic Gardens

Atlas Coffeehouse   COFFEE

(✉ 6314 2674; www.atlascoffeehouse.com.sg; 6 Duke's Rd; ⊘ 8am-6.30pm Tue-Sun; Ⓜ Botanic Gardens) This airy industrial-styled coffeehouse has caffeine lovers lining up for the in-house Guatemalan and Brazilian bean blend by Two Degrees North Coffee Co. Like your coffee served cold? Try the Black Bird, a taste flight of cold brew, nitro brew and iced black – perfect for a hot day.

Wala Wala Café Bar   BAR

(✉ 6462 4288; www.walawala.sg; 31 Lorong Mambong; ⊘ 4pm-1am Mon-Thu, to 2am Fri, 3pm-2am Sat, 3pm-1am Sun; Ⓜ Holland Village) Perennially packed at weekends (and most evenings, in fact), Wala Wala has live music on the 2nd floor, with warm-up acts Monday to Friday from 7pm and main acts nightly from 9.30pm. Downstairs it pulls in football fans with its large sports screens. As at most nearby places, tables spill out onto the street in the evenings.

Eastern Singapore

Cider Pit   BAR

(Map p510; ✉ 6440 0504; www.eastofavalonwines.com; 328 Joo Chiat Rd; ⊘ 3pm-1am, from 1pm Sat & Sun; 🐾; Ⓜ Paya Lebar) Wedged in a nondescript concrete structure, Cider Pit is easy to miss. Don't. This watering hole offers an extensive range of ciders on tap, and speciality beers such as Australia's Little Creatures. It's a refreshingly casual, unfussy kind of place, ideal for easygoing drinking sessions among expats in shorts, tees and flip-flops.

Coastal Settlement   BAR

(✉ 6475 0200; www.thecoastalsettlement.com; 200 Netheravon Rd; ⊘ 10.30am-11pm Tue-Thu, to midnight Fri, from 8.30am Sat & Sun; 🐾; 🚌 29) In a black-and-white colonial bungalow on verdant grounds, this cafe-bar-restaurant is ideal for unhurried idling. It's like a hipster op shop, packed with modernist furniture, the odd Vespa and cabinets filled with retro gizmos. The fresh juices are delicious and the coffee is top-notch; food options cover most bases, from pastas and pizzas to a wagyu-beef cheeseburger.

Catch the metro to Tampines MRT station and then take bus 29.

Little Island Brewing Co.   BREWERY

(✉ 6543 9100; www.libc.co; 01-01/02, 6 Changi Village Rd; ⊘ noon-11pm, to midnight Fri & Sat; 🐾; 🚌 2) A perfect spot to perch after a trip to nearby **Pulau Ubin** (✉ 1800 471 7300; www.nparks.gov.sg; ⛴ from Changi Village). This rustic, shed-like, microbrewery serves six in-house brews as well as international craft beers and even wines on tap. Purchase a top-up card at the counter, then use it to dispense the exact amount of beer you'd like – well, to the card's value at least.

Leave a little room in your tank for the tasty pub grub – our picks are the tender 15-hour smoked wagyu beef brisket and the crispy fish and chips.

Sentosa Island

★ Tanjong Beach Club   BAR

(Map p516; ✉ 6270 1355; www.tanjongbeachclub.com; 120 Tanjong Beach Walk; ⊘ 11am-10pm, from 10am Sat, from 9am Sun; 🐾; 🚌 Tanjong Beach) Generally cooler than the bars on Siloso Beach, Tanjong Beach Club is an evocative spot, with loungers on the sand, a small, stylish pool for guests, and a sultry, lounge-and-funk soundtrack. The restaurant serves trendy beachside fare, and a kick-ass weekend-brunch menu. Some of the island's hottest parties happen on this shore; check the website for details.

FOC Sentosa   BAR

(Map p516; ✉ 6100 1102; www.focsentosa.com; 110 Tanjong Beach Walk; ⊘ 11.30am-11pm Tue-Sun; 🚌 Palawan Beach) A tiny slice of Barcelona on Palawan Beach, this vibrantly striped hangout is perfect for lazing the afternoon away either by the compact infinity pool or ensconced on a lounger on the sand. Tummy rumbling? Pick a few bites from the menu of seafood-heavy tapas, and wash it down with a refreshing cocktail – our pick is the 'never ending summer', made with vodka, strawberry and watermelon.

Check the website for upcoming events from sunset DJ sessions to bootcamp workouts – the monthly Beach Brunch Beats is legendary.

☆ Entertainment

The city's performing-arts hub is **Esplanade – Theatres on the Bay** (Map p492; ✔6828 8377; www.esplanade.com; 1 Esplanade Dr; ✆box office noon-8.30pm; Ⓟ; ⓂEsplanade, City Hall), which also hosts regular free music performances. The venue is also home to the Singapore Symphony Orchestra. Broadway musicals take to the stage at Marina Bay Sands, while independent theatre companies like Wild Rice and Singapore Repertory Theatre perform at various smaller venues.

An enthusiastic local music scene thrives (to a point) and homegrown talent is sometimes showcased at unexpected venues. Tickets to most events are available through **SISTIC** (Map p506; ✔6348 5555; www.sistic. com.sg; Level 4 Concierge, ION Orchard, 2 Orchard Turn; ⓂOrchard). To see what's on, scan Singapore broadsheet *Straits Times* or check www.timeout.com/singapore.

☆ Chinese Opera

Chinese Theatre Circle   OPERA
(Map p500; ✔6323 4862; www.ctcopera.com; 5 Smith St; show & snacks S$25, show & dinner S$40; ✆7-9pm Fri & Sat; ⓂChinatown) Teahouse evenings organised by this nonprofit opera company are a wonderful, informal introduction to Chinese opera. Every Friday and Saturday at 8pm there is a brief talk on Chinese opera, followed by a 45-minute excerpt from an opera classic, performed by actors in full costume. You can also opt for a pre-show Chinese meal at 7pm. Book ahead.

☆ Live Music

Singapore Symphony Orchestra   CLASSICAL MUSIC
(SSO; Map p492; ✔6602 4245; www.sso.org.sg; 01-02 Victoria Concert Hall, 9 Empress Pl; ✆box office 9am-6.30pm Mon-Fri, 1hr before performances at Victoria Concert Hall; ⓂRaffles Place, City Hall) The neoclassical **Victoria Theatre & Concert Hall** (Map p492; ✔6908 8810; www. vtvch.com; 9 Empress Pl; ✆10am-9pm; ⓂRaffles Place, City Hall) is home to Singapore's well-respected flagship orchestra, which makes its performing home at the 1800-seat state-of-the-art Esplanade – Theatres on the Bay. It plays at least weekly; check the website or SISTIC for details and book ahead, there is a box office on-site. Student and senior (55 plus) discounts available; kids under six years not permitted.

Singapore Chinese Orchestra CLASSICAL MUSIC
(Map p500; ✔6557 4034; www.sco.com.sg; Singapore Conference Hall, 7 Shenton Way; ✆box office 10am-6.45pm Mon-Fri, 6-9pm SCO concert nights; ⓂTanjong Pagar, Downtown) Using traditional instruments such as the *liuqin, ruan* and *sanxian,* the SCO treats listeners to classical Chinese concerts throughout the year. Concerts are held at the SCO Concert Hall as well as at various venues around the city, with occasional collaborations showcasing jazz musicians. Tickets can be purchased via SISTIC or at the on-site box office. Check the website for upcoming performances.

BluJaz Café   LIVE MUSIC
(Map p504; ✔6292 3800; www.blujazcafe.net; 11 Bali Lane; ✆9am-12.30am Mon & Tue, to 1am Wed-Thu, to 2.30am Fri & Sat, noon-midnight Sun; 🛜; ⓂBugis) Bohemian pub BluJaz is one of the best options in town for live music, with regular jazz jams, and other acts playing anything from blues to rockabilly. Check the website for the list of events, which includes DJ-spun funk, R&B and retro nights, as well as 'Talk Cock' open-mic comedy nights on Wednesday and Thursday. Cover charge for some shows.

☆ Theatre, Comedy & Dance

★**Singapore Dance Theatre**   DANCE
(Map p492; ✔6338 0611; www.singaporedance theatre.com; 07-02/03, Bugis+, 201 Victoria St; ⓂBugis) This is the headquarters of Singapore's premier dance company, which keeps fans swooning with its repertoire of classic ballets and contemporary works, many of which are performed at Esplanade – Theatres on the Bay. The true highlight is the group's Ballet under the Stars season at Fort Canning Park (p497), which usually runs midyear. See the website for program details.

Singapore Repertory Theatre   THEATRE
(Map p492; ✔6221 5585; www.srt.com.sg; KC Arts Centre, 20 Merbau Rd; ⓂFort Canning) Based at the KC Arts Centre but also performing at other venues, the SRT produces international repertory standards as well as mod-

ern Singaporean plays. Check the website for upcoming productions.

Comedy Masala · COMEDY
(Map p492; 8525 7414; www.comedymasala. com; 69 Circular Rd; adult/student S$25/15; 8pm Tue; Raffles Place, Clarke Quay) Need a good belly laugh? Head to Hero's bar on a Tuesday night to watch comics from far and wide. The good times keep rolling with a live band once the laughs have died down. It's usually standing room only, so if you'd like a place to park your derrière, book via the website; tickets are a few dollars cheaper, too.

Necessary Stage · THEATRE
(Map p510; 6440 8115; www.necessary.org; B1-02 Marine Parade Community Bldg, 278 Marine Parade Rd; 12, 16, 36, 196) Since the theatre's inception in 1987, artistic director Alvin Tan has collaborated with resident playwright Haresh Sharma to produce over 60 original works. Innovative, indigenous and often controversial, the Necessary Stage is one of Singapore's best-known theatre groups. Productions are performed at the Necessary Stage Black Box and other venues; check the website for current shows and purchase tickets through Sistic.

Wild Rice · THEATRE
(Map p504; 6292 2695; www.wildrice.com.sg; 65 Kerbau Rd; Little India) Singapore's sexiest theatre group is based in Kerbau Rd but performs shows elsewhere in the city (as well as abroad). A mix of homegrown and foreign work, productions range from farce to serious politics, fearlessly wading into issues not commonly on the agenda in Singapore.

Many performances take place at the LASALLE College of the Arts, located at 1 McNally St, just steps from the Rochor MRT station.

Shopping

While its shopping scene mightn't match the edge of Hong Kong's or Bangkok's, Singapore is no retail slouch. Look beyond the malls and you'll find everything from sharply curated local boutiques to vintage map peddlers and clued-in contemporary galleries.

Prices are usually fixed, except at markets and some shops in touristy areas. If you do haggle, stay good-humoured and don't get petty, causing everyone to lose face. Singapo-

rean shops don't accept returns. Exchanges are accepted if items have original tags and packaging.

Colonial District, the Quays & Marina Bay

Basheer Graphic Books · BOOKS
(Map p492; 6336 0810; www.basheergraphic. com; 04-19 Bras Basah Complex, 231 Bain St; 10am-8pm Mon-Sat, 11am-6.30pm Sun; Bugis, Bras Basah) Spruce up your coffee table at this temple to design books and magazines. Located inside Bras Basah Complex (locally dubbed 'Book City'), it has everything from fashion tomes to titles on art, architecture and urban planning. The shop also does a brisk mail-order business, so if you're mid-visit and want to have something posted to you, the staff are happy to help.

Kapok · GIFTS & SOUVENIRS
(Map p492; 9060 9107; www.ka-pok.com; 01-05 National Design Centre, 111 Middle Rd; 11am-8pm; Bugis, Bras Basah) Inside the National Design Centre, Kapok showcases beautifully designed products from Singapore and beyond. Restyle your world with local jewellery from Amado Gudek and Lorem Ipsum Store and flattering dress by GIN-LEE Studio. Imports include anything from seamless Italian wallets to British striped tees and Spanish backpacks. When you're shopped out, recharge at the on-site cafe.

Raffles Hotel Arcade · MALL
(Map p492; 6337 1886; www.rafflessingapore. com; 1 Beach Rd; City Hall, Esplanade) Part of the hotel complex, Raffles Hotel Arcade has been home to some of the world's most notable retailers. This famous shopping destination welcomes big spenders and big browsers alike.

Raffles Hotel Gift Shop · GIFTS & SOUVENIRS
(Map p492; 6337 1886; www.rafflessingapore. com; 3 Seah St; 9am-8pm; City Hall, Esplanade) It might sound like a tourist trap, but the Raffles Hotel gift shop is a good spot for quality souvenirs, whatever your budget. Remaining open while the hotel undergoes renovation, it has moved to 3 Seah St. Pick up anything from vintage hotel posters to handcrafted silk cushions, and branded Raffles stationery, tea sets and toiletries.

Cat Socrates · GIFTS & SOUVENIRS
(Map p492; 6333 0870; www.cat-socrates. myshopify.com; 02-25 Bras Basah Complex, 231

Bain St; ⊘ noon-8pm Mon-Sat, 1-7pm Sun; M Bugis, Bras Basah) Can't find that retro Chinese toy car? What about Pan Am wrapping paper? Chances are you'll find them at this quirky shop, inside the bookworm heaven that is the Bras Basah Complex. Expect anything from felt laptop sleeves and quirky totes to supercool Singapore souvenirs, such as city-themed graphic postcards and neighbourhood sketchbooks.

🔒 Chinatown & the CBD

⭐ Tong Mern Sern Antiques — ANTIQUES
(Map p500; ☑ 6223 1037; www.tmsantiques.com; 51 Craig Rd; ⊘ 9.30am-5.30pm Mon-Sat, from 1.30pm Sun; M Outram Park) An Aladdin's cave of dusty furniture, books, records, woodcarvings, porcelain and other bits and bobs (we even found an old cash register), Tong Mern Sern is a curious hunting ground for Singapore nostalgia. A banner hung above the front door proclaims: 'We buy junk and sell antiques. Some fools buy. Some fools sell'. Better have your wits about you.

Utterly Art — ART
(Map p500; ☑ 6226 2605; www.facebook.com/utterlyart; Level 3, 20B Mosque St; ⊘ 2-8pm Mon-Sat, noon-5.30pm Sun; M Chinatown) Climb the stairs to this tiny, welcoming gallery for works by emerging contemporary Singaporean and Asian artists. While painting is the gallery's focus, exhibitions dabble in sculpture, photography and ceramics on occasion; check the Facebook page for current and upcoming exhibitions. Opening times can be a little erratic, so always call ahead if making a special trip.

innit — FASHION & ACCESSORIES
(Map p500; ☑ 9781 7496; www.innitbangkok.com; 13 Ann Siang Hill; ⊘ 11am-8pm Wed-Sat; M Chinatown, Telok Ayer) Singaporean fashionistas swoon over the flowing fabrics and perfect pleating of Thai fashion house Innit. Pieces are easily mixed and matched, plus the high-quality artisanship means you'll get plenty of wear from each item.

Anthony the Spice Maker — SPICES
(Map p500; ☑ 9117 7573; www.anthonythespicemaker.com; B1-169 Chinatown Complex, 335 Smith St; ⊘ 8.15am-3.30pm Tue-Sun; M Chinatown) If you want to recreate the aromas and tastes of Singapore at home, make a beeline for this tiny stall where little brown airtight packets, which don't allow even the slightest whiff of the heady spices to escape, are uniformly lined up. Anthony is only too happy to help you choose, but we can personally recommend the meat *rendang* blend.

🔒 Little India & Kampong Glam

⭐ Sifr Aromatics — PERFUME
(Map p504; ☑ 6392 1966; www.sifr.sg; 42 Arab St; ⊘ 11am-8pm Mon-Sat, to 5pm Sun; M Bugis) This Zen-like perfume laboratory belongs to third-generation perfumer Johari Kazura, whose exquisite creations include the heady East (30mL S$125), a blend of oud, rose absolute, amber and neroli. The focus is on custom-made fragrances (consider calling ahead to arrange an appointment), with other heavenly offerings including affordable, high-quality body balms, scented candles and vintage perfume bottles.

---

❶ TAXES & REFUNDS

Departing visitors can get a refund of the 7% GST on their purchases, under the following conditions:

➡ Minimum spend of $100 at one retailer on the same day for no more than three purchases.

➡ You have a copy of the eTRS (Electronic Tourist Refund Scheme) ticket issued by the shop. Alternatively you can use a debit or credit card as a token to track your purchases; no need to pay with the card, it will just keep a tally.

➡ You scan your eTRS ticket or token debit/credit card at the self-help kiosks at the airport or cruise terminal. If physical inspection of the goods is required as indicated by the eTRS self-help kiosk, you will have to present the goods, together with the original receipt and your boarding pass, at the Customs Inspection Counter.

You will need to show your passport at the store when purchasing. Smaller stores may not participate in the GST refund scheme.

Supermama GIFTS & SOUVENIRS
(Map p504; ☑ 6291 1946; www.supermama.sg; 265 Beach Rd; ☺ 11am-8pm; Ⓜ Bugis) Tucked around the corner from Arab St, this gallery-esque store is a treasure trove of contemporary giftware. Circle the huge central bench while you pore over the Singapore-inspired wares, most created by local designers. The blue-and-white fine-porcelain dishes, made in Japan, are the headliners.

Haji Lane FASHION, HOMEWARES
(Map p504; Haji Lane; Ⓜ Bugis) Narrow, pastel-hued Haji Lane harbours a handful of quirky boutiques and plenty of colourful street art. Shops turn over fast due to exorbitant rents. For a sweet treat, stop off at whimsical **Windowsill Pies** (Map p504; ☑ 9004 7827; www.windowsillpies.sg; 17 Haji Lane; pie slices S$7-8; ☺ 11am-8pm Tue-Thu & Sun, to 10pm Fri & Sat; ☎; Ⓜ Bugis).

Rugged Gentlemen Shoppe FASHION & ACCESSORIES
(Map p504; ☑ 6396 4568; www.tuckshopsundry supplies.com; 8 Perak Rd; ☺ noon-8pm Mon-Sat, by appointment Sun; Ⓜ Rochor, Jalan Besar) A vintage-inspired ode to American working-class culture, this little menswear store offers a clued-in selection of rugged threads and accessories, including Red Wing boots, grooming products and made-in-house leather goods. Stock up on plaid shirts, sweat tops and harder-to-find denim from brands like Japan's Iron Heart and China's Red Cloud.

Bugis Street Market MARKET
(Map p504; ☑ 6338 9513; www.bugisstreet.com. sg; 3 New Bugis St; ☺ 11am-10pm; Ⓜ Bugis) What was once Singapore's most infamous sleaze pit – packed with foreign servicemen on R&R, gambling dens and 'sisters' (transvestites) – is now its most famous undercover street market, crammed with cheap clothes, shoes, accessories and manicurists, and especially popular with teens and 20-somethings. In a nod to its past, there's even a sex shop.

⌂ Orchard Road

ION Orchard Mall MALL
(Map p506; ☑ 6238 8228; www.ionorchard.com; 2 Orchard Turn; ☺ 10am-10pm; ☎; Ⓜ Orchard) Rising directly above Orchard MRT station, futuristic ION is the cream of Orchard Rd malls. Basement floors focus on mere-mortal high-street labels like Zara and Uniqlo, while upper-floor tenants read like the index of *Vogue*. Dining options range from food-court bites to posher nosh, and the attached 56-storey tower offers a top-floor viewing gallery. **ION Sky** (Map p506; ☑ 6238 8228; www.ion orchard.com/en/ion-sky.html; Level 56, ION Orchard, 2 Orchard Turn; ☺ 2-8.30pm; Ⓜ Orchard) **FREE**.

Antiques of the Orient ANTIQUES
(Map p506; ☑ 6734 9351; www.aoto.com.sg; 02-40 Tanglin Shopping Centre, 19 Tanglin Rd; ☺ 10am-5.30pm, 11am-3.30pm Sun; Ⓜ Orchard) Snugly set in a mall filled with Asian arts and crafts shops, Antiques of the Orient is a veritable treasure chest of original and reproduction vintage prints, photographs and maps from across the continent. Especially beautiful are the richly hued botanical drawings commissioned by British colonist William Farquhar.

Ngee Ann City MALL
(Map p506; ☑ 6506 0461; www.ngeeanncity.com. sg; 391 Orchard Rd; ☺ 10am-9.30pm; Ⓜ Somerset) It might look like a forbidding mausoleum, but this marble-and-granite behemoth promises retail giddiness on its seven floors. International luxury brands compete for space with sprawling bookworm nirvana **Kinokuniya** (Map p506; ☑ 6737 5021; www. kinokuniya.com.sg; 04-20/21 Ngee Ann City, 391 Orchard Rd; ☺ 10am-9.30pm; Ⓜ Orchard) and upmarket Japanese department store **Takashimaya** (Map p506; ☑ 6738 1111; www. takashimaya.com.sg; Ngee Ann City, 391 Orchard Rd; ☺ 10am-9.30pm; ☎; Ⓜ Somerset), home to Takashimaya Food Village, one of the strip's best food courts.

Pedder On Scotts SHOES
(Map p506; ☑ 6244 2883; www.pedderonscotts. com; Level 2, Scotts Sq, 6 Scotts Rd; ☺ 10am-9pm; Ⓜ Orchard) Even if you're not in the market for high-end heels and bags, Pedder On Scotts thrills with its creative, whimsical items. The store hand picks only the most unique pieces from leading designers, and displays them in separate 'zones' – each more creative than the next. Accessories include statement jewellery fit for a modern gallery.

⌂ Dempsey Hill & the Botanic Gardens

Many parts of Dempsey Hill's former British Army barracks are home to long-established art and antique shops, selling anything from teak furniture to landscaping ornaments and ancient temple artefacts. See www. dempseyhill.com for a complete rundown.

SINGAPORE SHOPPING

★**Bynd Artisan**   ARTS & CRAFTS
(☑6475 1680; www.byndartisan.com; 01-54, 44 Jln Merah Saga; ⊙noon-9pm, from 10am Sat & Sun; Ⓜ Holland Village) Connoisseurs of bespoke stationery and leather will love this sublime store that prides itself on artisanal excellence. Select from the range of handmade journals or spend time customising your own; don't forget to deboss your name. Other items include leather travel accessories and jewellery pieces. For the complete artist experience, sign up for a course (from S$78) in leather crafting or bookbinding.

Shang Antique   ANTIQUES
(☑6388 8838; www.shangantique.com.sg; 01-03, Block 26, Dempsey Rd; ⊙10am-7pm; ☐7, 75, 77, 105, 106, 123, 174) Specialising in antique religious artefacts from Cambodia, Laos, Thailand, India and Burma, as well as reproductions, Shang Antique has items dating back nearly 2000 years – with price tags to match. Those with more style than savings can pick up old bronze gongs, beautiful Thai silk scarves or Burmese ornamental rice baskets for under S$50.

Em Gallery   FASHION, HOMEWARES
(☑6475 6941; www.emtradedesign.com; 01-03A Block 26, Dempsey Rd; ⊙10am-7pm, from 11am Sat & Sun; ☐7, 75, 77, 105, 106, 123, 174) Singapore-based Japanese designer Emiko Nakamura keeps Dempsey's society women looking whimsically chic in her light, sculptural creations. Emiko also collaborates with hill tribes in Laos to create naturally dyed hand-woven handicrafts, such as bags and cushions. Other homewares might include limited-edition (and reasonably priced) pottery from Cambodia.

Eastern Singapore

★**Rumah Bebe**   CLOTHING, HANDICRAFTS
(Map p510; ☑6247 8781; www.rumahbebe.com; 113 East Coast Rd; ⊙9.30am-6.30pm Tue-Sun; ☐10, 14, 16, 32) Bebe Seet is the owner of this 1928 shophouse and purveyor of all things Peranakan. She sells traditional *kebayas* (Nonya-style blouses with decorative lace) with contemporary twists and beautifully beaded shoes. If you've got time and the inclination, you can take one of the beading classes run by Bebe, including a two-session beginners' course (S$450).

Tours of the shophouse are also available; check the website for details.

Kim Choo Kueh Chang   FOOD, HANDICRAFTS
(Map p510; ☑6741 2125; www.kimchoo.com; 109-111 East Coast Rd; ⊙9am-9pm; ☐10, 14, 16, 32) Joo Chiat (Katong) is stuffed with bakeries and dessert shops, but few equal old-school Kim Choo. Pick up traditional pineapple tarts and other brightly coloured Peranakan *kueh* (bite-sized snacks), and stop by the adjoining boutique for colourful Peranakan ceramics, clothing and accessories. Fashion designer Raymond Wong runs Peranakan-beading workshops (S$65), with each session lasting 1½ hours.

SURVIVAL GUIDE

❶ Directory A–Z

ACCESSIBLE TRAVEL

Ramps, lifts and other facilities are common on the island. The footpaths in the city are nearly all immaculate, MRT stations all have lifts and some buses and taxis are equipped with wheelchair-friendly equipment.

Visit Singapore (http://www.visitsingapore.com/travel-guide-tips/getting-around/accessibility.html) gives further information about and links to accessibility on different modes of transport and the built environment.

The government maintains the **Friendly Built Environment Portal** (http://www.bca.gov.sg/friendlyBuilding/FindBuilding/FriendlyFeatures.aspx): a search engine for accessible buildings with a variety of filters, including type of building, user group (not only various disabilities, but also families with children and/or pushchairs), friendly features, and level of friendliness!

The **Disabled People's Association Singapore** (www.dpa.org.sg) can provide information on accessibility in Singapore.

Download Lonely Planet's free Accessible Travel guides from http://lptravel.to/AccessibleTravel.

CUSTOMS REGULATIONS

You are not allowed to bring tobacco into Singapore unless you pay duty. You will be slapped with a hefty fine if you fail to declare and pay.

You are permitted 1L each of wine, beer and spirits duty free. Alternatively, you are allowed 2L of wine and 1L of beer, or 2L of beer and 1L of wine. You need to have been out of Singapore for more than 48 hours and to anywhere but Malaysia.

It's illegal to bring chewing gum, firecrackers, obscene or seditious material, gun-shaped cigarette lighters, endangered species or their by-products and pirated recordings or publications with you.

DISCOUNTS
If you arrived on a Singapore Airlines or SilkAir flight, you can get discounts at shops, restaurants and attractions by presenting your boarding pass. See www.singaporeair.com/boardingpass for information.

ELECTRICITY
Plugs are of the three-pronged, square-pin type used in Malaysia and the UK. Electricity runs at 230V and 50 cycles.

EMBASSIES & CONSULATES
For a full list of foreign embassies and consulates in Singapore, check out the website of the Ministry of Foreign Affairs (www.mfa.gov.sg).

INTERNET ACCESS
Most hotels offer internet access. All backpacker hostels offer free internet access and wi-fi. Unlike many other modern, major cities around the world, very few cafes offer free wi-fi.

SingTel (www.singtel.com), StarHub (www.starhub.com) and M1 (www.m1.com.sg) are local providers of broadband internet via USB modem dongles. Bring your own or buy one from them. You can get prepaid data SIM cards if you have your own dongle.

LEGAL MATTERS
Singapore's reputation for harsh laws is not undeserved: don't expect any special treatment for being a foreigner. Despite the surprisingly low-key police presence on the street, they appear pretty fast when something happens. Police have broad powers and you would be unwise to refuse any requests they make of you. If you are arrested, you will be entitled to legal counsel and contact with your embassy.

Don't even think about importing or exporting drugs. At best, you'll get a long jail term; at worst, you'll get the death penalty.

Serious issues with retailers are unlikely (the worst you'll probably get is lethargic service), but if you've been ripped off or taken for a ride, contact the **Small Claims Tribunal** (Map p492; ☑6587 8423; www.statecourts.gov.sg; State Courts, 1 Havelock Sq; ⊘8.30am-1pm & 2-6pm Mon-Thu, to 5.30pm Fri; Ⓜ Chinatown). Tourist complaints are usually heard within two or three days.

MEDICAL SERVICES
Singapore's medical institutions are first-rate and generally cheaper than private healthcare in the West. But needless to say, travel insurance is advisable. Check with insurance providers as to which treatments and procedures are covered before you leave home.

Your hotel or hostel should be able to direct you to a local GP: there are plenty around. There are several 24-hour emergency rooms.

Gleneagles Hospital (Map p506; ☑6470 5688; www.gleneagles.com.sg; 6A Napier Rd; ⊘24hr; ☑7, 75, 77, 106, 123, 174)

International Medical Clinic (Map p506; ☑6733 4440; www.imc-healthcare.com; 14-06 Camden Medical Centre, 1 Orchard Blvd; ⊘8am-5.30pm Mon-Fri, 9am-1pm Sat; Ⓜ Orchard) Specialising in family and travel medicine.

International Medical Clinic (☑6465 4440; www.imc-healthcare.com; 02-04 Jelita Shopping Centre, 293 Holland Rd; ⊘9am-5.30pm, to 1pm Sat; ☑7, 61, 75, 165,) International standard medical care.

Raffles Medical Clinic (Map p504; ☑6311 2233; www.rafflesmedicalgroup.com; Level 2, Raffles Hospital, 585 North Bridge Rd; ⊘8am-10pm; Ⓜ Bugis) A walk-in clinic at Raffles Hospital.

Singapore General Hospital (☑6222 3322; www.sgh.com.sg; Block 1, Outram Rd; Ⓜ Outram Park) Also has an emergency room.

MONEY
The country's unit of currency is the Singapore dollar (S$), locally referred to as the 'sing dollar', which is made up of 100 cents. Singapore uses 5¢, 10¢, 20¢, 50¢ and S$1 coins, while notes come in denominations of S$2, S$5, S$10, S$50, S$100, S$500 and S$1000. The Singapore dollar is a highly stable and freely convertible currency.

ATMs
Cirrus-enabled ATMs are widely available at malls, banks, MRT stations and commercial areas.

Changing Money
Banks change money, but virtually nobody uses them for currency conversion because the rates are better at the moneychangers dotted all over the city. These tiny stalls can be found in just about every shopping centre (though not necessarily in the more modern malls). Rates can be haggled a little if you're changing amounts of S$500 or more.

SINGAPORE DIRECTORY A–Z

Credit Cards

Credit cards are widely accepted, apart from at local hawkers and food courts.

Tipping

Tipping is generally not customary. It's prohibited at Changi Airport.

Restaurants Many add a 10% service charge, so tipping is discouraged. A small tip is still appreciated when staff have gone out of their way. Don't tip at hawker centres and food courts.

Hotels At higher-end establishments tip porters S$2 to S$5 and housekeeping S$2.

Taxis It's courteous to round up or tell the driver to keep the change.

OPENING HOURS

Banks 9.30am to 4.30pm Monday to Friday (some to 6pm or later); 9.30am to noon or later Saturday

Government and Post Offices Between 8am and 9.30am to 4pm and 6pm Monday to Friday; 8am or 9am to 11.30am or 1.30pm Saturday.

Restaurants Generally noon to 2.30pm and 6pm to 11pm. Casual restaurants and food courts open all day.

Shops 10am or 11am to 6pm; larger shops and department stores til 9.30pm or 10pm. Some smaller shops in Chinatown and Arab St close Sunday.

POST

Postal delivery in Singapore is very efficient. Call 1605 to find the nearest post office or check www.singpost.com.sg.

PUBLIC HOLIDAYS

The only holiday that has a major effect on the city is Chinese New Year, when virtually all shops shut down for two days. Public holidays are as follows:

New Year's Day 1 January

Chinese New Year Two days in January/February

Good Friday March/April

Labour Day 1 May

Vesak Day May

Hari Raya Puasa June

National Day 9 August

Hari Raya Haji August

Deepavali October

Christmas Day 25 December

SMOKING

Smoking is prohibited in most indoor locations. Fines for smoking in prohibited places range from S$200 up to S$1000.

TELEPHONE

➡ Singapore's country code is 65.

➡ There are no area codes within Singapore; telephone numbers are eight digits unless you are calling toll-free (1800).

➡ You can make local and international calls from public phone booths. Most phone booths take phonecards.

➡ Singapore also has credit-card phones that can be used by running your card through the slot.

➡ Calls to Malaysia (from Singapore) are considered to be STD (trunk or long-distance) calls. Dial the access code 020, followed by the area code of the town in Malaysia that you wish to call (minus the leading zero) and then the phone number. Thus, for a call to 346 7890 in Kuala Lumpur (area code 03) you would dial 02-3-346 7890.

Mobile Phones

Mobile-phone numbers start with 9 or 8.

You can buy tourist SIM cards for around S$15 from post offices, convenience stores and telco stores – by law you must show your passport. Local carriers include:

M1 (www.m1.com.sg)

SingTel (www.singtel.com)

StarHub (www.starhub.com)

TIME

Singapore is eight hours ahead of GMT/UTC (London), two hours behind Australian Eastern Standard Time (Sydney and Melbourne), 13 hours ahead of American Eastern Standard Time (New York) and 16 hours ahead of American Pacific Standard Time (San Francisco and Los Angeles).

So, when it's noon in Singapore, it is 8pm in Los Angeles and 11pm in New York the previous day, and 4am in London and 2pm in Sydney and Melbourne.

TOILETS

Free public toilets are plentiful in Singapore and are usually of the sit-down variety. In some

---

EATING PRICE RANGES

Bear in mind that most restaurant prices will have 17% added to them at the end: a 10% service charge plus 7% for GST. You'll see this indicated by ++ on menus. The following price ranges represent the cost of a single dish or a main course, including service charge and GST.

$ less than S$10

$$ S$10–30

$$$ more than S$30

hawker centres you will be asked to pay a small fee; usually 10¢ per entry.

TOURIST INFORMATION

Singapore Visitors Centre @ Orchard (Map p506; ☑1800 736 2000; www.yoursingapore. com; 216 Orchard Rd; ⊗8.30am-9.30pm; ☎; Ⓜ Somerset) This main branch is filled with knowledgeable staff who can help you organise tours, buy tickets and book hotels.

There is a large Singapore Visitors Centre branch in **Chinatown** (Map p500; ☑1800 736 2000; www.yoursingapore.com; 2 Banda St; ⊗9am-9pm; ☎; Ⓜ Chinatown), and a small outlet in **ION** (Map p506; ☑1800 736 2000; www.yoursingapore.com; Level 1 Concierge, ION Orchard, 2 Orchard Turn; ⊗10am-10pm; ☎; Ⓜ Orchard), on Orchard Rd.

Before your trip, a good place to check for information is the website of the Singapore Tourism Board.

VISAS

Citizens of most countries are granted 90-day entry on arrival. Citizens of India, Myanmar and certain other countries must obtain a visa before arriving.

Visa extensions can be applied for at the **Immigration & Checkpoints Authority** (Map p504; ☑6391 6100; www.ica.gov.sg; Level 4, ICA Bldg, 10 Kallang Rd; ⊗8am-4pm Mon-Fri; Ⓜ Lavender) website.

ⓘ Getting There & Away

Singapore is one of Asia's major air hubs, serviced by both full-service and budget airlines. The city state has excellent and extensive regional and international connections. You can also catch trains and buses to Malaysia and Thailand.

For more on the overland transport connections between Singapore and Malaysia see p244.

AIR

Changi Airport (☑6595 6868; www.changi airport.com; Airport Blvd; ☎; Ⓜ Changi Airport), 20km northeast of Singapore's central business district (CBD), has four main terminals (the latest opened in 2017) and a fifth already in the works. Regularly voted the world's best airport, it is a major international gateway, with frequent flights to all corners of the globe. You'll find free internet, courtesy phones for local calls, foreign-exchange booths, medical centres, left luggage, hotels, day spas, showers, a gym, a swimming pool and no shortage of shops.

The **Jewel Changi Airport** is a 10-storey complex featuring attractions such as a canopy park, forest and rain vortex, as well as retail, accommodation and dining offerings.

ⓘ PRACTICALITIES

Newspapers English daily newspapers in Singapore include broadsheets the *Straits Times* and *Business Times,* and afternoon tabloid the *New Paper.*

Magazines Pornographic publications are strictly prohibited, but toned-down local editions of *Cosmopolitan* are allowed.

Weights and measures The metric system is used.

LAND

The Causeway linking Johor Bahru (JB) in Malaysia with Singapore handles most traffic between the countries. Trains and buses run from all over Malaysia straight through to Singapore, or you can get a taxi or bus to/from JB. There's also a crossing called the Second Link linking Tuas, in western Singapore, with Geylang Patah in Malaysia – some buses to Melaka and Malaysia's west coast head this way.

Bus

Numerous private companies run comfortable bus services between Singapore and many destinations in Malaysia, including Melaka and Kuala Lumpur, as well as to/from destinations such as Hat Yai in Thailand. Many of these services run from **Golden Mile Complex** (5001 Beach Rd; Ⓜ Bugis, Nicoll Hwy). The terminal is home to numerous bus agencies specialising in journeys between Singapore and Malaysia, and Singapore and Thailand (shop around). You can also book online at www.busonlineticket.com.

Train

It's no longer possible to catch a direct train from Singapore to Kuala Lumpur. Instead, Malaysian KTM (www.ktmb.com.my) operates a shuttle train from **Woodlands Train Checkpoint** (11 Woodlands Crossing; ☐170, Causeway Link Express from Queen St terminal) to JB Sentral with a connection to Kuala Lumpur. Tickets for the shuttle (S$5) can be bought at the counter. Trains leave from here to Kuala Lumpur, with connections on to Thailand. You can book tickets at the Woodlands or JB Sentral stations or online at www.easybook.com.

A handful of times a year, the luxurious **Eastern & Oriental Express** (☑6395 0678; www. belmond.com/eastern-and-oriental-express) connects Singapore with Malaysia and Thailand.

SEA

Ferry services from Malaysia and Indonesia arrive at various ferry terminals in Singapore. **Changi Point Ferry Terminal** (☑6545 2305; 51 Lorong Bekukong; ⊗24hr; ☐2)

FERRIES TO RIAU ARCHIPELAGO (INDONESIA)

Direct ferries run between the Riau Archipelago islands of Pulau Batam and Pulau Bintan and Singapore. The ferries are modern, fast and air-conditioned. A small ferry also runs to Tanjung Belungkor in Malaysia.

BatamFast (☑6270 2228; www.batamfast.com; 02-50/51 Harbourfront Centre, 1 Maritime Sq) Ferries from Batam Centre, Sekupang and Harbour Bay in Pulau Batam terminate at Harbourfront Ferry Terminal. Ferries from Nongsapura, also in Pulau Batam, terminate at the **Tanah Merah Ferry Terminal** (☑6542 6310; www.batamfast.com; 50 Tanah Merah Ferry Rd).

Bintan Resort Ferries (☑6542 4369; www.brf.com.sg; 01-21 Tanah Merah Ferry Terminal, 50 Tanah Merah Ferry Rd; ☺7am-8pm, 6.30am-8pm Sat & Sun; ⓜTanah Merah, then bus 35) Ferries to Bandar Bentan Telani in Pulau Bintan depart from Tanah Merah Ferry Terminal.

Sindo Ferries (☑HarbourFront terminal 6331 4123, Tanah Merah terminal 6331 4122; www.sindoferry.com.sg; 01-15 Tanah Merah Ferry Terminal, 50 Tanah Merah Ferry Rd; ⓺35) Ferries to Batam Centre, Sekupang and Tanjung Balai depart from HarbourFront Ferry Terminal. Ferries to Tanjung Pinang depart from Tanah Merah Ferry Terminal.

Limbongan Maju Ferry Services (☑Tangjung Belungkor 07-827 8001; www.limbongan maju.com) Ferries from Tanjung Belungkor, Malaysia, arrive at Changi Point Ferry Terminal.

HarbourFront Cruise & Ferry Terminal
(☑6513 2200; www.singaporecruise.com; 1 Maritime Sq; ☎; ⓜHarbourFront)
Tanah Merah Ferry Terminal (☑6513 2200; www.singaporecruise.com.sg; 50 Tanah Merah Ferry Rd; ⓺35)

ℹ Getting Around

Singapore is the easiest city in Asia to get around. For online bus information, including the useful IRIS service (which offers live next-bus departure times), see www.sbstransit.com.sg or download the 'SBS Transit iris' app. For train information, see www.smrt.com.sg. For consolidated transport information, see www.mytransport.sg.

BICYCLE

Avoid cycling on roads. Drivers are sometimes aggressive and the roads themselves are uncomfortably hot. A much safer and more pleasant option for cyclists is Singapore's large network of parks and park connectors, not to mention the dedicated mountain-biking areas at Bukit Timah Nature Reserve, Tampines and Pulau Ubin.

Other excellent places for cycling include East Coast Park, Sentosa, Pasir Ris Park and the route linking Mt Faber Park, Telok Blangah Hill Park and Kent Ridge Park.

Only fold-up bikes are allowed on trains and buses, with only *one* fold-up bike allowed on buses at any time, so you might as well ride if you have to.

Bikes can be rented at several places along East Coast Park and on Sentosa Island and Pulau Ubin, with adult prices starting from S$7 a day on Pulau Ubin and around S$12 an hour elsewhere.

Bike-sharing platforms made an appearance in Singapore in 2017 and they're already extremely popular. So far there are two players in the market, **Mobike** (www.mobike.com) and **ofo** (www.ofo.so) – each are still working out the kinks in their systems but basically you download the app, pay a deposit (between S$40 and S$50), find a bike and off you go. You're charged for the time you ride.

BOAT

Visit the Southern Islands of Singapore from the Marina South Pier. There are regular **bumboat** (one-way S$3, bicycle surcharge S$2; ☺24hr; ⓺2) (motorised sampan) services from Changi Point Ferry Terminal to **Pulau Ubin** (S$3). To get there, take bus 2 from Tanah Merah MRT.

BUS

Singapore's extensive bus service is clean, efficient and regular, reaching every corner of the island. The two main operators are **SBS Transit** (☑1800 225 5663; www.sbstransit.com.sg) and **SMRT** (☑1800 336 8900; www.smrt.com.sg). Both offer similar services. For information and routes, check the websites. Alternatively download the 'SG Buses' smartphone app, which will give you real-time bus arrivals.

Bus fares range from S$1 to S$2.10 (less with an EZ-Link card). When you board the bus, drop the exact money into the fare box (no change is given), or tap your EZ-Link card or Singapore Tourist Pass on the reader as you board, then again when you get off.

Train operator SMRT also runs late-night bus services between the city and various suburbs from 11.30pm to 4.35am on Fridays, Saturdays and the eve of public holidays. The flat rate per journey is S$4.50. See the website for route details.

Tourist Buses

SIA Hop-On (Map p492; ☑ 6338 6877; www.siahopon.com; Suntec Hub, Suntec Mall; 24hr ticket adult/child S$39/29; ⊙ 8.30am-6pm) Singapore Airlines' tourist bus traverses the main tourist arteries every 15 to 60 minutes daily, over four different lines. Trips start from Suntec Hub, with the first bus departing at 9am and the last bus departing at 6pm, terminating back at Suntec Hub at 7.10pm. Buy tickets from the driver; see the website for route details. Half-price for SIA passengers.

CAR & MOTORCYCLE

Singaporeans drive on the left-hand side of the road and it is compulsory to wear seat belts in the front and back of the car. The *Mighty Minds Singapore Street Directory* (S$16.90) is invaluable and available from petrol stations, bookshops, FairPrice supermarkets and stationery stores. However, the island has good internet coverage so Google Maps is also a reasonable option.

Driving Licence

If you plan on driving in Singapore, bring your current home driver's licence. Some car-hire companies may also require you to have an international driving permit.

Hire

If you want a car for local driving only, it's worth checking smaller operators, where the rates are often cheaper than the big global rental firms. If you're going into Malaysia, you're better off renting in Johor Bahru, where the rates are significantly lower (besides which, Malaysian police are renowned for targeting Singapore licence plates).

Rates start from around S$60 a day. Special deals may be available, especially for longer-term rental. Most rental companies require that drivers are at least 23 years old.

All major car-hire companies have booths at Changi Airport as well as in the city.

Avis (☑ 6305 3183; www.avis.com.sg; 01-07 Waterfront Plaza, 390A Havelock Rd; ⊙ 9am-5pm; ☒ 5, 16, 75, 175, 195, 970)

Hawk (☑ 6431 0299; www.hawkrentacar.com.sg; 04-64, Pioneer Centre, 1 Soon Lee St; ⊙ 9am-6pm Mon-Fri, to 1pm Sat; Ⓜ Pioneer)

Hertz (☑ 6542 5300; www.hertz.com; Terminals 2 & 3, Changi Airport; ⊙ 7am-11pm; Ⓜ Changi Airport)

Restricted Zone & Car Parking

At various times through the day, from Monday to Saturday, much of central Singapore is considered a restricted zone. Cars are free to enter but they must pay a toll. Vehicles are automatically tracked by sensors on overhead Electronic Road Pricing (ERP) gantries, so cars must be fitted with an in-vehicle unit, into which drivers must insert a cash card (available at petrol stations and 7-Elevens). The toll is extracted from the card. The same system is also in operation on certain expressways. Rental cars are subject to the same rules. Check www.onemotoring.com.sg for ERP rates and hours of operation.

Parking in the city centre is expensive, but relatively easy to find – almost every major mall has a car park. Many car parks are now using the same in-vehicle unit and cash card as the ERP gantries. Outdoor car parks and street parking spaces are usually operated by the government – you can buy booklets of parking coupons, which must be displayed in the window, from petrol stations and 7-Elevens; however, these are being phased out in favour of the 'Parking SG' smartphone app.

MASS RAPID TRANSIT (MRT)

The efficient Mass Rapid Transit (MRT) subway system is the easiest, quickest and most comfortable way to get around Singapore. The system operates from 5.30am to midnight, with trains at peak times running every two to three minutes, and off-peak every five to seven minutes.

In the inner city, the MRT runs underground, emerging overground out towards the suburban housing estates. It consists of six colour-coded lines: North–South (red), North–East (purple), East–West (green), Circle Line (orange), Downtown (blue) and Thomson–East Coast (brown).

You'll find a map of the network at www.smrt.com.sg.

Fares & Fare Cards

Single-trip tickets cost from S$1.40 to S$2.50, but if you're using the MRT a lot it can become a hassle buying and refunding tickets for every journey. A lot more convenient is the EZ-Link card. Alternatively, a **Singapore Tourist Pass** (www.thesingaporetouristpass.com.sg) offers unlimited train and bus travel (S$10 plus a S$10 refundable deposit) for one day.

➔ If you're staying in Singapore for more than a day or two, the easiest way to pay for travel on public transport is with the EZ-Link card (www.ezlink.com.sg). The card allows you to travel by train and bus by simply swiping it over sensors as you enter and leave a station or bus.

➔ EZ-Link cards can be purchased from the customer service counters at MRT stations for S$12 (this includes a S$5 nonrefundable deposit).

➔ The card can also be bought at 7-Elevens for S$10 (including the S$5 nonrefundable deposit).

➔ Cards can be topped up with cash or by ATM cards at station ticket machines. The minimum

TRISHAWS

Trishaws peaked just after WWII when motorised transport was practically nonexistent and trishaw drivers could make a tidy income. Today there are only around 250 trishaws left in Singapore, mainly plying the tourist routes. Trishaws have banded together and are now managed in a queue system by **Trishaw Uncle** (Map p504; 🕿 6337 7111; www. trishawuncle.com.sg; Albert Mall Trishaw Park, Queen St; 30min tour adult/child from S$39/29, 45min tour S$49/39; M Bugis).

You can also find freelance trishaw riders outside the Raffles Hotel (p532). Always agree on the fare beforehand: expect to pay S$40 for 30 minutes.

top-up value is S$10 while the maximum stored value allowed on your card is S$500.

TAXI

You can flag down a taxi any time, but in the city centre taxis are technically not allowed to stop anywhere except at designated taxi stands.

Finding a taxi in the city at certain times is harder than it should be. These include during peak hours, at night, or when it's raining. Many cab drivers change shifts between 4pm and 5pm, making it notoriously difficult to score a taxi then.

The fare system is also complicated, but thankfully it's all metered, so there's no haggling over fares. The basic flagfall is S$3 to S$3.40 then S$0.22 for every 400m.

There's a whole raft of surcharges to note, among them:

➡ 50% of the metered fare from midnight to 6am

➡ 25% of the metered fare between 6am and 9.30am Monday to Friday, and 6pm to midnight daily

➡ S$5 for airport trips from 5pm to midnight Friday to Sunday, and S$3 at all other times

➡ S$3 city-area surcharge from 5pm to midnight

➡ S$2.30 to S$8 for telephone bookings

Payment by credit card incurs a 10% surcharge. You can also pay using your EZ-Link transport card. For a comprehensive list of fares and surcharges, visit www.taxisingapore.com.

Comfort Taxi & CityCab (🕿 6552 1111; www.cdgtaxi.com.sg)

Premier Taxis (🕿 6363 6888; www.premiertaxi.com.sg)

SMRT Taxis (🕿 6555 8888; www.smrt.com.sg)

Also download Grab, which is Singapore's answer to Uber.

Understand Malaysia, Singapore & Brunei

HISTORY 564

These three countries emerged from and were forged by the lucrative trade in spices, rubber and oil around the Malay Peninsula.

PEOPLE, CULTURE & POLITICS...............576

Malays, Chinese and Indians mingle in these multicultural nations. There are also scores of indigenous people, particularly on Borneo.

RELIGION 582

Islam is the region's main religion but Hinduism predates it in these parts. Christianity and the various Chinese beliefs are also present.

ARTS, ARCHITECTURE & MEDIA..............586

Malaysia and Singapore's contemporary art and architecture scenes are thriving. However in all three nations media freedom in curtailed.

ENVIRONMENT...........................592

The conservation of mega-diverse environments in the region is balanced with economic development.

History

As the countries we know today, Malaysia, Singapore and Brunei have been around since 1963, 1965 and 1984 respectively. The region's history, of course, stretches back much further, although pinning down exactly how far back is tricky due to a lack of archaeological evidence and early written records. Events from the rise of the Melaka Sultanate in the 16th century, however, were well documented locally and by the nations that came to trade with, and later rule over, the peninsula and Borneo.

The Negrito & Early Migrants

Discovered in 1991, the complete 11,000-year-old skeleton 'Perak Man' has genetic similarities to the Negrito, ethnic ancestors of the Semang tribe of Orang Asli who still live in the mountainous rainforests of northern Malaysia. The Negrito were joined by Malaysia's first immigrants, the Senoi, from southern Thailand, and later by the Proto-Malay, ancestors of today's Malays, who came by sea from Indonesia between 1500 BCE and 500 BCE.

By the 2nd century Malaya was known as far away as Europe. Ptolemy, the Greek geographer, labelled it Aurea Chersonesus (Golden Chersonese); Indian traders, who came in search of precious metals, tin and aromatic jungle woods, referred to the land as Savarnadvipa (Land of Gold).

It's thought that the word Malay (or Melayu) is based on the ancient Tamil word *malia*, meaning 'hill'. Other Malay words like *bahasa* (language), *raja* (ruler) and *jaya* (success) are Sanskrit terms imported to the area by Indian visitors as early as the 2nd century CE.

Early Trade & Empires

The first formalised religions on the peninsula – Hinduism and Buddhism – arrived with the Indian traders in the 2nd century, giving rise to the first recorded Hindu kingdom on the peninsula, Langkasuka (from the Sanskrit for 'resplendent land').

From the 7th century to the 13th century, the area fell under the sway of the Srivijaya Empire, based in southern Sumatra. This Buddhist empire controlled the entire Malacca Straits, Java and southern Borneo and became fabulously rich through trade with India and China. Under the protection of the Srivijayans, a significant Malay trading state grew up in the Bujang Valley area in the far northwest of the Thai–Malay peninsula.

TIMELINE	CE 150	200	600
	European knowledge of the Malay peninsula is confirmed in Ptolemy's book *Geographia*. It's likely that Romans visited the region during trading expeditions to India and China.	Langkasuka, one of the first Hindu-Malay kingdoms, is established on the peninsula around the area now known as Kedah. It lasted in one form or another until the 15th century.	From their base in southern Sumatra, most likely around modern-day Palembang, the Buddhist Srivijaya Empire dominates Malaya, Singapore, Indonesia and Borneo for another six centuries.

THE ADOPTION OF ISLAM

Peninsular Malaysia was Buddhist and Hindu for a thousand years before the local rulers adopted Islam. The religion is believed to have spread through contact with Indian Muslim traders; in 1136 the *Kedah Annals* record that Hindu ruler Phra Ong Mahawangsa converted to Islam and founded the sultanate of Kedah, the oldest on Peninsular Malaysia.

The first sultan of Brunei, Muhammad Shah, converted to Islam in 1363 upon his marriage to a princess from Johor-Temasik. Maharaja Mohammed Shah of Melaka, who reigned between 1424 and 1444, also converted. The maharaja's son, Mudzaffar Shah, later took the title of sultan and made Islam the state religion. With its global trade links, Melaka became a regional hub for the dissemination of Islam and the Malay language.

The growing power of the southern Thai kingdom of Ligor and the Hindu Majapahit Empire of Java finally led to the demise of the Srivijayans in the 14th century.

The Melaka Empire

The history of the Malay state begins in earnest in the late 14th century when Parameswara, a renegade Hindu prince/pirate from a little kingdom in southern Sumatra, washed up around 1401 in the tiny fishing village that would become Melaka. As a seafarer, Parameswara recognised a good port when he saw it and he immediately lobbied the Ming emperor of China for protection from the Thais in exchange for generous trade deals. Thus the Chinese came to Malaysia.

Equidistant between India and China, Melaka became a major stop for freighters from India loaded with pepper and cloth, and junks from China loaded with porcelain and silks, which were traded for local metal and spices. Business boomed as regional ships and *perahu* (Malay-style sampans) arrived to take advantage of trading opportunities. The Melakan sultans soon ruled over the greatest empire in Malaysia's history.

A History of Malaysia by Barbara and Leonard Andaya brilliantly explores the evolution of 'Malayness' in Malaysia's history and the challenges of building a multiracial, post-independence nation.

Portuguese & Dutch Rule

By the 15th century, Europe had developed an insatiable appetite for spices, which were conveyed there via a convoluted trade route through India and Arabia. The Portuguese decided to cut out the intermediary and go directly to the source: Melaka. Reaching the Malay coast in 1509, the Portuguese were greeted warmly by the local sultan, but relations soon soured. The invaders laid siege to Melaka in 1511, capturing the city and driving the sultan and his forces back to Johor.

The Portuguese secured Melaka by building the robust Porta de Santiago (A'Famosa fortress) and their domination lasted 130 years, though the entire period was marked by skirmishes with local sultans. Com-

1402	1446	1485	1509
Hindu prince and pirate Parameswara (1344–1414) founds the great trading port and sultanate of Melaka; seven years later he marries a Muslim princess and adopts the Persian title Iskandar Shah.	A naval force from Siam (Thailand) attacks Melaka. Warded off, the Siamese return in 1456 but are again rebuffed. Such attacks encourage Melaka's rulers to develop closer relations with China.	Sultan Bolkiah of Brunei controls land as far south as present-day Kuching in Sarawak and north towards the islands of the Philippines.	Portuguese traders sail into Melaka. Although at first greeted warmly, acting on the advice of his Indian Muslim councillors, the Melakan sultan later attacks the Portuguese ships, taking 19 prisoners.

Sejarah Melayu (Malay Annals), a literary work covering the establishment of the Melaka sultanate and 600 years of Malay history, is believed to have been compiled by Tun Sri Lanang, the *bendahara* (chief minister) of the Johor Royal Court in the early 17th century.

pared with Indian Muslim traders, the Portuguese contributed little to Malay culture; attempts to introduce Christianity and the Portuguese language were never a big success, though a dialect of Portuguese, Kristang, is still spoken in Melaka.

Vying with the Portuguese for control of the spice trade, the Dutch formed an allegiance with the sultans of Johor to oust the Portuguese from Melaka. A joint force of Dutch and Johor soldiers and sailors besieged Melaka in 1641 and wrested the city from the Portuguese. In return for its cooperation, Johor was made exempt from most of the tariffs and trade restrictions imposed on other vassal states. Despite maintaining control of Melaka for about 150 years, the Dutch never really realised the full potential of the city. High taxes forced merchants to seek out other ports and the Dutch focused their main attention on Batavia (now Jakarta) as their regional headquarters.

Enter the East India Company

British interest in the region began with the need for a halfway base for East India Company (EIC) ships plying the India–China maritime route. The first base was established on the island of Penang in 1786.

Meanwhile, events in Europe were conspiring to consolidate British interests on the Malay peninsula. When Napoleon overran the Netherlands in 1795, the British, fearing French influence in the region, took over Dutch Java and Melaka. When Napoleon was defeated in 1818, the British handed the Dutch colonies back – but not before leaving the A'Famosa fortress in ruins.

THE NAVEL OF THE MALAY COUNTRIES

'It is impossible to conceive a place combining more advantages...it is the Navel of the Malay countries', wrote a delighted Stamford Raffles soon after landing in Singapore in 1819. This statement proves his foresight because at the time the island was an inhospitable swamp surrounded by dense jungle, with a population of 150 fishermen and a small number of Chinese farmers. Raffles returned to his post in Bencoolen, Sumatra, but left instructions on Singapore's development as a free port with the new British Resident, Colonel William Farquhar.

In 1822 Raffles returned to Singapore and governed it for one more year. He initiated a town plan that included levelling a hill to form a new commercial district (now Raffles Pl) and erecting government buildings around Forbidden Hill (now Fort Canning Hill). Wide streets of shophouses with covered walkways, shipyards, churches and a botanic garden were all built to achieve his vision of a Singapore that would one day be 'a place of considerable magnitude and importance'.

1511	1629	1641	1786
Following the Portuguese conquest of Melaka, the sultan and his court flee, establishing two new sultanates on the peninsula: Perak to the north and Johor to the south.	The Portuguese in Melaka and the sultanate of Johor unite to successfully defend themselves against the navy of Iskandar Muda, the sultan of Aceh in Sumatra, who had already conquered Kedah.	After a siege lasting several months, the Dutch, with the help of the Johor sultanate, wrest Melaka from the Portuguese. Melaka starts to decline as a major trading port.	British Captain Francis Light cuts a deal with the sultan of Kedah to establish a settlement on the largely uninhabited island of Penang. Under a free-trade policy the island's new economy thrives.

The British lieutenant-governor of Java, Stamford Raffles – yes, *that* Stamford Raffles – soon persuaded the EIC that a settlement south of the Malay peninsula was crucial to the India–China maritime route. In 1819, he landed in Singapore and negotiated a trade deal with Johor that saw the island ceded to Britain in perpetuity, in exchange for a significant cash tribute.

In 1824, Britain and the Netherlands signed the Anglo–Dutch Treaty, dividing the region into two distinct spheres of influence. The Dutch controlled what is now Indonesia, and the British controlled Penang, Melaka, Dinding (centred around Pulau Pangkor) and Singapore, which were soon combined to create the 'Straits Settlements'.

It was British colonial practice across the region to administer the population according to neat racial categories, with the Europeans, Indians, Chinese and Malays living and working in their own distinct quarters.

Borneo Developments

Britain did not include Borneo in the Anglo–Dutch treaty, preferring that the EIC concentrate efforts on consolidating its power on the peninsula rather than furthering their geographical scope. Into the breach jumped opportunistic British adventurer James Brooke. In 1841, having helped the local viceroy quell a rebellion, Brooke was installed as raja of Sarawak, with the fishing village of Kuching as his capital.

Through brutal naval force and skilful negotiation, Brooke extracted further territory from the Brunei sultan and eventually brought peace to a land where piracy, headhunting and violent tribal rivalry had been the norm. The 'White Raja' dynasty of the Brookes was to rule Sarawak until 1941 and the arrival of the Japanese.

Meanwhile, the once-mighty empire of Brunei, which had held sway over all the islands of Borneo and much of the present-day Philippines, continued to shrink. In 1865 the American consul to Brunei persuaded the ailing sultan to grant him what is now Sabah in return for an annual payment. The rights eventually passed to an Englishman, Alfred Dent. In 1881, with the support of the British government, Dent formed the British North Borneo Company to administer the new settlement. To prevent a scramble for Brunei's remains, in 1888 the British government acceded to a request by the sultan to declare his territory a British protectorate.

Sarawak's White Rajas – a dynasty of British rulers installed by the Sultan of Brunei – included tribal leaders in their ruling council, discouraged large European companies from destroying native jungle to plant massive rubber plantations and encouraged Chinese migration.

British Malaya

In Peninsular Malaya, Britain's policy of 'trade, not territory' was challenged when trade was disrupted by civil wars within the Malay sultanates of Negeri Sembilan, Selangor, Pahang and Perak. In 1874 the British started to take political control by appointing the first colonial governor of Perak. In 1896 Perak, Selangor, Negeri Sembilan and Pahang were united under the banner of the Federated Malay States, each governed by a British Resident.

1790	1819	1823	1826
The sultan of Kedah's attempt to retake Penang from the British fails. He is forced to cede the island to the British East India Company for 6000 Spanish dollars per annum.	By backing the elder brother in a succession dispute in Johor, Stamford Raffles gains sole rights to build a trading base on the island of Singapore.	The Johor sultan fully cedes Singapore to Britain. A year later the Dutch and British carve up the region into what eventually becomes Malaya and Indonesia.	Having swapped Bencoolen on Sumatra for the Dutch-controlled Melaka, the British East India Company combines this with Penang and Singapore to create the Straits Settlements.

Kelantan, Terengganu, Perlis and Kedah were then purchased from the Thais, in exchange for the construction of the southern Thai railway, much to the dismay of local sultans. The 'Unfederated Malay States' eventually accepted British 'advisers', though the sultan of Terengganu held out until 1919 – to this day, the states of the northeast peninsula form the heartland of the fundamentalist Malay Muslim nationalist movement.

Creating a Multicultural Nation

Although official British policy was that Malaya belonged to the Malays, colonial rule radically altered the ethnic composition of the country. Chinese and Indian migrant workers were brought into the country in droves, as they shared a similar economic agenda and had less nationalist grievance against the colonial administration than the native Malays.

The Chinese were encouraged to work the mines and the Indians to tap the rubber trees and build the railways. The Ceylonese were clerks in the civil service, and the Sikhs were employed in the police force.

Even though the 'better bred' Malays were encouraged to join a separate arm of the civil service, there was growing resentment among the vast majority of Malays that they were being marginalised in their own country. A 1931 census revealed that the Chinese numbered 1.7 million and the Malays 1.6 million. Malaya's economy was revolutionised, but the impact of this liberal immigration policy continues to reverberate today.

By the eve of WWII, Malays from all states were pushing for independence.

WWII PERIOD

A few hours before the bombing of Pearl Harbor in December 1941, Japanese forces landed on the northeast coast of Malaya. Within a few months they had taken over the entire peninsula and Singapore. The poorly defended Borneo states fell even more rapidly.

Singapore's new governor, General Yamashita, slung the Europeans into the infamous Changi Prison, and Chinese communists and intellectuals, who had vociferously opposed the Japanese invasion of China, were targeted for Japanese brutality. Thousands were executed in a single week. In Borneo, early resistance by the Chinese was also brutally put down.

The Japanese achieved very little in Malaya. The British had destroyed most of the tin-mining equipment before their retreat, and the rubber plantations were neglected. The Malayan People's Anti-Japanese Army (MPAJA), comprising remnants of the British army and Chinese from the fledgling Malayan Communist Party, waged a jungle-based guerrilla struggle throughout the war.

The Japanese surrendered to the British in Singapore in 1945. Despite the eventual Allied victory, Britain had been humiliated by the easy loss of Malaya and Singapore to the Japanese, and it was clear that their days of controlling the region were now numbered.

1839	1874	1888	1896
British buccaneer James Brooke lands in Sarawak and helps quell a local rebellion. In gratitude, the Brunei sultanate installs him as the first White Raja of Sarawak two years later.	British start to take control of Peninsular Malaysia after the Pangkor Treaty with the sultan of Perak; Sir James Birch is installed as Perak's first British Resident.	Having lost much territory to the British Empire, Brunei's sultan signs a treaty to make his country a British protectorate. A British Resident is installed in 1906.	Perak, Selangor, Negeri Sembilan and Pahang join as Federated Malay States; the sultans concede political power to British Residents but keep control of matters relating to Malay traditions and Islam.

Federation of Malaya

In 1946 the British persuaded the sultans to agree to the Malayan Union, which amalgamated all the Peninsular Malayan states into a central authority and offered citizenship to all residents regardless of race. In the process, the sultans were reduced to the level of paid advisers, the system of special privileges for Malays was abandoned and ultimate sovereignty passed to the king of England.

The normally acquiescent Malay population were less enthusiastic about the venture than the sultans. Rowdy protest meetings were held throughout the country, and the first Malay political party, the United Malays National Organisation (UMNO), was formed, leading to the dissolution of the Malayan Union and, in 1948, the creation of the Federation of Malaya, which reinstated the sovereignty of the sultans and the special privileges of the Malays.

Merdeka & Malaysia

Malaysia's march to independence from British rule was led by UMNO, which formed a strategic alliance with the Malayan Chinese Association (MCA) and the Malayan Indian Congress (MIC). The new Alliance Party led by Tunku Abdul Rahman, the Sultan of Kedah's son, won a landslide victory in the 1955 election and, on 31 August 1957, Merdeka (Independence) was declared. Sarawak, Sabah (then North Borneo) and Brunei remained under British rule.

In 1961 Tunku Abdul Rahman proposed a merger of Singapore, Malaya, Sabah, Sarawak and Brunei, which the British agreed to the following year. At the 11th hour Brunei pulled out of the deal, as Sultan Sri Muda Omar Ali Saifuddien III (and, one suspects, Shell Oil) didn't want to see the revenue from its vast oil reserves channelled to the peninsula.

When modern Malaysia was born in July 1963, it immediately faced a diplomatic crisis. The Philippines broke off relations, claiming that Sabah was part of its territory, while Indonesia laid claim to the whole of Borneo, invading parts of Sabah and Sarawak before finally giving up its claim in 1966.

The marriage between Singapore and Malaya was also doomed from the start. Ethnic Chinese outnumbered Malays in both Malaysia and Singapore and the new ruler of the island-state, Lee Kuan Yew, refused to extend constitutional privileges to the Malays in Singapore. Riots broke out in Singapore in 1964; in August 1965 Tunku Abdul Rahman was forced to boot Singapore out of the federation.

Ethnic Tensions

Impoverished Malays became increasingly resentful of the economic success of Chinese Malaysians, while the Chinese grew resentful of the

F Spencer Chapman's *The Jungle is Neutral* follows a British guerrilla force based in the Malaysian jungles during the Japanese occupation of Malaya and Singapore.

Revolusi '48 (www.revolusi48. blogspot.co.uk), the sequel to Fahmi Reza's doco *10 Tahun Sebelum Merdeka* (10 Years Before Merdeka), chronicles the largely forgotten armed revolution for national liberation launched against British colonial rule in Malaya.

HISTORY FEDERATION OF MALAYA

1909	1941	1942	1944
Britain does a deal with Thailand to gain control of Kelantan, Terengganu, Perlis and Kedah. Johor succumbs to a British Resident in 1914, completing the set of 'Unfederated Malay States'.	The Japanese land on Malaya's northeast coast. Within a month they've taken Kuala Lumpur, and a month later they are at Singapore's doorstep.	The British suffer a humiliating defeat in February as they capitulate Singapore to the Japanese. The occupiers rename it Syonan (Light of the South).	Z Special Unit parachute into Sarawak's Kelabit Highlands and win over the indigenous Dayak people. Armed with blowpipes and led by Australian commandos, this unlikely army scores several victories over the Japanese.

THE EMERGENCY

While the creation of the Federation of Malaya appeased Malays, the Chinese felt betrayed, particularly given their massive contribution to the war effort. Many joined the Malayan Communist Party (MCP), which promised an equitable and just society. In 1948 the MCP took to the jungles and embarked on a 12-year guerrilla war against the British. The insurrection was on par with the Malay civil wars of the 19th century; however, the British authorities downplayed it as an 'Emergency' so as to ensure that insurance of infrastructure remained valid.

The effects of the Emergency were felt most strongly in the countryside, where villages and plantation owners were repeatedly targeted by rebels. In 1951 the British high commissioner, Sir Henry Gurney, was assassinated on the road to Bukit Fraser (Fraser's Hill). His successor, General Sir Gerald Templer, set out to 'win the hearts and minds of the people'. Almost 500,000 rural Chinese were forcibly resettled into fortified *kampung baru* (new villages), restrictions were lifted on guerrilla-free areas, and the jungle-dwelling Orang Asli were co-opted to help the police track down the insurgents.

In 1960 the Emergency was declared over, although sporadic fighting continued and the formal surrender was signed only in 1989.

Singapore Story, the memoirs of Lee Kuan Yew, provides the official account on the birth and rise of the nation by the man who masterminded the whole thing.

political privileges granted to Malays. Things reached breaking point when the Malay-dominated government attempted to suppress all languages except Malay and introduced a national policy of education that ignored Chinese and Indian history, language and culture.

In the 1969 general elections, the Alliance Party lost its two-thirds majority in parliament and a celebration march by the opposition Democratic Action Party (DAP) and Gerakan (The People's Movement) in KL led to a full-scale riot, which Malay gangs used as a pretext to loot Chinese businesses, killing hundreds of Chinese in the process.

Stunned by the savageness of the riots, the government decided that if there was ever going to be harmony between the races then the Malay community needed to achieve economic parity. To this end the New Economic Policy (NEP), a socio-economic affirmative action plan, was introduced. The Alliance Party also invited opposition parties to join them and work from within, and the expanded coalition was renamed the Barisan Nasional (BN; National Front).

The First Mahathir Era

In 1981 former UMNO member Mahathir Mohamad became prime minister. Malaysia's economy went into overdrive, growing from one based on commodities such as rubber to one firmly rooted in industry and manufacturing. Government monopolies were privatised, and heavy industries like steel manufacturing (a failure) and the Malaysian car

1946	1948	1951	1953
The United Malays National Organisation (UMNO) is formed on 1 March, signalling the rise of Malay nationalism and a desire for political independence from Britain.	The Malaysian Communist Party (MCP) takes to the jungles and begins a 12-year guerrilla war against the British. Formal surrender is only signed in 1989.	Sir Henry Gurney, British high commissioner to Malaya, is assassinated by MCP rebels on the road to Bukit Fraser, a terrorist act that alienates many of the party's moderate Chinese members.	The Parti Perikatan (Alliance Party) is formed, an alliance between UMNO, the Malayan Chinese Association (MCA) and Malayan Indian Congress (MIC). Two years later the party wins Malaya's first national elections.

(successful but heavily protected) were encouraged. Multinationals were successfully wooed to set up in Malaysia, and manufactured exports began to dominate the trade figures.

One notable criticism of Mahathir's time as prime minister was that the main media outlets became little more than government mouthpieces. The sultans lost their right to give final assent on legislation, and the once proudly independent judiciary appeared to become subservient to government wishes, the most notorious case being that of Anwar Ibrahim. Mahathir also permitted widespread use of the Internal Security Act (ISA) to silence opposition leaders and social activists, most famously in 1987's Operation Lalang, when 106 people were arrested and the publishing licences of several newspapers were revoked.

Noel Barber's *The War of the Running Dogs* is a classic account of the 12-year Malayan Emergency. The title refers to what the communist fighters called the opposition who were loyal to the British.

Economic & Political Crisis

In 1997, after a decade of near constant 10% growth, Malaysia was hit by the regional currency crisis. Mahathir blamed it all on unscrupulous Western speculators deliberately undermining the economies of the developing world for their personal gain. He pegged the Malaysian ringgit to the US dollar, bailed out what were seen as crony companies, forced banks to merge and made it difficult for foreign investors to remove their money from Malaysia's stock exchange. Malaysia's subsequent recovery from the economic crisis, which was more rapid than that of many other Southeast Asian nations, further bolstered Mahathir's prestige.

Anwar Ibrahim, Mahathir's deputy prime minister and heir apparent, was at odds with Mahathir over how to deal with the economic crisis. Their falling out was so severe that in September 1998 Anwar was sacked and soon after charged with corruption and sodomy. Many Malaysians, feeling that Anwar had been falsely arrested, took to the streets chanting Anwar's call for *'reformasi'*. The demonstrations were harshly quelled and, in trials that were widely criticised as unfair, Anwar was sentenced to a total of 15 years' imprisonment. The international community rallied around Anwar, with Amnesty International proclaiming him a prisoner of conscience.

Dr Mahathir Mohamad's first book, *The Malay Dilemma*, in which he postulated that Malay backwardness was due to hereditary and cultural factors, was banned in 1970.

In the following year's general elections BN suffered huge losses, particularly in the rural Malay areas. The gainers were the fundamentalist Islamic party, PAS (Parti Islam se-Malaysia), which had vociferously supported Anwar, and a new political party, Keadilan (People's Justice Party), headed by Anwar's wife Wan Azizah.

Abdullah Badawi's Premiership

Mahathir retired in 2003 and his successor, the widely respected Abdullah Badawi, went on to lead BN to a landslide victory in the following year's election. In stark contrast to his feisty predecessor, the pious and

1957	1963	1965	1969
On 31 August Merdeka (independence) is declared in Malaya; Tunku Abdul Rahman becomes the first prime minister and the nine sultans agree to take turns as the nation's king.	In July the British Borneo territories of Sabah and Sarawak are combined with Singapore and Malaya to form Malaysia – a move that sparks confrontations with Indonesia and the Philippines.	In August, following Singapore's refusal to extend constitutional privileges to the Malays on the island and subsequent riots, Singapore is booted out of Malaysia. Lee Kuan Yew becomes Singapore's first prime minister.	Following the general election, on 13 March race riots erupt in KL, killing hundreds. In response the government devises the New Economic Policy of positive discrimination for Malays.

BUMIPUTRA PRIVILEGES

When introduced in 1971, the aim of the New Economic Policy (NEP) was that 30% of Malaysia's corporate wealth be in the hands of indigenous Malays and Orang Asli, or *bumiputra* (literally, sons of the soil), within 20 years. A massive campaign of positive discrimination began which handed majority control over the army, police, civil service and government to Malays. The rules extended to education, scholarships, share deals, corporate management and even the right to import a car.

By 1990 *bumiputra* corporate wealth had risen to 19%, but was still 11% short of the original target. Poverty in general fell dramatically, a new Malay middle class emerged and nationalist violence by Malay extremists receded. In the meantime, however, the *bumiputra* policy had led to cronyism, and discrimination against Indians and Chinese has increased.

Also, despite over 40 years of such government policies, there is still much to be done to improve the lives of the ethnic minorities of Sabah and Sarawak and the Orang Asli of Peninsular Malaysia – these *bumiptura* still lag far behind Malays in terms of poverty, employment, education and health care.

Sabri Zain's colourful website Sejarah Melayu: A History of the Malay Peninsula (www.sabrizain. org/malaya) contains a wealth of historical info including a virtual library of nearly 500 books and academic papers.

mild-mannered Abdullah impressed voters by taking a nonconfrontational, consensus-seeking approach. He set up a royal commission to investigate corruption in the police force (its recommendations have yet to be implemented) and called time on several of the massively expensive mega-projects that had been the hallmark of the Mahathir era, including a new bridge across the Strait of Johor to Singapore.

In the March 2008 election, UMNO and its coalition partners in BN saw their parliamentary dominance slashed to less than the customary two-thirds majority. Pakatan Rakyat (PR), the opposition People's Alliance, also took control of four of Malaysia's 13 states, including the key economic bases of Selangor and Penang. PR subsequently lost Perak following a complex power play between various defecting MPs.

In April 2008 Abdullah Badawi resigned in favour of his urbane deputy, Najib Razak. Son of Abdul Razak, Malaysia's second prime minister after independence and nephew of Razak's successor Hussein Onn, Najib had been groomed for this role ever since he first entered national politics at the age of 23 in 1976.

Anwar In & Out of Jail

Even though he had been released from jail in 2004, Anwar's return to national politics was delayed due to legal factors until after the March 2008 election. In August 2008 he won the by-election for the seat vacated by his wife and was declared leader of the opposition.

1974	1981	1984	1990
Following the formation of the Barisan Nasional (BN) in 1973, this new coalition led by Tun Abdul Razak wins the Malaysian general election by a landslide.	Dr Mahathir Mohamad becomes prime minister of Malaysia and introduces policies of 'Buy British Last' and 'Look East' to encourage the country to emulate Japan, South Korea and Taiwan.	A somewhat reluctant Sultan Hassanal Bolkiah leads Brunei to complete independence from Britain. The country subsequently veers towards Islamic fundamentalism, introducing full Islamic law in 1991.	After more than three decades in the job, Lee Kuan Yew steps down as prime minister of Singapore, handing over to Goh Chok Tong.

However, a month earlier a 23-year-old aide, Saiful Bukhari Azlan, had accused Anwar of sodomising him. The subsequent police investigation led to Anwar being arrested in August for a trial that did not start until February 2010. Anwar was acquitted of the charges in 2012, after the judge ruled DNA evidence had been tampered with.

The prosecution filed an appeal and in March 2014 the court overturned the verdict, sentencing Anwar to five years jail. He appealed but in February 2015, Malaysia's highest court upheld the conviction and sent the persecuted politician back to prison. Anwar's freedom was eventually secured three days after the opposition election victory of 2018, when he also received an official royal pardon.

GE13 & After

In the months leading up to Malaysia's 13th general election (GE13) in 2013, opposition parties, political commentators and the public had been calling attention to irregularities and unfairness in Malaysia's electoral system. Unbalanced constituency sizes, lack of access to the media for campaigning, and possibility of gerrymandering were the main concerns. Major rallies in KL saw tens, if not hundreds, of thousands marching for fair and free elections.

With the results in, BN had lost seven seats in the national parliament but emerged as the majority winner, thus again able to form a government with Najib Razak back as prime minister. The opposition coalition parties in PR won a majority of votes overall, but this counted for little given Malaysia's first past the post election system. PR did, however, hold onto government in Selangor, the state surrounding the federal territory of KL, which it had first won in the 2008 election.

On 8 May it was reported that 120,000 people gathered at a stadium just outside the city limits to protest the election results. However, a 'Malaysian Spring' was not in the offing. With racially divisive rhetoric in the air (Najib had referred to a 'Chinese tsunami' of voters as being responsible for the coalition's losses), people from all sides called for community harmony and the need to double down on the objectives of the 1Malaysia policy.

The Fate of Malaysia's Lost Flights

The discovery in July 2015 of plane debris on the Indian Ocean island of Reunion finally offered conclusive proof about the fate of Malaysian Airlines flight MH370, 16 months after its disappearance. Many questions about the final hours of MH370 and its 239 passengers still remain, not least of which is where the rest of the wreckage is. In January 2017, the biggest search in aviation history was called off and in August 2018, the

Brunei's ties with its former colonial master remain strong: UK judges sit in the High Court and Court of Appeal and a British Army Gurkha battalion is permanently stationed in Seria.

Covering events up to 2001, the second edition of Graham Saunders' *History of Brunei* is the only full-length study of how this tiny country came to be formed.

Amir Muhammad's 2009 documentary *Malaysian Gods* commemorates the decade after the Reformasi movement began with the sacking of Anwar Ibrahim as deputy prime minister in 1998.

1998	2003	2004	2007
Deputy prime minister Anwar Ibrahim, charged with corruption and sodomy, is sacked, arrested and jailed following disagreements with Dr Mahathir	Having announced his resignation the previous year, Dr Mahathir steps down as prime minister in favour of Abdullah Badawi. He remains very outspoken on national politics.	A month after the election in which BN takes 199 of 219 seats in the Lower House of parliament, Anwar Ibrahim sees his sodomy conviction overturned and is released from prison.	As Malaysia celebrates 50 years since independence it is also shaken by two anti-government rallies in November in which tens of thousands take to the streets of KL to protest.

MALAYSIA'S GOVERNMENT

Malaysia is made up of 13 states and three federal territories (Kuala Lumpur, Pulau Labuan and Putrajaya). Each state has an assembly and government headed by a *menteri besar* (chief minister). Nine states have hereditary rulers (sultans), while the remaining four have government-appointed governors, as do the federal territories. In a pre-established order, every five years one of the sultans takes his turn in the ceremonial position of Yang di-Pertuan Agong (king).

Malaysia has a two-house parliament: a 222-member House of Representatives (Dewan Rakyat) elected from single-member districts; and a 70-member Senate (Dewan Negara) with 26 members elected by the 13 state assemblies and 44 members appointed by the king on the prime minister's recommendation. National and state elections are held every five years.

1957–2007 Chronicle of Malaysia, edited by Philip Mathews, is a beautifully designed book showcasing 50 years of the country's history in news stories and pictures.

Malaysian government's 1500-page report on the crash was published. Investigators are still not certain what happened to the plane.

The scattered remains of Malaysia Airlines MH17, which crashed on 17 July 2014 in the Donetsk area of Ukraine with a loss of 298 lives, were all too apparent. The official Dutch Safety Board report on the causes of the crash, published in October 2015, confirmed that the flight was shot down by a surface-to-air missile.

While Malaysia gained much international sympathy for its handling of the MH17 tragedy, suspicion has lingered that the authorities could have done more in the early hours and days of MH370's disappearance. Confidence in Malaysian Airlines subsequently plummeted, necessitating its nationalisation and a major restructuring with a loss of 6000 jobs in 2015 when its chief executive Christoph Mueller declared the company 'technically bankrupt'.

Lee's Law: How Singapore Crushes Dissent, by Chris Lydgate, is a disturbing account of the rise and systematic destruction of Singapore's most successful opposition politician lawyer, JB Jeyaretnam.

Najib & 1MBD

In July 2015, Najib was implicated in an ongoing corruption scandal involving the government's 1MBD sovereign investment fund that aims to turn Kuala Lumpur (KL) into a global financial hub. The fund had racked up huge debts at the same time as it appears that nearly US$700 million had been transferred from it into Najib's personal bank accounts; subsequent news reports suggest the total may exceed US$1 billion.

Najib's denials of any wrongdoing were met by scepticism from the public, most of whom were shocked when the prime minister quashed local investigations into the affair, clamped down on media reporting and purged critics from his ruling party. Three years later, Najib and his government had their comeuppance when they lost the general election

2008	2009	2013	2014
In the March election BN retains power but suffers heavy defeats to the opposition coalition Pakatan Rakyat (PR); in August Anwar Ibrahim becomes PR leader following his re-election to parliament.	In April, Najib Razak succeeds Abdullah Badawi as prime minister; the 1Malaysia policy is introduced to build respect and trust between the country's different races.	General elections in May see BN hold on to power even though opposition parties in PR won a majority of votes overall	Malaysian Airlines suffers twin tragedies with the mysterious and as-yet-unexplained disappearance of MH370 and the loss of MH17 over Ukraine due to missile fire.

to a coalition of opposition parties led by that great survivor of Malaysian politics – Dr Mahathir Mohamad.

Najib's fall from grace has been swift. Multiple criminal charges were brought against both the former PM and his wife Rosmah Mansor, including ones for money laundering, as part of the 1MDB scandal. In July 2020, Najib was found guilty on all counts and sentenced to 12 years jail – a verdict that he is appealing at the time of research. The trial of his wife on charges of money laundering and tax evasion is set to start in November 2021.

Short-Lived Coalition

Less than two years after their historic victory, the Pakatan coalition collapsed in late February 2020, faultering on the bad history of 94-year-old PM Mahathir's relations with Anwar Ibrahim, leader of the Keadilan party. Into the breach stepped Muhyiddin Yassin, a career politician who had been a member of UMNO up until 2016. Defecting from the coalition along with over 30 other MPs, Muhyiddin formed an alliance with UMNO under which he was installed as Malaysia's new prime minister.

Barely weeks later the region was engulfed in the global COVID-19 pandemic, and borders were shut between Malaysia, Singapore and Brunei. In January 2021 a state of emergency was declared in Malaysia – its first in 50 years - that would run until 1 August or until COVID numbers significantly decreased. Critics have claimed that this draconian move, which saw parliament suspended, has allowed Muhyiddin's unstable government to cling on to power and evade scrutiny as it introduced new laws without parliamentary oversight.

Rehman Rashid's 2016 book *Peninsula: A Story of Malaysia*, the follow-up to *A Malaysian Journey*, published in 1993, provides an engagingly written overview of the country's recent political and social history.

Singapore: A Biography by Mark Ravinder Frost and Yu-Mei Balasingamchow is a well-written and handsomely illustrated history of Singapore.

2015	2018	2020	2021
Singapore mourns in March when Lee Kuan Yew, the nation's founding prime minister, dies at the age of 91. Later in the year Singapore celebrates 50 years of independence.	BN lose the general election to a coalition of opposition parties led by 93-year-old Mahathir Mohamad. Anwar Ibrahim is released from jail and Najib Razak is charged with corruption.	In the midst of the COVID pandemic, Singapore holds a general election. The ruling People's Action Party (PAP) returns to power, but with a reduced majority.	In January, Malaysia's king declares a state of emergency, under which parliament is suspended, and that would run until 1 August or until COVID cases are bought under control.

People, Culture & Politics

There's a strong sense of shared experience and national identity in Malaysia, Singapore and Brunei. Malays, Chinese and Indians live side by side with Peranakan (Straits Chinese) and other mixed race communities as well as the aboriginal nations – the Orang Asli of Peninsular Malaysia and Borneo's indigenous community. Ethnic diversity and harmony are touted as a regional strength, but none of these multicultural nations is the perfect melting pot. Religious and ethnic tensions remain a fact of life, particularly in Malaysia.

The Region's Peoples

The Malays

All Malays who are Muslims by birth are supposed to follow Islam, but many also adhere to older spiritual beliefs and *adat* (Malay customary law). With its roots in the Hindu period, *adat* places great emphasis on collective responsibility and maintaining harmony within the community – almost certainly a factor in the general goodwill between the different ethnic groups across the region.

Malaysian politicians have been known to call in a *bomoh* (a traditional spiritual healer and spirit medium) during election campaigns to assist in their strategy and provide some foresight.

The enduring appeal of the communal *kampung* (village) spirit shouldn't be underestimated – many an urban Malay hankers after it, despite the affluent Western-style living conditions they enjoy at home. In principle, villagers are of equal status, though a headman is appointed on the basis of his wealth, greater experience or spiritual knowledge. Traditionally the founder of the village was appointed village leader (*penghulu* or *ketua kampung*) and often members of the same family would also become leaders. A *penghulu* is usually a haji, one who has made the pilgrimage to Mecca.

The Muslim religious leader, the imam, holds a position of great importance in the community as the keeper of Islamic knowledge and the leader of prayer, but even educated urban Malaysians periodically turn to *pawang* (shamans who possess a supernatural knowledge of harvests and nature) or *bomoh* (spiritual healers with knowledge of curative plants and the ability to harness the power of the spirit world), for advice before making any life-changing decisions.

The Chinese

In Malaysia and Brunei, the Chinese represent the second-largest ethnic group after the Malays. In Singapore they are the largest. The Chinese immigrants are mainly, in order of largest dialect group, Hokkien, Hakka, Cantonese and Wu. They are also predominantly Buddhist but also observe Confucianism and Taosim, with a smaller number being Christian.

When Chinese people first began to arrive in the region in early 15th century they came mostly from the southern Chinese province of Fujian and eventually formed one half of the group known as Peranakans. They developed their own distinct hybrid culture whereas later settlers, from

Guangdong and Hainan provinces, stuck more closely to the culture of their homelands, including keeping their dialects.

The Indians

Like the Chinese settler, Indians in the region hail from many parts of the subcontinent and have different cultures depending on their religions – mainly Hinduism, Islam, Sikhism and Christianity. Most are Tamils, originally coming from the area now known as Tamil Nadu in South India where Hindu traditions are strong. Later, Muslim Indians from northern India followed along with Sikhs. These religious affiliations dictate many of the home life customs and practices of the region's Indians, although one celebration that all Hindus and much of the rest of the region takes part in is Deepavali.

A small, English-educated Indian elite has always played a prominent role in Malaysian and Singaporean society, and a significant merchant class exists. However, a large percentage of Indians – imported as indentured labourers by the British – remain a poor working class in both countries. There's a small population of Indians living in Brunei.

Status-conscious Malaysians love their honourable titles. At the federal level these include, in order of importance, Tun, Tan Sri and Datuk. At the state level you have Dato' Sri, Datuk Seri and Dato.

The Peranakans

Peranakan means 'half-caste' in Malay, which is exactly what the Peranakans are: descendants of Chinese immigrants who from the 16th century onwards principally settled in Singapore, Melaka and Penang and married Malay women.

The culture and language of the Peranakans is a fascinating melange of Chinese and Malay traditions. The Peranakans took the name and religion of their Chinese fathers, but the customs, language and dress of their Malay mothers. They also used the terms Straits-born or Straits Chinese to distinguish themselves from later arrivals from China.

The Peranakans were often wealthy traders who could afford to indulge their passion for sumptuous furnishings, jewellery and brocades. Their terrace houses were brightly painted, with patterned tiles embedded in the walls for extra decoration. When it came to the interior, Peranakan tastes favoured heavily carved and inlaid furniture.

Peranakan dress was similarly ornate. Women wore fabulously embroidered *kasot manek* (beaded slippers) and *kebaya* (blouses worn over a sarong), tied with beautiful *kerasong* (brooches), usually of fine filigree gold or silver. Men – who assumed Western dress in the 19th century, reflecting their wealth and contacts with the British – saved their finery for important occasions such as the wedding ceremony, a highly stylised and intricate ritual dictated by *adat*.

The Peranakan patois is a Malay dialect but one containing many Hokkien words – so much so that it is largely unintelligible to a Malay speaker. The Peranakans also included words and expressions of English and French, and occasionally practised a form of backward Malay by reversing the syllables. The language is very little used these days, but there are efforts to keep it alive via groups such as Singapore's Gunong Sayang Association, a cultural group which has staged productions in the patois since 1984.

Famous Singaporeans of Peranakan descent include Lee Kuan Yew (the first prime minister of Singapore), Dick Lee (singer, composer) and Goh Keng Swee (Singapore's deputy prime minister, 1973–1984).

Eurasians

If you meet a Malaysian or Singaporean whose surname is Clarke, de Souza or Hendricks, chances are they are Eurasian, a term used to describe people of mixed Asian and European descent. In the early colonial days, the majority of Eurasian migrants arrived from the Malaysian trading port of Melaka, which alongside Goa, Macau and Ceylon (modern Sri Lanka) claimed notable mixed-race communities, a legacy of Portuguese, Dutch and British colonisers marrying local women.

Shared Christian beliefs and shared cultural traditions created a firm bond between Singapore's British ruling class and the island's Eurasian community, and many Eurasians enjoyed privileged posts in the civil service. The bond would erode after the opening of the Suez Canal, when an increase in European arrivals saw the 'half Europeans' sidelined.

These days, the vast majority of Eurasians in Malaysia are found in Melaka. Here live around 37,000 Kristang, a group of people with predominantly mixed Portuguese and Malay blood, although a lot of other ethnic heritages are in there due to intermarriages down the generations.

In Singapore the Eurasian community is around 16,900 with many featuring prominently in the media and entertainment industries; they even have their own association (www.eurasians.org.sg). The Eurasians' mixed-race appearance is especially appealing to advertisers, who see it as conveniently encompassing Singapore's multiracial make-up. The majority of modern Singaporean Eurasians are of British descent, with English as their first language.

The Malay surname is the child's father's first name. This is why Malaysians will use your given name after Mr or Ms; to use your surname would be to address your father.

The Orang Asli

The indigenous people of Malaysia – known collectively as Orang Asli (Original People) – played an important role in early trade, teaching the colonialists about forest products and guiding prospectors to outcrops of tin and precious metals. They also acted as scouts and guides for anti-insurgent forces during the Emergency in the 1950s.

Despite this, the Orang Asli remain marginalised in Malaysia. In 2015, government figures put the population of Orang Asli in Peninsular Malaysia at just over 0.6% of the total population, or 178,197 people. The vast majority live below the poverty line. The tribes are generally classified into three groups: the Negrito; the Senoi; and the Proto-Malays, who are subdivided into 18 tribes, the smallest being the Orang Kanak, with just 238 accounted for in the 2010 census. There are dozens of different tribal languages and most Orang Asli follow animist beliefs, though there are vigorous attempts to convert them to Islam.

Since 1939 Orang Asli concerns have been represented and managed by a succession of government departments, the latest iteration being JAKOA (www.jakoa.gov.my), an acronym for Jabatan Kemajuan Orang Asli (Orang Asli Development Department), which came into being in 2011. The main goals of JAKOA are to provide protection to the Orang Asli and their way of life from exploitation by external parties and ensure there are adequate facilities and assistance for education, health and socio-economic development.

Borneo's indigenous community is comprised of scores of different tribal groups speaking around well over 100 languages and dialects.

In the past, Orang Asli land rights have often not been recognised, and when logging, agricultural or infrastructure projects require their land, their claims are generally regarded as illegal. Between 2010 and 2012 the Human Rights Commission of Malaysia (SUHAKAM; www.suhakam. org.my) conducted a national enquiry into the Land Rights of Indigenous Peoples and made various recommendations. This was followed up by government task force to study the finding and look at implementing the recommendations. The report was presented to government in September 2014, but has yet to be acted on.

The Dayaks & Peoples of Borneo

The term 'Dayak' was first used by colonial authorities in about 1840; it means upriver or interior in some local languages, human being in others. Not all of Borneo's indigenous tribes refer to themselves as Dayaks but the term usefully groups together peoples who have a great deal in common – and not just from an outsider's point of view.

Sabah

None of Sabah's 30-odd indigenous ethnicities are particularly keen on the term Dayak. The state's largest ethnic group, the Kadazan-Dusun, make up 18% of the population. Mainly Roman Catholic, the Kadazan and the Dusun share a common language and have similar customs; the former originally lived mainly in the state's western coastal areas and river deltas, while the latter inhabited the interior highlands.

The Murut (3.2% of the population) traditionally lived in the southwestern hills bordering Kalimantan and Brunei, growing hill-rice and hunting with spears and blowpipes. They were soldiers for Brunei's sultans, and the last group in Sabah to abandon head-hunting.

Sarawak

Dayak culture and lifestyles are probably easiest to observe and experience in Sarawak, where Dayaks make up about 48% of the population.

About 29% of Sarawakians are Iban, a group that migrated from West Kalimantan's Kapuas River starting five to eight centuries ago. Also known as Sea Dayaks for their exploits as pirates, the Iban are traditionally rice growers and longhouse dwellers. A reluctance to renounce head-hunting enhanced the Iban's ferocious reputation.

The Bidayuh (8% of the population), many of whom also trace their roots to what is now West Kalimantan, are concentrated in the hills south and southwest of Kuching. Few Bidayuh still live in longhouses and adjacent villages sometimes speak different dialects.

Upland groups such as the Kelabit, Kayan and Kenyah (ie everyone except the Bidayuh, Iban and coastal-dwelling Melenau) are often grouped under the term Orang Ulu ('upriver people'). There are also the Penan, originally a nomadic hunter-gatherer group living in northern Sarawak.

Brunei

Indigenous non-Malays, mainly Iban, Dusun and Melanau, account for around 6% of Brunei's population.

Some Dayak societies, such as the Iban and Bidayuh, are remarkably egalitarian, while others, including the Kayan, have a strict social hierarchy – now somewhat blurred – with classes of *maren* (nobles), *hipuy* (aristocrats), *panyin* (commoners) and *dipen* (slaves).

PEOPLE, CULTURE & POLITICS THE REGION'S PEOPLES

LONGHOUSE LIFE

One of the most distinctive features of Dayak life is the longhouse (*rumah batang* or *rumah panjai*), which is essentially an entire village under one seemingly interminable roof. Longhouses take a variety of shapes and styles, but all are raised above the damp jungle floor on hardwood stilts and most are built on or near river banks.

The focus of longhouse life is the covered verandah, known as a *ruai* to the Iban, an *awah* to the Bidayuh, and a *dapur* to the Kelabits; other groups use other terms. Residents use this communal space to socialise, engage in economic activities, cook and eat meals and hold communal celebrations.

One wall of the verandah, which can be up to 250m long, is pierced by doors to individual families' *bilik* (apartments), where there's space for sleeping and storage. If you ask about the size of a longhouse, you will usually be told how many doors – eg family units – it has.

Like the rest of us, Dayaks love their mod-cons, so longhouses where people actually live fuse age-old forms with contemporary conveniences. The resulting mash-up can see traditional bamboo slat floors mixed with corrugated iron, linoleum, satellite dishes, and a car park out the front.

Most young Dayaks move away from the longhouse to seek higher education and jobs in the cities, but almost all keep close ties with home, returning for major family and community celebrations.

Multiculturalism

From the ashes of Malaysia's interracial riots of 1969, when distrust between the Malays and Chinese peaked, the country has managed to forge a more tolerant multicultural society. The government's *bumiputra* policy (p572), which promotes positive discrimination to improve the economic status of indigenous Malays, has increased Malay involvement in the economy, albeit largely for an elite. This has helped defuse Malay fears and resentment of Chinese economic dominance, but at the expense of Chinese or Indian Malaysians being discriminated against by government policy.

A single 'Malaysian' identity continues to be a much-discussed and lauded concept. However, the reality is that Malaysia's different ethnic communities mostly coexist rather than mingle, intermarriage being rare. Education and politics are still largely split along ethnic lines.

Singaporean government policy has always promoted Singapore as a multicultural nation in which Chinese, Indians and Malays can live in equality and harmony while maintaining their distinct cultural identities. For example, each Housing Development Board (HDB) public housing complex is subject to ethnic-based quotas that reflect Singapore's demographic mix – one way to prevent the formation of 'ethnic enclaves'.

Imbalances in the distribution of wealth and power among Singapore's racial groups do exist, and tensions have boiled over on a couple of occasions: riots in 1969 when over 500 people were injured and 36 died in the clashes between Chinese and Malays; and in December 2013 when around 300 migrant labourers from the Indian subcontinent were involved in a riot in Little India following a fatal road accident in which a construction worker from Tamil Nadu was knocked down by a local bus driver. On the whole multiculturalism seems to work much better in small-scale Singapore than it does in Malaysia.

Similarly Brunei's small scale (not to mention great wealth) has allowed all its citizens, 33% of whom are not Muslim, to find common goals and live together harmoniously in a state run according to Islamic laws.

Young and Malay (2015; ed Ooi Kee Beng and Wan Hamidi Hamid) is a series of essays on what it's like to grow up in multicultural Malaysia.

Women in Malaysia, Singapore & Brunei

Women had great influence in pre-Islamic Malay society; there were female leaders and the descendants of the Sumatran Minangkabau in Malaysia's Negeri Sembilan still have a matriarchal society. The arrival of Islam weakened the position of women in the region. Nonetheless, women were not cloistered or forced to wear full purdah as in the Middle East, and today Malay women still enjoy more freedom than their counterparts in many other Muslim societies.

As you travel throughout the region you'll see women taking part in all aspects of society: politics, big business, academia and family life. However, Malaysia's Islamic family law makes it easier for Muslim men to take multiple wives, to divorce them and to take a share of their wives' property (similar laws exist in Brunei, where the Sultan has two wives). Around 40% of women over the age of 15 have been beaten by their partners in Malaysia. While the Domestic Violence Act does provide legal protection for abused women, it does not consider marital rape a crime.

In Chinese-dominated Singapore women traditionally played a small role in public life. In recent years women have started to take up key positions in government and industry – the current Singapore president is a woman, Halimah Yacob. However, as in Malaysia, women make up a tiny percentage of the numbers of members of parliament and top positions in companies.

A 2011 study by the University of Malaya indicated that as many as 93% of Malaysian Muslim women have undergone some form of Female Genital Mutilation (FGM). The practice isn't illegal in Malaysia, although public hospitals are prevented from offering such procedures.

In Islamic Brunei more women wear the *tudong* (headscarf) than in Malaysia. Many work and there are even one or two female politicians. Since 2002 female Bruneians have been able to legally transfer their nationality to their children if the father is not Bruneian.

The Region's Political Systems

Malaysia

Malaysia is made up of 13 states and three federal territories (Kuala Lumpur, Pulau Labuan and Putrajaya). Each state has an assembly and government headed by a *menteri besar* (chief minister). Nine states have hereditary rulers (sultans), while the remaining four have government-appointed governors, as do the federal territories. In a pre-established order, every five years one of the sultans takes his turn in the ceremonial position of Yang di-Pertuan Agong (king). The Sultan of Kelantan was king from December 2016 until unexpectedly abdicating in January 2019. The deputy king assumed official king duties until a new king is elected.

Malaysia has a two-house parliament: a 222-member House of Representatives (Dewan Rakyat) elected from single-member districts; and a 70-member Senate (Dewan Negara) with 26 members elected by the 13 state assemblies and 44 members appointed by the king on the prime minister's recommendation. National and state elections are held every five years. The current prime minister is Dr Mahathir Mohamad, who heads the coalition Pakatan Harapan (PH).

Singapore

Singapore is a parliamentary republic modelled on the UK's Westminster System. There are numerous political parties in Singapore, but one party, the People's Action Party (PAP), has dominated the political landscape since independence.

The President of Singapore (since 2017, Halimah Yacob) is the democratically elected head of state, a traditionally ceremonial role that has since 1991 included powers to veto a small number of decisions, largely related to security and the armed service. The president, who serves a six-year term, appoints a prime minister (currently Lee Hsien Loong) as the head of government. Legislative power is vested in both the government and the Parliament of Singapore.

Some critics say the electoral system makes it difficult for opposition parties to gain seats, entrenching the dominance of the PAP. This position is backed up by the strict (by Western standards) controls the government places on political assembly, freedom of expression and behaviours deemed antisocial. This said, the 2015 election, in which the PAP increased its share of the vote by nearly 10% over the 2011 poll, was the first in which opposition candidates were fielded in all constituencies. The election was a landslide win for the PAP, who gained 70% of the votes.

Brunei

Although internationally classified as a constitutional monarchy, Brunei officially deems itself a *Melayu Islam Beraja* (MIB; Malay Islamic Monarchy) and is, in many ways, an absolute monarchy. Sultan Hassanal Bolkiah has been in power since 1967; he appoints his advisory cabinet, privy council and council of succession. There is a 33-member legislative council, but those members are also appointed by and include the sultan; in 2004 there was talk of holding elections for 15 more seats, but those elections have never materialised.

To stem a booming population, Singapore's government encouraged birth control in the 1970s and 1980s. That plan worked so well that it now provides much encouragement, financial and otherwise, for its citizens to have more children.

Kiasu, a Hokkien word describing Singaporeans, literally means 'afraid to lose', but embraces a range of selfish and pushy behaviour in which the individual must not lose out at all cost.

Religion

Freedom of religion is guaranteed throughout this mainly Islamic region, although in Brunei the Baha'i faith is banned and you are unlikely to encounter many practising Jews. Hinduism's roots in the region long predate Islam, and the various Chinese religions are also strongly entrenched. Christianity has a presence, more so in Singapore than Peninsular Malaysia, where it has never been strong. In Malaysian Borneo many of the indigenous people have converted to Christianity, yet others still follow their animist traditions.

Islam

Islam most likely came to Malaysia, Singapore and Brunei in the 14th century with South Indian traders. It absorbed rather than conquered existing beliefs, and was adopted peacefully by the region's coastal trading ports. Islamic sultanates replaced Hindu kingdoms – though the Hindu concept of kings remained – and the Hindu traditions of adat continued despite Islamic law dominating.

Malay ceremonies and beliefs still exhibit pre-Islamic traditions, but most Malays are ardent Muslims – to suggest otherwise would cause great offence. With the rise of Islamic fundamentalism, the calls to introduce Islamic law and purify the practices of Islam have increased; yet, while the federal government of Malaysia is keen to espouse Muslim ideals, it is wary of religious extremism. In Brunei, Islam is the official religion and practised by nearly 83% of the population; in 2019 the final phase of sharia law was introduced. In Singapore, around 15% of the population is Muslim.

Sisters in Islam (www.sistersinislam.org.my) is an organisation run by and for Malaysian Muslim women who refuse to be bullied by patriarchal interpretations of Islam.

Key Beliefs & Practices

Most of the region's Muslims are Sunnis, but all Muslims share a common belief in the Five Pillars of Islam. The first is Shahadah (the declaration of faith): 'There is no God but Allah; Mohammed is his Prophet.' The second is *salat* (prayer), ideally done five times a day; the muezzin (prayer leader) calls the faithful from the minarets of every mosque. Third is *zakat* (tax), usually taking the form of a charitable donation, and fourth, *sawm* (fasting), which includes observing the fasting month of Ramadan. The last pillar is hajj (the pilgrimage to Mecca), which every Muslim aspires to do at least once in their lifetime.

Muslim dietary laws forbid alcohol, pork and all pork-based products. Restaurants where it's OK for Muslims to dine will be clearly labelled halal; this is a more strict definition than places that label themselves simply 'pork-free'.

Islam in Malaysia: Perceptions & Facts by Dr Mohd Asri Zainul Abidin, the former Mufti of Perlis, is a collection of articles on aspects of the faith as practised in Malaysia.

Chinese Religions

The Chinese in the region usually follow a mix of Buddhism, Confucianism and Taoism. Buddhism takes care of the afterlife, Confucianism looks after the political and moral aspects of life, and Taoism contributes animistic beliefs to teach people to maintain harmony with the universe. But to say that the Chinese have three religions is too simplistic a view

ISLAMIC FESTIVALS

Ramadan The high point of the Islamic festival calendar, Ramadan is when Muslims fast from sunrise to sunset. It always occurs in the ninth month of the Muslim calendar and lasts between 29 and 30 days, based on sightings of the moon. The start of Ramadan moves forward 11 days every year, in line with the Muslim lunar calendar – in 2022 it commences on 3 April, on 23 March in 2023, and on 11 March in 2024.

Nisfu Night Fifteen days before the start of Ramadan it is believed the souls of the dead visit their homes.

Laylatul Qadr (Night of Grandeur) During Ramadan, Muslims celebrate the arrival of the Quran on earth, before its revelation by the Prophet Mohammed.

Hari Raya Aidilfitri Hari Raya marks the end of the month-long fast, with two days of joyful celebration and feasting – this is the major holiday of the Muslim calendar. Starts on 3 May 2022, 22 April 2023 and 10 April 2024.

Mawlid al-Nabi Celebrating the birth of the Prophet Mohammed. Starts on 8 October 2022, 27 September 2023 and 16 September 2024.

Hari Raya Haji A two-day festival marking the successful completion of the hajj – the pilgrimage to Mecca – and commemorating the willingness of the Prophet Ibrahim (the biblical Abraham) to sacrifice his son. Many shops, offices and tourist attractions close and locals consume large amounts of cakes and sweets. Celebrated on 10 July 2022, 29 June 2023 and 17 June 2024.

Awal Muharram The Muslim New Year, which falls on 30 July 2022, 19 July 2023 and 8 July 2024.

of their traditional religious life. At the first level Chinese religion is animistic, with a belief in the innate vital energy in rocks, trees, rivers and springs. At the second level people from the distant past, both real and mythological, are worshipped as gods. Overlaid on this are popular Taoist, Mahayana Buddhist and Confucian beliefs.

On a day-to-day level most Chinese are much less concerned with the high-minded philosophies and asceticism of the Buddha, Confucius or Lao Zi than they are with the pursuit of worldly success, the appeasement of the dead and the spirits, and seeking knowledge about the future. Chinese religion incorporates elements of what Westerners might call 'superstition' – if you want your fortune told, for instance, you go to a temple. Chinese religion is polytheistic: apart from the Buddha, Lao Zi and Confucius, there are many divinities, such as house gods, and gods and goddesses for particular professions.

The most popular Chinese gods and local deities, or *shen*, are Kuan Yin, the goddess of mercy; Kuan Ti, the god of war and wealth; and Toh Peh Kong, a local deity representing the spirit of the pioneers and found only outside China.

Hinduism

Hinduism in the region dates back at least 1500 years and there are Hindu influences in cultural traditions, such as *wayang kulit* (shadow-puppet theatre) and the wedding ceremony. However, it is only in the past 100 years or so, following the influx of Indian contract labourers and settlers, that it has again become widely practised.

Hinduism has three basic practices: puja (worship), the cremation of the dead, and the rules and regulations of the caste system. Although still very strong in India, the caste system was never significant in Malaysia, mainly because the labourers brought there from India were mostly from the lower classes.

Hinduism has a vast pantheon of deities, although the one omnipresent god usually has three physical representations: Brahma, the creator; Vishnu, the preserver; and Shiva, the destroyer or reproducer. All three gods are usually shown with four arms, but Brahma has the added advantage of four heads to represent his all-seeing presence.

Animism

The animist religions of Malaysia's indigenous peoples are as diverse as the peoples themselves. While animism does not have a rigid system of tenets or codified beliefs, it can be said that animists perceive natural phenomena to be animated by various spirits or deities, and a complex system of practices is used to propitiate these spirits.

Ancestor worship is also a common feature of animist societies; departed souls are considered to be intermediaries between this world and the next. Examples of elaborate burial rituals can still be found in some parts of Sarawak, where the remains of monolithic burial markers and funerary objects still dot the jungle around longhouses in the Kelabit Highlands. However, most of these are no longer maintained and they're being rapidly swallowed up by the fast-growing jungle.

In Malaysian Borneo, Dayak animism is known collectively as Kaharingan. Carvings, totems, tattoos and other objects (including, in earlier times, head-hunting skulls) are used to repel bad spirits, attract good spirits and soothe spirits that may be upset. Totems at entrances to villages and longhouses are markers for the spirits.

Adat, with its roots in the region's Hindu period and earlier, is customary law that places great emphasis on collective rather than individual responsibility and on maintaining harmony.

Religious Issues
Islamic Conservatism in Malaysia

A radical Islamic movement has not taken serious root in Malaysia but religious conservatism has grown over recent years. For foreign visitors, the most obvious sign of this is the national obsession with propriety, which extends to newspaper polemics on female modesty and raids by the police on 'immoral' public establishments, which can include clubs and bars where Muslims may be drinking.

THAIPUSAM

The most spectacular Hindu festival in Malaysia and Singapore is Thaipusam, a wild parade of confrontingly invasive body piercings. The festival, which originated in Tamil Nadu (but is now banned in India), happens every year in the Hindu month of Thai (January/February) and is celebrated with the most gusto at the Batu Caves (p108), just outside Kuala Lumpur.

The greatest spectacle is the devotees who subject themselves to seemingly masochistic acts as fulfilment for answered prayers. Many carry offerings of milk in *paal kudam* (milk pots), often connected to the skin by hooks. Even more striking are the *vel kavadi* – great cages of spikes that pierce the skin of the carrier and are decorated with peacock feathers, pictures of deities, and flowers. Some penitents go as far as piercing their tongues and cheeks with hooks, skewers and tridents.

The festival is the culmination of around a month of prayer, a vegetarian diet and other ritual preparations, such as abstinence from sex, or sleeping on a hard floor. While it looks excruciating, a trance-like state stops participants from feeling pain; later the wounds are treated with lemon juice and holy ash to prevent scarring. As with the practice of firewalking, only the truly faithful should attempt the ritual. It is said that insufficiently prepared devotees keep doctors especially busy over the Thaipusam festival period with skin lacerations, or by collapsing after the strenuous activities.

Thaipusam is also celebrated in Penang at the Nattukottai Chettiar Temple and the Waterfall Hilltop Temple, and in Johor Bahru at the Sri Thandayuthabani Temple. Ipoh attracts a large number of devotees, who follow the procession from the Sri Mariamar Temple in Buntong to the Sri Subramaniar Temple in Gunung Cheroh. In Singapore, Hindus march from the Sri Srinivasa Perumal Temple on Serangoon Rd to the Chettiar Hindu Temple.

Omar Ali Saifuddien Mosque (p470), Bandar Seri Begawan

Freedom of Religion in Brunei

Brunei's constitution allows for the practice of religions other than the official Sunni Islam. However, as Freedom House (www.freedomhouse. org) reports, proselytising by non-Muslims is prohibited and other forms of Islam are actively discouraged. Christianity suffers censorship. Marriage between Muslims and non-Muslims is not allowed. With permission from the Ministry of Religious Affairs, Muslims can convert their faith, but in reality conversion is practically impossible.

Anti-Semitism

Penang once had a Jewish community large enough to support a synagogue (closed in 1976) and there's been a Jewish cemetery in George Town since 1805. Elsewhere in Malaysia, Jewish life is practically unknown.

Sadly, anti-Semitism, ostensibly tied to criticism of Israel, is a feature of Malaysia. Current prime minister Mahathir is the most infamously outspoken Malaysian anti-Semite: in 2003 he made a speech to an Islamic leadership conference claiming the USA is a tool of Jewish overlords, and he once cancelled a planned tour of Malaysia by the New York Philharmonic because the program included work by a Jewish composer.

A 2014 survey by the US-based Anti-Defamation League (ADL) found that nearly two in three Malaysians admit to being prejudiced against Jews, the highest proportion by far in the region. Israeli passport holders are not permitted to enter Malaysia without clearance from the Ministry of Home Affairs, and very few local Muslims differentiate between Israelis and Jews generally – something worth noting if you're Jewish and travelling in the region.

Dayak animism considers the hornbill a powerful spirit – the bird is honoured in dance and ceremony and its feathers are treasured.

The Jewish Welfare Board (www. singaporejews. com) contains information about the history of Jews in Singapore as well as details about the current community and its events.

Arts, Architecture & Media

Malaysia, Singapore and Brunei are not widely known for their arts, even though there is much creativity here, particularly in Malaysia and Singapore. Traditional art forms like *wayang kulit* (shadow puppetry) and *mak yong* (all-female dance and music performances) hang on alongside contemporary art, drama and filmmaking. The region's distinctive architecture ranges from Chinese shophouses and stately colonial buildings through to iconic hyper-modern constructions. Local authors and visual artists are also gaining attention in the wider world.

Arts

Literature

Writers W Somerset Maugham, Joseph Conrad and Noel Coward were inspired by the region in the early 20th century. The classic colonial expat experience is recounted by Anthony Burgess in *The Malayan Trilogy* written in the 1950s.

In recent decades locally born authors have been coming to the fore. Tash Aw's debut novel *The Harmony Silk Factory,* set in Malaysia of the 1930s and '40s, won the 2005 Whitbread First Novel Award. His latest work, *Five Star Billionaire* (2013), is about four expat Malaysians trying to make a go of it in contemporary Shanghai. Tan Twan Eng's debut novel *The Gift of Rain,* set in Penang prior to WWII, was long-listed for the Man Booker literature prize. His follow-up, *The Garden of Evening Mists,* winner of the Man Asian Literary Prize in 2012, takes the reader deep into the Cameron Highlands and the 1950s era of the Emergency. *Evening Is the Whole Day* (2008) by Preeta Samarasan looks at the experiences of an Indian immigrant family living on the outskirts of Ipoh in the early 1980s.

Brian Gomez's comedy-thriller *Devil's Place* (2008) is a fun read and very evocative of its KL setting. *Once We Were There* (2017) by Bernice Chauly is set in KL during the era of the *reformasi* protests from the late 1990s to the early 2000s. It shines a light into the city's darker corners, including the drug trade and babies stolen for adoption or worse.

In the late 1960s Paul Theroux lived in Singapore, which forms the backdrop to his novel *Saint Jack* (1973) and his short-story collection *The Consul's File* (1977). JG Farrell's *The Singapore Grip* (1978), about the decline of British colonialism in the region in the run-up to WWII, is considered a classic Singapore novel.

Catherine Lim's *Little Ironies* (1978) is a series of keenly observed short stories about Singaporeans from a prolific writer of novels, poetry and political commentary. Hwee Hwee Tan pinpoints the peculiar dilemmas and contradictions facing Singaporean youth in her novels *Foreign Bodies* (1999) and *Mammon Inc.* (2001). Singapore-born Kevin Kwan's witty satire on the lives of the island state's megarich in *Crazy Rich Asians* (2013) has been so successful it has spawned two sequels and a Hollywood movie.

Online Arts Resources

Arts.com.my (www.arts.com.my)

Malaysia Design Archive (www.malaysiadesignarchive.org)

National Arts Council Singapore (www.nac.gov.sg)

Bruneions (www.bruneions.com)

Arts Equator (www.artsequator.com)

Look out for books from local publisher Epigram Books (www.shop.epigrambooks.sg) – it sponsors a writing prize that has brought to public attention such talented writers as Sebastian Sim, whose *The Riot Act* was the 2017 winner. This darkly comic satire riffs on the causes of and fallout from the real-life riot in Little India in 2013.

Also short-listed for the Epigram Prize was Jeremy Tiang's outstanding *State of Emergency* (2017), which went on to win the Singapore Literature Prize in 2018, and Balli Kaur Jaswal for her 2015 novel *Sugarbread*. Also look out for Jaswal's debut *Inheritance* (2013) about a dysfunctional Punjabi Sikh family's trials and tribulations between 1970 and 1990. UK-based Singaporean writer Sharlene Teo's debut novel *Ponti* (2018) is about the relationship between a woman who once starred in cult horror movies, her daughter and her daughter's friend.

Drama & Dance

Traditional Malay dances include *menora,* a dance-drama of Thai origin performed by an all-male cast dressed in grotesque masks, and the similar *mak yong,* in which the participants are female. These performances often take place at Puja Ketek, Buddhist festivals held at temples near the Thai border in Kelantan. There's also the *rodat,* a dance from Terengganu, and the *joget,* an upbeat dance with Portuguese origins, often performed at Malay weddings by professional dancers; in Melaka it's better known as *chakunchak.*

The best chances of seeing performances are in Kuala Lumpur, George Town, Melaka and Kota Bharu.

When it comes to contemporary drama and dance, Singapore tends to have the edge. There's a lot of interesting work by local theatre companies such as Wild Rice, Necessary Stage and Singapore Repertory Theatre. Singapore's leading dance company, Singapore Dance Theatre, puts on performances ranging from classical ballet to contemporary dance.

Shadow Puppetry

It's in east-coast Peninsular Malaysia towns like Kota Bharu and Kuala Terengganu that you're most likely to see *wayang kulit* (performances), similar to those of Java in Indonesia, which retell tales from Hindu epic the Ramayana. It's a feat of endurance both for performer and audience since the shadow plays, which can take place at weddings or after the harvest, can last for many hours.

There are thought to be no more than 10 practising puppet masters *(dalang)* in Malaysia. The nongovernmental organisation Pusaka is working to keep Malaysian traditional arts, including *wayang kulit,* alive by introducing them to the general public with free shows, and by training a new generation of artists. Shows are by donation and often feature some outstanding older performers and the occasional young phenom.

Music
Traditional & Classical

Traditional Malay music is based largely on *gendang* (drums), but other percussion instruments include the gong and various tribal instruments made from seashells, coconut shells and bamboo. The Indonesian-style gamelan (a traditional orchestra of drums, gongs and wooden xylophones) also crops up on ceremonial occasions. The Malay *nobat* uses a mixture of percussion and wind instruments to create formal court music.

Islamic and Chinese influences are felt in the music of *dondang sayang* (Chinese-influenced romantic songs) and *hadrah* (Islamic chants, sometimes accompanied by dance and music). In Singapore,

Silat, or bersilat, is a Malay martial art that originated in 15th-century Melaka. Today it is a highly refined and stylised activity, more akin to dance than self-defence.

ARTS, ARCHITECTURE & MEDIA ARTS

CHINESE OPERA

In Malaysia and Singapore *wayang* (Chinese opera) is derived from the Cantonese variety. The performances mix dialogue, music, song and dance, and what they lack in literary nuance, they make up for with garish costumes and the crashing music that follows the action. Scenery and props are minimal; it's the action that is important, and even for the uninitiated it's usually easy to get the gist of the plot.

Performances can go for an entire evening. Even though the acting is very stylised, and the music can be discordant to Western ears, they are worth seeing. Free street performances are held in the Chinatown areas of Kuala Lumpur and Singapore, Melaka and Penang's George Town during important festivals like Chinese New Year (January/February), the Hungry Ghost Festival (August/September) and the Festival of the Nine Emperor Gods (September/October).

catch the well-respected Singapore Chinese Orchestra (www.sco.com.sg), which plays not only traditional and symphonic Chinese music but also Indian, Malay and Western pieces.

Popular Music

Snapping at the high heels of demure Malaysian pop songstress Siti Nurhaliza are Zee Avi, who was signed by the US label Bushfire Records for her eponymous debut CD, and Yuna, who has also cut a US record deal and is another of the talented vocalists and songwriters from the nation's new generation of musicians. Also look out for Najwa, whose slickly produced EP *Aurora* has garnered positive reviews; the MIA-style rapper Arabyrd; and the more retro guitar jingly pop stylings of Noh Salleh.

In 2015, indie rock band Kyoto Protocol, who have been steadily building their reputation since forming in 2008, finally released a full album, *Catch These Men,* after a series of singles and EPs in the past.

Local artists show up at music festivals in Malaysia such as Urbanscapes (p70) and the Rainforest World Music Festival (p404). A great resource for catching other up-and-coming local bands and singers is The Wknd (www.the-wknd.com).

Singapore's pop music scene creates only a small blip internationally. On the radar are rapper and hip-hop artists Thelioncityboy (www.facebook.com/thelioncityboy) and Shigga Shay (www.shiggashay.com) and singer-songwriters Jasmine Sokko (www.jasminesokko.com) and Inch Chua (www.thisisinch.com).

Visitors should look out for local festivals like the annual Baybeats at the Esplanade – Theatres on the Bay, showcasing alternative singers and bands.

In December 2017 Brunei hosted its first film festival, Brunei Film Blitz. You can view the short movies at https://progresif.com/brunei-film-blitz.

Cinema

Back in the 1950s, when Malaysia and Singapore were both part of the Federation of Malaya, P Ramlee dominated the silver screen. This Penang-born actor, singer and director started his movie career in Singapore in 1948 and moved back to Malaysia in the mid 1960s. His directorial debut, *Penarik Becha* (The Trishaw Man; 1955), is a classic of Malay cinema, and he would act in and direct scores more films before his death in 1973, aged just 44.

Like Ramlee, Yasmin Ahmad's movie career was also cut short. Her film *Sepet* (2005), about a Chinese boy and Malay girl falling in love, cuts across the country's race and language barriers, upsetting many devout Malays, as did her follow-up, *Gubra* (2006), which dared to take a sympathetic approach to prostitutes. Causing less of a stir were *Mukshin* (2007), a romantic tale about Malay village life, and *Talentime*

(2009), about an inter-school performing arts contest, and what would be Yasmin's final film before her death at 51 from a stroke the same year.

U-Wei Haji Saari was the first Malaysian director to show a film – *Kaki Bakar* (The Arsonist) – at the prestigious Cannes festival in 1995. His 2014 movie *Hanyut* (Drifting) is an adventure drama set in Malaya in the 19th century. Directed by Shanjhey Kumar Perumal and with a script in Tamil, *Jagat* (2015) is a crime drama set in Malaysia's poor and marginalised Indian community. It won the best film award at the 2016 Malaysia Film Festival.

Set in Kelantan, Dain Said's action-drama *Bunohan* (2012) did well at film festivals around the world, gaining it an international release – rare for a Malaysian movie. Said's 2016 movie *Interchange* is a noir–style supernatural thriller set in KL.

In 1979 when Hollywood director Peter Bogdanovich headed to Singapore to film *Saint Jack,* he had to submit a fake shooting script to the authorities so as to avoid having the production shut down. On its release the movie, about an American pimp in 1970s Singapore, was banned on the island state (the ban was lifted in 2006).

Local filmmakers are in a constant dance with government censors. The first locally made movie to gain international attention was Eric Khoo's debut feature *Mee Pok Man* (1995) about the relationship between a fish-ball noodle vendor and a troubled prostitute. Several of Khoo's subsequent films, including the animated *Tatsumi* (2011) and prison drama *Apprentice* (2016), have since featured in competition at Cannes.

Royston Tan's first feature *15* (2003), about teenage gangsters, fell foul of local censors and had 27 scenes snipped. In response, he produced the hilarious short music video *Cut* (which can be viewed on YouTube). Less controversial was *881* (2007), a campy musical comedy about the *getai* (stage singing) aspirations of two friends.

Anthony Chen's *Ilo Ilo* (2013) explores the relationship between a Singaporean family and their Filipino maid, topical given tensions between locals and foreign workers. Among the film's awards is the Camera d'Or from Cannes.

Hollywood was back in Singapore (with full government approval) in 2017 to film *Crazy Rich Asians* based on Kevin Kwan's best selller. Various locations, including Raffles Hotel, Marina Bay Sands and Newton Food Centre, feature in the movie.

Visual Arts

Latiff Mohidin, who is also a poet, is a Penang-based artist whose work spans several decades and has featured in a major retrospective at the National Visual Arts Gallery; he's considered a national treasure.

Other long-established artists include Hoessein Enas, who was commissioned by Shell Ltd in 1963 to produce a series of portraits celebrating the newly born country, and Amron Omar, who has focused throughout his career on *silat* (a Malay martial art) as a source of inspiration for his paintings.

Among notable contemporary Malaysian artists are Jalaini Abu Hassan ('Jai'), Wong Hoy Cheong, landscape painter Wong Perng Fey and multimedia artist Yee I-Lann. Work by Malaysian sculptor Abdul Multhalib Musa has won awards and he created several pieces in Beijing for the 2008 Olympics.

In Singapore the visual-arts scene is also vibrant, with painting, sculpture and multimedia the vehicles of choice for dynamic explorations into the tensions between Western art practices and the perceived erosion of traditional values. Highly regarded local artists include Tang Da Wu, Vincent Leow, Jason Lim and Zulkifle Mahmod. The National Gallery Singapore is aiming to be the region's leading visual arts institution.

Volunteer-run Gerai OA (www.facebook.com/geraioa) sells and promotes crafts by Malaysia's indigenous minorities. Its Facebook page lists the crafts markets in the Kuala Lumpur area and where you'll find them.

MALAYSIAN CARTOONISTS

The cartoonist and artist Lat is a national institution in Malaysia. His witty sketches turn up in the *New Straits Times* newspaper, advertisements and books including *Kampung Boy*.

Check out the works of political cartoonist Zunar (www.zunar.my). Under the previous government his works were considered seditious and he suffered arrests, the banning of his books and a travel ban outside of Malaysia. All charges against him were dropped in June 2018.

Traditional Crafts

The region's crafts have much rustic beauty and incorporate traditional designs.

Batik Produced by drawing or printing a pattern on fabric with wax and then dyeing the material, batik can be made into clothes and homewares, or simply be created as works of art. It's made across Malaysia, but Kelantan and Terengganu are its true homes.

Basketry & weaving The baskets of the Iban, Kayan, Kenyah and Penan are highly regarded. Weaving materials include rattan, bamboo, swamp nipah grass and pandanus palms. Related weaving techniques produce sleeping mats, seats and materials for shelters. While each ethnic group has certain distinctive patterns, hundreds or even thousands of years of trade and interaction has led to an intermixing of patterns.

Fabrics Gold and silver threads are hand-woven through the luxurious material *kain songket*, a speciality of Kelantan and Terengganu. Clothes made from it are usually reserved for important festivals and occasions. You can also buy pieces of the fabric for decorative purposes. Traditional weaving techniques are used to produce *pua kumbu*, a patterned, multicoloured cotton cloth, used by the Iban in Sarawak.

Kites & puppets The *wau bulan* (moon kite) of Kelantan is a traditional paper and bamboo crescent-shaped kite as large as 3m in length and breadth, while kite makers in Terengganu specialise in the *wau kucing* (cat kite). *Wayang kulit* are made from buffalo hide in the shape of characters from epic Hindu legends.

Metalwork Kelantan is famed for its silversmiths, who work in a variety of ways and specialise in filigree and repoussé work. In the latter, designs are hammered through the silver from the underside. Brasswork is an equally traditional skill in Kuala Terengganu. Objects crafted out of pewter (an alloy of tin) are synonymous with Selangor, where you'll find the Royal Selangor Pewter Factory as well as other pewter manufacturers.

Woodcarving The Orang Asli tribe of Hma' Meri, who live in a village on Pulau Carey, off the coast of Selangor, are renowned woodcarvers. In Malaysian Borneo the Kenyah and Kayan peoples are also skilled woodcarvers, producing hunting-charms and ornate knife-hilts known as *parang ilang*.

The Brunei Art Forum in Bandar Seri Begawan fosters international links and promotes local contemporary artists (mostly painters) including Zakaria Bin Omar, Haji Padzil Haji Ahmad and Teck Kwang Swee.

Architecture

Vividly painted and handsomely proportioned, traditional wooden Malay houses are also perfectly adapted to the hot, humid conditions of the region. Built on stilts, with high, peaked roofs, they take advantage of even the slightest cooling breeze. Further ventilation is achieved by full-length windows, no internal partitions, and lattice-like grilles in the walls. The layout of a traditional Malay house reflects Muslim sensibilities. There are separate areas for men and women, as well as distinct areas where guests of either sex may be entertained.

Although their numbers are dwindling, this type of house has not disappeared altogether. The best places to see examples are in the *kampung* (villages) of Peninsular Malaysia, particularly along the east coast in the states of Kelantan and Terengganu. Here you'll see that roofs are often tiled, showing a Thai and Cambodian influence. In Melaka, the Malay house has a distinctive tiled front stairway leading up to the front verandah – examples can be seen around Kampung Morten.

Few Malay-style houses have survived Singapore's rapid modernisation – the main place they remain is on Pulau Ubin. Instead, the island state has some truly magnificent examples of Chinese shophouse architecture, particularly in Chinatown, Emerald Hill (off Orchard Rd) and around Katong. There are also the distinctive 'black and white' bungalows built during colonial times; find survivors lurking in the residential areas off Orchard Rd.

Despite its oil wealth, there's little that's flashy in the architecture of Brunei's modest capital, Bandar Seri Begawan, where the city's skyline is dominated by the striking Omar Ali Saifuddien Mosque. About 3km outside of the capital is the sultan's opulent palace Istana Nurul Iman, while at Jerudong is the eye-boggling Empire Hotel.

Media

Malaysia, Singapore and Brunei all leave much to be desired when it comes to freedom of the press. In the Reports Without Borders rankings for 2018, the three countries placed 145, 151 and 153 respectively out of the 179 nations surveyed. All the countries have stringent publishing laws with the courts frequently used to silence critics and frighten journalists into self-censorship.

Following the 2018 general election, Malaysia's new government led by Pakatan Harapan has committed to allowing greater press freedom in the country. It repealed the previous government's controversial Anti-Fake News Act of 2018, which was used to stop coverage of the 1Malaysia Development Bhd scandal. However, freedom of expression in the country remains problematic, as lawyer Fadiah Nadwa Fikri discovered in July 2018 when she wrote a blog article questioning Malaysia's monarchy, describing it as incompatible with democracy. Following complaints she was questioned by the police under the investigation of breaking sections of the Sedition Act and Communication and Multimedia Act.

Singapore's government keeps a tight leash on local media through regulation and censorship. Prominent opposition bloggers such as Roy Ngerng are subject to persistent harassment including lawsuits and police questioning. A new anti-terrorism law in 2018 gives police special powers during terrorist attacks, including banning journalists and members of the public from reporting on the scene.

All this said, social media increasingly plays a part in Malaysia's, Singapore's and Brunei's mediascape, with local newspapers often quoting bloggers and reporting on issues generated on the internet and social media. Many people also go online to read news they are unlikely to see in print.

The Minangkabau-style houses found in Negeri Sembilan are the most distinctive of the *kampung* houses, with curved roofs resembling buffalo horns. The design is imported from Sumatra.

ARTS, ARCHITECTURE & MEDIA MEDIA

Environment

Many visitors come to Malaysia, Singapore and Brunei to experience first hand the region's amazing natural environment. However, these countries, like others the world over, are grappling with the sometimes conflicting demands of economic development and environmental conservation. Items on the local sustainability agenda include deforestation, a result of the rampant growth of palm-oil plantations in Malaysia; protection of endangered wildlife; cleaning up polluted waterways; and cutting the region's carbon footprint through innovative energy-efficiency projects.

Lay of the Land

Large parts of Peninsular Malaysia (132,090 sq km) are covered by dense jungle, particularly its mountainous, thinly populated northern half, although it's dominated by palm oil and rubber plantations. On the western side of the peninsula there is a long, fertile plain running down to the sea, while on the eastern side the mountains descend more steeply and the coast is fringed with sandy beaches. Jungle features heavily in Malaysian Borneo, along with many large river systems, particularly in Sarawak. Mt Kinabalu (4095m) in Sabah is Malaysia's highest mountain.

Singapore, consisting of the main, low-lying Singapore island and 63 much smaller islands within its territorial waters, is a mere 137km north of the equator. The central area is an igneous outcrop, containing most of Singapore's remaining forest and open areas. The western part of the island is a sedimentary area of low-lying hills and valleys, while the southeast is mostly flat and sandy. The undeveloped northern coast and the offshore islands are home to some mangrove forest.

The sultanate of Brunei covers just 5765 sq km (the Brunei government-owned cattle farm in Australia is larger than this!). The capital, Bandar Seri Begawan, overlooks the estuary of the mangrove-fringed Sungai Brunei (Brunei River), which opens onto Brunei Bay and the separate, eastern part of the country, Temburong, a sparsely populated area of largely unspoilt rainforest. Approximately 75% of Brunei retains its original forest cover.

Deforestation

According to WWF Malaysia, just under 60% of Malaysia is covered by forest. However, as the Malaysian Nature Society and others have pointed out, the problem is what this 'forest cover' is comprised of. Currently the government description includes rubber plantations. In many states old-growth forests are being cut down to plant rubber.

There's a disparity between government figures and those of environmental groups, but it's probable that up to 80% of Malaysia's rainforests have been logged. Government initiatives like the National Forestry Policy have led to deforestation being cut to 900 sq km a year, a third slower than previously. The aim is to reduce the timber harvest by 10% each year, but even this isn't sufficient to calm the many critics who remain alarmed at the rate at which Malaysia's primary forests are disappearing.

Online Resources

Malaysian Nature Society (www. mns.my)

Orangutan Foundation (www. orangutan.org.uk)

Sahabat Alam Malaysia (www. foe-malaysia.org)

WWF Malaysia (www.wwf.org.my)

WILDLIFE SMUGGLING

Malaysia's Wildlife Conservation Act includes fines of up to RM100,000 and long prison sentences for poaching, smuggling animals and other wildlife-related crimes. Even so, smuggling of live animals and animal parts remains a particular problem in the region. In July 2010 police looking for stolen cars also uncovered an illegal 'mini zoo' in a KL warehouse containing 20 species of protected wildlife, including a pair of rare birds of paradise worth RM1 million.

Pangolins, also known as scaly anteaters, are the most traded species, even though they are protected under Malaysian law. Their scales, believed to have medicinal properties, can fetch up to RM800 per kilogram.

After serving 17 months of a five-year sentence, Malaysia's most notorious animal smuggler Anson Wong – described as 'the Pablo Escobar of wildlife trafficking' in Bryan Christy's *The Lizard King* – was allegedly back in business in 2013 according to documentary screened by Al Jazeera in 2013.

It's not just live animals that are being smuggled. Malaysia has been fingered as a transit point for illegally traded ivory on its way to other parts of Asia. In August 2017, authorities seized ivory tusks and pangolin scales worth nearly US$1 million at a cargo warehouse at Kuala Lumpur International Airport.

Environmental groups like TREES (www.trees.org.my) have also been campaigning for the protection of the rainforests and water catchment area along the eastern flank of Selangor. In 2010, 930 sq km of these uplands were gazetted as the Selangor State Park making it the peninsula's third-largest protected area of forest after Taman Negara and Royal Belum State Park. Find out more at www.selangorstatepark.blogspot.com.

It's in Sarawak and Sabah that old-growth rainforests are under the most severe threat. The detrimental effects of past logging are still clearly being felt in the region, which now suffers unusually long floods during the wet season.

To afford a measure of protection, several national parks and reserves have been created or extended, such as the Maliau Basin Conservation Area and the Pulong Tau National Park. In 2007 the Heart of Borneo Initiative was signed by Malaysia, Brunei and Indonesia. The aim is to safeguard Borneo's biodiversity for future generations and ensure indigenous people's cultural survival by protecting 24,000 sq km of interconnected forest land in Sabah, Sarawak, Brunei and Kalimantan – altogether almost a third of the island.

For more on what the government is doing in relation to forest management, see the websites of the forestry departments of Peninsular Malaysia (www.forestry.gov.my), Sarawak (www.forestry.sarawak.gov.my) and Sabah (www.forest.sabah.gov.my). For the alternative point of view, read William W Bevis' award-winning *Borneo Log: The Struggle for Sarawak's Forests* (1995), an evocative narrative that starkly outlines the environmental and human impacts of the logging in Sarawak, and Lukas Straumann's *Money Logging: On the Trail of the Asian Timber Mafia* (2014), a damming account of former Sarawak chief minister Taib's alleged rape of the state's rainforests.

The Clouded Leopard Project (www.clouded leopard.org) has funded several conservation efforts on Malaysian Borneo for this beautiful animal that may be rarer than the Malayan tiger.

Palm-Oil Plantations

The oil palm, a native of West Africa that was introduced into Malaysia in the 1870s, is probably now the most common tree in Malaysia. The country's first palm-oil plantation was established in 1917. Today, according to the Malaysian Palm Oil Council (www.mpoc.org.my), Malaysia is the world's leading producer of palm oil, accounting for over 40% of global production. The oil is extracted from the orange-coloured fruit, which grows in bunches just below the fronds. It is used primarily for cooking, although it can also be refined into biodiesel – an alternative to fossil fuels.

For all the crop's benefits, there have been huge environmental consequences to the creation of vast plantations that have replaced the native jungle and previously logged forests; a UN Environment Program report in 2007 concluded that palm-oil plantations are the leading cause of rainforest destruction in Malaysia. The use of polluting pesticides and fertilisers in palm-oil production also undermines the crop's eco credentials. Palm-oil plantations convert land into permanent monoculture, reducing the number of plant species by up to 90%. Oil palms require large quantities of herbicides and pesticides that can seep into rivers; drainage may lower water tables, drying out nearby peat forests (and releasing huge quantities of greenhouse gases in the process). Plantations also fragment the natural habitats that are especially important to large mammals.

The Palm Oil Action Group (www.palmoilaction.org.au) is an Australian pressure group raising awareness about palm oil and the need to use alternatives. Roundtable on Sustainable Palm Oil (www.rspo.org) tries to look at the issue from all sides while seeking to develop and implement global standards. Proforest (www.proforest.net) has also been working with palm-oil producers in the region, to help growers to understand and adopt responsible production practices.

> The Sarawak Biodiversity Centre (www.sbc.org.my) carries out research on the state's biodiversity for potential commercialisation. If the multi-million-dollar cure for cancer or AIDS can be found in these forests, it might just be their partial saviour.

Cutting Carbon Emissions

Under the BN government's Green Technology Master Plan 2017–2030, the aim was to slash Malaysia's CO_2 emissions from a current eight metric tonnes (MT) per capita to six MT per capita by 2030.

In order to reach its stated goal the government has added green technology to the portfolio of the Ministry of Energy and Water. The details remain sketchy, however, and the overall aim sits awkwardly with the continuing expansion of local budget airlines such as AirAsia.

Melaka is creating a smart electricity grid, including the use of solar power, with the aim of becoming the country's first carbon-free city. The Carbon Trust (www.carbontrust.com) is also working with the local government of Petaling Jaya in Selangor to help develop its five-year carbon reduction strategy.

In the meantime the region's environment faces an ongoing threat from the so-called 'haze' – smoke from fires set by Indonesian farmers and plantation companies to clear land for agricultural purposes. The haze is at its worst around August/September.

> The Sarawak Report (www.sarawakreport.org) has called attention to issues such as deforestation and the impact of dam building in Malaysia.

Hydroelectric Dams

Hydoelectric dams are touted as sources of carbon-free energy, but these huge projects often have serious environmental impacts. In addition, indigenous people are often forcibly relocated to areas where they have difficulty earning a living or maintaining their traditions. Such is the case with the Murum Dam, located in a Penan area 60km upriver from Bakun in Sarawak, and the state's controversial Bakun Dam.

In October 2010 the 207m-high Bakun Dam structure began flooding a reservoir that covers an area of once-virgin rainforest about the size of Singapore (690 sq km). At full generating capacity, the second-highest concrete-faced rockfill dam in the world will produce 2400MW of emission-free clean energy – 2.5 times as many watts as Sarawak's current peak demand.

Malaysian and international watchdogs claim the whole Bakun Dam project – including contracts to clear the site of biomass, which involves logging old-growth jungle – has been shot through with corrupt dealings designed to benefit the business associates of local politicians.

Rivers

There has been some success in both Penang and Melaka when it comes to cleaning up polluted waterways. The Sungai Pinang that flows through the heart of George Town was once so filthy that it had a Class V classification, meaning it was unable to sustain life and contact with the water was dangerous. The state's clean-up program resulted in the waterway's pollution rating dropping to Class III in 2010, and in 2015, a family of 10 smooth-coated otters where regularly spotted in the river – a sign that fish have also returned to the waters. The long-term goal is to have the river rated Class I.

According to the Malaysian Nature Society, the revival of the once sludgy Sungei Melaka flowing through Melaka is also a model of how a river can be cleaned. Starting in 2005 the city invested about RM100 million in the project, which also included building grassy areas and walking paths along the river banks. A catamaran designed to clean up oil slicks was employed to remove rubbish then compress it into a material that could be used to reinforce the banks. The next step was the beautification of the banks, followed by domestic wastewater and cesspool treatment; reservoirs were built to trap scum, oil and refuse.

The focus has now turned to KL and the Klang Valley. The literal translation of Kuala Lumpur is 'muddy estuary'; anyone gazing on any of the milk-coffee-coloured waterways that flow through the city would still find that name highly appropriate. Following moves in 2010 by the Selangor state government to clean up a 21km stretch of the Sungei Klang around Klang, the much larger River of Life program now focuses antipollution efforts on the river's upper reaches. In 2011 the government allocated RM3 billion for the task of raising the river water quality from the current Class III and Class IV (not suitable for body contact) to Class IIb (suitable for body contact and recreational usage).

Up to three quarters of Kelantan's coast is under attack from erosion; in the worst cases the shoreline is retreating by up to 10m a year.

THE PLIGHT OF TASIK CHINI

Part of the Sungai Pahang (Pahang River) basin and with a catchment size of 45 sq km, Tasik Chini is just one of two Unesco Biosphere Reserves in Malaysia (the other is the Crocker Range in Sabah). As late as 10 years ago the lake was a major tourist draw for the lotus flowers that practically carpeted its surface. Today pollution of the lake (which is actually a freshwater swamp) has resulted in murky waters and the near extinction of the lotuses.

Problems began in the mid-1980s, when the state government began approving land development schemes around the lake. Things got worse when the federal government built a weir at the end of Sungai Chini in 1995 to facilitate the navigation of tourist boats, despite protests by the Orang Asli who live in six villages around Tasik Chini.

The weir raised the lake by at least 2m, submerging thousands of trees and many stands of rattan by the water's edge, as well endangering the survival of the lotus plants, which grow best in shallow water. The water, already spoiled by run-off from open-cut iron ore mines as close as 50m from the lake's edge, was further polluted by the methane and hydrogen sulphide that the dead vegetation in the lake produced as it rotted.

With the situation viewed as critical, Transparency International-Malaysia (TI-M) and environmental agencies including WWF Malaysia and Malaysian Nature Society are campaigning to Save Tasik Chini.

RESPONSIBLE TRAVEL

➡ Tread lightly and buy locally, avoiding (and reporting) instances where you see parts of or products made from endangered species for sale. In Malaysia call the 24-hour Wildlife Crime Hotline (019-356 4194) to report illegal activities.

➡ Visit nature sites, hire local trekking guides and provide custom for ecotourism initiatives. By doing so you're putting cash in local pockets and casting a vote for the economic (as opposed to the purely ecological) value of sustainability and habitat conservation.

➡ Sign up to be a voluntary forest monitor at Forest Watch, a Transparency International Malaysia project.

➡ Check out projects sponsored and promoted by the Ecotourism & Conservation Society Malaysia (www.ecomy.org), Wild Asia (www.wildasia.org) to learn more about responsible tourism in the region.

➡ Keep abreast of and support local campaigns by checking out the websites of organisations like WWF Malaysia (www.wwf.org.my), the Malaysian Nature Society (www.mns.my), EcoKnights (www.ecoknights.org.my), ECO Singapore (www.eco-singapore.org) and Green Brunei (www.green-brunei.com).

➡ Carbon-cutting overland travel to Peninsular Malaysia from Europe and most parts of Asia is possible as long as you're not in a hurry. See Man in Seat 61 (www.seat61.com/malaysia.htm) for how to reach Kuala Lumpur from London by a combination of trains and buses in 3½ weeks.

Green, Clean Singapore

Singapore's reputation as an efficiently run, squeaky clean place is well justified. The country has a vision of becoming a 'City in a Garden,' a cutting-edge role model of urban sustainability and biodiversity. A planned 35% improvement in energy efficiency between 2005 and 2030 led the government to introduce a sustainability rating system for buildings – the so-called Green Mark. Since 2008, all construction projects greater than 2000 sq metres (both new and retrofitted) are obliged to meet the Green Mark's minimum standards.

Singapore is steamrolling towards its target of 80% of buildings achieving Green Mark standards by 2030, with over 36% ticked off in 2018. Generous incentive schemes have encouraged an ever-growing number of buildings to incorporate sustainable design features, among them sun-shading exteriors, efficient water systems and carbon-emission-monitoring computers.

Singapore's incinerated waste is shipped off to Pulau Semakau, an island 8km south of the mainland. The 3.5 sq km landfill here is projected to meet the country's waste needs until 2045. More interestingly, the island itself has been much promoted by the government as an 'eco' hot spot. Rehabilitated mangrove swamps sit next to a coral nursery. In 2005, the island was also opened for recreation activities such as nature walks and fishing.

Though little of Singapore's original wilderness is left, growing interest in ecology has seen bird sanctuaries and parkland areas created, with new parks in the Marina Bay development as well as a series of connectors that link up numerous existing parks and gardens around the island.

Regional Environmental Awareness Cameron Highlands (REACH; www.reach.org.my) has been working since 2001 to preserve, restore and maintain this region as an environmentally sustainable agricultural area and tourist resort within a permanent nature reserve.

Survival Guide

DIRECTORY A–Z....598

Accessible Travel 598
Accommodation........ 598
Children 600
Customs
Regulations............ 600
Electricity 600
Embassies &
Consulates 600
Insurance...............601
Internet Access..........601
Legal Matters 601
LGBTIQ+ Travellers 601
Maps.................. 602
Money................. 602
Opening Hours 602
Photography 602
Post................... 602
Public Holidays........ 602
Safe Travel 603
Telephone 603
Time 603
Toilets................. 603
Tourist Information 604
Visas.................. 604
Volunteering 604

Women
Travellers.............. 605
Work 605

TRANSPORT 606

GETTING THERE
& AWAY 606
Entering Malaysia....... 606
Air 606
Land 606
Sea 607
GETTING AROUND.......607
Air 607
Bicycle 608
Boat 608
Bus 608
Car & Motorcycle....... 608
Hitching 609
Local Transport......... 609
Long Distance Taxis......610
Train 610

HEALTH 611

LANGUAGE 616

Directory A–Z

See the Directory sections of the Singapore (p556) and Brunei (p486) chapters for further information.

Accessible Travel

For those with mobility issues, Malaysia can be a nightmare. In many cities and towns there are often no footpaths, kerbs are very high, construction sites are everywhere, and crossings are few and far between.

While the 2008 Persons with Disabilities Act recognises the rights of people with disabilities to have equal access to public transport, among many other social goods, there is no penalty for noncompliance. The government does not mandate accessibility to transportation, and few older public facilities are adapted; new government buildings are generally more likely to be accessible.

The rights of air passengers were improved in 2016, meaning that people with a disability cannot be discriminated against and no longer need to notify an airline unless they are travelling with an electric mobility device, in which case 48 hours' notice is required. The only exception is if an aircraft's size or doors prevent boarding.

PRACTICALITIES

Electricity Connect to the reliable electricity supply (220V to 240V, 50 cycles) with a UK-type three-square-pin plug.

Newspapers English-language newspapers include the *New Straits Times* (www.nst.com.my), the *Star* (www.thestar.com.my) and the *Malay Mail* (www.malaymail.com).

Radio Listen to Traxx FM (90.3FM; http://traxxfm.rtm.gov.my), HITZ FM (92.9FM; www.hitz.com.my) and MIX FM (94.5FM; http://listen.mix.fm) for music, and BFM (89.9FM; www.bfm.my) or Fly FM (95.8FM; www.flyfm.com.my) for news.

TV You can watch the two government TV channels, TV1 and TV2, and the four commercial stations, TV3, NTV7, 8TV and TV9, as well as a host of satellite channels.

Weights and measures The metric system is used.

Ace Altair Travels (03-2181 8765; disabledtravelinmalaysia.weebly.com) Based in Kuala Lumpur, this is the only specialist accessible travel agent and tour operator in Malaysia. In addition to tours and hotel bookings, they offer wheelchair-accessible transfers (from the airport or door-to-door) and equipment rental.

Disabled Holidays (www.disabledholidays.com) This UK-based specialist accessible travel agent and tour operator has a range of offers covering both mainland and East Malaysia.

Malaysia's National Council for the Blind has some online information about tourism initiatives for the sight impaired across the country – see www.ncbm.org.my/index/tourism-in-malaysia for details.

Download Lonely Planet's free Accessible Travel guides from https://shop.lonelyplanet.com/categories/accessible-travel.com. Before setting off, get in touch with your national support organisation (preferably with the travel officer, if there is one).

Accommodation

Malaysia's accommodation options range from simple backpacker dorms to some of Asia's most luxurious resorts.

Outside the peak holiday seasons big discounts are frequently available – it's always worth asking about special offers.

A government tax of RM10 per room per night applies to all hotel rooms – check whether this is included in the quoted rates when booking. Almost all top-end hotels levy an additional 10% service charge on top of their rates, expressed as + on their rates. Credit cards are widely accepted, although at some cheaper places it's cash only.

Apart from for very specific places in the likes of national parks (where the accommodation options are limited) and during peak travel seasons (ie around major festivals such as Chinese New Year in January/February), it's not generally necessary to book in advance.

Apartment Rentals

In Malaysia's major cities and towns it's easy to find apartments and houses to rent – check the usual online sources. Rates can be very affordable and are comparable to midrange hotels although the level of facilities for individual properties can vary greatly. Key things to check include whether the property includes a swimming pool (many do), laundry facilities and unlimited wi-fi.

Camping

Many of Malaysia's national parks have official camping grounds and will permit camping in nondesignated sites once you are deep in the jungle. There are also many lonely stretches of beach that are ideal for camping. Likewise, it is possible to camp on uninhabited bays on many of Malaysia's islands. A two-season tent with mosquito netting is ideal. A summer-weight sleeping bag is OK, but the best choice is a lightweight bag-liner, since even the nights are warm.

Homestays

Staying with a Malaysian family will give you a unique experience many times removed from the fast-paced and largely recognisable life of the cities and towns. Enquire with Tourism Malaysia (www.tourism.gov.my) and each of the state tourism bodies about the homestay programs operating throughout the country in off-the-beaten-track *kampung* (villages).

Hostels & Guesthouses

At beach resorts and in the main tourist cities you will find a variety of cheap hostels and guesthouses as well as more modern hostels that cost a little more but offer better design and facilities. Dormitory accommodation is commonly available. Rooms may be spartan (with flimsy walls and sometimes no window) and have shared bathrooms, but this is the cheapest accommodation option around and a great place to meet fellow travellers. These places offer their customers lots of little extras to outdo the competition, such as free wi-fi, tea and coffee, bicycles and transport. Dorm beds cost anything between RM10 and RM50 depending on the location, a hotel-style room with air-con is RM20 to RM100.

Hotels

Standard rooms at top-end hotels are often called 'superior' in the local parlance. Most hotels have slightly more expensive 'deluxe' or 'club' rooms, which tend to

be larger, have a better view and include extras such as breakfast or free internet access. Many also have suites.

At the budget end of the scale are the traditional Chinese-run hotels usually offering little more than simple rooms with a bed, table and chair, and sink. The showers and toilets may be down the corridor. Note couples can sometimes economise by asking for a single, since in budget hotel language 'single' means one double bed, and 'double' means two beds. Don't think of this as being tight; in budget hotels you can pack as many into one room as you wish.

The main catch with these hotels is that they can sometimes be terribly noisy. They're often on main streets, and the cheapest ones often have thin walls that stop short of the ceiling – great for ventilation but terrible for acoustics and privacy.

Note, promotional deals at top-end hotels can bring their rates down to midrange levels.

Longhouses

A distinctive feature of indigenous Dayak life in Malaysian Borneo is the longhouse – essentially an entire village under one seemingly interminable roof. Contemporary longhouses fuse age-old forms with highly functional features such as corrugated-iron roofs and satellite dishes. According to longstanding Dayak tradition, anyone who shows up at a longhouse must be welcomed and given accommodation. However, these days turning up at a longhouse unannounced may be an unwelcome imposition on the residents – in short, bad manners. The way to avoid these pitfalls is to hire a locally savvy guide or tour company that can co-ordinate your visit and make introductions.

Resthouses

A handful of the old British-developed resthouses, set up during the colonial era to provide accommodation for travelling officials, are still operating. Many are still government owned but are privately operated. Some have been turned into modern midrange resorts, others retain colonial-era decor and are in poor health. Resthouses typically charge between RM60 and RM150 per room, usually including air-con and attached bathroom.

Children

Travelling with the kids in Malaysia is generally a breeze. For the most part, parents needn't be overly concerned, but it pays to lay down a few ground rules – such as regular hand-washing – to head off potential problems. Children should especially be warned not to play with animals, as rabies occurs in Malaysia.

Lonely Planet's *Travel with Children* contains useful advice on how to cope with kids on the road and what to

bring along to make things go more smoothly, with special attention paid to travelling in developing countries. Also useful for general advice is www.travelwithyourkids.com.

There are discounts for children for most attractions and for most transport. Many beach resorts have special family lodgings. Cots, however, are not widely available in cheaper accommodation. Public transport is comfortable and relatively well organised. Pushing a stroller around isn't likely to be easy given there are often no level footpaths and kerbs are high.

Baby formula, baby food and nappies (diapers) are widely available. However, it makes sense to stock up on these items before heading to remote destinations or islands. When breastfeeding a baby in public be sure to be discreet, covering your breasts with a scarf or towel.

Customs Regulations

The following can be brought into Malaysia duty free:

➡ 1L of alcohol

➡ 225g of tobacco (200 cigarettes or 50 cigars)

➡ souvenirs and gifts not exceeding RM200 (RM500 when coming from Labuan or Langkawi)

Cameras, portable radios, perfume, cosmetics and watches do not incur duty. Prohibited items include weapons (including imitations), fireworks and 'obscene and prejudicial articles' (pornography, for example, and items that may be considered inflammatory, or religiously offensive) and drugs. Drug smuggling carries the death penalty in Malaysia.

Visitors can carry no more than the equivalent of US$10,000 in ringgit or any other currency in and out of Malaysia.

Electricity

Type G
230V/50Hz

Embassies & Consulates

For a full list of Malaysian embassies and consulates outside the country check out www.kln.gov.my. Most foreign embassies are in Kuala Lumpur and are generally open 8am to 12.30pm and 1.30pm to 4.30pm Monday to Friday.

Australian High Commission (☎03-2146 5555; www.malaysia.highcommission.gov.au; 6 Jln Yap Kwan Seng; ⊗8.30am-4.30pm Mon-Fri; LRT KLCC)

Brunei High Commission (☎03-8888 7777; www.mofat.gov.bn; 2 Jln Diplomatik 2/5, Precint 15; ⊗8.30am-4.30pm Mon-Fri)

Canadian High Commission (☎03-2718 3333; www.canadainternational.gc.ca; 17th fl, Menara Tan & Tan, 207 Jln Tun Razak; ⊗8am-noon & 1-4.30pm Mon-Thu, 8am-12.30pm Fri; LRT Ampang Park)

Dutch Embassy (☑03-2168 6200; www.nederland wereldwijd.nl/landen/maleisie; 7th fl, South Block, The Amp Walk, 218 Jln Ampang; ☺8.30-11am Mon-Thu; LRT Ampang Park)

French Embassy (☑03-2053 5500; www.ambafrance-my. org; Level 31, Integra Tower, 348 Jln Tun Razak; ☺8.45am-1pm & 2-5.15pm Mon-Fri; LRT Ampang Park)

German Embassy (☑03-2170 9666; www.kuala-lumpur.diplo. de; 26th fl, Menara Tan & Tan, 207 Jln Tun Razak; ☺9am-noon Mon-Fri & 1-3pm Thu; LRT Ampang Park)

Indonesian Embassy (☑03-2116 4000; www.kemlu.go.id/ kualalumpur/en; 233 Jln Tun Razak; ☺9am-1pm & 2-5pm Mon-Thu, 9am-12.30pm & 2.30-5pm Fri; Ⓜ Tun Razak Exchange)

Irish Embassy (☑03-2167 8200; www.dfa.ie/irish-embassy/malaysia; 5th fl, South Block, The Amp Walk, 218 Jln Ampang; ☺9.30am-12.30pm daily, 2.30-3.30pm Mon-Thu; LRT Ampang Park)

New Zealand High Commission (☑03-2078 2533; www. nzembassy.com/malaysia; Level 21, Menara IMC, 8 Jln Sultan Ismail; ☺8.30am-12.30pm Mon-Fri; Ⓑ Bukit Nanas)

Singapore High Commission (☑03-2161 6277; www.mfa. gov.sg; 209 Jln Tun Razak; ☺8.30am-5pm Mon-Fri; LRT Ampang Park)

Thai Embassy (☑03-2145 8004; www.thaiembassy.org/ kualalumpur; 206 Jln Ampang; ☺9am-1pm & 2-5pm Mon-Fri; LRT Ampang Park)

UK High Commission (☑03-2170 2200; www.gov.uk/world/ malaysia; Level 27 Menara Binjai, 2 Jln Binjai; ☺8am-12.30pm daily, 1.15-4.30pm Mon-Thu; LRT Ampang Park)

US Embassy (☑03-2168 5000; https://my.usembassy. gov; 376 Jln Tun Razak; ☺7.45am-4.30pm Mon-Fri; LRT Ampang Park)

Insurance

It's always a good idea to take out travel insurance. Check the small print to see if the policy covers potentially dangerous sporting activities such as caving, diving or trekking, and make sure that it adequately covers your valuables. Health-wise, you may prefer a policy that pays doctors or hospitals directly rather than having to pay on the spot and claim later. If you have to claim later, make sure that you keep all documentation. Check that the policy covers ambulances, an emergency flight home and, if you plan trekking in remote areas, a helicopter evacuation.

A few credit cards offer limited, sometimes full, travel insurance to the holder.

Internet Access

Malaysia is blanketed with hot spots for wi-fi connections (usually free). Internet cafes are much less common these days, but do still exist if you're not travelling with a wi-fi enabled device. Only in the jungles and the most remote reaches of the peninsula and Malaysian Borneo are you likely to be without any internet access.

Legal Matters

In any dealings with the local police it will pay to be deferential. You're most likely to come into contact with them either through reporting a crime (some of the big cities in Malaysia have tourist police stations for this purpose) or while driving. Minor misdemeanours may be overlooked, but don't count on it.

Drug trafficking carries a mandatory death penalty. A number of foreigners have been executed in Malaysia, some of them for posses-sion of amazingly small quantities of heroin. Even possession of tiny amounts of classified drugs can bring down a lengthy jail sentence and a beating with the *rotan* (cane). Just don't do it.

LGBTIQ+ Travellers

Malaysia is a predominantly Muslim country and the level of tolerance for homosexuality is vastly different from its neighbours. It's illegal for men of any age to have sex with other men. In addition, the Islamic sharia laws (which apply only to Muslims) forbid sodomy and cross-dressing.

LGBTIQ+ travellers should avoid behaviour that attracts unwanted attention. The locals in the region are conservative about all displays of public affection regardless of sexual orientation. Although same-sex hand-holding is fairly common for men and women, this is rarely an indication of sexuality; an overtly gay couple doing the same would attract attention.

There's actually a fairly active LGBTIQ+ scene in KL and a slightly more discreet one in George Town. Start looking for information on www.utopia-asia.com, which provides good coverage of LGBTIQ+ events and activities across Asia.

EATING PRICE RANGES

The following price ranges refer to an average meal including a soft drink.

$ less than RM15

$$ RM15–60

$$$ more than RM60

Maps

Periplus (www.periplus publishinggroup.com) has maps covering Malaysia, Peninsular Malaysia and KL. Tourism Malaysia's free *Map of Malaysia* has useful distance charts, facts about the country and inset maps of many major cities.

For accurate maps of rural areas contact the **National Survey & Mapping Department** (Ibu Pejabat Ukur & Pemetaan Malaysia; ☎03-2617 0800; www.jupem.gov. my; Wisma JUPEM, Jln Sultan Yahya Petra, Kuala Lumpur; ⊙7.30am-5.30pm Mon-Thu, 7.30am-noon & 2.45-5.30pm Fri; ☒Damai).

Money

ATMs & Credit Cards

Mastercard and Visa are the most widely accepted brands of credit card. You can make ATM withdrawals with your PIN, or banks such as Maybank (Malaysia's biggest bank), HSBC and Standard Chartered will accept credit cards for over-the-counter cash advances. Many banks are also linked to international banking networks such as Cirrus (the most common), Maestro and Plus, allowing withdrawals from overseas savings or cheque accounts.

If you have any questions about whether your cards will be accepted in Malaysia, ask your home bank about its reciprocal relationships with Malaysian banks.

Currency

The ringgit (RM) is made up of 100 sen. Coins in use are 1 sen (rare), 5 sen, 10 sen, 20 sen and 50 sen; notes come in RM1, RM5, RM10, RM20, RM50 and RM100.

Older Malaysians sometimes refer to ringgit as 'dollars' – if in doubt ask if people mean US dollars

or 'Malaysian dollars' (ie ringgit).

Be sure to carry plenty of small bills with you when venturing outside cities – in some cases people cannot change bills larger than RM20.

Travellers Cheques & Cash

Banks in the region are efficient and there are plenty of moneychangers. For changing cash or travellers cheques, banks usually charge a commission (around RM10 per transaction, with a possible small fee per cheque), whereas moneychangers have no charges but their rates vary more. Compared with a bank, you'll generally get a better rate for cash at a money-changer – it's usually quicker too. Away from the tourist centres, moneychangers' rates are often poorer and they may not change travellers cheques.

All major brands of travellers cheques are accepted across the region. Cash in major currencies is also readily exchanged, though like everywhere else in the world, the US dollar has a slight edge.

Opening Hours

Banks 10am–3pm Monday to Friday, 9.30am–11.30am Saturday

Bars and clubs 5pm–5am

Cafes 8am–10pm

Restaurants noon–2.30pm and 6pm–10.30pm

Shops 9.30am–7pm, malls 10am–10pm

Photography

Malaysians are generally happy to be photographed, although of course it's polite to ask permission before doing so. Also ask before taking pictures in mosques or temples. For advice on taking better photos, Lonely

Planet's *Travel Photography: A Guide to Taking Better Pictures* is written by travel photographer Richard I'Anson.

Post

Pos Malaysia Berhad (☎1300 300 300; www.pos. com.my) runs an efficient postal system. Post offices are generally open 8.30am to 5.30pm from Monday to Friday, and until 1pm on Saturday.

Aerograms and postcards cost 50 sen to send to any destination. Letters weighing 20g or less cost RM1.40 to Asia, Australia or New Zealand, and RM2 to all other countries. Parcel rates range from around RM30 to RM80 for a 1kg parcel, depending on the destination. Main post offices sell packaging materials and stationery.

Public Holidays

In addition to national public holidays, each state has its own holidays, usually associated with the sultan's birthday or a Muslim celebration. Muslim holidays are 10 or 11 days earlier each year. Hindu and Chinese holiday dates also vary, but fall roughly within the same months each year.

As well as fixed secular holidays, various religious festivals (which change dates annually) are national holidays. These include Chinese New Year (in January/ February), the Hindu festival of Deepavali (in October/ November), the Buddhist festival of Wesak (April/May) and the Muslim festivals of Hari Raya Haji, Hari Raya Puasa, Mawlid al-Nabi and Awal Muharram (Muslim New Year).

Fixed annual holidays include the following:

New Year's Day 1 January

Federal Territory Day 1 February (in Kuala Lumpur and Putrajaya only)

Good Friday March or April (in Sarawak & Sabah only)

Labour Day 1 May

Yang di-Pertuan Agong's (King's) Birthday 1st Saturday in June

National Day (Hari Kebangsaan) 31 August

Malaysia Day 16 September

Christmas Day 25 December

School Holidays

Schools break for holidays five times a year. The actual dates vary from state to state but are generally in January (one week), March (two weeks), May (three weeks), August (one week) and October (four weeks).

Safe Travel

Animal Hazards

Rabies does occur in Malaysia, so any bite from an animal should be treated very seriously. In the jungles and mangrove forests, living hazards include leeches (annoying but harmless), snakes (some kinds are highly venomous), macaques (prone to bag-snatching in some locales), orangutans (occasionally aggressive) and, in muddy estuaries, saltwater crocodiles (deadly, if they drag you under).

Theft & Violence

Muggings do happen, particularly in KL and Penang, and physical attacks have been known to occur, particularly after hours and in areas of cities with limited infrastructure. Thieves on motorbikes particularly target women for grab raids on their handbags. Also don't drop your guard on holiday islands such as Langkawi and the Perhentians – never leave your belongings unattended while on the beach for example.

A small, sturdy padlock is well worth carrying, especially if you are going to be staying at any of the inexpensive huts found on Malaysia's beaches, where flimsy padlocks are the norm.

Telephone

Landline services are provided by the national monopoly Telekom Malaysia (TM; www.tm.com.my).

International Calls

The easiest and cheapest way to make international calls is to buy a local SIM card for your mobile (cell) phone. Only certain payphones permit international calls. You can make operator-assisted international calls from local TM offices. To save money on landline calls, buy a prepaid international calling card (available from convenience stores).

Local Calls

Local calls cost eight sen for the first two minutes. Payphones take coins or prepaid cards, which are available from TM offices and convenience stores. Some also take international credit cards. You'll also find a range of discount calling cards at convenience stores and mobile-phone counters.

Mobile (Cell) Phones

If you have arranged global roaming with your home provider, your GSM digital phone will automatically tune into one of the region's networks.

If not, buy a prepaid SIM card (passport required) for one of the local networks on arrival.

The rate for locals calls and text messages is around 36 sen.

There are three main mobile-phone companies, all with similar call rates and prepaid packages:

Celcom (www.celcom.com.my) This is the best company to use if you'll be spending time in remote regions of Sabah and Sarawak.

DiGi (http://new.digi.com.my)

Maxis (www.maxis.com.my)

Time

Malaysia is eight hours ahead of GMT/UTC (London). When it's noon in Malaysia it is:

Los Angeles	8pm previous day
New York	11pm previous day
London	4am
Sydney	2pm

Toilets

Although there are still some places with Asian squat-style toilets, you'll most often find Western-style ones these days. At public facilities toilet paper is not usually provided. Instead, you will find a hose which you are supposed to use as a bidet or, in cheaper places, a bucket of water and a tap. If you're not comfortable with this, remember to take

DIRECTORY A-Z TOURIST INFORMATION

packets of tissues or toilet paper wherever you go.

Tourist Information

Tourism Malaysia (www. tourism.gov.my) has a good network of overseas offices, which are useful for pre-departure planning. Unfortunately, its domestic offices are less helpful and are often unable to give specific information about destinations and transport. Nonetheless, they do stock some decent brochures as well as the excellent *Map of Malaysia*.

Within Malaysia there are also a number of state tourist-promotion organisations, which often have more detailed information about specific areas. These include:

Sabah Tourism (www.sabah tourism.com)

Pahang Tourism (www.pahang tourism.org.my)

Perak Tourism (www.perak tourism.com.my)

Sarawak Tourism (www. sarawaktourism.com)

Penang Global Tourism (www. mypenang.gov.my)

Tourism Johor (http://tourism. johor.my)

Tourism Selangor (www.tourism selangor.my)

Tourism Terengganu (http:// tourism.terengganu.gov.my)

Kelantan Tourism (http:// tourism.kelantan.my)

Visit Kedah (www.visitkedah. com.my)

Visit Kuala Lumpur (www. visitkl.gov.my/visitklv2)

Visas

Visitors must have a passport valid for at least six months beyond the date of entry into Malaysia. The following gives a brief overview of other requirements – full

details of visa regulations are available at www.kln. gov.my.

Depending on the expected length of their stay, most visitors are given a 30- or 60-day visa on arrival. As a general rule, if you arrive by air you will be given 60 days automatically, though coming overland you may be given 30 days unless you specifically ask for a 60-day permit. It's possible to get an extension at an immigration office in Malaysia for a total stay of up to three months. This is a straightforward procedure that is easily done in major Malaysian cities.

Only under special circumstances can Israeli citizens enter Malaysia.

Both Sabah and Sarawak retain a certain degree of state-level control of their borders. Tourists must go through passport control and have their passports stamped at the following occasions:

➡ arriving in Sabah or Sarawak from Peninsular Malaysia or the federal district of Pulau Labuan;

➡ exiting Sabah or Sarawak on the way to Peninsular Malaysia or Pulau Labuan;

➡ travelling between Sabah and Sarawak.

When entering Sabah or Sarawak from another part of Malaysia, your new visa stamp will be valid only for the remainder of the period left on your original Malaysian visa. In Sarawak, an easy way to extend your visa is to make a 'visa run' to Brunei or Indonesia (through the Tebedu–Entikong land crossing).

Volunteering

There are myriad volunteering organisations in the region, but be aware that so-called 'voluntourism' has become big business

and that not every organisation fulfils its promise of meaningful experiences. Experts recommend a minimum commitment of three months for positions working with children. Lonely Planet does not endorse any organisations that we do not work with directly, so it is essential that you do your own thorough research before agreeing to volunteer with any organisation.

All Women's Action Society Malaysia (www.awam.org.my) Aims to improve the lives of women in Malaysia by lobbying for a just, democratic and equitable society with respect and equality for both genders.

Ecoteer (www.ecoteer.com) Offers various volunteer projects including ones relating to turtle conservation in the Perhentians.

Free Tree Society (www.free treesociety.org; Jln Limau Purut, Bangsar; ⊙9.30-11.30am Tue & Sat; ◻822) This organisation is always on the lookout for green-fingered volunteers to take care of its plants.

The Great Projects (www. thegreatprojects.com) Organisation that places paying volunteers at the Matang Wildlife Centre in Sarawak as well as on other wildlife conservation projects around Malaysia.

Lang Tengah Turtle Watch (www.langtengahturtlewatch. org; Turtle Bay; per 2 weeks US$530) Help safeguard the turtles that come to lay their eggs on this east-coast peninsula island.

LASSie (www.langkawilassie. org.my) Dog and cat lovers can help out at the Langkawi Animal Shelter & Sanctuary Foundation.

Malaysian Nature Society (www.mns.my) Check its website or drop them a line to find out ways you can get involved in helping preserve Malaysia's natural environment.

Miso Walai Homestay Program (www.misowalaihomestay.

com) Gets travellers involved with local wetlands restoration projects.

PAWS (www.paws.org.my) Animal rescue shelter in Subang, about 30 minutes from central KL.

Sepilok Orangutan Rehabilitation Centre (SORC; ☑089-531189, emergency 089-531180; www.wildlife.sabah.gov.my; Jln Sepilok; adult/5-17yr RM30/15, camera fee RM10; ☺9am-noon & 2-4pm) ☞ Has one of Malaysia's best established volunteer programs for animal lovers.

Wild Asia (www.wildasia.org) A variety of volunteer options generally connected with the environment and sustainable tourism in the region.

Zoo Negara (National Zoo; ☑03-4108 3422; www.zoonegaramalaysia.my; Jln Ulu Kelang, Ampang Jaya; adult/child RM80/40.50; ☺9am-5pm; P; MWangsa Maju) It is possible to arrange to spend a day volunteering at Malaysia's national zoo.

Women Travellers

Be mindful of what's culturally appropriate. When visiting mosques, cover your head and limbs with a headscarf and sarong (many mosques lend these out at the entrance). At the beach, most Malaysian women swim fully clothed in T-shirts and shorts – while you might not want to follow suit, choosing a modest bathing costume will keep you in line with social customs.

Malaysia is generally a safe country but it is prudent to be proactive about personal safety. Treat overly friendly strangers, both male and female, with a good deal of caution. Take taxis after dark and avoid walking alone at night in quiet or less busy parts of town.

Work

There are possibilities for those who seek them out, from professional-level jobs in finance, journalism and the oil industry to temporary jobs at some guesthouses and dive centres in popular resort areas. Those with teaching credentials can find English-teaching jobs in Malaysia, though pickings are slim compared to Japan and Korea.

Depending on the nature of your job, you'll need either an Expatriate Personnel Visa or a Temporary Employment Visa. For details and requirements, check the website of the **Immigration Department of Malaysia** (www.imi.gov.my/index.php/ms).

Transport

See the Transport sections of the Singapore (p559) and Brunei (p480) chapters for further information.

GETTING THERE & AWAY

Entering Malaysia

The main requirements for entering Malaysia are a passport that's valid for travel for at least six months, proof of an onward ticket and adequate funds for your stay, although you will rarely be asked to prove this.

Flights, tours and tours can be booked online at www.lonelyplanet.com/bookings.

Air

Airports & Airlines

The bulk of international flights arrive at **Kuala Lumpur International Airport** (KLIA; ☑03-8777 7000; www.klia.com.my; ℝKLIA), 55km south of Kuala Lumpur (KL); it has two terminals with KLIA2 being used mainly by budget airlines (KLIA2 is AirAsia's hub). Some budget airlines with connections from Indonesia, Singapore and Thailand also fly into KL's **SkyPark Subang Terminal** (Sultan Abdul Aziz Shah Airport; ☑03-7845 1717; www.subangskypark.com; M17, Subang). There are also direct flights from Asia and Australia into Penang, Kuching, Kota Kinabalu and a few other cities.

Malaysia Airlines (MAS; ☑03-7843 3000, international 1300 883 000; www.malaysiaairlines.com) is the national carrier.

Tickets

When shopping for a ticket, compare the cost of flying into Malaysia versus the cost of flying into Singapore. From Singapore you can travel overland to almost any place in Peninsular Malaysia in less than a day, and Singapore also has direct flights to Malaysian Borneo and Brunei. KL and Singapore are also good places to buy tickets for onward travel.

Land

Brunei

Daily buses run from Bandar Seri Begawan (BSB) to Miri (Sarawak) and Kota Kinabalu (Sabah).

Indonesia

Several bus companies ply the route between Kuching Sentral bus terminal (and other cities along the Sarawak coast) and the West Kalimantan city of Pontianak (economy RM60, 1st class RM80, seven/10 hours via the new/old road), passing through the Tebedu (Malaysia) and Entikong (Indonesia) crossing 80km south of Kuching, the only official land border between

---

CLIMATE CHANGE & TRAVEL

Every form of transport that relies on carbon-based fuel generates CO_2, the main cause of human-induced climate change. Modern travel is dependent on aeroplanes, which might use less fuel per kilometre per person than most cars but travel much greater distances. The altitude at which aircraft emit gases (including CO_2) and particles also contributes to their climate change impact. Many websites offer 'carbon calculators' that allow people to estimate the carbon emissions generated by their journey and, for those who wish to do so, to offset the impact of the greenhouse gases emitted with contributions to portfolios of climate-friendly initiatives throughout the world. Lonely Planet offsets the carbon footprint of all staff and author travel.

Sarawak and Kalimantan. Travellers from 64 countries can sometimes get a one-month Indonesian visa on arrival at the Tebedu–Entikong crossing. However, as this situation can be liable to change, it's best to arrange an Indonesian visa at the Indonesian Consulate in Kuching before making the journey. The border crossing is open for all bus arrivals and departures.

Singapore

The Causeway linking Johor Bahru with Singapore handles most traffic between the countries.

From Johor Bahru, a shuttle train (RM5/S\$5, five minutes) operated by Malaysia's **KTM** (Keretapi Tanah Melayu; ☑03-2267 1200; www.ktmb.com.my; ☺call centre 7am-10pm) ferries commuters between the Woodlands Checkpoint on Singapore and JB Sentral between 14 and 17 times a day. Alternatively take one of the more frequent buses from JB to central Singapore or a taxi across the Causeway.

A good website with details of express buses between Singapore, Malaysia and Thailand is the Express Bus Travel Guide (www. singaporemalaysiabus.com).

There is also a causeway linking Tuas, in western Singapore, with Geylang Patah in JB. This is known as the Second Link, and some bus services to Melaka and up the west coast head this way; be prepared for delays at the immigration control. If you have a car, tolls on the Second Link are much higher than those on the main Causeway.

Thailand
BUS & CAR

You can cross the border by road into Thailand at Padang Besar, Bukit Kayu Hitam, Rantau Panjang (Sungai Golok on the Thai side) and Pengkalan Kubor.

TRAIN

The rail route into Thailand crosses the Malaysian border at Padang Besar. There is one direct train daily from Bangkok to Padang Besar in each direction, plus three others that shuttle between Padang Besar and Hat Yai on the Thai side of the border.

If you're planning on travelling to Thailand from Johor Bahru (just across the border from Singapore) then you'll now need to change trains: first Johor Bahru to Gemas, then from there to Padang Besar for a connection to Thailand. You will have to stop overnight en-route.

For more details on fares, timetables etc see KTM and www.seat61.com.

A handful of times a year, the opulent *Eastern & Oriental Express* (www.belmond. com/eastern-and-oriental-express) connects Singapore and Bangkok, making stops in KL and Butterworth (for Penang).

Sea
Brunei

There are at least two ferries (adult/child/car B\$18/10/58) each day departing from Serasa Ferry Terminal in Muara, about 25km northeast of Bandar Seri Begawan, to the Malaysian federal territory of Pulau Labuan (two hours), though only the car ferry is reliable.

Indonesia

The following are the main ferry routes between Indonesia and Malaysia:

➡ Bengkalis (Sumatra) to Melaka

➡ Pulau Batam to Johor Bahru

➡ Dumai (Sumatra) to Melaka

➡ Medan (Sumatra) to Penang

➡ Pekanbaru (Sumatra) to Melaka

➡ Tanjung Pinang Bintan to Johor Bahru

➡ Tanjung Balai (Sumatra) to Pelabuhan Klang and Kukup

➡ Tarakan (Kalimantan) to Tawau

Singapore

Limbongan Maju (www.limbon ganmaju.com) ferries connect Singapore's **Changi Point Ferry Terminal** (☑6545 2305; 51 Lorong Bekukong; ☺24hr; ☑2) with Tanjung Belungkor in Johor, Malaysia. The service, which takes 30 minutes and costs from S\$26 one-way, runs twice daily in both directions Monday to Friday and four times on weekends.

Thailand

Ferries connect Kuah on Pulau Langkawi with Satun on the Thai coast and, from November to mid-May, with Ko Lipe; make sure you get your passport stamped going in either direction.

GETTING AROUND

Air

The two main domestic operators are **Malaysia Airlines** (MAS; ☑03-7843 3000; international 1300 883 000; www. malaysiaairlines.com) and **AirAsia** (☑600 85 8888; www. airasia.com).

The Malaysia Airlines subsidiary **Firefly** (☑03-7845 4543; www.fireflyz.com.my) has flights from KL (SkyPark Subang Terminal) to Ipoh, Johor Bahru, Kerteh, Kota Bharu, Kuala Terengganu, Langkawi and Penang. It also runs connections between Penang and Langkawi, Kuantan and Kota Bharu, Ipoh and JB, and JB and Kota Bharu.

Malindo Air (☎03-7841 5388; www.malindoair.com) also has a wide range of connections between many Malaysian cities and towns.

In Malaysian Borneo, Malaysia Airlines' subsidiary **MASwings** (☎1300-88 3000; www.maswings.com. my) offers local flights within and between Sarawak and Sabah; its main hub is Miri. These services, especially those handled by 19-seat Twin Otters, are very much reliant on the vagaries of the weather. In the wet season (October to March in Sarawak and on Sabah's northeast coast; May to November on Sabah's west coast), places like Bario in Sarawak can be isolated for days at a time, so don't venture into this area if you have a tight schedule. These flights are completely booked during school holidays. At other times it's easier to get a seat at a few days' notice, but always book as far in advance as possible.

Discounts

All the airlines offer discounted tickets online, depending on how far in advance you book. A variety of other discounts (typically between 25% and 50%) are available for flights around Malaysia on Malaysia Airlines, including for families and groups of three or more. Student discounts are available, but only for students enrolled in institutions that are in Malaysia.

Bicycle

Bicycle touring around Malaysia is an increasingly popular activity. The main road system is well engineered and has good surfaces, but the secondary road system is limited. Road conditions are good enough for touring bikes in most places, but mountain bikes

are recommended for forays off the beaten track.

Top-quality bicycles and components can be bought in major cities, but generally 10-speed (or higher) bikes and fittings are hard to find. Bringing your own is the best bet. Bicycles can be transported on most international flights; check with the airline about extra charges and shipment specifications.

Cycling Kuala Lumpur (http://cyclingkl.blogspot.my) A great resource for cycling adventures in and around KL

Kuala Lumpur Mountain Bike Hash (www.klmbh.org) Details of the monthly bike ride out of KL.

Malaysia Cycling Events & Blogs (www.malaysiacycling. blogspot.co.uk) Includes listings of cycle shops around the country.

Boat

There are no services connecting Peninsular Malaysia with Malaysian Borneo. On a local level, there are boats and ferries between the peninsula and offshore islands, and along the rivers of Sabah and Sarawak. Note that some ferry operators are notoriously lax about observing safety rules, and local authorities are often nonexistent. If a boat looks overloaded or otherwise unsafe, *do not board it* – no one else will look out for your safety.

Bus

Bus travel in Malaysia is economical and generally comfortable. Seats can be paid for and reserved either directly with operators or via online sites such www. easybook.com. Some bus drivers speed recklessly, resulting in frequent, often fatal, accidents.

Konsortium Transnasional Berhad (www.ktb.com.my) is Malaysia's largest bus operator running services under

the **Transnasional** (☎03-4047 7878; www.trans nasional.com.my), **Nice** (☎03-2260 1185; www.nice-coaches. com.my; Mezzanine floor, Jln Sultan Hishamuddin, Kuala Lumpur; ⊠Kuala Lumpur), **Plusliner** (☎03-4047 7878; www.plusliner.com) and **Cityliner** (☎03-4047 7878; www.cityliner.com.my) brands. Its services tend to be slower than rivals, but its buses have also been involved in several major accidents. It has competition from a variety of privately operated buses on the longer domestic routes, including Aeroline (www.aeroline.com.my) and Super Nice (www.supernice. com.my). There are so many buses on major runs that you can often turn up and get a seat on the next bus.

Most long-distance buses have air-con, often turned to frigid, so bring a sweater!

In larger towns there may be a number of bus stations; local/regional buses often operate from one station and long-distance buses from another; in other cases, KL for example, bus stations are differentiated by the destinations they serve.

Bus travel off the beaten track is relatively straightforward. Small towns and *kampung* (villages) all over the country are serviced by public buses. Unfortunately, they are often poorly signed and sometimes the only way to find your bus is to ask a local. These buses are invariably dirt cheap and provide a great sample of rural life. In most towns there are no ticket offices, so buy your ticket from the conductor after you board.

Car & Motorcycle

Driving in Malaysia is fantastic compared with most Asian countries. There has been a lot of investment in the country's roads, which are generally of a high quality. New cars for hire are commonly available and fuel is inexpensive (RM2.20 per litre).

It's not all good news though. Driving in the cities, particularly KL, can be a nightmare, due to traffic and confusing one-way systems. Malaysian drivers aren't always the safest when it comes to obeying road rules – they mightn't be as reckless as drivers elsewhere in Southeast Asia, but they still take risks. For example, hardly any of the drivers keep to the official 110km/h speed limit on the main highways and tailgating is a common problem.

The Lebuhraya (North–South Hwy) is a six-lane expressway that runs for 966km along the length of the peninsula from the Thai border in the north to JB in the south. There are quite steep toll charges for using the expressway and these vary according to the distance travelled. As a result the normal highways remain crowded while traffic on the expressway is light.

Bring Your Own Vehicle

It's technically possible to bring your vehicle into Malaysia, but there are reams of red tape and the costs are prohibitively expensive – a hire car is a much better proposition.

Driving Licence

A valid overseas licence is needed to rent a car. An International Driving Permit (a translation of your state or national driver's licence and its vehicle categories) is usually not required by local car-hire companies, but it is recommended that you bring one. Most rental companies also require that drivers are at least 23 years old (and younger than 65) with at least one year of driving experience.

Hire

Major rent-a-car operations in Malaysia:

Avis (www.avis.com.my)

Hertz (www.simedarbycarrental. com)

Mayflower (www.mayflower carrental.com.my)

Orix (www.orixauto.com.my).

You'll also find local operators in individual cities.

Unlimited distance rates for a 1.3L Proton Saga, one of the cheapest and most popular cars in Malaysia, are posted at around RM190/1320 per day/week, including insurance and collision-damage waiver. The Proton is basically a Mitsubishi assembled under licence in Malaysia.

You can often get better prices, either through smaller local companies or when the major companies offer special deals. Rates drop substantially for longer rentals. The advantage of dealing with a large company is that it has offices all over the country, giving better backup if something goes wrong and allowing you to pick up in one city and drop off in another.

The best place to look for car hire is KL, though Penang is also good. In Sabah and Sarawak there is less competition and rates are higher, partly because of road conditions; there's also likely to be a surcharge if you drop your car off in a different city from the one you rented it in.

Insurance

Rental companies will provide insurance when you hire a car, but always check what the extent of your coverage will be, particularly if you're involved in an accident. You might want to take out your own insurance or pay the rental company an extra premium for an insurance excess reduction.

Road Rules & Hazards

➡ Cars are right-hand drive, and you drive on the left side of the road.

➡ The speed limit is 110km per hour on expressways, 50km per hour on *kampung* back roads.

➡ Wearing safety belts is compulsory.

➡ Watch out for stray animals, wandering pedestrians and the large number of motorcyclists.

➡ Malaysia drivers show remarkable common sense compared to other countries in the region. However, there are still plenty of drivers who take dangerous risks. Lane-drift is a big problem and signalling, when used at all, is often unclear. Giving a quick blast of the horn when you're overtaking a slower vehicle is common practice and helps alert otherwise sleepy drivers to your presence.

Hitching

Keep in mind hitching is never entirely safe, and we don't recommend it. Travellers who decide to hitch should understand that they are taking a small but potentially serious risk. People who do choose to hitch will be safer if they travel in pairs and let someone know where they are planning to go.

This said, Malaysia has long had a reputation for being a great place for hitchhiking, and it's generally still true, though with inexpensive bus travel, most travellers don't bother. Note that hitchers are banned from expressways.

Local Transport

Taxis are found in all large cities, and most have meters – although you can't always rely on the drivers to use them. Most people use the taxi app Grab.

Bicycle rickshaws (trishaws) supplement the taxi service in George Town and Melaka and are definitely handy ways of getting around the older parts of town, which have convoluted and narrow streets.

In major cities there are also buses, which are extremely cheap and convenient once you figure out which one is going which way. KL also has commuter trains, a Light Rail Transit (LRT), Mass Rapid Transit (MRT) and a monorail system.

In Malaysian Borneo, once you're out of the big cities, you're basically on your own and must either walk or hitch. If you're really in the bush, of course, riverboats and aeroplanes are the only alternatives to lengthy jungle treks.

Long Distance Taxis

As Malaysia has become a wealthier country, with more people owning their own cars, the long-distance taxi is becoming less of a feature of the transport landscape. However, in major towns and cities there will be a *teksi* stand for long-distance travel.

Taxis are available on a share basis for up to four people. As soon as a full complement of passengers turns up, off you go; alternatively, you can charter the whole taxi which is four times the single-fare rate. Early morning is generally the best time to find people to share a taxi, but enquire at the taxi stand the day before as to the best time to turn up.

Single fares are generally about twice the comparable bus fares. If you want to charter a taxi to an obscure destination, or by the hour, you'll probably have to do some negotiating. On the peninsula you're likely to pay around 50 sen per kilometre.

Taxi drivers often drive at frighteningly high speeds. They don't have as many head-on collisions as you might expect, but closing your eyes at times of high stress certainly helps! You also have the option of demanding that the driver slow down, but this can be met with varying degrees of hostility.

Train

Malaysia's national railway company is **KTM** (Keretapi Tanah Melayu; ☏03-2267 1200; www.ktmb.com.my; ◷call centre 7am-10pm). It runs a modern, comfortable and economical railway service, although there are basically only two lines.

One line runs up the west coast from Johor Bahru, through KL on into Thailand; there's a short spur off this line for Butterworth – the jumping off point for the island of Penang. Line two branches off the first line at Gemas and runs through Kuala Lipis up to the northeastern corner of the country near Kota Bharu in Kelantan. Often referred to as the 'jungle train', this line is properly known as the 'east line'.

On the west-coast line, a speedy electric train service now runs between Gemas and Padang Besar on the Thai border. .

In Sabah the North Borneo Railway (www.suteraharbour.com/north-borneo-railway), a narrow-gauge line running through the Sungai Padas gorge from Tenom to Beaufort, offers tourist trips lasting four hours on Wednesday and Saturday.

Services & Classes

There are two main types of rail services: express (ETS) and local trains. Express trains are air-conditioned and have 'premier' (1st class), 'superior' (2nd class) and sometimes 'economy' (3rd class) seats and, depending on the service, sleeping cabins. Local trains are usually economy class only, but some have superior seats.

Express trains stop only at main stations, while local services, which operate mostly on the east-coast line, stop everywhere, including the middle of the jungle, to let passengers and their goods on and off. Consequently local services take more than twice as long as the express trains and run to erratic schedules, but if you're in no hurry they provide a colourful experience and are good for short journeys.

Train schedules do change each year, so check the KTM website, where you can make bookings and buy tickets.

Health

BEFORE YOU GO

➡ Pack medications in their original, clearly labelled containers.

➡ Carry a signed and dated letter from your physician describing your medical conditions and medications, including their generic names.

➡ If you have a heart condition bring a copy of your ECG taken just prior to travelling.

➡ Bring a double supply of any regular medication in case of loss or theft.

Recommended Vaccinations

Proof of yellow-fever vaccination will be required if you have visited a country in the yellow-fever zone (such as Africa or South America) within the six days prior to entering the region. Otherwise, the World Health Organization (WHO) recommends the following vaccinations:

Adult diphtheria & tetanus Single booster recommended if none have been had in the previous 10 years.

Hepatitis A Provides almost 100% protection for up to a year. A booster after 12 months provides at least another 20 years' protection.

Hepatitis B Now considered routine for most travellers. Given as three shots over six months. A rapid schedule is also available, as is a combined vaccination with hepatitis A.

Measles, mumps & rubella (MMR) Two doses of MMR are required unless you have had the diseases. Many young adults require a booster.

Polio There have been no reported cases of polio in recent years. Only one booster is required as an adult for lifetime protection.

Typhoid Recommended unless your trip is less than a week and is only to developed cities. The vaccine offers around 70% protection, lasts for two to three years and comes as a single shot. Tablets are also available but the injection is usually recommended as it has fewer side effects.

Varicella If you haven't had chickenpox, discuss this vaccination with your doctor.

Online Resources

Centers for Disease Control & Prevention (CDC; www.cdc.gov) Check health conditions in all destinations and get up-to-date travel advice.

World Health Organization (WHO; www.who.int/ith) Has links to national travel and health websites.

It's also a good idea to consult your government's travel-health website, if one is available, before departure:

Australia (www.smartraveller. gov.au)

Canada (www.phac-aspc.gc.ca)

New Zealand (www.safetravel. govt.nz)

UK (www.gov.uk/foreign-travel-advice)

USA (wwwnc.cdc.gov/travel)

IN MALAYSIA, SINGAPORE & BRUNEI

Availability & Cost of Health Care

Malaysia The standard of medical care in the major centres is good, and most problems can be adequately dealt with in Kuala Lumpur.

Singapore Excellent medical facilities. You cannot buy medication over the counter without a doctor's prescription.

Brunei General care is reasonable. There is no local medical university, so expats and foreign-trained locals run the health-care system. Serious or complex cases are better managed in Singapore, but adequate primary health care and stabilisation are available.

BEDBUGS

Bedbugs live in the cracks of furniture and walls, and migrate to the bed at night to feed on you. They are a particular problem in the region and are more likely to strike in high-turnover accommodation, especially backpacker hostels, though they can be found anywhere. The room may look very clean but they can still be there. Protect yourself with the following strategies:

➡ Ask the hotel or hostel what they do to avoid bedbugs. It's a common problem and reputable establishments should have a pest-control procedure in place.

➡ Keep your luggage elevated off the floor to avoid having the critters latch on – this is one of the common ways bedbugs are spread from place to place.

➡ Check the room carefully for signs of bugs – you may find their translucent light brown skins or poppy seed–like excrement. Pay particular attention to places less likely to have seen a dusting from cleaning staff.

If you do get bitten:

➡ Treat the itch with antihistamine.

➡ Thoroughly clean your luggage and launder all your clothes, sealing them after in plastic bags to further protect them.

➡ Be sure to tell the management – if they seem unconcerned or refuse to do anything about it, complain to the local tourist office.

Infectious Diseases

The following are the most common for travellers:

Dengue fever Increasingly common in cities. The mosquito that carries dengue bites day and night, so use insect avoidance measures at all times. Symptoms can include high fever, severe headache, body ache, a rash and diarrhoea. There is no specific treatment, just rest and paracetamol – do not take aspirin as it increases the likelihood of haemorrhaging.

Hepatitis A This food- and water-borne virus infects the liver, causing jaundice (yellow skin and eyes), nausea and lethargy. All travellers to the region should be vaccinated against it.

Hepatitis B The only sexually transmitted disease (STD) that can be prevented by vaccination, hepatitis B is spread by body fluids, including sexual contact.

Hepatitis E Transmitted through contaminated food and water and has similar symptoms to hepatitis A, but it is far less common. It is a severe problem in pregnant women and can result in the death of both mother and baby. A vaccine has been developed and is licensed in China, but not elsewhere. Prevention is by following safe eating and drinking guidelines.

HIV Unprotected sex is the main method of transmission.

Influenza Can be very severe in people over the age of 65 or in those with underlying medical conditions such as heart disease or diabetes; vaccination is recommended for these individuals. There is no specific treatment, just rest and paracetamol.

Malaria Uncommon in the region but still present in Malaysian Borneo and deeply forested areas. Antimalarial drugs are rarely recommended for travellers. Remember that malaria can be fatal. Before you travel, seek medical advice on the right medication and dosage for you.

Rabies A potential risk, and invariably fatal if untreated, rabies is spread by the bite or lick of an infected animal – most commonly a dog or monkey. Pre-travel vaccination means the post-bite treatment is greatly simplified. If an animal bites you, gently wash the wound with soap and water, and apply an iodine-based antiseptic. If you are not pre-vaccinated you will need to receive rabies immunoglobulin as soon as possible.

Typhoid This serious bacterial infection is spread via food and water. Symptoms include high and slowly progressive fever, headache, a dry cough and stomach pain. Vaccination, recommended for all travellers spending more than a week in Malaysia, is not 100% effective so you must still be careful with what you eat and drink.

Traveller's Diarrhoea

By far the most common problem affecting travellers and commonly caused by a bacteria. Treat by staying well hydrated, using a solution such as Gastrolyte. Antibiotics such as Norfloxacin, Ciprofloxacin or Azithromycin will kill the bacteria quickly. Seek medical attention quickly if you do not respond to an appropriate antibiotic.

Loperamide is just a 'stopper', but it can be helpful in certain situations, such as if you have to go on a long bus ride.

Giardiasis is relatively common. Symptoms include nausea, bloating, excess gas, fatigue and intermittent diarrhoea. The treatment of choice is Tinidazole, with Metronidazole being a second option.

Environmental Hazards

Air Pollution

If you have severe respiratory problems, speak with your doctor before travelling to any heavily polluted urban centres. If troubled by the pollution, leave the city for a few days to get some fresh air.

Diving & Surfing

If planning on diving or surfing, seek specialised advice before you travel to ensure your medical kit also contains treatment for coral cuts and tropical ear infections. Have a dive medical before you leave your home country – there are certain medical conditions that are incompatible with diving. Hyberbaric chambers are located in Kuantan and Lumut on Peninsular Malaysia, Labuan on Malaysian Borneo, and Singapore.

Heat

It can take up to two weeks to adapt to the region's hot climate. Swelling of the feet and ankles is common, as are muscle cramps caused by excessive sweating. Prevent these by avoiding dehydration and excessive activity in the heat.

Dehydration is the main contributor to heat exhaustion. Symptoms include feeling weak, headache, irritability, nausea or vomiting, sweaty skin, a fast, weak pulse, and a normal or slightly elevated body temperature. Treat by getting out of the heat, applying cool, wet cloths to the skin, lying flat with legs raised, and rehydrating with water containing a quarter of a teaspoon of salt per litre.

Heat stroke is a serious medical emergency. Symptoms come on suddenly and include weakness, nausea, a body temperature of over 41°C, dizziness, confusion, loss of coordination, fits and, eventually, collapse and loss of consciousness. Seek medical help and commence cooling by getting out of the heat, removing clothes, and applying cool, wet cloths or ice to the body, especially to the groin and armpits.

Prickly heat – an itchy rash of tiny lumps – is caused by sweat being trapped under the skin. Treat by moving out of the heat and into an air-conditioned area for a few hours and by having cool showers. Creams and ointments clog the skin so they should be avoided.

Insect Bites & Stings

Lice Most commonly inhabit your head and pubic area. Transmission is via close contact with an infected person. Treat

---

LEECHES

You may not encounter any of these slimy little vampires while walking through the region's jungle, but if the trail is leafy and it's been raining, chances are you'll be preyed upon.

The local leeches are so small they can squeeze through tight-knit socks. They don't stay tiny for long, however, since once a leech has attached to your skin, it won't let go until it has sucked as much blood as it can hold.

Two species are common: the brown leech and the tiger leech. The tiger leech is recognisable by its cream and black stripes, but you'll probably feel one before you see it. Unlike the brown leech, whose suction is painless, tiger leeches sting a bit. Brown leeches hang around on, or near, the forest floor, waiting to grab onto passing boots or pants. Tiger leeches lurk on the leaves of small trees and tend to attack between the waist and neck, and that can mean any orifice there and around. Keep your shirt tucked in.

Leeches are harmless, but bites can become infected, so it's best to prevent them becoming attached in the first place. Insect repellent on feet, shoes and socks works temporarily; loose tobacco or washing powder in your shoes and socks is also said to help. Better yet, invest in some leech-proof socks that cover the foot and boot heel and fasten below the knees.

Safe and effective ways to dislodge leeches include flicking them off – try using a credit card to do this and aim for the mouth end as pulling a leech off by the tail can make it dig in harder. Tiger balm, iodine or medicated menthol oil will also get leeches off. Otherwise, succumb to your fate as a reluctant blood donor and they will eventually drop off.

with numerous applications of an anti-lice shampoo such as permethrin.

Ticks Contracted after walking in rural areas. If you are bitten and experience symptoms – such as a rash at the site of the bite or elsewhere, fever or muscle aches – see a doctor. Doxycycline prevents tick-borne diseases.

Bees or wasps If allergic to their stings, carry an injection of adrenaline (eg an Epipen) for emergency treatment.

Jellyfish Most are not dangerous. Note that vinegar is no longer recommended for treating some jellyfish stings, and putting alcohol or urine on the sting should also be avoided. Take painkillers, and seek medical advice if your condition worsens.

Skin Problems

There are two common fungal rashes that affect travellers in the tropics. The first occurs in moist areas that get less air, such as the groin, armpits and between the toes. It starts as a red patch that slowly spreads and is usually itchy. Treatment involves keeping the skin dry, avoiding chafing and using an antifungal

cream such as Clotrimazole or Lamisil. Tinea versicolour is also common – this fungus causes small, light-coloured patches, most commonly on the back, chest and shoulders. Consult a doctor.

Take meticulous care of any cuts and scratches to prevent infection. Immediately wash all wounds in clean water and apply antiseptic. If you develop signs of infection (increasing pain and redness), see a doctor. Divers and surfers should be particularly careful with coral cuts.

Snakes

Assume all snakes are poisonous. Always wear boots and long pants if walking in an area that may have snakes. First aid in the event of a snake bite involves pressure immobilisation via an elastic bandage firmly wrapped around the affected limb, starting at the bite site and working up towards the chest. The bandage should not be so tight that the circulation is cut off; the fingers or toes should be kept free so the circulation can be checked. Immobilise the limb with a splint and carry the

victim to medical attention. Don't use tourniquets or try to suck out the venom. Antivenin is available for most species.

Sunburn

Even on a cloudy day, sunburn can occur rapidly. Always use a strong sunscreen (at least SPF 30), making sure to reapply after a swim, and always wear a wide-brimmed hat and sunglasses outdoors. Avoid lying in the sun during the hottest part of the day (10am to 2pm). If you're sunburnt, stay out of the sun until you've recovered, apply cool compresses and take painkillers for the discomfort. Applied twice daily, 1% hydrocortisone cream is also helpful.

Travelling with Children

There are specific issues you should consider before travelling with your child:

➡ All routine vaccinations should be up to date, as many of the common childhood diseases that have been eliminated in the West are still present in parts of Southeast Asia. A travel-health clinic can advise on specific vaccines, but think seriously about rabies vaccination if you're visiting rural areas or travelling for more than a month, as children are more vulnerable to severe animal bites.

➡ Children are more prone to getting serious forms of mosquito-borne diseases such as malaria, Japanese B encephalitis and dengue fever. In particular, malaria is very serious in children and can rapidly lead to death – you should think seriously before taking your child into a malaria-risk area. Permethrin-impregnated clothing is safe to use, and insect repellents should contain between 10% and 20% DEET.

TAP WATER

➡ Never drink tap water unless you've verified that it's safe (many parts of Malaysia, Singapore and Brunei have modern treatment plants).

➡ Bottled water is generally safe – check the seal is intact at purchase.

➡ Avoid ice in places that look dubious.

➡ Avoid fruit juices if they have not been freshly squeezed or you suspect they may have been watered down.

➡ Boiling water is the most efficient method of purification.

➡ The best chemical purifier is iodine. It should not be used by pregnant women or those with thyroid problems.

➡ Water filters should also filter out viruses. Ensure your filter has a chemical barrier such as iodine and a small pore size (eg less than 4 microns).

➡ Diarrhoea can cause rapid dehydration and you should pay particular attention to keeping your child well hydrated. The best antibiotic for children with diarrhoea is Azithromycin.

➡ Children can get very sick, very quickly so locate good medical facilities at your destination and make contact if you are worried – it's always better to get a medical opinion than to try to treat your own children.

Women's Health

If travelling while pregnant:

➡ Find out about quality medical facilities at your destination and ensure you continue your standard antenatal care at these facilities. Avoid travel in rural areas with poor transport and medical facilities.

➡ Ensure travel insurance covers all pregnancy-related possibilities, including premature labour.

➡ Be aware that malaria is a high-risk disease in pregnancy. WHO recommends that pregnant women do not travel to areas with malaria resistant to chloroquine. None of the more effective antimalarial drugs is completely safe in pregnancy.

➡ Traveller's diarrhoea can quickly lead to dehydration and result in inadequate blood flow to the placenta. Many of the drugs used to treat various diarrhoea bugs are not recommended in pregnancy. Azithromycin is considered safe.

Additional considerations:

➡ In urban areas, supplies of sanitary products are readily available. Birth-control options may be limited so bring adequate supplies of your own form of contraception.

➡ Heat, humidity and antibiotics can all contribute to thrush. Treatment is with antifungal creams and pessaries such as clotrimazole. A practical alternative is a single tablet of Fluconazole (Diflucan).

➡ Urinary-tract infections can be precipitated by dehydration or long bus journeys without toilet stops; bring suitable antibiotics.

Traditional & Folk Medicine

Throughout Asia, traditional medical systems are widely practised. There is a big difference between these traditional healing systems and 'folk' medicine. Folk remedies should be avoided, as they often involve rather dubious procedures with potential complications. In comparison, traditional healing systems, such as traditional Chinese medicine, are well respected, and aspects of them are being increasingly utilised by Western medical practitioners.

All traditional Asian medical systems identify a vital life force, and see blockage or imbalance as causing disease. Techniques such as herbal medicines, massage and acupuncture bring this vital force back into balance or maintain balance. These therapies are best used for treating chronic disease such as chronic fatigue, arthritis, irritable bowel syndrome and some chronic skin conditions. Traditional medicines should be avoided for treating serious acute infections such as malaria.

Be aware that 'natural' doesn't always mean 'safe', and there can be drug interactions between herbal medicines and Western medicines. If you are using both systems, ensure you inform both practitioners as to what the other has prescribed.

Language

The national language of Malaysia is Malay, also known as Bahasa Malaysia. It's spoken with slight variations throughout Malaysia, Singapore and Brunei, although it's by no means the only language. Various dialects of Chinese are spoken by those of Chinese ancestry, and Mandarin is fairly widely used. Indian Malaysians also speak Tamil, Malayalam and other languages. In Singapore, the official languages alongside Malay (which is mostly restricted to the Malay community) are Tamil, Mandarin and English.

You'll find it easy to get by with English not only in Singapore and on mainland Malaysia, but also in Malaysian Borneo (Sabah and Sarawak) and Brunei. English is the most common second language for Borneo's ethnic groups and is often used by people of different backgrounds, like ethnic Chinese and ethnic Malays, to communicate with one another.

In Bahasa Malaysia, most letters are pronounced more or less the same as their English counterparts, except for the letter c which is always pronounced as the 'ch' in 'chair'. Nearly all syllables carry equal emphasis, but a good approximation is to lightly stress the second-last syllable.

Pronouns, particularly 'you', are rarely used in Bahasa Malaysia. *Kamu* is the egalitarian form designed to overcome the plethora of terms relating to a person's age and gender that are used for the second person.

QUESTION WORDS

How?	*Berapa?*
What?	*Apa?*
When?	*Bilakah?*
Where?	*Di mana?*
Who?	*Siapakah?*
Why?	*Mengapa?*

BASICS

Hello.	*Helo.*
Goodbye.	*Selamat tinggal/jalan.* (said by person leaving/ staying)
How are you?	*Apa kabar?*
I'm fine.	*Kabar baik.*
Excuse me.	*Maaf.*
Sorry.	*Maaf.*
Yes./No.	*Ya./Tidak.*
Please.	*Silakan.*
Thank you.	*Terima kasih.*
You're welcome.	*Sama-sama.*
What's your name?	*Siapa nama kamu?*
My name is ...	*Nama saya ...*
Do you speak English?	*Adakah anda berbahasa Inggeris?*
I don't understand.	*Saya tidak faham.*

ACCOMMODATION

Do you have any rooms available?	*Ada bilik kosong?*
How much is it per day/person?	*Berapa harga satu malam/orang?*
Is breakfast included?	*Makan pagi termasukkah?*
campsite	*tempat perkhemahan*
guesthouse	*rumah tetamu*
hotel	*hotel*
youth hostel	*asrama belia*
single room	*bilik untuk seorang*
room with a double bed	*bilik untuk dua orang*
room with two beds	*bilik yang ada dua katil*

air-con	pendingin udara
bathroom	bilik air
mosquito coil	obat nyamuk
window	tingkap

DIRECTIONS

Where is ...?	Di mana ...?
What's the address?	Apa alamatnya?
Could you write it down, please?	Tolong tuliskan alamat itu?
Can you show me (on the map)?	Tolong tunjukkan (di peta)?
Turn left/right.	Belok kiri/kanan.
Go straight ahead.	Jalan terus.
at the corner	di simpang
at the traffic lights	di tempat lampu isyarat
behind	di belakang
far (from)	jauh (dari)
in front of	di depan
near (to)	dekat (dengan)
opposite	berhadapan dengan

EATING & DRINKING

A table for (two), please.	Meja untuk (dua) orang.
What's in that dish?	Ada apa dalam masakan itu?
Bring the bill, please.	Tolong bawa bil.
I don't eat ...	Saya tak suka makan ...
chicken	ayam
fish	ikan
(red) meat	daging (merah)
nuts	kacang

Key Words

bottle	botol
breakfast	sarapan pagi
cold	sejuk
cup	cawan
dinner	makan malam
food	makanan
fork	garfu
glass	gelas
hot	panas

SIGNS

Buka	Open
Dilarang	Prohibited
Keluar	Exit
Lelaki	Men
Masuk	Entrance
Perempuan	Women
Tandas	Toilets
Tutup	Closed

knife	pisau
lunch	makan tengahari
market	pasar
menu	menu
plate	pinggan
restaurant	restoran
spicy	pedas
spoon	sedu
vegetarian	sayuran saja
with	dengan
without	tanpa

Meat & Fish

beef	daging lembu
chicken	ayam
crab	ketam
fish	ikan
lamb	anak biri-biri
mussels	kepah
pork	babi
shrimp	udang

Fruit & Vegetables

apple	epal
banana	pisang
carrot	lobak
cucumber	timun
jackfruit	nangka
mango	mangga
orange	jeruk oren
peanut	kacang
starfruit	belimbing
tomato	tomato
watermelon	tembikai

NUMBERS

1	satu
2	dua
3	tiga
4	empat
5	lima
6	enam
7	tujuh
8	lapan
9	sembilan
10	sepuluh
11	sebelas
12	dua belas
20	dua puluh
21	dua puluh satu
22	dua puluh dua
30	tiga puluh
40	empat puluh
50	lima puluh
60	enam puluh
70	tujuh puluh
80	lapan puluh
90	sembilan puluh
100	seratus
200	dua ratus
1000	seribu
2000	dua ribu

Other Foods

bread	roti
cheese	keju
egg	telur
ice	ais
rice	nasi
salt	garam
sugar	gula

Drinks

beer	bir
bottled water	air botol
citrus juice	air limau
coffee	kopi
milk	susu
tea	teh
water	air
wine	wain

EMERGENCIES

Help!	Tolong!
Stop!	Berhenti!
I'm lost.	Saya sesat.
Go away!	Pergi!
There's been an accident.	Ada kemalangan.
Call the doctor!	Panggil doktor!
Call the police!	Panggil polis!
I'm ill.	Saya sakit.
It hurts here.	Sini sakit.
I'm allergic to (nuts).	Saya alergik kepada (kacang).

SHOPPING & SERVICES

I'd like to buy ...	Saya nak beli ...
I'm just looking.	Saya nak tengok saja.
Can I look at it?	Boleh saya tengok barang itu?
How much is it?	Berapa harganya?
It's too expensive.	Mahalnya.
Can you lower the price?	Boleh kurang?
There's a mistake in the bill.	Bil ini salah.
ATM	ATM ('a-te-em')
credit card	kad kredit
internet cafe	cyber cafe
post office	pejabat pos
public phone	telpon awam
tourist office	pejabat pelancong

TIME & DATES

What time is it?	Pukul berapa?
It's (seven) o'clock.	Pukul (tujuh).
It's half past (one).	Pukul (satu) setengah.
in the morning	pagi
in the afternoon	tengahari
in the evening	petang
yesterday	semalam
today	hari ini
tomorrow	esok

Monday	hari Isnin	Sunday	hari Minggu
Tuesday	hari Selasa		
Wednesday	hari Rabu	January	Januari
Thursday	hari Kamis	February	Februari
Friday	hari Jumaat	March	Mac
Saturday	hari Sabtu	April	April

SINGLISH

One of the most intriguing things the visitor to Singapore will notice is the patois spoken by the locals. Nominally English, it contains borrowed words from Hokkien and Malay, such as *shiok* (delicious) and *kasar* (rough). Unnecessary prepositions and pronouns are dropped, word order is flipped, phrases are clipped short, and stress and intonation are unconventional, to say the least. The result is known locally as Singlish. Singlish is frowned upon in official use, though you'll get a good idea of its pervasive characteristics of pronunciation if you listen to the news bulletins on TV or the radio.

There are a number of interesting characteristics that differentiate Singlish from standard English. First off, there's the reverse stress pattern of double-barrelled words. For example, in standard English the stress would be '*fire*-fighter' or '*theatre* company' but in Singlish it's 'fire-*fighter*' and 'theatre *company*'. Word-final consonants – particularly *l* or *k* – are often dropped, and vowels are often distorted; a Chinese-speaking taxi driver might not understand 'Perak Road' since they pronounce it 'Pera Roh'. The particle *-lah* is often tagged on to the end of sentences as in, 'No good, *lah*', which could mean (among other things) 'I don't think that's such a good idea'. Requests or questions will often be marked with a tag ending, since direct questioning is considered rude. So a question such as 'Would you like a beer?' might be rendered as 'You want beer or not?', which, ironically, might come across to speakers of standard English as being rude. Verb tenses tend to be nonexistent – future, present or past actions are all indicated by time phrases, so in Singlish it's 'I go tomorrow' or 'I go yesterday'.

The following are some frequently heard Singlishisms:

ah beng – unsophisticated person with no fashion sense or style; redneck

Aiyah! – 'Oh, dear!'

Alamak! – exclamation of disbelief, frustration or dismay, like 'Oh my God!'

ayam – Malay word for chicken; adjective for something inferior or weak

blur – a slow or uninformed person

buaya – womaniser, from the Malay for 'crocodile'

Can? – 'Is that OK?'

Can! – 'Yes! That's fine.'

char bor – babe, woman

cheena – old-fashioned Chinese in dress or thinking (derogatory)

go stan – to reverse, as in 'Go stan the car' (from the naval expression 'go astern'; pronounced 'go stun')

heng – luck, good fortune (from Hokkien)

hiao – vain

inggrish – English

kambing – foolish person, literally 'goat' (from Malay)

kena ketuk – ripped off, literally 'get knocked'

kiasee – scared, literally 'afraid to die'; a coward

kiasu – selfish, pushy, always on the lookout for a bargain, literally 'afraid to lose'

lah – generally an ending for any phrase or sentence; can translate as 'OK', but has no real meaning; added for emphasis to just about everything

looksee – take a look

malu – embarrassed

minah – girlfriend

Or not? – general tag for questions, as in 'Can or not?' (Can you or can't you?)

see first – wait and see what happens

shack – tired

shiok – good, great, delicious

steady lah – well done, excellent; expression of praise

Wah! – general exclamation of surprise or distress

ya ya – boastful, as in 'He always *ya ya*'

KEY PATTERNS

To get by in Malay, mix and match these simple patterns with words of your choice:

When's (the next bus)?
Jam berapa (bis yang berikutnya)?

Where's (the station)?
Di mana (stasiun)?

I'm looking for (a hotel).
Saya cari (hotel).

Do you have (a local map)?
Ada (peta daerah)?

Is there (a lift)?
Ada (lift)?

Can I (enter)?
Boleh saya (masuk)?

Do I need (a visa)?
Saya harus pakai (visa)?

I'd like (the menu).
Saya minta (daftar makanan).

I'd like (to hire a car).
Saya mau (sewa mobil).

Could you (help me)?
Bisa Anda (bantu) saya?

May	*Mei*
June	*Jun*
July	*Julai*
August	*Ogos*
September	*September*
October	*Oktober*
November	*November*
December	*Disember*

TRANSPORT

At what time does the ... leave?	*Pukul berapa ... berangkat?*
boat	*kapal*
bus	*bas*
plane	*kapal terbang*
train	*kereta api*

I want to go to ...	*Saya nak ke ...*
Does it stop at ... ?	*Berhenti di ...?*
How long will it be delayed?	*Berapa lambatnya?*
I'd like to get off at ...	*Saya nak turun di ...*
Please put the meter on.	*Tolong pakai meter.*

Please stop here.	*Tolong berhenti di sini.*
I'd like a ... ticket.	*Saya nak tiket ...*
1st-class	*kelas pertama*
2nd-class	*kelas kedual*
one-way	*sehala*
return	*pergi balik*
the first	*pertama*
the last	*terakhir*
the next	*berikutnya*
bus station	*stesen bas*
bus stop	*perhentian bas*
cancelled	*dibatalkan*
delayed	*lambat*
platform	*landasan*
ticket office	*pejabat tiket*
ticket window	*tempat/kaunter tikit*
timetable	*jadual waktu*
train station	*stesen keretapi*
I'd like to hire a ...	*Saya nak menyewa ...*
bicycle	*basikal*
car	*kereta*
jeep	*jip*
motorbike	*motosikal*
diesel	*disel*
helmet	*topi keledar*
leaded petrol	*petrol plumbum*
unleaded petrol	*tanpa plumbum*
petrol	*petrol*
pump	*pam*
Is this the road to ...?	*Ini jalan ke ...?*
Where's a petrol station?	*Stesen minyak di mana?*
(How long) Can I park here?	*(Beberapa lama) Boleh saya letak kereta di sini?*
I need a mechanic.	*Kami memerlukan mekanik.*
The car has broken down at ...	*Kereta saya telah rosak di ...*
I have a flat tyre.	*Tayarnya kempis.*
I've run out of petrol.	*Minyak sudah habis.*
I've had an accident.	*Saya terlibat dalam kemalangan.*

GLOSSARY

adat – Malay customary law

adat temenggong – Malay law with Indian modifications, governing the customs and ceremonies of the sultans

air – water

air terjun – waterfall

alor – groove; furrow; main channel of a river

ampang – dam

ang pow – red packets of money used as offerings, payment or gifts

APEC – Asia-Pacific Economic Cooperation

arak – Malay local alcohol

arrack – see arak

Asean – Association of Southeast Asian Nations

atap – roof thatching

Baba-Nonya – descendants of Chinese immigrants to the Straits Settlements (namely Melaka, Singapore and Penang) who intermarried with Malays and adopted many Malay customs; also known as Peranakan, or Straits Chinese; sometimes spelt Nyonya

Bahasa Malaysia – Malay language; also known as Bahasa Melayu

bandar – seaport; town

Bangsawan – Malay opera

batang – stem; tree trunk; the main branch of a river

batik – technique of imprinting cloth with dye to produce multi-coloured patterns

batu – stone; rock; milepost

belukar – secondary forest

bendahara – chief minister

bendang – irrigated land

bomoh – spiritual healer

British Resident – chief British representative during the colonial era

bukit – hill

bumboat – motorised sampan

bumiputra – literally, sons of the soil; indigenous Malays

bunga raya – hibiscus flower (national flower of Malaysia)

dadah – drugs

dato', datuk – literally, grandfather; general male nonroyal title of distinction

dipterocarp – family of trees, native to Malaysia, that have two-winged fruits

dusun – small town; orchard; fruit grove

genting – mountain pass

godown – river warehouse

gua – cave

gunung – mountain

hilir – lower reaches of a river

hutan – jungle; forest

imam – keeper of Islamic knowledge and leader of prayer

istana – palace

jalan – road

kain songket – traditional Malay handwoven fabric with gold threads

kampung – village; also spelt kampong

kangkar – Chinese village

karst – characteristic scenery of a limestone region, including features such as underground streams and caverns

kedai kopi – coffee shop

kerangas – distinctive vegetation zone of Borneo, usually found on sandstone, containing pitcher plants and other unusual flora

khalwat – literally, close proximity; exhibition of public affection between the sexes, which is prohibited for unmarried Muslim couples

kongsi – Chinese clan organisations, also known as ritual brotherhoods, heaven-man-earth societies, triads or secret societies; meeting house for Chinese of the same clan

kopitiam – coffee shop

kota – fort; city

kramat – Malay shrine

KTM – Keretapi Tanah Melayu; Malaysian Railways System

kuala – river mouth; place where a tributary joins a larger river

laksamana – admiral

langur – small, usually tree-dwelling monkey

laut – sea

lebuh – street

Lebuhraya – expressway or freeway; usually refers to the North–South Highway, which runs from Johor Bahru to Bukit Kayu Hitam at the Thai border

lorong – narrow street; alley

LRT – Light Rail Transit (Kuala Lumpur)

lubuk – deep pool

macaque – any of several small species of monkey

mandi – bathe; Southeast Asian wash basin

masjid – mosque

MCP – Malayan Communist Party

Melayu Islam Beraja – MIB; Brunei's national ideology

merdeka – independence

Merlion – half-lion, half-fish animal; symbol of Singapore

MRT – Mass Rapid Transit (Singapore)

muara – river mouth

muezzin – mosque official who calls the faithful to prayer

negara – country

negeri – state

nonya – see Baba-Nonya

GLOSSARY

orang asing – foreigner

Orang Asli – literally, Original People; Malaysian aborigines

Orang Laut – literally, Coastal People; Sea Gypsies

Orang Ulu – literally, Upriver People

padang – grassy area; field; also the city square

pantai – beach

PAP – People's Action Party

parang – long jungle knife

PAS – Parti Islam se-Malaysia

pasar – market

pasar malam – night market

Pejabat Residen – Resident's Office

pekan – market place; town

pelabuhan – port

pencak silat – martial-arts dance form

penghulu – chief or village head

pengkalan – quay

Peranakan – literally, half-caste; refers to the Baba-Nonya or Straits Chinese

PIE – Pan-Island Expressway, one of Singapore's main road arteries

pua kumbu – traditional finely woven cloth

pulau – island

puteri – princess

raja – prince; ruler

rakyat – common people

rantau – straight coastline

rattan – stems from climbing palms used for wickerwork and canes

rimba – jungle

rotan – cane used to punish miscreants

roti – bread

sampan – small boat

samsu – Malay alcohol

sarong – all-purpose cloth, often sewn into a tube, and worn by women, men and children

seberang – opposite side of road; far bank of a river

selat – strait

semenanjung – peninsula

silat – see pencak silat

simpang – crossing; junction

songkok – traditional Malay headdress worn by males

Straits Chinese – see Baba-Nonya

sungai – river

syariah – Islamic system of law

tambang – river ferry; fare

tamu – weekly market

tanah – land

tanjung – headland

tasik – lake

teluk – bay; sometimes spelt telok

temenggong – Malay administrator

towkang – Chinese junk

tuai rumah – longhouse chief (Sarawak)

tuak – local 'firewater' alcohol (Malaysian Borneo)

tunku – prince

ujung – cape

UMNO – United Malays National Organisation

warung – small eating stalls

wayang – Chinese opera

wayang kulit – shadow-puppet theatre

wisma – office block or shopping centre

yang di-pertuan agong – Malaysia's head of state, or 'king'

yang di-pertuan besar – head of state in Negeri Sembilan

yang di-pertuan muda – under-king

yang di-pertuan negeri – governor

Behind the Scenes

SEND US YOUR FEEDBACK

We love to hear from travellers – your comments keep us on our toes and help make our books better. Our well-travelled team reads every word on what you loved or loathed about this book. Although we cannot reply individually to your submissions, we always guarantee that your feedback goes straight to the appropriate authors, in time for the next edition. Each person who sends us information is thanked in the next edition – the most useful submissions are rewarded with a selection of digital PDF chapters.

Visit **lonelyplanet.com/contact** to submit your updates and suggestions or to ask for help. Our award-winning website also features inspirational travel stories, news and discussions.

Note: We may edit, reproduce and incorporate your comments in Lonely Planet products such as guidebooks, websites and digital products, so let us know if you don't want your comments reproduced or your name acknowledged. For a copy of our privacy policy visit lonelyplanet.com/privacy.

OUR READERS

Many thanks to the travellers who used the last edition and wrote to us with helpful hints, useful advice and interesting anecdotes: Ameer Hamza, Andrew Lamère, Charlotte Crawford, Dale Follas, Edwin Heeregrave, Evelin Mueller, Hanna Becker, J Welch, Jean-Philippe Mauve, Ken Wilson, Nadia Vendrig, Nicolas Combremont, Owen Davies, Sally Arnold, Simone and Sergine Verswijveren, Steve Mair, Steven Hankey, Susanne Mathys, Tim Marlow, Tom Micciche.

WRITER THANKS

Simon Richmond

Terima kasih to the following who assisted with my research in Malaysia: Ng Seksan, Andrew Sebastian, Narelle, Brian and Andrew, Mei Yun (Elena), Melissa Low, Baida Herbus and Mienal Hussein.

Brett Atkinson

In Kuching, *terima kasih* to Donald and Marina, Wayne, Danny and Purdey, and thanks to Louise in Santubong. Around Batang Ai, Bading effortlessly led the way, and Lucy, David and Lian (x2) made visiting Bario an absolute highlight. Also in Bario it was good to meet the Mild Men of Borneo, Alasdair, Jason and Giles. Cheers also to Mr Lim, Daniel and Jason Brooke. Final thanks to Tanya Parker at Lonely Planet and my Borneo co-authors Anna and Paul.

Lindsay Brown

I am very grateful for the assistance provided by numerous friendly folks across Malaysia's northeast. In particular, I would like to thank Lorenz in Kuala Terengganu, Zeck in Kota Bharu and Bukhari 'Bob' Mat in Dabong. Thanks to Jenny for being the best travelling companion.

Austin Bush

Thanks to all the kind folks on the ground in Malaysia, in particular Bairavi Shanmugam, Narelle McMurtrie, Wanida Razali and the cats at Temple Tree.

Ria de Jong

Thank you to my destination editor Tanya Parker for all her help guiding me through my Lonely Planet adventure, and to all those I met along my travels who kindly shared their knowledge, time and Singapore secrets with me. Thanks also to Craig, Cisca and William, my travelling circus tribe.

Damian Harper

Many thanks to everyone who helped along the way, especially Allan Rodrigo Balang, Peck Choo Ho, Carl Lim, Celeste Brash, Shaowen, Ruth, Pei Lee Yeoh, Johnny Doran, Rupert Maconick, Sue, the helpful staff at Hotel Sentral Kuantan, Haziq, Rudin Zulkarnain Voon, Tim and Emma, and much gratitude and a tip of the hat to everyone else who proffered tips and suggestions along the way.

Anita Isalska

Big thanks to all the travellers who shared their travel tips and tribulations with me – you helped make this trip. I'm grateful for the local insights and advice of Val and the Father's Guesthouse team, Jason Marcus Chin, Andrew Sebastian, Jaja Taher, Jennifer Freely and Howard Tan – *terima kasih*. Special thanks to Normal Matt for facing highland roads (and his food demons) to join my research.

Anna Kaminski

Huge thanks to Tanya for entrusting me with Sabah and Brunei, and to everyone who's helped me along the way. In particular: Thanis Lim and Leslie in BSB; William, Wendy and Tom in KK; Shavez in Tawau

Hills; Itisha and Simon in Lahad Datu; Howard at the Tip of Borneo; Anton and Linn in Sandakan; Wong in Sepilok; Sitti in Deramakot; Afiq on the Kinabatangan; and my guides on Mt Kinabalu, in Danum Valley and Tabin Wildlife Reserve.

ACKNOWLEDGEMENTS

Climate map data adapted from Peel MC, Finlayson BL & McMahon TA (2007) 'Updated World Map of the Köppen-Geiger Climate Classification', *Hydrology and Earth System Sciences*, 11, 1633–44.

Cover photograph: Old rickshaw near Blue Mansion, George Town, Penang; Elena Ermakova/ Shutterstock ©

THIS BOOK

This 15th edition of Lonely Planet's *Malaysia, Singapore & Brunei* guidebook was curated by Simon Richmond, and researched and written by Simon, Brett Atkinson, Lindsay Brown, Austin Bush, Ria de Jong, Damian Harper, Anita Isalska and Anna Kaminski. The previous edition was also written by Simon, Brett, Lindsay, Austin, Ria, Damian, Anita and Anna. This guidebook was produced by the following:

Senior Product Editor Daniel Bolger

Product Editor Bruce Evans

Book Designer Virginia Moreno

Assisting Editors Sarah Bailey, Andrew Bain, James Bainbridge, Judith Bamber, Nigel Chin, Michelle Coxall, Jacqueline Danam, Anne Mulvaney, Rosie Nicholson, Monica Woods

Cartographer Julie Sheridan

Cover Researcher Gwen Cotter

Thanks to Victoria Harrison, Karen Henderson, Sonia Kapoor, Genna Patterson, Kirsten Rawlings

Index

A

Abai 361-3
accessible travel 598
  Singapore 556
accommodation 22, 598-600, see also individual locations, accommodation types
  booking 599
  budgeting 71, 600
  language 616-17
activities 34-41, see also individual activities
adventure sports 517
AIDS 612
Air Itam 183-4
air travel 606, 607-8
airports 21
Alor Gajah 236
Alor Setar 209-12, **211**
ambuyat 44, 477, **45**
amusement parks
  Escape 187
  Jerudong Park Playground 474
  Legoland 241
  Melaka Wonderland 235-6
  Skytrex Melaka 235
  Sunway Lagoon 115
  Universal Studios 515-16
animals 12, 337, 521-30, see also individual species
animism 584
Annah Rais Longhouse 420-1
anti-Semitism 585
apartments 599
  George Town 173
  Kuala Lumpur 75
aquariums
  Aquaria KLCC 59
  SEA Aquarium 515
  Underwater World 193
architecture 16-17, 590-1
  Minangkabau 122

Map Pages **000**
Photo Pages **000**

area codes 21
art galleries, see galleries
Art Printing Works (APW) 93
arts 586-90
asam laksa 44, **81**
Asian Civilisations Museum 15, 495-6, **15**
ayam percik 87, **86**
Ayer Keroh 235-6

B

Ba Kelalan 465
Badawi, Abdullah 571-2
Bako National Park 414-17
Bakun Dam 438
Balik Pulau 188-90
ballooning 114
Bandar Labuan 388-91, **389**
Bandar Seri Begawan 470-82, **472**, **585**
  accommodation 475-6
  activities 475
  drinking 478-9
  emergencies 479
  entertainment 479
  food 476-8
  internet access 479
  media 479
  medical services 479
  money 480
  nightlife 478-9
  postal services 480
  shopping 479
  sights 470-4
  telephone services 480
  tours 475
  travel to/from 480
  travel within 480-2
Bangar 484-5
bargaining 23
Bario 460-4
Bario rice 464
Batang Ai 429-30
Batang Duri 485
Batang Rejang 434-8
batik courses 69, 268, 286
bats 444, 525, **525**, **529**

Batu Caves 19, 25, 108-9, **2-3**, **19**
Batu Ferringhi 184-6
Batu Gajah 135
Batu Maung 190
Batu Punggul 385
Bau 423-4
Bawang Assan Longhouse Village 430
beaches
  Batu Ferringhi 184-6
  Beserah Beach 264
  Pantai Cahaya Bulan 291-2
  Pantai Cenang 193
  Pantai Kok 195-6
  Pantai Pasir Hitam 197
  Pantai Pasir Tengkorak 196
  Pantai Seri Kenangan 482
  Pantai Tengah 194-5
  Peranginan Pantai Muara 474
  Pulau Libaran 357
  Pulau Mamutik 330
  Pulau Manukan 330
  Pulau Perhentian 296
  Pulau Sapi 330
  Sentosa Island 515
  Tanjung Aru 320, 326
  Teluk Kumbar 190
  Tempurung 386
  Tip of Borneo 343
bears 352
Beaufort 385-6
Beaufort Division 385-7
bedbugs 612
bees 614
Belaga 437-8
Belait 482-3
Belum-Temenggor Rainforest 156-7
Besar 296-8
bicycle travel 608, see also cycling
Bidong Island 308
Bilit 361
Bintulu 438-41, **440**
birds 525
birds' nests 38, 359, 444

bird-watching
  Danum Valley Conservation Area 366
  Gunung Mulu National Park 453
  Jurong Bird Park 513
  KL Bird Park 61
  Labuan Bird Park 389
  Vale Eco Center 143
boat travel 607, 608
boat trips
  Bako National Park 415-16
  Bandar Seri Begawan 475
  Kuching 402
  Sabah 359
  Similajau National Park 441
  Taman Negara 275
boating 41
books 580, 582
  history 565, 566, 569, 570, 571, 573, 575
border crossings
  Brunei Darussalam 391, 452, 480, 481
  Indonesia 234, 243, 379, 412, 465, 560
  Singapore 244
  Thailand 209, 212, 213, 291
Brickfields Street eateries 92
bridges
  Darul Hana Bridge 393
  Sultan Haji Omar Saifuddien Bridge 485
Brunei Darussalam 52, 468-87, **469**
  accommodation 468, 487
  budgeting 486-7
  climate 468
  emergencies 487
  food 468, 90
  highlights 469
  holidays 487
  legal issues 487
  LGBTIQ+ travellers 487
  media 591
  money 486
  people 579
  politics 581
  postal services 487

Brunei Darussalam *continued*
telephone services 487
time 487
tourist information 487
travel seasons 468
travel to/from 391, 452, 480, 481
visas 487
weather 468
women travellers 487
Buddhism 582-3
Buddhist temples
Buddha Tooth Relic Temple 499
Dhammikarama Burmese Buddhist Temple 168
Dharma Realm Guan Yin Sagely Monastery 60
Kek Lok Si Temple 19, 184
Kong Meng San Phor Kark See Monastery 512
Puh Toh Tze Buddhist Temple 319-20
Puu Jih Syh Temple 346
Sam Poh Temple 136
Sin Sze Si Ya Temple 61
Thean Hou Temple 64-5
Tumpat 292
Wat Buppharam 169
Wat Chayamangkalaram 167-8
Wat Nikrodharam 210
budgeting 21, 600, 601, *see also individual locations*
Bukit Fraser 110-13, **111**
Bukit Larut 156
Bukit Tambun 189
bumiputra 572
bus travel 606-7, 608
business hours 21, 602
butterflies 65, 188, 529, **528**
Butterworth 183

C
Cameron Highlands 18, 136-43, **138**, **18**
accommodation 139-41
drinking 141-3
food 141-3
hiking 137
information 142
sights 136-9
tours 139
travel to/from 142
travel within 143
camping 599
canopy walks 366
car travel 608-9

Map Pages **000**
Photo Pages **000**

carbon emissions 594, 606
cartoons 590
cathedrals, *see* churches & cathedrals
cats 401
caves
Agop Batu Tulug 358
Batu Caves 19, 25, 108-9, **2-3**, **19**
Clearwater Cave 454
Dabong 293
Deer Cave 454, 529
Fairy Cave 424
Gomantong Caves 358-9
Great Cave 443, 444
Gua Charas 266
Gua Kelam 214
Gua Tempurung 134
Kek Look Tong 128
Langang Cave 455
Lang Cave 454
Painted Cave 443
Perak Tong 128
Pungiton Caves 385
Sam Poh Tong 128
Sleeping Buddha Cave 266
Taman Negeri Perlis 214
Wind Cave (Bau) 423-4
Wind Cave (Gunung Mulu National Park) 454, **11**
caving 38-9, 424
cell phones 20
cemeteries
Bukit China 224
Chinese Cemetery (Sandakan) 346
Japanese Cemetery (Sandakan) 347
Labuan War Cemetery 389
Protestant Cemetery 167
char kway teow 44, **84**
Cherating 268-70, **269**
children, travel with 70, 600, 614-15
Chiling Waterfalls 112
China House 176
Chinatown
Kuala Lumpur 60-1, 71-4, 80-91, 96-7, 99-100
Kuala Terengganu 307-8
Kuching 399-400, 401
Melaka City 222-3
Singapore 499-501, 533-4, 538-41
Chinese opera 588
Chinese people 576
churches & cathedrals
All Saints Church 151
Christ Church 218
St Andrew's Cathedral 496
St Michael's & All Angels Church 347

St Paul's Church 218-19
St Peter's Church 224
cinema 588-9, *see also* films
clanhouses 161
climate 20, 26-7
climate change 606
clothing 22
clouded leopards 522, **523**
clubs 547
coffin caves 358
Confucianism 582-3
conservation, *see* environmental issues
consulates 600-1
cooking courses 43
George Town 169
Kota Bharu 286
Kota Kinabalu 321
Kuala Lumpur 69
Kuching 403
Melaka City 224-5
Penang 169
Singapore 520
coral 526, **526-7**
Coral Beach 143, 145, 147, **147**
courses, *see also individual locations*
batik 69, 268, 286
cooking 43, 69, 169, 224-5, 286, 321, 403, 520
COVID-19 24
crabs 545, **12**
crafts 590
Crazy Rich Asians 589
crocodiles 441
culture 15, 576-81
currency 20
customs regulations 600
cycling 35
Kuala Lumpur 68-9

D
Dabong 293
dams 594-5
dance 587
Danum Valley Conservation Area 365-7
bird-watching 366
Dayak people 578-9
deforestation 592-3
dengue fever 612
departure tax 607
Desaru Coast 25
diarrhoea 612-13
diving & snorkelling 39, 526, **40**, **526**
Bandar Labuan 389-90
Bandar Seri Begawan 475
Kota Belud 342
Miri 446
Pulau Kapas 304

Pulau Langkawi 200
Pulau Perhentian 294-5
responsible diving 41
safety 613
Semporna Archipelago 369
Tanjung Datu National Park 427
Tioman Island 254-6
Tip of Borneo 343
tours 320-2
drama 587
driving licences 609
durian 47, **46**

E
East Coast Malaysia, *see* northeast peninsular, Pahang, Tioman Island
East India Company 566-7
ecosystems 530
electricity 598, 600
elephants 271, 525, **524-5**
embassies 600-1
emergencies 21
language 618
Emergency, the 570
Endau-Rompin National Park 250-1, **251**
environment 592-6
environmental issues 592-6, 606
websites 593, 594, 596
Escape 187
etiquette 23, 44
Eurasian people 577-8
events, *see* festivals & events
exchange rates 21

F
fasting 48
festivals & events 26-7, *see also* music festivals, *individual locations, individual festivals*
food 42
Islamic 583
films 569, 573
fireflies 118, 312
fish 526, **527**
flying foxes 444, 525, **525**
folk medicine 615
food 14, 23, 81-90, **14**, **23**, **45**, **46**, **81**, **82-3**, **84-5** *see also individual foods, individual locations*
blogs 78
budgeting 601
Burmese 537
cooking courses 43
etiquette 44
festivals 42

food courts 543
language 617-18
street food 43-8, 177
Thai 537
Free Tree Society 94
fried carrot cake 89, **89**
fruit 47

G
gado gado 378
galleries, *see also* street art
Art Porters 501
Bank Negara Malaysia
Museum & Art Gallery 67
Batik Painting Museum
Penang 163-4
Galeri Petronas 59
Gillman Barracks 514
Hin Bus Depot 167
ILHAM 55
Junglebluesdream Art
Gallery 460
Kampong Ayer Cultural &
Tourism Gallery 471
National Gallery
Singapore 15, 495
National Visual Arts Gallery
65-7
Perakanan Photo
Gallery 308
Sabah Art Gallery 317
Sekeping Tenggiri 65
Zheng He Duo
Yun Xuan 223
gardens, *see* parks & gardens
Gardens by the Bay 18, 489,
494-5, **6-7**, **18**
Genting Highlands 109-10
geography 592
geology 332-3
George Town 160-83, **162-3**,
168
accommodation 171-4
drinking 178-9
entertainment 179-80
food 14, 175-8, **14**, **84-5**
internet access 181
medical services 181
money 181
nightlife 178-9
postal services 181
shopping 180-1
sights 160-9
tourist information 181
travel to/from 181-2
travel within 182-3
walking tours 166, **166**
gibbons 522
Gillman Barracks 514
Golden Mile Complex 537
golf 517
Gopeng 134-6

government 24, 574
guesthouses 599
Gunung Bengoh 424
Gunung Mulu National Park
11, 453-9, **11**, **37**

H
Hari Raya Aidil Fitri 471
hawker stalls, *see* street food
health 611-15
websites 611
heat 613
hepatitis A 612
hepatitis B 612
hepatitis E 612
high tea 538
hiking 34-5, 36
Bako National Park 415-16
Batang Ai National Park
429
Bukit Fraser 110-11
Cameron Highlands 137
Danum Valley Conservation
Area 365-6
guides 456, 462
Gunung Gading National
Park 425-6
Gunung Mulu
National Park 453-7
Kelabit Highlands 464-5
Kuala Lipis 279
Kubah National Park 422
Lambir Hills National
Park 445
Limbang Division 466
Maliau Basin Conservation
Area 380
Matang Wildlife Centre 423
Mt Kinabalu 333-7
Niah National Park 443
Penang National Park 187
preparation 276
Pulau Perhentian 295-6
safety 36, 256, 276
Similajau National
Park 441
Sungai Kinabatangan 360
Taman Negara 274-5
Tanjung Datu National
Park 427
Tioman Island 256
tours 320-2
Ulu Temburong National
Park 486
Hindu temples
Arulmigu Rajamariamman
Devasthanam 239
Arulmigu Sri
Rajakaliamman 239
Batu Caves 19, 25, 108-9,
2-3, **19**
Sri Mahamariamman
Temple 61

Sri Mariamman Temple 169
Sri Poyatha Venayagar
Moorthi Temple 223
Sri Srinivasa Perumal
Temple 503
Sri Subramaniam
Thuropathai Amman
Alayam 224
Sri Vadapathira Kaliamman
Temple 502
Sri Veeramakaliamman
Temple 502
Hinduism 583
historic buildings & sites
8 Heeren Street 223
Astana 402
Balai Besar 210
Balai Nobat 210
Batu Bersurat 145
Blue Mansion 160-1
Bukit Malawati 118
Fort Cornwallis 165
Hock Teik Cheng Sin
Temple 164
Kota Belanda 145
Loke Mansion 67
Master Mat's House 95
Old Court House
Complex 398
Old KL Train Station 65
Pinang Peranakan
Mansion 161-2
Porta de Santiago 222
Rumah Penghulu Abu
Seman 59
Sandakan Memorial
Park 346
St Francis' Institution
Melaka 219
Stadthuys 217-18
Teck Soon Heritage
House 307-8
TT5 Tin Dredge 135
Villa Sentosa 223
history 564-75
books 565, 566, 569, 571,
573, 575
Kedah 193
Kuala Lumpur 55
Melaka 216-17
Negeri Sembilan 108
Penang 159-60
Perak 127
Sabah 332
Sarawak 393
Selangor 108
Singapore 489
websites 569, 572
hitchhiking 609
HIV 612
holidays 602-3
homestays 362
honey 137-8

hor fun 85, **84**
hornbills 525, **524**
hostels 599
hotels 599

I
Ibrahim, Anwar 571-2
Imbak Canyon Conservation
Area 357
Indian people 577
Indonesia, travel to/from
234, 243, 379, 412,
465, 560
influenza 612
insurance 601
internet access 601
internet resources,
see websites
Ipoh 127-34, **130-1**
accommodation 129-31
activities 129
drinking 133
food 14, 131-3, **14**
nightlife 133
shopping 133
sights 128
tours 129
travel to/from 133-4
travel within 134
Islam 565, 582
Islamic Arts Museum 15,
61, **15**
Islamic festivals 583
islands 13, *see also* Pulau
itineraries 28-33, **28**, **29**, **30**,
31, **32-3**

J
Jalan Alor eateries 79
Jalan Labi 482-3
jellyfish 201
Jerantut 272-3, **273**
Jerudong 474
Johor 50, 237-51, **238**
accommodation 237
climate 237
food 87
highlights 238
travel seasons 237
weather 237
Johor Bahru 238-44, **240**
drinking & nightlife 242
eating 241
immigration 242-3
shopping 242
sights 239
sleeping 239
tourist inframation 243
jungles 522
Jurong Bird Park 513

K

Kampong Ayer 17, 470-1, **16-17**
Kampung Air Batang (ABC) 257, 258
Kampung Baru 95
Kampung Benuk 421
Kampung Genting 257, 260
Kampung Juara 257, 259
Kampung Kuala Tahan 276-7
Kampung Mukut 257, 260
Kampung Nipah 257, 260
Kampung Papan 135
Kampung Paya 257, 260
Kampung Pulau Betong 188-90
Kampung Salang 257, 258-9
Kampung Tekek 257, 257-8
Kangar 213-14
Kapit 435-7, **436**
kari kepala ikan 89, **88**
kayaking 39-41
Kebun-Kebun Bangsar 94
Kecil 298-301
Kedah 50, 191-213, **192**
  climate 191
  food 85
  highlights 192
  history 193
  travel seasons 191
  weather 191
Kelabit Highlands 459-65
Kelantan 283-92
Keningau 384
Kenong Rimba State Park 280
kerangas 530
kidnappings 374
Kinabalu National Park 332-9, **338**
Kinabatangan Orangutan Conservation Project 359
Kinabatangan River 358-63
Kinta Valley 135
Kiulu River 321, **40**
KL Bird Park 61
Klang 116-18
Kota Belud 341, 342
Kota Bharu 283-91, **287**, **292**
  accommodation 286-8
  courses 286
  drinking 290
  festivals & events 286
  food 288-90
  information 290
  nightlife 290
  shopping 290

sights 283-6
tours 286
travel to/from 290
travel within 291
Kota Kinabalu 316-29, **318**, **83**, **90**
  accommodation 322-3
  activities 320-2
  cuisine 324
  drinking 326
  emergencies 327
  food 323-6
  immigration 327
  laundry 327
  medical services 327
  money 327
  nightlife 326
  postal services 327
  shopping 326-7
  sights 316-20
  tourist information 327
  tours 320-2
  travel to/from 327-8
  travel within 328
Kota Tinggi 246
Kuala Besut 300
Kuala Kangsar 148-51, **150**
Kuala Kedah 212-13
Kuala Keniam 277
Kuala Kubu Bharu 112
Kuala Lipis 279-80
Kuala Lumpur 49, 54-105, **56-7**, **58**, **62-3**, **66**, **68**, **72-3**, **76**
  accommodation 54, 70-7, 103
  activities 67-9
  climate 54
  courses 69
  drinking 94
  entertainment 98-9
  festivals & events 70
  food 54, 77-80, 89, 91-4
  for children 70
  highlights 56-7
  history 55
  immigration 102
  internet access 102
  itineraries 60
  LGBTIQ+ travellers 98
  media 102
  medical services 102
  money 102
  nightlife 94
  postal services 102
  shopping 99-101
  sights 55-67
  tourist information 102
  travel seasons 54
  travel to/from 102-3
  travel within 103-5
  weather 54

Kuala Perkai 277
Kuala Pilah 121-2
Kuala Selangor 118-19
Kuala Sepetang 155-6
Kuala Terengganu 305-11, **306**
Kuantan 263-7, **264**
Kubah National Park 421-3
Kuching 393-413, **396-7**, **414**
  accommodation 404-6
  activities 402-3
  consulates 410
  drinking 409
  emergencies 410
  festivals & events 403-4
  food 406-9
  laundry 410
  medical services 410
  money 411
  nightlife 409
  police 411
  postal services 411
  safety 411
  shopping 409-10
  sights 393-402
  tourist information 411
  tours 403
  travel to/from 411-12
  travel within 412
  visas 411
Kuching Wetlands National Park 419
Kudat 342
kuih 83, **83**

L

Labuan Bird Park 389
Lahad Datu 363-4
Langkawi, *see* Pulau Langkawi
language 20, 23, 616-20
Layang Layang 345, **40**
Lee Kuan Yew 571
leeches 365, 613
legal issues 601
legends 202
Legoland 241
Lenggong Valley 149
leopards 522, **523**
LGBTIQ+ travellers 98, 487, 549, 601
lice 613-14
Limbang Division 465-7
literature 586-7, *see also* books
Long Pasia 383
longhouses 17, 579, 599-600, **17**
  Annah Rais Longhouse 420-1
  Bario Asal Longhouse 459

Batang Rejang basin 442
Bawang Assan Longhouse Village 430
Belaga 437
Labi Longhouses 482-3
Lundu 424-5

M

macaques 416, 522, 603, **11**
Mah Meri Cultural Village 117
Mahathir Mohamad 570-1
malaria 612
Malay people 576, **23**
Maliau Basin 381
  independent travel around 381
Maliau Basin Conservation Area 380-1
mangroves 530
maps 602
Marang 312-13
Marina Bay Sands 497
markets 100, **14**, **82-3**, **84-5**
  Bangsar Sunday Market 91
  Bau 424
  Bazaar Baru Chow Kit 100
  Chinatown Wet Market 100
  George Town 174, **14**, **84-5**
  Ipoh 127, **14**
  Kapit 435
  Kota Kinabalu 316, **83**
  Kuala Terengganu 307
  Kuching 402, 408
  Masjid India Pasar Malam 91
  Melaka City 230
  Miri 446
  Pudu Market 100
  Pulau Langkawi 206
  Singapore 503, 509, **14**
massage 517-19
media 591
medicine, traditional 615
mee jawa 378
mee rebus 87, **86-7**
megaliths
  Bario 461
  Pengkalan Kempas Megalith Site 123
Melaka 50, 215-36, **216**
  accommodation 215
  climate 215
  food 87
  highlights 216
  history 216-17
  travel seasons 215
  weather 215
Melaka City 217-35, **218**, **220-1**
  accommodation 226-8
  activities 224

drinking 231-2
entertainment 232
festivals & events 225-6
food 228-31
information 234
nightlife 231-2
shopping 232-4
sights 217-24
tours 225
travel to/from 234-5
travel within 235
Melaka Wonderland 235-6
memorials, see monuments & memorials
Merang 312
Mersing 246-8, **247**
MH17 574
MH370 573-4
Minangkabau people 122
Miri 446-53, **448**
mobile phones 20
money 20, 21, 602
bargaining 23
exchange rates 21
tipping 23
monkeys 353, 387, 416, 522, **11, 522**
monuments & memorials
Billionth Barrel Monument 483
German Girl Shrine 509
Great Cat of Kuching 401
Kota Mahsuri 197
Kranji War Memorial 515
Kucing Kucing 401
Kundasang War Memorial 340
Melaka Malay Sultanate Water Wheel 219
Memorial Stone 385
National Monument 64
Pialungan Sandakan-Ranau Death March Memorial 340
Sunsuron Guritom 383
Tom Harrisson Monument 460
mosques
Abdul Gafoor Mosque 503
City Mosque (Kota Kinabalu) 317-18
Indian Mosque 400
Masjid A R Rahman Pulau Perhentian 294
Masjid Diraja Sultan Suleiman 116
Masjid Jamek Sultan Abdul Samad 19, 60
Masjid Kampung Hulu 223
Masjid Kampung Kling 223
Masjid Kapitan Keling 165-7
Masjid Negara 65
Masjid Negeri Sembilan 120

Masjid Selat Melaka 217
Masjid Sultan Ahmad Shah 263
Masjid Sultan Salahuddin Abdul Aziz Shah 115
Masjid Tengku Tengah Zaharah 308
Masjid Ubudiah 149
Masjid Zahir 209
Mosque, Semporna 368
Omar Ali Saifuddien Mosque 470, **2**
Putra Mosque 113
Sultan Abu Bakar Mosque 239
Sultan Mosque 505
Tuanku Mizan Zainal Abidin Mosque 113
Zainal Abidin Mosque 308
mosquitoes 278
motorcycle travel 608-9
mountain climbing 35-8, 332-6
Mt Kinabalu 18, 332-9, 530, **335, 338, 18, 530**
accommodation 337-9
climbing 332-6
flora & fauna 337
food 339
geology 332-3
history 332
planning 333
travel to/from 339
Mt Trusmadi 383-4
Muar 244-6
multiculturalism 580
murals 245, 499, see also street art
museums
Agnes Keith House 346
Art Museum 401
Asia Camera Museum 164
Asian Civilisations Museum 15, 495-6, **15**
Baba House 499
Baba & Nyonya Heritage Museum 222-3
Bank Negara Malaysia Museum & Art Gallery 67
Battlebox 496
Brunei Darussalam Maritime Museum 473
Brunei Museum 472-3
Cathay Gallery 507
Changi Museum & Chapel 508
Cheng Ho Cultural Museum 223
Chetti Museum 224
Chinatown Heritage Centre 499
Chinese Heritage Museum 239

Chinese History Museum 398
Dusun Museum 383
Forestry Museum 483
Former Ford Factory 511-12
Fort Margherita 402
Fort Siloso 515
Fort Sylvia 435
Galeri Diraja Sultan Abdul Aziz 116
Galeri Sultan Abdul Halim 210
Galeria Perdana 197
House of Yeap Chor Ee 164
Images of Singapore Live 516
Indian Heritage Centre 501-2
Interpretation Centre (Bako National Park) 414
Interpretation Centre (Matang Wildlife Centre) 423
Interpretation Centre (Similajau National Park) 441
Islamic Arts Museum 15, 61, **15**
Islamic Heritage Museum 400
Istana Batu 286
Istana Heritage Gallery 507
Istana Jahar 283
Istana Kenangan 149
Istana Lama 122
Katong Antique House 509
Klang Fire Station 116-17
Komik Asia 167
Kompleks Muzium Negeri Terengganu 308
Labuan Marine Museum 388-9
Labuan Museum 388
Laman Padi 193
Lau King Howe Memorial Museum 430
Lee Kong Chian Natural History Museum 513-14
Lenggong Archaeological Gallery 149
Limbang Regional Museum 466
Mahathir's Birthplace 210
Malay Heritage Centre 505
Malay Technology Museum 471-2
Mari Mari Cultural Village 317
Maritime Museum & Naval Museum 218
Monsopiad Cultural Village 318-19
Mulu Discovery Centre 453
Museum of Islamic Civilisation 319

Muzium Darul Ridzuan 128
Muzium Diraja Kedah 210
Muzium Islam 283
Muzium Kota Kayang 213
Muzium Negeri 210
Muzium Negeri Kelanta 283
Muzium Negeri Sembilan 119-20
Muzium Padi 212
Muzium Perak 151
National Museum (Kuala Lumpur) 61
National Museum of Singapore 496
Natural History Museum 401
Niah Archaeology Museum 443
NUS Museum 513
Oil & Gas Discovery Centre 483
Pahang Art Museum 263
Penang Museum 165
Peranakan Museum 496
Petroleum Museum 446
Petrosains 59
Ranee Museum 398
Red Dot Design Museum 497
Royal Abu Bakar Museum 239
Royal Museum 65
Royal Regalia Museum 470
Rungus Museum 343
Sabah Museum 316-17
SAM at 8Q 498
Sarawak Cultural Village 417-18
Sarawak Museum Complex 25, 400
Sarawak Textile Museum 399
Sibu Heritage Centre 430
Singapore City Gallery 501
Sultan Azlan Shah Gallery 149
Sultanate Palace 222
Teochew Puppet & Opera House 164
music 587-8
music festivals
Borneo Jazz 447
Penang Island Jazz Festival 185
Rainforest World Music Festival 404

N
nasi kerabu 44, **45, 87**
nasi kuning 378
nasi lemak 47, 48, **2**
National Library (Singapore) 498

national parks & nature reserves 38, *see also* wildlife reserves & sanctuaries
Bako National Park 414, 415-16
Batang Ai National Park 429
Bukit Gemok Forest Reserve 376
Bukit Mas Nature Reserve 466
Bukit Patoi Recreational Park 484
Bukit Timah Nature Reserve 512
Cape Rachado Forest Reserve 123
Chek Jawa Wetlands 509
Crocker Range National Park 382
Danum Valley Conservation Area 365-7
Deramakot Forest Reserve 357-8
Endau-Rompin National Park 250-1
Forest Research Institute Malaysia 109
Gunung Gading National Park 425-7
Gunung Ledang National Park 245
Gunung Mulu National Park 453-9, **37**
Gunung Stong State Park 293
Habitat, The 184
Imbak Canyon Conservation Area 357
Kenong Rimba State Park 280
Kilim Karst Geoforest Park 196-7
Kinabalu National Park 332-9
Kubah National Park 421-3
Kuching Wetlands National Park 419
Labrador Nature Reserve 514
Labuan Marine Park 389
Lambir Hills National Park 445
Luagan Lalak Recreation Park 482
MacRitchie Reservoir 512
Maliau Basin Conservation Area 380-1
Niah National Park 443-5
Penang National Park 187

Pulau Selirong Recreational Park 485
Pulau Tiga National Park 387
Rainforest Discovery Centre 353
Royal Belum State Park 156-7
Similajau National Park 441-3
Soga Perdana Recreational Forest 246
Southern Ridges 513
Sungai Bantang Recreational Forest 246
Talang-Satang National Park 428-9
Taman Alam Kuala Selangor 118
Taman Negara 273-9
Taman Negeri Perlis 214
Tambunan Rafflesia Reserve 382-3
Tampat Do Aman Nature Reserve 343
Tanjung Datu National Park 427-8
Tanjung Piai National Park 246
Tawau Hills Park 379-80
Teluk Bahang Forest Reserve 187-8
Tunku Abdul Rahman National Park 329-31
Ulu Temburong National Park 11, 485-6, **11**
nature reserves, *see* national parks & nature reserves
Negeri Sembilan 49, 106-7, 119-24, **107**
accommodation 106
climate 106
food 89
highlights 107
history 108
travel seasons 106
weather 106
newspapers 598
northeast peninsula 51, 282-313, **284-5**
accommodation 282
climate 282
food 282
highlights 284-5
travel seasons 282
weather 282
notable buildings, *see also* historic buildings & sites, palaces
Atkinson Clock Tower 316
Bangunan Sultan Ibrahim 239
Emerald Hill Road 505
Heritage District (Johor Bahru) 239

Istana Kehakiman 113-14
Kampung Baru Gateway 67
King George V School 120
Kompleks Perdadanan Putrajaya 114
Kuching North City Hall 402
Menara Alor Setar 209
Menara Kuala Lumpur 60
Merdeka 118 24
Petronas Towers 17, 55, **17**
Putrajaya Convention Centre 114
Raffles Hotel 496
Sarawak State Assembly 402
State Library (Seremban) 120

O
Omar Ali Saifuddien Mosque 470, **2**
opening hours 21, 602
Orang Asli people 578
orangutans 351, 353, 423, 522, **12**, **522-3**
otak otak 85, **85**

P
Pahang 51, 252-81, **253**
accommodation 252
climate 252
food 87
highlights 253
travel seasons 252
weather 252
painting 589
palaces
Istana Besar 123
Istana Iskandariah 150
Istana Kenangan 149
Istana Lama 122
Istana Maziah 309
Istana Nurul Iman 471, 473-4
palm-oil plantations 593-4
Pa'Lungan 462-3
Pangkor Laut 147
Pangkor Town 148
pan mee 89, **88**
Pantai Cenang 193, **198**
Pantai Kok 195-6
Pantai Tengah 194-5, **198**
parks & gardens
Art & Garden by Fuan Wong 187
Botanical Garden (Kinabalu National Park) 340
Botanical Gardens (Penang) 184
Chestnut Park 512
China-Malaysia Friendship Garden 113

East Coast Park 508-9
Entopia by Penang Butterfly Farm 188
Fort Canning Park 497
Gardens by the Bay 489, 494-5, **6-7**, **18**
Kebun-Kebun Bangsar 94
KL Forest Eco Park 60
KLCC Park 55
Lake Gardens 120
Lake Gardens - Tun Abdul Razak Heritage Park 65
Marina Barrage 497
Melaka Botanical Garden 235
Miri City Fan 446
Monkeycup@Penang Hill 184
Orchid Garden 402
Perdana Botanical Garden 65
Rejang Esplanade 430
Singapore Botanic Gardens 507-8
Taman Botani 113
Taman Peranginan Tasek 474
Taman Tamadu Islam 308
Taman Tasik Taiping 151
Taman Tugu 61-4
Taman Wetland 113
Tanjung Emas Park 245
Titiwangsa Lake Gardens 67
Tropical Spice Garden 187
Pasir Bogak 146, 147
Pekan 262-3, **263**
Pelabuhan Klang 116-18
Penang 50, 158-90, **159, 84-5**
accommodation 158, 171-4
climate 158
courses 169
festivals & events 170-1
food 85
highlights 159
history 159-60
tours 169-70
travel seasons 158
weather 158
Penang Hill 183-4
Penarik 312
people 576-81, *see also individual peoples*
Perak 49, 125-57, **126**
climate 125
food 85
highlights 126
history 127
travel seasons 125
weather 125
Peranakan people 577

Perlis 50, 191-2, 213-14, **192**
climate 191
food 85
highlights 192
travel seasons 191
weather 191
Petaling Jaya 115-16
Petronas Towers 17, 55, **17**
photography 602
pineapples 464
planning 22-3
budgeting 21
calendar of events 26-7
checklist 22
itineraries 28-33, **28, 29, 30, 31**
Malaysia, Singapore & Brunei basics 20-1
Malaysia, Singapore & Brunei regions 49-52
travel seasons 20
websites 21
plants 337
politics 581
pollution 613
population 25
Port Dickson 123-4
postal services 602
proboscis monkeys 353, 387, 522, **522**
Pudu eateries 80
Pulau Aman 189
Pulau Aur 249-50
Pulau Banggi 344
Pulau Berhala 356
Pulau Besar 236, 248
Pulau Bidong 312, **526**
Pulau Carey 117
Pulau Dayang 249-50
Pulau Duyung 308-9
Pulau Gaya 331
Pulau Kapalai 375
Pulau Kapas 304-5
Pulau Ketam 117
Pulau Labuan 388-91
Pulau Langkawi 13, 50, 191-2, 193-209, **192, 194-5, 198**
accommodation 191, 200-4
activities 193-9, 200
climate 191
drinking 207
festivals & events 200
food 191, 204-7
highlights 192
internet access 208
legends 202
medical services 208
money 208
nightlife 207
shopping 207-8
sights 193-9

tourist information 208
tours 199-200
travel seasons 191
travel to/from 208
travel within 208-9
weather 191
Pulau Lang Tengah 302
Pulau Lankayan 356
Pulau Libaran 357
Pulau Mabul 374
Pulau Mamutik 330
Pulau Mantanan 344
Pulau Manukan 330
Pulau Mataking 375
Pulau Pangkor 143-8, **144**
Pulau Pemanggil 249-50
Pulau Perhentian 293-301, **294**
Pulau Pom Pom 375
Pulau Rawa 249
Pulau Redang 301-4, **526**
Pulau Sapi 330
Pulau Satang Besar 428
Pulau Selingan 356
Pulau Sibu 248-9
Pulau Sipadan 12
Pulau Sulug 331
Pulau Talang-Talang 428
Pulau Tinggi 249
Pulau Tioman 13, 51, 252-62, **253, 254, 13**
Pulau Ubin 13, 509
Purvis Street 539
Putrajaya 113-15
pygmy elephants 525, **524**

Q
quays, Singapore 498

R
rabies 612
radio 598
Raffles, Stamford 566, 567
rafflesia 382, 529, **528-9**
rafting, see white-water rafting
rainbow toads 529
Ramadan 48
Ranau 339
Raub 280-1
Razak, Najib 572, 574-5
religion 582-5
religious issues 584-5
resorts 129, 260-1
responsible travel 596
resthouses 600
rhinos 525
Riau Archipelago (Indonesia) 560
rice, Bario 464

River of Life project 61
rivers 595
road rules 609
rock climbing 35-8
Romol Eco Village 385
roti canai 324, **88-9**
roti prata 89

S
Sabah 51, 314-91, **315**
accommodation 314
art scene 317
boating 359
climate 314
driving tours 330
food 90
highlights 315
history 332
people 579
travel seasons 314
weather 314
safe travel 603, 609
crocodiles 441
diving 613
hiking 36
jellyfish 201
Johor Bahru 242
kidnappings 374
mosquitoes 278
Sepilok Orangutan Rehabilitation Centre 352
surfing 613
Tioman Island 256
salt 464
Sandakan 346-51, **348**
accommodation 348
drinking 350
food 349-50
information 350
nightlife 350
sights 346-7
tours 347-8
travel to/from 350
travel within 351
Sandakan Archipelago 356-7
Sandakan Death Marches 347
Santubong Peninsula 417-20
Sarawak 51, 392-467, **394-5**
accommodation 392
climate 392
food 90
highlights 394-5
history 393
people 579
travel seasons 392
weather 392
Sarawak Cultural Village 417-18, **17**
Sarawak Museum Complex 25, 400
satay celup 87, **86**

sculpture 589
Selangor 49, 106-7, 108-19, **107**
accommodation 106
climate 106
food 89
highlights 107
history 108
travel seasons 106
weather 106
Seletar Aerospace Park 544
Sematan 426
Semporna 367-9, **370**
Semporna Archipelago 369-76
Sentosa Island 515-16, 536, 545-6, 551-2, **516**
Sepilok 351-6, **354**
Seremban 119-21, **121**
Seria 483
Seributat Archipelago 248-50
shadow puppetry 587
Shah Alam 115-16
shopping, see also individual locations
language 618
Sibu 430-4, **433**
Singapore 52, 488-562, **490-1, 492-3, 500-1, 504, 506, 510, 516, 83**
accessible travel 556
accommodation 488, 531-6, 557
airport hotels 535
budgeting 557, 558
business hours 558
climate 488
consulates 557
courses 520
customs regulations 556
discounts 557
drinking 546-52
drinks 546
electricity 557
embassies 557
entertainment 552-3
festivals & events 520-31
food 14, 488, 89, 536-46, **14**
greening 596
highlights 490-1
history 489
holidays 558
internet access 557
itineraries 495
language 619
legal issues 557
LGBTIQ+ travellers 549
magazines 559
media 591
medical services 557
money 557

Singapore *continued*
newspapers 559
nightlife 546-52
opening hours 558
politics 581
postal services 558
Quays 498
shopping 553-6
sights 489-516
smoking 558
telephone services 558
time 558
toilets 558
tourist information 559
tours 520
travel seasons 488
travel to/from 559
travel within 560-2
visas 559
walking tours 518, **518**
weather 488
weights & measures 559
Singapore Zoo 12, 200,
511, **12**
Singlish 619
Siniawan Night Market 408
Sipadan 374, **526**
skin protection 614
Sky Mirror 25
Skytrex Melaka 235
snakes 614
snorkelling, *see* diving &
snorkelling
soto makassar 378
spas
Gunung Mulu National
Park 453
Kinabalu National
Park 340
Kuala Lumpur 67-9
Melaka City 224
Penang 185
Pulau Langkawi 193,
194-5, 197
Singapore 517-19
speakeasies 179, 548
Sri Menanti 122-3
statues, *see* monuments &
memorials
strawberries 139
street art
George Town 170
Kota Bharu 286
Kuala Lumpur 97
Melaka 225
Singapore 499
street festivals 171

street food 177
Kota Kinabalu 325
Kuala Lumpur 79
street names, George
Town 182
Sukau 360-1
Sultan of Brunei 471
sun bears 352
Sungai Kinabatangan 358-63
Sungai Klias 387
Sungai Lembing 266
Sunway Lagoon 115
Supertrees 489, 494-5,
6-7, 18
surfing 41
Cherating 268
Sabah 343
safety 613
swiftlets 359, 444
swimming
Singapore 519

T
Tabin Wildlife Reserve 367
Taiping 151-5, **152**
walking tours 154, **154**
Taman Negara 273-9, **275**, **11**
Taman Rekreasi Gunung
Lang 129, **521**
Tambunan 382-3
Tanah Rata 139-42, **140**
Tanjung Aru 320, 326
Tanjung Gemok 262
Tanjung Rhu 196-7
Tanjung Sipang
Mengayu 342-4
Taoism 582-3
Taoist temples, *see* temples
tapirs 525, **524**
Tasik Chini 271, 595
Tasik Kenyir 313
Tawau 376-9, **377**
taxes 554
taxis 609
long distance 610
tea plantations
Boh Sungei Palas Tea
Estate 142
Boh Tea Garden 138
Gaharu Tea Valley 134
Sabah Tea Garden 340
Tekka Centre 541
telephone services 603
Teluk Bahang 186-8
Teluk Datai 196
Teluk Kumbar 190
Teluk Nipah 145-6, 147, **147**
Temburong 483-6
Temerloh 270
temple caves 128

temples 19, *see also* Buddhist
temples, Hindu temples
Cheng Hoon Teng Temple
223
Foo Lin Kong 143
Hiang Thian Siang
Temple 400
Hin Ho Bio 400
Ho Ann Kiong 307
Hock Teik Cheng Sin
Temple 164
Hong San Si Temple 399
Johor Bahru Old Chinese
Temple 239
Kuan Yin Teng 167
Lian Shan Shuang Lin
Monastery 512
Lin Je Kong Temple 145
Sam Poh Footprint Temple
190
San Ching Tian Temple 446
Thian Hock Keng
Temple 499
Tiang Yun Dian Chinese
Temple 471
Tua Pek Kong Temple 400,
430, 446
Tempurung 386-7
Tenom 384-5
Terengganu 293-313
Thailand, travel to/from 209,
212, 213, 291
Thaipusam 584
ticks 614
tigers 522, **12**
time 20, 603
language 618
Tioman Island 252-62, **253**,
254, 13
accommodation 252
climate 252
food 252
highlights 253
hiking 256
travel seasons 252
weather 252
Tiong Bahru 503
Tip of Borneo 342-4
tipping 23
toads 529
toilets 603-4
tourist information 604, *see
also individual locations*
tours, *see also individual
locations*
adventure 320-2
diving 320-2
wildlife-watching 322
traditional medicine 615
train travel 329, 610
transit hotels 103, 535
transport 606-10
language 620

travel advisories 603
travel cards 105
travel to/from Malaysia, Singapore & Brunei 606-7
travel within Malaysia,
Singapore & Brunei 21,
607-10
Tringgus 424
trishaws 235, 562, 609-10
Tuaran 341
Tumpat 292
Tunku Abdul Rahman
National Park 329-31
turtles 526, **526-7**
Tutong 482
TV 598
typhoid 612

U
Ulu Temburong National Park
11, 485-6, **11**
Unesco World Heritage sites
central George Town
160-7, 167
central Melaka 217-22
Mt Kinabalu & Kinabalu
National Park 332-9
Singapore Botanic Gardens
507-8
Universal Studios 515-16

V
vacations 602-3
vaccinations 611
Vale Eco Center 143
Via Ferrata 336
viewpoints 18
Menara Taming
Sari 219-22
Pinnacle@Duxton 499
Signal Hill Observatory
Platform 316
Sky Tower Malacca 223-4
Top at KOMTAR 169
visas 20, 604
volunteering 256-7, 423,
604-5
East Coast islands 299

W
walking tours
George Town 166, **166**
Singapore 518, **518**
Taiping 154, **154**
wasps 614
water parks
Adventure Cove
Waterpark 519
Singapore Wake
Park 519
Wave House 520
water, tap 614

waterfalls
Chiling Waterfalls 112
Durian Perangin 197
Gunung Gading National Park 426
Lata Iskandar 137
Mahua Waterfall 383
Takah Berangin Falls 251
Takah Pandan Falls 251
Telaga Tujuh 195
Temurun Waterfall 196
Upeh Guling Falls 250-1
weather 20, 26-7
websites 21, 25, 572
environmental issues 593, 594, 596
health 611
history 569, 572
weights & measures 598
Weston 387
White Rajas 567
white-water rafting 39-41
Beaufort 386
Kuala Kubu Bharu 112

wildlife reserves & sanctuaries
Borneo Sun Bear Conservation Centre 352
Jurong Bird Park 513
Kinabatangan Orangutan Conservation Project 359
Kinta Nature Park 134
KL Bird Park 61-80
KL Butterfly Park 65
Kota Kinabalu Wetland Centre 317
Kudat Turtle Conservation Society 343
Labuk Bay Proboscis Monkey Sanctuary 353
Matang Wildlife Centre 423
National Elephant Conservation Centre 271
Penarik Firefly Sanctuary 312
Semenggoh Wildlife Centre 420
Sepilok Orangutan Rehabilitation Centre 12, 351

Sungei Buloh Wetland Reserve 514-15
Tabin Wildlife Reserve 367
wildlife smuggling 593
wildlife-watching 39
Bako National Park 414, 416
Cherating 268
Kampung Kuantan 118
Maliau Basin Conservation Area 380
Pulau Pangkor 146
Softwoods Plantation 376
tours 322
Zoo Negara 109
Wind Cave (Gunung Mulu National Park) 454, **11**
women in Malaysia, Singapore & Brunei 580-1
women travellers 605
women's health 615
work 605
WWII 347, 568
WWII sites & memorials
Battlebox 496

Changi Museum & Chapel 508
Kranji War Memorial 515
Kundasang War Memorial 340
Pialungan Sandakan-Ranau Death March Memorial 340
Sandakan Memorial Park 346
WWII Memorial (Labuan War Cemetery) 389

Z
Zhongshan building 101
zoos
Langkawi Wildlife Park 197
Singapore Zoo 12, 511, **12**
Zoo Negara 109
Zoo Taiping & Night Safari 151-2

Map Legend

Sights

- Beach
- Bird Sanctuary
- Buddhist
- Castle/Palace
- Christian
- Confucian
- Hindu
- Islamic
- Jain
- Jewish
- Monument
- Museum/Gallery/Historic Building
- Ruin
- Shinto
- Sikh
- Taoist
- Winery/Vineyard
- Zoo/Wildlife Sanctuary
- Other Sight

Activities, Courses & Tours

- Bodysurfing
- Diving
- Canoeing/Kayaking
- Course/Tour
- Sento Hot Baths/Onsen
- Skiing
- Snorkelling
- Surfing
- Swimming/Pool
- Walking
- Windsurfing
- Other Activity

Sleeping

- Sleeping
- Camping
- Hut/Shelter

Eating

- Eating

Drinking & Nightlife

- Drinking & Nightlife
- Cafe

Entertainment

- Entertainment

Shopping

- Shopping

Information

- Bank
- Embassy/Consulate
- Hospital/Medical
- Internet
- Police
- Post Office
- Telephone
- Toilet
- Tourist Information
- Other Information

Geographic

- Beach
- Gate
- Hut/Shelter
- Lighthouse
- Lookout
- Mountain/Volcano
- Oasis
- Park
- Pass
- Picnic Area
- Waterfall

Population

- Capital (National)
- Capital (State/Province)
- City/Large Town
- Town/Village

Transport

- Airport
- Border crossing
- Bus
- Cable car/Funicular
- Cycling
- Ferry
- Metro station
- Monorail
- Parking
- Petrol station
- Subway station
- Taxi
- Train station/Railway
- Tram
- Underground station
- Other Transport

Routes

- Tollway
- Freeway
- Primary
- Secondary
- Tertiary
- Lane
- Unsealed road
- Road under construction
- Plaza/Mall
- Steps
- Tunnel
- Pedestrian overpass
- Walking Tour
- Walking Tour detour
- Path/Walking Trail

Boundaries

- International
- State/Province
- Disputed
- Regional/Suburb
- Marine Park
- Cliff
- Wall

Hydrography

- River, Creek
- Intermittent River
- Canal
- Water
- Dry/Salt/Intermittent Lake
- Reef

Areas

- Airport/Runway
- Beach/Desert
- Cemetery (Christian)
- Cemetery (Other)
- Glacier
- Mudflat
- Park/Forest
- Sight (Building)
- Sportsground
- Swamp/Mangrove

Note: Not all symbols displayed above appear on the maps in this book

Austin Bush
Penang; Langkawi, Kedah & Perlis Austin originally went to Thailand in 1999 as part of a language study program hosted by Chiang Mai University. The lure of city life, employment and spicy food eventually led him to Bangkok and have managed to keep him there since. He works as a writer and photographer, and in addition to having contributed to numerous books, magazines and websites, he has contributed text and photos to more than 20 Lonely Planet titles, with a focus on food and Southeast Asia. Austin also wrote the Eat Like a Local and Regional Specialties sections of this book.

Ria de Jong
Singapore Ria started life in Asia, born in Sri Lanka to Dutch-Australian parents; she has always relished the hustle and excitement of this continent of contrasts. After growing up in Townsville, Australia, Ria moved to Sydney as a features writer before packing her bags for a five-year stint in the Philippines. Moving to Singapore in 2015 with her husband and two small children, Ria is loving discovering every nook and cranny of this tiny city, country, nation.

Damian Harper
Melaka; Johor; Pahang & Tioman Island With two degrees (one in modern and classical Chinese from SOAS), Damian has been writing for Lonely Planet for over two decades, covering destinations as diverse as China, Vietnam, Thailand, Ireland, Mallorca, Malaysia, Hong Kong and the UK. A seasoned guidebook writer, Damian also has penned articles for numerous newspapers and magazines, including the *Guardian* and the *Daily Telegraph*, and currently makes Surrey, England, his home. A self-taught trumpet novice, his other hobbies include collecting modern first editions, photography and taekwondo. Follow Damian on Instagram (damian.harper).

Anita Isalska
Perak; Selangor & Negeri Sembilan Anita Isalska is a travel journalist, editor and copywriter. After several merry years as a staff writer and editor – a few of them in Lonely Planet's London office – Anita now works freelance between San Francisco, the UK and any Baltic bolthole with good wi-fi. Anita specialises in Eastern and Central Europe, Southeast Asia, France and off-beat travel. Read her stuff on www.anitaisalska.com.

Anna Kaminski
Sabah; Brunei Darussalam Originally from the Soviet Union, Anna grew up in Cambridge, UK. She graduated from the University of Warwick with a degree in Comparative American Studies, a background in the history, culture and literature of the Americas and the Caribbean, and an enduring love of Latin America. Her restless wanderings led her to settle briefly in Oaxaca and Bangkok, and her flirtation with criminal law saw her volunteering as a lawyer's assistant in the courts, ghettos and prisons of Kingston, Jamaica. Anna has contributed to almost 30 Lonely Planet titles. When not on the road, Anna calls London home.

OUR STORY

A beat-up old car, a few dollars in the pocket and a sense of adventure. In 1972 that's all Tony and Maureen Wheeler needed for the trip of a lifetime – across Europe and Asia overland to Australia. It took several months, and at the end – broke but inspired – they sat at their kitchen table writing and stapling together their first travel guide, *Across Asia on the Cheap*. Within a week they'd sold 1500 copies. Lonely Planet was born.

Today, Lonely Planet has offices in the US, Ireland and China, with a network of over 2000 contributors in every corner of the globe. We share Tony's belief that 'a great guidebook should do three things: inform, educate and amuse'.

OUR WRITERS

Simon Richmond

Kuala Lumpur Journalist and photographer Simon Richmond has specialised as a travel writer since the early 1990s and first worked for Lonely Planet in 1999 on their Central Asia guide. He's long since stopped counting the number of guidebooks he's researched and written for the company, but countries covered include Australia, China, India, Iran, Japan, Korea, Malaysia, Mongolia, Myanmar (Burma), Russia, Singapore, South Africa and Turkey. For Lonely Planet's website he's penned features on topics from the world's best swimming pools to the joys of urban sketching. Simon also wrote most of the Plan Your Trip section and the Understand and Survival Guide sections of this book.

Brett Atkinson

Sarawak Brett Atkinson is based in Auckland, New Zealand, but frequently on the road for Lonely Planet. He's a full-time travel and food writer specialising in adventure travel, unusual destinations and surprising angles on more well-known destinations. Craft beer and street food are Brett's favourite reasons to explore places. He is featured regularly on the Lonely Planet website, and in newspapers, magazines and websites across New Zealand and Australia. Since becoming a Lonely Planet author in 2005, Brett has covered areas as diverse as Vietnam, Sri Lanka, the Czech Republic, New Zealand, Morocco, California and the South Pacific.

Lindsay Brown

Peninsular Malaysia's Northeast Lindsay started travelling as young bushwalker exploring the Blue Mountains west of Sydney. Then as a marine biologist he dived the coastal and island waters of southeastern Australia. He continued travelling whenever he could while employed at Lonely Planet as an editor and publishing manager. On becoming a freelance writer and photographer he has co-authored over 35 Lonely Planet guides to Australia, Bhutan, India, Malaysia, Nepal, Pakistan and Papua New Guinea.

OVER PAGE MORE WRITERS

Published by Lonely Planet Global Limited
CRN 554153
15th edition – December 2021
ISBN 978 1 78868 441 5
© Lonely Planet 2021   Photographs © as indicated 2021
10 9 8 7 6 5 4 3 2 1
Printed in Singapore